KNOW
YOUR
BOAT

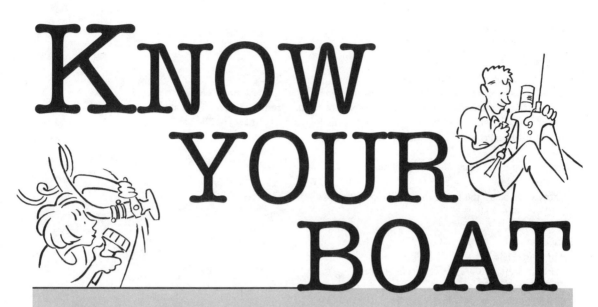

KNOW YOUR BOAT

THE GUIDE TO EVERYTHING THAT MAKES YOUR BOAT WORK

David Kroenke

Illustrations by Jim Sollers

INTERNATIONAL MARINE / McGRAW-HILL

Camden, Maine • New York • Chicago • San Francisco • Lisbon • London • Madrid • Mexico City
Milan • New Delhi • San Juan • Seoul • Singapore • Sydney • Toronto

International Marine
*A Division of The **McGraw·Hill** Companies*

10 9 8 7 6 5

Copyright © 2002 International Marine

Library of Congress Cataloging-in-Publication Data
Kroenke, David.
   Know your boat : the guide to everything that makes your boat work /
David Kroenke.
       p.   cm.
Includes index.
   ISBN 0-07-136134-0
   1. Boats and boating–Popular works. I. Title.
VM321 .K73 2002
   623.8′2–dc21   2001007296

Questions regarding the content of this book should be addressed to
International Marine
P.O. Box 220
Camden, ME 04843
www.internationalmarine.com

Questions regarding the ordering of this book should be addressed to
The McGraw-Hill Companies
Customer Service Department
P.O. Box 547
Blacklick, OH 43004
Retail customers: 1-800-262-4729
Bookstores: 1-800-722-4726

This book is printed on 60 lb. Computer Book by Quebecor World, Fairfield, PA
Design by Dede Cummings, DCDesigns
Production by Dede Cummings, DCDesigns, and Dan Kirchoff
Illustrations by Jim Sollers
Edited by Jon Eaton, David Brown, and Jennifer Elliott

CONTENTS

PREFACE

This book is intended to provide an easy-to-understand introduction to the major systems in a modern boat, whether power or sail. It's for that person who owns a boat, or who is about to purchase one, who pulls up a cabin-sole board, looks at the fittings, hoses, wires, pumps, etc., and begins to wonder whether owning a boat is such a good idea after all. "What is this stuff? What does it do? Should I be doing something to maintain it, and what do I do if it breaks?!"

Most boat systems are simple, and well within the grasp of anyone who can negotiate the labyrinth of vendors, salespeople, surveyors, loan officers, and insurance brokers required to buy a boat. *Know Your Boat* will guide you through the basic boat systems, explaining their functions, their components, a bit on how they work, what you need to do to maintain them, and when to call in a professional.

Even better, once you know something about these systems, you'll be more prepared when you're out on the water and something breaks; the knowledge you gain from this book will help you figure out what might be wrong, what you can do to fix it, and whether or not you need outside help.

And last, but far from least, working on your boat is one of the great joys of being a boatowner. It may not always seem that way, but over time, as you get to know your boat, you'll find greater and greater pleasure in just being aboard her, and you'll be able to enjoy the tremendous satisfaction of fixing a pump or repairing a connection out in the middle of nowhere.

So, read on . . . and have fun!

ACKNOWLEDGMENTS

This book would not exist without the vision and persistence of Jonathan Eaton, publisher, editor, and midwife. From the beginning, Jon had a vision for the art program that resulted in the superb illustrations throughout this book. To that end, tremendous thanks to Jim Sollers, who created the drawings and illustrations that so wonderfully capture both the facts and the spirit of the ideas. David Brown played a crucial role not only in helping me to understand the errors of my ways, but also in relaying what I was trying to say to both Jon and Jim and in working closely with both of them throughout the production process.

Here in Seattle, I thank the professionals who have helped me maintain my boat and have taught me so much over the years. Specifically I thank Tom Cooper, Max Heller, and Doc Doolittle of Seacraft Yacht Sales; Irvin Prichard of Gallery Marine; Carol Hasse of Port Townsend Sails; Don Forrest of Aquamarine; David Burch of Starpath Navigation; and Kent and Stephanie Williams and Rick Smith of Armchair Sailor, Seattle. All of these people are not only experts and consummate professionals in their fields; they're also fun, and patient with large doses of enthusiasm blended with ignorance.

Finally, I thank Lynda, my wife, and partner in the tales told here, and we both thank *Isla*, our Dulcinea, for many days and miles of safe voyaging and saltwater adventure.

DEDICATION

This book is dedicated to all brave souls who, in spite of fear and ignorance, pick up that screwdriver and wrench and manage to solve their own boat problems, somehow, one way or another, sooner or later, maybe this time, I hope. May none of your tools fall overboard, may none of your fittings corrode, and may you never drop that one, last essential screw into the black depths of the bilge!

1

WHAT WERE YOU THINKING?

Nobody should buy a boat. It makes no sense. Consider this multiple-choice question:

A boat is

a.   a fiberglass-lined hole in the water into which you pour money
b.   an acronym for Blow Off Another Thousand
c.   the world's most expensive way of traveling third-class
d.   all of the above

The answer is d, as we all know. This is obvious; we've heard it before. And did we listen?

No.

The fact is, owning a boat is a disease, an addiction. There should be organizations to help—places where people like you and me could stand up and say, "Hello, my name is David, and I own a boat." And where sympathetic and compassionate souls would gasp in surprise and amazement that people as normal looking as us could be so addicted. And they would help.

Instead, what do we find? An entire industry exists to feed this addiction, ensuring that people like us continue ~~to invest~~ to spend our hard-earned dollars. Open the current issue of *Yachting This Month* (or whatever your local monthly boating paper is called) and look at the pictures of new boat-owners in the "Recent Purchases" column. In my issue I see a picture of Selma and Harry Biffenbarfer, who look like a perfectly normal couple in their early fifties. The paper tells me that Selma and Harry just purchased a Dreamboat 40 that they hope to sail (after getting more experience locally) to Uruguay so Selma can connect with her long-lost relatives.

Now, the truth is Harry and Selma could save a lot of money if they just limo'ed on down to the airport, chartered their own 747, and flew to Uruguay while sipping hot-and-cold-running margaritas served by slavishly attentive butlers. A month in the Presidential Suite of the five-star Uruguanian Paradise Palace would be cheaper than the new rigging Harry and Selma are just about to find out they need for the Dreamboat 40.

Or, consider the picture of the next happy couple. Mary and Fred Had-

SomeSuccess have just purchased a 46-foot twin-diesel trawler, which they plan to take on their dream cruise to Glacier Bay, Alaska. The picture gives not a clue of the scene that will unfold several months down the road as Fred is frantically trying to reach his banker.

Fred and Mary are happily cruising the Inside Passage when they hear a god-awful noise in the engine room. They shut down the engines and manage, eventually, to limp into a remote coastal town. Do they feel humiliated and embarrassed while pushing their glorious twin-diesel beauty up to the dock with an inflatable rubber raft? Of course! But the locals are friendly and help Fred and Mary locate a diesel mechanic to diagnose the problem. They hear something like this: "Well, I can't be positive, but I think the flufflemuffle failed and caused the larkenshank to collapse into the ratsgable. I never seen anything like it before—I'm just surprised you didn't lose the whole shebang."

Ignoring the hollow feeling in the pit of his stomach, Fred bravely asks: "Can you fix it?"

"Well, we might be able to patch it together if we can get the parts."

"How long will it take?"

"Don't know—depends on when we can get the parts. Maybe a week. Maybe more."

Sure enough, ten days later, Fred and Mary are ready to continue their cruise, except that the yard won't accept a personal check and there's no bank to issue a cashier's check. The bill, totaling $17,314.87, is over the $15,000 limit on Fred's card. The tide's falling, and in another hour Fred won't be able to get his boat out of the slip (for which he's now paying $72.50 a day). Hence Fred's frantic call to his banker.

That's boating, fellow sufferer.

THE BEGINNING

It starts simply enough—very innocently, really. Perhaps you're at the grocery store and you absentmindedly pick up a boating magazine. Or, you're at the seashore and you watch the boats rounding the pier at sunset, and you imagine how great it must feel to con your own ship into harbor, basking in the admiration and respect of your family and friends. Or perhaps it's a beautiful day, you've just finished mowing the lawn, the barbecue is cleaned and ready for service, and you've got a few hours on your hands. You say, "Honey, why don't we go down to the marina and look at the boats?" (Why am I remembering those pamphlets in junior high school that warned, "One puff on a marijuana cigarette and the next thing you're a heroin addict"?)

Yes, that's how it starts, and soon you find yourself standing on the pier, looking at, yes, your Dulcinea.* There that beauty sits, riding so peacefully at the slip. One look into the pilothouse or cockpit and you envision yourself sitting in a quiet little anchorage, the children paddling the dinghy around the cove, piles of fresh-dug clams lying on the counter in the galley, crab pot over the side, and the smell of that perfect, fresh sea air. Or, you gaze at that beautiful wooden wheel and see yourself, steely eyed, impassively steering over the wine-dark sea, the boat heeling as you adjust the helm to pick up that extra puff in the spinnaker. Ah, yes, there she is: your Dulcinea!

So, in spite of the fact that nobody should own a boat, you buy her. Just like I did.

REALITY SETS IN

As we first gazed lovingly at our Dulcineas, there were one or two things we didn't know. Like the through-hull that tends to leak. Or the cutless bearing that's shot because the propeller shaft is out of alignment. Or the refrigerator that's never been able to freeze anything that wasn't already close to a temperature of absolute zero. Little things like that.

But unless we were completely bewitched by Dulcinea's beauty, we

*In case you missed it in Literature 101, Dulcinea was the love object of Don Quixote de la Mancha. Quixote imaged her as a beautiful aristocratic lady, the object of his undying love. She was, in fact, a barmaid of ill-repute, etc. Come to think of it, Don Quixote should have been a boatowner!

hired a surveyor who found many of these problems. However, the surveyor's job was just to find them. That's why surveyors are such a happy lot—they don't have to deal with what they discover.

One day, while I was still suffering withdrawal symptoms from a serious bout of buyer's addiction, I had lunch with the surveyor who'd just discovered that the starboard half of the interior core of the boat I'd almost bought was full of water. I asked the surveyor, "So, Bill, if you wanted to visit the midlatitudes of the world, what would you buy?" Perhaps it was the cold beer talking, but before he could stop himself, he replied, "A hell of a lot of airplane tickets!"

Undismayed, I continued my (ultimately sucessful) search for my Dulcinea. The upshot of the survey I had done was—surprise!—a list of items that needed to be fixed. Some of them the seller fixed before I bought the boat, others he credited against the purchase price; fixing them was up to me.

Which brings us to where we are today: we bought the boat, we've used it a few times, and we're beginning to get to know it. Like many relationships, however, we're beginning to realize that our dream—our Dulcinea—is more complicated than we thought.

In fact, go out some beautiful day and look at your gorgeous Dulcinea. As she bobs gently at her mooring, think about all of the systems she has: engine and propulsion; electrical generation, distribution, and use; water pressure, hot water, and possibly watermaking; plumbing and sewage; propane and refrigeration; steering and autopilot systems; heating and/or air conditioning; and, if a sailboat, sails and rigging. In truth, because Dulcinea was designed to be self-sufficient, she has all the characteristics of a small city. And you and I are the City Engineering Department.

If you spent the better part of your youth rebuilding automobile engines, or if you have an advanced degree in diesel engine design, or if you worked for ten years building the Alaskan pipeline, you probably aren't too fazed by the reality that's just beginning to set in. If, on the other hand, your expertise is in something like selling computer information systems to the insurance industry, the prospect of pulling up the cabin floor and figuring out what all those hoses, wires, pumps, valves, and mysterious boxes actually do may be daunting, even overwhelming. So, on your boating excursions, you turn keys and flip switches and just hope, hope, hope that everything works. And then there's another, darker phenomenon . . .

MECHANICAL IMPOTENCE

No, this is not a sexual problem. It's about that horrible feeling that comes when you turn the ignition key and nothing happens. Silence . . . click . . . silence. What do you do now? Or when you pull on the head pump handle and it won't budge; there are four people on your boat way out at Remote Island, and the head's broken. Or, just before that big trip you've been planning for weeks, you hear a new noise in the engine compartment. Is that a harmless squeak in a V-belt, a sign that the engine water pump is about to fail, or an indication that the valves are out of adjustment?

Or consider that lurking shadow of incompetence that flits by when you read in *Boating Today* that you should periodically inspect and clean your antisiphon valves. The truth is, you have no idea what or where they are. Does Dulcinea even have one? Or several? Or perhaps you're getting some toilet paper from the head locker and you see a hose that comes up from the bilge, makes a tight U-turn, and heads back down to the toilet fixture. What's *that* about? Did they have surplus hose in the boatyard, or is there something going on there that you should know about?

Maybe you overhear a conversation at the local yacht club bar about some unfortunate couple who just burned out the instruments on their brand-new boat. Eavesdropping with feigned nonchalance, you hear that their voltage regulator malfunctioned and sent 70 volts to their 12-volt instruments. Now, with $3,500 of damage, everyone is pointing the finger at everyone else. The voltage regulator people say the installer should have put an in-line fuse in the power supply circuit. The installer says the instrument installation instructions say nothing about an in-line fuse. The instrument manufacturer says that it relies on a safe power supply and any installer should know that. You, meanwhile are thinking, if 12 volts are

SHOWER INTERRUPTUS

One fall day, Lynda and I were motoring down Agamemnon Channel on our way into Pender Harbor, British Columbia. I was taking a shower while she was on watch (hand-steering, by the way, because our autopilot failed—but that's another story). Just as I got my hair shampooed, the shower stopped showering. We'd recently switched to a full water tank, so I knew we had plenty of water. "Oh, my goodness, what could be wrong?" I asked myself. (Well, words to that effect, anyway.) I knew I'd turned the water pressure circuit breaker on. "It must be a problem with the water pump."

So, shampoo and all, I dripped my way back to the cabin-sole board that covers the water pump and pulled it up. Bending over, I stuck my head down in the bilge to look at the pump (making no pretty sight, I'll tell you; I was glad Lynda was busy steering and wouldn't be popping around the corner at any moment). Sure enough, a wire connection to the pump was loose—the connector had corroded and broken. I used a paper clip to temporarily hold the wire onto its connection on the water pump, and hurray! The pump started up again. I went back to finish my shower, awfully proud of my diagnostic prowess.

Lynda knew nothing about this, and when she came off watch, her comment was, "Why is shampoo all over the cabin sole? What the heck have you been doing? And without me?"

"It wasn't that kind of thing," I said lamely.

good, why aren't 70 volts better? And what's an in-line fuse, and more to the point, does Dulcinea have them?

Listening to this, you begin to wonder if buying a boat was such a good idea after all. Isn't this supposed to be fun?

THE GOOD NEWS

Believe it or not, there's lots of good news. First, we're not talking about rocket science. You don't have to have a Ph.D. in mechanical engineering to understand Dulcinea because most boat systems are simple in concept.

They look complicated because they're intertwined all over the boat—one system lies next to, on top of, and/or is wound around another. Once you learn the basic components and their purpose, however, it's easy to decode the mystery of what's what and you'll find order in the maze of wires, hoses, clamps, and mystery objects under the cabin sole. It's far easier than filing your taxes, and a lot more enjoyable.

Second, for each of your boat's systems, there are certain basic maintenance tasks that need to be done. As we will say often, *the easiest way to solve a problem is not to have it*. And the best way to prevent problems is periodic maintenance. (I know, this sounds like floss your teeth, eat your vegetables, and get plenty of exercise—practical, boring advice. But there are several benefits to this, so keep reading!)

Each chapter in *Know Your Boat* discusses one or more of Dulcinea's major systems, including a description of basic maintenance tasks. You might consider doing at least some of those tasks yourself, but realize that, unless you're the Mozart of Mechanics, you'll make mistakes—lots of them— and that's OK. We all do. However, as Virginia Satir used to say, "I may be slow, but I'm educable."

Some boatowners have a lot more cash than time and may be tempted to call up their boatyard and ask them to change the fuel filters, check out the engine, or, more expensively, say, "John, get my boat ready for a trip to the San Juan's, will you?" Requests like those are an invitation to mechanical impotence.

In truth, if you aren't actively involved in the maintenance and servicing of your boat's systems, you're denying yourself one of the major pleasures of boating. When you're standing on your head with oil dripping in your eyes and you just dropped the gizmo to fix the whatchamacallit in the bilge for the third time, you'll curse this book for saying it, but it's true. There is tremendous enjoyment (and the pleasant glow that comes with self-sufficiency) in getting to know Dulcinea, understanding how everything fits together, and being able to fix things when you need to.

Which brings up the third bit of good news. Things break—it's inevitable. (This is good news?!) Boats are complicated, they're used in an unforgiving environment, they often sit unused for long periods of time, and then they're driven hard for short intervals—about the worst scenario you can imagine for mechanical systems. So, failure is not only likely, it's certain. The good news is that as you learn more and more about Dulcinea, you'll be able to fix more and more things. Even if you just make a temporary fix so you can limp into port, you're carrying on the self-sufficiency that's part of our pioneering heritage, but that modern life seldom requires.

Last week I helped moor a disabled boat that was being towed back to the marina. The owner had taken his family out to the islands for a weekend trip. When they started back, he heard a funny sound coming from the engine. Shutting it off, he opened the engine compartment to investigate. He found the wire harness to the alternator had somehow become entangled in the alternator's V-belt. The wires were torn, broken, and entangled in a rat's nest mess; there was no way he could repair them. So, he concluded that he couldn't run his boat and called for an (expensive) tow. His grandchildren were bouncing off the cabin headliner while they waited three hours for the tow to arrive and another six hours to get back to the marina.

However, as you'll learn in chapter 3, diesel engines don't need an alternator to run. All that long-suffering grandfather had to do was cut or tie the damaged wires so that they'd be out of the way of the V-belt, start the engine, and motor home. With the alternator out of service, he wouldn't be generating any 12-volt electricity while he was running, but it wouldn't have mattered as long as he didn't turn the engine off and restart it more than a few times. He could have saved money, time, and stress for everyone. Even better, he would have had that self-sufficient glow of self-sufficiency.

THE PROCESS FOR GETTING TO KNOW DULCINEA

My high school chemistry class had lab sessions in which we'd pour green stuff into red stuff and get blue stuff that we had to measure to get some kind of an answer. My lab partner and I figured out that life would be easier for us if we skipped the pouring stage and just looked up the answer in a chemical reference book. Then, we'd work backwards and make up a bunch of data to fit that answer. That way, we didn't even have to go to the lab.

Well, Mr. Johnson, our teacher, figured out what we were up to and called us into his office. I remember sitting there as he looked me in the eye and said, "David, this just won't do. I don't care if you learn what happens when you pour the green stuff into the red stuff. I don't even care that you remember the chemical symbol for the red stuff. But what I do care about, and what I want you to learn, is a process. Something called the 'scientific method.'"

Those words have stuck with me all these years, long after I could remember what the blue stuff was or even what Mr. Johnson looked like. Getting to know your Dulcinea is also a process—it's not the scientific method, but it is a process. And, as Mr. Johnson told us that day, if you follow that process, you'll have success far more frequently than if you don't.

THE EQUIPMENT INVENTORY

So, what is that process? It starts with making an inventory of all the equipment on your boat. For example, you probably know whether you have a gas or diesel engine. But, if it's a gas engine, does it have carburetors or fuel injectors? If it's a diesel engine, does it have a turbocharger or not? You can use the sample Equipment Inventory table to help you. You won't have all of the types of equipment in this table on your boat, but you'll have many of them, and you'll probably have other items that are not listed here. Add tanks, valves, hydraulics, electronics, and other items as appropriate and as desired. Don't get too obsessed with it. You want the list to be your servant, not your master. While you're looking at your boat's equipment, write down the make and model; on high-cost items like engines, generators, air conditioners, cabin heaters, watermakers, etc., record the serial number if you can find it easily.

Why serial numbers? While on a trip to Mexico, I needed to replace an injector for my diesel engine (see chapter 3). I have a Yanmar 4JH-TE

Equipment Inventory

	TYPE	MAKE	MODEL	SERIAL NUMBER	MANUALS	REMARKS
Engine(s)						If gas, fuel-injected or carbureted? If diesel, turbocharged?
Transmission(s)						
Propeller(s)						
Generator(s)						Output capacity?
Alternator(s)						Output capacity?
Voltage regulator						Single or multistage?
Batteries						Type? Voltage? Amp-hours? Age?
Battery chargers(s)						Single or multistage?
Inverter						Wattage?
Bilge pumps						
Foot pumps						
Wind generator						Capacity?
Solar panels						Capacity?
Cabin heater						
Air conditioner						
Water heater						Capacity?
Water pressure pump						
Watermaker						Capacity?
Head(s)						Type?
Stove/oven						Electric, propane, or other?
Barbecue						
Other propane appliances						
Refrigerator						12-volt? 120-volt? Engine-driven? Cold plates?
Freezer						
Steering systems						Wire or hydraulic?
Binnacle						
Compass						
Autopilot(s)						Linear-drive or hydraulic?
Roller furling						
Windlass						Location of circuit breaker?
Winches						
Anchor(s)						Weight?
Anchor chain						Length? Type?
Anchor rode (nylon line)						Length?

engine, and it turns out that engines of this model with serial numbers under 11,001 have one injector type, those with serial numbers between 11,002 and 12,000 have another type, and those with higher serial numbers have a third type. My serial number is 12,451, and because I didn't know about the serial number distinction, it took me three tries to get the right injector. So, while you're making your equipment inventory, it's a good idea to record the serial number. A little hand mirror like that on the back of a make-up compact can be useful for reading one in a hard-to-see spot.

You don't have to make the whole inventory at once. Take a few days (or weeks or months), relax, and just enjoy seeing Dulcinea from different perspectives. Lift up the cabin sole, open lockers, peer under settees, and look around. Tear up an old T-shirt and clean here and there as you go—this is a good opportunity to remove some surface dirt and grime. If you don't know what something is, just keep reading this book; we'll come to it eventually, and then you'll know what to look for.

WHAT'S WHAT?

Once you've made an inventory, the next step is to go through the boat and figure out what's what. This will be easier if you have the owner's manuals for your equipment, so before you start, check through your pile of owner's manuals to ensure you've got a manual for each piece of equipment in your inventory. Match up the manuals with the model identifications you found in your inventory. Make sure the manuals are for the equipment currently installed on your boat since a previous owner may have changed equipment since the boat was constructed.

If you're missing manuals, get on the Internet and search for the manufacturer and model. Send an e-mail requesting an owner's manual, and include your make, model, and serial number if you know them. For major equipment such as engines and generators, you might ask for a parts manual as well. You may have to pay a few dollars for the parts manual, but the owner's manual will probably be free.

You can use this book as a guide for navigating those manuals and getting to know Dulcinea. Read a chapter, read the owner's manual for the equipment involved, and then trace out the components of that system. For example, if you have an engine-driven refrigeration system, read chapter 7, look at the pictures of the equipment in your owner's manual, and then find all the parts. In this case, you'll be looking for the compressor, the condenser, the RFD, the pressure valve, and the cold plates. Trace the refrigerant hoses around the boat as you go.

We'll talk about electricity in chapter 4. For now, however, you should know that AC electricity (like what you get from shore power) is exceedingly dangerous, especially around water. Therefore, you should disconnect the shore-power cord at the dock while you're poking around. Don't just turn off the circuit breaker: unplug the plug. That way there's no connection from the shore power to your boat.

MAINTENANCE

By the time you've inventoried your boat and figured out what's what, you'll know a lot about Dulcinea. Now's the time to start performing some of the basic maintenance tasks. Read over the maintenance discussions and consult your owner's manuals. Then make a *maintenance schedule*—a list of tasks for the equipment on your boat. Put the list into spreadsheet form so you can sort it by type of equipment or by frequency. The screen shot next page shows a portion of a typical maintenance schedule.

If your Dulcinea doesn't have a repair and maintenance log, this is a good time to start one. I use a small notebook of lined pages and put four columns on each set of left- and right-hand pages. The headings for the columns read Date, Hours, Who, and Remarks (see page 15). The Date column has the date the maintenance was performed, and in the Hours column I record engine hours, generator hours, or watermaker hours, depending what I'm working on. The Who column has either my initials or the name of the person who did the maintenance or repair. The first time someone works on my boat, I record his or her company name, phone, address, and e-mail. Later, if I'm off in some remote spot and need to reach someone with a question, I'm sure to have all their

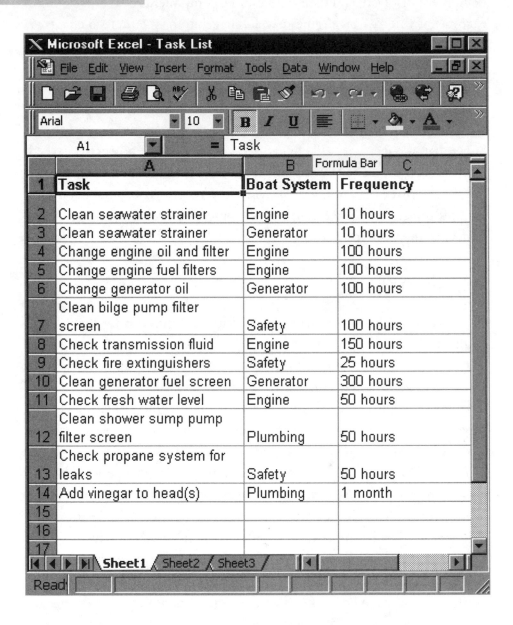

Task	Boat System	Frequency
Clean seawater strainer	Engine	10 hours
Clean seawater strainer	Generator	10 hours
Change engine oil and filter	Engine	100 hours
Change engine fuel filters	Engine	100 hours
Change generator oil	Generator	100 hours
Clean bilge pump filter screen	Safety	100 hours
Check transmission fluid	Engine	150 hours
Check fire extinguishers	Safety	25 hours
Clean generator fuel screen	Generator	300 hours
Check fresh water level	Engine	50 hours
Clean shower sump pump filter screen	Plumbing	50 hours
Check propane system for leaks	Safety	50 hours
Add vinegar to head(s)	Plumbing	1 month

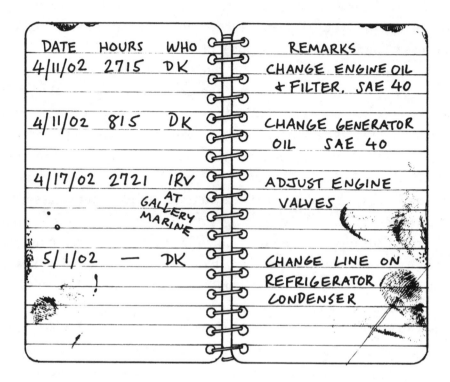

DATE	HOURS	WHO	REMARKS
4/11/02	2715	DK	CHANGE ENGINE OIL + FILTER, SAE 40
4/11/02	815	DK	CHANGE GENERATOR OIL SAE 40
4/17/02	2721	IRV AT GALLERY MARINE	ADJUST ENGINE VALVES
5/1/02	—	DK	CHANGE LINE ON REFRIGERATOR CONDENSER

contact information on the boat. The Remarks column has comments about the work that has been done.

I use this log to record all repairs, maintenance, fuel tank fillings, watermaker operations, and anything else I may need to know about the boat. Someday, when I sell Dulcinea, this log should add to the boat's value because the future owner(s) will be able to see exactly what was done to the boat, who did it, when, and why.

REPAIRS

Once you have an inventory, you know what's what, and you've been actively involved in maintaining Dulcinea's systems, you'll be in a position to make many repairs yourself. Here we'll describe a general process—like Mr. Johnson's scientific method—that most professionals use.

When something appears to be broken, the first thing to do is to make sure it's being operated correctly. Are the necessary circuit breakers on? Does the boat have power? Are all valves open that need to be open? And so forth. Find the owner's manual and go through the start-up procedures documented there. Nine times out of ten, something's not turned on correctly.

If you still have a problem, the next step is to think about what's happened since the last time you used the now-broken system. This is especially true if the problem appeared suddenly. Has the boat been bounced hard in rough weather? Did water splash on a circuit board? Did you pack clothes into a locker where wiring could have been disturbed? Events like these may point you to the cause of the problem.

Look in the owner's manual for the troubleshooting guide. Is your problem discussed there? If so, do you have the parts and tools you need to do the job? Do you want to tackle it where you are? Before starting on any but the smallest repair, it's worth asking if you can get back home without the use of the broken system. If not, patch together some sort of a fix with which to limp home.

Every moment you spend working with Dulcinea will better prepare you for problems that will inevitably occur. When problems do develop, take some time to think through the repair process before you grab your toolbag. For any such tasks, remember that if you're not sure what to do, hire a professional and work with him or her. Watch how they do the task and learn the tools and tricks they use for shortcuts. If the task seems complicated, make a video as they work. Above all, get involved and ask questions; you'll learn more and more about your Dulcinea.

TOOLS

If you're going to perform maintenance and repair tasks on Dulcinea, you'll need a set of good tools. It doesn't necessarily have to be an elaborate set, but don't use cheap tools. They'll make a hash out of Dulcinea's screws, nuts, bolts, and other components, and they're very hard to work with. SnapOn tools are the Rolls-Royce of tools. They're incredibly well crafted and very expensive. They also can be heartbreaking to use on a boat because it's agonizing to watch your $35 screwdriver take a graceful dive overboard. A good choice for tools for most boatowners are those from Sears, but there are a number of other brands that are equally as good. A key quality test is whether the manufacturer will replace it for free if it breaks. Quality used tools that have been well cared for can be a great buy. Also, you can

Cloth Toolbag

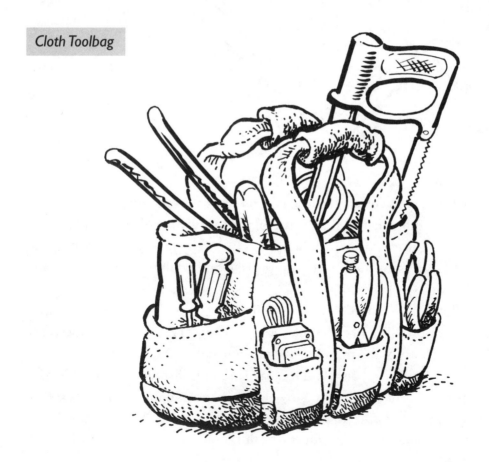

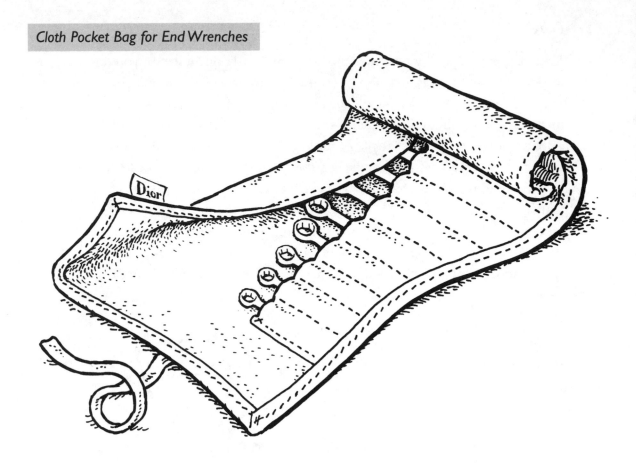

sometimes get a substantial discount on tools at home shows, auto shows, race car events, and the like. Be careful to buy only brand-name, high-quality tools, however; it's much better to buy a few quality tools than it is to buy a large assortment of cheap tools. Good tools are a joy to use and make your work much easier.

While you're buying tools, set some of your budget aside to acquire a good cloth toolbag like the one shown on page 17. You don't want to use a metal toolbox aboard a boat because it will scratch surfaces and will quickly rust. When your cloth toolbag runs out of space, try a set of small-ish plastic toolboxes. I put all my electrical tools in one, all my sockets in another, and so forth. Store your end wrenches in a cloth pocket bag. Lynda made the one shown here for my birthday one year.

Caring for your tools is important, especially since the wet (and possibly salty) environment is hazardous to their health. Whenever your tools are exposed to salt water, be sure to rinse them off with freshwater as soon as you can to avoid rust, and spray a mist of WD-40 on them. Some people like to place a slightly oily cloth in their toolbox or wrap their tools in an oily cloth (don't use linseed oil; it can be a fire hazard). I've found that my tools don't corrode as long as I put them away dry and keep them in a dry locker. (See appendix 2 for tool suggestions.)

LEGEND

1. toilet (seawater) intake
2. toilet (waste) outlet through-hull
3. engine cooling water intake
4. bilge pump discharge
5. engine exhaust
6. manual bilge pump
7. cockpit drain
8. electric bilge pump
9. holding tank
10. holding tank pumpout
11. seacock
12. cockpit drain through-hull
13. shaft through-hull
14. stuffing box
15. rudderstock through-hull
16. rudderstock stuffing box
17. exhaust line shutoff valve
18. sink drain through-hull
19. vented loop with anti-siphon valve

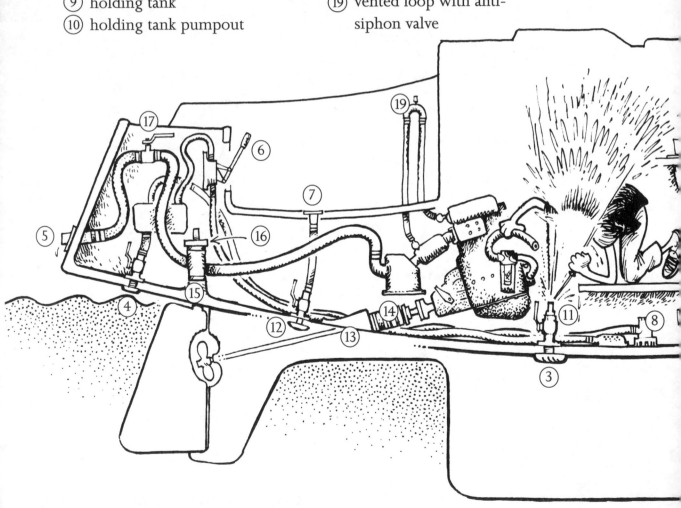

2

KEEPING
YOUR BOAT
AFLOAT

What makes a boat a boat? While there's little agreement on the characteristics of a good boat, we can all agree on one key element: it *floats*. But what makes a boat float? It doesn't seem surprising that a wooden canoe floats, but why does an aircraft carrier float? How do you make steel or concrete or engines, for that matter, float?

The basic principle was discovered by Archimedes back in 246 B.C. As you may recall from Mr. Gazernenplatz, your 11th grade physics teacher, Archimedes shouted "Eureka!" when he figured it out while taking a bath. The idea is this: when you place an object in water, it pushes water aside. The amount of water that is pushed aside is called the *displacement* of the object. An object will sink if it weighs more than the weight of the water it displaces; if it weighs less, it will float and displace water just to the point where the weight of the water displaced equals the weight of the object.

To see this principle in action, take an empty soda bottle, cork it, and put it in water. It will sink slightly into the water and then float. The weight of the water displaced by the part of the bottle that's underwater will be equal to the weight of the bottle. Next, take the soda bottle, fill it with sand, cork it, and put it in water. It will sink. The weight of the soda bottle and the sand is more than the weight of the water that the bottle can displace. Extrapolating your findings to aircraft carriers, you'll see that they float because they're so huge. They take up such an enormous volume of water that the weight of the water displaced is equal to the weight of the carrier—plus the weight of the airplanes, pilots, tools, doughnuts, etc., on board.

Your boat has an advertised weight, its displacement, that the boat's designer calculated from obscure formulas. That displacement is likely to be less than the actual weight of your boat because the marketplace gives incentives for underestimating the displacement, and also because you add weight to your boat with fuel, water, sewage, people, food, scuba gear, fishing poles, dirty clothes, etc. The only thing you can be certain of is, if Dulcinea is floating, her actual weight will be exactly the weight of the water that she displaces.

While we're on this topic, be aware that your Dulcinea was designed to carry only a certain amount of weight. As long as she sits above the original waterline (some of her bottom paint shows above the water), she's not loaded beyond her designed limit, and you're OK. While you can put even more weight into her—even raising the waterline above the original manufacturer's line—this is a bad idea. For one, it will slow her down; for another, it can make her less safe in a stormy sea.

Also, think about where you put additional weight. In general, the farther the weight is from the center of the boat, the greater the impact that weight will have on Dulcinea's performance. Excess weight in the bow is particularly bad. If she was designed to carry 250 feet of chain in her bow, but you put 900 feet of chain in the bow locker, that excess weight will have a terrible impact on her seaworthiness. Similarly, tying many diesel and water cans up on the deck, along the toerail, will impact her ability to recover from a roll. In general, if you store the toilet paper in the upper forward lockers and the canned goods low and toward the center of the boat, Dulcinea will be happier, faster, and give a better ride!

THROUGH-HULLS

Boat manufacturers go to great lengths to create watertight hulls, ensure the various layers of fiberglass stay bonded to one another, and ensure the deck-to-hull bond is strong and watertight. Having done that, they then start boring holes into the hull: holes for the propeller shaft, seawater intakes, drains, instruments, etc. Most of these holes are then lined with a bronze or plastic fixture called a *through-hull fitting*, the outside end of which is flanged to seat firmly against the hull's outside surface. Through-hulls that pass fluids carry a thread on the stempiece sticking up into the hull. A *seacock*, which is a valve that can be closed to seal off the hole, is threaded onto the stempiece, as shown in the illustration on page 24.

Often, no distinction is made between the hole, the through-hull fitting, and the seacock, and the whole arrangement is simply called a *through-hull*. Thus, one hears, "Honey, would you please open the engine through-hull

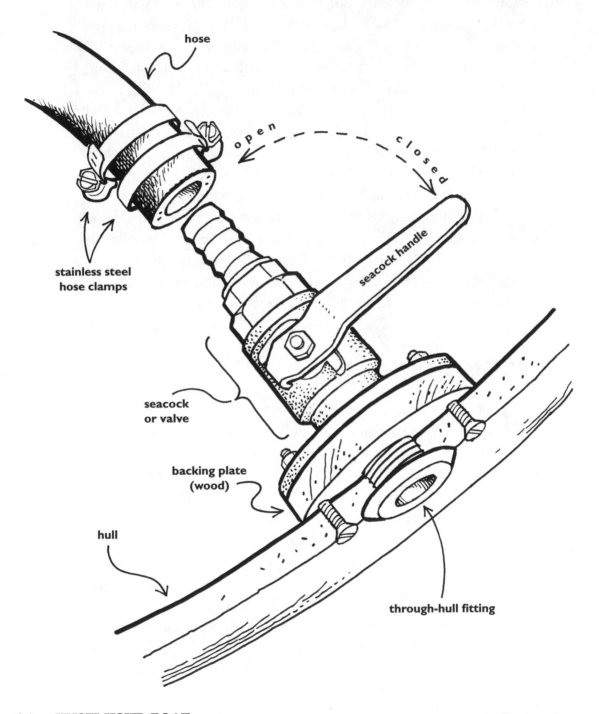

hose

open — closed

stainless steel
hose clamps

seacock handle

seacock
or valve

backing plate
(wood)

hull

through-hull fitting

as fast as you can?" Instead of, "Honey, would you please open the seacock that is threaded into the through-hull fitting that fills the through-hull where we're supposed to be sucking water at this very minute lest our engine impeller dry out and burn up?" You get the picture. But, to get you in the habit of using the correct terminology, we'll use the following terms: *through-hull* for the hole, *through-hull fitting* for the device that lines the hole, and *seacock* for the valve that opens and closes to allow fluids to pass through.

Other than damage caused by running into something hard like a reef, a rock, or another boat, any problems you have with water coming into your boat will likely occur around a through-hull. Thus, the first thing

Sample Through-Hull Diagram

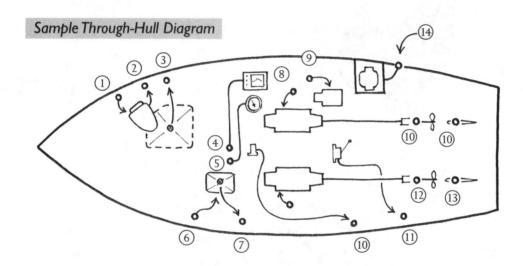

LEGEND

① head intake
② head discharge
③ shower drain discharge
④ depth instrument
⑤ speed instrument
⑥ galley seawater intake
⑦ galley sink drain

⑧ engine cooling intake (2)
⑨ generator cooling intake
⑩ electric bilge pump discharge
⑪ manual bilge pump discharge
⑫ propeller shaft (2)
⑬ rudderstock (2)
⑭ drain for propane locker

you should do when getting to know your boat is to find out how many through-hulls you have and where they're located. Even if the manufacturer of your boat created a through-hull diagram for you, you should still verify its accuracy since your boat may have a different number of through-hulls than the standard model. A prior owner may have added (or removed) equipment that required more through-hulls be put in (or that old ones be filled in). Make a diagram of their locations, or correct the existing dia-

Seacock with Tied-On Bung

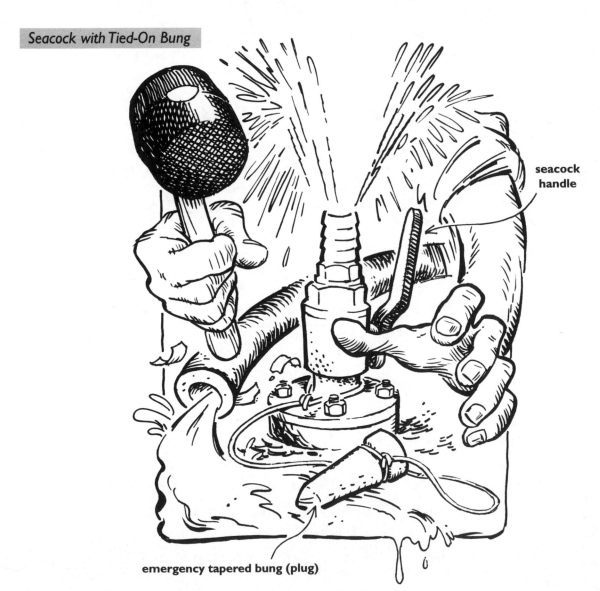

seacock handle

emergency tapered bung (plug)

gram (see illustration on page 25), and put it in a safe yet easily accessible place. You should also have a plan for what to do if a particular through-hull starts leaking, but more on that later.

Disaster can strike a through-hull in several ways. One (highly unlikely) possibility is failure of a through-hull fitting. In the worst case, a through-hull fitting could fall out of the hole (very unlikely unless there has been a corrosion problem). Another possibility is that a seacock will fail and leak. Or the hose clamps will fail, the hose will come off, and water will start shooting out of the seacock. (To increase the horror of this scenario, assume you locate the spurting hole, try to turn the seacock handle, and it sticks!)

In any of these cases, you would need to find something slightly larger than the hole and jam that something into the hole. Experienced boat-owners prepare ahead of time and have a wooden bung of just the right size stored near each through-hull. A bung is a wooden cone with a tip slightly smaller than the hole in the seacock fitting and an end larger than the diameter of the through-hull. You can use string to tie the bung to something nearby (see illustration opposite) so it will be close at hand in the event you need it.

Because you may need to get to your through-hulls in a hurry, make sure they're not obstructed by stowed gear or anything else. Also make sure that gear cannot move around and inadvertently open, close, or break a seacock by sliding onto the seacock handle.

As stated in chapter 1, the very best way to solve a problem is not to have it. Two ways to prevent through-hull disasters are to periodically open and close every seacock in the boat to ensure none of them sticks or leaks, and inspect the hose clamps to ensure they're tight and not worn or corroded. The surveyor should have performed this inspection when your boat was surveyed, but you should make this one of your routine maintenance tasks.

HOSE CLAMPS

Most experienced boaters agree that when leaving their Dulcinea unattended in the water, it's important to close as many through-hulls as possible, especially those that exit below the waterline. Assuming you leave your bilge pumps on automatic, you should not, of course, close the bilge pump hose seacocks. Nor should you ever close the seacock that vents your propane locker, if you have one, or those that empty your cockpit drains. But all the others—head, galley sink, shower, engine, generator, etc.—should be closed.

This is a sound practice. The only problem is remembering to open the seacocks next time you use Dulcinea. Engine impeller pumps (see next chapter) cannot be run when dry: more of them are ruined by boaters forgetting to reopen the engine seacock than for any other reason. Therefore, leave a note to remind yourself to open the engine intake seacock before you start the engine. I know one boater who ties the ignition start key to the closed seacock when he leaves his boat so he has to look at the closed seacock before he can even get the key. He also leaves a note to this effect for anyone else who needs to start his engine.

When you buy hose clamps, make sure that the metal band, the screw housing, and the screw are all made of stainless steel (they should be marked with the words "stainless steel," the letters "SS," or something similar). Conscientious boat manufacturers put two hose clamps on any hose fitting that is below the waterline (including those that may be below the waterline when Dulcinea rolls or heels). If this hasn't been done on your boat, you might want to install a second hose clamp on such fittings. If you do this, however, make sure that the *hose barb* (the ridged tube coming out of the seacock) is longer than the width of two hose clamps plus half an inch or so. To be sure, close the seacock, loosen the hose clamp, remove the hose from the fitting, and look. If the barb is too short, don't put on the second clamp—it will just crimp down on and partially close the hose when you tighten it.

TYPES OF SEACOCKS

Ball valves are the most common seacocks (see illustration). They contain a ball with a hole bored through it that rests in two Teflon seals. When the handle of the valve is turned so that it's parallel to the valve body and the tailpiece to which the hose attaches, the hole lines up with the openings in the valve and fluid can flow through. When the handle is turned so that it is perpendicular to the valve body, the hole is at right angles to the valve openings and is closed.

Ball valves can be made out of either bronze or plastic. Bronze valves are stronger and won't melt in a fire, but they are susceptible to corrosion. For this reason, you may find that bronze valves and through-hull fittings are connected to the boat's grounding system. By the way, whenever you replace a seacock, make sure that the replacement is a valve designed for its intended purpose.

Ball-Valve Seacock in the Open and Closed Positions

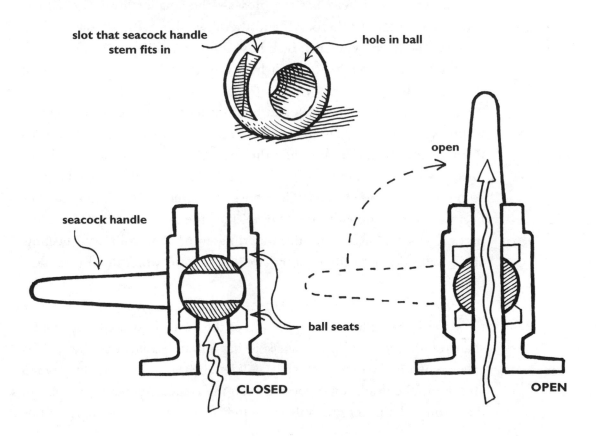

On an older boat you may encounter *tapered-plug seacocks*, which are usually bronze and function like ball valves. Another type is *gate-valve seacocks*, which use a handle that resembles a faucet to lower a metal disk that obstructs the through-hull passage. These are fragile, cranky, and liable to jam, and it's difficult to tell whether they're open or closed; they have no place on your Dulcinea.

ANTISIPHON LOOPS

If the seacock and the equipment that uses it are both below the waterline (or could be when rolling or heeling), then something has to be done to keep water from pouring into the boat when the seacock is opened. Consider, for example, the marine toilet, or *head*. As you'll learn in chapter 6, your head has two hoses—the smaller hose, the *water-in hose*, brings water to the bowl, and the larger hose, the *contents-out hose*, removes the bowl's contents. Each hose leads to a different through-hull. Normally the water-in through-hull is forward of the contents-out through-hull.

Assume that the toilet itself and both through-hulls are below the waterline (which is usually the case). If either hose ran straight from its through-hull to the head, when the seacock on that through-hull was open, water would flow into the bowl, fill it, and overflow into the boat. To prevent this, these hoses are led above the waterline into U-shaped connectors and then down to the fixture. Thus, the hoses make a loop, some part of which is well above the waterline even when rolling or heeling. Since water doesn't naturally flow uphill, the head won't flood (see illustration).

However, there's a problem. Under certain circumstances, it's possible for water to be siphoned over the top of the loop. To prevent this, the U-shaped connector (called a *vented loop*) has an *antisiphon valve* at its top. This valve, when it's working correctly, will let air in but not out. Thus, when you pump the head, water goes through the U-shaped connector and out the through-hull. Since the valve won't let air (or water) out, there will be

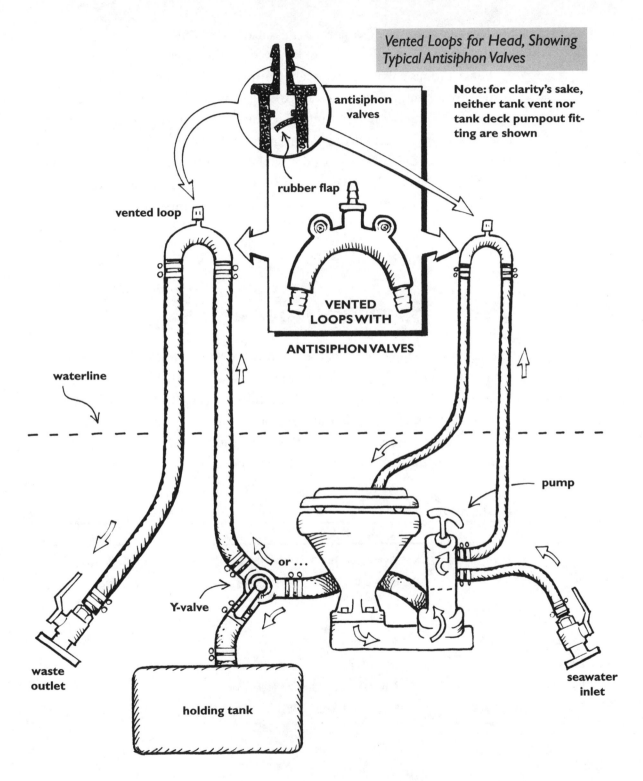

Note: for clarity's sake, neither tank vent nor tank deck pumpout fitting are shown

antisiphon valves

rubber flap

vented loop

VENTED LOOPS WITH

ANTISIPHON VALVES

waterline

pump

or ...

Y-valve

waste outlet

seawater inlet

holding tank

no leaks. If water were to start to move backward due to siphoning, however, the valve would let air in and thus break the siphon.

Vented loops solve one problem but present another: the water must somehow be pumped over the loop. In the case of the head, this happens when you pump the head manually to flush it. In the engine cooling system, seawater is driven from the engine's exhaust manifold up over the vented loop in the raw-water outlet by the raw-water pump. In the case of other vented loops, however, a pump must be added to the system. For shower stall drains, for example, a small electric pump is normally added to remove the water and pump it through the vented loop and out the through-hull.

TYPES OF THROUGH-HULLS

The accompanying table lists the various types of through-hulls used by various types of equipment. Most of Dulcinea's through-hulls are designed to let something pass in or out of the hull, so each of these will have a seacock in the through-hull fitting. The seacock will be connected to a hose that will lead to the equipment that uses the through-hull passage, as shown in the illustration on page 24. In some cases, a through-hull is used

Types of Through-Hulls	
TYPE	CONNECTED TO
Seawater intake	Engine(s), toilets, sink faucets, generator, watermaker, air conditioner
Seawater drain	Galley and head sinks, shower drains, head, bilge pumps, watermaker, air conditioner
Cockpit and deck drains	Cockpit and deck
Propane locker vent drain	Propane locker
Exhaust	Engine(s), generator
Instrument	Boat speed sensor, depth-sounder, sonar
Shaft	Propeller and rudder shafts

for more than one purpose and there will be a T- or Y-connection inboard of the through-hull, from which two hoses lead to the two devices. There could even be several hoses connected to the same hole in a pipe assembly referred to as a *manifold*.

DECK AND COCKPIT DRAINS

Some boats have deck drains that empty via through-hulls, and all boats with cockpits near the waterline have cockpit drains that empty similarly. Usually such through-hulls are above the waterline, but they're low enough that they're easily submerged when rolling, heeling, or underway in any kind of sea. Consequently, you should inspect them as well.

If the bottom of the cockpit is close to the waterline, water can flow backward through the cockpit drain to flood the bottom of the cockpit. This is especially true for sailboats when they're heeling. Two different approaches are commonly taken to solve this problem: One is to plumb the cockpit drain so that the starboard drains are connected to a port-side through-hull and the port drains are connected to a starboard-side through-hull. This way, when the boat is heeled over so that one of the cockpit drains is below the waterline, the through-hull to which it's connected (on the opposite side of the boat) has been lifted clear of the water on the boat's windward side.

The other approach is to close the cockpit drain seacocks. *This is very dangerous!* If the boat takes a wave in the cockpit with the drains closed, it is possible for the stern to be submerged and sink the boat. If I had a boat with a wet cockpit problem, I would replumb the cockpit drains to connect to through-hulls on the opposite side.

PROPANE LOCKER DRAIN

As we discuss in chapter 7, propane is very dangerous. One of its dangers is that it's heavier than air. This means that if you have a propane leak, propane gas (which is incredibly flammable) will sink to the lowest spot it can and sit there waiting to cause an explosion. Therefore, the bottoms of all propane lockers contain an overboard drain so that if there is a leak, the propane will flow out of the locker and overboard.

Depending on the location of your propane locker, this drain may simply be a through-hull hole in the propane locker itself, or it may connect to a hose that connects to a through-hull opening (normally without a seacock). If there's a hose, you should regularly inspect it and its connections to the locker drain and the through-hull fitting. The hose should slope continually downward from the locker to the discharge so that it can't trap moisture or leaking gas. In all cases the discharge must be above the *static*, or normal, waterline, and it should be above the heeled waterline if at all possible (see illustration on page 172). If the outlet isn't above the heeled waterline, ABYC (American Boat and Yacht Council) standards require a seacock. If your boat has a seacock in the propane locker drain, you must ensure that it's open except when in danger of shipping water through it. When the seacock is closed, any leaking gas can accumulate in the locker and present a serious hazard. Sailing with this outlet continually submerged may also restrict the venting of any leaking gas.

ENGINE THROUGH-HULLS

The hose for engine and generator through-hulls usually runs from the through-hull into a seawater strainer (more on this in the next chapter). From the seawater strainer, the hose runs through a pump on the engine and then to the vented loop (see illustration). This siphon breaker can also be located in the line from the heat exchanger to the exhaust. If your engine is below the waterline (or could be when rolling or heeling), it's very important that you periodically check the antisiphon valve because if it freezes shut, your engine could fill with seawater, which will ruin it.

All of the connections from the engine through-hull to the vented loop are probably below the waterline, so you should regularly check the hose clamps on all of them. You might want to add a second hose clamp, if nec-

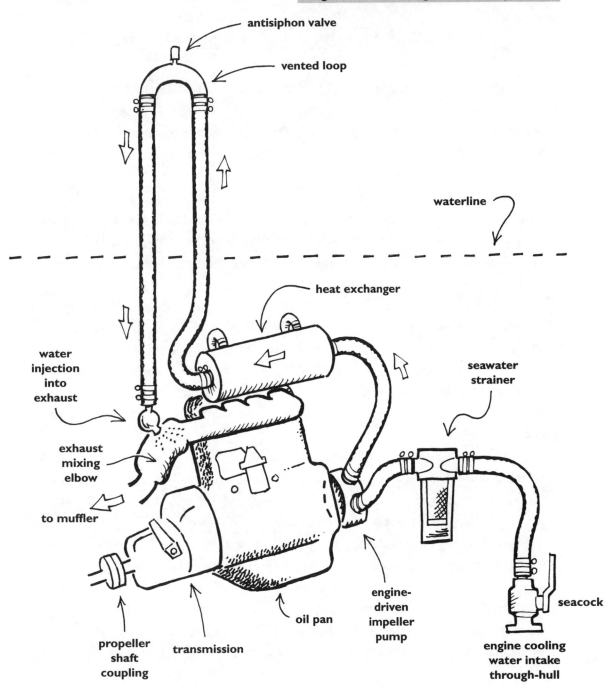

antisiphon valve

vented loop

waterline

heat exchanger

water injection into exhaust

seawater strainer

exhaust mixing elbow

to muffler

engine-driven impeller pump

propeller shaft coupling

transmission

oil pan

seacock

engine cooling water intake through-hull

SEAFOOD À LA SEACOCK

Several years ago, Lynda and I were cruising the Inside Passage of British Columbia, and motoring our sailboat through a narrow passage called the Blow Hole. All was well until the engine exhaust started sounding funny—a different pitch—and black smoke began to pour out the exhaust. There was no water splashing with the exhaust gas and the engine temperature gauge moved up to the red line. We shut down the engine.

Ironically, several days earlier we'd been asking ourselves what we would do if we lost the engine in a tight spot. We'd decided we'd get the jib up as fast as we could if there was wind and, if not, we'd try to anchor. That day there was a slight breeze behind us, so we put up the jib and sailed slowly into a bay wide enough so Lynda could tack back and forth while I went down below to see what I could do.

Since there was no water splashing out with the exhaust, I figured there had to be a problem in the seawater intake line. Leaving the engine cooling seawater intake seacock open, I slowly took off the top of the seawater strainer. If the line between the through-hull and the strainer wasn't clogged, then water would've been leaking out of the strainer. No water, even with the top of the strainer off. OK, I thought, the blockage has to be in the hose ahead of the strainer. (I also heaved a sigh of relief, because if the problem had been in the engine, at that time I wouldn't have had any idea what to do.)

I put the top back on the strainer and closed the seacock. Next, I removed the hose clamps, pulled the hose off the seacock and looked inside the hose; OK as far as I could see. I slowly opened the seacock with the hose removed. Nothing. Eureka! Archimedes! It had to be in the through-hull itself! Maybe there was a plastic bag over it or something else plugging it.

But then I made a mistake. I looked around for something I could stick into the open valve and found the bottom part of a wooden coat hanger. Getting my face down close to the through-hull, I poked the wooden stick into the seacock tube, and the remains of a fingerling salmon shot out of the hole, followed by a gush of cold water. Groping around, blinded by dead fish and salty water, I finally found the seacock handle and closed it. Then I put everything back together, started the engine, and off we went. Other than the dead fish, the wet cabin, and the broken coat hanger, we were fine.

essary, as explained above. The engine exhaust hose is another potential problem. Even though the engine exhaust through-hull exits the transom above the waterline, it's possible for water to enter the exhaust hose and work its way back into the engine. The likelihood of this depends upon the location of the through-hull, the run of the hose, and the size and location of the water muffler. Many boats have a plastic or rubber flap that lies over the exhaust through-hull hole. Exhaust gas and water push the flap open, but the flap is pushed closed by a following sea. If there's any chance of water entering your engine via the exhaust, such a flap is a cheap safeguard, as is an above-waterline loop in the exhaust hose, and, in sailboats, a shutoff valve in the top of the loop that can be closed in following seas when the engine is shut down.

SHAFT THROUGH-HULLS

Since moving parts pass through shaft through-hulls, they need to be sealed to keep water out. The traditional *packing gland seal* (see illustration next page) has a fiber packing around the shaft. The packing is contained in a recess in the stuffing box housing and is compressed by a movable part called the *gland*. The nuts that draw the gland into the packing should be tightened so that the seal drips slightly while the shaft is turning; one or two drips per minute is typical. Overtightening these nuts will cause excessive wear and possibly dangerous temperatures. Your boat's documentation should give you the appropriate drip rate for your shaft through-hull seals.

As Dulcinea ages with use, you'll eventually reach the point where you can't compress the gland any more—it's been drawn up into the packing as far as it will go and the box still drips too much. At this point, you'll have to pull Dulcinea out of the water, remove what remains of the old stuffing material, and replace it with new. In theory, you can do this job yourself, but you probably don't want to because this is one of those jobs that turn boatyard workers gray before their time. You'll have to hang by your knees from the cabin sole, contorting your body into weird pretzel-

Shaft Through-Hull Seals: A Traditional Packing Gland Seal (Stuffing Box)

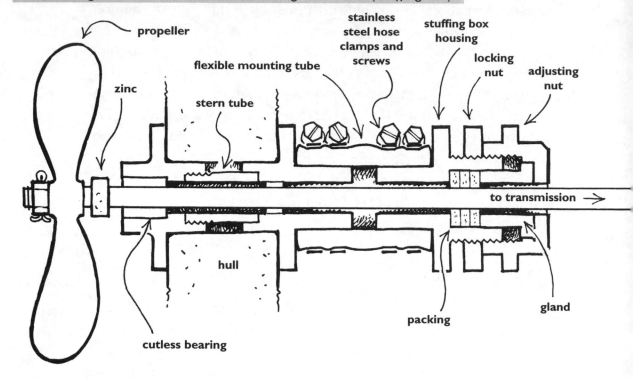

propeller

zinc

stern tube

flexible mounting tube

stainless steel hose clamps and screws

stuffing box housing

locking nut

adjusting nut

to transmission →

hull

cutless bearing

packing

gland

Shaft Through-Hull Seals: A Dripless Seal

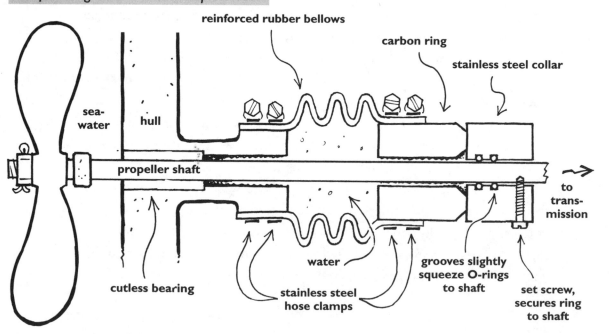

reinforced rubber bellows

carbon ring

stainless steel collar

sea-water

hull

propeller shaft

to trans-mission

cutless bearing

stainless steel hose clamps

water

grooves slightly squeeze O-rings to shaft

set screw, secures ring to shaft

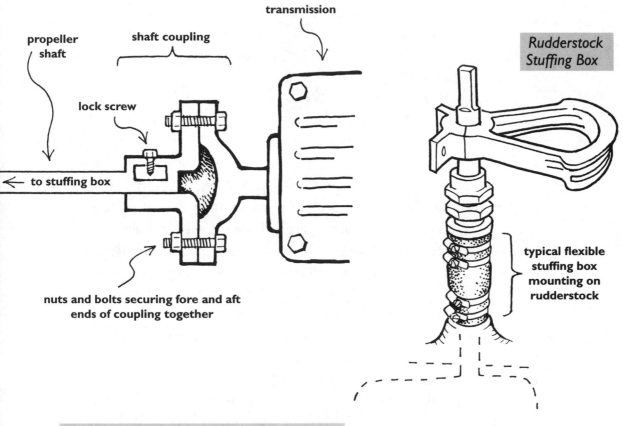

propeller shaft

shaft coupling

transmission

lock screw

← **to stuffing box**

nuts and bolts securing fore and aft ends of coupling together

Rudderstock Stuffing Box

typical flexible stuffing box mounting on rudderstock

Shaft Through-Hull Seals: Mounting Variations

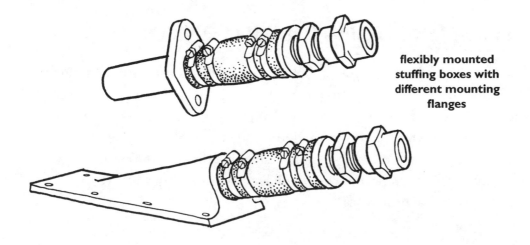

flexibly mounted stuffing boxes with different mounting flanges

like shapes, while you discover that you don't have the right tools and really, truly have no idea what you're doing. All the while wondering whether you're going to have leaks when you put her back in the water (which will necessitate another pullout). Therefore, hire a professional; he or she will also check propeller shaft alignment, which might be the real problem, anyway.

The second, newer type of seal is designed not to drip and (not surprisingly) is called a *dripless shaft seal.* As shown in the illustration on page 38, a bellows pushes a carbon disk up against a metal disk mounted on the shaft. To work properly, the disks must be very smooth and stay very smooth as they are used and wear. As long as this kind of seal is not dripping or overheating, it doesn't require any maintenance. But any time you take your boat out of the water, you need to *burp* the bellows (allow cooling water to enter the bellows) when you put the boat back in the water and before you start the engine. A number of different dripless shaft seals are now available that are designed differently than the one shown here. If you have one of these newer designs, see the documentation for your seal to learn if it needs to be maintained and whether (and how) it should be burped.

The through-hull on your rudderstock(s) is almost certain to be of the traditional packing gland type (see illustration). It should drip only when the rudder is being moved.

THE THROUGH-HULL INVENTORY

OK, you're ready. Put on your grubbies, pull up the floorboards, and start looking. Find every through-hull in your boat, determine its type and what it's connected to, examine the hose clamps, check for the presence of a bung, see if there's an antisiphon loop, and if so, note the type of antisiphon valve. Record the results in a table like the one shown here. By recording the hose size and type, you'll know what to buy when you need spares or replacement hoses.

Dulcinea's Through-Hull Inventory

LOCATION	TYPE	PURPOSE	SEACOCK TYPE?	DOES SEACOCK OPEN AND CLOSE?	HOSE CLAMPS OK?	BUNG(S) NEARBY?	ANTI-SIPHON TYPE?	HOSE TYPE AND SIZE?
Sink	Seacock	Drain	Ball-valve	Yes	Yes	Yes	No	Rubber-no wire, 1¼-inch ID*
Engine	Seacock	Seawater intake	Ball-valve	Yes	Yes	Yes	Yes	Rubber-wire, 1-inch ID*

*ID = inner diameter of hose

When inspecting hose clamps, close the seacock and then unscrew and retighten the clamps, watching for rust and corrosion inside the barrel of the hose clamp screw housing. Replace the clamp if you suspect interior corrosion that you cannot see. You should plan to inspect all seacocks, clamps, hoses, and through-hull fittings at least once a year. You'll also want to buy or make bungs if you don't have them, and deal with any antisiphon valve problems you discover.

When you've finished this inspection, sit back and give yourself a pat on the back. This was a dirty job—hoses can be stiff and hard to work with—but now you know where the through-hulls are and have some idea of what to do if you have problems with them.

MAINTENANCE

Periodic maintenance tasks for through-hulls and vented loops are summarized in the table on pages 42–43.

In addition to these scheduled tasks, I've formed the habit over the years of opening and closing a seacock whenever I happen to notice it. This action keeps the seacocks working easily and prevents marine organisms from growing inside and freezing the ball closed. If that happens, the seacock handle usually breaks off and the seacock has to be replaced.

Through-Hull Maintenance Tasks

TYPE	TASK	FREQUENCY	REMARKS
Through-hulls with seacocks	Open and close.	Monthly	Open and close several times to keep free of marine growth. Don't force them. If they won't move, they'll have to be repaired, perhaps replaced. Boat should be pulled from water to do this. Always ensure propane and bilge pump seacocks are open.
	Inspect for leaks.	Monthly	If through-hull leaks, replace it. Pull boat from water. Leak in seacock itself may be repairable without pulling boat from water. Get professional help the first time.
	Check hose clamps.	Yearly	Replace as necessary.
	Remove ball, inspect, and lubricate.	Yearly?	Boat must be out of water. If seacock operates smoothly, may not be necessary.
	Check antisiphon valves	Quarterly	Remove and inspect. Replace as necessary.
Engine through-hulls	All tasks above.	As above	As above
	Check antisiphon valves.	Monthly	Check more frequently if you've ever had problems. Replace at least once a year.
	Other tasks discussed in next chapter.		
Shaft through-hulls	Check prop packing gland/stuffing box for correct drip rate.	Monthly	Adjust as necessary. If glands can't be tightened further, you need to add and/or replace packing material. Get professional help the first time.
	Check dripless seal for no drips and no evidence of excessive heat.	Monthly	Get professional help for any type of trouble. Do not ignore!
	Burp dripless seal according to user's manual whenever boat is pulled from water.	As needed	
	Check and adjust rudder-stock packing gland/stuffing box for slight drip when rudder is turned.	Quarterly (unless excessive water appears in bilge)	Adjust as necessary. Get help if need to add packing material. May need to pull boat from water.

Through-Hull Maintenance Tasks

TYPE	TASK	FREQUENCY	REMARKS
Instrument through-hulls	Check for leaks.	Monthly	If leaking, pull boat from water and repair as necessary. Get professional help.
	Clean speed instrument paddle.	As needed	Do this in the water only if you have the plug for the speed instrument through-hull that is provided by the instrument manufacturer.
All	Thoroughly check all through-hull fittings. Open and close seacocks. Inspect for leaks or looseness.	Whenever boat is out of water	Replace through-hull fitting if any doubt. Get professional help.
	Check packing material in traditional shaft seals.	Whenever boat is out of water	Add packing material if in doubt.
	Burp dripless shaft seal when back in water.		

At least once a quarter, check the valves in the antisiphon loops to ensure that they're working properly. They should be intact, not corroded, and flexible, and should let air in but not out. You should carry spare valves or valve parts for each type of antisiphon valve in your boat; every now and then, you should replace them. If your engine(s) are below the waterline, inspect those antisiphon valves even more frequently (say once a month).

I like Hal Roth's* idea about spares: When you buy a spare, remove the current component (even if it's working) and replace it with the spare. Then, carry the original component as the spare. That way you know you have the correct spare, you have all of the tools you need, and you can do the job before you need to. See the appendices for more on spare parts and tools.

*Hal and Margaret Roth were one of the first cruising couples. Hal has written many books, one of which is After 50,000 Miles.

If you're out in Dulcinea a lot, you should inspect the shaft seals at least once a month. Make sure the drip rate of traditional seals is correct and feel the seal while underway to ensure it's not too hot. Examine dripless seals to ensure they're dripless. Don't ignore any problems with these seals: get professional help if you have any doubts at all; many boats have sunk from shaft-seal failure!

By the way, use special care anytime you're around a moving propeller shaft. Make sure you're not wearing any loose clothing that could be caught in the shaft. Station yourself in a stable position so that you cannot fall onto the shaft, even if the boat heels or lurches. And take your time.

There isn't much you need do to instrument through-hulls. If you have a paddle-type speed indicator, you may find that marine growth develops around it to the point that the paddle won't move. If you have a plug for the paddle through-hull fitting (not a bung—this is one provided by the instrument manufacturer), you can pull the paddle from inside the boat. Working quickly (water will be pouring in the boat), fill the hole with its special plug. Now you can clean the paddle at your leisure and then replace it by pulling the plug and reinserting the paddle.

Whenever your boat is pulled out of the water, schedule enough time to thoroughly inspect each of your through-hull fittings. Go around the boat and make sure none of them has been damaged and that each one is tight. Look for pitting from corrosion or damage from other sources. Clean out any growth inside the through-hull, being careful not to damage the valve or fitting inside it. If you find any suspicious through-hull fittings, have them replaced. Since having a watertight through-hull fitting is so important, replacing one is not a job for the amateur: hire a qualified professional. When your boat is put back in the water, don't forget to burp dripless shaft seals as necessary.

3 ENGINE BASICS

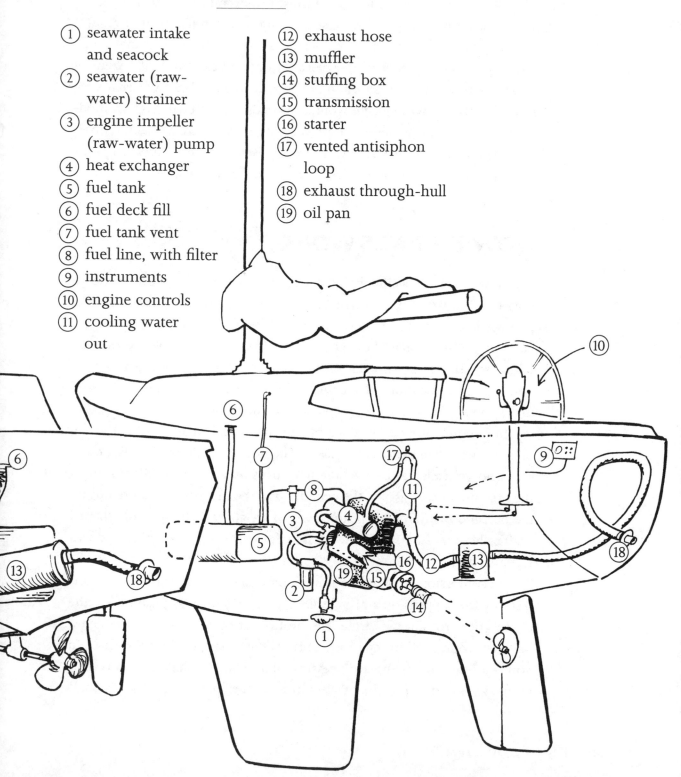

Your engine is probably the most important safety device aboard your boat. Even if you lose steering, you can use your engine(s) to control and maneuver the boat. There will also be times when the loss of engine power would be catastrophic; I can think of dozens of rocky, narrow entrances along the Inside Passage to Alaska where loss of power at just the wrong time would mean loss of the boat. Even in moderate conditions, loss of engine power can be an expensive (and embarrassing) inconvenience. Happily, most engines will run for a very long time with only a modest amount of regular care and maintenance.

HOW ENGINES WORK

Before we turn to specific maintenance tasks, we'll spend a little time on how engines work, which will help you to make sense of the tasks that follow. Also, situations will crop up that differ from any described in this book. If you understand how engines work, you may be able to come up with a solution to a particular problem. In any case, this basic knowledge will help you to communicate with mechanics and other specialists and make you appear less like a sheep ready for fleecing!

Your engine propels Dulcinea by burning fuel. It does this by igniting fires in small chambers called *cylinders*. The floor of each cylinder is a movable plunger called a *piston*. As the fire burns inside the cylinder, it raises the pressure of the gases in the cylinder, and the increased pressure pushes the piston downward. The pistons, which are attached to an oddly shaped shaft called a *crankshaft*, cause the crankshaft to turn as they are pushed down (see illustration).

The conversion of the up-and-down motion to a circular motion is similar to what happens on a bicycle. On a bike, as your legs push down, the chain goes around in a circle. The motion of one leg pushes the chain halfway around and in the process brings the other pedal up. Similarly, in your engine, the downward pressure of a piston pushes the crankshaft halfway around and in the process moves other pistons up. In this anal-

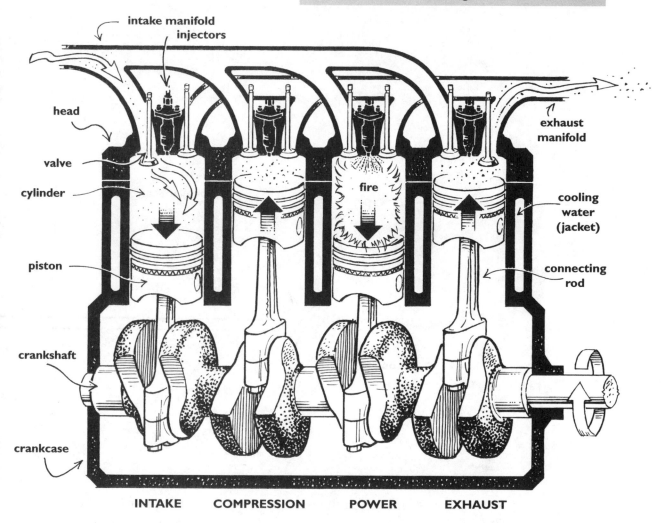

intake manifold
injectors

head

valve

cylinder

piston

crankshaft

crankcase

fire

exhaust
manifold

cooling
water
(jacket)

connecting
rod

INTAKE   COMPRESSION   POWER   EXHAUST

ogy, the bike is like a two-cylinder engine. Your engine probably has three or
four (or six or even more) cylinders, so the situation is more complicated,
but this basic concept still applies. On a boat, the crankshaft is connected
to a *transmission*, which is connected to the *propeller shaft*, which is connected to
the *propeller*. The whole arrangement serves to convert energy from burning
fuel into the rotation of your propeller (see illustration pages 50–51).

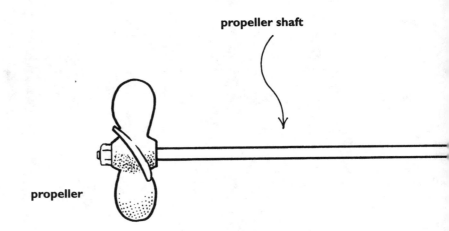

propeller shaft

propeller

All of this is simple enough to say, but how does it happen? Your engine has to start a fire just when the piston is near the top of its motion. The fire has to be just large enough to push the piston down the cylinder with the correct force. Then, the leftover gases in the cylinder have to be expelled as exhaust. To make it more complicated, this process has to be repeated many times per second. For example, in a four-stroke engine operating at 2,400 rpm (revolutions per minute), each piston fires 2,400 ÷ 2, which is 1,200 times per minute or 20 times per second! That's a lot of fire-starting and exhaust-expelling!

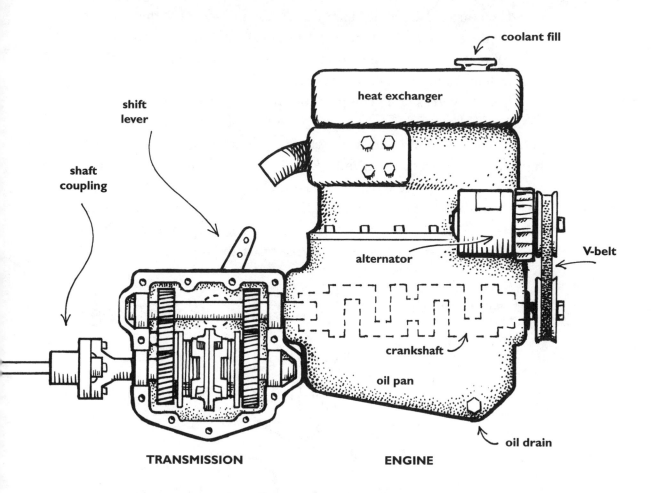

coolant fill

heat exchanger

shift
lever

shaft
coupling

alternator

V-belt

crankshaft

oil pan

oil drain

TRANSMISSION

ENGINE

DIESEL VS. GASOLINE ENGINES

Your Dulcinea uses one of two fundamentally different types of engine: diesel or gasoline. These engine types differ not only in the kind of fuel they use, but also in how they cause that fuel to burn. In both types, the fuel and oxygen are ignited by a high temperature source. Diesel engines create the high temperature by compressing the air to something like $\frac{1}{20}$ of its original volume. When compressed this much, the temperature of the air rises above that required for diesel fuel to burn. As the piston reaches the top of the cylinder, a device called a *fuel injector* sprays a fine mist of precisely timed and metered diesel fuel into the hot, compressed air in the cylinder. Because the temperature of that compressed air is above the combustion point of diesel, the mist immediately catches fire. Presto, the gases expand and push the piston back down the cylinder.

Gasoline engines don't compress the air as much as diesel engines—something closer to $\frac{1}{8}$ of the original volume. Because of this, the temperature of the compressed air is not high enough to ignite the gasoline. Instead, the fuel inside the cylinder is ignited by an electrical spark from a spark plug, which is screwed into the top of the cylinder. The spark must arrive at the spark plug at just the right moment—when the fuel is in the cylinder and the piston is at the top—and so a complex array of electrical paraphernalia is required to ensure correct spark timing.

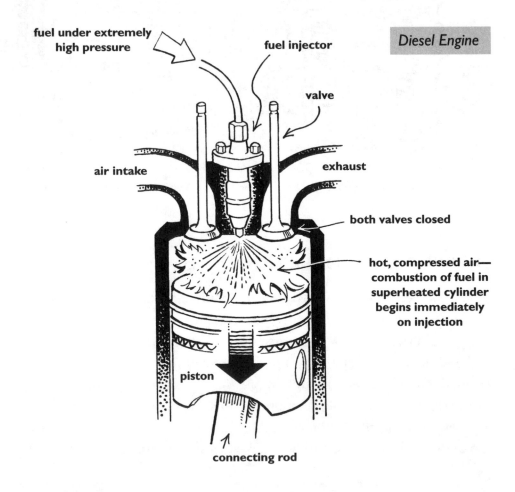

fuel under extremely high pressure

fuel injector

Diesel Engine

valve

air intake

exhaust

both valves closed

hot, compressed air—combustion of fuel in superheated cylinder begins immediately on injection

piston

connecting rod

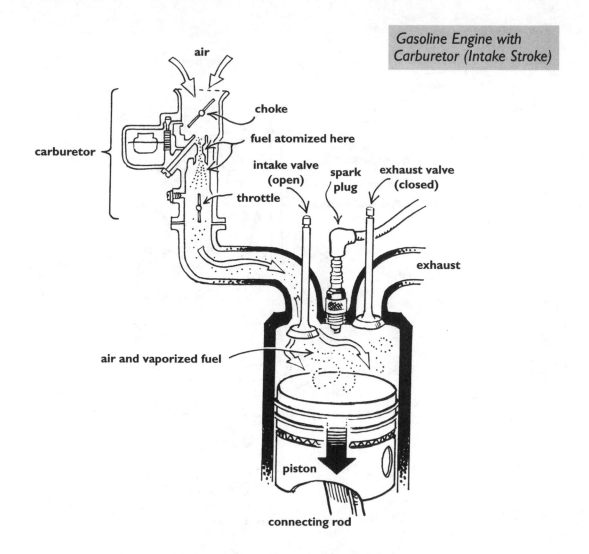

air

choke

fuel atomized here

carburetor

intake valve
(open)

spark
plug

exhaust valve
(closed)

throttle

exhaust

air and vaporized fuel

piston

connecting rod

While some gasoline engines have fuel injectors that spray a mist of gasoline into the air in a manner similar to diesel engines, many others do not. Instead, air and gasoline are blended in a device called a *carburetor* and the blend is compressed by the piston. Such devices are cheaper than fuel injection but perform a similar function. If you have a gasoline engine, check your owner's manual to see if you have fuel injection or a carburetor(s).

As you can see, diesel engines don't have spark plugs and once you get a diesel engine started, it doesn't need electricity to run. This means that

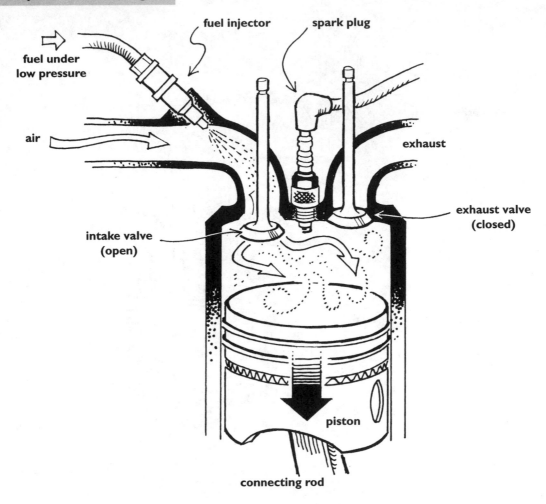

fuel injector

spark plug

**fuel under
low pressure**

air

exhaust

**exhaust valve
(closed)**

**intake valve
(open)**

piston

connecting rod

you can't shut down a diesel engine by turning off the start key—that may disconnect the charging circuit and, for reasons described in chapter 4, possibly ruin the alternator. Instead, diesel engines are shut down by starving them for fuel. We'll say more about that on page 72.

On the bright side, if your electrical system fails, you don't need to worry about your engine quitting. You'll only need electricity after you shut the engine off and try to restart it.* Further, if there's no other load on the engine battery, you can probably restart your engine five, ten, or even more times without ever charging the battery. And if you have a generator, solar panel, or other external charger, you can charge the engine's start battery with them and run indefinitely with a defective alternator.

Advantages and Disadvantages of Diesel Engines

Diesel engines enjoy a number of advantages over gasoline engines, one of which is better fuel economy. That's why they're almost always used in commercial vehicles and machines where fuel economy is important: trucks, buses, construction equipment, and workboats. For pleasure boats, this advantage translates into savings on fuel expense and a greater cruising range. Another advantage, as mentioned above, is that traditional diesel engines only need electrical power for starting, which is very useful if you need to run without power. Diesel engines also avoid the hazards of gasoline (see next page). Finally, because diesel engines don't have spark plugs (and related equipment) or carburetors, they don't require tune-ups. This makes them easier to own and cheaper to maintain, and ultimately, they last longer.

Few things are perfect, however, and diesels also have disadvantages. First, they're more expensive: the basic engine structure must be stronger to withstand the higher compression pressures, and they must be larger than a gasoline engine to deliver the same power because they have lower operating speeds than gasoline engines. They also require sophisticated fuel systems—just the right amount of diesel fuel must be delivered into the cylinder at very high pressure in a particular spray pattern. This pressure misting must be done during the hottest, highest-pressure part of the combustion cycle. To do this, diesel fuel pumps and injectors require a precision that would make a Swiss watchmaker weep. Diesels are also bigger and heavier than gasoline engines of comparable power, and they generate more noise, vibration, smoke, and odor.

Well, this isn't true if you have a large 21st-century powerboat with a power plant that's electronically controlled. Your engines will need electricity for all that modern, solid-state logic. In that case, however, you'll probably have several engines and/or generators, and this advantage wouldn't matter, anyway.

Advantages and Disadvantages of Gasoline Engines

Gasoline engines are cheaper since they don't have to be as beefy as diesels and even if a gasoline engine is fuel injected, the injectors and related equipment are not nearly as complicated as those for a diesel engine. Also, the designs of many marine gasoline engines are adaptations of successful automotive engines, which reduces their development cost. Gasoline engines are smaller and lighter since they don't need the high compression diesels require, and because they run at higher rpms. This means a small boat can use a more powerful engine.

The biggest disadvantage of gasoline engines is that they burn gasoline with all of the hazards mentioned below. Also, they are less fuel efficient, meaning greater fuel costs and a shorter cruising range.

WARNING FOR BOATS WITH GASOLINE ENGINES

Gasoline engines work because gasoline is very volatile (read: flammable) and because it has a low combustion temperature (read: flammable). *This means gasoline is very dangerous!* To add anxiety, gasoline fumes can ignite all by themselves. Any sort of spark near gasoline fumes—even dropping a screwdriver on metal—can ignite them and cause a fire or explosion. These dangers are exacerbated on boats because gasoline fumes are heavier than air and will sink to the lowest part of the bilge. Therefore, if you have a gasoline engine, you must be *very, very careful* with both the fuel and its fumes. Before starting the engine, always use a *blower*, or bilge fan, to disperse any fumes. Above all, use your nose: we all know what gasoline fumes smell like, so if you smell them, *don't start the engine!*

The manufacturer of your boat should provide detailed safety procedures for fueling your boat and starting your engine(s): *these are important!* You and anyone who may ever start your boat's engines must understand and be able to follow those instructions. Never start someone else's gasoline-powered boat unless you know the correct starting procedure since it may differ from how you start your engine.

So What's the Bottom Line?

Well, in truth, we probably will do a careful analysis of all these factors but then buy the engine that happens to come with the boat we fall in love with. But, given a choice, most cruising boaters choose a diesel. Cost is a factor, though, and your budget will probably determine whether you choose a gasoline- or diesel-powered boat.

FUEL DOCK DOS & DON'TS

Never put the wrong fuel in your boat. Diesel engines run *only* on diesel and gasoline engines run *only* on gasoline. *Never* pump the wrong fuel into your boat; if you do, you'll have to pump it out of your tanks before you start the engine. This is a mess and an environmental hazard. Remember, the best way to solve a problem is not to have it.

Not pumping the wrong fuel may seem obvious, but it happens all the time. The attendant doesn't know what kind of fuel you need, so make sure you tell him or her. Better yet, always fuel your boat yourself—that's what I do, and I always follow the hose with my eyes from the nozzle all the way back to the pump and verify that the pump is labeled with the type of fuel I need (in my case, diesel). And before I put the nozzle into the fuel deck fill, I fix the attendant with one of my best steely-eyed looks and ask, "This is diesel, right??," and wait for an affirmative response before I proceed.

Make sure you put the fuel into the fuel tank and not into water tanks or waste tanks. This also may seem silly to say, but again, it happens all the time.

Make sure your deck fills are clearly labeled with the name of what should go in them: "water," "fuel," and "waste." Most well-designed boats physically separate the fuel intakes from the water-tank intakes and waste-tank drain. If this isn't the case on your boat, paint them different colors or do something else to clearly indicate which is which. Don't scoff at this simple task: just imagine yourself (at the dark end of the dock) filling the fuel tank at 11:30 at night after a long weekend on the water; rain is pouring over your hat, your glasses are fogged over, and your spouse is asking you what you did with the car keys. Now, can you be absolutely sure you're filling the fuel tank and not the water tank? Well-labeled deck fills will help!

CLEANING UP THE CAMPFIRE

So far we've learned about the fire-starting process, but what about the exhaust-expelling process? You'll recall that the piston slides up the cylinder to compress the air, a fire is started, and the piston is pushed down by the high pressures created by the fire. At this point, the cylinder is full of waste gas that must be expelled before the cylinder can fire again. To do this, the *exhaust valve* is opened in the cylinder to create a hole that leads to the *exhaust manifold* (a pipe assembly that collects gases from all the cylinders and directs them out the exhaust hose). As the piston returns to the top of the cylinder, it pushes the waste products out of the cylinder through the exhaust valve.

Continuing the process, the exhaust valve is closed, the intake valve is opened, and the piston is pulled back to the bottom of the cylinder. As it's pulled back, it draws fresh air into the cylinder. In a gas engine, a mist of air and fuel is pulled into the cylinder as well. In a diesel engine, no fuel is added until the air has been compressed in the next stroke.

As illustrated previously (see pages 52, 53, and 54), the fuel mixture enters the cylinder either via the injector (fuel injection) or via an intake valve (carburetor), the spark plug (gasoline only) ignites the fuel, and the exhaust valves open to allow the residue to be expelled. Note that engine valves don't look like valves on seacocks or water hoses, but more like large golf tees. The tapered tees slide down and up to plug and unplug the intake and exhaust ports. Since the piston and cylinder go through four phases or strokes—*compression* (up), *power* (down), *exhaust* (up), and *intake* (down)—such engines are known as *four-stroke* or *four-cycle engines*.

There is another engine type, the *two-stroke engine*, in which the cylinder fires every time the piston comes to the top. Small outboard engines are usually two-stroke. Such engines are always powered by gasoline, and require that you mix oil with the gas before putting it into the tank. We won't say more about them in this book.

By now you're beginning to see that there's a little symphony going on inside your engine: The pistons slide up and down, and, at just the right time, the injector squirts mist into the cylinder. On a gas engine, the spark plug fires at just the right moment. Gases in the cylinder ignite and the piston is pushed down. As the piston comes back up, the exhaust valves open and the exhaust is expelled. Air is then drawn back into the cylinder. And, in most cases, the action of three or four (or six or eight or more) cylinders must be coordinated. Unlike a symphony, however, engines don't have a conductor—the whole process is coordinated by chains and belts that are connected to the crankshaft and other gadgetry. With any luck, you should never have to deal with any of this coordinating equipment.

THE DOWNSIDE: HEAT AND FRICTION

The problem with generating power from fires is that only a fraction of the fire's energy goes into propelling your boat. Depending on the efficiency of your engine, something like 20 percent of the energy is used for propulsion. The rest is turned into heat, and that heat is conducted to the pistons, cylinder walls, crankshaft, and other engine elements. If something isn't done to cool the engine, it will eventually melt, or become so hot it starts a fire in your boat. Additionally, as the pistons move up and down the cylinder, they generate friction. Rub your hands together quickly and you'll see that friction, too, generates heat. Friction also causes wear and reduces the life of engine parts. So, the designers of your engine had to do something to combat both heat and friction. We'll consider heat first.

Cooling Your Engine

Like your car engine, your boat engine is cooled with water. Little channels, called *water jackets*, surround the walls of the cylinders and other parts of your engine, and freshwater in a closed circuit is pumped through those channels. This engine cooling water absorbs the heat in your engine, becoming quite hot itself. For this system to work, that water must be cooled.

In your car, hot engine water is cooled by passing it through a radiator. The radiator is located in the front of your car so that air flows over it as you drive. The radiator is a collection of long thin tubes with cooling fins arranged so that air can flow through gaps in the winding. Air carries heat away from the water as it passes through the gaps and over the thin tubes. If you're driving slowly, a fan pulls air through the radiator to maintain air flow.

In a boat, there's no place for a radiator, so another solution is needed. Stand in your cockpit and look around for a place to dump a lot of heat; you'll soon see that the water on which you're floating is ideal. Obviously, the colder the water the better the heat transfer, but even tropical waters are cooler than your engine. Instead of a radiator, your boat engine has a *heat exchanger*. Like a radiator, a heat exchanger has tubes through which the engine cooling water flows in a closed circuit. Seawater is pumped through to

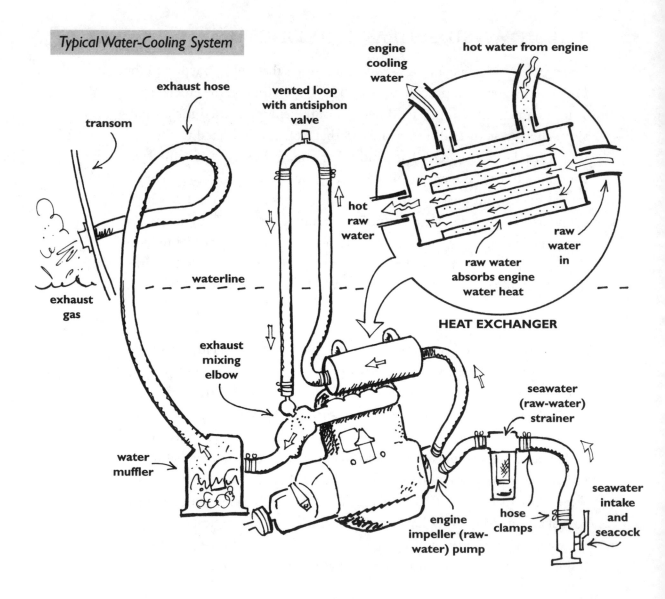

Typical Water-Cooling System

transom

exhaust hose

vented loop with antisiphon valve

engine cooling water

hot water from engine

hot raw water

exhaust gas

waterline

raw water absorbs engine water heat

raw water in

HEAT EXCHANGER

exhaust mixing elbow

seawater (raw-water) strainer

water muffler

engine impeller (raw-water) pump

hose clamps

seawater intake and seacock

the heat exchanger and over the tubes that contain the hot engine water to carry heat away from the engine water and from the engine.

Once the seawater has passed through the heat exchanger, it has one more role to play. When we were discussing the burning of gas in the cylinders, we left the exhaust gases in limbo—pushed out of the cylinder through the exhaust valves and collected into the exhaust manifold. To finish the process, the exhaust gases are then combined with the seawater that exits the heat exchanger. The combined gas and water is pushed through a water muffler to reduce noise, and then out of the boat through the exhaust hose.

Engine Cooling Water vs. Seawater

It's important to emphasize that two different kinds of water are used in your boat's engine: *engine cooling water* and *seawater*, or as the latter is sometimes called, *raw water*. Engine cooling water, which is always freshwater, flows through the water jackets around the engine, then passes through tubes in the heat exchanger where it's cooled by the seawater, and then flows back into the engine, all in a closed circuit. Depending on your boat, it may also flow through a hot water heater for your boat's freshwater system (see chapter 5). None of the engine water is used up in this process. The engine cooling water and the seawater pass by each other in the tubes in the heat exchanger, but they never mix.

Normally, antifreeze is added to engine cooling water because water expands when it freezes, and the water jackets in your engine would be severely damaged if that water ever froze. Antifreeze solutions also contain rust inhibitors, so it's a good idea to add antifreeze to the engine cooling water even in tropical climates.

When your engine is hot, the engine cooling water is under pressure. Therefore, *never attempt to remove the engine-water fill cap from a hot engine!*—you could be sprayed with scalding water. Wait until the engine is cool to the touch before removing the fill cap.

Seawater, unlike the engine cooling water, passes through the heat exchanger just once. A pump, called an *impeller pump*, sucks seawater into the through-hull and then through a seawater strainer. The water then passes through the impeller pump and is pushed through the heat exchanger to a vented loop and a muffler, and then out the exhaust through-hull (see illustration on page 60). Seawater obviously contains no antifreeze or anything similar. It may, however, contain foreign substances like seaweed, twigs, cigarette butts, fishing line, animal parts, or plastic bags; hence the need for the seawater strainer. This is another good reason, by the way, to encourage everyone aboard your boat not to throw trash into the water—the trash you suck in may be your own!

The *impeller* of an impeller pump is a small wheel to which flexible paddles are connected, like those on a paddle wheel (see page 80). As the pump turns, the paddles are compressed as they rub against the inside of the pump, with the water acting as a lubricant. If the impeller is ever run without water, it can be severely damaged. If your engine intake through-hull is clogged, you must *immediately* shut down your engine. Also, whenever you start your engine, be sure you've remembered to open the engine intake seacock! Listen and look for the splashing of water out the exhaust every time you start your engine; if you don't hear and see the splash, shut the engine down.

It's also possible to have too much water. Any time your engine is difficult to start—you run the starter motor more than 5 to 10 seconds—you should shut the engine intake seawater seacock. Cranking the engine with the starter motor pulls seawater in, but if the engine doesn't start, the seawater won't be expelled. If you crank the engine repeatedly, seawater builds up in the muffler and will eventually backfill into the engine, with disastrous effects. Be especially wary of this possibility on sailboats where the muffler may be mounted very low in the boat and the exhaust hose led high to exit well above the waterline. In normal operation, you should never need to close the seacock when starting your engine; do it only when you have a problem getting the engine to start.

Reducing Friction

Friction is the bane of all engines: it creates heat, causes wear on parts, and reduces engine efficiency. Because there are so many moving parts in an engine, friction cannot be eliminated, so engine designers try to reduce friction by lubricating moving parts with oil.

Without getting too detailed, the bottom of your engine is enclosed with a sheet of metal bent into a panlike shape called the *engine pan*. This pan forms a reservoir of oil that lubricates the sides of the cylinders, the crankshaft, the bearings, and other engine parts. An *oil pump* pumps oil from the reservoir under pressure through channels to these parts of your engine. It also sends oil through an *oil filter*, a mesh that traps particles of dirt in the oil.

Proper oil pressure is critical to engine operation and longevity. The manufacturer of your engine put an oil pressure gauge on the control panel to your engine that measures the oil pump output pressure. Read your engine operation manual and determine the acceptable range of oil pressure for your engine. If the oil pressure ever drops below the minimum, *stop your engine immediately*—loss of oil pressure can cause sudden, major (and expensive) engine damage.

If the oil becomes dirty, friction will increase, so it's critical to keep your oil clean by regularly changing both it and the oil filter. Also, do everything you can to keep dirt out of your engine. Most engine oils contain detergents to help clean your engine. Those specially formulated for diesel engines contain more detergent than those for gasoline engines, but unlike fuel, if you have to, you can use either type of oil in either type of engine.

You can also buy oil that contains no detergents. Such oil is used for specialty applications like a high-pressure pump for a watermaker. In a pinch, you can use nondetergent oil in place of detergent oil, but this is not recommended. *You can never substitute detergent oil for nondetergent oil.* You'll never get the detergents out of whatever gizmo you put it into. To be safe, for any engine or piece of equipment, use only the type of oil recommended by the manufacturer.

Oil comes in different, standardized weights. Typical weights are 10, 20, 30, and 40. Ten-weight (10W) oil is thin and is intended for use in very cold climates, like the north slope of Alaska. Forty-weight (40W) oil is much thicker and is intended for use in tropical waters. You can buy oil that changes its consistency less as its temperature changes. An example is 10W30 oil—the consistency changes from 10- to 30-weight as the temperature increases.

According to the engine manufacturer Yanmar, mixing oil weights reduces lubricating capability, so avoid mixing them if possible. However, if you have 30W oil in your engine and you need to add some, but all you have is 40W, then add it. Certainly the mixture has more lubricating properties than no oil at all! Also, as you sail into warmer (or colder) climates, you might want to change all of the oil to a different weight. Do that when you change your oil and filter.

MAINTENANCE

Congratulations! You've made it through a long section on how engines work. As a typical boatowner, there isn't anything you'll need to do to maintain the components we have talked about so far. Every 600 hours or so (depending on your engine), the valves will need to be adjusted, but unless you are very mechanically adept, this is a job you should leave for a professional—a mistake on valve adjustment is costly. Also, on a fuel-injected engine, every several thousand hours the injectors will need to be replaced, but again, that's a job for a professional.

On a gas engine, the carburetor may need to be serviced from time to time, but this is also a job for a professional. See your owner's manual for information. Also, the spark plugs will periodically need to be replaced, and that is a task you might want to take on. Hire a mechanic to do it the first time, and watch. Then you can decide whether you want to do it yourself after that.

In this section, we'll describe tasks that you can do yourself. As you can see in the following table, many tasks need to be done after so many engine hours. To track engine hours, almost every boat engine has an hour meter that runs whenever the engine switch is on. You should have a meter for each engine. Whenever you perform a maintenance task, record the date and engine hours in your maintenance log as mentioned in chapter 1.

If your engine(s) doesn't have an hour meter, or if that meter isn't working, you'll need to record the number of engine hours in your ship's log.

Engine Maintenance Tasks

TASK	FREQUENCY
Check oil level; add oil if necessary. Check to be sure oil has no gooey white substance; change if necessary.	Before starting engine.
Check (listen and look) for presence of water in exhaust as it exits through-hull. If you don't hear/see it, shut off engine.	When starting engine, and periodically when engine is running.
Check and clean seawater strainer.	Before starting engine first time each day.
Check engine cooling water level. Add distilled water as necessary.	Once a week; more frequently if leak is suspected.
Check vented loop antisiphon valve.	Once a month.
Add antibacterial substance to fuel.	When adding fuel as directed on additive bottle.
Change oil and filter.	As recommended by engine manufacturer, or about every 100 hours.
Change fuel filters.	As recommended by engine manufacturer, or about every 150 hours.
Replace heat exchanger zinc.	Depends on boat and environment, or between once a month and once every two years.
Adjust valves.	As recommended by engine manufacturer, or about every 600 hours.
Check tightness of hose clamps and engine hoses for wear. Replace as necessary.	Once a year.
Check seawater through-hull and seacock, and exhaust through-hull and seacock. Replace as necessary.	During haulout; close and inspect once a month.
Replace spark plugs (gasoline only).	As recommended by engine manufacturer, or about every two years.
Replace impeller in impeller pump.	As needed, or once every 2,000 hours.

continued page 66

Engine Maintenance Tasks (continued)	
TASK	FREQUENCY
Replace injectors.	As recommended by engine manufacturer, or about every 2,000 to 4,000 hours.
Change engine cooling water and antifreeze.	When you buy boat and then every two years.

Make an entry each time you use your boat or run your engine(s). You can then use that log to keep a running total of engine hours.

We can divide engine maintenance tasks into three categories: fuel, lubrication, and cooling.

MAINTAINING YOUR FUEL SYSTEM

The single most important thing you can do to keep your engine in great shape is to keep your fuel clean. On a diesel engine, the gap in the injectors through which the fuel passes may be less than 0.003 inch in width. This means that the tiniest particle of dust or grime or bacterial growth can become a problem.

Fuel cleanliness starts at the fuel dock. Buy fuel only from docks that are known to keep their fuel clean. Ask around among fishermen or other boaters if you are unsure about a particular fuel dock. Generally, the best bets are docks that service fishing or other commercial boats and sell a lot of fuel.

Before you open the fuel deck fill, clean the deck area surrounding it. Avoid fueling if the wind is blowing dust or dirt into the air. If it's raining, place a tarp or other protection over the deck fill to keep water from entering the tanks as you fuel. Once you've finished, immediately close the deck fill valve—make sure it seals correctly.

Fuel docks can be beehives of activity. Once you're tied up at the fuel dock, ignore the commotion and concentrate on the task at hand. Make sure you're filling the right tanks with the proper fuel. Take the time to observe all fuel handling and engine starting precautions at the fuel dock: this is doubly important if you have a gasoline engine.

Try to keep your tanks full, especially if you're going to leave your boat unused in cold weather when water can condense on the inside of your tank and drip into your fuel. If the tank is full, there's no room for the condensation to form. Many people think it's a good idea to pour a bacteria-retarding additive into your fuel. This is especially important in tropical climates, but many boaters use additives even in colder climates. Read the instructions on the product to determine the correct amount to add.

In the typical layout for fuel lines in a fuel-injected boat (which includes any boat with a diesel engine), a fuel line runs from the tank to an independent filter like that shown in the illustration on page 69. If your engine is above the tanks, there will likely be a fuel lift pump that pushes or pulls fuel through this filter. If your tanks are above your engine, no such auxiliary pump will be necessary. From there, the fuel line goes to the engine's fuel pump and then to a second filter also mounted on the engine. Fuel passes to the injector pump and injectors and then unused fuel is returned back to the tank. There may be shutoff valves on both the feed and return fuel lines.

Fuel Filters

Most boats have two or more fuel filters per engine. These filters need to be changed periodically. I have a Yanmar diesel engine, and I change my filters every 100 to 150 engine hours. Check the documentation for your engine for the manufacturer's recommendation. If you've taken on dirty fuel, or if dirt has somehow entered your fuel lines, you must change the filters immediately. Hire a mechanic to change your filters the first time. Take notes or even better, film the process with a video camera. Changing the filters is easy—it's the elimination of the air that you introduce into the lines that can be hard (see page 70).

In general, if your engine is running well and suddenly quits or runs in a ragged fashion, a dirty fuel filter should be your first suspect. The most common cause of a sudden engine problem, especially for diesels, is a clogged filter. This is even more likely if you have been out in rough water for the first time. Many older boats have accumulated dirt in the bottom of their fuel tanks. Bouncing around in rough water stirs up the dirt, which then enters the fuel lines and clogs the fuel filter. If this happens, change the filters. Be prepared to change them several times if a lot of dirt has entered the fuel lines. You should always travel with at least three sets of spare fuel filters. If this happens over and over, get professional help to clean your fuel tanks and/or take other corrective action.

The first fuel filter is usually independent of the engine and is mounted separately from it. Such a fuel filter acts as both a filter and a device for separating water out of the fuel. Because of the popularity of the Racor brand, these filters are sometimes called Racor-type filters. For some of these filters, the filter element is threaded onto the holding bracket and a plastic see-through bowl is then threaded onto the filter element as shown in the illustration. Because you thread them on, these are called *spin-on filters*. Another version of the Racor-type filter places the filter inside a canister. For these, remove the canister top and then take out the filter. There will be a gasket and an O-ring to replace as well. The bowl traps any water that may have entered with the fuel. Because water is heavier than diesel fuel, if this happens you'll see water in the bottom of the bowl with a clean line separating it from the diesel fuel.

If your fuel tanks are higher than your fuel filter, when you open the filter canister, fuel will start pouring out. Somewhere between the tank and the filter there is a shutoff valve; turn it off before you open the canister. This type of fuel filter element comes in three porosities, each a different color. You should use the type recommended by the boat's manufacturer. If you don't know, use the type that's already on your boat; if in doubt, use the finest porosity (brown for Racor filters). If your engine can't tolerate that porosity (it runs rough and sounds as if fuel isn't getting to it), try a filter of the next coarser porosity.

When you change the filter, make sure there's no water in the filter canister. Water is heavier than fuel and, if present, will appear as a separate layer of liquid on the bottom. If there is water in the canister, drain it

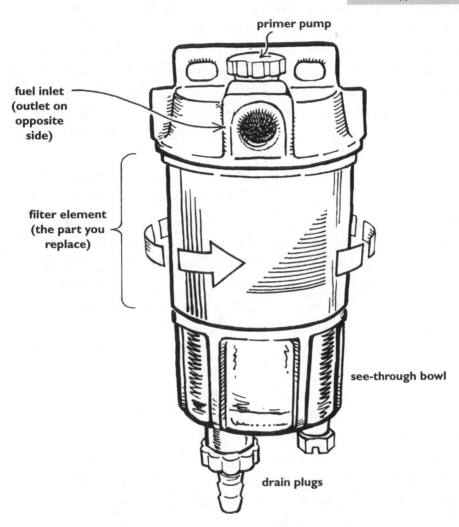

primer pump

fuel inlet
(outlet on
opposite
side)

filter element
(the part you
replace)

see-through bowl

drain plugs

through the plug in the button of the canister. (You should probably hire a mechanic to find out how the water got there in the first place.) Also clean any dirt out of the canister, if necessary.

The second fuel filter is usually mounted on the engine. Check the documentation of your engine to find the type and part number of the fuel filter you need. Generally, engine-mounted fuel filters screw into place. Twist the filter counterclockwise with a filter wrench (see illustration on page 77) to remove it. You can prevent a mess if you place a small plastic bag over (or a small plastic container under) the filter before you unscrew it to catch any fuel that slops down the side of the filter.

When you put the new filter on, follow the instructions that came with it. If there are none (or you've mislaid them), moisten the rubber gasket on the top of the filter with a small amount of fuel and then screw it on hand-tight. After you start the engine, check for leaks and tighten a bit more with the filter wrench, if necessary. It doesn't take much to tighten a filter so don't overdo it.

When you change fuel filters, air will enter the fuel lines. This is no problem for engines with carburetors, but for fuel-injected engines, you must remove (*bleed*) the air out of the lines before starting your engine. While you might be able to start your engine with air in the lines, as soon as the air reaches the injectors, the engine will quit. Engines vary in how difficult and elaborate the bleeding procedure is; with some self-bleeding engines, you just turn the start key halfway, wait a minute or two, and then start the engine. With others, you pump a small hand-operated pump for a few minutes, and there are some where you have to open cocks in the fuel lines, run the fuel pump in some fashion, utter various magic phrases, shake your left hand in a northerly direction, and make humble of-ferings and libations to the spirits of the engine world.* Again, the first time, hire a mechanic and watch carefully.

After you've changed the filters, open any closed fuel shutoff valves, start the engine, and check for leaks. Tighten the filter as necessary, but again, do not overtighten. If you have a leak, it's more likely a gasket didn't seat cor-rectly than the filter is undertightened.

If you have a gasoline engine, there may be additional fuel screens that act as filters. In some cases, there's a fuel screen rather than a filter on the engine. In this case, the screen only needs to be cleaned (unless the screen is torn, it shouldn't need to be replaced).

*Remember, if the engine won't start right away, close the seawater intake! (And don't forget to open it once the engine starts!)

Changing Injectors and Spark Plugs

Every 2,000 to 4,000 hours (that's a lot of boating!), diesel fuel injectors will need to be replaced. This is not a job for an amateur—hire a professional. However, if the injectors aren't too worn, you can save money by having them tested and rebuilt rather than replacing them with new ones.

If you have a gasoline engine, every 100 hours or so you will need to change spark plugs. Hire a professional to do it the first time and watch. After that, you may want to do the job yourself.

If you ever run out of fuel, you'll introduce air into your fuel lines. So after you add more fuel to the fuel tanks, if you have fuel injection, you may need to bleed your fuel lines. For this reason alone, you should learn how to do it. Also, if you ran out of fuel, there's a chance that your fuel pump sucked gunk or dirt off the bottom of your fuel tank, so check your fuel filters carefully and change them if needed.

Starting and Stopping Your Engine

The most important thing you can do to prolong your engine's longevity is to start it at the lowest possible rpm and let it run for 3 to 5 minutes before increasing them. Similarly, whenever you shut your engine off, run it at low rpm for a few minutes before stopping it. This ensures that the cooling fluids and oil are pumped through your engine as it's warming up and cooling down.

Irv Prichard, an experienced mechanic in Seattle, told me that he sees the worst engine problems on boats berthed in easy-access slips—the owners just start their engines and drive off. At the end of the day, they pull their boats into their slips at high speed, turn the hot engines off, and walk away. Damage results on both ends of the trip.

On the other hand, boats located in marinas where lots of slow engine work is required to get out of or into a slip, have far fewer problems because their engines are run at slow speeds at the start and end of the trip. Keep this in mind, too, when you pull into a fuel dock. If you've been running your engine hard, let it cool off before you shut it down at the dock.

As mentioned earlier, you can't shut down a diesel engine by turning off the start key because diesels don't need electricity to run. Instead, diesels are stopped by temporarily closing off the fuel supply either mechanically or electrically. The mechanical system consists of a cable that runs from the fuel line on the engine into the boat's cockpit. When you pull the cable handle, the fuel line is closed and the engine stops. After shutting down the engine, push the handle back to the original position or the engine won't start. (I once ruined an entire weekend trying to find a problem in my fuel line. On Monday I gave up and spent $273.84 to have one of Seattle's finest mechanics come to my boat, which was anchored out, to show me that the stop cable handle was caught in the out position in the zipper of the binnacle cover. Boy, did I feel like an idiot!)

If the stop cable breaks and you innocently pull the handle, the cable will come all the way out into your cockpit. You'll be holding a long greasy wire and your engine will continue to chug along. Instead of sitting in your cockpit waiting to run out of fuel, go down to your engine, find where the cable connects to the shutoff valve in the fuel line, manually pull the shutoff closed, and your engine will stop.

Some boats use an electrical circuit to energize a solenoid that shuts off the fuel supply. Such boats have a large, usually red, stop button. Push it, and the solenoid closes and temporarily closes the fuel line. If this system ever fails, just find the solenoid on the engine and push or pull the shutoff valve. If you cannot locate this device, have your mechanic show you where it is.

Of course, the time to be looking for all of these items is not when you're holding the greasy wire in your hand and your engine is chugging along. So, one of these days when you're visiting Dulcinea, take some time just to look at the engine. Turn the engine off and poke around to identify all the parts you can. See if you can locate the fuel filters and trace the run of the fuel hoses around from the tank, possibly through a lift pump, through the filters, to the injectors, and back to the tank.

At the same time, find the fuel shutoff mechanism, whether a mechanically activated cable or an electronic solenoid. Also locate the oil filter, dipstick, and any oil drain plugs that you may be able to use to drain your oil (see next section). Also find all the components in the seawater system. Trace the flow of raw water from the raw-water seacock, through the seawater strainer, to the impeller pump, over the antisiphon loop, and back to the mixing elbow. You may have trouble finding all of these components; if so, ask your mechanic for help the next time he or she is aboard Dulcinea. Your mechanic will also be able to point out any peculiarities in your engine and its installation.

CHECKING AND CHANGING ENGINE OIL

Check your oil every time before you start your engine: pull out the dipstick and check that the oil level is between the two marks etched on the dipstick—you want neither too much nor too little. If you need oil, add some, but don't try to bring the oil all the way up to the Full mark. If you do, you'll probably add too much oil, which you'll then have to drain out. This is a hassle, but it must be done. Too much oil can cause gaskets and other seals to fail, as well as other more dangerous problems. Try to keep the oil level up around two-thirds of the distance between the two marks on the dipstick.

While the dipstick is out, check for the presence of a soft, white goo on the dipstick, which indicates that water has somehow entered your engine. This isn't common, but it's *very* serious: Don't start the engine; that way, you'll avoid pumping the water through your engine, and possibly save a huge repair job. If you can, contact a mechanic immediately—the sooner you get the water out, the better. If you can't contact a mechanic, immediately change your oil. Don't start your engine to warm the oil, but drain as much of the cold oil out as you can. Add more oil, run the engine a minute or two, and then drain that oil. Do this three or four times until you no longer see the white goo. If the goo keeps appearing, water is leaking into your engine, and you must somehow get the boat to a qualified mechanic—but without running the engine.

Changing Your Oil

Every 100 hours of engine time or every six months*—whichever comes first—you should change your engine oil and oil filter since harmful acids build up over time. Warm the oil before you start to drain it. You can do this by taking your boat out for a short spin around the harbor. For smaller boats, you can also run your engine in gear at the dock (but first check the docklines to be certain your boat is securely tied). To properly warm the engine, put the boat in gear. Depending on how you're tied in your slip, put the boat into forward or reverse, and run the engine just above idle speed. Watch carefully to make certain your docklines are secure and have someone stand by to take the engine out of gear, if necessary. Run the engine this way for 5 minutes or so, and then feel the side of the oil filter. When the filter is warm to touch, take the boat out of gear and turn off the engine. Put on your grubby clothes and cover any upholstery and other vulnerable interior surfaces that could be splashed with oil.

If you're lucky, you'll have plenty of space in your engine room and you'll be able to drain the oil out of a drain plug in the bottom of your engine into a large pan. More likely, though, there's hardly any room, and you'll have to pump it out via the oil dipstick tube. In this case, you can buy a 12-volt oil-change pump from your local chandlery before you start. (You can pump the oil out by hand, but this is slow and messy, and you probably won't get all of the oil out.) Electric pumps aren't very expensive, and they're worth every penny.

Another option is to buy an *oil extractor*, which is an airtight container with a manual pump. Put the intake hose of the extractor down your oil dipstick tube, then pump the handle on the extractor several times. The pumping action creates a partial vacuum in the container, and air pressure forces the engine oil into the container. When you're done, just empty the container into the oil disposal tank.

*This is a general rule. To be safe, check the owner's manual for your engine to ensure that a more frequent change is not required.

DON'T BE FUELISH

Gasoline, diesel fuel, and lubricating oil are all flammable and environmentally hazardous. When working with them, take extra time and avoid spillage into the bilge. Put rags or plastic bags or containers under your work area. When you're done, properly dispose of rags and fluids. Don't just put them into the marina trash cans. Ask at your marina office about facilities and policies for disposing of fuel and oil. If your marina does not have proper facilities, ask them where to go with your old fuel and oil. You can also call your city's refuse and recycling department to find the location of city facilities. If you can't find the information you need, ask at the fire department.

Remember that oil- and fuel-soaked rags are a fire hazard. Above all, don't stuff them into a bag and shove them into one of Dulcinea's back corners. It is possible for such rags to sponta-neously ignite when confined this way. Again, talk to the marina, the city, or the fire department to find out how to dispose of these materials.

Changing Oil Filters and Adding Oil

To remove the oil filter, you'll need a filter wrench like the one shown on page 77. Unfortunately, you'll probably need two filter wrenches, a large one for the oil filter and a smaller one for your fuel filters. Place a small plastic container under the filter, if possible, or put a small plastic bag around the filter. If the filter is mounted on its side or at an angle, use a filter wrench to loosen the filter a quarter turn and let oil drip into the container or bag for a few minutes. Then remove the filter. If the filter is mounted straight up and down, carefully unscrew it and try to get any oil that drips over the edges to fall into the plastic container. Remove both the plastic container and the filter and place them in a plastic bag for proper disposal.

Install the new filter, following the directions provided. If there are no directions, rub a small amount of clean oil on the gasket on the top of the filter and screw it on hand-tight. Later, *after you have added oil*, run the engine, and if the filter leaks, turn it no more than a quarter turn with the filter wrench. Do not overtighten the oil filter as this will make the gasket leak.

Now, open the oil filler cap (*do not* confuse this cap with the engine water cap). Be very careful not to get any dirt into this hole; the interior of your engine should be as clean as possible. Use a small funnel to add the oil and add a little less oil than you removed. Put the filler cap back on and start the engine. Run it at the lowest possible rpm for a minute or two and then check the oil level. Add more oil if necessary, but do not overfill.

Clean up the mess and you're done! Be sure to properly dispose of your

Oil and Fuel Filter Wrenches

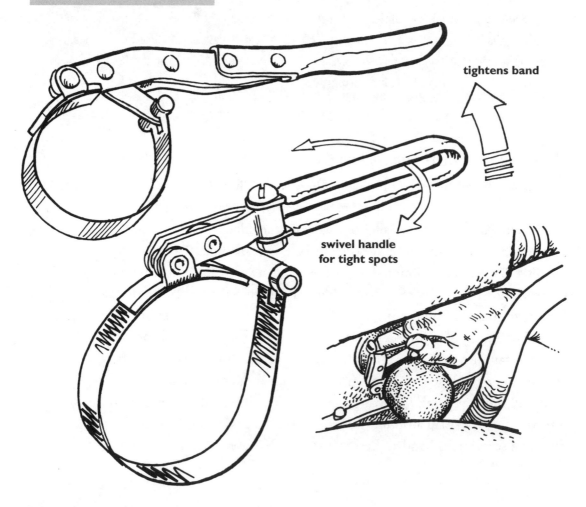

tightens band

swivel handle
for tight spots

waste. You can usually return used oil to the place where you bought the new oil.

THE ENGINE WATER SYSTEM

Once every two or three times you run your engine, check the fluid level to be certain that you're not losing water. If your engine has an overflow container, check the level against the low and high marks on that container. As with engine oil, there's no reason to keep the level at the high mark; just be sure that the level is between the two marks. When your engine is hot, the water level will be higher than when it's cold, so check the water level when the engine is cold. If the water level is low, add clean freshwater—distilled water is best.

If you find that you frequently have to add engine water, you may have a leak. Two common locations for water leaks are the water pump and the heat exchanger. The water pump is mounted on the front of the engine and is driven by a fan belt (usually called a *V-belt* on boats since there is no fan). Check around the front of the engine for stains that indicate water is dripping down the front of the engine. If you see evidence of leaks, it's likely someone overtightened the V-belt, and you'll need to call a mechanic to replace the water pump.

If you're losing engine water, but you don't see any stains on the front of your engine, then the leak is probably in your heat exchanger. Run your engine and watch the exhaust carefully—an unusual sheen on the water from your exhaust indicates such a leak. Or call a mechanic who will check for leaks in the heat exchanger with a pressure gauge. If it's leaking, it will have to be replaced.

Your heat exchanger may have a zinc that periodically needs to be replaced to prevent corrosion. Not all engines have a zinc, however, so check your owner's manual and/or ask a mechanic before you drive yourself crazy trying to find it. There is no hard-and-fast rule for how frequently this zinc needs to be replaced. If you keep your boat in freshwater, you'll almost never have to do it, but if your boat is in salt water, you may have to do it monthly, especially in the tropics.

Leakage problems are rare, however, and usually the only maintenance tasks you'll need to take care of are changing the water and the antifreeze. You should do this when you buy your boat and once every two years or so. Removing the fluid, properly disposing of it, determining the right amount of antifreeze, and bleeding the air out are a bit of a hassle and since you won't do it very often, I recommend hiring a mechanic.

The Seawater System

You should check and clean the seawater strainer frequently, some even say once each day you run your engine. To do this, close the seacock and unscrew the top of the seawater strainer as shown in the illustration on page 79. There is a special wrench, called a *spanner wrench*, for this job that has two pins that fit into the holed ears of the top of the strainer. If you can't find this wrench on your boat, ask for one at a chandlery.

Lift the strainer out and remove any debris. Also, look in the bottom of the strainer case and clean it out if necessary. There's a drain in the bottom of the case you can use if you need to. Replace the strainer basket and be certain that it seats properly in the groove in the bottom of the strainer case. You'll probably have to fuss with it a bit to make it drop down all the way. Replace the top and tighten; hand-tight should be good enough.

Reopen the seacock, check your engine oil, and then start your engine. Again, *every time you start your engine*, listen to and look at the exhaust. You should hear and see splashes of water exiting the exhaust fitting. If you don't, stop the engine and make sure the seacock is open. If it is, look for blockage in the seawater lines somewhere. (See the sidebar on page 36.)

If there's no water exiting your exhaust and no blockage in the sea-water lines, then probably your impeller pump has worn out or is damaged. You can repair the pump by replacing the rubber wheel (the impeller) inside it. The basic task is not difficult, but usually the impeller pump is located in a position that requires you to stand on your head to get to it. Because of this, you'll probably have to work by feel, and the task can be very frustrating if you haven't done it before. Therefore, especially the first time, hire a mechanic and watch. Make a sketch, and note the wrench types and sizes for the bolts and screws involved.

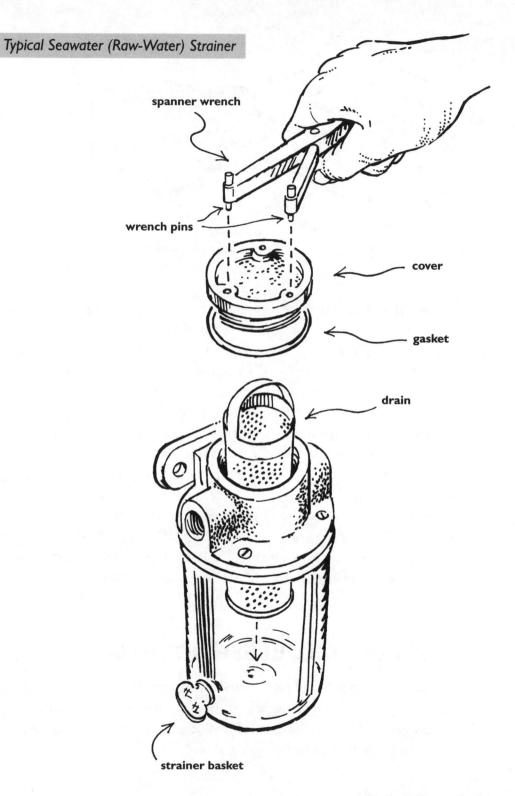

Typical Seawater (Raw-Water) Strainer

spanner wrench

wrench pins

cover

gasket

drain

strainer basket

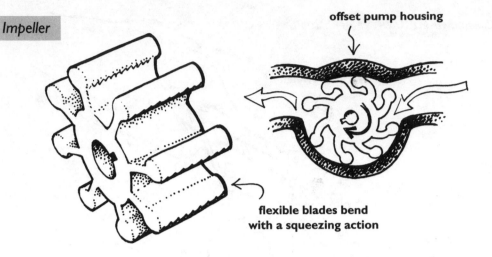

Impeller

offset pump housing

flexible blades bend
with a squeezing action

Even if you have no intention of ever replacing the impeller yourself, you should always carry spares. You can find a skilled mechanic in Klemtu, British Columbia, but you'll wait days for the proper impeller part to be delivered. They're not expensive, so buy one or two and keep them with your spare parts. When you buy it, ask if you also need an O-ring or gasket for it. (See appendix 1 for more on spare parts.)

You should change the impeller pump if you buy a used boat, and once every 2,000 engine hours or so. Additionally, the impeller can be ruined by running it dry, and by debris that gets past the seawater strainer. If this happens, you'll have to replace it, so check the seawater strainer frequently.

There's little downstream of the impeller pump that you need to worry about. Unlike the one on your car, your boat's exhaust muffler seldom wears out. Check the hose clamps on all the hoses in this system periodically. Under normal conditions, these hoses won't wear out.

ENGINE TROUBLESHOOTING

The table on pages 81 and 82 lists basic symptoms and remedies for engine problems. The goal here is to help you avoid a maintenance call for a simple problem. The owner's manual for your engine will have a similar, possibly more detailed, table. Consult it as well.

The left-hand column of this table breaks engine problems down into categories. If the engine isn't cranking, the problem is somewhere between the battery and the starter motor. Symptoms and remedies are shown for this category. When you have this type of problem, be sure you can find the emergency shutoff for your engine's electrical system since you'll need to use it if you hear a loud, continuous, whirring sound from the starter motor.

For starter solenoid problems, it's possible to bypass the starter solenoid by essentially hot-wiring the starter. This remedy is beyond the scope of this book. It can be done, however, and you might want to ask a mechanic to show you how to do it on your boat.

Engine Troubleshooting Guide

SYMPTOM	POSSIBLE CAUSE	REMEDY
Engine won't crank.	Starter switches not turned on properly.	Turn on proper switches (consult your owner's manual).
	Battery discharged.	Charge battery or turn battery switches to include house batteries in charging battery. If you get engine started, find out why battery was discharged. (See chapter 4.)
	Starter solenoid or starter defective.	Listen to starter motor when someone else turns ignition switch. If you hear a click and nothing happens, tap side of starter motor once with hammer while trying to start. The starter may start (this is only a temporary fix). Be ready to shut off emergency engine electricity if you hear a loud whirring hum, however. Call a professional.
	Loud, whirring hum.	Severe problem in starter. Turn off power to engine start circuit; use emergency switch if you have one. Don't use starter. Call a professional.
Engine cranks, but won't start.	Out of fuel.	Add fuel and bleed fuel lines if necessary.
	Fuel line valve closed.	Open valve.

continued page 82

Engine Troubleshooting Guide (continued)

SYMPTOM	POSSIBLE CAUSE	REMEDY
Engine cranks, but won't start. (continued)	Fuel shutoff cable is shutting off fuel.	Move shutoff cable to On position.
	Air in fuel line.	Bleed fuel lines.
	Blockage in fuel line.	Clear blockage.
	Very dirty fuel filters.	Change fuel filters.
No water exiting exhaust.	Water intake closed.	Open seawater intake seacock, fast!
	Blockage in seawater intake line.	Clear blockage.
	Defective impeller pump.	Replace impeller.
Engine runs ragged.	Dirty fuel.	Change fuel filters, change to different fuel tank if possible. Have professional clean tanks.
	Dirty fuel filters.	Change fuel filters.
	Blockage in fuel line.	Clear blockage.
	Fuel lift pump defective.	Replace fuel lift pump.
Engine smokes.	Defective injectors.	Replace injectors.
	Serious engine problem.	Call professional.
	Too much oil in engine.	Stop engine; pump excess oil out. Do not run engine in an excess-oil state: *Very dangerous!*

Additional Possibilities for Gasoline Engines

SYMPTOM	POSSIBLE CAUSE	REMEDY
Engine cranks, but won't start.	Defective spark plugs.	Replace spark plugs.
	Carburetor problem.	Call a professional.
	Engine timing problem.	Call a professional.
Engine runs ragged.	Defective spark plugs.	Replace spark plugs.
	Carburetor problem.	Call a professional.
	Engine timing problem.	Call a professional.

If a diesel engine cranks but won't start, the problem has to be in the fuel supply somewhere. Either there's no fuel, or something is inhibiting the flow of fuel to the injectors. You may need to bleed the fuel lines; also look for blockages in fuel lines or in the fuel filters.

A few of the possible causes and symptoms for smoking engines are also listed. Smoke is never a good sign; call a professional as soon as possible. Check your engine for too much oil. If that's the problem, especially on a diesel engine, *you must reduce the oil level before running the engine* (see page 73). Because gasoline engines are more complicated than diesel ones, there are more potential problems to check for when the engine cranks but won't start; some of these are listed in the the lower portion of the table.

ARE WE HAVING FUN YET?

This was a tough chapter—important, but tough. Don't get discouraged if there seems to be too much to learn and too much to do. Getting to know your boat is a process, one that takes months or even years. Every time you do something to Dulcinea—every time you change the oil, change a fuel filter, or figure out how to clear the engine seawater line—you'll know a little bit more about your boat. And you'll have gained that much more confidence to deal with whatever comes your way.

For now, put this book down, go aboard Dulcinea, and take a nap. You can figure out where everything goes tomorrow.

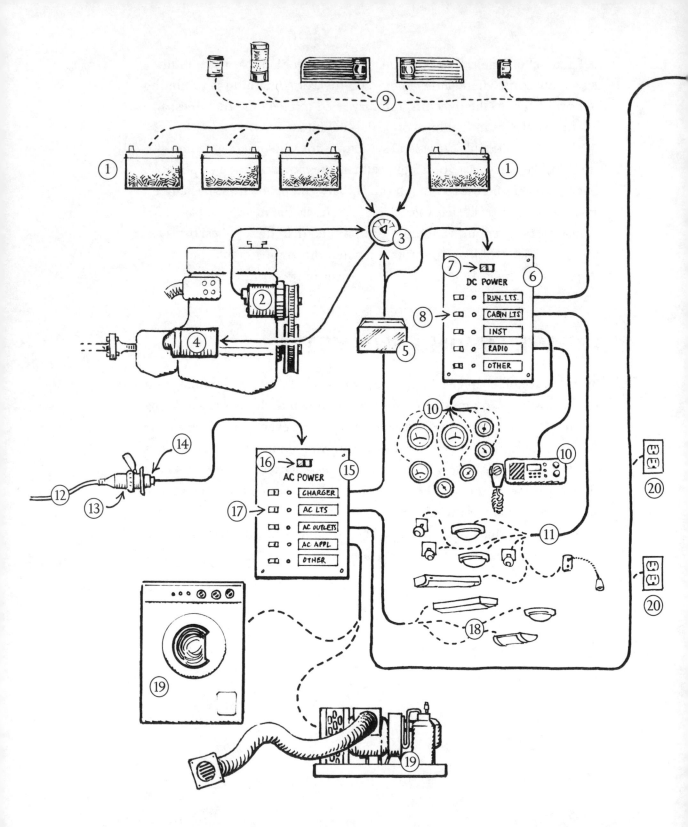

4

BOAT ELECTRICITY

LEGEND

1. 12-volt batteries
2. alternator
3. battery selector/ isolator switch
4. engine starter
5. battery charger
6. DC panel
7. main DC breaker
8. individual DC circuit breakers
9. running lights
10. instruments
11. cabin lights
12. shore power cable
13. AC shore power cable connector
14. connector on boat
15. main AC breaker
16. AC panel
17. individual AC circuit breakers
18. AC lights
19. AC appliances
20. AC outlets

Boats become more complex every year, and most of this complexity involves equipment that uses or generates electricity. Ten years ago, radar was rare; today, almost every boat has it. Hot water used to be a luxury, with hot showers a marina-only treat. Today, generators supply not only hot water, but also the ability to drive watermakers that make 20 (or more) gallons of water per hour. Even while Dulcinea hangs on the hook in a remote anchorage, you can take a hot shower in a head warmed by an electric heater.

Some purists say such a lifestyle defeats the purpose of cruising— it's getting away from it all by taking it all with you. And there's probably more truth to that than any of us would like to admit. But that's human nature, I guess. Over the years, I've added more and more equipment to my boat, and today it's quite a complicated assemblage of expensive components. I didn't mean to do it, and sometimes I wish I hadn't, but through a combination of curiosity, vulnerability to sales pitches, and a hatred of cold showers, I did. Whatever the reason for this complexity, we all can save considerable time, agony, and expense by learning how to use and maintain the electrical equipment on our boats. Even more important, *boat electrical systems are potentially dangerous if not properly used and maintained.*

BASIC IDEAS

Nothing in Dulcinea is more impressive than the electrical panel. Rows and rows of multicolored circuit breakers sport stark labels with impressive names, and the toggle switches are lined up like ships in Nelson's navy. This array testifies that this boat belongs to a serious and competent mariner. Perhaps, however, as you glance down at that ordered complexity on your way out to the cockpit, there's a small voice in the back of your head that says, "I wonder what all that stuff is for? I wonder if I should be doing something to it? I wonder if I'd be electrocuted if I opened that panel? I wonder what those impressive meters meter?"

TWO KINDS OF ELECTRICITY

To begin, Dulcinea can have two kinds of electricity: one is the same as that in your house and the other is same as that in your automobile. The house kind (which small boats may not have but which most others do) is called *120-volt AC*; the auto kind (which all boats have) is called *12-volt DC*. In practice, AC electricity varies from 110 to 125 volts; here we will refer to it as 120 volts, or more simply as just AC.

A *volt* is a measure of electrical pressure between two points; 120-volt electricity has ten times the pressure that 12-volt electricity does. If you've ever accidentally touched the bare wires in a 120-volt circuit (do *not* do this!), you felt a shock because there was sufficient electrical pressure to overcome the resistance in your skin and other tissues.

On the other hand, if you touch the bare wires in most 12-volt circuits, you won't normally feel a shock because there's insufficient pressure to overcome the resistance in your body. (Unless, of course, you're working in a tight spot on a very hot day when your skin is sweating profusely and you're holding the only tiny little nut you have for a particular job and you accidentally touch two wires in a 12-volt circuit with the back of your very sweaty hand. Then you might get a little buzz across the back of your hand; just enough to scare you into dropping that last little nut into the bilge.) Normally, you can't receive a shock from a 12-volt circuit, but read Electrical Hazards on page 90 before touching any wires.

House current is 120 volts, *AC*. The AC stands for *alternating current*, and with it, the voltage varies from plus to minus and back again. It does this 60 times per second and is hence called *60-cycle AC*. By the way, the rating of 120 volts is an average of voltage values computed from a standard formula. In a 120-volt AC circuit, the true voltage varies from +170 volts to −170 volts. It's these changes in voltage that are used by AC electrical appliances to accomplish work.

Unfortunately, alternating voltages are exceedingly dangerous to humans because they confuse the heart's electrical system. Even a very small amount of AC current passing through your chest can cause a heart attack (as could happen if you held a defective wire in one hand and a grounded fixture like the galley sink in the other). Therefore, as you work around Dulcinea's electrical system, always keep in mind that AC can kill you. In general, I believe only professionals should work on AC boat circuits. We amateurs should restrict ourselves to the 12-volt DC domain.

Auto electricity is 12-volt DC. The DC stands for *direct current*, and with it, the voltage is a constant 12 volts. It does not vary at all. Work is accomplished by the flow of electrons rather than by the changing of voltages. Most of the time, boat DC circuits are safer than AC circuits because the voltage does not vary and because the voltage is ten times less.

There is, however, more to the story. Voltage is a measure of the electrical pressure between two points. Mother Nature attempts to equalize that pressure by sending electrons from the higher voltage to the lower.* The number of electrons that pass a particular spot on a wire is referred to as *amperage* or more commonly as *amps*. If you could see electrons and count fast, you would find that when the current is 1 amp, 6.28 billion billion electrons pass by every second. This number is not important at all unless you're reading this book for a class. What is important, however, is that amps measure the flow of electricity through a wire.

The power of an electrical circuit, or the amount of work it can do, is the product of amperage times voltage. Such power is measured in units called *watts*. Thus

WATTS (POWER) = AMPERAGE × VOLTAGE

A 2-amp current flowing on a 120-volt circuit generates 2 × 120 or 240 watts of power. That same 2-amp current flowing on a 12-volt circuit generates 2 × 12 or 24 watts of power. You can work this equation back-

*Yes, if you're paying close attention you realize the electrons in an AC circuit are going to be schizophrenic because the voltage varies from high to low and low to high. Electrons in an AC circuit are therefore going to shuttle back and forth like lobbyists between New York City and Washington, D.C., at year-end. Let's simplify things and just consider DC current, but, as the lights at home show, it works for AC, too.

ward, too. For example, a heater that's rated at 1,200 watts of power will need, on a 120-volt circuit, 1,200 ÷ 120 or 10 amps of current.

Now, let's suppose that you want to use an electric motor to pump water to your galley sink. Suppose the motor requires 120 watts of power. You can supply this amount of power with 1 amp of 120-volt current or with 10 amps of 12-volt current. This is misleading, however, because common electric pumps are either AC or DC, but not both. Hence if you wanted to use 120-volt AC to power the pump, you'd need an AC pump; if you wanted to use 12-volt DC to power the pump, you'd need a DC pump.

Before moving on, there's one more term you need to learn. An *amp-hour* is the amount of electricity used when 1 amp of current flows for 1 hour. Thus, if you have a 3-amp light that burns for 7 hours, you'll have used 21 amp-hours of electricity.

On boats, AC is supplied by shore-power connections, by a device called an *inverter* that converts DC to AC, or by an AC generator. DC power is supplied from the boat's batteries, which are recharged by the engine's *alternator* when the engine is running, by a battery charger when shore power is connected, or possibly by solar panels or a wind-driven generator. If you have an AC generator, that can power the battery charger as well.

USES FOR DC AND AC POWER

The table on page 91 shows uses for 12-volt and 120-volt electricity on boats. Most of the applications in the 120-volt column require high power. A typical electric cabin heater, for example, requires 1,200 watts of power. This necessitates 10 amps of 120-volt power or 100 amps of 12-volt power. For reasons explained below, it's both unrealistic and unsafe to have more than 25 or 30 amps in a boat circuit, and so most applications that need higher power use 120 volts.

Some equipment—such as refrigerators and watermakers—comes in both 12-volt and 120-volt versions. The 12-volt versions always have less capacity. For example, a typical 12-volt watermaker can generate 80 gallons of water per day, while a typical 120-volt watermaker can generate 500 gallons or more per day.

Electrical Hazards

Alternating voltages are exceedingly dangerous to humans. Always keep in mind that AC can kill you. In general, I believe only professionals should work on AC boat circuits. While working on 12-volt DC systems, disconnect all AC sources since there could be a short circuit feeding AC current into the DC system. Unplug the power cord at the dock.

Get a detailed professional inspection of the electrical system. The hostile marine environment, improper repairs, wiring modifications, or "equipment upgrades" can all cause problems, so unless your boat is new and from a first-class builder, a professional inspection is a must.

Work safe. Sparking is a hazard, even with 12-volt circuits, and shorting at the battery connections can cause severe burns. Remove all jewelry before working on battery connections or on battery cables and be careful not to short-circuit these connections with your tools. *Never work on your electrical system until you are sure the bilge is free of any explosive vapor such as propane or gasoline fumes.*

Avoid overloading. Overloaded circuits, bad connections, or corroded wire or connections can cause overheating, which can ignite flammable materials, including your fiberglass boat. Properly sized fuses or circuit breakers are required to protect all circuits from overloading. A fuse or breaker must be in each hot wire as near the battery as practical.

Use batteries safely. Battery acid can burn holes in your clothes and your skin and cause permanent eye damage or blindness, so wear eye protection, keep your face away from open cells, and avoid spills and splashes. If you do come in contact with the acid, flush the area immediately with plenty of freshwater. Get medical attention for eye contact. Neutralize spills on clothes or the boat with baking soda *(DO NOT use on skin or eyes)*.

Batteries generate hydrogen and oxygen when charging, so the battery compartment must be well ventilated. Do not work on the electrical system when the battery is charging or use a match to check the electrolyte level.

Batteries need to be solidly anchored and contained. Plastic battery boxes are available and can contain spilled acid if the case cracks. A battery that comes loose can cause serious damage and injury, so secure straps or retaining rods are a must.

Applications for 12-Volt DC and 120-Volt AC Power	
APPLICATIONS USING 12-VOLT DC POWER	APPLICATIONS USING 120-VOLT AC POWER
Engine starter	Water heater
Water pumps	Microwave
Shower sump pumps	Electric cabin heaters
Bilge pumps	Shore-power charger
Bilge fans and blowers	Electric cooking range
Interior lights	Electric oven
Deck wash pumps	120-volt refrigerator
Deck lights	High-capacity watermaker
Running lights	Air conditioner
Propane solenoid	
Radar	
GPS	
VHF and SSB radios	
Instruments	
Anchor windlass	
Autopilot	
Low-capacity watermaker	
12-volt refrigerator	

So why not use 120 volts for everything? Because of the high pressure of 120-volt electricity, *short circuits*, or *shorts* occur more readily with 120-volt than with 12-volt electricity. *Shorts* happen when electrical current takes an unintended path and bypasses the equipment (or *load*) that it is supposed to power. If your stern light, for example, corrodes so that the two wires leading to it touch before they get to the light, electricity will bypass the load and current will build to the point that one of the safety devices (a fuse or circuit breaker) will cut off the flow of electricity. A 120-volt stern light could short even if the wires didn't touch because the electrical pressure is high enough so that something like moisture on the wire covers could cause the current to jump. Therefore, stern lights are not powered by 120 volts (even when it's available).

In most pleasure boats, then, equipment that is exposed to water or weather and equipment that must operate when underway is powered by 12-volt electricity. This is usually fine since most such equipment (lights, instruments, GPS, VHF radio) uses very little power.

Anchor windlasses are an exception. It takes a lot of power to pull up 200 feet of chain and a 75-pound anchor, so you would normally select a 120-volt motor for this job. The problem is that anchor windlasses are located out on the deck where water is certain to be present, and shorts (as well as shocks to the anchor-retriever) are likely. Therefore, anchor windlass motors are powered by 12 volts. Since such motors need 1,200 watts or so for the heavy lifting, the wires leading to the windlass may carry 100 amps (1,200 ÷ 12) or so of current. This is the one place where high amperage is allowed on a boat, and it necessitates special equipment (as we will discuss next and in chapter 8).

AMPERAGE, WIRE LENGTH, AND WIRE SIZE

Amperage is a measure of the number of electrons flowing in a circuit. Even though electrons are small, they do take up space. As amperage increases, the number of electrons increases, and if the space available for them is too small, they bump into one another and generate heat (which reduces voltage and power, too). If the wire is too small for the current trying to pass through it, it can heat up enough to start a fire or cause other damage.

Therefore, when running a wire from one place to another, you need to ensure that the wire is large enough in diameter for the expected current. Wire size, or diameter, is identified by *gauge*. Gauge numbers run backwards (the bigger the gauge number, the smaller the wire) and are printed on the wire's insulation. You also need to ensure that a fuse or circuit breaker is in place in case a short or other problem causes the amperage to exceed the safe capacity of the wire.

Fuses or circuit breakers break the circuit when the current exceeds their capacity. In a fuse, a small wire in the fuse melts and the fuse must be replaced (use only replacement fuses of the proper capacity; using a larger fuse will defeat the intended protection).

Circuit breakers trip an internal switch when an overload is sensed. The breaker's external handle moves from On to an intermediate position, identifying the tripped breaker. The breaker can be reset after the overload is removed.

Using our example of an anchor windlass, the wires that lead to it have to be large because they'll carry 100 amps or so of current. A circuit breaker should also be placed close to the battery on the windlass circuit just in case the amperage exceeds the designed amperage. For another example, the wires leading to the display light on your instrument panel might be quite small since they'll carry only a $\frac{1}{10}$ amp or less. They'll still need a fuse or circuit breaker, just in case a short causes that limit to be exceeded.

Note that the breakers in the panel are sized to protect the wire, not the device; these low-current devices often have their own small fuses in the connecting wire at the unit or in the unit itself.

Wire resists the flow of electrons. The farther the electrons have to travel, the more resistance they'll need to overcome. Resistance reduces the voltage in the wire so the longer the wire run, the greater the voltage drop, and the less power is available at the load. This power loss can be overcome by increasing the size of the wire.

Thus, the size of the wire you need depends both on the amperage to be carried and on the length of the run from the power source to the load. The table next page shows recommended wire sizes for different amperages and wire runs. Note that the run length includes the entire circuit—panel to load and back to the panel—and that the wire can be used for AC or DC current. (There are standards for color in DC circuits; however, without a current wiring diagram, they are not a reliable guide—colors may vary depending on who did the wiring and what color wire they had at the time!)

Wire sizes go down to 0 (spoken as "aught"); they don't become negative, however. Wires larger than 0 are 00, 000, and 0000 (spoken as "two aught," "three aught," and "four aught" by those who have been admitted to the inner sanctum). There is probably wire larger than this, but I've never seen it and I couldn't afford it, anyway. At the other end of the scale, ABYC standards require wires no smaller than 16 for most applications since smaller wires are just too dainty for boat service, although some 18-gauge wire is allowed in panels.

Wire Size (Gauge) Recommendations for 3 Percent Voltage Drop

AMPS	length of conductor in feet, from source to load and back to source							
	10	15	20	25	30	50	70	100
5	18*	16	14	12	12	10	8	6
10	14	12	10	10	10	6	6	4
15	12	10	10	8	8	6	4	2
20	10	10	8	6	6	4	2	2
25	10	8	6	6	6	4	2	1
30	10	8	6	6	4	2	1	0
50	6	6	4	4	2	1	00	000
70	6	4	2	2	1	00	000	—
100	4	2	2	1	0	000	—	—

*Only for instruments in panels.

Adapted from Nigel Calder, *Boatowner's Mechanical and Electrical Manual*, page 115

When you buy wire, keep in mind that both price and weight go up dramatically as the size increases. The gauge numbers are set so that each 3-gauge step doubles the wire's cross-sectional area. Thus, 8-gauge wire has nearly 6½ times as much metal as 16-gauge wire. The bottom line here is that you want wire just big enough to do the job—no more and no less. Also be aware that wire quality varies tremendously, so always buy wire specifically manufactured for marine purposes and rated for the temperature of its environment. Tell the chandlery your intended use and make sure they sell you wire appropriate for that use. Using cheap wire will lead to corrosion and other problems, and using inappropriate wire can be a fire hazard.

You can also see the need to keep wire runs as short as possible. When I bought my Dulcinea, 00 wire ran from the batteries under the forward bunks all the way aft to a cockpit locker, and then back forward to amidships and the engine alternator. This was nuts—the trip back to the cockpit locker was completely unnecessary. By relocating the cockpit locker connections to amidships, I removed 20 pounds of wire and considerably reduced the wire resistance that had to be overcome by my alternator.

A BASIC ELECTRICAL SYSTEM

The illustration on pages 96–97 shows the components of a basic boat electrical system. This and the illustration on pages 112–13 are organized with 12-volt DC power on the top half of the diagram and 120-volt AC power on the bottom half. Electrical sources are shown on the left-hand side and electrical loads (uses) are shown on the right-hand side. The rectangles to right of center represent the electrical panels.

SHORE POWER

Let's start with shore power. You plug your power cord into the marina's AC supply and bring, essentially, the shore power to your boat. The maximum amperage that is supplied varies from marina to marina; 15-, 20-, 30-, and 50-amp supplies are the most common. Each of these electrical supplies has a different type of plug. A 15-amp plug looks like a typical house plug, while the others look like varieties of the plugs on clothes dryers. Your power cord is made of wire of a particular gauge, and it's a certain length, so it can be used for a certain maximum amperage. Your cord will have the plug type that is appropriate for that maximum. The illustration on page 98 shows the common plug and receptacle configurations.

At some point, you'll pull into a lovely marina, step onto the dock, tie up in shipshape fashion, and pull your power cord over to the marina's power receptacle. It's getting a little dark, you don't see quite as well as you used to, and for some reason, you can't get the plug in. You guessed it! You've got a 30-amp power cord and they have a 20-amp power supply! The plugs won't fit no matter how many times you try.

You need an adapter. You can buy 15 to 30, 20 to 30, and even 50 to 30 adapters. You might even be able to borrow (rent?) one from the marina. Note, however, in the case of the 50 to 30 adapter, that you could possibly have 50 amps of current flowing through your 30-amp cord, which is dangerous. For this and other reasons, the main AC circuit breaker in your boat should be rated the same or less than the rating of your power cord. If you have a 30-amp main circuit breaker in your boat, you should

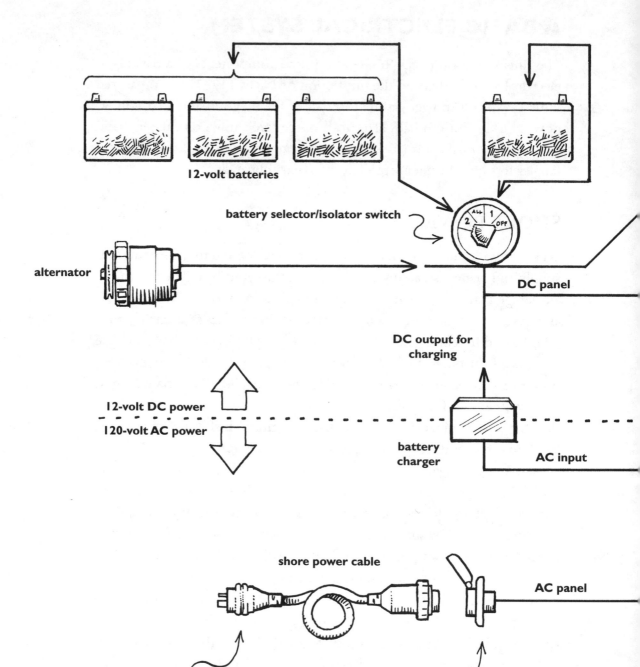

12-volt batteries

battery selector/isolator switch

alternator

DC panel

DC output for charging

12-volt DC power

120-volt AC power

battery charger

AC input

shore power cable

AC panel

connector to shore AC power

connector on boat

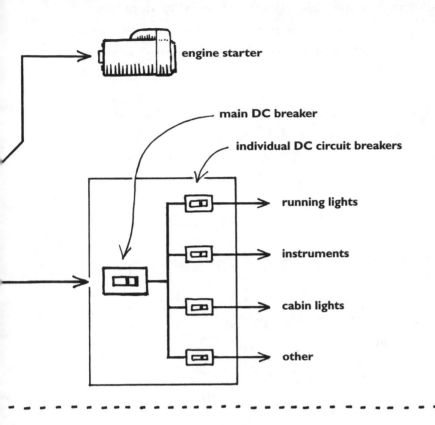

engine starter

main DC breaker

individual DC circuit breakers

running lights

instruments

cabin lights

other

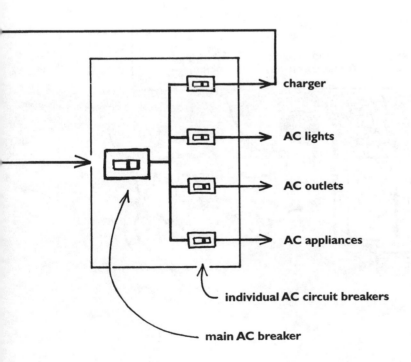

charger

AC lights

AC outlets

AC appliances

individual AC circuit breakers

main AC breaker

have a 30-amp or or more cord. This way, no matter what amperage is supplied by the marina, you'll never have more current coming into your boat than your power cord can handle. Note, too, if you connect your 30-amp boat to a 20-amp service and turn everything on, you may trip the breaker on the dock.

Shore-power cords and adapters, which you depend on for safe and reliable service, are exposed to all kinds of rough use and weather, so use cords designated type SO, ST, or STO. For a 30-amp service, #10 AWG (American Wire Gauge; see table on page 94) or larger is required. Comparing the price of these cords to the cord your local hardware or building supply store calls "heavy duty" is a bit of a jolt, but don't skimp: it

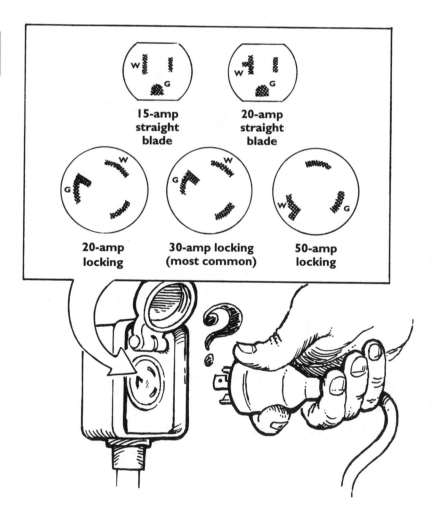

120-Volt Plug Types

may well save a much worse "shock" later. Commercial adapters are also expensive, but they're reliable and properly wired.

Make sure cords are connected properly as improper connections can cause severe shock and fire hazards. Inexpensive and easy-to-use circuit testers are sold at hardware stores. Plugging one into the dock service, with proper adapter (if required) will check the shoreside wiring (see illustration next page). If your boat has a polarity indicator, check it at each hookup. A hot power cord in the water or reversed polarity can be a shock hazard to swimmers as well as boaters. Check your connections and stay out of the water at marinas.

When you connect to the marina's power supply, you're also connecting—through the marina's wiring—to the electrical systems of nearby boats. If those boats have problems, those problems can be passed on to you (stray-current corrosion is the most common one). There's not much you can do about this in unfamiliar marinas; your only choice is not to hook into shore power at all. At your home port, you should regularly check your zincs.

Be aware that Dulcinea may have a device called a *galvanic isolator* to prevent stray-current corrosion. As part of your professional inspection, find out if you have one, if it's properly installed and sized, and how to check it periodically.

THE 120-VOLT AC ELECTRICAL PANEL

As shown in the illustration on pages 96–97, the 120-volt AC power is led from your shore-power connector into the AC electrical panel. On a well-designed boat, all of the AC circuit breakers will be placed adjacent to one another on the panel. For safety's sake, before you explore this panel, step out to the dock, turn off the circuit breaker to your boat, and unplug your power cord. Bring the cord back aboard so that no one can "help out" and reconnect it. Disconnect your inverter or generator if you have them.

Having done that, open your electrical panel and locate your AC breakers (they may be covered with a plastic shield so that you can't accidentally shock yourself). Mentally trace the power from the dock, through

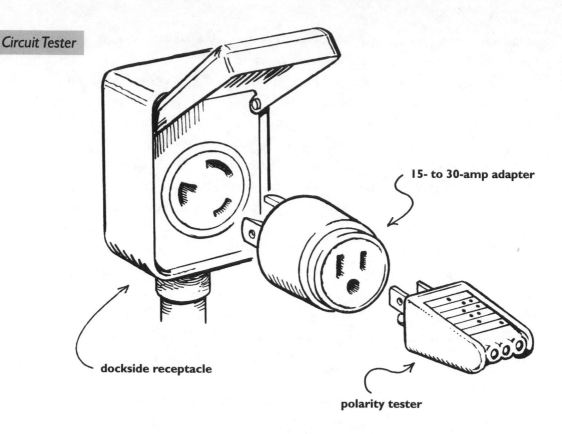

15- to 30-amp adapter

dockside receptacle

polarity tester

your power cord, into the electrical fitting on the exterior of your boat, through interior wires to the main AC circuit breaker, and finally to the AC circuit breakers. You may note that one side of the circuit breakers has a copper bar that runs across them. This bar, which is called a *bus*, distributes voltage to all of the breakers. A series of wires would do the same thing but would be messier.

Typical boats will have AC circuit breakers that lead to the water heater, the AC outlets in your boat, possibly to a microwave, watermaker, or trash compactor, and most certainly to a battery charger. Examine your electrical panel to see which of these you have. Breakers should be labeled with the circuits they serve. A typical AC circuit is shown in the bottom illustration on page 101. When you've finished your inspection, close up your panel, secure everything, and then reconnect to shore power.

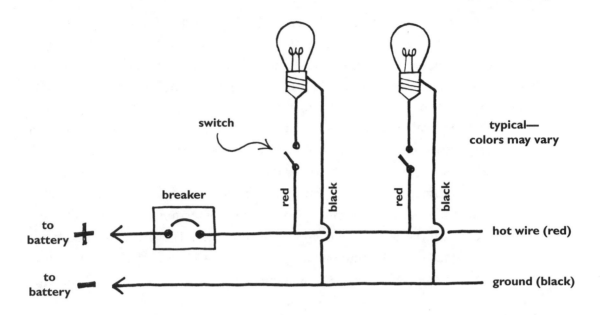

switch

typical—
colors may vary

breaker

red black red black

to
battery **+**

hot wire (red)

to
battery **–**

ground (black)

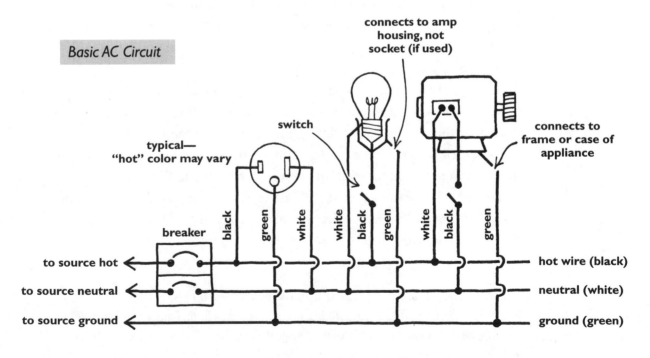

connects to amp
housing, not
socket (if used)

switch

typical—
"hot" color may vary

connects to
frame or case of
appliance

black green white white black green white black green

breaker

to source hot

hot wire (black)

to source neutral

neutral (white)

to source ground

ground (green)

BATTERIES AND BATTERY CHARGERS

On most boats, the batteries store 12-volt electricity. The capacity of a battery is rated in amp-hours, and batteries typically range from 100 amp-hours to 250 amp-hours, though both smaller and larger batteries are available. As stated earlier, an amp-hour is the electricity used when running a 1-amp load for 1 hour, or a 2-amp load for 30 minutes, etc.

Most likely you have two or more banks of batteries. The illustration on pages 96–97 shows two banks connected via a battery switch. Each bank consists of one or more batteries connected so they combine their stored amp-hours into one pool. To do this, the batteries are connected in *parallel*, which means all of the plus (positive) battery terminals are connected together onto one red cable, and all of the minus (negative) terminals are connected together onto one black cable. Three 12-volt 250-amp-hour batteries connected in this way will create a 12-volt bank having 750 amp-hours.*

Due to the heavier loads placed upon them, boat batteries are usually *deep-cycle* batteries, which means they're built to withstand more discharge and recharge cycles than auto batteries. Powering the boat when the engine is not running demands this kind of service.

There are two common types of batteries: *wet-cell* and *gel-cell*. Wet-cell batteries contain a watery mixture of sulfuric acid and they periodically need to have distilled water added through the removable cap provided on each cell. Gel-cell batteries contain a gelatinous ooze; they are sealed and you should never attempt to open them—you'll ruin them if you do.

There's a lot of mystique about batteries; my guess is that few people really understand them. I believe we can boil most of the hocus-pocus down to a few basic rules:

An alternative way of connecting batteries is in series. Here the positive terminal of one battery is connected to the negative terminal of the next and so forth. Batteries connected in this way combine their voltages but do not change their capacity. Three 12-volt 250-amp-hour batteries connected in series will create a 36-volt bank having 250 amp-hours.

1. Try to keep your batteries fully charged.
2. The fuller your battery is, the slower you must charge it.
3. Plan to use only half of your batteries' capacity.
4. If you have wet-cell batteries, check the water level periodically and add distilled water.
5. Your life will be simpler if all of the batteries on your boat are of the same type (gel-cell or wet-cell).

Rule 1 only pertains if you're not using your batteries. If you're on the hook or sailing for several days, you're obviously going to be running your batteries down. When you can, however, bring them back to full charge, or close to it. And if Dulcinea is sitting in the marina, try to keep her batteries charged.

Rule 2 is the bane of battery use and an opportunity for the engineering and marketing departments of battery charger manufacturers. The problem is this: when your batteries are substantially discharged, say 50 percent or so, they'll accept a large charging current. Depending on the capacity of your battery bank and the amount of discharge, you can put 50 to 100 amps into your batteries with no problem. However, as your batteries become charged, they'll accept less and less amperage. If you continue to put 100 amps into a nearly charged battery, most of the energy will go into heat and you'll boil the water or gel inside the battery and potentially ruin the battery or start a fire.

Therefore, most AC-powered (shore power or generator) battery chargers are *multistage* chargers. Three-stage chargers are common. There is a maximum phase that sends a large current to the battery when it's substantially discharged, a second phase that sends an intermediate amount of current, and a third stage that sends a modest current necessary for topping off the battery and maintaining its charge state. A similar multistage strategy is used with some engine alternators, as you'll learn below.

I don't know where rule 3 comes from; apparently you wear your batteries down much faster if you discharge them past the 50 percent mark. I trust that it's not the invention of battery manufacturers' sales and marketing departments. I would try to observe the rule to increase battery life; but, of course, if I were in a pinch, I'd use all the battery capacity I needed.

So, assuming you want to follow this rule, how do you know how much capacity you've used? You either have a meter on your boat that tells you how many amp-hours you've used, or keep rough calculations yourself. With powerboats, you only need to be concerned about usage while at anchor, when the engines aren't running. With sailboats, you need to consider time at anchor and time under sail. The table opposite shows a chart for a boat at anchor where a total of 279 amp-hours is used in 24 hours. Assuming the batteries are never discharged below 50 percent, a battery bank of 560 amp-hours is required if the batteries are charged after one day's use. A bank of 1,120 hours is required if the batteries are charged after two days' use.

Here's a second example of making rough usage calculations. Say you've been sailing for 24 hours since your last charge and you've been using your autopilot, which consumes, say, 10 amps. Additionally, you ran all night (say 10 hours) with four lights, each of which uses 1 amp. Additionally, you've been using your VHF radio (2 amps) and your GPS (less than 1 amp) and occasionally your freshwater pump, your propane solenoid, and a cabin light.

We can calculate the amp-hours used by each of these items by multiplying the amps used times the number of hours in use. Thus, the autopilot used 24 × 10 or 240 amp-hours. The running lights consumed 4 × 10 or 40 amp-hours. The VHF and GPS used less than 3 × 24 or 72 amp-hours. The other items used, let's say, less than 5 amp-hours. Altogether then you've used 240 + 40 + 72 + 5 or 357 amp-hours. If the capacity of your battery bank is 700 amp-hours, you're just under the 50 percent rule and it's time to recharge.

Rule 4 is straightforward for *wet-cell batteries only*; you should check your batteries frequently if you've been charging a lot. If you're using up a lot of water, your charger may be sending too much current into your batteries and you should adjust it as described in the charger's documentation.

Finally, rule 5 exists because gel-cell and wet-cell batteries accept charges at different rates. If all of the batteries on your boat are of the

Amp-Hour Requirements

APPLIANCE	AMP RATING	HOURS	AMP-HOURS
Cabin lights	3	8	24
Anchor lights	10	8	80
12-volt refrigerator	25	4	100
VHF	1	20	20
Stereo	1	5	5
Cabin heater	25	2	50
Total			279

same type, there's less chance that any of them will be charged too fast and your battery life will be longer.

THE ALTERNATOR

The alternator on your engine(s) provides a second way of generating electricity and charging your batteries. There are two parts to an alternator that you should know about, the alternator itself and the voltage regulator. To understand how these two interact, we need to consider a principle discovered by the Scot James Clerk Maxwell in the 19th century. Maxwell discovered that electricity and magnetism are different forms of the same thing. Ask a mathematician or physicist about this and they will expound at length about the beauty of what Maxwell did. If, like me, you don't understand a word they're saying, just nod your head and agree.

What this means is that we can rotate a magnet, the *rotor*, in close proximity to metal bands, the *stator*, that are connected to wires and generate electricity in the wires. We've all seen magnets as kids. What you might not know is that certain metals can be turned into a magnet by wrapping a wire around them and putting an electrical current through the wire. The rotor (magnet) inside your alternator is of this type.

Here's the gist of how your alternator works: A small amount of electricity is put into the rotor to energize the magnet. Then, using a V-belt off your engine's crankshaft, the rotor spins inside the stator, creating electricity. If you increase the amount of current going into the rotor, you increase the magnetic field, and consequently increase the output of the alternator. If you decrease the current going into the magnet, you decrease the magnetic field, and consequently decrease the output of the alternator.*

Your alternator has a *voltage regulator* that varies the amount of electricity going to the magnet and thus varies the output produced. On some engines, the regulator is built into the alternator, on others it is exterior to the alternator. All voltage regulators vary the amount of current going to the magnet to adjust the alternator's output. Some of them are even smarter, and provide three or more stages of output, depending on the load and the degree to which the batteries are discharged. These are similar to multistage battery chargers.

If you have a single-stage regulator, you'll have a low-capacity alternator, around 65 amps or so. You don't want to install a larger alternator with a single-stage regulator because you can overcharge your batteries. The disadvantage of this is that it may take a long time to recharge your batteries. For example, if your batteries are discharged 195 amp-hours, you'll need 3 hours (actually considerably more because of heat losses) to recharge your batteries with a 65-amp alternator.

On the other hand, if you have a multistage voltage regulator, you can have a very large alternator, 150 amps or more. The regulator will begin by causing the alternator to produce a lot of current and then taper off the output as the batteries reach a fully charged state. Charge time can be reduced by half or more. Be aware that large-capacity alternators can be physically huge—you may need a lot of room around your engine to install one. You'll also need multiple V-belts to drive it, which may involve other changes to pulleys on your engine and may cause damage to your engine's water pump. If you're thinking about installing such an alternator, think twice, and get the opinion of a boat electrician before proceeding. Use only ignition-protected alternators designed for marine service.

The electricity generated at the stator is AC electricity. Since we want the alternator to produce DC, additional circuitry, called a rectifier, is added to convert the AC to DC. All of this is hidden from us, however; as far as we can tell, the alternator produces DC current.

Further, don't be fooled into buying a small alternator that has been souped up to large-output capacity—you'll have constant problems with it. (I tried this, and now I know most of the places you can have an alternator rebuilt between Seattle and Sitka.)

If your alternator stops producing, the failure can be traced to either the alternator or the voltage regulator (see Electrical System Maintenance beginning on page 115). So, if you have a separate regulator, you might consider carrying a spare regulator. If you have the room and money, you might also want to carry a spare alternator, though not too many people do this because alternators can be repaired in most cities.

THE BATTERY SWITCH

The illustration next page shows a battery switch that can be used to manage two banks of batteries. Note that it can be set to select from bank 1, from bank 2, from both, or turned off. Why does such a seemingly unimportant device merit our attention? As always, the answer is in the small print. See where it says, "Stop engine before turning to Off"? This is important! Imagine the following scenario: you've just pulled out of an anchorage on a beautiful morning, motoring happily along with your engine at 2,000 rpm. Your multistage voltage regulator senses your batteries are low, and causes your (expensive) high-capacity alternator to put out 150 amps. All is perfect with the world until someone accidentally bumps into that little switch and turns it off.

Suddenly, the electrons that have been pouring out of your alternator have no place to go. They back up, and in an instant your alternator is crammed with electrons. Inside your alternator, in the device that converts AC to DC, one-way electrical gates called diodes are overwhelmed by the electron horde and they fail: your alternator has suffered death by electron suffocation.

So, now you know: that little message really has nothing to do with the engine; it really means, "Don't turn this switch off while the alternator is running or you'll ruin the alternator!"

There is a safety device called a Zap-Stop that you can put on your alternator to provide an emergency electron exit to prevent electron suffocation. These devices are cheap and easy to install, so next time you have a mechanic on your boat, ask him or her to install one.

If your Dulcinea has three or more banks of batteries, you may have two or more battery switches. In this case, as long as one pathway is open to a battery, it's OK to set all but one switch to Off. Be certain, however, you understand enough about your wiring to know that there will be one pathway open to some battery when you do this. If you're not sure, shut the engine off before turning the battery switch to Off. The bottom line: unless you know exactly what you're doing, don't ever set a battery switch to Off while the engine is running.

While we're on the subject of suffocation by electron, you should also know that similar problems can occur on diesel-powered boats if you turn the start key to Off while the engine is running. This action may not do as much damage as turning the battery switch to Off, but it is hard on the alternator, and it may damage the circuitry in your engine stop button too. So, get in the habit of leaving the key in the on position when your engine is running.

Battery Switch (Note Fine Print)

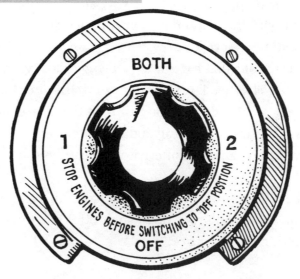

THE 12-VOLT DC ELECTRICAL PANEL

On a well-designed system, the 12-volt breakers will be physically separate from the AC breakers. You probably have a main 12-volt breaker that determines the maximum amount of 12-volt current that can run through your system. This main breaker then leads to the rows of 12-volt breakers, which are probably connected together with a copper bus along one side. Note that each breaker is labeled with its current limit; if you need to replace a breaker, be certain to replace it with a breaker having the same limit.

Circuit breakers generally have a long life. If you have a problem in a circuit that causes a breaker to switch off, wait a minute or two before trying to turn the breaker back on. A breaker generates a small amount of heat when it closes, and a small wire inside will fail if it's overheated by the breaker closing several times in quick succession. I learned this when we had a failure in a propane solenoid. We didn't know what the problem was, and Lynda and I kept turning the breaker back on while trying to light the stove. Eventually, the breaker failed, and then we had two problems—and still no coffee!

A MORE ELABORATE ELECTRICAL SYSTEM (WITH GENERATOR AND INVERTER)

The illustration on pages 112–13 shows an electrical system that's more complicated than the one shown on pages 96–97. There are three main differences. The first is that the more complicated system has a generator to produce 120-volt AC power. Note that this generator and the shore power share a special circuit breaker/transfer switch that allows only one of them to be on-line at a time. This is shown by the "OR" in the illustration. Otherwise, your generator would contribute its output to the city's power grid, which is probably not what you had in mind when you bought the generator. You'd also be creating serious onboard electrical problems as well as a severe shock hazard to anyone who happened to be working on the shoreside electrical system.

The second change is the replacement of the battery charger with an inverter-charger, usually just called an inverter, which can transform 12-volt DC into 120-volt AC; it can also transform 120-volt AC into 12-volt DC. For some reason, the process of converting from DC to AC is called *inverting*, and the process of converting from AC to DC is called *charging* or *rectifying*.

Typical marine inverters have a capacity of 1,500 to 3,000 watts. A 1,500-watt inverter can produce a maximum of $1,500 \div 120$ or 12.5 amps of AC power; a 3,000-watt inverter can produce a maximum of $3000 \div 120$ or 25 amps of AC power. (They actually produce somewhat less than this because 5 to 10 percent of the output is lost to heat.)

This sounds great, and it is, except for one important fact. Consider what's happening to your poor batteries while the inverter is doing its

ILLUMINATING ADVICE

Several years ago, I had to cut a large hole in the cabintop of my Dulcinea. I hate making holes in Dulcinea, but this had to be done. I borrowed a large drill and a hole-saw bit, measured twice, and drilled away. I was nearly through the cabintop when sparks, flashes, pops, crackles, and snaps erupted all over the place. Sure enough, I'd cut the wires that lead to the interior cabin lights. Luckily, I'd turned off the 120-volt AC power as a precaution, but I'd forgotten to turn off the DC circuit breakers.

Unfortunately, one of the broken wires led into a nearby light and was now too short to be spliced. So, I had to take down the light and pull it apart to replace the short end with a new, longer piece. The procedure was: Take the light down and cut the remaining wires. Then take out three little screws to pull the lens off and remove the lightbulb. Then take out two screws to pull the lightbulb holder off its bracket and unscrew the short wire. Then cut a new longer wire, and put it all back together. Finally, remount the light in the ceiling and, using the new longer wire, splice the cut wires back together.

So far, so good. But, I was mad at myself and in a hurry (always a good combination). All this electrical work was an unwelcome addition to the original job I'd been trying to do

thing. Pulling 3,000 watts out of your batteries is requiring the inverter to take 250 amps of 12-volt DC from the batteries. In 2 hours, you'll have taken 500 amp-hours out of the battery; if you have a 1,000 amp-hour battery system, it's time to recharge. The sudden rush of electrons out of your batteries will be hard on the batteries, too. So, the bottom line is that you only want to hook your inverter up to small to medium AC loads. It's great for powering the AC plugs so you can charge your computer, run your printer, and even run the microwave for short periods of time. You do not, however, want to try to run the water heater using your inverter; it will rapidly discharge your batteries.

For this reason, AC breakers are typically split into two groups: those having loads that can be powered by the inverter and those that can't. In the illustration on pages 112–13, there's a gap between the AC breakers for these two groups. Breakers above this line can be powered by the inverter;

when I cut the hole. While I was making the electrical repairs, I was muttering ugly things to myself. But, I finally got it all back together, turned on the power and flipped the light switch. Nothing. I thought perhaps my splice was bad, so I cut the wires and respliced them. Still nothing. Well, I thought, maybe I mixed up the wires when I spliced them together (there were four cut wires). I got out the multimeter and traced the wires around the cabin ceiling and back. Hmmm, no, it looked OK. I respliced the two wires leading into the light. Still no change.

Muttering even worse things to myself, I was about to take the light fixture apart again when I heard my friend Doc working on the boat next to mine. (Doc has been working on boats for many, many years, and has forgotten more than most of us will ever know.) "Hey, Doc," I yelled, "have you got a minute?" I met him on deck, showed him what had happened, and asked him to come below. I was explaining the wire runs in the ceiling when he reached over and picked something up. "Where does this go?" he asked, holding up the lightbulb. Silence. A deep, embarrassed silence.

I laughed feebly, wishing I could crawl into the crack between my cabin-sole boards. You guessed it, in my hurry to put the light back together, I'd forgotten to replace the bulb. With the bulb in, everything worked fine.

As the machinists say, "We don't have enough time to hurry."

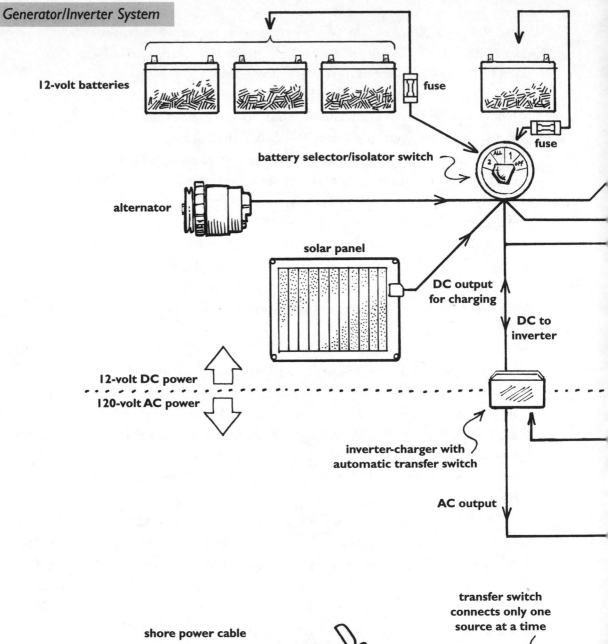

12-volt batteries

fuse

fuse

battery selector/isolator switch

alternator

solar panel

DC output
for charging

DC to
inverter

12-volt DC power

120-volt AC power

inverter-charger with
automatic transfer switch

AC output

transfer switch
connects only one
source at a time

shore power cable

OR

generator

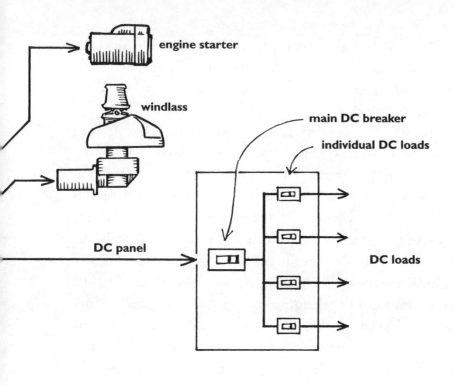

engine starter

windlass

main DC breaker

individual DC loads

DC panel

DC loads

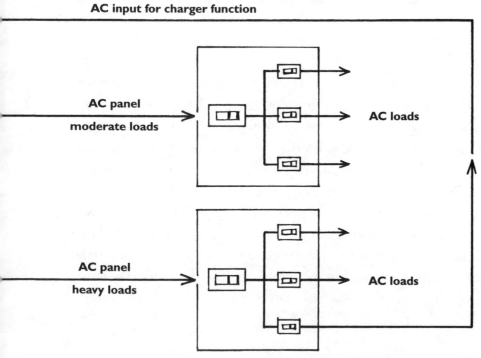

AC input for charger function

AC panel
moderate loads

AC loads

AC panel
heavy loads

AC loads

those below that line can by powered only by shore power or by the generator. Like the generator, the inverter is a source of potentially lethal AC current: it must be off when any electrical work is done. Also, don't put metal objects in the same locker as the inverter.

AC from shore power or a generator flows to your electrical panel. From there, some of it goes to the inverter, and some of it goes directly to the high loads that cannot be powered by the inverter. The AC that goes to the inverter is used to charge the batteries, and some of it is *passed through* to run the other AC loads. Thus, when a source of AC power is available, the inverter does not take power from the batteries—it simply passes the AC through to run the other loads via an automatic transfer switch.

The third change between the illustrations on pages 96–97 and 112–13 is the addition of additional DC charging equipment. Solar panels, wind generators, and the like can be added as sources of DC. If the system includes an inverter, solar or wind power can be transformed into AC. Again, however, only small AC loads should be used. Running the microwave will use up many, many days of sunshine on the solar panel!

Your system may differ, depending on the particular equipment installed. Consult your manuals and a qualified electrician to ensure a proper system.

SOLENOIDS

A *solenoid* is a device that accepts a small electrical current and electromagnetically closes or opens a circuit or makes or unmakes some other connection, such as a valve (see illustration on page 116). I have three types of solenoids on my boat. One is on the engine starter; when I turn the key, a small current goes to the starter solenoid and closes a switch on a second circuit so that a huge amount of current will flow from the battery to the engine starter. In this way, large 00 cable need not run all the way from the battery to my cockpit and back to the engine's starter. The large cable runs just to the starter. Small wires can run from the solenoid to the engine start switch in the cockpit because the solenoid doesn't take much current. This arrangement is also safer because I don't have high currents flowing all over the boat.

There's a second solenoid on my engine for shutting it down. I have a diesel engine, so to stop it, I need to stop the fuel flow. When I push the shutoff button, this solenoid closes and pulls the fuel shutoff lever closed.

The third solenoid is for our propane tank. When current flows to this solenoid, it opens a valve that allows propane to flow into our propane lines. Thus, this solenoid is used to open rather than to close a connection.

Another application for solenoids is *battery isolation switches*. These use several solenoids to replace a battery switch with an electrical switch. I had nothing but trouble with mine, and finally removed them and replaced them with a normal battery switch. My experience seems to be a common one; the experts I queried on this topic agreed that isolation switches are failure prone, and have other disadvantages such as a loss of voltage. In general, they're not recommended.

ELECTRICAL SYSTEM MAINTENANCE

There really isn't much routine maintenance required on your electrical system other than watching your electrical consumption and keeping your batteries charged. When you're anchored or sailing for long periods of time, make sure you don't run your batteries down to the point where you can't start your engine(s). To prevent this, some boatowners dedicate a battery bank for engine-starting. Battery switches can be set to isolate this bank from the house bank when anchored. Doing so will probably isolate them from charging as well, so when you start charging the house batteries, you'll need to bring the engine batteries back on-line, too.

ELECTRICAL TROUBLESHOOTING

Do not work on AC circuits: they're too dangerous for anyone but professionals. When you're working on Dulcinea's 12-volt DC circuits, always disconnect the AC power first. Don't just turn off the shore-power circuit breaker: disconnect the power cord at the boat or on the dock. Then start on the 12-volt problem.

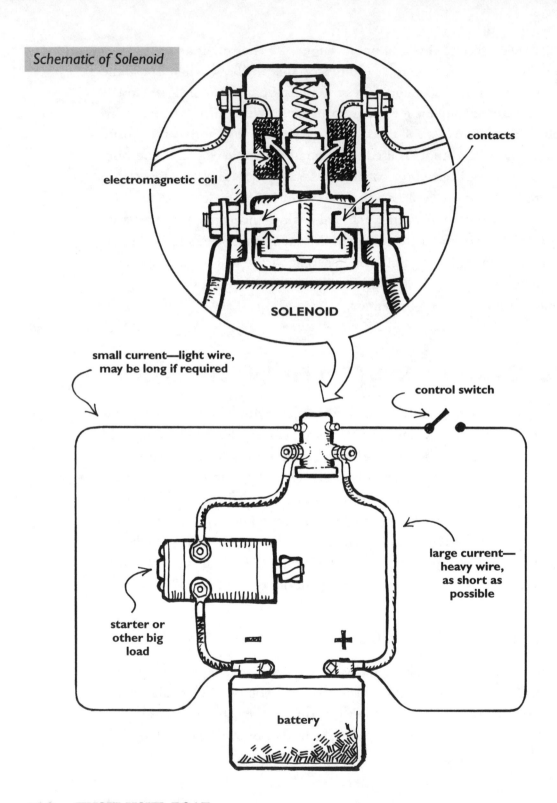

Schematic of Solenoid

contacts

electromagnetic coil

SOLENOID

small current—light wire,
may be long if required

control switch

large current—
heavy wire,
as short as
possible

starter or
other big
load

battery

Most electrical maintenance is an exception—that is, you'll know you need to do it when something breaks. Thankfully, many problems are simple ones like loose or corroded connections or defective switches and the like, and you should be able to diagnose and fix many of the electrical problems on your boat yourself. Even if you can't fix them, you can save money by eliminating some possibilities before you call an expert.

Remember that neatness counts! As you're working on your boat, keep an eye out for wiring that's not neatly secured in a wiring harness or wire tie. You don't want any wires to be snagged, chafed, or caught in anything else. Buy wire ties and clips of various sizes and use them to secure safely all of Dulcinea's wiring. The builder probably did a neat and proper job, but subsequent work may not have been of the same quality.

Note: In this book we only scratch the surface of working on electrical systems. The objective for now is to introduce you to your electrical system, not to make you intimate with it. We leave that for other books.

Measuring DC Voltage

In order to work on Dulcinea's 12-volt system, you need to buy a small, inexpensive multimeter like the one shown on page 119. You can get them at RadioShack, auto-parts stores, and similar places. Get a digital meter with "auto ranging." As the name implies, multimeters can be used for a variety of purposes; most can measure DC voltage and amperage, AC voltage, and resistance. (We won't be using the AC feature here.)

Find a flashlight battery of any size. Set the multimeter on DC voltage and hold the black (negative) probe on the flat bottom of the battery while you touch the red (positive) probe to the button on the top. Your multimeter will read 3, or 1.5, or whatever the battery's voltage happens to be.

Why is a multimeter useful on a boat? Suppose your masthead anchor light is not working. Before crawling up there to change the bulb, you can check to see if voltage is being correctly supplied to that fixture. First, check the panel to see if the circuit breaker for the light is tripped. If it is, a short is most likely (see Finding Short Circuits on pages 120–21). If the breaker isn't tripped, get your multimeter (disconnect the AC before proceeding).

Suppose the wires coming out of the masthead are connected to a terminal block or other connector at the foot of the mast. In this case, turn on the anchor light switch and place the black probe of the multimeter (on DC voltage setting) on the black wire going to the light and the red probe of the multimeter on the colored (probably red) wire going to the light. A little bit of bare wire is probably showing right at the terminal block screw. If not, place the probes on the heads of the screws that are holding the wires in place. You should get a reading of 12 or 13 volts or something similar, indicating voltage is being delivered to the masthead line. If you don't, then the problem is not the bulb and you don't need to crawl up the mast. If voltage is being delivered to the mast line, it's probably the bulb or possibly a break in that part of the circuit.

Measuring Resistance

You can use your multimeter to determine if wires have been cut or whether switches are defective. When you do this, however, there must be no current on the wire you are testing—if there is, you'll ruin your multimeter. To measure resistance, first turn your multimeter to ohms (a symbol like Ω on your multimeter). Now, touch the two probes of the meter to a piece of wood. The resistance reading will be either a very large number like 999999 or it will be 0; either value indicates there is infinite resistance (wood does not conduct electricity) and therefore no electrical connection between the probes of the meter. Now touch the two probes to each other. There is a solid connection and you should see a number like 1, which indicates there is nearly no resistance. (Check the user's manual for your meter because you may see some other small number like 0.7 or 0.8.)

To return to the anchor light example, suppose you suspect that the positive wire from the anchor light circuit breaker to the block at the foot of the mast has been cut. To check out this possibility, disconnect the red wire from the anchor light circuit breaker and from the terminal block at the foot of the mast. (Remember to disconnect the AC power before sticking your hands into the electrical panel.) Now, take a spare piece of wire that is long enough to reach from the foot of the mast to the circuit breaker. Temporarily connect this spare piece of wire to one end of the suspect anchor light wire. At the other end, place one of the multimeter probes on the spare wire and the other on the suspect wire. If you get a 1 or a reading like the one when you touched the probes together, maybe 0.8 or 0.9, the wire is probably OK. If you get a 0 or 999999, it has been cut (assuming your temporary connection is a good connection).

Assume that the anchor light wire is OK. Perhaps now you suspect the circuit breaker itself. To check it, turn off the main breaker or disconnect the breaker to be tested. (Voltage at the test breaker can damage your meter when it is set on ohms.) Put one of the probes on the screw on one side of the breaker and the other on the other side. You should get a 0 or

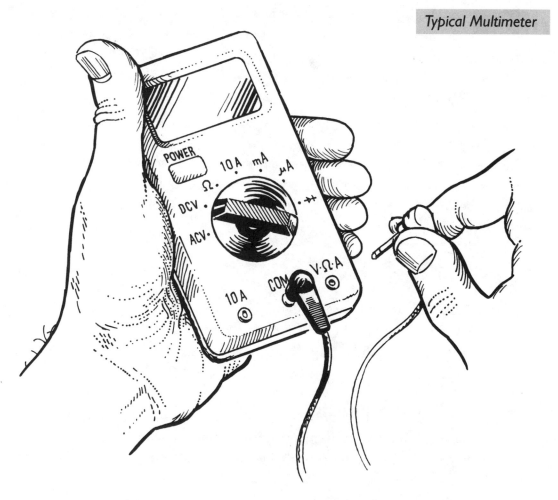

Typical Multimeter

HOW MUCH IS ENOUGH?

By now, you should be getting a sense of how each boat system influences every other boat system. It's good to keep this in mind when you're tempted to add new equipment to your boat.

For example, there are some excellent diesel heaters on the market; perhaps you're thinking of getting one for Dulcinea. Before writing the check, however, think about the heater's impact on the rest of your boat. You'll need to tap into your diesel fuel supply, but you probably won't use too much fuel. You'll need to run heating ductwork through your boat; that may or may not be a problem.

The problem, if there is one, is likely to be electrical consumption. Your heater will draw, say, 10 amps an hour. Running it 5 hours a day at anchor will use 50 amp-hours. Do you have sufficient battery capacity? If not, will you need to run your engine while you run your heater? Now we're talking fuel usage!

Or maybe you think it's time to increase your battery capacity. OK, but where will you put the new batteries and what will that do to your ballast situation? Also, how are you going to charge those new batteries? With a bigger alternator? Now we're talking lots of work and expense!

And we haven't mentioned that you'll need to learn how to use and maintain your heater. You'll have to get it fixed from time to time, and you'll need to carry spare parts for it. It still might be worthwhile, but thinking through all of this, you may decide that a colorful blanket would be a better choice!

999999 reading indicating no electrical connection (open circuit). Now, holding the probes in place, flip the test breaker on. You should now get a reading like 1, indicating that there is a connection. If not, the breaker is defective.

Finding Short Circuits

A short circuit is an unintended path to ground, allowing the current to bypass the load and probably blow the breaker or fuse. We can use the multimeter to find this low-resistance path, or short. Remember, power must be disconnected when measuring ohms. Also disconnect the device (light, motor, or whatever) from both the hot wire (red) and the ground (black).

With the meter's red lead on the red wire and the black lead on the connected portion of the black wire, measure the resistance. An open circuit shows no connection, no short; a low resistance (1 ohm or so) indicates a short. If a short is found, disconnect the red wire at any switches, terminal blocks, or other connections and test each isolated section in turn to find the one with the short. Also check the device for resistance across its terminals. A similar low resistance here indicates an internal short.

After the short is found and fixed, check again with the meter, and also inspect the wire run from the short back to the source for any overheating damage caused by the high current.

Measuring Amperage

This is a bit more involved and risky to your multimeter since the current will run through it, so we won't describe that process here. See the user's manual for your multimeter to learn how.

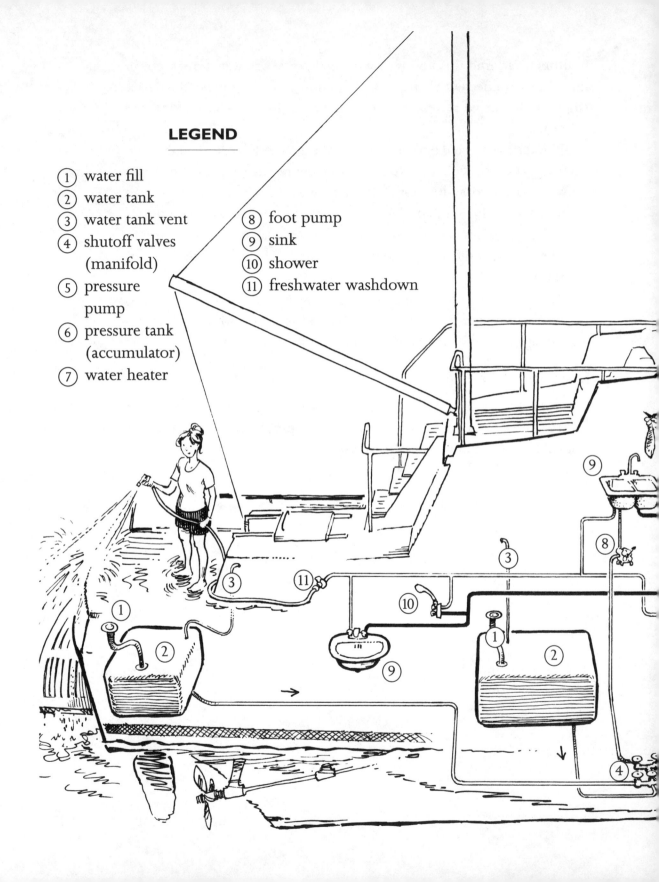

LEGEND

1. water fill
2. water tank
3. water tank vent
4. shutoff valves (manifold)
5. pressure pump
6. pressure tank (accumulator)
7. water heater
8. foot pump
9. sink
10. shower
11. freshwater washdown

FRESHWATER PLUMBING AND WATERMAKERS

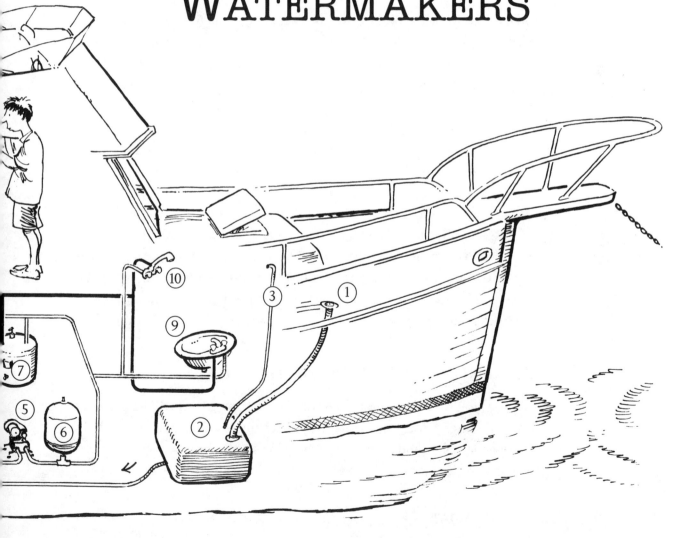

About the only thing more frustrating than running out of water or losing water pressure is having problems with the head. We'll deal with freshwater plumbing here and save the head and related systems for the next chapter. The good news is that water problems aren't usually too hard to fix and, except for watermakers, water systems and their components are simple, especially when compared to engines and electricity.

UNDERSTANDING YOUR FRESHWATER SYSTEM

You can save yourself a lot of trouble by making a diagram of the arrangement of tanks, hoses, pumps, water heater, faucets, etc., aboard Dulcinea. It will help you understand why filling one tank fills (or doesn't fill) another tank, where to look for leaks, and assorted idiosyncrasies (like when you run out of water and switch tanks, you have to open the head faucet before the water pump stops running). A fringe benefit is that you can inspect the system as you go, and also make a list of spares to carry.

Because you'll be lifting cushions and pulling up cabin-sole boards, pick a day when you have the boat to yourself. Go down to the boat, open a few hatches, let the fresh air flow in. Then, find your favorite bunk, and before you pull that cushion up, lie down and take a nap. It's good preparation for making the water diagram, and besides, one of the greatest pleasures of owning a boat is taking an afternoon nap on a nice day when the water is calm and the boat rocks ever so gently at its mooring. And, if you don't get to the diagram, well, it's a big job and tomorrow is another day.

MAKING A WATER-FLOW DIAGRAM

OK, now you're ready to start. Each water tank in your boat will have at least three openings: water-in, water-out, and a vent. It will probably also have an inspection plate, and it may have a dipstick as well. The first thing you need to do is find all of your tanks and figure out the location of these three openings on each one. The water-in and vent will be on the top of the tank and the water-out will be on the bottom. Try to follow the water-in and vent hoses up to the deck so you'll know for sure which deck fills and vent openings lead to which tanks. Make sketches and notes of what you find.

While you're at it, inspect the tanks, hoses, and hose clamps, though I don't recommend undoing any clamps (unless they look suspect) as that may cause water leaks. If you can see the hose as it leads to the deck, check to be sure that it doesn't have any kinks in it. If it does, try to smooth them out because if you don't, when you fill that tank the kink may cause the water to back up, making you think the tank is full when it's not.

If the tanks are plastic or fiberglass, they should be in fine shape. Metal tanks may develop corrosion along the welds and seams. Brush the seam with a brass wire brush to see how deep the corrosion is. If the corrosion is deep or if the tank starts to leak after you brush it, you'll need to replace the tank. This is often a painful and expensive job, and I hope none of it pertains to your Dulcinea.

Once you've found all the tanks, try to figure out how they're connected. They may be connected so that filling one fills them all, but it's more likely that they're separated in some way. I have five water tanks in my boat and three water deck fills. The three tanks on the port side are connected so they can be filled from the port-side deck fill. The two tanks on the starboard side are separate, and each has its own starboard-side deck fill. The advantage of separated tanks is that if you develop a leak in one, you won't lose all of your water. My system was designed for the days before watermakers, when it was sometimes necessary to take on water of questionable quality; separate tanks meant that if you happened to get some bad water, it wouldn't contaminate all of your tanks.

All of the water-out hoses will lead to a set of valves or a manifold like that shown in the chapter-opening illustration. If you have trouble finding these, try looking in or around the galley. By turning these on, you can select the tank that is connected to the house water system. These valves are most likely ball valves like those described for seacocks in chapter 2; when the handle is parallel to the valve, it's open; when it crosses the valve at a right angle, it's closed.

For the system shown, you could have more than one tank on-line at a time, but this is usually a bad idea since using two or more tanks simultaneously makes it hard to know how much water you have left. If several of your tanks are connected together, taking water from the lowest tank may take water from all of them; you may think you've used the water from only one tank, when you've actually used the water from several. If several tanks are connected together, they probably have a valve between them; you can shut this if you want to ensure that you're using water from a particular tank.

SAMPLE WATER FLOW DIAGRAM

The illustration opposite shows a freshwater diagram for a boat with two water tanks. Each tank has a water-in line, a vent, and a water-out line. The tanks on this system are connected by two shutoff valves to the main house water supply line. That line is extended to a *foot pump* at the galley sink. There's probably also a line to foot pumps at the head sink(s) as well, but adding them to this diagram just confuses the issue.

A second water supply line is taken from the main house line and leads to a *water pressure pump*. This pump has a *pressure switch* that senses the pressure in the hose between it and the *accumulator*. While you're making your diagram, notice the wiring arrangement between the pressure pump and the pressure switch. A 12-volt wire leads from the water pressure circuit breaker to the pressure switch, and another wire leads from the switch to the pump. In most setups, when necessary, the pressure switch can be replaced separately from the pressure pump. The accumulator is essentially an empty tank that works something like a balloon. It levels out changes in pressure so that your water pipes don't bang like those in an old apartment building, and so that the water pressure pump is not constantly cycling on and off.

All water lines after the pump have pressurized water in them, so be sure to turn off the water pressure circuit breaker before loosening any connections downstream of the pump. Then with the pump off, open a faucet to release the pressure in the accumulator before disconnecting anything.

In the illustration opposite, the pressurized cold water line runs from the accumulator tank to the faucet. A second pressurized line runs to the

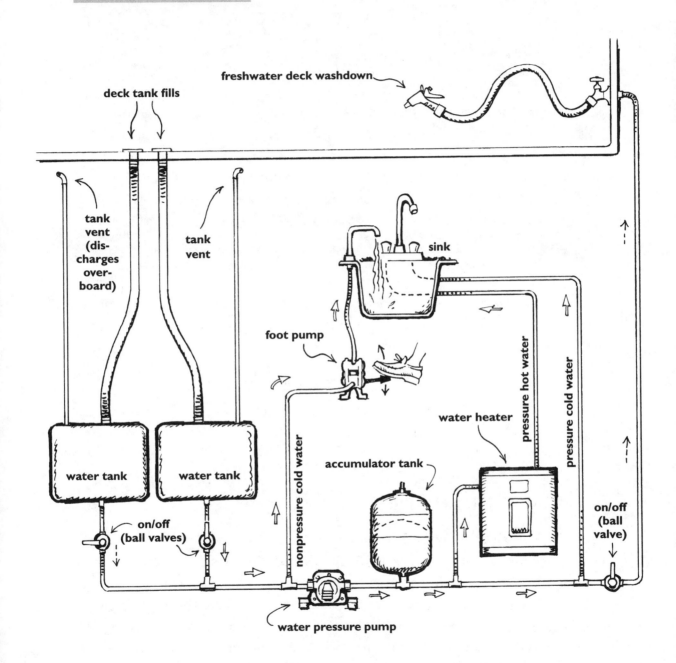

freshwater deck washdown

deck tank fills

tank vent (discharges overboard)

tank vent

sink

foot pump

pressure hot water

pressure cold water

water heater

accumulator tank

water tank

water tank

nonpressure cold water

on/off (ball valves)

on/off (ball valve)

water pressure pump

GOOD TO THE (NEXT TO) LAST DROP

Like everything else on your deck, be sure your washdown hoses are clearly labeled, especially if your boat has both fresh- and saltwater washdown hose fittings. A friend of mine had anchored out in San Diego Bay for his last night before starting a passage to Cabo San Lucas. In the morning, he pulled up his anchor and blithely used his washdown hose to clean the anchor, all the chain, the foredeck, etc. You guessed it: he used the wrong hose and went through almost all of the water in one set of tanks. Luckily, it was only 40 miles back to the dock and more water.

hot water heater and then to the hot water side of the faucet. Again, you'll also have lines that run to faucets in the sinks and showers in the head(s). Finally, you may have a pressure line that runs to your deck washdown. If so, you should also have a shutoff valve that you normally keep off. If not, consider adding one so you don't lose water through it if the cap is not securely on. In the Pacific Northwest, where the decks are usually wet, it's hard to know when you have a leak in the deck washdown system.

WATER PUMPS

The accompanying illustration shows the basic design of a diaphragm pump; all of the pumps in Dulcinea's freshwater system are a variation of this design. There is a pump housing that encloses a space where the pumping action occurs. The inflow hose has a flap of rubber (or something similar) that covers the inflow hole from the inside of the pump housing. The outflow hose has a similar flap that covers the outflow hose from the outside of the pump housing.

The pump works like this: When you raise the pump handle, you extend

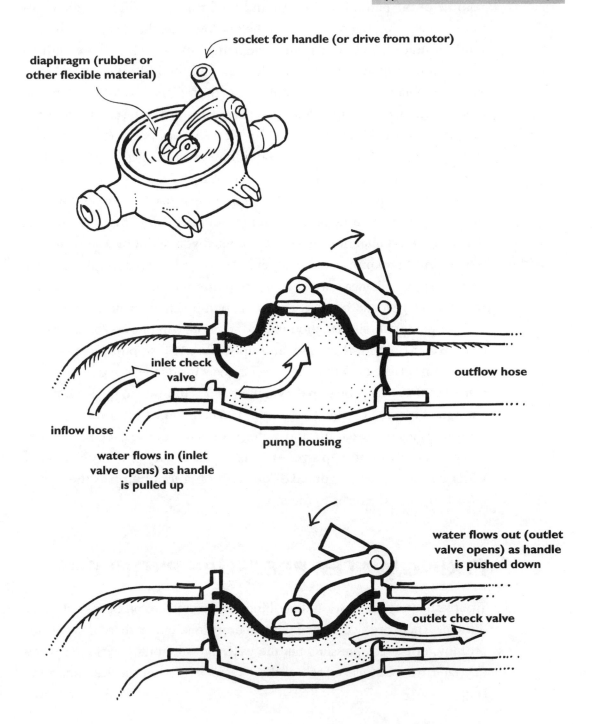

socket for handle (or drive from motor)

diaphragm (rubber or other flexible material)

inlet check valve

outflow hose

inflow hose

pump housing

water flows in (inlet valve opens) as handle is pulled up

water flows out (outlet valve opens) as handle is pushed down

outlet check valve

the *diaphragm* (rubbery sheet) that's attached to the handle, increasing the volume of the pump housing. Air and fluid rush in to fill the added volume and equalize the pressure. On the outflow side, the suction of air and fluid causes the flap to pull against the pump housing, closing the outflow hose. On the inflow side, the inrush of air and fluid fills the pump housing with whatever it is you're pumping (in this case, water). When you push down on the pump handle, you place pressure on the air and water in the pump housing. This causes the flap on the inflow opening to fall down and cover the inflow hole. The air and fluid push the flap on the outflow side open, and the air and fluid are pumped out.

One of the advantages of diaphragm pumps is that, unlike the impeller pump in your engine, diaphragm pumps can be run dry. This doesn't mean that you should intentionally run them when you're out of water, but you won't ruin the pump if that happens. Almost all water pumps have this basic design. Dulcinea's water pressure pump includes an electric motor with a large gear and belt that drives the pump handle up and down.

Foot pumps are similar, though they are more complicated because they draw water on both the down and up strokes. A foot pump is basically two pumps placed back to back. The chambers inside the foot pump are designed so that when you step down, the water is directed to the front pump (designed to draw on the down stroke). When you let up, a spring in the pump pushes the pedal up, and water is directed to the back pump (designed to draw on the up stroke). This explains why one more spurt of water comes out when you take your foot off a foot pump as the spring returns the pedal returns to the top.

FIXING WATER PRESSURE PROBLEMS

Troubleshooting (or at least, describing) water pressure problems isn't very difficult. There are two basic kinds of problems: either there is no water pressure, or there is pressure, but the water pressure pump cycles on when no water has been used. Each of these cases is listed in the accompanying table.

Freshwater System Troubleshooting Guide

PROBLEM	POSSIBLE CAUSE	REMEDY
No water pressure; pump is running.	Out of water.	Switch tanks.
	Air in water hose.	While pump is running, open faucets in galley and head for 10 seconds or so. Then shut off. Pump will stop running.
	Pump motor is running but belt drive is not moving.	Allen screws on pump gears are loose or belt is defective. Turn off water pressure switch and tighten screws or replace belt.
	Water hose disconnected from fitting. Freshwater flowing into bilge.	Turn off pump. Reconnect hose.
No water pressure; pump not running.	Water pressure circuit breaker not on.	Turn breaker on.
	House power not on.	Turn house power on.
	Faulty electrical connections to pump or pressure switch.	Fix connections.
	12-volt power not reaching pump.	Open faucet. With circuit breaker on, check voltage into pressure switch. If voltage around 12 volts, likely problem is defective pressure switch. If no voltage to pressure switch, problem is in wiring to pressure switch or in circuit breaker.
Pressure leak: water pump cycles on every now and then when water has not been used.	Faucet or valve to watermaker partially open.	Close all faucets and valves.
	Leak in water hose.	Find and fix leak. Check hoses into hot water tank first.
	Dirt or grit in water pump flap seats.	Take pump apart and clean flaps and flap seats.
	Faulty pump flaps.	Replace flaps.

continued page 132

Freshwater System Troubleshooting Guide (continued)

PROBLEM	POSSIBLE CAUSE	REMEDY
Pressure leak: water pump cycles on every now and then when water has not been used. (continued)	Leak in accumulator tank.	Replace accumulator.
Water heater not working	Problem in 120-volt AC water heater.	Call a professional. *Do not attempt to fix AC wiring around water!!!!*

If the water pressure pump is running but there is no pressure, the most likely causes are that you're out of water or there's air in the pressure system hoses. In the latter case, you can bleed the air out by opening the faucets in all the heads and the galley for 10 seconds or so. Then shut them off and the pressure should build in the water system.

If this doesn't work, examine the water pump to see if the belt between the motor and the pump is moving while the motor runs. If not, turn off the power and tighten the Allen screws on the gears on both the motor and the pump. Also check the belt to make sure that it's not broken.

One other possibility is that a hose has popped off a connection and the pump is filling your bilge with freshwater. If this is the case, shut off the pump and reconnect the hose. This is a good reason to keep your water pressure pump circuit breaker off when you're not using the water pressure system. The noise from your engine or from wind and waves can make it hard to hear your pump running—the first sign that you're pumping freshwater into the bilge could be water coming over the cabin sole!

PUMP REPAIR

Little needs to be done to most water pumps because the fluid they pump is clean. However, if you don't have water pressure and the pump isn't running, first check to make sure the circuit breaker is on and house power is on. If they are and the pump motor doesn't run with a faucet open, check the connections going into the pressure switch and from the pressure switch to the motor. If they're OK, turn on the water pressure circuit breaker (*keep hands and tools out of the way of the belt just in case the motor suddenly comes on!*) and use your multimeter to check for the presence of something close to 12 volts on the wires going into the pressure switch. To do this, place the red probe on the wire going into the pressure switch and the black probe on the black wire terminal on the pump. If there's no voltage going into the switch, then something is wrong between the circuit breaker and the pressure switch. Check again to make sure the correct circuit breaker is on and that the boat has DC power.

If power is on and you still have no voltage at the pressure switch, look for a loose connection or break in the 12-volt wire from the panel to the pressure switch. If there are 12 volts or so going into the pressure switch, then turn on water somewhere in the boat and check for the presence of 12 volts coming out of the water pressure switch. Do this by moving the red probe of the multimeter to the wire coming out of the pressure switch. If there's voltage going in and none coming out, then the problem is in the switch. If there's voltage coming out of the switch, then there's either a problem in the wiring or in the pressure pump motor.

Of course, if your pump is leaking, then you'll need to rebuild it. The first thing to do is examine the pump and find the name of the manufacturer and the model number. Then, search the Internet for that manufacturer and model. You'll most likely find both a diagram of your pump and a list of available repair kits. Take the part number of the repair kit to your local chandlery and buy that kit. The kit will include instructions for repairing your pump.

From the illustration on page 129 you can see that if anything interferes with the flaps—say a piece of string or a toothpick—and keeps them from sealing their holes, then the pump won't work. This is seldom a problem with water pumps, though, because nothing like string or toothpicks should be in your water system. With your head pumps, however . . . but we'll wait until the next chapter for that story.

FIXING PRESSURE LEAKS

Every now and then your Dulcinea's freshwater system may develop a pressure leak. You'll know this is occurring if your water pressure pump comes on from time to time when no one has used any water. If you develop a pressure leak, before doing anything else, check all of the faucets to make sure that none of them is partially on or leaking, which would cause the water pressure pump to cycle. Also make sure that any pressurized deck fittings are closed, and if you have a watermaker (more about them later in this chapter), ensure that connections to it from the pressure side of your water system are fully closed. If you've done all this, and you still have a leak, the problem is probably at a hose clamp. The fewer clamps you have, the better, so when you have equipment added to your water system, don't let the installer add any splices or more clamps than necessary. Replace splices in water hose with longer, whole pieces of hose, if necessary.

The first hose clamps to check are those on the hot water tank, especially if you've just turned on the hot water (or run the engine) for the first time in a while. The alternate heating and cooling of the hot water line is perfect for developing a hose leak. If you find a hose fitting that's obviously loose or one with water oozing out, you can bet that the leak is there. In fact, for a water pressure leak, there must be water accumulating somewhere. Dry your hands and rub them over all the water hoses until you find where the leak might be. If you don't know what else to do, tighten all the hose clamps.

Often all you need to do to stop a leak is tighten the hose clamp a bit. If that doesn't work, and if the hose is otherwise in good shape, heat the end that's leaking with a heat gun until it becomes limp (but don't burn it). While it's still hot, tighten the hose clamp down. This should stop the leak. (If you don't have a heat gun, put boiling water in a small pan and stick the end of the hose in the boiling water for a minute or so. When it gets soft, put it back on the fitting and tighten the clamp while the hose is still hot. That should do the trick. I tried a microwave once, but with a very unsatisfactory result, so I don't recommend it.)

If heating it doesn't work, you may have to cut the hose to get fresh material for the clamp to bite on. Cut an inch or so off the end of the hose, reattach it to the fitting, and tighten the hose clamp. If the hose is too short to cut, you'll have to replace it. Before doing that, however, give the heat trick one more try.

If you can't find a leak around any of your hose clamps, then it's possible that some dirt or grit is keeping the pump flaps from seating correctly. To find out, you'll have to take the pump apart, and while you're at it, you might as well replace the flaps using the proper repair kit.

If you still have a pressure leak after repairing your pressure pump, then the only thing left to try is the accumulator tank. This is a long shot, however, and before buying a new one, splice a section of hose to bypass the accumulator tank and see if the pressure leak goes away. If it does, the leak is in the tank and you'll need to replace it. It would be worthwhile to check all of the faucets and everything else one more time before buying a new accumulator. I recommend turning the pump off and getting a good night's rest before even thinking about this problem again—maybe your subconscious will come up with a solution while you sleep.

WATERMAKERS

Ah, watermakers. When they work, they're wonderful—fulfilling the alchemical dreams of seafarers through the ages by turning salt water into fresh, sweet water, freeing us from the dock, from questionable water supplies, and from schlepping 5-gallon cans from the boat to the beach in the dinghy, up to the water supply, and back to the boat. Showers every day, even offshore—what luxury! But can they be hard to keep running! They're complicated; they work at high pressures; bacteria want to grow in them; minerals and little pieces of dirt and oil want to fill them; and chlorine from the city's water supply or other sources wants to destroy them. And leaks! But for any type of extended cruising today, you can't live with 'em and you can't live without 'em.

So, buy the highest quality system you can afford and treat it with kid gloves.

WATERMAKER BASICS

The idea behind a watermaker (sometimes called a *reverse osmosis watermaker*) is to take raw seawater and filter it to remove as much junk and as many impurities as possible. Then this filtered seawater is led to a *membrane*, a long tube that contains a smaller tube inside. The smaller tube is made of a mesh of very small holes just large enough to let freshwater through but keep salt and bacteria out.

When raw seawater is pumped between the outer tube and the inner tube, its flow is constricted downstream of the membrane, and the pressure inside the membrane increases to the point where some water will be forced from the outer tube, through the mesh, and inside the second tube. Eureka! This is freshwater that can then be led to a test station at a sink and to the boat's water tanks. The higher the pressure, the more freshwater will be forced through the mesh and the greater the output of the watermaker. However, higher pressures necessitate a more powerful high-pressure pump and they place more force on the high-pressure components. This means higher quality components and, of course, greater expense. Also, such a high-pressure pump will need to be driven either by the engine or by 120-volt AC power; 12-volt electricity doesn't have enough power to drive a higher pressure pump.

The reliability of the system can be greatly increased if the membrane, the high-pressure pump, and the other components exposed to seawater are flushed with freshwater after watermaking. This means using some of the water that was just produced, but, especially with high-capacity watermakers, it's well worth the investment. Around 5 gallons of water are normally used for this flushing process, so flushing lower capacity systems that make 2 gallons an hour just isn't practical.

If you're not going to use the watermaker for some time—more than a month or so—then a solution of chemicals to prevent algae growth, etc, must be pumped into the membrane. This process is referred to as *pickling* the watermaker. Once the watermaker has been pickled, it can remain unused for a year or so, but before you use it again, the pickling solution must be removed and the system flushed for 30 to 40 minutes or more (depending on the watermaker).

WATERMAKER COMPONENTS

The illustration on pages 138–39 shows the design of a high-quality watermaking system. Not all systems have all these features, but higher quality, more reliable systems do. This illustration is complicated because it shows three different systems in one diagram. There's one system for obtaining raw seawater, filtering it, and delivering it to the membrane (the solid line). There's a second system for producing water, testing it, and storing it in your boat's tanks (the dashed line). And there's a third system for flushing the components with freshwater after using the watermaker (the short-long dashed line). We'll consider each of these in turn.

Seawater Delivery

The solid line shows the path of seawater to the membrane. The water enters the boat through a through-hull seacock and flows through a seawater strainer like that on your engine. A low-pressure pump then pushes the water through one or two filters; the illustration shows a 20-micron filter followed by a 5-micron filter (this just means a coarser one followed by a finer one). These filters need to be cleaned and replaced periodically; if you forget, your produced water will start to smell like rotten eggs, which probably won't hurt you, but it makes for bad coffee.

From here, the filtered raw water enters the high-pressure pump. Look at the right-hand side of the illustration to find the *regulator valve*. If this valve is left fully open, there will be no additional pressure on the raw water, and it will simply flow through the membrane, around the outside of the mesh, and out of the boat through a through-hull. The gauge should show zero pressure or close to it when this is the case.

Water that passes through the outside of the membrane is referred to as *brine water*. With the valve open, all of the raw water will be brine water.

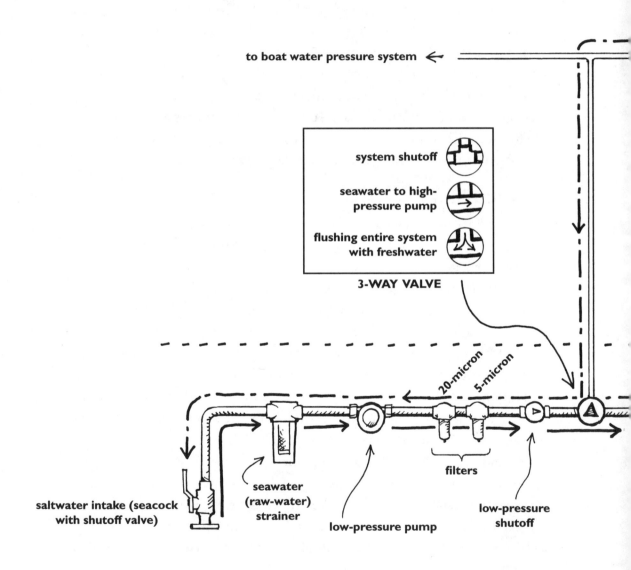

to boat water pressure system

system shutoff

seawater to high-pressure pump

flushing entire system with freshwater

3-WAY VALVE

20-micron

5-micron

filters

saltwater intake (seacock with shutoff valve)

seawater (raw-water) strainer

low-pressure pump

low-pressure shutoff

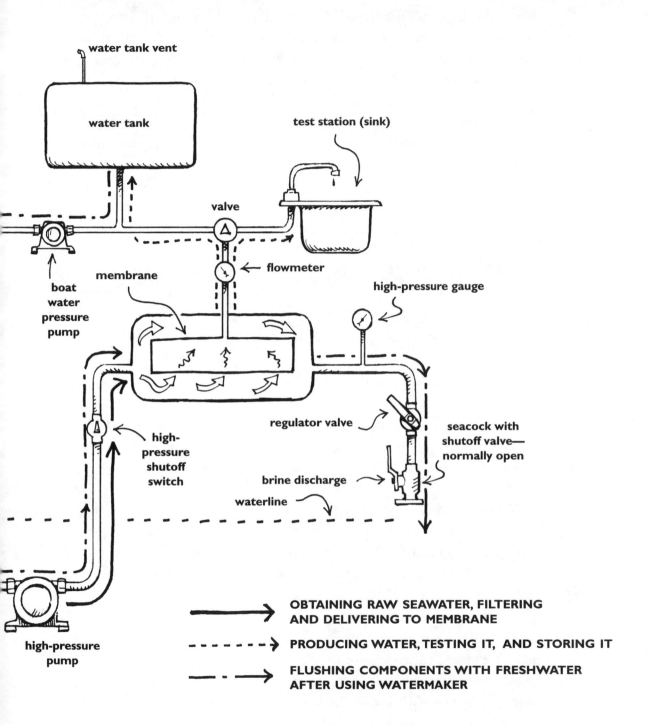

water tank vent

water tank

test station (sink)

valve

boat water pressure pump

membrane

flowmeter

high-pressure gauge

high-pressure shutoff switch

regulator valve

seacock with shutoff valve— normally open

brine discharge

waterline

high-pressure pump

OBTAINING RAW SEAWATER, FILTERING AND DELIVERING TO MEMBRANE

PRODUCING WATER, TESTING IT, AND STORING IT

FLUSHING COMPONENTS WITH FRESHWATER AFTER USING WATERMAKER

Note that the brine discharge through-hull must be above the waterline and open for the brine to exit; if closed, the brine water will back up and the system will shut down (or a hose will pop off, or worse, depending on the design of your watermaker). I normally leave my brine-exit through-hull open all the time.

This system also has two safety switches; one protects the watermaker and one protects both the watermaker and the watermakee. The low-pressure (shutoff) switch ensures that sufficient raw water is entering the system to make water. The high-pressure (shutoff) switch ensures that pressure inside the membrane never exceeds the safe limit of the membrane and system components.

Producing Freshwater

The dashed line shows the components that come into play when making water. First, set the valve (to the left of the sink in the illustration) so that the produced water will go to a test spigot at the sink. Then, slowly tighten the regulator valve, causing pressure to rise in the high-pressure hoses and the membrane. Tighten the valve in stages—maybe 100 psi (pounds per square inch) at a time—and pause at each stage to let any air bubbles in the system work their way out. Tighten the valve until it reaches the designed rating of the watermaker, probably around 900 psi. At this point, water will be flowing out of the test spigot. The flow meter will indicate the amount of water that is being produced.

When you start a watermaker, the water produced at first will be saltier than when the system has been running for awhile. Therefore, it's a good idea to let the water run for a few minutes and taste it before turning the valve to send the water to the tank. You can also purchase a small device that will test the water to determine its salt content. Anything less than 500 parts per million is considered potable water.

Now, just sit back and relax (if you can—high pressure pumps are noisy) and let that freshwater flow into your tanks. Make sure that your water storage tanks have a vent and that you *always have a tank open* for the water to flow to. Otherwise, the high pressure will build . . . and build . . . and build . . . and . . . in my watermaker, a high-pressure hose will pop off and spray water all over the place! Not that I've ever done that, of course.

Flushing the System

When you've finished making water, the last step is to flush the system with freshwater. As shown by the short-long dashed line, water from the tank is pumped by your boat's water pressure pump through all the lines and components that had contained raw (salty water). With my water-maker, this is done in two phases. First, the freshwater is pumped through the high-pressure pump, the membrane, and out the brine discharge through-hull. I pump at least 3 or 4 gallons out this way. During the second stage, freshwater is pumped back through the filters, the low-pressure pump, the seawater strainer, and then out the intake through-hull. This takes another 2 gallons or so.

WATERMAKER TROUBLESHOOTING AND USE

The instructions for your watermaker will include a troubleshooting guide. When you have problems, you need to consult it. Watermakers are so different from each other that it's almost impossible to offer troubleshooting guidelines other than those of the "buy low, sell high" variety that follow.

For watermakers, it's especially true that the best way to solve a problem is not to have it. Do not run your watermaker when Dulcinea is sitting in water that's full of dirt or grime. *Especially do not run it when there is evidence of oil or diesel fuel on the water.* These two statements mean that you generally should not run your watermaker in a marina. (I know, who'd want to anyway? I mean, not everyone is using his or her holding tank. The manufacturer of my watermaker tells me that no bacteria can get through the membrane, so the least of my fears in running the watermaker in a marina should be illness. I still don't like the thought of drinking water made from marina water.)

Chlorine will ruin your watermaker's membrane. Never run city water into your watermaker, and never use city water from your tanks for back-flushing. Some say that you can use chlorinated water that's been in your tanks for more than a week or so for backflushing because the chlorine will have decomposed in that time. I say avoid the whole issue and use only water that you've made for backflushing. If you have no made water on hand when you need to backflush, buy 5 to 10 gallons of distilled water, put it into an empty tank, and use it.

You want to do all you can to keep dirt and debris from the membrane, so change your prefilters often. There is a type of prefilter that can be cleaned and reused. If you have that type, clean your filters often. Otherwise replace them often. Remove dirt from the bottom of the filter canister when you change the filters. Also, if your watermaker requires you to fill your prefilter canisters with water when you change filters, be sure to use salt water or water you have made yourself. If you use city dock-water for filling those canisters, you'll be introducing chlorine into your system, which you do not want to do!

Also, keep in mind that pickling your watermaker always leaves a small amount of pickling solution in your system. It is impossible to remove all of that solution by rinsing. Some of it will lodge in the small valves and springs in pressure switches and some will lodge in the bottom of the flow meter, etc. Therefore, pickle your watermaker as little as you can. While the general advice is to pickle if you're not going to make water for a month, you might want to stretch that to two months if you can. If you try this, double-backflush your system with made water beforehand.

In theory, you can rejuvenate a membrane that's clogged with bacteria and minerals. The process involves running very, very acidic water (pH 2, if you're a chemist) through the membrane for 15 minutes or so, rinsing the membrane, and then running very, very basic water for another 15 minutes, and rinsing again. I've never done this because I don't have the knowledge or skill to work with such dangerous chemicals. Much damage to you, the boat, and the watermaker can be caused by mishandling such strong acids and bases. When I needed a new membrane, I just bit the bullet and bought a new one.

If you're a professional chemist and you know what you're doing, you might try it. A better idea, however, if you don't want to buy a new membrane, is to send your old one back to the factory for reconditioning. Check with the manufacturer first, however, because they will have requirements for how you package the membrance before you ship it.

Watermakers are a pain, no doubt about it. But Lynda and I cruised in Mexico for two and a half years and never were sick. We think one reason is that we lived all that time on water that we made ourselves. Also, having a watermaker makes it possible to hang out in remote, dry places like the Sea of Cortez for long periods of time. You can also trade water for fish and give it away in times of drought. And there's nothing like a shower when you're covered with salt from swimming (or grime from fixing your watermaker . . .)

6

MARINE TOILETS

LEGEND

1. seawater in
2. pump assembly
3. flush water to bowl
4. vented antisiphon loops
5. waste out
6. Y- or diverter valve
7. holding tank
8. through-hulls with seacocks
9. holding tank deck pumpout
10. holding tank vent

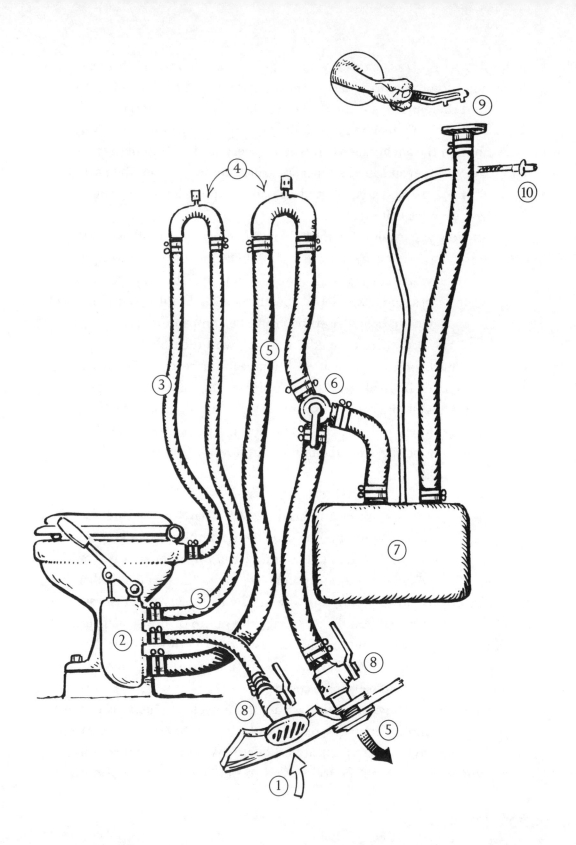

FRANKLY, YESTERDAY WAS A BIT FRIGHTENING—that pea-soup fog came up so fast in the afternoon, and then you had to find the entrance to the anchorage by radar. And the wind was blowing, too, maybe 25 or 30 knots. But now you're here. Even though the anchorage is crowded—everyone's hiding here from the wind—you found a quiet spot that's removed from the pack, dropped the hook, got a good set, and—snug as a bug in a rug—you slept well all night.

Now you're admiring the light in the trees as you mull over yesterday's trip, sipping your first cup of coffee out in the cockpit. "This is what cruising is all about," you think. The quiet soothes your nerves, and a wonderful contentment soaks into your bones as your teenage daughter erupts from the companionway.

"Dad, Dad, there's something wrong with the toilet!"

Your happy reverie shattered, you leap up, ready to berate the messenger, but realize in the nick of time that you need perspective. After all, she could be saying, "Dad, I'm pregnant!" Or, "Dad, I had a little problem with the car and the police want to talk to you!" Yes, perspective's the thing right now.

As you're about to learn, head problems have one of three causes: the head's being used incorrectly; something's blocking a valve or line; or a valve, diaphragm, piston, or other part is worn or broken. Of the three causes, the good news about the first two is that you don't need to buy anything to fix them. The bad news about the second one, however, is that you'll have to take the pump or hoses apart to find and fix the problem. The very bad news about the third one is that you have to have parts and you have to take the toilet apart. We'll discuss these further in the Toilet Problems section.

So, the first thing to do after getting the unwelcome news is to finish your coffee and reflect: How many heads do you have? Do you have to fix this one? What spare parts are on board? Where's everyone going to go while you work on the toilet? And so on. The first thing you might want to do is inflate the dinghy so everyone can go ashore—meaning they'll be able to use bathrooms there and be out of your way while you work.

USING YOUR HEAD

Marine toilets, unlike those on shore, are composed of many small components that can be easily damaged or clogged. Thus, the general rule for head usage is *never put anything into a marine head that you didn't eat*. That rule includes used or unused toilet paper, and some boats have a small receptacle near the toilet for all paper products. Other boaters are not quite so extreme—small amounts of marine toilet paper* are OK, but nothing else; no sanitary napkins or tampons, tissues, candy wrappers, or baseball cards.

Following this rule is generally not a problem for family members, who understand the need for it. A bigger problem can be adult guests who may be too modest to ask and child guests who just don't know to ask. Therefore, although it can be a bit awkward, always take the time to instruct your guests and their children on the use of the toilet. The best policy may be to tell visiting children not to flush the toilet, just to let you know when they've used it. Another good idea is to post a note somewhere visible in the head on proper toilet usage.

To prolong your head's life, *use only mild cleaners and cleansers*. The rubber seals and valves used on toilet parts can be damaged by most household cleaners, so don't use any of the drain cleaners you use at home. Peggie Hall, a recognized expert in this field, says not to use detergent, bleach, dish soap, or other cleaners, especially cleaners that contain pine oil, petroleum, or alcohol. Instead, follow the directions for cleaning and maintenance that are provided in the users' manual for your head. You can also find specially formulated toilet cleaners at marine stores. To prevent calcium

*Marine toilet paper is nothing more than inexpensive, single-ply toilet paper you can find at grocery stores (it's a lot cheaper there than at marine stores).

buildup in your head, once a month or so pour a ½ cup of vinegar down it, flush with a quart or two of water and wait—as long as overnight if you can. It's possible the acid in the vinegar will react with calcium that could become a problem. For calcium buildup in the head that's attached to your shoulders, industry experts recommend two jiggers of rum, a lime . . . oh, never mind.

When sailing offshore, we've always had the rule that everyone sits down when using the head. It's just too hard to reliably hit the toilet when standing and the boat is lurching around. When we noticed how much cleaner (and sweeter smelling) our head stayed, we decided to extend the rule to all situations. While this won't prolong the life of your toilet, it does make a world of difference in the cleanliness of the head.

Finally, remember to feed everyone a healthy high-fiber diet with lots of fruits, vegetables, and grains so that they'll have soft, easily flushed stools.

BASIC HEAD DESIGN

The illustration shows the basic components of a marine head system. There are two kinds of hoses used: those for bringing flushing water into the toilet fixture are usually ¾-inch inner diameter, and those for discharging waste material are typically 1½-inch inner diameter. If the toilet is located below the waterline (and most are), then antisiphon valves will be necessary on both hoses, as shown in the illustration.

The discharge line is connected to a Y-valve that directs the outflow to either a holding tank or directly overboard. Move the Y-valve back and forth now and then to make sure it doesn't get stuck. The drawing shows the Y-valve ahead of the holding tank; other designs run the outflow of the toilet directly into the holding tank and place the Y-valve between the holding tank deck pumpout and the head outflow through-hull.

While we're on this topic, there are federal and state laws about dumping sewage overboard. According to the Federal Clean Water Act of 1972, sewage cannot be dumped overboard when the boat is within 3

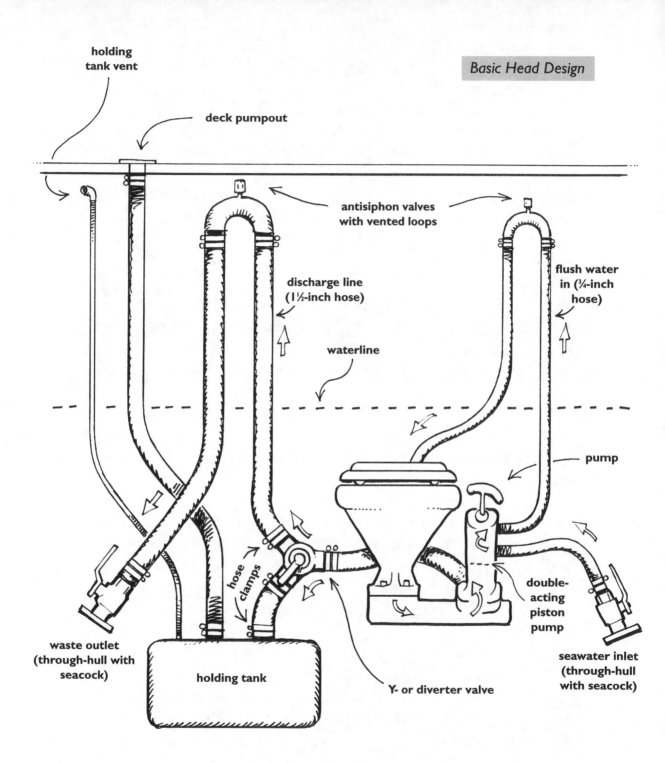

holding tank vent

deck pumpout

antisiphon valves
with vented loops

discharge line
(1½-inch hose)

flush water
in (¾-inch
hose)

waterline

pump

hose
clamps

double-
acting
piston
pump

waste outlet
(through-hull with
seacock)

holding tank

Y- or diverter valve

seawater inlet
(through-hull
with seacock)

Keeping It Legal

According to the Federal Clean Water Act of 1972 (amended in 1987) boaters operating within 3 nautical miles of a U.S. shoreline are required to use one of three types of marine sanitation devices. Boats 65 feet or less can use any of the three types, but boats 66 feet or more must use either a type 2 or type 3 device. Any state can petition the Environmental Protection Agency to classify a body of water as a *No-Discharge Zone*, where only type 3 devices are allowed.

Type 1 devices treat sewage so that discharges have no visible solid, floating material and meet specified levels for bacteria count. They use a combination of salt water, chemicals, and electricity to macerate and clean sewage. They typically cost about $1,000 and consume around 45 amps of 12-volt electricity for 3 minutes after each flush. They may not be used in any No-Discharge Zone.

Type 2 devices are similar to type 1, but have higher standards for cleanliness. Since they're more complicated and require more power, prices start around $5,000. They may not be used in No-Discharge Zones.

Type 3 devices are holding tanks used to hold sewage. They can be emptied only at dockside pumpout stations or discharged overboard when the boat is more than 3 nautical miles offshore. They must have some means of detecting when they're two-thirds or more full. If the tank and its contents are visible, it complies with this rule; otherwise, some type of level-indicating device is required. Holding tanks cost about $200 to $300.

Any device that complies with the MSD standards is required to have a label that indicates this fact. This law pertains only to heads that are attached to a boat. A portable toilet, if it isn't attached in any way to a boat, is exempt. Direct human deposits into the water are also exempt (although you may be subject to indecent exposure laws and the ridicule of your anchorage neighbors).

nautical miles of shore, nor can it be dumped overboard in any location designated as a No-Discharge Zone. Instead, you are required to use a type 1 or 2 marine sanitation device (MSD) or to pump your sewage into a holding tank (a type 3 MSD) and to empty its contents using a pumpout facility located at a fuel dock, marina, or other location (see sidebar).

Judging by the large number of boats on the water and the few boats that actually use a pumpout, these discharge laws are frequently violated. In the Pacific Northwest, most boaters consider it gross and inappropriate to pump sewage overboard in any anchorage. On the other hand, while underway in deep water (400 feet or more), where there's lots of tidal current, most boaters pump away. It's hard to argue with this when the city of Victoria, British Columbia, pumps its raw sewage directly into the Strait of Juan de Fuca. Still, others argue that any exceptions increase water pollution and contribute to the problem, no matter who else may be polluting. And such overboard discharge, while it may be an accepted local custom, is still illegal.

One thing is certain: Nothing is more disgusting than waking up in an otherwise beautiful anchorage that is covered with sewage from boats that have thoughtlessly pumped their waste overboard. And never, ever, pump raw sewage overboard in a marina, if for no other reason than consideration for the hardworking people who clean the bottom of your boat!

TOILET PUMPS

As shown in the illustration on page 149, there are two requirements for toilet pumps: putting flush water (seawater coming from a through-hull) into the toilet fixture, and pumping wastes out of the fixture. Given this two-part need, some early marine toilet designs used two separate pumps, a small pump to fill the bowl, and a larger one to empty it. These toilets used either diaphragm pumps like the one illustrated on page 129 or simple piston pumps, like the pump described in the next section. Since such toilets are now rare, we will skip them here.

HEAD GAMES

One of the items on our surveyor's list when we bought our Dulcinea was a stuck Y-valve. The handle was broken and it seemed to me the easiest course would be to replace the valve. So, on a day when I couldn't think of anything else I had to do, I put on a pair of heavy rubber gloves and got to work.

Each of the three hoses attached to the Y-valve had two hose clamps, and even though the Y-valve was mounted up underneath the head sink, it wasn't too much trouble to loosen all six clamps. The next step, however, was a problem. The hoses were old and stiff—no way were they going to come apart. But, I thought, maybe if I could get one of them loose, there would be room to wiggle the Y-valve to loosen the other two.

I pulled, I pushed, I pleaded. Nothing. (Since those days, I've learned that sometimes you can loosen a hose fitting by heating the hose with a heat gun.) So I pushed and pulled some more. Nothing. Each of the hoses was mounted to the bulkhead a few inches from the Y-valve with plastic straps. I undid each of those straps. (By now, sweat was dripping down my face and my rubber gloves were starting to tear from the sharp edges of the hose clamps.) Nothing. I rested a bit, and then with one giant heave-ho, I pushed and pulled and pushed and pulled . . . and the Y-valve broke loose, sending me across the head and into a heap at the bottom of the shower stall. Eureka! Except I soon realized three important things: 1) the Y-valve must be under the waterline because water was pouring into the boat; 2) I had no idea where the seacock for the toilet discharge was located; and 3) the shower was pouring cold water into my lap. During my flight from under the sink to the bottom of the shower, I'd apparently sideswiped the shower faucet, and turned it on.

Well, the boat didn't sink, I didn't sustain any (permanent) injury, and the toilet has worked fine since then. That was when I began to understand the importance of knowing where every one of my through-hulls was located!

Double-Acting Piston Pumps

The most common toilet pump is the double-acting piston pump (see illustration on page 154), so called because each stroke accomplishes two tasks at once. Pushing down on the handle pushes discharge water out of the pump and pulls flushing water into the pump; pulling up on the handle pushes flushing water into the fixture and pulls discharge water out of the fixture.

The four valves are the key to understanding the operation of this pump. Each of them will allow fluid to pass one way, but not the other. As the pump plunger is pushed down (bottom portion of illustration), wastewater in the bottom of the pump housing is pushed out of the pump. At the same time, a vacuum is created in the top of the pump and clean seawater is drawn into the pump. Valve 1 is pushed open by the entering clean water and valve 4 is pushed open by the departing wastewater. During this phase, nothing enters or leaves the toilet fixture because the vacuum sucks valve 2 closed and the water exiting the pump pushes valve 3 closed. At the end of this cycle, the pump is full of clean water and contains no wastewater.

As the pump plunger is being pulled up (top portion of illustration), the clean water in the top of the pump is pushed into the toilet fixture. At the same time, a vacuum is created in the bottom of the pump and wastewater is pulled from the toilet fixture and into the bottom of the pump. Valve 1 is pushed shut, valve 2 is pushed open, valve 3 is pulled open, and valve 4 is pulled shut. By repeating the up-and-down motion, the clean water is drawn into the pump, pushed into the fixture, drawn out of the fixture, and pushed out of the pump. Of course, when the clean water shutoff valve is closed, no clean water can enter the pump, and the up-and-down motion simply empties the toilet fixture.

Diaphragm Pumps (Lavac Vacuum Toilets)

The illustration on page 155 shows a much simpler (read: better) toilet design. With the Lavac vacuum toilet, the toilet seat and toilet cover both have rubber seals on their undersides so when the seat and cover are down,

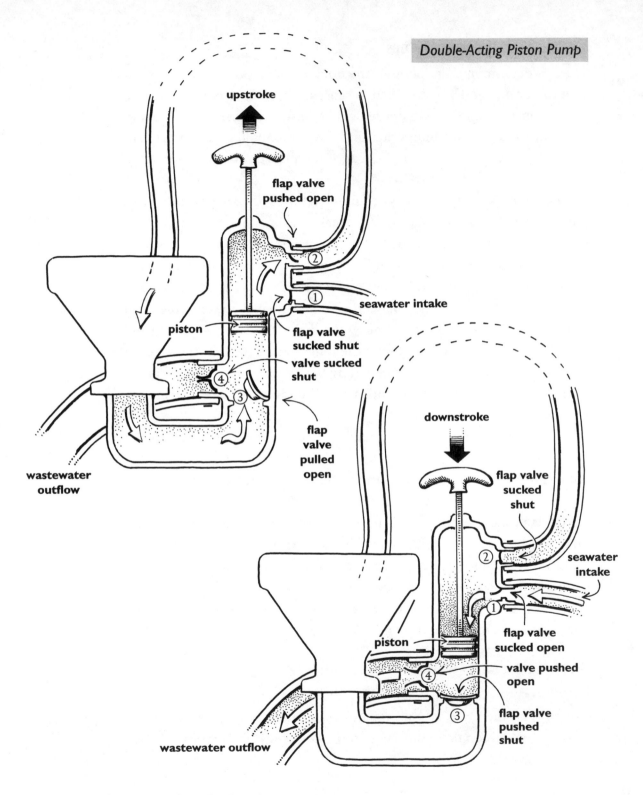

Double-Acting Piston Pump

upstroke

flap valve
pushed open

②

① seawater intake

piston

flap valve
sucked shut

valve sucked
shut

④

③

flap
valve
pulled
open

wastewater
outflow

downstroke

flap valve
sucked
shut

②

seawater
intake

①

piston

flap valve
sucked open

valve pushed
open

④

③

flap valve
pushed
shut

wastewater outflow

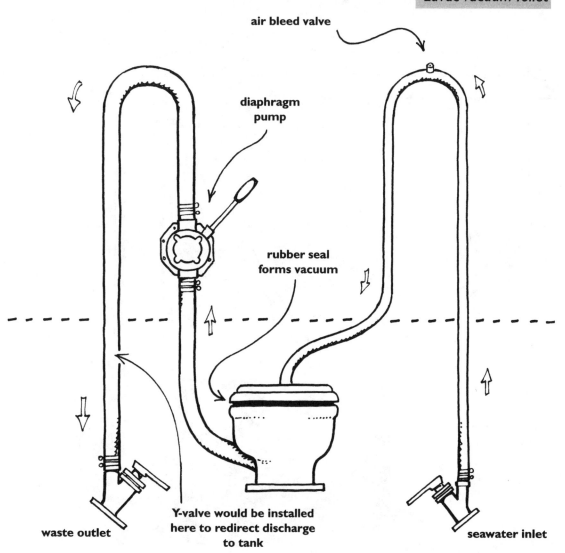

air bleed valve

diaphragm
pump

rubber seal
forms vacuum

waste outlet

Y-valve would be installed
here to redirect discharge
to tank

seawater inlet

the seals form an airtight chamber in the toilet fixture. To flush the toilet, a
diaphragm pump (either manual or electric with a manual backup) is used
to evacuate the toilet bowl contents. Because of the vacuum in the fixture, as
the bowl is emptied, clean flushing water is drawn into the fixture. If the

Marine Toilets   155

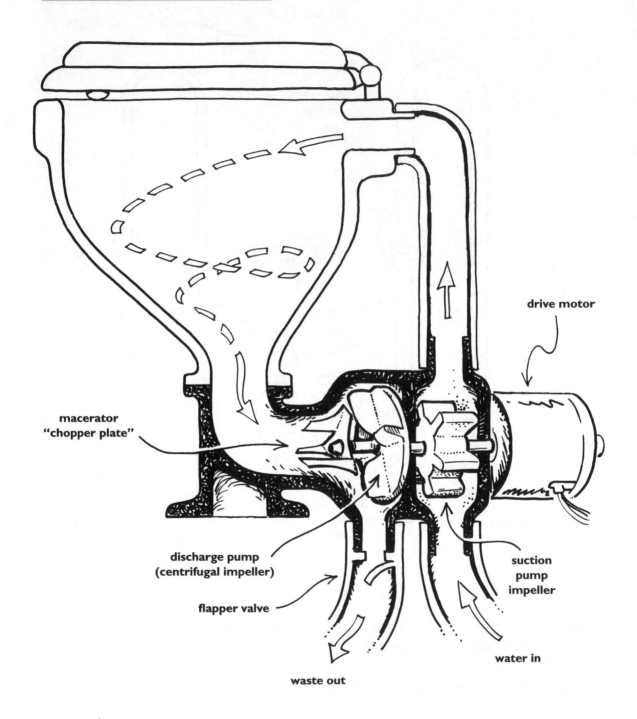

Electric Toilet with Macerator Pump

macerator
"chopper plate"

drive motor

discharge pump
(centrifugal impeller)

suction
pump
impeller

flapper valve

water in

waste out

pump is operated with the lid open, the bowl is simply emptied. Because diaphragm pumps are simple, this system is more reliable than the more complicated double-acting piston pumps. It's also easier to repair when it breaks.

Electric Toilet Pumps

Of the two types of electric toilets, the simplest just substitutes an electric motor for the human to operate the pump. The double-acting piston pump (see illustration on page 154) can be driven by an electric motor that moves the piston up and down. Similarly, the diaphragm pump in a vacuum toilet can be electrified as well. For these toilets, the motor is just an add-on to the manual toilet.

The other type is purpose-built for electrical operation. With such pumps, the electric motor is attached to a shaft that drives an impeller pump to push freshwater into the fixture. The shaft is also connected to a macerator pump that removes waste from the fixture (see illustration opposite). There are several kinds of macerator pumps. One uses a small chopper plate in front of an impeller pump; the waste is chopped and then removed by the impeller. Another uses a worm-drive gear to push waste into a chopper (similar to a meat grinder) and then remove the waste with an impeller or other type of pump.

Opinions vary on the desirability of electric heads. When they work, they're convenient, but they're also one more thing to maintain and repair. They also consume electric power, but unless your entire family comes down a violent stomach flu, they're not likely to be a serious power drain. If your Dulcinea has electric heads, you're not likely to replace them with manual toilets unless you've had lots of problems. Personally, they're on my not-worth-it list.

TOILET PROBLEMS

Meanwhile, back at your pristine anchorage, we left you jarred out of your reverie by your daughter's news of the nonfunctioning head. As you'll recall, there are three possibilities: incorrect usage, blockage, or broken part(s). First let's try and eliminate category one. Are all the seacocks open that are supposed to be? Is the water-inlet seacock open? Is the holding tank full?

Speaking of full holding tanks, how can you tell if your holding tank is full? Some tanks have a meter that displays the holding tank level. Others have an inspection plate that you can open (phew!) to look. With still others, the only way you know if the tank is full is if sewage is appearing out the holding tank vent pipe—not recommended, since sewage may remain in the vent, stop it up, and cause odor problems (see Foul Odors on pages 161 and 163–64). If your holding tank doesn't have a meter, you can guesstimate its level by knowing the capacity of your tank and the amount of water discharged each time you use the head (your owner's manual for the head may give you a range). Of course, the more water pumped through the head, the more will be deposited in the holding tank. In any case, you can determine how close your tank is to full by multiplying the number of flushes times the amount of water per flush and comparing that to the holding tank's capacity.

If you have an electric toilet that won't work, check its battery bank for a charge and ensure that all circuit breakers are on that need to be. Also check to ensure the battery switch is in the correct position and whether or not there's a tripped circuit breaker or blown fuse.

If the toilet is being used correctly and still won't work, you need to decide if you want to try to tackle the problem yourself. If you're out for the afternoon, or if you have more than one toilet and won't be out for too long, you might want to save the problem for a professional when you get back to port. If you're out for a longer time, have only one toilet, or just feel curious (or masochistic?), then you may want to proceed yourself.

You won't know ahead of time whether the problem will require spare parts, but once you have the toilet apart, you'll probably want to finish the job, so it's a good idea to have a spare-parts repair kit for your toilet on board. Even if you don't intend to fix head problems yourself, it's still a good idea to carry spare parts; while you may find some qualified person to repair your toilet in Barre de Navidad, you may not be able to get the spare parts. (See appendix 1 for more on spare parts.) Also consider carrying a spare replacement pump. That way, if you figure out that the problem has to be in the pump, you don't have to tear the pump apart on the boat. Just take it out, install the new one, and put the old one in a plastic bag to take to someone else when you get home.

As with other boat components, you can find repair kits by searching on the Web. Enter the brand and model of your head into your favorite Internet search engine. You should find Web pages with parts diagrams and a list of available repair kits. Take the part number of the kit you want to your local chandlery to buy it. This is generally money well spent.

TOILET TROUBLESHOOTING

The table on pages 162–63 lists common toilet problems and their possible causes. Since most of these problems can be caused by one form of calcification or another, before doing anything try the vinegar remedy described on pages 147–48. You can try stronger acids if you know what you're doing, but that's a job better left to a professional.

If the toilet has been working normally and the problem developed suddenly, you've probably got something blocking a hose or valve, or a broken part. So, don your strongest, disposable rubber gloves and get to work. Close any seacocks that aren't protected by antisiphon loops before removing any hoses (remember you've closed them when checking things later).

If clean water won't enter the bowl (the first row of the table), and all of the seacocks were open, then the cause is either a defective shutoff valve, a block in the intake hose, or something interfering with the intake flap valves. If this is the case, you can still operate the toilet without a repair— just pour a bucket of seawater to flush it and then pump it away.

To proceed with the repair, close the intake seacock (if you haven't already) and pull the hose off the fitting. Gradually open the seacock to see if it's blocked. If it's not, examine the hose opening to see if it's clogged. If it is, it's probably clogged close to the through-hull end. If the seacock and hose are OK at that end, I'd suspect the pump valves and check those next. However, if you have reason to believe the hose is clogged elsewhere, then remove the hoses from the antisiphon valve and pour water down each side to see which, if either, side is clogged.

If the problem is not a clogged hose, then it's probably a badly fitting or damaged pump valve. You can either replace the complete pump if you have a spare on board, or take the pump apart and examine each of the valves. Something (like a mat of hair) may be preventing a valve from seating correctly, or a valve could be broken.

If the pump handle moves but nothing happens, you can try the vinegar trick, but if the problem occurred suddenly, calcification is unlikely. It's more likely that one of the valves is clogged, stuck, or defective and you'll need to either replace the pump or take it apart to find the problem. If the valve is just clogged or stuck, you won't need any spare parts, but if it's damaged, you'll have to replace it. Other culprits could be a damaged diaphragm or a piston that's fallen off the plunger. If you have a spare-parts kit, follow the instructions for taking apart and rebuilding your pump. If you don't have the instructions, don't start the job unless the pump is simple or you're mechanically adept.

If the handle won't move, it's most likely that the seacock is closed or the holding tank is full. Otherwise, a clogged discharge line is your next suspect. Since head discharge hoses don't suck water in from the outside, the blockage is more likely to be near the toilet than the through-hull. Pull the discharge hose off the toilet and inspect it. If your head is above the waterline, the discharge line has no antisiphon loop, and the holding tank is below the toilet (or if the Y-valve is set to overboard), slowly pour water down the line to see if it clears. If it doesn't, the hose is blocked. If your head is below the waterline or above, but has an antisiphon loop, then you have a more difficult problem. Try disconnecting the hose at the antisiphon loop and slowly pouring water from the high end of the hose to the lower to check for blockage.

If the problem is not a blocked hose, it's probably a damaged or broken piston or plunger. In this case, you'll have to replace the pump or take it apart. If the toilet fills faster than it discharges, the discharge line is partially blocked. Proceed as described above.

If the bowl fills when the toilet is not in use, you need to determine if the leakage is occurring from the seawater side or the discharge side. Shut off the seawater intake seacock and observe the toilet for a period of time. If water leaks in, the problem is on the discharge side and is most likely a partially blocked valve. But if no water enters with the seawater intake seacock closed, the problem is on the intake side. A defective shutoff valve or a stuck antisiphon valve could be allowing water to siphon back into the boat. Either way, you can fix the problem now, or you can continue to use the head. If you want to keep using the head, just shut the seawater intake seacock after every use; make sure everyone who uses the head knows that this needs to be done and how to do it.

If you have a piston-type pump and water is leaking around the seals at the top, the seals need to be replaced; buy a repair kit and follow the instructions for rebuilding the pump. This is definitely a job that can wait for a more convenient time because the water that's leaking out of the top is seawater and won't hurt anything if left to drip. Turn the seawater intake seacock off when the toilet is not in use.

If you have an electric toilet that won't work, besides the problems described above, you could have an electrical problem. If it's easy to disconnect the motor from the toilet, do so, and try to operate the toilet by hand. If the toilet doesn't work, then proceed as above. If it does work manually, you have an electrical problem. If the solution is obvious (tripped circuit breaker, blown fuse), make the repair (although the tripped breaker may mean you have a plumbing problem if it keeps tripping). Or, since you can operate your toilet manually, you can wait for a professional repair back home.

FOUL ODORS

Heads should be nearly odor free, so if you have an odor problem, don't despair. The first culprit to check is the holding tank—pump it out as

Head Troubleshooting Guide

SYMPTOM	POSSIBLE CAUSE	REMEDY
Clean water won't enter bowl.	Seawater seacock closed.	Open seacock.
	Seawater shutoff valve closed.	Open valve.
	Seawater shutoff valve broken.	Fix valve.
	Blockage in seawater line.	Remove blockage (see pages 159–60).
Pump handle moves but nothing happens.	Blocked flap valves.	Disassemble pump and clean valves.
	Calcified flap valves.	Put vinegar in toilet, wait, hope, and flush. Or, replace valves.
	For diaphragm pumps, tear in diaphragm.	Replace diaphragm.
	For piston pumps, piston dropped off shaft or seals worn out.	Replace or rebuild pump.
Pump handle won't move.	Seacocks or other valves not open.	Open seacocks.
	Holding tank full.	Empty tank—check vent line for blockage.
	Blockage in discharge line.	Clear line.
	Piston calcified in place.	Replace or rebuild pump.
	Piston mechanism broken.	Replace or rebuild pump.
Bowl fills faster than it empties.	Discharge flap valve blocked or calcified.	Try vinegar. Or, disassemble and clean valve. Or, rebuild or replace pump.
Bowl fills when not in use.	Leak in seawater valves.	Rebuild or replace pump.
	Leak in discharge water valves.	Rebuild or replace pump.
	Seawater shutoff valve in line broken.	Fix valve.

Head Troubleshooting Guide

SYMPTOM	POSSIBLE CAUSE	REMEDY
Seawater leaks out of top of piston.	Worn seals (but note leaking water is fresh!).	Do nothing, close seawater intake seacock when head not in use. Later, rebuild pump.
Electric toilet not operating.	Fuse blown or circuit breaker tripped.	Replace fuse or reset circuit breaker. If it happens again, check for blockage. Use pump manually if you can.
	Wiring problem.	Call a professional.
Foul odors.	Holding tank not empty.	Always empty holding tank when able.
	Holding tank vent line kinked or clogged.	Fix or clean vent line.
	Improper hoses.	Replace hoses.
	Antisiphon valve on discharge hose leaking.	Repair or replace antisiphon valve.
	Leaking hose connections.	Tighten hose clamps.

often as you can. Rinse the tank out by emptying it, filling it partially with water (seawater is OK), and emptying it again. You can use holding tank deodorizing chemicals in this process, although some experts think they do more harm than good (see below). Also check that the holding tank vent is unclogged; if the tank has been overfilled, contents may have solidified in this vent line. You can usually tell if the vent is clogged by standing near it when someone else pumps water from the head into the holding tank. If the vent is open, you should smell head odor near the vent exit. The vent line may also have a kink in it.

Peggie Hall has done extensive research on marine sanitation systems and claims that there are two types of bacteria in holding tank contents: aerobic (which thrive in oxygen environments) and anaerobic (which thrive in oxygen-starved environments). According to her, only the anaerobic variety cause foul odors; if your holding tank has plenty of ventilation, it shouldn't smell. She recommends a vent hose of at least ¾ inch in diameter, and possibly two vents to get cross-ventilation. (Can a holding tank windscoop be far away?) She also claims that chemical additives kill both the good and bad bacteria and shouldn't to be used. She's developed a product (K.O., sold by Raritan) containing live bacteria that enhance the action of the odor-destroying bacteria. K.O. is supposed to work better as the temperature rises.

Hose is another source of foul odor. Place a wet rag on the side of the hose and then (carefully!) smell the rag. If it smells bad, odors are permeating the hose. Replace the hose with one designed for head applications. (The September 2000 issue of *Practical Sailor* reported superior odor blocking in a hose called OdorSafe, sold by SeaLand Corporation. It's expensive, but probably worth it.) Hose will only smell if sewage is allowed to remain in the hose. If you can eliminate low spots in your hose installation, this problem will be reduced. Also, be sure to flush sufficient clean water through the toilet after each use to clear the hoses of sewage.

Seawater can also be an odor source if seaweed or other organisms are left to decay in the toilet bowl, pumps, or hoses. To counteract this possibility, some people fill the toilet bowl with freshwater and pump that water into the hoses after using the head, or before leaving the boat for any period of time.

If the head only smells when you pump it, then the problem is either discharge from the antisiphon valve or a leak in the hoses or connections. In the first case, you should replace the antisiphon valve. In the second case, you'll need to tighten hose clamps or take other action as appropriate. Then, clean the outside of the dirty hose with soap and water (throw the rags away).

HEAD-HUNTING

So how does your story end? In the best of all possible worlds, you chuckle comfortably and say to your daughter, "Sorry, sweetums, I forgot to open the head intake seacock. The head works fine now." Then you wash your hands, pour yourself another cup of coffee, and settle back into your peaceful reverie.

In the world that most of us live in, though, you grumble exasperatedly, "I have no idea what's wrong. I'll have to take it apart to see. Sure wish I'd brought that spare pump. And where the heck did I put those heavy-duty rubber gloves?"

That's boating, fellow sufferer.

7

STOVES, SINKS, AND REFRIGERATION

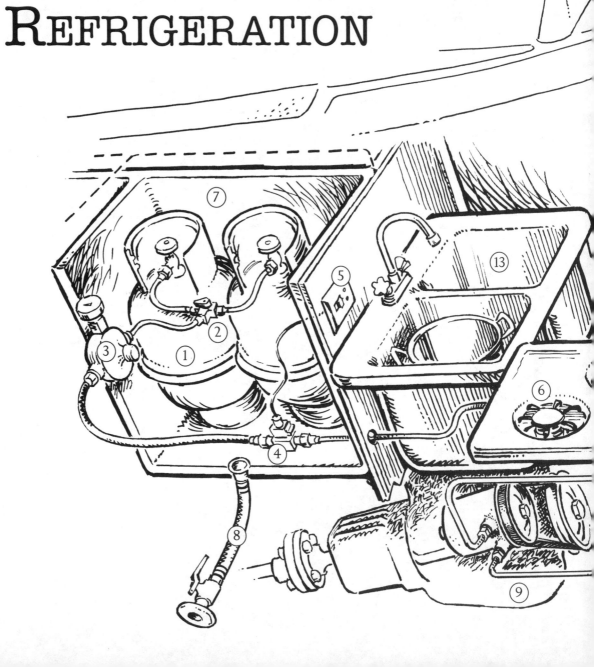

LEGEND

1. propane tank
2. selector valve
3. regulator
4. solenoid shutoff
5. solenoid valve control panel
6. propane stove
7. propane locker
8. locker drain; if below heeled waterline, needs seacock
9. engine-driven compressor
10. condenser
11. RFD (receiver-filter-dryer)
12. cold plate
13. galley sink

It's the galley that differentiates boating from camping. An easy-to-use stove, deep sinks with pressurized freshwater, and reliable refrigeration all make food preparation and cleanup easier and enjoyable, even in a seaway. We've come to rely on these systems and have forgotten that only a few years ago, people cooked with kerosene, washed dishes in seawater, and did without a refrigerator. Today, we feel abused when these systems don't work. That's progress (I guess). In any case, there are several important things to know and understand about Dulcinea's galley. Let's start with stoves and ovens.

STOVES AND OVENS

Stoves and ovens are available in a wide array of choices. You can choose from the simplest one-burner alcohol stove to a multiburner electric range, oven, and broiler combination that would daunt even Julia Child. Stove fuels vary widely as well; alcohol, kerosene, diesel, compressed natural gas (CNG—like gas at home), liquid propane gas (LPG), and electricity are all used.

For a variety of reasons—ease of starting and use, smell, lack of fuel availability, and safety—most boats today use one of three types. Smaller boats with reduced cooking needs are sometimes equipped with a one- or two-burner nonpressurized alcohol stove. With these, the alcohol is poured into a fuel container that has a wicking material that delivers alcohol to the burners. Because no pressure is required to operate the stove, they are easier to start and safer to use.

At the other end of the spectrum, medium and large powerboats with substantial electrical generation capability use modern electric stoves, just like those in the finest home kitchen. Most boats lie between these two alternatives and rely on propane, or LPG, to fuel their stoves and ovens. Because propane is the most popular alternative, we will discuss it in more detail.

PROPANE

First, the most important thing to know about propane is that it's *exceedingly dangerous*—much more dangerous than the natural gas you have at home. It's not just that propane is highly flammable; we expect that in a fuel. The danger is that propane, unlike natural gas, is heavier than air. If you ever have a propane leak, the gas will sink to the lowest spot in Dulcinea's bilge and sit there until something like a spark, engine starter, or other form of heat ignites it into a fire or explosion. To prevent this, Dulcinea's propane system has been designed with multiple safeguards. Your job is to understand those safeguards, use them correctly, and test them periodically.

Therefore, read all of the instructions for all of the propane equipment Dulcinea has. If you no longer have the instructions, search the Internet for the manufacturer of your equipment and contact them via e-mail. Send them the model and serial number of your appliance and ask them to send you the user's manual and safety instructions. They will be happy to comply because for them, too, the easiest way to solve a problem is not to have it. Also, read any information from the manufacturer of your boat regarding Dulcinea's propane system.

PROPANE TANKS

Propane is stored in the familiar metal containers like the one shown on page 170. The tanks have a small wheel on top that turns a valve to open and close the tank. As you would expect, close the valve by turning clockwise and open it by turning counterclockwise.

Now, however, for one of life's surprises. The propane tank has a threaded fitting that connects the tank to Dulcinea's propane hose. The threads on this fitting (not the wheel, I mean the hole into which the propane hose goes) are BACKWARD! The first time I tried to remove the hose fitting from a propane tank, I nearly stripped the threads on the fitting. So, the fittings on propane tanks loosen clockwise (to the right)

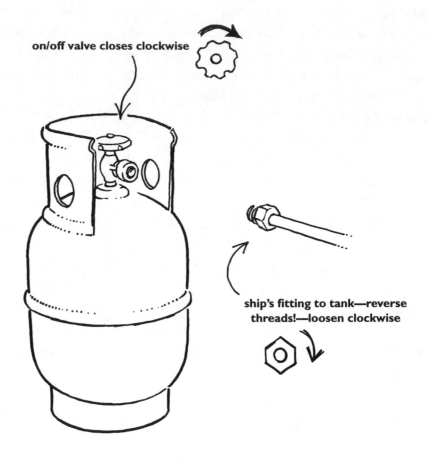

on/off valve closes clockwise

ship's fitting to tank—reverse threads!—loosen clockwise

and tighten counterclockwise (to the left). Life is full of mysteries.*

While we're on this topic, when you remove the fitting from the propane tank, hold it in position with one hand while you unscrew it with the other. Try not to bang up the threads, the O-ring (if you have one), or the inside of the fitting. Also, don't let dirt get into either end of the fitting. Work slowly and carefully because any of these problems can cause a leak at the fitting. And—very important—every time you loosen and tighten this fitting you must check for leaks as described below.

Apparently, this was done so that propane tanks could not be used for any other purpose.

Propane tanks should be white or silver. Never paint your propane tank(s) a dark color because 1) the tank will more readily overheat from sunlight, and 2) no reputable propane dealer will fill a nonwhite or non-silver tank. When you have a tank filled, take it immediately from your car or truck to a shady open area or install it in your boat's propane locker. Don't leave it in the sun, in your car trunk, or in some other enclosed hot space. Propane is a gas that will expand under pressure and eventually, the pressure will cause the safety cap on the bottle to dump propane out of the container and into your car or enclosed space. *Very dangerous!*

PROPANE LOCKER

Dulcinea must have a propane locker that is self-contained and separate from the rest of your boat. If not, your surveyor should have picked that fact up as a deal-killer when you bought your boat. The bottom of the propane locker must have a drain that leads directly overboard. This drain may be a hole through the hull into the locker, or it may be connected to a hose that leads to a through-hull above the waterline. In the latter case, if that through-hull has a seacock (required if it's below the heeled waterline), then you must ensure that the seacock is always open. Be certain that you open, close, and open this seacock when you inspect the others so it doesn't freeze from calcification or corrosion, however. Also check the hoses and their connections on a regular basis.

If you're planning extended trips, you should have room for two propane tanks in your locker. It's not that you will necessarily use all of the propane in one tank on your trip. Rather, you need two tanks in case one of them develops a leak while you're a long way from store or shore.

A typical propane tank setup is shown in the illustration next page. The tank is connected to a (reverse-thread!) fitting that is in turn connected to a pressure gauge, which is connected to a pressure regulator. The pressure regulator is connected to a solenoid-operated valve that leads out of the propane locker and into your boat. All of these fittings are located in the propane locker for a good reason: if any of them leak, the gas will flow overboard and not into Dulcinea's bilge.

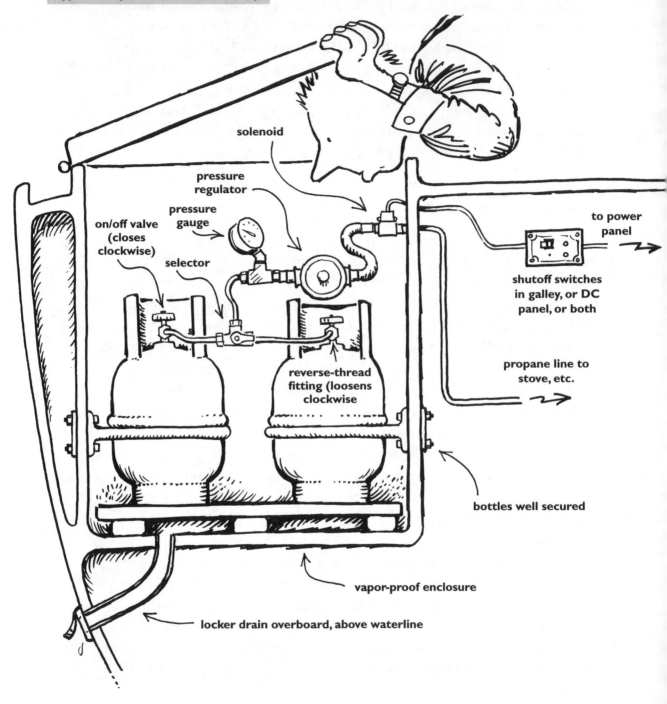

solenoid

pressure regulator

pressure gauge

on/off valve (closes clockwise)

selector

reverse-thread fitting (loosens clockwise)

to power panel

shutoff switches in galley, or DC panel, or both

propane line to stove, etc.

bottles well secured

vapor-proof enclosure

locker drain overboard, above waterline

By the way, the pressure gauge cannot be used to determine how much propane you have. The only reliable way to do that is to weigh the container. Sometimes you can see the level of liquid in the tank if you squirt cold water on it, but this is unreliable. So, if the gauge is not used to measure the propane level, what is it for? It's used to check for leaks as we will describe below.

SOLENOIDS AND SAFETY

Dulcinea must have the solenoid valve just described in the propane locker. The valve is "normally closed"—that is, the valve opens only when the soleniod is energized. The valve is opened and closed by a clearly labeled switch panel near the stove. The panel also contains an indicator light to show when the valve is open.

To light the stove: In the propane locker, open the valve on top of the propane tank that is connected by the selector valve. In the galley, turn on the solenoid valve control switch in the panel (light comes on). Light the stove according to the manufacturer's instructions. Most stoves have an additional safety device that will require you to hold in or turn the knob on the stove for a few seconds, until the burner is warm. See your instructions.

As soon as you are finished with the stove, turn off the switch on the galley panel to close the soleniod valve (the indicator light will go off). Keep in mind that as long as the soleniod valve is open, pressurized propane resides in all the hoses and fittings inside your boat. A dangerous leak is always possible. Form a habit of checking that this switch is off each time you pass.

On this same topic, whenever you leave the boat, turn the valve(s) on the propane tank(s) off. This ensures that no propane can leak into your boat if you have a defective soleniod valve or have mistakenly left the solenoid valve on (very dangerous). If you want to be very safe, turn the solenoid switch on, light a burner, and close the propane tank valve. The stove will burn all of the propane out of the hoses. Now turn the solenoid switch off.

CHECKING FOR LEAKS

You should check for leaks every time you remove and install the hose fitting on your propane tank. You should also check for leaks the first time you're using your boat after an extended period, and at least once a month or more when you're using your boat.

First, make sure the solenoid switch is off inside the boat and open the propane tank valve. Note the reading on the pressure gauge. Now, close the tank valve and wait 10 minutes or so. The reading on the pressure gauge shouldn't decrease during this period. If it does, this means Dulcinea has a propane leak somewhere between the gauge and the propane solenoid. Check the hose fitting on the tank and retest. If the pressure still drops, call a technician to have the leak fixed. A propane leak anywhere is dangerous. Shut all tank valves until the leak is fixed.

If the reading on the pressure gauge is unchanged, open the propane tank valve, turn the solenoid switch on, and note the reading on the pressure gauge. Close the propane tank valve, and watch the gauge reading. 10 minutes or so. The pressure reading should not decrease. If it does, and if the first test was successful, then there's a propane leak somewhere between the solenoid valve and the stove. Such a leak is *VERY DANGEROUS!* Do not use your propane system until a qualified, licensed technician has found and fixed the leak!

If you discover no leaks and want to test your solenoid valve and switch for normal operation, open the valve on top of the propane tank and ensure the switch on the galley panel is off. Try to light a stove burner. You should not be able to do so. If you can, either the switch or the valve is defective.

If the burner did not light, good; turn on the panel switch (indicator light comes on) and light a burner. Now, turn off the panel switch. This should extinguish the burner.

If the solenoid switch indicator light turns on but the burner will not ignite, doublecheck that the tank valve you opened is the one selected by the selector switch. If the solenoid switch wil not turn on (indicator light remains off), check the solenoid breaker on the DC panel. If it was in the On position but is now off, it must have tripped for a reason. Suspect a short somewhere in the current.

SNIFFING OUT TROUBLE

Any boat that has gasoline engines that run while people are sleeping should have a carbon monoxide alarm. Better yet, any boat that has a gasoline engine should have such an alarm. You should also have an alarm if you have a propane heater. Many people choose to have such devices on their boats even if all they have are propane stoves.

The reason is that burning fuel for heat or to run engines converts the oxygen in the air to carbon dioxide. This conversion is usually incomplete, which creates carbon monoxide as well as carbon dioxide. Since most boat cabins are small, enclosed spaces, oxygen levels can be dangerously depleted, and carbon monoxide poisoning can result. Carbon monoxide has no odor, color, or taste, and it weighs about the same as air, so it won't sink to your bilges or rise out of your cabin. If you breathe it, the oxygen-carrying slots in your red blood cells fill up with carbon monoxide, your bloodstream loses its capacity to carry oxygen, and suffocation results. Small amounts of carbon monoxide absorbed over a long period of time are just as deadly as a large amount absorbed in a short period of time, so a warning system is critical.

The best carbon monoxide alarms measure not only the amount of carbon monoxide in the air, but also the amount that has been in the air over a period of time so they're able detect a slow but dangerous buildup of carbon monoxide in the air. Consult a professional for the best kind of alarm to buy (you'll probably need more than one), and the most appropriate places to install them in your boat.

Important Note: If your propane system leaks or malfunctions, do not use your propane stove or other propane appliances. Turn off all propane tanks and call a licensed technician. Propane equipment is too dangerous to be worked on by anyone other than a qualified, licensed technician.

SINKS

As long as your sink is mounted substantially above Dulcinea's waterline, there isn't much to say about it. It will have hoses that are connected to a seacock on a through-hull below the waterline. In general, you should keep this seacock closed, except when you're using your boat. However, in some boats, the galley sink through-hull is used for secondary purposes, such as a bilge pump or a drain for a vented loop from a generator or engine. If this is the case, then you need to consider those additional uses and leave the seacock open accordingly.

In a sailboat, however, there's a good chance that the sink is close to the waterline. If so, as you load the boat, there's a chance that you'll have an inch or two of standing water in the bottom of the sink. If this is a possibility, the manufacturer of your boat may have added a macerator pump as shown in the illustration on page 177. You can use a sink with such a setup in one of two modes. When Dulcinea is slightly loaded and the sink bottom is above the waterline, close the hose to the macerator pump, open the seacock to the lower through-hull and wash away! After you've put all those canned goods and your scuba equipment aboard, the sink bottom is now below the waterline, and standing water is a problem. Under these conditions, close the bottom seacock, open the seacock to the macerator pump, open its seacock, and run the pump to eliminate water and waste from the sink.

A macerator pump has a chopper-grinder in front of an impeller pump. The chopper-grinder chews up food particles from the sink that would otherwise ruin the impeller pump blades.

One aggravating situation that develops with galley sinks is that any cooking oil that finds its way down your sink will float on top of the water in the hose because oil is lighter than water. Over time, oil will build up in the top of each of your galley sink drains. The only way to remove this oil is to suction it out with a turkey baster or a hand pump; if your sink has a macerator pump, you can use that also.

Remember to check under your galley sinks for leaks from time to time. The space under galley sinks is tight, and is often used to store bottles of soap, detergent, bleach, rolls of foil, collections of plastic bags, etc. As these items are pushed and pulled in and out, it's easy for them to knock hoses and hose clamps around.

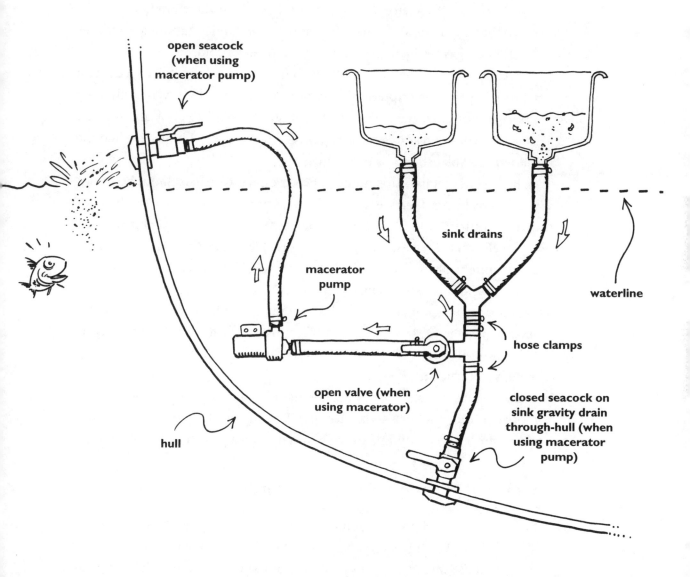

open seacock
(when using
macerator pump)

sink drains

waterline

macerator
pump

hose clamps

open valve (when
using macerator)

closed seacock on
sink gravity drain
through-hull (when
using macerator
pump)

hull

REFRIGERATION

This is the chapter for life's great mysteries. We've already encountered one mystery: the reverse threads on the propane tank fitting. That mystery, however, is nothing compared to the next one: refrigeration. How in the world does a refrigerator work? Did you know that there are home appliances that use natural gas to refrigerate? I can understand a gas clothes dryer, but a gas refrigerator? How does heat make cold?

The instructions that came with the refrigerator on our Dulcinea contain a two-paragraph description of how refrigeration works. It was written by a refrigerator engineer with a Ph.D. in physics. Gobbledygook about latent heat, superheat, pressure changes, patented nozzles, etc. I hope you find the following explanation less confusing.

Before we get into this mystery, however, it's worth asking whether or not you really need refrigeration. After all, sailors cruised the ocean blue for many centuries without it. If you cruise in a moderately cool climate such as the Northeast or Northwest of the United States or Canada, you can get along quite well with an ice block in an icebox. The ice will last several days to a week, and it's easy to buy more.

Another question is, What is that you need to refrigerate? On a twenty-six-day passage to Hawaii, I found that most of what I wanted to refrigerate was spoiled after two weeks, anyway. There wasn't much left to refrigerate, so I turned it off.

Still, many cruisers want the benefits of onboard refrigeration, and it's more common on boats today than not. If yours breaks, you might try running without it for a while to see if you can get by with an ice block.

HOW REFRIGERATORS WORK

Refrigerators work by combining two phenomena from chemistry: First, when a liquid changes to gas, it takes heat away. That's why Mother Nature created sweat. As the moisture on our skin evaporates, it takes heat away, thus making us cooler. Put some rubbing alcohol on your skin and you can feel it take heat away as it evaporates.

This is not to say there are thousands of sweating, invisible people on the plates inside your refrigerator. No. But it is true that the plates inside your refrigerator get cold because there's a lot of liquid changing to gas inside them.

Here's the second phenomenon: you can make a liquid change into a gas (or the reverse) just by changing its pressure. You don't have to change the temperature. The air pressure in the Mile High City of Denver, Colorado, is much less than that in sea-level Miami. Consequently, water boils at about 202°F in Denver but at 212°F in Miami. Now, this means if we had a jar full of 200°F water in Miami and we instantaneously moved it to Denver, some of it would boil and change to gas (steam). The change would be caused by the decrease in air pressure. And, from phenomenon 1, as the water changed to steam, the jar would become colder.

Similarly, if we had a jar full of 202°F steam in Denver and we instantaneously moved it to Miami, the steam would change to water. The change would be caused by the increase in air pressure between Denver and Miami. And, although we didn't say it before, when the steam condensed to water, the jar would get hotter.

One more fact before the secret of refrigeration is revealed before your very eyes. The refrigerator has a substance called a *refrigerant* that flows through its pipes and hoses. Unlike water, which changes from liquid to gas at a high temperature, the refrigerant changes from a liquid to a gas at a very low temperature, something like −21°F. This means, among other things, that when the refrigerant turns from liquid to gas, it is very cold gas.

OK, this is how it all works: Dulcinea's refrigeration system has a *compressor* that takes the refrigerant in gas form and pressurizes it (see illustration next page). The refrigerant gets hot in the process, so it's run through a *condenser* to make it cooler and condense it to liquid. The cooled, liquid refrigerant then goes to an *expansion valve* near your refrigerator. There, the liquid is sprayed into the *cold plates* (evaporators) and the pressure is allowed to drop. As the pressure drops, the liquid changes to gas (like moving hot water from Miami to make steam in Denver) and becomes cold. This makes the plates freeze. When the refrigerant leaves the cold plates, it is now a gas under lower pressure and it returns back to the compressor where it is compressed and then condensed back to liquid and so forth.

Typical Refrigeration Cycle

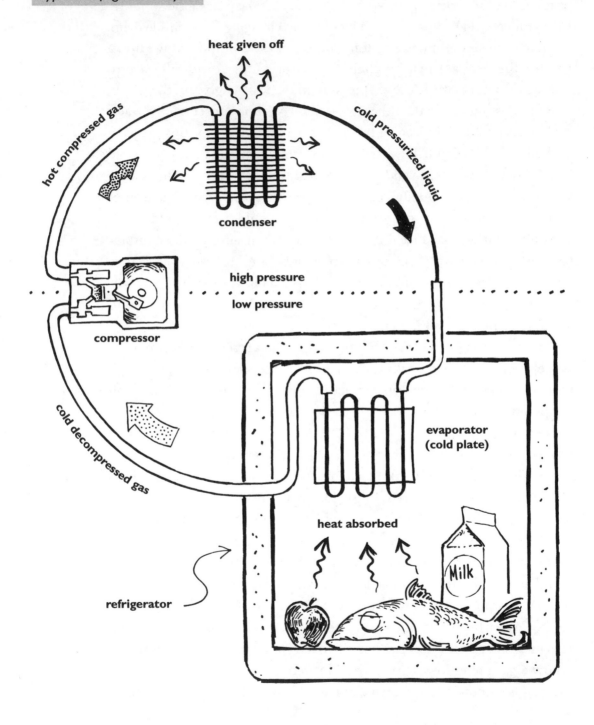

heat given off

hot compressed gas

cold pressurized liquid

condenser

high pressure

low pressure

compressor

cold decompressed gas

evaporator
(cold plate)

heat absorbed

Milk

refrigerator

Refrigerant

The refrigerant operates like a conveyor belt for heat. It goes into the cold plates in liquid form, changes to gas, and in the process sucks heat out of the plates. The heat is carried away in the energy of gas molecules bouncing around. When the compressor compresses the gas, the energy of the bouncing molecules is turned into a higher temperature of the refrigerant. But that heat is then transferred to water (or in some cases, air) in the condenser. Thus, the whole system works to move heat out of the refrigerator and into the condenser, where it's transferred to outside air or water.

In the past, chlorinated fluorocarbon (CFC) was almost universally used as a refrigerant. CFC, also known as R-12, and by its DuPont trade name Freon, is known to cause a reduction in the earth's ozone layer. Consequently, its use has been made illegal for new refrigerators. Refrigeration systems today use CFC-free refrigerants, of which there are many. Typical names are: R-134a, R-401a, R-406a, FR-12, and still others. When adding refrigerant, you need to know which kind of refrigerant you have and use only that kind or one that is compatible with the kind you have. Because of environmental hazards, in the United States and Canada, only licensed technicians are allowed to buy and work with Freon.

COLD PLATE ENGINE-DRIVEN REFRIGERATORS

The illustration on page 182 depicts a typical engine-driven compressor refrigeration system. The compressor is driven by a V-belt off the boat's engine. The compressed hot gas is cooled in a condenser filled with seawater. Here the condenser taps into the raw-water cooling line for the engine. In other systems, the condenser has a raw-water system of its own. Because the refrigerant lines are metal and in contact with seawater, corrosion is a potential problem. The condenser therefore has a zinc that must be changed from time to time. The instructions in your refrigeration manual will explain how to do this.

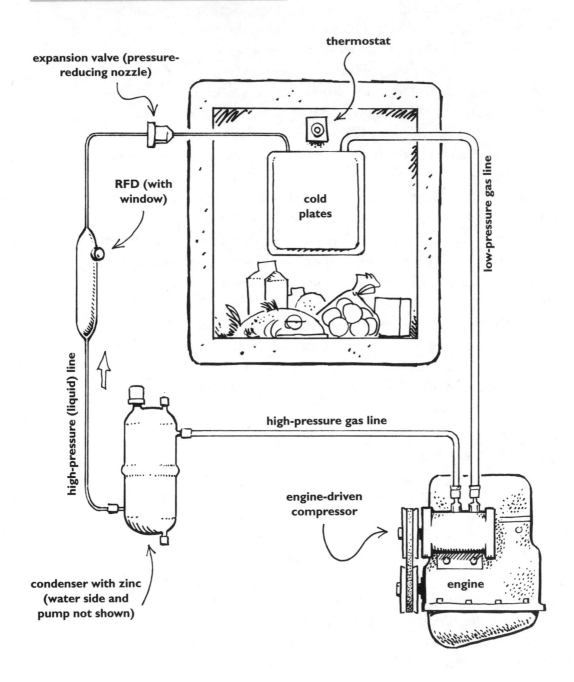

thermostat

expansion valve (pressure-
reducing nozzle)

RFD (with
window)

cold
plates

low-pressure gas line

high-pressure (liquid) line

high-pressure gas line

engine-driven
compressor

condenser with zinc
(water side and
pump not shown)

engine

The cooled liquid refrigerant flows from the condenser to a device called an RFD, which stands for receiver-filter-dryer. This device holds a reservoir of refrigerant. It also contains a screen for filtering out particles that get into the refrigerant and some desiccant that removes moisture. None of this is particularly important to us as users of refrigerators. What is important about the RFD is that it has a window that is used to check the level of refrigerant as described below.

The cooled, cleaned liquid refrigerant flows from the RFD into an expansion valve or a pressure-reducing nozzle, which sprays the liquid into the cold plates. The system shown here has one plate; other systems have two and some have three or more.

Inside the plates, there's a long folded tube that looks a lot like a car's radiator (see illustration below). The refrigerant is sprayed into that long folded tube. Interwoven around that tube is a second set of tubes that contains a liquid that is frozen by the refrigerant.

Typical Cold Plate

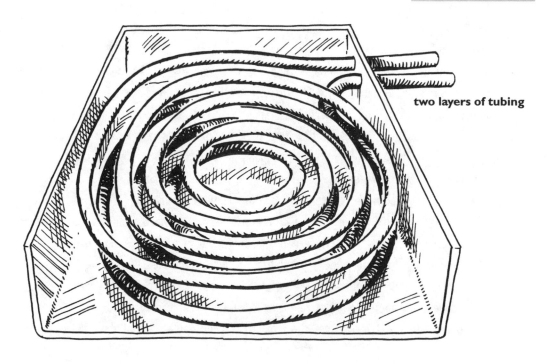

two layers of tubing

THAT ZINC-ING FEELING

We have an engine-driven compressor on our Dulcinea and our condenser is located underneath the cabin sole. The condenser has a pencil zinc threaded into the bottom of the condenser, just like that shown in the illustration on page 182. If I lie on the cabin floor and extend my arm just as far as it will go, I can just reach the fitting on the zinc. Just barely.

A couple of days before departing on a trip, I decided that I needed to check that zinc. This time, I remembered to close the seacock and then I lay down flat on the floor, extended my arm as far as I could, and managed to get a wrench on the nut that holds the zinc. Slowly, I loosened it, pulled it out, and sure enough, it needed to be replaced.

"Good job," I thought, as turned the old pencil zinc out of the plug and replaced it with a new one. Thank heavens there was enough of the old zinc left to get pliers on it to turn it out of the plug. (The plug has two parts; the plug body that threads into the condenser, and the zinc, which threads into the inside of the plug.) Since the old zinc was shot, it was difficult to tell if the new zinc was the right length, but it seemed about right and I proceeded.

Back on the floor, with my face scrunched into the top of the compressor motor, I slipped the zinc back in the condenser and started to tighten it. The instructions clearly say not to overtighten the plug because it's a tapered fitting and the metal plug can crack the plastic case of the condenser. So, I was careful to notice any resistance as I tightened the plug. Turning and turning, nothing happened until I felt (maybe heard?) a slight crunch. What was that?

Aware that I didn't want to overtighten the fitting, I backed the plug out to see what was the matter, and guess what? No new zinc. It was apparently too long, it hit the condenser coils on the inside, and being a weak metal, as I tightened the plug, it broke off right where it entered the plug fitting.

Now I had two problems! The broken-off zinc inside the condenser and a zinc plug with the butt of the broken-off zinc threaded into it. The break was flush with the plug, so there was no way to remove the butt of the zinc to expose the threads to fit a new zinc into the plug.

Well, to make a long story short, you can melt zinc out of the plug. I took the plug home, put it in a vise, and heated it with a propane torch. The zinc melted before the plug and I was able to clean the zinc out of the plug with a small wire brush.

OK, so far, but now I had to get the broken part of the zinc out of the condenser. Ugh.

Back to the cabin floor, head scrunched into the compressor motor, feeling around inside with my little finger trying to get the zinc piece up and down so that it would fall out of the zinc's hole in the condenser like some child's puzzle toy. Again and again with no success until I noticed that there's a drain plug in the bottom of the condenser. I pulled that plug out and in another 20 minutes, with little fingers in each of the holes, and the V-belt of the compressor in my teeth, I got the zinc pieces out.

This time I measured the amount of free space between the plug and the coils inside the condenser, and cut the second new zinc to the right length. All's well, except that it's about time to change that zinc again! And where did I write down the right length of the zinc?

While we're on this subject, once the interior liquid of the plates has been frozen, there is no reason to continue to run the compressor. The plates are as cold as they're going to get. Therefore, it is better to run the compressor for say, 20 minutes twice a day than for 40 minutes once a day. Run it once in the morning to freeze the plate(s). During the day, the plates will gradually defrost. You can then freeze them again by running the compressor at the end of the day.

Once the now gaseous refrigerant leaves the cold plates, it flows back to the compressor and the cycle starts again.

CHECKING THE LEVEL OF REFRIGERANT

It is important to check the level of refrigerant in your system once a month or even more frequently because running the refrigerator with insufficient refrigerant can ruin the compressor. This is bad news not only because new compressors are expensive, but also the work must be done by a licensed (hence expensive) technician.

You check the refrigerant level by watching the window in the RFD. If the refrigerator has the correct amount of refrigerant, when you first turn the compressor on, a series of bubbles will appear in the RFD window.

Within 10 seconds or so, the bubbles should disappear. If they do not, or if they do not appear in the first place, then refrigerant level is too low.

Checking the refrigerant level is a two-person job. Start your engine, and run it at about 1,200 rpm. While looking in the window of the RFD, ask someone else to start the refrigerator. You should hear the engine rpm decrease a bit as the compressor load kicks in and then you should see a series of bubbles that gradually disappear. See your manual for more instructions on this process. It is important to do it, however. Again, running the refrigerator with too little refrigerant can ruin the compressor.

If you need to add refrigerant, you probably should call a licensed technician. If your refrigerator uses Freon, and if you live in the United States or Canada, you are legally required to call a licensed technician.

12-VOLT DC REFRIGERATORS

DC refrigerators are smaller, cheaper, and less complicated. Since they're smaller, they need to be run more frequently. Some DC refrigerators have cold plates, but others just have a series of cold coils similar to those in a household refrigerator. Cold coils also require the refrigerator to be run more frequently, and may pose a serious challenge to the capacity of your battery system.

The condenser for DC refrigerators is almost always air-cooled, and there will be no zinc to check. Also, it may not be possible to check the refrigerant level in a DC refrigeration system. See your owner's manual for more information.

120-VOLT AC REFRIGERATORS

So-called *assist refrigerators* are meant to back up an engine-driven compressor system when the boat is tied to the dock. They have a small capacity, use an air-cooled condenser, and are designed to run almost continuously, similar to a household refrigerator. If the main refrigeration system uses cold plates, then the assist refrigerator will use them as well. Note, too, that there will be two completely separate refrigerant systems. One set of

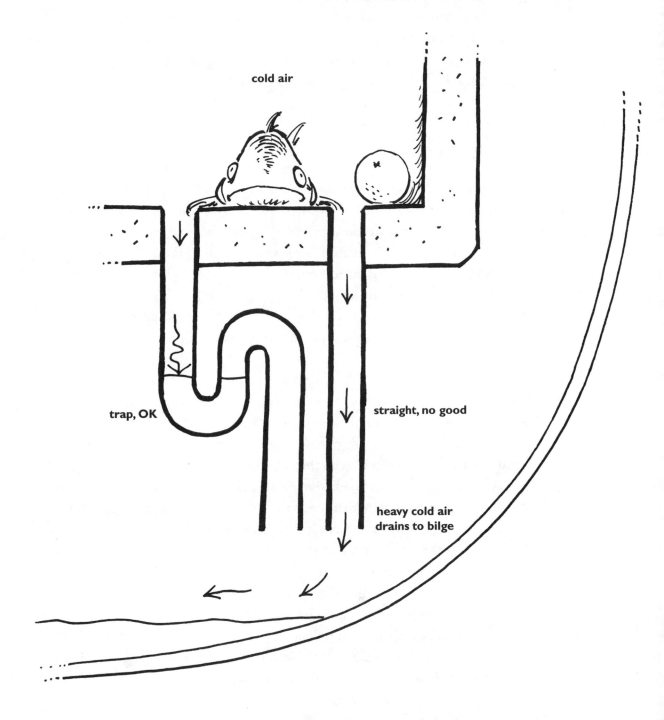

cold air

trap, OK

straight, no good

heavy cold air
drains to bilge

hoses and pipes will lead to the backup AC refrigerator and a second set will lead to the engine-driven compressor.

The second type of AC refrigerator is designed to run with a generator. This type is essentially the same as the engine-driven compressor system except that here the compressor is driven by a large AC motor instead of the engine. Such systems have a water-cooled condenser and an RFD for checking the refrigerant level.

INSULATION

To provide effective service, even the highest capacity refrigerator needs a box that is well insulated. If you have difficulty keeping your refrigerator cold, you probably have insufficient insulation around the box. Unfortunately, replacing this insulation will require pulling the box out and may even require rebuilding it. Sometimes it is possible to improve insulation by lining the box on the inside.

New vacuum-packed insulation materials provide superior insulation (R-50, which is a higher insulation rating than is required in a house attic) with an inch or two of material. See the Glacier Bay Web site, www.glacierbay.com, for information on their insulation products.

Since cold air is heavier than warm air, opening your refrigerator from the top will not allow cold air out. However, if your cold box has a side entry door, every time you open it, cold air will flow out of the cold box onto the floor. Therefore, keep the use of such side doors to a minimum. Plan to use those doors just before or during the time when you run your compressor. Also, ensure that the seals are tight on all of your refrigerator doors, but especially on the side doors. To determine if there is extra play in the seal, close the door on a piece of paper or a dollar bill and move it around the seal. It should be difficult to remove the paper at all parts of the seal. If not, replace the seal or adjust the settings on the door hinges.

If your refrigerator has a drain at the bottom, the drain should have a cold-air trap (see illustration on page 187). If the drain is straight, cold air will continuously flow out of the cold box and into your bilge. Also, ensure that the holes admitting hoses into your box are insulated as well.

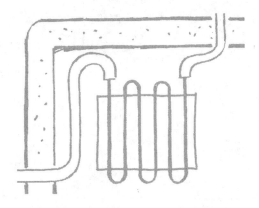

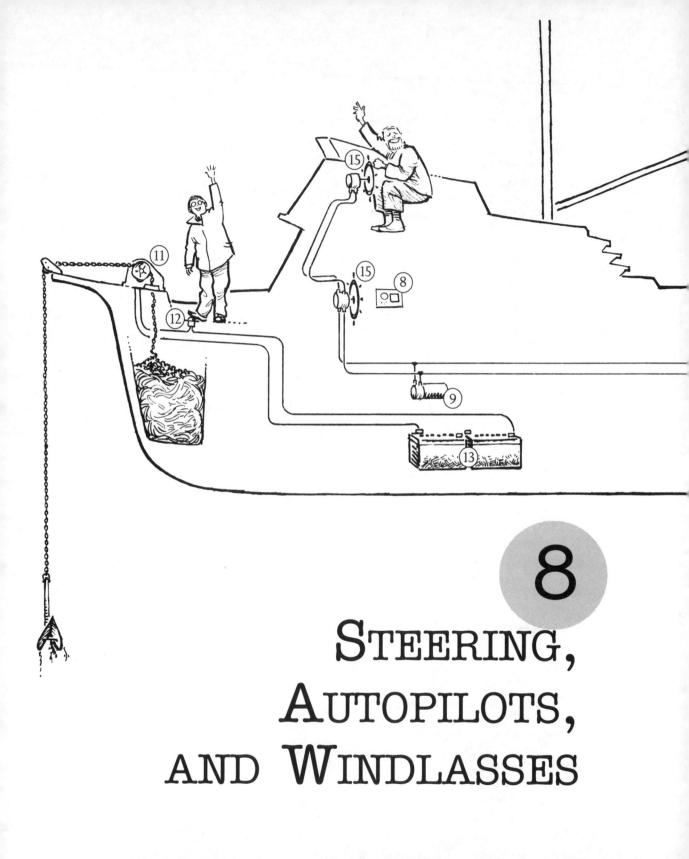

8

STEERING, AUTOPILOTS, AND WINDLASSES

LEGEND

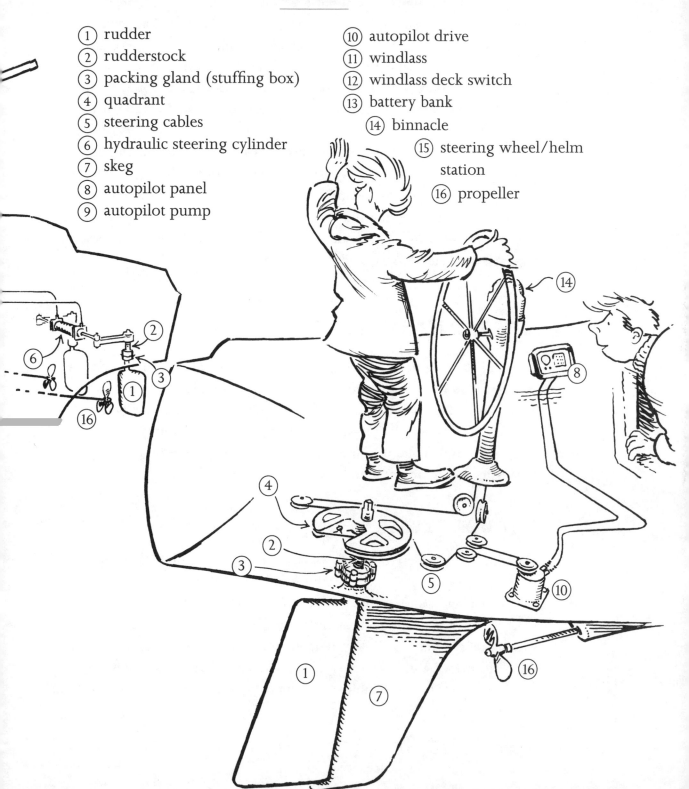

1. rudder
2. rudderstock
3. packing gland (stuffing box)
4. quadrant
5. steering cables
6. hydraulic steering cylinder
7. skeg
8. autopilot panel
9. autopilot pump
10. autopilot drive
11. windlass
12. windlass deck switch
13. battery bank
14. binnacle
15. steering wheel/helm station
16. propeller

L oss of steering is just about everybody's worst nightmare. There you are cruising up Nightmare Channel into Calamity Bay, when all of a sudden, you turn the wheel and nothing, I mean *nothing*, happens. You turn the wheel back and forth and it's just like one of those toy trucks you give your kids—the wheel turns freely, but nothing happens. In this dreadful nightmare, you're usually standing nude at the wheel while . . .

Fortunately, with proper maintenance, this scenario will remain only a nightmare. And the maintenance isn't too demanding, either: inspection, lubrication, occasional tightening, and you should never need to use Dulcinea's emergency steering system. While we're talking about steering, in this chapter we'll also discuss autopilots and, while we've got the grease, rags, and lube gun out, we'll address windlasses as well.

STEERING SYSTEMS

While all boats are steered by rotating one or more rudders, there are many different rudder designs and many different steering system designs. There's been a loud debate raging for many years regarding the best underbody and rudder design; we'll just note that any of the following rudder types can be great if well designed and constructed—or a source of headaches and problems if not.

RUDDER TYPES

The oldest rudder design, a *rudder mounted on a full keel* (see illustration opposite), is common on sailboats with full or cutaway keels. The end of the keel forms the *rudderpost*, to which the rudder is mounted. This design provides the most protection for the rudder and, if properly made, can be very strong. Such an underbody, however, doesn't provide the best upwind sailing performance, and most newer sailboats have a different design. Also, this design isn't feasible for semidisplacement or planing powerboat hulls. The

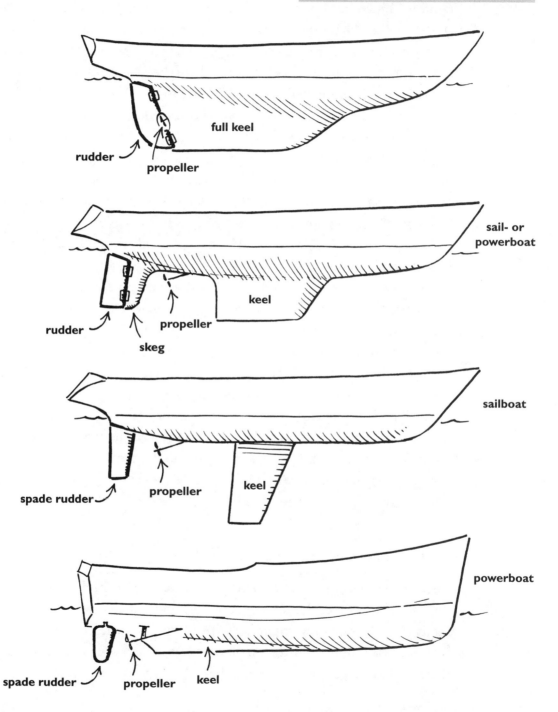

full keel

rudder

propeller

sail- or powerboat

rudder

skeg

propeller

keel

sailboat

spade rudder

propeller

keel

powerboat

spade rudder

propeller

keel

illustration also shows a *skeg-mounted rudder* that can be used on either sail- or powerboats. With this type, the trailing edge of the skeg contains the reinforced material to which the rudder is mounted. This design provides protection for the rudder, can be strong, and results in better performance for sailboats. It can also be used for displacement and semidisplacement powerboats. The third type, the *spade rudder* (shown on both a sail- and a powerboat), is supported only by the *rudderstock*, which is used both to mount the rudder and to rotate it for steering. While such rudders provide the best performance for sailboats and can be used for planing and twin-engine powerboats, they're vulnerable to logs, reefs, fishing nets, and other hazards. Consequently, some people believe they are poorly suited for nonperformance applications. Others claim that spade rudderstocks can be made strong enough to withstand serious blows without harm.

In all of these designs, the rudderstock extends through the hull and is connected to the steering system. As we discussed in chapter 2 (see pages 37–40), and also as shown in the illustration next page, a packing gland (stuffing box) allows the rudder to turn while at the same time keeps water from entering the boat. You may need to tighten the nuts on the packing gland occasionally to keep water out, but don't tighten too much or steering will become difficult. After several thousand hours of use, the nuts may be as tight as they'll go; if so, you'll have to have the packing material replaced. The rudderstock may be supported by one or more bearing rings (one is shown near the top of the stock in the illustration). The ring is likely to have a grease nipple; every season or so, you should grease the nipple with marine-grade grease while you inspect the steering system as described below.

STEERING SYSTEM DESIGNS

Steering systems are usually *hydraulic* or *mechanical*. Hydraulic systems use fluid like auto brakes do, but they use it to transfer steering wheel movement into rudder movement. They're often used on powerboats and large sailboats. In the illustration on page 196, when the wheel is turned, it drives an attached pump. Fluid is forced down the appropriate hose to

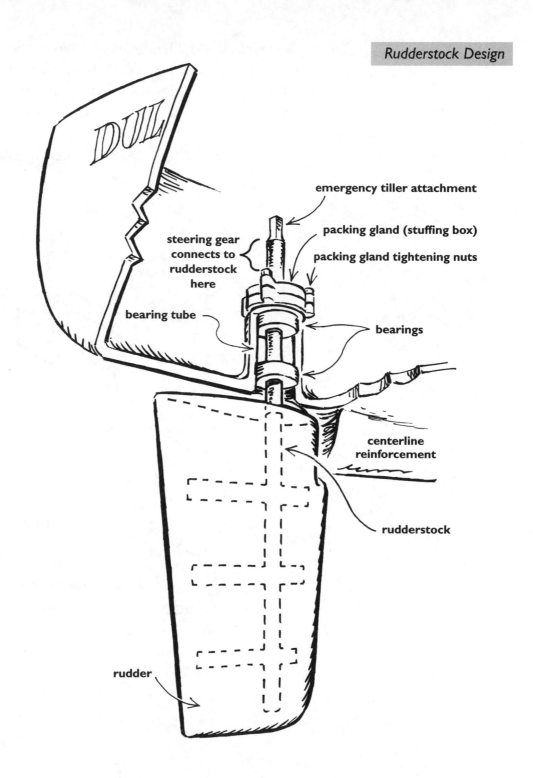

emergency tiller attachment

packing gland (stuffing box)

packing gland tightening nuts

steering gear connects to rudderstock here

bearing tube

bearings

centerline reinforcement

rudderstock

rudder

the *actuator cylinder*, which turns the rudder. Excess fluid from the other end of the cylinder returns through the other hose. In some cases, an electric pump is used to move the piston (like power brakes in a car). There is little most boatowners can do to maintain a hydraulic system. The

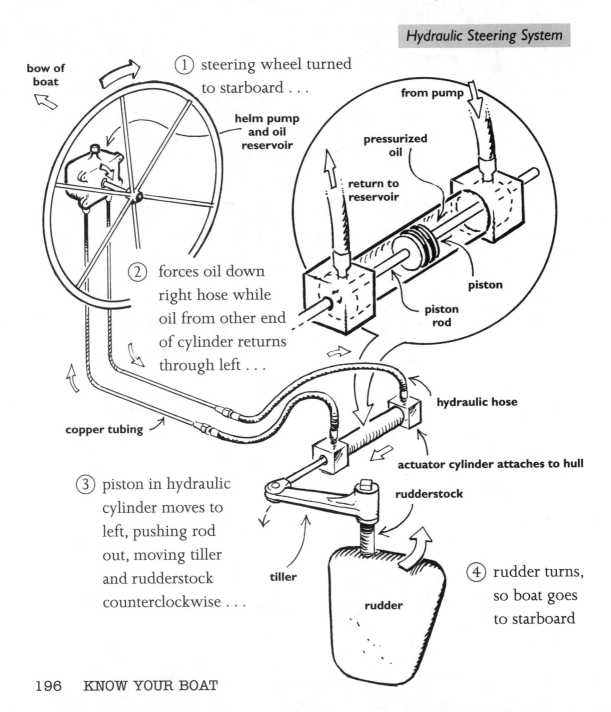

Hydraulic Steering System

bow of boat

① steering wheel turned to starboard . . .

helm pump and oil reservoir

from pump

pressurized oil

return to reservoir

piston

② forces oil down right hose while oil from other end of cylinder returns through left . . .

piston rod

hydraulic hose

copper tubing

actuator cylinder attaches to hull

③ piston in hydraulic cylinder moves to left, pushing rod out, moving tiller and rudderstock counterclockwise . . .

rudderstock

tiller

④ rudder turns, so boat goes to starboard

rudder

most important task is to inspect the fittings, hoses, and lines for evidence of leaks every month or so (hydraulic fluid is dark with a slight reddish tinge to it). Such leaks should be rare, however—think how seldom a hydraulic leak occurs in your car.

Mechanical steering systems are more common on sailboats and smaller powerboats. The most common type uses cables to transfer wheel movement into rudder movement. The cables are run from the steering wheel to an assembly mounted on the rudderstock. (There are many variations on this theme; take the time to figure out which variant your Dulcinea uses.) The illustration on page 198 shows a *quadrant* steering system, common on sailboats and many powerboats because it requires the least space near the rudder(s). The steering wheel is connected to a chain sprocket inside the binnacle. A chain runs over this sprocket and its ends are connected to steering cables. There are two cables: one cable runs down the starboard side of the binnacle, and the other runs down the port side. The cables run through a series of pulleys (sheaves) and then wrap around the quadrant, which is shaped like a quarter of a pie (hence its name).

The cables are subject to wear, so they should be greased (with a waterproof, multipurpose grease) where they run through the pulleys. Also, inspect the cables for wear—broken strands and the like. If you see any evidence of wear, replace the cable, which is a lot easier to do at the dock than at sea. If you need to replace a cable, try to find out what caused the wear and fix the cause as well. While you're at it, check the cables for tightness because cables, especially new ones, stretch under load. The end of the cable that attaches to the quadrant will have a threaded eyebolt or similar attachment. Tighten the cables by moving the nuts out on the eyebolt; you want the cables snug enough so that they can't fall out of the pulleys but not so tight as to cause excessive wear.

A steering cable will likely give you plenty of notice before it breaks—signs include rust, broken strands, squeaks, and awkward wheel motion—so if you inspect your cable system at least once a season and before any long trips or passages, it's unlikely you'll ever have a steering cable problem.

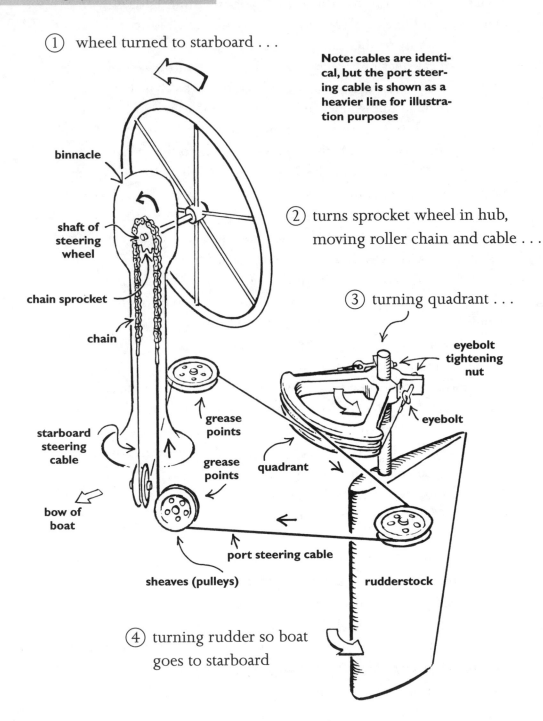

(1) wheel turned to starboard . . .

Note: cables are identical, but the port steering cable is shown as a heavier line for illustration purposes

binnacle

(2) turns sprocket wheel in hub, moving roller chain and cable . . .

shaft of steering wheel

(3) turning quadrant . . .

chain sprocket

eyebolt tightening nut

chain

grease points

starboard steering cable

grease points

quadrant

eyebolt

bow of boat

port steering cable

sheaves (pulleys)

rudderstock

(4) turning rudder so boat goes to starboard

EMERGENCY STEERING SYSTEMS

With proper maintenance, steering problems are unlikely, but even so, it is worthwhile to think about what you would do should your steering system fail. Most boats have some type of emergency steering—a right-angled steel lever, for example, that inserts into a fitting on the top of the rudderstock. You should determine what type of emergency system your Dulcinea has, and, some warm day when your boat is far from any hazard, practice using it. That way, if you ever have to use it for real, you'll know where the parts are, how it fits together, and what, realistically, you can expect from it.

If you have an autopilot, you can use it for emergency steering, as long as whatever problem caused your steering to fail doesn't make the autopilot inoperable as well. You might develop an emergency procedure that says that in the event of a steering problem, you'll first try the autopilot. If that doesn't work, you'll rig the emergency steering next.

Again, however, the best way to solve a problem is not to have it. With proper maintenance, your steering system should work well for all the years you cruise with Dulcinea.

AUTOPILOTS

Autopilots are wonderful; they're like having an extra crew member who's always available, and who doesn't eat, mess up the cabin, use the head, or complain. Unfortunately, they're also prone to failure. I don't think there's any other piece of boat equipment that varies more in quality and performance, so if you're choosing or replacing an autopilot, be sure to research the manufacturers and models. Read publications like *Practical Sailor* (a consumer's guide to boating equipment), surf the Internet, post questions on boating message boards, and talk to experienced sailors who have your type of boat.

But before you choose an autopilot, you have to understand your requirements. If you're looking for one to steer on calm waters for short periods of time, you can get by with a cheaper, less robust model. If you're

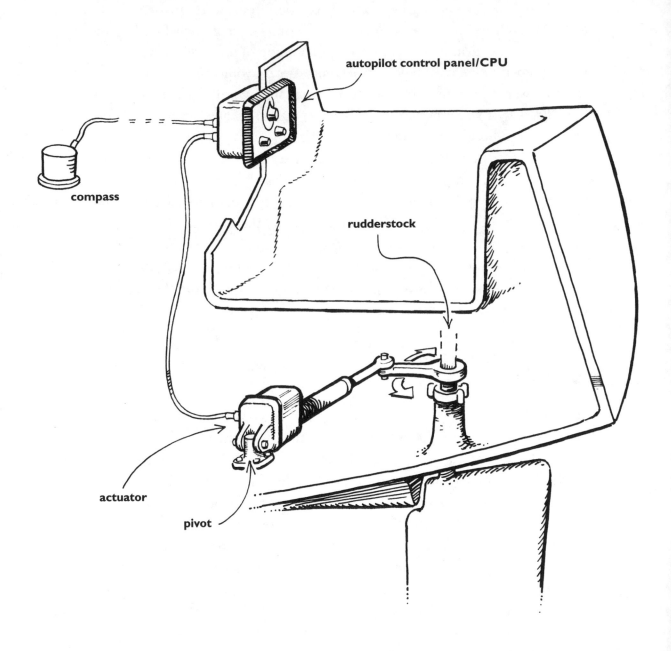

autopilot control panel/CPU

compass

rudderstock

actuator

pivot

looking for one to drive day after day through large seas, then you need to pick the highest quality system you can find. Autopilot reliability is a function of both design and construction. A well-designed but poorly built autopilot will give more problems than a less-well-designed but better-built one. It doesn't matter if you can afford it; just buy it. Sell the house, mortgage the kids, but buy the best.

I say all of this because I've had nothing but problems with autopilots, and I'm not the only one. On a recent trip to Mexico, autopilots were the most complained-about equipment among the cruisers we met.

Every autopilot consists of four basic components: drive unit, compass, computer, and control unit.

DRIVE UNITS

The drive unit is a mechanical or hydraulic unit that receives commands from the computer and drives the boat's steering system. Drive units take the most abuse and thus are most likely to have problems. The simplest (and least powerful) drive units are belt-driven attachments to the wheel and are designed for limited use on small boats on calm waters. Other types of drive units connect to an extension bar (tiller) that's attached to the boat's rudderstock as shown in the illustration opposite. The arm of the drive unit moves the rudder by contracting and expanding in and out.

In a mechanical drive unit, some type of worm gear moves the arm in and out. These drive units are much stronger than wheel-mounted ones, but the races, pins, and bearing stops are still likely to fail. If you use one on an extended cruise, give serious thought to bringing along a replacement, even though the replacement may cost $1,500 or more. It's possible to replace the whole unit, even at sea.

The most powerful drive units are hydraulically driven. Since hydraulic fluid replaces the gears, bearings, etc., there are few moving parts, but the hydraulic pump can be noisy. This is not a problem in a powerboat or when motor-sailing because the noise of the engine will drown out the noise of the autopilot. It can be an aggravating, however, to listen to the constant "eeengh-eeengh" when under sail.

An Autocracy of Autopilots

My battle with autopilots began on a trip from Seattle to Hawaii in 1994. Ten days out, the drive unit fell off its bulkhead mounting and broke the pin that rode in the worm gear. The design of this particular autopilot required a 2-ton hydraulic press to pull the drive-unit shell housing apart. I didn't have one of those aboard, so I tried to jury-rig it. But the bearings kept falling out, so I eventually gave up. No wind vane meant the two of us hand-steered the rest of way—15 days of 2 hours on and 2 hours off. It also meant I had lots of time to ponder my stupidity in not bringing along a backup or having a wind vane.

My next autopilot adventure was on a trip to the Queen Charlotte Islands in 1996. Lynda and I were departing a lovely little anchorage on the southeast side of Moresby Island when I tried to engage the autopilot. Nothing. When we got back to Seattle—after 12 days of hand-steering down the Inside Passage—we found out it was a bad computer component.

My third autopilot failure was off Cabo Blanco on the Oregon coast in the fall of 1999. Lynda and I were caught between the North Pacific High and a thermal low coming up from California, and the sustained 40- to 50-knot winds raised enormous seas (or so they seemed to us). A wave broke over the stern and damaged the wind vane, so we turned on the autopilot. It worked as best it could for 12 hours or so, but gave up the ghost when the bearings in the drive unit fell off their race and jammed the autopilot and rudder. I don't really blame the autopilot for that one, though, because the waves were huge and it was a mechanical (instead of hydraulic) unit, and probably not designed for those conditions.

My most recent autopilot experience occurred on a trip from San Francisco to La Paz, Mexico. Two days out of San Francisco the computer and/or compass went haywire and the boat started going in circles. We were baffled; the flux-gate compass seemed fine (there was nothing metal or magnetic near it—honest!), and the computer had been recently checked out by the manufacturer (because we'd doused it with water in the storm off Oregon). We never did figure out what happened, but we had great winds, so we used the wind vane all the time and hardly missed the autopilot.

These (mis)adventures occurred with two different brands of autopilots on two different boats. We've recently installed a third brand with a hydraulic drive unit, and we're going to give it a try on a trip to the Marquesas. We're keeping our fingers crossed . . .

COMPASSES

Almost all autopilots use a *flux-gate compass*, which determines direction by electronically sensing the earth's magnetic field. It should be installed inside the boat, near the boat's center, both fore and aft and side to side, and away from large amounts of metal (including your pots and pans) and magnets. If you move it, consult your autopilot manual for how to adjust the compass to your boat's magnetic environment.

Audio speakers, by the way, have magnets inside them as I learned once when I nearly ran aground in the shallows southwest of Vancouver, British Columbia. I was following a compass course with a portable radio temporarily tied to the binnacle to listen to the Seahawks football game—back when there was a good reason to listen to a Seahawks football game. Anyway, don't place audio speakers near your flux-gate compass, either.

THE COMPUTER AND CONTROL UNIT

Autopilot technology has benefited from the computer revolution and models that are only a year or two newer than others can have significantly improved features and reliability. All newer autopilots can be connected to GPS devices so the autopilot can steer a course as directed by the GPS waypoint or route course. To learn how to do this, look in your autopilot user's manual under National Marine Electronics Association (NMEA) connections. NMEA, by the way, is the group that sponsored the development of a protocol for navigation communication devices, so any NMEA-compliant device (autopilots, GPS, radar, chartplotters, etc.) can communicate with any other such device, even if they're from different manufacturers.

The computer should be mounted in a dry location so that it will never get wet (unless it's specifically designed to be weatherproof). One of our autopilot computers was mounted inside the starboard cockpit locker, which seemed safe enough. In a big blow, however, we took a wave in the cockpit and the locker lid latches were not locked. Sure enough, water entered the locker and doused the computer, although we didn't know this had happened until the autopilot failed. We hand-steered into port, pulled the computer apart, and dried the circuit boards with a hair dryer. This enabled that particular autopilot to work well enough to seduce us into trying it a little bit longer.

Beyond keeping the computer dry, though, there isn't any maintenance that boatowners can or should do to the computer. Leave that to the professionals.

The control unit is used to start and stop the autopilot and to set and adjust the course. With some autopilots, the control unit engages and disengages the drive unit automatically, but for others, you have to manually pull or push a handle.

AUTOPILOT POWER CONSUMPTION

Autopilots consume considerable 12-volt electrical power, using as much as 20 amps. Even if the average consumption is less, say 15 amps, that requirement translates into 15×24 or 360 amp-hours per day when cruising offshore. Of course, if you're under power, the engine's alternator will generate more than sufficient electricity to power the autopilot. If the alternator fails, the autopilot will eventually be unusable. And under sail, using the autopilot means frequent battery charges with the engine or a generator. So, when you're thinking about adding or replacing an autopilot, first find out how much power it uses. Compute the amp-hour requirements and be sure you have sufficient battery and generating capability for the new unit. If you have a sailboat and are planning on cruising offshore, you might also want to consider a wind vane.

WIND VANES

A wind vane is a mechanical device that uses the wind direction to steer a course. As mechanical devices, wind vanes use no electricity and unlike electronic circuits, they can often be repaired at sea.

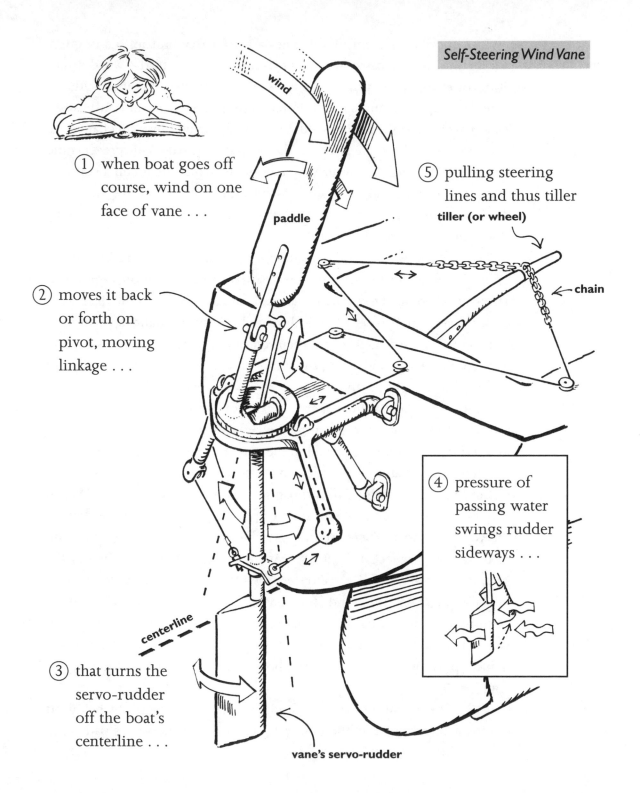

Self-Steering Wind Vane

wind

① when boat goes off course, wind on one face of vane . . .

paddle

⑤ pulling steering lines and thus tiller

tiller (or wheel)

← **chain**

② moves it back or forth on pivot, moving linkage . . .

④ pressure of passing water swings rudder sideways . . .

centerline

③ that turns the servo-rudder off the boat's centerline . . .

vane's servo-rudder

Steering, Autopilots, and Windlasses   205

Even more important, wind vanes are safer than autopilots in gusty wind conditions because they steer a course relative to the wind direction. For example, suppose you set a wind vane to steer a course with the wind at a particular angle over the starboard quarter. If a wind gust causes a sudden change in apparent wind direction, the wind vane will change the boat's course to keep the wind on the starboard quarter. This prevents the accidental jibes that can occur with autopilots, which maintain a constant magnetic course regardless of the wind's direction. Be aware, however, that with a gradual change in wind direction, the wind vane will gradually change the boat's direction.

The *vane* of a wind vane is a paddle, usually made of wood, that sticks up in the wind at the stern of your boat (see illustration on page 205). The vane is mounted to a device that can be rotated through 360 degrees in either direction. You set the wind-vane direction by hand-steering the boat on the desired course, and then rotating the vane so that it's parallel to the wind. In this position, the wind vane is neutral to the wind, and will remain straight up and down.

Now, if the boat veers off the course for which the vane is set, the wind will push the vane down to the right or left. The vane is attached to a rod that is, in turn, attached to the vane's servo-rudder, which is submerged in the water. When the vane is pushed down, it pushes the attaching rod down, which in turn causes the servo-rudder to turn. When the servo-rudder turns, it's pushed to port or starboard by the flow of the water against it. There are lines attached to the servo-rudder that run to the steering wheel or boat tiller. As the servo-rudder is pushed to the side, the lines are pulled so as to steer the boat back on the correct course. When that occurs, the wind stops pushing the vane down, which stops pushing the rod, which causes the servo-rudder to turn straight ahead, which brings the lines that are attached to the wheel or tiller back to the neutral position, which causes the boat to steer straight on the original course.

Voilà! The pressure of the wind on the vane from the boat's being off course is physically amplified by water pressure on the vane's paddle, to turn the boat back on course. And, even better, the stronger the wind, the stronger the forces pushing the vane's paddle, and the stronger the pull on the steering wheel. In fact, the only downside to a wind vane is sailing in light winds where there may not be enough wind to drive the system.

It truly is amazing to watch!

The only difficulty in using a wind vane is learning how to set it up on your Dulcinea. Every boat is different, and slight adjustments one way or another are often required to get the vane to hold a course. The lines to the wheel have to be just the right tension (neither too tight nor too loose, but looser rather than tighter), the vane has to be in just the right position relative to the wind on the stern (which because of junk hanging on the stern pulpit may be different than that on your wind instrument), and you have to talk to the wind vane with kindness and just the right amount of reverence, but with authority, too.

The first time you use your vane, make sure you have a good wind—15 knots or so—and sail without the main to avoid accidental jibes. You might put your boat on a beam reach or some other easy-to-sail point of wind, and experiment away. Make small adjustments in the vane direction until you know how it all works. It will work, but it's an art form, too.

WINDLASSES

Windlasses retrieve anchor rode, chain, and anchors, and can be manual or power. Some only raise the gear, others will raise and lower it. Unless your boat (and anchor) is very small, or you never anchor out, or you're a champion weight lifter, I think a power windlass is mandatory; I'd even go so far as to say it's a mandatory piece of *safety* equipment. Boating purists may scoff at that, but one night I had to set the anchor fourteen times (Lynda kept count) before we got a set that seemed strong and safe, and there's no way that I could have done that with a manual windlass.

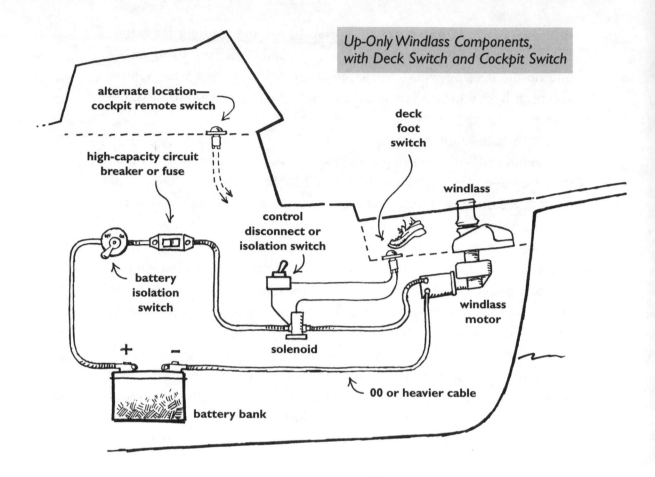

alternate location— cockpit remote switch

deck foot switch

windlass

high-capacity circuit breaker or fuse

control disconnect or isolation switch

battery isolation switch

windlass motor

+ −

solenoid

00 or heavier cable

battery bank

POWER WINDLASSES

As mentioned in chapter 4, windlasses need strong motors, but because of their exposed location, they must be powered by 12 rather than 120 volts. Since windlass motors need 1,200 watts of power or more, they can draw 100 amps of current or more. That's a lot! From page 94 this means wiring into windlasses needs to be large 00 cable.

The illustration above shows the arrangement of components in a typical up-only windlass system. A large cable leads from the battery bank to the windlass and a large-capacity circuit breaker is placed in this line, as close to the batteries as possible in case of a short (so only a short run will be unprotected). Usually these circuit breakers have a red light to indicate they're on. As with a propane solenoid, only turn this breaker on when you need to.

Since this windlass is wired for up-only, the positive-side cable is led to a foot switch on the deck and then to the windlass. The illustration also shows a remote switch in the cockpit in addition to the foot switch. A solenoid, much like the one on your starter motor (see chapter 4), is used to save running heavy-duty cable and power all the way back to the cockpit. The cockpit switch should be a positive switch, meaning it's on only when it's being pushed. When on, it activates the solenoid that closes the circuit and causes the windlass to operate.

An up-and-down windlass (see illustration below) has a two-way motor with two wires leading out of it. The large cable from the battery is run

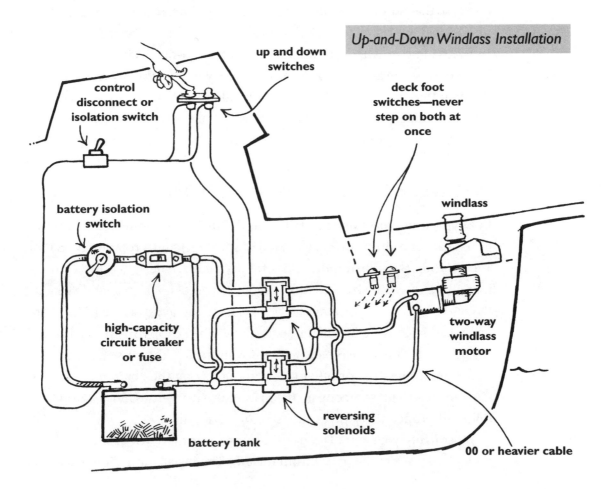

Up-and-Down Windlass Installation

control disconnect or isolation switch

up and down switches

deck foot switches—never step on both at once

windlass

battery isolation switch

high-capacity circuit breaker or fuse

two-way windlass motor

reversing solenoids

battery bank

00 or heavier cable

to two different solenoids. The first solenoid has the positive wire going to the left-hand terminal of the windlass motor and the negative wire going to the right-hand terminal. The second solenoid is just the opposite. When you step on the left-hand foot switch, the first solenoid is energized, opens, and sends positive current to the left-hand terminal, causing the motor to turn in one direction. When the user steps on the right-hand foot switch, the second solenoid is energized, opens, and positive current is sent to the right-hand terminal, causing the motor to turn in the opposite direction. If you step on both pedals at the same time, though, you'll cause a short (the circuit breaker should trip and turn off), which in a circuit with this much current is dangerous, so the foot switches should be far enough apart so that it's impossible to step on both of them at the same time. They should also have covers so that only one of them is uncovered at a time. Some newer units have interlocked up-and-down controls that eliminate this problem.

I've had boats with both up-and-down and up-only windlass switches. Once I got some anchoring experience, I never used the down switch on the boat that had one, and our current Dulcinea only has an up switch. A down switch is probably safer because you don't have chain rattling out of the chain locker at a high speed, but I try not to let that happen, anyway.

WINDLASS DECK INSTALLATION

In a typical windlass deck installation, the motor is connected to a set of gears that drive the chain gypsy (a kind of sprocket) and a rotating barrel for anchor rode (see illustration opposite). Gypsies are designed for a particular range of chain size and link lengths. If you change to a larger or different type of chain, you might have to change the gypsy as well. The chain gypsy can be loosened from the shaft (done when dropping the anchor using gravity). This is also handy if you want to use the rode barrel to lift someone up the mast or other task without having the chain move. Using the windlass to lift someone up the mast is also dangerous. Ensure you have followed proper safety precautions before doing this.

Most likely your windlass has a locking lever that provides a mechanical lock to prevent the gypsy from turning. The installation shown also has

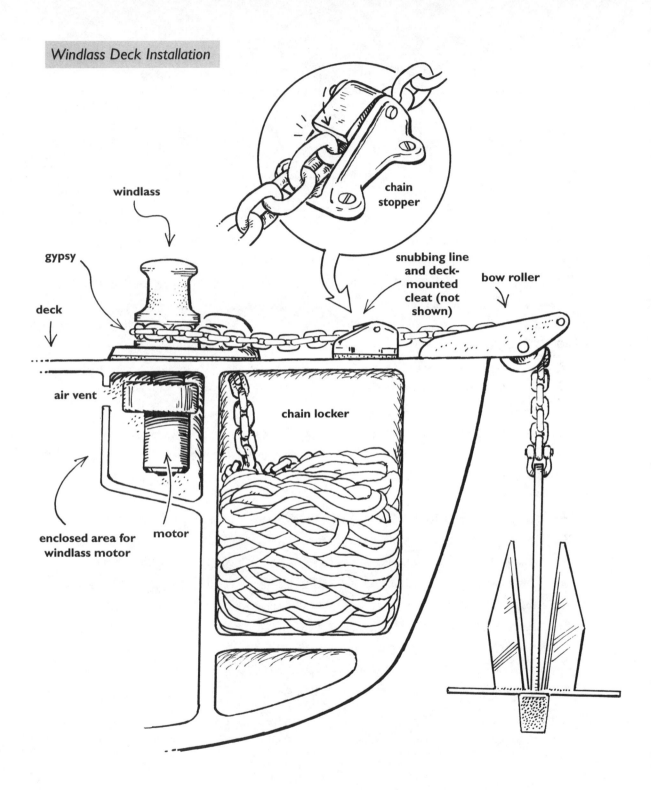

Windlass Deck Installation

chain
stopper

windlass

gypsy

snubbing line
and deck-
mounted
cleat (not
shown)

bow roller

deck

air vent

chain locker

enclosed area for
windlass motor

motor

Windlasses
Are
Dangerous!

Windlasses are dangerous! I once saw the mangled hand of one boater who caught his hand between the running windlass motor and the chain. He'd lost two fingers and his hand was an angry mass of scar tissue. Therefore, *locate your foot switches well away from the windlass*; the best distance is far enough apart so that you can't reach both the foot switch and the windlass at the same time. In this way, you can either work with the chain or rode, or use the windlass, but never both.

In a similar vein, don't allow other people near the foot switch when you're working with the windlass. If the boat rolls or lurches, it's very easy for someone to step on the foot switch while catching his or her balance. For this and other reasons as well, don't allow children on the foredeck when you're using the windlass.

Finally, if you have a remote windlass switch, don't allow anyone to use it when you're on the foredeck working with the windlass. Don't ask anyone to use it while you're up there either, because communication between the foredeck and cockpit is notoriously bad. Just ask any happy boating couple!

This is a different subject, but a good set of hand signals goes a long way toward marital bliss (and safety). It's just too hard to hear from the foredeck. Lynda and I have developed a system that allows us to anchor in what must appear to be a pantomime of deaf-mutes. From the time I leave the cockpit to the time we shut the engine off, we don't need to say a word. It's fun, actually, and I suppose we're more than a bit vain when we enjoy pulling into a crowded anchorage, dropping the hook with a good set, and cooperatively doing all tasks required without saying a word.

But, when we're tired after a long day, it's raining and cold, and the wind's howling, such signals are not only fun, they're a godsend to safe boating.

a chain stop block (chain stopper) that accomplishes the same purpose. We have both of these features on our Dulcinea, but when we're anchored, we also put out a three-part nylon snubber line that hooks the chain and is tied to a deck cleat. The snubber line takes the constant pulling force that occurs when anchored in a windy or rolly anchorage.

Most windlasses have a grease fitting for lubricating the spindle. This fitting may be above or below the deck, depending on your windlass. Every season (or more frequently if you use your windlass a lot), you should take the windlass apart and clean and regrease it. See the windlass user's manual for information on how to do this. You can get it from the manufacturer if you don't have it by searching the Internet as we've described before.

May your first set be a good one—and keep your hands and feet away from the windlass!

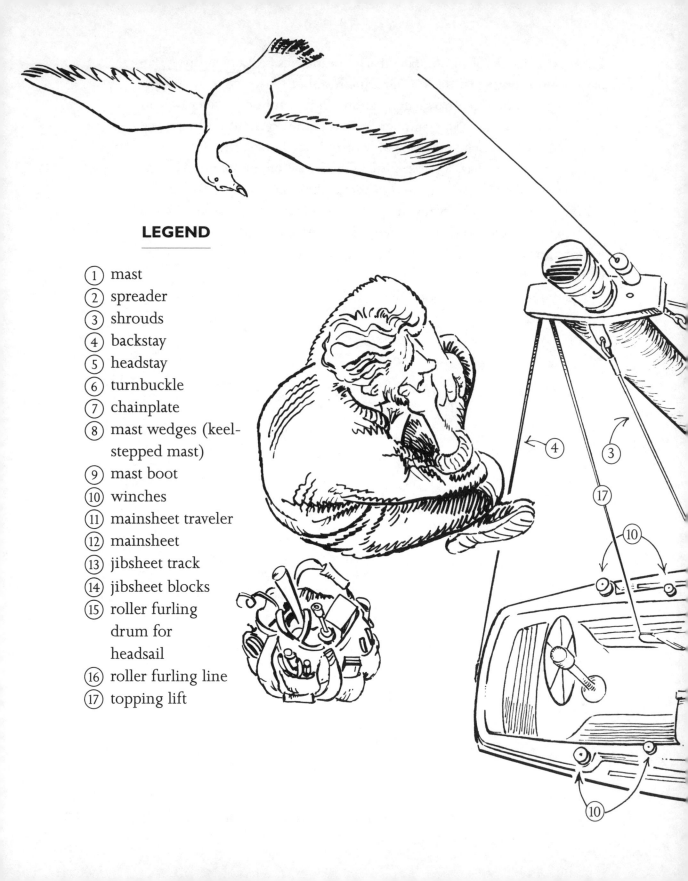

LEGEND

1. mast
2. spreader
3. shrouds
4. backstay
5. headstay
6. turnbuckle
7. chainplate
8. mast wedges (keel-stepped mast)
9. mast boot
10. winches
11. mainsheet traveler
12. mainsheet
13. jibsheet track
14. jibsheet blocks
15. roller furling drum for headsail
16. roller furling line
17. topping lift

9

SAILBOAT RIGGING

The secret to a happy rig is inspection, inspection, inspection. Listen to any seasoned, experienced sailor and you'll hear, "Inspect your rig. Every season, before every big passage, inspect your rig."

This sounds like nothing more than "always wear clean underwear" or some of Mother's other sensible advice until you look at what holds your rig together. I once rebuilt my mast, and I was stunned to see, firsthand, how tiny little parts hold slightly larger parts, that hold slightly larger parts, etc. If you look closely at your rig, you'll see small cotter pins that hold slightly larger clevis pins that hold the even larger spreaders in place so they can hold the even larger shrouds in place so they can hold up the mast. And, the failure of the cotter pin, could, conceivably, bring the whole mess down! It never does—at least, it almost never does—but that's why inspection is so important. With the rig, little problems always lead to big ones, and again, the easiest way to solve a problem is not to have it.

The question is, what do we inspect and how? Answering that question is the prime goal of this chapter.

STANDING RIGGING

Standing rigging is rigging that doesn't move. It is the fore- and back-stays, shrouds, and the fittings that hold the assembly together. The designers of these components face a serious challenge. The standing rigging should be lightweight yet strong and corrosion resistant. Accordingly, most masts are made from aluminum and most of the other rigging is made of stainless steel. Right there we have a problem, because aluminum and stainless steel are different metals and can react with one another in a process called *galvanic corrosion*.

LOOKING FOR CORROSION

So, when inspecting the rig, you need to be on the lookout for evidence of corrosion, especially where two different metals come together. When

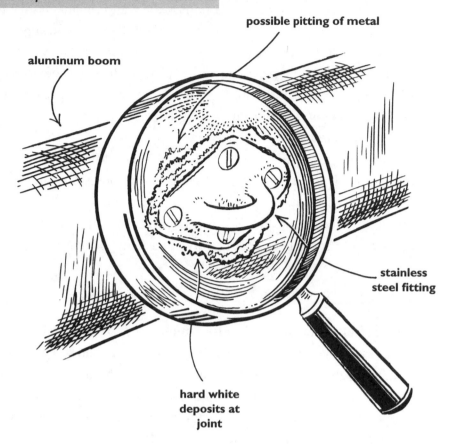

possible pitting of metal

aluminum boom

stainless
steel fitting

hard white
deposits at
joint

two different metals are in contact, especially in the presence of salt water, one of the metals will lose electrons (and mass) to the other. In the case of an aluminum mast with stainless steel rivets or other fittings, it's the aluminum that gives up mass to the stainless steel. Normally, this is not a problem because there's much more aluminum in the mast than there is stainless steel in the fitting, and the mast has sufficient electrons to give some away without suffering damage. If there's a nick or pinprick in the paint on the mast, it may be only the aluminum in that nick or pinprick that is under attack. Over time, the exposed aluminum will suffer damage and the hole or pinprick will become larger.

As shown in the illustration on page 217, corrosion looks like a bad skin rash. The surface will be bubbled and powdery, and the metal may be pitted. In bad cases, the corrosion will have worked all the way through the surface to create a hole. In some cases, screws, rivets, and bolts may come loose.

You want to find and fix corrosion problems before they get to the hole-in-the-surface stage. A little sluffing paint, even a little pitting, isn't a problem, as long as you attend to it. Letting it go, however, is an invitation to greater problems and expense.

Whenever I use fasteners (screws, bolts, rivets) for fittings that involve different metals, I put some type of goop (LanoCote is one brand) on the fastener that will help insulate one metal from the other. Riggers do the same thing with stainless steel fittings before installing them. Doing this also makes life easier later when removing a screw or bolt.

STAINLESS STEEL

Stainless steel is strange stuff. As its name implies, it does resist corrosion, but the small print of that statement is that it will only do so in the presence of oxygen. Since you're probably thinking of doing most of your sailing in the presence of oxygen, that doesn't sound like too much of a limitation. But, put a small amount of water down the creases of a fitting where there's not much room for air, and corrosion can develop, even in stainless steel. So, as described below, it's important to take stainless steel fittings apart from time to time, clean them up, and ensure that oxygen-starvation corrosion has not begun.

Such corrosion can also occur on your stainless steel prop shaft. As long as you're using your boat, the prop shaft will turn and be exposed to oxygen in the water. If Dulcinea sits for a long time, however, and the prop shaft does not turn, the stainless steel under the ribs of your cutless bearings (see the illustrations on page 38) will be starved for oxygen. Corrosion is possible. If none of this makes sense, just be sure that somebody runs Dulcinea's engine(s) at least once a month and puts her into gear, even if it's only at the dock.

Stainless steel is also susceptible to something called *galling*, which is a type of cold-welding. A stainless steel turnbuckle, for example, can start to gall as you turn it. What happens is that friction develops from dirt or damage in the threads, heat builds up, and the stainless steel threads are welded together. To prevent galling, first clean the threads of any fitting you're about to turn. If you feel an increase in friction as you're turning the threads, STOP! Further action with that big wrench will just make things worse, a lot worse!

Instead, apply a lubricant containing molybdenum disulfide (like McLube) or another lubricant recommended for stainless steel. Then back the threads off, apply lubricant to the part of the threads just exposed, wait a bit, and try again. Gently move the fitting, working it back and forth, until the bind goes away. Do not use excessive force; if you do the result will be a welded fitting or broken part.

Finally, not all stainless steel is the same. It varies in the degree of purity, resistance to corrosion, strength, and cost. Thus, when you buy stainless steel rope (wire is called rope on a boat), you should specify the type you want. Ask a professional for advice because higher grades aren't always better for all applications.

STAINLESS STEEL MAINTENANCE

Because of the possibility of corrosion and of galling, it's a good idea to lubricate all fittings, especially turnbuckles on shrouds, stays, and lifelines. Products containing molybdenum disulfide are particularly recommended, but they can be messy. Other products formulated for stainless steel can also be used, but be certain they are intended to be used in the marine (saltwater) environment.

Sooner or later some of Dulcinea's stainless will show rust stains. You might see, for example, a light spiral of rust on a stainless shroud. This doesn't necessarily mean inferior material; in the saltwater environment, some staining is unavoidable. Rust stains can be removed with mild cleaners, including those specifically designed for rust removal. After cleaning, rinse well with freshwater. Don't use anything that scratches the surface because those new scratches will be the site of the next stain. Above all, *do not* use steel wool. Bits of it will tenaciously adhere to the surface and start a bigger rust stain. The best prevention is to keep your stainless steel clean and let that oxygen in!

Proper Clevis Pin Sizing

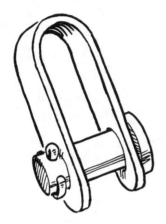

clevis pin held by cotter pin

clevis pin held by ring

clevis-pin diameter too small

clevis pin too long

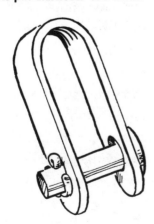

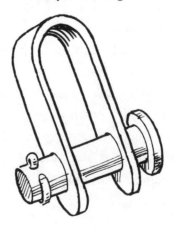

INSPECTING STAYS, SHROUDS, AND THEIR FITTINGS

Many rigging components are held together with clevis pins like the ones shown opposite. The pin goes through a hole in the fitting, then is secured with either a cotter pin or a ring. The cotter pin should be bent so that it cannot work its way out under load or vibration. The clevis pin should be just small enough to fit into the hole in the fitting. If it's too small, the pin can bend under load. Also, the pin should be just long enough to do the job. As you inspect your rig, ensure that all pins are in place, their cotter pins or rings are in place, and that the pins are the correct size and length.

If the pin is located where lines, sails, clothing, or bodies can snag on it, the cotter pin or ring can be covered with tape. If you do this, at least once a year you should remove the tape and inspect the fitting. Because of the possibility of oxygen-starvation corrosion, it's also a good idea to remove the clevis pin completely, clean and lubricate it and the fitting, and put it all back together.

Turnbuckles

The question is, with tension on a shroud or stay, how am I going to loosen the fitting to inspect it? The answer, of course, is to loosen the turnbuckles. Before doing that, however, you need to mark how tight the turnbuckle is so that you can, as they say, "return it to its original upright position." So, before loosening the turnbuckle, wrap tape around the top and bottom of the screws (see illustration next page).

Important Note: Assuming your Dulcinea has at least three shrouds on each side of the boat, you can remove one of them at a time without a problem. However, your Dulcinea only has one backstay. Therefore, if you're going to remove it, find some way to hold the mast in place while you work. If you have running backstays, install them. Otherwise, bring a halyard aft and tie it to a cleat to hold the mast in place. As long as it's not blowing a gale, you don't need much, but you do want something to keep the mast from wandering forward. The same, but opposite, is true for the forestay.

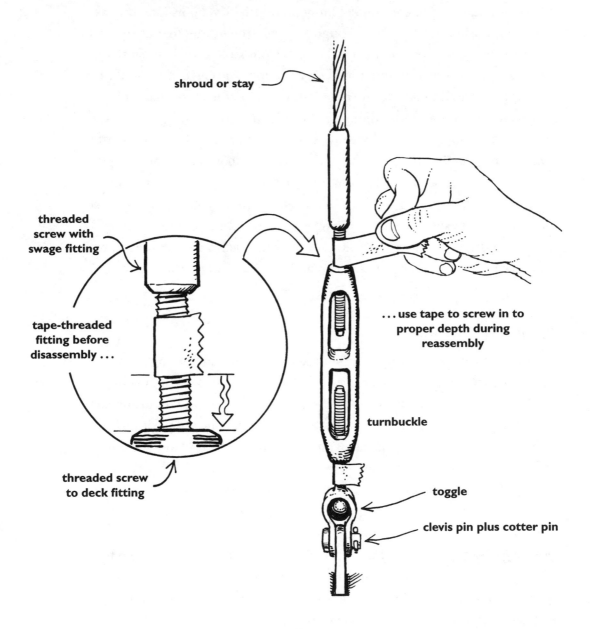

shroud or stay

threaded
screw with
swage fitting

tape-threaded
fitting before
disassembly . . .

threaded screw
to deck fitting

. . . use tape to screw in to
proper depth during
reassembly

turnbuckle

toggle

clevis pin plus cotter pin

Clean the turnbuckle threads as best you can and apply a bit of McLube or other lubricant to the threads inside the turnbuckle. Now, put a long screwdriver in the turnbuckle and turn to loosen it. Some turnbuckles loosen clockwise and other loosen counterclockwise. Turn the turnbuckle a bit one way or the other and watch the threads to see whether it's tightening or loosening. Be aware of galling and stop if you feel any increased friction. If you do, proceed for galling as described on page 219. While you're loosening or tightening your turnbuckles, hold the upper screw with a wrench so as not to twist the shroud.

You don't have to take the turnbuckle all the way off. Just loosen it enough so that you can remove the clevis pin to inspect and clean the fitting. Examine all parts for bends, cracks, corrosion, or any other sign of weakness or damage. If you find any, replace the part. In the case of weird bends or kinks, see if you can figure out why the bend occurred. Something may be installed incorrectly. Again, get professional help if necessary because it is important that all standing rigging parts come into alignment under load with no bending.

This discussion assumes that you're starting with the turnbuckles in place. If you ever need to start threading a turnbuckle, as for example with new lifelines, here's a trick. Thread the turnbuckle onto one of the fittings for several turns and then thread it onto the other fitting. That way, when you later remove the turnbuckle, when you get to the end, the fittings won't both fall out at the same time, leaving you with the turnbuckle and two fittings to try to hold at the same time. That's three loose items with just two hands . . . explaining why the bottom under most marinas looks like a parts warehouse.

SWAGES AND OTHER FITTINGS

The wire rope is connected to the turnbuckle via a *swage* or other type of fitting. Swage fittings are made by pressing the fitting around the wire rope using tremendous pressure in a swaging machine. Without such a machine, you cannot make swage fittings; they have to be made by specialized companies.

Two other kinds of fittings are Sta-Lok and Norseman. These fittings, which accomplish the same purpose as a swage fitting, can be done with normal tools, even aboard the boat. Each terminal is packed with instructions, but it's a good idea to hire a rigger to show you how to do it and make notes. It's not hard to do, but there several small parts that need to be put on in just the right way. Invariably, those small parts want to jump overboard, as well.

Most production rigging uses swage fittings because they're cheaper. If you're going on a long trip, however, you should be prepared to replace them. Take a piece of wire rope as long and strong as Dulcinea's longest stay, a pair of Sta-Lok or Norseman fittings, some sturdy shackles, and any other necessary fittings. You'll also need a suitable cable cutter. Check with your rigger on the selection and use of this hardware.

The major problem with swage fittings is that it's difficult to tell if they've been damaged or weakened internally. You can and should inspect each of your swage fittings at the top rim and edge, where the wire goes into the fitting. If you find small cracks on the edge or side as shown (see illustration), replace the shroud or stay. Also, if you find even one strand of broken wire, replace the stay. The same is true for weird bends or kinks at the swage

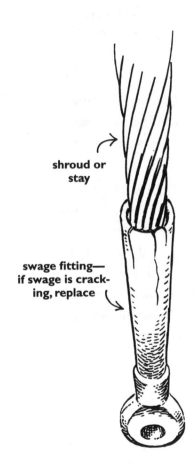

Swage Fitting Inspection

shroud or stay

swage fitting— if swage is cracking, replace

fitting. If the stay has been stressed that hard, there's a good chance the swage fitting has internal damage.

Because we can't inspect the fittings internally, most people replace their rigging after so many years. Opinions vary on how many years, however. It depends on how and where you've used your boat. Obviously, if most of the time you've been motoring up the Inside Passage, with your rigging cleaned by a soft Northwest rain every other day, then your rigging is going to last a lot longer than if you specialize in open-ocean racing in the south South Pacific. The best plan is to ask experienced riggers and sailors in the area where you sail, and check with your boat manufacturer. Most of us should replace our stainless shrouds and stays every 10 to 15 years.

CHAINPLATES

While inspecting your standing rigging, you should also examine your chainplates. Check for evidence of corrosion on the plates themselves as well as on the bolts that fasten the chainplates to the hull. Ensure that the bolts are tight and there is no evidence of movement in the plates or fastenings.

This is a good time to check inside Dulcinea for evidence of leakage where the chainplates pass through the deck (if they pass through the deck on your boat). If you see rust stains or other evidence that water is leaking into the boat, then you'll need to clean the old caulk where the chainplates pass through the deck and replace it with new. When you do this, be sure to clean out *all* of the old caulk. Otherwise, the new caulk will not bed properly and the leak will reappear.

MASTS

There are two kinds of masts: *deck-stepped* and *keel-stepped*. A deck-stepped mast rests on the deck and doesn't go through to the cabin. A keel-stepped mast extends through the deck, through the cabin sole, and rests on the keel. The advantages of a deck-stepped mast are that it's easier to install and remove, and because it doesn't go through the deck, leaks are rare. The advantage of a keel-stepped mast is that it's stronger; for boats over 40 feet, it's the only choice because it's just about impossible to beef up the deck enough to take the load of a large deck-stepped mast. If well designed and constructed, either type works well, though the inspection is slightly different.

Inspecting the Foot of the Mast

Start the mast inspection at the foot. On a keel-stepped mast, check for standing water and corrosion in the mast step. Water will inevitably work its way inside the mast, and it needs a channel in the bottom of the mast to flow out. If there's no such channel, bore ¼-inch (or smaller) holes in the fore, aft, and sides of the mast, about ½ inch from the bottom, to let water out. Be careful when you do this, however, so that you don't bore holes in part of the shoe fitting that holds the mast in place. If in doubt, check with an expert.

When you pull your mast for other reasons, paint the bottom of its edges and the bottom inside of the mast with zinc chromate. Paint the area where the mast touches the keel with it as well. This will help to retard corrosion in the mast foot.

Check the supporting area around the mast step for cracks, bends, or other evidence of damage due to compression. This is especially important if you have a hydraulic backstay tensioner. If the stay has been overtensioned, compression damage can occur at the mast base. Bring in outside expertise if you find any such evidence.

A few inches above the mast foot, wires will exit from inside the mast. While you've got the cabin sole up, check these wires for abrasion and repair them, if necessary.

Where it passes through the deck, the mast is wedged in place in the *mast partner*, a reinforced collar in the deck (see illustration opposite). The wedges are usually J-shaped pieces of softwood or plastic. A *mast boot* surrounds the mast and covers the wedges and any gaps in the hole. The boot is sealed to the mast and to the deck fitting, often held in place by hose clamps.

Ideally, you should inspect the partner underneath the mast boot, but if the boot isn't leaking, I wouldn't mess with it. Try to look at the wedges from

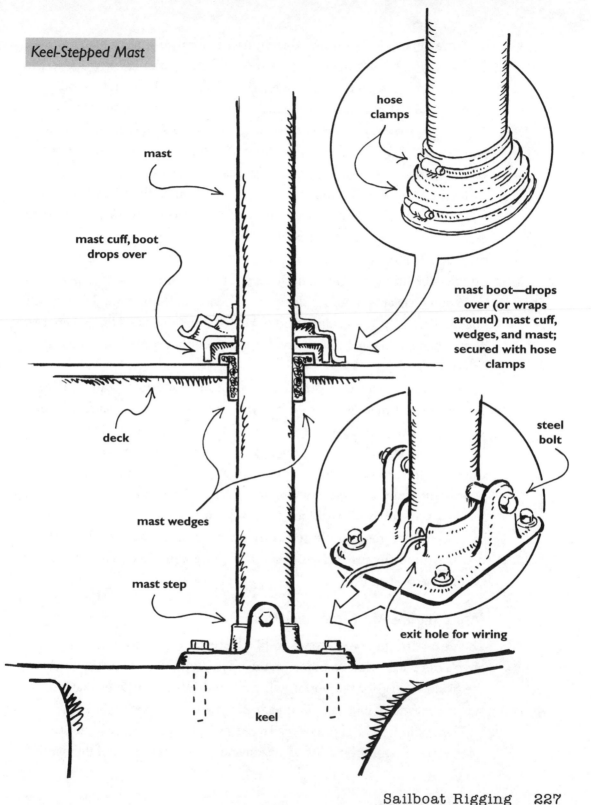

Keel-Stepped Mast

hose clamps

mast

mast cuff, boot drops over

mast boot—drops over (or wraps around) mast cuff, wedges, and mast; secured with hose clamps

deck

steel bolt

mast wedges

mast step

exit hole for wiring

keel

underneath, inside the cabin (you may have to remove interior molding). Of course, if you have evidence of a partner problem (splinters of wood in the cabin, weird noises out of the mast at the deck), you should take a look.

By the way, the best time to install a mast boot is when the mast is out of the boat. That way, you don't have to cut the boot to get it around the mast; you can just slide it up from the bottom. While you can cut a mast boot and wrap it around the mast in place, the seams always leak.

If your mast is deck-stepped, check for corrosion on the edges of the mast where its stepped on the deck. There should be some means for water to exit the mast, similar to that described for keel-stepped masts (see illustration on page 227). The mast is held in place by the compression from the shrouds on the deck fitting. Normally, no bolts or other fasteners hold it in place.

When inspecting your rig, look for evidence that something has recently changed. Usually there is dirt or oil or rust or some mark and line where two components come together. Look for evidence that something has shifted its position.

For example, on a deck-stepped mast, examine the area around the deck fitting to see if there is any evidence that the mast could be shifting either sideways or up and down as you sail. If so, the rigging is likely way too loose and needs to be tuned. I once saw a boat with rigging so badly out of tune that the deck-stepped mast popped out of the deck fitting and fell overboard—not only a serious but also an expensive problem!

On a keel-stepped mast, look for cracks or lines in the deck around the mast boot that might indicate that the deck is pumping (moving up and down around the mast) as you sail. If so, hire a professional to help you correct the problem.

Inspecting the Mast from the Deck

The next part of the mast to inspect is the section from the deck to as high as you can reach while standing on the boom. Typically, this section includes the *gooseneck* fitting for the boom, winches, and fittings for lines that run inside the mast (see illustration on page 230).

The boom is held in place by a large clevis pin, which is held in place by a cotter pin. Examine both for corrosion and wear. This section of the mast of-

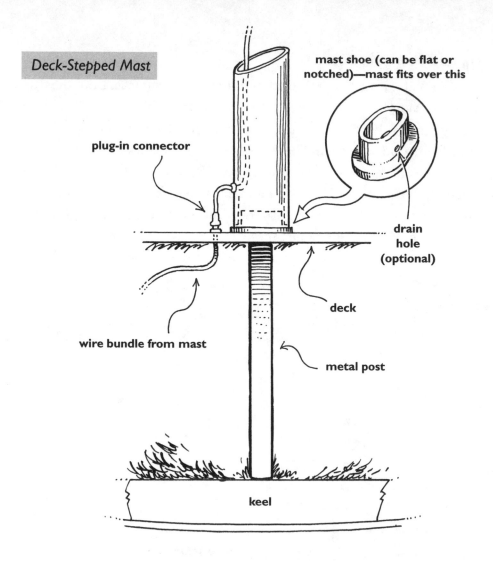

Deck-Stepped Mast

mast shoe (can be flat or notched)—mast fits over this

plug-in connector

drain hole (optional)

deck

wire bundle from mast

metal post

keel

ten connects to a boom vang as well. Check the pins and fittings of the vang while you're here. Ensure that the pins and rings are in place and that the screw fittings are tight. Again, the best procedure for stainless fittings is to remove, clean, and apply lubricant to them.

Winches are made of stainless steel and are typically installed with stainless steel screws into the aluminum mast, so corrosion is a possible problem where the winches meet the mast. The fittings for lines that run inside the mast are also typically made of stainless steel. They may be held in place by stainless steel screws or by stainless steel or aluminum rivets. In any case, check these for corrosion as well.

Up and Down the Mast

You can make a cursory examination of the rest of the mast from the deck or dock using binoculars. It's cursory, however, so before every offshore passage and at least once a year, you or your rigger should inspect the mast from a bosun's chair. There are a number of ways to make this job safer; have an experienced rigger show you how to go up the mast before you do it the first time. Check your local chandlery for books and videos on this topic as well. Lynda and I use the windlass to lift each other up the mast (no, not both at the same time).

Inspect as you go up the mast. At the spreaders, look at the clevis pins

Gooseneck Fitting

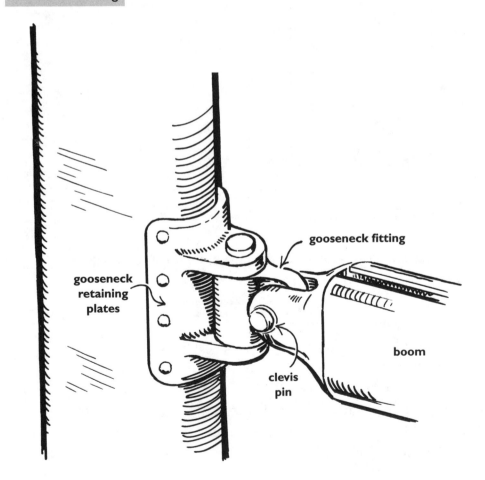

gooseneck fitting

gooseneck retaining plates

clevis pin

boom

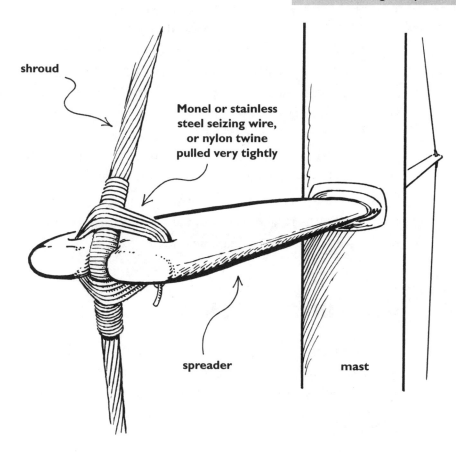

shroud

Monel or stainless steel seizing wire, or nylon twine pulled very tightly

spreader

mast

that hold the butts of the spreaders to the mast. Inspect the cotter pins and washers for corrosion and wear. Replace the cotter pins, if necessary. (Now, by the way, is not the time to think, "I wish I'd brought some cotter pins with me.") If you have a cutter rig, inspect the cutter stay fitting on the mast. Also, inspect the swage fittings on the stays. If you have a radar deflector, a radar, or other equipment mounted on the mast, inspect those fastenings as well. Check the mast and swage fittings on the lower and intermediate shrouds, if any, as you go up.

When you check the spreader fittings, move the spreaders up and down slightly to determine if the shrouds are free to move independently of the spreaders. If you have any doubt, move out to the end of the spreaders, remove the plastic covers, if any, and check. Monel seizing wire should wrap around the shrouds to hold them in place as shown in the illustration on page 231. If this wire seems doubtful, replace it.

Check everything at the top of the mast. Make sure the wind instruments and wind indicator are in place and that their fasteners are tight and in good condition. Ensure the masthead lights are securely fastened; fill any wiring holes with a marine sealant. Inspect the connections of both the forestay and backstay. Ensure all cotter pins are properly in place and in good condition. Examine all swage fittings at the top of the mast. This is also a good time to check or change masthead lightbulbs.

Slowly work your way back down the mast. Depending on how your bosun's chair is rigged, you can sometimes inspect one side of the mast on the way up and the other side on the way down.

RUNNING RIGGING

Running rigging is rigging that moves. It includes halyards, sheets, outhauls, vangs, travelers, and all of the blocks, cleats, and fittings used to manage them. Here, we'll include winches, though some would disagree and say winches belong in a category of their own.

LINES

The hardest part about inspecting lines is remembering to do it. It's not so hard for jibsheets that are in your face every time you get on or off the boat, but it's harder to remember to look at lines—like the jib halyard—that are hidden at the top of your roller-furling jib. That halyard, like all halyards, is subject to wear where it goes over the sheave or blocks at the top of the mast. So, when you do your inspection, you should endeavor to look at every line on your boat. Take every halyard down and take a look.

When to replace a line? That's a tough call. Clearly, if the outer layer of a double-braid line is cut or damaged, or there's substantial wear where the line runs over a sheave, it's time to replace or splice the line. Unlike swage fittings, though, if everything looks good from the outside, it's probably good on the inside. One trick is to reverse, or *end-for-end*, the line so you move the wear spots to a different part of the line. You can do this with halyards, for example, where the deck end of the halyard has little or no wear and the halyard top has a lot.

If you do swap ends on a halyard, however, there's a problem if you have a shackle spliced into the line. You want to move the shackle to the opposite end of the halyard, but tying eyesplices in two-part line is tricky, and can be especially difficult with used line. So, unless you're skilled at such splices, when you swap ends of the halyard, just tie the halyard to the head of the sail with a bowline. If you do this make sure the knot doesn't interfere with the rotation of the roller furling at the top of the mast.

Speaking of splices, there's a tremendous pleasure in learning how to make them. Making splices in three-part nylon line is easy. You can learn how to tie eyesplices and short and long splices from any good rigging book. Splices in double-braid line that has a cover and a core are difficult, however. You can learn to do it in a seminar or by hiring a rigger to show you.

BLOCKS, SLIDES, AND ROLLER FURLING

So, you're out for a sail one fine day. As you motor out of the marina, you realize you're going to have a perfect 15-knot breeze right on your beam. The sun's shining, and you're happy as a pig in mud as you raise Dulcinea's sails. All's well with the world as the boat picks up speed under her own sails—until you realize that you forgot to move the jibsheet block forward. (In the marina, you keep it back to make it easier to board the boat.) OK, no problem.

"Honey, will you bear up into the wind as I go move that block forward?"

Up you go, water splashing over the rail and onto your new,

dry deck shoes; but the water this time of year is almost warm and at least you're still as happy as a pig in moist dirt. The love of your life bears Dulcinea up into the wind, the sail starts flogging, the sheet flies in your face, and you push on that block. Nope, no way. It's not gonna slide.

You're pointed straight at shore. The sail's cracking in the wind as you start to kick that block. Bam, bam, with your brand-new, now very wet deck shoes. Your toes are killing you, the love of your life is frustrated because she/he doesn't like flogging the sail like that, either. Meanwhile, you've managed to move the block just far enough forward so that it's out of its locking hole. Bam, bam. Now you're about as happy as a pig in a serious drought. You remember that you varnished the toerail last week and realize that the edge of that block is caught on little varnish drips underneath the rail.

During your inspection, move all the moving blocks up and down their tracks. If they're caught on last week's varnish, remove it while you're still tied to the dock. You might spray silicone on the slides, but don't do this if you step on the slides when getting on or moving around the boat.

This is a good time, too, to lubricate the sheaves in the boom and the blocks in the boom sheet, and any blocks at the foot of the mast.

However, my best sources tell me to avoid the impulse to lubricate the bearings in your roller furling. Check your owner's manual, but some say lubricating those bearings just leads to trouble. Instead, every time you wash your boat, squirt a good spray of freshwater into the bearings in the roller furling (to the joy of the person who just washed and waxed the boat moored across the dock). Every now and then, lower the jib and wash out the bearings on the fitting at the top of your roller furling as well.

Check your owner's manual for maintenance on mainsail furling. Each system is different, but there are undoubtedly fittings to clean and lubricate these as well.

WINCHES

You should lubricate your winches at least once a year, and more often if they're frequently used. If they're in really bad shape, you'll know it because they'll start to sound like marbles dropping on a tin floor every time you use them. Short of that, however, a good test is to stick your thumb in the winch where the winch handle goes and try to turn the winch with just your thumb. If you can, the winch doesn't yet need to be lubricated.

Otherwise, it's time to clean and relubricate your winches. You'll need a supply of clean rags, some cleaning solvent, an old toothbrush, and some specially formulated winch grease. (I assume that special grease is necessary; at least I use it. It's incredibly expensive and since it's sold by winch manufacturers, my paranoid mind starts to wonder.) Anyway, you shouldn't have to use *that* much of it.

Winch parts, especially the springs in pawls, love to jump overboard. Therefore, before you start taking your winch apart, drape an old beach towel over the lifeline opposite the winch. Cover your cockpit drains, too, if there's a danger of a winch part falling in.

The owner's manual for your winch will show you how to take it apart, clean, and regrease it. Contact the winch manufacturer for such a manual if you don't have yours. The idea is to remove all of the parts, clean the grit and grime out of them, and lubricate the gears and bearings with that special grease. You want to put on a medium coat of grease; too much will make the winch hard to turn. The pawls, their springs, and the notch that catches the pawls *should not be greased*. Instead, put a light coating of oil on them. Grease can bunch up inside the notch and make it so the pawl can't catch on the side of the cup—barked knuckles at best for the poor soul who's cranking on the winch.

10 GETTING READY FOR THE BIG TRIP

There's tremendous pleasure in getting ready for the Big Trip (BT). It's tempting to say almost as much as making it, but that's not true. It's all fun.

So, what's a BT? Well, it depends on your perspective and experience. If you're just getting started in boating, then a week on the Chesapeake Bay or in the San Juan Islands is a BT. If you've done those trips for a while, then a month circumnavigating Vancouver Island, or cruising from San Diego to Ensenada, Mexico, or sailing from Newport, Rhode Island, to the Maine coast is a BT. After some experience with trips like that, a BT becomes a cruise from San Diego to the Mexican mainland, or from New England to the Caribbean, or from Florida to South America, or any offshore passage. But for certain, any destination where you can't readily get parts or find repair services is a BT!

THE SCHEDULE

The most important part about planning for a BT is to set a departure date (DD). Everyone who's made a BT agrees that the hardest part is untying from the dock. And the bigger your BT is, the more important this becomes. It's not too hard to take your annual vacation on your boat. But, getting away from work for an entire summer, for example, for a BT from Seattle to Alaska, well, that's a lot harder. Jobs/responsibilities/bills/kids/house all conspire to make your BT difficult, if not impossible.

So, with all of that resistance, if you don't have a departure date, the BT is unlikely to happen. So the first thing you need to do is to sit down with your spouse, family, partner, and/or friends, and set the departure date! Not something vague like early summer, but a specific date, like June 3.

Now having set that date, it becomes apparent you've got zillions of tasks to accomplish. Buy charts, pilots, and guidebooks. Plan, acquire, and store food. Acquire safety equipment; register the radios and EPIRB. Do something with the house. Explain/arrange/quit work. Do something about the kids' school. And, not least, the subject of this book, *get the boat ready.*

The following is written assuming you're leaving for six months or so on your BT. If you're going for less time, then what's described here is overkill. Just cut this discussion down to the size that's appropriate for your BT. So here we go!

DEPARTURE DATE (DD) MINUS SIX MONTHS

At six months away, you may think you have a lot of time, but really, you don't, so don't hesitate to get started. Begin by making a list of all of the major equipment aboard Dulcinea. If you made the inventory while reading chapter 1, use it.

Otherwise, fill out a form like the one shown next page. You need to list the manufacturer, model, and serial number for all major equipment aboard Dulcinea. Now, look through your boat's documentation and make sure you have at least the users' manuals for each. For major items, it's also good to have an installation and repair manual. I also carry a parts list manual for my engine. If you don't have these, search the Internet for the part, manufacturer, and model, and e-mail the manufacturer requesting the information you need. Start this process early, so you have time for mailing delays, etc.

If you're planning on adding any new major equipment (like a generator, autopilot, watermaker, or inverter), purchase it and, if possible, install it now. Plan time for test-runs before heading out to sea with your new major item.

Finally, crank up your spreadsheet again and start making a to-do list like the one shown on pages 241–43. Work through the systems we've discussed in this book. Drag out your last survey and read through it. Are there any items there that you need to think about? If so, add them to the list. Go through each of the items in the major equipment list and see if they suggest any tasks you need to do.

Major Equipment List

	TYPE	MANUFACTURER	MODEL	SERIAL NUMBER	MANUALS ON BOARD
Engine(s)					
Transmission(s)					
Propeller(s)					
Bilge pumps					
Generator					
Batteries					
Battery charger					
Inverter					
Water pressure pump					
Foot pumps					
Water heater					
Watermaker					
Toilet(s)					
Stove/oven					
Barbeque					
Other propane appliances					
Refrigerator(s)					
Freezer(s)					
Binnacle					
Compass					
Steering systems					
Autopilot(s)					
Windlass					
Roller furling					
Winches					
Electronics					

Equipment Task List

TASK	DO-BY DATE	STATUS
THROUGH-HULLS (SEACOCKS)		
Make diagram.		Done
Inspect each.	I March	
Get missing bungs.	I April	
BILGE PUMPS		
Test switches.		Monthly
Test pumps.		Monthly
ENGINE		
Change oil.	15 April	
Change fuel filters.	15 April	
Replace zinc.	15 April	
Adjust valves.	21 March	
Replace impeller.	21 March	
Have injectors rebuilt/replaced.	21 March	
Change antifreeze.	21 March	
Rebuild starter motor.		
Check propeller shaft alignment.		
TRANSMISSION		
Change fluid.	Etc.	
Check shaft alignment.		
ELECTRICAL		
Check batteries; replace if necessary.		
Test alternator; rebuild if necessary.		
Test inverter/battery charger.		
Test all solenoids.		
Test navigation lights; replace masthead lights if old (assuming this is easier now than later).		
FRESHWATER		
Make diagram.		
Check hoses.		
Open/close valves.		
Unpickle watermaker.		
Install new watermaker filters.		
Inspect water tanks; repair if necessary.		

continued page 242

Equipment Task List (continued)

TASK	DO-BY DATE	STATUS
HEAD		
Check Y-valve operation.		
Test toilet pump.		
Test holding tank pump.		
Treat with detergent.		
Treat with vinegar.		
Check for leaks.		
Inspect holding tank.		
Ensure holding tank vent is clear.		
PROPANE		
Test for leaks.		
Test appliances.		
Fill tanks.		
SINKS		
Check for leaks.		
Clean as necessary.		
REFRIGERATION		
Test compressor operation.		
Check refrigerant level.		
Clean the ugly mess out.		
STEERING SYSTEM		
Check packing gland, tighten as necessary.		
Lubricate grease fittings.		
Check cables, tighten as necessary.		
AUTOPILOT		
Test.		
Think about backup???		
WINDLASS		
Lubricate grease fittings.		
Disassemble, clean, and regrease.		
Check electrical connections.		

Equipment Task List

TASK	DO-BY DATE	STATUS
STANDING RIGGING		
Inspect fittings.		
Inspect shrouds, stays, swages, and turnbuckles.		
Apply LanoCote as necessary.		
Inspect mast.		
Obtain spares kit from rigger and learn how to use it.		
RUNNING RIGGING		
Check and replace halyards as necessary.		
Check and replace sheets as necessary.		
Check and lubricate blocks and slides.		
Regrease winches.		
SAILS		
Order and obtain any new sails.		
Inspect and repair as necessary.		
GROUND TACKLE		
Inspect chain; replace or turn end-for-end as necessary.		
Inspect swivels and seizing wire.		

If you live in a coastal area, this is a good time to attend seminars put on by marine stores, yacht clubs, and at boat shows. Check your local yachting news. You can find seminars on engine care, trip planning, rigging, safety, etc. Your local college may have an extension program for diesel repair that might be fun to take. Likely it will include a lot you don't need, but it still could be interesting. And, in all of these places, you'll meet fellow boaters to learn from and commiserate with.

DD MINUS FOUR MONTHS

Between six months and four months, just keep adding tasks to your list. I organize mine by major system when I'm creating it, but then I copy and sort it by Do-By Date to get some idea of what to do next.

Read through appendices 1 and 2 and make a list of spares and tools you need. From your Internet searches, obtain manufacturer's part numbers of spare parts and spare part kits. A VP of marketing from a large company once told me that she was certain that 50 percent of her company's advertising was wasted. Unfortunately, she said, she didn't know which half. Well, like her, at least half of your spares will be unnecessary, but unfortunately, you can't tell which half.

When you think you have your parts list complete, you can save yourself money and time by faxing it to two or three local chandlers and asking for a bid. It's likely you'll have several hundred to a thousand dollars or more of parts in that list, and you may be able to obtain a good discount. Even if not, if you can get them to fill your order, that will save you from running around their stores trying to find items like the Par Pump Repair Kit Number 13254, which is now sold under a different name and number. You'll still have to run around to find things you forgot, but this at least gives you a starting point.

About now, unless you have a *very* large boat, you're wondering where in the heck to put all this stuff? And, of course, at the same time, you're acquiring food, clothes, equipment, an inflatable kayak, the computer, books, and a bottle or two of wine. That feeling of panic and despair is normal. Take deep breaths. It's been done before and you can do it as well.

We have four standing lockers in our boat, and since we don't have that many standing clothes, we decided to convert two of them to shelved closets. We don't regret it. Lynda, however, was moving into the shelves before I had them finished, and so once they were done, we had serious negotiating to do. I finally got one of the new shelved lockers for tools and spare parts, but I had to give up three prime main saloon lockers, two drawers in the aft cabin, and agree to . . . oh, never mind.

In any case, I have a shelved locker where I keep tools and all but the largest and least-needed spare parts. It's been very handy. By the way, it's unrealistic to think you'll have the best arrangement of tools and spares the first time you organize them. As you use them, you'll find that some things need to be always accessible and others less so. I think I've re-arranged my tools and lockers four times in the three years we've been on our BT.

Anyway, now's the time to build shelves and start thinking about where things will go. And, unfortunately, you can't avoid the Chinese puzzle aspect of this. In order to get to the spare steering cable, I need to pull up the port settee cushion. But to do that, I have to slide the table over, which means I need to put the computer on the chart table. Then I need to set the cushion aside, pull up the locker cover and supports, and place them somewhere where I won't scar the cabin sole or get dirt on the clothes ly-ing on the starboard settee. Unfortunately, the cable is caught under the standing part of the storm anchor that is tied with webbing to the locker side, so . . . This is why I inspect my steering cable on a regular basis.

Some people have success with part/equipment/food/inventory lists that state where everything is located in the boat. They keep it on a com-puter and print the list from time to time. If you can do it, great, but I'm just not that organized. I keep tools and parts together by theme; all elec-trical parts and spares, for example, are in the same plastic fishing box. That seems to work so far, but you haven't seen the spare pawls for the large winches have you?

DD MINUS THREE MONTHS

Now's the time to get major maintenance done on the engine or genera-tor. This includes jobs like adjusting the valves, replacing injectors, rebuild-ing the starter or alternator, and similar major items. If possible, get tasks like this finished this month. Again, getting them done now will give you a chance to take off for a trial run or two before you disappear on your BT.

Keep adding to your task list. Don't be surprised if the list is getting longer rather than shorter. It will keep doing this until it collapses (along with you and yours) at the very end.

DD MINUS TWO MONTHS

Try to have all major maintenance tasks finished by now. You should have most of the spares purchased and on the boat or ready to put on the boat. Have all the other maintenance tasks scheduled for at least a week prior to your departure.

If possible, take a trip on the boat for a long weekend or more to test new equipment and any major repairs that have been done. Also, getting away will cause you to use your boat and equipment and jog your memory for tasks that you've forgotten like having the dinghy motor serviced and painting length markers on your anchor chain. Add these tasks to your list.

There's a good chance about now that you're doubting the whole enterprise. All the strings from normal life are pulling on you, the tasks to be done seem insurmountable, and you're writing (large) checks like some speeded up person in a movie.

Your BT was and is a good idea, and when you get to wherever your BT is leading, you'll be delighted you did it. Keep the faith, keep writing those checks, and stay calm. Remember, you can't take it with you and great memories truly are priceless.

DD MINUS ONE MONTH

By now you should have completed all of the major maintenance tasks. This month you can do last-minute maintenance like changing the oil, the oil filter, and the fuel filters. Move all of the spare parts and tools onto your boat. You'll probably also be moving a lot of stuff off the boat—clothes you won't need, the tortilla maker, the second blender, and all those cans and jars of leftover sealant and paint that are all dried up anyway.

Most of the BT tasks that occur in this month don't concern the boat. More likely you'll be down at Costco, buying cases and cases of whatever. In fact, you won't have much time for boat tasks at this end of the schedule. And, the last thing you want to do is have the boat torn apart, getting a new inverter installed while trying to store that third case of canned tomatoes. Try to have almost everything done on the boat prior to this month!

DD PLUS ONE DAY

After you've gotten everything aboard, said good-bye to friends and family, and had your bon voyage party, take Dulcinea around the corner to an anchorage a half-day or so away and stop. Spend a few days recuperating. Take the time to say hello to your spouse. Rearrange things for the third or fourth time. Hang out, and don't tell anyone where you are. Rest up. Then start your BT. And Bon Voyage!

YOUR LIST

Ah, the list. Of course, not everything on your list got done. It probably won't matter. Take your list with you and keep on going. As long as you own a boat, you'll have that list. It will get longer and shorter, fill with critical items and those that are just inconvenient. Some won't matter at all. You'll fix some of the items the first time and other items you'll "fix" again and again and again, until you finally figure out what was really wrong. Some items you'll decide never to fix and some you'll never figure out how to fix. Every now and again you'll have the crazy idea of adding a new piece of equipment and you'll do it. Then, you'll have even more items on that list as you work through the bugs of the new gizmo.

And, I'm told, some day you'll look at that list and say to yourself, "I just don't want to fix stuff anymore." With any luck, you'll have been to Bali and back by then, or to wherever your hopes lead you. Thankfully, it hasn't happened to me yet, but when it does, it's time to swallow the anchor. Meanwhile, I've got to change the watermaker prefilters, and I still haven't found the pawls for the large winches . . .

APPENDIX 1
SPARE PARTS

You know you need an inventory of spare parts aboard Dulcinea; the questions are, which parts and how many? In general, the farther and more remote your destination, the greater the parts inventory you need. On the other hand, you don't want to turn Dulcinea into a parts warehouse, and after buying your spare parts, you'd like to have some money left over for actually going somewhere.

The best advice is to read through lists like the one that follows and then adjust it after talking with people who have equipment like yours. For example, one popular cruising book advises its readers to carry a spare engine thermostat. I talked with my engine mechanic, who said that in thirty years of working on engines like mine, he'd never seen a thermostat problem. "I've seen lots of impeller problems, some of which looked like thermostat problems, but they never were. Instead, take several spare impellers—and gaskets to go with them, too." Of course, now that I've written that, the next problem I have will be with my thermostat. Oh, well.

Another consideration is vulnerability. What happens if something breaks and you don't fix it until you get home? You can probably cruise a long way without the galley foot pump or a closet light. Most of us could probably cruise without refrigeration. God forbid, but we might even make it without air conditioning or the trash compacter. An engine on the other hand . . .

So read the following list, talk with friends and professionals, and carry only what's appropriate for your destinations.

CATEGORY	SPARE PART	REMARKS
Engine	Fuel filters	Yes, three for each filter on boat—maybe more if hard to find.
	Oil filters	Yes, at least three.
	Oil	Yes, enough for at least two changes.
	Transmission fluid	Maybe—for remote destinations.
	Antifreeze	Maybe for long trips to remote destinations. (In a pinch, unless it's freezing, can use distilled water instead.)
	Impeller pump insert	Yes, two or three for medium to long trips. Also gasket or O-ring if necessary.
	Impeller pump	(The whole pump, housing and all.) Maybe, but only for remote destinations. Ask your mechanic.
	V-belts	Yes, two or three sets.
	Injectors	Maybe for remote destinations. At $125 or more apiece, possibly just take one.
	Spare spark plugs (gasoline engine)	Yes, if rare type. Otherwise, maybe one set if trip is remote from marine services.
	Heat exchanger zinc (if you have one)	Yes, two or three.
	Starter solenoid	Yes, for long trips to remote destinations.
	Starter motor	The whole motor—maybe for long trips to remote destinations—but probably not. Ask owners of your boat type/engine.
	Hoses	Possibly for trips to remote destinations.
	Shift and shutoff cables	Spare shift cable for remote destinations. Shutoff cable, maybe—you can always shut the engine off by hand, in a pinch.
	Engine thermostat	I doubt it, but ask around.
	Oil change pump	For medium to long trips away from marine services.
	Fuel biocide	Yes.
Electrical	Fuses	Yes, three for each size and type of fuse on your boat.
	Alternator	Only for long trips to remote destinations where repairs are unlikely.

CATEGORY	SPARE PART	REMARKS
	Voltage regulator (if regulator is external to alternator)	Maybe for remote destinations.
	Butt connectors, ring connectors, wire.	Only if you plan to make small electrical repairs yourself. Will need these for 10–12 gauge, and 14–16 gauge. Don't work on AC circuits!
	Spares for generator	See Engine list opposite.
	Lightbulbs	Yes, for navigation and anchor lights. Maybe, for cabin lights.
	Circuit breaker	Maybe, for long trips to remote destinations; will need several of different amperage ratings.
Plumbing	Pump repair kits	For medium to long trips. One kit for each pump aboard boat. Search Internet using pump brand and model for spare part kit number.
	House water pump pressure switch	Maybe, for long trips to remote destinations. Not if you could manage without water pressure.
	House water pump	The whole unit. Maybe, if pump is critical (say for backflushing watermaker on a trip where you must make water).
	Head pump	The whole thing, so that you don't have to repair yourself. Probably for medium to long trips away from marine service centers. Or just take repair kit and strong rubber gloves . . .
	Antisiphon valves	For engine/generator, at least one. For others, only for long trips or remote destinations.
	Washers	For all faucets on boat. Can buy a washer pack. Not expensive and worth having even for shorter trips.
	O-rings	Yes, various sizes.
Sailboat rigging	Stainless steel cotter pins and rings	Several for each pin and ring type on boat. Inexpensive and useful.
	Spare shackles, turnbuckles, wire, and Norseman-type ends	For long trips and trips to remote destinations. Ask your rigger to put a kit together. Particulars depend on your Dulcinea's standing rigging.
	Winch grease and winch repair kit	Yes, if you grease your own winches.

continued page 252

CATEGORY	SPARE PART	REMARKS
Sailboat rigging (cont.)	Spare winch handle	Two or three.
	Sail repair tape	Yes.
	Sail repair kit	For medium to long trips. Can be simple or elaborate depending on your skill and interest. For long trips, take sail repair class before departure.
	Spare halyard	For medium to long trips, as long as longest halyard on boat.
Miscellaneous	Hose clamps	Yes! Many, all stainless steel, different sizes, several of each size. Very useful.
	Hose mender fittings	For repairing leaks in hoses. Need two for each size of hose. Only for remote destinations.
	Hose	For remote destinations, maybe a few sections of hose of different types and sizes for making repairs. Only useful if you have hose mender fittings for that hose.
	Spare steering cable and end fittings	For medium to long trips, if you have this type of steering and make sure emergency tiller works.
	Zincs	For engine, generator, propeller shaft, refrigerator condenser, boat hull, rudder, and any others. Several of each type, maybe more for long trips to remote destinations.
	Monel seizing wire	Yes, for securing shackles on anchor chain/rode, and shackles on halyard.
	Duct tape	Yes.
	White tape	Yes.
	Spray silicone	Very slippery—watch overspray on decks or cabin sole.
	Corrosion Block	Great for protecting electrical connections. Will remove some corrosion. Use instead of WD-40.
	Grease and grease gun with zerk fitting if needed.	For use on windlass and rudder bearings on long trips.
	Silicone sealant	Small tubes, several for medium to long trips to remote destinations.
	Winch grease	Yes.
	McLube or similar	For stainless steel turnbuckles.
	5-minute epoxy	Yes, very useful for minor repairs.

APPENDIX 2

TOOL KIT

I love tools; I'm a sucker for them. In fact, I'm a danger to our retirement program every time I get near a tool shop. In moments of sanity, however, I know that for most of what I do, I need only a few basic, high-quality tools. See the Tools section in chapter 1 for more on this topic.

The following list constitutes the minimum for anyone who performs basic maintenance and simple repairs. The tools you need depend on the equipment on your boat. If you have a Japanese or European engine and a U.S. boat, you'll need both U.S. and metric wrenches.

Of course, if you find a beautiful tool that isn't on this list that you just absolutely have to have, then buy it. You can always justify it to your spouse as necessary for "safety reasons." In my experience that only works once or twice, however.

TOOL	REMARKS
Cloth toolbag	Buy a strong, durable bag.
Plastic toolboxes	After your cloth bag overflows.
Screwdrivers	Your most important tool. Buy high-quality ones that won't turn Dulcinea's screw heads into hash. Buy three or four sizes of both slotted and Phillips heads.
Combination screwdriver	A screwdriver handle with interchangeable bits. Necessary if Dulcinea has screws with square-drive or other exotic heads.

continued page 254

TOOL	REMARKS
Pliers	You need one each of four types: regular, locking (Vise-Grip), expandable, Channellock (open to 2 inches or so), and needlenose. Over time, you'll use all four types.
Allen wrenches	A set of medium sizes, $\frac{1}{16}$ to $\frac{1}{4}$ inch or so. You may need a set of larger ones for your winches. You may need both U.S. and metric sizes.
End wrenches	Buy the type that has an open wrench on one end and a box (enclosed circle on the other. You may need both U.S. and metric. Sizes depend on your equipment. You probably need from $\frac{1}{4}$ inch to 1 inch, and 5 mm to 18 mm (thereabouts, depending on your equipment and what sizes are offered in sets). If possible, buy short wrenches (5 inches or so in length); these are easier to use in tight spots and make it less likely you'll apply too much force.
Socket wrenches	Same sizes as end wrenches. These come in $\frac{1}{4}$-, $\frac{3}{8}$-, and $\frac{1}{2}$-inch drives. You want either $\frac{1}{4}$ or $\frac{3}{8}$ for most work. Buy a set of extensions of various lengths.
Crescent wrench	Adjustable to different sizes. Buy one that opens to, say, $\frac{7}{8}$ inch or so.
Pipe wrench	One that opens to $2\frac{1}{2}$ inches or so.
Hacksaw	Buy lots of extra blades. You can cut anything metal and wood with a hack saw—it may be inefficient on wood, but it will work.
Hammer	Not the typical household claw hammer. Buy a 3- to 5-pound (or so) hammer for heft when you need it.
Chisels	At least two—one wood chisel $\frac{3}{8}$-inch or so wide; another cold chisel for metal (for use with hammer).
Files	Several of different sizes, shapes, and coarseness.
Putty knife	1 inch or so.
Wire cutters	Quality that won't dull on first use.
Crimper and wire stripper	For electrical repairs. (Don't work on AC circuits!)

TOOL	REMARKS
Multimeter	See chapter 4.
Oil and fuel filter wrenches	As needed for your filters.
Spanner wrench	For opening seawater strainers and like fittings.
Tape measure	About 16 feet. Buy one with U.S. scale on one edge and metric on the other.
Cordless drill	⅜-inch chuck.
Drill bits	At least sizes ¹⁄₁₆ to ⅜-inch. Probably not worth buying expensive bit for marine use. They rust and wear out quickly on stainless steel even if they are expensive. Buy medium quality. Also ¾-inch wood bit.
Bronze brush	Don't use a steel brush on a boat. You'll be finding rust spots for months afterward.
Painting equipment	For whatever tasks Dulcinea requires.

METRIC CONVERSIONS

$(°F − 32) \times 0.555 = °C$

$(°C \times 1.8) + 32 = °F$

feet $\times$ 0.3 = meters

inches $\times$ 2.54 = centimeters

pounds $\times$ 0.454 = kilograms

U.S. gallons $\times$ 3.785 = liters

cups $\times$ 2.4 = deciliters

pounds per square inch $\times$ 0.7031 = kilograms per square centimeter

INDEX

Numbers in **bold** refer to pages with illustrations

roller furling, 234
Roth, Hal, 43
rudderposts, 192
rudderstocks, **39**, 40, 194, **195**
rudder types, 192–94, **193**
running rigging. *See also* standing
  rigging
  blocks, slides, and roller furl-
    ing, 234
  lines, 232–33
  spare parts for, 251–52
  winches, 229, 235

S
seacocks, about, 23–27, **24**, **26**
  clogged, 36
seacocks, types of
  ball-valve, 28–**29**
  gate-valve, 30
  tapered-plug, 30
seawater. *See also* watermakers
  and engine cooling, 61–62
  as odor source, 164
seawater strainer, 78, **79**
self-sufficiency, pride in, 8–10
serial numbers, importance of
  recording, 10, 12, 239
sewage
  disposing of, 148, 150, 151
  odor control, 161, 163–64
shaft through-hulls, 37–40, **38**,
  39, 42, 44
shore power, 95, 98–99. *See also*
  AC (120-volt) power
  inverters, 89, 110–11, 114
  120-volt electrical panel,
    99–100
short circuits, 91, 120–21
sinks, galley, 175–76, **177**

slides, 234
skeg-mounted rudder, **193**, 194
solenoids, **116**
  battery isolation switch, 115
  engine, 81, 114–15
  fuel line, 72–73
  power windlass, **209**, 210
  propane tank, 115
spade rudder, **193**, 194
spanner wrench, 78, **79**
spare parts, 43, 249
  electrical, 250–51
  engine, 250
  impeller pump, 80
  organizing, 245
  marine toilet, 158–59
  plumbing, 251
  purchasing, 244
  rigging, 251–52
spark plugs, 52, 53, 64
  changing, 71
speed indicator, paddle type, 44
spin-on fuel filters, 68
spreaders, on mast, 230–32, **231**
stainless steel
  and corrosion, 216–20, **217**,
    229
  hose clamps, 28
  maintenance, 219–20
Sta-Lok fittings, 224
standing rigging. *See also* corrosion; masts; running rigging
  chainplates, 225
  clevis pins, **220**, 221
  diagram of typical, **214–15**
  inspecting, 221
  spare parts for, 251–52
  swages, 223–25, **224**
  turnbuckles, 221–23, **222**

steering systems. *See also* autopilots
  diagram of typical, **190–91**
  emergency, 199
  hydraulic, 194, **196**, 198
  mechanical, 194, 197, **198**
stoves, 168
  propane, 173
stuffing box. *See* packing
  glands
surveys, of boat, 5, 27, 239
swages, 223–25, **224**

T
tanks. *See* holding tanks; propane
  tanks; water tanks
tapered-plug seacocks, 30
through-hull fittings, 23–27,
  24, **25**, **26**
through-hulls, about, 23–27,
  24, **26**
  diagram of typical, **25**
  inventory of, 40–41
  maintenance, 41–44
through-hulls, types of, **20–21**,
  32–33
  deck and cockpit drains, 33
  engine, 34, **35**, 37, 42, 62
  instrument, 43, 44
  propane locker drains,
    33–34, 171
  shaft, 37–40, **38**, **39**, 42, 44
toolbags, cloth, **17**
  pocketed, **18**, 253
tools
  organizing, 245, 253
  selection and care, **17–19**
  suggested, 253–55
transmission, 49, **51**

www.wadsworth.com

www.wadsworth.com is the World Wide Web site for Wadsworth and is your direct source to dozens of online resources.

At *www.wadsworth.com* you can find out about supplements, demonstration software, and student resources. You can also send email to many of our authors and preview new publications and exciting new technologies.

www.wadsworth.com
Changing the way the world learns®

LIBERTY

EQUALITY

POWER

A HISTORY OF THE AMERICAN PEOPLE
VOLUME I: TO 1877

FOURTH EDITION

JOHN M. MURRIN Princeton University

PAUL E. JOHNSON University of South Carolina

JAMES M. McPHERSON Princeton University

GARY GERSTLE University of Maryland

EMILY S. ROSENBERG Macalester College

NORMAN L. ROSENBERG Macalester College

THOMSON

WADSWORTH

Australia • Canada • Mexico • Singapore • Spain
United Kingdom • United States

THOMSON

WADSWORTH

Publisher: Clark Baxter
Senior Development Editor: Margaret McAndrew Beasley
Senior Assistant Editor: Julie Yardley
Editorial Assistant: Anne Gittinger
Senior Technology Project Manager: Melinda Newfarmer
Executive Marketing Manager: Caroline Croley
Marketing Assistant: Mary Ho
Advertising Project Manager: Brian Chaffee
Project Manager, Editorial Production: Kimberly Adams
Print/Media Buyer: Barbara Britton
Permissions Editor: Joohee Lee

Production Service: Lachina Publishing Services
Text Designer: Norman Baugher
Photo Researcher: Lili Weiner
Musical Consultant: Harvey Cohen
Copy Editor: Ginjer Clarke
Production Specialist: Sona Lachina
Cover Designer: John Walker and Lisa Devenish
Cover Image: © Francis G. Mayer/CORBIS
Printer: Quebecor World/Versailles
Compositor: Lachina Publishing Services

Library of Congress Control Number: 2003116388
Student Edition: ISBN 0-534-62731-5

Wadsworth/Thomson Learning
10 Davis Drive
Belmont, CA 94002-3098
USA

Asia
Thomson Learning
5 Shenton Way #01-01
UIC Building
Singapore 068808

Australia/New Zealand
Thomson Learning
102 Dodds Street
Southbank, Victoria 3006
Australia

Canada
Nelson
1120 Birchmount Road
Toronto, Ontario M1K 5G4
Canada

Europe/Middle East/Africa
Thomson Learning
High Holborn House
50/51 Bedford Row
London WC1R 4LR
United Kingdom

Latin America
Thomson Learning
Seneca, 53
Colonia Polanco
11560 Mexico D.F.
Mexico

Spain/Portugal
Paraninfo
Calle Magallanes, 25
28015 Madrid, Spain

About the Authors

THE AUTHOR TEAM

From left: Norman Rosenberg, Emily Rosenberg, Paul Johnson, Gary Gerstle, John Murrin, and Jim McPherson.

One of the pleasures of this textbook project, now 15 years old, is the opportunity it has given us to work with each other. Before starting work on a new edition, we all gather for a lengthy period of time to evaluate past editions, discuss reviews that we have solicited from our textbook readers, and brainstorm about ways to improve our book and to make our history more lively, accurate, and up to date. These meetings are always interesting and energizing. After we scatter, the discussions continue through extensive e-mail and phone conversations in which we test and refine the initiatives that we have developed. The volume and richness of this communication over the years have deepened the collective nature of our endeavor and strengthened the quality of the history that we write. We are all proud to be part of the *Liberty, Equality, Power* author team.

JOHN M. MURRIN *Princeton University, Emeritus*
John M. Murrin is a specialist in American colonial and revolutionary history and the early republic. He has edited one multivolume series and five books, including two co-edited collections, *Colonial America: Essays in Politics and Social Development,* Fifth Edition (2001), and *Saints and Revolutionaries: Essays in Early American History* (1984). His own essays on early American history range from ethnic tensions, the early history of trial by jury, the rise of the legal profession, and the political culture of the colonies and the new nation, to the rise of professional baseball and college football in the 19th century. Professor Murrin

served as president of the Society for Historians of the Early American Republic in 1998–99.

PAUL E. JOHNSON *University of South Carolina*
A specialist in early national social and cultural history, Paul E. Johnson is also the author of *Sam Patch, the Famous Jumper* (2003); *A Shopkeeper's Millennium: Society and Revivals in Rochester, New York, 1815–1837,* 25th Anniversary Edition (2004); co-author (with Sean Wilentz) of *The Kingdom of Matthias: Sex and Salvation in 19th-Century America* (1994); and editor of *African-American Christianity: Essays in History* (1994). He has been awarded

the Merle Curti Prize of the Organization of American Historians (1980), the Richard P. McCormack Prize of the New Jersey Historical Association (1989), a John Simon Guggenheim Memorial Fellowship (1995), and the Gilder Lehrman Fellowship (2001).

JAMES M. McPHERSON *Princeton University*
James M. McPherson is a distinguished Civil War historian and was president of the American Historical Association in 2003. He won the 1989 Pulitzer Prize for his book *Battle Cry of Freedom: The Civil War Era*. His other publications include *Marching Toward Freedom: Blacks in the Civil War*, Second Edition (1991); *Ordeal by Fire: The Civil War and Reconstruction*, Third Edition (2001); *Abraham Lincoln and the Second American Revolution* (1991); *For Cause and Comrades: Why Men Fought in the Civil War* (1997), which won the Lincoln Prize in 1998; and *Crossroads of Freedom: Antietam* (2002).

GARY GERSTLE *University of Maryland*
Gary Gerstle—a specialist in labor, immigration, and political history—has published four books: *Working-Class Americanism: The Politics of Labor in a Textile City, 1914–1960* (1989); *The Rise and Fall of the New Deal Order, 1930–1980* (1989); *American Crucible: Race and Nation in the Twentieth Century* (2001), which won the Saloutos Prize in 2001 for the best work in immigration and ethnic history; and *E Pluribus Unum: Immigrants, Civic Culture, and Political Incorporation* (2001). His articles have appeared in the *American Historical Review, Journal of American History, American Quarterly,* and other journals.

His honors include a National Endowment for the Humanities Fellowship for University Teachers and a John Simon Guggenheim Memorial Fellowship.

EMILY S. ROSENBERG *Macalester College*
Emily S. Rosenberg specializes in U.S. foreign relations in the 20th century and is the author of *Spreading the American Dream: American Economic and Cultural Expansion, 1890–1945* (1982); *Financial Missionaries to the World: The Politics and Culture of Dollar Diplomacy* (1999), which won the Ferrell Book Award; and *Pearl Harbor in American Memory* (2004). Her other publications include (with Norman L. Rosenberg) *In Our Times: America Since 1945,* Seventh Edition (2003), and numerous articles dealing with foreign relations in the context of international finance, American culture, and gender ideology. She has served on the board of the Organization of American Historians, on the board of editors of the *Journal of American History,* and as president of the Society for Historians of American Foreign Relations.

NORMAN L. ROSENBERG *Macalester College*
Norman L. Rosenberg specializes in legal history with a particular interest in legal culture and First Amendment issues. His books include *Protecting the "Best Men": An Interpretive History of the Law of Libel* (1990) and (with Emily S. Rosenberg) *In Our Times: America Since 1945,* Seventh Edition (2003). He has published articles in the *Rutgers Law Review, UCLA Law Review, Constitutional Commentary, Law & History Review,* and many other journals and law-related anthologies.

Contents in Brief

Contents in Detail

Features

Maps

Americans Abroad

History through Film

Link to the Past

Musical Link to the Past

To the Student: Why Study History?

WHY TAKE A COURSE in American history? This is a question that many college and university students ask. In many respects, students today are like the generations of Americans who have gone before them: optimistic and forward looking, far more eager to imagine where we as a nation might be going than to reflect on where we have been. If anything, this tendency has become more pronounced in recent years, as the Internet revolution has accelerated the pace and excitement of change and made even the recent past seem at best quaint, at worst uninteresting and irrelevant.

But it is precisely in these moments of great change that a sense of the past can be indispensable in terms of guiding our actions in the present and future. We can find, in other periods of American history, moments, like our own, of dizzying technological change and economic growth, rapid alterations in the concentration of wealth and power, and basic changes in patterns of work, residence, and play. How did Americans at those times create, embrace, and resist these changes? In earlier periods of American history, the United States was home, as it is today, to a remarkably diverse array of ethnic and racial groups. How did earlier generations of Americans respond to the cultural conflicts and misunderstandings that often arise from conditions of diversity? How did immigrants perceive their new land? How and when did they integrate themselves into American society? To study how ordinary Americans of the past struggled with these issues is to gain perspective on the opportunities and problems that we face today.

History also provides an important guide to affairs of state. What should the role of America be in world affairs? Should we participate in international bodies such as the United Nations or insist on our ability to act autonomously and without the consent of other nations? What is the proper role of government in economic and social life? Should the government regulate the economy? To what extent should the government enforce morality regarding religion, sexual practices, drinking and drugs, movies, TV, and other forms of mass culture? And what are our responsibilities as citizens to each other and to the nation? Americans of past generations have debated these issues with verve and conviction. Learning about these debates and how they were resolved will enrich our understanding of the policy possibilities for today and tomorrow.

History, finally, is about stories—stories that we all tell about ourselves; our families; our communities; our ethnicity, race, region, and religion; and our nation. They are stories of triumph and tragedy, of engagement and flight, and of high ideals and high comedy. When telling these stories, "American history" is often the furthest thing from our minds. But, often, an implicit sense of history informs what we say about grandparents who immigrated many years ago; the suburb in which we live; the church, synagogue, or mosque that we attend; or the ethnic or racial group to which we belong. But how well do we really understand these individuals, institutions, and groups? Do we tell the right stories about them, ones that capture the complexities of their past? Or have we wittingly or unwittingly simplified, altered, or flattened them? A study of American history first helps us to ask these questions and then to answer them. In the process, we can engage in a fascinating journey of intellectual and personal discovery and situate ourselves more firmly than we had ever thought possible in relation to those who came before us. We can gain firmer self-knowledge and a greater appreciation for the richness of our nation and, indeed, of all humanity.

Preface

WE ARE PLEASED to present the fourth edition of *Liberty, Equality, Power*. Like the first three editions, this one captures the drama and excitement of America's past, from the pre-Columbian era through our own time. It integrates social and cultural history into a political story that is organized around the themes of liberty, equality, and power, and synthesizes the finest older historical scholarship with the best of the new to create a narrative that is balanced, lively, and accessible to a broad range of students.

The *Liberty, Equality, Power* Approach

In this book, we tell many small stories, and one large one: how America transformed itself, in a relatively brief era of world history, from a land inhabited by hunter-gatherer and agricultural Native American societies into the most powerful industrial nation on earth. This story has been told many times before, and those who have told it in the past have usually emphasized the political experiment in liberty and equality that took root here in the 18th century. We, too, stress the extraordinary and transformative impact that the ideals of liberty and equality exerted on American politics, society, and economics during the American Revolution and after.

We show how the creation of a free economic environment—one in which entrepreneurial spirit, technological innovation, and industrial production have flourished—underpinned American industrial might. We have emphasized, too, the successful struggles for freedom that, over the course of the last 225 years, have brought—first to all white men, then to men of color, and finally to women—rights and opportunities that they had not previously known.

But we have also identified a third factor in this pantheon of American ideals—that of power. We examine power in many forms: the accumulation of vast economic fortunes that dominated the economy and politics; the dispossession of American Indians from land that they regarded as theirs; the enslavement of millions of Africans and their African American descendants for a period of almost 250 years; the relegation of women and of racial,

ethnic, and religious minorities to subordinate places in American society; and the extension of American control over foreign peoples, such as Latin Americans and Filipinos, who would have preferred to have been free and self-governing. We do not mean to suggest that American power has always been turned to these negative purposes. Subordinate groups have themselves marshaled power to combat oppression, as in the abolitionist and civil-rights crusades, the campaign for woman suffrage, and the labor movement. The state has used its power to moderate poverty and to manage the economy in the interests of general prosperity. And it has used its military power to defeat Nazi Germany, World War II Japan, the Cold War Soviet Union, and other enemies of freedom.

The invocation of power as a variable in American history forces us to widen the lens through which we look at the past and to complicate the stories we tell. Ours has been a history of freedom and domination; of progress toward realizing a broadly democratic polity and of delays and reverses; of abundance and poverty; of wars for freedom and justice and for control of foreign markets. In complicating our master narrative in this way, we think we have rendered American history more exciting and intriguing. Progress has not been automatic, but the product of ongoing struggles.

In this book, we have also tried to capture the diversity of the American past, both in terms of outcomes and in terms of the variety of groups who have participated in America's making. American Indians, in this book, are not presented simply as the victims of European aggression but as a people remarkably diverse in their own ranks, with a variety of systems of social organization and cultural expression. We give equal treatment to the industrial titans of American history—the likes of Andrew Carnegie and John D. Rockefeller—and to those, such as small farmers and poor workers, who resisted the corporate reorganization of economic life. We celebrate the great moments of 1863, when African Americans were freed from slavery, and of 1868, when they were made full citizens of the United States. But we also note how a majority of African Americans had to wait another 100 years, until the civil-rights movement of the 1960s, to gain full access to American freedoms. We tell similarly complex stories about women, Latinos, and other groups of ethnic Americans.

Political issues, of course, are only part of America's story. Americans have always loved their leisure and have created the world's most vibrant popular culture. They have embraced technological innovations, especially those promising to make their lives easier and more fun. We have, therefore, devoted considerable space to a discussion of American popular culture, from the founding of the first newspapers in the 18th century and the rise of movies, jazz, and the comics in the early 20th century, to the cable television and Internet revolutions in recent years. We have pondered, too, how American industry has periodically altered home and personal life by making new products—such as clothing, cars, refrigerators, and computers—available to consumers.

In such ways, we hope to give our readers a rich portrait of how Americans lived at various points in our history.

New to the Fourth Edition

The third edition won praise for its successful integration of political, cultural, and social history; its thematic unity; its narrative clarity and eloquence; its extraordinary coverage of pre-Columbian America; its extended treatment of the Civil War; its history of economic growth and change; and its excellent map and illustration programs. It also received high marks for its History through Film series, which discusses 31 different films (one per chapter) that treat important aspects of the American past. This very popular feature encourages students to think critically about what they see on screen and allows instructors to stimulate students' historical interest through a medium that they enjoy. The third edition earned plaudits, finally, for the inclusion of chapter outlines and focus questions at the beginning of each chapter and for the decision to move the Chronology boxes to each chapter's fore. We have preserved and enhanced all these strengths of the third edition in the fourth, and are pleased to announce that our History through Film series includes discussions of two new films, *The Gangs of New York* and *High Noon*. In preparing for this revision, we solicited feedback from professors and scholars throughout the country, many of whom have used the third edition of *Liberty, Equality, Power* in their classrooms. Their comments proved most helpful, and many of their suggestions have been incorporated into the fourth edition. For example, in response to reviewer comments, we have added captions to our outstanding map program, so that each map now comes with a brief commentary on how to interpret the geographical and topographical data it contains. Many of the maps are now animated on the Companion Web Site. We have also updated and condensed Suggested Readings and moved them to each chapter's end. Extensive bibliographic essays for each chapter are still available on the Web site. We have revised our Link to the Past feature so that the text of each focuses more on specific primary sources, offering quotes, commentary, and questions while still linking these sources to online documents, images, or video or sound recordings. We think these improvements in the Links will add to their appeal.

In addition to making these pedagogical changes, we scrutinized each page of the textbook, making sure our prose was clear, the historical issues well presented, and the scholarship up to date. This review, guided by the scholarly feedback we received, caused us to make numerous revisions and additions throughout the textbook. We have also worked hard to bring our story to the present. Because of the changes in the final chapters, we now offer students historical perspective on such important recent events as George W. Bush's election in 2000, the destruction of the World Trade Center towers on September 11, 2001, and the war on terrorism and against Iraq.

Although a list of all the notable substantive changes appears below, we want to highlight one concentrated area of revision—the period from the 1880s through the 1930s, encompassing chapters 18–25. Although reviewers praised the high quality of the political history contained in these pages, some asked us to add more cultural and social history to the narrative mix. We have taken this request seriously, and have introduced more than 5,000 words of social and cultural commentary, much of it focusing on the following topics: the growth of the American middle class in both white and African American communities during the Gilded Age; middle-class patterns of urban living and consumption; the significance of the Philadelphia Centennial Exposition of 1876, the Chicago World's Fair of 1893, and museum exhibitions to late 19th century culture; turn-of-the-century changes in literary culture; the changing circumstances of women; Chinese and Japanese immigration to the United States in the late 19th and early 20th centuries; the decline of feminism in the 1920s; and the effects of the Great Depression on literary, cinematic, and musical culture during the 1930s. So as not to make the chapters in this time period overly long, we have made careful cuts in those chapters' political coverage; the net addition of text is much less than 5,000 words. The result, we believe, is a balanced and integrated political, social, and cultural history of the United States between the Civil War and the Second World War.

New Feature: Americans Abroad

We have also gone beyond our reviewers' suggestions and, in our group meetings to prepare for the fourth edition, committed ourselves to two new features for the textbook. The first, Americans Abroad, appearing in each chapter, focuses on an American who spent a significant portion of his or her life abroad. Some of those profiled carried U.S. political and cultural influence to other countries, while others became conduits through which foreign ideas and influences entered the United States. With our 31 features on both kinds of individuals, we wish to stress the interconnections between American history and world history, and examine the people who forged them. We have chosen a broad range of interesting and important figures—from Pocahontas to Thomas Jefferson, from the explorer Henry Morton Stanley to the anthropologist Margaret Mead, from the American industrialist Francis Cabot Lowell to the African American entertainer Josephine Baker, and from Civil War general Daniel Sickles to Secretary of State Madeleine Albright. We think students will both enjoy learning about these fascinating Americans, their travels, and their influence, and begin to develop, through such knowledge, a sense for the international context in which U.S. history has always unfolded. In the past, Americans (historians among them) have often ignored that context. But, as the events of September 11, 2001, tragically demonstrated, we ignore that context at our peril.

New Feature: Musical Link to the Past

Across their 200 plus years as a people, Americans have produced an extraordinarily rich and varied musical heritage. With the second new feature, Musical Link to the Past, we have embarked on a special effort to make aspects of this musical heritage integral to the history we present to our readers. In 15 features, we examine songs—the lyrics, the music, the performers, the historical context—from the middle of the 18th century to the present. These pieces range from revolutionary era odes to American liberty to 20th century country music laments about women's domestic burdens. Represented in this textbook are pieces by artists as diverse as Stephen Foster and Joni Mitchell, John Philip Sousa and Bob Dylan, Duke Ellington and Grandmaster Flash. All have made important contributions to the history of American music and enriched our musical heritage.

We hope that instructors and students alike will respond enthusiastically to our Musical Links to the Past. To make this feature come alive in classrooms, we have assembled a CD containing the musical selections that we discuss. All instructors who adopt our textbook will, upon request, receive a free copy of this CD, and will, as a result, be able to play the music in their classrooms. For a small fee, students will be able to acquire their own CD copy.

In preparing this feature, we turned to Dr. Harvey Cohen, a cultural historian and music expert who teaches U.S. history at the University of Maryland. Possessing an extraordinary knowledge of the history of American music, and being an accomplished musician in his own right, Harvey was the ideal scholar to guide our choice of songs. He also drafted the texts of the 15 features, and, in the process, labored hard and imaginatively to turn his musical knowledge into history that, we think, will appeal to students. His work has been indispensable to us, and we are deeply grateful to him.

Specific Revisions to Content and Coverage

Chapter 2 New discussions of 1) how New France's Indian alliances drew the colony into the Indian slave trade by the early 18th century; 2) the recovery of the Massachusetts economy from the disastrous slump of 1641; and 3) the Indian slave trade in South Carolina.

Chapter 3 New material on the origins of the Yamasee War of 1715–17 that almost destroyed South Carolina. This chapter also contains new arguments about the contrasting origins and development of racism toward Indians and Africans in the southern colonies.

Chapter 4 New material on the Virginia slave revolt of 1730, the biggest one in the colony's history.

Supplements

For the Instructor

Instructor's Manual/Test Bank, Vols. I & II The Instructor's Manual portion contains Chapter Outlines, Chronologies, Thematic Topics for Enrichment (critical thinking questions that could be used for classroom discussion or exams), Suggested Essay Topics, Comprehensive Lecture Outlines, and a Teaching Resources section that provides video ideas for lecture enrichment. The Test Bank section includes for each chapter: 50 multiple choice questions, 40 true/false questions, and approximately 10 fill-in-the-blank questions. All three of these question types are classified by type of question, whether they are analytical or factual, and the level of difficulty. Also included in the Test Bank are approximately 10 identification questions per chapter as well as five to seven short essays and two to four long essay questions with answers provided. The IM/TB is also available electronically on the Instructor's Resource CD and the pin-coded text Web site.

Instructor's Resource CD with ExamView (Windows/Macintosh)
Includes the Instructor's Manual, Resource Integration Grid, ExamView® testing, and PowerPoint® slides with lecture outlines and images that can be used as offered, or customized by importing personal lecture slides or other material. ExamView allows you to create, deliver, and customize tests and study guides (both print and online) in minutes with this easy-to-use assessment and tutorial system. It offers both a Quick Test Wizard and an Online Test Wizard that guide you step by step through the process of creating tests, while its "what you see is what you get" capability allows you to see the test you are creating on the screen exactly as it will print or display online. You can build tests of up to 250 questions using up to 12 question types. Using ExamView's complete word processing capabilities, you can enter an unlimited number of new questions or edit existing questions.

New! Musical Links to the Past CD
Available free to adopters and for a small fee to students, this CD contains audio recordings of nearly all of the musical selections from the text's new Musical Link to the Past feature.

WebTutor Toolbox on WebCT or Blackboard
This online ancillary helps students succeed by taking the course beyond classroom boundaries to a virtual environment rich with study and mastery tools, communication tools, and course content. Professors can use WebTutor to provide virtual office hours, post their syllabi, set up threaded discussions, and track student progress with the quizzing material. For students, WebTutor offers real-time access to a full array of study tools, including flashcards (with audio), practice quizzes and tests, online tutorials, exercises, discussion questions, Web links, and a full glossary. Professors can customize the content in any way they choose, from uploading images and other resources, to adding Web links, to creating their own practice materials.

Transparency Acetates with Commentary for U.S. History
Contains more than 150 four-color map images from all of Wadsworth's U.S. History Texts.

Packages are three-hole punched and shrink-wrapped. Correlation Guides for specific texts are included.

Wadsworth History Resource Center & *Liberty, Equality, Power* Companion Web Site

http://history.wadsworth.com/murrin_LEP4e

Provocative, exciting, and interactive, this site has something for everyone: instructors, students, and U.S. history buffs. Includes a wealth of documents and visuals with related activities, interactive maps (Timeline Maps and Discovery Maps), tutorial quiz questions, hyperlinks, and Internet and InfoTrac® College Edition exercises for each chapter. Also features activities utilizing American Journey Online for each chapter of the text. Each chapter includes Chapter Outlines, Learning Objectives, Glossaries (including flashcards with audio), Tutorial Quizzes (20 multiple choice, 5 to 10 fill-in-the-blank or true/false, and 5 essay/ short answers per chapter), Final Exam (incorporates all the quizzes by chapter into one "final" exam), Internet Exercises (centered around the *Liberty, Equality, Power* theme), InfoTrac Exercises, and Web Links.

Online Instructor's Resources include detailed plans and instructions for three Group Projects for classroom use: 1) Re-creating the '60s: Teaching History through Teach-ins; 2) Commemorating the Boston Massacre: Teaching History through Public Memory; and 3) Reconstruction and the Meaning of Freedom: Teaching History through Public Debate. In each of the projects, students examine the choices facing people in a particular era from the various perspectives of the different groups involved in the historical event.

Core Concept Lecture Launcher Videos
The Core Concept video package was created exclusively for *Liberty, Equality, Power* by Films for the Humanities. Each video contains eight segments that include introductions by the respective author, concept clues, brief video segments, and concluding questions that take the student from image to text. Video segments are arranged chronologically and relate to topics of importance in the text. The video package is available free to instructors with adoption of the text.

Supplements are available to qualified adopters. Please consult your local sales representative for details.

For the Student

History Interactive: A Study Tool for *Liberty, Equality, Power*
This valuable resource for students includes chapter summaries, chapter outlines, identification terms and definitions, fill-in-the-blank and multiple choice

quizzes, and extensive bonus materials including source readings, maps, and images. Also included are interactive versions of the text's maps plus Link to the Past and Americans Abroad features; two HistoryNOW modules; and a complete catalog of HistoryNOW interactive modules available for students and correlated chapter by chapter to *Liberty, Equality, Power.*

U.S. History Atlas An invaluable collection of more than 50 clear and colorful historical maps covering all major periods in American history.

Wadsworth History Resource Center & *Liberty, Equality, Power* **Companion Web Site**

http://history.wadsworth.com/murrin_LEP4e

See description above.

American Journey Online Database

http://ajaccess.wadsworth.com

This text comes with free access to American Journey Online—16 primary source collections that capture the landmark events and major themes of the American experience through words and images from those who lived it. Each key topic in American history and culture addressed by the series encompasses hundreds of carefully selected rare documents, pictures, and archival audio and video, while essays, headnotes, and captions by scholars set the sources in context. Full text searchability and extensive hyperlinking provide fast and easy access and cross referencing. A new module on the Second World War is now available. For more information on how to search the database, please download the free User Guide, which highlights key features of American Journey Online including search tips for each module, exercises, activities, and more.

U.S. History Documents Package The Documents Package, edited by Mark W. Beasley of Hardin-Simmons University, has been expanded to include more than 250 primary source documents interspersed with political cartoons and advertisements. Chapter openers and notes for each selection introduce the documents, provide essential background, and tie in the themes of liberty, equality, and power. Chapter discussion questions ask students to think critically about the ways the documents relate to each other and the text. The two-volume package is available to bundle with the textbook.

WebTutor Toolbox on WebCT or Blackboard See description above.

Acknowledgments

We recognize the contributions of reviewers who read portions of the manuscript in various stages:

William Allison, Weber State University
Angie Anderson, Southeastern Louisiana University
Kenneth G. Anthony, University of North Carolina, Greensboro
Paul R. Beezley, Texas Tech University
David Bernstein, California State University at Long Beach
Michael R. Bradley, Motlow College
Betty Brandon, University of South Alabama
Daniel Patrick Brown, Moorpark College
Ronald G. Brown, College of Southern Maryland
Phil Crow, North Harris College
Lorenzo M. Crowell, Mississippi State University
Amy E. N. Darty, University of Central Florida
Thomas M. Deaton, Dalton State College
Norman C. Delaney, Del Mar College
Ted Delaney, Washington and Lee University
Andrew J. DeRoche, Front Range Community College
Bruce Dierenfield, Canisius College
Brian R. Dirck, Anderson University
Maura Doherty, Illinois State University
R. Blake Dunnavent, Lubbock Christian University
Eileen Eagan, University of Southern Maine
Derek Elliott, Tennessee State University
B. Jane England, North Central Texas College
Van Forsyth, Clark College
Michael P. Gabriel, Kutztown University of Pennsylvania
Gary Gallagher, Pennsylvania State University
Gerald Ghelfi, Santa Ana College
Michael Goldberg, University of Washington, Bothell
David E. Hamilton, University of Kentucky
Michael J. Haridopolos, Brevard Community College
Mark Harvey, North Dakota State University
Mark Huddle, University of Georgia
Samuel C. Hyde, Jr., Southeastern Louisiana University
Thomas N. Ingersoll, Ohio State University
Frank Karpiel, Ramapo College of New Jersey
Michael Kazin, American University
Michael King, Moraine Valley Community College
Michael Krenn, Appalachian State
Frank Lambert, Purdue University
Pat Ledbetter, North Central Texas College
Jan Leone, Middle Tennessee State University
Craig Livingston, Montgomery College
Robert F. Marcom, San Antonio College
Suzanne Marshall, Jacksonville State University

Jimmie McGee, South Plains College
Nora E. McMillan, San Antonio College
Jerry Mills, Midland College
Charlene Mires, Villanova University
Rick Moniz, Chabot College
Michael R. Nichols, Tarrant County College, Northwest
Linda Noel, University of Maryland
Richard B. Partain, Bakersfield College
William Pencak, Penn State University, University Park Campus
Teresa Thomas Perrin, Austin Community College
David Poteet, New River Community College
Jonathan Rees, University of Southern Colorado
Anne Richardson, Texas Christian University
Lelia M. Roeckell, Molloy College
Roy Scott, Mississippi State University
Reynolds J. Scott-Childress, University of Maryland
Katherine A. S. Sibley, St. Joseph's University
Herb Sloan, Barnard College
John Smolenski, University of California, Davis
Jennifer Stollman, University of Mississippi
Siegfried H. Sutterlin, Indian Hills Community College
John Wood Sweet, The Catholic University of America
Xiansheng Tian, Metro State College of Denver
Vincent Vinikas, University of Arkansas, Little Rock
Vernon Volpe, University of Nebraska
Harry L. Watson, The University of North Carolina at Chapel Hill
William Benton Whisenhunt, College of DuPage
Laura Matysek Wood, Tarrant County College, Northwest

We wish to thank the members of the Wadsworth staff who embraced our textbook wholeheartedly when they inherited it from Harcourt and who have expertly guided the production of this fourth edition. Marcus Boggs, vice president and editor-in-chief, made it clear to us from the moment of acquisition that Wadsworth's support for this textbook would be strong. Clark Baxter, publisher, has brought great vision, enthusiasm, and savvy to this project and kept watch on the many different individuals in various locations who had responsibilities to this edition. Caroline Croley, executive marketing manager, has proven to be shrewd and imaginative in her efforts to make the match between our book and teachers of U.S. history a good one. Jennifer Ellis and Melinda Newfarmer, technology project managers, have helped us to glimpse vistas of multimedia use that we did not know existed. Kim Adams, production project manager, has expertly guided this book through the necessary stages from man-

uscript to finished book, while Ronn Jost, a project editor at Lachina Publishing Services, Inc., has expeditiously handled the complicated and seemingly endless tasks of copyediting, composition, proofreading, and indexing. Finally, a big thanks to all the Wadsworth salesmen and women who, from the moment we first presented our book to them in September 2001, have worked hard and creatively to generate interest in our book among university, college, and high school teachers across America. May this be one of many editions that we produce under the Wadsworth imprint.

We have been fortunate to be able, in this edition, to keep working with two freelancers who have made important contributions to several previous editions. Our photo editor, Lili Weiner, continues to dig up scores of new and interesting photographs and illustrations for us to examine. And our longtime developmental editor, Margaret McAndrew Beasley, has provided indispensable continuity and calm in a complicated time of transition. Margaret's editing skills, organizational expertise, good sense, and belief in this book and its authors keep us going.

In addition, each of us would like to offer particular thanks to those historians, friends, and family members who helped to bring this project to a successful conclusion.

JOHN M. MURRIN Mary R. Murrin has read each chapter, offered numerous suggestions, and provided the kind of moral and personal support without which this project would never have been completed. James Axtell and Gregory Evans Dowd saved me from many mistakes about Indians. John E. Selby and the late Eugene R. Sheridan were particularly helpful on what are now chapters 5 and 6. At an early phase, William J. Jackson and Lorraine E. Williams offered some very useful suggestions. Fred Anderson and Virginia DeJohns Anderson offered many acute suggestions for improvement. I am deeply grateful for their advice. Several colleagues and graduate students also have contributed in various ways, especially Stephen Aron, Ignacio Gallup-Diaz, Evan P. Haefeli, Geoffrey Plank, Nathaniel J. Sheidley, Jeremy Stern, and Beth Lewis Pardse.

PAUL E. JOHNSON My greatest debt is to the community of scholars who write about the United States between the Revolution and the Civil War. Closer to home, I owe thanks to the other writers of this book—particularly to John Murrin. The Department of History at the University of South Carolina provided time to work, while my wife, Kasey Grier, and a stray dog we named Lucy provided the right kinds of interruptions.

JAMES M. McPHERSON My family provided an environment of affection and stability that contributed immeasurably to the writing of my chapters, while undergraduate students at Princeton University who have taken my courses over the years provided feedback, questions, and insights that helped me to understand what students know and don't know, and what they need to know.

GARY GERSTLE When first drafting my parts of this textbook, I benefited enormously from the input of Roy Rosenzweig and Tom Knock, who gave each of my chapters an exceptionally thorough, thoughtful, and insightful critique. Kathleen Trainor was a gifted research assistant: She researched subjects I knew too little about, contributed to the design of charts and maps, checked facts, and solved countless thorny problems. To all these tasks she brought imagination, efficiency, and good cheer. Jerald Podair helped me to compile chapter bibliographies, offered me excellent ideas for maps and tables, and, on numerous occasions (and at all hours of the day and night), allowed me to draw on his encyclopedic knowledge of American history.

Reynolds Scott-Childress wrote the initial drafts for the new sections on cultural and social history in chapters 18 and 19 (and for the latter's Americans Abroad feature), while Linda Noel helped to research and write the Americans Abroad features for chapters 20–25. Kelly Ryan helped me to assemble the Link to the Past features, while Robert Chase worked to streamline and update the bibliographies. Marcy Wilson helped me out in a pinch with some quick and careful proofreading. All of the last five individuals acknowledged are either recent Ph.D.s at the University or Maryland or soon will finish their degrees there. Four of them have taught for me in my U.S. history survey at Maryland and have used *Liberty, Equality, Power* in their sections. They know the book well (too well, some of them would say!), and the feedback they have given me over the years has helped to guide revisions. I thank them for their many contributions to this book. Finally, I thank my fellow authors for their intelligence, wit, and deep commitment to this project. By the time this book comes out, we will have been a team for 15 years. It has been an interesting, challenging, and satisfying journey.

EMILY AND NORMAN ROSENBERG We would like to thank our children—Sarah, Molly, Ruth, and Joe, who provided expert assistance on our charts. Students at Macalester College also deserve thanks, especially Sonya Michlin, Lorenzo Nencioli, Katie Kelley, Justin Brandt, Jessica Ford, and Mariah Howe. Paul Solon, a colleague at Macalester, provided his expertise in commenting on the maps. Anthony Todd, our research assistant at Macalester, made many important contributions to the fourth edition. We also want to acknowledge all of the people who offered their responses to the previous editions, including the historians who adopted the book and the students, especially those at San Diego State University, who read and evaluated it. Gary Gerstle, our collaborator, the late Richard Steele, a colleague at San Diego State, and Bruce Dierenfield provided wonderfully critical readings, and this edition is much better for their assistance.

Finally, no project of this scope is completely error free. We welcome all corrections and suggestions for improvement. Please send comments to:

Clark Baxter, Publisher
Wadsworth-Thomson
27R West Street #8
Beverly Farms, MA 01915

John M. Murrin, Paul E. Johnson, James M. McPherson,
Gary Gerstle, Emily S. Rosenberg, Norman L. Rosenberg

LIBERTY

EQUALITY

POWER

Chapter 1

When Old Worlds Collide: Contact, Conquest, Catastrophe

HISTORY ON CANVAS
Cortés Scuttles Ship (left), by O. Graeff, circa 1805. Nezahualcoyotzin (right), ruler of Texcoco from approximately 1431 to 1472, painted in battle array by a late 16th- or early 17th-century Mexican Indian who had mastered European artistic techniques.

CHAPTER OUTLINE

When Christopher Columbus crossed the Atlantic, he did not know where he was going, and he died without realizing where he had been. Yet he changed history forever. In the 40 years after 1492, European navigators mastered the oceans of the world, joining together societies that had lived in isolation for thousands of years. European invaders conquered the Americas, not just with sails, gunpowder, and steel, but also with their plants and livestock and, most of all, their diseases. They brought staple crops and slavery with them as well. By 1600, they had created the first global economy in the history of humankind and had inflicted upon the native peoples of the Americas—unintentionally, for the most part—the greatest known catastrophe that human societies have ever experienced.

In the 15th century, when all of this started, the Americas were in some ways a more ancient world than Western Europe. For example, the Portuguese, Spanish, French, and English languages were only beginning to assume their modern forms during the century or two before and after Columbus's voyage. Centuries earlier, when Rome was falling into ruins and Paris and London were little more than hamlets, huge cities were thriving in the Andes and Mesoamerica (the area embracing Central America and southern and central Mexico). Which world was old and which was new is a matter of perspective. Each already had its own distinctive past.

♦ What enabled relatively backward European societies to establish dominance over the oceans of the world?

♦ Why were the native peoples of the Americas extremely vulnerable to European diseases, instead of the other way around?

♦ Why did Western Europe, a free-labor society, generate systems of unfree labor overseas?

♦ What was the Columbian Exchange, and how important has it been?

Peoples in Motion

Like all other countries of North and South America, the United States is a nation of immigrants. Even the native peoples were once migrants who roamed their way through a strange new land.

Long before Europeans discovered and explored the wide world around them, many different peoples had migrated thousands of miles over thousands of years across oceans and continents. Before Columbus sailed west from Spain in 1492, five distinct waves of immigrants had already swept over the Americas. Three came from Asia. The fourth, from the Pacific Islands, or Oceania, may have just brushed America. The last, from northern Europe, decided not to stay.

From Beringia to the Americas

Before the most recent Ice Age ended about 12,000 years ago, glaciers covered huge portions of the Americas, Europe, and Asia. The ice captured so much of the world's water that sea level fell drastically and created a land bridge 600 miles wide across the Bering Strait between Siberia and Alaska. For more than 10,000 years after 23,000 B.C., this exposed area—geographers call it Beringia—was dry land on which plants, animals, and humans could live. Starting about 14,000 years ago, people drifted in small bands from Asia to North America. No doubt many generations lived on Beringia, although the harsh environment of this land on the edge of the Arctic Circle would have required unusual skills just to survive. These first humans to reach the Americas hunted animals for meat and furs and probably built small fishing vessels that could weather the Arctic storms. Faced with impassable glaciers to the north and east, they made snug homes to keep themselves warm through the fierce winters. Their numbers were, in all likelihood, quite small.

By 12,000 B.C., humans definitely were living in eastern Siberia, western Alaska, and Beringia. (Because Berin-

12,000 B.C. Migration to the Americas begins

9000 B.C. Shenandoah Valley occupied

9000–7000 B.C. Most large American mammals become extinct

5000–700 B.C. Cultures of the Red Paint People and the Louisiana mound builders thrive

1600 B.C. Polynesian migrations begin (reaching Hawaii by A.D. 100)

500 B.C.–A.D. 400 Adena-Hopewell mound builders emerge in Ohio River valley

874 Norsemen reach Iceland

900–1250 Toltecs dominate the Valley of Mexico • Cahokia becomes largest Mississippian mound builders' city • Anasazi culture thrives in American Southwest

982 Norse settle Greenland

1001–14 Norse found Vinland on Newfoundland

1400s Incas begin to dominate the Andes; Aztecs begin to dominate Mesoamerica (1400–50) • Cheng Ho makes voyages of exploration for China (1405–34) • Portuguese begin to master the Atlantic coast of Africa (1434) • First Portuguese slave factory established on African coast (1448) • Dias reaches Cape of Good Hope (1487) • Columbus reaches the Caribbean (1492) • Treaty of Tordesillas divides non-Christian world between Portugal and Spain (1494) • da Gama rounds Cape of Good Hope and reaches India (1497–99)

1500s Portuguese discover Brazil (1500) • Balboa crosses Isthmus of Panama to the Pacific (1513) • Magellan's fleet circumnavigates the globe; Cortés conquers the Aztec empire (1519–22) • de Vaca makes overland journey from Florida to Mexico (1528–36) • Pizarro conquers the Inca empire (1531–32) • de Soto's expedition explores the American Southeast (1539–43) • Coronado's expedition explores the American Southwest (1540–42) • Jesuit mission established at Chesapeake Bay (1570–71) • Philip II issues Royal Order for New Discoveries (1573) • Philip II unites Spanish and Portuguese empires (1580)

gia is once again under water, it cannot be easily studied, although fossils of mammoths have been found on the ocean floor.) As the glaciers receded for the last time, these people spread throughout the Americas. By 8000 B.C., they had reached all the way to Tierra del Fuego off the southern tip of South America. Near the eastern coast of North America, the Thunderbird dig in Virginia's Shenandoah Valley shows signs of continuous human occupation from before 9000 B.C. until the arrival of Europeans.

These Asians probably came in three waves. Those in the first wave spread over most of the two continents and spoke "Amerind," the forerunner of most American

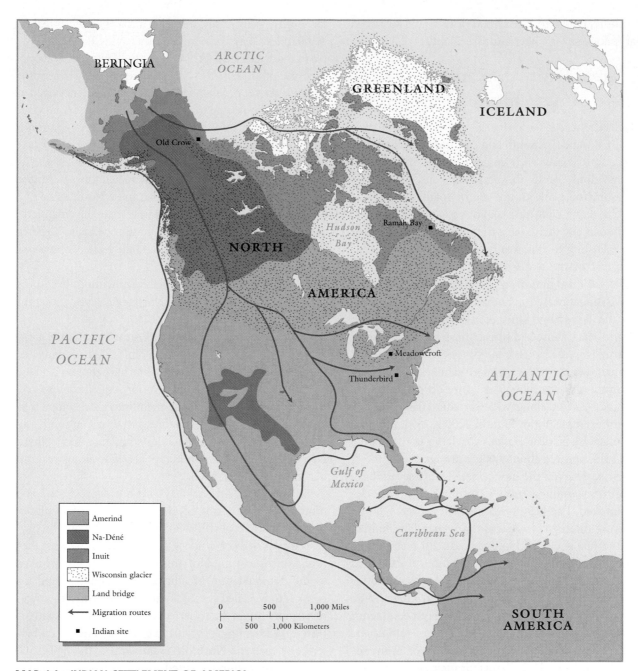

MAP 1.1 INDIAN SETTLEMENT OF AMERICA
The probable routes that people followed after they left Beringia and spread throughout the Americas.

Indian languages on both continents. The Algonquian, Iroquoian, Muskogean, Siouan, Nahuatl (Aztec), Mayan, and all South American tongues derive from this source. Those in the middle wave, which came a few thousand years later, spoke what linguists call "Na-Déné," which eventually gave rise to the various Athapaskan languages of the Canadian Northwest as well as the Apache, Navajo, and related tongues in the American Southwest. The last to arrive, the ancestors of the Inuits (called Eskimos by other Indians), crossed after 7000 B.C., when Beringia was again under

water. About 4,000 years ago, these people began to migrate from the Aleutian Islands and Alaska to roughly their present sites in the Americas. Unlike their predecessors, they found the Arctic environment to their liking and migrated across the northern rim of North America and then across the North Atlantic to Greenland, where they encountered the first Europeans migrating westward—the Norsemen. Somehow, the Inuits maintained at least limited contact with one another across 6,000 miles of bleak Arctic tundra. The Thule, or final pre-Columbian phase of

Inuit culture, lasted from A.D. 1000 to 1700 and sustained similar folkways from Siberia to Greenland.

The Great Extinction and the Rise of Agriculture

As the glaciers receded and the climate warmed, the people who had wandered south and east found an attractive environment teeming with game. Imperial mammoths, huge mastodons, woolly rhinoceroses, a species of enormous bison, and giant ground sloths roamed the plains and forests, along with camels and herds of small horses. These animals had thrived in a frigid climate, but they had trouble adjusting to hot weather. They also had no instinctive fear of the two-legged intruders, who became ever more skillful at hunting them. A superior spear point, the Clovis tip, appeared in the area of present-day New Mexico and Texas some time before 9000 B.C., and within a thousand years its use had spread throughout North and South America. As it spread, the big game died off along with horses, which were small and valued only as food. Overhunting cannot explain the entire extinction, but it was a major factor, along with climatic change. Mammoths, for example, survived until 2000 B.C. on uninhabited Wrangell Island near Alaska. Most large animals of the Americas disappeared about 9,000 years ago.

Their passing left the hemisphere with a severely depleted number of animal species. Nothing as big as the elephant survived. The largest beasts left were bears, bison, and moose; the biggest cat was the jaguar. The human population had multiplied and spread with ease so long as the giant species lasted. Their extinction probably led to a sharp decline in population as people scrambled for new sources of food. Some Indians raised guinea pigs, turkeys, or ducks, but apart from dogs on both continents, they domesticated no large animals except in South America, where they used llamas to haul light loads in mountainous terrain and raised alpacas for their wool. In Eurasia, with its numerous domesticated animals, the killer diseases such as smallpox and bubonic plague took hold first among domestic animals and then spread among humans. Disease by disease, the survivors developed immunities over a long period of time. No comparable process occurred in the Americas, where few animals were domesticated.

One North American culture, adapting to the new demands of a world with few large animals, displayed an energy that archaeologists are only now beginning to recognize. About 5000 B.C., along the northeast coast, a gifted maritime people emerged who ventured onto the Atlantic to catch swordfish and, probably, whales. They carried on a vigorous trade from Labrador to Maine and perhaps as far south as New Jersey, spanning a coastline of more than 1,500 miles. They are sometimes called the Red Paint People (a more technical term is Maritime Archaic) because of their use of red ocher in funeral ceremonies. Their burial mounds are the oldest yet found in America. They lived in multiroom houses up to 100 yards long. Most remarkable of all, the motifs on their religious monuments—mounds and stone markers—resemble others found in Brittany and Norway, but the American monuments are several hundred years older than the most ancient ones yet found in Europe. It is barely possible that these North American seafarers followed the Gulf Stream across the Atlantic to Europe thousands of years before Europeans voyaged to America. This culture collapsed 4,000 years ago. No one knows why.

Some native peoples settled down without becoming farmers. Those in the Pacific Northwest developed complex art forms that fascinate modern collectors and sustained themselves through fishing, hunting, and the gathering of nuts, berries, and other edible plants. Men fished and hunted; women gathered. California peoples sustained some of the densest populations north of Mexico by collecting acorns and processing them into meal, which they baked into cakes. In the rain forests of Brazil, in south and central Florida, and in the cold woodlands of northern New England, hunter-gatherers also got along without becoming farmers.

Most North Americans could not depend solely on hunting and gathering food, however. In a few places, some of them, probably women, began to plant and harvest crops instead of simply gathering and eating what they found. In Asia and Africa, this practice was closely linked to the domestication of animals and happened quickly enough to be called the Neolithic (new or late Stone Age) revolution. But in the Americas the rise of farming had little to do with animals, occurred gradually, and might better be termed the Neolithic *evolution*. For the first 3,500 years, farming supplemented a diet that still depended mostly on fishing and hunting, although now of smaller animals. Somewhere between 4000 and 1500 B.C., permanent farm villages began to dominate parts of Peru, south-central Mexico, northeast Mexico, and the southwestern United States. Their crops were different from those of Europe, the Middle East, or East Asia. The first American farmers grew amaranth (a cereal), manioc (familiar to modern Americans as tapioca), chili peppers, pumpkins, sweet potatoes, several varieties of beans, and, above all, maize, or Indian corn, which slowly became a staple throughout most of the Americas. Indians also raised white potatoes and tomatoes. The spread of these crops launched another population surge that was great enough to support cities in some areas.

The Polynesians and Hawaii

Asians migrating across Beringia were not the only people on the move. Polynesians sailed out from Southeast Asia into the Pacific about 1600 B.C., and during the next 2,000 years, they settled hundreds of islands scattered across more than 30 million square miles of ocean. Their ability to carry families and plants safely across thousands of miles of open sea in what were essentially large dugout canoes with sails and attached outriggers was the greatest maritime feat of the era. Nearly all of their settlements were on tropical islands. By the first century A.D., Fiji had become a kind of cultural and linguistic center, and the Polynesians had reached as far as Hawaii, nearly 2,500 miles to the northeast. By A.D. 300, they had colonized Easter Island, more than 4,000 miles to the east and only 2,000 miles off the coast of South America. Before A.D. 1000, they had also settled New Zealand, far to the south of Fiji. Hawaii's population, organized into stratified societies and multiple chiefdoms, would grow to 800,000 before the first Europeans arrived in the 1770s.

Did Polynesians ever reach the American mainland in prehistoric times? It seems hard to believe that such daring mariners would not have sailed on beyond Hawaii and Easter Island. And yet, if some of them did reach the Americas, they left no discernible influence on the Indian societies already there. Someone—either an Indian or a Polynesian—must have brought the sweet potato from South America to Easter Island. Yet the culture of Easter Island was Polynesian, whereas those of South America remained thoroughly Indian.

The Norsemen

About the time that Polynesians were settling Easter Island, Europeans also began trekking long distances. Pushed by fierce invaders from central Asia, various Germanic tribes overran the western provinces of the Roman Empire. The Norse, a Germanic people who had occupied Scandinavia, were among the most innovative of these invaders. For centuries their Viking warriors raided the coasts of the British Isles and France. Their sleek longboats, propelled by both sails and oars, enabled them to challenge the contrary currents of the north Atlantic. Some of them began to gaze westward across the ocean.

Beginning in A.D. 874, Vikings occupied Iceland. In 982 and 983, Erik the Red, who had been accused of manslaughter in Norway and outlawed for committing more mayhem in Iceland, led his Norse followers farther west to Greenland. There the Norse made Europe's first contact with Inuits and established permanent settlements.

Leif, Erik's son, sailed west from Greenland in 1001 and began to explore the coast of North America. He made three more voyages, the last in 1014, and started a colony that he called "Vinland" on the northern coast of Newfoundland at a place now named L'Anse aux Meadows. The local Indians (called "Skrellings" by the Norse, which means "barbarians" or "weaklings") resisted vigorously. In one engagement, just as the Norse were about to be routed, Freydis, the bastard daughter of old Erik, and the first European woman known to North American history, saved the day by baring her breasts, slapping them with a sword, and screaming ferociously. Awed, the Skrellings fled. Nevertheless, the Norse soon quarreled among themselves and destroyed the colony. During the 1014 voyage, Freydis and her husband murdered her brother and seized his ship. When Leif found out, he cursed Freydis's offspring, who, Norse poets assure us, never amounted to anything after that. The Norse abandoned Vinland, but they continued to visit North America for another century, probably to get wood. A 12th-century Norse coin, recovered from an Indian site in Maine, gives proof of their continuing contact with North America.

About 500 years after Erik the Red's settlement, the Norse also lost Greenland. There, not long before Columbus sailed in 1492, the last Norse settler died a lonely death. In the chaos that followed the Black Death in Europe and Greenland after 1350, the colony had suffered a severe population decline, gradually lost regular contact with the homeland, and slowly withered away. Despite their spectacular exploits, the Norse had no impact on the later course of American history. They had reached a dead end.

☛ Europe and the World in the 15th Century

Nobody in the year 1400 could have foreseen the course of European expansion that was about to begin. Europe stood at the edge, not the center, of world commerce. It desired much that others possessed but made little that those others wished to have.

China: The Rejection of Overseas Expansion

By just about every standard, China under the Ming dynasty was the world's most complex culture. In the 15th century, the government of China, staffed by well-educated bureaucrats, ruled 100 million people, a total half again as large as the combined populations of all European states west of Russia. The Chinese had invented the compass, gunpowder, and early forms of printing and paper money. Foreigners coveted the silks, teas, and other fine products available in China, but they had little to offer in exchange. Most of what Europe knew about China came from *The Travels of Marco Polo,* written by a merchant from the Italian city-state of Venice who at age 17 journeyed overland with his father and uncle to the Chinese court, which he reached in 1271, and then served the emperor, Kublai Khan, for the next 20 years. This "Great Khan is the mightiest man, whether in respect of subjects or of territory or of treasure, who is in the world today or who ever has been, from Adam our first parent down to the present moment," Marco assured Europe. The Khan's capital city (today's Beijing) was the world's largest and grandest, Marco insisted, and received 1,000 cartloads of silk a day. In brief, China outshone Europe and all other cultures.

The Chinese agreed. Between 1405 and 1434, a royal eunuch, Cheng Ho, led six large fleets from China to the East Indies and the coast of East Africa, trading and exploring along the way. His biggest ships, 400 feet long, displaced 1,500 tons and were certainly large enough to sail around the southern tip of Africa and "discover" Europe. Had China thrown its resources and talents into overseas expansion, the subsequent history of the world would have been vastly different, but most of what the Chinese learned about the outside world merely confirmed their belief that other cultures had little to offer their Celestial Kingdom. No one followed Cheng Ho's lead after he died. Instead, the emperor banned the construction of ocean-going ships and later forbade anyone to own a vessel with more than two masts. China, a self-contained economic and political system, turned inward. It did not need the rest of the world.

Europe versus Islam

Western Europe was a rather backward place in 1400. Compared with China or the Islamic world, it suffered severe disadvantages. Its location on the Atlantic rim of the Eurasian continent had always made access to Asian trade difficult and costly. Islamic societies controlled overland trade with Asia and the only known seaborne route to Asia through the Persian Gulf. As of 1400, Arab mariners were the world's best.

Europeans desired the fine silks of China. They also coveted East Indian spices to enliven their food and help preserve it through the long winters. But because Europeans produced little that Asians wished to buy, they had to pay for these imports with silver or gold, both of which were scarce.

In fact, while Europe's sphere of influence was shrinking and while China seemed content with what it already had, Islamic states were well embarked on another great phase of expansion. Europe's mounted knights in heavy armor failed to stop the Ottoman Turks, who took Constantinople in 1453, overran the Balkans by the 1520s, and even threatened Vienna. The Safavid Empire in Iran (Persia) rose to new splendor at the same time. Other Moslems carried the Koran to Indonesia and northern India, where their powerful Mogul empire formed the basis for the modern states of Pakistan and Bangladesh.

Yet Europe had certain advantages, too. The European economy had made impressive gains in the Middle Ages, primarily because of agricultural advances, such as improved plows, that also fostered population growth. By 1300, more than 100 million people were living in Europe. Europe's farms could not sustain further growth, however. Lean years and famines ensued, leaving people undernourished. In the late 1340s, the Black Death (bubonic plague) reduced the population by more than one-third. Recurring bouts of plague kept population low until about 1500, when vigorous growth resumed. But during the long decline of the 15th century, overworked soil regained its fertility, and per capita income rose considerably among people who now had stronger immunities to disease.

By then, European metallurgy and architecture were quite advanced. The Renaissance, which revived interest in the literature of ancient Greece and Rome, also gave a new impetus to European culture, especially after Johannes Gutenberg invented the printing press and movable type in the 1430s. Soon information began to circulate more rapidly in Europe than anywhere else in the world. This revolution in communications permitted improvements in ship design and navigational techniques to build on each other and become a self-reinforcing process. The Arabs, by contrast, had borrowed block printing from China in the 10th century, only to give it up by 1400.

Unlike China, none of Europe's kingdoms was a self-contained economy. All had to trade with one another and with the non-Christian world. Although in 1400 this need was a drawback, between the 15th and 17th centuries it slowly became an asset. No single state had a monopoly on the manufacture of firearms or on the flow of capital, and European societies began to compete with one another in gaining access to these resources and in mastering new maritime and military techniques. European armies were far more formidable in 1520 than they had been in 1453, and by then European fleets could outsail and outfight all rivals.

The Legacy of the Crusades

Quite apart from the Norse explorers, Europe had a heritage of expansion that derived from the efforts of the crusaders to conquer the Holy Land from Islam. Crusaders had established their own Kingdom of Jerusalem, which survived for more than a century but was finally retaken in 1244. Thereafter, while a new wave of Islamic expansion seemed about to engulf much of the world, Christian Europe gained only a few Mediterranean and Atlantic islands before 1492 but learned some important lessons in the process. To make Palestine profitable, the crusaders had taken over sugar plantations already there and had worked them with a combination of free and slave labor. After they were driven from the Holy Land, they retreated to the Mediterranean islands of Cyprus, Malta, Crete, and Rhodes, where they used slaves to grow sugar cane or grapes.

Long before Columbus, these planters had created the economic components of overseas expansion. They assumed that colonies should produce a staple crop, at least partly through slave labor, for sale in Europe. The first slaves were Moslem captives. In the 14th and 15th centuries, planters turned to pagan Slavs (hence the word *slave*) from the Black Sea area and the Adriatic. Some black Africans were also acquired from Arab merchants who controlled the caravan trade across the Sahara Desert, but these early plantations never exploited their laborers with the intensity that would later become routine in the Americas.

The Unlikely Pioneer: Portugal

It seemed highly improbable in 1400 that Europe was standing on the threshold of a dramatic expansion. That Portugal would lead the way seemed even less likely. Portugal, a small kingdom of fewer than a million people, had been united for less than a century. Lisbon, with 40,000 people, was the only city of any size. Portugal's maritime traditions lagged well behind those of the Italian states, France, and England. Its merchant class was tiny, and it had little capital.

Yet Portugal had some advantages. It enjoyed internal peace and an efficient government at a time when its neighbors were beset by war and internal upheaval. Moreover, Portugal's location at the intersection of the Mediterranean and Atlantic worlds prompted its mariners to ask how they could transform the Atlantic from a barrier into a highway.

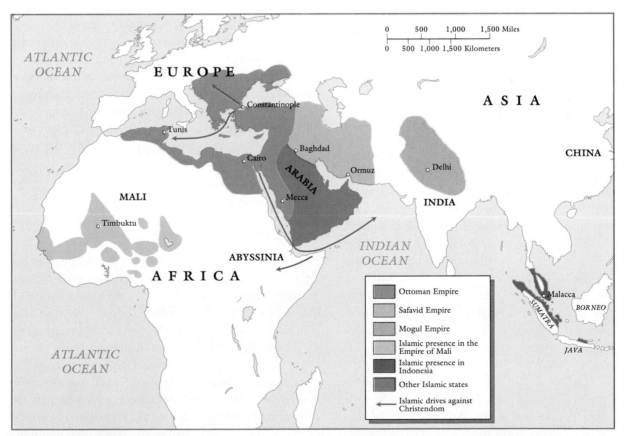

MAP 1.2   EXPANSION OF ISLAM

While Europeans were beginning to move overseas, Islam was also expanding into southeastern Europe, various parts of Africa, the Indian subcontinent, and the East Indies.

At first, they were interested in short-term gains, rather than in some all-water route to Asia. The Portuguese knew that Arab caravans crossed the Sahara to bring gold, slaves, and ivory from black Africa to Europe. Arab traders spoke of how King (or *Mansa*) Musa (d. 1332) of the Mandingo empire of Mali controlled more gold than any other ruler in the world and of how he could field an army of 100,000 men. These reports reached Europe, where Musa was described as "the richest and most noble lord of all this region on account of the abundance of gold which is gathered in his kingdom." The Portuguese believed that an Atlantic voyage to coastal points south of the Sahara would undercut Arab traders and bring large profits. The greatest problem they faced in this quest was Cape Bojador, with its treacherous shallows, awesome waves, and strong northerly winds. Several bold captains had sailed around the cape, but none had returned.

A member of the Portuguese royal family, Prince Henry, challenged this barrier. In 1420, he became head of the crusading Order of Christ and used its revenues to sponsor 15 voyages along the African coast. In 1434, one of his captains, Gil Eannes, finally succeeded. After passing the cape and exploring the coastline, Eannes sailed west into the Atlantic beyond the sight of land until he met favorable winds and currents that carried him back to Europe. Having launched Portugal's era of expansion, Henry soon lost interest in it. While he indulged in costly and futile crusades against Morocco, less exalted men pushed farther south along the African coast. Only after they made it beyond the Sahara did their efforts begin to pay off.

During the 15th century, Portugal vaulted past all rivals in two major areas—the ability to navigate the high seas beyond sight of land, and the capacity to defeat any non-European fleet on the world's oceans. Portuguese (and later Spanish) navigators mapped the prevailing winds and currents on the high seas over most of the globe. They collected geographic information from classical sources, foreigners, and modern navigators. They studied the superior designs of Arab vessels, copied them, and improved on them. They increased the ratio of length to beam (width at the broadest point of the hull) from 2:1 to 3:1, borrowed the lateen (triangular) sail from the Arabs, and combined it with square rigging in the right proportion to produce a superb oceangoing vessel, the caravel. A caravel could make from 3 to 12 knots and could beat closer to a head wind than any other sailing ship. Portuguese captains also used the compass and adopted the Arabs' astrolabe, a device that permits accurate calculation of latitude, or distances north and south. (The calculation of longitude—distances east and west—is much more

THE CARAVEL: A SWIFT OCEANGOING VESSEL
This caravel is a modern reconstruction of the 15th-century *Niña*, which crossed the Atlantic with Columbus in 1492.

© Jon Adkins/National Geographic Society.

difficult and was not mastered until the 18th century.) As they skirted the African coast, these Portuguese sailors made precise charts and maps that later mariners could follow.

The Portuguese also learned how to mount heavy cannon on the decks of their ships—a formidable advantage in an age when others fought naval battles by grappling and boarding enemy vessels. Portuguese ships were able to stand farther off and literally blow their opponents out of the water.

As the 15th century advanced, Portuguese mariners explored ever farther along the African coast, looking for wealth and eventually a direct, cheap route to Asia. South of the Sahara they found the wealth they had been seeking—gold, ivory, and slaves. These riches kept the enterprise alive.

Africa, Colonies, and the Slave Trade

West Africa was inhabited by a mostly agricultural population that also included skilled craftsmen. West Africans probably learned how to use iron long before Europeans did, and they had been supplying Europe with most of its gold for hundreds of years through indirect trade across the desert. West Africa's political history had been marked by the rise and decline of a series of large inland states. The most recent of these, the empire of Mali, was already in decline by 1450. As the Portuguese advanced past the Sahara, their commerce began to pull trade away from the desert caravans, which further weakened Mali and other interior states. By 1550, the empire had fallen apart.

The Portuguese also founded offshore colonies along the way. They began to settle the uninhabited Madeira Islands in 1418, took possession of the Azores between 1427 and 1450, occupied the Cape Verde group in the 1450s, and took over São Tomé in 1470. Like exploration, colonization also turned a profit. Lacking investment capital and experience in overseas settlement, the Portuguese drew on Italian merchants for both. In this way, the plantation complex of staple crops and slavery migrated from the Mediterranean to the Atlantic. Beginning in the 1440s, Portuguese island planters produced sugar or wine, increasingly with slave labor imported from nearby Africa. Some plantations, particularly on São Tomé, kept several hundred slaves at work growing and processing sugar.

At first, the Portuguese acquired their slaves by landing on the African coast, attacking agricultural villages, and carrying off everyone they could catch, but these raids enraged coastal peoples and made other forms of trade more difficult. In the decades after 1450, the slave trade assumed its classic form. The Portuguese established small posts, or "factories," along the coast or, ideally, on small offshore islands, such as Arguin Island near Cape Blanco, where they built their first African fort in 1448. Operating out of these bases, traders would buy slaves from the local rulers, who usually acquired them by waging war. During the long history of

MADEIRA

This modern photograph of Madeira conveys something of what the Portuguese saw when they first visited the island in the early 15th century— an uninhabited, mountainous, and heavily forested landscape.

the Atlantic slave trade, nearly every African shipped overseas had first been enslaved by other Africans.

Slavery had long existed in Africa, but in a form less brutal than that which the Europeans would impose. When the Atlantic slave trade began, no African middleman could have foreseen how the enslavement of Africans by Europeans would differ from the enslavement of Africans by Africans. These differences were crucial. In Africa, slaves were not forced to toil endlessly to produce staple crops, and their descendants often became fully assimilated into the captors' society. Slaves were not isolated as a separate caste. By the time African middlemen learned about the cruel conditions of slavery under European rule, the trade had become too lucrative to stop, although several African societies tried. They discovered, however, that those who refused to participate in the trade were likely to become its victims. When the rulers of the Kongo embraced Catholicism in the 16th century, they protested against the Atlantic slave trade, only to see their own people become vulnerable to enslavement by others. The non-Christian kingdom of Benin learned the same lesson.

The Portuguese made the slave trade profitable by exploiting rivalries among the more than 200 small states of West and Central Africa. This part of Africa was divided into more language groups and small states than Europeans would find anywhere else in the world. Despite many cultural similarities among these groups, West Africans had never thought of themselves as a single people. Nor did they share a universal religion that might have restrained them from selling other Africans into slavery.

THE PORTUGUESE SLAVE-TRADING FORTRESS OF ELMINA

Located on the Gold Coast of West Africa, the fortress was built in 1481.

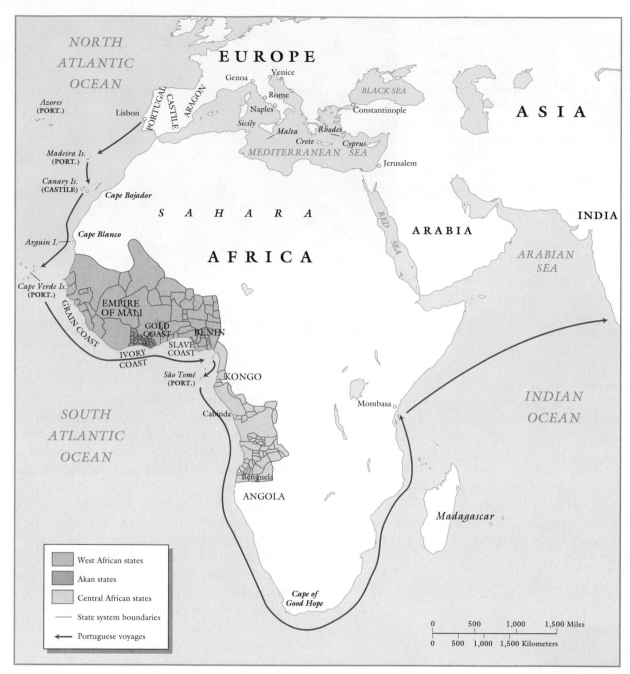

MAP 1.3   AFRICA AND THE MEDITERRANEAN IN THE 15TH CENTURY

The Mediterranean islands held by Europeans in the late Middle Ages, the Atlantic islands colonized by Portugal and Spain in the 15th century, the part of West Africa from Cape Blanco to Angola that provided the main suppliers of the Atlantic slave trade, and the Portuguese all-water route to India after 1497.

 View an animated version of this map or related maps at **http://history.wadsworth.com/murrin_LEP4e.**

Moslems believed it sinful to enslave a fellow believer. Western Europeans, although they were quite capable of waging destructive wars against one another, strongly believed that enslaving fellow Christians was immoral. Enslaving pagan or Moslem Africans was another matter. Some Europeans even persuaded themselves that they were doing Africans a favor by buying them and making their souls eligible for salvation.

Portugal's Asian Empire

Portuguese exploration continued, paying for itself through gold, ivory, and slaves. In the 1480s, the government decided to support the quest for an all-water route to Asia. In 1487, Bartolomeu Dias reached the Cape of Good Hope at the southern tip of Africa and headed east toward the Indian Ocean, but his crew rebelled in those stormy waters, and he turned back. Ten years later, Vasco da Gama led a small fleet around the Cape of Good Hope and sailed on to the Malibar Coast of southwestern India. In a voyage that lasted more than two years (1497–99), da Gama bargained and fought for spices that yielded a 20-to-1 profit for his investors.

Da Gama opened the way for Portugal's empire in the East. To secure their Asian trade, the Portuguese established a chain of naval bases that extended from East Africa to the mouth of the Persian Gulf, then to Goa on the west coast of India, and from there to the Moluccas, or East Indies. Portuguese missionaries even penetrated Japan. The Moluccas became the Asian center of the Portuguese seaborne empire, with their spices yielding most of the wealth that Portugal extracted from its eastern holdings. As early as 1515, African and Asian trade was providing two-thirds of Portugal's state revenues.

Beyond assuring its continued access to spices, Portugal made little effort to govern its holdings, and thus its eastern empire never became colonies of settlement. In all of their Asian holdings, the Portuguese remained heavily outnumbered by native peoples. Only in the Western Hemisphere—in Brazil, which was discovered accidentally by Pedro Álvares Cabral in 1500 when he was blown off course while trying to round the Cape of Good Hope—had settlement become a major goal by the late 16th century.

Early Lessons

As the Norse failure showed, the ability to navigate the high seas, although an impressive feat in itself, gave no guarantee of lasting success. Sustained expansion overseas required the support of a home government and ready access to what other states had learned. Italian merchants in nearby Rhodes or Cyprus passed their experiences on to the Portuguese to be applied in the Atlantic islands of Madeira or the Azores. And the lessons learned there were then relayed to distant Brazil. The Portuguese drew on Italian capital and maritime skills, as well as on Arab learning and technology, in launching their ventures. Spaniards, in turn, would learn much from the Portuguese, and the French, Dutch, and English would borrow from Italians, Portuguese, and Spaniards.

© Archivo Iconografico, S.A./Corbis.

THE LISBON WATERFRONT IN THE 16TH CENTURY

Although other European cities were larger than Lisbon, it became the first port to establish direct trade between Europe, Africa, South and East Asia, and the Americas.

The economic impulse behind colonization was thus in place long before Columbus sailed west. The desire for precious metals provided the initial stimulus, but staple crops and slavery kept that impetus alive. Before the 19th century, more than two-thirds of the people who crossed the Atlantic were slaves who were brought to America to grow sugar or other staples. The Atlantic slave trade was not some unfortunate exception to a larger story of liberty. For three and a half centuries, it was the norm.

Few Europeans who crossed the ocean expected to work. Early modern Europe was a hierarchical society in which men with prestige and wealth did virtually no physical labor. Upward social mobility meant advancing toward the goal of "living nobly," without the need to labor. In both Portugal and Spain, the social barriers between aristocrats and commoners had been flexible for some time. Professional men, famous soldiers, and rich merchants could acquire titles and begin to "live nobly." The opening of the Americas offered even greater possibilities for men to succeed by forcing others to toil for them.

🌐 Spain, Columbus, and the Americas

While the Portuguese surged east, Spaniards moved more sluggishly to the west. Just as Portugal gained experience by colonizing Madeira and the Azores, the Spanish kingdom of Castile sent its first settlers to the Canary Islands shortly after 1400. They spent the last third of the 15th century conquering the local inhabitants, the Guanches, a Berber people who had left North Africa before the rise of Islam and had been almost completely cut off from Africa and Europe for a thousand years. By the 1490s, the Spanish had all but exterminated them, the first people to face virtual extinction in the wake of European expansion.

Except for seizing the Canaries, the Spaniards devoted little attention to exploration or colonization. Instead, for most of the 15th century, the Iberian kingdoms of Aragon and Castile warred with other powers, quarreled with each other, or dealt with internal unrest. But in 1469, Prince Ferdinand of Aragon married Princess Isabella of Castile. They soon inherited their respective thrones and formed the modern kingdom of Spain, which had a population of about 4.9 million by 1500. Aragon, a Mediterranean society, had made good on an old claim to the Kingdom of Naples and Sicily and thus already possessed a small imperial bureaucracy

with experience in administering overseas possessions. Castile, landlocked on three sides, was larger than Aragon but in many ways more parochial. Its people, although suspicious of foreigners, had turned over much of their small overseas trade to merchants and mariners from Genoa in northern Italy who had settled in the port of Seville. Crusading Castilians, not traders, had taken the lead in expelling the Moors from the Iberian peninsula. Castilians, who were more likely than the Portuguese to identify expansion with conquest instead of trade, would lead Spain overseas.

In January 1492, Isabella and Ferdinand completed the reconquest of Spain by taking Granada, the last outpost of Islam on the Iberian peninsula. Flush with victory, they gave unconverted Jews six months to become Christians or be expelled from Spain. Just over half of Spain's 80,000 Jews fled, mostly to nearby Christian lands, including Portugal, that were more tolerant than Spain. A decade later, Ferdinand and Isabella also evicted all unconverted Moors. Spain entered the 16th century as Europe's most fiercely Catholic society, and this attitude accompanied its soldiers and settlers to America.

Columbus

A talented navigator from Genoa named Christopher Columbus promptly sought to benefit from the victory at Granada. He had served the Portuguese Crown for several years, had engaged in the slave trade between Africa and the Atlantic islands, had married the daughter of a promi-

Leonardo Torriani, Die Kanarischen Inseln und ihre Urbewohner [1590], ed. Dominik Wölfel (Leipzig: K. F. Koehler, 1940), Plate X.

TWO GUANCHES

In the late 15th century, Spaniards all but exterminated these people, of Berber descent, on the Canary Islands.

nent Madeira planter, and may even have sailed to Iceland. He had been pleading for years with the courts of Portugal, England, France, and Spain to give him the ships and men to attempt an unprecedented feat: He believed he could reach eastern Asia by sailing west across the Atlantic.

Columbus's proposed voyage was controversial, but not because he assumed the earth was round. Learned men at that time agreed on that point, but they disagreed about the earth's size. Columbus put its circumference at only 16,000 miles. He proposed to reach Japan or China by sailing west a mere 3,000 miles. The Portuguese scoffed at his reasoning. They put the planet's circumference at about 26,000 miles, and they warned Columbus that he would perish on the vast ocean if he tried his mad scheme. Their calculations were, of course, far more accurate than those of Columbus; the circumference of the earth is about 25,000 miles at the equator. Even so, the fall of Granada gave Columbus another chance to plead his case. Isabella, who now had men and resources to spare, grew more receptive to his request. She put him in charge of a fleet of two caravels, the *Niña* and the *Pinta*, together with a larger, square-rigged vessel, the *Santa María*, which Columbus made his flagship.

Columbus's motives were both religious and practical. He believed that the world was going to end soon, perhaps in 1648, but that God would make the Gospel available to all humankind before the last days. As the "Christ-bearer" (the literal meaning of his first name), Columbus was convinced that he had a role to play in bringing on the Millennium, the period at the end of history when Jesus would return and rule with his saints for 1,000 years; however, he was not at all averse to acquiring wealth and glory along the way.

Embarking from the port of Palos in August 1492, Columbus headed south to the Canaries, picked up provisions, and sailed west across the Atlantic. He kept two ship's logs, one to show his men, in which he underestimated the distance they had traveled, and the other for his

---

LINK TO THE PAST

Misunderstanding Columbus

On Christopher Columbus's third voyage to the Americas (1498–1500), he was sailing near a Caribbean island, possibly Trinidad, when he encountered a canoe manned by 24 Indians. His effort to bring the canoe close enough to trade with its occupants indicates how wide were the cultural misunderstandings between these two very different peoples.

*A*s this canoe approached, they shouted to us from a distance, but neither I nor anyone else understood them. I gave orders, however that they should be signalled to approach, and more than two hours passed in this way. Each time they came a little nearer, they immediately sheered off again. I ordered pans and other shining objects to be displayed in order to attract them and bring them closer, and after a while they came nearer. . . . I greatly desired conversation with them, but it seemed that I had nothing left to show them which would induce them to come nearer still. So I had a tambourine brought up to the poop [deck] and played, and made some of the young men dance, imagining that the Indians would draw closer to see the festivities. On observing the music and dancing, however, they dropped their oars, and picked up their bows, and strung them. Each one seized his shield, and they began to shoot arrows at us. I immediately stopped the music and dancing and ordered some crossbows to be fired. The Indians then put off, making for another caravel, and hastily sheltered under its stern. The pilot hailed them and gave a coat and hat to the man who seemed to be their chief, and arranged with him that he would meet and talk with them on the beach, to which they immediately rowed their canoe to await him. But he did not wish to go without my permission. When they saw him come to my ship in his boat, they got back into their canoe and rowed away, and I never saw them again or any other inhabitant of this island.*

From Columbus's account of his third voyage,
in *The Life of the Admiral by his Son, Hernando Colon*

1. Why do you suppose the Indians failed to connect the crew of the other European vessel with Columbus, and what do you think they were most afraid of?

For additional sources related to this feature, visit the *Liberty, Equality, Power* Web site at:

http://history.wadsworth.com/murrin_LEP4e

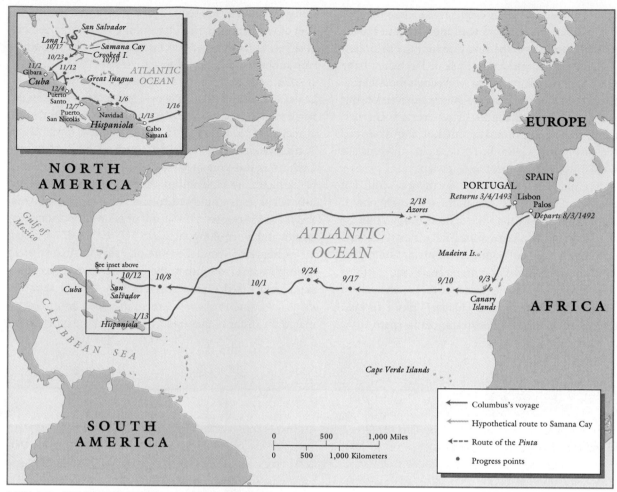

MAP 1.4   COLUMBUS'S FIRST VOYAGE, 1492

The route taken by Columbus from Palos, Spain, to the Canary Islands, then to San Salvador or possibly Samana Cay (see insert map), and finally back to Europe.

eyes only. (Ironically, the false log turned out to be more accurate than the official one.) He promised a prize to the first sailor to sight land. Despite his assurances that they had not sailed far, the crews grew restless in early October. Columbus pushed on. When land was spotted, on October 12, he claimed the prize for himself. He said he had seen a light in the distance the previous night.

The Spaniards splashed ashore on San Salvador, now Watling's Island in the Bahamas. (A few historians argue for Samana Cay, 60 miles south of San Salvador, as the site of the first landfall.) Convinced that he was somewhere in the East Indies, near Japan or China, Columbus called the local inhabitants "Indians," a word that meant nothing to them but one that has endured. When the peaceful Tainos (or Arawaks) claimed that the Carib Indians on nearby islands were cannibals, Columbus interpreted their word for "Carib" to mean the great "Khan" or emperor of China, known to him through Marco Polo's *Travels*. Columbus set out to find the Caribs. For several months he poked

about the Caribbean, mostly along the coasts of Cuba and Hispaniola. Then, on Christmas, the *Santa María* ran onto rocks and had to be abandoned. A few weeks later, Columbus sailed for Spain on the *Niña*. Some historians speculate that he had arranged the Christmas disaster as a way of forcing some of the crew to stay behind as a garrison on Hispaniola, but by then even the gentle Tainos had seen enough. By the time Columbus returned on his second voyage in late 1493, they had killed every man he had left.

The voyage had immediate consequences. In 1493, Pope Alexander VI (a Spaniard) issued a bull, *Inter Caeteras*, which divided all non-Christian lands between Spain and Portugal. A year later, in the Treaty of Tordesillas, the two kingdoms adjusted the dividing line, with Spain eventually claiming most of the Western Hemisphere, plus the Philippines, and Portugal most of the Eastern Hemisphere, including the African coast, plus Brazil. As a result, Spain never acquired direct access to the African slave trade.

Columbus made three more voyages in quest of China and also served as governor of the Spanish Indies. But Castilians never really trusted this Genoese opportunist, who spoke their language with a Portuguese accent and was a poor administrator to boot. The colonists often defied him, and after his third voyage, they shipped him back to Spain in chains in 1500. Although later restored to royal favor, he died in 1506, a bitter, disappointed man.

Spain and the Caribbean

By then, overseas settlement had acquired a momentum of its own as thousands of ex-soldiers, bored *hidalgos* (minor nobles with little wealth), and assorted adventurers drifted across the Atlantic. They carried with them seeds for Europe's cereal crops and livestock, including horses, cows, sheep, goats, and pigs. On islands without fences, the animals roamed freely, eating everything in sight, and soon threatened the Tainos' food supply. Unconcerned, the Spaniards forced the increasingly malnourished Indians to work for them, mostly panning for gold. Under these pressures, even before the onset of major infectious diseases, the native population fell catastrophically throughout the Caribbean. By 1514, only 22,000 able-bodied adults remained on Hispaniola, from an initial population of perhaps one million. The native people died even more rapidly than the meager supply of placer gold disappeared. This story was soon repeated on Cuba, Jamaica, and other islands. A whole way of life all but vanished from the earth to be replaced by sugar, slaves, and livestock as the Spaniards despaired of finding other forms of wealth. African slaves, acquired from the Portuguese, soon arrived to replace the dead Indians as a labor force.

The Spaniards continued their New World explorations: Juan Ponce de León tramped through Florida in quest of a legendary fountain of youth, shrewdly calculating that such an elixir would bring a handsome price in Europe. Vasco Núñez de Balboa became the first European to reach the Pacific Ocean, after crossing the Isthmus of Panama in 1513. Even so, as late as 1519—a full generation after Columbus's first voyage—Spain had gained little wealth from these new possessions, whatever and wherever they turned out to be. One geographer concluded that Spain had found a whole new continent, which he named "America" in honor of his informant, the explorer Amerigo Vespucci. For those who doubted this claim, Ferdinand Magellan, a Portuguese mariner serving the king of Spain, settled the issue when his fleet sailed around the world between 1519 and 1522. Magellan himself never completed the voyage. He was killed in the Philippines.

During the same three years, Hernán Cortés sailed from Cuba, invaded Mexico, and found the treasure that Spaniards had been seeking. In 1519, he landed at a place he named Veracruz (The True Cross) and over the next several months succeeded in tracking down the fabulous empire of the Aztecs, high in the Valley of Mexico. When his small army of 400 men first laid eyes on the Aztec capital of Tenochtitlán (a metropolis of 200,000, much larger than any city in Western Europe), they wondered if they were dreaming. But they marched on. Moctezuma (or Montezuma II), the Aztec "speaker," or ruler, sent rich presents to persuade the Spaniards to leave, but the gesture had the opposite effect. "They picked up the gold and fingered it like monkeys," an Aztec later recalled, "Their bodies swelled with greed, and their hunger was ravenous. . . . They snatched at the golden ensigns, waved them from side to side and examined every inch of them." Cortés had stumbled upon a wholly different world in the Americas, one with its own long and varied past.

The Emergence of Complex Societies in the Americas

The high cultures of the Americas had been developing for thousands of years before Cortés found one of them. Their ways were ancient, and they were proud of their past. Their wealth fired the imagination of Europe and aroused the envy of Spain's enemies. The fabulous Aztec and Inca empires became the magnets that turned European exploration into rival empires of permanent settlement.

The Rise of Sedentary Cultures

After 4000 B.C., agriculture transformed the lives of most Indians. As farming slowly became the principal source of food in the Americas, settled villages in a few locations grew into large cities. Most of them appeared in the Valley of Mexico, Central America, or the Andes. For centuries, however, dense settlements also thrived in Chaco Canyon in present-day New Mexico and in the Mississippi River valley. Meanwhile, farming continued to spread. By the time Columbus sailed, most Indians were raising crops.

Indians became completely sedentary (nonmigratory) only in the most advanced cultures. Most of those north of Mexico lived a semisedentary life—that is, they were migratory for part of each year. After a tribe chose a site, the men chopped down some trees, girded others, burned away the underbrush, and often planted tobacco, a mood-altering sacred crop grown exclusively by men. Burning the underbrush fertilized the soil with ash and gave the community years of high productivity. Meanwhile, women

© North Wind Picture Archives.

© Stock Montage, Inc.

© Historical Picture Archive/Corbis.

LONGHOUSE, WIGWAM, AND TEPEE
The longhouse (top right), made from bark or mats stretched over a wooden frame, was the standard communal dwelling of the Iroquois and Huron peoples. Most Algonquian peoples of the eastern woodlands lived in wigwams (top left), such as this undated example. Wigwams were made by bending the boughs of trees into a frame to be covered with animal skins. West of the Mississippi, most Plains Indians lived in small but strong tepees (bottom left), which were usually made from poles covered with buffalo hides. All of these dwellings were constructed by women.

erected the dwellings (longhouse, wigwam, tepee) and planted and harvested food crops, especially corn. Planting beans among the corn helped maintain good crop yields. In the fall, either the men alone or entire family groups went off hunting or fishing.

Under this "slash and burn" system of agriculture, farming became women's work, beneath the dignity of men, whose role was to hunt, fish, and make war. Because this system slowly depleted the soil, the whole tribe had to move to new fields after a decade or two, often because accessible firewood had been exhausted. In this semi-sedentary way of life, few Indians cared to acquire more personal property than the women could carry from one place to another, either during the annual hunt or when the whole community had to move. This limited interest in consumption would profoundly condition their response to capitalism after contact with Europeans.

Even sedentary Indians did not own land as individuals. Clans or families guarded their "use rights" to land that had been allocated to them by their chiefs. In sedentary societies, both men and women worked in the fields, and families accumulated surpluses for trade. Not all sedentary peoples developed monumental architecture and elaborate state forms. The Tainos of the Greater Antilles in the Caribbean were fully sedentary, for example, but they never erected massive temples or created powerful states. But, with a few striking exceptions, such examples of cul-

tural complexity emerged primarily among sedentary populations. In Mesoamerica and the Andes, intensive farming, cities, states, and monumental architecture came together at several different times to produce distinctive high cultures.

The spread of farming produced another population surge among both sedentary and semisedentary peoples. Estimates vary greatly, but according to the more moderate ones, at least 50 million people were living in the Western Hemisphere by 1492—and perhaps as many as 70 million, or one-seventh of the world's population. High estimates exceed 100 million. The Valley of Mexico in 1500 was one of the most densely inhabited regions on Earth.

Despite their large populations, even the most complex societies in the Americas remained Stone Age cultures in their basic technology. The urban societies of Mesoamerica and the Andes became the largest and most complex Stone Age cultures in the history of the world. The Indians made some use of metals, although more for decorative than practical purposes. This metalworking skill originated in South America and spread to Mesoamerica a few centuries before Columbus. By 1520, Indians had amassed enough gold and silver to provide dozens of plundering Europeans with princely fortunes. As far north as the Great Lakes, copper had been discovered and fashioned into fishing tools and art objects since the first millennium B.C. Copper was traded over large areas of North

INDIAN WOMEN AS FARMERS

In this illustration, a French artist depicted 16th-century Indian women in southeastern North America.

America, but Indians had not learned how to make bronze (a compound of copper and tin) nor found any use for iron. Nearly all of their tools were made of stone or bone, and their sharpest weapons were made from obsidian, a hard, glassy, volcanic rock. Nor did they use the wheel or devices based on the wheel, such as pulleys or gears. They knew how to make a wheel—they had wheeled toys—but they never found a practical purpose for this invention, probably because North America had no draft animals, and South Americans used llamas mostly in steep, mountainous areas where wheeled vehicles would have made no sense.

The Andes: Cycles of Complex Cultures

Despite these technological limitations, Indians accomplished a great deal. During the second millennium B.C., elaborate urban societies began to take shape both in the Andes and along Mexico's gulf coast. Because no Andean culture had become literate before the Europeans arrived, we know much less about events there than we do about Mesoamerica, but we do know that ancient Andean societies devised extremely productive agricultural systems at 12,000 feet above sea level, far above the altitude at which anyone else has ever been able to raise crops. In the 1980s, when archaeologists rebuilt part of the prehistoric Andean irrigation system according to ancient specifications, they discovered that it was far more productive than a system using modern fertilizers and machines. The Andean system could produce 10 metric tons of potatoes per hectare

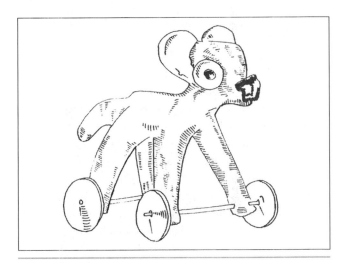

MESOAMERICAN TOY DEER

This sketch of a toy deer shows that Mesoamerican people did understand the principle of the wheel, but they found no practical use for it.

(about 2.4 acres), as against 1 to 4 tons on nearby modern fields. Lands using the Andean canal system never had to lie fallow. This type of irrigation took hold around Lake Titicaca about 1000 B.C. and spread throughout the region. It was abandoned around A.D. 1000, apparently in response to a monster drought that endured, with only brief intermissions, for two centuries.

Monumental architecture and urbanization appeared in the Andes even before the canal system at Lake Titicaca was created. Between 3000 and 2100 B.C., both took hold along the Peruvian coast and in the interior. The new

COMPLEX CULTURES OF PRE-COLUMBIAN AMERICA

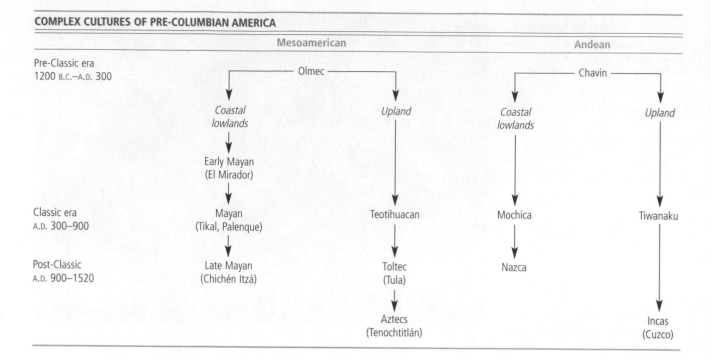

	Mesoamerican		Andean	
Pre-Classic era 1200 B.C.–A.D. 300	Olmec		Chavin	
	Coastal lowlands	*Upland*	*Coastal lowlands*	*Upland*
	Early Mayan (El Mirador)			
Classic era A.D. 300–900	Mayan (Tikal, Palenque)	Teotihuacan	Mochica	Tiwanaku
Post-Classic A.D. 900–1520	Late Mayan (Chichén Itzá)	Toltec (Tula)	Nazca	
		Aztecs (Tenochtitlán)		Incas (Cuzco)

communities were built around a U-shaped temple about three stories high. Some of the earliest temples were pyramids, the oldest of which are as ancient as those of Egypt. In later centuries, as more people moved into the mountains, some pyramids became immense. The one at Sechin Alto near Lima, more than 10 stories high, was built between 1800 and 1500 B.C. Eventually, these accomplishments merged into what archaeologists call the Pre-Classic Chavin culture, which was well established by 1000 B.C., only to collapse suddenly about 300 B.C. In all probability, no single state ever dominated this culture.

Chavin culture had two offshoots: one on the coast and one in the mountains. Together they constitute the Classic phase of pre-Columbian history in South America. The Mochica culture, which emerged about A.D. 300 on the northwest coast of Peru, produced finely detailed pottery, much of it erotic, and built pyramids as centers of worship. At about the same time, another Classic culture arose in the mountains around the city of Tiwanaku, 12,000 feet above sea level. The people of this society grew a great variety of food plants, both tropical and temperate. Terraces, laid out at various altitudes on the mountainside, enabled the community to raise crops from different climatic zones, all a few hours distant from one another. At the lowest levels, Tiwanakans planted cotton in the hot, humid air. Farther up the mountain, they raised maize (corn) and other crops suitable to a temperate zone. At still higher elevations, they grew potatoes and grazed their alpacas and llamas. They even invented freeze-dried food

© Ancient Art & Architecture Collection.

TERRACED AGRICULTURE OF THE ANDES

This example is from the Incas, but the technology was much older than the Inca civilization.

by carrying it far up the mountains to take advantage of the frost that fell most nights of the year.

The Tiwanaku Empire, with its capital on the southern shores of Lake Titicaca, flourished until even its sophisticated irrigation system could not survive the horrendous drought that began at the end of the 10th century A.D. The Classic Andean cultures collapsed between the 6th and 11th centuries A.D., possibly after a conquest of the Mochica region by the Tiwanakans, who provided water to the coastal peoples until they too were overwhelmed by the drought.

The disruption that followed this decline was temporary because complex Post-Classic cultures soon thrived both north and west of Tiwanaku. The coastal culture of the Nazca people has long fascinated both scholars and tourists because of its exquisite textiles, and above all because of a unique network of lines they etched in the desert. Some lines form the outlines of birds or animals, but others simply run straight for miles until they disappear at the horizon. Only from the air are these patterns fully visible.

Inca Civilization

Around A.D. 1400, the Inca (the word applied both to the ruler and to the empire's dominant nation) emerged as the new imperial power in the Andes. They built their capital at Cuzco, high in the mountains. From that upland center, the Incas controlled an empire that eventually extended more than 2,000 miles from south to north, and they bound it together with an efficient network of roads and

INCA *QUIPU*
The accounting device pictured here is based on a decimal system developed by the Incas.

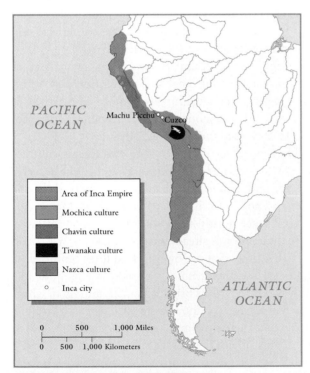

MAP 1.5 INCA EMPIRE AND PRINCIPAL EARLIER CULTURES
The Pacific coast of South America showing the location of the Mochica, Chavin, Tiwanaku, and Nazca cultures and finally the Inca empire, which covered a much larger area.

suspension bridges. Along these roads, the Incas maintained numerous storehouses for grain. They had no written language, but high-altitude runners, who memorized the Inca's oral commands with perfect accuracy, raced along the roads to relay their ruler's decrees over vast distances. The Incas also invented a decimal system and used it to keep records of the tribute they levied upon subject peoples. They used a device they called a *quipu*. By 1500, the Inca empire ruled perhaps 8 to 12 million people. No other nonliterate culture has ever matched that feat.

Mesoamerica: Cycles of Complex Cultures

Mesoamerica experienced a similar cycle of change, but over a somewhat shorter period. Its own Pre-Classic, Classic, and Post-Classic cultures also comprised both upland and lowland societies.

The Olmecs, who appeared along the Gulf Coast about 1200 B.C., became the parent culture for the region. It centered on three cities. The oldest, San Lorenzo (names are modern, as is "Olmec," which means "people of rubber," for the rubber trees that thrive in this tropical region), flourished from 1200 to 900 B.C., when it was conquered by invaders. Olmec influence reached its zenith during the domination of La Venta, which became an urban center about 1100 B.C., reached its peak 300 years later, and declined. After La Venta was demolished between 500 and 400 B.C., leadership passed to the city of Tres Zapotes, which thrived for another four centuries.

These three Olmec centers, with permanent populations of only about 1,000, were too small to sustain large armies. The colossal stone heads that honored their rulers were the most distinctive Olmec artifacts, but they appeared only in the homeland. Other aspects of Olmec culture became widely diffused throughout Mesoamerica. The Olmecs built the first pyramids and the first ballparks in Mesoamerica. Their game, played with a heavy rubber ball, spread into what is now the southwestern United States. The losers were, at least on certain religious occasions, beheaded.

The Olmecs also learned how to write and developed a dual calendar system that endured through the Aztec era. At the end of a 52-year cycle, the first day of the "short" calendar would again coincide with the first day of the "long" one. Olmecs faced the closing days of each cycle with dread, lest the gods allow the sun and all life on earth to be destroyed—something that, Olmecs believed, had already happened several times. They believed that the sacrifice of a god had been necessary to set the sun in motion

EL CARACOL, A LATE MAYAN OBSERVATORY AT CHICHÉN ITZÁ

Astronomy was highly developed in all of the pre-Columbian high cultures of Mesoamerica; however, if the Mayans used any specialized instruments to study the heavens, we do not know what they were.

in each new creation cycle and that only the blood of human sacrifice could placate the gods and keep the sun moving.

These beliefs endured in Mesoamerica for perhaps 3,000 years, regardless of the rise and fall of empires and cities. The essentials may even be older than Olmec culture. The creation myths of both Mesoamerican and Andean peoples are similar, which may suggest a common origin in the distant past, perhaps as far back as Beringia, where the sun did disappear for part of each year. Olmec beliefs retained immense power. The arrival of Cortés created a religious as well as a political crisis, because 1519 marked the end of a 52-year cycle.

The Olmecs were succeeded by two Classic cultures, both of which created great cities and studied the heavens. The city and empire of Teotihuacan emerged in the mountains not far from modern Mexico City. Mayan culture took shape mostly in the southern lowlands of Yucatán. Teotihuacan was already a city of 40,000 by A.D. 1 and grew to five times that size over the next three centuries. Its temples included enormous pyramids, but its most impressive art form was its brightly painted murals, of which only a few survive. Teotihuacan invested resources in comfortable apartment dwellings for ordinary residents, not in monuments or inscriptions to rulers. It probably had a form of senate government, not a monarchy. The city extended its influence throughout Mesoamerica and remained a powerful force until its sudden destruction in about A.D. 750, apparently by conquest because its shrines were toppled and the city was abandoned. In all likelihood, Teotihuacan's growth had so depleted the resources

OLMEC STONE HEAD
This giant head of stone is 9 feet 4 inches tall.

Reconstruction by Tatiana Proskouriakoff. From the Fall of the Ancient Maya by David Webster, published by Thames & Hudson, London and New York.

COPAN'S TEMPLE OF THE HIEROGLYPHIC STAIRWAY

It is an exceptional example both of Mayan architecture and Mayan literacy.

© Boltin Picture Library.

THE TEMPLE OF THE SUN AT TEOTIHUACAN

The giant, stepped pyramid shown here is one of pre-Columbian America's most elegant pyramids.

of the area that the city could not have sustained itself much longer. Modern beliefs to the contrary, Indians enjoyed no mystical protection from ecological disasters.

In the lowlands, Classic Mayan culture went through a similar cycle from expansion to ecological crisis. It was also urban but less centralized than that of Teotihuacan, although some Mayan temples were just as monumental. For more than 1,000 years, Mayan culture rested on a network of competing city-states, which, as in ancient Greece, shared similar values. One of the largest Mayan cities, Tikal, arose on the plateau separating rivers flowing into the Caribbean from rivers emptying into the Gulf of Mexico. It controlled commerce with Teotihuacan. Tikal housed 100,000 at its peak before A.D. 800. Twenty other cities, most about one-fourth the size of Tikal, flourished throughout the region. Mayan engineers built canals to water the crops needed to support this urban system, which was well established by the first century B.C. The Danta pyramid, completed in the second century B.C. at the Pre-Classic city of El Mirador, was probably the most massive architectural structure in pre-Columbian Mesoamerica. El Mirador declined before the Classic era began.

The earliest Mayan writings date to 50 B.C., but few survive from the next 300 years. About A.D. 300, Mayans began to record their history in considerable detail. Since 1960, scholars have deciphered most Mayan inscriptions, which means that the Classic phase of Mayan culture is completing a shift from a prehistoric to a historic (or written) past. Mayan texts are now studied much like those of Europe. Mayan art and writings reveal the religious beliefs of these people, including the place of human sacrifice in their cosmos and the role of ritual self-mutilation, particularly among the elite, in their worship. Scholars have learned, for example, about the long reign of Pacal the Great, king (or "Great Sun") of the elegant city of Palenque, who was born on March 26, 603, and died on August 31, 683. His sarcophagus lists his ancestors through six generations. Other monuments tell of the Great Suns of other cities whom Pacal vanquished and sacrificed to the gods.

Classic Mayan culture began to collapse about 50 years after the fall of Teotihuacan, which disrupted Mayan trade with the Valley of Mexico. The crisis spread rapidly. Palenque and a half-dozen other cities were abandoned between 800 and 820. The last date recorded at Tikal was in 869; the last in

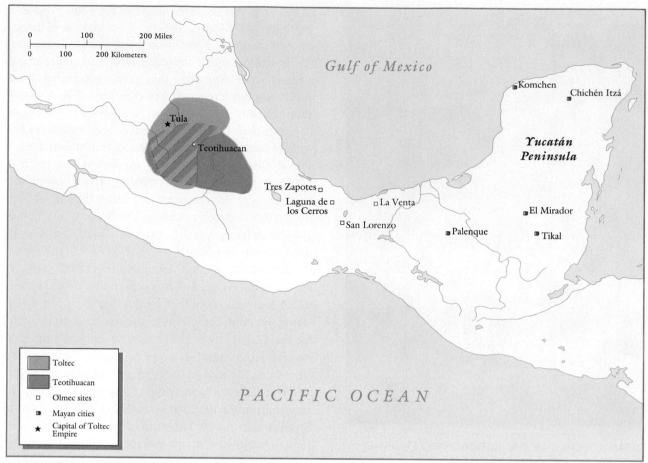

MAP 1.6 ANCIENT MESOAMERICA
The location of the three principal Olmec cities, Teotihuacan, several major Mayan cities, and the Toltec capital of Tula.

the southern lowlands came 40 years later. The Mayan aristocracy had grown faster than the commoners could support it, until population outstripped local resources and generated irreversible ecological decay. Frequent wars hastened the decline. Trade with the Valley of Mexico, although diminished, shifted north to other cities. With the collapse of the southern cities, the population of the region fell drastically, partly through emigration northward.

After A.D. 900, the Post-Classic era saw a kind of Mayan renaissance in the northern lowlands of the Yucatán, where many refugees from the south had fled. Chichén Itzá, a city that had existed for centuries, preserved many distinctive Mayan traits but merged them with new influences from the Valley of Mexico, where the Toltecs had become dominant in the high country and may even have conquered Chichén Itzá. The Toltecs were a fierce warrior people whose capital at Tula, with 40,000 people, was one-fifth as large as Teotihuacan at its peak. They prospered from the cocoa trade with tropical low-

lands but otherwise did nothing to expand the region's food supply. They controlled the Valley of Mexico for almost three centuries, until about A.D. 1200, when they too declined. They left a legacy of conquest to later rulers in the valley, all of whom claimed descent from Toltec kings.

The Aztecs and Tenochtitlán

By 1400, power in the Valley of Mexico was passing to the Aztecs, a warrior people who had migrated from the north about two centuries earlier and had settled, with the bare sufferance of their neighbors, on the shore of Lake Texcoco. They built a great city, Tenochtitlán, out on the lake. Its only connection with the mainland was by several broad causeways. The Aztecs raised their agricultural productivity by creating highly productive *chinampas*, or floating gardens, right on the lake. Yet their mounting population strained the food supply. In the 1450s, the threat of famine was severe.

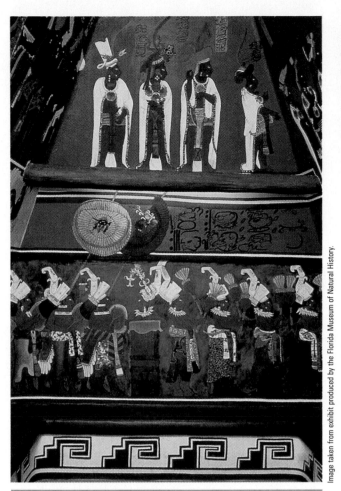

Image taken from exhibit produced by the Florida Museum of Natural History.

WALL PAINTINGS AT BONAMPAK

The wall paintings at Bonampak from the Teotihuacan era are a spectacular example of pre-Columbian art.

© Boltin Picture Library.

MAYAN SACRIFICIAL VICTIM

Human sacrifice played a major role in Mesoamerican religion. The artist who crafted this disemboweled man recognized the agony of the victim.

Tenochtitlán, with a population of something over 200,000, had forged an alliance with Texcoco and Tlacopan, two smaller lakeside cities. Together they dominated the area, but by the second quarter of the 15th century, leadership was clearly passing to the Aztecs. As newcomers to the region, the Aztecs felt a need to prove themselves worthy heirs to Teotihuacan, Tula, and the ancient culture of the Valley of Mexico. They adopted the old religion but practiced it with a terrifying intensity. They waged perpetual war, usually with neighboring cities, to gain captives for their ceremonies. They built and constantly rebuilt and enlarged their Great Pyramid of the Sun. At its dedication in 1487, they sacrificed—if we can believe later accounts—about 14,000 people in a ceremony that went on for four days until the priests dropped from exhaustion. Each captive climbed the steep steps of the pyramid and was held by his wrists and ankles over the sacrificial slab while a priest cut open his breast, ripped out his heart, held it up

to the sun, placed it inside the statue of a god, and then rolled the carcass down the steps so that parts of the body could be eaten, mostly by members of the captor's family, but never by the captor. He fasted instead and mourned the death of a worthy foe.

Human sacrifice was an ancient ritual in Mesoamerica, familiar to everyone, but the Aztecs practiced it on a scale that was unparalleled anywhere else in the world. The need for thousands of victims each year created potential enemies everywhere. Although neighboring peoples shared the religious beliefs of the Aztecs, they nevertheless hated these conquerors from the north. After 1519, many Indians in Mesoamerica would help the Spaniards bring down the Aztecs. By contrast, the Spanish found few allies in the Andes, where resistance in the name of the Inca would persist for most of the 16th century and would even revive in the late 18th century, 250 years after the conquest.

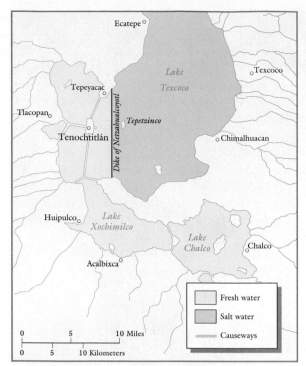

MAP 1.7 VALLEY OF MEXICO, 1519

Lake Texcoco and its principal cities, especially Tenochtitlán (built on the lake itself) and its allies, Tlacopan and Texcoco.

WOODCUT OF A QUEEN, OR THE WIFE OF A "GREAT SUN" OF THE MISSISSIPPI MOUND BUILDERS, BEING CARRIED ON A LITTER

This 16th-century engraving is by Theodore de Bry.

North American Mound Builders

North of Mexico, from 3000 B.C. to about A.D. 1700, three distinct cultures of "mound builders" succeeded each other and exerted a powerful influence over the interior of North America. Named for the huge earthen mounds they erected, these cultures arose near the Ohio and Mississippi rivers and their tributaries. The earliest mound builders became semisedentary even before learning to grow crops.

Fish, game, and the lush vegetation of the river valleys sustained them for most of the year and enabled them to erect permanent dwellings.

The oldest mound-building culture appeared among a preagricultural people in what is now northeastern Louisiana about 3400 B.C., at a site called Watson Break. Later, just 40 miles away, early mound builders flourished from 1500 B.C. to 700 B.C. at Poverty Point (named for a 19th-century plantation), a center that contained perhaps 5,000 people at its peak in about 1000 B.C. The second mound-building culture, the Adena-Hopewell, emerged between 500 B.C. and A.D. 400 in the Ohio River valley. Its mounds were increasingly elaborate burial sites, indicating belief in an afterlife. Mound-building communities participated in a commerce that spanned most

THE GREAT SERPENT MOUND

Located near Chillicothe, Ohio, this mound is about 1,200 feet long and is one of the most spectacular mounds to survive from the Adena-Hopewell era.

of the continent between the Appalachians and the Rockies, the Great Lakes and the Gulf of Mexico. Obsidian from the Yellowstone Valley in the Far West, copper from the Great Lakes basin, and shells from the Gulf of Mexico have all been found buried in the Adena-Hopewell mounds. Both the mound building and the long-distance trade largely ceased after A.D. 400, for reasons that remain unclear. The people even stopped growing corn for a few centuries. Yet the mounds were so impressive that when American settlers found them after the Revolution, they refused to believe that "savages" could have built them.

Mound building revived in a third and final Mississippian phase between A.D. 1000 and 1700. This culture dominated the Mississippi River valley from modern St. Louis to Natchez, with the largest center at Cahokia in present-day Illinois and another important one at Moundville in Alabama. Ordinary people became "stinkards" in this culture, while some families had elite status. The "Great Sun" ruled with authority and was transported by litter from place to place. When he died, some of his wives, relatives, and retainers even volunteered to be sacrificed at his funeral and join him in the afterlife. Burial mounds thus became much grander in Mississippian communities. The Indians topped the mounds in which their rulers were interred with elaborate places of worship and residences for the priests and Great Suns of these highly stratified societies.

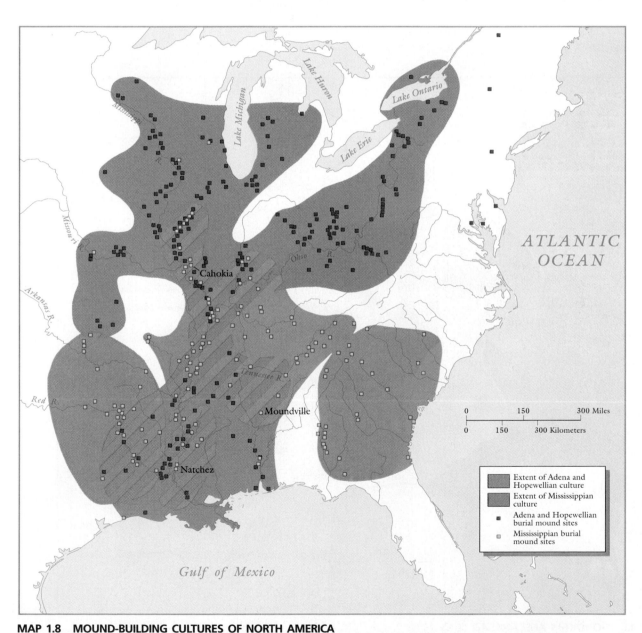

MAP 1.8 MOUND-BUILDING CULTURES OF NORTH AMERICA
Early Adena and Hopewell burial sites and later Mississippian sites and the areas that these cultures influenced.

Painting by Lloyd K. Townsend. Cahokia Mounds Historic Site.

CAHOKIA

The largest Mississippian mound-building site was Cahokia, in Illinois near St. Louis. Depicted here is the city's sacred, ceremonial center facing toward Monk Mound in the distance.

The city of Cahokia, near modern St. Louis, flourished from A.D. 900 to 1250 and may have had 30,000 residents at its peak, making it the largest city north of Mexico and almost as populous as the contemporary Toltec capital at Tula. Cahokia's enormous central mound, 100 feet high, is the world's largest earthen work. Similarities with Mesoamerican practices and artifacts have led many scholars to look for direct links between the two cultures. Yet although travel was possible between Mesoamerica and the Mississippi valley, no Mesoamerican artifacts have been found in the southeastern United States.

Urban Cultures of the Southwest

Other complex societies emerged in North America's semi-arid Southwest—among them the Hohokam, the Anasazi,

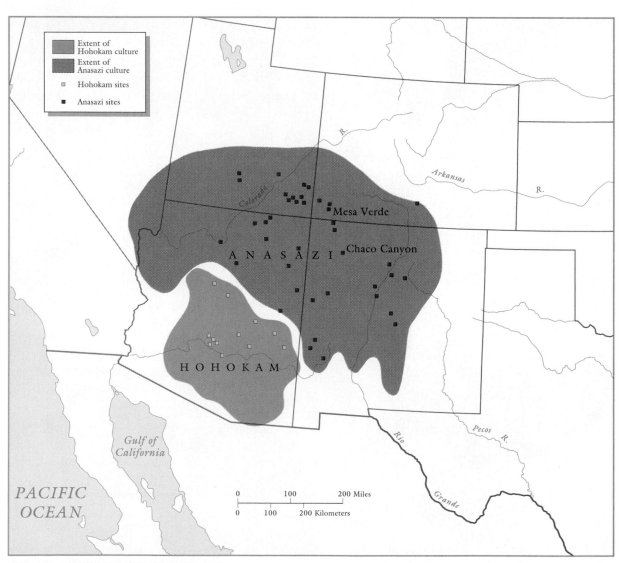

MAP 1.9   HOHOKAM AND ANASAZI SITES

These cultures in the Southwest combined irrigation and road building with sophisticated architecture.

and the Pueblo. The Hohokam Indians settled in what is now central Arizona somewhere between 300 B.C. and A.D. 300. Their irrigation system, consisting of several hundred miles of canals, produced two harvests per year. They wove cotton cloth and made pottery with a distinctive red color. They traded with places as distant as California and Mesoamerica and even imported a version of the Mesoamerican ball game. Perhaps because unceasing irrigation had increased the salinity of the soil, this culture, after enduring for more than 1,000 years, had gone into irreversible decline by 1450.

Even more tantalizing and mysterious is the brief flowering of the Anasazi (a Navajo word meaning "the ancient ones"), a cliff-dwelling people who have left behind some remarkable artifacts at Chaco Canyon in New Mexico, at Mesa Verde in Colorado, and at other sites. In their caves and cliffs, they constructed apartment houses five stories high with as many as 500 dwellings and with elegant and spacious *kivas,* or meeting rooms for religious functions. The Anasazi were superb astronomers. Through an arrangement of rock slabs, open to the sun and moon at the mouth of a cave, and of spirals on the interior wall that plotted the movement of the sun and moon, they created a calendar that could track the summer and winter solstices and even the 19-year cycles of the moon, an astronomical refinement Europeans had not yet achieved. They traveled to their fields and brought in lumber and other distant supplies on a network of roads that ran for scores of miles in several directions. They achieved most of these feats over a period of about two centuries, although Anasazi pottery has been found that dates from much earlier times. In the last quarter of the 13th century, apparently overwhelmed by a prolonged drought and by hostile invaders, they abandoned their principal sites. Pueblo architecture resembles that of the Anasazi, and the Pueblo Indians claim descent from them.

Contact and Cultural Misunderstanding

After the voyage of Columbus, the peoples of Europe and America, both with ancient pasts, confronted each other. Mutual understanding was unlikely except on a superficial level. Nothing in the histories of Europeans or Indians had prepared either of them for the encounter. The humanists of Renaissance Europe, avidly studying ancient Greece and Rome, were uncovering the huge differences between those pagan cultures and the Christian values of the Middle Ages and were developing a strong sense of history, an awareness that their past had been quite different from their present. They were also used to dealing with Moslem "infidels," whom they regarded as terribly alien but whose monotheistic beliefs were not all that different from their own. They also understood that East Asia was neither classical nor Christian, not Islamic or "barbaric." Even so, none of this experience prepared them for what they found in America.

Religious Dilemmas

Christians had trouble understanding how Indians could exist at all. The Bible, they were certain, recorded the creation of all humankind, but it never mentioned the Indians. From which of the sons of Noah had they descended? Were they the "lost 10 tribes" of Israel, perhaps? This idea was first suggested by Spanish missionaries and would later appeal to British Protestants. Some theologians, such as Spaniard Juan Ginés de Sepúlveda, tried to resolve this dilemma by arguing that Indians were animals without souls, not human beings at all. The pope and the royal courts of Portugal and Spain listened instead to a Dominican missionary, Fray Bartolomé de Las Casas, who insisted on the Indians' humanity. But, asked Europeans, if Indians (and Asians) did possess immortal souls, would a compassionate God have left them in utter darkness for centuries without making the Gospel known to them? Rejecting that possibility, some early Catholic missionaries concluded that one of the apostles must have visited America (and India) and that the Indians must have

MODERN RESTORATION OF AN ANASAZI *KIVA*

This *kiva,* or meeting room of the Anasazi, was located underground and was accessed by a ladder through a hole in the ceiling.

© David Muench.

TENOCHTITLÁN

This painting by Ignacio Marquina conveys a sense of the city's spectacular size and its monumental architecture.

rejected his message. The Portuguese announced in the 1520s that they had discovered the tomb of St. Thomas the Doubter in India, and then in 1549, a Jesuit claimed to have found Thomas's footprint in Brazil. If only to satisfy the spiritual yearnings of Europeans overseas, St. Thomas got around!

To Europeans, the sacrificial temples, skull racks, and snake motifs of Mesoamerica led to only one conclusion: The Aztecs worshiped Satan. Their statues and even their writings had to be destroyed. Human sacrifice and ritual cannibalism were widespread throughout the Americas, although nowhere else on the two continents did the scale approach that practiced by the Aztecs. The Incas, whose creation myth resembled that of Mesoamerica, offered an occasional victim to the sun or to some other god. The Indians of eastern North America frequently tortured to death their adult male captives, and every Indian warrior learned from boyhood how to endure such torments. Christians were shocked by human sacrifice and found cannibalism revolting, but Indians regarded certain European practices with equal horror. Between 1500 and 1700, Europeans burned or hanged perhaps 50,000 to 100,000 people, usually old women, for conversing with the wrong

spirits—that is, for witchcraft. The Spanish Inquisition burned thousands of heretics. To the Indians, such executions looked like human sacrifices to placate an angry Christian God.

The dilemma that Indians posed for Europeans emerged almost at once. On his second voyage, Columbus brought the first missionaries to the Americas. After one of them preached to a group of Tainos and presented them with some holy images, the Indians, records relate, "left the chapel, . . . flung the images to the ground, covered them with a heap of earth, and pissed upon it." The governor, a brother of Columbus, had them burned alive. The Indians probably saw this punishment as a form of human sacrifice to a vengeful god. They had no way of grasping the Christian distinction between human sacrifice and punishment for desecration.

Even the Christians' moral message was ambiguous. Missionaries eagerly brought news of the Christ, how he had died to save humankind from sin. Catholic worship, then as now, centered on the Mass and the Eucharist, in which a priest transforms bread and wine into the literal body and blood of Christ. "Except ye eat the flesh of the Son of man, and drink his blood," Jesus told his disciples

(John 6:53), "ye have no life in you." Most Protestants also accepted this sacrament but interpreted it symbolically, not literally. To the Indians, Christians seemed to be a people who ate their own god but grew outraged at the lesser matter of sacrificing a human being to please an Indian god.

When Europeans tried to convert Indians to Christianity, the Indians concluded that the converts would spend the afterlife with the souls of Europeans, separated forever from their own ancestors, whose memory they revered. Neither side fully recognized these obstacles to mutual understanding. Although early Catholic missionaries converted thousands of Indians, the results were mixed at best. Some Indians willingly abandoned their old beliefs, but others resisted Christian doctrines. Most converts adopted some Christian practices and continued many of their old rituals, often in secret.

Moctezuma's Mexico, by David Carrasco and Eduardo Mato Moctezuma, © 1992 University Press of Colorado. Photographs by Salvador Guil'liem Arroyo.

AZTEC SKULL RACK ALTAR

This rack held the skulls of hundreds of sacrificial victims and shocked the invading Spaniards.

War as Cultural Misunderstanding

Such misunderstandings multiplied as Indians and Europeans came into closer contact. Both waged war, but with different objectives. Europeans tried to settle matters on the battlefield and expected to kill many enemies. Indians fought mostly to obtain captives, whether for sacrifice (as with the Aztecs) or to replace tribal losses through adoption (as with the Iroquois). To them, massive deaths on the battlefield were almost a blasphemy, an appalling waste of life that could in no way appease the gods. Europeans and Indians also differed profoundly on what acts constituted atrocities. The torture and ritual sacrifice of captives horrified Europeans; the slaughter of women and children, which Europeans brought to America, appalled Indians.

Gender and Cultural Misunderstanding

Indian social organization also differed fundamentally from that of Europeans. European men owned almost all property, set the rules of inheritance, farmed the land, and performed nearly all public functions. Among many Indian peoples, especially those first encountered by Europeans north of Mexico, descent was matrilineal (traced through the maternal line), and women owned nearly all movable property. European men felt incomplete unless they acquired authority over other people, especially the other members of their households. They also expected social inferiors to obey superiors. Indian men had none of these patriarchal ambitions. Chiefs governed more through persuasion and example than through command. Women did the farming in semisedentary Indian cultures, and they often could demand a war or try to prevent one, although the final decision rested with men. When Europeans tried to change warriors into farmers, Indian males protested that they were being turned into women. Only over fully sedentary peoples could Europeans impose direct rule by building on the social hierarchy, division of labor, and system of tribute already in place.

🌎 Conquest and Catastrophe

Spanish *conquistadores,* or conquerors, led small armies that rarely exceeded 1,000 men. Yet, because they were also able to raise large Indian armies as allies, they subdued two empires much larger than Spain and then looked around for more worlds to overrun. There, beyond the great empires, Indians had more success in resisting them.

The Conquest of Mexico and Peru

When Cortés entered Tenochtitlán in 1519, he seized Moctezuma, the Aztec ruler, as prisoner and hostage. Although overwhelmingly outnumbered, Cortés and his

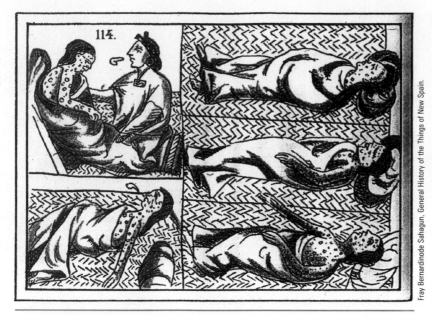

Fray Bernardinode Sahagun, General History of the Things of New Spain.

THE RAVAGES OF SMALLPOX

These drawings show the devastation of smallpox among the Aztecs, as depicted in the Aztec Codex, one of the few surviving collections of Aztec writing.

destroyed Tenochtitlán. He had hoped to leave the great city intact, not wreck it, but he and the Aztecs found no common understanding that would enable them to stop fighting before the city lay in ruins. "We have chewed dry twigs and salt grasses," mourned one Aztec poet after the fall of the city; "we have filled our mouths with dust and bits of adobe; we have eaten lizards, rats and worms." With royal support from Spain, the *conquistadores* established themselves as new imperial rulers in Mesoamerica, looted all the silver and gold they could find, and built Mexico City on the ruins of Tenochtitlán.

Rumors abounded about an even richer civilization far to the south, and in 1531 and 1532, Francisco Pizarro finally located the Inca empire high in the Andes. Smallpox had preceded him and killed the reigning Inca. In the civil war that followed, Atahualpa had defeated his brother to become the new Inca. Pizarro captured Atahualpa, held him hostage, and managed to win a few allies from among the Inca's recent enemies. Atahualpa filled his throne room with precious metals as a truly royal ransom, but Pizarro had him strangled anyway. Tens of thousands of angry Indians besieged the Spaniards for months in Cuzco, the Inca capital, but Pizarro, although vastly outnumbered, managed to hold out and finally prevailed. After subduing the insurgents, the Spanish established a new capital at Lima on the coast.

men began to destroy Aztec religious objects, replacing them with images of the Virgin Mary or other Catholic saints. In response, while Cortés was away, the Aztecs rose against the intruders, Moctezuma was killed, and the Spaniards were driven out with heavy losses. But then, the smallpox the Spaniards left behind soon began killing Aztecs by the thousands. Cortés found refuge with the nearby Tlaxcalans, a proudly independent people who had never submitted to Aztec rule. With thousands of their warriors, he returned the next year, built several warships armed with cannon to dominate Lake Texcoco, and

Folding Screen: The Encounter of Cortes and Moctezuma (obverse); The Four Continents (reverse). Collection Banco Nacional de Mexico, Mexico City.

THE ENCOUNTER OF CORTÉS AND MOCTEZUMA

Spain understood that the conquest of Mexico dramatically changed the history of the world and made possible a global empire. Juan Correa, a Mexican artist, painted this scene on a Japanese *biamba*, or folding screen, sometime between 1645 and 1650. On the other side of the screen he painted *The Four Continents* (Europe, Asia, Africa, and America).

TRIBUTE LABOR (*MITA*) IN THE SILVER MINES

The silver mines of Potosí, in the Andes, are about two miles above sea level. The work, as depicted in this 1603 engraving by Theodore de Bry, was extremely onerous and often dangerous.

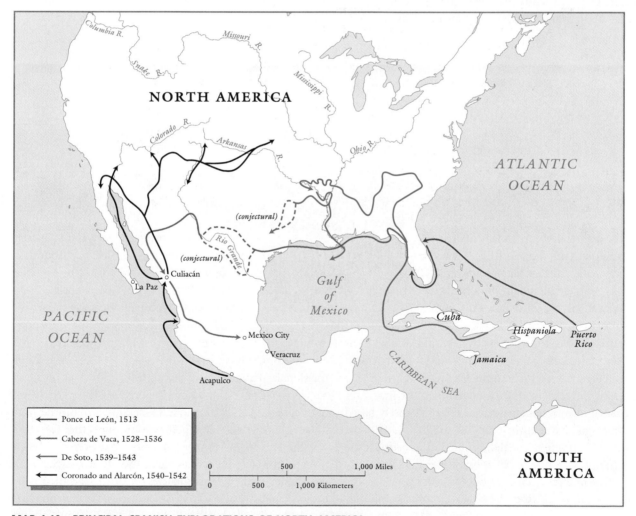

MAP 1.10   PRINCIPAL SPANISH EXPLORATIONS OF NORTH AMERICA

Four Spanish expeditions marched through much of the interior of North America between 1513 and 1543.

 View an animated version of this map or related maps at http://history.wadsworth.com/murrin_LEP4e.

In a little more than 10 years, some hundreds of Spanish soldiers with thousands of Indian allies had conquered two enormous empires with a combined population perhaps five times greater than that of all Spain. But only in the 1540s did the Spanish finally locate the bonanza they had been seeking. The fabulous silver mines at Potosí in present-day Bolivia and other smaller lodes in Mexico became the source of Spain's wealth and power for the next 100 years. So wondrous did the exploits of the *conquistadors* seem by then that anything became believable, including rumors that cities of pure gold lay somewhere in the interior of North America.

North American *Conquistadores* and Missionaries

Alvar Núñez Cabeza de Vaca was one of four survivors of Pánfilo de Narváez's disastrous 1528 expedition to Florida. Cabeza de Vaca made his way back to Mexico City in 1536 after an overland journey that took him from Florida through Texas and northern Mexico. In a published account of his adventures, he briefly mentioned Indian tales of great and populous cities to the north, and this reference soon became stories of "golden cities." Hernando de Soto landed in Florida in 1539 and roamed through much of the southeastern United States in quest of these treasures, leaving disease and mayhem in his wake. He crossed the Mississippi in 1541, wandered through the Ozarks and eastern Oklahoma, and marched back to the great river. He died there in 1542. His companions continued to explore for another year before returning to Spanish territory. Farther west, Francisco Vasquez de Coronado marched into New Mexico and Arizona, where he encountered several Pueblo towns but no golden cities. The expedition reached the Grand Canyon, then headed east into Texas and as far north as Kansas before returning to Mexico in 1542. North of Mexico, Indians menaced and sometimes even defeated Spanish soldiers, who finally gave up, but left their diseases behind. There were no cities of gold.

HISTORY THROUGH FILM

The Mission (1986)

Directed by Roland Joffé. Starring Jeremy Irons (Father Gabriel), Robert De Niro (Mendoza), and Liam Neeson (Father Fielding).

This film passionately portrays the destruction of the Jesuit missions in 18th-century Paraguay. Their success and communal prosperity (which included abolishment of private property) aroused the envy and the enmity of neighboring Portuguese settlers. Some of their churches were as large and as beautifully adorned as European cathedrals. When the Crown of Spain transferred the Guaraní territory to the Crown of Portugal in a 1750 treaty, the settlers and the government of Brazil got their chance to move against the missions. Loosely based on the Portuguese war against the Guaraní in the 1750s, the film is really a tribute to the dedication and sincerity of the Jesuit order, the colonial era's most successful missionary organization in either North or South America.

The screenplay by Robert Bolt, well known for his play and film of *A Man for All Seasons* (1966) and his film script for *Dr. Zhivago* (1965), telescopes the events of one and a half centuries into what seems to be only a year or so. In the 17th century, Portuguese slavers raided even Jesuit missions and carried off thousands of Indians to a life of toil in Brazil. The Guaraní War was not about enslavement but about the campaign to seize the native inhabitants' land and communal property. Bolt puts both events in the 18th century and provides a dramatic climax.

The film stars Jeremy Irons as Gabriel, a Spanish Jesuit missionary who uses the Guaraní Indians' love of music as a means of converting them. Robert De Niro plays Mendoza, a reformed slaver who has killed his own brother in a lovers' quarrel and then repents by joining Father Gabriel's mission. When the European courts and even the Jesuit order command the missionaries not to resist the Portuguese takeover, the missionaries refuse to leave their people but split over how to resist. Gabriel chooses nonviolence. Mendoza and Father Fielding (Liam Neeson) take up arms. All of them are killed. Jesuit involvement in the Guaraní War gave the Catholic monarchs of Europe the

After the *conquistadores* departed, Spanish priests did their best to convert thousands of North American Indians to the Catholic faith. These efforts extended well north of New Spain (Mexico). In 1570, the Jesuits even established a mission in what is now Virginia, but local Indians soon wiped it out.

After the failure of the Jesuit mission, Spain decided to treat the Indians of Florida and New Mexico with decency and fairness and eventually came to rely on these missions for protection against English and French intruders. The Jesuits withdrew, and Franciscans took their place. In 1573, King Philip II (1556–98) issued the Royal Orders for New Discoveries, which made it illegal to enslave Indians or even attack them. Instead, unarmed priests were to bring Indians together in missions and convert them into peaceful Catholic subjects of Spain. The Franciscans quickly discovered that, without military support, they were more likely to win martyrdom than converts. They reluctantly accepted military protection, but they tried to make sure that none of

the few soldiers who accompanied them behaved like *conquistadores.*

Missionary work demanded commitment and faith. The Franciscans had both. A belief in miracles also sustained them. In 1631, a mystical nun in Castile, María de Jesús de Agreda, claimed that angels had carried her across the Atlantic, where she preached to Indians in their own languages. When Pueblo Indians reported that a "Lady in Blue" once preached to them, the Franciscans put the two accounts together into a miraculous event that enchanted thousands for a century, even though the nun retracted most of her story in 1650.

Franciscans had no success among the nomadic residents of central and southern Florida. They had to build their missions within the permanent villages of northern Florida or the Pueblo communities of New Mexico. The Spanish incursion into New Mexico began quite badly with the slaughter of perhaps 800 Indian men, women, and children in 1599, but then relations softened. At first, Indian women willingly supplied the labor needed to

excuse they needed to expel the Jesuits from their kingdoms and then to persuade the pope to disband the order.

By telescoping events that occurred decades apart into a short period, Bolt intensifies the drama but also suggests that some Europeans, especially Jesuits, did consistently and over a long period place the welfare of Indians above all other values. In a poignant final scene, many mission children, now completely naked, are rowing back into the wilderness to escape enslavement. The settlers, Bolt insists, would not allow them to become civilized.

Filmed on location above and below magnificent Agazzu Falls, one of the most spectacular sights in South America, the film won the 1986 Cannes Film Festival's award for best picture and an Oscar for best cinematography. British director Roland Joffé had already earned acclaim for *The Killing Fields* (1983), a stark depiction of the near-genocidal atrocities in Cambodia after the Vietnam War. He later directed *Fatman and Little Boy* (1989), a dramatization of the birth of the atomic bomb.

Kobal Collection/Warner Bros.

In this scene, Father Gabriel plays the flute to attract a Guaraní audience.

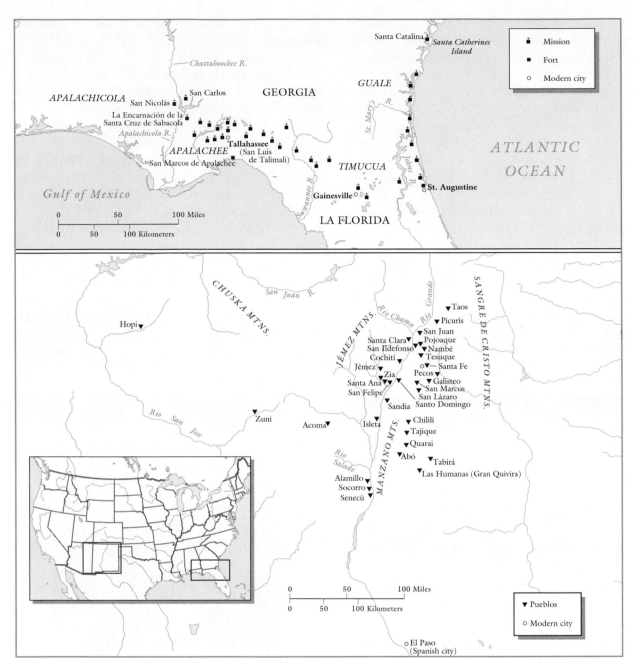

MAP 1.11 SPANISH MISSIONS IN FLORIDA AND NEW MEXICO CIRCA 1675
Franciscan friars established missions in Florida from the Atlantic to the Gulf of Mexico and in New Mexico along the Rio Grande Valley and, in a few cases, farther inland.

build and sustain these missions. By 1630, about 86,000 Pueblo, Apache, and Navajo Indians of New Mexico had accepted baptism. They lived in a chain of missions north and south of Santa Fe, 1,500 arduous and dusty miles from the colonial capital at Mexico City. By midcentury, 30 missions in Florida contained about 26,000 baptized Indians and covered an area extending some 250 miles from the Atlantic coast of what is now Georgia westward into the Florida panhandle. The Franciscans also urged their converts, with limited success, to wear European cloth-

ing. In 1671, when a bishop counted 4,081 newly converted women in Florida who went about topless and with their lower legs exposed, he ordered them to cover up.

The Spanish Empire and Demographic Catastrophe

By the late 16th century, the Spanish Empire had emerged as a system of direct colonial rule in Mexico and Peru, where the conquerors took over and used existing systems

A Chesapeake Warrior Challenges the Spanish Empire

In 1561, an Algonquian Indian chief brought his son aboard a Spanish vessel trading in Chesapeake Bay. The teenager seemed of such "fine presence and bearing" that the Spaniards asked to take him to Spain and present him to the royal court. They promised to return him with wealth and honors. In Spain, the expedition's commander, Pedro Menéndez de Avilés, introduced him as a "*cacique* or important lord from Florida." The young man learned Spanish, studied Christianity, and was baptized as Don Luis de Velasco in honor of the Spanish viceroy in Mexico, who became his godfather. Don Luis sailed to Mexico with Menéndez in 1563, then returned to Spain, and this time Don Luis studied with the Jesuits, whom Menéndez had been urging to establish a mission in the Chesapeake Bay region.

In September 1570, with Father Juan Baptista de Segura in charge, two priests, three brothers, three novices, a boy, and Don Luis, who was expected to act as interpreter, landed, probably near modern Williamsburg. The missionaries assumed that the young Indian had been appropriately awed by Spanish might. After 10 years' absence, his relatives were astonished to see him and at first believed that the Jesuits had awakened him from the dead. But this initial awe quickly turned sour because the newcomers expected the Indians to feed them after a season of drought. A younger brother of Don Luis had become chief and offered to yield the position to him, but Don Luis declined the honor. He soon reverted to Indian folkways by agreeing to take several wives. When Segura publicly humiliated him for engaging in these sinful practices, Don Luis deserted the mission in October. After four months, the Spaniards sent a small expedition to find him. He promised to come back, but instead, accompanied by several warriors, he followed the party and killed its members on February 4, 1571. Five days later, his men wiped out all of the survivors

except the boy. Don Luis had been impressed by Spanish power, but the result was not what the missionaries had hoped.

Menéndez took fearful vengeance in 1572. A barrage of harquebuses tore into a crowd of Indians. After the survivors refused to surrender Don Luis to Spanish justice, Menéndez hanged eight Indian hostages. Don Luis was very likely related to Powhatan and Opechancanough, the paramount sachems of the Powhatan Indians of "Virginia" between the founding of Jamestown in 1607 and Opechancanough's death in 1646. One historian has even argued that Don Luis was Opechancanough, an Algonquian word that meant "he whose soul is white" and who was described in the 1640s as more than a hundred years old. But if Opechancanough had lived among Europeans for 10 years as Don Luis, he would hardly have been so fascinated with a lock and key as to lock and unlock it a hundred times a day, according to an English missionary, for "he thought no device in all the world comparable to it."

DON LUIS DE VELASCO MURDERING THE JESUITS, 1571

This engraving by Melchior Küssell was published in 1675 and portrays the victims as martyrs who died for their faith. There is no reason to assume that the artist knew what Don Luis looked like.

of tribute. These core holdings were protected by a strong defensive perimeter in the Caribbean and surrounded by a series of frontier missions, extending in the north into Florida and New Mexico. The Spaniards also brought new systems of labor and new religious institutions to their overseas colonies, although in time both were altered by local conditions.

The first Spanish rulers in Mexico and Peru relied on a form of labor tribute that had helped to depopulate the West Indies. Called *encomienda,* this system permitted the holder, or *encomendero,* to claim labor from an Indian district for a stated period. *Encomienda* worked because it resembled the way the Aztecs and the Incas had routinely levied labor for their own massive public buildings and irrigation projects. In time, the king intervened to correct abuses and to limit labor tribute to projects that the Crown initiated, such as mining and the construction of churches or other public buildings. Spanish settlers resisted the reforms at first but slowly shifted from demanding labor to claiming land. In the countryside, the *hacienda,* a large estate with its own crops and herds, became a familiar institution.

Although the Church never had enough clergy to meet its needs, it became a massive presence during the 16th century. Yet America changed it, too. As missionaries acquired land and labor, they began to exhibit less zeal for Indian souls. The Franciscans—in Europe, the gentlest of Catholic religious orders—brutally and systematically tortured their Mayan converts in the 1560s whenever they caught them worshiping their old gods. To the Franciscans, the slightest lapse could signal a reversion to Satan worship, with human sacrifice a likely consequence. They did not dare to be kind.

Most important, the Spaniards brought deadly microbes with them. Smallpox, which could be fatal but which most Europeans survived in childhood, devastated the Indians, who had almost no immunity to it. Even measles could be fatal, and common colds easily turned into pneumonia. When Cortés arrived in 1519, the native population of Mexico probably exceeded 15 million. In the 1620s, after waves of killing epidemics, it bottomed out at 700,000 and did not regain its pre-Spanish level until the 1950s. Peru suffered nearly as horribly. Its population fell from about 10 million in 1525 to 600,000 a century later. For the hemisphere as a whole, any given region probably lost 90 or 95 percent of its population within a century of sustained contact with Europeans. Lowland tropical areas usually suffered the heaviest casualties; in some of these places, all of the Indians died. Highland areas and sparsely settled regions fared somewhat better.

The Spanish Crown spent much of the 16th century trying to keep abreast of these changes, but eventually it imposed administrative order on the unruly *conquistadores* and brought peace to its colonies. At the center of the imperial bureaucracy, in Seville, stood the Council of the Indies. The council administered the three American viceroyalties of New Spain, Peru, and eventually New Granada, which were further subdivided into smaller *audiencias,* executive and judicial jurisdictions supervised by the viceroys. The Council of the Indies appointed the viceroys and other major officials, who ruled from the new cities that the Spaniards built with local labor at Havana, Mexico City, Lima, and elsewhere. Although centralized and autocratic in theory, the Spanish Empire allowed local officials a fair degree of initiative, if only because months or even years could elapse in trying to communicate across its immense distances. "If death came from Spain," mused one official, "we should all live long lives."

Brazil

Portuguese Brazil was theoretically autocratic, too, but it was divided into 14 "captaincies," or provinces, and thus was far less centralized. The Portuguese invasion did not lead to the direct rule of native societies but to their displacement or enslavement. After the colonists on the northeast coast turned to raising sugar in the late 16th century, Brazilian frontiersmen, or *bandeirantes,* foraged deep into the continent to enslave more Indians. They even raided remote Spanish Andean missions, rounded up the converts, and dragged them thousands of miles across mountains and through the jungle to be worked to death on the sugar plantations. On several occasions, while Brazil was ruled by Spain (see the discussion that follows), outraged missionaries persuaded the king to abolish slavery altogether. Not even absolutism could achieve that goal. Slavery continued without pause, and Africans gradually replaced Indians as the dominant labor force. Brazil was the major market for African slaves until the 1640s, when demand in West Indian sugar islands became even greater.

Global Colossus, Global Economy

American silver made the king of Spain the most powerful monarch in Christendom. Philip II commanded the largest army in Europe, held the Turks in check in the Mediterranean, and tried to crush the Protestant Reformation in northern Europe (see chapter 2). He had other ambitions as well. In 1580, after the king of Portugal died with no direct heir, Philip claimed his throne, thus uniting under his own rule Portugal's Asian empire, Brazil, Spain's American possessions, and the Philippines. This colossus was the greatest empire the world had ever seen. It also sustained the first truly global economy, because the Portuguese used Spain's American silver to pay for the spices and silks they imported from Asia. The union of Spain and Portugal lasted until the 1640s, when Portugal revolted and regained its independence.

The Spanish colossus became part of an even broader economic pattern. Serfdom, which tied peasants to their lords and to the land, had been Europe's predominant labor system in the early Middle Ages. Although peasants could not move, neither could they be sold; they were not slaves. Serfdom had been declining in Western Europe since the 12th century and was nearly gone by 1500. A system of free labor arose in its place, and overseas expansion strengthened that trend within Western Europe. Although free labor prevailed in the Western European homeland, unfree labor systems took root all around Europe's periphery, both overseas and in Eastern Europe, and the two systems were structurally linked. In general, free labor reigned where populations were dense and still growing. Large pools of labor kept wages low, but around the periphery of Western Europe, where land was cheap and labor expensive, coercive systems became the only efficient way for Europeans to extract from those areas the goods they desired.

The forms of unfree labor varied greatly across space and time, from slavery to less brutal systems. In New Spain, as the native population dwindled, the practice of *encomienda* slowly yielded to debt peonage. Unpayable debts kept Indians tied to the *haciendas* of the countryside. The mining of precious metals, on the other hand, was so dangerous and unpleasant that it almost always required a large degree of physical coercion, a system of labor tribute called *mita* in the Andes. Similarly, any colonial region that devoted itself to the production of staple crops for sale in Europe also turned to unfree labor and eventually to overt slavery. Sugar production first reduced Indians to bondage in the Caribbean and Brazil and later, as they died off, led to the importation of African slaves by the millions. Other staples—tobacco, rice, cotton, coffee—later followed similar patterns. At first these crops were considered luxuries and commanded high prices, but as they became widely available on the world market, their prices fell steeply, profit margins contracted, and planters turned overwhelmingly to coerced labor. Even in Eastern Europe, which began to specialize in producing cereal crops for sale in the more diversified West, serfdom revived. In Russia, where the Orthodox Church never condemned the enslavement of fellow Christians, the condition of a serf came to resemble that of a slave in one of the Atlantic empires. Some serfs were even bought and sold.

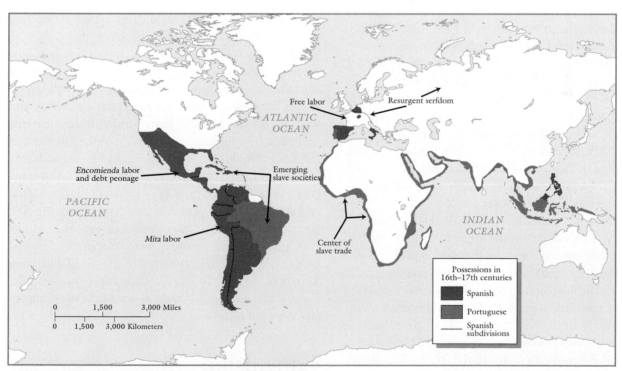

MAP 1.12 SPANISH EMPIRE AND GLOBAL LABOR SYSTEM

While Western European states were becoming free-labor societies, they created or encouraged the establishment of societies built on or providing laborers for various unfree labor systems in the Americas, the Caribbean, Africa, and Eastern Europe.

Spain's rise had been spectacular, but its empire was vulnerable. Although silver from the Americas vastly enhanced the Crown's ability to wage war, the costs of continuous conflict, the inflation generated by a steady influx of silver, and the need to defend a much greater perimeter absorbed Spain's new resources and a great deal more. Between 1492 and 1580, Spain's population grew from 4.9 million to 8 million, but over the course of the following century, it fell by 20 percent, mostly because of the escalating costs, both financial and human, of Spain's wars. As population declined, taxes rose. Castile grew poorer, not richer, in its century and a half of imperial glory. Most of the wealth of the Indies went elsewhere to pay for goods or services that Spain failed to provide for itself—to merchants in Genoa, to manufacturers in Lombardy and the Low Countries, and to bankers in Augsburg.

Explanations: Patterns of Conquest, Submission, and Resistance

By the middle of the 18th century, Europeans who thought seriously about the discovery of America and its global implications generally agreed that the whole process had been a moral outrage, possibly the worst in history. Conquest and settlement had killed millions of Indians, had enslaved millions of Africans, and had degraded Europeans. The benefits seemed small by comparison, even though economic gains were undeniably large by 1750. If the cruelest of the conquerors had been able to foresee the results of this process, asked the Abbé Raynal, would he have proceeded? "Is it to be imagined that there exists a being infernal enough to answer this question in the affirmative!" The success of the American Revolution, with its message of freedom and human rights, quieted such thinking for a time, but the critique has revived in recent years, especially in the developing world.

Modern historians, less moralistic than Raynal, also realize that he considerably underestimated the death toll. Even so, they are more interested in asking how and why these things happened. One major reason is geographical. The Eurasian land mass, the world's largest, follows an east-west axis that permits life forms and human inventions to travel immense distances without going through forbidding changes of climate. Chinese inventions eventually reached Europe. By contrast, the Americas, and sub-Saharan Africa, lie along north-south axes that do impose such barriers. Another compelling explanation for European success focuses on the prolonged isolation of the Americas from the rest of the world. If two communities of equal ability are kept apart, that with the larger and more varied population will be more inventive than the other, and its people will learn more rapidly from one another over time. For example, the use of iron spread gradually throughout nearly all of Asia, Africa, and Europe. And even though Europeans knew little about China, they slowly acquired Chinese inventions such as paper, the compass, and gunpowder. More than any other technological edge, far more than firearms or even horses, steel made military conquest possible. European armor stopped enemy spears and arrows, and European swords killed opponents swiftly without any need to reload.

The biological consequences of isolation were even more momentous than the technological barriers. The devastation European microbes inflicted upon the Indian population is the greatest tragedy in the history of humankind. The Indians' genetic makeup was more uniform than that of Europeans, Africans, or Asians. Indians were descended from a rather small sample of the total gene pool of Eurasia. Centuries spent in frigid Beringia had weeded out weaker people and killed the microbes that produce most diseases. The Indians first encountered by Europeans were bigger, stronger, and—at first contact—healthier than the newcomers, but they died in appalling numbers because they had almost no resistance to European diseases.

European plants also thrived at the expense of native vegetation. For example, when British settlers first crossed the Appalachian mountains, they marveled at the lush Kentucky bluegrass. They did not realize that they were looking at an accidental European import that had conquered the landscape even faster than they had. European animals also prevailed over potential American rivals. Horses multiplied at an astonishing rate in America, and wild herds moved north from Mexico faster than the Spaniards, transforming the way of life of the Apaches and the Sioux. The lowly sparrow never had it so good until someone turned a few loose in North America. But some life forms also moved from the Americas to Europe, Asia, and Africa. Indians probably gave syphilis to the first Europeans they met. Other American exports, such as corn, potatoes, and tomatoes, were far more benign and have enriched the diet of the rest of the world. Historian Alfred W. Crosby has called this larger process "the Columbian exchange." It ranks as one of the most important events of all time.

Conclusion

Americans like to believe that their history is a story of progress. They are right about its European phase. After its tragic beginnings in conquest, depopulation, and enslavement, things had to improve.

For thousands of years, the Americas had been cut off from the rest of the world. The major cultures of Eurasia and Africa had existed in relative isolation, engaging in direct contact with only their immediate neighbors. Islamic societies that shared borders with India, the East Indies, black Africa, and Europe had been the principal mediators among these cultures and, in that era, were more tolerant than most Christian societies.

In just 40 years, daring European navigators, supported by the Crowns of Portugal and Spain, joined the world together and challenged Islam's mediating role. Between 1492 and 1532, Europe, Africa, Asia, the Spice Islands, the Philippines, the Caribbean, Aztec Mexico, Inca Peru, and other parts of the Americas came into intense and often violent contact with one another. A few individuals gained much, and Spain acquired a military advantage within Europe that endured into the 1640s. Nearly everybody else suffered, millions horribly, especially in the Americas and Africa. And Spain spent the rest of the 16th century trying to create an imperial system that could impose order on this turbulent reality.

But Spain had many enemies. They too would find the lure of wealth and land overseas irresistible.

SUGGESTED READINGS

Two recent general surveys of early American history provide excellent coverage up to Independence: **Alan Taylor,** *American Colonies* (2001); and **Richard Middleton,** *Colonial America: A History, 1565–1776,* 3rd ed. (2002). For a useful collection of essays, see **Stanley N. Katz, John M. Murrin, and Douglas Greenberg, eds.,** *Colonial America: Essays in Politics and Social Development,* 5th ed. (2001).

Brian M. Fagan, *The Great Journey: The Peopling of Ancient America* (1987) is a fine introduction to pre-Columbian America. See also **David Webster,** *The Fall of the Ancient Maya: Solving the Mystery of the Maya Collapse* (2002). **Jared Diamond,** *Guns, Germs, and Steel: The Fates of Human Societies* (1997) is provocative and challenging in its global perspective. For the age of explorations, see **Peter Russell,** *Prince Henry 'the Navigator': A Life* (2000); **G. V. Scammell,** *The First Imperial Age: European Overseas Expansion c. 1400–1715* (1989); and **Alfred W. Crosby's** classic synthesis, *The Columbian Exchange: Biological and Cultural Consequences of 1492* (1972). For the slave trade, see **John Thornton,** *Africa and Africans in the Making of the Modern World, 1400–1800,* 2nd ed. (1998), which insists that Africans retained control of their affairs, including the slave trade, through the 17th century; and **Patrick Manning,** *Slavery and African Life: Occidental, Oriental, and African Slave Trades* (1990), which emphasizes the devastating impact of the slave trade in the 18th and 19th centuries. **Ira Berlin's** *Many Thousands Gone:*
The First Two Centuries of Slavery in North America (1998) is an effective and comprehensive synthesis of a huge subject.

James Lockhart and Stuart B. Schwartz, *Early Latin America: A History of Colonial Latin America and Brazil* (1983) is an outstanding introduction to the Iberian empires. **J. H. Parry's** *The Spanish Seaborne Empire* (1966) retains great value. **David J. Weber's** *The Spanish Frontier in North America* (1992) is easily the best introduction to its subject. For Brazil, see **John Hemming,** *Red Gold: The Conquest of the Brazilian Indians, 1500–1760* (1978).

 AMERICAN JOURNEY ONLINE
AND
INFOTRAC® COLLEGE EDITION

Visit the source collections at www.ajaccess.wadsworth.com and infotrac.thomsonlearning.com and use the Search function with the following key terms to explore documents, images, audio and video clips, articles, and commentary related to the material in this chapter.

Inca	Hernán Cortés
Maya	Tenochtitlán
Olmec	Anasazi
Mesoamerica	Cahokia
Aztecs	Christopher Columbus

GRADE AIDS

Visit the Liberty Equality Power Companion Web Site for resources specific to this textbook: http://history.wadsworth.com/murrin_LEP4e

 The CD in the back of this book and the U.S. History Resource Center at http://history.wadsworth.com/u.s./ offer a variety of tools to help you succeed in this course, including access to quizzes; images; documents; interactive simulations, maps, and timelines; movie explorations; and a wealth of other sources.

Chapter 2

The Challenge to Spain and the Settlement of North America

© SEF/Art Resource, NY.

MODERN VIEW OF MEXICO CITY
The conquest of Mexico made Spain the richest European empire and prompted it to think in grandiose terms. This view juxtaposes the Aztec ruins of Tlateloco in the foreground against a Spanish church that is far more imposing than anything built in the English or French colonies before 1776, but their people were eager to challenge Spanish power. In the background are modern high-rise apartments.

CHAPTER OUTLINE

Catholic France and two Protestant countries, the Dutch Republic and England, challenged Spanish power in Europe and overseas. None of them planted a permanent settlement in North America before 1600. In the quarter-century after 1600, they all did. The French converted thousands of Indians. The French and Dutch brought Indian hunters into the world market by trading European goods for their furs. By 1700, the English, who coveted the land itself, had founded 12 permanent colonies in North America and others in the West Indies.

These American colonies differed as much from one another as they did from their parent cultures in Europe. Europeans, Indians, and Africans interacted in contrasting ways in this strange "New World." In Mexico and Peru, the Spaniards had set themselves up as a European ruling class over a much larger Indian population of farmers, artisans, and miners. Spain's rivals created colonies of different kinds. Some, such as Virginia and Barbados, grew staple crops with indentured servants and African slaves. New France and New Netherland developed a prosperous trade with the Indians without trying to rule them. In New England, the Puritans relied on free labor provided by hardworking family members. After 1660, the English state conquered New Netherland, and English Quakers created another free-labor society in the Delaware valley, dedicated, more than any of the others, to human equality and complete religious liberty.

C H A P T E R   F O C U S

♦ Why did more Indians choose to become Catholics rather than Protestants?

♦ Why did Englishmen, crossing the Atlantic at nearly the same time, create such radically different societies in the Chesapeake colonies, the West Indies, and New England?

♦ How did England's Restoration colonies differ from those founded before 1660?

♦ If Pennsylvania really was the political failure described by many contemporaries, how could it have become such a spectacular economic success?

⚫ The Protestant Reformation and the Challenge to Spain

Spain, the most militantly Catholic society in Europe, did its best to crush the Protestant Reformation. Many of Spain's European enemies became Protestants during the 16th century and had strong religious motives for exposing Spanish "cruelties" in the Americas. Most Protestants, however, proved no more humane than the Spaniards in their own dealings with Indians.

By the time Spain's enemies felt strong enough to challenge Spain overseas, the Protestant Reformation had shattered the religious unity of Europe. In November 1517, not long before Cortés landed in Mexico, Martin Luther nailed his 95 Theses to the cathedral door at Wittenberg in the German electorate of Saxony and touched off the Reformation. No human act, or "good work," Luther insisted, can be meritorious in the sight of God. Salvation comes through faith alone, and God grants saving faith only to those who hear his Word preached to them, struggle to understand it, and admit that, without God's grace, they are damned. Within a generation, the states of northern Germany and Scandinavia had embraced Lutheranism, but the Lutheran Church never played a major role in founding colonies overseas. Calvinism did.

John Calvin, a French Protestant, also embraced justification by faith alone and put his own militant principles into practice in the Swiss canton of Geneva. The Huguenot movement in France, the Dutch Reformed Church in the Netherlands, and the Presbyterian Kirk (or Church) of Scotland all embraced Calvin's principles, as set forth in *The Institutes of the Christian Religion* (1536). In England, the Anglican Church adopted Calvinist doctrines but not forms of worship, a compromise that prompted the Puri-

C H R O N O L O G Y

1517 Luther begins the Protestant Reformation

1577–80 Drake circumnavigates the globe

1580s Gilbert claims Newfoundland for England (1583) • Ralegh twice fails to colonize Roanoke Island (1585–87) • England repels attack by the Spanish Armada (1588)

1607 English settlement established at Jamestown

1608 Champlain founds Quebec

1609 Virginia receives sea-to-sea charter

1613–14 Rolfe grows tobacco, marries Pocahontas

1618 Sandys implements London Company reforms

1619 First Africans arrive in Virginia • House of Burgesses and Headright system created

1620s Pilgrims adopt Mayflower Compact, land at Plymouth (1620) • Dutch West India Company chartered (1621) • Opechancanough launches war of extermination in Virginia (1622) • King assumes direct control of Virginia (1624) • Minuit founds New Amsterdam (1626)

1630s Puritans settle Massachusetts Bay (1630) • Maryland chartered (1632) • Williams founds Providence; Hooker founds Hartford (1636) • Anne Hutchinson banished to Rhode Island; Minuit founds New Sweden (1638) • New Haven Colony founded (1639)

1640s Massachusetts "Body of Liberties" passed (1641) • English civil wars begin (1642) • Pavonia Massacre in New Netherland (1643) • Charles I beheaded (1649)

1655 New Netherland conquers New Sweden • Quakers invade New England

1660s Charles II restored to English throne (1660) • Puritans institute Half-Way Covenant (1662) • First Carolina charter granted (1663) • New Netherland surrenders to the English (1664) • New Jersey becomes a separate colony (1665) • Carolina's Fundamental Constitutions proposed (1669)

1670s First permanent English settlement established in South Carolina (1670) • Dutch retake New York (1673–74) • West New Jersey approves Concessions and Agreements (1677)

1680s Charleston founded (1680) • Pennsylvania charter granted (1681) • New York and Pennsylvania each adopt a Charter of Liberties (1683)

1705 Virginia adopts comprehensive slave code

tan reform movement toward a more thoroughly Calvinist Church of England. Calvinists won major victories over Catholics in Europe in the last half of the 16th century. After 1620, Puritans carried their religious vision across the Atlantic to New England.

Calvinists rejected papal supremacy, the seven sacraments (they kept only baptism and the Lord's Supper),

Theodore de Bry.

SPANIARDS TORTURING INDIANS, AS DEPICTED BY THEODORE de BRY, LATE 16TH CENTURY

Among Protestants in northern Europe, images such as this one merged into a "black legend" of Spanish cruelty, which in turn helped justify their own challenge to Spanish power overseas. But in practice, the behavior of Protestant settlers toward Indians was often as harsh as anything the Spaniards had done.

clerical celibacy, veneration of the saints, and the acts of charity and the penitential rituals by which Catholics tried to earn grace and store up merits. They denounced these rites as "work righteousness." Calvin gave central importance to predestination. According to that doctrine, God decreed, even before creating the world, who will be saved and who will be damned. Christ died, Calvin insisted, not for all humankind, but only for God's elect. Calvinists kept the Lord's Supper, but in denying that Christ is actually present in the bread and wine, they broke with Luther as well as with Rome. Because salvation and damnation were beyond human power to alter, Calvinists—especially English Puritans—felt a compelling inner need to find out whether they were saved. They struggled to recognize in themselves a conversion experience, the process by which God's elect discovered that they were among the chosen.

France, the Netherlands, and England, all with powerful Protestant movements, challenged Spanish power in Europe. Until 1559, France was the main threat, with Italy as the battleground, but Spain won that phase. In the 1560s, with France embroiled in its own Wars of Religion, a new challenge came from the 17 provinces of the Netherlands, which Spain ruled. The Dutch rebelled against the heavy taxes and severe Catholic orthodoxy imposed by Philip II. As Spanish armies put down the rebellion in

the 10 southern provinces (modern Belgium), merchants and Protestants fled north. Many went to Amsterdam, which replaced Spanish-controlled Antwerp as the economic center of northern Europe. The seven northern provinces gradually took shape as the Dutch Republic, or the United Provinces of the Netherlands. The Dutch turned their resistance into a war for independence from Catholic Spain. The conflict lasted 80 years until 1648, drained Spanish resources, and spread to Asia, Africa, and America. England long remained on the edges of this European struggle, only to emerge in the end as the biggest winner overseas.

New France

About 16 million people lived in France in 1500, more than three times the population of Spain. The French made a few stabs at overseas expansion before 1600, but with little success. "The sun shines for me as for the others," growled King Francis I (1515–47) when reminded that the pope had divided all non-Christian lands between Spain and Portugal. "I should like to see the clause of Adam's will which excludes me from a share of the world."

Early French Explorers

In 1524, Francis sent Giovanni da Verrazano, an Italian, to America in search of a northwest passage to Asia. (Magellan's voyage had shown how difficult it was to sail around South America and across the Pacific.) Verrazano explored the North American coast from the Carolinas to Nova Scotia and noted Manhattan's superb potential as a harbor but found no passage to Asia. Between 1534 and 1543, Jacques Cartier made three voyages to North America. He sailed up the St. Lawrence River in search of Saguenay, a wealthy kingdom rumored to be in the interior. Instead, he discovered the severity of a Canadian winter and gave up. For the rest of the century, the French ignored Canada, except for a few fur traders and for fishermen who descended on Newfoundland each year in growing numbers. By the 1580s, the Canadian fisheries rivaled New Spain in the volume of shipping they employed.

After 1550, the French turned to warmer climates. Some Huguenots briefly challenged the Portuguese in Brazil. Others sacked Havana, prompting Spain to turn it into a fortified, year-round naval base under the command of Admiral Pedro Menéndez de Avilés. Still others planted a settlement on the Atlantic coast of Florida. Menéndez attacked them in 1565, talked them into surrendering, and then executed every man who refused to accept the Catholic faith. He did spare some women and children.

In France, the Wars of Religion blocked further efforts at expansion for the rest of the 16th century. King Henry IV (1589–1610), a Protestant, converted to Catholicism and granted limited toleration to Huguenots through the Edict of Nantes in 1598, thus ending the civil wars for the rest of his reign. Henry was a *politique;* he insisted that the survival of the state take precedence over religious differences. Moreover, he believed in toleration for its own sake. Another *politique* was the Catholic soldier and explorer Samuel de Champlain.

Missions and Furs

Champlain, whose mother may have been a Huguenot, believed that Catholics and Huguenots could work together, Europeanize the Indians, convert them, and even marry them. Before his death in 1635, he made 11 voyages to Canada. During his second trip (1604–06), he planted a predominantly Huguenot settlement in Acadia (Nova Scotia). In 1608, he sailed up the St. Lawrence River, established friendly relations with the Montagnais, Algonquin, and Huron Indians, and founded Quebec. "Our sons shall wed your daughters," he told them, "and we shall be one people." Many Frenchmen cohabited with Indian women, but only 15 formal marriages took place between them in the 17th century. Champlain's friendliness toward the Indians of the St. Lawrence valley also had some unpleasant consequences: It drew him into their wars against the Iroquois Five Nations farther south. At times, Iroquois hostility almost destroyed New France.

Champlain failed to unite Catholics and Protestants in mutual harmony. Huguenots in France were eager to trade with Canada, but few settled there. Their ministers showed no interest in converting the Indians, whereas Catholic priests became zealous missionaries. In 1625, the French Crown declared that only the Catholic faith could

HISTORY THROUGH FILM

Black Robe (1991)

Directed by Bruce Beresford. Starring Lothaire Bluteau (Father Laforgue), Aden Young (Daniel), Jean Brusseau (Samuel de Champlain), and Sandrine Holt (Annuka).

In *Black Robe*, director Bruce Beresford has given us the most believable film portrayal of 17th-century North America—both the landscape and its peoples—yet produced. This Canada–Australia co-production won six Genie Awards (Canada's equivalent of the Oscar), including best picture, best director, and best cinematography.

The film is based on Brian Moore's novel of the same title, and Moore wrote the screenplay. It was filmed on location amid the spectacular scenery in the Lac St. Jean/Saguenay region of Quebec.

In New France in the 1630s, Father Laforgue (Lothaire Bluteau), a young Jesuit, and Daniel (Aden Young), his teenaged assistant and translator, leave on Laforgue's first mission assignment. Samuel de Champlain (Jean Brusseau), the governor of the colony, has persuaded the Algonquin tribe to convey the two to their mission site among the Hurons, far in the interior.

Before long, Daniel falls in love with Annuka (Sandrine Holt), the beautiful daughter of Algonquin chief Chomina (August Schellenberg). When the priest inadvertently watches the young couple make love, he knows that, according to his faith, he has committed a mortal sin. From that point, his journey into the North American heartland threatens to become a descent into hell.

The Algonquins, guided by a dream quest, pursue a logic that makes no sense to the priest. Conversely, his religious message baffles them. Even so, when Chomina is wounded and Laforgue and Daniel are captured by the Iroquois, Annuka seduces their lone guard, kills him, and enables all four of them to escape. Chomina dies of his wounds, politely but firmly rejecting baptism until the end. What Indian, he asks, would want to go to the Christian heaven, populated by many black robes but none of his ancestors?

With the priest's approval, Daniel and Annuka go off by themselves. Laforgue reaches the mission, only to find many of the Indians dead or dying from some European disease. As the film closes, we learn that smallpox would

be practiced in New France, thus ending Champlain's dream of a colony that was more tolerant than France. Acadia soon became Catholic as well.

Early New France is a tale of missionaries and furs, of attempts to convert the Indians and of efforts to trade with them. The career of Etienne Brûlé, the first French *coureur de bois* (roamer of the woods), illustrates how incompatible these goals could be. Champlain left this teenage lad with the Indians in the winter of 1610 to learn their languages and customs. Brûlé absorbed more than that. He enjoyed hunting, the sexual permissiveness of Indian culture, and the chance to go where no European had ever been. He soon forgot most of his Christian training. Once, when he was about to be tortured to death by Indians, he tried to cry out to God, but the only prayer he could recall was, ominously, grace before meals. Desperate, he flashed a religious medal, and, when a thunderclap signaled divine approval, the Indians released him. Brûlé

apparently learned little from that experience. In 1632, he was caught robbing an Indian grave and was executed and eaten by the offended tribe. *Coureurs de bois,* such as Brûlé, did much for the fur trade but made life difficult for the missionaries.

After 1630, Jesuit missionaries made heroic efforts to bring Christian salvation to the wilderness. The Society of Jesus, or Jesuits, emerged in the 16th century as the Catholic Church's best-educated and most militant religious order. Uncompromising in their opposition to Protestants, Jesuits proved remarkably flexible in dealing with non-Christian peoples, from China to North America. Other missionaries insisted that Indians must be Europeanized before they could be converted, but the Jesuits disagreed. They saw nothing contradictory about a nation of Christians that retained its Indian culture. The Jesuits also tried to protect their converts from contamination by the *coureurs de bois.*

Black Robe, **based on Brian Moore's novel of the same title, is set in 17th-century North America.**

Kobal Collection/Alliance/Goldwyn.

devastate the mission in the following decade, and the Jesuits would abandon it in 1649.

Brian Moore's realism romanticizes nobody but treats both the Jesuits and the Algonquins with great respect. The screenplay drew criticism for its harsh depiction of the Iroquois, but it portrayed them through the eyes of the people they planned to torture. A smaller criticism is that Laforgue

is the lone priest on the journey during which he commits the sin of watching Daniel and Annuka make love. Jesuits, however, traveled in pairs precisely so they would always be accompanied by someone who could hear their confessions. Bruce Beresford, an Australian, directed *Breaker Morant* (1979), a highly acclaimed film set in the Boer War a century ago, and also *Driving Miss Daisy* (1989).

Theodore de Bry.

After learning to speak several Algonquian and Iroquoian dialects, the Jesuits began to convert the five confederated Huron nations and baptized several thousand of their members. The Jesuits mastered Indian languages, lived in Indian villages, accepted most Indian customs, and converted 10,000 Indians in 40 years, but this success antagonized Indians who were still attached to their own rituals. When smallpox devastated the Hurons in the 1640s, Jesuits baptized hundreds of dying victims to ensure their salvation. Many of the Indian survivors noticed that death usually followed this mysterious rite. Suspecting witchcraft, their resistance grew stronger. A second disaster occurred when the Iroquois attacked, defeated, and scattered the Hurons. Despite these setbacks, the Jesuits' courage remained strong. They were the only Europeans who measured up to Indian standards of bravery under torture. Some of them, such as Isaac Jogues and Jean de Brebeuf, died as martyrs. Even so, their efforts slowly lost ground to the fur trade, especially after the Crown assumed control of New France in 1663.

New France under Louis XIV

Royal intervention transformed Canada after 1663 when Louis XIV and his minister, Jean-Baptiste Colbert, took charge of the colony and tried to turn it into a model absolutist society—peaceful, orderly, deferential. Government was in the hands of two appointive officials: a governor-general responsible for military and diplomatic affairs, and an *intendant* who administered justice. Justice was made affordable to everyone, partly by banning lawyers. The people paid few taxes, and the church tithe was set at half its rate in France.

The governor appointed all militia officers and granted promotion through merit, not by selling commissions. When the Crown sent professional soldiers to New France after 1660, the governor put them under the command of Canadian officers, who knew the woodlands—a decision that had no parallel in the English colonies. Colbert also sent 774 young women to the St. Lawrence, to provide brides for settlers and soldiers. He offered bonuses to couples who produced large families and fined fathers whose children failed to marry while still in their teens. Between 1663 and 1700, the population of New France increased from 3,000 to about 14,000, even though close to 70 percent of 10,000 immigrants throughout the colonial era went back to France, usually to claim a tiny inheritance. About one-fourth of the population concentrated in three cities—Quebec, Three Rivers, and Montreal. Montreal, the largest, became the center of the fur trade.

Farming took hold in the St. Lawrence valley, and by the 1690s, Canada was growing enough wheat to feed itself and to give its *habitants,* or settlers, a level of comfort about equal to that of contemporary New Englanders. A new class of *seigneurs,* or gentry, claimed most of the land between Quebec and Montreal, but they had few feudal privileges and never exercised the kind of power wielded by aristocrats in France. Few of them even became militia captains, an office open to *habitants.* Yet when the Church was also the *seigneur,* as often happened near Quebec and

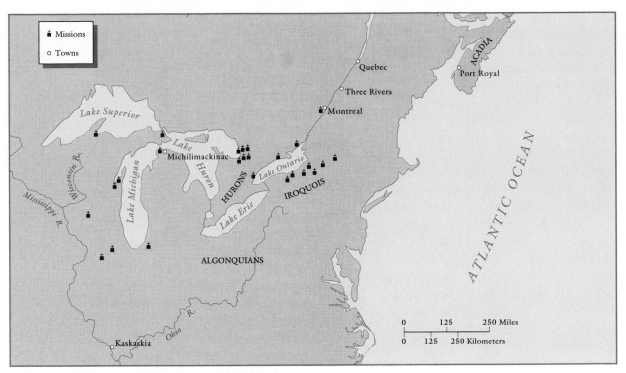

MAP 2.1 NEW FRANCE AND THE JESUIT MISSIONS
The Jesuits established Indian missions near Montreal and far into the interior of North America, most of them well beyond the range of French military aid in any emergency.

Montreal, the obligations imposed on farmers could be heavy.

Colbert even tried to ban Frenchmen from Indian territory by limiting the fur trade to annual fairs at Montreal and Quebec, thus bringing the Indians to the settlers, not the settlers to the Indians. Still, he failed to rein in the *coureurs de bois,* although a stint in the forests was becoming something a man did just once or twice in his youth, before settling down. Colbert's policy failed and, by 1700, even led to a quiet rebellion in the west. Hundreds of Frenchmen settled in the Mississippi River valley between the missions of Cahokia and Kaskaskia in what became the Illinois country. By 1750, these communities contained 3,000 residents. The settlers rejected *seigneurs,* feudal dues, tithes, and compulsory militia service. They did, however, import African slaves from Louisiana. Most settlers prospered as wheat farmers, and many married Christian Indian women from the missions.

But Canada did not long remain the center of French overseas activity. Like other Europeans, most of the French who crossed the Atlantic preferred the warmer climes of the Caribbean. At first, the French in the West Indies joined with other enemies of Spain to prey upon Spanish colonies and ships, contributing the word "buccaneer" *(boucanier)* to the English language. Then they trans-

formed the island colonies of Saint-Domingue (modern Haiti), Guadeloupe, and Martinique into centers of sugar or coffee production, where a small planter class prospered from the labor of thousands of slaves. The sugar islands were worth far more than Canada. By the late 18th century, Saint-Domingue was generating more wealth than any other colony in the world.

The Dutch and Swedish Settlements

For most of the 17th century, the Dutch were more active overseas than the French. In alliance with France during Europe's Thirty Years' War (1618–48), the Dutch wore down and finally destroyed Spain's bid for "universal monarchy" in Europe. The Netherlands, the most densely populated part of Europe, surpassed northern Italy in manufacturing and moved ahead of all competitors in finance, shipping, and trade. The Dutch Republic, with a population of 2 million by 1600, offered an ideological as well as a political challenge to Spanish absolutism.

In contrast to Spain, which stood for Catholic orthodoxy and the centralizing tendencies of Europe's "new monarchies," Dutch republicanism emphasized local liberties, prosperity, and, in major centers such as Amsterdam, informal religious toleration. Political power was decentralized to the cities and their wealthy merchants, who favored religious toleration, tried to keep trade as free as possible, and resisted the monarchical ambitions of the House of Orange. The prince of Orange usually served as *stadholder* (captain general) of Holland, the richest province, and commanded its armies, and sometimes those of other Dutch provinces as well.

The Dutch Republic—with Protestant dissenters from many countries, a sizable Jewish community, and a Catholic minority that exceeded 30 percent of the population—was actually a polyglot confederation. Amsterdam's merchant republicanism competed with the Dutch Reformed Church for the allegiance of the people. Only during a military crisis could the prince of Orange mobilize the Dutch Reformed clergy and impose something like Calvinist orthodoxy, even on the cities. The States General, to which each province sent representatives, became a weak central government for the republic. The broader public did not vote or participate actively in public life. The tension between tolerant merchant republicanism and Calvinist orthodoxy carried over into New Netherland.

Profit was the dominant motive in Dutch expansion overseas. By 1600, Dutch commercial assets were already enormous. The Bank of Amsterdam, founded in 1609, was the most important financial institution in Europe for the next century. By 1620, Dutch foreign trade probably exceeded that of the rest of Europe combined. Even during the long war with Spain, the Dutch traded with Lisbon and Seville for products from the East Indies and America. This effrontery so annoyed Philip II that he twice committed a grave blunder in the 1590s, when he confiscated all of the Dutch ships crowding his ports. The Dutch retaliated by sailing into the Atlantic and Indian Oceans to acquire colonial goods at the source. Spanish power finally crumbled. The Dutch threat forced Spain to use expensive convoys to protect the silver fleets crossing the Atlantic. Spain's supply of precious metals, after peaking in the 1590s, fell sharply in the 1630s, as the rapidly declining Indian population reduced the labor supply for the silver mines.

The East and West India Companies

In 1602, the States General chartered the Dutch East India Company, the richest corporation the world had yet seen. It pressured Spain where it was weakest, in the Portuguese East Indies. Elbowing the Portuguese out of the Spice Islands and even out of Nagasaki in Japan, the Dutch set up their own capital at Batavia (now Jakarta) on the island of Java.

The Atlantic and North America also attracted the Dutch, although never as strongly as did the East Indies. In 1609, during a 12-year truce between Spain and the Netherlands, Henry Hudson, an Englishman in Dutch service, sailed up what the Dutch called the North River (the English later renamed it the Hudson) and claimed the whole area for the Netherlands. In 1614, some Lutheran refugees from Amsterdam built a fort near modern Albany to trade with the Mahicans and Iroquois for furs, but they did not occupy the site on a year-round basis.

In 1621, when the truce expired between the Netherlands and Spain, the States General chartered the Dutch West India Company and gave it jurisdiction over the African slave trade, Brazil, the Caribbean, and North America. The West India Company harbored strong Orangist sympathies and even some Calvinist fervor, sustained by refugees fleeing from the Spanish army. Within the company, other activities—such as Piet Heyns's capture of the entire Spanish treasure fleet in 1627—were more attractive than opportunities in North America. The company took over Portugal's slave-trading posts in West Africa and for a while even dominated Angola. It also occupied the richest sugar-producing region of Brazil until the Portuguese took it back, as well as Angola, in the 1640s.

In North America, the Dutch claimed the Delaware, the Hudson, and the Connecticut river valleys. The company put most of its effort, and some of its religious fervor, into the Hudson valley. The first permanent settlers arrived in 1624. Two years later, Deacon Pierre Minuit, leading 30 Walloon (French-speaking) Protestant refugee families, bought Manhattan Island from the Indians and founded the port of New Amsterdam. The Dutch established Fort Orange (modern Albany) 150 miles upriver for trade with the Iroquois. Much like New France, New Netherland depended on the goodwill of nearby Indians, and the fur trade gave the colony a similar urban flavor. But unlike the settlers of New France, few Dutchmen ventured into the deep woods. There were no *coureurs de bois* and hardly any missionaries. The Indians brought their furs to Fort Orange and exchanged them for firearms and other goods that the Dutch sold more cheaply than anyone else.

In other ways, New Netherland resembled New France. In the 1630s, decades before the French created *seigneuries* in the St. Lawrence valley, the Dutch established "patroonships," vast estates under a single landlord, mostly along the Hudson. But patroonships never thrived, largely because few Dutch settlers had much interest in becoming peasants. The one exception was Rensselaerswyck, a gigantic estate on both banks of the Hudson above and below Fort Orange, which exported wheat and flour to the Caribbean.

New Netherland as a Pluralistic Society

New Netherland became North America's first experiment in ethnic and religious pluralism. The Dutch were a mixed people with a Flemish majority and a Walloon minority. Both came to the colony. So did Danes, Norwegians, Swedes, Finns, Germans, and Scots. One observer in the 1640s counted 18 languages spoken by the 450 inhabitants of New Amsterdam.

The government of the colony tried to utilize this diversity by drawing on two conflicting precedents from the Netherlands. On the one hand, it appealed to religious refugees by emphasizing the company's Protestant role in the struggle against Spain. This policy, roughly speaking, reflected the Orangist position in the Netherlands. On the other hand, the West India Company sometimes recognized that acceptance of religious diversity might stimulate trade. The pursuit of prosperity through toleration was the normal role of the city of Amsterdam in Dutch politics. Minuit and Pieter Stuyvesant represented the religious formula for unity, and they resisted toleration even in the name of commerce.

After Minuit returned to Europe in 1631, the emphasis shifted rapidly from piety to trade. The Dutch sold muskets to the Iroquois to expand their own access to the fur trade. They began to export grain to the Caribbean, a more elusive goal in which the patroonships were supposed to give the colony a strong agricultural base. In 1643, however, Willem Kieft, a stubborn and quarrelsome governor, slaughtered a tribe of Indian refugees to whom he had granted asylum from other Indians. This Pavonia Massacre, which took place across the Hudson from Manhattan, set off a war with nearby Algonquian nations that nearly destroyed New Netherland. By the time Stuyvesant replaced Kieft in 1647, the colony's population had fallen to about 700 people. An autocrat, Stuyvesant made peace and then strengthened town governments and the Dutch Reformed Church. During his administration, the population rose to more than 6,000 by 1664, twice that of New France. Most newcomers arrived as members of healthy families who reproduced readily, enabling the population to double once every generation.

Swedish and English Encroachments

Back in Europe, Minuit organized another refugee project, this one for Flemings who had been uprooted by the Spanish war. When Dutch authorities refused to back him, he turned for support to the Protestant kingdom of Swe-den. Financed by private Dutch capital, he returned to America in 1638 with Flemish and Swedish settlers to found New Sweden, with its capital at Fort Christina (modern Wilmington) near the mouth of the Delaware River, on land claimed by New Netherland. After Minuit died on his return trip to Europe, the colony became less Flemish and Calvinist and more Swedish and Lutheran, at a time when Stuyvesant was trying to make New Netherland an orthodox Calvinist society. The Swedes and Dutch lost another common bond in 1648 when their long war with Spain finally ended. In 1654, the Swedes seized Fort Casimir, a Dutch post that provided access to the Delaware. In response, Stuyvesant took over all of New Sweden the next year, and Amsterdam sent over settlers to guarantee Dutch control. Stuyvesant actively persecuted Lutherans in New Amsterdam but had to tolerate them in the Delaware Valley settlements. Orthodoxy and harmony were not easily reconciled.

The English, already entrenched around Chesapeake Bay to the south and New England to the east (discussed in the next section), threatened to overwhelm the Dutch as they moved from New England onto Long Island and into what is now Westchester County, New York. Kieft welcomed them in the 1640s and gave them local privileges greater than those enjoyed by the Dutch, in the hope that their farms and herds would give the colony valuable exports to the Caribbean. Stuyvesant regarded these "Yankees" (a Dutch word that probably meant "land pirates") as good Calvinists, English-speaking equivalents of his Dutch Reformed settlers. They agitated for a more active role in government, but their loyalty was questionable. If England attacked the colony, would these Puritans side with the Dutch Calvinists or the Anglican invaders? Which ran deeper, their religious or their ethnic loyalties? Stuyvesant learned the unpleasant answer when England attacked him in 1664.

☙ The Challenge from Elizabethan England

England's interest in America emerged slowly, even though ships from Bristol may have reached North America several years before Columbus's first voyage. If so, the English did nothing about it. In 1497, Henry VII (1485–1509) sent Giovanni Cabato (John Cabot), an Italian mariner who had moved to Bristol, to search for a northwest passage to Asia. Cabot probably reached Newfoundland, which he took to be part of Asia. He sailed again in 1498 with five ships but was lost at sea. Only one vessel returned, but Cabot's voyages gave England a vague claim to portions of the North American coast.

The English Reformation

When interest in America revived during the reign of Elizabeth I (1558–1603), England was rapidly becoming a Protestant kingdom. Elizabeth's father, Henry VIII (1509–47), desperate for a male heir, had broken with the pope to divorce his queen and had remarried. He proclaimed himself the "Only Supreme Head" of the Church of England, confiscated monastic lands, and opened the way for serious Protestant reformers. Under Elizabeth's younger brother, Edward VI (1547–53), the government embraced Protestantism. When Edward died, Elizabeth's older sister, Mary I (1553–58), reimposed Catholicism, burned hundreds of Protestants at the stake, and drove thousands into exile, where many of them became Calvinists. Elizabeth, however, accepted Protestantism, and in her reign the exiles returned. The Church of England, as reconstituted under Elizabeth, became an odd compromise—Calvinist in doctrine and theology, but still largely Catholic in structure, liturgy, and ritual. By the time of Elizabeth's death, England's Catholics were a tiny, fitfully persecuted minority, but one with powerful allies abroad, especially in Spain.

Some Protestants demanded a more complete reformation—the eradication of Catholic vestiges and the replacement of the Anglican Book of Common Prayer with sermons and psalms as the dominant mode of worship. These "Puritans," also called Non-Separatists, insisted they were loyal to the true Church of England and resisted any relaxation of Calvinist rigor. They would play a major role in English expansion overseas. More extreme Protestants, called Separatists, denied that the Church of England was a true church and began to set up independent congregations of their own. Some of them would found the small colony of Plymouth.

Hawkins and Drake

In 1560, England was a rather backward country of 3 million people. Its chief export was woolen cloth, most of which was shipped to the Netherlands, where the Dutch turned it into finished textiles. During the 16th century, the numbers of both people and sheep grew rapidly, and they sometimes competed for the same land. When farms were enclosed for sheep pasture, laborers were set adrift and often faced bleak prospects, creating the impression that England was overpopulated. Even without the enclosures, internal migration was becoming routine for a great many people. Thousands headed for London. Although deaths greatly outnumbered births in London, new arrivals lifted the city's population from 50,000 in 1500 to 200,000 in 1600 and, including the suburbs, to 575,000 by 1700. By then London was the largest city in Western Europe, containing more than 10 percent of England's population of 5 million. After 1600, internal migration fueled overseas settlement. Before then, interest in America centered not in London, but in the southwestern ports already involved in the Newfoundland fisheries.

Taking advantage of friendly relations that still prevailed between England and Spain, John Hawkins of Plymouth made three voyages to New Spain between 1562 and 1569. On his first trip, he bought slaves from the Portuguese in West Africa and sold them to the Spaniards in Hispaniola where, by paying all legal duties, he tried to set himself up as a legitimate trader. Spanish authorities disapproved, and on his second voyage he had to trade at gunpoint. On his third trip, the Spanish viceroy, in command of a much larger fleet, trapped his six vessels in a Mexican port. After promising Hawkins quarter, the viceroy sank four of his ships. Hawkins and his young kinsman Francis Drake escaped, both vowing vengeance.

Drake even began to talk of freeing slaves from Spanish tyranny. His most dramatic exploit came between 1577 and 1580, when he rounded Cape Horn and plundered Spanish possessions along the undefended Pacific coast of Peru. Knowing that the Spaniards would be waiting for him if he returned by the same route, he sailed north, explored San Francisco Bay, and continued west around the world to England—the first circumnavigation since Magellan's voyage more than half a century earlier. Elizabeth rewarded him with a knighthood.

Gilbert, Ireland, and America

By the 1560s, the idea of permanent colonization intrigued several Englishmen. England had a model close at hand in Ireland, which the English Crown had claimed for centuries. As of 1560, however, England had achieved little direct control over Ireland, except around Dublin. After 1560, the English tried to impose their agriculture, language, local government, legal system, aristocracy, and religion on the clan-based, mostly pastoral and Gaelic-speaking Irish. The Irish responded by becoming more intensely Roman Catholic than ever.

The English formed their preconceptions about American Indians largely from contact with the Irish who, claimed one Elizabethan, "live like beasts, void of law and all good order" and are "more uncivil, more uncleanly, more barbarous and more brutish in their customs and demeanors, than in any part of the world that is known." The English tried to conquer Ulster in the northeast and Munster in the southwest, the most Gaelic provinces.

In Ulster, the Protestant invaders drove out most of the residents and took over the land. In Munster, they ejected the Catholic leaders and tried to force the remaining Catholic Irish to become tenants under Protestant landlords. Terror became an acceptable tactic, as when the English slaughtered 200 Irish at a Christmas feast in 1574.

Sir Humphrey Gilbert, a well-educated humanist, was one of the most brutal of Elizabeth's captains in the Irish wars of the 1560s. "He thought his dogs' ears too good to hear the speech of the greatest nobleman amongst them," one admirer noted. In subduing Munster in 1569, Gilbert killed nearly everyone in his path and destroyed all of the crops, a strategy that the English later employed against Indians. Massacring women and children "was the way to kill the men of war by famine," explained one apologist. For 80 years after 1560, Ireland attracted more English settlers than all American and Caribbean colonies combined. Only after 1641, when the Irish rose and killed thousands of English settlers, did the Western Hemisphere replace Ireland as a preferred site for English colonization.

Fresh from his Irish exploits, Gilbert began to think about colonizing America. In an essay titled "A Discourse How Her Majesty May Annoy the King of Spain" (1577), he proposed that England grab control of the Newfoundland fisheries, a nursery of seamen and naval power. He urged the founding of settlements close enough to New Spain to provide bases for plundering. He obtained a royal patent in 1578 and sent out a fleet, but his ships got into a fight somewhere short of America and limped back to England. He tried again in 1583. This time his fleet sailed north to claim Newfoundland. The crews of 22 Spanish and Portuguese fishing vessels and 18 French and English ships listened in astonishment as he read his royal patent to them, divided up the land among them, assigned them rents, and established the Church of England among this mostly Catholic group. He then sailed away to explore more of the American coast. His own ship went under during a storm.

Ralegh, Roanoke, and War with Spain

Gilbert's half-brother, Sir Walter Ralegh (or Raleigh), obtained his own patent from the queen and tried twice to plant a colony in North America. In 1585, he sent a large expedition to Roanoke Island in Pamlico Sound, but the settlers planted no crops and exasperated the Indians with demands for food during a time of drought. In June 1586, the English killed the local chief, Wingina, whose main offense was apparently a threat to resettle his people on the mainland and leave the colonists to starve—or work. Days later, when the expected supply vessels failed to arrive on schedule, the colonists sailed back to England on the ships of Sir Francis Drake, who had just burned the Spanish city of St. Augustine with the support of Florida Indians, whom he freed from service to the Spanish. The supply ships reached Roanoke a little later, only to find the site abandoned. They left a small garrison there and sailed off in quest of Spanish plunder. The garrison was never heard from again.

Ralegh sent a second expedition to Roanoke in 1587, one that included some women—an indication that he envisioned a permanent colony, not just an outpost for raiding New Spain. When Governor John White went back to England for more supplies, his return to Roanoke was delayed by the assault of the Spanish Armada on England in 1588. By the time he reached Roanoke in 1590, the settlers had vanished, leaving a cryptic message— "CROATOAN"—carved on a tree. The colonists may have settled among the Chesapeake nation of Indians near the entrance to Chesapeake Bay. Sketchy evidence suggests that the Powhatans, the most powerful Indians in the area, wiped out the Chesapeakes, along with any English living with them, in spring 1607, just as an English fleet arrived in the bay.

The Spanish Armada touched off a war that lasted until 1604. The exploits of Hawkins, Drake, and Ralegh helped provoke this conflict, as did Elizabeth's intervention in the Dutch war against Spain. The loss of the Armada, first to nimbler English ships in the English Channel and then to fierce storms off the Irish coast, crippled Spain. The war also strained England's resources.

By 1600, Richard Hakluyt the elder and his cousin Richard Hakluyt the younger were publishing accounts of English exploits overseas and offering advice on how to make future colonization efforts more successful. The Hakluyts celebrated the deeds of Hawkins, Drake, Gilbert, and Ralegh, who were all West Country men with large ambitions and limited financial resources. Although their plundering exploits continued to pay, they could not afford to sustain a colony such as Roanoke until it could return a profit. But beginning in the 1590s, London became intensely involved in American affairs by launching privateering fleets against Spain. Even though London merchants remained more interested in trade with India, the Mediterranean, and Muscovy than in North American projects, the city's growing involvement with Atlantic privateering marked a significant shift. The marriage of London capital to West Country experience would permit Virginia to succeed where earlier settlements had failed.

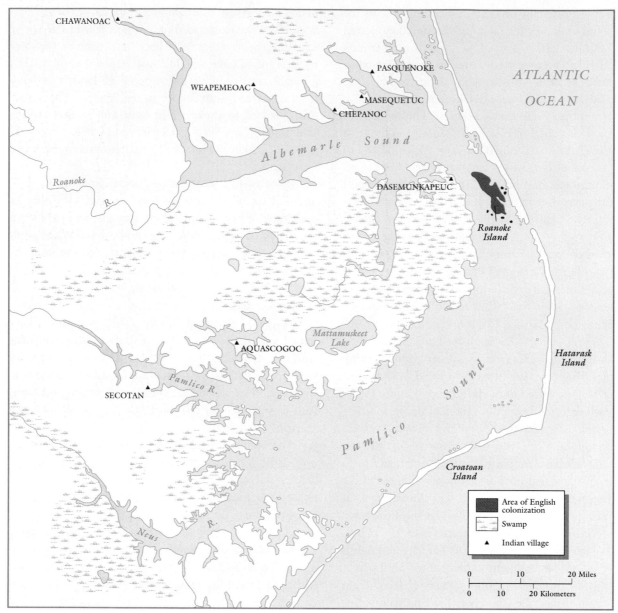

MAP 2.2   ROANOKE COLONY, 1584–1590
Roanoke marked the first English attempt to plant a permanent colony in North America.

The Swarming of the English

In the 17th century, more than 700,000 people sailed from Europe or Africa to the English colonies in North America and the Caribbean. Most of the European migrants were unmarried younger sons. With no inheritance at home, they hoped to improve their lot in a warmer climate. Instead, most spent their time trying to stay alive under the threat of malaria, typhoid fever, and other lethal maladies. Most of the Europeans arrived as servants. At first, at least some of the Africans were regarded as servants rather than slaves. Most of the men, whether Europeans or Africans, never fathered children.

The Europeans who settled in New England or the Hudson and Delaware valleys were the most fortunate. Because Puritans and Quakers migrated as families into wholesome and healthy regions, their population expanded at a rate far beyond anything known in Europe. The descendants of this small, idealistic minority soon became a substantial part of the total population, and they played a role in American history far out of proportion to their original numbers. As the accompanying table shows, the New England and Middle Atlantic colonies together attracted only 5.4 percent of the immigrants, but by 1700, they contained 37 percent of all the people in the English colonies and 55 percent of the Europeans.

THE PATTERN OF SETTLEMENT IN THE ENGLISH COLONIES UP TO 1700

Region	Who Came (in thousands)		Population in 1700 (in thousands)	
	Europeans	Africans	Europeans	Africans
West Indies	220 (29.6%)	316 (42.5%)	33 (8.3%)	115 (28.8%)
South	135 (18.1%)	30 (4.0%)	82 (20.5%)	22 (5.5%)
Mid-Atlantic	20 (2.7%)	2 (0.3%)	51 (12.8%)	3 (0.8%)
New England	20 (2.7%)	1 (0.1%)	91 (22.8%)	2 (0.5%)
Total	395 (53.1%)	349 (46.9%)	257 (64.4%)	142 (35.6%)

The Chesapeake and West Indian Colonies

In 1606, King James I of England (1603–25) chartered the Virginia Company with authority to colonize North America between the 34th and 45th parallels. The company had two headquarters. One, in the English city of Plymouth, raised only a small amount of capital but won jurisdiction over the northern portion of the grant. Known as the Plymouth Company, it carried on the West Country expansionist traditions of Gilbert and Ralegh. In 1607, it planted a colony at Sagadahoc on the coast of Maine. But the colonists found the cold winter intimidating, and when the Abenaki Indians refused to trade with them, they abandoned the site in September 1608. The Plymouth Company ran out of money and gave up.

The other branch, which had its offices in London, decided to colonize the Chesapeake Bay area. In 1607, the London Company sent out three ships carrying 100 men and 4 boys. They sailed up the Powhatan River (which they renamed the James), landed at a defensible peninsula, built a fort and other crude buildings, and called the place Jamestown. The investors hoped to find gold or silver, a northwest passage to Asia, a cure for syphilis, or other valuable products for sale in Europe. The settlers expected to persuade or compel local Indians to work for them, much as the Spanish had done. If the Indians proved hostile, the settlers were told to form alliances with more distant Indians and subdue those who resisted. Company officials did not realize that a war chief named Powhatan ruled virtually all of the Indians below the fall line.[1] He

had no rival within striking distance. The company's other expectations proved equally skewed.

The Jamestown Disaster

Jamestown was a deathtrap. Every summer, the James River became contaminated around Jamestown and sent out killing waves of dysentery and typhoid fever. Before long, malaria also set in. Only 38 of the original 104 colonists survived the first year. Of the 325 who came before 1609, fewer than 100 remained alive in the spring of that year.

The survivors owed their good fortune to the resourcefulness of Captain John Smith, a soldier and adventurer who outmaneuvered other members of the colony's ruling council and took charge. When his explorations uncovered neither gold or silver nor any quick route across the continent to Asia, he concentrated instead on sheer survival. He tried to awe Powhatan, maintain friendly relations with him, and buy corn. Powhatan captured Smith in December 1607, and they worked out an uneasy truce, but Powhatan was deeply suspicious. "Some doubt I have of your coming hither, that makes me not so kindly seeke to relieve you," he declared, ". . . for many do informe me, your coming is not for trade, but to invade my people and possesse my Country." But food remained scarce among the English. The colony had too many gentlemen and specialized craftsmen (including a perfumer) who considered farming beneath their dignity. Over their protests, Smith set them to work raising grain for four hours a day.

In 1609, the London Company sent out 600 more settlers under Lieutenant Governor Thomas Gates, but his ship ran aground on Bermuda, and the crew spent a year building another vessel. About 400 new settlers reached Virginia before Gates arrived. After suffering a severe injury in an explosion, Smith was shipped back to England, and the colony lacked firm leadership for the next year. Wearying Powhatan with their endless demands for corn at a time of severe drought, the settlers provoked the

---

[1] The *fall line*, defined by the first waterfall encountered on each river by a vessel sailing inland from the sea, marked a significant barrier to penetration of the continent. In the South, the area below the falls is called the *tidewater*. The land between the falls and the Appalachians is called the *piedmont*.

The Toast of London: Pocahontas

By all accounts, Pocahontas was the favorite daughter of her father, Powhatan, the most powerful Indian chief between the fall line and Chesapeake Bay south of the Potomac River as of 1607. After Indians captured Captain John Smith in December 1607, the 11- or 12-year-old girl may have saved his life and impelled Smith and Powhatan toward a mutual understanding, but if so Smith never mentioned the incident until 1624, years after her death. She clearly grew fond of Smith and visited him often in Jamestown.

After Smith returned to England, war broke out between Powhatan's people and the settlers in 1609 and lasted intermittently until 1614. Probably to protect Pocahontas, Powhatan placed her with the distant Potomac Indians, but they were eager to trade with the English and betrayed her to them. Carried as a prisoner to Jamestown, she charmed the widower John Rolfe so completely that he fell in love with her and, after she promised to become a Christian, he married her with the governor's permission. She took Rebecca as her Christian name. The wedding improved relations between the settlers and Powhatan, and they made peace.

Rolfe also developed a strain of tobacco milder than the local variety, shipped it to England, and got an excellent price for it. In effect, he started Virginia's first export boom, for the whole colony soon took to raising tobacco.

In 1616, Rolfe and Pocahontas sailed for England. For nearly a year they became one of London's top sensations, welcome at court, moving in the most prestigious social circles, and attending the theater. The couple also had a son whom they named Thomas. After nearly a year in the capital, the two decided to return to Virginia, but Pocahontas became seriously ill before the ship could reach the English Channel. She was taken ashore at Gravesend, where she died on March 21, 1617. By then she was already the best known Indian in the English-speaking world. Rolfe left Thomas with an uncle in England and returned to Virginia. Thomas, in turn, fathered numerous descendants.

The inscription around the portrait says "Matoaka [one of her Indian names] alias Rebecca [her baptismal name] daughter of the powerful Prince Powhatan, Emperor of Virginia."

Indian war that Smith had avoided. They almost starved during winter 1610. One settler was executed for cannibalizing his wife. Two were tied to posts and left to starve to death for raiding company stores. Some escaped to the Indians, but those who were caught fleeing were executed.

When Gates finally reached Jamestown with 175 colonists in June 1610, he found only 60 settlers alive (plus a garrison at Point Comfort) and the food supply nearly exhausted. Gates despaired, packed everyone aboard ship, and started downriver. Virginia was going the way of Roanoke and Sagadahoc, despite its greater resources. Instead, the small fleet came abreast of the new governor, Thomas West, baron de la Warr, sailing up the James with 300 new colonists. They all went back to Jamestown, and the colony managed to survive.

De la Warr and Gates found themselves in the middle of the colony's first Indian war, which lasted from 1609 to 1614. Powhatan's warriors picked off any settlers who strayed far from Jamestown. The English retaliated by slaughtering whole villages and destroying crops, as they had in Ireland. In August 1610, for example, Commander George Percy attacked the Paspahegh Indians, who had

CAPTAIN JOHN SMITH SUBDUING OPECHANCANOUGH, THE WARRIOR CHIEF OF THE PAMUNKEY INDIANS, 1608

Note the difference in height between Opechancanough and Smith, even as depicted by a European artist.

William C. Clements Library, University of Michigan, Ann Arbor.

refused to give the colonists more corn and had sheltered runaways. He burned the Paspahegh's crops, massacred most of them, captured the "queen" and her children, and started back to Jamestown by boat. When the soldiers murmured because "the queen and her children were spared," Percy had the children thrown overboard and let his men shoot "out their brains in the water." At Jamestown, a settler suggested burning the queen alive. Percy, feeling merciful, had her put to the sword instead. Percy's strategy was terroristic. The slaughter of one tribe might intimidate others. The war finally ended after the English captured Pocahontas, Powhatan's favorite daughter, and used her as a hostage to negotiate peace.

Despite the Indian war, the colony's prospects improved after 1610. The governors imposed martial law on the settlers and sent some of them to healthier locations, such as Henrico, 50 miles upstream. Through the efforts of John Rolfe, the colony began to produce a cash crop. In 1613, Rolfe imported a mild strain of tobacco from the West Indies. It brought such a good price in England that the king—who had insisted no one could build a colony

"upon smoke"—was proved wrong. Soon, settlers were even growing tobacco in the streets of Jamestown.

Reorganization, Reform, and Crisis

In 1609, a new royal charter extended Virginia's boundaries to the Pacific, although no one yet knew how far away that was. A third charter in 1612 made the London Company a joint-stock company. It resembled a modern corporation except that each stockholder had only one vote regardless of how many shares he owned. The stockholders met quarterly in the company's General Court but entrusted everyday management to the company's treasurer, who until 1618 was Sir Thomas Smyth, a wealthy London merchant. The lack of profits led to turmoil among the stockholders, who replaced Smyth in 1618 with Sir Edwin Sandys, the Puritan son of the archbishop of York.

In 1618, the company adopted an ambitious reform program for Virginia. It encouraged economic diversification, such as glassblowing, planting grape vines, and raising silkworms. English common law replaced martial law. The settlers were allowed to elect their own assembly, the House of Burgesses, to meet with the governor and his council and make local laws. Finally—the most popular reform—settlers were permitted to own land. Under this "headright" system, a colonist received 50 acres for each person whose passage to Virginia he financed. By 1623, Sandys had shipped 4,000 settlers to Virginia, but the economic diversification program failed. Only tobacco found a market. Corn still provided most of the food. Instead of growing silkworms and grapes, Virginians raised Indian crops with Indian methods, which meant using hoes instead of plows.

The flood of newcomers strained the food supply and soured relations with the Indians, especially after Powhatan died and was succeeded by his militant brother, Opechancanough. On Good Friday in March 1622, the new chief launched an attack that was intended to wipe out the whole colony. Without a last-minute warning from a friendly Indian, Jamestown might not have survived. As it turned out, 347 settlers were killed that day, and most of the outlying settlements were destroyed. Newcomers who arrived in subsequent months had nowhere to go and, with food again scarce, hundreds died over the winter. "Oh, that you did see my daily and hourly sighs, groans, and tears, and thumps that I afford my own breast, and rue and curse the time of my birth, with holy Job," complained Richard Frethorne, a servant, to his parents a year after the massacre. "I thought no head had been able to hold so much water as hath and doth daily flow from mine eyes."

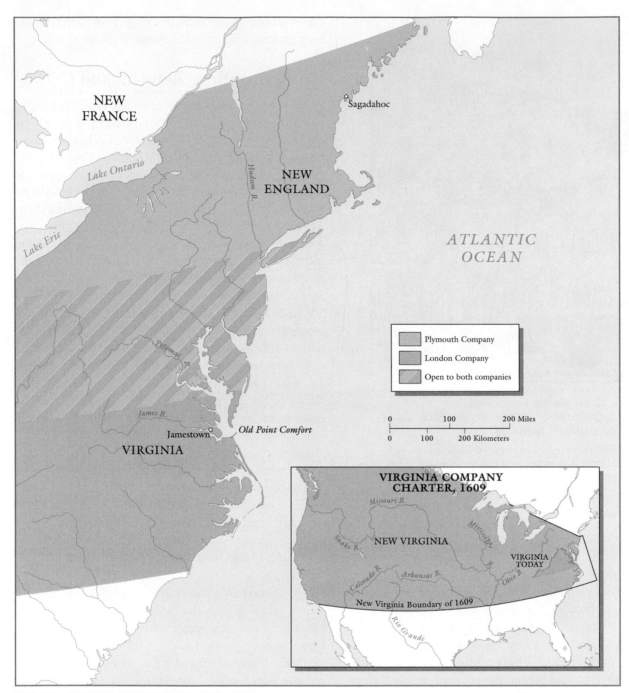

MAP 2.3   VIRGINIA COMPANY CHARTER, 1606

This charter gave the Plymouth Company jurisdiction over what would become New England and New York, and the London Company jurisdiction over most of what became Virginia and North Carolina. They shared jurisdiction over the intervening area. The insert map shows Virginia's revised sea-to-sea boundaries laid out in the 1609 charter.

Back in London, Smyth and his allies turned against Sandys, withdrew their capital, and asked the king to intervene. A royal commission visited the colony and found only 1,200 settlers alive out of the 6,000 sent over since 1607. In 1624, the king declared the London Company bankrupt and assumed direct control of Virginia, making it the first royal colony, with a governor and council appointed by the Crown. The London Company had invested some £200,000 in the enterprise, equal to £1,400 or £1,500 for every surviving settler, at a time when skilled English craftsmen were lucky to earn £50 per year. Such extravagance guaranteed that future colonies would be organized in different ways.

Tobacco, Servants, and Survival

Between Opechancanough's 1622 attack and the 1640s, Virginia proved that it could survive. Despite an appalling death rate, about a thousand new settlers came each year, and population grew slowly, to 5,200 by 1634 and 8,100 by 1640. For 10 years, the settlers warred against Opechancanough. In 1623, they poisoned 200 Indians they had invited to a peace conference. In most years, they attacked the Indians just before harvest time, destroying their crops and villages. By the time both sides made peace in 1632, all Indians had been expelled from the peninsula between the James and York rivers below Jamestown.

That area became secure for tobacco, and the export of tobacco financed the importation of indentured servants, even after the price of tobacco fell sharply in the 1630s. Most servants were young men, often desperate, who agreed to work for a term of years in exchange for the cost of passage, for bed and board during their years of service, and for modest freedom dues when their term expired. Those signing indentures in England usually had valuable skills and negotiated terms of four or five years. Those arriving without an indenture, most of whom were younger and less skilled, were sold by the ship captain to a planter. Those older than age 19 served five years, whereas those younger than 19 served until age 24. The system turned servants into freemen who hoped to prosper on their own. Most former servants became tenants for several years while they tried to save enough to buy their own land. Better tobacco prices enabled many to succeed between 1640 and 1660, but those who imported the servants were always in a stronger economic position, collecting the headright of 50 acres for each one. Because deaths still outnumbered births, the colony needed a steady flow of newcomers to survive.

In 1634, Virginia was divided into counties, each with its own justices of the peace, who sat together as the county court and, by filling their own vacancies, soon became a self-perpetuating oligarchy. Most counties also became Anglican parishes, with a church and a vestry of prominent laymen, usually the justices. The vestry managed temporal affairs for the church, including the choice of the minister. Although the king did not recognize the House of Burgesses until 1639, it met almost every year

THE OPECHANCANOUGH MASSACRE OF 1622

This famous event, as portrayed in an engraving from the workshop of Theodore de Bry, depicts the warriors as treacherous, bloodthirsty savages and the settlers as innocent victims.

after 1619 and was well established by 1640. Before long, only a justice could hope to be elected as a burgess.

Until 1660, many former servants managed to acquire land, and some even served on the county courts and in the House of Burgesses. As tobacco prices fell after 1660, however, upward mobility became more difficult. Political offices usually went to the richest 15 percent of the settlers, those able to pay their own way across the Atlantic. They, and eventually their descendants, monopolized the posts of justice of the peace and vestryman, the pool from which burgesses and councillors were normally chosen. Virginia was becoming an oligarchy, and after 1660, resentments became increasingly acute among those shut off from power and unable to prosper.

Maryland

Maryland had different origins but became much the same kind of society as Virginia. It grew out of the social and religious vision of Sir George Calvert and his son Cecilius, both of whom became Catholics and looked to America as a refuge for persecuted English and Irish people of that faith. Sir George, a prominent officeholder, had invested in the London Company. When he resigned his royal office because of his Catholicism, King James I made him baron Baltimore in the Irish peerage. Both James and Charles I (1625–49) encouraged his colonial projects.

TOBACCO LABORER, ST. MARY'S CITY, MARYLAND

St. Mary's City has been reconstructing the 17th-century Chesapeake world through archaeology and other modern scholarship. This scene illustrates labor patterns during the era of indentured servitude.

The Maryland charter of 1632 made Baltimore "lord proprietor" of the colony. It came close to making Baltimore king within Maryland, the most sweeping delegation of power that the Crown could grant. After 1630, most new colonies were proprietary projects, often with the Maryland charter as a model. Many of them embodied the distinctive social ideals of their founders.

George Calvert died as the Maryland patent was being issued, and Cecilius inherited Maryland and the peerage. Like Champlain, he believed that Catholics and Protestants could live in peace in the same colony, but he expected the servants, most of whom were Protestants, to continue to serve the Catholic gentlemen of the colony after their indentures expired. Baltimore made the gentlemen manor lords, with the power to preside over courts leet and courts baron, feudal tribunals that were nearly obsolete in England.

Those plans were never fulfilled. The condition of English Catholics improved under Charles I and his queen, Henrietta Maria, a French Catholic for whom the province was named. Because few Catholics emigrated, most settlers were Protestants. The civil war that erupted in England in 1642 (see following discussion) soon spread to Maryland. Protestants overthrew Lord Baltimore's regime several times between 1642 and 1660, but the English state always sided with him, even when the Puritans were in power there. During these struggles, Baltimore conceded a bicameral legislature to the colony, knowing that Protestants would dominate the elective assembly and that Catholics would control the appointive council. He also approved the Toleration Act of 1649, which granted freedom of worship to Christians (but not to Maryland's tiny Jewish minority).

The manorial system did not survive these upheavals. Protestant servants, after their indentures expired, acquired their own land rather than become tenants under Catholic manor lords, most of whom died or returned to England. When Maryland's unrest ended around 1660, the colony was raising tobacco, corn, and livestock and was governed by county courts similar to those in Virginia. If anything, the proprietary family's Catholicism and its claims to special privileges made the Maryland assembly more articulate than the Virginia House of Burgesses in demanding the liberties of Englishmen. Otherwise, religion provided the biggest difference between the two colonies. Virginia was Anglican, but Maryland had no established church and no vestries. Most Maryland Protestants had to make do without ministers until the 1690s.

Chesapeake Family Life

In the 1620s, European men outnumbered women in Virginia by at least 5 to 1. Among new immigrant servants as late as the 1690s, the ratio was still 5 to 2. Population became self-sustaining about 1680, when live births finally began to outnumber deaths. Among adults, this transition made little difference before 1700. Until then, most prominent people were immigrants.

Life expectancy slowly improved as the colonists planted orchards to provide wholesome cider to drink, but it still remained much lower than in England, where those who survived childhood could expect to live into their

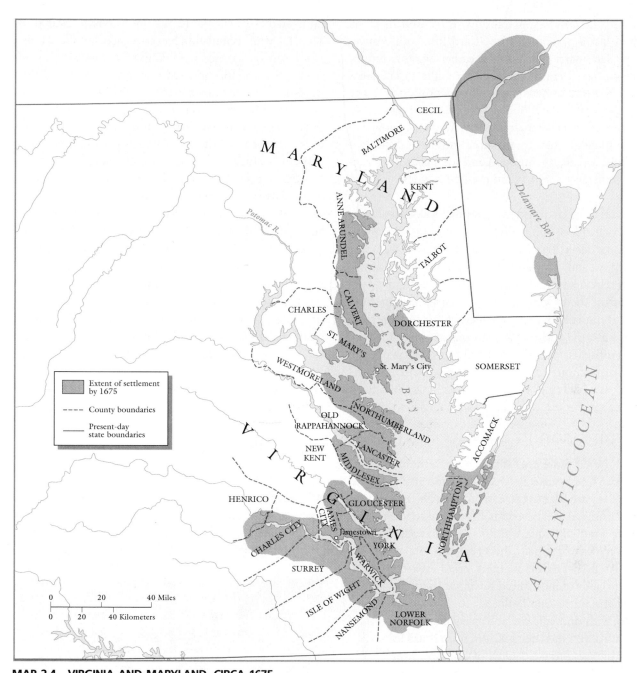

MAP 2.4 VIRGINIA AND MARYLAND, CIRCA 1675
Nearly 70 years after the founding of Jamestown, settlement remained confined to the tidewater and the eastern shore.

fifties. The Chesapeake immigrants had survived childhood diseases in Europe, but men at age 20 could expect to live only to about 45, with 70 percent dead by age 50. Women died at even younger ages, especially in areas ravaged by malaria, a dangerous disease for pregnant women. In those places, women rarely lived to age 40. England's patriarchal families found it hard to survive in the Chesapeake. About 70 percent of the men never married or, if they did, produced no children. Most men waited years after completing their service before they could marry.

Because women could not marry until they had finished their indentures, most spent a good part of their childbearing years unwed. About one-fifth had illegitimate children, despite severe legal penalties, and roughly one-third were pregnant on their wedding day. Virtually all women married, most as soon as they could.

In a typical Chesapeake marriage, the groom was in his thirties and the bride eight or ten years younger. Although men outlived women, this age gap meant that the husband usually died before his wife, who then quickly remarried. In one Virginia county, three-fourths of all children lost a parent, and one-third lost both. Native-born settlers married at a much earlier age than immigrants; women were often in their middle to late teens when they wed. Orphans were a major community problem. Stepparents were common because surviving spouses with property usually remarried. Few lived long enough to become grandparents. By the time the oldest child in a household was 20, the husband and wife, because of successive remarriages, might not even be that child's blood relatives.

Under these circumstances, family loyalties tended to focus on other kin—on uncles, aunts, cousins, older stepbrothers or stepsisters—thus contributing to the value that Virginia and Maryland placed on hospitality. Patriarchalism remained weak. Because fathers died young, even members of the officeholding elite that took shape after 1650 had difficulty passing on their status to their sons. Only toward the end of the 17th century were the men holding office likely to be descended from fathers of comparable distinction.

The West Indies and the Transition to Slavery

Before 1700, far more Englishmen went to the West Indies than to the Chesapeake. Between 1624 and 1640, they settled the Leeward Islands (St. Christopher, Nevis, Montserrat, and Antigua) and Barbados, tiny islands covering a little more than 400 square miles. In the 1650s, England seized Jamaica from Spain, increasing this total by a factor of 10. At first, English planters grew tobacco, using the labor of indentured servants. Then, beginning around 1645 in Barbados, sugar replaced tobacco, with dramatic social consequences. The Dutch, who were then being driven from Brazil by the Portuguese, provided some of the capital for this transition, showed the English how to raise sugar, introduced them to slave labor on a massive scale, and for a time dominated the exportation and marketing of the crop.

Sugar became so valuable that planters imported most of their food from North America rather than divert land and labor from the cash crop. Sugar required a heavy investment in slaves and mills, and large planters with many slaves soon dominated the islands. Ex-servants found little employment, and most of them left after their terms expired. Many joined the buccaneers or moved to the mainland. Their exodus hastened the transition to slavery. In 1660, Europeans out-numbered slaves in the islands by 33,000 to 22,000. By 1700, the white population had stagnated, but the number of slaves had increased sixfold. By 1775, they would triple again. Planters appropriated about 80 percent of their slaves' labor for their own profit, a rate of exploitation that had probably never been reached anywhere else. They often worked their slaves to death and then bought others to replace them. Of the 316,000 Africans imported before 1700, only 115,000 remained alive in that year.

Observers were depressed by the moral climate on the islands, where underworked and overfed planters arrogantly dominated their overworked and underfed slaves. Some of the islands were "of no advantage," remarked one governor, who thought they were "better under water than above." In 1671, another governor canvassed 40 parishes in the Leeward Islands and found just "one drunken orthodox [Anglican] priest, one drunken sectary priest, and one drunken parson." Yet the islands generated enormous wealth for the English empire, far more than the mainland colonies well into the 18th century. Around 1700, the islands sent sugar worth £710,000 per year to England at a time when Chesapeake planters were getting only £230,000 for their tobacco.

The Rise of Slavery in North America

Africans first came to Virginia in 1619 when, John Rolfe reported, a Dutch ship "sold us twenty Negars." Their status remained ambiguous for decades, even after slavery had been sharply defined in the West Indies. In Virginia

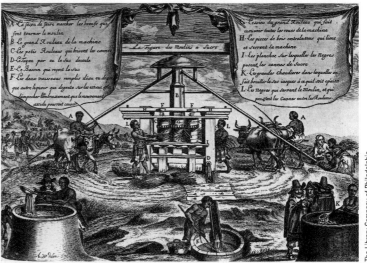

SUGAR MILL

This 1665 engraving shows an animal-powered sugar mill, worked by African slaves, in one of the French West Indian islands.

The Library Company of Philadelphia.

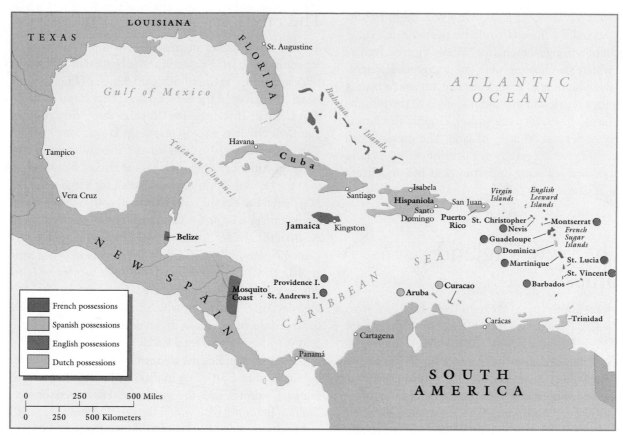

MAP 2.5   PRINCIPAL WEST INDIAN COLONIES IN THE 17TH CENTURY
Spain retained control of the large islands of Cuba, Hispaniola, and Puerto Rico while its English, French, and Dutch rivals settled the smaller but fertile islands east of Puerto Rico or south of Cuba.

and Maryland, many of the first Africans had Hispanic names. They were Creoles who had acquired a great deal of intercultural experience around the Atlantic world and were in a stronger position to negotiate with their masters than those who came later would be. Some Africans were treated as servants and won their freedom after several years. On Virginia's eastern shore, where as late as the 1660s perhaps 30 percent of African people were free, one "Anthony Johnson Negro" even became the master of other Africans, one of whom complained that Johnson held him beyond the term of his indenture. (The court backed Johnson.) But other Africans in the early years were already serving for life, and this pattern prevailed by the end of the 17th century.

This uncertainty about status is understandable. Because the English had no experience with slavery at home, a rigid caste system took time to crystallize. When Hugh Davis was whipped in 1630 "for abusing himself to the dishonor of God and shame of Christians, by defiling his body in lying with a negro," his offense may have been sodomy rather than miscegenation. The record is unclear.

Fifty years later, when Katherine Watkins, a white woman, accused John Long, a mulatto, of raping her, the neighbors (both men and women) blamed her, not him, for engaging in seductive behavior, which they described in lurid detail. The case of Elizabeth Key, a mulatto, a Christian, and the bastard daughter of Thomas Key, shows similar ambiguity. In 1655, when she claimed her freedom, her new owner fought to keep her enslaved. William Greensted, who had fathered two children by her, sued on her behalf, won, and then married her. One settler had no qualms about keeping her in bondage because of her dark skin, despite the known wishes of her deceased father. Another—Greensted—fell in love with her.

In the generation after 1680, the caste structure of the Chesapeake colonies became firmly set. Fewer indentured servants reached the Chesapeake from England, as the Delaware valley and the expanding English army and navy competed more successfully for the same young men. Slaves took their place. Some of the emerging great planters, such as William Byrd I and William Fitzhugh, made a deliberate choice after 1680 to replace indentured servants with enslaved Africans. They cost more to buy, but they served for life and could be treated more ruthlessly than other Englishmen. In 1705, the Virginia legislature, in which slaveholders were gaining greater weight, forbade the whipping of a white servant without a court's permission, a restriction that did not apply to the punishment of slaves. To attract more whites, Virginia also promised every ex-servant 50 acres of land. The message was obvious: Every white was now superior to any black. Racial caste was replacing opportunity as the organizing principle of Chesapeake society.

🫖 The New England Colonies

Captain John Smith coined the term "New England" years before the first Puritans left for America. It became an apt phrase. Other Europeans founded colonies to engage in economic activities they could not pursue at home, but the New England settlers reproduced the mixed economy of old England, with minor variations. Their family farms raised livestock and European grains, as well as corn. Their artisans specialized in many crafts, from carpentry and shipbuilding to printing. Their quarrel with England was over religion, not economics. They came to America, they insisted, to worship as God commanded, not as the Church of England required. That imperative made them critical of other English practices as well. Driven by a radical communitarian vision, the first settlers created towns, congregations, and law courts well suited to Puritan purposes while changing the English models on which they drew. Later generations were less certain of their place in the world, less eager to question English ways, and more inclined to drift back toward English models. They wanted to preserve what had already been accomplished. They became conservative communitarians.

The Pilgrims and Plymouth

As mentioned earlier in this chapter, the Pilgrims were Separatists who left England for the Netherlands between 1607 and 1609, convinced that the Church of England was no true daughter of the Reformation. They hoped to worship freely in Holland. After 10 years there, they realized that their children were growing up Dutch, not English. That fear prompted a minority of the congregation to move to America. After negotiating rather harsh terms with the London Company, they sailed for Virginia on the *Mayflower*. But the ship was blown off course late in 1620, landing first on Cape Cod and then on the mainland well north of the charter boundaries of Virginia, at a place they named Plymouth. Two-thirds of the settlers were not Separatists; they had been added to the passenger list by London investors. Before landing, the 100 passengers agreed to the Mayflower Compact, which bound them all to obey the decisions of the majority, an essential precaution in a colony with uncertain legal status.

Short on supplies, the colonists suffered keenly during the first winter. Half of them died, including all but three married women and the governor. His successor was William Bradford, who would be reelected annually for all but five years until his death in 1656. The settlers fared much better when spring came. The Patuxet Indians of the area had been wiped out by disease in 1617, but their fields were ready for planting. Squanto, the only Patuxet to survive, had been kidnapped in 1614 by coastal traders and carried to England. He had just made his way home and showed up at Plymouth one day in March 1621. He taught the settlers Indian methods of fishing and growing corn. He also introduced them to Massasoit, the powerful Wampanoag sachem (or chief), whose people celebrated the first thanksgiving feast with the settlers after the 1621 harvest. After a decade, the settlers numbered about 300. By paying off their London creditors, they gained political autonomy and private ownership of their flourishing

MASSASOIT'S PIPE

This rather whimsical artifact, popularly known as Massasoit's pipe, comes from an elite Indian grave in the Narragansett-Wampanoag country, mid-17th century, about the time that Massasoit died. He celebrated the first thanksgiving with the Pilgrims.

Museum of the American Indian/Heye Foundation, NY.

farms. During the 1630s, they founded several new towns and sold their surplus crops to the colonists flooding into Massachusetts.

Covenant Theology

A much larger Puritan exodus settled Massachusetts Bay between 1630 and 1641. The best-educated English group yet to cross the Atlantic, 130 of them had attended a university, most often Cambridge, a Puritan center. Puritans distrusted Charles I and his courtiers, especially William Laud, bishop of London and then archbishop of Canterbury, whom they accused of Catholic sympathies and of Arminianism, a heresy named for a Dutch theologian who had challenged strict Calvinists a generation earlier. To Puritans, the stakes were high indeed by the late 1620s. During that early phase of the Thirty Years' War (1618–48), Catholic armies seemed about to crush the German Reformation. Charles I blundered into a brief war against both Spain and France, raised money for the war by dubious methods, and dissolved Parliament when it protested. Puritans complained that Laud punished them for their piety but left blatant sinners alone. God's wrath would descend on England, they warned.

These matters were of genuine urgency to Puritans, who embraced what they called "covenant theology." According to this system, God had made two personal covenants with humans: the covenant of works and the covenant of grace. In the covenant of works, God had promised Adam that if he kept God's law he would never die—but Adam ate of the forbidden fruit, was expelled from the Garden of Eden, and died. All of Adam's descendants remained under the same covenant, but because of his Fall would never be capable of keeping the law. All humans deserved damnation, but God was merciful and answered sin with the covenant of grace. God would save his chosen people: "I will be their God, and they shall be my people" (Jeremiah 31:34). Everyone else would be damned: "Saith the Lord: yet I loved Jacob, and I hated Esau" (Malachi 1:3). Even though the covenant of works could no longer bring eternal life, it remained in force and established the strict moral standards that every Christian must strive to follow, before and after conversion. A Christian's inability to keep the law usually triggered the conversion experience by demonstrating that only faith, not works, could save.

At this level, covenant theology merely restated Calvinist orthodoxy, but the Puritans gave it a novel social

---

LINK TO THE PAST

A City upon a Hill

Governor John Winthrop preached a lay sermon entitled "A Model of Christian Charity" to his fellow passengers aboard the Arbella as they sailed to New England in 1630. The following passage has become the most famous part of any sermon by a New Englander in the 17th century.

For we must consider that we shall be as a City upon a Hill, the eyes of all people are upon us; so that if we shall deal falsely with our God in this work we have undertaken, and so cause Him to withdraw His present help from us, we shall be made a story and a by-word through the world. We shall open the mouths of enemies to speak evil of the ways of God and all professors [i.e., professing Christians] for God's sake; we shall shame the faces of many of God's worthy servants, and cause their prayers to be turned into Curses upon us till we be consumed out of the good land where we are going. . . . Beloved, there is now set before us life and good, death

and evil, in that we are commanded this day to love the Lord our God, and to love one another, to walk in His ways and to keep His Commandments and His Ordinances and His Laws, and the Articles of our Covenant with Him that we may live and be multiplied, and that the Lord our God may bless us in the land where we go. . . .

---

1. American popular culture regards this sermon as a celebration of the Puritan sense of mission, but why did Winthrop issue such a stark warning about the consequences of failure?

For additional sources related to this feature, visit the *Liberty, Equality, Power* Web site at:

http://history.wadsworth.com/murrin_LEP4e

dimension by pairing each personal covenant with a communal counterpart. The social equivalent of the covenant of grace was the church covenant. Each congregation organized itself into a church, a community of the elect. The founders, or "pillars," of each church, after satisfying one another of their own conversions, agreed that within their church the Gospel would be properly preached and discipline would be strictly maintained. God, in turn, promised to bestow saving grace within that church—not to everyone, of course, but presumably to most of the children of the elect. The communal counterpart of the covenant of works was the key to secular history. Puritans called it the "national" covenant. It determined not who was saved or damned, but the rise and fall of nations or peoples. As a people, New Englanders agreed to obey the law, and God promised to prosper them. They, in turn, covenanted with their magistrates to punish sinners. If magistrates enforced God's law and the people supported these efforts, God would not punish the whole community for the misdeeds of individuals. But if sinners escaped public account, God's anger would be terrible toward his chosen people of New England. God gave them much and demanded much in return.

For New Englanders, the idea of the covenant became a powerful social metaphor, explaining everything from crop failures and untimely deaths to Indian wars and political contention. Towns and militia companies used covenants to organize themselves. If only because a minister could always think of something that had missed proper correction, the covenant generated an almost automatic sense of moral crisis. It had a built-in dynamic of moral reform that was becoming obvious even before the migrants crossed the ocean.

In England, the government had refused to assume a godly role. Puritans fleeing to America hoped to escape the divine wrath that threatened England and to create in America the kind of churches that God demanded. A few hoped to erect a model "city upon a hill" to inspire all humankind. Governor John Winthrop developed this idea in a famous sermon of 1630, but this theme seldom appeared in the writings of other founders. It became more common a generation later when, ironically, any neutral observer could see that the rest of the world no longer cared what New Englanders were doing.

Massachusetts Bay

In 1629, several English Puritans obtained a charter for the Massachusetts Bay Company, a typical joint-stock corporation except for one feature: The charter did not specify where the company was to be located. Puritan investors going to New England bought out the other stockholders. Led by Winthrop, they carried the charter to America, beyond the gaze of Charles I. They used it not to organize a business corporation, but as the constitution for the colony. In the 1630s, the General Court created by the charter became the Massachusetts legislature. New England settlers came from the broad middle range of English society—few rich, few very poor. Most had owned property in England. When they sold it to go to America, they probably liquidated far more capital than the London Company had invested in Virginia. A godly haven was expensive to build.

An advance party that sailed in 1629 took over a fishing village on the coast and renamed it Salem. The Winthrop fleet brought 1,000 settlers in 1630. In small groups, they scattered around the bay, founding Dorchester, Roxbury, Boston, Charlestown, and Cambridge. Each town formed around a minister and a magistrate. The local congregation was the first institution to take shape. From it evolved the town meeting, as the settlers began to distinguish more sharply between religious and secular affairs. Soon the colonists were raising European livestock and growing English wheat and other grains, along with corn. Perhaps 30 percent of them perished during the first winter. A few hundred others grew discouraged and returned to England. Conditions after that rapidly improved, as they had at Plymouth a decade earlier. About 13,000 settlers came to Massachusetts by 1641, most as families—a unique event in Atlantic empires to that time.

Settlers did a brisk business selling grain to the newcomers arriving each year. When the flow of immigrants ceased in 1641, that trade collapsed, creating a crisis that lessened as towns improved their economic infrastructure by increasing their capacity to build ships or to raise sheep and produce woolen textiles. Towns also adopted the "warning out" system. It prohibited newcomers from settling in a town without the permission of the authorities. By limiting the mobility of labor, it kept wages below their market value. Ironically, Europe's first overseas free-labor society needed this coercive mechanism to get itself started. The region began to prosper after 1650 as Boston merchants opened up West Indian markets for New England grain, lumber, and fish. The economic success of the region depended on its ability to ship food and lumber products to colonies that grew staple crops. The very existence of colonies committed to free labor was an oddity. To prosper, they had to trade with more typical colonies, the societies elsewhere in the hemisphere that raised tobacco and sugar with unfree labor.

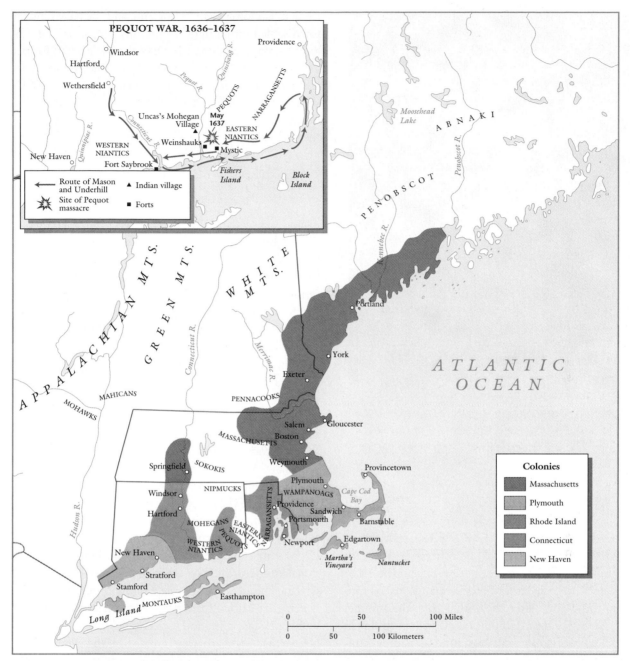

MAP 2.6   NEW ENGLAND IN THE 1640S

The five Puritan colonies spread over the Atlantic coast and nearby islands, the shores and islands of Narragansett Bay, both sides of Long Island Sound, and much of the Connecticut Valley. Although New Hampshire and Maine (not named as such on this map) were not founded by Puritans, Massachusetts extended its government over their settlers during the English civil wars. The insert map shows the principal military campaign of the Pequot War.

The region's economy imperiled Puritan orthodoxy. Few Boston merchants and almost no fishermen could meet the religious standards of a Puritan society. Although few of these men became church members in the first generation, the colony needed their services and had to put up with them. The fishing towns of Marblehead and Gloucester did little to implement Puritan values or even to found churches in the early decades, while Boston merchants increasingly favored toleration of Protestant dissenters because it would be good for business. Although these contrasts softened with time, Puritan orthodoxy was mostly a rural phenomenon.

Photograph © 2003 Museum of Fine Arts, Boston.

PORTRAIT OF ROBERT GIBBS (1670)
New Englanders did not provide distinctive garments for small boys and girls. They wore the same clothes.

Puritan Family Life

In rural areas, New Englanders soon observed a remarkable fact. After the first winter, deaths were rare. Mariners sailing to the Chesapeake noted the contrast between the sickly Virginians and the robust New Englanders. "The air of the country is sharp, the rocks many, the trees innumerable, the grass little, the winter cold, the summer hot, the gnats in summer biting, the wolves at midnight howling," one woman complained. But the place was undeniably healthy, and families grew rapidly as 6 or even 10 children reached maturity. The settlers had left most European diseases behind and had encountered no new ones in the bracing climate. For the founders and their children, life expectancy far exceeded the European norm. More than one-fifth of the men who founded Andover lived past age 80. Infant mortality fell, and few mothers died in childbirth. Because people lived so long, New England families became intensely patriarchal. Many fathers refused to grant land titles to their sons before their own deaths. In the early years, settlers often moved, looking for the richest soil, the best neighbors, and the most inspiring minister. By about 1645, most of them had found what they wanted. Migration into or out of country towns be-

came much lower than in England, and the New England town settled into a tight community that slowly became an intricate web of cousins. Once the settlers had formed a typical farming town, they grew reluctant to admit "strangers" to their midst. New Englanders largely avoided slavery, not out of sympathy for Africans or hatred of the institution, but to keep outsiders from contaminating their religion.

Conversion, Dissent, and Expansion

Among serious Puritans, competing visions of the godly society became divisive enough to spawn several new colonies. The vital force behind Puritanism was the quest for conversion. Probably because of John Cotton's stirring sermons in Boston, the settlers crossed an invisible boundary in the mid-1630s. As Cotton's converts described their religious experiences, their neighbors turned from analyzing the legitimacy of their own conversions to assessing the validity of someone else's. Afraid that Cotton's ecstatic converts had not scrutinized their own hearts with sufficient rigor, Thomas Shepard and other nearby ministers began to impose tests for regeneracy, and the standards of acceptance escalated rapidly.

The conversion experience was deeply ambiguous to a Puritan. Anyone who found no inner trace of saving grace was damned. Anyone who was absolutely certain of salvation had to be relying on personal merit and was also damned. Conversion took months, even years to achieve. It began with the discovery that one could not keep God's law and that one *deserved* damnation, not for an occasional misdeed, but for what one was at one's best—a wretched sinner. It progressed through despair to hope, which always arose from passages of scripture that spoke to that person's condition. A "saint" at last found reason to believe that God had saved him or her. The whole process involved a painful balance between assurance and doubt. A saint was sure of salvation, but never too sure.

This quest for conversion generated dissent and new colonies. The founders of Connecticut feared that Massachusetts was becoming too severe in certifying church members. The founders of the New Haven Colony worried that the Bay Colony was too lenient. The first Rhode Islanders disagreed with all of them.

In the mid-1630s, Reverend Thomas Hooker, alarmed by Cotton's preaching, led his people west to the Connecticut River, where they founded Hartford and other towns south of the charter boundary of Massachusetts. John Winthrop, Jr., built Saybrook Fort at the mouth of the river, and it soon merged with Hooker's towns into the colony of Connecticut. In 1639, an affluent group planted the New Haven Colony on Long Island Sound. The leaders were Theophilus Eaton, a wealthy London merchant, and Reverend John Davenport, who imposed the strictest requirements for church membership in New England.

The residents of most towns agreed on the kind of worship they preferred, but some settlers, such as Roger Williams and Anne Hutchinson, made greater demands. Williams, who served briefly as Salem's minister, was a Separatist who refused to worship with anyone who did not explicitly repudiate the Church of England. Nearly all Massachusetts Puritans were Non-Separatists who claimed only to be reforming the Anglican Church. In 1636, after Williams challenged the king's right as a Christian to grant Indian lands to anyone at all, the colony banished him. He fled to Narragansett Bay with a few disciples and founded Providence. He developed eloquent arguments for religious liberty and the complete separation of church and state.

Anne Hutchinson, a merchant's wife and an admirer of John Cotton, claimed that virtually all other ministers were preaching only the covenant of works, not the covenant of grace, and were leading people to hell. She won a large following in Boston. At her trial there, she claimed to have received direct messages from God (the Antinomian heresy). Banished in 1638, she and her followers also fled to Narragansett Bay, where they founded Newport and Portsmouth. These towns united with Providence to form the colony of Rhode Island and accepted both the religious liberty and the separation of church and state that Williams advocated.

Much of this territorial expansion reflected not just religious idealism, but also a quest for more land that threatened the neighboring Indians. Connecticut and Massachusetts waged a war of terror and annihilation against the Pequot Indians, who controlled the fertile Thames River valley in Connecticut. In May 1637, New England soldiers debated with their chaplain which of two Pequot forts to attack, the one held by warriors or the one with women, children, and the elderly. He probably told them to remember Saul and the Amalekites because, with horrified Narragansett Indians looking on as nominal allies of the settlers, the Puritan army chose the second fort, set fire to all the wigwams, and shot everyone who tried to flee. The godly had their own uses for terrorism.

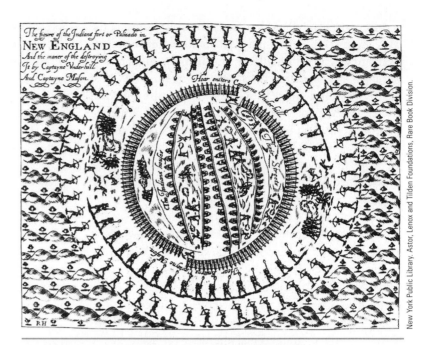

THE PURITAN MASSACRE OF THE PEQUOT INDIANS, 1637
The massacre took place at what is now Mystic, Connecticut. Most of the victims were women and children. The Indians shown in the outer circle were Narragansett allies of the settlers and were appalled by the carnage.

Congregations, Towns, and Colony Governments

These struggles helped shape New England's basic institutions. Congregations abolished the distinctive rites of Anglicanism—vestments, incense, the Book of Common Prayer, church courts, bishops. The sermon became the center of worship, and each congregation chose and ordained its own minister. No singing was permitted, except of psalms, with each worshiper warbling in his or her own key. Congregations sometimes sent ministers and laymen to a synod, but its decisions were advisory, not binding. A 1648 synod issued the Cambridge Platform, which defined Congregationalist worship and church organization.

By then the town had become something distinct from the congregation. Some towns chose independent farms at the outset, but many adopted a medieval system that appeared nowhere else in colonial America: open-field agriculture. In that system, farmers owned scattered strips of land within a common field, and the town decided what crops to grow. Although this emphasis on communal cooperation may have appealed to the founders, who were also short of oxen and plows at first and had to share them, the open-field system did not survive the first generation.

Town meetings decided who got how much land. It was distributed broadly but never equally. In Springfield, at one extreme, the Pynchon family controlled most of the land and most of the labor as well. In other towns, such as Dedham, the distribution was much more equitable. In some villages, town meetings occurred often, made most of the decisions, and left only the details to a board of elected "selectmen." In others, the selectmen did most of the governing. All adult males usually participated in local decisions, but Massachusetts and New Haven restricted the vote for colonywide offices to men who were full church members, a decision that greatly narrowed the electorate by the 1660s.

Massachusetts had a bicameral legislature by the 1640s. Voters in each town chose representatives who met as the Chamber of Deputies, or lower house. Voters also elected the governor and the magistrates, or upper house (the Council or, in its judicial capacity, the Court of Assistants). The magistrates also staffed the county courts. The Court of Assistants heard major criminal cases and appeals from the counties. Final appeals were heard by the General Court, with both houses sitting together to decide judicial questions.

Massachusetts defined its legal system in the "Body of Liberties" of 1641 (which may actually be history's first bill of rights) and in a comprehensive law code of 1648 that was widely imitated in other colonies. Massachusetts sharply reduced the number of capital offenses under English law and listed them in the order of the Ten Commandments. Unlike England, Massachusetts seldom executed anyone for a crime against property. Other distinctive features of the legal system included an explicit recognition of the liberties of women, children, servants, foreigners, and even "the Bruite Creature," or animals; a serious effort to ban professional lawyers; and the swift punishment of crime.

New England also transformed the traditional English jury system. New Haven abolished juries altogether because the Bible does not mention them. But the other colonies vastly expanded the role of civil (noncriminal) juries, using them even to decide appeals, something that never happened in England. Except in capital trials, however, the criminal jury—a fixture of English justice—almost disappeared in New England. The punishment of sin involved fidelity to the covenant and was too important to leave to 12 ordinary men. This system worked well because even sinners shared its values. Most offenders appeared in court and accepted their punishments. Acquittals were rare, almost unheard of in New Haven. Yet hardly anyone ran away to avoid trial or punishment.

Infant Baptism and New Dissent

Although most of the founders of the New England colonies became church members during the fervor of the 1630s, their children had trouble achieving conversion. They had never lived as part of a beleaguered minority in England, nor had they experienced the joy of joining with other holy refugees in founding their own church. They had to find God on their own and then persuade their elders—who were on guard because leniency had let Williams, Hutchinson, and other deviants through—that their conversions were authentic. Most failed. They grew up, married, and requested baptism for their children. The

BOSTON TOWN HOUSE

Erected in 1657, the Town House was probably the most imposing European structure in the region at the time.

© Bettmann/Corbis.

Cambridge Platform declared that only "saints" (the converted) and their children could be baptized. But what about the grandchildren of the saints if their own parents had not yet experienced conversion? By 1660, this problem was becoming acute.

Dissenters offered two answers, and the ministers a third. In the 1640s, some settlers became Baptists. Noting that scripture contains no mandate to baptize infants, they argued that only converted adults should receive that rite. Their position challenged the logic of a covenanted community by implying that New England was no different from Europe. The community was a mass of sinners from whom God would randomly choose a few saints. Samuel Gorton, a Baptist expelled from Massachusetts and Plymouth (he denounced the magistrates as "just asses"), founded Warwick, Rhode Island, in the 1640s. When Massachusetts arrested him, accused him of blasphemy, and put him on trial for his life, the legislature banished him instead, but Gorton appealed to Parliament in England, and Massachusetts backed down. Baptist principles also attracted Henry Dunster, the able president of Harvard College, which had been founded in 1636 to educate ministers and magistrates for a Puritan society. When the courts began to harass Baptists, Dunster left for more tolerant Plymouth.

Even more alarming to the Puritan establishment were the Quakers, who invaded the region from England in the 1650s (to be discussed later in the chapter). Quakers found salvation within themselves—through God, the Inner Light present in all people if they will only let it shine forth. To Puritans, the Quaker answer to the conversion dilemma seemed blasphemous and Antinomian. Massachusetts hanged four Quakers who refused to stop preaching, including Mary Dyer, who was once a disciple of Anne Hutchinson.

The clergy's answer to the lack of conversions, worked out at a synod in 1662, became known as the Half-Way Covenant. Parents who had been baptized but had not yet experienced conversion could bring their children before the church, "own the covenant" (that is, subject themselves and their offspring to the doctrine and discipline of the church), and have their children baptized. In practice, women often experienced conversion before age 30, men closer to 40, but many never did. In most churches, women also began to outnumber men as full members. For 15 or 20 years after 1662, most churches were still dominated by the lay members of the founding generation. Despite the urging of the clergy (by then most ministers were young Harvard graduates, not venerable saints), aging church members resisted implementation of the Half-Way Covenant. But as the founders died off in the 1670s and 1680s, the covenant took hold and soon led to something like universal baptism. Almost every child had an ancestor who had been a full church member.

Dissent persisted anyhow. The orthodox colonies were divided over whether to persecute or to ignore their Baptist and Quaker minorities. Ministers preached "jeremiads," shrill warnings against any backsliding from the standards of the founding generation, but many laypeople disliked the persecution of conscientious Protestants. By the 1670s, innovation seemed dangerous and divisive, but the past was also becoming a burden that no one could shoulder.

The English Civil Wars

The 1640s were a critical decade in England and the colonies. From 1629 to 1640, Charles I governed without Parliament, but when he tried to impose the Anglican Book of Common Prayer on Presbyterian Scotland, his Scottish subjects rebelled and even invaded England. Needing revenue, Charles summoned two Parliaments in 1640 only to find that many of its members, especially the Puritans, sympathized with the Scots. In 1641, Irish Catholics launched a massive revolt against the Protestant colonizers of their land. King and Parliament agreed that the Irish must be crushed, but neither dared trust the other with the men and resources to do the job. Instead, they began to fight each other.

In 1642, the king and Parliament raised separate armies and went to war. Parliament gradually won the military struggle and then had to govern most of England without a king. In January 1649, after its moderate members had been purged by its own New Model Army, Parliament beheaded Charles, abolished the House of Lords, and proclaimed England a Commonwealth (or republic). Within a few years, Oliver Cromwell, Parliament's most successful general, dismissed Parliament, and the army proclaimed him "Lord Protector" of England. He convened several of his own Parliaments, including one that consisted entirely of godly men, but these experiments failed. The army, even when it drafted a written constitution for England, could not win legitimacy for a government that ruled without the ancient trinity of "King, Lords, and Commons." Cromwell also faced a challenge outside Parliament from "levelers," "diggers," and "ranters" who claimed to speak for "the people" while demanding sweeping social reforms.

Cromwell died in September 1658, and his regime collapsed. Part of the army invited Charles II (1660–85) back from exile to claim his throne. After 20 years of turmoil, this Restoration government did its best to restore the old order. It brought back the House of Lords. The Church of England was reestablished under its episcopal form of government. The English state, denying any right of dissent, persecuted both Catholics and Protestant dissenters: Presbyterians, Congregationalists, Baptists, and Quakers. This persecution drove thousands of Quakers to the Delaware valley after 1675.

The First Restoration Colonies

England had founded 6 of the original 13 colonies before 1640. Six others were founded or came under English rule during the Restoration era (1660–88). The last, Georgia, was settled in the 1730s (see chapter 4). Most of the new colonies shared certain common features and also differed in some respects from earlier settlements. All were proprietary in form. As with Maryland earlier, a proprietary charter enabled the organizers to pursue daring social experiments. Except for Pennsylvania, the Restoration colonies were all founded by men with big ideas and small purses. The proprietors tried to attract settlers from the older colonies because importing them from Europe was too expensive.

The most readily available prospects were servants completing their indentures in the West Indies and being driven out by the sugar revolution. The most prized settlers, however, were New Englanders. Although the proprietors distrusted both their piety and their politics, New Englanders had built the most thriving colonies in North America. Cromwell had tried but failed to attract New Haven settlers to Jamaica. Few New Englanders would go farther south than New York or New Jersey. Settlers from the West Indies would populate South Carolina.

The Restoration colonies made it easy for settlers to acquire land, and they competed with one another by offering newcomers strong guarantees of civil and political liberties. They all promised either toleration or full religious liberty, at least for Christians. Whereas Virginia and New England (except Rhode Island) were still homogeneous societies, the Restoration colonies all attracted a mix of religious and ethnic groups. None of them found it easy to translate this human diversity into political stability.

Most of the new proprietors were "cavaliers" who had supported Charles II and his brother James, duke of York, during their long exile. Charles owed them something, and a colonial charter cost nothing to grant. Many proprietors took part in more than one project. The eight who obtained charters for Carolina in 1663 and 1665 were also prominent in organizing the Royal African Company, which soon made England a major participant in the African slave trade. Two of the Carolina proprietors obtained a charter from the duke of York for New Jersey as

well. William Penn, although the son of a Commonwealth admiral, became a friend of James and invested in West New Jersey before acquiring Pennsylvania from the king.

Far more than New England or Virginia, the Restoration colonies foreshadowed the diversity that would characterize the United States after 1790. South Carolina became the first home of the cotton kingdom. The Middle Atlantic provinces set much of the tone for the Midwest.

Carolina, Harrington, and the Aristocratic Ideal

In 1663, eight courtiers obtained a charter by which they became the board of proprietors for a colony to be founded south of Virginia. Calling their province Carolina in honor of the king, they tried to colonize the region in the 1660s but achieved little success until the following decade. Most of the settlers came from two sources. Former servants from Virginia and Maryland, many in debt, hoped that they would be left alone if they claimed land around Albemarle Sound in what eventually became North Carolina. Another wave of former servants came from Barbados. They settled the area that became South Carolina, 300 miles south of Albemarle, and began to export grain and meat to the West Indies.

To the proprietors in England, these scattered settlements made up a single colony called Carolina. Led by Anthony Ashley-Cooper, later the first earl of Shaftesbury and the principal organizer of England's Whig Party, the proprietors drafted the Fundamental Constitutions of Carolina in 1669, an incredibly complex plan for organizing the new colony. Philosopher John Locke, Shaftesbury's young secretary, helped write the document.

The Fundamental Constitutions drew on the work of Commonwealth England's most prominent republican thinker, James Harrington, author of *Oceana* (1656). He tried to design a republic that could endure—unlike ancient Athens or Rome, which had finally become despotic states. Harrington argued that how land was distributed ought to determine whether power should be lodged in one man (monarchy), a few men (aristocracy), or many (a republic). Where ownership of land was widespread, he insisted, absolute government could not prevail. He proposed several other devices to prevent one man, or a few, from undermining a republic, such as frequent rotation of officeholders (called "term limits" today), the secret ballot, and a bicameral legislature in which the smaller house would propose laws and the larger house approve or reject them. Harrington had greater impact on colonial governments than any other thinker of his time.

Shaftesbury believed that Harrington had uncovered the laws of history. By emphasizing Henry VIII's confiscation of monastic lands and their sale to an emerging gentry, Harrington seemed to have an explanation for the decline of the monarchy, England's civil wars, and the execution of Charles I—an explanation that was anathema to the king because, if Harrington was correct, the monarchy was still in trouble. English writers dared not discuss these ideas openly in the 1660s, but by applying Harrington's principles at a safe distance of 3,000 miles, the Carolina proprietors could choose the kind of society they desired and devise institutions to ensure its success. Well aware that the House of Lords had been abolished for 11 years after 1649, they were not yet certain whether the English aristocracy could survive at home. In Carolina, they hoped to create a thriving aristocratic society.

The Fundamental Constitutions proposed a government that was far more complex than any colony could sustain. England had three supreme courts; Carolina would have eight. A Grand Council of proprietors and councillors would exercise executive power and propose all laws. Their bills would have to pass a Parliament of commoners and nobles (called "landgraves" and "casiques"). The nobles would control 40 percent of the land. In a later version of the text, a noble who lost his land or permanently left the colony would forfeit his title, an application of Harrington's warning not to divorce power from land. A distinct group of manor lords would also have large estates. The document guaranteed religious toleration to all who believed in God, but everyone had to join a church or lose his citizenship. The document also envisioned a class of lowly whites, "leetmen," who would live on small tracts and serve the great landlords—and it accepted slavery. "Every Freeman of Carolina shall have absolute Power and Authority over his Negro Slaves," declared Article 110.

Conditions were bleak on Barbados for ex-servants, but not bleak enough to make the Fundamental Constitutions attractive to the Barbadians who settled in Carolina. Between 1670 and 1700, the proprietors tried several times, without success, to win their approval of the document. In the 1680s, weary of resistance from the predominantly Anglican Barbadians, the proprietors shipped 1,000 dissenters from England and Scotland to South Carolina. These newcomers formed the nucleus of a proprietary party in South Carolina politics and made religious diversity a social fact, but their influence was never strong enough to win approval for the Fundamental Constitutions. The Barbadians remained in control.

Carolina presented its organizers with other unanticipated obstacles to these aristocratic goals. The proprietors assumed that land ownership would be the key to everything else, including wealth and status, but many settlers prospered in other ways. Some of them, especially in Albe-

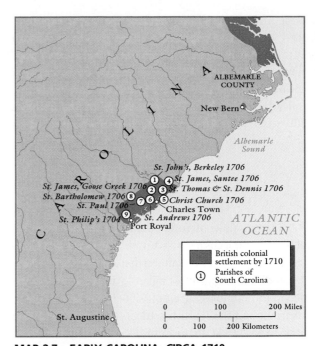

MAP 2.7 EARLY CAROLINA, CIRCA 1710
The first nine parishes of South Carolina and the English settlements along Albemarle Sound that became North Carolina.

marle, exploited the virgin forests all around them to produce masts, turpentine, tar, and pitch for sale to English shipbuilders. Other settlers raised cattle and hogs by letting them run free on open land. Some of South Carolina's African slaves were probably America's first cowboys. The settlers also traded with the Indians, usually for deerskins, often acquired west of the Appalachians. As in New France and New Netherland, the Indian trade sustained a genuine city, Charleston, the first in the American South, founded in 1680 at the confluence of the Ashley and Cooper rivers. The Indian trade also became something more dangerous than hunting or trapping animals. Carolina traders allied themselves with some Indians to attack others and drag the captives, mostly women and children, to Charleston for sale as slaves. Until 1715, the Indian slave trade was the colony's biggest business. South Carolina exported more enslaved Indians to other colonies than it imported Africans for its emerging plantations.

In the early 18th century, South Carolina and North Carolina became separate colonies, and South Carolina's economy began to move in a new direction. For two decades, until the mid-1720s, a parliamentary subsidy sustained a boom in the naval stores industry, which in turn stimulated a large demand for slaves, but Charleston merchants increasingly invested their capital, acquired in the Indian trade, in rice plantations. In the 1690s, planters learned how to grow rice from slaves who had cultivated it in West Africa. It gradually became the staple export of South Carolina and triggered a sharp growth of African slavery. In 1700, more than 40 percent of the colony's population of 5,700 were African or Indian slaves engaged in a wide variety of activities. The Indian slave trade collapsed after 1715. By 1730, two-thirds of the colony's 30,000 people were African slaves, most of whom toiled on rice plantations.

New York: An Experiment in Absolutism

In 1664, James, duke of York, obtained a charter from his royal brother for a colony between the Delaware and Connecticut rivers. Charles II claimed that the territory of New Netherland was rightfully England's because it was included in the Virginia charter of 1606. James sent a fleet to Manhattan, and the English settlers on Long Island rose to support his claim. Reluctantly, Stuyvesant surrendered without resistance. The English renamed the province New York. New Amsterdam became New York City, and Fort Orange became Albany. The Dutch ceded New Netherland with few regrets. It had never been profitable anyway. New York took over all of Long Island, most of which had been ruled by Connecticut, but never made good on its claim to the Connecticut River as its eastern boundary. New York also inherited New Netherland's role as mediator between the settlers and the Iroquois Five Nations. In effect, the duke of York's autocratic colony assumed most of the burdens of this relationship while unintentionally conferring most of the benefits on the Quakers who would begin to settle the Delaware valley a decade later. The shield provided by New York and the Iroquois would make the Quaker experiment in pacifism a viable option.

Richard Nicolls, the first English governor of New York, planned to lure Yankees to the Jersey coast as a way of offsetting the preponderance of Dutch settlers in the Hudson valley. Although English soldiers abused many Dutch civilians, official policy toward the Dutch was conciliatory. Those who chose to leave could take their property with them. Those who stayed retained their property and were assured of religious toleration. Most stayed. Except in New York City and the small Dutch portion of Long Island, Dutch settlers still lived under Dutch law. Dutch inheritance practices, which were far more generous to women than English law, survived in New York well into the 18th century. England also expected to take over the colony's trade with Europe, but New York's early governors realized that a total ban on commerce with Amsterdam could ruin the colony. Under various legal subterfuges, they allowed this trade to continue.

The duke boldly tried to do in New York what he and the king did not dare attempt in England—to govern without an elective assembly. This policy upset English settlers on Long Island far more than the Dutch, who had no experience with representative government. Governor Nicolls compiled a code of laws (the Duke's Laws) that were culled mostly from New England statutes. With difficulty, he secured the consent of English settlers to this code in 1665, but thereafter he taxed and governed on his own, seeking only the advice and consent of his appointed council and of a court of assize, also appointive, that dispensed justice, mostly to the English settlers.

This policy made it difficult to attract English colonists to New York, especially after New Jersey became a separate proprietary colony in 1665. The two proprietors, Sir George Carteret and John, baron Berkeley, granted settlers the right to elect an assembly, which made New Jersey far more attractive to English settlers than New York. The creation of New Jersey also slowed the flow of Dutch settlers across the Hudson and thus helped to keep New York Dutch.

The transition from a Dutch to an English colony did not go smoothly. James expected his English invaders to assimilate the conquered Dutch, but the reverse was more common for two or three decades. Most Englishmen who settled in New York after the conquest married Dutch women (few unmarried English women were available) and sent their children to the Dutch Reformed Church. In effect, the Dutch were assimilating the English. Nor did the Dutch give up their loyalty to the Netherlands. In 1673, when a Dutch fleet threatened the colony, the Dutch refused to assist the English garrison of Fort James at the southern tip of Manhattan. Eastern Long Island showed more interest in reuniting with Connecticut than in fighting the Dutch. Much like Stuyvesant nine years earlier, the English garrison gave up without resistance. New York City now became New Orange and Fort James was renamed Fort William, both in honor of young William III of Nassau, Prince of Orange, the new *stadholder* (military leader) of the Dutch Republic in its struggle with France. Thus James and William became antagonists in New York 15 years before the Glorious Revolution, in which William would drive James from the English throne (see chapter 3).

New Orange survived for 15 months, until the Dutch Republic again concluded that the colony was not worth what it cost and gave it back to England at the end of the war. The new governor, Major Edmund Andros, arrested seven prominent Dutch merchants and tried them as aliens after they refused to swear an oath of loyalty to England that might oblige them to fight other Dutchmen. Faced with the confiscation of their property, they gave in. Andros also helped secure bilingual ministers for Dutch

MAP 2.8 THE DUKE OF YORK'S COLONIAL CHARTER

This map shows the boundary of New York as set forth in the charter of 1664, the compromise boundary the first English governor negotiated with Connecticut, and the principal manors created in the 17th century.

Reformed pulpits. These preachers made a great show of their loyalty to the duke, a delicate matter now that James, in England, had openly embraced the Catholic faith. Ordinary Dutch settlers looked with suspicion on the new ministers and on wealthier Dutch families who socialized with the governor or sent their sons to New England to learn English.

English merchants in New York City resented the continuing Amsterdam trade and the staying power of the Dutch elite. They believed the colony had to become more English to attract newcomers. When Andros failed to renew the colony's basic revenue act before returning to England in 1680, the merchants refused to pay any duties not voted by an elective assembly. The court of assize, supposedly a bastion of absolutism, supported the tax strike, convicted the duke's customs collector of usurping authority, and sent him to England for punishment where, of course, James exonerated him. The justices also fined several Dutch officeholders for failing to respect English liberties. The English (but not Dutch) towns on Long Island joined in the demand for an elective assembly, an urgent matter now that William Penn's much freer colony on the Delaware threatened to drain away the small English population of New York. Several prominent merchants did move to Philadelphia.

The duke finally relented and conceded an assembly. When it met in 1683, it adopted a Charter of Liberties that proclaimed government by consent. It also imposed English law on the Dutch parts of the province. Although the drain of English settlers to Pennsylvania declined, few immigrants came to New York at a time when thousands were landing in Philadelphia. Philadelphia's thriving trade cut into New York City's profits. New York remained a Dutch society with a Yankee enclave, governed by English intruders. In 1689, when James and William fought for the English throne, their struggle would tear the colony apart.

🌎 Brotherly Love: The Quakers and America

The most fascinating social experiment of the Restoration era took place in the Delaware valley where Quakers led another family-based, religiously motivated migration of more than 10,000 people between 1675 and 1690. Founded by George Fox during England's civil wars, the Society of Friends expanded dramatically in the 1650s as it went through a heroic phase of missionaries and martyrs, including the four executed in Massachusetts. After the Restoration, Quakers faced harsh persecution in England and finally began to seek refuge in America.

Quaker Beliefs

Quakers infuriated other Christians. They insisted that God, in the form of the Inner Light, is present in all people, who can become good—even perfect—if only they will let that light shine forth. They took literally Jesus's advice to "Turn the other cheek." They became pacifists, enraging Catholics and most other Protestants, all of whom had found ways to justify war. Quakers also obeyed Jesus's command to "swear not." They denounced oathtaking as sinful. Again, other Christians reacted with horror because their judicial systems rested on oaths.

Although orderly and peaceful, Quakers struck others as dangerous radicals whose beliefs would bring anarchy. For instance, slavery made them uncomfortable, although the Friends did not embrace abolitionism until a century later (see chapter 5). Furthermore, in what they called "the Lamb's war" against human pride, Quakers refused to doff

their hats to social superiors. More than any other simple device, hats symbolized the social hierarchy of Europe. Every man knew his place so long as he understood whom to doff to, and who should doff to him. Quakers also refused to accept or to confer titles. They called everyone "thee" or "thou," familiar terms used by superiors when addressing inferiors, especially servants.

Although Quakers disliked theological speculation, the implications of their beliefs appalled other Christians. Without the bother of a refutation, the Inner Light seemed to obliterate predestination, original sin, maybe even the Trinity. Quakers had no sacraments, not even an organized clergy. They denounced Protestant ministers as "hireling priests," no better than the "papists." Other Protestants retorted that the Quakers were conspiring to return the world to "popish darkness" by abolishing a learned ministry. (The terms "papists" and "popish" were abusive labels applied to Catholics by English Protestants.) Quakers also held distinctive views about revelation. If God speaks directly to Friends, that Word must be every bit as inspired as anything in the Bible. Quakers compiled books of their "sufferings," which they thought were the equal of the "Acts of the Apostles," a claim that seemed blasphemous to others.

Contemporaries expected the Society of Friends to fall apart as each member followed his or her own Light in some unique direction, but it did nothing of the kind. In the 1660s, Quakers found ways to deal with discord.

North Wind Picture Archives.

HEXAGONAL QUAKER MEETING HOUSE
This unique design emphasizes the Quaker belief in the fundamental equality of all souls under God. The interior has no altar or pulpit, no front or back. All worshippers are equally close to God.

The heart of Quaker worship was the "weekly meeting" of the local congregation. There was no sermon or liturgy. People spoke whenever the Light inspired them. But because a few men and women spoke often and with great effect, they became recognized as "public friends," the closest the Quakers came to having a clergy. Public friends occupied special, elevated seats in some meetinghouses, and many went on missionary tours in Europe or America. The weekly meetings within a region sent representatives to a "monthly meeting," which resolved questions of policy and discipline. The monthly meetings sent delegates to the "yearly meeting" in London. At every level, decisions had to be unanimous. There is only one Inner Light, and it must convey the same message to every believer. This insistence on unanimity provided strong safeguards against schism.

Quaker Families

Quakers transformed the traditional family as well. Women enjoyed almost full equality, and some of them, such as Mary Dyer, became exceptional preachers, even martyrs. Women held their own formal meetings and made important decisions about discipline and betrothals. Quaker reforms also affected children, whom most Protestants saw as tiny sinners whose wills must be broken by severe discipline. But once Quakers stopped worrying about original sin, their children became innocents in whom the Light would shine if only they could be protected from worldly corruption. In America, Quakers created affectionate families, built larger houses than non-Quakers with equivalent resources, and worked hard to acquire land for all their children. Earlier than other Christians, they began to limit family size to give more love to the children they did have. After the missionary impulse declined, Quakers seldom associated with non-Quakers, and the needs of their own children became paramount. To marry an outsider meant expulsion from the Society, a fate more likely to befall poor Friends than rich ones. Poor Quakers had difficulty finding spouses precisely because their children might never receive the advantages that most Friends had come to expect.

Persecution in England helped drive Quakers across the ocean, but the need to provide for their children was another powerful motive for emigration. By 1700, about half of the Quakers in England and Wales had moved to America.

West New Jersey

In 1674, the New Jersey proprietors split their holding into two colonies. Sir George Carteret claimed what he now called East New Jersey, a province near New York City with half a dozen towns populated by Baptist, Quaker, Puritan, and Dutch Reformed settlers. Lord Berkeley claimed West New Jersey and promptly sold it to the Quakers, who then founded two colonies in America: West New Jersey and Pennsylvania. In the 1680s, when Quakers bought out the proprietor of East New Jersey and also gained power in Delaware (formerly New Sweden), they seemed poised to dominate the entire region between Maryland and New York. The West Jersey purchasers divided their proprietary into 100 shares. Two of the organizers were Edward Byllinge, a former "leveler," and William Penn, an admirer of Harrington. They revived in West Jersey many radical ideals of the English Commonwealth era.

In 1676, Byllinge drafted a document, the West New Jersey Concessions and Agreements, which was approved by the first settlers in 1677. It lodged legislative power in a unicameral assembly, elected by secret ballot, and it empowered voters to instruct their representatives. In the court system, juries would decide both fact and law. Judges would merely preside over the court and, if asked by a juror, offer advice. Although the document was never fully implemented, it made West Jersey the most radical political experiment attempted in America before the Revolution. West Jersey Quakers believed that godly people could live together in love—without war, lawyers, or internal conflict. They kept government close to the people, made land easy to acquire, and promised freedom of worship to everyone. In the 1680s, lawsuits often ended with one litigant forgiving the other, and criminal trials sometimes closed with the victim embracing the perpetrator. But as social and religious diversity grew, the system broke down. Non-Quakers increasingly refused to cooperate. In the 1690s, the courts became impotent, and Quaker rule collapsed some years before the Crown took over the colony in 1702.

Pennsylvania

By 1681, Quaker attention was already shifting to the west bank of the Delaware River. There, William Penn launched a much larger, if rather more cautious, "holy experiment" in brotherly love. The son of a Commonwealth admiral, Penn grew up surrounded by privilege. He knew well both Charles II and the duke of York, attended Oxford and the Inns of Court (England's law schools), went on the grand tour of Europe, and began to manage his father's Irish estates. Then something happened that embarrassed his family. "Mr. William Pen," reported a neighbor in December 1667, ". . . is a Quaker again, or some very melancholy thing." Penn often traveled to the continent on behalf of the Society of Friends, winning converts and recruiting settlers in the Netherlands and Germany. In England he was jailed several times for his beliefs, and in the so-called

PENN'S TREATY WITH THE INDIANS, BY BENJAMIN WEST

This 1771 painting celebrates William Penn's efforts, nearly a century earlier, to establish peaceful relations with the Delaware Indians.

© Bettmann/Corbis.

Penn-Meade trial of 1670, he challenged a judge's right to compel a jury to reconsider its verdict. In a landmark decision, a higher court vindicated him.

A gentleman and a Quaker, Penn was no ordinary colonizer. Using his contacts at court, he converted an old debt (owed to his father by the king) into a charter for a proprietary colony that Charles named Pennsylvania in honor of the deceased admiral. The emerging imperial bureaucracy disliked the whole project and, after failing to block it, inserted several restrictions into the charter. Penn agreed to enforce the Navigation Acts (see chapter 3), to let the Crown approve his choice of governor, to submit all legislation to the English Privy Council for approval, and to allow appeals from Pennsylvania courts to the Privy Council in England.

Contemporaries said little about the most striking innovation attempted by the Quaker colonists. They entered America unarmed. Pennsylvanians did not even organize a militia until the 1740s. Friendly relations with Indians were essential to the project's success, and Penn was careful to deal fairly with the Lenni Lenape, or Delaware Indians. They liked him and called him "Miquon," their word for "quill" and thus a pun on "Penn."

More thought went into planning Pennsylvania than into the creation of any other colony. Twenty drafts survive of Penn's First Frame of Government, his 1682 constitution for the province. It evolved from what was a larger version of the West Jersey Concessions and Agreements into something more Harringtonian but still quite

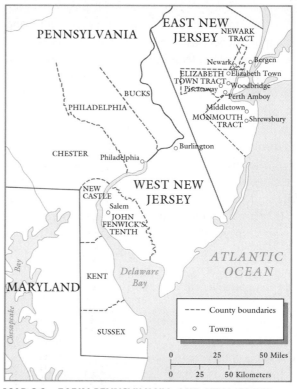

MAP 2.9   EARLY PENNSYLVANIA AND NEW JERSEY, CIRCA 1700

This map shows the first three counties of Pennsylvania and its capital of Philadelphia, the three counties of what would soon become Delaware, the colony of West New Jersey and its capital of Burlington, and the early towns of East New Jersey including its capital of Perth Amboy.

From the Collections of the Library of Congress (left). Hans Oswald Wild/TimePix (right).

WILLIAM PENN IN ARMOR AND PENN'S CELL IN THE TOWER OF LONDON

The son of an English admiral, William Penn was not always a pacifist. In the 1660s, an unknown artist painted him in this military pose. After his conversion to the Society of Friends, Penn paid a steep price for his religious convictions. Accused of blasphemy, he was imprisoned in this bleak cell from December 1668 to July 1669.

liberating. The settlers would elect a council of 72 men to staggered three-year terms. The council would draft all legislation and submit copies to the voters. In the early years, the voters would meet to approve or reject these bills in person. Penn anticipated that as the province expanded, such meetings would become impractical. Voters would then elect an assembly of 200, which would increase gradually to 500, about the size of the House of Commons, although for a much smaller population. Government would still remain close to the people. Penn gave up the power to veto bills but retained control of the distribution of land. Capital punishment was abolished for crimes against property and most other offenses, except murder. Religious liberty, trial by jury, and habeas corpus all received strong guarantees.

Settlers had been arriving in Pennsylvania for a year when Penn landed in 1682 with his First Frame of Government. Some lived in caves along the river. Others, imitating the nearby Swedes, built log cabins. The colonists persuaded Penn that the First Frame was too cumbersome for a small colony, and the first legislature worked with him to devise a simpler government. In what became known as the Second Frame, or the Pennsylvania Charter of Liberties of 1683, the council was reduced to 18 men and the assembly to 36. The assembly's inability to initiate legislation soon became a major grievance.

Penn laid out Philadelphia as "a green country town" and organized other settlements. Although an idealist, he hoped that land sales and other revenues would provide a handsome support for his family. Then, in 1684, he returned to England to answer Lord Baltimore's complaint that Philadelphia fell within the charter boundaries of Maryland, a claim that was soon verified. This dispute troubled the Penn family until the 1760s, when the Mason-Dixon line finally established the modern boundary.

In England, persecution had kept Quaker antiauthoritarianism in check, at least in relations with other Friends. In the colony, these attitudes soon became public. Penn expected his settlers to defer to the leaders among them. He created the Free Society of Traders to control commerce with England and gave high offices to its members.

From the start, however, wealth in Pennsylvania rested on trade not with England, but with other colonies, especially in the Caribbean. That trade was dominated by Quakers from Barbados, Jamaica, New York, and Boston. These men owed little to Penn and became an opposition faction in the colony. They and others demanded more land, especially in Philadelphia. They claimed that they could not afford to pay Penn's quitrents,[2] and they quarreled more often than was seemly for men of brotherly love.

In exasperation, Penn finally appointed John Blackwell, an old Cromwellian soldier, as governor in 1688, ordering him to end the quarrels and collect quitrents but to rule "tenderly." Boys jeered Blackwell as he tried to enter Penn's Philadelphia house, and the council refused to let him use the colony's great seal. Debate in the legislature became angrier than ever. After 13 months, Blackwell resigned. Each Quaker, he complained, "prayed for the rest on the First Day [of the week], and preyed on them the other six." The local mosquitoes, he added, "were worse than armed men but not nearly so nettlesome as the men without Armes." Because Penn had supported James II in England, he lost control of the colony between 1691 and 1693.

In 1691, the Society of Friends suffered a brief schism in the Delaware valley. A Quaker schoolteacher, George Keith, urged all Quakers to systematize their beliefs and even wrote his own catechism, only to encounter the opposition of the public friends, who included the colony's major officeholders. When he attacked them directly, he was convicted and fined for abusing civil officers. He claimed that he was being persecuted for his religious beliefs, but the courts insisted that his only crime was his attack on public authority. In contrast to Massachusetts in the 1630s, no one was banished, and Pennsylvania remained a haven for all religions. The colony's government

changed several more times before 1701, when Penn and the assembly finally agreed on the Fourth Frame, or Charter of Privileges, which gave Pennsylvania a unicameral legislature, but its politics remained turbulent and unstable into the 1720s.

Despite these controversies, Pennsylvania quickly became an economic success, well established in the Caribbean trade as an exporter of wheat and flour. Quaker families were thriving, and the colony's policy of religious liberty attracted thousands of outsiders. Some were German pacifists who shared the major goals of the Society of Friends. Others were Anglicans and Presbyterians who warned London that Quakers were unfit to rule—anywhere.

Conclusion

In the 16th century, France, the Netherlands, and England all challenged Spanish power in Europe and across the ocean. After 1600, all three founded their own colonies in North America and the Caribbean. New France became a land of missionaries and traders and developed close ties of cooperation with most nearby Indians. New Netherland also was founded to participate in the fur trade. Both colonies slowly acquired an agricultural base.

The English, by contrast, desired the land itself. They founded colonies of settlement that threatened nearby Indians, except in the Delaware valley, where Quakers insisted on peaceful relations. The southern mainland and Caribbean colonies produced staple crops for sale in Europe, first with the labor of indentured servants and then with enslaved Africans. The Puritan and Quaker colonies became smaller versions of England's mixed economy, with an emphasis on family farms. Maintaining the fervor of the founders was a problem for both. After conquering New Netherland, England controlled the Atlantic seaboard from Maine to South Carolina, and by 1700 the population of England's mainland colonies was doubling every 25 years. England was beginning to emerge as the biggest winner in the competition for empire.

---

[2] A feudal relic, a *quitrent* was an annual fee, usually small, required by the patent that gave title to a piece of land. It differed from ordinary rents in that nonpayment led to a suit for debt, not ejection from the property.

SUGGESTED READINGS

W. J. Eccles, *The French in North America, 1500–1783,* rev. ed. (1998) is a concise and authoritative survey. **C. R. Boxer,** *The Dutch Seaborne Empire, 1600–1800* (1965) is still the best synthesis of Dutch activity overseas. **Joyce E. Chaplin's** *Subject Matter: Technology, the Body, and Science on the Anglo-American Frontier, 1500–1676* (2001), and **Karen O. Kupperman,** *Indians and English: Facing Off in Early America* (2000) are efforts to keep Indians and the settlers of early Virginia and New England within a common focus. **Edmund S. Morgan's** *American Slavery, American Freedom: The Ordeal of Colonial Virginia* (1975) has become a classic, but **Thad W. Tate and David L. Ammerman, eds.,** *The Chesapeake in the Seventeenth-Century: Essays on Anglo-American Society* (1979) is also indispensable. For the West Indies, see **Richard S. Dunn,** *Sugar and Slaves: The Rise of the Planter Class in the English West Indies, 1624–1713* (1972). **Winthrop Jordan's** *White over Black: American Attitudes toward the Negro, 1550–1812* (1968) retains its freshness and acuity.

Edmund S. Morgan's *Visible Saints: The History of a Puritan Idea* (1963) is a brief and accessible introduction to Puritan values in New England's first century. **Carla G. Pestana's** *Quakers and Baptists in Colonial Massachusetts* (1991) deals with the principal dissenters from the New England Way. **Daniel Vickers,** *Farmers and Fishermen: Two Centuries of Work in Essex County, Massachusetts, 1630–1850* (1994) is an outstanding introduction to the New England economy.

For the Restoration colonies, see especially **Robert C. Ritchie,** *The Duke's Province: A Study of New York Politics and Society, 1664–1691* (1977); **Gary B. Nash,** *Quakers and Politics: Pennsylvania Politics, 1681–1726* (1968); **Barry J. Levy,** *Quakers and the American Family: British Settlement in the Delaware Valley* (1988); **Peter H. Wood,** *Black Majority: Negroes in Colonial South Carolina from 1670 through the Stono Rebellion* (1974); and **Alan Gallay,** *The Indian Slave Trade: The Rise of the English Empire in the American South, 1670–1717* (2002).

AMERICAN JOURNEY ONLINE
AND
INFOTRAC COLLEGE EDITION

Visit the source collections at www.ajaccess.wadsworth.com and infotrac.thomsonlearning.com and use the Search function with the following key terms to explore documents, images, audio and video clips, articles, and commentary related to the material in this chapter.

Protestant Reformation	Massachusetts Bay Company
Sir Walter Ralegh	Quaker
Jamestown	Anne Hutchinson
John Smith	New York
Pilgrims	William Penn
Plymouth	

GRADE AIDS

Visit the **Liberty Equality Power Companion Web Site for resources specific to this textbook:** http://history.wadsworth.com/murrin_LEP4e

The CD in the back of this book and the U.S. History Resource Center at http://history.wadsworth.com/u.s./ offer a variety of tools to help you succeed in this course, including access to quizzes; images; documents; interactive simulations, maps, and timelines; movie explorations; and a wealth of other sources.

Chapter 3

England Discovers Its Colonies: Empire, Liberty, and Expansion

THE KINGFISHER ENGAGING THE BARBARY PIRATES ON 22 MAY, 1681, BY WILLEM VAN DE VELDE THE YOUNGER
By the end of the 17th century, England had become the greatest naval power in the world, a position that Great Britain would maintain until overtaken by the United States in the Second World War.

CHAPTER OUTLINE

In 1603, when James VI of Scotland ascended the throne of England as King James I (1603–25), England was still a weak power on the fringes of Europe with no colonies except in Ireland. By 1700, England was a global giant, able to tip Europe's balance of power. It possessed 20 colonies in North America and the Caribbean, controlled much of the African slave trade, and had muscled its way into distant India. Commerce and colonies had vastly magnified England's power in Europe.

This transformation occurred during a century of political and religious upheaval at home. King and Parliament fought over their respective powers—a long struggle that led to civil war and the execution of one king in 1649 and to the overthrow of another in 1688. The result was a unique constitution that rested on parliamentary supremacy and responsible government under the Crown.

This upheaval produced competing visions of politics and the good society. At one extreme, the ruling Stuart dynasty often seemed to be trying to create an absolute monarchy, similar to that of Spain or France. Opponents of absolutism groped for ways to guarantee government by consent without undermining public order. England's colonies shared in the turmoil. Yet by 1700, all of them had begun to converge around the newly defined principles of English constitutionalism. All adopted representative government at some point during the century. All affirmed the values of liberty and property under the English Crown.

England also quarreled with the colonies, whose sheer diversity daunted anyone who hoped to govern them. The colonies formed not a single type, but a spectrum of settlement with contrasting economies, social relationships, and institutions. Yet by 1700, England had created a system of regulation that respected colonial liberties while asserting imperial power.

CHAPTER FOCUS

♦ What were the major colonial goals of English mercantilists, and how close to success did they come?

♦ What enabled the Middle Colonies to avoid the Indian wars that engulfed New England and Virginia in the mid-1670s?

♦ On what common principles did English political culture begin to converge in both the mother country and the colonies after the Glorious Revolution?

♦ What enabled sparsely settled New France to resist British expansion with great success for more than half a century, whereas Spanish Florida seemed almost helpless against the same threat?

The Atlantic Prism and the Spectrum of Settlement

Over thousands of years, the Indians of the Americas, at first a fairly homogeneous people, had become diversified into hundreds of distinct cultures and languages. The colonists of 17th-century North America and the Caribbean were following much the same course. America divided them. The Atlantic united them. Their connection with England gave them what unity they could sustain.

As long as population remained small, no colony could duplicate the complexity of England. The settlers had to choose what to bring with them and what to leave behind, what they could provide for themselves and what they would have to import—choices dictated both by their motives for crossing the ocean and by what the new environment would permit. The colonists sorted themselves out along a vast arc from the cold North to the subtropical Caribbean. If we can imagine England as a source of white light and the Atlantic as a prism refracting that light, 17th-century America becomes a spectrum of settlement, with each color merging imperceptibly into the shade next to it. Each province had much in common with its neighbors but shared few traits with more distant colonies. At the extremes, the sugar and slave society of Barbados had almost nothing in common with Puritan Massachusetts. Nor did Canada share many characteristics with the French West Indies.

CHRONOLOGY

1642	Civil war erupts in England • Miantonomo abandons planned war of extermination
1643	New England Confederation created
1644	Opechancanough's second massacre in Virginia
1649	England becomes a commonwealth
1651	Parliament passes first Navigation Act
1652–54	First Anglo-Dutch War
1660	Charles II restored to English throne • Parliament passes new Navigation Act
1662	Charles II grants Rhode Island Charter
1663	Staple Act passed • Charles II grants Connecticut Charter
1664	English conquest of New Netherland
1670	First permanent English settlement established in South Carolina
1673	Plantation Duty Act passed • Dutch retake New York for 15 months
1675	Lords of Trade established • Metacom's War breaks out in New England
1676	Bacon's Rebellion breaks out in Virginia
1678	Popish Plot crisis begins in England
1680	Pueblos revolt in New Mexico
1684	Massachusetts Charter revoked
1685	Louis XIV revokes Edict of Nantes
1686	Dominion of New England established
1688–89	Glorious Revolution occurs in England
1689	Anglo-French wars begin • Glorious Revolution spreads to Massachusetts, New York, and Maryland
1691	Leisler executed in New York
1692	19 people hanged for witchcraft in Salem
1696	Parliament passes comprehensive Navigation Act • Board of Trade replaces Lords of Trade
1699	French establish Louisiana • Woolens Act passed
1701	Iroquois make peace with New France
1702–04	Carolina slavers destroy Florida missions
1707	Anglo-Scottish union creates kingdom of Great Britain
1713	Britain and France make peace
1714	George I ascends British throne
1715	Yamasee War devastates South Carolina

Demographic Differences

The most pronounced differences involved life expectancy, the sex ratio (the ratio of men to women in any society), and family structure. At one extreme were the all-male, multiethnic buccaneering societies in the Caribbean that lived only for plunder. In the sugar colonies, European men often died by age 40, and slaves even sooner. Because women settlers were scarce at first, the family itself seemed an endangered institution. Even when the sex ratio evened out and families began to emerge, couples had few children. Life expectancy in early South Carolina was slightly better than in the islands, slightly lower than in the Chesapeake Bay area. In the Chesapeake colonies, men who survived childhood diseases lived to an average age of about 45 years during the last half of the 17th century, still less than in England, where life expectancy exceeded 50. In Virginia and Maryland, as natural increase replaced immigration as the main source of population growth after 1680, women became more numerous, married much earlier, and raised larger families.

The northern colonies were much healthier. In the Delaware valley, a man who reached adulthood could expect to live past 60. In New Netherland, life expectancy and family size exceeded Europe's by 1660, and men outnumbered women among the newcomers by only 2 to 1. On Long Island in the 1680s, one woman claimed that she had more than 300 living descendants. New England was one of the healthiest places in the world. Because the sex ratio rapidly approached equality and because the thriving economy permitted couples to marry perhaps two years earlier than in England, population growth exploded. Canada followed a similar pattern. In the late 17th century, the birthrate in New France caught up with New England's, and population grew at a comparable pace.

These demographic differences had significant consequences. For example, the Caribbean and southern colonies were youthful societies in which men with good connections could expect to achieve high office while in their thirties, or even their twenties. By contrast, the New England colonies gradually became dominated by grandfathers. A man rarely became even a selectman before his forties. Magistrates were even older. Simon Bradstreet was almost 90 when he completed his last term as governor of Massachusetts in 1692. Despite the appalling death rate in the sugar and tobacco colonies, young men remained optimistic and upbeat, as they looked forward to challenging the world and making their fortunes. But in New England, people grew more despondent as the century progressed,

THE SPECTRUM OF SETTLEMENT: DEMOGRAPHY, ETHNICITY, ECONOMY, 1650–1700

Category	West Indies	Lower South	Chesapeake	Mid-Atlantic	New England	New France
Life expectancy for men, age 20	40	42	45	60+	Late 60s	60s
Family size	Below replacement rate	About two children	Rising after 1680	Very large	Very large	Very large
Race and ethnicity	Black majority by circa 1670s	Black majority by circa 1710	Growing black minority	Ethnic mix, N.W. Europe, English a minority	Almost all English	Almost all French
Economy	Sugar	Rice, 1690s ff	Tobacco	Furs, farms	Farms, fishing, shipbuilding	Furs, farms

THE SPECTRUM OF SETTLEMENT: RELIGION AND GOVERNMENT, CIRCA 1675–1700

Category	West Indies	Lower South	Chesapeake	Mid-Atlantic	New England	New France
Formal religion	Anglican Church establishment	Anglican Church establishment by circa 1710	Anglican Church establishment (after 1692 in Md.)	Competing sects, no established church	Congregational Church established	Catholic Church established
Religious tone	Irreverent	Contentious	Low-church Anglican	Family-based piety, sectarian competition	Family-based piety, intensity declining	Intensely Catholic
Local government	Parish	Parish and phantom counties (i.e., no court)	County and parish	County and township	Towns and counties; parishes after 1700	Cities
Provincial government	Royal	Proprietary	Royal (Va.), proprietary (Md.)	From proprietary to royal, except in Pa.	Corporate, with Mass. and N.H. becoming royal	Royal absolutism

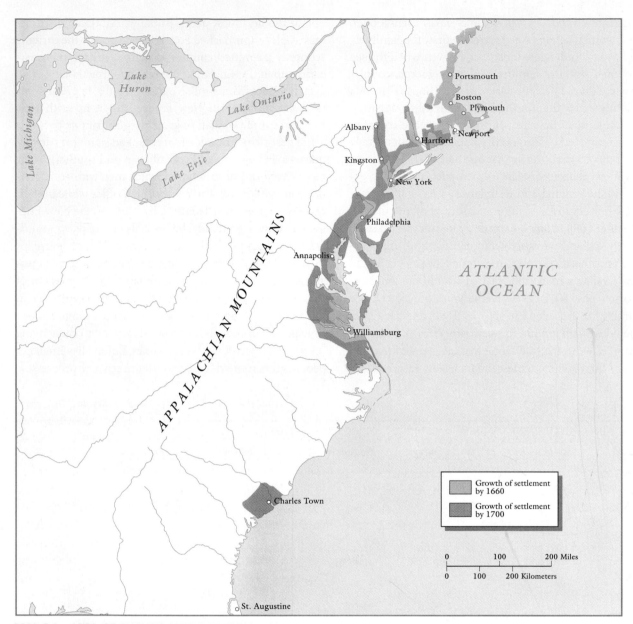

MAP 3.1 AREA OF ENGLISH SETTLEMENT BY 1700

This map differentiates the areas settled before 1660 from those settled between 1660 and 1700, or roughly the Restoration era.

even though they lived much longer. The typical sermon was a gloomy jeremiad that deplored the failings of the rising generation.

Race, Ethnicity, and Economy

The degree of racial and ethnic mixture also varied from region to region, along with economic priorities. The West Indies already had a large slave majority by 1700 and were well on their way to becoming a New Africa, except that the European minority had a firm grip on wealth and

power. In 1700, English settlers were still a clear majority in the southern mainland colonies, but African slaves became a majority in South Carolina around 1710 and were increasing rapidly. They would comprise 40 percent of Virginia's population by the 1730s. Africans were less numerous in the Delaware and Hudson valleys, although slavery became deeply entrenched in New York City and parts of New Jersey.

In the Middle Atlantic region, settlers from all over northwestern Europe were creating a new ethnic mosaic, especially in New Jersey and Pennsylvania. English colonists were probably always a minority, outnumbered at first by the Dutch, and later by Germans, Scots, and Irish. But New England was in every sense the most English of the colonies. In ethnic composition, it may have been more English than England, which by 1700 had sizable Dutch Reformed, French Huguenot, and Scottish Presbyterian minorities. New France was as French as New England was English. The farther south one went, the more diverse the population; the farther north, the more uniform.

Slavery and staple crops went together. The slave societies raised sugar, rice, or tobacco for sale in Europe. General farming and family labor also went together. By 1700, the Middle Atlantic was the wheat belt of North America. The New Englanders farmed and exported fish and lumber to the West Indies.

Religion and Education

With the exception of Spanish Florida, the intensity of religious observance varied immensely across the spectrum of settlement, ranging from irreverence and indifference in the West Indies to intense piety in New England and New France. Because formal education in the 17th century nearly always had a religious base, literacy followed a similar pattern. Colonists everywhere tried to prevent slaves from learning to read, and low literacy prevailed wherever slavery predominated. Chesapeake settlers provided almost no formal schooling for their children before the founding of the College of William and Mary in 1693 and of a Latin grammar school in Annapolis at about the same time. Even some of the justices of the peace in Maryland and Virginia were unable to write. By contrast, the Dutch maintained several good schools in New Netherland. Massachusetts founded Harvard College in 1636 and in 1642 required every town to have a writing school, and larger towns to support a Latin grammar school, in order to frustrate "ye old deluder Satan," as a 1647 school law phrased it. The Jesuits founded a college (actually more akin to a secondary school) in Quebec a few years before Harvard opened. France sent a bishop to Quebec in 1659, and he established a seminary (now Laval University) in the 1660s. Along the spectrum, piety, literacy, and education all grew stronger from south to north, although laymen in New France never became as literate as in New England.

Public support for the clergy followed the same pattern. By 1710, the established church of the mother country was the legally established church in the West Indies and in the southern mainland colonies. Establishment and dissent fought to a standstill in the Middle Atlantic, with toleration claiming the real victory in New York and full religious liberty in Pennsylvania. In New England, Old World dissent became the New World establishment. Public support for the clergy was much greater in the north than in the south. The sugar islands had the most wealth, but they maintained only one clergyman for every 3,000 to 9,000 people, depending on the island. In the Chesapeake, the comparable ratio was about one for every 1,500 people by 1700. It was perhaps one for every 1,000 in New York, one for every 600 in New England, and still lower in New France.

Moral standards also rose from south to north. New Englanders boasted that they were far more godly than all other colonists. The Puritans "give out that they are Israelites," reported a Dutch visitor to Connecticut, "and that we in our colony are Egyptians, and that the English in the Virginias are also Egyptians." As early as 1638, one Marylander quipped that a neighbor deserved to be "whippt at virginea" or "hanged in new England."

Local and Provincial Governments

Forms of government also varied. Drawing on their English experience, settlers could choose from among parishes, boroughs (towns), and counties. A colony's choices depended on its location along the spectrum of settlement.

The only important local institution in the sugar islands and in South Carolina was the parish, which took on many secular functions, such as poor relief. The Chesapeake colonies relied primarily on the county but also made increasing use of the parish. Few parishes were ever organized in the Middle Atlantic colonies, but the county as a form of government arrived with the English conquest of New Netherland in 1664 and became a powerful institution. Townships also appeared. New England's most basic local institution was the town. Massachusetts created counties in the 1640s, followed 20 years later by Connecticut and in the 1680s by Plymouth. Rhode Island and New Hampshire waited until the 18th century before creating counties. After 1700, towns large enough to support more than one church also adopted the parish system. In local government as in its economy, New England's use of the full range of parishes, towns, and counties made the region more fully English than other colonies.

The West Indian colonies all had royal governments by the 1660s (see the subsection "The Lords of Trade and Imperial Reform" later in this chapter). Proprietary forms dominated the mainland south of New England, except for royal Virginia. Until the 1680s, New England relied on corporate forms of government in which all officials, even governors, were elected. This system survived in Connecticut and Rhode Island until independence and beyond.

Unifying Trends: Language, War, Law, and Inheritance

Despite all this diversity, the 17th century produced a few trends toward greater homogeneity. For instance, language became more uniform in America than in England. True, the New England dialect derived mostly from East Anglia, the southern accent from southern and western England, and Middle Atlantic speech from north-central England. But Londoners went to all of the colonies (in England, people went to London), and London English affected every colony and softened the contrasts among the emerging regional dialects.

Another area of uniformity was the manner in which the settlers waged war: They did it in their own way, not with the professional armies that were just taking hold in Europe, but with short-term volunteers for whom terror against Indian women and children was often the tactic of choice. Europe was moving toward limited wars; the colonists demanded quick and total victories.

In the colonies, law became a simpler version of England's complex legal system. Justice was local and uncomplicated—in fact, an organized legal profession did not emerge until the 18th century. The absence of lawyers pleased most settlers.

Finally, no mainland American colony rigidly followed English patterns of inheritance. Instead, the colonies were developing their own practices. Some women had a chance to acquire property, usually by inheritance from a deceased husband, particularly in the Chesapeake colonies during the long period when men greatly outnumbered women. The single women who crossed the Atlantic as servants were desperate people who had hit bottom in England. Those who survived enjoyed a fantastic chance at upward mobility. Many won a respectability never available to them in England. In every colony, younger sons also found their situation improved. They played a huge role in settling the colonies, especially among the Chesapeake elite, and they showed little inclination to preserve institutions that had offered them no landed inheritance in England. Most families made no distinction between the eldest and other sons, except in New England. The Puritan colonies honored a biblical mandate to give the eldest son a double share. That practice strengthened patriarchy in the region, but it was much less discriminatory than primogeniture, which in England gave all land to the eldest son.

The Beginnings of Empire

In the chaotic 1640s, the English realized that their colonies overseas were bringing them few benefits. England had no coherent colonial policy.

Upheaval in America: The Critical 1640s

England's civil wars rocked its emerging empire, politically and economically. As royal power collapsed in the 1640s, the West Indian colonies demanded and received elective assemblies. The Dutch, taking advantage of the chaos in England, helped finance the sugar revolution in Barbados and seized control of trade in and out of England's West Indian and Chesapeake colonies. By 1650, most sugar and tobacco exports were going to Amsterdam, not London.

During the civil wars, nobody in England exercised effective control over the colonies. The king had declared that their trade was to remain in English hands, but no agency existed to enforce that claim. The new elective assemblies of Barbados and the Leeward Islands preferred to trade with the Dutch, even after the English Crown took over those colonies in 1660. The mainland colonies had been organized by joint-stock companies or proprietary lords under royal charters, but there the colonists governed themselves. As the New England settlements expanded, the new colonies of Connecticut, Rhode Island, and New Haven did not even bother to obtain royal charters. On the mainland, only Virginia had a royal governor.

The chaos of the 1640s gave Indians a unique opportunity to resist the settlers. As civil war disrupted trade with England and threatened to cut off regular supplies of muskets and gunpowder, the Indians gained a powerful advantage over the settlements. That danger seemed so ominous that Rhode Island ordered young men to learn how to use bows and arrows. Although the Indians of the eastern woodlands never united into an effective league, many of them, such as Miantonomo in New England and Opechancanough in Virginia, began to think of driving the Europeans out altogether.

Indians greatly outnumbered settlers, except in eastern New England and the Virginia tidewater. Between 1643 and 1647, the Iroquois nearly wiped out New France, and the Hudson valley Algonquians almost destroyed New Netherland. Maryland, beset by conflicts with Susquehannock Indians and by civil war among its colonists, nearly ceased to exist. The number of settlers there may have fallen to 300 by 1648. In Virginia, the aging warrior

Opechancanough staged another massacre, killing 500 settlers without warning on a holy day in 1644. This time the settlers recovered more quickly, took Opechancanough prisoner in 1646, and murdered him. They broke up his chiefdom and made its member tribes accept treaties of dependency.

Only New England avoided war with the Indians—just barely. Miantonomo, sachem of the Narragansetts, called for a war of extermination against the settlers, to be launched by a surprise attack in 1642. He abandoned the plan when settlers got wind of it. The colonists created their own defensive alliance in 1643, the New England Confederation, which united the four orthodox colonies of Massachusetts, Plymouth, Connecticut, and New Haven. Rhode Island was not invited to join. The confederation persuaded the Mohegans to kill Miantonomo, and tensions with the Narragansett Indians remained high. The Narragansetts controlled some of the finest land in New England. Massachusetts, Plymouth, and Connecticut all wanted that land, but the Narragansetts were still too powerful to intimidate. When threatened, they withdrew into inaccessible places that terrified most of the settlers. After the Narragansetts made it clear that they would fight if they had to, the Puritans backed down.

What happened in the colonies seemed of little interest to the English people in the turbulent 1640s. Later, as the debris of civil war was cleared away and the extent of Dutch commercial domination became obvious, the English turned their eyes westward once again. In a sense, England first discovered its colonies and their importance around 1650.

Mercantilism as a Moral Revolution

During the 17th century, most of the European powers adopted a set of policies now usually called mercantilism. The decline of the Spanish Empire persuaded many observers that the power of a state depended more on its underlying economy than on armies or the silver that paid for them. Mercantilists argued that power derived ultimately from the wealth of a country, that the increase of wealth required vigorous trade, and that colonies had become essential to that growth. Clearly, a state had to control the commerce of its colonies. Mercantilists, however, disagreed over the best ways to promote economic growth. The Dutch favored virtual free trade within Europe. England preferred some kind of state regulation of the domestic and imperial economy.

After a century of religious wars, neither Catholics nor Protestants had won a decisive victory in Europe. To European statesmen of the time, these conflicts merely confirmed their belief that governments reflected the passions of men. Philosophers agreed that the major passions are glory, love, and greed. Glory seemed nobler than carnal love, and love more inspiring than greed, which in any case was beneath the dignity of a gentleman. Still, the endless wars, driven by the quest for glory and the love of holy

---

A Desperate Strategy

During the slaughter of the Pequots at Mystic Fort in 1637, the Narragansett Indians had been allies of the Puritans, and they witnessed the massacre. By 1642, their principal sachem, Miantonomo, had reached a grim conclusion about the only proper way to deal with the settlers encroaching upon their lands:

O*ur fathers had plenty of deer and skins, our plains were full of deer, as also our woods, and of turkies, and our coves full of fish and fowl. But these English have gotten our land, they with scythes cut down the grass, and with axes fell the trees; their cows and horses eat the grass, and their hogs spoil our clam banks, and we shall be starved; therefore . . . When you see the three fires that will be made forty days hence, in a clear night, then do as we, and the next day fall on and kill men, women, and children, but no cows, for they will serve to eat till our deer be increased again.*

1. Why did both Opechancanough and Miantonomo decide that their best chance of survival lay in annihilating all Europeans?

For additional sources related to this feature, visit the *Liberty, Equality, Power* Web site at:

http://history.wadsworth.com/murrin_LEP4e

causes, had crippled Spain, killed one-third of the German people, and nearly destroyed the English state.

As time passed, statesmen began to look more favorably upon greed, a passion in which they found interesting properties. The pursuit of glory or love inspires intense but unpredictable activity, followed by relaxation or even exhaustion. Greed, because it is insatiable, fosters *predictable* behavior—namely, the pursuit of self-interest, a softer term than greed and one that most people preferred to use. By creating economic incentives, then, a state could induce its people to work to increase not only their own wealth and power but also that of the whole country. Likewise, by imposing import duties and other disincentives, the state could discourage actions detrimental to its power.

At first these ideas were as gloomy as the world in which they arose. Early mercantilists assumed that the world contained a fixed supply of wealth. A state, to augment its own power, would have to expropriate the wealth of a rival. Trade wars would replace religious wars, although presumably they would be less destructive, which they usually were. Gradually, however, a more radical idea took hold: The growth of trade might multiply the wealth of the whole world, with all nations benefiting and becoming so interdependent that war between them would be recognized as suicidal. That vision of peace and unending growth has never been realized, but it still inspires people today.

Mercantilism marked a major breakthrough toward modernity. It gradually became associated with the emerging idea of unending progress, and it made statesmen rethink the role of legislation in their societies.

Europeans were already familiar with two kinds of progress, one associated with Renaissance humanism, the other explicitly Christian. The opening of the Americas had already reinforced both visions. Humanists knew that the distant ancestors of Europeans had all been "barbarians" who had advanced over the centuries toward "civility." Their own encounters with the indigenous peoples of Africa, Ireland, and America underscored this dualistic view by revealing new "savages" who seemed morally and culturally inferior to the "civilized" colonists. Most Christians shared these convictions, but they also believed that human society was progressing toward a future Millennium in which Christ will return to earth and reign with his saints in perfect harmony for 1,000 years. To missionaries, both Catholic and Protestant, the discovery of millions of "heathens" in the Americas stimulated millennial thinking. God had chosen this moment to open a new hemisphere to Christians, they explained, because the Millennium was near. Both the humanist and the Christian notions of progress were static concepts, however.

© The British Museum.

A PICTISH MAN HOLDING A HUMAN HEAD,
BY JOHN WHITE, LATE 16TH CENTURY

In the ancient world, the Picts were among the ancestors of the English and the Scots. John White, who painted many Indian scenes on Roanoke Island in the 1580s, believed that the English had been "savages" not all that long ago and that American Indians, like the English, could progress to "civility." America made him think of "progress."

Humanity would advance to a certain level, and progress would cease. Mercantilism, by contrast, marked a revolution of the human imagination precisely because it could arouse visions of endless progress.

Mercantilism also promoted a more modern concept of law. In the past, most jurists believed that legislation merely restated natural laws or immemorial customs in written form. Mercantilists, on the other hand, saw law as an agent of change. They intended to modify behavior, perhaps even transform society. They had no illusions about achieving perfection, however. At first, they probably considered anything that made their exhausted world less terrible to be a triumph. But as the decades passed, mercantilists became more confident of their ability to improve society.

The First Navigation Act

English merchants began debating trade policy during a severe depression in the 1620s. They agreed that a nation's wealth depended on its balance of trade, that a healthy nation ought to export more than it imports, and that the difference—or balance—could be converted into military strength. They also believed that a state needed colonies to produce essential commodities that were unavailable at home. And they argued that a society ought to export luxuries, not import them. English merchants observed Dutch commercial success and determined that it rested on a mastery of these principles. For England to catch up, Parliament would have to intervene.

With the close of the Thirty Years' War in Europe in 1648, the three major Protestant powers—Sweden, the Netherlands, and England—no longer had reason to avoid fighting one another. England reacted quickly after the execution of Charles I. London merchants clamored for measures to stifle Dutch competition. Parliament listened to them, not to Oliver Cromwell and other Puritans who regarded war between two Protestant republics as an abomination. The merchants got their Navigation Act—and their naval war.

In 1650, Parliament banned foreign ships from English colonies. A year later, it passed the first comprehensive Navigation Act, aimed at Dutch competition. Under this act, Asian and African goods could be imported into the British Isles or the colonies only in English-owned ships, and the master and at least half of each crew had to be Englishmen. European goods could be imported into Britain or the colonies in either English ships or the ships of the producing country, but foreigners could not trade between one English port and another.

This new attention from the English government angered the colonists in the West Indies and North America. Mercantilists assumed that the colonies existed only to enrich the mother country. Why else had England permitted them to be founded? But the young men growing sugar in Barbados or tobacco in Virginia hoped to prosper on their own. Selling their crops to the Dutch, who offered the lowest freight rates, added to their profits. Although New England produced no staple that Europeans wanted except fish, Yankee skippers cheerfully swapped their fish or forest products in the Chesapeake for tobacco, which they then carried directly to Europe, usually to Amsterdam.

Barbados greeted the Navigation Act by proclaiming virtual independence. Virginia recognized Charles II as king and continued to welcome Dutch and Yankee traders. In 1651, Parliament dispatched a naval force to America. It compelled Barbados to submit to Parliament and then sailed to the Chesapeake, where Virginia and Maryland capitulated in 1652. In return, the Virginians received the right to elect their own governor, a privilege that the restored Crown revoked in 1660. Without resident officials to enforce English policy, however, trade with the Dutch continued.

By 1652, England and the Netherlands were at war. For two years, the English navy—trim and efficient after a decade of struggle against the king—dealt heavy blows to the Dutch. Finally, in 1654, Cromwell sent Parliament home and made peace. A militant Protestant, he preferred to fight Catholic Spain rather than the Netherlands. In the tradition of Drake, Gilbert, and Ralegh, he sent a fleet to take Hispaniola. It failed in that mission, but it seized Jamaica in 1655.

Restoration Navigation Acts

By the Restoration era, mercantilist thinking had become widespread. Although the new royalist Parliament invalidated all legislation passed during the Commonwealth period, these Cavaliers promptly reenacted and extended the original Navigation Act in a series of new measures. The Navigation Act of 1660 required that all colonial trade be carried on English ships (a category that included colonial vessels but now excluded the Scots), but the master and *three-fourths* of the crew had to be English. The act also created a category of "enumerated commodities," of which sugar and tobacco were the most important, permitting these products to be shipped from the colony of origin *only* to England or to another English colony—the intent being to give England a monopoly over the export of major staples from every English colony to Europe and to the rest of the world. The colonists could still export nonenumerated commodities elsewhere. New England could send fish to a French sugar island, for example, and Virginia could export wheat to Cuba, provided the French and the Spanish would let them.

In a second measure, the Staple Act of 1663, Parliament regulated goods going to the colonies. With few exceptions, products from Europe, Asia, or Africa had to land in England before they could be delivered to the settlements.

A third measure, the Plantation Duty Act of 1673, required captains of colonial ships to post bond in the colonies that they would deliver all enumerated commodities to England, or else pay on the spot the duties that would be owed in England (the "plantation duty"). England hoped that this measure would eliminate all incentives to smuggle. To make it effective, England sent customs officers to the colonies for the first time to collect the duty and prosecute all violators. Because the only income

MIRROR OF THE FRENCH TYRANNY (1673)

When Louis XIV sent the French army into the Netherlands, France replaced Spain as Europe's most militant Catholic power, as this Protestant view suggests.

of these officials came from fees and from their share of condemned vessels, their livelihood was precarious. At first, colonial governments regarded customs collectors as parasites. Maryland officials even murdered one of them in the 1680s.

Parliament intended nothing less than a revolution in Atlantic trade. Properly enforced, the Navigation Acts would dislodge the Dutch and establish English hegemony over Atlantic trade, and that is what happened in the next half-century. In 1600, about 90 percent of England's exports consisted of woolen cloth. By 1700, colonial and Asian commerce accounted for 30 to 40 percent of England's overseas trade, and London had become the largest city in Western Europe. As the center of England's colonial trade, its population tripled during the 17th century.

Enforcement long remained uneven, but in the 1670s, a war between France and the Netherlands diverted critical Dutch resources from trade to defense, thus helping England catch up with the Dutch. By 1700, Brit-

ain had the most powerful navy in the world. By 1710 or so, virtually all British colonial trade was carried on British ships. Sugar, tobacco, and other staple crops all passed through Britain on their way to their ultimate destination. Nearly all of the manufactured goods consumed in the colonies were made in Britain. Most products from Europe or Asia destined for the colonies passed through Britain first, although some smuggling of these goods continued.

Few government policies have ever been as successful as England's Navigation Acts, but England achieved these results without pursuing a steady course toward increased imperial control. For example, in granting charters to Rhode Island in 1662 and to Connecticut in 1663, Charles II approved elective governors and legislatures in both colonies. (The Connecticut charter also absorbed the New Haven Colony into the Hartford government.) These elective officials could not be dismissed or punished for failure to enforce the Navigation Acts. Moreover, the Crown also chartered several new Restoration colonies (see chapter 2), whose organizers had few incentives to obey the new laws. Making the empire work would take time.

Indians, Settlers, Upheaval

As time passed, the commercial possibilities and limitations of North America were becoming much clearer. The French and Dutch mastered the fur trade because they controlled the two all-water routes to the interior, via the St. Lawrence system and the Hudson and Mohawk valleys. South Carolinians could go around the southern extreme of the Appalachians. They all needed Indian trading partners.

As of 1670, no sharp boundaries yet existed between Indian lands and colonial settlements. Boston, the largest city north of Mexico, was only 15 miles from an Indian village. Connecticut valley towns were surrounded by Indians. The outposts on the Delaware River were islands in a sea of Indians. In the event of war, nearly every European settlement was vulnerable to attack.

Indian Strategies of Survival

By the 1670s, most of the coastal tribes in regular contact with Europeans had already been devastated by disease or soon would be. European diseases, by magnifying the depleted tribes' need for captives, also increased the intensity of wars among Indian peoples, probably to their highest point ever. The Iroquois, for example, although hard hit by smallpox and other ailments, acquired muskets from the Dutch and used them, first to attack other Iroquoian peoples and then Algonquians. These "mourning wars" were often initiated by the widow or bereaved mother or sister of a deceased loved one. She insisted that her male relatives repair the loss. Her warrior relatives then launched a raid and brought back captives. Adult male prisoners, who might take revenge if allowed to live, were usually tortured to death. Most women and children were adopted and assimilated. Adoption worked because the captives shared the cultural values of their captors. They became Iroquois. As early as the 1660s, most Indians in the Five Nations were adoptees, not native-born Iroquois. In this way, the confederacy remained strong while its rivals declined. In the southern piedmont, the warlike, Sioux-speaking Catawba Indians also assimilated thousands from other tribes. Further into the southern interior, the nations that were becoming Creeks assimilated adoptees from a wide variety of ethnic backgrounds. They and other southern

nations also became adept at playing off the Spaniards against the English (and later the French).

In some ways, America became as much a new world for the Indians as it did for the colonists. European cloth, muskets, hatchets, knives, and pots were welcomed among the Indians and spread far into the interior, but they came at a price. Indians who learned to use them gradually abandoned traditional skills and became increasingly dependent on trade with Europeans, a process that was not complete until the 19th century. Alcohol, the one item always in demand, was also dangerous. Indian men drank to alter their mood and achieve visions, not for sociability. Drunkenness became a major, if intermittent, social problem.

Settlers who understood that their future depended on the fur trade, as in New France, tried to stay on good terms with the Indians. Pieter Stuyvesant put New Netherland on such a course, and the English governors of New York followed his lead after 1664. Edmund Andros, governor from 1674 to 1680, cultivated the friendship of the Iroquois League, in which the five member nations had promised not to wage war against one another. In 1677, Andros and the Five Nations agreed to make New York the easternmost link in what the English called the Covenant Chain of peace, a huge defensive advantage for a lightly populated colony. Thus, while New England and Virginia fought bitter Indian wars in the 1670s, New York avoided conflict. The Covenant Chain later proved flexible enough to incorporate other Indians and colonies as well.

Where the Indian trade was slight, war became more likely. In 1675, it erupted in both New England and the Chesapeake. In the 1640s, Virginia had negotiated treaties of dependency with the member nations of the Powhatan chiefdom, in the hope of keeping them loyal in the event of war with other Indians. The New England colonies had similar understandings with the large non-Christian nations of the region, but the Puritan governments placed even greater reliance on a growing number of Christianized Indians.

Puritan Indian Missions

Serious efforts to convert Indians to Protestantism began in the 1640s on the island of Martha's Vineyard under Thomas Mayhew, Sr., and Thomas Mayhew, Jr., and in Massachusetts under John Eliot, pastor of the Roxbury church. Eliot tried to make the nearby Indian town of Natick into a model mission community.

The Mayhews were more successful than Eliot, although he received most of the publicity. They worked with local sachems and challenged only the tribal powwows

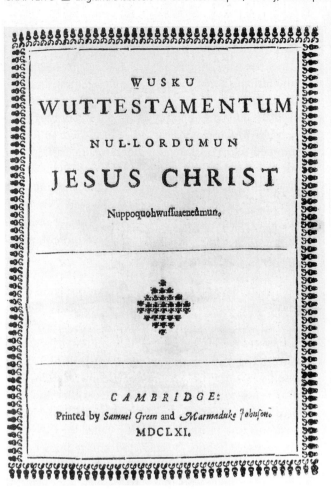

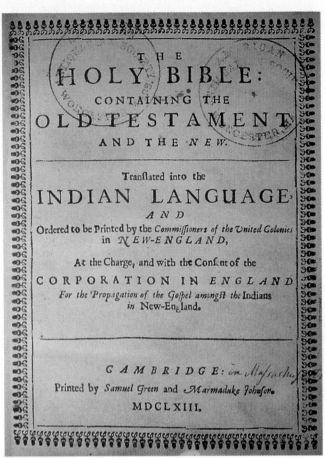

TITLE PAGES OF JOHN ELIOT'S INDIAN BIBLE

On the left is the New Testament (1661); on the right is the complete Bible (1663). Eliot's translation took many years to complete. Most copies of the Indian Bible were destroyed in Metacom's War of 1675–76.

(prophets or medicine men) and even converted some of them when they proved unable to cure smallpox. The Mayhews encouraged Indian men to teach the settlers of Martha's Vineyard and Nantucket how to catch whales, an activity that made them a vital part of the settlers' economy without threatening their identity as men. Eliot, by contrast, attacked the authority of the sachems as well as the powwows, challenged the traditional tribal structure, and insisted on turning Indian men into farmers, a female role in Indian society. Yet he did translate the Bible and a few other religious works into the Massachusett language.

By the early 1670s, more than 1,000 Indians, nearly all of them survivors of coastal tribes that had been decimated by disease, lived in a string of seven "praying towns," and Eliot was busy organizing five more, mostly among the Nipmucks of the interior. By 1675, about 2,300 Indians, perhaps one-quarter of all those living in southeastern New England, were in various stages of conversion to Christianity. But only 160 of them had achieved the kind of conversion experience that Puritans required for full membership in a church. Indians did not share the Puritan sense of sin. They could not easily grasp why their best deeds should stink in the nostrils of the Lord. The more powerful nations felt threatened by this pressure to convert, and resistance to Christianity became one cause of the war that broke out in 1675. Other causes were the settlers' lust for Indian lands, the intrusion of their livestock onto Indian cornfields, and the fear, especially among younger warrior-hunters, that their whole way of life was in danger of extinction.

Metacom (whom the English called King Philip) was one of those Indians. He was sachem of the Wampanoags and the son of Massasoit, who had celebrated the first thanksgiving feast with the Pilgrims. Metacom once remarked that if he became "a praying sachem, I shall be a poor and weak one, and easily be trod upon."

Metacom's (or King Philip's) War

War broke out shortly after Plymouth executed three Wampanoags accused of murdering John Sassamon, a Harvard-educated Indian preacher who may have been spying on Metacom. The fighting began in the frontier town of Swansea in June 1675, after settlers killed an Indian they found looting an abandoned house. When the Indians demanded satisfaction the next day, the settlers laughed in their faces. The Indians took revenge, and the violence escalated into war.

The settlers, remembering their easy triumph over the Pequots a generation earlier (see chapter 2), were confident of victory. But, since the 1630s, the Indians had acquired firearms. They had built forges to make musket balls and repair their weapons. They had even become marksmen with the smoothbore musket by firing several smaller bullets, instead of a single musketball, with each charge. The settlers, who had usually paid Indians to do their hunting for them, were terrible shots. In the tradition of European armies, they discharged volleys without aiming. To the shock of the colonists, Metacom won several engagements against Plymouth militia, usually by ambushing the noisy intruders. He then escaped from Plymouth Colony and headed toward the upper Connecticut valley, where he burned five Massachusetts towns in three months.

Massachusetts and Connecticut joined the fray. Rather than attack Metacom's Wampanoags, they went after the Narragansetts, who had accepted some Wampanoag refugees but were trying to remain neutral. Many prominent settlers dreamed of acquiring their fertile lands. In the Great Swamp Fight of December 1675, a Puritan army, with the aid of Indian guides, attacked an unfinished Narragansett fort and massacred hundreds of Indians, most of them women and children, but not before the Indians had picked off a high percentage of the officers. The surviving warriors joined Metacom and showed that they too could use terror. They torched more frontier settlements. Altogether, about 800 settlers were killed, and two dozen towns were destroyed or badly damaged in the war.

Atrocities were common on both sides. When one settler boasted that his Bible would save him from harm, the Indians disemboweled him and stuffed the sacred book in his belly. At least 17 friendly Indians were murdered by settlers, some in cold blood before dozens of witnesses, but for more than a year New England juries refused to convict anyone. On one occasion, when some Maine Indians were brought to Marblehead as prisoners, the women of that fishing village literally tore them to pieces with their bare hands.

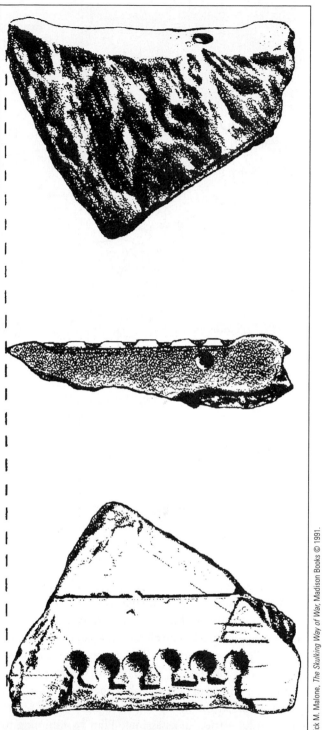

Patrick M. Malone, *The Skulking Way of War*, Madison Books © 1991.

BULLET MOLD IN USE AMONG NEW ENGLAND INDIANS, CIRCA 1675

Indians could make bullets and repair muskets, but they remained dependent on Europeans for their supply of gunpowder. In early 1676, the Indian leader Metacom ran low on gunpowder after failing to acquire more from New France. Over the next several months, he lost the war.

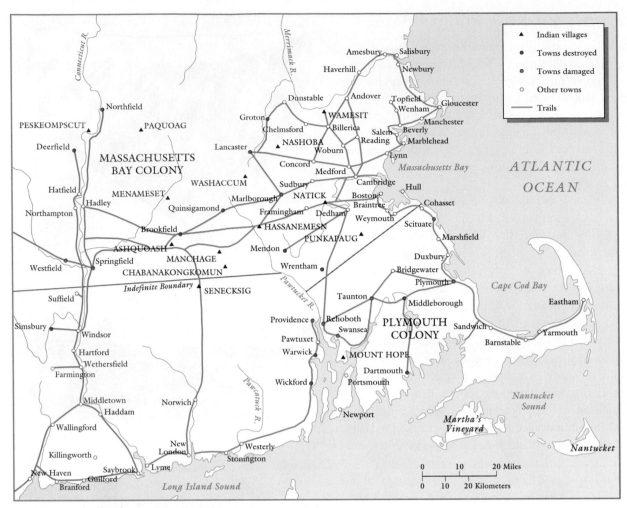

MAP 3.2 NEW ENGLAND IN METACOM'S WAR, 1675–1676
This map locates Indian villages and New England towns, and it indicates which towns were destroyed, damaged, or unscathed during the war.

Frontier settlers demanded the annihilation of all nearby Indians, even the Christian converts. The Massachusetts government, shocked to realize that it could not win the war without Indian allies, did what it could to protect the "praying" Indians. The magistrates evacuated them to a bleak island in Boston harbor, where they spent a miserable winter of privation but then enlisted to fight against Metacom in the spring campaign. Some settlers may even have tried to assassinate Eliot by ramming his boat in Boston harbor. The accused men, who insisted that the collision was accidental, were acquitted.

The war nearly tore New England apart, and it did split the clergy. Increase Mather, a prominent Boston minister, saw the conflict as God's judgment on a sinful people and warned that no victory would come until New England repented and reformed. At first, the Massachusetts General Court agreed. It blamed the war on young men who wore their hair too long, on boys and girls who took leisurely horse rides together, on people who dressed

above their station in life, and on blaspheming Quakers. Quakers, in turn, saw the war as divine punishment for their persecution by the Puritans. In Connecticut, which stopped hounding Quakers during the war, only one town was destroyed. Another Boston minister, William Hubbard, insisted that the war was only a brief testing time, after which the Lord would lead his saints to victory over the heathen. To Daniel Gookin, a magistrate committed to Eliot's mission work, the war was an unspeakable tragedy for both settlers and Indians.

Despite their disagreements, the settlers pulled together and won the war in 1676. Governor Andros of New York persuaded the Mohawks to attack Metacom's winter camp and disperse his people, who by then were short of gunpowder. The New Englanders, working closely with Mohegan and Christian Indian allies, then hunted down Metacom's war parties, killed hundreds of Indians, including Metacom, and sold hundreds more into West Indian slavery. Some of those enslaved had not even been party to the conflict and had actually requested asylum from it. As the tide turned, the Massachusetts government sided with Hubbard by ordering a day of thanksgiving, but Increase Mather's church observed a fast day instead. The colony had not reformed adequately, he explained.

Virginia's Indian War

In Virginia, Governor Sir William Berkeley, who had led the colony to victory over Opechancanough 30 years earlier, rejoiced in the New Englanders' woes. Metacom's War was the least they deserved for the way the Puritans had ripped England apart and executed Charles I during the civil wars. Then Virginia began to have troubles of its own.

In 1675, the Doegs, a dependent Indian nation in the Potomac valley, demanded payment of an old debt from a local planter. When he refused, they ran off some of his livestock. After his overseer killed one of them, the others fled but later returned to ambush and kill the man. The county militia mustered and followed the Doegs across the Potomac into Maryland. At a fork in the trail, the militia split into two parties. Each found a group of Indians in a shack a few hundred yards up the path it was following. Both parties fired at point-blank range, killing 11 at one cabin and 14 at the other. One of the bands was indeed Doeg; the other was not: "Susquehannock friends," blurted one Indian as he fled.

The Susquehannocks were a strong Iroquoian-speaking people with firearms; they had moved south to escape Iroquois attacks. At Maryland's invitation, they had recently occupied land north of the Potomac. Berkeley, still hoping to avoid war, sent John Washington (ancestor of George) with some Virginia militia to investigate the killings and, if possible, to set matters right.

Washington preferred vengeance. His Virginia militia joined with a Maryland force, and together they besieged a formidable Susquehannock fort on the north bank of the Potomac. The fort was too strong to take without artillery even though the attackers had a huge edge in numbers. When the Indians sent out five or six sachems to negotiate, the militia murdered them and then laid siege to the fort for the next six weeks. The Indians, short of provisions, finally broke out one night with all their people, killing several militiamen. After hurling taunts of defiance and promises of vengeance, they disappeared into the forest. Apparently blaming Virginia more than Maryland, they killed more than 30 Virginia settlers in January 1676. The colonists began to panic.

Berkeley favored a defensive strategy against the Indians; most settlers wanted to attack. In March 1676, the governor summoned a special session of the Virginia legislature to approve the creation of a string of forts above the fall line of the major rivers, with companies of "rangers" to patrol the stretches between them. Berkeley also hoped to maintain a distinction between the clearly hostile Susquehannocks and other Indians who might still be neutral or friendly. Frontier settlers, mostly former servants frustrated by low tobacco prices and unable to acquire tidewater lands because established planters had bought them up, demanded war against all Indians. Finally, to avoid further provocation, Berkeley restricted the fur trade to a few of his close associates. To the men excluded from that circle, his actions looked like favoritism. To settlers in frontier counties, whose access to new lands was blocked by the Indians and who now had to pay higher taxes, Berkeley's strategy seemed intolerable, ineffective, and needlessly expensive.

In both the Second (1665–67) and Third (1672–74) Anglo-Dutch Wars, Berkeley had built costly forts to protect the colony from the Dutch navy, but Dutch warships had sailed around the forts and mauled the tobacco fleet anyway. Accordingly, colonists denounced the building of any more forts and demanded an offensive campaign waged by unpaid volunteers, who would take their rewards by plundering and enslaving Indians. In April, the frontier

CRUDE HOUSING FOR SETTLERS IN NORTH AMERICA
When the first settlers came to North America, their living quarters were anything but luxurious. The crude housing shown in this modern reconstruction of Jamestown remained typical of Virginia and Maryland through the 17th century.

settlers found a reckless leader in Nathaniel Bacon, a young newcomer to the colony with a scandalous past and £1,800 to invest. Using his political connections (he was the governor's cousin by marriage), he managed an appointment to the council soon after his arrival in the colony in 1674. Bacon, the owner of a plantation and trading post in Henrico County at the falls of the James River (now Richmond), was one of the men excluded from the Indian trade under Berkeley's new rules.

Bacon's Rebellion

Ignoring Berkeley's orders, Bacon marched his frontiersmen south in search of the elusive Susquehannocks. After several days, his weary men reached a village of hospitable Occaneechees, who offered them shelter, announced that they knew where to find a Susquehannock camp, and even offered to attack it. The Occaneechees surprised and defeated the Susquehannocks and returned with their captives to celebrate the victory with Bacon. But after the Occaneechees had fallen asleep, Bacon's men massacred them and seized their furs and prisoners. On their return to Henrico in May, the Baconians boasted of their prowess as Indian killers.

By then, Berkeley had outlawed Bacon, dissolved the legislature, and called the first general election since 1661. The 1661 assembly had recently imposed a property requirement for voting, but Berkeley suspended it and asked the burgesses to bring their grievances to Jamestown for redress at the June assembly. "How miserable that man is," he complained, "that Governes a People where six parts of seaven at least are Poore Endebted Discontented and Armed."

As one measure of their resentment against elite planters, voters elected a fair number of burgesses who were not JPs, almost unheard of since mid-century. Henrico's voters elected Bacon to the assembly. Berkeley had him arrested when he reached Jamestown and made him go down on his knees before the governor and council and apologize for his disobedience. Berkeley then forgave him and restored him to his seat in the council. By then, even the governor had abandoned his effort to distinguish between hostile and friendly Indians, but he still favored a defensive war. While the burgesses were passing laws to reform the county courts, the vestries, and the tax system, Bacon slipped away to Henrico, summoned his followers again, and marched on Jamestown. At gunpoint, he forced Berkeley to commission him as general of volunteers and compelled the legislature to authorize another expedition against the Indians.

Berkeley retreated downriver to Gloucester County and mustered its militia, but they refused to follow him against Bacon. They would fight only Indians. Mortified, Berkeley fled to the eastern shore, the only part of the colony that was safe from Indian attack and thus still loyal to him. Bacon hastened to Jamestown, summoned a meeting of planters at the governor's Green Spring mansion, made them swear an oath of loyalty to him, and ordered the confiscation of the estates of Berkeley's supporters, who were men in the process of becoming great planters.

HENRY LATROBE'S SKETCH OF GREEN SPRING, THE HOME OF GOVERNOR SIR WILLIAM BERKELEY, AT THE TIME OF BACON'S REBELLION
Green Spring was one of the first great houses built in Virginia. Latrobe made this drawing in the 1790s.

Meanwhile, Berkeley raised his own force on the eastern shore by promising the men an exemption from taxes for 21 years and the right to plunder the rebels.

Royal government collapsed. During summer 1676, hundreds of settlers set out to make their fortunes by plundering Indians, other colonists, or both. Bacon's Rebellion was the largest upheaval in the American colonies before 1775. Later legends to the contrary, it had little to do with liberty but a lot to do with class resentments.

Bacon never did kill a hostile Indian. While he was slaughtering and enslaving the unresisting Pamunkeys along the frontier, Berkeley assembled a small fleet and retook Jamestown in August. Bacon rushed east, exhibiting his Indian captives along the way, and laid siege to James-

town. He captured the wives of prominent Berkeley supporters and forced them to stand in the line of fire as he dug his trenches closer to the capital. After suffering only a few casualties, the governor's men grew discouraged, and in early September the whole force returned to the eastern shore. Bacon then burned Jamestown to the ground. He also boasted of his ability to hold off an English army, unite Virginia with Maryland and North Carolina, and win Dutch support for setting up an independent Chesapeake republic. Instead he died of dysentery in October.

Berkeley soon regained control of Virginia. Using the ships of the London tobacco fleet, he overpowered the plantations that Bacon had fortified. Then, in January 1677, a force of 1,000 redcoats arrived, too late to help but

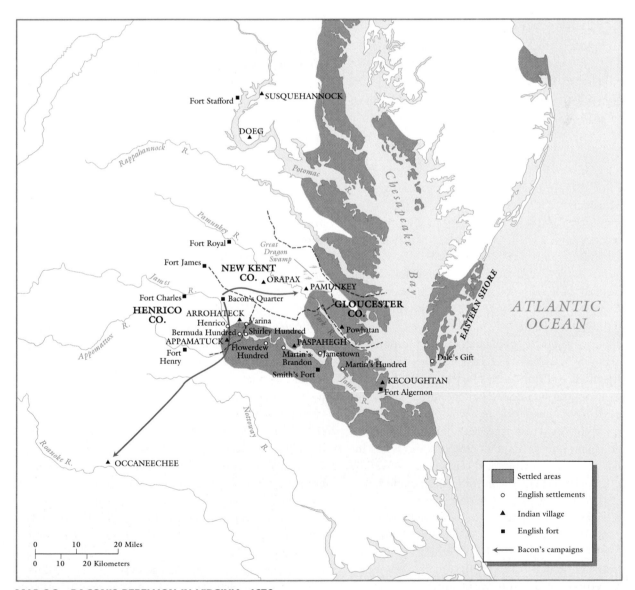

MAP 3.3 BACON'S REBELLION IN VIRGINIA, 1676
Settlement had just reached the fall line by the 1670s. The map also shows Bacon's two military campaigns, against the Occaneechees and the Pamunkeys.

in time to strain the colony's depleted resources. Ignoring royal orders to show clemency, Berkeley hanged 23 of the rebels. A new assembly repudiated the reforms of 1676, and in many counties the governor's men used their control of the courts to continue plundering the Baconians through confiscations and fines. Summoned to England to defend himself, Berkeley died there in 1677 before he could present his case.

Crisis in England and the Redefinition of Empire

Bacon's Rebellion helped trigger a political crisis in England. Because Virginia produced little tobacco in 1676 during the uprising, English customs revenues fell sharply, and the king was obliged to ask Parliament for more money. Parliament's response was tempered by the much deeper problem of the royal succession. Charles II had fathered many bastards, but his royal marriage was childless. After the queen reached menopause in the mid-1670s, his brother James, duke of York, became his heir. By then, James had become a Catholic. When Charles dissolved the Parliament that had sat from 1661 until 1678, he knew he would have to deal with a new House of Commons terrified by the prospect of a Catholic king.

The Popish Plot, the Exclusion Crisis, and the Rise of Party

In this atmosphere of distrust, a cynical adventurer, Titus Oates, fabricated the sensational story that he had uncovered a sinister "Popish Plot" to kill Charles and bring James to the throne. In the wake of these accusations, the king's ministry fell, and the parliamentary opposition won majorities in three successive elections between 1678 and 1681. Organized by Lord Shaftesbury (the Carolina proprietor), the opposition demanded that James, a Catholic, be excluded from the throne in favor of his Protestant daughters by his first marriage, Mary and Anne. It also called for a guarantee of frequent elections and for an independent electorate not under the influence of wealthy patrons. The king's men began castigating Shaftesbury's followers as Whigs, the name of an obscure sect of Scottish religious extremists who favored the assassination of both Charles and James. Whigs in turn denounced Charles's courtiers as Tories, a term for Irish Catholics who murdered Protestant landlords. Like Puritan, Quaker, Papist, and other terms of abuse, both words stuck.

England's party struggle reflected a deep rift between Court and Country forces. As of 1681, Tories were a Court party. They favored the legitimate succession, a standing army with adequate revenues to maintain it, the Anglican Church without toleration for Protestant dissenters, and a powerful monarchy. The Whigs were a Country opposition that stood for the exclusion of James from the throne, a decentralized militia rather than a standing army, toleration of Protestant dissenters but not of Catholics, and an active role in government for a reformed Parliament. During this struggle, James fled to Scotland in virtual exile. But Charles, after getting secret financial support from King Louis XIV of France, dissolved Parliament in 1681 and ruled without one for the last four years of his reign.

The Lords of Trade and Imperial Reform

English politics of the 1670s and 1680s had a profound impact on the colonies. The duke of York emerged from the Third Anglo-Dutch War as the most powerful shaper of imperial policy. At his urging, the government created a new agency in 1675, the Lords Committee of Trade and Plantations, or more simply, the Lords of Trade. This agency, a permanent committee of the Privy Council, enforced the Navigation Acts and administered the colonies. Although Virginia was the oldest royal colony, the West Indies became the object of most of the new policies, simply because the Caribbean remained a much more important theater of international competition and wealth. The instruments of royal government first took shape in the islands and were then extended to the mainland.

In the 1660s, the Crown took control of the governments of Barbados, Jamaica, and the Leeward Islands. The king appointed the governor and upper house of each colony; the settlers elected an assembly. The Privy Council in England reserved to itself the power to hear appeals from colonial courts and to disallow colonial legislation after the governor had approved it. The Privy Council also issued a formal commission and a lengthy set of instructions to each royal governor. In the two or three decades after 1660, these documents became standardized, especially after the Lords of Trade began to apply the lessons learned in one colony to problems anticipated in others.

The king's commission defined a governor's powers. From the Crown's point of view, the commission *created* the constitutional structure of each colony, a claim that few settlers accepted. The colonists believed they had an inherent right to constitutional rule even without the king's explicit warrant.

Written instructions told each royal governor how to use his broad powers. They laid out what he must do, such as command the militia, and what he must avoid, such as approving laws detrimental to English trade. Despite some confusion at first, Crown lawyers eventually agreed that these instructions were binding only on the governor, not on the colony as a whole. In other words, royal instructions never acquired the force of law.

London also insisted that each colony pay the cost of its own government. Ironically, this requirement strengthened colonial claims to self-rule. After a long struggle in Jamaica, the Crown imposed a compromise in 1681 that had broad significance for all of the colonies. The Lords of Trade threatened to make the Jamaica assembly as weak as the Irish Parliament, which could debate and approve only those bills that had first been adopted by the English Privy Council. Under the compromise, the Jamaica assembly retained its power to initiate and amend legislation, in return for agreeing to a permanent revenue act, a measure that freed the governor from financial dependence on the assembly.

Metacom's War and Bacon's Rebellion lent urgency to these reforms and speeded up their use in the mainland colonies. The Lords of Trade ordered soldiers to Virginia, along with a royal commission to investigate grievances there. In 1676, they also sent an aggressive customs officer, Edward Randolph, to Massachusetts. His lengthy reports recommended that the colony's charter be revoked. The Lords of Trade viewed New England and all proprietary colonies with deep suspicion, although they failed to block the founding of Pennsylvania as a new proprietary venture. They had reason for concern. As late as 1678, Virginia remained the only royal colony on the mainland. The Lords of Trade might enforce compliance with the Navigation Acts elsewhere, but they possessed no effective instruments for punishing violators in North America. The king could demand and reprimand, but not command.

The Jamaica model assumed that each royal governor would summon an assembly on occasion, although not often. In the 1680s, the Crown imposed a similar settlement on Virginia—an occasional assembly with full powers of legislation in exchange for a permanent revenue act. Although New York had been an experiment in autocracy since the English conquest of 1664, James conceded an assembly to that colony, too, in exchange for a permanent revenue act in 1683. The Jamaica model was becoming the norm for the Lords of Trade. James's real preference emerged after the English Court of Chancery revoked the Massachusetts Charter in 1684. Charles II died and his brother became King James II in early 1685. The possibility of a vigorous autocracy in America suddenly reappeared.

The Dominion of New England

Absolutist New York now became the king's model for reorganizing New England. James disallowed the New York Charter of Liberties of 1683 (see chapter 2) and abolished the colony's assembly but kept the permanent revenue act in force. In 1686, he sent Sir Edmund Andros, the autocratic governor of New York from 1674 to 1680, to Massachusetts to take over a new government called the Dominion of New England. James added New Hampshire, Plymouth, Rhode Island, Connecticut, New York, and both Jerseys to the Dominion. Andros governed this vast domain through an appointive council and a superior court that rode circuit dispensing justice. There was no elective assembly. Andros also imposed religious toleration on the Puritans, even forcing one Boston church to let Anglicans use its meetinghouse for public worship for part of each Sunday.

At first, Andros won support from merchants who had been excluded from politics by the Puritan requirement that they be full church members, but his rigorous enforcement of the Navigation Acts soon alienated them too. When he tried to compel New England farmers to take out new land titles that included annual quitrents, he enraged the whole countryside. His suppression of a tax revolt in Essex County, Massachusetts, started many people thinking more highly of their rights as Englishmen than of their peculiar liberties as Puritans. By 1688, government by consent probably seemed more valuable than ever.

☙ The Glorious Revolution

Events in England and France undermined the Dominion of New England. James II proclaimed toleration for Protestants and Catholics and began to name Catholics to high office, in violation of recent laws. In 1685, Louis XIV revoked the 1598 Edict of Nantes that had granted toleration to Protestants, and he launched a vicious persecution of the Huguenots. About 160,000 fled the kingdom, the largest forced migration of Europe's early modern era. Many went to England; several thousand settled in the English mainland colonies. James II tried to suppress the news of Louis's persecution, which made his own professions of toleration seem hypocritical, even though his commitment was probably genuine. In 1688, his queen gave birth to a son who would clearly be raised Catholic, thus imposing a Catholic *dynasty* on England. Several Whig and Tory leaders swallowed their mutual hatred and invited William of Orange, the *stadholder* of the Netherlands, to England. The husband of the king's older Protestant daughter Mary, William had become the most prominent Protestant soldier in Europe during a long war against Louis XIV.

William landed in England in November 1688. Most of the English army sided with him, and James fled to France in late December. Parliament declared that James

CALVINISM ON ITS DEATHBED AND LE ROY DE FRANCE
Louis XIV's persecution of the Huguenots led his supporters to hope that France would soon be rid of all Protestants. In *Le Roy de France*, the Dutch Protestant response to the persecution depicts Louis, the sun king, as death.

had abdicated the throne and named William III (1689–1702) and Mary II (1689–94) as joint sovereigns. It also passed a Toleration Act that gave Protestant dissenters (but not Catholics) the right to worship publicly and a Declaration of Rights that guaranteed a Protestant succession and condemned as illegal many of the acts of James II. This Glorious Revolution also brought England and the Netherlands into war against Louis XIV, who supported James.

The Glorious Revolution in America

The Boston militia overthrew Andros on April 18 and 19, 1689, even before they knew whether William had succeeded James. Andros's attempt to suppress the news that William had landed in England convinced the Puritans that he was part of a global Popish Plot to undermine Protestant societies everywhere. After some hesitation, Massachusetts resumed the forms of its old charter government. The other New England colonies followed its example. In May and June, the New York City militia took over Fort James at the southern tip of Manhattan and renamed it Fort William. To hostile observers, this action seemed almost a replay of the events of 1673, when the Dutch had reconquered New York and renamed the fort

for William. Francis Nicholson, lieutenant governor in New York under Andros, refused to proclaim William and Mary as sovereigns without direct orders from England and soon sailed for home. The active rebels in New York City were nearly all Dutch who had little experience with traditional English liberties. Few had held high office. Their leader, Jacob Leisler, dreaded conquest by Catholics from New France and began to act like a Dutch *stadholder* in a nominally English colony.

Military defense became Leisler's highest priority, but his demands for supplies soon alienated even his Yankee supporters on Long Island. Although he summoned an elective assembly, he made no effort to revive the Charter of Liberties of 1683 while continuing to collect duties under the permanent revenue act of that year. He showed little respect for the legal rights of his opponents, most of whom were English or were Dutch merchants who had served the Dominion of New England. He jailed several Anti-Leislerians for months without bringing them to trial, and when his own assembly raised questions about their legal rights, he sent it home. Loud complaints against his administration reached the Crown in London.

In Maryland, Protestants overthrew Lord Baltimore's Catholic government in 1689. The governor of Maryland had refused to proclaim William and Mary, even after all of the other colonies had done so. To Lord Baltimore's dismay, the messenger he sent from London to Maryland with orders to accept the new monarchs died en route. Had he arrived, the government probably would have survived the crisis.

The English Response

England responded in different ways to each of these upheavals. The Maryland rebels won the royal government they requested from England and soon established the Anglican Church in the colony. Catholics could no longer worship in public, hold office, or even expect toleration. Most prominent Catholic families, however, braced themselves against the Protestant storm and remained loyal to their faith.

In New York, the Leislerians suffered a deadly defeat. Leisler and his Dutch followers, who had no significant contacts at the English court, watched helplessly as their enemies, working through the imperial bureaucracy that William inherited from James, manipulated the Dutch king of England into undermining his loyal Dutch supporters in New York. The new governor, Henry Sloughter, named prominent Anti-Leislerians to his council, arrested Leisler and his son-in-law in 1691, tried both for treason, and had them hanged, drawn, and quartered. The assembly elected that year was controlled by Anti-Leislerians, most of whom were English. It passed a modified version of the Charter of Liberties of 1683, this time denying toleration to Catholics. Like its predecessor, this charter was later disallowed. Bitter struggles between Leislerians and Anti-Leislerians would characterize New York politics until after 1700.

Another complex struggle involved Massachusetts. In 1689, Increase Mather, acting as the colony's agent in London, failed to persuade Parliament to restore the charter of 1629. Over the next two years, he negotiated a new charter, which gave the Crown what it had been demanding since 1664—the power to appoint governors, justices, and militia officers, and the power to veto laws and to hear judicial appeals. The 1691 charter also granted toleration to all Protestants and based voting rights on property qualifications, not church membership. In effect, liberty and property had triumphed over godliness.

While insisting on these concessions, William also accepted much of the previous history of the colony, even if it did not augur well for the emerging model of royal government. The General Court, not the governor as in other

THE FORT PROTECTING NEW YORK CITY, AS SEEN FROM BROOKLYN HEIGHTS, 1679
This sketch, probably by Jasper Danckaerts or Peter Sluyter, two Dutch visitors, shows the fort at the southern tip of Manhattan Island. When the English conquered New Netherland in 1664, the fort was renamed for James, the lord proprietor of what now became New York. When the Dutch retook the fort in 1673, they changed its name to Fort William (for William of Orange). When the English regained control in 1674, they again renamed it Fort James, but when James II was overthrown in the Glorious Revolution of 1688–89, the settlers named it for William once again. Thereafter, the fort took the name of the reigning British monarch.

royal colonies, retained control over the distribution of land. The council remained an elective body, although it was chosen annually by the full legislature, not directly by the voters. The governor could veto any councillor. Massachusetts also absorbed the colonies of Plymouth and Maine. New Hampshire regained its autonomy, but until 1741 it usually shared the same royal governor with Massachusetts. Rhode Island and Connecticut resumed their charter governments.

The Salem Witch Trials

When Mather sailed into Boston harbor with the new charter in May 1692, he found the province besieged by witches. The accusations arose in Salem Village (modern Danvers) among a group of girls that included a young daughter and a niece of the local minister, Samuel Parris, and then spread to older girls, some of whom had been orphaned during the Indian wars. The girls howled, barked, and stretched themselves into frightful contortions. At first, Parris treated the outbursts as cases of demonic possession, but after weeks of prayer sessions brought no improvement, he accepted a diagnosis of witchcraft. With adult encouragement, the girls accused many village residents of witchcraft. The accusers came from families that

HISTORY THROUGH FILM

Three Sovereigns for Sarah (1986)

This film, originally a PBS American Playhouse miniseries, is the most powerful and effective dramatization ever made of the Salem witch trials of 1692. The three principal actresses were all previous Academy Award winners. When this series appeared, British director Philip Leacock was perhaps best known in the United States for *The War Lover* (1962) and *The Daughters of Joshua Cabe* (1972).

The screenplay by Victor Pisano, who also produced the film, concentrates on the three Towne sisters: Sarah Cloyse (Vanessa Redgrave), Rebecca Nurse (Phyllis Thaxter), and Mary Easty (Kim Hunter). Rebecca Nurse's ordeal became a major turning point in the Salem tragedy. Hers was one of the early trials, and at first the jury acquitted her, only to be urged by the judges to reconsider the verdict. They did, and she was hanged. After this reversal, no one else was acquitted. Mary Easty, after she too had been convicted, sent a petition to the magistrates, one of the most eloquent documents ever written in colonial America. As a committed Christian, she accepted her own death, but she urged the judges to reconsider their procedures because she knew that she was innocent, and so must be many of the other condemned witches. She was hanged.

Of the three sisters, only Sarah Cloyse survived the trials. The film focuses on Cloyse's lifelong efforts to vindicate the reputations of her two sisters. Vanessa Redgrave's portrayal of her suffering and her resistance to the whole appalling affair is one of the most compelling performances of her long and distinguished career.

The screenplay, by concentrating on the three sisters and their families, brings home the human tragedy that the trials became. This emphasis forced Pisano to leave out other important victims. For example, the Reverend George Burroughs, the only minister executed in the trials (or in any New England colony in the 17th century, for that matter), is not even mentioned. In addition, Pisano never explains that Sarah Cloyse survived because the grand jury refused to indict her. Grand juries were exempt from explaining their decisions to anyone else, and so we do not know why she became an exception, but evidently the jurors believed

Directed by Philip Leacock. Starring Vanessa Redgrave (Sarah Cloyse), Phyllis Thaxter (Rebecca Nurse), and Kim Hunter (Mary Easty).

that she was too dedicated a Christian woman to sell her soul to the devil. Finally, the screenplay attributes the onset of the crisis to fortune telling in the Samuel Parris household by Tituba, an Indian slave from South America who reached the village via Barbados. Guilt for indulging in this occult activity presumably triggered the seizures of the afflicted girls. Several historians have demolished this interpretation since the film appeared. We simply do not know what set off the girls' fits.

Three Sovereigns for Sarah is a grim, compelling, relentless drama. It romanticizes nothing and makes clear, unlike some Hollywood depictions of these events, that nothing about the trials was sexy. The accusation scenes, dominated by girls, convey the madness of the whole affair. Most of those accused and executed were grandmothers. When they are turned off the ladder, their bodies bounce as the nooses take hold. This film is a cinematic triumph.

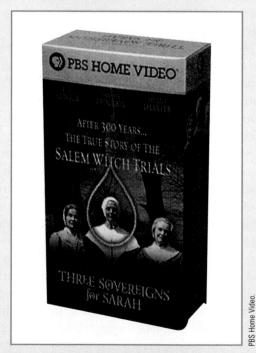

PBS Home Video.

Three Sovereigns for Sarah brings home the human tragedy of the Salem witch trials of 1692.

strongly supported Parris. Most of the accused were old women in families that had opposed his appointment as village minister. The number of the accused escalated sharply, and the crisis spread far beyond the village after 14-year-old Abigail Hobbs confessed in April that she had made a compact with the devil in Maine at age 10 just before the Indian war broke out. New England seemed on the edge of a calamity—an external enemy of Indians, ruled by Satan and supported by missionaries and gunpowder from Catholic New France, had joined with an internal enemy of numerous witches to destroy Massachusetts. By 1692, the Abenakis Indians had devastated the northern frontier, and Massachusetts had not found any effective way to strike back.

In June, the trials began in Salem Town. The court, composed mostly of judges who had compromised their Puritanism through willing service to the Dominion of New England, hanged 19 people, pressed one man to death because he refused to stand trial, and allowed several other people to die in jail. All of those executed insisted on their innocence. Nobody who confessed was hanged. Many of the victims were grandmothers, several quite conspicuous for their piety. One was a former minister at Salem Village who had become a Baptist. The governor finally halted the trials after the girls accused his wife of witchcraft. By then, public support for the trials was collapsing. The trials, along with the new charter, brought the Puritan era to a close.

The Completion of Empire

The Glorious Revolution killed absolutism in English America and guaranteed that royal government would be representative government in the colonies. Both Crown and colonists took it for granted that any colony settled by the English would elect an assembly to vote on all taxes and consent to all local laws. Governors would be appointed by the Crown or a lord proprietor. (Governors were elected in Connecticut and Rhode Island.) But royal government soon became the norm, especially after the New Jersey proprietors surrendered their powers of government in 1702, and the Carolina proprietors followed suit after their last governor was deposed by the settlers in 1719. On the other hand, the Crown restored proprietary rule in Maryland in 1716, after the fifth Lord Baltimore converted to the Church of England. By the 1720s, however, Maryland and Pennsylvania (along with Delaware, which became a separate colony under the Penn proprietorship in 1704) were the only surviving proprietary provinces on the mainland, and their proprietors were usually careful to abide by the rules of imperial administration.

This transition to royal government seems smoother in retrospect than it did at the time. London almost lost control of the empire in the 1690s. Overwhelmed by the pressures of the French war, the Lords of Trade could not keep pace with events in the colonies. When French

MATTHEW HOPKINS, *DISCOVERIE OF WITCHES* (1647)

This woodcut depicts activities that New Englanders associated with the behavior of witches, including flying through the air on poles or brooms.

privateers disrupted the tobacco trade, Scottish smugglers stepped in and began to divert it to Glasgow in defiance of the Navigation Acts. New York became a haven for pirates. The northern colonies could not cooperate effectively in the war against New France. Parliament, suspecting William of favoring Dutch interests over English, even threatened to take control of the colonies away from the king.

William took action in 1696. With his approval, Parliament passed a new, comprehensive Navigation Act that plugged several loopholes in earlier laws and extended to America the English system of vice admiralty courts, which dispensed quick justice without juries. When the new courts settled routine maritime disputes or condemned enemy merchant ships captured by colonial privateers, their services were highly regarded by the settlers.

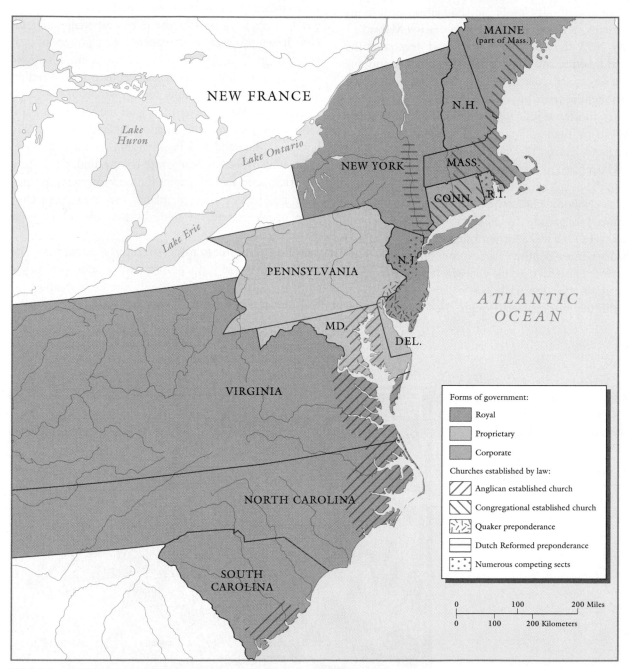

MAP 3.4   GOVERNMENT AND RELIGION IN THE BRITISH COLONIES, 1720

This map shows which colonies were royal, proprietary, or corporate in structure and whether Anglican or Congregational churches were established by law or whether, instead, the Quakers or the Dutch Reformed church predominated or numerous sects competed for the loyalties of the settlers.

But when the courts tried to assume jurisdiction over the Navigation Acts, they aroused controversy.

William also replaced the Lords of Trade in 1696 with a new agency, the Board of Trade. Its powers were almost purely advisory. It corresponded with governors and other officials in the colonies, listened to lobbyists in England, and made policy recommendations to appropriate governmental bodies, whether Parliament, the Treasury, or a secretary of state. The board tried to collect information on complex questions and to offer helpful advice. It was, in short, an early attempt at government by experts. John Locke, England's foremost philosopher and an able economist, was one of the board's first members.

Another difficult problem was resolved in 1707 when England and Scotland agreed to merge their separate parliaments and become the single kingdom of Great Britain. At a stroke, the Act of Union placed Scotland inside the Navigation Act system, legalized Scottish participation in the tobacco trade, and opened numerous colonial offices to ambitious Scots. By the middle of the 18th century, most of Scotland's growing prosperity derived from its trade with the colonies. In a very real sense, the tobacco trade built Glasgow.

Imperial Federalism

The transformations that took place between 1689 and 1707 defined the structure of the British Empire until the American Revolution. Although Parliament claimed full power over the colonies, in practice it seldom regulated anything colonial except Atlantic commerce. Even the Woolens Act of 1699, designed to protect the English woolens industry from Irish and colonial competition, did not prohibit the manufacture of woolen textiles in the colonies. It simply prohibited their export. The Hat Act of 1732 was similarly designed, except for a clause limiting the number of apprentices or slaves a colonial hatter could maintain. Nobody enforced that provision.

When Parliament regulated oceanic trade, its measures were usually enforceable. But compliance was minimal to nonexistent when Parliament tried to regulate inland affairs through statutes protecting white pines (needed as masts for the navy) or through the Iron Act of 1750, which prohibited the erection of certain types of new iron mills. To get things done within the colonies, the Crown had to win the settlers' agreement through their lawful assemblies and unsalaried local officials. In effect, the empire had stumbled into a system of de facto federalism, an arrangement that no one could quite explain or justify. Parliament exercised only limited powers, and the colonies controlled the rest. What seemed an arrangement of convenience in London soon acquired overtones of right in America, the right to consent to all taxes and local laws.

The Mixed and Balanced Constitution

The Glorious Revolution transformed British politics in a way that profoundly affected the colonies after 1700. To Europe's surprise, Britain, whose government had seemed wildly unstable for half a century, quickly became a far more powerful state under its limited government after 1689 than the Stuart kings had been able to sustain with their pretensions to absolute monarchy. The British constitution, which made ministers legally responsible for their public actions, proved remarkably stable. Before long, many Englishmen were celebrating this achievement as the wonder of the age. In the ancient world, as had been pointed out by republican thinker James Harrington (see chapter 2), free societies had degenerated into tyrannies. Liberty had always been fragile and was easily lost. Yet England had retained its liberty and grown stronger in the process. England had defied history.

The explanation, nearly everyone agreed, lay in England's "mixed and balanced" constitution, which embraced Harrington's ideas about republican liberty but absorbed them into a monarchical framework. Government by King, Lords, and Commons mirrored society itself—the monarchy, aristocracy, and commonality—and literally embodied all three in its structure. As long as each freely consented to government measures, English liberty would be secure because each had voluntarily placed the public good ahead of its own interests. But if either the Crown, the Lords, or the Commons acquired the power to dominate or manipulate the other two, English liberty would be in peril. That danger fueled an unending dialogue in 18th-century Britain. The underlying drama was always the struggle of power, especially royal patronage, against liberty, and liberty usually meant a limitation of governmental power.

Power had to be controlled, or liberty would be lost. Nearly everyone agreed that a direct assault on Parliament through a military coup was highly unlikely. The real danger lay in corruption, in the ability of Crown ministers to undermine the independence and integrity of the House of Commons.

The wars with France made Britain a great power, but they also aroused acute constitutional anxieties. After 1689, England raised larger fleets and armies than it had ever mobilized before. To support them, the kingdom created for the first time a funded national debt, in which the state agreed to pay the interest due to its creditors

In London, Harvard's Best Undermines Yale's Orthodoxy

Jeremiah Dummer, colonial agent, was the son of Jeremiah and Ann, or Hannah, Atwater Dummer. His father, a Boston silversmith and engraver, became the first native-born painter of significant ability. The son was born in 1681 and, according to President Increase Mather, became the ablest student at Harvard College in his generation. After graduating in 1699, he sailed for the Netherlands, where he arrived in 1702. He studied at the University of Leyden and the University of Utrecht, which awarded him both an A.M. and a Ph.D. degree in 1703. He was the first native-born American to receive a doctorate of philosophy. He returned to Boston a year later but was unable to get an appointment either to the Harvard faculty or to a conventional pulpit. His exceptional learning evidently intimidated others.

JEREMIAH DUMMER

This portrait by Sir Godfrey Kneller reveals the extent to which Dummer had become an English gentleman during his long residence in London. His periwig would have scandalized pious New Englanders.

Dummer returned to London in 1708 and stayed in Europe for the rest of his life. He soon ingratiated himself with the Tory Party, which remained in power until the death of Queen Anne in 1714. When the Board of Trade contemplated the revocation of all colonial charters in 1715, Dummer wrote *The Defence of the New England Charters,* which he finally published in London in 1721. It was promptly reprinted in Boston and again in 1745 and 1765. It was also reprinted twice in London during the decade before the Revolutionary War broke out. New England patriots held that pamphlet in high regard.

Dummer secured an appointment as the colonial agent for both Massachusetts and Connecticut, a position that he filled quite ably for two decades. His most significant accomplishment came when he persuaded an English gentleman, Elihu Yale, to donate his large personal library to the Connecticut college that had

been founded in 1701 and, two decades later, was in the process of moving to New Haven. In gratitude, the institution changed its name to Yale College, but because nearly all of the religious volumes were Anglican, the Yale faculty read them and, except for Tutor Jonathan Edwards, converted to the Church of England in 1722.

Although Dummer earned fame on a visit to Paris by openly challenging a Jesuit over the propriety of invoking the saints, his puritan convictions grew more relaxed in Europe, and rumors reached Boston that he might even have his own harem. He died in 1739. "He had an elegant Taste both in Men and Books," reported the *Gentleman's Magazine,* "and was a Person of excellent Learning, solid Judgment, and polite Conversation, without the least Tincture of Political or Religious Bigotry."

ahead of all other obligations. This simple device gave Britain enormous borrowing power. In 1694, the government created the Bank of England to facilitate its own finances; the London Stock Exchange also emerged in the 1690s. Parliament levied a heavy land tax on the gentry and excises on ordinary people to meet wartime expenses. Together, debt, bank, stock market, and new sources of

revenue added up to a financial revolution that enabled England to outspend France, despite having only one-fourth of France's population. These resources and a sharp expansion of offices during the wars vastly increased patronage. By giving offices to members of Parliament, Crown ministers were almost assured of majority support for their measures.

HAMPTON COURT PALACE

This elegant palace near London was one of Queen Anne's residences. Court architecture and protocol were hierarchical and designed to be awesome.

VIEW OF THE HARVESTING FIELD OF JAMES HIGFORD'S MANOR, DIXTON, GLOUCESTERSHIRE (CIRCA 1725–35)

The Country wing of British politics was dominated by landed gentlemen who owned great estates. The men who actually worked their fields seldom had a voice in politics.

As during the controversy over the Popish Plot, public debates still pitted Court against Country. The Court favored policies that strengthened its war-making capabilities. The Country stood for liberty. Each of the parties, Whig and Tory, had Court and Country wings. Between 1680 and 1720, however, they reversed their polarities. Although the Tories had begun as Charles II's Court party, by 1720 most of them were a Country opposition. Whigs had defended Country positions in 1680, but by 1720 most of them were strong advocates for the Court policies of George I (1714–27). Court spokesmen defended the military buildup, the financial revolution, and the new patronage as essential to victory over France. Their Country opponents denounced standing armies, attacked the financial revolution as an engine of corruption, favored an early peace with France, demanded more frequent elections, and tried to ban placemen (officeholders who sat in Parliament) from the House of Commons.

Court Whigs emerged victorious during the long ministry of Sir Robert Walpole (1721–42), but their opponents were more eloquent and controlled more presses. By the 1720s, the opposition claimed many of the kingdom's best writers, especially Tories Alexander Pope, Jonathan Swift, John Gay, and Henry St. John, viscount Bolingbroke. Their detestation of Walpole was shared by a smaller band of radical Whigs, including John Trenchard and Thomas Gordon, who wrote *Cato's Letters*, four volumes of collected newspaper essays. The central theme of the opposition was corruption—the indirect and insidious means by which ministers threatened the independence of Parliament and thus English liberty. This debate over liberty soon reached America. *Cato's Letters* were especially popular in the northern colonies, while Bolingbroke won numerous admirers among the gentry in the southern colonies.

🌐 Contrasting Empires: Spain and France in North America

After 1689, Britain's enemies were France and Spain, Catholic powers with their own American empires. Until 1689, the three empires had coexisted in America without much contact among them, but Europe's wars soon engulfed them all. Spain and France shared a zeal for converting Indians that exceeded anything displayed by English Protestants, but their American empires had little else in common.

The Pueblo Revolt

In the late 17th century, the Spanish missions of North America entered a period of crisis. Franciscan zeal began to slacken, and fewer priests took the trouble to master Indian languages, insisting instead that the Indians learn Spanish. For all of their good intentions, the missionaries regarded Indians as children and often whipped or even shackled them for minor infractions. They refused to trust them with firearms. Disease also took a heavy toll. A declining Indian population led to more pressing labor demands by missionaries, and despite strong prohibitions, some Spaniards enslaved some Indians in Florida and New Mexico. After 1670, Florida also feared encroachments by English Protestants out of South Carolina, who were eager to enslave unarmed Indians, whether or not they had embraced Christianity. By 1700, the European refusal to enslave other Christians protected only white people.

The greatest challenge to the Spanish arose in New Mexico, where the Pueblo population had fallen from 80,000 to 17,000 since 1598. A prolonged drought, together with Apache and Navajo attacks, prompted many Pueblos to abandon the Christian God and resume their old forms of worship. Missionaries responded with whippings and even several executions in 1675. Popé, a San Juan Pueblo medicine man who had been whipped for his beliefs, moved north to Taos Pueblo, where he organized the most successful Indian revolt in American history. In 1680, in a carefully timed uprising, the Pueblos killed 400 of the 2,300 Spaniards in New Mexico and destroyed or plundered every Spanish building in the province (see the chapter 1 map, "Spanish Missions in Florida and New Mexico, circa 1675"). They desecrated every church and killed 21 of New Mexico's 33 missionaries. "Now," they exulted, "the God of the Spaniards, who was their father, is dead," but the Pueblos' own god, whom they obeyed, "[had] never died." Spanish survivors fled from Santa Fe down the Rio Grande to El Paso.

Popé lost his influence when the traditional Pueblo rites failed to end the drought or stop the attacks of hostile Indians. When the Spanish returned in the 1690s, this time as conquerors, the Pueblos were badly divided. Most villages yielded without much resistance, and Spain accepted their submission, but Santa Fe held out until December 1693. When it fell, the Spanish executed 70 men and gave 400 women and children to the returning settlers as their slaves. The Hopi Indians to the west, however, never again submitted to Spanish rule.

Before these crises, missionaries in both Florida and New Mexico had often resisted the demands of Spanish governors. By 1700, the state ruled and missionaries obeyed.

Spain's daring attempt to create a demilitarized Christian frontier was proving to be a tragic failure for both Indians and Franciscans.

New France and the Middle Ground

A different story unfolded along the western frontier of New France over the same decades. There the Iroquois menace made possible an unusual accommodation between the colony and the Indians of the Great Lakes region. The survival of the Iroquois Five Nations depended on their ability to assimilate captives seized from other nations through incessant warfare. Their raiders, armed with muskets, terrorized western Indians, carried away thousands of captives, and left behind grisly trophies of their cruelty to discourage revenge. The Iroquois wars depopulated nearly all of what is now the state of Ohio and much of the Ontario peninsula. The Indians around Lakes Erie and Huron either fled west to escape these horrors or were absorbed by the Iroquois. The refugees, mostly Algonquian-speaking peoples, founded new communities farther west. Most of these villages contained families from several different tribes, and village loyalties gradually supplanted older tribal (or ethnic) loyalties, which often broke down under Iroquois pressure. When the refugees disagreed with one another or came into conflict with the Sioux to their west, the absence of traditional tribal structures made it difficult to resolve their differences. Over time, French soldiers, trappers, and missionaries stepped in as mediators.

The French were not always welcome. In 1684, the only year for which we have a precise count, the Algonquians killed 39 French traders. Yet the leaders of thinly populated New France were eager to erect an Algonquian shield against the Iroquois and, in later decades, against the British. They began by easing tensions among the Algonquians while supplying them with firearms, brandy, and other European goods. In fact, to the exasperation of missionaries, brandy became the lubricant of the fur trade by keeping the warriors hunting for pelts and dependent on French traders. New France, in turn, provided the resources that the Algonquians needed to strike back against the Iroquois. By 1701, Iroquois losses had become so heavy that the Five Nations negotiated a peace treaty with the French and the western Indians. The Iroquois agreed to remain neutral in any war between France and England. France's Indian allies, supported by a new French fort erected at Detroit in 1701, began returning to the fertile lands around Lakes Erie and Huron. That region became the Great Lakes Middle Ground, over which no one could

IROQUOIS WARRIORS LEADING AN INDIAN PRISONER INTO CAPTIVITY, 1660s

Because Indian populations had been depleted by war and disease, a tribe's survival became dependent on its ability to assimilate captives. This is a French copy of an Iroquois pictograph.

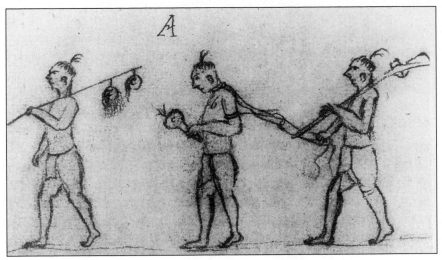

Archives Nationales.

wield sovereign power, although New France exercised great influence within it. France always ran a deficit in supporting the fur trade but kept the trade going mostly to block British expansion.

France's success in the interior rested more on intelligent negotiation than on force. Officials who gave orders instead of fostering negotiations merely alienated France's Indian allies. Blind obedience to commands, grumbled the warriors, was slavery. Hugely outnumbered, the French knew that they could not impose their will on the Indians. Indians respected those Frenchmen who honored their ways. The French conducted diplomacy according to Indian, not European rules. The governor of New France became a somewhat grander version of a traditional Indian chief. Algonquians called him Onontio ("Great Mountain"), the supreme alliance chief who won cooperation through persuasion and who had learned that, among the Indians, persuasion was always accompanied by gifts. The respect accorded to peacetime chiefs was roughly proportionate to how much they gave away, not to how much they accumulated. The English, by contrast, tried to "buy" land from the Indians and regarded the sale of both the land and of the Indians' right to use it as irrevocable. The French understood that this idea had no place in Indian culture. Agreements were not final contracts but required regular renewal, always with an exchange of gifts. The strongest party had to be more generous than all others.

Middle Ground diplomacy came at a price. It involved New France in the Indian slave trade even though Louis XIV expressly forbade the enslavement of Indians, a command finally rescinded in 1709. Because Indians fought wars mostly to acquire captives, Onontio's western allies frequently presented captives to French traders who realized that to refuse the gift would be an insult and could jeopardize New France's alliances with the western nations.

By the 1720s, up to 5 percent of the colony's population consisted of enslaved Indians. In the most commercial neighborhood of Montreal, every other household owned one or two slaves.

French Louisiana and Spanish Texas

The pattern worked out by the French and the Indians on the Great Lakes Middle Ground also took hold, although in a more fragile form, in the lower Mississippi valley. In quest of a passage to Asia, Father Jacques Marquette and trader Louis Joliet paddled down the Mississippi to its juncture with the Arkansas River in 1673. But once they became convinced that the Mississippi flowed into the Gulf of Mexico and not the Pacific, they turned back. Then, in 1682, René-Robert Cavelier, *sieur* de La Salle traveled down the Mississippi to its mouth, claiming possession of the entire area for France and calling it Louisiana (for Louis XIV). But when La Salle returned in 1684 by way of the Gulf of Mexico to plant a colony there, he overshot the mouth of the Mississippi, landed in Texas, and wandered around for three years in search of the great river until his exasperated men murdered him.

In 1699, during a brief lull in the wars between France and England, the French returned to the Gulf of Mexico. Pierre le Moyne d'Iberville, a Canadian, landed with 80 men at Biloxi, built a fort, and began trading with the Indians. In 1702, he moved his headquarters to Mobile, closer to the more populous nations of the interior, especially the Choctaws, who were looking for allies against the English. The Choctaws could still field 5,000 warriors but had suffered heavy losses from slaving raids organized by South Carolinians and carried out mostly by that colony's

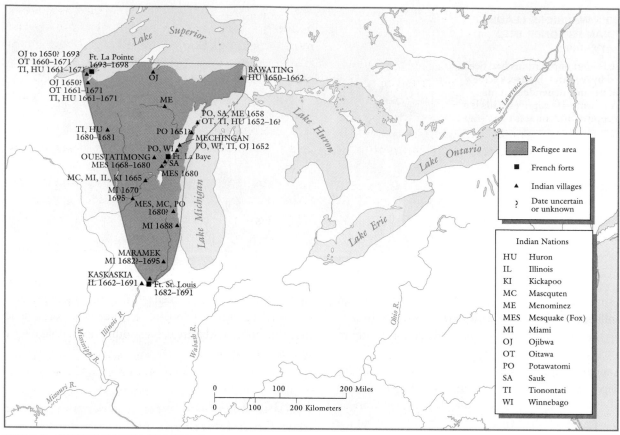

MAP 3.5 FRENCH MIDDLE GROUND IN NORTH AMERICA CIRCA 1700

French power in North America rested mostly on the arrangements French governors worked out with refugee Algonquian Indians trying to resist Iroquois raids in the Great Lakes region.

Chickasaw and Creek allies. About 1,800 Choctaws had been killed and 500 enslaved during the preceding decade. Using the Choctaws to anchor their trading system, the French created a weaker, southern version of the Great Lakes Middle Ground, acting as mediators and trading brandy, firearms, and other European products for furs and food. Often, during the War of the Spanish Succession (1702–13), the French received no European supplies, and they remained heavily outnumbered by the Indians. Although European diseases had been ravaging the area since the 1540s, the Indians of the lower Mississippi valley still numbered about 70,000. In 1708, the French numbered fewer than 300, including 80 Indian slaves. The French were lucky to survive at all. They did so, in large part, by trying to protect their allies from South Carolina slavers and by refusing to enslave other Indians.

Spain, alarmed at any challenge to its monopoly on the Gulf of Mexico, founded Pensacola in 1698, more to counter the English than the French. Competition from France prompted the Spanish to move into Texas in 1690,

where they established missions near the modern Texas–Louisiana border. At first, the missionaries were cordially received by the Tejas (Texas) Indians, but they brought smallpox with them. The Indians rejected their explanation that the epidemic was God's "holy will" and told the missionaries to get out or be killed. They departed in 1693, leaving Texas to the Indians for another 20 years.

An Empire of Settlement: The British Colonies

By 1700, 250,000 settlers and slaves were already living in England's mainland colonies, and the population was doubling every 25 years. New France matched that pace, but with only 14,000 people in 1700, it could not close the gap. By contrast, the population of the Spanish missions continued to decline. In the struggle for empire, a growing population became Britain's greatest advantage.

The Engine of British Expansion: The Colonial Household

Virginia's Robert "King" Carter, who died in 1730, became the first settler to acquire a thousand slaves and several hundred thousand acres of land. His household differed strikingly from that of an ordinary Pennsylvania or New England farmer, but both had something in common that distinguished them from households in England. With few exceptions, colonial families rejected the English customs of entail and primogeniture. *Entail* prohibited a landowner, or his heir, from dividing up his landed estate (that is, selling part of it) during his lifetime. *Primogeniture* obliged him to leave all of his land to his eldest surviving son. Under this system, younger sons clearly ranked below the oldest son, and daughters usually ranked behind both unless one of them could marry a man who would bring new resources into the family. Primogeniture and entail became more common in the 18th-century colonies than they had been before, but until the late colonial period they failed to structure social relations the way they did in England. A Virginia planter, for example, might entail his home plantation (the one on which he had erected his big house) and bequeath it to his oldest son, but he would also leave land and slaves, sometimes whole plantations, to his other sons. The primacy of the eldest son was far more sentimental than structural. By contrast, the patriarchs of colonial households tried to pass on their status to all of their sons and to provide dowries that would enable all of their daughters to marry men of equal status. Until 1750 or so, these goals were usually realistic.

For younger sons, then, the colonies presented a unique opportunity. Benjamin Franklin began his *Autobiography*, colonial America's greatest success story, by boasting that he was "the youngest Son of the youngest Son for 5 Generations back." Despite those odds, Franklin became a gentleman with an international reputation. He made enough money to retire as a printer, commissioned a genteel portrait of himself, engaged in scientific experiments, and entered public life. He no longer worked with his hands.

English households had become Americanized in the colonies during the earliest years of settlement, as soon as Virginia and Plymouth made land available to nearly all male settlers. By the mid-18th century, the question was whether that system could survive the pressures of a rising population. Social change began to drive American households back toward English practices. Only continual expansion onto new lands would allow the colonial household to provide equal opportunity for all sons, much less for all daughters.

Colonial households were patriarchal. The father expected to be loved and revered by his wife and children but insisted on being obeyed. A man's standing in the community depended on his success as a master at home. A mature male was expected to be the master of others. In New England and Pennsylvania, typical householders probably thought they were the rough equals of most other householders. Above all, a patriarch strove to perpetuate his household into the next generation and to preserve his own economic independence, or autonomy. Of course, complete independence was impossible. Every household owed small debts or favors to its neighbors, but these obligations seldom compromised the family's standing in the community.

Although farmers rarely set out to maximize profits, they did try to grow an agricultural surplus, if only as a hedge against drought, storms, and other unpredictable events. For rural Pennsylvanians, this surplus averaged about 40 percent of the total crop. With the harvest in, farmers marketed their produce, often selling it to merchants in Boston, New York, or Philadelphia for local consumption or for export to the West Indies or Europe. Farmers used the proceeds to pay taxes or their ministers' salaries and to buy British imports. Although these arrangements sometimes placed families in short-term debt to merchants, most farmers and artisans managed to avoid long-term debt. Settlers accepted temporary dependency among freemen—of sons on their parents, indentured servants on their masters, or apprentices and journeymen on master craftsmen. Sons often worked as laborers on neighboring farms, as sailors, or as journeymen craftsmen, provided that such dependence was temporary. A man who became permanently dependent on others lost the respect of his community.

The Voluntaristic Ethic and Public Life

Householders carried their quest for independence into public life. In entering politics and in waging war, their autonomy became an ethic of voluntarism. Few freemen could be coerced into doing something of which they disapproved. They had to be persuaded or induced to volunteer. "Obedience by compulsion is the Obedience of Vassals, who without compulsion would disobey," explained one essayist. "The Affection of the People is the only Source of a Cheerful and rational Obedience." Local officials serving without pay frequently ignored orders contrary to their own interests or the interests of their community.

Most young men accepted military service only if it suited their future plans. They would serve only under officers they knew, and then for only a single campaign. Few reenlisted. To the exasperation of professional British soldiers, provincials, like Indians, regarded blind obedience to commands as slavery. They did not enlist in order to become soldiers for life. After serving, they used their bonus and their pay, and often the promise of a land grant, to speed their way to becoming masters of their own households. Military service, for those who survived, could lead to land ownership and an earlier marriage. For New England women, however, war reduced the supply of eligible males and raised the median age of marriage by about two years, which meant, in effect, one fewer pregnancy per marriage.

Three Warring Empires, 1689–1716

When the three empires went to war after 1689, the Spanish and French fought mostly to survive. The British fought to expand their holdings. None of them won a decisive advantage in the first two wars, which ended with the Treaty of Utrecht in 1713.

Smart diplomacy with the Indians protected the western flank of New France, but the eastern parts of the colony were vulnerable to English invasion. The governors of New France knew that Indian attacks against English towns would keep the English colonies disorganized and

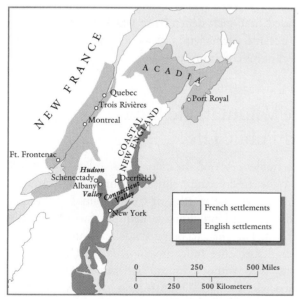

MAP 3.6 NORTHEASTERN THEATER OF WAR, 1689–1713

For a quarter of a century, the colonies north of the Quaker settlements in the Delaware Valley were locked in a brutal and costly struggle against the French and Indians to their north and west.

make them disperse their forces. Within a year after the outbreak of war between France and England in 1689, Indians had devastated most of coastal Maine and parts of New Hampshire and had burned the Mohawk valley town of Schenectady, killing 60 and taking 27 captives.

In each of the four colonial wars between Britain and France, New Englanders called for the conquest of New France, usually through a naval expedition against Quebec, combined with an overland attack on Montreal. In King William's War (1689–97), Sir William Phips of Massachusetts forced Acadia to surrender in 1690 (although the French soon regained it) and then sailed up the St. Lawrence, where his force proved inadequate to take the heavily fortified city of Quebec. The overland attack on Montreal had already collapsed amid intercolonial bickering and an outbreak of smallpox. French attacks, with Indians providing most of the fighters, continued to ravage the frontier.

In 1704, during Queen Anne's War (1702–13), the French and Indians destroyed Deerfield, Massachusetts, in a winter attack and marched most of its people off to captivity in Canada. Hundreds of New Englanders from Deerfield and other towns spent months or even years as captives. One of them was Eunice Williams, young daughter of John Williams, the pastor of Deerfield. Refusing to return to New England when the town's captives were released, she remained in Canada, became a Catholic, and married an Indian. Another New England woman who refused to return was Esther Wheelwright, daughter of a prominent Maine family. Captured by the Abenakis, she was taken to New France, where she also refused repatriation, converted to Catholicism, became a nun (Esther Marie Joseph de L'Enfant Jésus), and finally emerged as mother superior of the Ursuline Order in Canada—surely an unlikely career for a Puritan girl!

As the war dragged on, New Englanders twice failed to take Port Royal in Acadia, but a combined British and colonial force finally succeeded in 1710, renaming the colony Nova Scotia. An effort to subdue Quebec the following year met with disaster when many of the British ships ran aground in a treacherous stretch of the St. Lawrence River.

Farther south, the imperial struggle was grimmer and even more tragic. The Franciscan missions of Florida were already in decline, but mission Indians still attracted Carolina slavers, who invaded Florida between 1702 and 1704 with a large force of Indian allies, wrecked the missions, dragged off 4,000 women and children as slaves, and drove 9,000 Indians from their homes, some of whom then joined their attackers and got firearms. The invaders failed to take the Spanish fortress of St. Augustine, but slaving raids spread devastation as far west as the lands of the Choctaws and far south along the Florida peninsula.

Courtesy Massachusetts Historical Society.

PORTRAIT OF ESTHER WHEELWRIGHT

Esther Wheelwright (1696–1780), an English Puritan who was captured by the French and Indians during Queen Anne's War, converted to Catholicism and became Sister Esther Marie Joseph de L'Enfant Jésus and eventually Mother Superior of the Ursuline nuns in New France.

Illustrated London News.

SOUTH CAROLINA COLONISTS ENSLAVING AN INDIAN

The colony enslaved thousands of Indians from 1680 through 1715, a practice that was finally abandoned after the Yamasee War nearly destroyed the colony.

South Carolina's greed for Indian slaves and other abuses finally alienated the colony's strongest Indian allies, the Yamasees. Traders frequently abused Indian women, including some of high status, an offense almost unknown within Indian communities. In addition, faltering Atlantic markets during wartime compelled Indian hunters to bring in more deerskins for smaller returns, and many hunters fell deeply in debt, a process that could lead to enslavement. In 1707, to resolve disputes between traders and Indians, South Carolina created the office of Indian agent, which was held first by John Wright and then Thomas Nairne. They belonged to rival factions of Indian traders, and their controversies paralyzed the colony's gov-

ernment. In late 1714, Wright's bloc filed so many lawsuits against Nairne that for six months he could not leave Charleston to address Yamasee grievances. When the exasperated Indians threatened war, the government sent both Nairne and Wright to resolve the crisis in April 1715. Nairne brought a message of peace; Wright privately threatened war, which would most likely lead to enslavement. Taking no chances, the Yamasees killed both men and all the other traders who had just arrived to collect their debts. Throughout the Southeast, all other Indian nations trading with South Carolina, except the Chickasaws, followed the Yamasees' example, wiping out nearly all of the colony's experienced traders and launching a war

BRITISH WARS AGAINST FRANCE (AND USUALLY SPAIN), 1689–1763

European Name	American Name	Years	Peace
War of the League of Augsburg	King William's War	1689–1697	Ryswick
War of the Spanish Succession	Queen Anne's War	1702–1713	Utrecht
War of Jenkins' Ear, merging with		1739–1748	
War of the Austrian Succession	King George's War	1744–1748	Aix-la-Chapelle
Seven Years' War	French and Indian War	1754–1763*	Paris

*The French and Indian War began in America in 1754 and then merged with the Seven Years' War in Europe, which began in 1756.

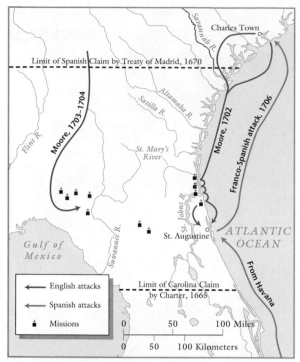

MAP 3.7 SOUTHEASTERN THEATER OF WAR, 1702–13

In this theater, the English and their Indian allies did most of the attacking, destroyed Spain's Florida missions, and enslaved thousands. Spain and France tried to attack Charleston, South Carolina, but their 1706 expedition failed after it was ravaged by disease.

that almost destroyed the colony before the Yamasees were thrust back and nearly exterminated. Some Yamasees and some escaped African slaves fled as refugees to Spanish Florida.

The wars of 1689–1716 halted the movement of British settlers onto new lands in New England and the Carolinas. Only four Maine towns survived the wars; by 1720, after half a century, South Carolina still had only 5,200 settlers (and 11,800 enslaved Africans and Indians). In Pennsylvania, Maryland, and Virginia—colonies that had not been deeply involved in the wars—the expansive thrust continued.

Conclusion

The variety and diversity of the colonies posed a huge challenge to the English government. After 1650, it found ways to regulate colonial trade, mostly for the mutual ben-

efit of both England and the colonies. The colonies, often beset by hostile Indians and internal discord, began to recognize that they needed protection that only England could provide. Once the Crown gave up its claims to absolute power, the two sides discovered much on which they could agree.

Political values in England and the colonies began to converge during the Glorious Revolution and its aftermath. Englishmen throughout the empire insisted that the right to property was sacred, that without it liberty could never be secure. They celebrated liberty under law, government by consent, and the toleration of all Protestants. They barred Catholics from succession to the throne and loaded them with severe disabilities of other kinds. In an empire dedicated to "liberty, property, and no popery," Catholics became big losers.

So did Indians and Africans. Racism directed against Indians mostly welled up from below, taking root among ordinary settlers who competed with Indians for many of the same resources, especially land, and then bore the brunt of Indian reprisals. Colonial elites tried, often ineffectually, to contain this popular rage that nearly tore apart both New England and Virginia in 1675–76. By contrast, racism directed against enslaved Africans was typically imposed from above and increasingly enforced by law. Ordinary settlers and Africans knew one another by name, made love, sometimes even married, stole hogs together, ran away together, and even fought together under Nathaniel Bacon's leadership. The men in the process of becoming great planters used their power in the legislature to criminalize all of these activities because they were terrified by the upheaval that ex-servants could create and hoped for greater stability from a labor force serving for life. They rewarded small planters and servants with white supremacy.

By the 18th century, the British colonists, despite or perhaps even because of their growing racism, had come to believe they were the freest people on earth. They attributed this fortune to their widespread ownership of land and to the English constitutional principles they had incorporated into their own governments. When George I became king in 1714, they proudly proclaimed their loyalty to the Hanoverian dynasty that guaranteed a Protestant succession to the British throne. In their minds, the British empire had become the world's last bastion of liberty.

SUGGESTED READINGS

The most comprehensive account of the Navigation Acts and England's instruments of enforcement is still **Charles M. Andrews, *The Colonial Period of American History,* vol. 4** (1938). **Ian K. Steele's *The English Atlantic, 1675–1740: An Exploration of Communication and Community*** (1986) is careful and original.

    Daniel K. Richter's *The Ordeal of the Longhouse: The People of the Iroquois League in the Era of European Coloni-zation* (1992); **Richard W. Cogley's *John Eliot's Mission to the Indians before King Philip's War*** (1999); **Jill Lepore's *The Name of War: King Philip's War and the Origins of American Identity*** (1998); and **Wilcomb Washburn, *The Governor and the Rebel: A History of Bacon's Rebellion in Virginia*** (1957) are all essential to understanding the crisis of the 1670s. For the transition to slavery after Bacon's Rebellion, see **Anthony S. Parent, Jr., *Foul Means: The Formation of a Slave Society in Virginia, 1660–1740*** (2003).

    For the Dominion of New England and the Glorious Revolution in the colonies, see **Richard R. Johnson, *Adjustment to Empire: The New England Colonies, 1675–1715*** (1981); **John M. Murrin, "The Menacing Shadow of Louis XIV and the Rage of Jacob Leisler: The Constitutional Ordeal of Seventeenth-Century New York," in Stephen L. Schechter and Richard B. Bernstein, eds., *New York and the Union: Contributions to the American Constitutional Experience*** (1990), pp. 29–71; and **Lois G. Carr and David W. Jordan, *Maryland's Revolution of Government, 1689–1692*** (1974). The best study of Salem witch-craft, which is also a superb introduction to the Indian wars in northern New England, is **Mary Beth Norton, *In the Devil's Snare: The Salem Witchcraft Crisis of 1692*** (2002).

For the French and Spanish colonies in these critical decades, see especially **Richard White, *The Middle Ground: Indians, Empires, and Republics in the Great Lakes Region, 1650–1815*** (1991); **Ramón Gutiérrez, *When Jesus Came, the Corn Mothers Went Away: Marriage, Sexuality, and Power in New Mexico, 1500–1846*** (1992), particularly on the Pueblo revolt; and **Daniel H. Usner, Jr., *Indians, Settlers, & Slaves in a Frontier Exchange Economy: The Lower Mississippi Valley before 1783*** (1992).

    On the householder economy in English North America, see **Laurel Thatcher Ulrich's *Good Wives: Images and Reality in the Lives of Women in Northern New England*** (1982), and **Mary M. Schweitzer, *Custom and Contract: Household, Government, and the Economy in Colonial Pennsylvania*** (1987).

AMERICAN JOURNEY ONLINE AND INFOTRAC COLLEGE EDITION

Visit the source collections at www.ajaccess.wadsworth.com and infotrac.thomsonlearning.com and use the Search function with the following key terms to explore documents, images, audio and video clips, articles, and commentary related to the material in this chapter.

Iroquois
Algonquians
Navigation Act
Metacom's War
   (or King Philip's War)

Bacon's Rebellion
Glorious Revolution
Salem witch trials
Pueblo Revolt

GRADE AIDS

Visit the Liberty Equality Power Companion Web Site for resources specific to this textbook: http://history.wadsworth.com/murrin_LEP4e

The CD in the back of this book and the U.S. History Resource Center at http://history.wadsworth.com/u.s./ offer a variety of tools to help you succeed in this course, including access to quizzes; images; documents; interactive simulations, maps, and timelines; movie explorations; and a wealth of other sources.

Chapter 4

Provincial America and the Struggle for a Continent

WATSON AND THE SHARK
John Singleton Copley's 1778 painting, dramatically depicting a young man's rescue from
shark attack, began the democratization of heroism. Note that a black man holds the traditional
central and elevated place of honor in the painting, and that only one person on the rescue boat
is a "gentleman." In this work, Copley announced that ordinary men can be heroes.

CHAPTER OUTLINE

The British colonists believed they were the freest people on earth. Yet during the 18th century they faced a dilemma peculiarly their own. To maintain the opportunity that settlers had come to expect, the colonies had to expand onto new lands. But provincial society also increasingly emulated the cultural values of Great Britain—its architecture, polite learning, evangelical religion, and politics. Relentless expansion made this emulation difficult because the two often worked at cross purposes: An anglicized province would become far more hierarchical than the colonies had so far been and might not even try to provide a rough equality of opportunity. The settlers tried to sustain both, an effort that brought brutal conflict with their neighbors—the Indians, the Spanish, and the French.

When the British again went to war against Spain and France after 1739, the settlers joined in the struggle and declared that liberty itself was at stake. Less fortunate people among them disagreed. Slaves in the southern colonies saw Spain, not Britain, as a beacon of liberty. In the eastern woodlands, most Indians identified France, not Britain, as the one ally genuinely committed to their survival and independence.

CHAPTER FOCUS

♦ Why was it difficult to sustain both continual expansion and the anglicization of the colonies in the 18th century?
♦ How were the colonists able to embrace both the enlightenment and evangelical religion at the same time?

♦ How could both the royal governors and the colonial assemblies grow stronger at the same time?

♦ What made the War for North America (1754–63) so much more decisive than the three earlier Anglo-French conflicts?

Expansion versus Anglicization

In the 18th century, as the British colonists sought to emulate their homeland, many of the institutions and material goods they had left behind in the 17th century began to reappear. After 1740, for example, imports of British goods grew spectacularly, even faster than population. The gentry dressed in the latest London fashions and embraced that city's standards of taste and elegance. Between 1720 and 1750, wealthy settlers built handsome mansions in the older portions of the colonies. Virginia planters erected "big houses," such as Mount Vernon, built by Lawrence Washington and bequeathed to his half-brother George. In Boston, on Beacon Hill, the merchant Thomas Hancock built a stylish residence that later passed to his nephew John. Newspapers and learned professions based on English models proliferated after 1700, and colonial seaports began to resemble Bristol and other provincial cities in England.

But the population of British North America doubled every 25 years. Each new generation required twice as many colleges, ministers, lawyers, physicians, craftsmen, printers, sailors, and unskilled laborers as the preceding generation. Without them, standards of "civility" would decline. None of these institutions could meet colonial needs unless it continued to grow. As the 18th century progressed, the colonies became the scene of a contest between the unrelenting pace of raw expansion and these newer, anglicizing tendencies.

Colonies that looked only to England, or even Europe, to satisfy their needs for skilled talent could no longer attract as many people as they needed. In 1700, for example, Oxford and Cambridge universities in England had managed to fill the colonies' needs for Anglican clergymen by sending over those graduates who were unable to find parishes at home. Most of them went to the southern colonies. By 1750, the colonial demand far exceeded what stagnant Oxford and Cambridge could supply, and the colonies were also importing Scottish and Irish clergymen. Before long, those sources also proved inadequate. By contrast, northern colonies trained their own ministers, lawyers, and doctors in their own colleges, as well as their own printers, shipwrights, and other skilled craftsmen. Although still colonies, they were becoming Amer-

C H R O N O L O G Y	
1690	Massachusetts invents fiat money
1704	*Boston News-Letter* founded
1712	Slaves revolt in New York City
1716	Spanish begin to settle Texas
1718	Beginning of Scots-Irish emigration to North America
1721	Boylston introduces smallpox inoculation in Boston
1730	300 slaves revolt in Virginia, and 29 are hanged
1732	Georgia charter granted by Parliament
1733	Molasses Act passed
1734	Edwards launches massive religious revival in the Connecticut valley
1735	Zenger acquitted of seditious libel in New York
1738	Spanish found Mose in Florida
1739	Slaves revolt in Stono, South Carolina
1739–41	Whitefield launches Great Awakening
1741	New York slave conspiracy trials lead to 35 executions
1745	New England volunteers take Louisbourg
1747	Ohio Company of Virginia founded • Anti-impressment rioters in Boston resist Royal Navy
1750	Massachusetts converts from paper money to silver
1754	Washington attacks French patrol near the forks of the Ohio River • Albany Congress proposes plan for colonial union
1755	Braddock suffers disaster near Fort Duquesne • British expel Acadians from Nova Scotia
1756–57	Loudoun antagonizes the colonies as commander-in-chief
1756	French take Oswego
1757	French take Fort William Henry • Pitt becomes Britain's war minister
1758	British take Fort Duquesne • British take Fortress Louisbourg and Fort Frontenac • French repel British attack at Ticonderoga
1759	British take Ticonderoga and Crown Point • Wolfe dies taking Quebec; Montcalm also killed
1760	Montreal falls; Canada surrenders to the British
1760–61	Cherokee War devastates South Carolina backcountry
1762	Spain enters war, loses Havana and Manila
1763	Peace of Paris ends Seven Years' War

ica's first modernizing societies. They learned to do for themselves what Britain had to do for the southern colonies.

Much of this change occurred during prolonged periods of warfare. War interrupted expansion, which then resumed at an even more frantic pace with the return of peace. By midcentury, the wars were becoming a titanic struggle for control of the North American continent. Gradually, Indians realized that they would be the ultimate victims of British victory. Constant expansion for British settlers meant unending retreat for them.

Threats to Householder Autonomy

As population rose, some families acquired more prestige than others. Although the status of "gentleman" was less rigid in the colonies than in Britain, it usually implied a man who performed no manual labor, and such men began to dominate public life. Before 1700, ordinary farmers and small planters had often sat in colonial assemblies. In the 18th century, the assemblies grew much more slowly than the overall population. In the five colonies from New York to Maryland, they remained almost unchanged in size despite enormous population growth. The men who took part in public life above the local level came, more and more, from a higher social status. They had greater wealth, a more impressive lineage, and a better education than ordinary farmers or craftsmen. Unlike their counterparts in England, however, few colonial gentlemen enjoyed a patron–client relationship with the voters. In England, one or two families dominated each of the "pocket boroughs" that elected most members of Parliament. In the colonies, most voters remained independent.

By midcentury, despite the high value that colonists placed on householder autonomy, patterns of dependency were beginning to emerge. In tidewater Virginia by 1760, about 80 percent of the land was entailed. Younger sons had to look west for an inheritance. In one Maryland county, 27 percent of the householders were tenants who worked small tracts of land without slaves, or were men who owned a slave or two but had no claim to land. Such families could not satisfy the ambitions of all their children. In Pennsylvania's Chester County, a new class of married farm laborers arose. Their employers, without granting them title or lease, would let them use a small patch of land on which they could build a cottage and raise some food. Called "inmates" in Chester County records (or "cottagers" in England), such people made up 25 percent of the county population. Tenants on New York manors had to accept higher rents and shorter leases after 1750. In Chebacco Parish in Ipswich, Massachusetts, half of the farmers had land enough for only some of their sons by 1760.

Families that could not provide for all of their children reverted to English social norms. A father favored his sons over his daughters, unless he could marry a daughter to a wealthy suitor. In Connecticut, from the 1750s to the 1770s, about 75 percent of eligible sons inherited some land, but for daughters the rate fell from 44 to 34 percent. When a father could not support all his sons, he favored the eldest over the younger sons. The younger sons, in turn, took up a trade or headed for the frontier. To increase their resources, many New England farmers added a craft or two to the household. The 300 families of Haverhill, Massachusetts, supported 44 workshops and 19 mills by 1767. In Northampton, more than one-third of all the farming families also practiced a craft. Families in the town of Lynn began making shoes in quantity, many for export. Most families added a craft in order to sustain household autonomy. The goal of independence continued to exercise great power, but it was under siege. The fear of imperiled autonomy energized the whole westward movement (see chapter 7).

Anglicizing the Role of Women

The changing role of women provides a dramatic example of the anglicizing tendencies of the 18th century. When they married, most women received a dowry from their father, usually in cash or goods, not land. Under the common law doctrine of coverture, married women could not make a contract. The legal personality of the husband "covered" the wife, and he made all legally binding decisions. If he died first, his widow was entitled to dower rights, usually one-third of the estate, which passed, after her death, to the couple's surviving children.

Women in many, perhaps most, households had to work harder to maintain the family status—at the spinning wheel, for example. New England women did virtually all of the region's weaving, a male occupation in other colonies. In a sense, women were becoming more English, thus reversing some earlier trends. Until 1700, many Chesapeake widows inherited all of their husbands' property and administered their own estates. After 1700, such arrangements were rare. In the Hudson valley, Dutch law had been much more generous than English common law in bestowing property rights on women, but during the 18th century, English law gradually prevailed. In New England, too, as Puritan intensity waned, women suffered losses. Before 1700, courts had routinely punished men for sexual offenses, such as fornication, and many men had pleaded guilty and accepted their sentence. After 1700, almost no man would plead guilty to a sexual offense, except perhaps that of making love to his wife before their wedding day. However, to avoid a small fine, some husbands humiliated their wives by denying that charge, even if their wives had already pleaded guilty after giving birth to a child that had obviously been conceived before marriage. Courts rarely convicted men of sex offenses, not even serious crimes such as rape. The European double standard of sexual behavior, which punished women for their indiscretions while tolerating male infractions, had been in some jeopardy under the Puritan regime. It now revived.

Expansion, Immigration, and Regional Differentiation

The end of the wars encouraged renewed expansion. After 1715, the settled portions of North America enjoyed their longest era of peace since the arrival of Europeans. The wars had emptied the borderlands of most of their inhabitants. Until midcentury, people poured into these areas without provoking the strong Indian nations of the interior. As the colonies expanded, they fitted, more or less snugly, into distinct regions, although only New Englanders had acquired a self-conscious sense of regional identity before independence.

Emergence of the Old South

Renewed immigration, free and unfree, drove much of the postwar expansion. After 1730, the flow became enormous. In that year, about 630,000 settlers and slaves lived in the mainland colonies. By 1775, another 248,000 Africans and 284,000 Europeans had landed, including 50,000 British convicts, shipped mostly to Maryland and Virginia, where they served long indentures. During this period, the African slave trade to North America reached its peak. Most of the 210,000 voluntary immigrants settled in the middle or southern colonies. Free migration decisively outweighed the influx of slaves only after 1763.

Almost 90 percent of the slaves went to the southern colonies. At least 84,000 slaves went to Charleston, 70,000 to Virginia, and 25,000 to Maryland. One-eighth of the slaves went to northern colonies. New England had 15,000 blacks by 1770, New York had 19,000, and New Jersey, Pennsylvania, and Delaware had a combined total of 16,000. About 80 percent of the slaves arrived from Africa on overcrowded, stinking, British-owned vessels. Most of the rest came, a few at a time, from the West Indies on smaller New England ships.

This massive influx of slaves created the Old South, a society consisting of wealthy slaveholding planters, a much larger class of small planters, and thousands of slaves. By 1720, slaves made up 70 percent of South Carolina's population. By 1740, they made up 40 percent of Virginia's and 30 percent of Maryland's. Slaves performed most of the manual labor in the southern colonies.

Their arrival transformed the social structure of the southern colonies. In 1700, most members of Virginia's House of Burgesses were small planters who raised tobacco with a few indentured servants and perhaps a slave or two. After 1730, the typical burgess was a great planter who owned at least 20 slaves. And by 1750, the rice planters of South Carolina were richer than any other group in British North America. Tobacco and rice planters had few contacts with each other, except in North Carolina, where they seldom got along well. They did not yet think of themselves as southerners.

The life of slaves in the upper South (Maryland, Virginia, and the Albemarle region of North Carolina) differed considerably from the life of slaves in the lower South (from Cape Fear in North Carolina through South Carolina and

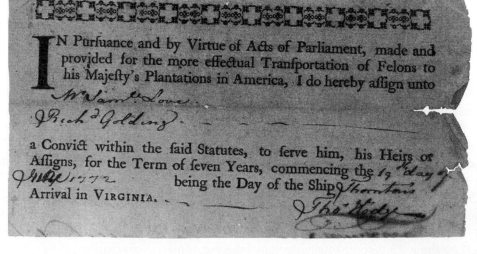

CONTRACT FOR THE CONVICT TRADE

The convict trade, which provided long-term servants for American colonists, became quite well organized in the 18th century.

Chicago Historical Society.

After John Barbot, from Churchill's Voyages.

THE GOLD COAST OF AFRICA AT THE HEIGHT OF THE SLAVE TRADE
This 18th-century view of the Gold Coast shows five European slaving posts, including "Mina" or Elmina, the Portuguese fortress built in 1481 and captured by the Dutch in the 17th century.

eventually Georgia). The Chesapeake tobacco planters organized their slaves into gangs, supervised them closely, and kept them in the fields all day, weather permitting. To make their plantations more self-sufficient, they also trained perhaps 10 percent of their slaves as blacksmiths, carpenters, coopers, or other skilled artisans. The planters, who saw themselves as benevolent paternalists, encouraged family life among their workers, who by the 1720s were beginning to achieve a rate of reproduction that almost equaled that of the settlers. Slaveholders even explained brutal whippings as fatherly efforts to correct the behavior of members of their household.

Paternalism soon extended to religion. In the 1720s, for the first time on any significant scale, many Virginia planters began to urge their slaves to convert to Christianity. At first, only adults who had a good command of the catechism, which they had to learn orally because they were not allowed to become literate, were accepted into the church, but by the 1730s, growing numbers of infants were also baptized. These efforts continued to expand despite a massive slave uprising. A rumor spread that the British government had promised emancipation to any slave who converted but that the colony was suppressing the news. On a Sunday in September 1730, about 300 slaves, mostly from Norfolk and Princess Anne counties, tried to escape through the Great Dismal Swamp. The planters hired Indians to track them, crushed the rebels, and hanged 29 of them. Yet the conversion effort continued to gain momentum mostly, it seems, because planters

hoped that Christian slaves would be more docile and dutiful.

South Carolina planters began with similar paternalistic inclinations, but the rice swamps and mosquitoes defeated them. "Carolina is in the spring a paradise, in the summer a hell, and in the autumn a hospital," claimed one visitor. Whites who supervised slave gangs in the rice fields quickly caught malaria. Although malaria was seldom fatal, it left its victims vulnerable to other diseases that often killed them. Many rice planters relocated their big houses to higher ground, at a safe distance from their rice fields. With only a few exceptions, they showed no inclination to Christianize their laborers.

Africans fared much better than whites in the marshy rice fields. (Modern medicine has shown that many Africans possess a "sickle cell" in the blood that grants them protection against malaria but can also expose their children to a deadly form of inherited anemia.) As the ability of Africans to resist malaria became evident, Carolina planters seldom ventured into the rice fields and became less paternalistic than their Virginia counterparts except toward their household servants. After midcentury, many of them chose to spend their summers in Charleston or else found summer homes on high ground in the interior. Others vacationed in Newport, Rhode Island.

This situation altered work patterns. To produce a crop of rice, planters devised the task system, in which the slaves had to complete certain chores each day, after which their time was their own. Slaves used their free time to raise crops, hunt, or fish, activities that enabled them to create a largely invisible economy of their own. The South Carolina planters relied on a large class of white artisans in Charleston for local manufacturing such as blacksmithing, coopering, and carpentry.

Thus, while many Chesapeake slaves were acquiring the skills of artisans, Carolina slaves were heading in the other direction. Before rice became the colony's staple, they had performed a wide variety of tasks. But the huge profits from rice now condemned nearly all of them to monotonous, unpleasant labor in the marshes, even though they were freed from the direct oversight of their masters. Rice culture also left Africans with low rates of reproduction. Yet because the task system gave them more control over their own lives, slaves preferred it to gang labor.

This freedom meant slower assimilation into the British world. African words and customs survived longer in South Carolina than in the Chesapeake colonies. Newly imported slaves spoke Gullah, originally a pidgin language (that is, a simple second language for everyone who spoke it). Gullah began with a few phrases common to many West African languages, gradually added English words, and became the natural language of subsequent generations. Modern black English, which developed from Gullah, was born in the Carolina rice fields.

The South Carolina slave population failed to grow by natural increase until perhaps the 1770s, a half-century later than in the tobacco colonies. Even South Carolina planters had difficulty replacing themselves before 1760. But by the Revolution, the American South was becoming the world's only self-sustaining slave society. Nowhere else could staple colonies reproduce their enslaved labor force without continuous imports from Africa.

Everywhere that slavery took hold, the system required a great deal of brute force to maintain it. Slaves convicted of arson were often burned at the stake, an unthinkable punishment to inflict on a white person. Whippings were frequent, and the master or overseer determined the number of stripes. In South Carolina, one overseer killed five slaves in two or three years before 1712. When one slave fell asleep and lost a parcel of rice in the

The Granger Collection.

A TOBACCO PLANTATION

This illustration shows the owner and perhaps his overseer or factor supervising the completion of wooden hogsheads to hold the year's tobacco crop. The white men are dressed as gentlemen. The African laborers wear hardly any clothing at all. Note the ships off in the distance.

river, he chained him, whipped him twice a day, refused to give him food, and confined him at night in a "hellish Machine contrived by him into the Shape of a Coffin where [he] could not stir." The victim finally obtained a knife from one of his children and committed suicide.

If extreme cruelty of this sort was rare, random acts of violence were common and, from a slave's perspective, unpredictable. In Virginia, William Byrd II was one of the most refined settlers in the colony and owned its largest library. His diary reveals that when he and his wife, Lucy, disagreed, the slaves could suffer. "My wife and I had a terrible quarrel about whipping Eugene while Mr. Mumford was there but she had a mind to show her authority before company but I would not suffer it, which she took very ill." On that occasion, Eugene was spared, but slaves were not always so lucky. On another occasion, "My wife caused Prue to be whipped violently notwithstanding I desired not, which provoked me to have Anaka whipped likewise who had deserved it much more, on which my wife flew into such a passion she hoped she would be revenged of me." This time both slaves were whipped, apparently for minor infractions. The Byrds also quarreled about whether Lucy could beat Jenny with the fire tongs. House servants must have dreaded the days that Byrd spent in Williamsburg, leaving Lucy in charge of the plantation.

The southern colonies prospered in the 18th century by exchanging their staple crops for British imports. By midcentury, much of this trade had been taken over by Scots. Glasgow became the leading tobacco port of the Atlantic. Although tobacco profits remained precarious before 1730, they improved in later decades, partly because Virginia guaranteed a high-quality leaf by passing an inspection law in 1730 (Maryland followed suit in 1747), and partly because a tobacco contract between Britain and France brought lucrative revenues to both governments and opened up a vast continental market for Chesapeake planters. By 1775, more than 90 percent of their tobacco was reexported to Europe from Britain.

Other exports and new crafts also contributed to rising prosperity. South Carolina continued to export provisions to the sugar islands and deerskins to Britain. Indigo, used as a dye by the British textile industry, received a cash bounty from Parliament and emerged at midcentury as a second staple crop, pioneered by a woman planter, Eliza Lucas Pinckney. North Carolina, where the population increased fivefold between 1720 and 1760 and more than doubled again by 1775, sold naval stores (pitch, resin, turpentine) to British shipbuilders. Many Chesapeake planters turned to wheat as a second cash crop. It required mills to grind it into flour, barrels in which to pack it, and ships to carry it away. It did for the Chesapeake what tobacco had failed to do: It created cities. Norfolk and Baltimore had nearly 10,000 people by 1775, and smaller cities, such as Alexandria and Georgetown, were also thriving. Shipbuilding, closely tied to the export of wheat, became an important Chesapeake industry.

The Mid-Atlantic Colonies: The "Best Poor Man's Country"

The mid-Atlantic colonies had been pluralistic societies from the start. Immigration added to this ethnic and religious complexity after 1700. The region had the most prosperous family farms in America and, by 1760, the two largest cities, Philadelphia and New York. Pennsylvania outpaced New York in the competition for immigrants. Mostly in the 1680s and 1690s, New York governors had granted their political supporters enormous manorial estates that dominated the Hudson valley and discouraged immigration. As late as 1750, the small colony of New Jersey had as many settlers as New York but fewer slaves. Pennsylvania's growth exploded, driven by both natural increase and a huge surge of immigration. The 12th colony to be founded out of the original 13, Pennsylvania was the second most populous by 1770, surpassed only by Virginia.

After 1720, Ireland and Germany replaced England as the source of most voluntary immigrants. About 70 percent of Ireland's emigrants came from Ulster. They were Presbyterians whose forebears had come to Ireland from Scotland in the 17th century. (Historians now call them the Scots-Irish, a term that was seldom used at the time.) Most of them left for America to avoid an increase in rents and to enjoy greater trading privileges than the British Parliament allowed Ireland. The first Ulsterites sailed for New England in 1718. They expected a friendly reception from fellow Calvinists, but the Yankees treated them with suspicion. Some of them stayed and introduced linen

JOHN HANCOCK'S BOSTON MANSION

Located on Beacon Hill, the mansion was an excellent example of the elegant houses that wealthy Americans aspired to own.

North Wind Picture Archives.

manufacturing in New Hampshire, but after 1718, most immigrants from Ulster headed for the Delaware valley. About 30 percent of Irish immigrants came from southern Ireland. Most of these were Catholics, but perhaps one-quarter were Anglicans. They too headed for the mid-Atlantic colonies. Altogether, some 80,000 Irish reached the Delaware valley before 1776.

Perhaps 70,000 of the free immigrants were Germans. Most of them arrived as families, often as "redemptioners," a new form of indentured service that was attractive to married couples because it allowed them to find and bind themselves to their own masters. Families could stay together. After redemptioners completed their service, most of them streamed into the interior of Pennsylvania, where Germans outnumbered the original English and Welsh settlers by 1750. In an outburst that he later regretted, Benjamin Franklin complained that German "boors" were taking over the colony. Other Germans moved to the southern backcountry with the Irish. The mid-Atlantic colonies, already North America's breadbasket, were the favored destination of free immigrants because the expanding economies of the region offered many opportunities.

These colonies grew excellent wheat and built their own ships to carry it abroad. At first, New York flour outsold Pennsylvania's, but Pennsylvania gained the edge in the 1720s after it instituted a new system of public inspection and quality control. When Europe's population started to surge after 1740, the middle colonies began to ship flour across the Atlantic. Before 1760, both Philadelphia and New York City overtook Boston's stagnant population of 15,000. Philadelphia, with 32,000 people, was the largest city in British North America by 1775.

The Backcountry

Many of the Scots-Irish, together with some of the Germans, pushed west into the mountains and up the river valleys into the interior parts of Virginia and the Carolinas. In South Carolina, about 100 miles of pine barrens stood between these backcountry settlements and the rice plantations along the coast. Most of the English-speaking colonists were immigrants from Ulster, northern England, or lowland Scotland who brought their folkways with them and soon gave the region its own distinctive culture. Although most of them farmed, many turned to hunting or raising cattle. Unlike the coastal settlements, the backcountry showed few signs of anglicizing. It had no newspapers, few clergymen or other professionals, and little elegance. Some parts, especially in South Carolina, had almost no government. A visiting Anglican clergyman bemoaned "the abandon'd Morals and profligate Principles" of the settlers. In 1768, he preached to a gathering who had never before heard a minister, or even the Lord's Prayer. "After the Service," he wrote, "they went out to Revell[in]g, Drinking, Singing, Dancing and Whoring, and most . . . were drunk before I quitted the Spott." Refined easterners found the backcountry more than a little frightening.

Backcountry settlers were clannish and violent. They drank heavily and hated Indians. After 1750, the situation became quite tense in Pennsylvania, where the Quaker legislature insisted on handling differences with the Indians through peaceful negotiation, even though few Quakers lived on the frontier. (The Moravian Brethren, a pacifist German sect, maintained Indian missions in Pennsylvania and North Carolina but had little impact on other colonists.) Once fighting broke out against the Indians, most backcountry residents demanded their extermination. Virginia and South Carolina faced the same problem.

© Corbis Engraving.

MORAVIAN BETHLEM

The Moravian Brethren made Bethlehem, Pennsylvania, their main settlement in the northern colonies. They erected some of the largest structures in the mainland colonies. This engraving is from a painting by Thomas Pownall, royal governor of New Jersey and Massachusetts in the 1750s.

New England: A Faltering Economy and Paper Money

New England was a land of farmers, fishermen, lumberjacks, shipwrights, and merchants and still considered itself more pious than the rest of the British Empire, but the region faced serious new problems. Few immigrants, either slave or free, went there. In fact, since about 1660, more people had been leaving the region, mostly for New York and New Jersey, than had been arriving.

New England's relative isolation in the 17th century began to have negative social and economic effects after 1700. Life expectancy declined as diseases from Europe, especially smallpox and diphtheria, invaded the region by way of Atlantic commerce. The first settlers had left these diseases behind in Europe, but lack of exposure in childhood made later generations vulnerable. When smallpox threatened to devastate Boston in 1721, Zabdiel Boylston, a self-taught doctor, began inoculating people with the disease on the theory that healthy people would survive the injection and become immune. Although the city's leading physicians opposed the experiment as too risky, it worked and soon became a regular feature of public health in many colonies. Even so, a diphtheria epidemic in the 1730s and high military losses after 1740 reduced population growth. New England's rate of growth fell behind that of other regions.

After the earlier wars ended in 1713, New England's economy began to weaken. The region had prospered in the 17th century, mostly by exporting cod, grain, and barrel staves to the West Indies. After 1700, however, Yankees had trouble feeding themselves, much less others. A blight called the "wheat blast" first appeared in the 1660s and slowly spread until cultivation of wheat nearly ceased. Because Yankees preferred wheat bread to cornbread, they had to import flour from New York and Pennsylvania and, eventually, wheat from the Chesapeake colonies. Poverty became a huge social problem in Boston, where by the 1740s about one-third of all adult women were widows, mostly poor. Poor relief became a major public expense.

After grain exports declined, the once-profitable West Indian trade barely broke even. Yet its volume remained large, especially when enterprising Yankees opened up new markets in the lucrative French sugar islands. Within the West Indian market, competition from New York and Philadelphia grew almost too severe for New Englanders to meet, because those cities had flour to export and shorter distances over which to ship it. Mostly, the Yankees shipped fish and forest products to the islands in exchange for molasses, which they used as a sweetener (cheaper than sugar) or distilled into rum. Rum joined cod and lumber as a major export. British West Indian planters, alarmed

by the flood of cheap French molasses, urged Parliament to stamp out New England's trade with the French West Indies. Parliament passed the Molasses Act of 1733, which placed a prohibitive duty of six pence per gallon on all foreign molasses. Strictly enforced, the act would have strangled New England trade; instead, it gave rise to bribery and smuggling, and the molasses continued to flow.

Shipbuilding gave New England most of its leverage in the Atlantic economy. Yankees made more ships than all of the other colonies combined, although the Chesapeake colonies and the Delaware valley were closing the gap by the 1760s. New England ships earned enough from freight in most years to offset losses elsewhere, but Boston merchants often had to scramble to pay for their imports. New England ran unfavorable balances with nearly every trading partner, especially England. Yankees imported many British products but produced little that anybody in Britain wanted to buy. Whale oil, used in lamps, was an exception. A prosperous whaling industry emerged on the island of Nantucket, where surviving Indians taught settlers how to use harpoons and actively participated in the trade until they were decimated by disease. But the grain trade with the mid-Atlantic and Chesapeake colonies was not profitable. Settlers there eagerly bought rum and a few slaves from Yankee vessels that stopped on their way back from the West Indies. Newport even became deeply involved in slave trading along the African coast. Although that traffic never supplied a large percentage of North America's slaves, it contributed to the city's growth.

New England's experience with paper money illustrates these economic difficulties. In response to a military emergency in 1690, Massachusetts invented fiat money—that is, paper money backed, not by silver or gold, but only by the government's promise to accept it in payment of taxes. This system worked well enough until serious depreciation set in after the Treaty of Utrecht. The return of peace in 1713 meant that nearly all paper money would be retired within a few years through taxes already pledged for that purpose. To sustain its paper currency, the Massachusetts legislature created four land banks between 1714 and 1728. Settlers could borrow paper money using their land as security and pay off the debt over 10 years at 5 percent interest. But when the value of New England's currency declined steadily in relation to the British pound, most Boston merchants turned against paper money. They sold many of their wares on credit only to be repaid in depreciated paper. Farmers, who had originally been suspicious of land banks, became strong advocates after they discovered that they could benefit as debtors. When Britain forbade the governor to consent to any new public land banks, the countryside organized a private land bank that issued huge amounts of paper in 1741, provoking a major crisis. Parliament intervened to crush the bank. But as the bank's supporters pointed out, land banks worked quite well in colonies outside New England, such as Pennsylvania, where Franklin became an eloquent supporter.

The declining value of money touched off a fierce debate that raged from 1714 until 1750. Creditors attacked paper money as fraudulent: Only gold and silver, they claimed, had real value. Defenders retorted that, in most other colonies, paper was holding its value. The problem, they insisted, lay with the New England economy, which could not generate enough exports to pay for the region's imports. The elimination of paper, they warned, would only deepen New England's problems. War disrupted shipping in the 1740s, and military expenditures sent New England currency to a new low. Then, in 1748, Parliament agreed to reimburse Massachusetts for these expenses at the 1745 exchange rate. Governor William Shirley and House Speaker Thomas Hutchinson, an outspoken opponent of paper money, barely persuaded the legislature to use the grant to retire all paper and convert to silver money. That decision was a drastic example of anglicization. Although fiat money was the colony's own invention, Massachusetts repudiated its own offspring in 1750 in favor of orthodox methods of British public finance. As Hutchinson's critics had warned, however, silver gravitated to Boston and back to London to pay for imports. New England's economy entered a deep depression in the early 1750s, from which it did not revive until after 1755, when the wars resumed.

☙ Anglicizing Provincial America

Forms of production made these regions diverse. What made them more alike was what they retained or acquired from Britain, not what they found in America. Although each region exported its own distinctive products, patterns of consumption became quite similar throughout the colonies. In the mid-1740s, the mainland colonies and the West Indies consumed almost identical amounts of British imports. Just 10 years later, the mainland provinces had forged ahead by a margin of two to one. Their ability to consume ever larger quantities of British goods was making the mainland colonies more valuable to the empire than the sugar islands.

In the 18th century, printing and newspapers, the learned professions, and the intellectual movement known as the Enlightenment all made their mark on British North America. The new colony of Georgia was in many ways a by-product of the English Enlightenment. A powerful transatlantic religious revival, the Great Awakening, swept across Britain and the colonies in the 1730s and 1740s. And colonial political systems tried to recast themselves in the image of Britain's mixed and balanced constitution.

The World of Print

Few 17th-century American settlers owned books, and except in New England, even fewer engaged in the intellectual debates of the day. For most of the century, only Massachusetts had printing presses, first in Cambridge to serve Harvard College, the clergy, and the government, and then in Boston beginning in 1674. For the next century, Boston remained the printing capital of North America. In the 1680s, William Bradford became Philadelphia's first printer, but after a Quaker controversy drove him from the colony, he moved to New York. By 1740, Boston had eight printers; New York and Philadelphia each had two. No other community had more than one.

WOODEN PRESS IN A COLONIAL PRINT SHOP
Modern drawing by Edwin Tunis.

The American Power of an English Education

The son of Stephen DeLancey, a Huguenot refugee who fled the persecution of Louis XIV and became a prominent New York City merchant in the 1690s, James DeLancey was born in 1703 and was sent by his parents to England for his education. At Cambridge University, his tutor was Thomas Herring, who rose in the hierarchy of the Church of England until he became Archbishop of Canterbury. After leaving Cambridge, DeLancey studied law at Lincoln's Inn and established contacts with several prominent London merchants. His English friends gave him a degree of influence with the British government that probably no other American-born public official could match. DeLancey's life became a study in the use of power.

Back in New York, James completed the anglicization of his family by marrying the wealthy heiress of Caleb Heathcote, whose brother had been one of the founders of the Bank of England. At age 26, he was appointed to the New York Council. In 1732, a new governor, William Cosby, insisted that his predecessor, Lieutenant Governor Rip Van Dam, turn over half of his salary from the time of Cosby's appointment until his arrival in New York. When Van Dam refused, Cosby sued him in equity before the New York Supreme Court to avoid a jury trial. After Chief Justice Lewis Morris sided with Van Dam, Cosby dismissed him, appointed DeLancey chief justice, and won a favorable judgment. Morris retaliated by establishing *The New York Weekly Journal* as an opposition newspaper with John Peter Zenger as printer. Using materials supplied by two lawyers, James Alexander and William Smith, Jr., the *Journal* attacked the governor and his inner circle as corrupt.

Chief Justice DeLancey twice asked a grand jury to indict Zenger for "seditious libel," the crime of criticizing the government, but it refused. The attorney general then filed an "information" against Zenger to bring him to trial. DeLancey set his bail at £400, a gigantic sum, and then disbarred Alexander and Smith, Zenger's attorneys, when they objected to two of the judges. The Morrisites brought Andrew Hamilton, Philadelphia's most prominent lawyer and the speaker of the Pennsylvania assembly, to New York to defend Zenger. He persuaded the jury to decide the general issue, guilty or not guilty, instead of a narrow verdict on whether Zenger had published the objectionable issues, which would have allowed the judges to determine whether they were seditious. Zenger was acquitted in August 1735.

Despite this setback, DeLancey's power continued to grow. His supporters dominated the assembly and made life so miserable for Governor George Clinton in the 1740s that he resolved to sail for Britain and make his case to London in person. Instead, he learned that DeLancey's friends had won him a commission as lieutenant governor. If Clinton left the colony, DeLancey would take over. And indeed, after Clinton's successor as governor committed suicide shortly after arriving in New York, Lieutenant Governor DeLancey finally took charge in 1753. He summoned the Albany Congress that met a year later and became a major force in organizing New York's war effort against New France. He served as acting governor from 1753–55 and again from 1757–60. He died in office.

A BRIEF

NARRATIVE

OF THE

CASE *and* TRYAL *of* JOHN PETER ZENGER, *Printer*
of the NEW-YORK *Weekly Journal.*

A BRIEF NARRATIVE OF THE CASE AND TRYAL OF JOHN PETER ZENGER (NY, 1736)

James DeLancey presided over this famous trial and did everything in his power to secure Zenger's conviction for seditious libel, but the jury acquitted him. The narrative was written by James Alexander, one of Zenger's lawyers.

Not surprisingly, Boston also led the way in newspaper publishing. John Campbell, the city's postmaster, established the *Boston News-Letter* in 1704, only a few years after provincial newspapers had begun to appear in England. By the early 1720s, two more papers had opened in Boston, and Philadelphia and New York City had each acquired one. The *South Carolina Gazette* was founded in Charleston in 1732 and the *Virginia Gazette* at Williamsburg in 1736. By then, Boston had added several more. Benjamin Franklin took charge of the *Pennsylvania Gazette* in 1729, and John Peter Zenger launched the controversial *New York Weekly Journal* in 1733 and won a major victory for freedom of the press when a jury acquitted him of "seditious libel," the crime of criticizing government officials.

These papers were weeklies that devoted nearly all of their space to European affairs. Before midcentury, they rarely reported local news because they assumed their readers already knew it. At first, they merely reprinted items from the *London Gazette*. Beginning in the 1720s, however, the *New England Courant,* under James Franklin, also began to reprint Richard Steele's essays from the *Spectator,* Joseph Addison's pieces from the *Tatler,* and the angry, polemical writings, mostly aimed at religious bigotry and political and financial corruption, of "Cato," a pen name used jointly by John Trenchard and Thomas Gordon. *Cato's Letters,* which Gordon later published in four volumes, became immensely popular among colonial printers and readers. In short, newspapers began to spread the English Enlightenment throughout the North American colonies.

Benjamin Franklin personified the Enlightenment values that the newspapers were spreading. As a boy, although raised in Puritan Boston, he skipped church on Sundays to read Addison and Steele and to perfect his prose style. As a young printer with the *New England Courant* in the 1720s, he helped publish the writings of John Checkley, an Anglican whom the courts twice prosecuted in a vain attempt to silence him. Franklin joined the Church of England after moving to Philadelphia. After 1729, he made his *Pennsylvania Gazette* the best-edited paper in America. It reached 2,000 subscribers, four times the circulation of a Boston weekly.

Franklin was always looking for ways to improve society. In 1727, he and some friends founded the Junto, a debating society that met Friday evenings to discuss literary and philosophical questions. It later evolved into the American Philosophical Society, which still thrives near Independence Hall. Franklin was a founder of North America's first Masonic lodge in 1730, the Library Company of Philadelphia a year later, the Union Fire Company in 1736, the Philadelphia Hospital in 1751, and an academy that became the College of Philadelphia (now the University of Pennsylvania) in the 1750s. Besides his famous electrical experiments, he invented the Franklin stove (much more efficient than a fireplace) and the lightning rod. By the 1760s, he had become the most celebrated North American in the world and was thinking of retiring to England.

The Enlightenment in America

The English Enlightenment, which rejected a vengeful God and exalted man's capacity for knowledge and social improvement, grew out of the rational and benevolent piety favored by Low Church (latitudinarian) Anglicans in Restoration England. These Anglicans disliked rigid doctrine, scoffed at conversion experiences, attacked superstition, and rejected all "fanaticism," whether that of High Church Laudians, who had brought on England's great crisis of 1640–42, or that of the Puritans, who had dismantled the monarchy. High Church men, a small group after 1689, stood for orthodoxy, ritual, and liturgy.

SEA CAPTAINS CAROUSING IN SURINAM

This painting by John Greenwood (ca. 1750) suggests the condescension that refined people could bestow on those who did the basic work of the empire. Although the captains are well dressed, they all seem determined to get as drunk as possible when not at sea.

Enlightened writers greeted Sir Isaac Newton's laws of motion as one of the greatest intellectual achievements of all time, joined the philosopher John Locke in looking for ways to improve society, and began to suspect that moderns had surpassed the ancients in learning and wisdom. John Tillotson, archbishop of Canterbury until his death in 1694, embodied this "polite and Catholick [that is, universal] spirit." He preached morality rather than dogma and had a way of defending the doctrine of eternal damnation that left his listeners wondering how a merciful God could possibly have ordained such a cruel punishment.

Enlightened ideas won an elite constituency in the mainland colonies even before newspapers began publishing and circulating these new views. Tillotson had a huge impact on America. His sermons appeared in numerous southern libraries and made a deep impression at Harvard College, beginning with two young tutors, William Brattle and John Leverett, Jr. After Leverett replaced Samuel Willard as college president in 1708, Tillotson's ideas became entrenched in the curriculum. For the rest of the century, most Harvard-trained ministers, although still claiming to be Calvinists, embraced Tillotson's latitudinarian piety. They stressed the similarities, not the differences, between Congregationalists and Anglicans and favored broad religious toleration. After 1800, most Harvard-educated ministers became Unitarians who no longer believed in hell or the divinity of Jesus.

In 1701, largely in reaction against this trend at Harvard, a new college was founded as a bastion of orthodoxy in Connecticut, becoming Yale College when it finally settled in New Haven. Sadly for orthodox Congregationalists,

most of the faculty converted to the Church of England in 1722 and sailed for England to be ordained by the bishop of London. Their leader, Timothy Cutler, became the principal Anglican spokesman in Boston. Samuel Johnson, another defector, became the first president of King's College (now Columbia University) in New York City in the 1750s and won a considerable reputation as a moral philosopher.

Lawyers and Doctors

The rise of the legal profession helped spread Enlightenment ideas. Before 1700, most colonists despised lawyers as men who took advantage of the misery of others and who deliberately stirred up discord. Virginia and Massachusetts briefly abolished the legal profession. Only in Maryland did it take firm hold before 1700, but then it began to spread everywhere. In 1692, three English lawyers handled nearly all of the cases in the province of New York; by 1704, there were eight. In Boston, the legal profession seemed disreputable as late as 1720. Three British immigrants, all of them Anglicans, handled most cases. When a Congregational clergyman resigned his Connecticut pulpit and moved to Boston to practice law, he too joined Anglican King's Chapel. Benjamin Gridley, a Harvard man famous for his impiety, took up law and wrote enlightened essays for Boston newspapers in the 1730s, turned his office into an informal law school, and set up a debating society, the Sodalitas, in which students disputed legal questions within the context of contemporary oratory and philosophy. By then, a college education was almost a prerequisite to a legal career in New England.

Most Massachusetts lawyers before 1760 were either Anglicans or young men who had rejected the Congregational ministry as a career. Some were scoffers and skeptics, and most probably thought of themselves as a new learned elite. By the 1790s, lawyers saw themselves as the cultural vanguard of the new republic. Poet John Trumbull, playwright Royall Tyler, and novelist Hugh Henry Brackenridge all continued to practice law while writing on the side. Poet William Cullen Bryant, writer Washington Irving, and novelist Charles Brockden Brown turned from the law to full-time writing. Clearly, law and the Enlightenment rode together in 18th-century America.

Medicine also became an enlightened profession, with Philadelphia setting the pace. William Shippen earned degrees at Princeton and Edinburgh, the best medical school in the world at the time, before returning to Philadelphia in 1762, where he became the first American to lecture on medicine, publish a treatise on chemistry, and dissect human cadavers—a practice that shocked the unenlightened. His student John Morgan became the first professor of medicine in North America when the College of Philadelphia established a medical faculty a few years later.

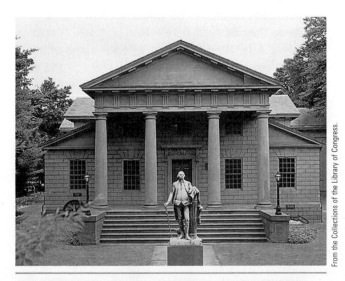

From the Collections of the Library of Congress.

THE REDWOOD LIBRARY, NEWPORT, RHODE ISLAND
Designed by architect Peter Harrison and erected between 1748 and 1750, this elegant building was named for Abraham Redwood, who donated £500 for the purchase of books in 1747.

Benjamin Rush, who also studied at Princeton and Edinburgh, brought the latest Scottish techniques to the newly founded Philadelphia Hospital. He too became an enlightened reformer. He attacked slavery and alcohol and supported the Revolution. Many colonial physicians embraced radical politics.

Georgia: The Failure of an Enlightenment Utopia

In the 1730s, Anglican humanitarianism and the Enlightenment belief in the possibility of social improvement converged in Britain to provide support for the founding of Georgia, named for King George II (1727–60). The sponsors of this project had several goals. They hoped to create a society that could make productive use of England's "worthy" poor (but not the lazy or criminal poor). Believing that South Carolina might well be helpless if attacked by Spain, they also intended—with no sense of irony—to shield that colony's slave society from Spanish Florida by populating Georgia with disciplined, armed free men. The founders of Georgia were appalled by what cheap English gin was doing to the sobriety and industry of the working people of England. They hoped to produce silk and wine, items that no other British colony had yet succeeded in making. They prohibited hard liquor and slavery. Slaves would make Georgia a simple extension of South Carolina, with all of its vulnerabilities.

A group of distinguished trustees, including members of both houses of Parliament, set themselves up as a nonprofit corporation and announced that they would give land away, not sell it. Led by James Oglethorpe, the

---

MUSICAL LINK TO THE PAST

He Could Make a Lass Weep

**Composers: Francis Hopkinson (music),
            Thomas Parnell (lyrics)**

**Title: "My Days Have Been So Wondrous
        Free" (1759)**

Until almost the American Revolution, American music was European music, especially English music, and most of it was church music. Thomas Hopkinson was America's earliest secular songwriter, and "My Days Have Been so Wondrous Free" was probably the first American secular song. Although the title and the song's rhythm suggest a jaunty mood, the song is not as upbeat as a superficial listen might indicate. Francis Hopkinson's music complimented and added depth to the lyrics written decades earlier by Thomas Parcell. A romantic and bittersweet yearning permeates the song, although whether such yearning is directed toward communing with nature or with a romantic companion is uncertain.

Hopkinson worked in an environment where no American song tradition, no American publishing companies, and no consumer demand for American secular songs existed. He was a multitalented Renaissance man in the style of his contemporaries and friends Thomas Jefferson and Benjamin Franklin, exhibiting expertise in the fields of music, painting, inventing, writing, the law, and politics (he was a delegate to the Continental Congress and signed the Declaration of Independence).

"My Days" also represented an early example of two important traditions in American songwriting. First, Hopkinson purposely crafted compositions that untrained amateurs could perform and enjoy. "The best of [my songs] is that they are so easy that any Person who can play at all may perform them without much Trouble, & I have endeavour'd to make the melodies pleasing to the untutored Ear," he explained. Second, his songs meant to provoke emotion and emanated from "the Imagination of an Author who composes from his Heart, rather than his Head."

Although Hopkinson's songs did not attain large popularity, they did fulfill his elevated purposes in at least one family. After Hopkinson sent Jefferson some of his songs, Jefferson replied: "Accept my thanks . . . and my daughter's . . . I will not tell you how much they have pleased us, nor how well the last of them merits praise for its pathos, but relate a fact only, which is that while my elder daughter was playing it on the harpsichord, I happened to look toward the fire, & saw the younger one in tears. I asked her if she was sick? She said 'no; but the tune was so mournful.'"

1. Why do you think the colonists took more than a hundred years to develop their own popular songs, relying instead on material imported from England and the rest of Europe?

Listen to an audio recording of this music on the Musical Links to the Past CD.

trustees obtained a 20-year charter from Parliament in 1732, raised money from Anglican friends, and launched the colony on land claimed by both Spain and Britain. The trustees recruited foreign Protestants, including some Germans who had just been driven out of Salzburg by its Catholic bishop, a small number of Moravian Brethren (a German pacifist sect, led by Count Nicholas von Zinzendorf), and French Huguenots. In England, they interviewed many prospective settlers to distinguish the worthy poor from the unworthy. They engaged silk and wine experts and recruited Scottish Highlanders as soldiers.

But the trustees refused to consult the settlers on what might be good for them or for Georgia. As refined men of the Enlightenment, they believed they knew what the colony needed. They created no elective assembly, nor did they give the British government much chance to supervise them. Under their charter, Georgia laws had to be approved by the British Privy Council. Therefore the trustees passed only three laws during their 20 years of rule. One laid out the land system, and the others prohibited slavery and hard liquor. The trustees governed through regulations instead of laws. An elective assembly, the trustees promised, would come later, after Georgia's character had been firmly set.

In 1733, the first settlers laid out Savannah, a town with spacious streets. Within 10 years, 1,800 charity cases and just over 1,000 self-supporting colonists reached Georgia. The most successful were the Salzburgers, who agreed with the prohibitions on slavery and alcohol and built a thriving settlement at Ebenezer, farther up the Savannah River. The Moravian Brethren left for North Carolina after five years rather than bear arms. A group of Lowland Scots known as the Malcontents grew disgruntled and, after Oglethorpe ignored their complaints, left for South Carolina.

The land system never worked as planned. The trustees gave 50 acres to every male settler whose passage was paid for out of charitable funds. Those who paid their own way could claim up to 500 acres. Ordinary farmers did poorly; they could not support a family on 50 acres of the sandy soil around Savannah. Because the trustees envisioned every landowner as a soldier, women could not inherit land, nor could landowners sell their plots.

The settlers were unable to grow grapes or to persuade the sickly worms that survived the Atlantic crossing to make silk out of mulberry leaves. They clamored for rum, smuggled it into the colony when they could, and insisted that Georgia would never thrive until it had slaves. By the mid-1740s, enough people had died or left to reduce the population by more than half, and by 1752, the population had dropped below the 2,800 who had first settled the colony.

Between 1750 and 1752, the trustees gave up. They dropped their ban on alcohol, allowed the importation of slaves, summoned an elective assembly (but only to consult, not legislate), and finally surrendered their charter to Parliament. The establishment of royal government in 1752 at last gave Georgia an elective assembly with full powers of legislation, and Georgia became what it was never meant to be, a smaller version of South Carolina, producing rice and indigo with slave labor. By then, however, in one of the supreme ironies of the age, the colony had done more to spread religious revivalism than to vindicate Enlightenment ideals. Georgia helped turn both

A VIEW OF SAVANNAH ON MARCH 29, 1734

This painting by Peter Gordon emphasizes the wide streets and spacious atmosphere of this planned city.

John Wesley and George Whitefield into the greatest revivalists of the 18th century.

⬤ The Great Awakening

Between the mid-1730s and the early 1740s, an immense religious revival, the Great Awakening, swept across the Protestant world. Within the British Empire, it affected some areas more intensely than others. England, Scotland, Ulster, New England, the mid-Atlantic colonies, and for a time South Carolina responded warmly to emotional calls for a spiritual rebirth. Southern Ireland, the West Indies, and the Chesapeake colonies remained on the margins until Virginia and Maryland were drawn into a later phase of revivalism in the 1760s and 1770s. The Great Awakening shattered some denominational loyalties in the colonies and enabled the Methodists and the Baptists to surge ahead of all Protestant rivals in the generation after 1780.

Origins of the Revivals

Some of the earliest revivals arose among the Dutch in New Jersey. Guiliam Bertholf, a farmer and cooper (barrel maker), was a lay reader who had been ordained in an obscure corner of the Netherlands in 1694 (Amsterdam did not approve) and returned to preach to his former neighbors in Hackensack and Passaic. His emotional piety won many adherents. After 1720, Theodorus Jacobus Frelinghuysen sparked several revivals in his congregation in New Brunswick, New Jersey. The local Presbyterian pastor, Gilbert Tennent, watched and learned.

Tennent was a younger son of William Tennent, Sr., an Anglican-turned-Presbyterian minister who had moved from Ulster to America. At Neshaminy, Pennsylvania, he set up the Log College, where he trained his sons and other young men as evangelical preachers. The Tennent family dominated the Presbytery of New Brunswick, used it to ordain ministers, and sent them off to any congregation that requested one, even in other presbyteries. That practice angered the Philadelphia Synod, the governing body of the Presbyterian church in the colonies. Most of its ministers emphasized orthodoxy over a personal conversion experience. In a 1740 sermon, *The Dangers of an Unconverted Ministry*, Gilbert Tennent denounced those preachers for leading their people to hell. His attack split the church. In 1741, the outnumbered revivalists withdrew and founded their own Synod of New York.

In New England, Solomon Stoddard of Northampton presided over six revivals, which he called "harvests of souls," between the 1670s and his death in 1729. Jonathan Edwards, his grandson and successor—the only member of the Yale faculty who had not defected to the Anglicans in 1722—touched off a revival in 1734 and 1735 that rocked dozens of Connecticut valley towns. The revival ended suddenly when a prominent man, overwhelmed by the burden of his sins, slit his own throat. Edwards's *A Faithful Narrative of the Surprising Work of God* (1737) explained what a revival was—an emotional response to God's Word that brought sudden conversions to scores of people. He described these conversions in acute detail and won admirers in Britain as well as in New England.

In England, John Wesley and George Whitefield set the pace. At worldly Oxford University, Wesley and his brother

In actuality, some presbyteries had more churches than others. Arrows indicate descending lines of authority.

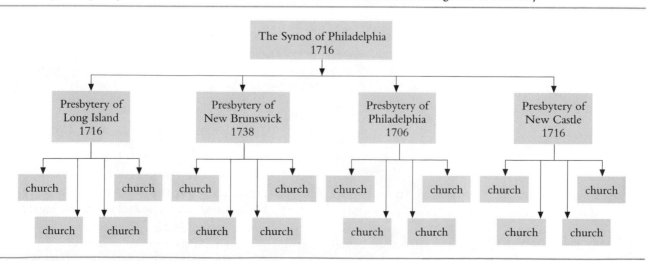

THE SYNOD OF PHILADELPHIA BY 1738

Charles founded the Holy Club, a High Church society whose members fasted until they could barely walk. One even lay prostrate for hours on the frigid earth, lost in prayer while his hands turned black. These methodical practices prompted scoffers to call them Methodists. Still dissatisfied with the state of his soul, Wesley went to Georgia as a missionary in 1735, an unhappy experience for him. He fell in love with a woman who did not return his affection, and the settlers rejected his ascetic piety. In 1737, on the return voyage to England, some Moravians convinced him that, for all his zeal, he had never grasped the central Protestant message, justification by faith alone. Some months later, he was deeply moved by Edwards's *Faithful Narrative*. Soon, Wesley found his life's mission, the conversion of sinners, and it launched him on an extraordinary preaching career of more than 40 years.

George Whitefield, who had been a talented amateur actor in his youth, joined the Holy Club at Oxford and became an Anglican minister. He followed Wesley to Georgia, founded an orphanage, then returned to England and preached all over the kingdom to raise money for it. He had the power to move masses of people through a single sermon, and he too began to preach the "new birth"—the necessity of a conversion experience. When many pastors banned him from their pulpits, he responded by preaching in open fields to anyone who would listen. Newspapers reported the controversy, and soon Whitefield's admirers began to notify the press where he would be on any given day. Colonial newspapers, keenly sensitive to the English press, also reported his movements.

Whitefield Launches the Transatlantic Revival

In 1739, Whitefield made his second trip to America, ostensibly to raise funds for his orphanage at Bethesda, Georgia. Everyone knew who he was from newspaper accounts, and thousands flocked to hear him preach. After landing in Delaware, he preached his way northward through Philadelphia, New Jersey, and New York City, and then headed south through the Chesapeake colonies and into South Carolina. In September 1740, he sailed to Newport and for two months toured New England. During his travels, he met Benjamin Franklin, Gilbert Tennent, and Jonathan Edwards. In the cities he sometimes attracted as many as 30,000 people, or twice the population of Boston. His voice was so musical, claimed one observer, that he could seduce a crowd just by the way he said "Mesopotamia." Using his acting skills, he imitated Christ on the cross, shedding "pious tears" for poor sinners. Or he became God at the Last Judgment, thundering: "Depart from me ye accursed into everlasting fire!" When he wept,

his audience wept with him. When he condemned them, they fell to the ground in agony.

Although Whitefield wore the surplice of an Anglican minister and carried the *Book of Common Prayer* when he preached, Anglicans treated him with reserve or hostility. In Charleston and New York City, the official spokesmen for the bishop of London denounced him, but Presbyterians, Congregationalists, and Baptists embraced him, at least until some of them began to fear that he was doing more harm than good. To many he embodied the old Non-Separatist ideal that all English Protestants were really members of the same church.

Disruptions

When other preachers tried to take up Whitefield's role after he moved on, they aroused fierce controversy. In South Carolina, Hugh Bryan, a Savannah River planter, began preaching the evangelical message to his slaves. In 1742, not long after a major slave revolt had rocked the colony, he denounced slavery as a sin and warned that God would pour out his wrath on the planters unless they rejected it. Proclaiming himself an American Moses, he attempted to part the waters of the Savannah River and lead the slaves to freedom in Georgia. Instead, he almost drowned. He then confessed publicly that he had been deluded. This fiasco discredited evangelicalism among the planters of the lower South for another generation, but Bryan and his family continued to convert their own slaves. African American evangelical piety, including some of the first black preachers, took root from these efforts.

Whitefield's successors caused severe disturbances in New England. Gilbert Tennent preached there for months. Lacking Whitefield's musical voice and Oxford diction, Tennent spoke with a Scottish burr and specialized in Holy Laughter, the scornful peals of a triumphant God as sinners tumble into hell. He abandoned the usual garb of a minister for a robe and sandals and let his hair grow long, thereby proclaiming himself a new John the Baptist heralding the Second Coming of Christ. Many ecstatic followers believed that the biblical Millennium was at hand.

James Davenport, who succeeded Tennent, denounced unregenerate ministers by name. He liked to preach by eerie candlelight, roaring damnation at his listeners, even grabbing Satan and wrestling him back to hell. He advised his admirers to drink rat poison rather than listen to another lifeless sermon. In 1743, he established the Shepherd's Tent in New London to train awakened preachers. This outdoor school abandoned the classical curriculum of colleges and insisted only on a valid conversion experience. He organized a book-burning, in which titles by Increase Mather and other New England dignitaries went up in flames, and he threw his britches on the fire, declaring them a mark of human vanity. A New England grand jury, asked to indict him, proclaimed him mad instead. Like Bryan in South Carolina, he repented and claimed that he had been deluded. The Shepherd's Tent collapsed.

Long-Term Consequences of the Revivals

The revivals had dramatic consequences. As time passed, they feminized evangelical churches. Amid the enthusiasm of Whitefield's tour, more men than usual had joined a church, but after another year or two, men became difficult to convert. The number of women church members began to soar, however, until by 1800 they often formed a majority of 3 or 4 to 1, and in some congregations acquired an informal veto over the choice of the minister.

Partly in reaction to the revivals, thousands of men became Freemasons, often instead of joining a church. After 1730, the Masons made some headway among the merchants and professionals of Philadelphia and Boston, but during and after the Revolution, their membership grew spectacularly. They appealed to men of all denominations, accepting even a few Catholics, Jews, and Indians. Artisans began to dominate city lodges, and the Masons penetrated deeply into the countryside as well. They very nearly turned their order into a religion of manliness, complete with secret and mysterious rituals. They extolled sobriety, industry, brotherhood, benevolence, and citizenship. At first, most clergymen saw Masons as a force for good, but by the 1820s, the order would be drawing angry criticism.

The revivals shattered the unity of New England's Congregational Church. Evangelicals seceded from dozens of congregations to form their own "Separate" churches. Many of those that survived went Baptist by the 1760s, thereby gaining protection under the toleration statutes of the New England colonies. In the middle colonies, the revivals strengthened denominational loyalties and energized the clergy. In the 1730s, most people in the region, particularly in New Jersey and Pennsylvania, had never joined a church. The revivals prompted many of them to become New Side (evangelical) Presbyterians, Old Side (antirevival) Presbyterians, or nonevangelical Anglicans. Similar cleavages ran through the German population. The southern colonies were less affected, although evangelical Presbyterians made modest gains in the Virginia backcountry after 1740. Finally, in the 1760s, the Baptists began to win thousands of converts, as did the Methodists after 1776, whose numbers surpassed the Baptists a few decades later.

The revivals broke down localism by creating new cosmopolitan links with Britain and between colonies. Whitefield ran the most efficient publicity machine in the Atlantic world. In London, Glasgow, and Boston, periodicals called the *Christian History* carried news of revivals occurring anywhere in the empire. For years, London evangelicals held regular Letter Days, at which they read accounts of revivals in progress. Revivalists wrote often to one another. When fervor declined in New England, Jonathan Edwards organized a Concert of Prayer with his Scottish correspondents, setting regular times for them all to beseech the Lord to pour out his grace once more. As Anglicans split into Methodists and Latitudinarians, Congregationalists into New Lights (prorevival) and Old Lights (antirevival), and Presbyterians into comparable New Side and Old Side synods, evangelicals discovered that they had more in common with revivalists in other denominations than with antirevivalists in their own. When New Side Presbyterians chose a new president of the College of New Jersey in 1757, they saw nothing strange in naming a Congregationalist, Jonathan Edwards.

Edwards was the most able apologist for revivals in Britain or America and probably the most profound theologian that North America has yet produced. When Boston's Charles Chauncy (very much a man of the Enlightenment) attacked the revivals as frauds because of their emotional excesses, Edwards replied with *A Treatise concerning Religious Affections* (1746), which displayed his own mastery of Enlightenment sources, including Newton and Locke. Although admitting that no emotional response, however intense, was proof by itself of the presence of God in a person's soul, he insisted that intense feeling must always accompany the reception of divine grace. That view upset people who believed that a rational God must have established a polite and genteel religion. For Edwards, an unemotional piety could never be the work of God. In effect, Edwards countered Chauncy's emotional defense of reason with his own rational defense of emotion.

New Colleges

The Great Awakening also created several new colleges. Each was set up primarily by a single denomination, but all admitted other Protestants. In 1740, North America had only three colleges: Harvard, William and Mary, and Yale. Although Yale eventually embraced the revivals, all three opposed them at first. In 1746, middle colony evangelicals, eager to show their commitment to classical learning after the fiasco of the Shepherd's Tent, founded the College of New Jersey. It graduated its first class in

1748 and settled in Princeton in 1756. Unlike the older colleges, it drew students from all 13 colonies and sent its graduates throughout America, especially to the middle and southern colonies. It also reshaped the Presbyterian Church. When Presbyterians healed their schism and reunited in 1758, the New Siders set the terms. Outnumbered in 1741, they held a large majority of ministers by 1758. Through control of Princeton, their numbers had increased rapidly. The Old Side, still dependent on the University of Glasgow in Scotland, could barely replace those who died.

New Light Baptists founded the College of Rhode Island (now Brown University) in the 1760s. Dutch Reformed revivalists established Queens College (now Rutgers University) in New Jersey, mostly to train evangelical ministers who could preach in English. Eleazer Wheelock opened an evangelical school for Indians in Lebanon, Connecticut. After his first graduate, Samson Occum, raised £12,000 in England for the school, Wheelock moved to New Hampshire and used most of the money to found Dartmouth College instead. By 1790, Dartmouth was turning out more graduates, and far more ministers, than any other American college.

In the 1750s, Anglicans countered with two new colleges of their own: the College of Philadelphia (now the University of Pennsylvania), which also had Old Side Presbyterian support, and King's College (now Columbia University) in New York. Their undergraduate programs remained small, however, and few of their students chose a ministerial career. In the competition for student loyalties, nonevangelicals could not yet compete effectively with revivalists.

The Denominational Realignment

The revivals transformed American religious life. In 1700, the three strongest denominations had been the Congregationalists in New England, the Quakers in the Delaware valley, and the Anglicans in the South. By 1800, all three had lost ground to newcomers: the Methodists, who grew at an astonishing rate as the Church of England collapsed during the Revolution; the Baptists, who leaped into second place; and the Presbyterians. Methodists and Baptists did not expect their preachers to attend college, and they recruited ministers from a much broader segment of the population than their rivals could tap. Although they never organized their own Shepherd's Tent, they embraced similar principles, demanding only personal conversion, integrity, knowledge of the Bible, and a talent for preaching.

Antirevivalist denominations, especially Anglicans and Quakers, lost heavily. New Light Congregationalists made only slight gains because, when their people left behind the established churches of New England and moved west, they usually joined a Presbyterian church, which provided a structure and network of support that isolated congregations in a pluralistic society could not sustain.

☙ Political Culture in the Colonies

In politics as in other activities, the colonies became more like Britain during the 18th century. A quarter-century of warfare after 1689 convinced the settlers that they needed the protection of the British state and strengthened their admiration for its parliamentary system. Most colonial voters and assemblymen were more "independent" than their British counterparts, who lived in a hierarchical world of patrons and clients. Still, provincial politics began to absorb many of the values and practices that had taken hold in Britain after the Glorious Revolution. Colonists agreed that they were free because they were British, because they too had mixed constitutions that united monarchy, aristocracy, and democracy in almost perfect balance.

By the 1720s, every colony except Connecticut and Rhode Island had an appointive governor, either royal or proprietary, plus a council and an elective assembly. The governor stood for monarchy and the council for aristocracy. In Massachusetts, Rhode Island, and Connecticut, the council or upper house was elected (indirectly in Massachusetts). In all other colonies except Pennsylvania, an appointive council played an active legislative role. The office of councillor was not hereditary, but many councillors served for life, especially in Virginia, and some were succeeded by their sons.

THE SPECTRUM OF COLONIAL POLITICS

Constitutional Type	Successful	Unsuccessful
Northern "Court"	New York, circa 1710–28 New Hampshire after 1741 Massachusetts after 1741 New Jersey after 1750	New York after 1728 Pennsylvania (successful in peace, ineffective in war)
Southern "Country"	Virginia after 1720 South Carolina after 1730 Georgia after 1752	Maryland North Carolina

Connecticut and Rhode Island never really belonged to this system.

The Rise of the Assembly and the Governor

In all 13 colonies, once the Crown took over Georgia, the settlers elected the assembly, which embodied a colony's "democratic" elements. The right to vote in the colonies, although narrowing as population rose, was more widely shared than in England, where two-thirds of adult males were disenfranchised, a ratio that continued to rise. By contrast, something like three-fourths of free adult white men could vote in the colonies, and a fair number of those who were ineligible at any given time would win that right by acquiring property as they grew older. The frequency of elections varied—from every seven years in New York (from the 1740s on) and Virginia, as well as in Britain, to at least once a year in five colonies. As the century advanced, legislatures sat longer and passed more laws. The lower house—the assembly—usually initiated major bills. The rise of the assembly was a major political fact of the era. It made most of its gains at the expense of the council.

Every royal colony except New York and Georgia already had an assembly with a strong sense of its own privileges when the first royal governor arrived, but the governors in most colonies also grew more effective as time passed. Because the governor's instructions usually challenged some existing practices, clashes often occurred in which the first royal governors never got all of their demands. Nevertheless, they did win concessions and became much more effective over the years. In almost every colony, the most successful governors were men who served between 1730 and 1765. Most of them had learned by then that their success depended less on their prerogatives (specific royal powers embodied in their commissions) than on their ability to win over the assembly through persuasion or patronage.

Early in the century, conflicts between the governor and an assembly majority tended to be legalistic. Each side cited technical precedents to justify the governor's prerogatives or the assembly's traditional privileges. Later on, when conflict spilled over into pamphlets and newspapers, it often pitted an aggrieved minority (unable to win a majority in the assembly) against both governor and assembly. These contests were ideological. The opposition accused the governor of corruption, of threatening the colonists' liberties, and he denounced the opposition as a "faction." Everyone condemned factions, or political parties, as self-interested and destructive. "Party is the madness of many for the gain of a few," declared poet Alexander Pope. Hardly anyone claimed to be a party leader; the other side was the faction.

"Country" Constitutions: The Southern Colonies

Although the colonies were all aware of the ideological currents in British politics, they reacted to them in different ways. In most southern colonies, the Country principles of the British opposition (see chapter 3) became the common assumptions of public life, acceptable to both governor and assembly, typically after a failed attempt to impose the Court alternative. When a governor, such as

THE GOVERNOR'S PALACE AT WILLIAMSBURG, VIRGINIA

The governor's palace was built during the term of Governor Alexander Spotswood (1710–22) and restored in the 20th century. For Spotswood, the palace was an extension of royal might and splendor across the ocean. He set a standard of elegance that many planters imitated when they built their own great houses in the second quarter of the 18th century.

Colonial Williamsburg Foundation.

Virginia's Alexander Spotswood (1710–22), used his patronage to fill the assembly with his own "placemen," the voters turned them out at the next election. Just as Spotswood learned that he could not manipulate the house through patronage, the assembly discovered that it could not coerce a governor who had a permanent salary. Accordingly, Virginia and South Carolina cultivated a "politics of harmony," a system of ritualized mutual flattery. Governors found that they could accomplish more through persuasion than through patronage, and the assemblies responded by showing their appreciation. The planters of Virginia and South Carolina concluded that their societies embodied almost exactly what British opposition writers had been demanding. Factions disappeared, allowing the governor and the assembly to pursue the "common good" in an atmosphere free of rancor or corruption. Georgia adopted similar practices in the 1750s.

This system worked well because the planters were doing what Britain wanted them to do: shipping staple crops to Britain. Both sides could agree on measures that would make this process more efficient, such as the Virginia Tobacco Inspection Act of 1730. In Virginia, public controversy actually ceased. Between 1720 and 1765, particularly during the able administration of Sir William Gooch (1727–49), the governor and House of Burgesses engaged in only one public quarrel, an unparalleled record of political harmony. South Carolina's politics became almost as placid from the 1730s into the 1760s, but harmony there masked serious social problems that were beginning to emerge in the unrepresented backcountry. By contrast, the politics of harmony never took hold in Maryland, where the lord proprietor always tried to seduce assemblymen with his lavish patronage, nor in factional North Carolina, where the tobacco and rice planters continually wrangled, and the growing backcountry distrusted both sides.

"Court" Constitutions: The Northern Colonies

With many economic interests and ethnic groups to satisfy, the northern colonies often produced political factions. Governors with a large vision of the public welfare could win support by using patronage to reward some groups and to discipline others. William Shirley, governor of Massachusetts from 1741 to 1756, used judicial and militia appointments and war contracts to build a majority in the assembly. Like Sir Robert Walpole in Britain, he was a master of Court politics. In New Hampshire, Benning Wentworth created a political machine that rewarded just about every assemblyman between 1741 and 1767. An ineffective opposition in both colonies accused the governors of corrupting the assembly, but Shirley and Wentworth each claimed that his actions were essential to his colony's needs. Both governors remained in tight control.

The opposition, although seldom able to implement its demands at the provincial level, was important nonetheless. It kept settlers alert to any infringements on their liberties. It dominated the town of Boston from 1720 on, and it reminded people that resistance to authority might be the only means to preserve liberty. Boston artisans engaged in ritualized mob activities that had a sharp political edge. Every year on Guy Fawkes Day (November 5), a North End mob and a South End mob bloodied each other for the privilege of burning effigies of the pope, the devil, and the Stuart pretender to the British throne. These men were raucously celebrating liberty, property, and no popery—the British constitution as they understood it. The violence made many wealthy merchants nervous, and by 1765 some of them would become its targets.

New York's governors, particularly Robert Hunter (1710–19), achieved great success even before 1720, mostly by playing off one faction against another in a colony that had been fiercely divided since Leisler's rebellion of 1689. Hunter's salary and perquisites became more lucrative than those attached to any other royal office in North America, and after 1716 he and his successor were so satisfied with their control of the assembly that they let 10 years pass without calling a general election. During the 25 years after 1730, later governors lost these advantages, primarily because London gave the governorship to a series of men who were eager to rebuild their tattered fortunes at New York's expense. This combination of greed and need gave new leverage to the assembly, and it attacked many royal prerogatives during the 1740s. Of the mainland colonies, only the governor of New York emerged weaker by 1760 than he had been in 1730.

Pennsylvania, by contrast, kept its proprietary governor weak well into the 1750s. After three decades of factionalism, a unified Quaker Party won undisputed control of the assembly during the 1730s. The governor, who by this time was never a Quaker, had a lot of patronage to dispense. He found it useless in controlling the Quaker assemblymen, who had lost interest in becoming judges if that meant administering oaths. Nor could he win these pacifists over with military commissions or war contracts, no matter how lucrative. The colonists, both north and south, absorbed the ideology of the British opposition, which warned that those in power were always trying to destroy liberty and that corruption was power's most dangerous weapon. By 1776, that view would justify independence and the repudiation of a "corrupt" king and Parliament. Before the 1760s, however, it served different purposes. In the south, this ideology celebrated both the political success of Virginia and South Carolina and Anglo-American harmony. In the north, it replicated its role in Britain and became the language of frustrated minorities unable to defeat the governor or control the assembly.

The Renewal of Imperial Conflict

A new era of imperial war began in 1739 and continued, with only a brief interruption, until 1763. The British colonies, New Spain, and New France all became involved, and eventually so did all the Indians of the eastern woodlands. By 1763, France had been expelled from North America. Britain controlled the continent east of the Mississippi, and Spain claimed the land west of it.

Challenges to French Power

In the decades of peace after 1713, the French tried, with mixed results, to strengthen their position in North America. At great cost, they erected the continent's most formidable fortress, Louisbourg, on Cape Breton Island. A naval force stationed there could protect the French fishery and guard the approaches to the St. Lawrence River. The French also built Fort St. Frédéric (the British called it Crown Point) on Lake Champlain and maintained their Great Lakes posts at Forts Frontenac, Michilimackinac, and Detroit. To bolster its weak hold on the Gulf of Mexico, France created the Company of the Indies, which shipped 7,000 settlers and 2,000 slaves to Louisiana between 1717 and 1721 but then failed to supply them. By 1726, half had starved to death or had fled. Another 5,000 slaves, but few settlers, reached the colony by 1730. The French founded New Orleans, which became the capital of Louisiana in 1722.

Despite these efforts, the French hold on the interior began to weaken, both north and south. From all points of the compass, Indians returned to the Ohio valley, mostly to trade with pacifist Pennsylvania or with Fort Oswego, a new British post on Lake Ontario. Compared with the French, the British were often clumsy in their dealings with Indians, but they had one advantage: British trade goods were cheaper than French goods, although no better in quality. Many of the Indians founded what the French disparagingly called "republics," villages outside

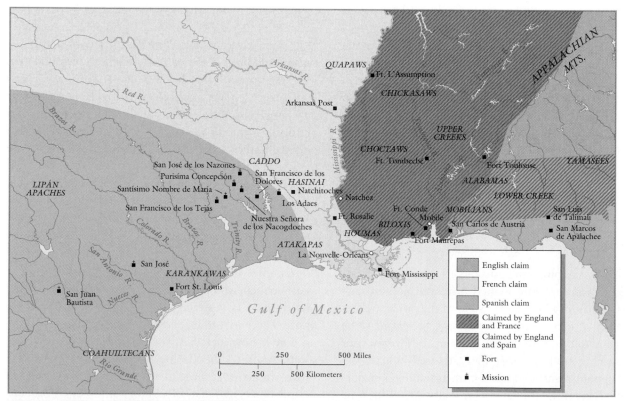

MAP 4.1 FRENCH LOUISIANA AND SPANISH TEXAS, CIRCA 1730

In this part of North America, French and Spanish settlers and missionaries were spread quite thinly over a vast area and surrounded by much larger numbers of Indian peoples.

View an animated version of this map or related maps at http://history.wadsworth.com/murrin_LEP4e.

the French alliance system that were willing to trade with the British. The chiefs at Venango, Logstown, and other republics accepted people from all tribes—Delawares from the east, Shawnees from the south and east, Mingoes (Iroquois who had left their homeland) from the north, and other Algonquians of the Great Lakes region to the west. Because the inhabitants of each new village had blood relatives living among all of the nearby nations, the chiefs welcomed Pennsylvania traders and hoped that none of their neighbors would endanger their own relatives by attacking them.

Sometimes even the French system of mediation broke down. In the northwest from 1712 to 1737, the French and their Algonquian allies fought a long, intermittent war with the Fox nation. In the southwest, an arrogant French officer decided to take over the lands of the Natchez Indians (the last of the Mississippian mound builders) and ordered them to move. While pretending to comply, the Natchez planned a counterstroke and, on November 28, 1729, killed every French male in the vicinity. In the war that followed, the French and their Choctaw allies destroyed the Natchez as a distinct people, although some Natchez refugees found homes among the Chickasaws or the Creeks.

During the war, in 1730, the French barely averted a massive slave uprising in New Orleans. To stir up hatred between Indians and Africans, the French turned over some of the African leaders of the revolt to the Choctaws to be burned alive. They also encouraged hostilities between the Choctaws and the Chickasaws, largely because they could not afford enough gifts to hold an alliance with both nations. This policy did serious damage to the French. Instead of weakening the pro-British Chickasaws, it touched off a civil war among the Choctaws, and France lost both influence and prestige.

The Danger of Slave Revolts and War with Spain

To counter the French, Spain sent missionaries and soldiers into Texas between 1716 and 1720 and founded a capital at Los Adaes, a few miles from the French trading post at Natchitoches. To prevent smuggling, Spain refused to open a seaport on the Gulf Coast. As a result, its tiny outposts had to depend on French trade goods for supplies, sometimes even for food. The Texas missions won few converts and suffered frequent depredations by Indians carrying French muskets. In 1719, the survivors of these attacks abandoned their missions in eastern Texas and fled west to San Antonio, which eventually became the capital.

The Spanish presence in Florida proved troublesome to the British, especially in South Carolina. In the 16th century, Francis Drake had proclaimed himself a liberator when he attacked St. Augustine and promised freedom to Indians and Africans groaning under Spanish tyranny (see chapter 2). By the 1730s, the roles had been reversed. On several occasions after 1680, Spanish Florida had promised freedom to any slaves who escaped from Carolina and were willing to accept Catholicism. In 1738, the governor established, just north of St. Augustine, a new town, Gracia Real de Santa Teresa de Mose (or Mose for short, pronounced Moe-shah). He put a remarkable African in charge, a man who took the name Francisco Menéndez at baptism. He had escaped from slavery, had fought with the Yamasees against South Carolina in 1715, and had fled to Florida, only to be enslaved again. Yet he became literate in Spanish and, while still a slave, rose to the rank of militia captain. After winning his freedom, he took charge of Mose in 1738 and made it the first community of free blacks in what is now the United States. The very existence of Mose acted as a magnet for Carolina slaves.

In 1739, the governor of Spanish Florida offered liberty to any slaves from the British colonies who could make their way to Florida. This manifesto, and rumors about Mose, touched off the Stono Rebellion in South Carolina, the most violent slave revolt in the history of the 13 colonies. Some of the rebellion's leaders were Catholics from the African Kingdom of the Kongo, which Portuguese missionaries had converted in the 16th century.

On Sunday morning, September 9, 1739, a force of 20 slaves attacked a store at Stono (south of Charleston), killed the owner, seized weapons, and moved on to assault other houses and to attract new recruits. Heading toward Florida, they killed about 25 settlers that day and nearly captured Lieutenant Governor William Bull, who happened to be riding by and just managed to gallop away. When the rebels reached the Edisto River, they stopped, raised banners, and shouted "Liberty," hoping to begin a general uprising. There the militia caught them and killed about two-thirds of the growing force. In the weeks that followed, the settlers killed another 60. None of the rebels reached Florida, but, as the founders of Georgia had foreseen, South Carolina was indeed vulnerable in any dispute with Spain.

In 1739, at almost the same moment, the War of Jenkins's Ear, derisively named for a ship captain who displayed his severed ear to Parliament as proof of Spanish cruelty, broke out between Britain and Spain. The war cost Britain dearly because Spanish defenses held everywhere. Some 3,000 men from the 13 colonies, eager for plunder, joined expeditions in 1741 and 1742 against the seaport of Cartagena, New Granada (now Colombia), and against Cuba and Panama. All were disasters (see map on p. 143).

CHRISTIAN BURIAL IN THE KONGO, 18TH CENTURY

At least some of the Africans who organized the Stono rebellion in South Carolina in 1739 were Catholics from the kingdom of the Kongo.

Most of the men died of disease; only 10 percent of the volunteers returned home. But one of the survivors, Lawrence Washington, so admired the British naval commander, Edward Vernon, that he named his Virginia plantation Mount Vernon. Britain also experienced a surge of patriotic fervor from the war. Both "God Save the King" and "Rule Britannia" were written during the struggle.

Georgia was supposed to protect South Carolina. General Oglethorpe, its governor, retaliated against the Spanish by invading Florida in 1740. He dispersed the black residents of Mose and occupied the site, but the Spaniards mauled his garrison in a surprise counterattack. Oglethorpe retreated without taking St. Augustine and returned to Georgia with disturbing reports. Spain, he said, was sending blacks into the British colonies to start slave uprisings. And Spanish priests in disguise were intermingled with the black conspirators and would try to destroy British fortifications. This news set off panics in the rice and tobacco colonies, but it had its biggest impact in New York City.

Back in 1712, a slave revolt had shaken the city. After setting fire to a barn one night, slaves had shot 15 settlers who rushed to put out the blaze, killing nine. Twenty-one slaves were executed, some after gruesome tortures.

By 1741, New York City's 2,000 slaves were the largest concentration of blacks in British North America outside of Charleston. On March 18, Fort George burned down in what was probably an accident, but when a series of suspicious fires broke out, the settlers grew nervous. Some of the fires probably provided cover for an interracial larceny ring that operated out of the tavern of John Hughson, a white man. When the New York Supreme Court offered freedom to Mary Burton, a 16-year-old Irish servant girl at the tavern, in exchange for her testimony, she swore that the tavern was the center of a hellish "popish plot" to murder the city's whites, free the slaves, and make Hughson king of the Africans. Several free black Spanish sailors, who had been captured and enslaved by privateers, also were accused, although apparently their only crime was to insist that they were free men. After Oglethorpe's warning reached New York in June, the number of the accused escalated, and John Ury, a recently arrived High Churchman and a Latin teacher, was hanged as the likely Spanish priest.

The New York conspiracy trials, which continued from May into August of 1741, reminded one observer of the Salem witch frenzy of 1692, in which the testimony of several girls had led to 19 hangings. The toll in New York was worse. Four whites and 18 slaves were hanged, 13

SAVAGES OF SEVERAL NATIONS, NEW ORLEANS, 1735

This painting by Alexandre de Batz depicts a multiethnic Indian village near New Orleans. The woman at lower left was a Fox Indian who had been captured and enslaved. The African boy was an adoptee.

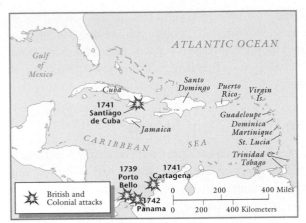

MAP 4.2 CARIBBEAN THEATER OF WAR, 1739–1742
Spanish defenses held up remarkably well against repeated
and very costly British attacks.

slaves were burned alive, and 70 were banished to the West
Indies. The judges spoke pompously about the sacred
rights of Englishmen, again in danger from popish conspirators, and grew enraged at any African who dared to
imperil what the colony would not let him share.

In 1742, King Philip V of Spain nearly accomplished
what Oglethorpe and the New York judges dreaded. He
sent 36 ships and 2,000 soldiers from Cuba with orders to
devastate Georgia and South Carolina, "sacking and burning all the towns, posts, plantations, and settlements" and
freeing the slaves. Although the invaders probably outnumbered the entire population of Georgia, Oglethorpe
raised 900 men and met them on St. Simons Island in July.
After he ambushed two patrols, Spanish morale collapsed.
When a British soldier deserted to the Spanish with word
of how weak Georgia really was, Oglethorpe arranged to
have the Spanish intercept a letter that implicated the de-
serter as a spy sent to lure them to their destruction. They
departed in haste, leaving British North America as a safe
haven once more for liberty, property, no popery—and
slavery.

Britain did achieve one other success against Spain.
Between 1740 and 1744, Commodore George Anson
rounded Cape Horn, plundered and burned a small port
in Peru, captured several prizes, and then sailed across
the Pacific, where he captured the Manila galleon, the
world's richest ship, loaded with silver that sailed annually

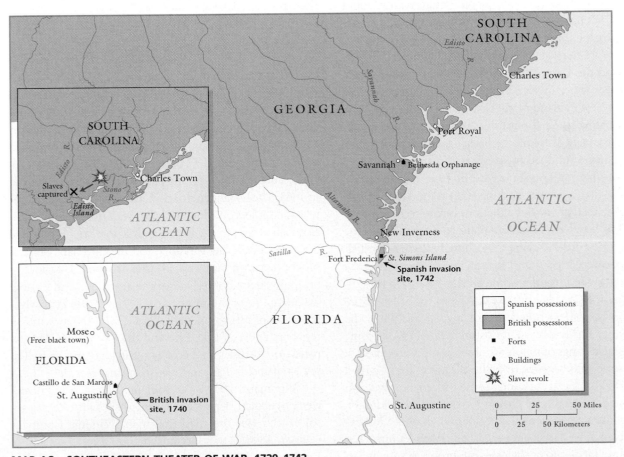

MAP 4.3 SOUTHEASTERN THEATER OF WAR, 1739–1742
Florida's defenders repelled a British attack led by James Oglethorpe, and then Oglethorpe turned back a much larger
Spanish invasion of Georgia.

from Mexico to the Philippines. Anson completed his circumnavigation of the globe and returned to England with 1.3 million Spanish silver dollars and more than 35,000 ounces of unminted silver. Even though only one of Anson's six ships completed the voyage, his success alarmed the Spanish about the security of their lightly defended Pacific possessions. Spain would be reluctant to challenge Britain in the next war.

France versus Britain: King George's War

In 1744, France joined Spain in the war against Britain. The main action then shifted to the north. When the French laid siege to Annapolis Royal, the capital of Nova Scotia, Governor William Shirley of Massachusetts intervened just in time to save the small garrison, and the French withdrew. Shirley then planned his own offensive, a rash attack on Fortress Louisbourg on Cape Breton Island. With only a few lightly armed Yankee vessels at his disposal, he asked the commander of the British West Indian squadron, Sir Peter Warren, for assistance. But Shirley's expedition, which included about one-sixth of all the adult males of Massachusetts, set out before Warren could respond. With no heavy artillery of his own, Shirley ordered the expedition to take the outer batteries of the fortress, capture their guns, and use them to knock down its walls. Had the Yankees met a French fleet instead of the Royal Navy, which arrived in the nick of time, nearly every family in New England might have lost a close relative. The most amazing thing about this venture is that it worked. The British navy drove off the French, and untrained Yankee volunteers subdued the mightiest fortress in America with its own guns. Louisbourg fell on June 16, 1745.

After that, however, nothing went right. Hundreds of volunteers died of various afflictions before regular troops arrived to take over. Elaborate plans to attack Quebec by sea in 1746 and 1747 came to nothing because no British fleet appeared. French and Indian raiders devastated the weakly defended frontier, while Shirley held back most of his men for a Canada offensive that never took place. Bristol County farmers rioted against high taxes. When the Royal Navy finally docked at Boston in late 1747, its commander sent gangs of sailors ashore to compel anyone they could seize into serving with the fleet. An angry crowd descended on the sailors, took some officers hostage, and controlled the streets of Boston for three days before the naval commander relented and released all of the Massachusetts men he had impressed. (The rioters let him keep outsiders.) Finally, to offset losses in Europe, Britain had to return Louisbourg to France under the Treaty of Aix-la-Chapelle, which ended the war in 1748. New England had suffered enormous losses and had gained nothing except pride. Yet well into 1747, public opinion had strongly supported the war. The clergy, in particular, saw it as an apocalyptic struggle of free British Protestants against popish tyranny.

The Impending Storm

The war had driven back the frontiers of British settlement in North America, but the colonies had promised land grants to many volunteers. Thus peace touched off a frenzy of expansion that alarmed Indians and French alike. The British, aware that their hold on Nova Scotia was feeble, recruited 2,500 Protestants from the continent of Europe to populate the colony and sent four regiments of redcoats to accompany them. In 1749, they founded the town of Halifax, which became the new capital of Nova Scotia. The governor also emphasized that his colony would be European, not Indian, by offering bounties for Indian scalps even though the war had ended. When the Micmac Indians, who had lived in peace with French settlers for more than a century, turned to the Acadians for support, the British relented. The Acadians were still too numerous to challenge.

In the 13 colonies, settlers eagerly pressed on to new lands. Yankees swarmed north into Maine and New Hampshire and west into the middle colonies, creating serious tensions. By refusing to pay rent to the manor lords of the Hudson valley, they sparked a tenant revolt in 1753 that the wealthy Livingston family had difficulty subduing. A year later, Connecticut's delegation to the Albany Congress (discussed in the next section) used bribes to acquire an Indian title to all of northern Pennsylvania, which Connecticut claimed on the basis of its sea-to-sea charter of 1663. The blatant encroachments of New York speculators and settlers on Mohawk lands west of Albany so infuriated the Mohawks' Chief Hendrik that he bluntly told the governor of New York in 1753, "the Covenant Chain is broken between you and us [the Iroquois League]. So brother you are not to hear of me any more, and Brother we desire to hear no more of you." New York, Pennsylvania, and Virginia competed for trade with the new Indian republics between Lake Erie and the Ohio River. The expansionist thrust pitted colony against colony, as well as settler against Indian, and British against French.

Virginians, whom the Indians called "long knives," were particularly aggressive. Citing their own 1609 sea-to-sea charter (see the chapter 2 map, "Virginia Company Charter, 1606"), they organized the Ohio Company of Virginia in 1747 to settle the Ohio valley and established their first outpost at the place where the Monongahela and Allegheny rivers converge to form the Ohio River (the site

PORTRAIT OF CHIEF HENDRIK OF THE MOHAWKS
Hendrik's ultimatum to New York in 1753 precipitated the summoning of the Albany Congress a year later.

Collection of The New-York Historical Society.

way, Blainville buried plaques, claiming the area for France. The Indians removed them. Marquis Duquesne sent 2,000 Canadians, with almost no Indian support, to erect a line of posts from Fort Presque Isle (now Erie, Pennsylvania) to Fort Duquesne (now Pittsburgh).

The French clearly intended to prevent British settlement west of the Alleghenies. Duquesne thought this policy so obviously beneficial to the Indians that it needed no explanation. Yet the Mingoes warned him not to build a fort in their territory, and a delegation of Delawares and Shawnees asked the Virginians if they would be willing to expel the French from the Ohio country and then go back home. The Indians did not like Virginia's response. In 1753, Virginia sent Washington to the Ohio country to warn Duquesne to withdraw, and a small Virginia force began building its own fort at the forks of the Ohio. Washington was not the man to win over the Indians, who, he declared, had "nothing human except the shape." Duquesne ignored Washington, advanced toward the Ohio, expelled the Virginians, took over their site, and finished building the fort. Virginia sent Washington back to the Ohio in 1754. On May 28, after discovering a French patrol nearby, Washington launched an attack. That order set off a world war.

of modern Pittsburgh). The company hired George Washington as a surveyor. Farther south, encroachments upon the Cherokees almost provoked war with South Carolina in 1750.

The French response to these intrusions verged on panic. The fall of Louisbourg had interrupted the flow of French trade goods to the Ohio country for several years, and the men who had long been conducting Indian diplomacy had either died or left office by the late 1740s. Authoritarian newcomers from France replaced them and began giving orders to Indians instead of negotiating with them. The French did, however, make some constructive moves. They rebuilt Louisbourg and erected Fort Beauséjour on the neck that connects mainland Canada to Nova Scotia. In 1755, they erected Fort Carillon (Ticonderoga to the British) on Lake Champlain to protect Crown Point.

Far more controversial was the new French policy in the area between the Great Lakes and the Ohio. Without trying to explain themselves to the Indians, they launched two expeditions into the area. In 1749, Pierre-Joseph Céloron de Blainville led several hundred men down the Allegheny and the Ohio, then up the Miami and back to Canada. He ordered western Indians to join him, but most of them refused. To the Indians, the French were acting like British settlers, intruding on their lands. Along the

🌎 The War for North America

Beginning in 1755, the modernizing British state with its professional army came into direct contact with the householder society and the voluntaristic ethic of the colonists. The encounter was often unpleasant, but the gap between the two sides lessened as each became more familiar with the other. At first, the war with France generated fierce tensions between Britain and the colonies, but both sides learned to cooperate effectively until together they achieved victory.

Of the four wars fought between Britain and France from 1689 to 1763, only the last began in America. That conflict, popularly known as the French and Indian War, was also the biggest and produced the most sweeping results. Among all of America's wars from 1750 to the present, according to unpublished calculations by Thomas L. Purvis, it achieved the fourth highest rate of mobilization and, measured by casualties per capita (excluding Indians), it was the third bloodiest contest Americans have ever fought. Only World War II, the Civil War, and the Revolution put a higher percentage of men under arms. Only the Civil War and the Revolution killed a higher percentage of those mobilized.

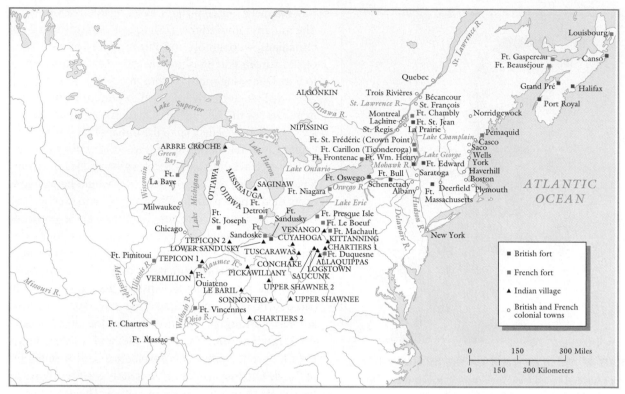

MAP 4.4 FRANCE VERSUS BRITAIN IN NORTH AMERICA BY 1755

North of the Ohio River, much of North America was becoming a series of fortresses along the frontiers separating New France from the British colonies.

The Albany Congress and the Onset of War

In spring 1754, both New France and Virginia were expecting a limited clash at the forks of the Ohio River. Neither anticipated the titanic struggle that encounter would set off, nor did the French and British governments, which hoped to limit any conflict to a few strategic points in North America. New Englanders, however, saw an apocalyptic struggle in the making between "Protestant freedom" and "popish slavery," with the North American continent as the battleground. "The continent is not wide enough for us both," declared one preacher, "and they [the French] intend to have the whole."

Britain, fearful that the Six Nations (the Tuscaroras had joined the original Five Nations by the 1720s) might side with New France, ordered New York to host an intercolonial congress at Albany to meet with the Iroquois and redress their grievances. The governor invited every colony as far south as Virginia, except nonroyal Connecticut and Rhode Island. Virginia and New Jersey declined to attend. Governor Shirley of Massachusetts, on his own initiative, invited Connecticut and Rhode Island to participate, and the Massachusetts legislature instructed its delegates to work for a plan of intercolonial union.

In Philadelphia, Benjamin Franklin too was thinking about colonial union. On May 9, 1754, his *Pennsylvania Gazette* printed the first political cartoon in American history, with the caption "Unite or die." A month later, he drafted his "Short Hints towards a Scheme for Uniting the Northern Colonies," which he presented to the Albany Congress in June. His plan called for a "President General" to be appointed by the Crown as commander-in-chief and to administer the laws of the union, and for a "Grand Council" to be elected for three-year terms by the lower houses of each colony. Deputies would be apportioned according to tax receipts. The union would have the power to raise soldiers, build forts, levy taxes, regulate the Indian trade when it touched the welfare of more than a single colony, purchase land from the Indians, and supervise western settlements until the Crown organized them as new colonies. To take effect, the plan would require ap-

North Wind Picture Archives.

BENJAMIN FRANKLIN'S SNAKE CARTOON

The first newspaper cartoon in colonial America, this device appeared in the *Pennsylvania Gazette* in spring 1754. The cartoon called for colonial union on the eve of the Albany Congress and drew on the folk legend that a snake, cut into pieces, could revive and live if it somehow joined its severed parts together before sundown.

proval by the Crown and by each colonial legislature and presentation to Parliament for its consent. The Albany Congress adopted an amended version of Franklin's proposal.

Both Shirley and Franklin were far ahead of public opinion. Newspapers did not even discuss the Albany Plan. Every colony rejected it, most with little debate, some unanimously. The voting was close only in Massachusetts, which had borne the heaviest burden in the three earlier wars with New France. As Franklin later explained, the colonies feared that the president general might become too powerful, but they also distrusted one another. Despite the French threat, they were not ready to patch up their differences and unite. They did not yet see themselves as "Americans."

The Board of Trade responded by drafting its own plan of union. Its plan resembled Franklin's, except that the Grand Council could only requisition—instead of tax—and colonial union would not require Parliament's approval. After news arrived that Washington had surrendered his small force to the French at Great Meadows in July 1754, Britain decided that the colonies were incapable of uniting in their own defense. Even if they could, the precedent would be dangerous. London sent redcoats to Virginia instead—two regiments, commanded by General Edward Braddock. For Britain, colonial union and direct military aid were policy *alternatives*. Although military aid would cost the British government more than the proposed union, it seemed the safer choice. By winter of 1754–55, colonial union was a dead issue on both sides of the ocean.

Yet the Albany Congress achieved one major objective. Addressing Iroquois grievances against New York, it urged the Crown to take charge of relations with all west-

ern Indians. London created two Indian superintendencies—one south of the Ohio, which went first to Edmund Atkin and then John Stuart; and one north of the Ohio, which went to William Johnson, an Irish immigrant to New York who had influence with the Mohawks. These offices would survive the war.

Britain's Years of Defeat

In 1755, London hoped that a quick victory by Braddock at the forks of the Ohio River would keep the war from spreading. Braddock's regiments landed in Virginia, a signal that London probably intended to let Virginia, rather than Quaker Pennsylvania, control the upper Ohio valley, including what is now Pittsburgh. At a council of high officials called by Braddock at Alexandria, Virginia, Governor Shirley persuaded him to accept New England's much broader war objectives. Instead of a single expedition aimed at one fort, to be followed by others if time permitted, the campaign of 1755 became four distinct offensives designed to crush the outer defenses of New France and leave it open to British invasion. Braddock was so impressed with Shirley that he named him second in command of the British army in North America, not bad for an English lawyer with no military training who had arrived almost penniless in Boston 25 years earlier.

Braddock and Shirley tried to make maximum use of both redcoats and provincials. The redcoats were highly disciplined professional soldiers who served long terms and had been trained to fight other professional armies. Irregular war in the forests of North America made them uneasy. Provincials, by contrast, were recruited by individual colonies. They were volunteers, often quite young, who usually enlisted only for a single campaign. They knew little about military drill, expected to serve under the officers who had recruited them, and sometimes refused to obey orders that they disliked. Provincials admired the courage of the redcoats but were shocked by their irreverence and by the brutal discipline imposed on them by their officers. Nevertheless, thousands of colonists also enlisted in the British army, providing up to 40 percent of its strength in North America by 1760.

Under the enlarged plan for 1755, the redcoats in Nova Scotia together with New England provincials would assault Fort Beauséjour, where the Acadian peninsula joins mainland Canada. New England and New York provincials would attack Crown Point, and Shirley, commissioned as a British colonel, would lead two regiments of redcoats (recently recruited in New England) to Niagara and cut off New France from the western Indians. Braddock, with the strongest force, would attack Fort Duquesne.

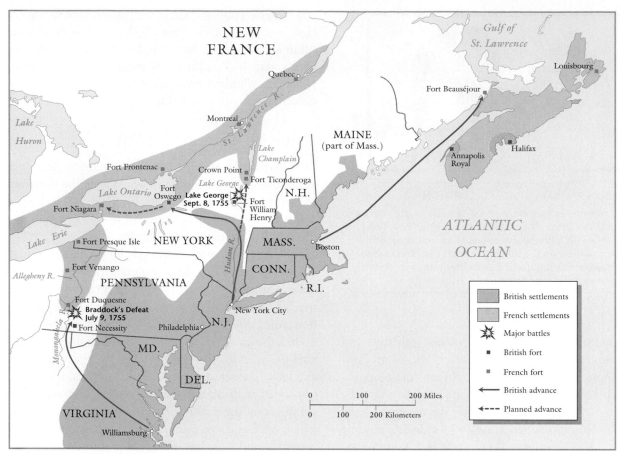

MAP 4.5   BRITISH OFFENSES, 1755

The British launched four major offenses against the French: in Nova Scotia, at Lake George, at Fort Oswego, and at the Forks of the Ohio River, where Edward Braddock led his men to disaster.

Instead, Braddock alienated the Indians and marched to disaster on the Monongahela. The western Delawares asked him whether their villages and hunting rights would be secure under the British. He replied, "No Savage Should Inherit the Land." The chiefs retorted that "if they might not have Liberty To Live on the Land they would not Fight for it." Braddock declared that he "did not need their Help." It took Braddock several months to hack a road through the wilderness wide enough for his artillery. He took care to prevent ambushes at two fords of the Monongahela, and as he crossed that stream on July 9, he pushed on, confident that he had overcome all obstacles.

At Fort Duquesne, the French commander, Liénard, *sieur* de Beaujeu, could muster only 72 French, 146 Canadians, and 637 Indians against the 1,400 regulars under Braddock and 450 Virginia provincials. Beaujeu had planned to attack the British at the fords of the Monongahela, but the Indians thought such an assault would be suicidal and refused. "Will you allow your father to act

alone?" he finally asked melodramatically. "I am sure to defeat them." As Beaujeu marched out, the reluctant Indians followed. Too late to attack at the fords, the French ran into the British vanguard a few miles southeast of the fort. They clashed along a narrow path with thick forest and brush on either side. Beaujeu was killed at once, and his men almost broke, but they rallied and took cover on the British flanks. Braddock's rear elements rushed toward the sound of the guns and there, massed together, the redcoats formed a gigantic bull's-eye. The Indians and the French poured round after round into them, while the British fired wild volleys at the invisible enemy. The British lost 977 killed or wounded, along with their artillery. Braddock was killed. Only 39 French and Indians were killed or wounded. The redcoats finally broke and ran. Washington, who had fought as a Virginia volunteer, reported that offensive operations would be impossible for the rest of the year. Braddock's road through the wilderness now became a highway for the enemy. For the first time in the history of Quaker Pennsylvania, its settlers faced the horrors of a frontier war.

In Nova Scotia, Fort Beauséjour fell on June 17, 1755. Then the commanders did something to indicate that this war would not be a conventional, limited struggle. When the Acadians refused to take an oath that might have obliged them to bear arms against other Frenchmen, the British and Yankees responded with an 18th-century version of ethnic cleansing. They rounded up between 6,000 and 7,000 Acadians, forced them aboard ships, and expelled them from the province, to be scattered among the 13 colonies, none of which was prepared for the influx. A second roundup in 1759 caught most of the families that had evaded the first one. The British also resumed their merciless war against the Micmac Indians.

The officers who organized these expulsions insisted that they had found a humane way of compelling French Catholics to assimilate with the Protestant majority. Reasoning also that the Acadians were not British subjects because they had not taken the oath, and that only British subjects could own land in a British colony, the government of Nova Scotia confiscated the land the Acadians had farmed for generations and redistributed it to Protestant settlers, mostly from New England. About 3,000 of the Acadian refugees, after spending miserable years as unwanted Catholic exiles in a Protestant world, finally made it to French Louisiana, where their descendants became known as Cajuns. Others went to France, and some even made their way back to Nova Scotia or what later became New Brunswick. Few remained in the 13 colonies.

In the principal northern theater of war in 1755, William Johnson led his provincials against Crown Point. The French commander, Jean-Armand, baron Dieskau, hoping to repeat the French success against Braddock, attacked a body of provincials on September 8 and drove it back in panic to its base camp, the improvised Fort William Henry near Lake George. French regulars assailed the fort but were driven off with heavy losses in a six-hour struggle. Colonial newspapers proclaimed the battle a great victory because the provincials had not only held the field but had also wounded

and captured Dieskau. Johnson probably could have taken poorly defended Crown Point, but he too had been wounded and was content to hold Fort William Henry and nearby Fort Edward at the headwaters of the Hudson. It took a more professional eye than his to distinguish the carnage of victory from the carnage of defeat.

Farther west, Shirley's Niagara campaign reached Oswego on Lake Ontario and then stopped for the winter, held in check by the French at Fort Frontenac on the lake's northern shore. Oswego was soon cut off by heavy snows. Malnutrition and disease ravaged the garrison.

A World War

With the death of Braddock and the capture of Dieskau, military amateurs took over both armies: Shirley in the British colonies and Governor-General Pierre de Rigaud de Vaudreuil in New France. Vaudreuil, a Canadian, understood his colony's weakness without Indian support. First, the white population of the 13 colonies outnumbered that of New France by 13 to 1; Massachusetts alone had nearly three times as many settlers as New France. Second, Vaudreuil knew that if the redcoats and the British colonies could concentrate their resources in a few critical places, they had a good chance of overwhelming New France. Therefore, a frontier war that pitted New France primarily against ordinary settlers—horrible though it was—remained the most effective way to force the British colonies to scatter their resources over a vast area.

© Hulton Archive/Getty Images.

THE ENGLISH LION DISMEMBER'D (1756)
This striking cartoon reflects British consternation during the first half of the Seven Years' War. France had just taken the Mediterranean island of Minorca from the British.

As long as Vaudreuil was in charge, New France kept winning. Indian attacks devastated frontier settlements, especially in Pennsylvania, a pacifist colony without even a militia when the war began. Even so, the French government decided that New France needed a professional general and sent Louis-Joseph, marquis de Montcalm, in 1756. Shocked and repelled by the brutality of frontier warfare, Montcalm tried to turn the conflict into a traditional European struggle of sieges and battles in which the advantage (as Vaudreuil well understood) would pass to the British. Nevertheless, Montcalm won several major successes. Oswego fell in summer 1756. When Fort William Henry surrendered to him a year later, he promised the garrison the honors of war, which meant that it could keep its property and march unmolested to Fort Edward. But France's Indian allies considered this agreement a betrayal of their customs. They killed or carried off 308 of the 2,300 prisoners, an event that colonial newspapers called the Fort William Massacre. Most of those killed were trying to save their property, which the Indians considered their rightful plunder. Montcalm lost heavily at Fort William Henry. He never again managed to raise sizable bodies of Indian allies, and because the British blamed him for the "massacre," they refused to grant the honors of war to any French force for the rest of the conflict.

HISTORY THROUGH FILM

The Last of the Mohicans (1992)

Directed by Michael Mann. Starring Daniel Day-Lewis (Hawkeye), Russell Means (Chingachgook), Eric Schweig (Uncas), Steven Waddington (Major Heyward), Madeleine Stowe (Cora), Jodhi May (Alice), and Wes Studi (Magua).

This movie, the most recent and most effective film version of James Fenimore Cooper's immensely successful 1826 novel of the same title, centers on the siege and capture of Fort William Henry in 1757, an event that had enormous consequences for everyone involved. During the Seven Years' (or French and Indian) War, the French, accompanied by a huge contingent of Indian allies, besiege this British fort at the northern tip of Lake George in New York. Hawkeye (Daniel Day-Lewis) is a frontiersman reared among Indians, who include his two closest friends, Chingachgook (Russell Means) and Chingachgook's son, Uncas (Eric Schweig). The trio are escorting to the fort a party that includes British Major Heyward (Steven Waddington) and Cora (Madeleine Stowe) and Alice (Jodhi May), the two daughters of Colonel Munro (Maurice Reyes), the commander of the fort. Heyward plans to marry Cora. Through the treachery of another Indian, Magua (Wes Studi), the party is ambushed, but the trio of escorts rescues the major and the two women and leads them safely to the fort just as the siege begins.

Fort William Henry soon falls to the French. General Montcalm (Patrick Chereau) accepts the formal surrender of the British garrison and promises them the "honors of war," the right to march away with their unloaded muskets and their personal possessions. Instead, Magua defies Montcalm and leads a murderous assault against the column as it tries to retreat to Fort Edward at the head of the Hudson River. In a climactic action sequence, Heyward is captured and is being tortured to death when Hawkeye shoots him to end his misery. Alice leaps off a cliff rather than submit to Magua, who has already killed Uncas. Chingachgook then kills Magua. Along with Hawkeye and Cora, Chingachgook survives, thus becoming the last of the Mohicans.

Cooper gave the Iroquois the role of the attacking Indians, probably because most of them did side with the British during the American Revolution. But in the Seven Years' War, most of those who fought were on the British side. The film version addresses this problem by making the Hurons, by then a minor nation, into the pro-French Indians, thereby providing a rare example of a movie being more historically accurate than the novel on which it rests. The film, like Cooper, makes the massacre far more destructive than it actually was. Most of the settlers killed or captured that day were trying to protect their personal

Meanwhile, Braddock's defeat, combined with the British loss of Minorca in the Mediterranean, convinced the British government that the struggle with France could not be limited to a few outposts. Britain declared war on France in 1756, and the French and Indian War in the colonies merged with a general European struggle—the Seven Years' War (1756–63)—involving France, Austria, and Russia against Prussia, which was heavily subsidized by Britain. Although religion had little to do with the war in Europe, the Seven Years' War aligned coalitions of Protestant states against Catholic states in a way not seen there for a century. To many North American clergymen, a Protestant victory might herald the onset of the Millen-

nium. The conflict spread even to India, where British forces expelled the French from nearly all of that vast subcontinent.

Reluctant to antagonize Britain, Spain remained neutral for most of the war, a choice that had huge implications within North America. In the previous war, Spain had been able to turn the slaves of South Carolina against their masters and to create unrest even in New York. At a minimum, Spanish hostilities early in the war would have forced the British to fight in another theater of conflict. Instead, Spain's neutrality permitted Britain to concentrate its resources against New France. By 1762, when Spain finally entered the war in a vain effort to prevent a total

The Last of the Mohicans tells of the siege and capture of Britain's Fort William Henry in 1757, during the French and Indian War.

property, which the Indians regarded as their rightful plunder. The French had traditionally raised Indian forces with the promise of loot and captives. Montcalm's attempt to impose European standards of war by intervening on the British soldiers' and settlers' behalf meant that he broke faith with his Indian allies and was never again able to raise a force of comparable size. That the massacre occurred at

all meant that he lost credibility with the British and their settlers. For the rest of the conflict, the British never again granted a French force the honors of war. Montcalm's great victory became, in the long run, a severe defeat for France.

In 1979, director Michael Mann won an award as best director from the Directors' Guild of America for *The Jericho Mile*.

Kobal Collection/20th Century Fox/Morgan Creek.

British victory, the French had already surrendered Canada, and Britain's seasoned army and navy easily rolled over Spain's less experienced forces.

Imperial Tensions: From Loudoun to Pitt

In 1755, London, to its dismay, realized that Shirley, an amateur, had taken command of the British army in North America. The government dispatched an irascible Scot, John Campbell, earl of Loudoun, to replace him and began pouring in reinforcements. Loudoun had a special talent for alienating provincials. Colonial units did not care to serve under his command and sometimes bluntly rejected his orders. Provincials believed they had a contractual relationship with *their* officers; they had never agreed to serve under Loudoun's professionals. They refused to serve beyond their term of enlistment, most of which expired on November 1 or December 1 of each year. Even when the British ordered them to stay longer, many of them defiantly marched home.

In fact, many British officers despised the provincials, especially their officers. "The Americans are in general the dirtiest most contemptible cowardly dogs that you can conceive," snarled General James Wolfe; "They fall down dead in their own dirt and desert by battalions, officers and all." General John Forbes was usually more positive, but he too once suggested "shooting dead a Dozen of their cowardly Officers at the Head of the Line." Other British officers held more favorable opinions. Horatio Gates, Richard Montgomery, Hugh Mercer, and Arthur St. Clair all remained in America after the war and became generals in the American army during the Revolution. Colonel Isaac Barré praised American courage in the House of Commons in 1765 and even coined the phrase "Sons of Liberty" to describe them—a label instantly adopted by men who resisted Britain's postwar policies.

As the new commander-in-chief, Loudoun faced other problems—the quartering (or housing) of British soldiers, the relative rank of British and provincial officers, military discipline, revenue, and smuggling. He tried to impose authoritarian solutions on them all. When he sent redcoats into a city, he demanded that the assembly pay to quarter them or else he would take over buildings by force. He tried to make any British captain superior in rank to any provincial officer, a rule that antagonized such experienced New England officers as General John Winslow and his six colonels. Loudoun ordered New England troops to serve directly under British officers and to accept the harsh discipline of the British army, an arrangement that New Englanders thought violated the terms of their enlistment. They refused to cooperate. When some colonial assemblies refused to vote adequate supplies, Loudoun urged Parliament to tax the colonies directly. Shocked that the molasses trade with the French West Indies was proceeding as usual, he urged the navy to stamp it out or imposed embargoes on colonial shipping, an action that punished fair traders as well as smugglers. Loudoun built up his forces but otherwise achieved little.

In 1757, William Pitt came to power as Britain's war minister and found workable voluntaristic solutions to the problems that had defeated Loudoun's authoritarian methods. Pitt understood that consent worked better than coercion in the colonies. Colonial assemblies built barracks to house British soldiers. Pitt declared that every provincial officer would rank immediately behind the equivalent British rank but above all lesser officers, British or provincial. He then promoted every British lieutenant colonel to the rank of "colonel in America only." That decision left only about 30 British majors vulnerable to being ordered about by a provincial colonel, but few of them had independent commands anyway. Provincial units under the command of their own officers cooperated with the British army, and the officers began to impose something close to British discipline on them, including hundreds of lashes for routine offenses.

Rather than impose a parliamentary tax, Pitt set aside £200,000 beginning in 1758 (later reduced to £133,000) and told the colonies that they could claim a share of it in proportion to their contribution to the war effort. In effect, he persuaded the colonies to compete voluntarily in support of his stupendous war effort. The subsidies covered something less than half of the cost of fielding 20,000 provincials each year from 1758 to 1760, and rather smaller numbers in 1761 and 1762 as operations shifted to the Caribbean. Smuggling angered Pitt as much as it did anyone else, but British conquests soon reduced that problem. By 1762, Canada, Martinique, and Guadeloupe, as well as Spanish Havana, were all in British hands. Few places were any longer worth smuggling to, except Saint-Domingue.

Pitt had no patience with military failure. After Loudoun called off his attack on Louisbourg in 1757, Pitt replaced him with James Abercrombie. He also put Jeffrey Amherst in charge of a new Louisbourg expedition, with James Wolfe as one of his brigadiers. By 1758, the British Empire had finally put together a military force capable of overwhelming New France and had learned how to use it. In the last years of the war, cooperation between redcoats and provincials became routine and devastatingly effective.

The Years of British Victory

By 1758, the Royal Navy had cut off Canada from reinforcements and even from routine supplies. Britain had sent more than 30 regiments to North America. Combined with 20,000 provincials, thousands of bateau men rowing supplies into the interior, and swarms of privateers preying on French commerce, Britain had mustered perhaps 60,000 men in North America and in nearby waters. Most of them now closed in on the 75,000 people of New France. Montcalm, who in any case was running out of goods for use in the Indian trade, refused to encourage more Indian attacks on the frontier and prepared to defend the approaches to Canada at Forts Duquesne, Niagara, Frontenac, Ticonderoga, Crown Point, and Louisbourg.

Spurred on by Quaker mediators, the British and colonial governments came to terms with the western Indians in 1758, promising not to seize their lands after the war and arranging an uneasy peace. Few settlers or officials had yet noticed a new trend that was emerging dur-

ing the conflict: Before the 1750s, Indian nations had often waged terrible wars against one another. Now, however, few Indians in the northeastern woodlands were willing to attack others. In 1755, for example, some Senecas fought with New France and some Mohawks with the British, but they maneuvered carefully to avoid confronting each other. This Iroquois sense of solidarity was beginning to spread. Iroquois and western Algonquians, once deadly enemies, saw real advantages in cooperation. A sense of pan-Indian identity was beginning to emerge. Although most Indians regarded the French as far less dangerous than the British and even fought alongside the French, they were never French puppets. They fought, negotiated, and made peace in 1758 to preserve their own hold on the land.

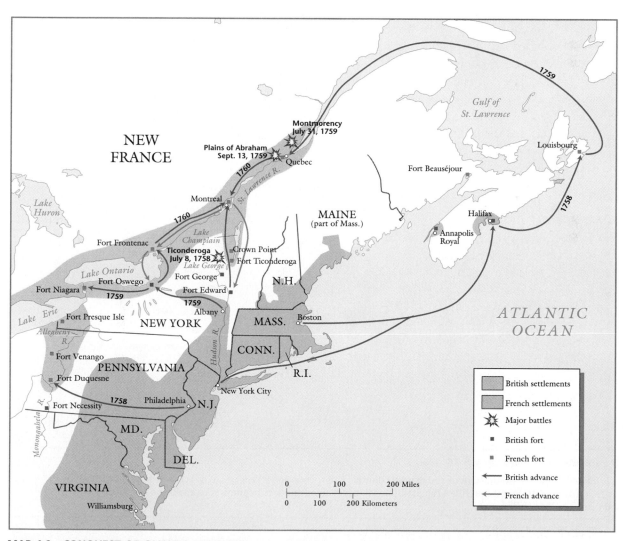

MAP 4.6   CONQUEST OF CANADA, 1758–1760

In three campaigns, the British with strong colonial support first subdued the outer defenses of New France, then took Quebec in 1759 and Montreal in 1760.

 View an animated version of this map or related maps at http://history.wadsworth.com/murrin_LEP4e.

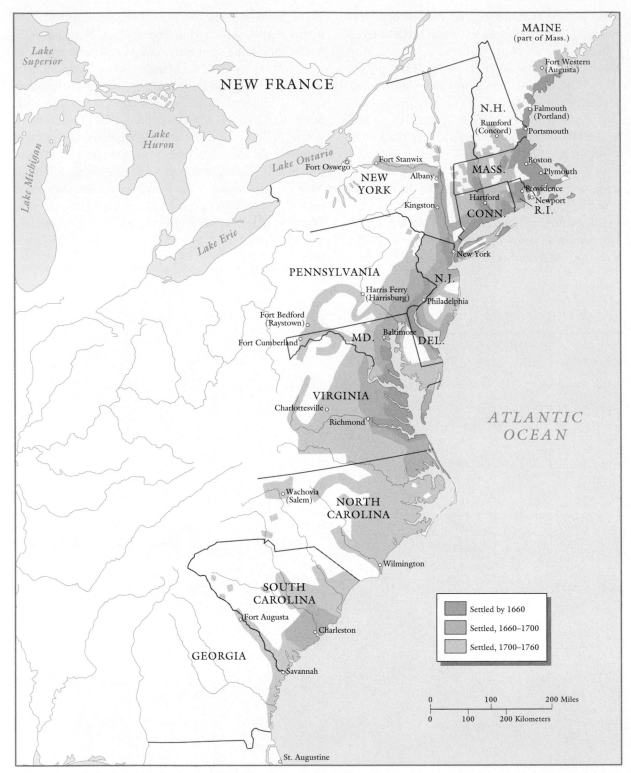

MAP 4.7 GROWTH OF POPULATION TO 1760

Between 1700 and 1760, the population of the British colonies had increased by more than a factor of six, from 250,000 to almost 1.6 million. Settlement had filled the piedmont in most areas and was beginning to cross the Appalachian watershed into the Ohio Valley.

Peace with the western Indians in 1758 permitted the British to revive the grand military plan of 1755, except that this time the overall goal was clear—the conquest of New France. Amherst and Wolfe, with 9,000 regulars and 500 provincials, besieged Louisbourg for 60 days. It fell in September, thus adding Cape Breton Island to the British province of Nova Scotia. A force of 3,000 provincials under Colonel John Bradstreet advanced to Lake Ontario, took Fort Frontenac, and began building a fleet. This victory cut off the French in the Ohio valley from their supplies. A powerful force of regulars under John Forbes and provincials under Washington marched west, this time through Pennsylvania, to attack Fort Duquesne, but the French blew up the fort and retreated north just before they arrived. The British erected Fort Pitt on the ruins.

The only British defeat in 1758 occurred in northern New York when Abercrombie sent 6,000 regulars and 9,000 provincials against Ticonderoga (Carillon), defended by Montcalm and 3,500 troops. Instead of waiting for his artillery to arrive or trying to outflank the French, Aber-crombie ordered a frontal assault against a heavily fortified position. His regulars were butchered by the withering fire, and after witnessing the carnage for several hours, the horrified provincials fled. Like Indians, they regarded such attacks as sheer madness. When Pitt heard the news, he sacked Abercrombie, put Amherst in charge of the New York theater of war, and left Wolfe at Louisbourg to plan an attack up the St. Lawrence River against Quebec.

In 1759, while the provincials on Lake Ontario moved west and took Niagara, Amherst spent the summer cautiously reducing Ticonderoga and Crown Point. (Pitt expected him to reach Montreal.) The most dramatic campaign occurred farther east. In June, Wolfe ascended the St. Lawrence River with 8,000 redcoats and colonial rangers and laid siege to Quebec, defended by Montcalm with 16,000 regulars, Canadian militia, and Indians. When an attack below the city failed, Wolfe mounted howitzers on high ground across the river from Quebec and began reducing most of the city to rubble. Frustrated by the French refusal to come out and fight, he turned loose his

Clements Library, University of Michigan, Ann Arbor.

DEATH OF GENERAL WOLFE (1771)

Benjamin West, who was born in Pennsylvania, taught himself to paint, opened a studio in Philadelphia, and then went to Europe. He studied the great Italian masters for several years and then settled in London, where he became the first American artist to have an enormous impact. Contemporary heroes were displayed in classical attire, but West used their actual uniforms. George III was so impressed that he made West the history painter to the royal court.

American rangers ("the worst soldiers in the universe," he boasted), who ravaged and burned more than 1,400 farms. Anyone who resisted was shot and scalped. Still the French held out.

By September, both Wolfe and Montcalm realized that the British fleet would soon have to depart or risk being frozen in during the long winter. Wolfe made a last desperate effort, preferring to die rather than fail. His men silently sailed up the river, climbed a formidable cliff above the city in darkness, and on the morning of September 13, 1759, deployed on the Plains of Abraham behind Quebec. Montcalm panicked. Instead of using his artillery to defend the walls from inside (Wolfe's force had been able to drag only two guns with them), he marched out of Quebec onto the plains. Both generals now had what they craved most, a set-piece European battle that lasted about 15 minutes. Wolfe and Montcalm were both mortally wounded, but the British drove the French from the field and took Quebec. After the fall of Montreal in 1760, Canada surrendered.

The Cherokee War and Spanish Intervention

In December 1759, as the British were completing their triumph over France, the Cherokees, who had been allies and trading partners of South Carolina, reacted to a long string of violent incidents by attacking backcountry settlers. Within a year, they drove the frontier back 100 miles. South Carolina appealed to Amherst for help, and he sent regular soldiers who laid waste to the Cherokee Lower Towns in the Appalachian foothills. When that expedition failed to bring peace, another one the next year devastated the Middle Towns farther west, while Virginia threatened the Overhill Towns. The Cherokees made peace in December 1761, but the backcountry settlers, left brutalized and lawless, soon became severe political problems for South Carolina's government.

Only then, in January 1762, after the French and the Cherokees had been defeated, did Spain finally enter the war. British forces quickly took Havana and even Manila in the distant Philippines. France and Spain sued for peace.

The Peace of Paris

In 1763, the Peace of Paris ended the war. Britain returned Martinique and Guadeloupe to France. France surrendered to Great Britain several minor West Indian islands and all of North America east of the Mississippi, except New Orleans. In exchange for Havana, Spain ceded Florida to the British and also promised to pay a large ransom for the return of Manila. To compensate its Spanish ally, France gave all of Louisiana west of the Mississippi and New Orleans to Spain. Most of the Spanish and African occupants of Florida withdrew to other parts of the Spanish empire, but nearly all French settlers remained behind in Canada, the Illinois country, and what was now Spanish Louisiana.

The British colonists were jubilant. The age of warfare and frontier carnage seemed over at last. Britain and the colonies could now develop their vast resources in an imperial partnership and would share unprecedented prosperity. But the western Indians angrily rejected the peace settlement. No one had conquered them, and they denied the right or the power of France to surrender their lands to Great Britain. They began to plan their own war of liberation.

Conclusion

Between 1713 and 1754, expansion and renewed immigration pushed North American settlement ever farther into the interior. With a population that doubled every 25 years, many householders no longer enjoyed the opportunity to give all of their sons and daughters the level of economic success that they were enjoying. By midcentury, many families took up a trade or looked westward for what their old community could not provide. Women worked harder just to sustain levels of opportunity for their households. Many families had to favor sons over daughters and the eldest son over his younger brothers, reluctantly following practices used in England.

The colonies anglicized in other ways as well. Newspapers and the learned professions spread the English Enlightenment to the colonies. English revivalists, especially George Whitefield, had a tremendous impact in North America. The northern colonies borrowed Court politics from Walpole's Britain, while most southern colonies favored politics as envisioned by the Country opposition in Britain. Both considered themselves the freest people on earth. When expansion and imperial rivalries again led to war after 1739, the colonists discovered that enslaved Africans associated Spain with liberty, whereas most eastern woodland Indians looked to New France for support. The threat of internal upheaval kept King George's War indecisive in the 1740s. Taking advantage of Spain's neutral position when Britain and France went to war after 1754, the British Empire mobilized its full resources and conquered New France.

The French and Indian War left behind vivid memories. Provincials admired the courage of the redcoats and the victories they won but hated their brutal discipline and arrogant officers. British officials greatly exaggerated what military force alone could accomplish and underestimated colonial contributions to the imperial cause. The concord and prosperity that were supposed to follow Britain's great triumph yielded instead to bitter strife.

SUGGESTED READINGS

The best study of 18th-century immigration is **Bernard Bailyn, *Voyagers to the West: A Passage in the Peopling of America on the Eve of the Revolution*** (1986). **A. Roger Ekirch, *Bound for America: The Transportation of British Convicts to the Colonies*** (1987) is also important. For gentility and the Enlightenment, excellent studies include **Richard L. Bushman, *The Refinement of America: Persons, Houses, Cities*** (1992); **Ned Landsman, *From Colonials to Provincials: Thought and Culture in America, 1680–1760*** (1998); **David S. Shields, *Civil Tongues & Polite Letters in British America*** (1997); and **Charles E. Clark, *The Public Prints: The Newspaper in Anglo-American Culture, 1665–1740*** (1994). For early Georgia, see **Harold E. Davis, *The Fledgling Province: Social and Cultural Life in Colonial Georgia, 1773–1776*** (1976); and **Larry E. Ivers, *British Drums on the Southern Frontier: The Military Colonization of Georgia, 1733–1749*** (1974). **Frank J. Lambert's *"Pedlar in Divinity": George Whitefield and the Transatlantic Revivals*** (1994) provides a strong introduction to the Great Awakening. **Bernard Bailyn's *The Origins of American Politics*** (1968) touched off a considerable debate. See especially **Jack P. Greene, "Political Mimesis: A Consideration of the Historical and Cultural Roots of Legislative Behavior in the British Colonies in the Eighteenth Century,"** with a comment by Bailyn and a reply by Greene, in ***American Historical Review,*** 75 (1969), 333–367.

For the renewal of imperial conflict after 1739, see **T. J. Davis, *A Rumor of Revolt: The "Great Negro Plot" in Colonial New York*** (1985); **Fred Anderson, *Crucible of War: The Seven Years War and the Fate of Empire in British North America, 1754–1766*** (2000); **Timothy J. Shannon, *Indians and Colonists at the Crossroads of Empire: The Albany Congress of 1754*** (2000); and **Ian K. Steele, *Betrayals: Fort William Henry and the "Massacre"*** (1990).

 AMERICAN JOURNEY ONLINE AND INFOTRAC COLLEGE EDITION

Visit the source collections at www.ajaccess.wadsworth.com and infotrac.thomsonlearning.com and use the Search function with the following key terms to explore documents, images, audio and video clips, articles, and commentary related to the material in this chapter.

John Peter Zenger
Francisco Menéndez
Albany Congress
French and Indian War
Enlightenment

Great Awakening
King George's War
Cherokee War
Peace of Paris

 GRADE AIDS

Visit the Liberty Equality Power Companion Web Site for resources specific to this textbook: http://history.wadsworth.com/murrin_LEP4e

The CD in the back of this book and the U.S. History Resource Center at http://history.wadsworth.com/u.s./ offer a variety of tools to help you succeed in this course, including access to quizzes; images; documents; interactive simulations, maps, and timelines; movie explorations; and a wealth of other sources.

Chapter 5

Reform, Resistance, Revolution

ENGAGEMENT AT THE NORTH BRIDGE IN CONCORD, APRIL 19, 1775
This 1775 painting by Ralph Earl is quite accurate in its details. It shows the first American military victory in the war when the militia drove the British back from Concord Bridge and eventually through Lexington and all the way to Boston.

CHAPTER OUTLINE

Britain left an army in North America after 1763 and taxed the colonies to pay part of its cost. The colonists agreed that they should contribute to their own defense but insisted that taxation without representation violated their rights as Englishmen. Three successive crises shattered Britain's North American empire by 1776.

In the first, the Stamp Act crisis, the colonists began by petitioning for a redress of grievances. When that effort failed, they nullified the Stamp Act and continued their resistance until Parliament repealed the tax in 1766. The jubilant colonists celebrated their victory. In the second, the Townshend crisis of 1767–70, Parliament imposed new taxes on certain imported goods. The colonists petitioned and resisted simultaneously, mostly through an intercolonial nonimportation movement. The British sent troops to Boston. After several violent confrontations, the soldiers withdrew, and Parliament modified but did not repeal the Townshend Revenue Act. The duty on tea remained. Repeal of the other duties broke the back of the nonimportation movement. This time nobody celebrated. The Tea Act of 1773 launched the third crisis, and it quickly escalated. Boston destroyed British tea without bothering to petition first. When Parliament responded with the Coercive Acts of 1774, the colonists created the Continental Congress to organize further resistance. Neither side dared back down, and the confrontation careened toward military violence. The war broke out in April 1775. Fifteen months later, the colonies declared their independence.

CHAPTER FOCUS

♦ Why, in 1766, did the colonists stop resisting and rejoice over the repeal of the Stamp Act, even though the Revenue Act of 1766 continued to tax molasses?

♦ Why did the colonists start a revolution after the government lowered the price of tea through the Tea Act of 1773?

♦ In 1775, Lord North promised that Parliament would not tax any colony that paid its share of the costs of imperial defense and gave adequate salaries to its civil officers, but the Second Continental Congress rejected the proposal out of hand. Had George Grenville offered something of the kind between 1763 and 1765, could Britain have averted the Revolution?

♦ How and why did a resistance movement, dedicated to protecting the colonists' rights as Englishmen, end by proclaiming American independence instead?

🌎 Imperial Reform

In 1760, George III (1760–1820) inherited the British throne at the age of 22. The king's pronouncements on behalf of religion and virtue at first won him many admirers in North America, but the political coalition leading Britain to victory over France fell apart. The king's new ministers set out to reform the empire.

From Pitt to Grenville

The king, along with his tutor and principal adviser, John Stuart, earl of Bute, feared that the Seven Years' War would bankrupt Britain. From 1758 on, despite one victory after another, George and Bute grew increasingly despondent. When William Pitt, the king's war minister, urged a preemptive strike on Spain before Spain could attack Britain, Bute forced him to resign in October 1761, even though Pitt had become the most popular official of the century. Bute soon learned that Pitt had been right. Spain entered the war in January 1762. In May, Bute replaced Thomas Pelham-Holles, duke of Newcastle and the most powerful politician of the previous 25 years, as first lord of the treasury. To economize, Bute next reduced Britain's subsidies to Prussia, its only major ally in Europe. So eager were the king and Bute to end the war that they gave back to France the wealthy West Indian islands of Guadeloupe and Martinique.

The British press harshly denounced Bute. As soon as Parliament approved the Treaty of Paris, Bute dismayed the king by resigning. He had had enough. In April 1763, George Grenville (Pitt's brother-in-law) became first lord of the treasury, although the king distrusted him and found him only marginally acceptable. Pitt and Newcastle, who blamed Grenville for having sided with Bute against them, would have nothing at all to do with him.

The Grenville Ministry

Grenville spent most of his first year coping with a crisis at home that later dovetailed with events in the colonies. John Wilkes, a radical journalist, questioned the king's

CHRONOLOGY

1745–55	Land riots rock New Jersey
1760–61	Cherokee War devastates South Carolina backcountry
1760	George III becomes king of Great Britain
1761	Pitt resigns as war minister
1763	Grenville ministry takes power • Wilkes publishes *North Briton* No. 45 • Pontiac's War begins • King issues Proclamation of 1763
1764	Parliament passes Currency and Sugar Acts
1765	Parliament passes Quartering Act • Stamp Act passed and nullified • Rockingham replaces Grenville as prime minister
1766	Parliament repeals Stamp Act, passes Declaratory Act and Revenue Act of 1766 • Chatham (Pitt) ministry takes power
1767	Parliament passes New York Restraining Act and Townshend Revenue Act
1768	Massachusetts assembly dispatches Circular Letter • Wilkes elected to Parliament • Massacre of St. George's Fields occurs in England • Massachusetts refuses to rescind Circular Letter • *Liberty* riot occurs in Boston • Governors dissolve assemblies that support Circular Letter • Redcoats sent to Boston
1769	Nonimportation becomes effective • Regulators achieve major goals in South Carolina
1770	North becomes prime minister • Boston Massacre • Townshend Revenue Act partially repealed • Nonimportation collapses
1771	North Carolina regulators defeated at Alamance Creek
1772	*Gaspée* affair in Rhode Island increases tensions
1772–73	Twelve colonies create committees of correspondence
1773	Tea Act passed • Boston Tea Party protests tea duty • Wheatley's poetry published in London
1774	American Quakers prohibit slaveholding • Parliament passes Coercive Acts and Quebec Act • First Continental Congress convenes in Philadelphia
1775	Revolutionary War begins at Lexington and Concord • Second Continental Congress creates Continental Army • Olive Branch Petition fails • George III issues Proclamation of Rebellion
1775–76	Americans invade Canada
1776	Paine publishes *Common Sense* • British evacuate Boston • Continental Congress approves Declaration of Independence

integrity in the 45th number of the *North Briton*, a newspaper founded to vilify Bute, a Scot (or "North Briton"). The government used a general warrant (one that specified neither the person nor place to be searched) to invade the newspaper's offices and arrest Wilkes, a member of Parliament as well as a journalist. He was charged with publishing a seditious libel. But Chief Justice Charles Pratt, an admirer of Pitt, declared general warrants illegal and freed Wilkes. The government promptly arrested Wilkes on a special warrant, but Pratt again freed him, declaring that parliamentary privilege extended to seditious libels. London artisans shouted lustily for "Wilkes and Liberty!" Grenville had given the opposition two popular issues, and its leaders expected to overturn him during the winter session of Parliament. Grenville triumphed, however. A reading of Wilkes's pornographic *Essay on Woman* to a shocked and amused House of Lords got Grenville enough votes in the Commons for an unexpectedly huge victory on parliamentary privilege. Months later, after the shock had faded, Grenville also managed a narrow win on general warrants. Wilkes fled to France and was outlawed in Britain, but "45" became a symbol of liberty on both sides of the ocean.

As the Wilkes affair subsided, Grenville turned his attention to the colonies. Britain's national debt had nearly doubled during the last war with France and stood at £130 million. Interest on the debt absorbed more than half of annual revenues, and Britain was already one of the most heavily taxed societies in the world. The sheer scale of Britain's victory required more revenue just to police the conquered colonies. In 1762 and 1763, Bute and Grenville decided to leave 20 battalions with about 7,000 men in America, mostly in Canada and Florida, with smaller garrisons scattered throughout Indian territory. Because the colonists would receive the benefit of this protection, Grenville argued, they ought to pay a reasonable portion of the cost, and eventually all of it. He never asked the settlers to contribute anything to Britain's national debt or to Britain's heavy domestic needs, but he did insist that the colonies begin to pay toward their own defense.

Instead of building on the voluntaristic measures that Pitt had used to win the war, Grenville reverted to the demands for coercive reforms that had crisscrossed the Atlantic during Britain's years of defeat from 1755 to 1757. London, he believed, must gain effective centralized control over the colonies. To the settlers, victory over France would mean new burdens, not relief. To Grenville, the willing cooperation of the colonies after 1758 reflected the empire's weakness, not its strength. He thought Britain had won the war, not with the cooperation of the colonies, but despite their obstruction. He believed that the British government had to act quickly to establish its authority before the colonies, with their astonishing rate of growth, slipped completely out of control. In effect, he set in motion a self-fulfilling prophecy in which the British government brought about precisely what it was trying to prevent. Nearly every step it took undermined the colonies' loyalty to Britain.

Indian Policy and Pontiac's War

The king's Proclamation of 1763 set up governments in Canada, Florida, and other conquered colonies, and it honored wartime commitments to the western Indians. It tried to regulate the pace of western settlement by laying out the so-called Proclamation Line along the Appalachian watershed. No settlements could be planted west of that line unless Britain first purchased the land by treaty from the Indians. Settlers would be encouraged to move instead to Nova Scotia, northern New England, Georgia, or Florida. Because most Iroquois land lay east of the line, the Six Nations felt threatened by the new policy, even though Sir William Johnson, the northern superintendent, upheld their claims. General Amherst's decision in 1760 to cut back sharply on gifts to Indians angered many of them. His contempt for Indian customs deprived the government of its major leverage with Indians, at a time when their ability to unite had become stronger than ever.

In 1761, Neolin, a western Delaware, reported a vision in which God commanded Indians to return to their ancestral ways. Neolin called for an end to Indian dependence on the Anglo-Americans, although he did accept Christian ideas of heaven and hell. European vices, he said, especially drinking rum, blocked the path to heaven. "Can ye not live without them?" he asked. God was punishing Indians for accepting European ways: "If you suffer the English among you, you are dead men. Sickness, smallpox, and their poison will destroy you entirely." Neolin stopped short of condemning the French, who were still living in the Great Lakes region. Many of his followers even hoped that their display of unity would attract the support of King Louis XV of France (1715–74), restore the friendly relations of the past, and halt British expansion.

With a unity never seen before, the Indians struck in 1763. The conflict became known as Pontiac's War, named for an Ottawa chief. Senecas, Mingoes, Delawares, Shawnees, Wyandots, Miamis, Ottawas, and other nations attacked 13 British posts in the West. Between May 16 and June 20, all of the forts fell except Niagara, Pitt, Detroit, and a tiny outpost on Green Bay that the Indians did not bother to attack. For months, the Indians kept Forts Detroit and Pitt under close siege, something Indians were supposed to be incapable of doing. They hoped to drive British settlers back to the Eastern seaboard.

Enraged by these successes, Amherst ordered Colonel Henry Bouquet, commander at Fort Pitt, to distribute smallpox-infested blankets among the western nations, touching off a lethal epidemic in 1763 and 1764. "You will do well to try to Inoculate the Indians by means of Blankets," he wrote to Bouquet, "as well as to Try Every other Method that can serve to Extirpate this Execrable

MAP 5.1   PONTIAC'S WAR AND THE PROCLAMATION LINE OF 1763
Britain claimed possession of North America east of the Mississippi only to face an extraordinary challenge from the Indians of the interior, who wiped out eight garrisons but could not take Detroit, Niagara, or Fort Pitt.

 View an animated version of this map or related maps at http://history.wadsworth.com/murrin_LEP4e.

Race." In 1764, British and provincial forces ended resistance and restored peace. The British then reluctantly accepted the role that the French had played in the Great Lakes region by distributing gifts and mediating differences.

But 10 years of conflict had brutalized the frontiersmen. Perhaps sensing the Indians' growing revulsion against warring with one another, many settlers began to assume that all Indians must be the enemies of all whites.

In December 1763, the Scots-Irish of Paxton Township, Pennsylvania, murdered six unarmed Christian Indians—two old men, three women, and a child—at nearby Conestoga. Two weeks later, the "Paxton Boys" slaughtered 14 more Christian Indians who had been brought to Lancaster for protection. After Governor John Penn removed 140 Moravian mission Indians to Philadelphia for safety, the Paxton Boys marched on the capital determined to kill them all.

Denouncing the Paxton Boys as "Christian white Savages," Benjamin Franklin led a delegation from the assembly that met the marchers at Germantown and persuaded them to go home after they presented a list of their grievances. The Moravian Indians had been spared. All efforts to bring the murderers to justice failed, however, and the frontiersmen of Pennsylvania and Virginia virtually declared an open season on Indians that continued for years. Settlers in Augusta County, Virginia, slaughtered nine Shawnees in 1765. Frederick Stump, a Pennsylvanian, murdered 10 more in 1768 but could not be convicted in his frontier county. Such atrocities kept western Indians smoldering. London had hoped that its officials would bring even-handed justice to the frontier. Indians had won real benefits from the superintendents, such as protection from land speculators, but otherwise they found little to choose between Amherst's smallpox blankets and the murderous rage of the Paxton Boys and their imitators.

ANTI-FRANKLIN CARTOON

Pontiac's War and the Paxton riots inspired this anti-Franklin cartoon in which Quakers and Franklin protect Indians from settlers instead of settlers from Indians.

Colonial Williamsburg Foundation.

The Sugar Act

In a step that settlers found ominous, Grenville's Sugar Act of 1764 proclaimed it "just and necessary, that a revenue be raised . . . in America for defraying the expenses of defending, protecting, and securing" the colonies. The act placed duties on Madeira wine, coffee, and other products, but Grenville expected the greatest revenue to come from the molasses duty of three pence per gallon. The Molasses Act of 1733 had been designed to keep French molasses out of North America by imposing a prohibitive duty of six pence per gallon. Instead, by paying a bribe of about a penny per gallon, merchants got French molasses certified as British. By 1760, more than 90 percent of all molasses imported into New England came from the French islands. Planters in the British islands gave up, lost interest in New England markets, and turned their molasses into quality rum for sale in Britain and Ireland. Nobody, in short, had any interest in stopping the trade in French molasses. New England merchants said they were willing to pay a duty of one pence (the current cost of bribes), but Grenville insisted on three. He hoped to raise £100,000 per year from the molasses duty, although in public he seldom put the figure above £40,000.

The Sugar Act also launched Grenville's war against smugglers. It vastly increased the amount of paperwork required of ship captains and permitted seizures of ships for what owners considered mere technicalities. In effect, Grenville tried to make it more profitable for customs officers to hound the merchants than to accept bribes from them. The Sugar Act encouraged them to prosecute violators in vice admiralty courts, which did not use juries, rather than in common law courts, which did. Prosecutors were virtually immune from any suit for damages, even when the merchant won an acquittal, so long as the judge certified "probable cause" for the seizure.

The Currency Act and the Quartering Act

Grenville passed several other imperial measures. The Currency Act of 1764 responded to wartime protests of London merchants against Virginia's paper money, which had been issued for the colony's defense. (That money had lost almost 15 percent of its value between 1759 and 1764.) The act forbade the colonies to issue any paper money as legal tender. The money question had become urgent because the Sugar Act (and, later, the Stamp Act) required that all duties be paid in specie (silver or gold). Supporters of those taxes argued that the new duties would keep the specie in America to pay the army, but the colonists replied that the drain of specie from some colonies would put impossible constraints on trade. Boston and Newport, for instance, would pay most of the molasses tax, but the specie collected there would follow the army to Quebec,

New York, the Great Lakes, and Florida. Grenville saw "America" as a single region in which specie would circulate to the benefit of all. The colonists knew better. As of 1765, "America" existed only in British minds, not yet in colonial hearts.

Another reform measure was the Quartering Act of 1765, requested by Sir Thomas Gage, Amherst's successor as army commander. Gage asked for parliamentary authority to quarter soldiers in private homes, if necessary, when on the march and away from their barracks. Parliament ordered colonial assemblies to vote specific supplies, such as beer and candles, for the troops, which the assemblies were willingly doing already. It also required the army to quarter its soldiers only in public buildings, such as taverns, which existed in large numbers only in cities. The Quartering Act solved no problems, but it created several new ones.

The Stamp Act

In early 1764, when Parliament passed the Sugar Act, Grenville announced that a stamp tax on legal documents and on publications might also be needed. The army in North America was costing Britain £225,000 per year. Other expenses, including the navy, transport, and Indian gifts, brought the annual total closer to £400,000. Grenville needed more revenue, and a stamp tax seemed the best way to raise it. No one in the House of Commons, he declared, doubted Parliament's right to impose such a tax. Because Parliament had never levied a direct tax on the colonies, however, he also knew that he must persuade the settlers that a stamp tax would not be a constitutional innovation. His supporters insisted that the measure did not violate the principle of no taxation without representation. Each member of Parliament, they argued, represented the entire empire, not just a local constituency. The colonists were no different from the large nonvoting majority of subjects within Great Britain. All were "virtually" represented in Parliament. Grenville also denied that there was any legal difference between external taxes (port duties, such as that on molasses) and internal (or inland) taxes, such as the proposed stamp tax.

Grenville put off passage of the Stamp Act while he collected more complete information about legal forms in the colonies. He also indicated that, if the colonies could devise a revenue plan better than a stamp tax, he would listen. His offer created confusion and became a public relations disaster for the government. All 13 colonial assemblies drafted petitions objecting to the Stamp Act as a form of taxation without representation. Most of them also attacked the duties imposed by the Sugar Act. They too rejected the distinction between internal and external taxes

(for revenue, as against for the regulation of trade). Both kinds, they declared, violated the British constitution. While agreeing that they ought to contribute to their own defense, they urged the government to return to the traditional method of requisitions, in which the Crown asked a colony for a specific sum, and the assembly decided how (or whether) to raise it. Colonists feared that taxation by Parliament might tempt Britain to rule them without consulting their assemblies.

When these petitions began to reach London, Parliament refused to receive them, citing a standing rule that prohibited petitions against money bills and declaring that any petition challenging the right of Parliament to pass such a tax was simply inadmissible. To Grenville, requisitions were not a better idea. They had often been tried, had never worked efficiently, and never would. He rejected the petitions with a clear conscience. But to the colonists, he seemed to have acted in bad faith all along. He had asked their advice and had then refused even to consider it.

The Stamp Act passed in February 1765, to go into effect on November 1. All contracts, licenses, commissions, and most other legal documents would be void unless they were executed on officially stamped paper. Law courts would not recognize any document that lacked the proper stamp, and the colonists would quietly if grudgingly accept Parliament's power to tax them. The act would almost enforce itself. A stamp duty was also put on all newspapers and pamphlets, a requirement likely to anger every printer in the colonies. Playing cards and dice were also taxed.

When the Stamp Act became law, most colonial leaders resigned themselves to a situation that seemed beyond their power to change. Daniel Dulany, a Maryland lawyer who did more than any other colonist to refute the argument for virtual representation, drew a line short of overt resistance. "I am upon a Question of *Propriety*, not of Power," he wrote; ". . . at the same Time that I invalidate the Claim upon which [the Stamp Act] is founded, I may very consistently recommend a Submission to the Law, whilst it endures." Instead, ordinary settlers decided to take direct action to prevent implementation of the act.

☝ The Stamp Act Crisis

Resistance to the Stamp Act began in spring 1765 and continued for nearly a year, until it was repealed. Patrick Henry, a newcomer to the Virginia House of Burgesses, launched the first wave by introducing five resolutions on May 30 and 31. His resolves passed by margins ranging between 22 to 17 and 20 to 19; one was rescinded and expunged from the record the next day. Henry had two more in his pocket that he decided not to introduce. Over the summer, the *Newport Mercury* printed six of Henry's seven resolutions, and the *Maryland Gazette* printed all of them. Neither paper reported that some of the seven had not passed. To other colonies, Virginia seemed to have taken a far more radical position than it actually had. The last resolve printed in the *Maryland Gazette* claimed that anyone defending Parliament's right to tax Virginia "shall be Deemed, an Enemy to this his Majesty's Colony."

In their fall or winter sessions, eight colonial legislatures passed new resolutions condemning the Stamp Act. Nine colonies sent delegates to the Stamp Act Congress, which met in New York in October. It passed resolutions affirming colonial loyalty to the king and "all due subordination" to Parliament but condemned the Stamp and Sugar Acts. By 1765, nearly all colonial spokesmen agreed that the Stamp Act was unconstitutional, that colonial representation in Parliament (urged by a few writers) was impractical because of the distance and the huge expense, and that therefore the Stamp Act had to be repealed. They accepted the idea of virtual representation *within* the colonies—their assemblies, they said, represented both voters and nonvoters—but the colonists ridiculed the argument when it was applied across the Atlantic. A disenfranchised Englishman who acquired sufficient property could become a voter, pointed out Daniel Dulany, in a pamphlet that was widely admired, even in Britain. But, Dulany explained, no colonist, no matter how wealthy he became, could vote for a member of Parliament. Members of Parliament paid the taxes that they levied on others within Britain, but they would never pay any tax imposed on the colonies.

Nullification

No matter how eloquent, resolutions and pamphlets alone could not defeat the Stamp Act. Street violence might, however, and Boston showed the way, led by men calling themselves Sons of Liberty. On August 14, the town awoke to find an effigy of Andrew Oliver, the stamp distributor, hanging on what became the town's Liberty Tree (the gallows on which enemies of the people deserved to be hanged). The sheriff admitted that he dared not remove the effigy. After dark, a crowd of men roamed the streets, shouted defiance at the governor and council, and demolished a new building Oliver was erecting that "they called the Stamp Office," beheaded and burned Oliver's effigy, and finally invaded Oliver's home, "declaring they would kill Him." He had already fled to a neighbor's home. Thoroughly cowed, he resigned.

On August 26, an even angrier crowd all but demolished the elegant mansion of Lt. Governor Thomas Hutch-

inson. Most Bostonians believed that, in letters to British friends, Hutchinson had defended and even helped to draft the Stamp Act. In fact, he had quietly opposed it. Shocked by the destruction of property, the militia finally appeared to police the streets, but when Governor Sir Francis Bernard tried to arrest those responsible for the first riot, he got nowhere. Bostonians deplored the events of August 26 but approved those of August 14. No one was punished for either event, although the whole city knew that Ebenezer McIntosh, a poor shoemaker and a leader of the annual Pope's Day (Guy Fawkes Day) processions, had organized both riots.

Everywhere except Georgia, the stamp master was forced to resign before the law took effect on November 1. With no one to distribute the stamps, the act could not be

LORD BUTE AND GEORGE GRENVILLE HANGED IN EFFIGY, 1765 OR 1766

Bute and Grenville were always unpopular in the colonies, but even more so after passage of Grenville's Stamp Act. This image, which shows both men (Bute wears a kilt) chained to the devil, borrowed from the popular rites of Pope's Day (Guy Fawkes Day), November 5. Especially in Boston, images of the pope, the Stuart pretender to the British throne, and the devil were destroyed each year on this day. Bute was especially vulnerable because his family name was Stuart.

implemented. Merchants adopted nonimportation agreements to pressure the British into repeal. Following Boston's lead, the Sons of Liberty took control of the streets in other cities. After November 1, they agitated to open the ports and courts, which had closed down rather than operate without stamps. Neither the courts nor the customs officers had any stamps to use because nobody dared distribute them. As winter gave way to spring, most ports and some courts resumed business. Only Newport matched Boston's level of violence, but in New York City a clash between the Sons of Liberty and the British garrison grew ugly and almost escalated into an armed encounter. Violent resistance worked. The Stamp Act was nullified—even in Georgia, eventually.

Repeal

The next move was up to Britain. For reasons that had nothing to do with the colonies, the king dismissed Grenville in summer 1765 and replaced his ministry with a narrow coalition organized primarily by William Augustus, duke of Cumberland, the king's uncle. An untested young nobleman, Charles Watson-Wentworth, marquess of Rockingham, took over the treasury. This Old Whig ministry had to deal with the riots in America, and Cumberland—the man who had sent Braddock to America in winter 1754–55—may have favored a similar use of force in late 1765. If so, he never had a chance to issue the order. On October 31, minutes before an emergency cabinet meeting on the American crisis, he died of a heart attack, leaving Rockingham in charge of the government. At first, Rockingham favored amending the Stamp Act, but by December he had decided on repeal. To win over the other ministers, the king, and Parliament, he would need great skill.

To Rockingham, the only alternative to repeal seemed to be a ruinous civil war in America, but as the king's chief minister, he could hardly tell Parliament that the world's greatest empire must yield to unruly mobs. He needed a better reason for repeal. Even before the first American nonimportation agreements reached London on December 12 (New York City's) and December 26 (Philadelphia's), he began to mobilize the British merchants and manufacturers who traded with America. They petitioned Parliament to repeal the Stamp Act. They condemned the Grenville program as an economic disaster, and their arguments gave Rockingham the leverage he needed.

Rockingham won the concurrence of the other ministers by promising to support a Declaratory Act affirming Parliament's sovereignty over the colonies. When William Pitt eloquently demanded repeal in the House of Commons on January 14, 1766, Rockingham gained a powerful, although temporary, ally. "I rejoice that America has resisted," declared Pitt. "Three millions of people, so dead to all the feelings of liberty, as voluntarily to submit to be slaves, would have been fit instruments to make slaves of the rest." Parliament "may bind [the colonists'] trade, confine their manufactures, and exercise every power whatsoever," Pitt declared, "except that of taking their money out of their pockets without their consent."

Rockingham still faced resistance from the king, who hinted that he favored "modification" rather than repeal. George III appeared willing to repeal all the stamp duties except those on dice and playing cards, the two levies most difficult to enforce. Only Grenville, however, was ready to use the army to enforce even an amended Stamp Act. Rockingham brought the king around by threatening to resign, which would have forced the king to bring back Grenville, whom he hated. Many pro-American witnesses appeared before Parliament to urge repeal, including Benjamin Franklin, who gave a masterful performance. Slowly, Rockingham put together his majority.

Three pieces of legislation ended the crisis. The first, the Declaratory Act, affirmed that Parliament had "full power and authority to make laws and statutes of sufficient force and validity to bind the colonies and people of America . . . in all cases whatsoever." Rockingham resisted pressure to insert the word "taxes" along with "laws and statutes." That omission permitted the colonists, who drew a sharp distinction between legislation (which, they conceded, Parliament had a right to pass) and taxation (which it could not), to interpret the act as an affirmation of their position, while nearly everyone in Britain read precisely the opposite meaning into the phrase "laws and statutes." Old Whigs hoped that Parliament would never again have to proclaim its sovereign power over America. Like the royal veto of an act of Parliament, that power existed, explained Edmund Burke; and like the veto, which had not been used for 60 years, it should never again be invoked. The colonists agreed. They read the Declaratory Act as a face-saving gesture that made repeal of the Stamp Act possible.

The second measure repealed the Stamp Act because it had been "greatly detrimental to the commercial interests" of the empire. The third, which modern historians call the Revenue Act of 1766, even though its preamble described it as a regulation of trade, reduced the duty on molasses from three pence per gallon to one penny, but imposed the duty on all molasses, British or foreign, imported into the mainland colonies. Although the act was more favorable to the molasses trade than any other measure yet passed by Parliament, it was also, beyond any doubt, a revenue measure, and it generated more income for the empire than any other colonial tax. Few colonists

The European Power of a Self-Taught American

The youngest son of a youngest son for five consecutive generations, Benjamin Franklin was born into a tradesman's family in Boston in 1706. His father apprenticed him to his older brother, James, a printer who founded *The New England Courant* in 1721. Benjamin even took over briefly as publisher and editor of the paper after James was jailed for criticizing the government. But Benjamin considered James a harsh master, and in 1723, he fled from his brother and made his way to Philadelphia, where he became a journeyman printer. In 1724, he sailed to London, where he read widely and improved his writing and printing skills. Back in Philadelphia by 1726, he set up his own press and founded *The Pennsylvania Gazette,* which soon became the best-edited newspaper in British North America. He did his best to support causes that would improve the city. Having earned enough to live comfortably, he retired in 1747. Only then did he begin the active pursuit of science and public service.

Franklin's electrical experiments earned him a towering reputation throughout the Atlantic world. He also won election to the Pennsylvania assembly, where he soon emerged as the leader of the moderate wing of the Quaker Party by urging it to organize the province for defensive war against the French and Indians, who began devastating Pennsylvania's frontier settlements in 1755. These commitments made him a dangerous opponent of the Penn family, who angrily resisted all attempts to tax their extensive lands and help pay for the war. Franklin grew so exasperated with the Penns that he carried the struggle against them to London in 1757.

He spent 24 of the last 33 years of his life abroad—in London from 1757–62 and again from 1765–75, and in Paris from 1776–85. Those cities and Philadelphia sustained the most vigorous attacks on slavery in the north Atlantic world, and by 1776, Franklin had embraced the cause. In Britain he was quite well received most of the time. Oxford University and the St. Andrews University in Scotland granted him honorary doctorates, and he was a welcome guest in many of Britain's finest country houses. In both 1757 and 1765, he arrived in London as an outspoken defender of the British empire and looked as though he would become an overt loyalist, but the Townshend Crisis (1767–70) changed his mind. He concluded that the men administering the colonies could not be trusted, and he did his best to warn them through satirical publications, such as *Rules by Which a Great Empire May Be Reduced to a Small One* (1773).

After returning to Philadelphia in 1775, Franklin served in the Second Continental Congress, including the committee that drafted the Declaration of Independence. He then became the United States' first minister to France, took Paris by storm, negotiated the treaty of alliance in 1778, and played a major role in drafting the Peace of Paris that ended the war in 1783. Back in America, he served as a delegate to the Philadelphia Convention in 1787 and, in his last composition, one that appeared shortly before his death in 1790, he published an eloquent protest against slavery. His service abroad was probably indispensable to the success of the new nation.

Benjamin West's *Benjamin Franklin Drawing Electricity from the Sky* (ca. 1817).

"THE REPEAL OR THE FUNERAL OF MISS AMERIC-STAMP"

This London cartoon of 1766 shows George Grenville carrying the coffin of the Stamp Act with Lord Bute behind him. Contemporaries would easily have identified the other personalities.

attacked it for violating the principle of no taxation without representation. In Britain, it seemed that the colonists objected to internal taxes but would accept external duties.

Against the advice of British friends, the colonists greeted repeal with wild celebrations. Over the next decade, many communities observed March 18 as the anniversary of the Stamp Act's repeal. Neither side fully appreciated the misunderstandings that had made repeal possible or their significance. In the course of the struggle, both sides, British and colonial, had rejected the distinction between external and internal taxes. They could find no legal or philosophical basis for condemning the one while approving the other. Hardly anyone except Franklin noticed in 1766 that the difference was quite real and that the crisis had in fact been resolved according to that distinction. Parliament had tried to extend its authority over the internal affairs of the colonies and had failed, but it continued to collect port duties in the colonies, some to regulate trade, others for revenue. No one knew how to justify this division of authority, but the external–internal cleavage marked, even defined, the power axis of the empire, the boundary between what Parliament could do on its own and what, internally, only the Crown could do, and then only with the consent of the colonists.

Another misunderstanding was equally grave. Only the riots had created a crisis severe enough to push Parliament into repeal. Both sides, however, preferred to believe that economic pressure had been decisive. For the colonies, this conviction set the pattern of resistance for the next two imperial crises.

🌐 The Townshend Crisis

The goodwill created by repeal did not last. In 1766, the king again replaced his ministry. This time he persuaded William Pitt to form a government. He and Pitt shared a contempt for the aristocratic families that had governed Britain since 1714, most of whom were now Rockingham Whigs. Both the king and Pitt considered factions immoral and put their faith in a government of "measures, not men." Pitt appealed to men of goodwill from all parties, but few responded. His ministry, which included many supporters of the Grenville program, faced serious opposition within Parliament. Pitt compounded that problem by accepting a peerage as earl of Chatham, a decision that removed his compelling oratory from the House of Commons and left Charles Townshend as his spokesman in that chamber. A witty, extemporaneous speaker, Townshend had betrayed every leader he ever served. The only point of real consistency in his political career had been his hard-line attitude toward the colonies.

The Townshend Program

New York had already created a small crisis for the new earl of Chatham by objecting to the Quartering Act as a disguised form of taxation without consent. Under the old rules, the army asked for quarters and supplies and the assembly voted them. Consent was an integral part of the process. Now one legislature (Parliament) was telling others (the colonial assemblies) what they must do. New York refused. In 1767, Parliament passed the New York Restraining Act, which forbade New York's governor to sign any law until the assembly complied with the Quartering Act. The crisis fizzled out when the governor bent the rules and announced that the assembly had already complied with the substance (if not all the specifics) of the Quartering Act before the Restraining Act went into effect. In the end, instead of helping the army, the Quartering Act weakened colonial loyalty to Britain.

Chatham soon learned that he could not control the House of Commons from his position in the House of

Lords. During the Christmas recess of 1766–67, he saw the extent of his failure and began to slip into an acute depression that lasted more than two years. He refused to communicate with other ministers or even with the king. The colonists, who admired him more than any other Englishman of the day, expected sympathy from his administration. Instead, they got Townshend, who took charge of colonial policy in spring 1767.

As chancellor of the exchequer, Townshend presented the annual budget to the House of Commons. A central aspect of that year's budget, the Townshend Revenue Act of 1767, imposed new duties in colonial ports on certain imports that the colonies could legally buy only from Britain: tea, paper, glass, red and white lead, and painter's colors. But Townshend also removed more duties on tea within Britain than he could offset with the new revenue collected in the colonies. Revenue, clearly, was not his object. The statute's preamble stated his real goal: To use the new American revenues to pay the salaries of governors and judges in the colonies, thereby freeing them from dependence on the assemblies. This devious strategy aroused suspicions of conspiracy in the colonies. Many sober provincials began to believe that, deep in the recesses of the British government, men really were plotting to deprive them of their liberties.

Other measures gave appellate powers to the vice admiralty courts in Boston, Philadelphia, and Charleston and created a separate American Board of Customs Commissioners to enforce the trade and revenue laws in the colonies. The board was placed in Boston, where resistance to the Stamp Act had been fiercest, rather than in Philadelphia, which had been rather quiet in 1765 and would have been a much more convenient location. Townshend was eager for confrontation.

The British army also began to withdraw from nearly all frontier posts and concentrate near the coast. Although the primary motive was to save money, the implications were striking. It was one thing to keep an army in

MUSICAL LINK TO THE PAST

An American Heart of Oak

**Composers: William Boyce (music),
John Dickinson (lyrics)
Title: "Liberty Song" (1768)**

Within weeks of publication, this sprightly tune spread throughout the colonies, along with the political message embedded in its lyrics. It formed part of the attack by John Dickinson against the Townshend Revenue Act. Dickinson's pamphlet *Letters from a Farmer in Pennsylvania* argued that the Act went against traditional English philosophies of government because "no tax designed to produce revenue can be considered constitutional unless a people's elected representatives voted for it." But to reach those colonists who did not read pamphlets or newspapers, Dickinson also used popular song.

"Liberty Song" repeats Dickinson's written sentiments in a more rousing manner, and one can imagine the lyrics sung loudly by carousers in a public tavern or meeting place: "This bumper I crown for our Sov'reign's health / and this for Britannia's glory and wealth / That wealth, and that glory immortal may be / If she is but just, and if we are but free." These lines demonstrate that, like most colonists, Dickinson viewed himself as a loyal and patriotic British subject. In his song and pamphlet, he made no arguments for independence. He claimed that if Britain treated her subjects in a "just" manner, they would continue to loyally serve the government. But this relatively new and controversial insistence on a more equal two-way relationship between Britain and its American colonies, instead of a paternalistic relationship, provoked increasing friction with the mother country, presaging more open oppositions such as the Boston Tea Party and, eventually, the Revolution.

Dickinson penned his "Liberty Song" lyrics to fit a popular 1750s British patriotic stage tune entitled "Heart of Oak" that celebrated the navy's victories in the Seven Years' War, and they helped the song achieve quick popularity. It was also telling that "Liberty Song" was based on music from Europe. European music enjoyed a pervasive and dominating influence in the colonies. A distinctly American music would not make a significant appearance for at least another half-century.

1. Do you think that the medium of popular song is effective for spreading political messages?
2. Why do so few popular songs on today's best-selling charts feature political content?

Listen to an audio recording of this music on the Musical Links to the Past CD.

America to guard the frontier and then ask the colonists to pay part of its cost, but an army far distant from the frontier presumably existed only to police the colonists. Why should they pay any part of its cost if its role was to enforce policies that would deprive them of their liberties?

Townshend ridiculed the distinction between internal and external taxes, a distinction that he attributed to Chatham and the colonists, but he declared that he would honor it anyway. After winning approval for his program, he died suddenly in September 1767 and passed on to others the dilemmas he had created. Frederick, Lord North, became chancellor of the exchequer. Chatham resigned, and Augustus Henry Fitzroy, duke of Grafton, became prime minister.

Resistance: The Politics of Escalation

The external–internal distinction was troublesome for the colonists. Since 1765, they had objected to all taxes for revenue, but in 1766, they had accepted the penny duty on molasses with few complaints. Defeating the Townshend Revenue Act would prove tougher than nullifying the Stamp Act. Parliament had never been able to impose its will on the internal affairs of the colonies, as the Stamp Act fiasco demonstrated, but it did control the seas. Goods subject to duties might arrive aboard any of hundreds of ships from Britain each year, but screening the cargo of every vessel threatened to impose an enormous, perhaps impossible burden on the Sons of Liberty. A policy of general nonimportation would be easier to implement, but British trade played a bigger role in the colonial economy than North American trade did in the British economy. To hurt Britain a little, the colonies would have to harm themselves a lot.

The colonists divided over strategies of resistance. The radical *Boston Gazette* called for complete nonimportation of all British goods. The merchants' paper, the *Boston Evening Post,* disagreed. In October, the Boston town meeting encouraged greater use of home manufactures and authorized voluntary nonconsumption of British goods. But there was no organized resistance against the new measures, and the Townshend duties became operative in November 1767 with little opposition. A month later, John Dickinson, a Philadelphia lawyer, tried to rouse his fellow colonists to action through 12 urgent letters printed in nearly every colonial newspaper. These *Letters from a Farmer in Pennsylvania* denied the distinction between internal and external taxes, insisted that all parliamentary taxes for revenue violated the colonists' rights, and speculated darkly about Townshend's real motives.

Massachusetts again set the pace of resistance. In February 1768, its assembly petitioned the king, not Parliament, against the new measures. Without waiting for a reply, it also sent a Circular Letter to the other assemblies, urging them to pursue "constitutional measures" of resistance against the Quartering Act, the new taxes, and the use of Townshend revenues to pay the salaries of governors and judges. The implication was that, because Britain responded only to resistance, the colonies had better work together.

The British ministry got the point and did not like it. Wills Hill, earl of Hillsborough and secretary of state for the American colonies (an office created in 1768), responded so sharply that he turned tepid opposition into serious resistance. He ordered the Massachusetts assembly to rescind the Circular Letter and instructed all governors to dissolve any assembly that dared to accept it. In June 1768, the Massachusetts House voted 92 to 17 not to rescind. Most other assemblies had shown little interest in the Townshend program, particularly in the southern colonies where governors already had fixed salaries. Even so, they bristled at being told what they could or could not debate. All of them took up the Circular Letter or began to draft their own. One by one, the governors dissolved their assemblies until government by consent really seemed in peril.

The next escalation again came from Boston. On March 18, 1768, the town's celebration of the anniversary of the Stamp Act's repeal grew so raucous that the governor and the new American Board of Customs Commissioners asked Hillsborough for troops. He ordered General Gage, based in New York, to send two regiments from Nova Scotia to Boston. On June 10, before Gage could respond, a riot broke out in Boston after customs collectors seized John Hancock's sloop *Liberty* for having smuggled Madeira wine (taxed under the Sugar Act) on its *previous* voyage. By waiting until the ship had a new cargo, informers and customs officials could split larger shares when the sloop was condemned. Terrified by the fury of the popular response, the commissioners fled to Castle William in Boston harbor and again petitioned Hillsborough for troops. He sent two more regiments from Ireland.

At about this time, nonimportation at last began to take hold. Two dozen Massachusetts towns adopted pacts in which they agreed not to consume British goods. Boston merchants drafted a nonimportation agreement on March 1, 1768, conditional on its acceptance by New York and Philadelphia. New York agreed, but Philadelphia balked, preferring to wait and see whether Parliament would make any effort to redress colonial grievances. There the matter rested until the *Liberty* riot prompted most Boston merchants to agree to nonimportation, effective January 1. New York again concurred, but Philadelphia held out until early 1769, when it became obvious that Parliament would make no concessions.

Spurred on by the popular but mistaken belief that the nonimportation agreements of 1765 had forced Parliament to repeal the Stamp Act, the colonists again turned to a strategy of economic sanctions. Nonimportation affected only imports from Britain. Tea, consumed mostly by women, was the most objectionable import of all. No one tried to block the importation of West Indian molasses, which was essential to the rum industry of Boston and Newport and which brought in about £30,000 a year under the Revenue Act of 1766. Rum was consumed mostly by men. Some women resented the disproportionate sacrifices they were asked to make. On the other hand, the Sons of Liberty knew that virtually all molasses came from the French islands, and that nonimportation would injure only French planters and American manufacturers and consumers and put no pressure on Parliament or British merchants. The only proven way to resist the penny duty was through smuggling.

Believing that he held the edge with the army on its way, Governor Bernard leaked this news in late August 1768. The public response stunned him. The Boston town meeting asked him to summon the legislature, which Bernard had dissolved in June after it stood by its Circular Letter. When Bernard refused, the Sons of Liberty asked the other towns to elect delegates to a "convention" in Boston. The convention contained most of the radical members of the House of Representatives but not the conservatives. It had no legal standing in the colony's royal government. Boston, professing alarm over the possibility of a French invasion, urged its citizens to arm themselves. When the convention met, it accepted Boston's definition of colonial grievances but refused to sanction violence. Boston had no choice but to go along. It could not call the shots for the whole colony. Instead, the *Boston Gazette* portrayed the city as an orderly community (which it usually was) that had no need of British troops.

An Experiment in Military Coercion

The British fleet entered Boston harbor in battle array by October 2, 1768, and landed 1,000 soldiers, sent by General Gage from Nova Scotia. They soon discovered that

PAUL REVERE'S ENGRAVING OF THE BRITISH ARMY LANDING IN BOSTON, 1768

The navy approached the city in battle array, a sight familiar to veterans of the French wars. To emphasize the peaceful, Christian character of Boston, Revere exaggerated the height of the church steeples.

their most troublesome enemy was not the Sons of Liberty but the Quartering Act, which required that British soldiers be lodged in public barracks where available. Massachusetts had built such barracks—in Castle William, miles away on an island in Boston harbor, where the soldiers could hardly function as a police force. According to the act, any attempt to quarter soldiers on private property would expose the officer responsible to being cashiered from the army, after conviction before any two justices of the peace. And several prominent patriots, such as John Adams and James Otis, Jr., were justices. The soldiers pitched their tents on Boston Common. Seventy men deserted in the first week, about 7 percent of the force. Eventually, the soldiers took over a building that had been the Boston poorhouse. The regiments from Ireland joined them later.

To warn the public against the dangers posed by a standing army in time of peace, the patriots compiled a "Journal of the Times" describing how British soldiers were undermining public order in Boston—clashing with the town watch, endangering the virtue of young women, disturbing church services, and picking fights. The "journal" always appeared first as a newspaper column in some other city, usually New York. Only later was it reprinted in Boston, after memories of any specific incident had grown hazy. Yet violence against customs officers ceased for many months. John Mein (pronounced "mean"), loyalist editor of the *Boston Chronicle*, caricatured leading patriots (John Hancock's generosity, for example, made him "the milch-cow of the disaffected") and began to publish customs records that exposed merchants who were violating the nonimportation agreement. This information could undermine intercolonial resistance by discrediting its Boston leaders. Yet Britain's experiment in military coercion seemed successful enough to justify withdrawal of half the soldiers in summer 1769.

Meanwhile, when news of the Massachusetts convention of towns reached Britain, the House of Lords promptly escalated the crisis another notch by drafting a set of resolutions calling for the deportation of colonial political offenders to England for trial. Instead of quashing dissent, this threat to colonial political autonomy infuriated the southern colonies, which had not been deeply involved in resistance to the Townshend duties. Virginia, Maryland, and South Carolina now adopted nonimportation agreements. In the Chesapeake, the movement had more support among planters than among tobacco merchants, most of whom were Scots loyal to their parent firms. No enforcement mechanism was ever put in place. Charleston, however, took nonimportation seriously. Up and down the continent, the feeble resistance of mid-1768 was becoming formidable by 1769.

The Second Wilkes Crisis

In 1768, just as the Townshend Crisis was brewing up, George III dissolved Parliament and issued writs for the usual septennial elections. John Wilkes, an outlaw since 1763, returned from France and won a seat for the English county of Middlesex. He then received a one-year sentence in King's Bench Prison. Hundreds of supporters gathered to chant "Wilkes and Liberty!" or even "No Wilkes? No King!" On May 10, 1768, as the new Parliament convened, Wilkites just outside the prison clashed with soldiers who fired into the crowd, killing six and wounding 15. Wilkes denounced "the massacre of St. George's Fields."

The House of Commons expelled Wilkes and ordered a new election, but the voters chose him again. Two more expulsions and two more elections took place the next year, until April 1769 when, after Wilkes won again by 1,143 votes to 296, the exasperated House of Commons voted to seat the loser.

Wilkes had created a constitutional crisis. His adherents founded "the Society of Gentlemen Supporters of the Bill of Rights," which raised money to pay off his huge debts and organized a national campaign on his behalf. About one-fourth of the voters of the entire kingdom signed petitions demanding a new general election. Wilkites called for a reduction of royal patronage and major reforms of the electoral system. They also began the regular publication of parliamentary debates and sympathized openly with North American protests. Colonial Sons of Liberty began to identify strongly with Wilkes. If he lost, they warned, their own liberties would be in danger. The Wilkite number "45" (issue number of the *North Briton* in which his notorious anti-Bute essay had appeared), often combined with the number "92" (number of members in the Massachusetts House who stood by the Circular Letter), became sacred in America. Boston even printed a Wilkite parody of the Apostles' Creed. It began: "I believe in Wilkes, the firm patriot, maker of number 45. Who was born for our good. Suffered under arbitrary power. Was banished and imprisoned." It ended with a hope for "the resurrection of liberty, and the life of universal freedom forever. Amen." In South Carolina, Wilkes was hailed as the "unshaken colossus of freedom; the patriot of England, the rightful and legal representative of Middlesex; the favourite of the people; the British Hercules, that has cleaned a stable fouler than the Augean." In 1769, the South Carolina assembly borrowed £1,500 sterling from the colony's treasurer and donated it to Wilkes. When the assembly passed an appropriation to cover the gift, the council rejected the bill. Because neither side would yield, the assembly voted no taxes after 1769 and passed no laws after 1771. Royal government broke down over the Wilkes question.

The Townshend crisis and the Wilkite movement became an explosive combination. For the first time, many colonists began to question the decency of the British government and its commitment to liberty. That a conspiracy existed to destroy British and colonial liberty began to seem quite credible.

The Boston Massacre

In late 1769, the Boston Sons of Liberty turned to direct confrontation with the army, and the city again faced a serious crisis. The redcoats had intimidated Boston for nearly a year. Now Boston reciprocated. The town watch clashed with the army's guard posts because the watch, when challenged by the redcoats' call "Who goes there?" refused to give the required answer: "Friends." Under English common law, soldiers could not fire on civilians without an order from a civil magistrate, except in self-defense when their lives were in danger. By the fall of 1769, no magistrate dared issue such a command. Clashes between soldiers and civilians grew frequent, and justices of the peace singled out the soldiers for punishment. At one point, when town officials tried to arrest a British officer who was commanding the guard at Boston Neck, Captain Ponsonby Molesworth intervened to confront a stone-throwing crowd. Molesworth ordered the soldiers to bayonet anyone throwing stones who moved too close. Later, a Boston justice told him that under common law a bayonet thrust was not an act of self-defense against a stone, which was not a lethal weapon. Had a soldier killed anyone, Molesworth could have been tried for his life for issuing the order.

By 1770, the soldiers often felt under siege. When rioters drove editor John Mein out of town, the army offered him no protection. "Go, Mein, to some dark corner of the world repair," mocked one poet, "And spend thy life in horror and despair." Once again the Sons of Liberty freely intimidated merchants who violated nonimportation. They nearly lynched Ebenezer Richardson, a customs informer who fired shots from his home into a stone-throwing crowd and killed an 11-year-old boy. The lad's funeral on February 26, 1770, became an enormous display of public mourning. Several hundred schoolboys marched ahead of the bier, which was carried by six youths and followed by 30 coaches and thousands of mourners. Richardson, although convicted of murder, was pardoned by George III.

After the funeral, tensions between soldiers and citizens reached a fatal climax. Off-duty soldiers tried to supplement their meager wages with part-time employment, a practice that angered local artisans who resented the competition in the city's depressed economy. On Friday, March 2, 1770, three soldiers came to John Hancock's wharf looking for work. "Soldier, will you work?" asked Samuel Gray, a rope maker. "Yes," replied one. "Then go and clean my shit house," sneered Gray. After an ugly brawl, Gray's employer finally persuaded Colonel William Dalrymple to confine his men to barracks. Peace prevailed through the Puritan sabbath that ran from Saturday night to sunrise on Monday, but everyone expected trouble on Monday, March 5.

After dark on Monday, fire bells began ringing throughout the town, and civilians and soldiers clashed at several places. A crowd hurling snowballs and rocks closed in on the lone sentinel guarding the hated customs house, where the king's revenue was stored. The guard called for help. A corporal and seven soldiers, including two who had participated in the wharf brawl, rushed to his aid and loaded their weapons. Captain Thomas Preston took command and ordered the soldiers to drive the attackers slowly back with fixed bayonets. The crowd taunted the soldiers, daring them to fire. One soldier apparently slipped, discharging his musket into the air as he fell. The others then fired into the crowd, killing five and wounding six. One of the victims was Samuel Gray; another was Crispus Attucks, a man of African and Indian ancestry.

With the whole town taking up arms, the soldiers were withdrawn to Castle William in Boston harbor where, the Sons of Liberty insisted, they had always belonged. Preston and six of his men stood trial for murder and were defended, brilliantly, by two radical patriot lawyers, John Adams and Josiah Quincy, Jr., who believed that every accused person ought to have a proper defense. Preston and four of the soldiers were acquitted. The other two were convicted only of manslaughter, which permitted them to plead a legal technicality called "benefit of clergy." They were branded on the thumb and released.

The Boston Massacre, as the Sons of Liberty called this encounter, became the colonial counterpart to the Massacre of St. George's Fields in England. It marked the failure of Britain's first attempt at military coercion.

Partial Repeal

The day of the massacre marked a turning point in Britain as well, for on March 5, Lord North asked Parliament to repeal the Townshend duties, except the one on tea. North wanted them all repealed, but the cabinet had rejected complete repeal by a 5-to-4 vote back on May 1, 1769. As with the Stamp Act, Britain had three choices: enforcement, repeal, or modification. The ministry feared that Parliament would lose all credibility in North America if it retreated as far as it had in 1766. In effect, North chose the middle ground that had been rejected in 1766—modification instead of full repeal or enforcement. In public, he claimed to be retaining only a preamble without a statute,

Colonial Williamsburg Foundation.

"THE COLOSSUS OF THE NORTH; OR THE STRIDING BOREAS"
This print was an opposition cartoon condemning the corruption of Lord North's ministry while Britannia complains that "Those that should have been my Preservers have been my Destroyers."

a vestige of the Townshend Revenue Act, while repealing the substance. In fact, he did the opposite. Tea provided nearly three-fourths of the revenue under the act. North kept the substance but gave up the shadow.

This news reached the colonies just after nonimportation had achieved its greatest success in 1769 (see the accompanying table). The colonies reduced imports by about one-third from what they had been in 1768, but the impact on Britain was slight, partly because Britain had found a lucrative market for textiles by selling new uniforms to the Russian army. North had hoped that partial repeal, although it would not placate all of the colonists, would at least divide them. It did. Most merchants favored renewed importation of everything but tea, while the Sons of Liberty, most of whom were artisans, still supported complete nonimportation, a policy that would increase demand for their own manufactures.

Resistance collapsed first in Newport, where smuggling had always been the preferred method of challenging British authority. It spread to New York City, where the boycott on imports had been most effective. Soon Philadelphia caved in, followed by Boston in October 1770. By contrast, nonimportation had hardly caused a ripple in the import trade of the Chesapeake colonies. North's repeal was followed by an orgy of importation of British goods, setting record highs everywhere.

Disaffection

Repeal in 1770 lacked the impact that it had in 1766. There was no public rejoicing, not even when Lord North's government (he had replaced Grafton as prime minister in January 1770) took further steps to reduce tension. The Quartering Act expired quietly in 1770, some of the more objectionable features of the vice admiralty courts were softened, and the Currency Act of 1764 was repealed in stages between 1770 and 1773, as even London began to

recognize that it was harming trade. Yet North failed to restore confidence in the justice and decency of the British government. To a degree that is difficult to appreciate today, the empire ran on voluntarism, on trust, or what people at the time called "affection." Its opposite, *dis*affection, had a more literal and dangerous meaning to them than it does now.

Many colonists blamed one another for failing to win complete repeal of the duties. A Philadelphian attacked the "little dirty colony of Rhode Island" for yielding first. Bostonians lamented the "immortal shame and infamy" of New Yorkers for abandoning resistance: "Let them . . . be despised, hated, detested, and handed down to all future ages as the betrayers of their country." A New Yorker retaliated by calling Boston "the common sewer of America into which every beast that brought with it the unclean thing has disburthened itself." These recriminations, gratifying as they must have been to British officials, actually masked a vast erosion of trust in the imperial government. The colonists were angry with one another for failing to appreciate how menacing British policy still was. The tea duty continued to proclaim Parliament's sovereignty over the colonies. It remained a sliver in a wound that would not heal.

That fear sometimes broke through the surface calm of the years from 1770 to 1773. Rhode Islanders had often clashed with customs officers and had even fired on the king's ships once or twice without stirring much interest in other colonies. Then, in 1772, a predatory customs vessel, the *Gaspée*, ran aground near Providence while pursuing some peaceful coastal ships. After dark, men with blackened faces boarded the *Gaspée*, wounded its captain, and burned the ship. Britain sent a panel of dignitaries to the colony with instructions to send the perpetrators to England for trial. The inquiry failed because no one would talk.

Twelve colonial assemblies considered this threat so ominous that they created permanent committees of

EXPORTS IN £000 STERLING FROM ENGLAND AND SCOTLAND TO THE AMERICAN COLONIES, 1766–75										
Colony	1766	1767	1768	1769	1770	1771	1772	1773	1774	1775
New England	419	416	431	224	417	1,436*	844	543	577	85.0
New York	333	424	491	76	480	655*	349	296	460	1.5
Pennsylvania	334	383	442	205	140	747*	526	436	646	1.4
Chesapeake†	520	653	670	715	997*	1,224*	1,016	589	690	1.9
Lower South‡	376	292	357	385*	228	515*	575*	448	471	130.5
Totals	1,982	2,168	2,391	1,605	2,262	4,577*	3,310	2,312	2,844	220.3

Average total exports, 1766–68 = £2,180
1769 = 73.6% of that average, or 67.1% of 1768 exports
1770 = 103.8% of that average, or 94.6% of 1768 exports
*These totals surpassed all previous highs
†Chesapeake = Maryland and Virginia
‡Lower South = Carolinas and Georgia

correspondence to keep in touch with one another and to *anticipate* the next assault on their liberties. Even colonial moderates now believed that the British government was conspiring to destroy liberty in America. When Governor Hutchinson announced in 1773 that, under the Townshend Act, the Massachusetts Superior Court justices would receive their salaries from the imperial treasury, Boston created its own committee of correspondence and urged other towns to do the same. Boston's role in the "patriot" cause had grown dramatically since the convention of 1768, and Bostonians such as John Adams had become the major spokesmen for the resistance movement. A plot to destroy their liberties now seemed plausible to many colonials. Hutchinson, amused at first, grew alarmed when most towns of any size followed Boston's lead.

The Boston Massacre trials and the *Gaspée* affair convinced London that it was pointless to prosecute individuals for politically motivated crimes. Whole communities would have to be punished. That choice brought the government to the edge of a precipice. Was the empire held together by law and consent, or only by force? The use of force against entire communities could lead to outright war, and war is not and cannot be a system of justice. The spread of committees of correspondence within Massachusetts and throughout the colonies suggested that settlers who had been unable to unite against New France at Albany in 1754 now deemed unity against Britain essential to their liberties. By 1773, several New England newspapers were calling on the colonies to create a formal union.

In effect, the Townshend crisis never ended. With the tea duty standing as a symbol of Parliament's right to tax the colonies without their consent, genuine imperial harmony was becoming impossible. North's decision to retain the tea tax in 1770 did not guarantee that armed resistance would break out five years later, but it severely narrowed the ground on which any compromise could be built. The price of miscalculation had grown enormously.

Internal Cleavages: The Contagion of Liberty

Any challenge to British authority carried high risks for prominent families in the colonies. They depended on the Crown for their public offices, official honors, and government contracts, which in turn ratified their status at the top of society. After the Stamp Act crisis, these families faced a dilemma. The Hutchinsons of Massachusetts kept on good terms with Britain while incurring the scorn and even hatred of many of their neighbors. John Hancock, the Livingstons of New York, and most of the great planters in the southern colonies championed the grievances of their communities but alienated British authorities. The Townshend crisis was a far more accurate predictor of future behavior than response to the Stamp Act had been. Nearly everyone had denounced the Stamp Act, including such future loyalists as Daniel Dulany of Maryland. By contrast, the merchants and lawyers who resisted nonimportation in 1768 were likely to become loyalists by 1775. Artisans, merchants, and lawyers who supported the boycotts, especially those who favored continuing them past 1770, became patriots.

But the patriot leaders also faced challenges from within their own ranks. Artisans, who had mobilized to resist Britain in 1765 and 1769, demanded more power, and tenant farmers in the Hudson valley protested violently against their landlords. In Boston, where the economy had been faltering since the 1740s while taxes remained high, Britain's policies bore hard on the town and gave an angry edge to its protests. Boston's radical artisans set the pace of resistance in every imperial crisis. In New York City, Philadelphia, and Charleston, artisans began to play a much more assertive role in public affairs. Could the new and fragile social hierarchy of the 18th century withstand these strains?

The Feudal Revival and Rural Discontent

Tensions increased in the countryside as well as in the cities. Three processes intensified discontent in rural areas: a revival of old proprietary charters, massive foreign immigration, and the settlement of the backcountry.

Between about 1730 and 1750, the men who owned 17th-century proprietary or manorial charters began to see, for the first time, the prospect of huge profits by enforcing these old legal claims. The great estates of the Hudson valley had attracted few settlers before the mid-18th century, and those who arrived first had received generous leases. By the 1750s, however, a typical manor lord was taking in between £1,000 and £2,000 per year, while the Livingston and Van Rensselaer families did much better. As leases became more restrictive and as New Englanders swarmed into New York, discontent increased. In 1753, the proprietor of Livingston Manor had difficulty putting down Yankee rioters, and discontent spread throughout the Hudson valley over the next decade. In 1766, several thousand angry farmers, inspired by the Stamp Act riots, took to the fields and the roads to protest the terms of their leases. They threatened to kill the lord of Livingston Manor or to pull down the mansions of absentee landlords in New York City. Supported by some of the city's most prominent Sons of Liberty, the colony called in redcoats to suppress them. New York's experience exposed the difficulties of uniting urban and rural radicals in a common cause. But when New York landlords also tried to make good their claims to the upper Connecticut valley, the Yankee settlers utterly defied them, set up their own government, and, after a long struggle, ultimately became the independent state of Vermont.

The proprietors of East New Jersey claimed much of the land being worked by descendants of the original settlers of Newark and Elizabethtown, who thought they owned their farms. The proprietors, in firm control of the law courts, planned to sell or lease the land, either to the current occupants or to newcomers. After they expelled several farmers and replaced them with tenants, the farmers retaliated. A succession of land riots, in which farms were burned and jails were broken open, rocked much of northern New Jersey for 10 years after 1745. The proprietary intruders were driven out, and the riots stopped, but tensions remained high.

Maryland and Pennsylvania had brought few returns to the Calvert and Penn families before 1730, but over the next three or four decades, both families organized land sales much more carefully and began to collect quitrents. Frederick, the seventh and last Lord Baltimore, milked Maryland for the princely income of £30,000 sterling per year until his death in 1771. The Penns enjoyed similar gains in Pennsylvania, although more slowly. Their landed income rose to about £15,000 or £20,000 in the 1760s and then soared to £67,000 in 1773, only to fall sharply as the Pennsylvania government disintegrated over the next three years. With more than half of their land still unsettled, they seemed about to turn their colony into the most lucrative piece of real estate in the Atlantic world. But their reluctance to contribute to the war effort in the 1750s had so angered Benjamin Franklin that, with the assembly's support, he went to London to urge the Crown to make Pennsylvania a royal colony. This effort weakened the colony's resistance to both the Stamp Act and the Townshend Act. Meanwhile Connecticut settlers, who claimed they had bought Pennsylvania's Wyoming valley from the Indians at the Albany Congress of 1754, rejected the Penns' authority, claimed all of northern Pennsylvania on the basis of Connecticut's sea-to-sea charter and, aided by the Paxton Boys, set off a small civil war in the 1770s.

In Virginia, Thomas, the sixth baron Fairfax, acquired title to the entire northern neck of the colony (the land between the Potomac and the Rappahannock rivers), which Charles II had granted to two courtiers in the mid-17th century. By 1775, the Fairfax estate's 5 million acres contained 21 counties. He received £5,000 per year from his holdings, but he muted criticism by moving to the colony and setting himself up as a great planter and a patron of youthful George Washington.

In North Carolina, John Carteret, earl of Granville—the only heir of the original Carolina proprietors who refused to sell his share to the Crown in the 1720s—consolidated his claim as the Granville District after 1745. Although still living in England, he received an income of about £5,000 per year. The Granville District embraced more than half of North Carolina's land and two-thirds of its population, deprived the colony of revenue from land sales and quitrents within the district, and forced North Carolina to resort to direct taxation. For several years after Granville's death in 1763, his land office remained closed. Disgruntled settlers often rioted when they could not gain title to their lands.

Taken together, the claims of New York's manor lords, the New Jersey proprietors, and the Penn, Baltimore, Fairfax, and Granville families blanketed the colonies from New York to North Carolina. They were the biggest winners in America's feudal revival, the use of old charters to pry income from the settlers.

The Regulator Movements in the Carolinas

Massive immigration from Europe, mostly through Philadelphia, and the settlement of the backcountry created severe social tensions. Most immigrants were Scottish or Scots-Irish Presbyterians, Lutherans, or German Reformed Protestants. They were dissenters from the prevailing faith in the colonies they entered, whether it was the Quaker religion in Pennsylvania or the Church of England from Maryland to Georgia. They angered Indians by squatting on their land and, quite often, by murdering those who were in their way—behavior that the Paxton Boys' march on Philadelphia in 1763 attempted to justify. In the Carolina backcountry, the newcomers provoked the Cherokee War of 1759–61, which brutalized and demoralized the whole region.

After the Cherokee War, bands of outlaws, men who had been dislocated by the war, began roaming the countryside, plundering the more prosperous farmers and often raping their wives and daughters. As the violence peaked between 1765 and 1767, the more respectable settlers organized themselves as "regulators" (a later generation would call them "vigilantes") to impose order in the absence of any organized government. Although South Carolina claimed jurisdiction over the backcountry, the colony's law courts were located in Charleston, more than 100 miles to the east. Even though most of the white settlers now lived in the backcountry, they elected only 2 of the 48 members of South Carolina's assembly. In effect, they had no local government.

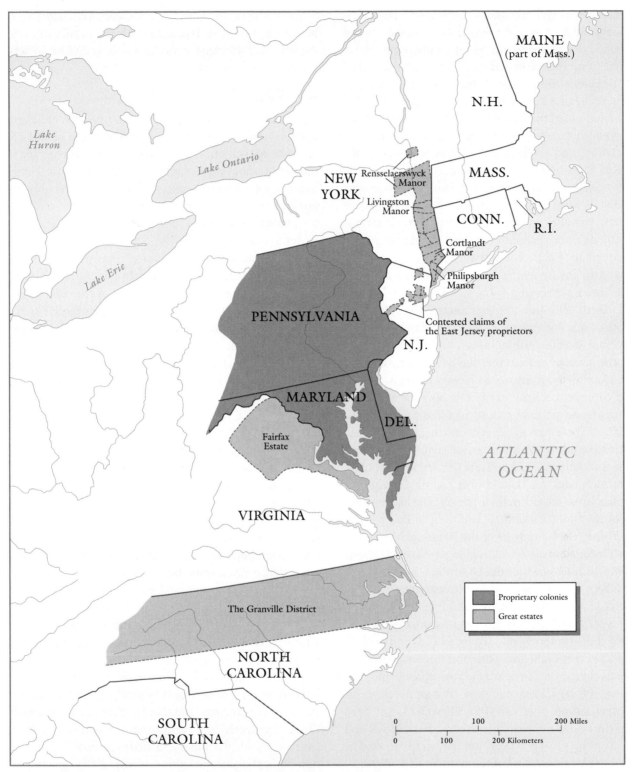

MAP 5.2 FEUDAL REVIVAL: GREAT ESTATES OF LATE COLONIAL AMERICA

On the eve of the Revolution, more than half of the land between the Hudson Valley and North Carolina was claimed by men who had inherited various kinds of 17th-century charters or patents.

After obtaining commissions from Charleston as militia officers and justices of the peace, the regulators chased the outlaws out of the colony, many of them into North Carolina. They then imposed order on what they called the "little people," poor settlers who often made a living as hunters, many of whom may have aided the outlaws. The discipline imposed by the regulators, typically whippings and forced labor, outraged their victims, who organized as "moderators" and got their own commissions from the governor. With both sides claiming legality, about 600 armed regulators confronted an equal force of moderators at the Saluda River in 1769. Civil war was avoided only by the timely arrival of an emissary from the governor bearing a striking message: South Carolina would finally bring government to the backcountry by providing a circuit court system for the entire colony. Violence ebbed, but tensions remained severe.

In North Carolina, the backcountry's problem was corruption, not the absence of government. The settlers, mostly immigrants pushing south from Pennsylvania, found the county courts under the control of men with strong blood or business ties to powerful families in the eastern counties. Because county officials were appointed by the governor, political success required gaining access to his circle. These justices, lawyers, and merchants seemed to regard county government as an engine for fleecing farmers through regressive poll taxes, fees, and court costs, and through suits for debt. North Carolina's regulator movement arose to reform these abuses. The backcountry counties contained more than half the colony's population, but they elected only 17 of the 78 assemblymen.

In 1768, the regulators refused to pay taxes in Orange County, which was part of the Granville District. Governor William Tryon mustered 1,300 eastern militiamen, one-sixth of whom were officers, including more than half of the assemblymen from the eastern counties. With 8 generals and 14 colonels, and led by an elite unit of Gentlemen Volunteer Light Dragoons, this force overawed the regulators for a time. Then, in a bid for a voice in the 1769 assembly, the regulators managed to capture six seats. These new assemblymen called for the secret ballot, fixed salaries (instead of fees) for justices and other officials, and a land tax rather than poll taxes. But they were outvoted by the eastern majority. After losing ground in the 1770 election, they stormed into Hillsborough, closed the Orange County Court, and whipped Edmund Fanning, a Yale graduate whose lust for fees had made him the most detested official in the backcountry. They also seized the court docket and scribbled unflattering comments next to many of the names of their creditors. Tryon responded by marching 1,000 militiamen westward, who defeated a force of more than 2,000 poorly armed regulators in early 1771

at the battle of Alamance Creek. Seven regulators were hanged, and many fled the colony. North Carolina entered the struggle for independence as a bitterly divided society.

Slaves and Women

In Charleston, South Carolina, in 1765, the Sons of Liberty marched through the streets chanting "Liberty and No Stamps." To their amazement, slaves organized a parade of their own, shouting, "Liberty! Liberty!" Merchant Henry Laurens tried to convince himself that they probably did not know the meaning of the word.

About the middle of the 18th century, slavery came under serious attack for the first time. An antislavery movement arose on both sides of the Atlantic and attracted both patriots and loyalists. In the 1740s and 1750s, Benjamin Lay, John Woolman, and Anthony Benezet urged fellow Quakers to free their slaves. In the 1750s, the Quaker Yearly Meeting placed the slave trade off limits and finally, in 1774, forbade slaveholding altogether. Any Friend who failed to comply by 1779 was disowned. Britain's Methodist leader John Wesley, in almost every other respect a social conservative, also attacked slavery, as did several colonial disciples of Jonathan Edwards. Two and three decades after the Great Awakening, many evangelicals began to agree with the message of South Carolina's Hugh Bryan in 1742, that slavery was a sin.

By the 1760s, supporters of slavery found that they now had to defend the institution. Hardly anyone had bothered to do so earlier, because a social hierarchy seemed necessary and inevitable, and slavery simply marked one extreme of that hierarchy. As equal rights became a popular topic, however, some began to suggest that *all* people could claim these rights, and slavery came under attack. In Scotland, Adam Smith, the most original economist of the age, praised African slaves for their "magnanimity," which, he claimed, "the soul of the sordid master is scarce capable of conceiving." Arthur Lee, a Virginian, defended the character of his fellow planters against Smith's charge but discovered that he could not justify slavery, "always the deadly enemy to virtue and science." Patrick Henry agreed. Slavery, he wrote, "is as repugnant to humanity as it is inconsistent with the Bible and destructive of liberty." He himself kept slaves, but only because of "the general inconvenience of living without them. I will not, I cannot justify it." In England, Granville Sharp, an early abolitionist, brought the Somerset case before the Court of King's Bench in 1771 and compelled a reluctant Chief Justice William Murray, baron Mansfield, to declare slavery incompatible with the "free air" of England. That decision gave England's 10,000 or 15,000 blacks a chance to claim their freedom.

"A SOCIETY OF PATRIOTIC LADIES AT EDENTON IN NORTH CAROLINA"

This 1775 London cartoon satirized the active role of women in resisting British policies.

From the Collections of the Library of Congress.

New Englanders began to head in similar directions. Two women, Sarah Osborn and Phillis Wheatley, played leading roles in the movement. Osborn, an English immigrant to Newport, Rhode Island, and a widow, opened a school in 1744 to support her family. A friend of revivalist George Whitefield, she also taught women and blacks and began holding evening religious meetings, which turned into a big local revival. At one point in the 1760s, about one-sixth of Newport's Africans were attending her school. That made them the most literate African population in the colonies, although they were living in the city most deeply involved in the African slave trade. Osborn's students supported abolition of the slave trade and, later, of slavery itself.

In 1761, an eight-year-old girl who would become known as Phillis Wheatley arrived in Boston from Africa and was purchased by wealthy John Wheatley as a servant for his wife, Susannah, who treated her more like a daughter than a slave, taught her to read and write, and emancipated her when she came of age. In 1767, Phillis published her first poem in Boston, and in 1773, a volume of her poetry was printed in London, making her a transatlantic celebrity by age 20. Her poems deplored slavery but rejoiced in the Christianization of Africans. Some of them supported the patriot cause, but she withheld those from the London edition.

Soon many of Boston's blacks sensed an opportunity for emancipation. On several occasions in 1773 and 1774, they petitioned the legislature or the governor for freedom,

PHILLIS WHEATLEY

Engraving of Phillis Wheatley opposite the title page of her collected poems, published in 1773.

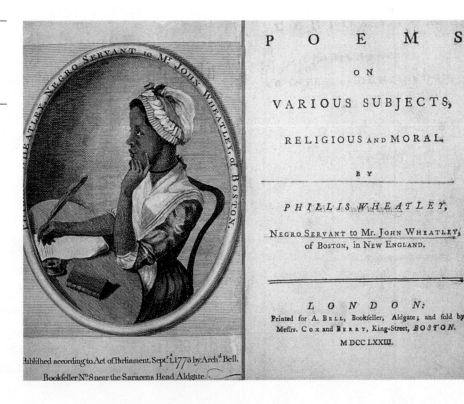

American Antiquarian Society.

pointing out that, although they had never forfeited their natural rights, they were being "held in slavery in the bowels of a free and Christian Country." When the legislature passed a bill on their behalf, Governor Hutchinson vetoed it. Boston slaves made it clear to General Gage, Hutchinson's successor, that they would serve him as a loyal militia in exchange for their freedom. In short, they offered allegiance to whichever side supported their emancipation. Many patriots began to rally to their cause. "If we would look for Liberty ourselves," the town of Medfield declared in 1773, ". . . we ought not to continue to enslave others but immediately set about some effectual method to prevent it for the future."

The patriots could look to another group of allies as well. Many women became indispensable to the broader resistance movement. They could not vote or hold office, but without their willing support, nonimportation would have been not just a failure, but a fiasco. In thousands of households, women joined the intense discussions about liberty and agreed to make homespun clothing to take the place of imported British textiles.

Freedom's ferment made a heady wine. After 1773, any direct challenge to British power would trigger enormous social changes within the colonies.

The Last Imperial Crisis

The surface calm between 1770 and 1773 ended when Lord North moved to save the East India Company, Britain's largest corporation, from bankruptcy. The company was being undersold in southeastern England and the colonies by low-priced, smuggled Dutch tea, which left the East India Company's warehouses bulging with millions of unsold pounds of tea. North's main concern was the company, not colonial resistance to Townshend's tea duty. Without solving the company's problems, he created a colonial crisis too big for Britain to handle.

The Tea Crisis

North decided to rescue the East India Company by empowering it to undersell its rivals, the smugglers of Dutch tea. Benjamin Franklin, who was still in London as a colonial agent, reminded North that he could achieve that goal in the colonies by repealing the Townshend duty for sound economic reasons. North rejected that idea. The settlers, he thought, would hardly revolt if he somehow managed to give them cheap tea. His Tea Act of 1773 repealed import duties on tea in England but retained the Townshend duty in the colonies. In both places, North estimated, legal tea would be cheaper than anyone else's. The company would be saved, and the settlers, by willingly buying legal tea, would accept Parliament's right to tax them.

Another aspect of the Tea Act antagonized most merchants in the colonies. The company had been selling tea to all comers at public auctions in London, but the Tea Act gave it a monopoly on the shipping and distribution of tea in the colonies. Only company ships could carry it, and a few consignees in each port would have the exclusive right to sell it. The combined dangers of taxation and monopoly again forged the coalition of artisans and merchants that had helped defeat the Stamp Act by 1766 and resist the Townshend Act by 1769. Patriots saw the Tea Act as a Trojan horse that would destroy liberty by seducing the settlers into accepting parliamentary sovereignty. Unintentionally, North gave a tremendous advantage to those determined to resist the Tea Act. He had devised an oceanic, or external, measure that the colonists could actually nullify despite British control of the seas. No one would have to police the entire waterfront looking for tea importers. The patriots had only to wait for the specially chartered tea ships and prevent them from landing their cargoes.

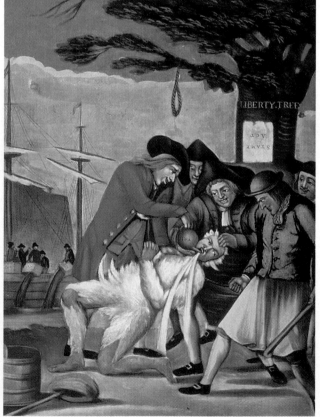

Courtesy of the John Carter Brown Library at Brown University.

"THE BOSTONIANS PAYING THE EXCISE-MAN, OR TARRING AND FEATHERING"
This London cartoon of 1774 satirizes the Sons of Liberty.

Direct threats usually did the job. As the first tea ship approached Philadelphia, the Sons of Liberty greeted the skipper with a rude welcome: "What think you Captain, of a halter around your neck—ten gallons of liquid tar decanted on your pate—with the feathers of a dozen wild geese laid over that to enliven your appearance? Only think seriously of this—and fly to the place from whence you came—fly without hesitation—without the formality of a protest—and above all, . . . let us advise you to fly without the wild geese feathers." The ship quickly departed.

Similar scenes took place in every port except Boston. There, Governor Hutchinson, whose sons were the local tea consignees, decided to face down the radicals. He refused to grant clearance papers to three tea ships that, under the law, had to pay the Townshend duty within 21 days of arrival or face seizure. Hutchinson meant to force them to land the tea and pay the duty. This timetable led to urgent mass meetings for several weeks and generated a major crisis. Finally, convinced that they had no other way to block the landing of the tea, Boston radicals disguised themselves as Indians and threw 342 chests of tea, worth about £11,000 sterling (more than $700,000 in 2004 dollars), into Boston harbor on the night of December 16, 1773.

Britain's Response: The Coercive Acts

This willful destruction of private property shocked both Britain and America. Convinced that severe punishment was essential to British credibility, Parliament passed four Coercive Acts during spring 1774. The Boston Port Act closed the port of Boston until Bostonians paid for the tea. A new Quartering Act allowed the army to quarter soldiers on civilian property if necessary. The Administration of Justice Act (a response to the Boston Massacre trials) permitted a British soldier or official who was charged with a crime while carrying out his duties to be tried either in another colony or in England. Most controversial of all was the Massachusetts Government Act. It overturned the Massachusetts Charter of 1691, made the council appointive, and restricted town meetings. In effect, it made Massachusetts like other royal colonies. Before it passed, the king named General Gage, already the commander of the British army in North America, as the new governor of Massachusetts, with the clear implication that he could use military force against civilians.

THE MASSACHUSETTS CALENDAR; OR AN ALMANACK (1774)
In the era of witch trials, engravings of devils were meant to be taken literally. By the Revolution, they had become symbolic. The cover of this almanac castigates Governor Thomas Hutchinson of Massachusetts who, it suggests, deserves damnation.

Parliament also passed a fifth law, unrelated to the Coercive Acts but significant nonetheless. The Quebec Act established French civil law and the Roman Catholic Church in the Province of Quebec, provided for trial by jury in criminal but not in civil cases, gave legislative power (but not the power to tax) to an appointive governor and council, and extended the administrative boundaries of Quebec to the area between the Great Lakes and the Ohio River, saving only the legitimate charter claims of other colonies. Historians now regard the act as a farsighted measure that gave French Catholics the toleration that the empire had denied to Acadians 20 years earlier, but settlers from New England to Georgia were appalled. Instead of conciliation and toleration, they saw a deliberate revival of the power of New France and the Catholic Church on their northern border, this time bolstered by Britain's naval and military might. The Quebec Act added credibility to the fear that evil ministers in London were conspiring to destroy British and colonial liberties. Many British colonists suspected that the autocratic government of Quebec might become a model for restructuring their own provinces. The settlers lumped the Quebec Act together with the Coercive Acts and coined their own name for all of them: the Intolerable Acts.

The Radical Explosion

The interval between passage of the Boston Port Act in March 1774 and the Massachusetts Government Act in May permits us to compare the response that each provoked. The Port Act was quite enforceable and immune to nullification by the colonists. It led to another round of nonimportation and to the summoning of the First Continental Congress. But the Government Act *was* nullified by the colonists. It led to war. The soldiers marching to Concord on April 19, 1775, were trying to enforce that act against settlers who absolutely refused to obey it.

Gage took over as governor of Massachusetts in May 1774, before Parliament passed the Massachusetts Government Act. In June, he closed the ports of Boston and Charlestown, just north of Boston. The navy gave him more than enough power to do so. At first, Boston split over the Port Act. Many merchants wanted to abolish the Boston Committee of Correspondence and pay for the tea

to avoid an economic catastrophe, but they were badly outvoted in a huge town meeting. Boston then called for a colonial union and for immediate nonimportation and nonconsumption of British goods. By then, some radicals were losing patience with nonimportation as a tactic. Parliament had already shut Boston down.

Discouraging news arrived from elsewhere. A mass meeting in New York City rejected immediate nonimportation in favor of an intercolonial congress. Philadelphia followed New York's lead. In both cities, cautious merchants hoped that a congress might postpone or prevent radical measures of resistance.

This was only a momentary success. North assumed that the Coercive Acts would isolate Boston from the rest of the province, Massachusetts from the rest of New England, and New England from the other colonies, a goal that Britain would pursue through 1777. Instead, contributions began pouring in from all of the colonies to help Boston survive. The Stamp Act crisis and the Townshend crisis had been largely urban affairs. The Intolerable Acts politicized the countryside on a scale never seen before. When royal governors outside Massachusetts dismissed their assemblies to prevent them from joining the resistance movement, colonists there did what Massachusetts had done in 1768: They elected "provincial congresses," or conventions, to organize resistance. These bodies were much larger than the legal assemblies they displaced, and they mobilized far more people. As the congresses took hold, royal government began to collapse almost everywhere.

Numerous calls for a continental congress made the movement irresistible. By June, it was also obvious that any congress would adopt nonimportation. Except for some details, that issue had been settled, even before the

"THE ABLE DOCTOR, OR AMERICA SWALLOWING THE BITTER DRAUGHT"

This 1774 engraving by Paul Revere used "The Bostonians Paying the Excise-Man" as a model but turned it into a patriot statement. In Revere's version, the British are forcing tea down the throat of America (represented by a ravished lady, Liberty). The British are also imposing martial law in Boston.

© Bettmann/Corbis.

congress met, by mandates that the delegates brought with them.

Despite these signs of disaffection, Gage remained optimistic through most of the summer. Then news of the Massachusetts Government Act arrived on August 6. Gage's authority disintegrated when he tried to enforce the act, which marked the most dramatic attempt yet made by Parliament to control the internal affairs of the colonies. The "mandamus councillors," whom Gage appointed to the new upper house under the act, either resigned their seats or fled to Boston to seek protection from the army. The Superior Court could not hold its sessions, even in Boston under the guns of the army, because jurors refused to take an oath under the new act. At the county level (the real center of royal power in the colony), popular conventions closed the courts and took charge in August and September. Gage was beginning to realize that none of his major objectives was achievable.

Before this explosion of radical activity, Gage had called for a new General Court to meet in Salem in October. Many towns sent representatives, but others followed

© The Granger Collection.

A POLITICAL LESSON (1774)
When General Sir Thomas Gage replaced Thomas Hutchinson as royal governor of Massachusetts in 1774, he closed the port of Boston and moved the capital to Salem. This cartoon shows him thrown from his horse, presumably representing the people.

© North Wind Picture Archives.

THE PATRIOTICK BARBER OF NEW YORK (1775)
British army and navy officers who came to New York often disguised themselves as civilians when dealing with tradesmen. This cartoon shows what happened when one officer was outed while dealing with a barber who was also a Son of Liberty.

the lead of the Worcester County Convention, which in August urged all towns to elect delegates to a provincial congress in Concord, 17 miles inland, out of range of the navy. Although Gage revoked his call for a General Court, about 90 representatives met at Salem anyway. When Gage refused to recognize them, they adjourned to Concord in early October and joined the 200 delegates already gathered there as the Massachusetts Provincial Congress. That body became the de facto government of the colony and implemented the radical demands of the Suffolk County Convention (representing Boston and its hinterland), which included a purge of unreliable militia officers, the creation of a special force of armed "minutemen" able to respond rapidly to any emergency, and the payment of taxes to the congress in Concord, not to Gage in Boston. The Provincial Congress also collected military stores at Concord and created an executive arm, the Committee of Public Safety. North assumed that Gage's army would uphold the new Massachusetts government. Instead, Gage's government survived only where the army could protect it.

The alternative to government by consent was becoming no British authority at all in the colony. For example, in the predawn hours of September 1, Gage dispatched soldiers to confiscate 250 half-barrels of gunpowder stored a few miles outside Boston. He got the powder, but the foray started one-third of the militia of New England marching toward Boston. They turned back when they were assured that no one had been killed. In later raids on other stores, the colonists always beat the redcoats to the powder. By October, Gage's power was limited to the Boston area, which the army held. Unable to put his 3,000 soldiers to any positive use, he wrote North on October 30 that "a small Force rather encourages Resistance than terrifys." He then stunned North by asking for 20,000 redcoats, nearly as many as had been needed to conquer Canada.

The First Continental Congress

From 1769 into 1774, colonial patriots had looked to John Wilkes in London for leadership. At the First Continental Congress, they began relying on themselves. Twelve colonies (all but Georgia) sent delegates. In September 1774, they met at Philadelphia's Carpenters' Hall, a center of artisan strength. They scarcely even debated nonimportation. The southern colonies insisted, and the New Englanders agreed, that nonimportation finally be extended to molasses, which continued to generate revenue under the penny duty of 1766. The delegates were almost unanimous in adopting nonexportation if Britain did not redress colonial grievances by September 1775. Nonexportation was a much more radical tactic than nonimportation because it contained the implicit threat of repudiating debts to British merchants, which were normally paid off with colonial exports.

Joseph Galloway, a Pennsylvania loyalist, submitted a plan of imperial union that would have required all laws affecting the colonies to be passed by both Parliament and an intercolonial congress, but his proposal was tabled by a vote of 6 colonies to 5. The Congress spent three weeks trying to define colonial rights. Everyone agreed that the Coercive Acts, the Quebec Act, and all surviving revenue acts had to be repealed and that infringements on trial by jury had to be rejected. The delegates generally agreed on what would break the impasse, but they had trouble finding the precise language for their demands. They finally affirmed the new principle of no *legislation* without consent—but added a saving clause that affirmed colonial assent to existing acts of Parliament that regulated their trade.

Congress petitioned the king rather than Parliament because patriots no longer recognized Parliament as a legitimate legislature for the colonies. Congress explained its position in separate addresses to the people of the 13 colonies, the people of Quebec, and the people of Great Britain. It took two other radical steps: It agreed to meet again in May 1775 if the British response was unsatisfactory, and it created the Association—with citizen committees in every community—to enforce its trade sanctions against Britain. Most towns and counties heartily embraced the idea, and perhaps 7,000 men served on such committees during winter 1774–75. In approving the Association, Congress began to act as a central government for the United Colonies.

Toward War

The news from Boston and Philadelphia shook the North ministry. "The New England Governments are in a State of Rebellion," George III told North; "blows must decide whether they are to be subject to this Country or independent." Although Franklin kept assuring the British that Congress meant exactly what it said, both North and the opposition assumed that conciliation could be achieved on lesser terms. Edmund Burke, who had been out of office since 1766, urged a return to pre-1763 understandings without explaining how to restore the loyalty that had made them workable. "A great empire and little minds go ill together," he cautioned in an eloquent speech urging conciliation. Lord Chatham (William Pitt) introduced a bill to prohibit Parliament from taxing the colonies, to recognize the Congress, and even to ask Congress to provide revenue for North American defense and to help pay down the national debt. When a spokesman for North's ministry challenged him, Chatham retorted that his plan, if implemented, "must annihilate your power . . . and at once reduce you to that state of insignificance for which God and nature designed you." Neither plan passed.

The initiative lay, of course, with Lord North. An amiable man, he still had vague hopes for a peaceful solution to the crisis. But in January 1775, he took a step that made war inevitable. He ordered Gage to send troops to Concord, destroy the arms stored there, and arrest John Hancock and Samuel Adams. Only after sending this dispatch did he introduce his own Conciliatory Proposition. Parliament pledged that it would tax no colony that met its share of the cost of imperial defense and paid proper salaries to its royal officials, but Britain would use force against delinquent colonies. To reassure hard-liners that he was not turning soft, he introduced the New England Restraining Act on the same day. It barred New Englanders from the Atlantic fisheries and prohibited all commerce between New England and any place except Britain and the British West Indies, precisely the trade routes that

Congress had resolved to block through nonimportation. Both sides were now committed to economic sanctions.

North's orders to Gage arrived before his Conciliatory Proposition reached America, and Gage obeyed. He hoped to surprise Concord with another predawn march, but Boston radicals knew about the expedition almost as soon as the orders were issued. They had already made careful preparations to alert the whole countryside. Their informant, in all likelihood, was Gage's wife, Margaret Kemble Gage, a New Jerseyan by birth. At 2 A.M. on the night of April 18–19, about 700 grenadiers and light infantry began their march toward Concord. Paul Revere, a Boston silversmith who had done as much as anyone to create the information network that he now set in motion, went dashing west with the news that "The redcoats are coming!" When he was captured past Lexington by a British patrol, Dr. Samuel Prescott, returning from a lady friend's house at the awkward hour of 1 A.M., managed to get the message through to Concord. As the British approached Lexington Green at dawn, they found 60 to 70 militiamen drawn up to face them. The outnumbered militia began to withdraw when somebody—probably a colonial bystander and possibly also a British soldier—fired the first shot. Without orders, the British line opened fire, killing eight and wounding nine. From every direction, like angry bees, the countryside surged toward them. Secrecy had become pointless, and the British broke out their regimental fifes and drums. Cheered by the tunes, they marched west toward Concord and into another world war.

☞ The Improvised War

In April 1775, neither side had a plan for winning a major war. Gage's soldiers were trying to enforce acts of Parliament. The militia were fighting for a political regime that Parliament was determined to change. They drove the British from Concord Bridge and pursued them all the way to Boston. Suffering only 95 casualties, the militia inflicted 273 on the British. Had a relief force not met the battered British survivors east of Lexington, all of them might have been lost.

Lacking an adequate command or supply structure, the colonists besieged Boston. After two months, Gage finally declared that all settlers bearing arms, and those who aided them, were rebels and traitors. He offered to

The Granger Collection, New York.

THE BATTLE OF LEXINGTON, APRIL 19, 1775

Ralph Earl's painting, which was engraved by Amos Doolittle in 1775, portrays the opening shots of the Revolutionary War. The British are firing a volley into the Lexington militia, who are trying to leave the field without offering resistance. In fact, the first British soldiers who fired did so without orders, possibly in response to a shot from a colonial bystander. The militia was indeed trying to withdraw.

pardon anyone who returned to his allegiance, except John Hancock and Samuel Adams. Instead of complying, the besiegers escalated the struggle two days later. They fortified the high ground on Breed's Hill (next to Bunker Hill) near Charlestown and overlooking Boston. The British sent 2,400 men, one-fifth of the garrison, to take the hills on June 17. Merely by seizing Charlestown Neck, a smaller force could have cut off the Yankee militia at low risk to itself. Instead, to prove that civilians had no chance against a regular army, General William Howe launched three frontal attacks. Secure behind their defenses, the settlers shot more than 1,000 of the attackers, including 92 officers (about one-sixth of those lost in the entire war), before they ran out of ammunition and withdrew. The defenders suffered about 370 casualties, nearly all during the retreat.

For the moment at least, patriotism seemed to make colonial farmers and artisans a match for Britain's professional army. But as the war progressed, "Bunker Hillism" became a dangerous delusion. Time after time, Americans fortified a hill and then waited for the stupid frontal assault that never came. The British got the message at Bunker Hill. A few more such victories, reflected one of them, and no one would be left alive to carry the news to London.

Well into 1776, both sides fought an improvised war. In May 1775, Vermont and Massachusetts militia took Fort Ticonderoga on Lake Champlain and seized the artillery and gunpowder that would be used months later in the siege of Boston. Crown Point also fell. With nearly

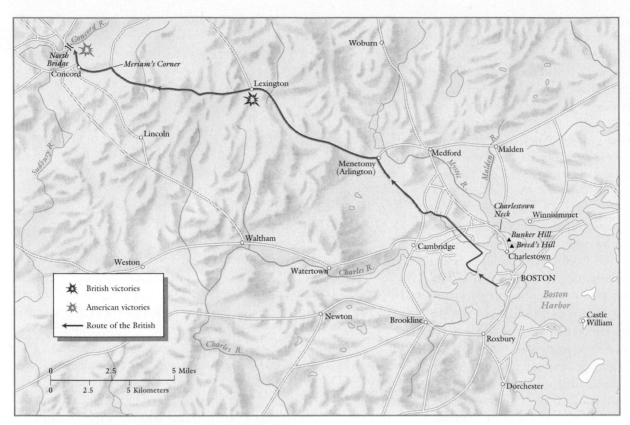

MAP 5.3 LEXINGTON, CONCORD, AND BOSTON, 1775

The British march to Lexington and Concord on April 19, 1775, touched off the Revolutionary War. The colonists drove the redcoats back to Boston and then besieged the city for 11 months until the British withdrew.

all of their forces in Boston, the British were too weak to defend other positions or to intervene in the short Indian conflict, Lord Dunmore's War, that broke out in the upper Ohio valley in 1774. The collapse of royal government meant that the rebels now controlled the militia and most of the royal powderhouses.

The militia became the key to political allegiance. Compulsory service with the militia politicized many waverers, who decided that they really were patriots when a redcoat shot at them or when they drove a loyalist into exile. The militia kept the countryside committed to the Revolution wherever the British army was too weak to overwhelm them.

The Second Continental Congress

When the Second Continental Congress met in May 1775, it inherited the war. For months it pursued the conflicting strategies of resistance and conciliation. It voted to turn the undisciplined men besieging Boston into a Continental Army. As in earlier wars, the soldiers were volunteers who expected to serve for only a few months, or a single campaign. In the absence of royal authority, they elected their officers, who tried to win their obedience through persuasion, not command. Supplying the soldiers with food and munitions became a huge problem.

Most of the men were Yankees who would have preferred to serve under their own officers, but Congress realized that a successful war effort would have to engage the other colonies as well. On June 15, at the urging of John Adams of Massachusetts, Congress made George Washington of Virginia commanding general. When Washington took charge of the Continental Army, he was appalled at the poor discipline among the soldiers and their casual familiarity with their officers. He insisted that officers behave with a dignity that would instill obedience, and as the months passed, most of them won his respect. As the year ended, however, nearly all of the men went home, and Washington had to train a new army for 1776. But enthusiasm for the cause remained strong, and fresh volunteers soon filled his camp.

In June 1775, fearing that the British might recruit French Canadians to attack New York or New England, Congress authorized an invasion of Canada, designed to win over the French before they could side with the British. Two forces of 1,000 men each moved northward. One, under General Richard Montgomery, took Montreal in November. The other, commanded by Colonel Benedict Arnold, advanced on Quebec through the Maine wilderness and laid siege to the city, where Montgomery joined Arnold in December. With enlistments due to expire at year's end, they decided to assault the city, partly to get maximum service out of their men and partly to inspire some of them to reenlist. Their attack on December 31 was a disaster. Nearly half of the 900 men still with them were killed, wounded, or captured. Montgomery was killed and Arnold wounded. Both were hailed as American heroes.

The colonial objective in this fighting was still to restore government by consent under the Crown. After rejecting Lord North's Conciliatory Proposition out of hand, Congress approved an Olive Branch Petition to George III on July 5, 1775, in the hope of ending the bloodshed. Moderates, led by John Dickinson, strongly favored the measure. The petition affirmed the colonists' loyalty to the Crown, did not even mention "rights," and implored the king to take the initiative in devising "a happy and permanent reconciliation." Another document written mostly by Thomas Jefferson, "The Declaration of the Causes and Necessities of Taking Up Arms," set forth the colonies' grievances and justified their armed resistance. "We have counted the cost of this contest," Jefferson proclaimed, "and find nothing so dreadful as voluntary slavery." Like the Olive Branch Petition, the declaration assured the British people "that we mean not to dissolve that Union which has so long and so happily subsisted between us." The king's refusal even to receive this moderate petition strengthened colonial radicals. It reached London along with news of Bunker (Breeds) Hill. George III replied with a formal proclamation of rebellion on August 23.

Congress began to function more and more like a government, but with few exceptions, it assumed royal rather than parliamentary powers, which were taken over by the individual colonies. Congress did not tax or regulate trade, beyond encouraging nonimportation. It passed no laws. It took command of the Continental Army, printed paper money, opened diplomatic relations with Indian nations, took over the postal service, and decided which government was legitimate in individual colonies—all functions previously performed by the Crown. In short, Congress thought of itself as a temporary plural executive for the continent, not as a legislature.

War and Legitimacy, 1775–1776

Throughout 1775, the British reacted with fitful displays of violence and grim threats of turning slaves and Indians against the settlers. When the weak British forces could neither restore order nor make good on their threats, they conciliated no one, enraged thousands, and undermined British claims to legitimacy. The navy burned Falmouth (now Portland), Maine, in October. On November 7, John Murray, earl of Dunmore and governor of Virginia, offered freedom to any slaves of rebel planters who would join his 200 redcoats. About 800 slaves mustered under his banner only to fall victim to smallpox after the Virginia militia defeated them in a single action. On January 1, Dunmore bombarded Norfolk in retaliation, setting several buildings ablaze. The patriot militia, who considered Norfolk a loyalist bastion, burned the rest of the city and then blamed Dunmore for its destruction. Overall, his campaign undermined whatever loyalist sentiment survived among Virginia planters beyond Norfolk.

British efforts suffered other disasters in Boston and the Carolinas. The greatest colonial victory came at Boston, where most of the British army lay virtually imprisoned. On March 17, 1776, after Washington fortified Dorchester Heights south of the city and brought heavy artillery (from Ticonderoga) to bear on it, the British pulled out and sailed for Nova Scotia. A loyalist uprising by Highland Scots in North Carolina was crushed at Moore's Creek Bridge on February 27, and a British naval expedition sent to take Charleston was repulsed with heavy losses in June. Cherokee attacks against Virginia failed in 1776 because they occurred after Dunmore had left and did not fit into any larger general strategy. Before spring turned to summer, patriot forces had won control of the territory of all 13 colonies. Except in East and West Florida, Quebec, and Nova Scotia, the British had been driven from the continent.

Independence

George III's dismissal of the Olive Branch Petition left moderates no option but to yield or fight. In late 1775, Congress created a committee to correspond with foreign powers. By early 1776, the delegates from New England, Virginia, and Georgia already favored independence, but they knew that unless they won over all 13 colonies, the British would have the leverage to divide them. The British attack on Charleston in June nudged the Carolinas toward independence.

Resistance to independence came mostly from the mid-Atlantic colonies, from New York through Maryland. Elsewhere, provincial congresses had supplanted the colonial assemblies in 1774 and 1775. In the middle colonies, however, both assemblies and congresses met and competed for the loyalties of the people. None of the five legal assemblies in the mid-Atlantic region ever repudiated the Crown. All of them had to be overthrown along with royal (or proprietary) government itself. The last royal governor to be driven from his post was New Jersey's William Franklin, Benjamin's natural son, who was arrested on June 19, 1776, to prevent him from summoning a new session of the regular assembly.

In the struggle for middle colony loyalties, Thomas Paine's pamphlet, *Common Sense,* became a huge success. First published in Philadelphia in January 1776, it sold more than 100,000 copies within a few months and reached more people than any other colonial tract ever had. Paine, a recent immigrant from England who had waged his own contests with the British government, wasted no reverence on Britain's mixed and balanced constitution. To him, George III was "the Pharaoh of England" and "the Royal Brute of Great Britain." Paine attacked monarchy and aristocracy as degenerate institutions and urged Americans to unite under a simple republican government of their own. "Reconciliation and ruin are nearly related," he insisted. "There is something very absurd, in supposing a Continent to be perpetually governed by an island."

The British continued to alienate the colonists. The king named Lord George Germain, a hard-liner, as secretary of state for the American colonies, and thus as war minister. Germain tried to hire 20,000 Russian mercenar-

HISTORY THROUGH FILM

1776 (1972)

1776 does not pretend to be a historical re-creation of actual events. It is, rather, an intelligent, off-beat, winning fantasy conceived by Northeasterners at the expense, mostly, of Virginians. *1776* is a screen adaptation of a musical comedy produced on the New York stage by Stuart Ostrow. Some scenes were filmed on location at Independence Hall in Philadelphia. Sherman Edwards's lively music and lyrics carry the drama from May 1776 to the signing of the Declaration of Independence on July 4.

Director Peter Hunt made his motion picture debut with *1776*. He also directed *Give 'Em Hell, Harry* in 1975 and the 1997 Broadway version of *The Scarlet Pimpernel*, along with various films made for television.

The movie opens with John Adams (William Daniels) trying to force the Second Continental Congress into a serious debate on independence. The delegates respond in a fulsome chorus, shouting: "Sit down, John! Sit down,

Directed by Peter H. Hunt. Starring William Daniels (John Adams), Virginia Vestoff (Abigail), Ken Howard (Thomas Jefferson), Howard da Silva (Benjamin Franklin), and Blythe Danner (Martha).

John! For God's sake, John, sit down!" while some of them complain about the flies and the oppressive heat. Adams stalks out and then unburdens himself to his wife, Abigail (Virginia Vestoff), who is still at home in Massachusetts. Abigail in her reply urges him to "Tell the Congress to declare / independency. / Then sign your name, get out of there / And hurry home to me."

With Benjamin Franklin's help, Adams finally achieves his goal. The film's bite derives from its determination to move Adams to the center of the story, rather than Thomas Jefferson (Ken Howard), whom Adams and Franklin (Howard da Silva) finally maneuver into writing the first draft of the Declaration, much against his will. Adams declines to write the actual Declaration because, as he explains to Franklin and Jefferson, "If I'm the one to do it / They'll run their quill pens through it. / I'm obnoxious and disliked, / You know that, Sir."

ies, who, smirked one British official, would make "charming visitors at New York and civilize that part of America wonderfully." When that effort failed, the British bought 17,000 soldiers from Hesse and other north German states. (The colonists called them all "Hessians.") To Jefferson, that action was "the last stab to [the] agonizing affection" that had once bound together the people of Britain and North America. Disturbing (although false) rumors suggested that Britain and France were about to sign a "partition treaty" dividing the eastern half of North America between them. Many congressmen concluded, some of them sadly, that only independence could counter these

dangers by engaging Britain's European enemies on America's side. As long as conciliation was the goal, France would not participate, because American success would mean restoring the British Empire to its former glory. But Louis XVI (1774–93) might well help the colonies win their independence if that meant crippling Britain.

From April to June, about 90 communities issued calls for independence. Most of them looked no further back than 1775 to justify their demand. The king had placed the colonists outside his protection, was waging war against them, and had hired foreigners to kill them. Self-defense demanded a permanent separation.

Jefferson also declines at first because he pines for Martha (Blythe Danner), his young bride, who is still in Virginia. "Mr. Adams, damn you Mr. Adams! / . . . once again you stand between me and my lovely bride. / Oh, Mr. Adams you are driving me to homicide!"

This outburst prompts the other members of the drafting committee to chorus: "Homicide! Homicide! We may see murder yet!" But instead, Jefferson accepts the burden. When he is unable to write, Adams and Franklin bring Martha to Philadelphia so that he can concentrate his energies on the Declaration.

Some of the delegates appear as mere caricatures, especially Richard Henry Lee of Virginia and James Wilson of Pennsylvania, two articulate delegates who, in real life, played important roles in creating the new republic. The film addresses the slavery question by showing South Carolina's fierce opposition to inclusion of an antislavery clause, a point on which Adams, Jefferson, and Franklin reluctantly yield. The film, like the play on which it is based, works well to deliver an articulate, entertaining taste of history.

Kobal Collection/Columbia.

1776 **is a lively musical depicting events from May 1776 to the signing of the Declaration of Independence on July 4.**

Congress finally broke the mid-Atlantic stalemate. On May 15, 1776, it voted to suppress "every kind of authority" under the British Crown, thus giving radicals an opportunity to seize power in Pennsylvania and New Jersey. Moderates remained in control in New York, Delaware, and Maryland, but they reluctantly accepted independence as inevitable. In early June, Congress postponed a vote on independence but named a committee of five, including Jefferson, John Adams, and Franklin, to prepare a declaration that would vindicate America's decision to the whole world.

On July 2, with the necessary votes in place, Congress passed Richard Henry Lee's resolution "that these United colonies are, and of right, ought to be, Free and Independent States; . . . and that all political connexion between them, and the state of Great Britain, is, and ought to be, totally dissolved." Two days later, 12 colonies, with New York abstaining for the time being, unanimously approved Jefferson's Declaration of Independence, as amended by Congress.

"We hold these truths to be self-evident, that all men are created equal, that they are endowed by their Creator with certain unalienable Rights, that among these are Life, Liberty, and the pursuit of Happiness," Congress proclaimed in what is perhaps the most famous statement ever made in American public life. Whenever "any Form of Government becomes destructive of these ends, it is the Right of the People to alter or to abolish it, and to institute new Government, laying its foundation on such principles . . . as to them shall seem most likely to effect their Safety and Happiness." The longest section of the Declaration indicted George III as a tyrant.

During the three days that Congress was proclaiming American independence, the first ships of the largest armada yet sent across the Atlantic by any European state began landing British soldiers on Staten Island. Americans celebrated the creation of their new republic at the very moment that they faced a military challenge more ominous than any they had ever confronted before.

Conclusion

Between 1763 and 1776, Britain and the colonies became trapped in a series of self-fulfilling prophecies. The British feared that without major reforms to guarantee Parliament's control of the empire, the colonies would drift toward independence. Colonial resistance to the new policies convinced the British that a movement for independence really was under way, a perception that led to even sterner measures. Until a few months before it happened, nearly all colonists denied that they desired independence, but they began to fear that the British government was determined to deprive them of their rights as Englishmen. Britain's policy drove them toward a closer union with one another and finally provoked armed resistance. With the onset of war, both sides felt vindicated. The thousands of redcoats heading toward America did not bode well for colonial liberties. When the colonists finally did leave the empire, British ministers believed that their predictions had finally come true.

Both sides were wrong. The British had no systematic plan to destroy liberty in North America, and until winter 1775–76, hardly any colonists favored independence. But the three imperial crises undermined mutual confidence and brought about what no one had desired in 1765, or even 1774—an independent American nation. Unable to govern North America, Britain now faced the grim task of conquering it instead.

SUGGESTED READINGS

The best one-volume narrative history of the coming of the Revolution remains **Merrill Jensen's *The Founding of a Nation: A History of the American Revolution, 1763–1776*** (1968). **Bernard Bailyn's *The Ideological Origins of the American Revolution*** (1967) has had an enormous impact. **Gregory Evans Dowd** provides a fresh perspective in ***War under Heaven: Pontiac, the Indian Nations, and the British Empire*** (2002).

On the three imperial crises, **Edmund S. and Helen M. Morgan's *The Stamp Act Crisis, Prologue to Revolution,*** 3rd ed. (1953, 1995) has lost none of its saliency. Nor has **John Shy's *Toward Lexington: The Role of the British Army in the Coming***

of the American Revolution (1965). **Pauline Maier's *From Resistance to Revolution: Colonial Radicals and the Development of American Opposition to Britain, 1765–1776*** (1972) and **Richard D. Brown's *Revolutionary Politics in Massachusetts: The Boston Committee of Correspondence and the Towns*** (1970) are both excellent on the process of disaffection. **David Ammerman's *In the Common Cause: American Response to the Coercive Acts of 1774*** (1974) is especially strong on the First Continental Congress and its aftermath. **David Hackett Fischer's *Paul Revere's Ride*** (1994) is a rare combination of exhaustive research and stirring prose. **Pauline Maier's**

American Scripture: Making the Declaration of Independence (1997) uses 90 local declarations of independence issued in spring 1776 to give context to Jefferson's famous text.

Important studies of internal tensions include **Gary B. Nash, *The Urban Crucible: Social Change, Political Consciousness, and the Origins of the American Revolution*** (1979); **Woody Holton's** imaginative *Forced Founders: Indians, Debtors, Slaves, and the Making of the American Revolution in Virginia* (1999); **James P. Whittenburg's** "Planters, Merchants, and Lawyers: Social Change and the Origins of the North Carolina Regulation," *William and Mary Quarterly*, 3d ser., 34 (1977): 214–38; and **Richard M. Brown, *The South Carolina Regulators*** (1963). **David Grimsted's** "Anglo-American Racism and Phillis Wheatley's 'Sable Veil,' 'Length'ned Chain,' and 'Knitted Heart,'" in **Ronald Hoffman and Peter J. Albert, eds., *Women in the Age of the American Revolution*** (1989) is a superb study of the emerging antislavery movement and the role of women in it.

AMERICAN JOURNEY ONLINE
AND
INFOTRAC COLLEGE EDITION

Visit the source collections at www.ajaccess.wadsworth.com and infotrac.thomsonlearning.com and use the Search function with the following key terms to explore documents, images, audio and video clips, articles, and commentary related to the material in this chapter.

Stamp Act	Battle of Lexington
Proclamation of 1763	Battle of Concord
Pontiac	Phillis Wheatley
William Pitt	First Continental Congress
George Grenville	Second Continental Congress
Boston Massacre	Declaration of Independence
Boston Tea Party	

GRADE AIDS

Visit the Liberty Equality Power Companion Web Site for resources specific to this textbook: http://history.wadsworth.com/murrin_LEP4e

The CD in the back of this book and the U.S. History Resource Center at http://history.wadsworth.com/u.s./ offer a variety of tools to help you succeed in this course, including access to quizzes; images; documents; interactive simulations, maps, and timelines; movie explorations; and a wealth of other sources.

Chapter 6

The Revolutionary Republic

THE PASSAGE OF THE DELAWARE
This painting by Thomas Sully, completed in 1818, celebrates George Washington's attack on the Hessian garrison of Trenton, New Jersey, on December 26, 1776, as a turning point of the Revolutionary War.

The Revolutionary War killed a higher percentage of Americans who fought in it than any other American conflict except the Civil War. It was a civil war in its own right. Neighbors were more likely to shoot at neighbors during the Revolution than they were between 1861 and 1865, when the geographical line separating the two sides would be much sharper. Twice, in 1776 and 1780, the British had a chance to win a decisive victory, but in both campaigns the Americans somehow rallied. The Americans won only by bringing in France as an ally, and France brought in Spain.

During the war, ever more Americans began to think in crude racial categories. Ideas about racial inferiority clashed sharply with claims of universal rights and human equality. As settlers and Indians, whites and blacks redefined their differences, they often resorted to racial stereotypes. Most Indians and enslaved Africans hoped that Britain would win the war.

Even as the war raged and the economy disintegrated, Americans drafted state constitutions and eloquent bills of rights that reached far beyond the racism many of them felt. They knew they were attempting something daring—the creation of a stable, enduring republic. Some European monarchies were 1,000 years old. No republic had ever lasted that long. Educated people knew a great deal about the city-states of classical Greece and about republican Rome—how they had called forth the noblest sentiments of patriotism for a time and then decayed into despotisms. Still, once Americans broke with Britain, they warmly embraced republicanism and never looked back. They were able to build viable republican governments because they grasped the voluntaristic dynamics of their society. They knew they had to restructure their governments through persuasive means. The use of force against armed fellow citizens would be self-defeating.

The war also demonstrated how weak Congress was, even after ratification of the Articles of Confederation in 1781. Congress could not pay its debts. It could not expel the British from their western military posts or defeat the Indians of the Ohio country. In the Northwest Ordinance of 1787, Congress nevertheless announced plans to create new western states and to admit them to the Union as full equals of the original 13. During that same summer, the Philadelphia Convention drafted a new Constitution for the United States. After ratification by 11 states in 1787 and 1788, it went into effect in April 1789. The federal system it created was the most distinctive achievement of the Revolutionary generation.

CHAPTER FOCUS

♦ How did American constitutionalism after 1776 differ from the British constitutional principles that the colonists had accepted and revered before 1776?

♦ Why, given that the Declaration of Independence proclaimed that all men are created equal, did most Indians and blacks, when given the chance, side with Britain?

♦ In what ways did the values shared by independent householders limit the reforms that the Revolution could offer to other Americans?

♦ The Articles of Confederation generally favored small states, especially in giving all states one vote in Congress. Why then did large states ratify quickly while three small states held up final ratification for years? The Constitution shifted power to large states. Why then did most small states ratify quickly while every large state except Pennsylvania came close to rejecting the new government?

Hearts and Minds: The Northern War, 1776–1777

Because the men who ruled Britain believed that the loss of the colonies would be a fatal blow to British power, the price of patriotism escalated once independence became the goal. Britain raised more soldiers and larger fleets than ever before and more than doubled its national debt. Americans, too confident after their early successes, staggered under the onslaught.

The British Offensive

The first setback came in Canada. The Americans, devastated by smallpox, had to retreat from Quebec when a

CHRONOLOGY	
1769	Spanish found San Diego
1775	Settlement of Kentucky begins
1776	Virginia becomes first state to adopt a permanent constitution and bill of rights • British forces land on Staten Island • Declaration of Independence adopted • Pennsylvania constitution creates unicameral legislature • British win battle of Long Island; New York City falls • Washington wins at Trenton
1777	Washington wins at Princeton • Howe takes Philadelphia • Burgoyne surrenders at Saratoga • Congress completes the Articles of Confederation
1778	Franco-American alliance negotiated
1779	Indians form confederation from the Gulf to the Great Lakes • Spain declares war on Britain • Continental dollar collapses
1780	Massachusetts constitution approved • Pennsylvania adopts gradual emancipation • British take Charleston and overrun South Carolina • Gordon riots in London discredit other reformers • Arnold's treason uncovered • Americans win at King's Mountain
1781	Continental Army mutinies • Americans win at Cowpens • Congress creates executive departments • Articles of Confederation ratified • Cornwallis surrenders at Yorktown
1782	Gnadenhutten massacre leaves 100 unarmed Indians dead
1783	Peace of Paris recognizes American independence
1785	Congress passes Land Ordinance
1786	Virginia passes Statute for Religious Freedom • Annapolis convention meets
1786–87	Shays's Rebellion in Massachusetts protests taxes and economic woes
1787	Congress passes the Northwest Ordinance • Philadelphia Convention drafts a new federal Constitution
1787–88	Eleven states ratify the Constitution
1789	First federal Congress sends Bill of Rights to the states
1799	New York adopts gradual emancipation
1804	New Jersey adopts gradual emancipation

fresh British force sailed up the St. Lawrence River in May 1776. By July, Sir Guy Carleton drove them back into northern New York, to Fort Ticonderoga on Lake Champlain. Both sides built ships to control that strategic waterway. Largely through Benedict Arnold's efforts, the Americans held, and Carleton returned to Canada for the winter.

Farther south, Richard, viscount Howe, admiral of the British fleet, and his brother General William Howe prepared an awesome striking force on Staten Island. They also acted as peace commissioners, with power to restore whole colonies to the king's peace and to pardon individual rebels. They hoped to avoid using their huge army, but when they wrote George Washington to open negotiations, he refused to accept the letter because it did not address him as "General." To do so would have recognized the legitimacy of his appointment. Benjamin Franklin, an old friend of the Howes, wrote that "it must give your lordship pain to be sent so far on so hopeless a business." Unable to negotiate, the Howes had to fight.

Since spring, Washington had moved his army from Boston to New York City, where he had about 19,000 men to face more than 30,000 redcoats and Hessians. Early successes had kept morale high among American forces and helped to sustain the *rage militaire* (warlike enthusiasm) that had prompted thousands to volunteer in 1775 and 1776, including 4,000 veterans of 1775 who reenlisted for 1776. Although some served in the Continental Army and others with state militia units, the difference between the two forces was still minimal. Neither of them gave formal military training, and the men in both served only for short terms.

Washington, who knew that civilian morale could be decisive, was reluctant to abandon any large city. Against conventional military wisdom, he divided his inferior force and sent half of it from Manhattan to Long Island. Most of the men dug in on Brooklyn Heights, just two miles from lower Manhattan, and waited for a frontal attack. The British invaded Long Island, a loyalist stronghold, and on August 27, 1776, sent a force around the American left flank through unguarded Jamaica Pass. While Hessians feinted a frontal assault, the flanking force crushed the American left and rear and sent the survivors reeling.

The Howes did nothing to prevent the evacuation of the rest of the American army to Manhattan, even though the navy could have cut them off. Instead, the British opened informal talks with several members of Congress on Staten Island on September 11, without acknowledging Congress's legality. The talks collapsed when the Americans insisted that the British recognize their independence before discussing substantive issues. Washington evacuated lower Manhattan. The British took New York City, much of which was destroyed by an accidental fire on September 21. The Howes then appealed directly to the people to lay down their arms and return to British allegiance within 60 days in exchange for a full pardon. In southern New York state, thousands complied.

In October, the Howes drove Washington out of Manhattan and Westchester and then turned on two garrisons he had left behind. On November 16, at a cost of 460 casualties, the British forced 3,000 men to surrender at Fort Washington on the Manhattan side of the Hudson River. General Nathanael Greene, a lame Rhode Island Quaker who had given up pacifism for soldiering, saved his men on the New Jersey side by abandoning Fort Lee, including all of his supplies.

The Howes probably could have destroyed Washington's army on Long Island or Manhattan, but they knew what they were doing. British victories and the American reliance on short-term volunteers were destroying Washington's army. British success seemed to prove that no American force could stand before a properly organized British army. But to capture Washington's entire army would have been a political embarrassment, leading to massive treason trials, executions, and great bitterness. Instead, Britain's impressive victories demoralized Americans and encouraged them to go home, many with their muskets. In September, 27,000 Americans stood fit for duty in the northern theater (including the Canadian border); by December, only 6,000 remained, most of whom intended to leave when their enlistments expired on December 31.

The Howes' strategy nearly worked. In December, British forces swept across New Jersey as far south as Burlington. They captured Charles Lee, next in command after Washington, and Richard Stockton, a signer of the Declaration of Independence. Several thousand New Jersey residents, including Stockton, took the king's oath. To seal off Long Island Sound from both ends, the Howes also captured Newport, Rhode Island. Many observers thought the war was all but over as sad remnants of the Continental Army crossed the Delaware River into Pennsylvania, confiscating all boats along the way so that the British could not follow them. One general believed that the time had come to "bargain away the Bubble of Independency for British Liberty well secured." Charles Carroll, another signer of the Declaration, agreed. Even Jefferson began to think about the terms on which a restoration of the monarchy might be acceptable.

The Trenton-Princeton Campaign

Washington knew he had to do something dramatic to restore morale and encourage his soldiers to reenlist. On the night of December 25, 1776, he crossed the ice-choked Delaware and marched south, surprising the Trenton garrison at dawn. At almost no cost to the attackers, 1,000 Hessians, suffering from Christmas hangovers, surrendered. The British sent their most energetic general, Charles, earl Cornwallis, south with 8,000 men to "bag the fox"— Washington and the 5,000 Continentals and militia still with him. Cornwallis caught him at Trenton near sunset on January 2 but decided to wait until dawn before attacking. British patrols watched the Delaware to prevent another escape across the river, but Washington tried

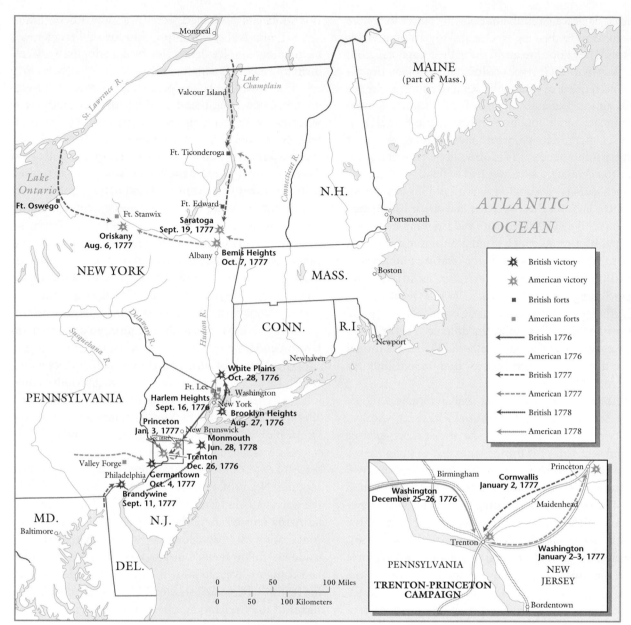

MAP 6.1   REVOLUTIONARY WAR IN THE NORTHERN STATES

This map shows the campaigns in New York and New Jersey in 1776–77, in northern New York and around Philadelphia in 1777, and at Monmouth, New Jersey, in 1778. The inset shows Washington's Trenton and Princeton campaigns after Christmas 1776.

 View an animated version of this map or related maps at http://history.wadsworth.com/murrin_LEP4e.

nothing of the kind. Leaving his campfires burning, he muffled the wheels of his wagons and guns and stole around the British left flank, heading north. At dawn, he met a British regiment just beginning its march from Princeton to Trenton. The Battle of Princeton amounted to a series of sharp clashes in which the Americans, with a 5-to-1 edge, mauled yet another outpost.

Washington's two quick victories had an enormous impact on the war, although they inspired few reenlistments. The Howes, who until January had shown a firm grasp of revolutionary warfare, blundered in not hounding Washington's remnant of an army to its destruction after Princeton. Instead, afraid that Washington might pick off their outposts one at a time, they called in their garrisons and concentrated the army along the Raritan River from New Brunswick to the sea. As the British departed, the militia returned, asking who had sworn oaths to the king. Those who had taken the oath now groveled, as the price of acceptance, or fled to British lines. The Howes had encouraged loyalists to come forward and then abandoned them to the king's enemies. The Hessians had aroused fierce hatred by looting and raping their way across New Jersey. Together, the British and the Hessians had lost the hearts and minds of the settlers. In Howe's 1777 campaign, few would be willing to declare for the Crown. The Revolution survived.

The Campaigns of 1777 and Foreign Intervention

Britain's thoughtful strategy of 1776 gave way to incoherence in 1777. The Howes again had a plan for winning the war, but it required 20,000 reinforcements that did not exist. Instead, Lord George Germain, Britain's war minister, ordered the Howes to take Philadelphia. He also sent John Burgoyne, a poet and playwright as well as a general, to Canada with orders to march his army south and link up with the garrison of New York City, commanded by Sir Henry Clinton. A small force under Barry St. Leger was to march down the Mohawk valley and threaten Albany from the west. When few reinforcements reached the Howes, they rejected an overland march to Philadelphia as too risky and decided to invade by sea, a decision that allowed Washington to shift men north to oppose Burgoyne.

The British campaign made little sense. If the point of Burgoyne's march was to move his army to New York City, he should have gone by sea. If the point was to force a battle with New Englanders, his army should have been larger. And if Howe's army—Britain's largest—would not challenge Washington's, who would?

The Loss of Philadelphia

After Trenton and Princeton, Washington recruited a virtually new army in 1777. He demanded stricter discipline and longer terms of enlistment. Congress responded by raising the number of lashes a soldier could receive from 39 to 100 and by promising a cash bonus to anyone enlisting for three years and a land bounty to anyone serving for the duration. Congress never came close to raising the 75,000 men it hoped for, but these new policies did create a solid foundation for the Continental Line, or Army. Longer terms made military training a real possibility, which in turn made the Continentals much more professional than the militia. These improvements took time, however, and did not fully take hold until 1778 and later, after the first year of service.

The Continental Army acquired its own distinctive character. The men who signed up were often poor. About half of the New Jersey Line came from families that were not on the tax rolls. Some recruits were British deserters. Short-term militia, by contrast, usually held a secure place in their communities and were more likely than the Continentals to be church members. As the 1777 recruits came in, the two northern armies, swelled by militia, grew to about 28,000 men fit for duty—17,000 in northern New York and 11,000 under Washington.

The Howes sailed south from New York with 13,000 men. When river pilots could not guarantee a safe ascent up the Delaware against American fire, the fleet sailed on to Chesapeake Bay and landed the troops at Head of Elk, Maryland, on August 24. The British marched toward Philadelphia through southeastern Pennsylvania, a region thickly populated with loyalists and neutral Quakers. Few militia turned out to help Washington, but most residents, aware of the atrocities committed by the Hessians in New Jersey, fled rather than greet the British army as liberators. The British burned many of their abandoned farmhouses.

After his experience in New York, Washington was wary of being trapped in a city. Instead of trying to hold Philadelphia, he took up strong positions at Brandywine

CONGRESS FLEEING PHILADELPHIA BY BALLOON, 1777
This British cartoon mocked Congress as it fled from the British army in the 1777 campaign. Hot air balloon flights, still experimental, were becoming a popular rage in France and Britain. The first flight across the English Channel would occur in 1783.

Creek along the British line of march. On September 11, Howe again outmaneuvered him, drove in his right flank, inflicted 1,000 casualties while suffering 500, and forced the Americans to retreat. Congress fled to Lancaster, and the British occupied Philadelphia on September 26. Eight days later, Washington surprised an outpost at Germantown, but the British rallied from early losses and drove him off.

Washington headed west to Valley Forge, where the army endured a miserable winter. There, Frederich Wilhelm, baron von Steuben, a Prussian serving with the Continental Army who would soon become a major general, devised a drill manual based on Prussian standards that he modified for use by the Americans. Through his efforts, the Continentals became far more soldierly. Other European volunteers also helped. From France came the marquis de Lafayette and Johann, baron de Kalb. The Poles sent Thaddeus Kosciuszko (a talented engineer) and Casimir, count Pulaski. De Kalb and Pulaski died in American service. By the last years of the war, perhaps one-fifth of all Continental officers were professional soldiers from Europe, who gave the American officer corps an aristocratic tone that alarmed civilians.

Saratoga

In northern New York, Fort Ticonderoga fell to Burgoyne on June 2, 1777, but little went right for the British after that. Colonel St. Leger, with 900 soldiers and an equal number of Indians, reached Fort Schuyler in the Mohawk valley in August and defeated 800 militia at Oriskany, but when Benedict Arnold approached with an additional

---

HISTORY THROUGH FILM

Mary Silliman's War (1993)

Directed by Stephen Surjik. Starring Nancy Palk (Mary Silliman), Richard Donat (Selleck Silliman), Paul Boretski (David Holly), Joanne Miller (Amelia), Elias Williams (Peter), and Allan Royal (Thomas Jones)

Strong movies about the Revolutionary War are hard to find. *Mary Silliman's War* is the rare exception. It rests on the outstanding research of Joy Day Buel and Richard Buel, Jr., on the life of an articulate woman, Mary Fish Noyes Silliman Dickinson, a woman who was widowed three times in the course of a long life (1736–1818). She left behind numerous letters and journals that make possible the reconstruction and dramatization of her life. Steven Schechter, who co-produced the film, also wrote most of the screenplay. It picks up Mary's story in 1779 when she was living in Fairfield, Connecticut, with her second husband, Gold Selleck Silliman, and their children. Selleck commanded the militia that had to respond to emergencies, and he also served as prosecuting attorney in his civilian capacity. In the northern states, the Revolutionary War had become mostly a series of destructive raids, with the British and loyalists based on Long Island and the patriots on the mainland. For good reason, both sides worried about traitors and spies in their midst.

As the film opens, Selleck is successfully prosecuting two loyalist townsmen. When they are sentenced to death, Mary objects that the war is turning neighbor against neighbor, but Selleck will not relent. In retaliation, the loyalists stage a night raid on the Silliman home, capture Selleck, and take him to New York City, which was the headquarters of the British army. The message seemed clear. If the Fairfield loyalists were to be executed, Selleck would also die. Thomas Jones, a magistrate and perhaps the most prominent loyalist living on Long Island, had known Selleck since their undergraduate days at Yale College. He acted as an intermediary. When George Washington refused to exchange a captured British officer for Selleck because he was not an officer in the Continental Army, Mary had to face an unpleasant dilemma. An American privateer, Capt. David Holly, offered to raid Long Island, capture Judge Jones, and force the British to negotiate an exchange. Mary disliked privateers and did not approve of Holly, but after the British raided Fairfield

1,000 men, the Indians fled and St. Leger withdrew to Oswego.

Burgoyne's army of 7,800, advancing from Ticonderoga toward Albany, was overwhelmed in the upper Hudson valley. As his supply line to Canada grew longer, American militia swarmed behind him to cut it. When he detached 700 Hessians to forage in the Green Mountains, they ran into 2,600 militia raised by John Stark of New Hampshire. On August 16 at Bennington, Vermont, Stark killed or captured nearly all of them. A relief force of 650 Hessians was also mauled. By the time Burgoyne's surviving sol-diers reached the Hudson and started toward Albany, the Americans under Horatio Gates outnumbered them 3 to 1. The British got as far as Bemis Heights, 30 miles north of Albany, but failed to break through in two costly battles on September 19 and October 7, with Arnold again distinguishing himself. Burgoyne retreated 10 miles to Saratoga, where he surrendered his entire army on October 17.

French Intervention

Colonial resistance delighted the French court, which was still recovering from its defeats in the Seven Years' War. In May 1776, Louis XVI authorized secret aid to the American rebels. A French dramatist, Pierre-Augustin Caron de Beaumarchais, author of *The Barber of Seville* (1775) and *The Marriage of Figaro* (1784), set up the firm of Roderique Hortalez et Compagnie to smuggle supplies through Britain's weak blockade of the American coast. (The British navy had deployed most of its ships to transport and supply the army and had few left for blockade duty.)

and burned most of the town, she consented. The rest of the story explores the consequences of this decision. Mary's deep religious convictions are emphasized throughout the film.

The screenplay telescopes the chronology of these events somewhat, invents a romance between Amelia (a servant in the Silliman household) and Captain Holly, and uses the slave Peter to illustrate the dilemmas that African Americans faced during the war. But the central plot line follows a drama that is well-documented in the historical record and exposes a side of the Revolutionary War that few Americans are even vaguely aware of. The struggle was a long, brutal conflict that brought liberty to many and equality to smaller numbers but also turned some neighbors against others.

Mary Fish Silliman at age 58, four years after the death of her second husband, Gold Selleck Silliman.

Fairfield Historical Society.

About 90 percent of the gunpowder used by Americans from 1775 to 1777 came either from captured British supplies or from abroad. Hortalez et Compagnie's 14 ships brought in most of what arrived from Europe. Without this aid, the Americans could not have continued the war.

In December 1776, Benjamin Franklin arrived in France as an agent of the American Congress. Although the French court could not officially receive him without risking a declaration of war by Britain, the 70-year-old Franklin took Parisian society by storm by adopting simple clothes, replacing his wig with a fur cap, and playing to perfection the role of an innocent man of nature. Through Beaumarchais, he kept the supplies flowing and organized privateering raids on British commerce, which the French court claimed it could not stop.

The fall of Philadelphia and Burgoyne's surrender at Saratoga persuaded the French to intervene openly. The loss of Philadelphia alarmed Foreign Minister Charles Gravier, comte de Vergennes. He feared that Congress might give up unless France entered the war. But Burgoyne's defeat convinced Louis that the Americans could win and that intervention was a good risk. Franklin and Vergennes signed two treaties in February 1778. One, a commercial agreement, granted Americans generous trading terms with France. In the other, France made a perpetual alliance with the United States, recognized American independence, agreed to fight until Britain conceded independence, and disavowed all territorial ambitions on the North American continent. Americans could not have hoped for more. Vergennes also brought Spain into the war a year later.

The Franco-American treaties stunned London. Lord North put together a plan of conciliation that conceded virtually everything but independence and sent a distinguished group of commissioners under Frederick Howard, earl of Carlisle, to present it to Congress and block the French alliance. In 1775, such terms would have resolved the imperial crisis, but in June 1778, Congress recognized them as a sign of British desperation and rejected them out of hand.

Americans now expected a quick victory, while the British regrouped. George III declared war on France, recalled the Howe brothers, and ordered General Clinton to abandon Philadelphia. Wary of being caught at sea by the French, Clinton marched overland to New York in June 1778. Washington's newly disciplined army attacked his rear at Monmouth, New Jersey, and almost drove the British

from the field, but the redcoats rallied and won a draw. Fearing a French invasion of the British Isles while most of the Royal Navy was in American waters, the British redeployed their forces on a global scale. They stood on the defensive in America through most of 1778 and 1779 and even evacuated Newport, but loyalists often raided Connecticut and New Jersey from their bases in New York City, Staten Island, and Long Island.

Spanish Expansion and Intervention

Like France, Spain was eager to avenge old defeats against Britain. The Spanish king, Charles III (1759–88), had endured the loss of Florida shortly after ascending the throne but had received Louisiana from France in compensation. Spanish rule there did not begin smoothly. In 1769, Spain suppressed a small revolt against its restrictions on trade, but in later years, when its trade policy became more favorable, Louisiana enjoyed a level of prosperity it had never before known. The province attracted 2,000 immigrants from the Canary Islands, perhaps 3,000 Acadian refugees, and other French settlers from the Illinois country, some of whom founded St. Louis in 1764. Louisiana remained heavily French even under Spanish rule.

During this time, Spaniards also moved into California, partly in response to the migration of Russian hunters into Alaska. Spain founded San Diego in 1769. In the next few years, Spaniards explored the Pacific coastline as far north as southern Alaska, set up an outpost at San Francisco Bay, and built a series of Franciscan missions under Junípero Serra. With little danger from other Europeans, Spain sent relatively few soldiers to California. In fact, its

© Alon Reininger/Woodfin Camp.

THE MISSION OF SAN CARLOS BORROMEO
The Spanish mission at Carmel, California, was founded in 1770.

California frontier duplicated many aspects of the earlier Florida missions. For the last time in the history of North America, missionaries set the tone for a whole province. As in Florida, the Indians died in appalling numbers from European diseases, and many objected to the harsh discipline of the missions.

Charles III recognized the danger of one imperial power urging the subjects of another to revolt and never made a direct alliance with the United States, but in 1779, he joined France in its war against Britain, hoping to retake Gibraltar and to stabilize Spain's North American borders. Although Spain failed to take Gibraltar, it overran British West Florida. At the end of the war, Britain ceded East Florida as well. By 1783, for the first time in a century, Spain once again controlled the entire coastline of the Gulf of Mexico.

☞ The Reconstitution of Authority

In 1776, the prospect of independence touched off an intense debate among Americans on constitutionalism. They agreed that every state needed a written constitution to limit the powers of government in terms more explicit than the precedents, statutes, and customs that made up Britain's unwritten constitution. They moved toward ever-fuller expressions of popular sovereignty—the theory that all power must be derived from the people. For four years, these lively debates sparked a learning process until, by 1780, Americans knew what they meant when they insisted that the people of a republic must be their own governors.

John Adams and the Separation of Powers

No one learned more from this process than John Adams. When Thomas Paine advocated a simple, unicameral legislature to carry out the people's will, Adams took alarm. He replied in *Thoughts on Government,* a tract that influenced the men drafting Virginia's constitution, which other states then imitated.

In 1776, Adams was already moving away from the British notion of a "mixed and balanced" constitution, in which government by King, Lords, and Commons embodied the distinct social orders of British society. He was groping toward quite a different notion, the separation of powers. Government, he affirmed, should be divided into three branches—an executive armed with veto power, a legislature, and a judiciary independent of both. The legislature, he insisted, must be bicameral, so that each house could expose the failings of the other. A free government need not embody distinct social orders to be stable. It could uphold republican values by being properly balanced within itself.

Governments exist to promote the happiness of the people, Adams declared, and happiness depends on "virtue," both public and private. Public virtue meant "patriotism," the willingness of independent householders to value the common good above their personal interests and even to die for their country. The form of government that rests entirely on virtue, Adams argued, is a republic. Americans must elect legislatures that would mirror the diversity of society. Britain had put the nobility in one house and the commoners in another, but in America, everyone was a commoner. America had no social orders. In what sense, then, could any government reflect American society? Adams came close to saying that the legislature should represent the "interests" of its citizens, but he did not face the implications of that argument. Should citizens enter politics to pursue selfish interests? What then of selfless patriotism?

In 1776, Adams knew only that the legislature should mirror society and that the structure of a republic should be more complex and balanced than what Paine advocated. Unicameral legislatures, which Georgia, Pennsylvania, and Vermont all adopted, horrified him: "A single assembly, possessed of all the powers of government, would make arbitrary laws for their own interest, execute all laws arbitrarily for their own interest, and adjudge all controversies in their own favor," he warned.

Adams had not yet found a way to distinguish between everyday legislation and the power to create a constitution, and neither had his admirers. While struggling to define what a republic ought to be, they could not escape two assumptions on which European politics rested— that government itself must be sovereign, and that it alone could define the rights of the people. A few ordinary settlers had already spotted the dangers of those assumptions. As the citizens of Concord, Massachusetts, warned in October 1776: "A Constitution alterable by the Supreme Legislative [Power] is no Security at all to the Subject against any Encroachment of the Governing part on . . . their Rights and Privileges."

This concern would eventually prompt Americans, including Adams, to invent the embodiment of popular sovereignty in its purest form, the constitutional convention. But meanwhile, in 1776, most Americans still assumed that governments must be sovereign. In the early state constitutions, every state lodged sovereign power in its legislature and let the legislature define the rights of citizens. In 1776, the American reply to Britain's sovereign Parliament was 13 sovereign state legislatures—14, with Vermont.

The Virginia Constitution

Only years of struggle exposed the inadequacy of the assumptions that the government possesses supreme authority and that the rights of the people must be defined by the government. In June 1776, Virginia became the first state to adopt a permanent, republican constitution. The provincial congress (called a "convention" in Virginia), which had assumed full legislative powers, affirmed "that the legislative and executive powers . . . should be separate and distinct from the judiciary"—but then wrote a constitution that made the legislature sovereign. The legislature chose the governor, the governor's council, and all judges above the level of justice of the peace. The governor had no veto and hardly any patronage. The lower house faced annual elections, but members of the upper house served four-year terms.

George Mason drafted a declaration of rights that the Virginia delegates passed before approving the constitution, on the theory that the people should define their rights before empowering the government. The amended text affirmed human equality but was carefully worded to exclude enslaved people. It upheld the right to life, liberty, property, and the pursuit of happiness. It condemned hereditary privilege, called for rotation in office, provided strong guarantees for trial by jury and due process, and extolled religious liberty. Legally, Virginia's bill of rights was merely a statute, with no more authority than any other law, but it was eloquent, and many states copied it.

Other states adopted variations of the Virginia model. Because America had no aristocracy, uncertainty about the proper makeup of the upper house was widespread. Some states imposed higher property qualifications on "senators" than on "representatives." In three states, the lower house elected the upper house. Maryland chose state senators through an electoral college, but most states created separate election districts for senators. Most states also increased the number of representatives in the lower house. Inland counties, which were underrepresented in most colonial assemblies, became better represented, and men of moderate wealth won a majority of seats in most states, displacing the rich, who had been winning most colonial elections. Most states also stripped the governor of patronage and of royal prerogatives, such as the power to dissolve the legislature. At this stage, only New York empowered the governor, in conjunction with a Council of Revision, to reject bills passed by the legislature.

The Pennsylvania Constitution

Many states disagreed sharply on constitutional issues. Pennsylvania learned how troubling these questions could become. Radicals there overthrew Crown, proprietor, and assembly in June 1776, rejected the leadership of both the old Quaker and Proprietary parties, and elected artisans to office in Philadelphia and ordinary farmers in rural areas. Until 1776, most officeholders had been either Quakers or Anglicans. Now, Scots-Irish Presbyterians and German Lutherans or Calvinists replaced most of them and drafted a new constitution in their own quest for legitimacy.

In 1776, Pennsylvania came closer than any other state to recognizing the constitutional dangers of resting sovereignty solely in the government—and government's arm, the legislature—rather than in the citizens. The radicals even summoned a special convention whose only task was to write a constitution. That document established a unicameral assembly and a plural executive of 12 men, one of whom would preside and thus be called "president." All freemen who paid taxes, and their adult sons living at home, could vote. Elections were annual, voting was by secret ballot, legislative sessions were open to the public, and no representative could serve for more than four years out of any seven. All bills were to be published before passage for public discussion throughout the state. Only at the next session of the legislature could they be passed into law, except in emergencies. Pennsylvania also created a Council of Censors to meet every seven years to determine whether the constitution had been violated. It could also recommend amendments.

The Pennsylvania constitution, however, never worked as planned and generated intense conflict in late 1776 as the British army drew near. In this emergency, the convention that drafted the constitution also began to pass laws, destroying any distinction between itself and the legislature it had created. Likewise, the convention and the legislatures that eventually succeeded it rarely delayed the enactment of a bill until after the voters had had time to discuss it. The war lent a sense of emergency to almost every measure. Even more alarming, many residents condemned the new constitution as illegitimate. The men driven from power in 1776 never consented to it and saw no good reason why they should accept it. The radicals, calling themselves Constitutionalists, imposed oaths on all citizens obliging them to uphold the constitution and then disenfranchised those who refused to support it, such as Quakers.

These illiberal measures gave radicals a majority in the legislature into the 1780s and kept voter turnout low in most elections, although some men (mostly leaders of the old Proprietary Party) took the oaths only to form an opposition party. Called Anticonstitutionalists at first (that is, opponents of the 1776 constitution), they soon took the name Republicans. After the war, as the disenfranchised regained the right to vote, Republicans won a solid majority in the legislature. In 1787, they won ratification of the federal Constitution, and then, in 1790, they replaced the

1776 state constitution with a new one that created a bicameral legislature and an elective governor with a veto that could be overridden. By then, Massachusetts had created the definitive model of constitution-making.

Massachusetts Redefines Constitutionalism

Another bitter struggle occurred in Massachusetts that finally generated a new consensus about what a constitution should be. After four years of intense debate, Massachusetts found a way to lodge sovereignty with the people and not with government—that is, a way to distinguish a constitution from simple laws.

In response to the Massachusetts Government Act passed by Parliament in 1774 (see chapter 5), the colonists had prevented the royal courts from sitting. In the three western counties of Worcester, Hampshire, and Berkshire, they had ousted from office a group of wealthy, intermarried families (called "river gods" in Connecticut valley towns), most of whom became loyalists. The courts remained closed until the British withdrew from Boston in March 1776, and the provincial congress moved into the city and reestablished itself as the General Court under the royal charter of 1691. The legislature then reapportioned itself. Under the old system, most towns elected a single representative. A few (such as Salem) chose two. Only Boston could elect four. The new system let towns choose representatives in proportion to population. It rewarded the older, populous eastern towns at the expense of the lightly settled western towns.

When the General Court also revived royal practice by appointing its own members as county judges and justices of the peace, the western counties exploded. Their hatred of the river gods extended to eastern gentlemen as well. Denouncing the "antient Mode of Government among us which we so much detest and abhor," they attacked the reapportionment act and refused to reopen the courts in Hampshire and Berkshire counties. Most of Berkshire's radicals were Baptists in religion and Lockeans in politics. They insisted on contracts or compacts as the basis of authority in both church and state and continued to use county conventions in place of the courts. To the Berkshire Constitutionalists, a "convention" was becoming the purest expression of the will of the people, superior to any legislature. These uneducated farmers set the pace in demanding a formal constitution for the state.

In fall 1776, the General Court asked the towns to authorize it to draft a constitution. By a 2-to-1 margin, the voters agreed, a result that reflected growing *distrust* of the legislature. Six months earlier, hardly anyone would have questioned such a procedure. The legislature drafted a constitution over the next year and then, in an unusual precaution, asked the towns to ratify it. The voters rejected it by the stunning margin of 5 to 1. Some towns objected to the lack of a bill of rights, and a few insisted that it should have been drafted by a separate convention. Several towns wanted the governor to be directly elected by the people, but most gave no reason for their disapproval. Voters angry with a particular clause were likely to condemn the whole document.

Chastened, the General Court urged the towns to postpone the question until after the war. Hampshire County reopened its courts in April 1778, but Berkshire County threatened to secede from the state unless the legislature summoned a constitutional convention. Drawing upon John Locke, these farmers insisted that they were now in a "state of nature," subject to no legitimate government. They might even join a neighboring state that had a proper constitution. At a time when Vermont was making good its secession from New York, theirs was no idle threat.

The General Court gave in, and a convention met in Boston in December 1779. John Adams drafted a constitution that the convention used as its starting point. A constitution now had to be drafted by a convention, elected for that specific purpose, and then ratified by the people. The people would then be the source of all legitimate authority.

In the four years since 1776, Adams's thoughts on the separation of powers and bicameralism had matured. Like the Virginia constitution, the Massachusetts constitution began with a bill of rights. Both houses would be elected annually. The House of Representatives would be chosen by the towns, as reapportioned in 1776. Senators would be elected by counties and apportioned according to property values, not population. The governor would be elected by the people and would have a veto that two-thirds of both houses could override. Property qualifications rose as a man's civic duties increased. Voters must own £50 of real property or £100 of personal property, representatives must have £100 in land or £200 in other property, senators must have £300 in land or £600 in total wealth, respectively, and the governor had to own £1,000 in landed property. He also had to be a Christian. For purposes of ratification only, all free adult males were eligible to vote. In accepting the basic social compact, everyone (that is, all free men) would have a chance to consent. Voters were asked to vote on each article separately, not on the document as a whole.

During spring 1780, town meetings began the ratification process. The convention tallied the results and declared that the constitution had received the required two-thirds majority, but it juggled the figures on two articles, both involving religion, to get this result. Those articles provided for the public support of ministers and required the governor to be a Christian. Baptists objected to all taxes for the support of religion, and many Protestants wanted to exclude Catholics from the governorship. The new constitution promptly went into effect and, although it has often been amended, is still in force today, making it the world's oldest written constitution. Starting with New Hampshire in 1784, other states adopted the Massachusetts model.

Confederation

The states' creativity had no counterpart in the Continental Congress, which met almost continuously during the war. Before independence, hardly anyone had given serious thought to how an American nation ought to be governed. Dozens of colonists had drafted plans of conciliation with Britain, some quite innovative, but through 1775 only Benjamin Franklin and Connecticut's Silas Deane had presented plans for an American union. Franklin's was an updated version of the Albany Plan of 1754 (see chapter 4). Another anonymous proposal appeared in an American newspaper, but none of the three plans attracted public comment. Colonists passionately debated the empire and their state governments, but not America.

Congress began discussing the American union in summer 1776 but did not produce the final text of what became the "Articles of Confederation and perpetual Union" until a year and a half later. Congress had been voting by state since the First Continental Congress in 1774. Delegates from large states favored representation according to population, but no census existed to give precise numbers, and the small states insisted on being treated as equals. As long as Britain was ready to embrace any state that defected, small states had great leverage: The tail could wag the dog. In one early draft of the Articles of Confederation, John Dickinson rejected proportional representation in favor of state equality. He enumerated the powers of Congress, which did not include levying taxes or regulating trade. To raise money, Congress would have to print it or requisition specific amounts from the states. Congress then split over how to apportion these requisitions. Northern states wanted to count slaves in computing the ratios. Southern states wanted to apportion requisitions on the basis of each state's free population.

Western lands were another tough issue. States with fixed borders pressured states with boundary claims stretching into the Ohio or Mississippi valleys to surrender their claims to Congress. Many speculators favored the land cessions. Congress could not resolve these issues in 1776.

Debate resumed after Washington's victories at Trenton and Princeton. Thomas Burke of North Carolina introduced a resolution that eventually became part of the Articles of Confederation: "Each state retains its sovereignty, freedom and independence, and every power, jurisdiction, and right, which is not by this confederation expressly delegated to the United States in Congress assembled." The acceptance of Burke's resolution, with only Virginia dissenting, ensured that the Articles would contain a firm commitment to state sovereignty. Only after Saratoga, however, was Congress able to complete the Articles. In the final version, Congress was given no power over western land claims, and requisitions would be based on each state's free population. In 1781, Congress tried to change the formula so that each slave was counted as three-fifths of a person for the purpose of apportioning requisitions, but this amendment was never ratified.

In November 1777, Congress asked the states to ratify the Articles by March 10, 1778, but only Virginia met the deadline. Most states tried to attach conditions, which Congress rejected, but by midsummer 10 had ratified. The three dissenters were Delaware, New Jersey, and Maryland—all states without western land claims who feared their giant neighbors. Maryland held out for more than three years, until Virginia agreed to cede its land claims north of the Ohio River to Congress. The Articles finally went into force on March 1, 1781.

By then, the Continental Congress had lost most of its power. Some of its most talented members, including Jefferson and Samuel Adams, had returned home to help reshape their state governments. Others, such as Washington, had taken army commands, and some, including Benjamin Franklin, John Adams, and John Jay, had departed on diplomatic assignments. The congressional effort to manage everything through committees created impossible bottlenecks. In 1776, the states had looked to Congress to confer legitimacy on their new governments, especially in the middle colonies, but as the states adopted their own constitutions, their legitimacy became more obvious than that of Congress. Even more alarming, by the late 1770s, Congress simply could not pay its bills.

☙ The Crisis of the Revolution, 1779–1783

Americans expected a quick victory under the French alliance. Instead, the struggle turned into a grim war of attrition, testing which side would first exhaust its resources or lose the will to fight. Loyalists became much more important to the British war effort, both as a source of manpower and as the main justification for continuing the war. Most settlers, argued Lord North, were still loyal to Britain. They could turn the contest around. To abandon them would be dishonorable and might lead to a bloodbath. The British began to look to the Deep South as the likeliest recruiting ground for armed loyalists. The Carolinas, bitterly divided by the regulator movements and vulnerable to massive slave defections, seemed a promising source.

The Loyalists

Most loyalists were committed to English ideas of liberty. Many of them had objected openly to the Stamp Act and other British measures but doubted that Parliament intended to undermine government by consent in the colonies. They also thought that creating a new American union was a far riskier venture than remaining part of the British empire. For many, the choice of loyalties was painful. Some waited until the fighting reached their neighborhood before deciding which soldiers to flee from and which to shoot at. The loyalists then learned a stark truth: They could not fire at their neighbors and expect to retain their homes except under the protection of the British army. The British, in turn, were slow to take advantage of the loyalists. In the early years of the war, British officers regarded the loyalists' military potential with the same disdain that they bestowed on the patriots. As the war continued, however, the loyalists, who stood to lose everything in an American victory, showed that they could be fierce soldiers.

About one-sixth of the white population chose the British side in the war, and 19,000 men joined more than 40 loyalist military units, mostly after 1778 when Britain grew desperate for soldiers. Unlike most patriots, loyalists served long terms, even for the duration, because they could not go home unless they won. By 1780, the number of loyalists under arms exceeded the number of Continentals by almost two to one. State governments retaliated by banishing prominent loyalists under pain of death and by confiscating their property.

Loyalist Refugees, Black and White

When given the choice, most slaves south of New England sided with Britain. In New England, where they sensed that they could gain freedom by joining the rebels, many volunteered for military service. Elsewhere, although some fought for the Revolution, they realized that their best chance of emancipation lay with the British army. During the war, more than 50,000 slaves (about 10 percent) fled their owners; of that total, about 20,000 were evacuated by the British. The decision to flee carried risks. In South Carolina, hundreds reached the sea islands in an effort to join the British during Clinton's 1776 invasion, only to face their owners' wrath when the British failed to rescue them. Others approached British units only to be treated as contraband (property) and to face possible resale. Most slaves who reached British lines won their freedom, however, even though the British army never became an instrument of systematic emancipation.

When the British withdrew after the war, blacks went with them, many to Jamaica, some to Nova Scotia, others to London. In the 1780s, the British even created a colony for former slaves at Sierra Leone in West Africa.

The war, in short, created an enormous stream of refugees, black and white. In addition to 20,000 former slaves, some 60,000 to 70,000 colonists left the states for other parts of the British empire. The American Revolution created 30 refugees for every 1,000 people, compared with 5 per 1,000 created by the French Revolution in the 1790s. About 35,000 settlers found their way to Nova Scotia, the western part of which became the province of New Brunswick in the 1780s. Another 6,000 to 10,000 fled to Quebec, settled upriver from the older French population,

---

AN OFFER OF FREEDOM

An American newspaper reported on British efforts to gain the support of slaves by offering them freedom.

Extract of a letter from Monmouth county, June 12.
" Ty, with his party of about 20 blacks and whites, last Friday afternoon took and carried off prisoners, Capt. Barns Smock and Gilbert Vanmater; at the same time spiked up the iron four pounder at Capt. Smock's house, but took no ammunition: Two of the artillery horses, and two of Capt. Smock' horses, were likewise taken off."
The above-mentioned Ty is a Negroe, who bears the title of Colonel, and commands a motly crew at Sandy-Hook.

National Archives of Canada/C-002001.

ENCAMPMENT OF LOYALISTS AT JOHNSTON, ONTARIO, JUNE 6, 1784
This painting by James Peachey depicts the arrival of loyalist exiles in Upper Canada.

and in 1791 became the new province of Upper Canada (later Ontario). A generous land policy, which required an oath of allegiance to George III, attracted thousands of new immigrants to Canada from the United States in the 1780s and 1790s. By the War of 1812, four-fifths of Upper Canada's 100,000 people were American-born. Although only one-fifth of them could be traced to loyalist resettlement, the settlers supported Britain in that war. In a real sense, the American Revolution laid the foundation for two new nations—the United States and Canada—and competition between them for settlers and loyalties continued long after the fighting stopped.

The Indian Struggle for Unity and Survival

Indians of the eastern woodlands also began to play a more active role in the war. For them the stakes were immense. Most of them saw that an American victory would threaten their survival as a people on their ancestral lands. Nearly all of them sided with Britain in the hope that a British victory might stem the flood of western expansion. In the final years of the war, they achieved a level of unity without precedent in their history.

At first, most Indians tried to remain neutral. The British were rebuffed when they asked the Iroquois to fight against the colonists. The Delawares and the Shawnees, defeated in Lord Dunmore's War in 1774, also stood neutral. Only the Cherokees took up arms in 1776. Short on ammunition and other British supplies, they took heavy losses before making peace and accepting neutrality. The

Chickamaugas, a splinter group, continued to resist. In the Deep South, only the Catawbas—by now much reduced in number—fought on the American side.

Burgoyne's invasion brought the Iroquois into the war in 1777. The Mohawks in the east and the Senecas in the west sided with Britain under the leadership of Joseph Brant, a literate and educated Mohawk and a Freemason. His sister, Mary Brant, emerged as a skillful diplomat in the alliance between the Iroquois and the loyalists. A minority of Oneidas and some Tuscaroras fought with the Americans. Most of them were becoming Christians under a patriot Presbyterian missionary, Samuel Kirkland. Despite severe strains during the Revolution, the Iroquois League was not shattered until after the war, when those who fought for Britain migrated to Canada.

A minority of Shawnees, led by Cornplanter, and of Delawares, led by White Eyes and Killbuck, also pursued friendly relations with the Americans. They provided intelligence to American forces and served as wilderness guides, but they refused to fight other Indians and did their best to preserve peace along the frontier. Christian Moravian Indians in the Ohio country took a similar stance. The reluctance of Indians to kill other Indians, already evident during the Seven Years' War, became even more obvious during the Revolution. Loyalists and patriots were far more willing than Indians to kill one another.

Frontier racism, already conspicuous in Pontiac's War, became more vicious than ever and made Indian neutrality all but impossible. Backcountry settlers from Carolina through New York refused to accept the neutrals on their own terms. Indian warriors, especially young men

JOSEPH BRANT, PORTRAIT BY GILBERT STUART (1786)

Brant, a Mohawk and a Freemason, was one of Britain's most effective commanders of loyalist and Indian forces. After the war, he led most of the Six Nations to Canada for resettlement.

New York State Historical Association, Cooperstown, New York.

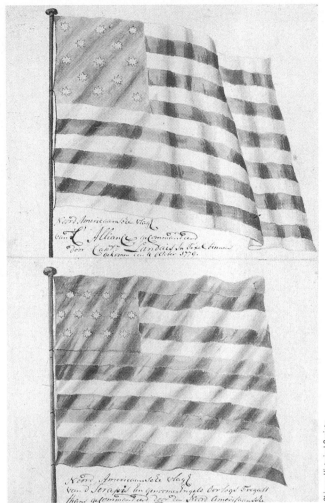

Chicago Historical Society.

AMERICAN FLAGS, 1779

Even three years after independence, no standardized version of the flag had yet taken hold. People were still experimenting with their own patterns.

strongly influenced by nativist prophets, increasingly believed that the Great Spirit had created whites, Indians, and blacks as separate peoples who ought to remain apart. Their militancy further enraged the settlers. Young white hunters, disdained by many easterners as "near savages," proved their worth as "whites" by killing Indians.

The hatred of Indians grew so extreme that it threatened to undercut the American war effort. In 1777, a Continental officer had Cornplanter murdered. In 1778, American militia killed White Eyes. Four years later, Americans massacred 100 unarmed Moravian mission Indians at Gnadenhutten, Ohio. Nearly all of them were women and children, who knelt in prayer as, one by one, their skulls were crushed with mallets. This atrocity brutalized Indians as well as settlers. Until then, most Indians had refrained from the ritual torture of prisoners, but after Gnadenhutten they resumed the custom, not as a general practice, but to punish atrocities. When they captured known leaders of the massacre, they burned them alive.

Faced with hatred, Indians united to protect their lands. They won the frontier war north of the Ohio River. The Iroquois ravaged the Wyoming valley of Pennsylvania in 1778. When an American army devastated Iroquoia in 1779 and committed many atrocities along the way, the Indians fell back on the British post at Niagara and continued the struggle. In 1779, nearly all Indians, from the Creeks on the Gulf Coast to the nations of the Great Lakes, exchanged emissaries and planned an all-out war along the frontier. George Rogers Clark of Virginia thwarted their offensive with a daring winter raid in which he captured Vincennes and cut off the western nations from British supplies. But the Indians regrouped and by 1782 drove the Virginia "long knives" out of the Ohio country.

Attrition

After 1778, George III's determination to continue the war bitterly divided his kingdom. Much of the British public doubted that the war could be won. Trade was disrupted,

MAP 6.2 WAR ON THE FRONTIER, 1777–82

Indian unity during the Revolution exceeded even what had been achieved in Pontiac's War.

thousands of ships were lost to privateers, taxes and the national debt soared, military recruits became harder to find, and a French invasion became a serious threat. Political dissent rose and included widespread demand for the reduction of royal patronage and for electoral reforms. A proposal to abolish Lord George Germain's office, clearly an attack on the American war, failed in the House of Commons by only 208 votes to 201 in March 1780. A resolve condemning the influence of the Crown carried in

April, 233 to 215. The king had great difficulty persuading North not to resign.

Desperate for men, the British army had been quietly recruiting Irish Catholics, and North supported a modest degree of toleration for English and Scottish Catholics. This leniency produced a surge of Protestant violence culminating in the Gordon riots, named for an eccentric agitator, Lord George Gordon. For a week in June 1780, crowds roared through the streets of London, smashing

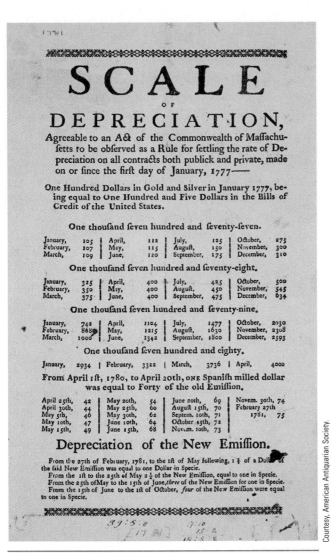

DEPRECIATION OF THE DOLLAR

By 1779, the dollar had become all but worthless.

Catholic chapels attached to foreign embassies, liberating prisoners from city jails, and finally attacking the Bank of England. The army, supported by Lord Mayor John Wilkes, put down the rioters. This spectacular violence discredited the demands for reform that had seemed on the verge of toppling North. The riots gave him one more chance to win the war.

Attrition also weakened the United States. Indian raids reduced harvests, and military levies kept thousands of men away from productive work. Loyalist raids into Connecticut and New Jersey wore down the defenders and destroyed a great deal of property. A 1779 raid on Virginia carried off or destroyed property worth £2 million. Merchants lost most of their European and West Indian markets, although a few of them made huge profits through blockade running or privateering. Average household income plunged by more than 40 percent. Even some American triumphs came at a high price. Burgoyne's surrender left Americans with the burden of feeding his army for the rest of the war. When a French fleet called at Boston, the crews devoured an alarming share of available provisions, as did the French army that landed at Newport in 1780.

These heavy demands led to the collapse of the Continental dollar in 1779–80. Congress had been printing money to pay its bills, using the Spanish dollar as its basic monetary unit. With the French alliance bolstering American credit, this practice worked reasonably well into 1778. The money depreciated but without causing widespread dissatisfaction. As the war ground on, though, the value of Continental money fell to less than a penny on the dollar in 1779. Congress agreed to stop the printing presses and to rely instead on requisitions from the states and on foreign and domestic loans, but without paper it could not even pay the army. Congress and the army had to

THE PRESENT STATE OF GREAT BRITAIN (1779?), PROBABLY BY JAMES GILLRAY

The war is going badly for weary John Bull (England). America, the Indian, is stealing liberty, the Dutch are lifting Britain's purse, and the French are attacking. Only a surly Scot is defending John Bull, and he may lose his dagger.

requisition supplies directly from farmers in exchange for certificates geared to an inflation rate of 40 to 1, well below its true rate. Many farmers, rather than lose money on their crops, simply cut back production. William Beadle, a Connecticut shopkeeper, tried to fight inflation by accepting Continental money at face value until he saw the consequences. Rather than leave his wife and children impoverished, he slit their throats and shot himself.

Continental soldiers—unpaid, ill-clothed, and often poorly fed—grew mutinous. As they became more professional through frequent drill, they also became contemptuous of civilians. The winter of 1779–80, the worst of the century, marked a low point in morale among the main force of Continentals snowed in with Washington at Morristown, New Jersey. Many deserted. In May 1780, two Connecticut regiments of the Continental Line, without food for three days, threatened to go home, raising the danger that the whole army might dissolve. Their officers barely managed to restore control. On paper, Washington had 16,000 men. His real strength was 3,600 men and not even enough horses to move his artillery.

◕ The British Offensive in the South

Sensing a unique opportunity in 1780, the British attacked in the Deep South with great success. The Revolution entered its most critical phase and nearly collapsed. "I have almost ceased to hope," Washington confessed at one point. In December 1778, a small British amphibious force had taken Savannah and had held it through 1779 against an American and French counterthrust. The British even restored royal government with an elective assembly in Georgia between 1780 and 1782. By early 1780, they were ready to move from this enclave and launch a general offensive. Their commander, General Clinton, was a cautious man who had been in charge of Britain's war effort since 1778. He had exasperated loyalist supporters by remaining on the defensive in New York City. By the time he took command in Georgia in January 1780, he had finally devised a strategy for winning the war, but he revealed its details to no one.

Clinton's New York army would invade South Carolina, take Charleston, and unleash armed loyalists to pacify the countryside. Part of the regular forces would remain in the Carolinas to deal with any other army the Americans might field. Clinton would sail with the rest back to New York and land on the Jersey coast with a force three times larger than Washington's at Morristown. By dividing this army into two columns, Clinton could break through both passes of the Watchung Mountains leading to Morristown. Washington must either hold fast and

be overwhelmed or else abandon his artillery for lack of horses and attack one of the invading columns on unfavorable terms. Either way, Clinton reasoned, the Continental Army would be destroyed. He was also negotiating secretly with Benedict Arnold for the surrender of West Point, which would open the Hudson River to British ships as far north as Albany. Arnold, who thought that Congress had never adequately rewarded his heroism, had begun trading intelligence for cash in 1779. Finally, if the French landed in Newport, as everyone expected, Clinton would then move against them with nearly his entire New York fleet and garrison. If he succeeded there too, he would have smashed every professional force in North America within a year's time. His remaining task would then be pacification, which he could pretty much leave to loyalists.

Clinton's invasion of South Carolina began with awesome successes. While the British navy sealed off Charleston from the sea, an army of 10,000 closed off the land approaches to the city and trapped Benjamin Lincoln and 5,000 defenders. Their surrender on May 12 gave Britain its largest haul of prisoners in the entire war. Clinton had already turned loose his angry, well-trained loyalists under Banastre Tarleton and Patrick Ferguson. Tarleton caught the 350 remaining Continentals at the Waxhaws near the North Carolina border on May 29 and, in what became infamous as "Tarleton's quarter," killed them all.

The calculated brutality of Britain's pacification policy was designed to terrorize civilians into submission. It succeeded for a time, but Thomas Sumter began to fight back after loyalists burned his plantation. His mounted raiders attacked British outposts and terrorized loyalists. At Hanging Rock on August 6, Sumter's 800 men scattered 500 loyalists, killing or wounding nearly half of them before Sumter's own men embarked on an orgy of looting and drinking. All participants on both sides were colonists.

Leaving Cornwallis in command of 8,300 men in South Carolina, Clinton sailed north with one-third of his Carolina army, only to learn that his plans for New Jersey had gone awry. During his absence, the leading loyalists, fearing that he would never take the initiative in the north, had persuaded Wilhelm, baron von Knyphausen, the temporary commander, to land in New Jersey with 6,000 men on the night of June 6–7, 1780. Even a force that small would pose a grave threat to Washington unless the militia came to his aid. Most loyalists hoped that the militia was so weary from the harsh winter and numerous raids that they would not turn out. Some companies had even begun to muster women. To the dismay of the British, however, the militia appeared in force on June 7.

Only then, after an inconclusive engagement, did Knyphausen learn that Clinton was on his way with his own plan of attack. The British pulled back to the coast and waited, but they had lost the element of surprise.

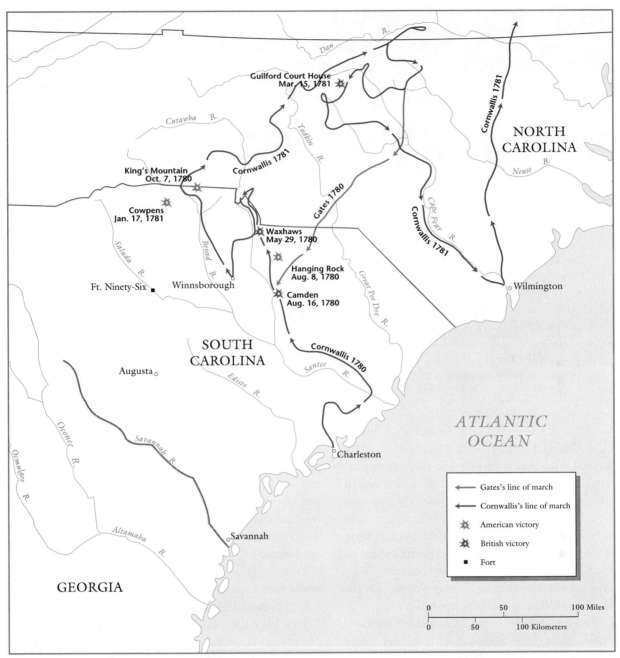

MAP 6.3 WAR IN THE LOWER SOUTH, 1780–81

British victories in 1780 nearly restored Georgia and South Carolina to the Crown, but after Guilford Court House in March 1781, the Americans regained the advantage throughout the region.

 View an animated version of this map or related maps at http://history.wadsworth.com/murrin_LEP4e.

Clinton attacked at Springfield on June 23 while loyalists set fire to the village. The battle became America's civil war in miniature. New Jersey loyalist regiments attacked the New Jersey regiments of the Continental Line, who were assisted by New Jersey militia. The defense was stout enough to persuade Clinton to withdraw to New York.

With Washington's army still intact, Clinton ignored the French when they landed at Newport. After June 1780, the British put all of their hopes on the southern cam-

paign. Even Arnold's attempt to betray West Point was thwarted in September. Clinton's agent, John André, was caught and hanged, but Arnold escaped to British lines and became a general in the British army.

Despite Sumter's harassment, Cornwallis's conquest of the Carolinas proceeded rapidly. Congress scraped together 900 tough Maryland and Delaware Continentals, put Horatio Gates, the hero of Saratoga, in command, and sent them south against Cornwallis. Bolstered by 2,000

SELF-PORTRAIT OF JOHN ANDRÉ
André, a talented amateur artist, sketched this self-portrait after he had been condemned to hang for his role in the treason of Benedict Arnold.

Yale University Art Gallery, Gift of Ebenezer Baldwin, B.A. 1808.

Virginia and North Carolina militia, Gates rashly offered battle at Camden on August 16 even though many of his men had been up all night with diarrhea after eating half-baked bread. The militia, who lacked bayonets, fled in panic at the first British charge. The exposed Continentals fought bravely but were crushed. Gates rode an astonishing 240 miles away from the scene in three days and, from Hillsborough, North Carolina, informed Congress that he had suffered "total Defeat." Two days after Camden, Tarleton surprised Sumter's camp at Fishing Creek, near the Waxhaws, killing 150 men and wounding 300.

In four months, the British had destroyed all the Continental forces in the Deep South, mauled Sumter's band of partisans, and left North Carolina open to invasion. These victories seemed to fulfill Clinton's boast that he would strip "three stripes . . . from the detestable thirteen." When the French foreign minister heard the news, he quietly inquired whether Britain would make peace, with each side keeping what it currently possessed. Cornwallis turned the pacification of South Carolina over to his loyalists, many of whom were exiles from other states, and marched confidently on to "liberate" North Carolina.

The Partisan War

Yet resistance continued. Tarleton and Sumter fought one battle to a draw. Farther west, frontier riflemen, angered by Britain's alliance with the Indians, crossed the Blue Ridge

1,800 strong to challenge Patrick Ferguson's loyalists at King's Mountain near the North Carolina border on October 7, 1780. Nearly all of the combatants on both sides were Americans. Losing only 88 men, rebel marksmen picked off many defenders, advanced from tree to tree, and finally overwhelmed the loyalists, killing 160 men, including Ferguson, and capturing 860. They shot many prisoners and hanged a dozen, their answer to "Tarleton's quarter." This victory, the first major British setback in the Deep South, stung Cornwallis, who halted his drive into North Carolina.

In October 1780, Congress sent Nathanael Greene to the Carolinas with a small Continental force. When Sumter withdrew for several months to nurse a wound, Francis Marion took his place. A much abler leader, Marion (who became known as the Swamp Fox) operated from remote bases in the swampy low country. Yet Greene's prospects seemed desperate. The ugliness of the partisan war—the mutilation of corpses, killing of prisoners, and wanton destruction of property—shocked him. The condition of his own soldiers appalled him. Yet Greene and Marion devised a masterful strategy of partisan warfare that finally wore out the British.

In the face of a greatly superior enemy, Greene ignored a standard maxim of war and split up his force of 1,800 Continentals. In smaller bands they would be easier to feed, but Greene's decision involved more than supplies. He sent 300 men east to bolster Marion and ordered Daniel Morgan and 300 riflemen west to threaten the British outpost of Ninety-Six. Tarleton urged Cornwallis to turn and crush the 1,000 men still with Greene, but Greene had no intention of engaging a superior force. Cornwallis worried that after Morgan's King's Mountain victory, he might raise the entire backcountry against the British, and so he divided his own army. He sent Tarleton with a mixed force of 1,100 British and loyalists after Morgan, who decided to stand with his back to a river at a place called Cowpens, where a loyalist kept cattle. Including militia, Morgan had 1,040 men.

Tarleton attacked on January 17, 1781. In another unorthodox move, Morgan sent his militia out front as skirmishers. He ordered them to fire two rounds and then redeploy in his rear as a reserve. Relieved of their fear of a bayonet charge, they obeyed. As they pulled back, the British rushed forward into the Continentals, who also retreated at first, then wheeled and discharged a lethal volley. After Morgan's cavalry charged into the British left flank, the militia returned to the fray. Although Tarleton escaped, Morgan annihilated his army. For the first time in the war, an American force had clearly outfought a British army without an advantage of numbers or terrain.

As Morgan rejoined Greene, Cornwallis staked everything on his ability to find Greene and crush him, precisely what he had failed to do to Washington after Trenton and Princeton four years earlier. But Greene outthought him. He placed flatboats in his rear at major river crossings and then lured Cornwallis into a march of exhaustion. In a race to the Dan River, Cornwallis burned his baggage in order to travel lightly. Greene escaped on his flatboats across the Yadkin River, flooded with spring rains, just ahead of Cornwallis—who had to march to a ford 10 miles upstream, cross the river, and then march back while Greene rested. Greene repeated this stratagem all the way to the Dan until he judged that Cornwallis was so weak that the Americans could offer battle at Guilford Court House on March 15, 1781. With militia, he outnumbered Cornwallis 4,400 to 1,900. Although the British retained possession of the battlefield, they lost one-quarter of their force and the strategic initiative. Cornwallis retreated to Wilmington to refit. He then marched north into Virginia—the seat of southern resistance, he told Clinton, the one place where Britain could achieve decisive results. Instead of following him, Greene returned to South Carolina, where he and Marion took the surviving British outposts one by one. After the British evacuated Ninety-Six on July 1, 1781, they held only Savannah and Charleston in the Deep South. Against heavy odds, Greene had reclaimed the region for the Revolution.

Mutiny and Reform

After the Camden disaster, army officers and state politicians demanded reforms to strengthen Congress and win the war. State legislatures sent their ablest men to Congress. Maryland, the last state to hold out, finally completed the American union by ratifying the Articles of Confederation.

Before any reforms could take effect, discontent again erupted in the army. Insisting that their three-year enlistments had expired, 1,500 men of the Pennsylvania Line got drunk on New Year's Day 1781, killed three officers, and marched out of their winter quarters at Morristown. General Clinton sent agents from New York to promise them a pardon and their back pay if they defected to the British, but instead the mutineers marched south toward Princeton and turned Clinton's agents over to Pennsylvania authorities, who executed them. Congress, reassured, negotiated with the soldiers. More than half of them accepted discharges, and those who remained in service got furloughs and bonuses for reenlistment. Encouraged by this treatment, 200 New Jersey soldiers at Pompton also mutinied, but Washington used New England units to disarm them and had two of the leaders executed. The army held together, but well into 1781 more loyalists were still serving with the British than Continentals with Washington.

Civilian violence, such as the "Fort Wilson" riot in Philadelphia, also prompted Congress to change policies. Radical artisans blamed the city's rich merchants for the rampant inflation of 1779 and demanded price controls as a remedy. The merchants blamed paper money. In October, several men were killed when the antagonists exchanged shots near the fortified home of James Wilson, a wealthy lawyer. Spokesmen for the radicals deplored the violence and abandoned the quest for price controls. For city dwellers rich and poor, sound money was becoming the only solution to the devastating inflation.

Congress interpreted these disturbances as a call for reform at the national level. While armed partisans were making the war more radical, politics veered in a conservative direction, toward the creation of European state forms, such as executive departments and a bank. Patriot leaders gave up efforts at price control and allowed the market to set prices and the value of money. Congress stopped printing money, abandoned its cumbersome committee system, and created separate executive departments of foreign affairs, finance, war, and marine. Robert Morris, a Philadelphia merchant, became the first secretary of finance, helped organize the Bank of North America (America's first), and made certain that the Continental Army was clothed and well fed, although it still was not paid. Congress began to requisition revenue from the states. The states began to impose heavy taxes but could never collect enough to meet both their own and national needs. Congress tried to amend the Articles of Confederation in 1781 and asked the states to accept a 5 percent duty on all imports. Most states quickly ratified the "impost" amendment, but Rhode Island rejected it in 1783. Amendments to the Articles needed unanimous approval by the states, and this opposition killed the impost. A new impost proposal in 1783 was defeated by New York in 1786.

The reforms of 1781 just barely kept a smaller army in the field for the rest of the war, but the new executive departments had an unforeseen effect. Congress had been a plural executive, America's answer to the imperial Crown. But once Congress created its own departments, it looked more like a national legislature, and a feeble one at that, because it still had no power to compel obedience. It began to pass, not just "orders" and "resolves," but also "ordinances," which were intended to be permanent and binding. It still could not punish anyone for noncompliance, which may be why it never called any of its measures "laws."

From the Ravaging of Virginia to Yorktown and Peace

Both Cornwallis and Washington believed that events in Virginia would decide the war. When a large British force raided the state in late 1780, Governor Thomas Jefferson called up enough militia to keep the British bottled up in Portsmouth, while he continued to ship men and supplies to Greene in the Carolinas. Thereafter, the state's ability to raise men and supplies almost collapsed.

In January 1781, Clinton sent Arnold by sea from New York with 1,600 men, mostly loyalists. They sailed up the James, took the new capital of Richmond almost without resistance, and gutted it. When Jefferson called out the militia, few responded. Virginia had not experienced the partisan struggles that drew men to both sides in New Jersey and the Carolinas. The state provided a different kind of test for American values under stress. The voluntaristic ethic nearly failed to get the state through a long war. Most Virginia freemen had already done service, if only as short-term militia, thousands of them in response to the 1780 raid. In 1781, they thought it was now someone else's turn. For months, there was no one else. Cornwallis took command in April, and Arnold departed for New York. But the raids continued into summer, sweeping as far west as Charlottesville, where Tarleton, who had recruited a

new legion since Cowpens, scattered the Virginia legislature and came within minutes of capturing Jefferson on June 3. Many of Jefferson's slaves greeted the British as liberators. Washington sent Lafayette with 1,200 New England and New Jersey Continentals to contain the damage, while Cornwallis, on Clinton's orders, withdrew to Yorktown.

At last, Washington saw an opportunity to launch a major strike. He learned that a powerful French fleet under François, comte de Grasse, would sail with 3,000 soldiers from Saint-Domingue on August 13 for Chesapeake Bay. Cooperating closely with the French army commander, Jean Baptiste Donatien, comte de Rochambeau, Washington sprang his trap. Rochambeau led his 5,000 soldiers from Newport to the outskirts of New York, where they joined Washington's 5,000 Continentals. After feinting an attack to freeze Clinton in place, Washington led the combined French and American armies 400 miles south to tidewater Virginia, where they linked up with Lafayette's Americans and the other French army brought by de Grasse. After de Grasse's fleet beat off a British relief force at the Battle of the Capes on September 5, Washington cut off all retreat routes and besieged Cornwallis in Yorktown. On October 19, 1781, Cornwallis surrendered his entire army of 8,000 men. Many escaped slaves had died during the siege, most from smallpox, but Virginia planters hovered nearby to reclaim the survivors.

Yorktown brought down the British government in March 1782. Lord North resigned, and George III even drafted an abdication message, although he never released it. The new ministry, committed to American independence as the price of peace, continued to fight the French

"THE AMERICAN RATTLE SNAKE"
This 1782 cartoon celebrated the victory of Yorktown, the second time in the war that an entire British army had surrendered to the United States.

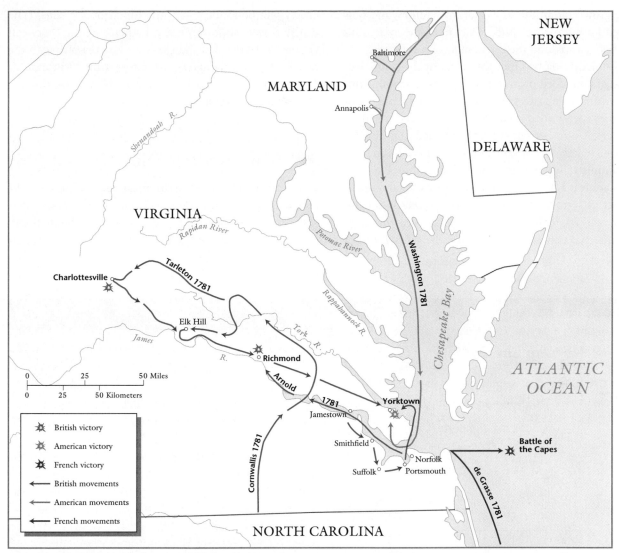

MAP 6.4 VIRGINIA AND THE YORKTOWN CAMPAIGN
After the British ravaged much of Virginia, Washington and a French fleet and army were able to trap Lord Cornwallis at Yorktown, force his surrender, and guarantee American independence.

in the Caribbean and the Spanish at Gibraltar, but the British evacuated Savannah and Charleston and concentrated their remaining forces in New York City.

Contrary to the French Treaty of 1778, and against Franklin's advice, John Jay and John Adams opened secret peace negotiations in Paris with the British. They won British recognition of the Mississippi, but without New Orleans, as the western boundary of the new republic. New Englanders retained the right to fish off Newfoundland. The treaty recognized the validity of prewar transatlantic debts, and Congress promised to urge the states to restore confiscated loyalist property. These terms gave American diplomats almost everything they could have desired. After the negotiations were far advanced, the Americans told Vergennes, the French foreign minister,

what they were doing. He feigned indignation, but the threat of a separate peace gave him the leverage he needed with Spain. Spain stopped demanding that France keep fighting until Gibraltar surrendered. The Treaty of Paris, although not ratified for months, ended the war in February 1783.

Western Indians were appalled to learn that the treaty gave their lands to the United States. They had not been conquered, whatever European diplomats might say. Their war for survival continued with few breaks into 1795.

Congress still faced ominous problems. In March 1783, many Continental officers threatened a coup d'état unless Congress granted them generous pensions. Washington, confronting them at their encampment at Newburgh, New York, fumbled for his glasses and remarked,

"I have grown old in the service of my country, and now find that I am growing blind." Tears filled the eyes of his comrades in arms, and the threat of a coup vanished.

In Philadelphia two months later, unpaid Pennsylvania soldiers marched on the statehouse where both Congress and the state's executive council sat. Ignoring Congress, they demanded that Pennsylvania redress their grievances. Congress felt insulted and left the city for Princeton, where it reconvened in Nassau Hall. Its archives and administrative departments remained in Philadelphia. "I confess I have great apprehensions for the union of the states," wrote Charles Thomson, secretary to Congress since 1774, "& begin to fear that America will experience internal convulsions, and that the fabrick of her liberty will be stained with the blood of her sons." The British threat, Thomson knew, had created the American Union. He feared that the Union would dissolve with the return of peace. Congress moved on from Princeton to Annapolis and eventually settled in New York, but the Union's survival remained uncertain.

A Revolutionary Society

Independence transformed American life. The biggest winners were free householders, who gained enormous benefits from the democratization of politics and the chance to colonize the Great West. Besides the loyalists, the biggest

MUSICAL LINK TO THE PAST

No King but God!

Composer: William Billings
Title: "Independence" (1778)

William Billings, America's most important musical figure during its first two decades of independence, was the first native-born composer to spend all of his time on music, a luxury both then and now. Billings was also the first person, and perhaps the only one, to compose songs inspired by the Revolution. While John Dickinson and Thomas Jefferson established political justifications for the American break with Great Britain, Billings in "Independence" offered a religious justification: "To the King they shall sing hallelujah / And all the continent shall sing: down with this earthly King / No King but God." Billings insisted that Americans were not impetuous in declaring independence because they exhibited a great respect for God and proper social institutions. In this view, Britain and King George III placed themselves in a position above God by depriving Anglo-Americans of their rights as British subjects. For a new country that already had a long history of passionate commitment to religion, this argument for American independence was probably quite convincing.

Although the idea that Americans could create art equal to or of more worth than Europeans would not become commonplace until the 20th century, Billings viewed himself as a serious American artist. Billings was also the first major American composer to lobby for a copyright law. The lack of a copyright law cost Billings a fortune when his defiant song "Chester" became the most popular song of the American Revolution, and numerous publishers bootlegged his song without permission. Under pressure from Billings and a similarly plagiarized Noah Webster (the author of America's first dictionary), Congress passed its first copyright law in 1790. Because it failed to provide any U.S. protection for foreign artists and composers, however, American publishers released and promoted floods of European works on which they did not have to pay royalties. Because Congress was unable to protect what is now known as intellectual property, William Billings, the author of "Independence," did not make a living commensurate to the musical contribution he made to his country.

1. Early American artists such as William Billings had to decide what the role of an artist in a democracy should be. Some American observers at the time and in the 19th century believed that creating art represented a frivolous and decadent occupation in the United States. Should artists in a democracy seek to create works that promote the goals and aspirations of the populace as a whole, or should they cultivate a more personal expression?

2. Do you think that today's practice of downloading music through the Internet presents a similar ethical problem to the unauthorized publishing of Billings's works that occurred during the early national period?

Listen to an audio recording of this music on the Musical Links to the Past CD.

losers were Indians, who continued to resist settler expansion. Many slaves won their freedom, and women struggled for greater dignity. Both succeeded only when their goals proved compatible with the ambitions of white householders.

Religious Transformations

During the Revolution, the Anglican Church, with George III as its "supreme head," became vulnerable. Although most Anglican clergymen supported the Revolution or remained neutral, an aggressive loyalist minority stirred the wrath of patriots. Religious dissenters disestablished the Anglican Church in every southern state. They deprived it of its tax support and other privileges, such as the sole right to perform marriages. In 1786, Virginia passed Thomas Jefferson's eloquent Statute for Religious Freedom, which declared that "God hath created the mind free" and that efforts to use coercion in matters of religion "tend only to beget habits of hypocrisy and meanness." In Virginia, church attendance and the support of ministers became voluntary activities. Religious liberty and the pluralism it created became not just tolerated but admired.

INTERIOR OF TOURO SYNAGOGUE IN NEWPORT, RHODE ISLAND

The synagogue shown here presents the best surviving example of Jewish artistic taste in 18th-century America.

Other states moved more slowly. In New England (except in Rhode Island), the Congregational churches were established by law. They had strongly supported the Revolution and were less vulnerable to attack. Their ministers' salaries continued to be paid out of public taxes, although lawful dissenters, such as Baptists, could insist that their church taxes go to their own clergy. The Congregational Church exercised other public or quasi-public functions, especially on thanksgiving, fast, and election days. Disestablishment did not become complete until 1818 in Connecticut and 1833 in Massachusetts.

Although most states still restricted officeholding to Christians or Protestants, many people were coming to regard the coercion of anyone's conscience as morally wrong. Jews and Catholics both gained from the new atmosphere of tolerance. When Britain recognized the Catholic Church in the Quebec Act of 1774, most Protestants had shuddered with anxiety, but in 1790, when John Carroll of Maryland became the first Roman Catholic bishop in the United States, hardly anyone protested. Before independence, an Anglican bishop had been an explosive issue in several colonies, but in the 1780s, the Church of England reorganized itself as the Protestant Episcopal Church and quietly began to consecrate its own bishops. Both Episcopalians and Presbyterians paid homage to republican values by adopting written constitutions for their churches.

The First Emancipation

The Revolution freed tens of thousands of slaves, but it also gave new vitality to slavery in the region that people were beginning to call "the South." Within a generation, slavery was abolished in the emerging "North." Race became a defining factor in both regions. In the South, most blacks remained slaves. In the North, they became free but not equal. The independent householder and his voluntaristic ethic remained almost a white monopoly.

Many slaves freed themselves. The British army enabled more than half the slaves of Georgia and perhaps one-quarter of those in South Carolina to win their freedom. A similar process was under way in Virginia in 1781, only to be cut off at Yorktown. Hundreds of New England slaves won their freedom through military service. They announced what they were fighting for in the surnames they chose. Jeffrey Liberty, Cuff Liberty, Dick Freeman, and Jube Freeman served in one Connecticut regiment. After the Massachusetts bill of rights proclaimed that all people were "born free and equal," Elizabeth (Bett) Freeman sued her master in 1781 and won her liberty. Thereafter, most of the slaves in Massachusetts and New Hampshire simply walked away from their masters.

Elsewhere, legislative action was necessary. Pennsylvania led the way in 1780 with the modern world's first gradual emancipation statute. It declared that all children born to Pennsylvania slaves after a given date would become free at age 28. In other words, slaves, not masters or taxpayers, had to pay the costs of their own emancipation. This requirement left them unable to compete on equal terms with free whites, who usually entered adult life with inherited property. Some masters shipped their slaves south before the moment of emancipation, and some whites kidnapped freedmen and sent them south. The Pennsylvania Abolition Society was organized largely to fight these abuses. By 1800, Philadelphia had the largest community of free blacks in America, with their own churches and other voluntary societies.

The Pennsylvania pattern took hold, with variations, in most other northern states until all of them had made provision for emancipation. Where slaves constituted more than 10 percent of the population, as in southern New York and northeastern New Jersey, slaveholders' resistance delayed legislation for years. New York yielded in 1799, and finally so did New Jersey in 1804.

In the upper South, many Methodists and Baptists supported emancipation in the 1780s, only to retreat in later years. Maryland and Virginia authorized the manumission of individual slaves. By 1810, more than one-fifth of Maryland's slaves had been freed, as had 10,000 of Virginia's 300,000 slaves, including more than 300 freed under Washington's will after he died in 1799. But slaves were essential to the plantation economy and were usually their masters' most valuable asset. In the South, emancipation would have amounted to a social revolution and the impoverishment of the planter class. Planters supported the Christianization of their slaves and other humane reforms, but they resisted emancipation, especially with the rise of cotton as a new cash crop after the war. Tragically, the slaves contributed a great deal to the acceptance of cotton as a new staple, which in turn guaranteed that their children and grandchildren would remain in bondage. Cut off from British textiles during the war, South Carolina slaves insisted on growing cotton as a substitute. Their owners quickly recognized the enormous potential of that crop.

Maryland and Virginia, where population growth among the slaves exceeded what the tobacco economy could absorb, banned the Atlantic slave trade, as had all states outside the Deep South. Georgia and South Carolina, to make good their losses during the war and to meet the demand for cotton after 1790, reopened the Atlantic slave trade. South Carolina imported almost 60,000 more Africans before Congress prohibited that traffic in 1808.

The Challenge to Patriarchy

Nothing as dramatic as emancipation altered relations between the sexes, although subtle changes did occur. With the men away fighting, many women were left in charge of the household, sometimes with interesting consequences. "I hope you will not consider yourself as commander in chief of your own house," Lucy Knox warned her soldier husband, Henry, in 1777, "but be convinced . . . that there is such a thing as equal command." Although some women acquired new authority, nearly all of them had to work harder to keep their households functioning. The war cut them off from most European consumer goods. Household manufactures, mostly the task of women, filled the gap. Women accepted these duties without insisting on broader legal or political rights, but soaring food prices made many women assertive. In numerous food riots through 1779, women tried to force merchants to lower prices or stop hoarding grain.

Attitudes toward marriage were also changing. The common-law rule of coverture (see chapter 4) still denied wives any legal personality, but some of them, citing their own support of the Revolution, persuaded state governments not to impoverish them by confiscating the property of their loyalist husbands. Many writers insisted that good marriages rested on mutual affection, not on property settlements. In portraits of wealthy northeastern families, husbands and wives were beginning to appear as equals. Parents were urged to respect the personalities of their children and to avoid severe discipline. Traditional reverence for the elderly was giving way to an idealization of youth and energy.

In 1780, to relieve the sufferings of Continental soldiers, Esther de Berdt Reed organized the Philadelphia Ladies Association, the first women's society in American history to take on a public role. Although few women yet demanded equal political rights, the New Jersey Constitution of 1776 let them vote if they headed a household (usually as a widow) and paid taxes. This right was revoked in 1807.

Especially in the Northeast, more women learned to read and write. Philosophers, clergymen, and even popular writers were beginning to treat women as morally superior to men, a sharp reversal of earlier teachings. The first female academies were founded in the 1790s. By 1830, nearly all native-born women in the Northeast had become literate. The ideal of the "republican wife" and the "republican mother" took hold, giving wives and mothers an expanding educational role within the family. They encouraged diligence in their husbands and patriotism in their sons. The novel became a major cultural form in the United States. Its main audience was female, as were many

WOMEN VOTING IN LATE 18TH-CENTURY NEW JERSEY

Alone among the 13 states, the New Jersey constitution of 1776 permitted women to vote if they were the heads of their households, a category that included mostly widows. This privilege was revoked in 1807.

of the authors. Novels cast women as central characters and warned young women to beware of suitors motivated only by greed or lust.

Western Expansion, Discontent, and Conflict with Indians

Westward expansion continued during the Revolutionary War. With 30 axmen, Daniel Boone, a North Carolina hunter, hacked out the Wilderness Road from Cumberland Gap to the Kentucky bluegrass country in early 1775. The first settlers called Kentucky "the best poor man's country" and challenged the speculative Transylvania Company, which claimed title to the land. They insisted that the land should belong to those who tilled its soil, not to nonresidents with paper titles from governments far to the east in Virginia or London.

Although few Indians lived in Kentucky, it was the favorite hunting ground of the Shawnees and other nations. Their raids often prevented the settlers from planting crops. The settlers hunted and put up log cabins against the inside walls of large rectangular stockades, 10 feet high and built from oak logs. At each corner, a blockhouse with a protruding second story permitted the defenders to fire along the outside walls. Three of these Kentucky stations were built—at Boonesborough, St.

Asaph, and Harrodsburg. They withstood Indian attacks until late in the war.

Because of the constant danger, settlement grew slowly at first. In 1779, when George Rogers Clark's victory at Vincennes provided a brief period of security, thousands of settlers moved in. After 1780, however, the Indians renewed their attacks, this time with British allies who could smash the stockades with artillery. Kentucky lived up to its old Indian reputation as the "dark and bloody ground." Only a few thousand settlers stuck it out until the war ended, when they were joined by swarms of newcomers. Speculators and absentees were already trying to claim the best bluegrass land. The Federal Census of 1790 listed 74,000 settlers and slaves in Kentucky and about half that many in Tennessee, where the Cherokees had ceded a large tract after their defeat in 1776. These settlers thrived both because few Indians lived there and because British and Spanish raiders found it hard to reach them.

To the south and north of this bulge, settlement was much riskier. After the war, Spain supplied arms and trade goods to Creeks, Cherokees, Choctaws, and Chickasaws who were willing to resist Georgia's attempt to settle its western lands. North of the Ohio River, where confederated Indians had won their military struggle, Britain refused to withdraw its garrisons and traders from Niagara,

Missouri Historical Society.

DANIEL BOONE PROTECTS HIS FAMILY

During and after the Revolution, family portraits in the Northeast began to place husband and wife on an equal level and to emphasize their role in nurturing children. But in the West, the husband and father remained the protector of his family. This 1874 lithograph was copied from an 1852 statue by Horatio Greenough that was meant to demonstrate, in the artist's words, "the superiority of the white man" over all other races. Contemporaries assumed that the central figure was Boone, who performs heroic deeds while his wife and child cower in fear.

Detroit, and a few other posts, even though, according to the Treaty of Paris, those forts now lay within the boundaries of the United States. To justify their refusal, the British pointed to Congress's failure to honor America's obligations to loyalists and British creditors under the treaty. When small groups of Indians sold large tracts of land to Georgia, Pennsylvania, and New York, as well as to Congress, the Indian nations repudiated those sales and, supported by either Spain or Britain, continued to resist into the 1790s.

During the Revolutionary War, many states and Congress had recruited soldiers with promises of land after the war ended, and now they needed Indian lands to fulfill these pledges. The few Indian nations that had supported the United States suffered the most. In the 1780s, after Joseph Brant led most of the Iroquois north to Canada, New York confiscated much of the land of the friendly Iroquois who stayed. South Carolina dispossessed the Catawbas of most of their ancestral lands. The states had a harder time seizing the land of hostile Indians, who usually had Spanish or British allies.

Secessionist movements arose in the 1780s when neither Congress nor eastern state governments seemed able to solve western problems. Some Tennessee settlers seceded from North Carolina and for a time maintained a separate state called Franklin. Separatist sentiment also ran strong in Kentucky. Even the settlers of western Pennsylvania thought of setting up on their own after Spain closed the Mississippi to American traffic in 1784. James Wilkinson explored the possibility of creating an independent republic west of the Appalachians under Spanish protection. When Congress refused to recognize Vermont's independence from New York, even the radical Green Mountain Boys sounded out Canadian officials about readmission to the British empire as a separate province.

The Northwest Ordinance

After Virginia ceded its land claims north of the Ohio River to Congress in 1781, other states followed suit. Jefferson offered a resolution in 1784 that would have created 10 or more new states in this Northwest Territory. Each state could adopt the constitution and laws of any of the older states and, when its population reached 20,000, could be admitted to the Union on equal terms with the original 13. The possibility that the northwestern states, plus Kentucky, Tennessee, and Vermont, might outvote the old 13 made Congress hesitate, and Jefferson's resolution was never implemented. In the Land Ordinance of 1785, however, Congress authorized the survey of the Northwest Territory and its division into townships six miles square,

each composed of 36 "sections" of 640 acres. Surveyed land would be sold at auction starting at a dollar an acre. Alternate townships would be sold in sections or as a whole, to satisfy settlers and speculators, respectively.

In July 1787, while the Constitutional Convention met in Philadelphia, Congress (sitting in New York) returned to the problem of governing the Northwest Territory. By then, Massachusetts veterans were organizing the Ohio Company under Manassah Cutler to obtain a huge land grant from Congress. Cutler joined forces with William Duer, a New York speculator who was organizing the Scioto Company. Together they pried from Congress 1.5 million acres for the Ohio Company veterans and an option on 5 million more acres, which the Ohio Company assigned to the Scioto Company. The Ohio Company agreed to pay Congress two installments of $500,000 in depreciated securities. To meet the first payment, Duer's backers lent Cutler's $200,000. Once again, speculators, rather than settlers, seemed to be winning the West.

In July, Congress passed the Northwest Ordinance of 1787 to provide government for the region. Rejecting Jefferson's earlier goal of 10 or more states, the ordinance authorized the creation of from 3 to 5 states, to be admitted to the Union as full equals of the original 13. The ordinance thus rejected colonialism among white people except as a temporary phase through which a "territory" would pass on its way to statehood. Congress would appoint a governor and a council to rule until population reached 5,000. At that point, the settlers could elect an assembly empowered to pass laws, although the governor (obviously modeled on earlier royal governors) had an absolute veto. When population reached 60,000, the settlers could adopt their own constitution and petition Congress for statehood. The ordinance protected civil liberties, made provision for public education, and prohibited slavery within the region.

Southern delegates all voted for the Northwest Ordinance despite its antislavery clause. They probably hoped that Ohio would become what Georgia had been in the 1730s, a society of armed free men able to protect vulnerable slave states, such as Kentucky, from hostile invaders. The Ohio valley was the republic's most dangerous frontier. Southern delegates also thought that most settlers would come from Maryland, Virginia, and Kentucky. Even if they could not bring slaves with them, they would have southern loyalties. New Englanders, by contrast, were counting on the Ohio Company to lure their own veterans to the region.

Finally, the antislavery clause may have been part of a larger Compromise of 1787, involving both the ordinance and the clauses on slavery in the federal Constitution. The

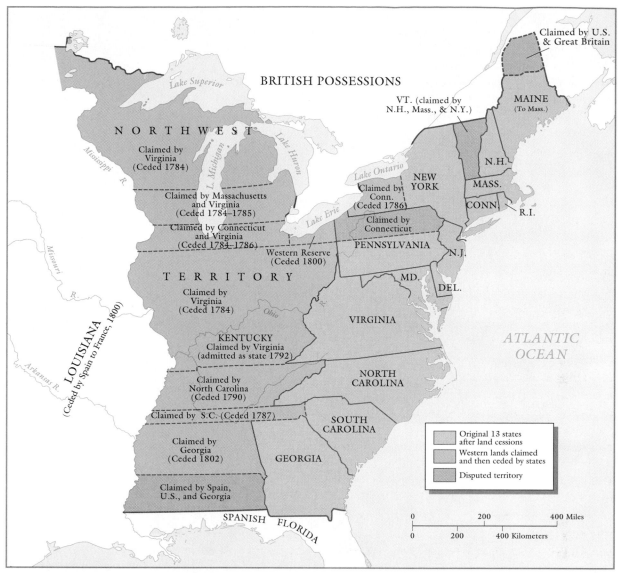

MAP 6.5 WESTERN LAND CLAIMS DURING THE REVOLUTION
One of the most difficult questions that Congress faced was the competing western land claims of several states. After Virginia ceded its claims north of the Ohio to Congress, other states followed suit, creating the national domain and what soon became the Northwest Territory.

 View an animated version of this map or related maps at http://history.wadsworth.com/murrin_LEP4e.

Philadelphia Convention permitted states to count three-fifths of their slaves for purposes of representation and direct taxation. The antislavery concession to northerners in the ordinance was made at the same time that southern states won this concession in Philadelphia. Several congressmen were also delegates to the Constitutional Convention and traveled back and forth between the two cities while these decisions were being made. They may have struck a deal.

Congress had developed a coherent western policy. After 1787, only the Indians, who drove away hundreds of squatters, stood in the way. Federal surveyors risked their lives in Ohio, and few buyers stepped forward when the first townships were offered for sale in late 1787. Yet by 1789, the Ohio Company had established the town of Marietta, Kentuckians had founded a town that would soon be called Cincinnati, and tiny outposts had been set up at Columbia and Gallipolis. But without massive help from the new federal government, the settlers had little chance of overcoming stout Indian resistance.

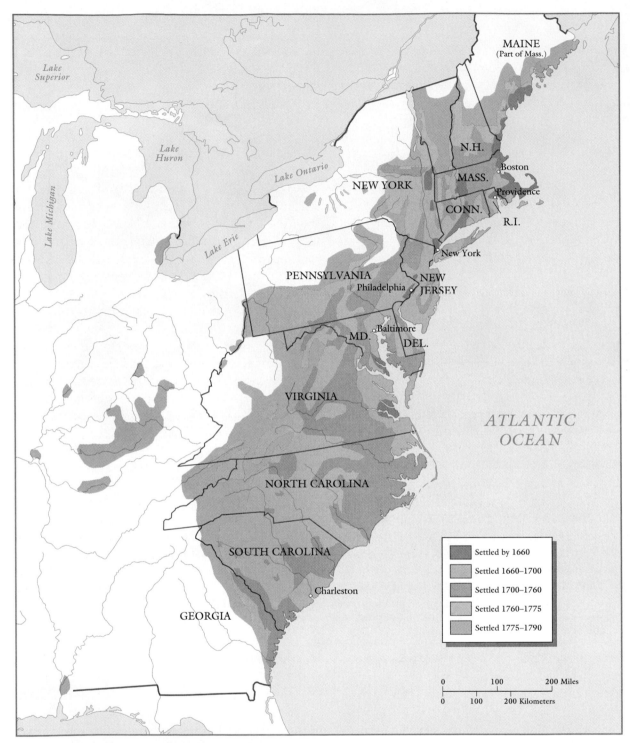

MAP 6.6   ADVANCE OF SETTLEMENT TO 1790

Between 1760 and 1790, America's population grew from nearly 1.6 million to almost 4 million. The area of settlement was spreading west of Pittsburgh and into much of Kentucky and parts of Tennessee.

 View an animated version of this map or related maps at http://history.wadsworth.com/murrin_LEP4e.

A More Perfect Union

The 1780s were difficult times. The economy failed to rebound, debtors fought creditors, and state politics became bitter and contentious. Out of this ferment arose the demand to amend or even replace the Articles of Confederation.

Commerce, Debt, and Shays's Rebellion

In 1784, British merchants flooded American markets with exports worth £3.7 million, the greatest volume since 1771. But Americans could not pay for them. Exports to Britain that year were £750,000—less than 40 percent of the £1.9 million of 1774, the last year of peace. When Britain invoked the Navigation Acts to close the British West Indies to American ships (but not to American goods), indirect returns through this once profitable channel also faltered. Trade with France closed some of the gap, but because the French could not offer the long-term credit that the British had provided, it remained disappointing. The American economy entered a depression that lifted only slightly in 1787 and 1788 before the strong recovery of the 1790s. British imports fell by 40 percent in 1785. Exports rose to almost £900,000 but remained far below prewar levels. Private debts became a huge social problem that the states, buried under their own war debts, could not easily mitigate. Merchants, dunned by British creditors, sued their customers, many of whom could not even pay their taxes. Farmers, faced with the loss of their crops, livestock, and even their farms, resisted foreclosures and looked to their state governments for relief.

About half of the states issued paper money in the 1780s, and many passed stay laws to postpone the date on which a debt would come due. Massachusetts, which remembered its fierce conflicts over paper money before 1750 (see chapter 4), rejected both options and raised taxes to new highs. In 1786, many farmers in Hampshire County took matters into their own hands. Crowds gathered to prevent the courts from conducting business, much as patriots had done against the British in 1774. Governor James Bowdoin insisted that acts of resistance that had been appropriate against a tyrannical monarch were unacceptable in a government elected by the people. But in early 1787, the protestors, loosely organized under a Continental Army veteran, Captain Daniel Shays, attacked the federal arsenal at Springfield. An army of volunteers under Benjamin Lincoln marched west with artillery and scattered the Shaysites. Even so, Shaysites won enough seats in the May assembly elections to pass a stay law. In Massachusetts, Shays's Rebellion converted into nationalists many gentlemen and artisans who until then had opposed strengthening the central government.

Cosmopolitans versus Localists

The tensions racking Massachusetts surfaced elsewhere as well. Crowds of debtors in other states closed law courts or even besieged the legislature. State politics reflected a persistent cleavage between "cosmopolitan" and "localist" coalitions. Merchants, professional men, urban artisans, commercial farmers, southern planters, and former Continental Army officers made up the cosmopolitan bloc. They looked to energetic government, both state and continental, to solve their problems. They favored aggressive trade policies, hard money, payment of public debts, good salaries for executive officials and judges, and leniency to returning loyalists. The localists were farmers, rural artisans, and militia veterans who distrusted those policies. They demanded paper money and debtor relief. They supported generous salaries for representatives, so that ordinary men could serve, which cosmopolitans resisted.

In most states, localists defeated their opponents most of the time. They destroyed the feudal revival (see chapter 5) by confiscating the gigantic land claims of the Granville District, the Fairfax estate, the Calvert and Penn proprietaries, and the manorial estates of New York loyalists. (Because their owners were patriots, Rensselaerswyck and Livingston Manor survived to become the site of agrarian violence into the 1840s, when the manors were finally abolished.) Except in Vermont, localists were much less adept at blocking the claims of land speculators, some of whom put together enormous tracts. Yet cosmopolitans lost so often that many of them despaired of state politics and looked to a strengthened central government for relief.

Congress faced its own fiscal problems. Between October 1781 and February 1786, it requisitioned $15.7 million from the states but received only $2.4 million. Its annual income had fallen to $400,000 at a time when interest on its debt approached $2.5 million and when the principal on the foreign debt was about to come due. Requisitions were beginning to seem as inefficient as George Grenville had proclaimed them to be when he proposed the Stamp Act.

Foreign relations also took an ominous turn. Without British protection, American ships that entered the Mediterranean risked capture by Barbary pirates and the enslavement of their crews. In 1786, Foreign Secretary John Jay

An American Views the French Revolution

Gouverneur Morris, the youngest son in one of provincial New York's most prominent families, was born in 1752 at the manor of Morrisania in what is now the Bronx. He attended the Academy of Philadelphia and then King's College (now Columbia University), studied law, and soon prospered in his profession. As the revolutionary crisis unfolded, he stood for conciliation until the fighting began and then sided with the patriots. During the drafting of New York's 1777 constitution, he advocated the abolition of slavery and toleration of Roman Catholics, but on other issues he was quite conservative. He favored a strong executive with an absolute veto, for example. In 1780, he broke his ankle, and his leg was amputated below the knee. Thereafter, he was as famous for his oaken stump as for his oratory. In 1787, just before departing for the Philadelphia Convention, he purchased Morrisania from an older brother.

At the Convention, he opposed the three-fifths clause, warned against what a later generation would call the "slave power," supported the creation of a powerful executive, and became perhaps the strongest advocate of the electoral college. But his most significant contribution came when the Committee on Style asked him to take the resolves that had been approved by the delegates and turn them into a single document, a constitution. He compressed the delegates' 23 articles into seven and wrote nearly all of the preamble, including "We the people of the United States," rather than enumerate the separate states as in the Articles of Confederation.

In December 1788, he sailed for France on business and landed in a kingdom that was about to explode in the most momentous revolution that Europe had ever seen. He became prominent enough to correspond directly with Louis XVI, and he sympathized deeply with Queen Marie Antoinette. He backed those who favored a moderate constitutional monarchy, and in 1792,

President George Washington secured his appointment as minister plenipotentiary to France. He kept a diary in these years and filled it with pungent comments about people and events. In the polemical debate between Edmund Burke and Thomas Paine, he sided with Burke, the conservative. He also used his diplomatic immunity to shield royalist refugees until the French republic asked for his recall in 1794. He crossed the Channel and for four years gave the British government advice on how to defeat revolutionary France.

After returning to the United States, he became a prominent Federalist who opposed Thomas Jefferson's Embargo and James Madison's drift into war with Britain by 1812. By 1814, although he had been one of America's foremost nationalists in the 1780s, he became so exasperated with Democratic-Republican policies that he urged the secession of New York and New England from the Union. With peace restored, however, he joined Governor DeWitt Clinton in urging New York State to build the Erie Canal. He died in 1816.

© Bettmann/Corbis.

GOUVERNEUR MORRIS IN A LITHOGRAPH ENGRAVED BY ALONZO CHAPPEL

The man who gave the federal Constitution its final stylistic form then went to Paris, where he witnessed the most radical phase of the French Revolution.

negotiated a treaty with Don Diego de Gardoqui, the Spanish minister to the United States. It offered northern merchants trading privileges with Spanish colonies in exchange for the closure of the Mississippi River to American traffic for 25 years. Seven northern states voted for the treaty, but all five southern states in Congress rejected these terms, thus defeating the treaty, which needed nine votes for ratification under the Articles of Confederation. Angry talk of disbanding the Union soon filled Congress. Delegates began haggling over which state would join what union if the breakup occurred. The quarrel became public in February 1787 when a Boston newspaper called for a dissolution of the Union.

By the mid-1780s, many cosmopolitans were becoming nationalists eager to strengthen the Union. Many of them had served long, frustrating years in the army or in Congress, unable to carry out measures that they considered vital to the Confederation. In 1785, some of them tried to see what could be done outside Congress. To resolve disputes about navigation rights on the Potomac River, George Washington invited Virginia and Maryland delegates to a conference at Mount Vernon, where they drafted an agreement that was acceptable to both states and to Congress. Prompted by James Madison, a former congressman, the Virginia legislature then urged all of the states to participate in a convention at Annapolis to explore ways to improve American trade.

Four states, including Maryland, ignored the call, and the New Englanders had not yet arrived when, in September 1786, the delegates from the four middle states and Virginia accepted a report drafted by Alexander Hamilton of New York. It asked all of the states to send delegates to a convention at Philadelphia the next May "to devise such further provisions as shall appear to them necessary to render the constitution of the Federal Government adequate to the exigencies of the Union." Seven states responded positively before Congress endorsed the convention on February 21, 1787, and five accepted later. Rhode Island refused to participate. Madison used the winter months to study the defects of classical and European confederacies and to draft a plan for a stronger American union.

The Philadelphia Convention

The convention opened in May 1787 with a plan similar to the Virginia constitution of 1776. It proposed an almost sovereign Parliament for the United States. By September, the delegates had produced a document that was much closer to the Massachusetts constitution of 1780, with a clear separation of powers. The delegates, in four months of secret sessions, repeated the constitutional learning process that had taken four years at the state level after 1776.

With Washington presiding, Governor Edmund Randolph proposed the Virginia, or "large state," plan. Drafted by Madison, it proposed a bicameral legislature, with representation in both houses apportioned according to

"THE HERO WHO DEFENDED THE MOTHERS WILL PROTECT THE DAUGHTERS"

Washington is hailed by young women near the bridge at Trenton on the way to his inauguration as first President of the United States, 1789.

© North Wind Picture Archives.

population. The legislature would choose the executive and the judiciary. It would possess all powers currently lodged in Congress and the power "to legislate in all cases to which the separate States are incompetent." It could "negative all laws passed by the several States, contravening in [its] opinion . . . the articles of Union." Remarkably, the plan did not include specific powers to tax or regulate trade. Madison apparently believed it wiser to be vague and sweeping, rather than explicit. His plan also required ratification by state conventions, not by state legislatures. Within two weeks, the delegates agreed on three-year terms for members of the lower house and seven-year terms for the upper house. The legislature would choose the executive for a single term of seven years.

In mid-June, delegates from the small states struck back. William Paterson proposed the New Jersey Plan, which gave the existing Congress the power to levy import duties and a stamp tax (as in Grenville's imperial reforms of 1764 and 1765), to regulate trade, and to use force to collect delinquent requisitions from the states (as in North's Conciliatory Proposition of 1775). Each state would have one vote. As another alternative, perhaps designed to terrify the small states into accepting the Virginia Plan, Hamilton suggested a government in which both the senate and the executive would serve "on good behavior"—that is, for life! To him, the British constitution still seemed the best in the world, but he never formally proposed his plan.

All of the options before the convention at that point seemed counterrevolutionary. Madison's Parliament for America, Paterson's emulation of Grenville and North, and Hamilton's enthusiasm for the British empire all challenged in major ways the principles of 1776. As the summer progressed, however, the delegates asked themselves what the voters would or would not accept and relearned the hard lessons of popular sovereignty that the state constitutions had taught. The result was a federal Constitution that was truly revolutionary.

Before the Constitution took its final shape, however, the debate grew as hot as the summer weather. The small states warned that their voters would never accept a constitution that let the large states swallow them. The large states insisted on proportional representation in both houses. "The Large States dare not dissolve the Confederation," retorted Delaware's Gunning Bedford in the most inflammatory outburst of the convention. "If they do, the small ones will find some foreign ally of more honor and good faith, who will take them by the hand and do them justice." Then the Connecticut delegates announced that they would be happy with proportional representation in one house and state equality in the other.

In mid-July, the delegates accepted this Connecticut Compromise and then completed the document by September. They finally realized that they were creating a government of laws, to be enforced on individuals through federal courts, and were not propping up a system of congressional resolutions to be carried out (or ignored) by the states. Terms for representatives were reduced to two years, and terms for senators to six, with each state legislature choosing two senators. The president would serve four years, could be reelected, and would be chosen by an Electoral College. Each state received as many electors as it had congressmen and senators combined, and the states were free to decide how to choose their electors. Each elector had to vote for two candidates, one of whom had to be from another state. This provision reflected the fear that localist impulses might prevent a majority vote for anyone. The delegates knew that Washington would be the first president, but there was no obvious choice after him.

In other provisions, free and slave states agreed to count only three-fifths of the slaves in apportioning both representation and direct taxes. The enumeration of congressional powers became lengthy and explicit and included taxation, the regulation of foreign and interstate commerce, and the catchall "necessary and proper" clause. Madison's negative on state laws was replaced by the gentler "supreme law of the land" clause. Over George Mason's last-minute objection, the delegates voted not to include a bill of rights.

With little debate, the convention approved a revolutionary proposal for ratifying the Constitution. This clause called for special conventions in each state and declared that the Constitution would go into force as soon as any nine states had accepted it, even though the Articles of Confederation required unanimous approval for all amendments. The delegates understood that they were proposing an illegal but peaceful overthrow of the existing legal order—that is, a revolution. They hoped that once nine or more states accepted the Constitution, the others would follow their example after the new government got under way and would make ratification unanimous. At that point, their revolution would become both peaceful and legal. The Constitution would then rest on popular sovereignty in a way that the Articles never had. The Federalists, as supporters of the Constitution now called themselves, were willing to risk destroying the Union in order to save and strengthen it. But they knew that they would have to use persuasion, not force, to win approval.

Ratification

When the Federalist delegates returned home, they made a powerful case for the Constitution in newspapers, most of which favored a stronger central government. Most Anti-Federalists, or opponents of the Constitution, were localists with few interstate contacts and only limited access to the press. The Federalists gave them little time to organize. The first ratifying conventions met in December. Delaware ratified unanimously on December 7, Pennsylvania by a 46-to-23 vote five days later, and New Jersey unanimously on December 18. Georgia ratified unanimously on January 2, and Connecticut soon approved, also by a lopsided margin.

Except in Pennsylvania, these victories were in small states. Ironically, although the Constitution was mostly a "large state" document, small states embraced it while large states hesitated. Small states, once they had equality in the senate, saw many advantages in a strong central government. Under the Articles, for example, New Jersey residents had to pay duties to neighboring states on foreign goods imported through New York City or Philadelphia. Under the new Constitution, import duties would go to the federal government, a clear gain for every small state but Rhode Island, which stood to lose import duties at both Providence and Newport.

By contrast, Pennsylvania was the only large state with a solid majority for ratification. But Anti-Federalists there eloquently demanded a federal bill of rights and major changes in the structure of the new government. Large states could think of going it alone. Small states could not—except for Rhode Island with its two cities and its long history of defying its neighbors.

The first hotly contested state was Massachusetts, which set a pattern for struggles in other divided states. Federalists there won by a slim margin (187 to 168) in February 1788. They blocked Anti-Federalist attempts to make ratification conditional on the adoption of specific amendments. Instead, the Federalists promised to support a bill of rights by constitutional amendment after ratification. But the Rhode Island legislature voted overwhelmingly not even to summon a ratifying convention. Maryland and South Carolina ratified easily in April and May, bringing the total to eight of the nine states required. Then conventions met almost simultaneously in New Hampshire, Virginia, New York, and North Carolina. In each, a majority at first opposed ratification.

As resistance stiffened, the ratification controversy turned into the first great debate about the American Union, over what kind of nation the United States should be. By summer 1788, Anti-Federalists were eloquent and well organized. They argued that the new government would be too remote from the people to be trusted with the broad powers specified in the Constitution. They warned that in a House of Representatives divided into districts of 30,000 people (twice the size of Boston), only prominent and wealthy men would be elected. The new government would become an aristocracy or oligarchy that would impose heavy taxes and other burdens on the people. The absence of a bill of rights also troubled them.

During the struggle over ratification, Hamilton, Madison, and Jay wrote a series of 85 essays, published first in New York newspapers and widely reprinted elsewhere, in which they defended the Constitution almost clause by clause. Signing themselves "Publius," they later published the collected essays as *The Federalist Papers,* the most comprehensive body of political thought produced by the Revolutionary generation. In *Federalist, no. 10,* Madison argued that a large republic would be far more stable than a small one. He challenged 2,000 years of accepted wisdom, which insisted that only small republics could survive. Small republics were inherently unstable, Madison insisted, because majority factions could easily gain power within them, trample on the rights of minorities, and ignore the common good. In a republic as huge and diverse as the United States, however, factions would seldom be able to forge a majority. "Publius" hoped that the new government would draw on the talents of the wisest and best-educated citizens. To those who accused him of trying to erect an American aristocracy, he pointed out that the Constitution forbade titles and hereditary rule.

Federalists won a narrow majority (57 to 46) in New Hampshire on June 21, and Madison guided Virginia to ratification (89 to 79) five days later. New York approved, by 30 votes to 27, one month later, bringing 11 states into the Union, enough to launch the new government. North Carolina rejected the Constitution in July 1788 but finally ratified in November 1789 after the first Congress had drafted the Bill of Rights and sent it to the states. Rhode Island, after voting seven times not to call a ratifying convention, finally summoned one that ratified by a vote of only 34 to 32 in May 1790.

Conclusion

Americans survived the most devastating war they had yet fought and won their independence, but only with massive aid from France. Most Indians and blacks who could do so sided with Britain. During the struggle, white

Americans affirmed liberty and equality for themselves in their new state constitutions and bills of rights, but they rarely applied these values to blacks and Indians, even though every northern state adopted either immediate or gradual emancipation. The discontent of the postwar years created the Federalist coalition, which drafted and ratified a new national Constitution to replace the Articles of Confederation. Federalists endowed the new central government with more power than Parliament had ever successfully exercised over the colonies but insisted that the Constitution was fully compatible with the liberty and equality proclaimed during the Revolution. Nothing resembling the American federal system had ever been tried before. Under this new system, sovereignty was removed from government and bestowed on the people, who then empowered separate levels of government through their state and federal constitutions. As the Great Seal of the United States proclaimed, it was a *novus ordo seclorum,* a new order for the ages.

SUGGESTED READINGS

Stephen Conway's *The War of American Independence, 1775–1783* (1995) is a recent history that is strong and accessible. **Charles Royster's** *A Revolutionary People at War: The Continental Army and American Character, 1775–1783* (1979) is the best study of its kind. The essays in **John Shy's** *A People Numerous and Armed: Reflections on the Military Struggle for American Independence,* rev. ed. (1990) have had a tremendous influence on other historians. For the critical 1776 and 1777 campaigns, see **Ira D. Gruber, *The Howe Brothers and the American Revolution*** (1972). **Judith L. Van Buskirk, *Generous Enemies: Patriots and Loyalists in Revolutionary New York*** (2002) analyzes patterns in America's most fiercely contested state and is quite insightful about Arnold's treason and André's execution. **Walter Edgar's *Partisans and Redcoats: The Southern Conflict That Turned the Tide of the American Revolution*** (2001) is a fresh study of the bitter partisan war in the Lower South. For the war's impact on slavery, see **Sylvia R. Frey, *Water from the Rock: Black Resistance in a Revolutionary Age*** (1991) and **Arthur Zilversmit, *The First Emancipation:***

The Abolition of Slavery in the North (1967). Of the numerous studies of loyalism, **Paul H. Smith's *Loyalists and Redcoats: A Study in British Revolutionary Policy*** (1964) remains one of the best.

The single most important book on emerging American constitutionalism remains **Gordon S. Wood, *The Creation of the American Republic, 1776–1787*** (1969). **H. James Henderson's** *Party Politics in the Continental Congress* (1974) is a major contribution. **Jackson Turner Main's *Political Parties before the Constitution*** (1973) carefully investigates postwar divisions within the states. **Jack N. Rakove** won a Pulitzer Prize for *Original Meanings: Politics and Ideas in the Making of the Constitution* (1996). **Saul Cornell** provides a thoughtful approach to *The Other Founders: Anti-Federalism and the Dissenting Tradition in America* (1999). **Stuart Leibiger, *Founding Friendship: George Washington, James Madison, and the Creation of the American Republic*** (1999) is insightful and original.

AMERICAN JOURNEY ONLINE
AND
INFOTRAC COLLEGE EDITION

Visit the source collections at www.ajaccess.wadsworth.com and infotrac.thomsonlearning.com and use the Search function with the following key terms to explore documents, images, audio and video clips, articles, and commentary related to the material in this chapter.

George Washington	Daniel Boone
Yorktown	Northwest Ordinance
Saratoga	Shays's Rebellion
General William Howe	

GRADE AIDS

Visit the Liberty Equality Power Companion Web Site for resources specific to this textbook: http://history.wadsworth.com/murrin_LEP4e

 The CD in the back of this book and the U.S. History Resource Center at http://history.wadsworth.com/u.s./ offer a variety of tools to help you succeed in this course, including access to quizzes; images; documents; interactive simulations, maps, and timelines; movie explorations; and a wealth of other sources.

The Democratic Republic, 1790–1820

WILLIAM RUSSELL BIRCH, *PREPARATION FOR WAR TO DEFEND COMMERCE*
International commerce made many great fortunes in the early republic, and shipbuilding ranked among the largest and best-developed manufacturing enterprises in America. Yet shipbuilders—like nearly all American craftsmen—continued to perform their work in traditional ways. Workers in this Philadelphia shipyard crafted each ship (and each part of it) individually and by hand—a job that required traditional craft skills, careful cooperation, and heavy physical labor. Large-scale machine industry remained decades in the future.

CHAPTER OUTLINE

George Washington assumed his duties as the first president under the Constitution in 1789. He and others who filled offices in the new government were members of the country's educated elite: planters and large farmers who grew staple crops for export, and merchants and financiers who organized America's export-based foreign trade. It was a thin upper crust. Most Americans were outside of or marginal to the Atlantic economy in which the elite made its money and its aspirations. Nine of ten Americans lived on farms. Most farmers provided for their own and their neighbors' needs, and then sent surpluses down rivers and over bad roads to a wider world that they seldom saw or thought about. Not all of them had taken part in the argument that established the Constitution. Of those who had, about half had opposed it. Yet the Founders insisted that their experiment depended on white property holders who were citizens—either as the docile electorate imagined by Washington and his friends, or as the active, "public spirited" (what they had earlier called "virtuous") citizenry imagined by James Madison and Thomas Jefferson. Much of this was beside the point: In 1789, the Founders did not know how citizens would behave.

Americans who were not citizens tended to live in households and under the patriarchal government of men who were. Women had no formal public role; their husbands and fathers spoke and acted for the household in public. One-fifth of the population was African Americans, nearly all of them slaves who had little reason to cheer the success of the slaveholding republic their masters had made. Many thousands more were Indians. Nearly all of those west of the Appalachians were unconquered (Indian peoples occupied more than half of what the maps said was the United States), and they were justifiably wary of the independent nation of land-hungry farmers to their east. Near the Indians and increasingly interspersed with them were white settlers who seemed, to the merchants and planters who ran the country, as ungovernable as the Indians themselves.

In the first 30 years of government under the Constitution, the Americans consolidated their republic and expanded their commerce with a war-torn Europe. In these years their population shot from 4 million to 10 million persons; their agrarian republic spilled across the Appalachians and reached the Mississippi River; their exports rose; and their seaport towns became cities. In the midst of this rapid change, the revolutionary republic drifted from its moorings in the patriarchal household. Increasing thousands of white men found it hard to maintain their status as propertied citizens or to pass that status on to new generations; others simply grew impatient with the responsibilities and constraints of rural patriarchy. The resultant erosion of authority, along with the increasingly equalitarian implications of revolutionary republicanism, encouraged women, slaves, and the growing ranks of propertyless white men to imagine that the revolutionary birthrights of liberty and equality—perhaps even power—might also belong to them. By 1820, the Founders' republic, which depended on widespread proprietorship and well-ordered paternal authority, was expanding, prosperous, and in deep trouble. An individualistic, democratic, and insecure order was taking its place.

CHAPTER FOCUS

♦ What was the nature of the American agricultural economy and of agricultural society in the years 1790 through 1815?

♦ What was the history of slavery in these years? In what areas (and in what ways) did it expand? In what areas (and, again, in what ways) was the slave system called into question?

♦ In what ways was the spread of evangelical Protestantism in these years beginning to shape American society and culture?

♦ Which Americans benefited from economic and social change between 1790 and 1815? Which did not?

The Farmer's Republic

In 1782, J. Hector St. John de Crèvecoeur, a French soldier who had settled in rural New York, explained American agrarianism through the words of a fictionalized farmer. First of all, he said, the American farmer owns his own land and bases his claim to dignity and citizenship on that fact. He spoke of "the bright idea of property," and went on: "This formerly rude soil has been converted by my father into a pleasant farm, and in return, it has established all our rights; on it is founded our rank, our freedom, our power as citizens, our importance as inhabitants of [a

CHRONOLOGY

1789	National government under the Constitution begins
1791	Vermont enters the union as the 14th state
1792	Kentucky enters the union as the 15th state
1793	Beginning of Anglo-French War • Eli Whitney invents the cotton gin
1794	Anthony Wayne defeats the northwestern Indians at Fallen Timbers • British abandon their forts in the Old Northwest
1795	Northwestern Indians cede most of Ohio at Treaty of Greenville
1796	Tennessee enters the union as the 16th state
1799	Successful slave revolution in Haiti
1800	Gabriel's Rebellion in Virginia
1801	First camp meeting at Cane Ridge, Kentucky
1803	Jefferson purchases the Louisiana Territory from France • Ohio enters the union as the 17th state
1805	Tenskwatawa's first vision
1810	Nationalist Cherokee chiefs depose old local leaders
1811	Battle of Tippecanoe
1812	Second war with Britain begins

rural neighborhood]." Second, farm ownership endows the American farmer with the powers and responsibilities of fatherhood. "Often when I plant my low ground," he said, "I place my little boy on a chair which screws to the beam of the plough—its motion and that of the horses please him; he is perfectly happy and begins to chat. As I lean over the handle, various are the thoughts which crowd into my mind. I am now doing for him, I say, what my father did for me; may God enable him to live that he may perform the same operations for the same purposes when I am worn out and old!"

Crèvecoeur's farmer, musing on liberty and property, working the ancestral fields with his male heir strapped to the plough, evokes a proud citizen of America's revolutionary republic. Few of Crèvecoeur's fellow citizens were as poetic as he, but they shared his concern with propertied independence and its social and political consequences. From New England through the mid-Atlantic and on into the southern Piedmont and backcountry, few farmers in 1790 thought of farming as a business. Their first concern was to provide subsistence for their households. Their second was to achieve long-term security and the ability to pass their farm on to their sons. The goal was to create what rural folks called a "competence": the ability to live up to neighborhood standards of material decency while protecting the long-term independence of their household—and thus the dignity and political rights of its head. Most of these farmers raised a variety of animals and plants, ate most of what they grew, traded much of the rest within their neighborhoods, and sent small surpluses into outside markets.

The world's hunger for American food, however, was growing. West Indian and European markets for American meat and grain had grown since the mid-18th century. They expanded dramatically between 1793 and 1815, when war disrupted farming in Europe. American farmers took advantage of these markets, but few gambled with local food supplies or neighborly relations. They continued to rely on family and neighbors for subsistence and risked little by sending increased surpluses overseas. Thus they profited from world markets without becoming dependent on them.

Households

Production for overseas markets after 1790 did, however, alter relationships within rural households. Farm labor in postrevolutionary America was carefully divided by sex.

Men worked in the fields, and production for markets both intensified that labor and made it more exclusively male. In the grain fields, for instance, the long-handled scythe was replacing the sickle as the principal harvest tool. Women could use the sickle efficiently, but the long, heavy scythe was designed to be wielded by men. At the same time, farmers completed the substitution of ploughs for hoes as the principal cultivating tools—not only because ploughs worked better but also because rural Americans had developed a prejudice against women working in the fields. By the early 19th century, visitors to the long-settled farming areas (with the exception of some mid-Atlantic German communities) seldom saw women in the fields. In his travels through France, Thomas Jefferson spoke harshly of peasant communities where he saw women doing field labor.

At the same time, household responsibilities multiplied and fell more exclusively to women. It was farm women's labor and ingenuity that helped create a more varied and nutritious rural diet in these years. Bread and salted meat remained staples. The bread was the old mix of Indian corn and coarse wheat ("rye and Injun," the

LINK TO THE PAST

Jefferson's Farmer-Patriots

In 1781, a French friend asked Thomas Jefferson 23 questions about Virginia. To a query about commerce and manufacturing, Jefferson answered that Virginians were farmers with little need for domestic manufactures or trade with each other, and explained why that was a good system for a republic:

*T*hose who labour in the earth are the chosen people of God, if ever he had a chosen people, whose breasts he has made his peculiar deposit for substantial and genuine virtue. It is the focus in which he keeps alive that sacred fire, which otherwise might escape from the face of the earth. Corruption of morals in the mass of cultivators is a phaenomenon of which no age nor nation has furnished an example. It is the mark set on those, who not looking up to heaven, to their own soil and industry, as does the husbandman, for their subsistence, depend for it on the casualties and caprice of customers. Dependence begets subservience and venality, suffocates the germ of virtue, and prepares fit tools for the designs of ambition. This, the natural progress and consequence of the arts, has sometimes perhaps been retarded by accidental circumstances:

but, generally speaking, the proportion which the aggregate of the other classes of citizens bears in any state to that of its husbandmen, is the proportion of its unsound to its healthy parts, and is a good-enough barometer whereby to measure its degree of corruption.

THOMAS JEFFERSON
From *Notes on the State of Virginia*

1. Jefferson insists that land-owning farmers are ideal citizens of a republic. Why was that so? And why were persons engaged in nonfarming occupations less suited to citizenship?
2. How does this statement reconcile with Jefferson's discussion of slavery and its cultural results in Queries XIV and XVIII?
3. What is the assumed role of international commerce in Jefferson's sociopolitical formulation?

For additional sources related to this feature, visit the *Liberty, Equality, Power* Web site at:

http://history.wadsworth.com/murrin_LEP4e

farmers called it), with crust so thick that it was used as a scoop for soups and stews. Although improved brines and pickling techniques augmented the supply of salt meat that could be laid by, farmers' palates doubtless told them that it was the same old salt meat. By the 1790s, however, other foods were becoming available. Improved winter feeding for cattle and better techniques for making and storing butter and cheese kept dairy products on the tables of the more prosperous farm families throughout the year. Chickens became more common, and farm women began to fence and manure their kitchen gardens, planting them with potatoes, turnips, cabbages, squashes, beans, and other vegetables that could be stored in the root cellars that were becoming standard features of farmhouses. By the 1830s, a resident of Weymouth, Massachusetts, claimed that "a man who did not have a large garden of potatoes, crooked-necked squashes, and other vegetables . . . was regarded [as] improvident." He might have added poultry and dairy cattle to the list, and he might have noted that all were more likely to result from the labor of women than from the labor of men.

Rural Industry

Industrial outwork provided many farmers with another means of protecting their independence by working their wives and children harder. From the 1790s onward, city merchants provided country workers with raw materials

---

HISTORY THROUGH FILM

A Midwife's Tale

Directed by Richard D. Rodgers (PBS).

The historian Laurel Thatcher Ulrich's *A Midwife's Tale* won the Pulitzer Prize for history and biography in 1991. Shortly thereafter, the Public Broadcasting System (PBS) turned the book into a documentary movie—a close and imaginative analysis of the diary of Martha Ballard, a Maine farm woman and midwife of the late 18th and early 19th centuries. Events are acted out on screen, and period modes of dress, housing, gardening, washing, coffin-making, spinning and weaving, and other details are reconstructed with labored accuracy.

The viewer hears the sounds of footfalls, horses, handlooms, and dishes, but the only human sounds are an occasional cough, exclamation, or drinking song. The principal narrative is carried by an actress who reads passages from the diary, and Thatcher occasionally breaks in to explain her own experiences with the diary and its interpretation. The result is a documentary film that knows the difference between dramatizing history and making it up. It also dramatizes the ways in which a skilled and sensitive historian goes about her work.

Martha Ballard was a midwife in a town on the Kennebec River. She began keeping a daily diary at the age of 50 in 1785, and continued until 1812. Most of the film is about her daily life: delivering babies, nursing the sick, helping neighbors, keeping house, raising and supervising the labor of her daughters and niece, gardening and tending cattle and turkeys. In both the book and the film, the busyness of an ordinary woman's days—and a sense of her possibilities and limits—in the early republic comes through in exhausting detail. The dailiness of her life is interrupted only occasionally by an event: a fire at her husband's sawmill, an epidemic of scarlet fever, a parade organized to honor the death of George Washington, the rape of a minister's wife by his enemies (including the local judge, who is set free), and a neighbor's inexplicable murder of his wife and six children.

There is also the process of getting old. At the beginning, Martha Ballard is the busy wife in a well-run household. As she ages and her children leave to set up households of their own, Ballard hires local girls who—perhaps

and paid them for finished shoes, furniture, cloth, brooms, and other handmade goods. In Marple, Pennsylvania, a farming town near Philadelphia, fully one-third of households were engaged in weaving, furniture making, and other household industry in the 1790s. As late as the 1830s, when the rise of the factory system had reduced the demand for household manufactures, 33,000 New England women were still weaving palm leaf hats at home. Most of the outwork was taken on by large, relatively poor families, with the work organized in ways that shored up the authority of fathers. When young Caleb Jackson and his brother began making shoes for a Massachusetts merchant in 1803, the account was carried in their father's name. When New Hampshire women and girls fashioned hats, the accounts were kept in the name of the husband or father. In general, household industry was part-time work performed only by the dependent women and children of the household. Even when it was the family's principal means of support, the work was arranged in ways that supported traditional notions of fatherhood and proprietorship.

In eastern Massachusetts in the 1790s, for instance, when thousands of farmers on small plots of worn-out land became household shoemakers, skilled men cut the leather and shaped the uppers, while the more menial tasks of sewing and binding were left to the women. In the town of North Reading, the family of Mayo Greanleaf Patch made shoes throughout the 1790s. Patch was a poor

because an increasingly democratic culture has made them less subservient than Ballard would like, perhaps because Ballard is growing old and impatient, perhaps both—tend to be surly. Her husband, a surveyor who works for merchants speculating in local land, is attacked twice in the woods by squatters and spends a year and a half in debtor's jail—not for his own debts but because, as tax collector, he failed to collect enough. While the husband is in jail and his aging wife struggles to keep the house going, their son moves his own family into the house and Martha is moved into a single room and is made to feel unwanted—a poignant and unsentimental case of the strained relations between generations that historians have discovered in the early republic.

A Midwife's Tale is a modest film that comes as close as a thorough and imaginative historian and a good filmmaker can to recreating the texture of lived experience in the northeastern countryside at the beginning of the 19th century. Students who enjoy the movie should go immediately to the book.

The PBS documentary movie *A Midwife's Tale* is based on the Pulitzer Prize–winning book of the same name by historian Laurel Thatcher Ulrich.

man who drank too much and lived on a small plot of land owned by his father-in-law; the family income came largely from shoemaking. Yet Patch, when asked to name his occupation, described himself as a "yeoman"—a fiction subsidized by the labor of Patch's wife and children.

Neighbors

The struggle to maintain household independence involved most farmers in elaborate networks of neighborly cooperation. Few farmers possessed the tools, labor, and food they would have needed to be truly independent. They regularly worked for one another, borrowed oxen and plows, and swapped surpluses of one kind of food for another. Women frequently traded ashes, herbs, butter and eggs, vegetables, seedlings, baby chicks, goose feathers, and the products of their spinning wheels and looms. Such exchanges of goods and services were crucial to the workings of a rural neighborhood, and the feminine character of those exchanges may have increased the authority of women within households and neighborhoods. Some cooperative undertakings—house and barn-raisings and husking bees, for example—brought the whole neighborhood together, transforming a chore into a pleasant social event. The gossip, drinking, and dancing that took place on such occasions were welcome rewards for neighborly cooperation.

Few neighborhood transactions involved money. In 1790, the states and federal government had not yet issued paper money, and the widespread use of Spanish, English,

Lewis Miller (1796–1882). The Historical Society of York County, PA.

OLD MRS. HANSMAN KILLING A HOG

This Pennsylvania farm wife seldom if ever worked in the fields, but her daily round of work was no dainty business. Along with other arduous and dirty labors, she killed and butchered hogs not only for her family but for some of her neighbors as well.

and French coins testified to the shortage of specie. In New England, farmers kept careful accounts of neighborhood debts. In the South and West, on the other hand, farmers used a "changing system" in which they simply remembered what they owed; they regarded the New England practice as a sign of Yankee greed and lack of character. Yet farmers everywhere relied more on barter than on cash: "Instead of money going incessantly backwards and forwards into the same hands," observed a French traveler in Massachusetts in 1790, "[Americans] supply their needs in the countryside by direct reciprocal exchanges. The tailor and the bootmaker go and do their work at the home of the farmer . . . who most frequently provides the raw material for it and pays for the work in goods. They write down what they give and receive on both sides, and at the end of the year they settle a large variety of exchanges with a very small quantity of coin." Such a system created an elaborate network of neighborhood debt. In Kent, Connecticut, for instance, the average farmer left 20 creditors when he died. The debts were indicators not of exploitation and class division, however, but of a highly structured and absolutely necessary system of neighborly cooperation.

Inheritance

The rural republicanism envisioned by men such as Jefferson and Crèvecoeur rested on widespread farm ownership and on a rough equality among adult male householders. Even as they were formulating that vision, however, its social base was disintegrating. Overcrowding and the growth of markets caused the price of good farmland to rise sharply throughout the older settlements. Young people could expect to inherit only a few acres of exhausted land or to move to wilderness land in the backcountry. Failing those options, they would quit farming altogether. Crèvecoeur's baby boy—who in fact ended up living in Boston—was in a more precarious position than his seat on his father's plough might have indicated.

In Revolutionary America, fathers had been judged by their ability to support and govern their households, to serve as good neighbors, and to pass land on to their sons and substantial dowries on to their daughters. After the war, fewer farm fathers could meet those expectations. Those in the old settlements had small farms and large families, which made it impossible for them to provide competence for all their offspring. Fathers felt that they had failed as fathers, and their daughters and sons, with no prospect of an adequate inheritance, were obliged to leave home. Most fathers tried valiantly to provide for all of their heirs (generally by leaving land to their sons and personal property to their daughters). Few left all of their land to one son, and many stated in their wills that the sons to whom they left the land must share barns and cider mills—even the house—on farms that could be subdivided no further. Such provisions suited a social system that guaranteed the independence of the household head through complex relations with kin and neighbors. They also indicated that the system had reached the end of the line.

Outside New England, farm tenancy was on the increase. In parts of Pennsylvania and in other areas as well, farmers often bought farms when they became available in the neighborhood, rented them to tenants to augment the household income, and then gave them to their sons

THE DINING ROOM OF DR. WHITBRIDGE, A RHODE ISLAND COUNTRY DOCTOR, CIRCA 1815

It is a comfortable, neatly furnished room, but with little decoration, and the doctor must sit near the fire in layered clothing to ward off the morning chill.

Old Dartmouth Historical Society/New Bedford Whaling Museum.

when they reached adulthood. The sons of poorer farmers often rented a farm in the hope of saving enough money to buy it. Some fathers bought tracts of unimproved land in the backcountry—sometimes on speculation, more often to provide their sons with land they could make into a farm. Others paid for their sons' educations or arranged apprenticeships to provide them with an avenue of escape from a declining countryside. As a result, more and more young men left home. The populations of the old farming communities grew older and more female, while the populations of the rising frontier settlements and seaport cities became younger and more male. The young men who stayed home often had nothing to look forward to but a lifetime as tenants or hired hands.

Standards of Living

The rise of markets in the late 18th and early 19th centuries improved living standards for some families but widened the disparity between prosperous farmers and their marginal and disinherited neighbors. Most farmhouses in the older rural areas were small, one-story structures. Few farmers, especially in the South and West, bothered to keep their surroundings clean or attractive. They repaired their fences only when they became too dilapidated to function. They rarely planted trees or shrubs, and housewives threw out garbage to feed the chickens and pigs that foraged near the house.

Inside, homes had few rooms and many people. Beds stood in every room, and few family members slept alone.

Growing up in Bethel, Connecticut, future show business entrepreneur P. T. Barnum shared a bed with his brother and an Irish servant; guests shared beds in New England taverns until the 1820s. The hearth remained the source of heat and light in most farmhouses. In the period from 1790 to 1810, more than half the households in central Massachusetts—an old and relatively prosperous area—owned only one or two candlesticks. One of the great disparities between wealthy families and their less affluent neighbors was that wealthy families could light their houses at night. Another disparity was in the outward appearance of houses. The wealthier families painted their houses white as a token of pristine republicanism, which stood in stark and unrepublican contrast to the weathered gray-brown clapboard siding of their neighbors.

Some improvements emerged in personal comfort. Beds in most houses may have been shared, but as time passed more of them had mattresses stuffed with feathers. At mealtimes, only the poorest families continued to eat with their fingers or with spoons from a common bowl. By 1800, individual place settings with knives and forks and china plates, along with chairs instead of benches, had become common in rural America. Although only the wealthiest families had upholstered furniture, ready-made chairs were widely available; the number of chairs per household in Massachusetts, for instance, doubled in the first third of the 19th century. Clocks, one of the first items to be mass produced in the United States, appeared in the more prosperous rural households: As early as the 1790s, fully 35 percent of the families in Chester County, Pennsylvania, owned at least one clock.

🌰 From Backcountry to Frontier

The United States was a huge country in 1790, at least on paper. In the treaty that ended the War of Independence in 1783, the British ignored Indian claims and ceded all of the land from the Atlantic Ocean to the Mississippi River to the new republic, with the exceptions of Spanish Florida and New Orleans. The states then surrendered their individual claims to the federal government, and in 1790, George Washington became president of a nation that stretched nearly 1,500 miles inland. Still, most white Americans lived on thin strips of settlement along the Atlantic coast and along the few navigable rivers that emptied into the Atlantic. Some were pushing their way into the wilds of Maine and northern Vermont, and in New York others set up communities as far west as the Mohawk Valley. Pittsburgh was a struggling new settlement, and two outposts had been established on the Ohio River: at Marietta and at what would become Cincinnati.

Farther south, farmers had occupied the Piedmont lands up to the eastern slope of the Appalachians and were spilling through the Cumberland Gap into the new lands of Kentucky and Tennessee. North of the Ohio River, however, the Shawnee, Miami, Delaware, and Potawatomie nations, along with smaller tribes, controlled nearly all of the land shown on the Northwest Ordinance's neatly gridded and largely fictitious map. To the south, Indians whom the whites called the "Five Civilized Tribes" still occupied much of their ancestral land: the Cherokees in the Carolinas and northern Georgia, the Creeks in Georgia and Alabama, the Choctaws and Chickasaws in Mississippi, and the Seminoles in southern Georgia and Spanish Florida. Taken together, Indian peoples occupied most of the land that treaties and maps showed as the interior of the United States.

The Destruction of the Woodland Indians

Although many of the woodland tribes were still intact and still living on their ancestral lands in 1790, they were in serious trouble. The members of the old Iroquois Federation had been restricted to reservations in New York and Pennsylvania; many had fled to Canada. The once-powerful Cherokees had been severely punished for fighting on the side of the British during the Revolution and by 1790 had ceded three-fourths of their territory to the

Americans. Like the Iroquois, by this time they were nearly surrounded by white settlements.

In the Old Northwest, the Shawnee, Miami, and other tribes—with the help of the British, who still occupied seven forts within what was formally the United States—continued to trade furs and to impede white settlement. Skirmishes with settlers, however, brought reprisals, and the Indians faced not only hostile pioneers but the U.S. Army as well. In the Ohio country, punitive expeditions led by General Josiah Harmar and General Arthur St. Clair failed in 1790 and 1791—the second ending in an Indian victory in which 630 soldiers died. In 1794, President Washington sent a third army, under General "Mad Anthony" Wayne, which defeated the Indians at Fallen Timbers, near present-day Toledo. The Treaty of Greenville forced the Native Americans to cede two-thirds of what are now Ohio and southeastern Indiana. At this point, the British decided to abandon their forts in the Old Northwest. Following their victory at Fallen Timbers, whites filtered into what remained of Indian lands. In 1796, President Washington threw up his hands and announced that "I believe scarcely any thing, short of a Chinese Wall, or a line of troops, will restrain Land Jobbers and the encroachment of settlers upon the Indian Territory." Five years later, Governor William Henry Harrison of Indiana Territory admitted that frontier whites "consider the murdering of the Indians in the highest degree meritorious."

Relegated to smaller territory but still dependent on the European fur trade, the natives of the Northwest now fell into competition with settlers and other Indians for the diminishing supply of game. The Creeks, Choctaws, and other tribes of the Old Southwest faced the same problem: Even when they chased settlers out of their territory, the settlers managed to kill or scare off the deer and other wildlife, thus ruining the old hunting grounds. When the Shawnee sent hunting parties farther west, they met irate western Indians. The Choctaws also sent hunters across the Mississippi, where they found both new sources of furs and angry warriors of the Osage and other peoples of Louisiana and Arkansas. The Indians of the interior now realized that the days of the fur trade, on which they depended for survival, were numbered.

Faced with shrinking territories, the disappearance of wildlife, and diminished opportunities to be traditional hunters and warriors, many Indian societies sank into despair. Epidemics of European diseases (smallpox, influenza, measles) attacked peoples who were increasingly sedentary and vulnerable. Old internal frictions grew nastier. In the Old Southwest, full-blooded Indians came into conflict with mixed-blood Indians, who often no longer spoke the native language and who wanted their people to

MAP 7.1 NATIVE AMERICA, 1783–1812

Native Americans had lost a lot before the American Revolution, but the losses grew worse as British, French, and Spanish traders, missionaries, and soldiers were replaced by a democratic republic of farmers who wanted Indian land. By 1812, Indian peoples in the Northwest were battered and increasingly threatened by settlement; Indians of the Southwest continued to occupy most of their old lands, but they would lose everything within the next generation.

adopt white ways. Murder and clan revenge plagued the tribes, and depression and suicide became more common. The use of alcohol, which had been a scourge on Indian societies for two centuries, increased. Indian males spent more time in their villages and less on the hunt, and by most accounts they drank more and grew more violent.

The Failure of Cultural Renewal

Out of this cultural wreckage emerged visionary leaders who spoke of a regenerated native society and the expulsion of all whites from the old tribal lands. One of the first was Chief Alexander McGillivray, a mixed-blood Creek who had sided with the British during the Revolution. Between 1783 and 1793, McGillivray tried to unite the Creeks under a national council that could override local chiefs and to form alliances with other tribes and with Spanish Florida. McGillivray's premature death in 1793, coupled with the mistrust with which many traditionalist Creeks viewed his schemes, prevented the realization of his vision.

The Cherokees north and east of the Creeks did succeed in making a unified state. Angered by the willingness of village chiefs to be bribed and flattered into selling land, and by the departure of tribe members to remote locations in the Appalachians or to government land in Arkansas, a group of young chiefs staged a revolt between 1808 and 1810. Previously, being a Cherokee had meant loyalty to one's clan and kin group and adherence to the tribe's ancient customs. Now it meant remaining on the tribe's ancestral land (migration across the Mississippi was regarded as treason) and unquestioning acceptance of the laws, courts, and police controlled by the national council. By 1810, the Cherokee had transformed themselves from a defeated and divided tribe into a nation within a nation.

Among the many prophets who emerged during these years, the one who came closest to military success was Tenskwatawa, a fat, one-eyed, alcoholic Shawnee who had failed as a warrior and medicine man. He went into a deep trance in 1805, and the people thought he was dead. During preparations for his funeral, he awoke and told them he had visited heaven and hell and had received a prophetic vision. First, all Indians must stop drinking and fighting among themselves. They must also return to their traditional food, clothing, tools, and hairstyles, and must extinguish all of their fires and start new ones without using European tools. All who opposed the new order (including local chiefs, medicine men, shamans, and witches) must be put down by force. When all of that had been done, God (a monotheistic, punishing God borrowed from the Christians) would restore the world that Indians had known before the whites came over the mountains.

The Granger Collection, New York.

TENSKWATAWA

The Shawnee prophet Tenskwatawa ("The Open Door"), brother of Tecumseh, was painted by George Catlin in 1836—long after the defeat of his prophetic attempt to unify American Indians.

Tenskwatawa's message soon found its way to the Delawares (who attacked the Christians among their people as witches) and other native peoples of the Northwest. When converts flooded into the prophet's home village, he moved to Prophetstown (Tippecanoe) in what is now Indiana. There, with the help of his brother Tecumseh, he created an army estimated by the whites at anywhere between 650 and 3,000 warriors and pledged to end further encroachment by whites. Tecumseh, who took control of the movement, announced to the whites that he was the sole chief of all the Indians north of the Ohio River; land cessions by anyone else would be invalid. Tenskwatawa's prophecy and Tecumseh's leadership had united the Indians of the Old Northwest in an unprecedented stand against white encroachment.

Tecumseh's confederacy posed a threat to the United States. A second war with England was looming, and Tecumseh was receiving supplies and encouragement from the British in Canada. He was also planning to visit the southern tribes in an attempt to bring them into his confederacy. The prospect of unified resistance by the western tribes in league with the British jeopardized every settler west of the Appalachians. In 1811, William Henry

Harrison led an army toward Prophetstown. With Tecumseh away, Tenskwatawa ordered an unwise attack on Harrison's army and was beaten at the Battle of Tippecanoe.

Tecumseh's still-formidable confederacy, joined by the traditionalist wing of the southern Creeks, fought alongside the British in the War of 1812 and lost (see chapter 8). The loss destroyed the military power of the Indians east of the Mississippi River. General Andrew Jackson forced the Creeks (including those who had served as his allies) to cede millions of acres of land in Georgia and Alabama. The other southern tribes, along with the members of Tecumseh's northern confederacy, watched helplessly as new settlers took over their hunting lands. Some of the Indians moved west, and others tried to farm what was left of their old land. All of them had to deal with settlers and government officials who neither feared them nor took their sovereignty seriously. By this time, most whites simply assumed that the Indians would have to move on to the barren land west of the Mississippi (see chapter 12).

The Backcountry, 1790–1815

To easterners, the backcountry whites who were displacing the Indians seemed no different from the defeated aborigines. In fact, in accommodating themselves to a borderless forest used by both Indians and whites, many settlers—like many Indians—had melded Indian and white ways. To clear the land, backcountry farmers simply girdled the trees and left them to die and fall down by themselves. They plowed the land by navigating between the stumps. To easterners' minds, the worst offense was that women often worked the fields, particularly while their men, as did Indians, spent long periods away on hunting trips for food game and animal skins for trade. The arch-pioneer Daniel Boone, for instance, braided his hair, dressed himself in Indian leggings, and, with only his dogs for company, disappeared for months at a time on "long hunts." When easterners began to "civilize" his neighborhood, Boone moved farther west.

Eastern visitors were appalled not only by the poverty, lice, and filth of frontier life but also by the drunkenness and violence of the frontiersmen. Americans everywhere drank heavily in the early years of the 19th century, but everyone agreed that frontiersmen drank more and were more violent when drunk than men anywhere else. Travelers told of no-holds-barred fights in which frontiersmen gouged the eyes and bit off the noses and ears of their opponents. No account was complete without a reckoning of the number of one-eyed, one-eared men the traveler had met on the frontier. Stories arose of half-legendary heroes such as Davy Crockett of Tennessee, who wrestled bears and alligators and had a recipe for Indian stew, and Mike Fink, a Pennsylvania boatman who brawled and drank his way along the rivers of the interior until he was shot and killed in a drunken episode that none of the participants could clearly remember. Samuel Holden Parsons, a New Englander serving as a judge in the Northwest Territory, called the frontiersmen "our white savages." Massachusetts conservative Timothy Pickering branded them "the least worthy subjects of the United States. They are little less savage than the Indians."

After 1789, settlers of the western backcountry made two demands of the new national government: protection from the Indians and a guarantee of the right to navigate the Ohio and Mississippi rivers. The Indians were pushed back in the 1790s and finished off in the War of 1812, and in 1803, Jefferson's Louisiana Purchase (see chapter 8) ended the European presence on the rivers and at the crucial chokepoint at New Orleans. Over these years, the pace of settlement quickened. In 1790, only 10,000 settlers lived west of the Appalachians—about 1 American in 40. By 1800, the number of settlers had risen to nearly 1 million. By 1820, 2 million Americans were westerners—one in five.

The new settlers bought land from speculators who had acquired tracts under the Northwest Ordinance in the

"Old Homestead, Late Residence of R. H. Constant." From Illustrated Atlas Map of Sangamon County, Ill. (Springfield, Ill.: Brink, McCormick & Co., 1874).

A NORTHWESTERN FARM

A settler, R. H. Constant, built this farm in pioneer Sangamon County, Illinois. The original house was a log cabin; a separate kitchen was added at a later date. Sangamon County was settled largely from the upper South, and Constant's farm, like most farms in the neighborhood, was surrounded by a traditional Virginia split-rail or "worm" fence—like those that Constant's younger neighbor, the rail-splitter Abraham Lincoln, helped to build.

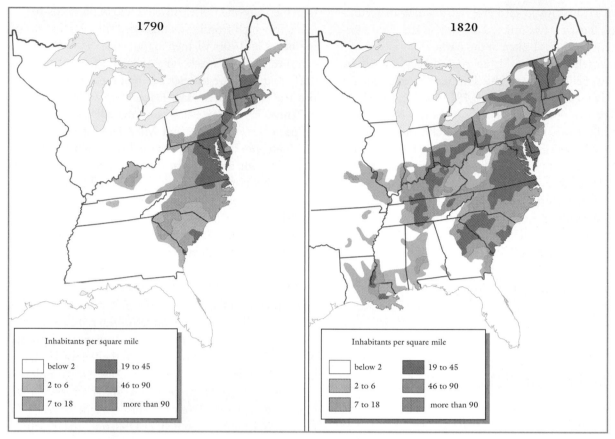

MAP 7.2 POPULATION DENSITY, 1790–1820

The population of the United States nearly doubled between 1790 and 1820, growing from 5.2 million to 9.6 million persons. In the South, an overwhelmingly rural population spread rapidly across space. The population of the Northeast and mid-Atlantic also occupied new territory over these years, but the rise of seaport towns and intensely commercialized (and often overcrowded) farming areas were turning the North into a much more densely settled region.

Northwest; from English, Dutch, and American land companies in western New York; and from land dealers in the Southwest and in northern New England. They built frame houses surrounded by cleared fields, planted marketable crops, and settled into the struggle to make farms out of the wilderness and to meet mortgage payments along the way. By 1803, four frontier states had entered the union: Vermont (1791), Kentucky (1792), Tennessee (1796), and Ohio (1803). Louisiana soon followed (1812), and when war ended in 1815, one frontier state after another gained admission: Indiana (1816), Mississippi (1817), Illinois (1818), Alabama (1818), Maine (1820), and Missouri (1821).

As time passed, the term *backcountry,* which easterners had used to refer to the wilderness and the dangerous misfits who lived in it, fell into disuse. By 1820, the term *frontier* had replaced it. The new settlements no longer represented the backwash of American civilization. They were its cutting edge.

The Plantation South, 1790–1820

In 1790, the future of slavery was uncertain in the Chesapeake (the states of Virginia, Maryland, and Delaware, where the institution first took root in North America). The tobacco market had been precarious since before the Revolution, and it continued to decline after 1790. Tobacco depleted the soil, and by the late 18th century, tidewater farms and plantations were giving out. As lands west of the Appalachians opened to settlement, white tenants, laborers, and small farmers left the Chesapeake in droves. Many of them moved to Kentucky, Tennessee, or the western reaches of Virginia. Many others found new homes in nonslave states north of the Ohio River. Faced with declining opportunities within the slave societies of the Chesapeake, thousands of the poorer whites had voted with their feet.

Slavery and the Republic

With slave labor becoming less necessary, Chesapeake planters continued to switch to grain and livestock—crops that required less labor than tobacco—and tried to think up new uses for slaves. Some planters divided their land into small plots and rented both the plots and their slaves to white tenant farmers. Others, particularly in Maryland, recruited tenants from the growing ranks of free blacks. Still others hired out their slaves as artisans and urban laborers. None of these solutions, however, could employ the great mass of slaves or repay the planters' huge investment in slave labor.

In this situation, many Chesapeake planters (who had, after all, fought a revolution in the name of natural rights) began to manumit their slaves. The farmers of Maryland and Delaware in particular set their slaves free; by the time those states sided with the North in 1861, more than half the blacks in Maryland and nine-tenths of those in Delaware were free. Virginia's economic and cultural commitment to the plantation was stronger, but even the Old Dominion showed a strong movement toward manumitting slaves. George Washington stated that he wished "to liberate a certain species of property," and manumitted his slaves by will. (The manumissions were to take place at the death of his widow—thus, as one wag declared, surrounding Mrs. Washington with 100 people who wanted her dead.) Robert Carter, reputedly the largest slaveholder in Virginia, also freed his slaves, as did many others. The free black population of Virginia stood at 2,000 in 1782, when the state passed a law permitting manumission. The number of free blacks rose to 12,766 in 1790, to 20,124 in 1800,

and to 30,570 in 1810. In all, the proportion of Virginia blacks who were free increased from 4 percent in 1790 to 7 percent in 1810.

There were, however, limits on the manumission of Virginia slaves. First, few planters could afford to free their slaves without compensation. Second, white Virginians feared the social consequences of black freedom. Thomas Jefferson, for instance, owned 175 slaves when he penned the phrase that "all men are created equal." He lived off their labor, sold them to pay his debts, gave them as gifts, and sometimes sold them away from their families as a punishment. Through it all, he insisted that slavery was wrong. He could imagine emancipation; however, only if freed slaves would be colonized far from Virginia. A society of free blacks and whites, Jefferson insisted, would end in disaster: "Deep rooted prejudices entertained by the whites; ten thousand recollections, by the blacks, of the injuries they have sustained; new provocations; the real distinctions which nature has made . . . [will] produce convulsions which will probably never end but in the extermination of the one or the other race." Near the end of an adult lifetime of condemning slavery but doing nothing to end it, Jefferson cried out that white Virginians held "a wolf by the ears": They could not hold onto slavery forever, and they could never let it go.

The Recommitment to Slavery

Jefferson's dilemma eased as cotton cultivation increased farther south. British industrialization created a demand for cotton from the 1790s onward, and planters knew they could sell all the cotton they could grow. But long-staple

GOING TO TENNESSEE

The Pennsylvanian Lewis Miller met with this group of slaves near Staunton, Virginia, in 1853. They were being sent from their old farms in Virginia to the slave markets of Tennessee and from there to the cotton fields of the newer southern states. In the years after 1820, hundreds of thousands of upper South slaves suffered this migration.

Abby Aldrich Rockefeller Folk Art Center, Williamsburg, VA.

cotton, the only profitable variety, was a delicate plant that thrived only on the Sea Islands off Georgia and South Carolina. The short-staple variety was hardier, but its sticky seeds had to be removed by hand before the cotton could be milled. One adult slave would work an entire day to clean a single pound of short-staple cotton—a profit-killing expenditure of labor. In 1790, the United States produced only 3,000 bales of cotton, nearly all of it on the plantations of the Sea Islands.

In 1793, Eli Whitney, a Connecticut Yankee who had come south to work as a tutor, set his mind to the problem. Within a few days, he had made a model of a cotton "gin" (a southern contraction of "engine") that combed the seeds from the fiber with metal pins fitted into rollers. Working with Whitney's machine, a slave could clean 50 pounds of short-staple cotton in a day. At a stroke, cotton became the great American cash crop and plantation agriculture was rejuvenated. Cotton production grew to 73,000 bales in 1800, to 178,000 bales in 1810, and to 334,000 bales in 1820. By 1820, cotton accounted for more than half the value of all agricultural exports.

Short-staple cotton grew well in the hot, humid climate and long growing season of the Lower South (roughly, the land below the southern borders of Virginia and Kentucky), and it grew almost anywhere: in the rolling Piedmont country east of the Appalachians, in the coastal lowlands, and—especially—in the virgin lands of the Old Southwest. It was also a labor-intensive crop that could be grown in either small or large quantities; farmers with few or no slaves could make a decent profit, and planters with extensive land and many slaves could make enormous amounts of money. Best of all, the factories of England and, eventually, of the American Northeast, had a seemingly insatiable appetite for southern cotton.

Plantation slavery, now rejuvenated, spread rapidly into the new cotton-growing regions of the South. Meanwhile, Chesapeake planters, who lived too far north to grow cotton, continued to diversify. To finance the transition to mixed agriculture, they sold their excess slaves at high prices to planters in the cotton frontier. Up until about 1810, most of the slaves who left Virginia had traveled to Kentucky or Tennessee with their masters. There-

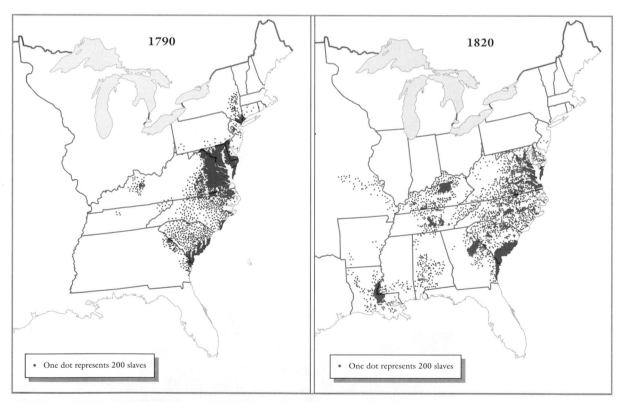

MAP 7.3 DISTRIBUTION OF SLAVE POPULATION, 1790–1820

In 1790, slaves were concentrated in the Chesapeake and in the South Carolina and Georgia low-country. Over the next 30 years, as a result of the decline of slave-based agriculture in Virginia and the beginnings of the cotton boom further south, Chesapeake planters were selling or freeing their slaves, whereas cotton farmers, through both the internal and international slave trade, were beginning to build a Black Belt that stretched through the interior of the Carolinas and on through the Southwest.

View an animated version of this map or related maps at http://history.wadsworth.com/murrin_LEP4e.

after, most of them left Virginia as commodities in the burgeoning interstate slave trade, headed for the new plantations of Georgia, Alabama, and Mississippi.

The movement of slaves out of the Chesapeake was immense. In the 1790s, about 1 in 12 Virginia and Maryland slaves was taken south and west. The figure rose to 1 in 10 between 1800 and 1810, and to 1 in 5 between 1810 and 1820. In 1790, planters in Virginia and Maryland had owned 56 percent of all American slaves; by 1860, they owned only 15 percent. The demand for slaves in the new cotton lands had thus provided many Chesapeake planters with a means of disposing of an endangered investment and with cash to pay for their transition to new crops.

The other center of slavery during the 18th century—coastal South Carolina and Georgia—made a massive recommitment to slave labor in the years after the Revolution. There, the principal crop, rice, along with other American foodstuffs, was experiencing a sharp rise in international demand. Most planters in this region were switching from indigo (a source of blue dye) to cotton as a secondary crop, creating an increase in the demand for slaves. Thousands of slaves in this region had either run away or been carried off by the British in the Revolution, and planters knew that the African slave trade was scheduled to end in 1808. With slave prices rising and slave-produced crops becoming steadily more profitable, they rushed to import as many African slaves as they could in the time remaining. Between 1788 and 1808, some 250,000 slaves were brought directly from Africa to the United States—nearly all of them to Charleston and Savannah. That figure equaled the number of Africans who had been brought to North America during the whole colonial period.

Race, Gender, and Chesapeake Labor

The transition to grain and livestock agriculture in the Chesapeake and the rise of the cotton belt in the Lower South imposed new kinds of labor on the slaves. The switch to mixed farming in Maryland and Virginia brought about a shift in the chores assigned to male and female slaves. Wheat cultivation, for example, meant a

Collection of the Maryland Historical Society, Baltimore.

AN OVERSEER DOING HIS DUTY

In 1798, the architect and engineer Benjamin Latrobe sketched a white overseer smoking a cigar and supervising slave women as they hoed newly cleared farmland near Fredericksburg, Virginia. A critic of slavery, Latrobe sarcastically entitled the sketch *An Overseer Doing His Duty.*

switch from the hoes used for tobacco to the plow and grain cradle—both of which called for the upper-body strength of adult men. The grain economy also required carts, wagons, mills, and good roads, and thus created a need for more slave artisans, nearly all of whom were men. Many of these slave artisans were hired out to urban employers and lived as a semifree caste in cities and towns. In the diversifying economy of the Chesapeake, male slaves did the plowing, mowing, sowing, ditching, and carting and performed most of the tasks requiring artisan skills. All of this work demanded high levels of training and could be performed by someone working either by himself or in a small group with little need for supervision.

Slave women were left with all of the lesser tasks. Contrary to legend, few slave women in the Chesapeake worked as domestic servants in the planter's house. A few of them worked at cloth manufacture, sewing, candle molding, and meat salting, but most female slaves still did farm work—hoeing, weeding, spreading manure, cleaning stables—monotonous work that called for little skill and was closely supervised. This new division of labor was clearly evident during the wheat harvest. On George Washington's farm, for example, male slaves, often working alongside temporary white laborers, moved in a broad line as they mowed the grain. Following them came a gang of children and women bent over and moving along on their hands and knees as they bound wheat into shocks. Similarly, Thomas Jefferson, who had been appalled to see

RICE FIELDS OF THE SOUTH

The rice fields of coastal South Carolina, with their complex systems of irrigation, were often created by Africans who had done similar work in West Africa before their enslavement.

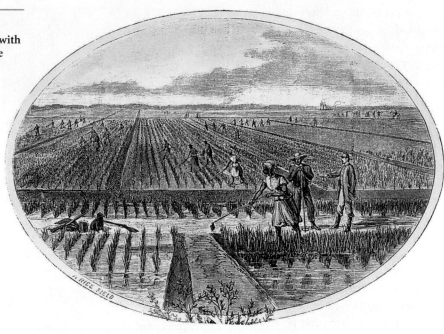

French women working in the fields, abandoned his concern for female delicacy when his own slaves were involved. At the grain harvest, he instructed his overseers to organize "gangs of half men and half women."

The Lowland Task System

On the rice and cotton plantations of South Carolina and Georgia, planters faced different labor problems. Slaves made up 80 percent of the population in this region, more than 90 percent in many parishes. Farms were large, and the two principal crops demanded skilled, intensive labor. The environment encouraged deadly summer diseases and kept white owners and overseers out of the fields. Planters solved these problems by organizing slaves according to the so-called task system. Each morning the owner or overseer assigned a specific task to each slave and allowed him to work at his own pace. When the task was done, the rest of the day belonged to the slave. Slaves who failed to finish their task were punished, and when too many slaves finished early, the owners assigned heavier tasks. In the 18th century, each slave had been expected to tend three to four acres of rice per day. In the early 19th century, with the growth of the rice market, the assignment was raised to five acres.

The task system encouraged slaves to work hard without supervision, and they turned the system to their own uses. Several slaves would often work together until all of their tasks were completed. Strong, young slaves would sometimes help older and weaker slaves after they had finished their own tasks. Once the day's work was done, the

slaves would share their hard-earned leisure out of sight of the owner. A Jamaican visitor remarked that South Carolina and Georgia planters were "very particular in employing a negro, without his consent, after his task is finished, and agreeing with him for the payment which he is to receive." Farther west, low-country slaves who were moved onto the cotton frontier often imposed the task system on new plantations, sometimes against the resistance of masters.

Slaves under the task system won the right to cultivate land as "private fields"—not the little garden plots common in the Chesapeake, but farms of up to five acres on which they grew produce and raised livestock for market. A lively trade developed in slave-produced goods, and by the late 1850s, slaves in the low-country not only produced and exchanged property but also passed it on to their children. The owners tolerated such activity because slaves on the task system worked hard, required minimal supervision, and made money for their owners. The rice and cotton planters in South Carolina and Georgia were among the richest men in the country.

The Seaport Cities, 1790–1815

When the first federal census takers made their rounds in 1790, they found 94 percent of the population living on farms and in rural villages. The remaining 6 percent lived in the 24 towns that had populations of more than 2,500 (a census definition of "urban" that included many communities that were, by modern standards, tiny). Only five communities had populations larger than 10,000: Baltimore (13,503), Charleston (16,359), Boston (18,038), New York (33,131), and Philadelphia (42,444). All five were seaport cities—testimony to the key role of international commerce in the economy of the early republic.

Commerce

These cities had grown steadily during the 18th century, handling imports from Europe and farm exports from America. With the outbreak of war between Britain and France in 1793—a world war that lasted until 1814—the overseas demand for American foodstuffs and for shipping to carry products from the Caribbean islands to Europe further strengthened the seaport cities. Foreign trade during these years was risky and uneven, subject to the tides of war and the strategies of the belligerents. French seizures of American shipping and the resulting undeclared war of 1798–1800, the 1805 British ban on America's reexport trade (the carrying of goods from French islands in the Caribbean), Jefferson's importation ban of 1806 and his trade embargo of 1807, and America's entry into the war in 1812 all disrupted the maritime economy and threw the seaports into periods of economic collapse (see chapter 8). But by 1815, wartime commerce had transformed the seaports and the institutions of American business. New York City had become the nation's largest city, with a population that had grown from 33,131 in 1790 to 96,373 in 1810. Philadelphia's population had risen to 53,722 by 1810, Boston's to 34,322, and Baltimore's to 46,555. Between 1800 and 1810, for the first time in American history, the growth of the urban population exceeded that of the rural population.

Seaport merchants in these years amassed the private fortunes and built the financial infrastructure that would soon take up the task of commercializing and industrializing the northern United States. Old merchants such as the Brown brothers of Providence and Elias Hasket Darby of Salem grew richer, and newcomers such as immigrant John Jacob Astor of New York City built huge personal fortunes. To manage those fortunes, new institutions emerged. Docking and warehousing facilities expanded dramatically. Bookkeepers were replaced by accountants who were familiar with the new double-entry system of accounting, and insurance and banking companies were formed to handle the risks and rewards of wartime commerce.

From the Collection of the New-York Historical Society.

A SCENE NEAR THE NEW YORK CITY DOCKS IN 1798 OR 1799

The large building on the left is the Tontine Coffee House, which housed the Stock Exchange and the principal insurance offices, at the corner of Water and Wall streets.

Rebecca Gore Imagines a House

The increase in commerce in early national America enabled rich Americans to live like English gentlemen. It also created cultural opportunities for wealthy women. Freed from the restrictions of colonial provincialism and not yet bound by the rules of 19th-century domesticity, many of them grasped new opportunities to cultivate themselves, and some became accomplished amateur painters, musicians, botanists, and writers. Rebecca Gore of Boston became an architect.

Rebecca Gore lived in London from 1796 through 1804 while her husband, the Federalist gentleman Christopher Gore, was a commissioner negotiating claims under the Jay Treaty. In 1799, they received news that their country house near Boston had burned down. Rebecca took on the responsibility for designing a new one. The couple visited English estates, and in 1801, they toured Holland, Belgium, and Switzerland, then lived in Paris for six months. During her travels, Rebecca Gore studied architecture. She particularly admired the work of Jacques-Guillaume Legrand in Paris. The Gores met Legrand, and Rebecca arranged to study with him. (Christopher Gore wrote a friend from Paris: "Mrs. G. is now with Monsieur Legrand in the adjoining parlour building houses.") Back in London, Rebecca drew up plans for the new country house and sent them back to Legrand. There is no further documentation of how the plans took shape, but the result was Gore Place in Waltham, one of the great showhouses of Federalist New England.

At first glance, Gore Place looked like an English country estate, with a high central block and lower wings. The broad front lawn, the carefully shaped woods, the large vegetable garden, and the two greenhouses were also English. So too were the field of English wheat and other agricultural experiments that Christopher Gore, aping the English aristocracy, conducted on the estate. But a closer look revealed the influence of Rebecca Gore's sojourn in Napoleon's Paris and her studies with the architect Legrand. Two simple front doors were placed symmetrically in the central façade. Inside, the back wall of the first room curved inward, and a door opened onto an oval parlor that looked out on the back garden. There was a skylight, and Rebecca insisted that a window be placed over one of the fireplaces, causing considerable concern for Christopher Gore and his American builders. These were all touches of the French Enlightenment, used frequently in Legrand's Paris buildings. There were also concessions to cost and to America's obligatory republican simplicity: the house was elegant with a minimum of ornament; the fireplaces were of Connecticut sandstone rather than the traditional marble, and while English gentlemen built their country houses of stone, the Gores built theirs of Boston brick. Gore Place, with its ties to English aristocracy, the French Enlightenment, and the American republic, was unique—largely because Rebecca Gore had had the opportunity to travel, to live in the highest circles of British and French society, and to study architecture and design a house for her family.

GORE PLACE IN WALTHAM, MASSACHUSETTS

The bustle of prosperity was evident on the waterfronts and principal streets of the seaport cities. An Englishman who visited the New York City docks during the wartime boom left this description:

> The carters were driving in every direction; and the sailors and labourers upon the wharfs, and onboard the vessels, were moving their ponderous burdens from place to place. The merchants and their clerks were busily engaged in their counting-houses, or upon the piers. The Tontine coffee-house was filled with underwriters, brokers, merchants, traders, and politicians. . . . The steps and balcony of the coffee-house were crowded with people bidding, or listening to the several auctioneers, who had elevated themselves upon a hogshead of sugar, a puncheon of rum, or a bale of cotton; and with Stentorian voices were exclaiming, "Once, twice. Once, twice." "Another cent." "Thank ye, gentlemen. . . ." The coffeehouse slip, and the corners of Wall and Pearl Streets were jammed up with carts, drays, and wheelbarrows; horses and men were huddled promiscuously together, leaving little or no room for passengers to pass. . . . Everything was in motion; all was life, bustle, and activity.

Poverty

Away from the waterfront, the main thoroughfares and a few of the side streets were paved with cobblestones and lined with fine shops and townhouses. In other parts of the cities, however, the boom was creating unprecedented poverty as well as wealth. Earlier in the 18th century, seaports had their share of poor people and depressed neighborhoods, but not on the scale that prevailed between 1790 and 1820. A few steps off the handsome avenues were narrow streets crowded with ragged children, browsing dogs, pigs, horses, and cattle, and garbage and waste-filled open sewers. Epidemics had become more frequent and deadly. New York City, for example, experienced six severe epidemics of yellow fever between 1791 and 1822. Each time, the disease entered through the seaport and settled in the slums. Life expectancy in Boston, reputedly the healthiest city in America, was three to five years lower than in the surrounding countryside.

The slums were evidence that money created by commerce was being distributed in undemocratic ways. Per capita wealth in New York rose 60 percent between 1790 and 1825, but the wealthiest 4 percent of the population owned more than half of that wealth. The wages of skilled and unskilled labor rose in these years, but the increase in seasonal and temporary employment, together with the recurring interruptions of foreign commerce, cut deeply into the security and prosperity of ordinary women and men. Added to the old insecurities of sickness, fire, accident, aging, and any number of personal misfortunes, these setbacks ate up the gains made by laborers, sailors, and most artisans and their families.

The Status of Labor

Meanwhile, the status of artisans in the big cities was undergoing change. In 1790, independent artisans demanded and usually received the respect of their fellow citizens. When a clerk in Boston refused to attend dancing classes that one of the town's master saddlers had joined, a newspaper scolded him (a mere "stockjobber's lackey") for considering himself the social superior of the saddler and other "reputable mechanics." Artisans constituted about half of the male workforce of the seaport cities, and their respectability and usefulness, together with the role they had played in the Revolution (see chapter 6), had earned them an honorable status.

That status rested largely on their independence. In 1790, most artisan workshops were household operations with at most one or two apprentices and hired journeymen, who looked forward to owning their own shops one day. Timothy Dwight, the conservative president of Yale College, observed that few of those "amphibious beings" in America remained journeymen for life. Most master craftsmen lived modestly (on the borderline of poverty in many cases) and aspired only to the ability to support their households in security and decency. They identified their way of life with republican virtue. A doggerel verse dedicated to New York's stonemasons in 1805 reflects their view of themselves:

> I pay my debts I steal from no man; would not cut a throat
> To gain admission to a great man's purse
> Or a whore's bed. I'd not betray my friend
> To get his place of fortune; I scorn to flatter
> A blown up fool above me or crush
> The wretch beneath me.

This was a classic statement of the republican honesty and virtue that characterized the self-descriptions of skilled workmen. Thomas Jefferson catered to these sensibilities when he pronounced artisans "the yeomanry of the cities."

As in the countryside, however, the patriarchal base of that republicanism was eroding. As the maritime economy grew, changes occurred in the nature of construction work, shipbuilding, the clothing trades, and other specialized crafts. Artisans were replaced by cheaper labor and were undercut by subcontracted "slop work" performed by semiskilled outworkers. Perhaps one in five master craftsmen entered the newly emerging business class. The others took work as laborers or journeymen (the term for wage-earning craftsmen). By 1815, most young craftsmen could no longer hope to own their own shops. About half of New York City's journeymen that year were older than 30 years; nearly one-quarter were older than 40. Most of them were married, and about half of them headed a household that included four or more dependents. In short, they had become wage earners for life. In the seaport cities between 1790 and 1820, the world of artisans such as Paul Revere, Benjamin Franklin, and Thomas Paine was passing out of existence and was being replaced by wage labor.

The loss of independence undermined the paternal status of artisan husbands and fathers. As wage earners, few could support their family unless the wife and children earned money to augment family income. Working-class women took in boarders and did laundry and found work as domestic servants or as peddlers of fruit, candy, vegetables, cakes, or hot corn. They sent their children out to scavenge in the streets. The descent into wage labor and the reliance on the earnings of women and children clashed sharply with the republican, patriarchal assumptions of fathers.

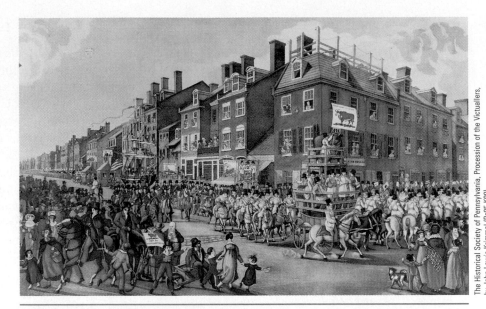

The Historical Society of Pennsylvania, Procession of the Victuallers, by John Lewis Krimmel (Bc85 K89).

PROCESSION OF VICTUALLERS, 1815

The frequent and festive parades in the seaport cities included militia companies, political officials, clergymen, and artisans organized by trade. In this Philadelphia parade celebrating the end of the War of 1812, the victuallers, preceded by militia cavalrymen, carry a penned steer and a craft flag high atop a wagon, while butchers in top hats and clean aprons ride below. Behind them, shipbuilders drag a ship through the streets. Such parades were vivid displays of the system of interlocking labors that made up the city and of the value of artisans within that system.

The Withering of Patriarchal Authority

In the 50 years following the Declaration of Independence, the patriarchal republic created by the Founding Fathers became a democracy. The decline of authority and deference and the rise of individualistic, democratic social and political forms had many roots—most obviously in rural overcrowding, the movement of young people west and into the towns, and, more happily, in the increasingly democratic implications of American Revolutionary ideology. Most Americans witnessed the initial stirrings of change as a withering of paternal authority in their own households. Some—slaves and many women in particular—welcomed the decline of patriarchy. Others (the fathers themselves, disinherited sons, and women who looked to the security of old ways) considered it a disaster of unmeasured proportions. Whether they experienced the transformation as a personal rise or fall, Americans by the early 19th century had entered a world where received authority and past experience had lost their power. A new democratic faith emerged, grounded in the experience, intellect, and intuition of ordinary people.

Paternal Power in Decline

The philosopher Ralph Waldo Emerson, who reached adulthood in the 1830s, later mused that he had had the misfortune to be young when age was respected and to have grown old when youth counted for everything. Arriving in America at about the time Emerson came of age, the French visitor Alexis de Tocqueville observed that paternal power was largely absent in American families. "All that remains of it," he said, "are a few vestiges in the first years of childhood. . . . But as soon as the young American approaches manhood, the ties of filial obedience are relaxed day by day; master of his thoughts, he is soon master of his conduct. . . . At the close of boyhood the man appears and begins to trace out his own path."

From the mid-18th century onward, especially after the Revolution, many young people grew up knowing that their fathers would be unable to help them and that they would have to make their own way in the world. The consequent decline of parental power became evident in many ways—perhaps most poignantly in changing patterns of courtship and marriage. In the countryside, young men knew that they would not inherit the family farm, and young women knew that their father would be able to provide only a small dowry. As a result, fathers exerted less control over marriage choices than when marriage entailed a significant transfer of property. Young people now courted away from parental scrutiny and made choices based on affection and personal attraction rather than on property or parental pressure. In 18th-century America, rural marriages had united families; now they united individuals. One sign of youthful independence (and of young people's lack of faith in their future) was the high number of pregnancies outside of marriage. Such incidents had been few in the 17th-century North, but in the second half of the 18th century and in the first decades of the 19th, the number of first births that occurred within eight months of marriage averaged between 25 and 30 percent, with the rates running much higher among poor couples. Apparently, fathers who could not provide for their children could not control them either.

The Alcoholic Republic

The erosion of the old family economy was paralleled by a dramatic rise in alcohol consumption. Americans had been drinking alcohol since the time of the first settle-ments. (The Puritan flagship *Arabella* had carried three times as much beer as water.) But drinking, like all other "normal" behaviors, took place within a structure of paternal authority. Americans tippled every day in the course of their ordinary activities: at family meals and around the fireside, at work, and at barn-raisings, militia musters, dances, court days (even judges and juries passed the bottle), weddings, funerals, corn-huskings—even at the ordination of ministers. Under such circumstances, drinking—even drunkenness—seldom posed a threat to authority or to the social order.

That old pattern of communal drinking persisted into the 19th century, but during the 50 years following the Revolution, it gradually gave way to a new pattern. Farmers, particularly those in newly settled areas, regularly produced a surplus of grain that they turned into whiskey. In Washington County in western Pennsylvania, for example, 1 family in 10 operated a distillery in the 1790s. Whiskey was safer than water and milk, which were often tainted, and it was cheaper than coffee or tea. It was also cheaper than imported rum, so Americans embraced

John Lewis Krimmel, American, 1786–1821 Village Tavern, 1813–14, oil on canvas, 16-7/8 x 22-1/2 in. (42.8 x 56.9 cm), The Toledo Museum of Art, Toledo, Ohio; Purchased with funds from the Florence Scott Libbey Bequest in Memory of her Father, Maurice A. Scott.

INTERIOR OF AN AMERICAN INN, 1813

In this democratic, neighborly scene in a country inn in the early republic, men of varying degrees of wealth, status, and inebriety are drinking and talking freely with each other. One man's wife and daughter have invaded this male domain, perhaps to question the time and money spent at the inn.

whiskey as their national drink and consumed extraordinary quantities of it. Per capita consumption of pure alcohol in all its forms increased by three to four gallons annually between 1790 and 1830. Most of the increase was in consumption of cheap and potent whiskey. By 1830, per capita consumption of distilled spirits was more than five gallons per year—the highest it has ever been, and three times what it is in the United States today. The United States had become, as one historian has said, an "alcoholic republic."

The nation's growing thirst was driven not by conviviality or neighborliness but by a desire to get drunk. Most Americans drank regularly, although with wide variations. Men drank far more than women, the poor and the rich drank more than the emerging middle class, city dwellers drank more than farmers, westerners drank more than easterners, and southerners drank a bit more than northerners. Throughout the nation, the heaviest drinking took place among the increasing numbers of young men who lived away from their families and outside the old social controls: soldiers and sailors, boatmen and other transport workers, lumberjacks, schoolmasters, journeyman craftsmen, college students. Among such men, the controlled tippling of the 18th century gave way to the binge and to solitary drinking. By the 1820s, American physicians were learning to diagnose delirium tremens—the trembling and the paranoid delusions brought on by withdrawal from physical addiction to alcohol. By that decade, social reformers branded alcohol as a threat to individual well-being, to social peace, and to the republic itself (see chapter 11).

The Democratization of Print

Of course, Americans freed from the comforts and constraints of patriarchal authority did more than fornicate and drink. Many seized more constructive opportunities to think and act for themselves. That tendency was

---

M U S I C A L   L I N K   T O   T H E   P A S T

The Minuet in America

Composer: Alexander Reinagle
Title: "Minuet and Gavotte" (c. 1800)

Like the quadrille, another European dance style popular at this time in the United States, the minuet and gavotte required dancers to learn highly complicated directions that took more time to master than most working people could spare. A strict formality reigned: The dances commenced with introductions and an exchange of courtesies, featured little if any contact between partners, and required balletlike technique that rendered them nearly impossible for casual, untrained dancers.

By 1800, the minuet and gavotte were becoming passé in the United States. Their stiff and formal qualities represented values of rank and privilege that reminded Americans of the monarchy they had cast aside. The newly emerging market revolution tended to reward those who worked the hardest or had the best ideas for products, not those from elite families. In the election of 1800, Americans seemed to embrace this ideal in their election of Thomas Jefferson to the presidency, over the more authoritarian and conservative "kingly" politics (according to Jefferson; see page 267) espoused by the incumbent Federalist party.

In the years surrounding the turn of the century, middle-class citizens became more involved than ever in all levels of government thanks to an increase in compensation for government positions, an explosion of voluntary political clubs, and a movement toward universal white male suffrage. The upshot of all these developments was that political, economic, and religious leadership in American society, once viewed as the province of the elite, increasingly fell to people of merit, not birthright, as it largely had been in English society. In this uniquely American atmosphere, rarefied and exclusive dance traditions such as the minuet and gavotte were rapidly losing popular favor. By the mid-19th century, these dance traditions virtually vanished in the United States.

1. Can popular dancing styles be used as evidence to document changes in American history and culture?
2. What do you think the dance crazes of today communicate about our current society?

Listen to an audio recording of this music on the Musical Links to the Past CD.

speeded by a rise in literacy and by the emergence of a print culture that catered to popular tastes. The literacy rate in the preindustrial United States was among the highest ever recorded. In 1790, approximately 85 percent of adult men in New England and 60 percent of those in Pennsylvania and the Chesapeake could read and write. The literacy rate was lower among women—about 45 percent in New England—but on the rise. By 1820, all but the poorest white Americans, particularly in the North, could read and write. The rise in literacy was accompanied by an explosive growth in the amount and kinds of reading matter that became available to the public. At its simplest and most intimate, this took the form of personal letters. Increased mobility separated families and friends and encouraged letter writing. In 1790, only 75 post offices operated in the United States. By 1800, 903 were open. The amount of mail increased similarly, and—if what has survived to the present is an indication—the proportion made up of family correspondence, and the proportion of that correspondence written and read by women, both increased dramatically.

Women also were the principal readers of novels, a new form of reading matter that Thomas Jefferson and other authorities denounced as frivolous and aberrant. The first best-selling novel in the United States was *The Power of Sympathy,* a morally ambiguous tale of seduction and betrayal that exposed hypocrisy in male authorities who punished (generally poor and vulnerable) women for their own seductions. Such tales were seen as dangerous not only because they contained questionable subject matter but also because girls and women read them silently and in private, without proper surveillance.

The most widely distributed publications, however, were newspapers. In 1790, 90 newspapers were being published in the United States. In 1830, 370 were in publication, and they had grown chattier and more informal. Still, even in New England, only 1 household in 10 or 12 subscribed to a newspaper. The papers were passed from hand to hand, read aloud in groups, and made available at taverns and public houses. Timothy Dwight, conservative president of Yale, hated newspapers and associated them with gambling, tavern-haunting, and drinking.

The increase in literacy and in printed matter accelerated the democratizing process. In the 18th century, when books and newspapers were scarce, most Americans had experienced the written word only as it was read aloud by fathers, ministers, or teachers. Between 1780 and 1820, private, silent reading of new kinds of texts—religious tracts, inexpensive Bibles, personal letters, novels, newspapers, and magazines—became common. No longer were authority figures the sole interpreters of the world for families and neighborhoods. The new print culture encouraged Americans to read, think, and interpret information for themselves.

Citizenship

The transition from republic to democracy—and the relation of that transition to the decline of rural patriarchy—took on formal, institutional shape in a redefinition of republican citizenship.

The revolutionary constitutions of most states retained colonial freehold (property) qualifications for voting. In the yeoman societies of the late 18th century, freehold qualifications granted the vote to between one-half and three-quarters of adult white men. Many of the disenfranchised were dependent sons who expected to inherit citizenship along with land. Some states dropped the freehold clause and gave the vote to all adult men who paid taxes, but with little effect on the voting population. Both the freehold and taxpaying qualifications tended to grant political rights to adult men who headed households, thus reinforcing classical republican notions that granted full citizenship to independent fathers and not to their dependents. Statesmen often defended the qualifications in those terms. Arthur St. Clair, the territorial governor of Ohio, argued for retention of the Northwest Ordinance's 50-acre freehold qualification for voting in territorial elections in set-piece republican language: "I do not count independence and wealth always together," he said, "but I pronounce poverty and dependence inseparable." When Nathaniel Macon, a respected old revolutionary from North Carolina, saw that his state would abolish property qualifications in 1802, he suggested that the suffrage be limited to married men. Like St. Clair's proposition, it was an attempt to maintain the old distinction between citizen-householders and disenfranchised dependents.

Between 1790 and 1820, republican notions of citizenship grounded in fatherhood and proprietorship gave way to a democratic insistence on equal rights for all white men. In 1790, only Vermont granted the vote to all free men. Kentucky entered the Union in 1792 without property or taxpaying qualifications; Tennessee followed with a freehold qualification, but only for newcomers who had resided in their counties for less than six months. The federal government dropped the 50-acre freehold qualification in the territories in 1812; of the eight territories that became states between 1796 and 1821, none kept a property qualification, only three maintained a taxpaying qualification, and five explicitly granted the vote to all white men. In the same years, one eastern state after another widened the franchise. By 1840, only Rhode Island retained a propertied electorate, primarily because Yankee farmers in that state wanted to retain power in a society made up more of urban, immigrant wage earners. (When Rhode Island finally reformed the franchise in 1843, the new law included a freehold requirement that applied only to the foreign-born.) With that exception, the white men of every state held the vote.

Early 19th-century suffrage reform gave political rights to propertyless men, and thus took a long step away from the Founding Fathers' republic and toward mass democracy. At the same time, however, reformers explicitly limited the democratic franchise to those who were white and male. New Jersey's revolutionary constitution, for instance, had granted the vote to "persons" who met a freehold qualification. This loophole enfranchised property-holding widows, many of whom exercised their rights. A law of 1807 abolished property restrictions and gave the vote to all white men; the same law closed the loophole that had allowed propertied women to vote. The question of woman suffrage would not be raised again until women raised it in 1848 (see chapter 11); it would not be settled until well into the 20th century.

New restrictions also applied to African Americans. The revolutionary constitutions of Massachusetts, New Hampshire, Vermont, and Maine—northeastern states with tiny black minorities—granted the vote to free blacks. New York and North Carolina laws gave the vote to "all men" who met the qualifications, and propertied African Americans in many states (a tiny but symbolically crucial minority) routinely exercised the vote. Postrevolutionary laws that extended voting rights to all white men often specifically excluded or severely restricted votes for blacks. Free blacks lost the suffrage in New York, New Jersey, Pennsylvania, Connecticut, Maryland, Tennessee, and North Carolina—all states in which they had previously voted. By 1840, fully 93 percent of blacks in the North lived in states that either banned or severely restricted their right to vote. And the restrictions were explicitly about race. A delegate to the New York constitutional convention of 1821, noting the movement of freed slaves into New York City, argued against allowing them to vote: "The whole host of Africans that now deluge our city (already too impertinent to be borne), would be placed upon an equal with the citizens." A Michigan legislator later confirmed the distinction between "Africans" and "citizens" when he insisted that neither blacks nor Indians belonged to the "great North American Family," and thus could never be citizens of the republic.

Thus the "universal" suffrage of which many Americans boasted was far from universal: New laws dissolved the old republican connections between political rights and property, and thus saved the citizenship of thousands who were becoming propertyless tenants and wage earners; the same laws that gave the vote to all white men, however, explicitly barred other Americans from political participation. Faced with the disintegration of Jefferson's republic of proprietors, the wielders of power had chosen to blur the emerging distinctions of social class while they hardened the boundaries of sex and race. The "democracy" of white men would return to this formula repeatedly as the 19th century unfolded.

Republican Religion

The Founding Fathers had been largely indifferent to organized religion, although a few were pious men. Some, like George Washington, a nominal Episcopalian, attended church out of a sense of obligation. Many of the better educated, including Thomas Jefferson, subscribed to deism, the belief that God had created the universe but did not intervene in its affairs. Many simply did not bother themselves with thoughts about religion. When asked why the Constitution mentioned neither God nor religion, Alexander Hamilton is reported to have smiled and answered, "We forgot."

The Decline of the Established Churches

In state after state, postrevolutionary constitutions withdrew government support from religion, and the First Amendment to the U.S. Constitution clearly prescribed the national separation of church and state. Reduced to their own sources of support, the established churches went into decline. The Episcopal Church, which had been the established Church of England in the southern colonies until the Revolution, went into decline. In Virginia, only 40 of the 107 Episcopal parishes supported ministers in the early 19th century. Nor did the Episcopal Church travel west with southern settlers. Of the 408 Episcopal congregations in the South in 1850, 315 were in the old seaboard states.

In New England, the old churches fared little better. The Connecticut Congregationalist Ezra Stiles reported in 1780 that 60 parishes in Vermont and an equal number in New Hampshire were without a minister. In Massachusetts, according to Stiles's reports, 80 parishes lacked a minister. In all, about one-third of New England's Congregational pulpits were vacant in 1780, and the situation was worse to the north and west. In Vermont between 1763 and 1820, the founding of churches followed the incorporation of towns by an average of 15 years, an indication that frontier settlement in that state proceeded almost entirely without the benefit of organized religion. In 1780, nearly all of the 750 Congregational churches in the United States were in New England. In the next 40 years, although the nation's population rose from 4 to 10 million, the number of Congregational churches rose by only 350. Ordinary women and men were leaving the churches that had dominated the religious life of colonial America, sometimes ridiculing the learned clergy as they departed. To Ezra Stiles and other conservatives, it seemed that the republic was plunging into atheism.

The Rise of the Democratic Sects

The collapse of the established churches, the social dislocations of the postrevolutionary years, and the increasingly antiauthoritarian, democratic sensibilities of ordinary Americans provided fertile ground for the growth of new democratic sects. These were the years of campmeeting revivalism, years in which Methodists and Baptists grew from small, half-organized sects into the great popular denominations they have been ever since. They were also years in which fiercely independent dropouts from older churches were putting together a loosely organized movement that would become the Disciples of Christ. At the same time, ragged, half-educated preachers were spreading the Universalist and Freewill Baptist messages in upcountry New England, while in western New York young Joseph Smith was receiving the visions that would lead to Mormonism (see chapter 10).

The result was, first of all, a vast increase in the variety of choices on the American religious landscape. Within that welter of new churches was a roughly uniform democratic style shared by the fastest-growing sects. First, they renounced the need for an educated, formally authorized clergy. Religion was now a matter of the heart and not the head; crisis conversion (understood in most churches as personal transformation that resulted from direct experience of the Holy Spirit) was a necessary credential for preachers; a college degree was not. The new preachers substituted emotionalism and storytelling for Episcopal ritual and Congregational theological lectures; stories attracted listeners, and they were harder for the learned clergy to refute. The new churches also held up the Bible as the one source of religious knowledge, thus undercutting all theological knowledge and placing every literate Christian on a level with the best-educated minister. These tendencies often ended in Restorationism—the belief that all theological and institutional changes since the end of biblical times were manmade mistakes, and that religious

organizations must restore themselves to the purity and simplicity of the church of the Apostles. In sum, this loose democratic creed rejected learning and tradition and raised up the priesthood of all believers.

Baptists and Methodists were by far the most successful at preaching to the new populist audience. The United States had only 50 Methodist churches in 1783; by 1820 it had 2,700. Over those same years, the number of Baptist churches rose from 400 to 2,700. Together, in 1820, these two denominations outnumbered Episcopalians and Congregationalists by 3 to 1, almost a reversal of their relative standings 40 years earlier. Baptists based much of their appeal in localism and congregational democracy. Methodist success, on the other hand, entailed skillful national organization. Bishop Francis Asbury, the head of the church in its fastest-growing years, built an episcopal bureaucracy that seeded churches throughout the republic and sent circuit-riding preachers to places that had none. These early Methodist missions were grounded in self-sacrifice to the point of martyrdom. Asbury demanded much of his itinerant preachers, and until 1810, he strongly suggested that they remain celibate. "To marry," he said, "is to locate." Asbury also knew that married circuit riders would leave many widows and orphans behind, for hundreds of them worked themselves to death. Of the men who served as Methodist itinerants before 1819, at least 60 percent died before the age of 40.

From seaport cities to frontier settlements, few Americans escaped the sound of Methodist preaching in the early 19th century. The Methodist preachers were common men who spoke plainly, listened carefully to others, and carried hymnbooks with simple tunes that anyone could sing. They also, particularly in the early years, shared traditional folk beliefs with their humble flocks. Some of the early circuit riders relied heavily on dreams; some could predict the future; many visited heaven and hell and returned with full descriptions. In the end, however, the hopefulness and simplicity of the Methodist message attracted ordinary Americans. The Methodists rejected the old terrors of Calvinist determinism and taught that although salvation comes only through God, men and women can decide to open themselves to divine grace and thus play a decisive role in their own salvation. They also taught that a godly life is a gradual, lifetime growth in grace—thus allowing for repentance for minor, and sometimes even major, lapses of faith and behavior. By granting responsibility (one might say sovereignty) to the individual believer, the Methodists established their democratic credentials and drew hundreds of thousands of Americans into their fold.

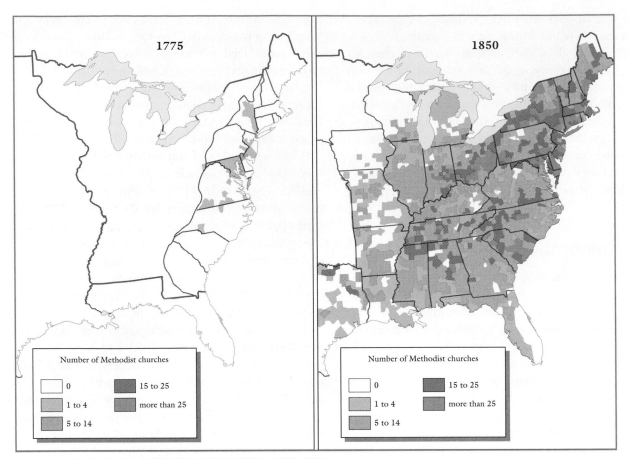

MAP 7.4 GROWTH OF AMERICAN METHODISM, 1775–1850

This is a county-by-county map of the rise of American Methodism from the Revolution through the eve of the Civil War. In 1775, Methodism was almost nonexistent in British North America. By 1850, the Methodists were the largest Protestant denomination in the United States, and they were truly a national faith: There were Methodist churches in almost every county in the country.

The Christianization of the White South

During these same years, evangelical Protestantism became the dominant religion of the white South. That triumph constituted a powerful assault on the prerevolutionary structure of authority, because the Baptists, Methodists, and evangelical Presbyterians who achieved it saw it as a revolt of poor and middling folk against the cultural dominance of the gentry. The essence of southern evangelicalism was a violent conversion experience followed by a life of piety and a rejection of what evangelicals called "the world." To no small degree, "the world" was the economic, cultural, and political world controlled by the planters. James McGready, who preached in rural North Carolina, openly condemned the gentry: "The world is in all their thoughts day and night. All their talk is of corn and tobacco, of land and stock. The price of merchandise and negroes are inexhaustible themes of conversation. But

for them, the name of Jesus has no charms; it is rarely mentioned unless to be profaned." In the 1790s, this was dangerous talk, as McGready learned when young rakes rode their horses through one of his outdoor meetings, tipped over the benches, set the altar on fire, and threatened to kill McGready himself.

Southern Baptists, Methodists, and Presbyterians spread their democratic message in the early 19th century through the camp meeting. Although its origins stretched back to the 18th century, the first full-blown camp meeting took place at Cane Ridge, Kentucky, in 1801. Here the annual "Holy Feast," a three-day communion service of Scotch-Irish Presbyterians, was transformed into an outdoor, interdenominational revival at which hundreds experienced conversion under Presbyterian, Methodist, and Baptist preaching. Estimates of the crowd at Cane Ridge ranged from 10,000 to 20,000 persons, and by all accounts the enthusiasm was nearly unprecedented. Some converts fainted; others succumbed to uncontrolled bod-

CAMP MEETING NEAR YORK, PENNSYLVANIA, 1808

Painting from memory, the local artist Lewis Miller portrayed a Methodist camp meeting at Codorus Creek in 1808, catching the evangelicals in their powerful combination of individual piety and public, democratic display. Miller remembered their tent city and the shanty from which the evangelists preached. In the center of the sketch, male and female converts revel together in public humiliation and spiritual triumph. A crowd in which men and women stand separately looks on.

ily jerkings, while a few barked like dogs—all of them visibly taken by the Holy Spirit. Such exercises fell upon women and men, whites and blacks, rich and poor, momentarily erasing southern social distinctions in moments of profound and very public religious ecstasy. A witness to a later camp meeting recounted that "to see a bold and courageous Kentuckian (undaunted by the horrors of war) turn pale and tremble at the reproof of a weak woman, a little boy, or a poor African; to see him sink down in deep remorse, roll and toss, and gnash his teeth, till black in the face, entreat the prayers of those he came to devour . . . who can say the change was not supernatural?"

Evangelicals and Slavery

Southern evangelicalism was a subversive movement from its origins before the Revolution into the early 19th century. Although it reviled worldliness, southern evangelicalism was at bottom conservative because it seldom questioned the need for social hierarchy. As the 19th century progressed, the Baptists, Methodists, and Presbyterians of the South, although they never stopped railing against greed and pride, learned to live comfortably within a system of fixed hierarchy and God-given social roles.

Slavery became the major case in point. For a brief period after the Revolution, evangelicals included slavery on their list of worldly sins. Methodists and Baptists preached to slaves as well as to whites, and Bishop Francis Asbury,

principal architect of American Methodism, was familiar with John Wesley's statement that slavery was against "all the laws of Justice, Mercy, and Truth." In 1780, a conference of Methodist preachers ordered circuit riders to free their slaves and advised all Methodists to do the same. In 1784, the Methodists declared that they would excommunicate members who failed to free their slaves within two years. Lay Methodists took the order seriously: On the Delmarva Peninsula (Delaware and the Eastern Shore of Maryland and Virginia), for instance, Methodist converts freed thousands of slaves in the late 18th century. Other evangelicals shared their views. As early as 1787, southern Presbyterians prayed for "final abolition," and two years later, Baptists condemned slavery as "a violent deprivation of the rights of nature and inconsistent with a republican government."

The period of greatest evangelical growth, however, came during the years in which the South was committing irrevocably to plantation slavery. As increasing numbers of both slaves and slave owners came within the evangelical fold, the southern churches had to rethink their position on slavery. The Methodists never carried out their threat to excommunicate slaveholders, confessing in 1816 that southerners were so committed to slavery that "little can be done to abolish the practice so contrary to moral justice." Similarly, the Baptists and Presbyterians never translated their antislavery rhetoric into action. By 1820, evangelicals were coming to terms with slavery. Instead of demanding freedom for slaves, they suggested, as the

Methodist James O'Kelly put it, that slave owners remember that slaves were "dear brethren in Christ" who should not be treated cruelly and who should be allowed to attend religious services. By the 1830s, with large numbers of the planter elite converted to the evangelical fold, this evolved into a full-scale effort to Christianize the institution of slavery (see chapter 10).

After 1820, few southern evangelicals spoke out against slavery. Those who held to their antislavery views were concentrated in the upcountry, where few whites owned slaves. Many of these were joining the stream of poor and middling whites who were moving to free states north of the Ohio River. A Kentucky farmer and carpenter named Thomas Lincoln, for instance, belonged to a Baptist congregation that had separated from its parent church over the question of slavery. When he moved his family to a site near Pidgeon Creek, Indiana, Lincoln helped build an antislavery Baptist church and served it as trustee. He also arranged a job as church sexton for his young son Abraham.

The Beginnings of African American Christianity

Slaves in America who were Christian in the 17th and 18th centuries mostly were converted by Anglican missions. Blacks participated in the revivals of the southern Great Awakening, and the number of Christian slaves increased steadily in the second half of the 18th century. In the slave communities of the Upper South, as well as the burgeoning free and semifree urban black populations of both the North and South, the evangelical revivals of the late 18th and early 19th centuries appealed powerfully to African Americans who sensed that the bonds of slavery were loosening. By 1820, most blacks outside the Deep South considered themselves Christians. In the South Carolina and Georgia low-country, however, few slaves were Christians before 1830.

From 1780 to 1820, for the first time, thousands of slaves embraced Christianity and began to turn it into a religion of their own. Slaves attended camp meetings (the Cane Ridge revival included a black preacher, probably from the independent church in Lexington), listened to itinerant preachers, and joined the Baptist and Methodist congregations of the southern revival.

Blacks were drawn to revival religion for many of the same reasons as whites. They found the informal, story-telling evangelical preachers more attractive than the old Anglican missionaries. The revivalists, in turn, welcomed slaves and free blacks to their meetings and sometimes recruited them as preachers. Evangelical, emotional preaching; the falling, jerking, and other camp-meeting "exercises"; and the revivalists' emphasis on singing and other forms of audience participation were much more attractive than the cold, high-toned preaching of the Anglicans. So were the humility and suffering of the evangelical whites. Slaves respected Methodist missionaries who entered their cabins and talked with them on their own terms; they listened more closely to men such as James McGready than to the slaveholders who rode horses through McGready's meetings. Finally, the slaves gloried in the evangelicals' assault on the slaveholders' culture and in the antislavery sentiments of many white evangelicals.

BETHEL AME CHURCH

Founded in 1794 by the Reverend Richard Allen and nine other blacks who resented discrimination at the hands of white Methodists, Philadelphia's Bethel African Methodist Episcopal Church became a cornerstone of the city's free black community.

Historical Commission, Mother Bethel AME Church, Philadelphia, PA.

The result was a huge increase in the number of African American Christians. Methodists, who counted converts more carefully than some others, claimed 20,000 black members in 1800—one in three American Methodists.

Neither antislavery beliefs nor openness to black participation, however, persisted long among white evangelicals. Although exceptions existed, most "integrated" congregations in both the North and South were in fact internally segregated, with blacks sitting in the back of the church or upstairs in the gallery, and with only whites serving in positions of authority. Blacks began organizing independent churches. In Philadelphia, black preachers Richard Allen and Absalom Jones rebelled against segregated seating in St. George's Methodist Church and, in 1794, founded two separate black congregations; by 1800, about 40 percent of Philadelphia's blacks belonged to one of those two churches. Similar secessions resulted in new churches farther south: in Baltimore; in Wilmington, Delaware; in Richmond; in Norfolk; and in the cluster of villages that had risen to serve the Chesapeake's new mixed economy. Even Charleston boasted an independent Methodist conference made up of 4,000 slaves and free blacks in 1815.

By 1820, roughly 700 independent black churches operated in the United States where there had been none at all 30 years earlier. Only after 1830 did an independent Christian tradition exist among the majority of blacks who remained plantation slaves (see chapter 10). The democratic message of the early southern revival, the brief attempt of white and black Christians to live out the implications of that message, and the independent black churches that rose from the failure of that attempt all left a permanent stamp on southern Protestantism, black and white.

Black Republicanism: Gabriel's Rebellion

Masters who talked of liberty and natural rights sometimes worried that slaves might imagine that such language could apply to themselves. The Age of Democratic Revolution took a huge step in that direction in 1789, when the French Revolution—fought in the name of "Liberty, Equality, and Fraternity"—went beyond American notions of restored English liberties and into the heady regions of universal natural rights. Among the first repercussions outside of France was a revolution on the Caribbean island of Hispaniola in the French colony of Saint-Domingue. That island's half-million slaves fought out a complicated political and military revolt that began with the events in Paris in 1789 and resulted—after the

defeats of Spanish, English, and French armies—with the creation of the independent black republic of Haiti on the western one-third of the island. Slave societies throughout the hemisphere heard tales of terror from refugee French planters and stories of hope from the slaves they brought with them (12,000 of these entered South Carolina and Louisiana alone). In 1800, a conservative Virginia white complained that "Liberty and Equality has been infused into the minds of the negroes." A South Carolina congressman agreed that "this newfangled French philosophy of liberty and equality" was stirring up the slaves. Even Thomas Jefferson, who applauded the spread of French republicanism, conceded that "the West Indies appears to have given considerable impulse to the minds of the slaves . . . in the United States."

Slaves from the 1790s onward whispered of natural rights and imagined themselves as part of the Democratic Revolution. This covert republic of the slaves sometimes came into the open, most ominously in Richmond in 1800, where a slave blacksmith named Gabriel hatched a well-planned conspiracy to overthrow Virginia's slave regime. Gabriel had been hired out to Richmond employers for most of his adult life; he was shaped less by plantation slavery than by the democratic, loosely interracial underworld of urban artisans. In the late 1790s, the repressive acts of the Federalist national government and the angry responses of the Jeffersonian opposition (see chapter 8), along with the news from Saint-Domingue (present-day Haiti), drove the democratic sensibilities of that world to new heights. Gabriel's plans took shape within that heated ideological environment.

Gabriel, working with his brother and other hired-out slave artisans, planned his revolt with military precision. Working at religious meetings, barbecues, and the grog shops of Richmond, they recruited soldiers among slave artisans, adding plantation slaves only at the last moment. Gabriel planned to march an army of 1,000 men on Richmond in three columns. The outside columns would set diversionary fires in the warehouse district and prevent the militia from entering the town. The center would seize Capitol Square, including the treasury, the arsenal, and Governor James Monroe.

Although his army would be made up of slaves, and although his victory would end slavery in Virginia, Gabriel hoped to make a republican revolution, not a slave revolt. His chosen enemies were the Richmond "merchants" who had controlled his labor. Later, a co-conspirator divulged the plan: The rebels would hold Governor Monroe hostage and split the state treasury among themselves, and "if the white people agreed to their freedom they would then hoist a white flag, and [Gabriel] would dine and drink with the merchants of the city on the day when it would be agreed to." Gabriel expected what he called "the poor white people" and "the most redoubtable republicans" to join him. He in fact had the shadowy support of two Frenchmen, and rumors indicated that other whites were involved, although never at levels that matched the delusions of the conspirators. Gabriel planned to kill anyone who opposed him, but he would spare Quakers, Methodists, and Frenchmen, for they were "friendly to liberty." Unlike those of earlier slave insurgents, Gabriel's dreams did not center on violent retribution or a return to or reconstruction of West Africa. He was an American revolutionary, and he dreamed of a truly democratic republic for Virginia. His army would march into Richmond under the banner "Death or Liberty."

Gabriel and his co-conspirators recruited at least 150 soldiers who agreed to gather near Richmond on August 30, 1800. The leaders expected to be joined by 500 to 600 more rebels as they marched upon the town. On the appointed day, however, it rained heavily. Rebels could not reach the meeting point, and amid white terror and black betrayals, Gabriel and his henchmen were hunted down, tried, and sentenced to death. In all, the state hanged 27 supposed conspirators, while others were sold and transported out of Virginia. The condemned carried their radical republican dreams to their graves. A white Virginian marveled that the rebels on the gallows displayed a "sense of their [natural] rights, [and] a contempt of danger." When asked to explain the revolt, one condemned man replied in terms that could only have disturbed the white republicans of Virginia: "I have nothing more to offer than what General Washington would have had to offer, had he been taken by the British and put to trial by them. I have adventured my life in endeavoring to obtain the liberty of my countrymen, and am a willing sacrifice in their cause."

Conclusion

Between 1790 and 1820, Americans had transformed their new republic—with paradoxical results. The United States more than doubled in both size and population during these years. American trade with Britain, continental Europe, and the Caribbean skyrocketed. Some Americans amassed fortunes, others made more modest gains, while still others saw their positions deteriorate. Nonwhite Americans experienced the expansion of the republic and the growth of commerce as unmixed catastrophes: Indians between the Appalachians and the Mississippi River lost everything; their hunting grounds became American farmland, much of it worked by slaves who now knew that their masters would never voluntarily free them.

The transformation stemmed both from American independence and from the expansion of agriculture and increased exports of American farm products. When Americans traded plantation staples and surplus food for European (largely British) manufactured goods and financial services, however, they deepened their colonial dependence on the old centers of the world economy—even as they insisted on their independence with a bellicose republican nationalism. This formed the cluttered backdrop of social change, economic and geographic growth, and continuing vulnerability to the whims and needs of the Old World powers against which Federalists and Jeffersonian Republicans fought each other to determine the ultimate outcome of the American Revolution.

SUGGESTED READINGS

Douglas C. North, *The Economic Growth of the United States, 1790–1860* (1961) is an economic overview of these years. On rural society in the North, see **Christopher Clark,** *The Roots of Rural Capitalism: Western Massachusetts, 1780–1860* (1990); **Laurel Thatcher Ulrich,** *A Midwife's Tale: The Life of Martha Ballard, Based on Her Diary, 1785–1812* (1990); **Martin Bruegel,** *Farm, Shop, Landing: The Rise of a Market Society in the Hudson Valley, 1780–1860;* and **Jack Larkin,** *The Reshaping of Everyday Life, 1790–1840* (1988). Good accounts of Native Americans in these years include **Anthony F. C. Wallace,** *The Death and Rebirth of the Seneca* (1969); and **Gregory Evans Dowd,** *A Spirited Resistance: The North American Indian Struggle for a New World* (1992). **Stephen Aron,** *How the West was Lost: The Transformation of Kentucky from Daniel Boone to Henry Clay* (1996), treats white settler societies. Economic change in the South is traced in **Robert William Fogel and Stanley L. Engerman,** *Time on the Cross: The Economics of American Negro Slavery* (1974). The social history of colonial and early national slavery is ably covered in **Ira Berlin,** *Many Thousands Gone: The First Two Centuries of Slavery in North America* (1998). On urban labor, see the early chapters of **Sean Wilentz,** *Chants Democratic: New York City and the Rise of the American Working Class* (1984). The study of religion in the postrevolutionary years begins with two books: **Nathan O. Hatch,** *The Democratization of American Christianity* (1989); and **Jon Butler,** *Awash in a Sea of Faith: Christianizing the American People* (1990). The concluding section of **Gordon Wood,** *The Radicalism of the American Revolution* (1992) discusses the "democratization of mind" during these years. Other important books on these topics are listed in the Suggested Readings for chapter 10.

AMERICAN JOURNEY ONLINE
AND
INFOTRAC COLLEGE EDITION

Visit the source collections at www.ajaccess.wadsworth.com and
infotrac.thomsonlearning.com and use the Search function with
the following key terms to explore documents, images, audio
and video clips, articles, and commentary related to the material
in this chapter.

Eli Whitney   Tenskwatawa
Cotton   James Monroe
Tecumseh   Gabriel's Rebellion

GRADE AIDS

**Visit the Liberty Equality Power Companion Web Site for resources specific to
this textbook:** http://history.wadsworth.com/murrin_LEP4e

The CD in the back of this book and the U.S. History Resource Center at
http://history.wadsworth.com/u.s./ offer a variety of tools to help you succeed in
this course, including access to quizzes; images; documents; interactive simulations,
maps, and timelines; movie explorations; and a wealth of other sources.

Chapter 8

Completing the Revolution, 1789–1815

Collections of Davenport West, Jr.

WE OWE ALLEGIANCE TO NO CROWN, A PATRIOTIC PAINTING
FROM THE WAR OF 1812
Liberty—portrayed, as always, by a pure and determined woman—holds a Liberty
Cap on a staff (the old symbol of international republicanism) and crowns an
embattled American seaman with a classical wreath. Here the war is portrayed
not only as a conflict between Britain and America but also as a contest between
monarchy and republicanism.

CHAPTER OUTLINE

Almost by acclamation, George Washington became the first president under the Constitution. Washington and his closest advisers (they would soon call themselves Federalists) believed that the balance between power and liberty had tipped toward anarchy after the Revolution; "local mischiefs," they said, had nearly destroyed the union of the states that had made independence possible. Federalists wanted the Constitution to counter democratic excesses. They came into office determined to make the national government powerful enough to command respect abroad and to impose order at home. For the most part, they succeeded, but in the process they aroused a determined opposition that feared the Federalists' consolidation of central power at the expense of the states and the citizenry. These self-styled Democratic Republicans (led almost from the beginning by Thomas Jefferson) were as firmly tied to revolutionary ideals of limited government and a citizenry of independent, public-spirited farmers as the Federalists were tied to visions of an orderly commercial republic with a powerful national state. The fight between Federalists and Democratic Republicans echoed the revolutionary contest between liberty and power—conducted this time against an ominous backdrop of international intrigue and war between France (which entered a republican revolution of its own in 1789) and Britain. Only when this Age of Democratic Revolution ended with the defeat of Napoleon in 1815 could the Americans survey the kind of society and government that their Revolution had made.

CHAPTER FOCUS

♦ What was the Federalist plan for organizing the national government and its finances? What were the Jeffersonian Republicans' principal objections to those plans?

♦ What was the nature of the governmental crisis of 1798–1800, and how was it resolved?

♦ What were the principal reforms of the national government during Thomas Jefferson's administration? What were the implications of those reforms for the nature of republican government?

♦ What was the situation of the United States within the international politics created by the Napoleonic Wars, and how did that situation degenerate into a second war with Britain?

CHRONOLOGY

1789	George Washington inaugurated as first president of the United States • Judiciary Act establishes the Supreme Court and federal circuit courts
1790	Hamilton delivers his Report on Public Credit to Congress • Congress drafts the Bill of Rights
1792	Revolutionaries proclaim the French Republic
1793	Anglo-French War begins
1794	Federalists' excise tax triggers Whiskey Rebellion
1796	Jay's Treaty and Pinckney's Treaty ratified • John Adams elected second president
1798	XYZ affair results in undeclared war with France • Alien and Sedition Acts passed by Congress
1799	Slave revolution in Haiti
1800	Thomas Jefferson defeats Adams for the presidency
1803	United States purchases Louisiana Territory from France • *Marbury* v. *Madison* establishes the doctrine of judicial review
1804	Twelfth Amendment to the Constitution passed by Congress
1806	Non-Importation Act forbids importation of many British goods into U.S.
1807	Congress passes Embargo Act • Chesapeake-Leopard affair ignites anti-British sentiment
1810	Congress passes Macon's Bill No. 2
1811	Henry Clay elected Speaker of the House
1812	War of 1812 begins
1814	Federalists call Hartford Convention • Treaty of Ghent ends War of 1812
1815	American victory at the Battle of New Orleans

🌐 Establishing the Government

George Washington left Mount Vernon for the temporary capital in New York City in April 1789. The way was lined with the grateful citizens of the new republic. Militia companies and local dignitaries escorted him from town to town, crowds cheered, church bells marked his progress, and lines of girls in white dresses waved demurely as he passed. At Newark Bay he boarded a flower-bedecked barge and, surrounded by scores of boats, crossed to New York City. There he was welcomed by jubilant citizens as he made his way to the president's house. He arrived on April 23 and was inaugurated seven days later.

The "Republican Court"

Reporting for work, President Washington found the new government embroiled in its first controversy—an argument over the dignity that would attach to his own office. Vice President John Adams had asked the Senate to create a title of honor for the president. Adams, along with many of the senators, wanted a resounding title that would reflect the power of the new executive. They rejected "His Excellency" because that was the term used for ambassadors, colonial governors, and other minor officials. Among the other titles they considered were "His Highness," "His Mightiness," "His Elective Highness," "His Most Benign Highness," "His Majesty," and "His Highness, the President of the United States, and Protector of Their Liberties." The Senate debated the question for a full month, then gave up when it became clear that the more democratic House

of Representatives disliked titles. They settled on the austere dignity of "Mr. President." A senator from Pennsylvania expressed relief that the "silly business" was over. Thomas Jefferson, who was not yet a member of the government, pronounced the whole affair "the most superlatively ridiculous thing I ever heard of."

Jefferson would learn, however, that much was at stake in the argument over titles. Although the Constitution provided a blueprint for the republic, George Washington's administration would translate the blueprint into a working state. Members of the government knew their decisions would set precedents. It mattered very much what citizens called their president, for that was part of the huge constellation of laws, customs, and forms of etiquette that would give the new government either a republican or (as many anti-Federalists feared) a courtly tone. Many of those close to Washington wanted to protect presiden-

GEORGE WASHINGTON IN 1796, NEAR THE END OF HIS PRESIDENCY

The artist here captured the formal dignity of the first president and surrounded him with gold, red velvet, a presidential throne, and other emblems of kingly office.

tial power from the localism and democracy that, they believed, had nearly killed the republic in the 1780s. Washington's stately inaugural tour, the high salaries paid to executive appointees, the endless round of formal balls and presidential dinners, the observance of the English custom of celebrating the executive's birthday, the appearance of Washington's profile on some of the nation's coins—all were meant to bolster the power and grandeur of the new government, particularly of its executive. When Jefferson became secretary of state and attended official social functions, he often found himself the only democrat at the dinner table. Aristocratic sentiments prevailed, said Jefferson, "unless there chanced to be some [democrat] from the legislative Houses." Thus the battle over presidential titles was not "silly business." It was a revealing episode in the argument over how questions of power and liberty that Americans had debated since the 1760s would finally be answered.

The First Congress

Leadership of the First Congress fell to James Madison, the Virginia congressman who had helped write the Constitution. Under his guidance, Congress strengthened the new national government at every turn. First it passed a tariff on imports, which would be the government's chief source of income. Next, it turned to amendments to the Constitution demanded by the state ratifying conventions.

Madison proposed 19 constitutional amendments to the House. The 10 that survived congressional scrutiny and ratification by the states became the Bill of Rights. They reflected fears raised by a generation of struggle with centralized power. The First Amendment guaranteed the freedoms of speech, press, and religion against federal interference. The Second and Third Amendments, prompted by old fears of a standing army, guaranteed the continuation of a militia of armed citizens and stated the specific conditions under which soldiers could be quartered in citizens' households. The Fourth, Fifth, Sixth, Seventh, and Eighth Amendments protected and defined a citizen's rights in court and when under arrest—rights whose violation had been central to the Revolution's list of grievances. The Ninth Amendment stated that the enumeration of specific rights in the first eight amendments did not imply a denial of other rights; the 10th Amendment stated that powers not assigned to the national government by the Constitution remained with the states and the citizenry.

Madison, a committed nationalist, had performed skillfully. Many doubters at the ratifying conventions had called for amendments that would change the government detailed in the Constitution. By channeling their fears into the relatively innocuous area of civil liberties, Madison soothed their mistrust while preserving the government of the Constitution. The Bill of Rights was an important guarantee of individual liberties. In the context in which it was written and ratified, it was an even more important guarantee of the power of the national government.

To fill out the framework of government outlined in the Constitution, Congress created the executive departments of war, state, and treasury and guaranteed that the heads of those departments and their assistants would be appointed solely by the president, thus removing them from congressional control. Congress next created the federal courts, which were demanded but not specified in the Constitution. The Judiciary Act of 1789 established a Supreme Court with six members, along with 13 district courts and 3 circuit courts of appeal. The act allowed certain cases to be appealed from state courts to federal circuit courts presided over by traveling Supreme Court justices, thus dramatizing federal power. As James Madison and other members of the intensely nationalist First Congress surveyed their handiwork, they could congratulate themselves on having strengthened national authority at every opportunity.

Hamiltonian Economics: The National Debt

Washington filled posts in what would become the cabinet with familiar faces. As secretary of war, he chose Henry Knox, an old comrade from the Revolution. The State Department went to his fellow Virginian, Thomas Jefferson. He chose Alexander Hamilton of New York, his trusted aide-de-camp during the Revolution, to head the Department of the Treasury.

The most single-minded nationalist in the new government, Hamilton was a brilliant economic thinker, an admirer of the British system of centralized government and finance, and a supremely arrogant and ambitious man. More than other cabinet members, and perhaps even more than Washington himself (he later referred to Washington's presidency as "my administration"), Hamilton directed the making of a national government.

In 1789, Congress asked Secretary of the Treasury Hamilton to report on the public debt. The debt fell into three categories, Hamilton reported. The first was the $11 million owed to foreigners—primarily debts to France incurred during the Revolution. The second and third— roughly $24 million each—were debts owed by the national and state governments to American citizens who had supplied food, arms, and other resources to the revolutionary cause. Congress agreed that both justice and the credibility of the new government dictated that the foreign debts be paid in full, but the domestic debts raised troublesome questions. Those debts consisted of notes issued during the Revolution to soldiers, and to merchants, farmers, and others who had helped the war effort. Over the years, speculators had purchased many of these notes at a fraction of their face value; when word spread that the Constitution would create a government likely to pay its debts, speculators and their agents fanned out across the countryside buying up all the notes they could find. By 1790, the government debt was concentrated in the hands of businessmen and speculators—most of them northeasterners— who had bought notes at prices only 10 to 30 percent of their original value. Full payment would bring them enormous windfall profits.

L I N K   T O   T H E   P A S T

Washington's "Republican Court"

George Washington did what he could to surround the office of the presidency with dignity and an aura of awe—something that more democratic members of the new government considered reminiscent of European court society. Here is a description of Washington at a formal reception:

[T]*he president was dressed] in black velvet; his hair in full dress, powdered and gathered behind in a large silk bag; yellow gloves on his hands; holding a cocked hat with cockade in it, and the edges adorned with a black feather about an inch deep. He wore knee and shoe buckles; and a long sword, with a finely wrought and polished steel hilt, which appeared at the left hip; the coat worn over the sword, so that the hilt, and the part below the folds of the coat behind, were in view. The scabbard was white polished leather.*

He stood always in front of the fireplace, with his face towards the door of entrance. . . . He received his *visitor with a dignified bow, while his hands were so disposed of as to indicate, that the salutation was not to be accompanied with shaking hands. This ceremony never occurred in these visits.*

WILLIAM SULLIVAN

1. Insofar as it can be discerned from this description, what was the public persona of America's first president? In what ways did he behave differently outside of official situations?
2. Why do you think he avoided shaking hands with his guests?

For additional sources related to this feature, visit the *Liberty, Equality, Power* Web site at:

http://history.wadsworth.com/murrin_LEP4e

The Revolutionary War debts of the individual states were another source of contention. Nationalists, with Hamilton at their head, wanted to assume the debts of the states as part of a national debt—a move that would concentrate the interests of public creditors, the need for taxation, and an expanded civil service in the national government. The state debts also had been bought up by speculators, and they posed another problem as well: Many states, including all of the southern states with the exception of South Carolina, had paid off most of their notes in the 1780s; the other states still had significant outstanding debts. If the federal government assumed the state debts and paid them off at the face value of the notes, money would flow out of the southern, middle, and western states into the Northeast, whose citizens would hold fully four-fifths of the combined national debt.

That is precisely what Hamilton proposed in his Report on Public Credit, issued in January 1790. He urged Congress to assume the state debts and to combine them with the federal government's foreign and domestic debts into a consolidated national debt. He agreed that the foreign debt should be paid promptly and in full, but he insisted that the domestic debt be a permanent, tax-supported fixture of government. Under his plan, the government would issue securities to its creditors and would pay an annual rate of interest of 4 percent. Hamilton's funding and assumption plans announced to the international community and to actual and potential government creditors that the United States would pay its bills, but Hamilton had domestic plans for the debt as well. A permanent debt would attract the wealthiest financiers in the country as creditors and would render them loyal and dependent on the federal government. It would bring their economic power to the government and at the same time would require a significant enlargement of the federal civil service, national financial institutions, and increased taxes. The national debt, in short, was at the center of Alexander Hamilton's plan for a powerful national state.

Hamiltonian Economics: The Bank and the Excise

As part of that plan, Hamilton asked Congress to charter a Bank of the United States. The government would store its funds in the bank and would supervise its operations, but the bank would be controlled by directors representing private stockholders. The Bank of the United States would print and back the national currency and would regulate other banks. Hamilton's proposal also made stock in the bank payable in government securities, thus (1) adding to the value of the securities, (2) giving the bank a powerful interest in the fiscal stability of the government, and (3) binding the holders of the securities even closer to the national government. Those who looked closely saw that Hamilton's Bank of the United States was a carbon copy of the Bank of England.

To fund the national debt, Hamilton called for a federal excise tax on wines, coffee, tea, and spirits. The tax on spirits would fall most heavily on the whiskey produced in abundance on the frontier. Its purpose, stated openly by Hamilton, was not only to produce revenue but also to establish the government's power to create an internal tax and to collect it in the most remote regions in the republic. The result, as we shall see later in this chapter, was a "Whiskey Rebellion" in the west and an overwhelming display of federal force.

Passed in April 1791, the national bank and the federal excise measures completed Hamilton's organization of government finances. Taken separately, the consolidated government debt, the national bank, and the federal excise tax ably solved discrete problems of government finance. Taken together, however, they constituted a full-scale replica of the treasury-driven government of Great Britain.

The Rise of Opposition

In 1789, every branch of government was staffed by supporters of the Constitution. The most radical anti-Federalists took positions in state governments or left politics altogether. Nearly everyone in the national government was committed to making the new government work. In particular, Alexander Hamilton at Treasury and James Madison in the House of Representatives expected to continue the political and personal friendship they had made while writing the Constitution and working to get it ratified. Yet in the debate over the national debt, Madison led congressional opposition to Hamilton's proposals. In 1792, Thomas Jefferson joined the opposition, insisting that Hamilton's schemes would dismantle the Revolution. Within a few short years, the consensus of 1789 had degenerated into an angry argument over what sort of government would finally result from the American Revolution. More than 25 years later, Jefferson still insisted that the battles of the 1790s had been "contests of principle between the advocates of republican and those of kingly government."

Hamilton presented his national debt proposal to Congress as a solution to specific problems of government finance, not as part of a blueprint for an English-style state. Madison and other southerners opposed it because they did not want northern speculators—many of whom had received information from government insiders—to reap fortunes from notes bought at rock-bottom prices from soldiers, widows, and orphans. He branded Hamilton's plan "public plunder."

At the urging of Jefferson and others, Madison and members of the congressional opposition compromised with Hamilton. In exchange for accepting his proposals on the debt, they won his promise to locate the permanent capital of the United States at a site on the Potomac River. The compromise went to the heart of American revolutionary republicanism. Hamilton intended to tie northeastern commercial interests to the federal government. If New York or Philadelphia became the permanent capital, political and economic power might be concentrated there as it was in Paris and London—court cities in which power, wealth, and every kind of excellence were in league against a plundered and degraded countryside. Benjamin Rush, a Philadelphian, condemned the "government which has begun so soon to ape the corruption of the British Court, conveyed to it through the impure channel of the City of New York." Madison and other agrarians considered Philadelphia just as bad and supported Hamilton's debt only on condition that the capital be moved south. The compromise would distance the commercial power of the cities from the federal government and would put an end to the "republican court" that had formed around Washington. This radically republican move ensured that the capital of the United States would be, except for purposes of government, a place of no importance.

Jefferson versus Hamilton

When Hamilton proposed the Bank of the United States, republicans in Congress immediately noted its similarity to the Bank of England and voiced deep suspicion of Hamilton's economic and governmental plans. Thomas Jefferson had joined the opposition, arguing that Congress had no constitutional right to charter a bank and that allowing Congress to do so would revive the popular fears of centralized despotism that had nearly defeated ratification of the Constitution. Hamilton responded with the first argument for expanded federal power under the clause in the Constitution empowering Congress "to make all laws which shall be necessary and proper" to the performance of its duties. President Washington and a majority in Congress ultimately sided with Hamilton.

Jefferson's strict constructionism (his insistence that the government had no powers beyond those specified in the Constitution) revealed his fears of the de facto constitution that Hamilton's system was making. Jefferson argued that the federal bank was unconstitutional, that a federal excise tax was certain to arouse public opposi-

tion, and that funding the debt would reward speculators and penalize ordinary citizens. More important, Jefferson argued, Hamilton used government securities and stock in the Bank of the United States to buy the loyalty not only of merchants and speculators but also of members of Congress. Thirty congressmen owned stock in the Bank of the United States, and many others held government securities or had close ties to men who did. Jefferson charged that this "corrupt squadron" of "paper men" in Congress was, in the classic fashion of evil ministers, enabling Hamilton to control Congress from his nonelective seat in the executive branch. "The ultimate object of all this," insisted Jefferson, "is to prepare the way for a change, from the present republican form of government, to that of a monarchy, of which the English constitution is to be the model."

For their part, Hamilton and his supporters (who by now were calling themselves Federalists) insisted that the centralization of power and a strong executive were necessary to the survival of the republic. The alternative was a return to the localism and public disorder of the 1780s and ultimately to the failure of the Revolution. The argument drew its urgency from the understanding of both Hamilton and his detractors that the United States was a small revolutionary republic in a world governed by kings and aristocrats, and that republics had a long history of failure. They all knew that Americans might yet lose their Revolution. Until late 1792, however, the argument over Hamilton's centralizing schemes remained mostly among government officials. Hamilton and his supporters tried to mobilize the commercial elite on the side of government, while Madison and Jefferson struggled to hold off the perceived monarchical plot until the citizens could be aroused to defend their liberties. As both sides began to mobilize popular support, events in Europe came to dominate the politics of the American republican experiment, to place that experiment in even greater jeopardy, and to increase the violence of American politics to the point at which the republic almost failed.

The Republic in a World at War, 1793–1800

Late in 1792, French revolutionaries rejected monarchy and proclaimed the French Republic. They beheaded Louis XVI in January 1793. Eleven days later, the French, already at war with Austria and Prussia, declared war on conservative Britain, thus launching a war between French republicanism and British-led reaction that, with periodic outbreaks of peace, would embroil the Atlantic world until the defeat of France in 1815.

Jefferson's French Revolution

Thomas Jefferson was Minister to France from 1785 through fall 1789. The erudite Jefferson enjoyed his sojourn in Paris. He bought books, attended salons, conversed with *philosophes*, and attended parties, concerts, and balloon ascensions. Then, in April 1788, he returned after an absence and found that "The gay and thoughtless Paris is become a furnace of Politics." The great Virginia republican became an eyewitness to the French Revolution.

Faced with horrendous government deficits and an overtaxed, underfed, and increasingly riotous population, King Louis XVI called the Estates General—the assembly of nobles, clergy, and people that served France's absolutist kings as a national legislature. Many in the Third Estate (representatives of the commoners) demanded the end of feudal privileges and a declaration of rights. Jefferson had his own plan for peaceful reform: The King should ally himself with the people and end the privileges of the nobility and clergy. The result— surprisingly conservative for the radical Jefferson—would be a solvent constitutional monarchy.

When the Estates General met in May 1789, Jefferson was there. He even took the liberty of drafting a charter of rights and passing it on to his friend Lafayette. The King, responding to a Third Estate that wanted to control the assembly (as well as to an aristocracy that was adamant in protecting its privileges), locked the Third Estate out of its hall. Retiring to an indoor tennis court, the self-proclaimed National Assembly swore to support a written constitution and a constitutional monarchy. The King sided with the nobles and began assembling troops. The Paris crowd responded with the storming of the Bastille, the King withdrew his troops, and Paris assumed government of itself. Jefferson ventured out to view the crowds and pronounced their actions "legitimate." "The National Assembly," Jefferson wrote, "have now as clean a canvas to work on here as we had in America." He went on: "I have so much confidence in the good sense of man, and his qualifications for self-government, that I am never afraid of the issue where reason is left free to exert her force; and I will agree to be stoned as a false prophet if all does not end well in this country. Nor will it end with this country. Here is but the first chapter of the history of European liberty."

THE STORMING OF THE BASTILLE

© Gianni Dagli/Corbis.

Americans and the French Revolution

Americans could not have escaped involvement even if they had wanted to. Treaties signed in 1778 allied the United States with France, although Federalists and Jeffersonians would argue whether those treaties applied to the new French Republic or became void with the execution of the monarch who had signed them. Americans had overwhelmingly supported the French Revolution of 1789 and had applauded the progress of French republicanism during its first three years. Both their gratitude for French help during the American Revolution and American hopes for international republicanism faced severe tests in 1793, when the French Republic began to execute thousands of aristocrats, priests, and other "counterrevolutionaries," and when the French threatened the sovereignty of nations by declaring a war of all peoples against all monarchies. The argument between Jeffersonian republicanism and Hamiltonian centralization was no longer a squabble within the

U.S. government. National politics was now caught up and subsumed within the struggle over international republicanism.

As Britain and France went to war in 1793, President Washington declared American neutrality, thereby abrogating obligations made in the 1778 treaties with the French. Washington and most of his advisers realized that the United States was in no condition to fight a war. They also wanted to stay on good terms with Great Britain. Ninety percent of American imports came from Britain, and 90 percent of the federal revenue came from customs duties on those imports. Thus both the nation's commerce and the financial health of the government depended on good relations with Great Britain. Moreover, Federalists genuinely sympathized with the British in the war with France. They regarded the United States as a "perfected" England and viewed Britain as the defender of hierarchical society and ordered liberty against the homicidal anarchy of the French.

Jefferson and his friends saw things differently. They applauded the French for carrying on the republican revolution Americans had begun in 1776, and they had no affection for the "monarchical" politics of the Federalists or for Americans' continued neocolonial dependence on British trade. The faction led by Jefferson and Madison wanted to abandon the English mercantile system and trade freely with all nations. They did not care if that course of action hurt commercial interests (most of which supported the Federalists) or impaired the government's ability to centralize power in itself. Although they agreed that the United States should stay out of the war, the Jeffersonians sympathized as openly with the French as the Federalists did with the British.

Citizen Genêt

Throughout the war years from 1793 to 1815, both Great Britain and France, by intervening freely in the internal affairs of the United States, made American isolationism impossible.

In April 1793, the French sent Citizen Edmond Genêt as minister to the United States. Genêt's ruling Girondists were the revolutionary faction that had declared the war on all monarchies; they ordered Genêt to enlist American aid with or without the Washington administration's consent. After the president's proclamation of neutrality, Genêt openly commissioned American privateers to harass British shipping and enlisted Americans in intrigues against the Spanish outpost of New Orleans. Genêt then opened France's Caribbean colonies to American shipping, providing American shippers a choice between French free trade and British mercantilism. Genêt's mission came to an abrupt end in summer 1793, when Robespierre and the

infamous Terror drove the Girondists from power. Learning that he would be guillotined if he returned to France, Genêt accepted the hospitality of Americans, married a daughter of George Clinton, the old anti-Federalist governor of New York, and lived out the rest of his life as an American country gentleman.

The British responded to Genêt's free-trade declaration with a promise to seize any ship trading with French colonies in the Caribbean. Word of these Orders in Council—almost certainly by design—reached the Royal Navy before American merchant seamen had learned of them, with the result that 250 American ships fell into British hands. The Royal Navy also began searching American ships for English sailors who had deserted or who had switched to safer, better-paying work in the American merchant marine. Inevitably, some American sailors were kidnapped into the British navy in a contemptuous and infuriating assault on American sovereignty. Meanwhile the British, operating from Canada and from their still-garrisoned forts in the Northwest, began promising military aid to the Indians north of the Ohio River. Thus, while the French ignored the neutrality of the United States, the English engaged in both overt and covert acts of war.

Western Troubles

The problems with France and on the high seas were accompanied by an intensified threat from British and Indian forces in the Northwest Territory, as well as from settlers in that region. The situation came to a head in summer and fall 1794. The Shawnee and allied tribes, emboldened by two victories over American armies, plotted with the British and talked of driving all settlers out of their territory. At the same time, frontier whites, sometimes with the encouragement of English and Spanish officials, grew increasingly contemptuous of a national government that could neither pacify the Indians nor guarantee their free use of the Mississippi River. President Washington heard that 2,000 Kentuckians were armed and ready to attack New Orleans—a move that would have started a war between the United States and Spain. Settlers in Georgia were making unauthorized forays against the Creeks. Worst of all, settlers up and down the frontier refused to pay the Federalists' excise tax on whiskey—a direct challenge to federal authority. In western Pennsylvania, mobs tarred and feathered excise officers and burned the property of distillers who paid the tax. In July 1794, near Pittsburgh, 500 militiamen marched on the house of General John Neville, one of the most hated of the federal excise collectors. Neville, his family, and a few federal soldiers fought the militiamen, killing two and wounding six before they abandoned the house to be looted and

MAP 8.1 THE WEST, 1790–1796

In 1790, the United States "owned" nearly all of its present territory east of the Mississippi River, but white Americans remained concentrated east of the Appalachians (see the map on population density, p. 242), and independent Indian peoples controlled most of the map of the United States. The Battle of Fallen Timbers and the resultant Treaty of Greenville pushed white settlement across Ohio and into Indiana, but the Indians of the Norwest remained intact, determined, and in touch with the British in Canada. Native Americans also controlled nearly all of the Southwest, and Florida and the Gulf Coast—including all outlets from the interior to the Caribbean—remained in Spanish hands. The American west was very far from secure in the 1790s.

burned. Two weeks later, 6,000 "Whiskey Rebels" met at Braddock's Field near Pittsburgh, threatening to attack the town.

Faced with serious international and domestic threats to his new government, Washington determined to defeat the Indians and the Whiskey Rebels by force, thus securing American control of the Northwest. He sent General "Mad"

Anthony Wayne against the northwestern tribes. Wayne's decisive victory at Fallen Timbers in August 1794—fought almost in the shadow of a British fort—ended the Indian-British challenge in the Northwest for many years (see chapter 7).

In September, Washington ordered 12,000 federalized militiamen from eastern Pennsylvania, Maryland, Virginia, and New Jersey to quell the Whiskey Rebellion. The president promised amnesty to rebels who pledged to support the government and prison terms to those who did not. As the army marched west from Carlisle, they found defiant liberty poles but no armed resistance. Arriving at Pittsburgh, the army arrested 20 suspected rebels—none of them leaders—and marched them back to Philadelphia for trial. In the end only two "rebels," both of them feebleminded, were convicted. President Washington pardoned them, and the Whiskey Rebellion was over.

The Jay Treaty

Although he sent armies against Indians and frontiersmen, President Washington capitulated to the British on the high seas. In 1794, he sent John Jay, chief justice of the Supreme Court, to negotiate the conflicts between the United States and Britain. Armed with news of Wayne's victory, Jay extracted a promise from the British to remove their troops from American territory in the Northwest. On every other point of dispute, however, he agreed to British terms. The Jay Treaty made no mention of impressment or other violations of American maritime rights, nor did it refer to the old issue of British payments for slaves carried off during the Revolution. The treaty did allow small American ships back into the West Indies, but only on terms that the Senate would reject. In short, Jay's Treaty granted British trade a most-favored-nation basis in exchange for the agreement of the British to abandon their northwestern forts. Given the power of Great Britain, it was the best that Americans could expect. Washington, obliged to choose between an unpopular treaty and an unwinnable war, passed Jay's Treaty on to the Senate, which, in June 1795, ratified it by a bare two-thirds majority.

During the fight over Jay's Treaty, dissension within the government was first aired in public. The seaport cities and much of the Northeast reacted favorably to the treaty. It ruled out war with England and cemented an Anglo-American trade relationship that strengthened both Hamilton's national state and the established commercial interests that supported it. Moreover, northeasterners held little enthusiasm for the French Revolution—particularly in New England, with its long history of colonial wars with France. The South, on the other hand, saw Jay's Treaty as a blatant sign of the designs of Britain and the Federalists to subvert republicanism in both France and the United States. The Virginia legislature branded the treaty as unconstitutional, and Republican congressmen demanded to see all documents relating to Jay's negotiations. Washington responded by telling them that their request could be legitimate only if the House was planning to initiate impeachment proceedings, thus tying approval of the treaty to his enormous personal prestige.

Meanwhile, on March 3, 1796, Washington released the details of a treaty that Thomas Pinckney had negotiated with Spain. In this treaty, Spain recognized American neutrality and set the border between the United States and Spanish Florida on American terms. Most important, the Pinckney Treaty put an end to Spanish claims to territory in the Southwest and gave Americans the unrestricted right to navigate the Mississippi River and to trans-ship produce at the Spanish port of New Orleans. Coupled with the victory at Fallen Timbers, the British promise to abandon their posts in the Northwest, and Washington's personal popularity, Pinckney's Treaty helped turn the tide in favor of the unpopular Jay's Treaty. With a diminishing number of hotheads willing to oppose Washington, western representatives joined the Northeast and increasing numbers of southerners to ratify Jay's Treaty.

Washington's Farewell

George Washington refused to run for reelection in 1796, thus setting a two-term limit observed by every president until Franklin Roosevelt (see chapter 25). Washington could be proud of his accomplishment. He had presided over the creation of a national government. He had secured American control over the western settlements by ending British, Spanish, and Indian military threats and by securing free use of the Mississippi River for western produce. Those policies, together with the federal invasion of western Pennsylvania, had made it evident that the government could and would control its most distant regions. He had also avoided war with Great Britain, although not without overlooking assaults on American sovereignty. As he was about to leave government, he wrote, with substantial help from Hamilton, his farewell address. In it he warned against long-term "entangling alliances" with other countries; America, he said, should stay free to operate on its own in international affairs—an ideal that many felt had been betrayed in Jay's Treaty. Washington also warned against internal political divisions. Of course, he did not regard his own Federalists as a "party"—they were simply friends of the government—but he saw the Democratic Republicans (the name by which Jefferson's allies called themselves) as a self-interested, irresponsible "faction," thus branding them, in the language of classical republicanism, as public enemies. Washington's call for national unity and an end to partisanship was in fact a parting shot at the Democratic Republican opposition.

The Election of 1796

Washington's retirement opened the way to the fierce competition for public office that he had feared; in 1796, Americans experienced their first contested presidential election. The Federalists chose as their candidate John Adams, an upright conservative from Massachusetts who had served as vice president. The Democratic Republicans nominated Thomas Jefferson. According to the gentlemanly custom of the day, neither candidate campaigned in person. Jefferson stayed home at Monticello and Adams retired to his farm near Boston, while friends of the candidates, the newspaper editors who enjoyed their patronage, and even certain European governments ensured that the election would be intensely partisan.

Adams would certainly carry New England and Jefferson would carry the South, which left the election to be decided in Pennsylvania and New York. Some states, most of them in the South, chose presidential electors by direct vote, but in most states, including the crucial mid-Atlantic states, state legislatures selected the presidential electors. The election of 1796 would be decided in elections to the legislatures of those states and in subsequent intriguing within those bodies. John Beckley, clerk of the House of Representatives, devised the Republican strategy in Pennsylvania. He secretly circulated a list of well-known and respected candidates for the state legislature who were committed to Jefferson's election as president. Discovering the Republican slate only when it was too late to construct a similar list, the Federalists lost the elections. In December, Beckley delivered all but one of Pennsylvania's electoral votes to Jefferson. New York, however, had no John Beckley. Adams took the state's electoral votes and won the national election. The distribution of electoral votes revealed the bases of Federalist and Republican support: Adams received only 2 electoral votes south of the Potomac, and Jefferson received only 18 (all but 5 of them in Pennsylvania) north of the Potomac.

The voting was over, but the intriguing was not. Alexander Hamilton, who since his retirement from the Treasury in 1795 had directed Federalist affairs from his New York law office, knew that he could not manipulate the independent and almost perversely upright John Adams. So he secretly instructed South Carolina's Federalist electors to withhold their votes from Adams. That would have given the presidency to Adams's running mate, Thomas Pinckney, relegating Adams to the vice presidency. (Before the ratification of the 12th Amendment in 1804, the candidate with a majority of the electoral votes became president,

and the second-place candidate became vice president.) Like some of Hamilton's other schemes, this one backfired. New England electors heard of the plan and angrily withheld their votes from Pinckney. As a result, Adams was elected president and his opponent Thomas Jefferson became vice president. Adams narrowly won the election, but he took office with a justifiable mistrust of many members of his own party and with the head of the opposition party as his second in command. It was not an auspicious beginning.

Troubles with France, 1796–1800

As Adams entered office, an international crisis was already in full swing. France, regarding Jay's Treaty as an Anglo-American alliance, had recalled its envoy in 1796 and had broken off relations with the United States. The French hinted that they intended to overthrow the reactionary government of the United States but would postpone taking action in the hope that a friendlier Thomas Jefferson would replace "old man Washington" in 1797. Then, during the crucial elections in Pennsylvania, they stepped up their seizures of American ships trading with Britain, giving the Americans a taste of what would happen if they did not elect a government that was friendlier to France. When the election went to John Adams, the French gave up on the United States and set about denying Britain its new de facto ally. In 1797, France expelled the American

North Wind Picture Archives.

WASHINGTON, D.C.

The Americans built a capital city that had no function other than republican government. It had no mercantile or financial establishments, no theaters, and no military fortress. Broad, straight streets stretched beyond the built-up areas of the town; visually as well as politically, Washington, D.C., was dependent upon and vulnerable to the countryside—the opposite of European court cities. It was the kind of capital that American republicans wanted.

minister and refused to carry on relations with the United States until it addressed French grievances.

The French ordered that American ships carrying "so much as a handkerchief" made in England be confiscated without compensation and announced that American seamen serving in the British navy would be summarily hanged if captured.

President Adams wanted to protect American commerce from French depredations, but he knew that the United States might not survive a war with France. He also knew that French grievances (including Jay's Treaty and the abrogation of the French-American treaties of 1778) were legitimate. He decided to send a mission to France, made up of three respected statesmen: Charles Cotesworth Pinckney of South Carolina, John Marshall of Virginia, and Elbridge Gerry of Massachusetts. When these prestigious delegates reached Paris, however, they were left cooling their heels in the outer offices of the Directory—the revolutionary committee of five that had replaced France's beheaded king. At last, three French officials (the correspondence identified them only as "X, Y, and Z"—and the incident later became known as the XYZ affair) discreetly hinted that France would receive them if they paid a bribe of $250,000, arranged for the United States to loan $12 million to the French government, and apologized for unpleasant remarks that John Adams had made about France. The delegates refused, saying "No, not a sixpence," and returned home. There a journalist transformed their remark into "Millions for defense, but not one cent for tribute."

President Adams asked Congress to prepare for war, and the French responded by seizing more American ships. Thus began, in April 1798, an undeclared war between France and the United States in the Caribbean. While the French navy dealt with the British in the North Atlantic, French privateers inflicted costly blows on American shipping. After nearly a year of fighting, with the British providing powder and shot for American guns, the U.S. Navy chased the French privateers out of the Caribbean.

The Crisis at Home, 1798–1800

The troubles with France precipitated a crisis at home. Disclosure of the XYZ correspondence, together with the quasi-war in the Caribbean, produced a surge of public hostility toward the French and, to some extent, toward their Republican friends in the United States. Many Federalists, led by Alexander Hamilton, wanted to use the crisis to destroy their political opponents. Without consulting President Adams, the Federalist-dominated Congress passed several wartime measures. The first was a federal property tax—graduated, spread equally between sections of the country, and justified by military necessity—nonetheless a direct federal tax. Congress then passed four laws known as the Alien and Sedition Acts. The first three were directed at immigrants: They extended the naturalization period from 5 to 14 years and empowered the president to detain enemy aliens during wartime and to deport those he deemed dangerous to the United States. The fourth law—the Sedition Act—set jail terms and fines for persons who advocated disobedience to federal law or who wrote, printed, or spoke "false, scandalous, and malicious" statements against "the government of the United States, or the President of the United States [note that Vice President Jefferson was not included], with intent to defame . . . or to bring them or either of them, into contempt or disrepute."

President Adams never used the powers granted under the Alien Acts, but the Sedition Act resulted in the prosecution of 14 Republicans, most of them journalists. William Duane, editor of the *Philadelphia Aurora,* was indicted when he and two Irish friends circulated a petition against the Alien Act on the grounds of a Catholic church. James Callendar, editor of a Jeffersonian newspaper in Richmond, was arrested, while another prominent Republican went to jail for statements made in a private letter. Jedediah Peck, a former Federalist from upstate New York, was arrested when he petitioned Congress to repeal the Alien and Sedition Acts. Matthew Lyon, a scurrilous and uncouth Republican congressman from Vermont, had brawled with a Federalist representative in the House chamber; he went to jail for his criticisms of President Adams, Federalist militarism, and what he called the "ridiculous pomp" of the national administration.

Republicans, charging that the Alien and Sedition Acts violated the First Amendment, turned to the states for help. Southern states, which had provided only 4 of the 44 congressional votes for the Sedition Act, took the lead. Jefferson provided the Kentucky legislature with draft resolutions, and Madison did the same for the Virginia legislature. These so-called Virginia and Kentucky Resolves restated the constitutional fundamentalism that had guided Republican opposition to the Federalists through the 1790s. Jefferson's Kentucky Resolves reminded Congress that the Alien and Sedition Acts gave the national government powers not mentioned in the Constitution and that the 10th Amendment reserved such powers to the states. He also argued that the Constitution was a "compact" between sovereign states and that state legislatures could "nullify" federal laws they deemed unconstitutional, thus anticipating constitutional theories that states'-rights southerners would use after 1830.

The Virginia and Kentucky Resolves demonstrated the extremes to which Jefferson and Madison might go. Beyond that, however, they had few immediate effects. Opposition to the Sedition Act ranged from popular attempts to obstruct the law to fistfights in Congress, and Virginia began calling up its militia. No other states followed the lead of Virginia and Kentucky, however, and talk of armed opposition to Federalist policies was limited to a few areas in the South.

The Politicians and the Army

Federalists took another ominous step by implementing President Adams's request that Congress create a military prepared for war. Adams wanted a stronger navy, both because the undeclared war with France was being fought on the ocean and because he agreed with other Federalists that America's future as a commercial nation required a respectable navy. Hamilton and others (who were becoming known as "High Federalists") preferred a standing army. At the urging of Washington and against his own judgment, Adams had appointed Hamilton inspector general. As such, Hamilton would be the de facto commander of the U.S. Army. Congress authorized a 20,000-man army, and Hamilton proceeded to raise it. Congress also provided for a much larger army to be called up in the event of a declaration of war. When Hamilton expanded the officer corps in anticipation of such an army, he excluded Republicans and commissioned only his political friends. High Federalists wanted a standing army to enforce the Alien and Sedition Acts and to put down an impending rebellion in the South. Beyond that, there was little need for such a force. The war was being fought at sea, and most Americans believed that the citizen militia could hold off any land invasion until an army was raised. The Republicans, President Adams, and many other Federalists now became convinced that Hamilton and his High Federalists were determined to destroy their political opponents, enter into an alliance with Great Britain, and impose Hamilton's statist designs on the nation by force. By 1799, Adams and many of his Federalist friends had come to see Hamilton and his supporters as dangerous, antirepublican militarists.

Adams was both fearful and angry. First the Hamiltonians had tried to rob him of the presidency, then they had passed the Alien and Sedition Acts, the direct tax, and plans for a standing army without consulting him. None of this would have been possible if not for the crisis with France.

Adams, who had resisted calls for a declaration of war, began looking for ways to declare peace. In a move that he knew would split his party and probably cost him reelection in 1800, he opened negotiations with France and stalled the creation of Hamilton's army while the talks took place. At first the Senate refused to send an envoy to France. The senators relented when Adams threatened to resign and leave the presidency to Vice President Jefferson. In the agreement that followed, the French canceled the obligations that the United States had assumed under the treaties of 1778. But they refused to pay reparations for attacks on American shipping since 1793—the very point over which many Federalists had wanted to declare war. Peace with France cut the ground from under the more militaristic and repressive Federalists and intensified discord among the Federalists in general. (Hamilton would campaign against Adams in 1800.) It also damaged Adams's chances for reelection.

The Election of 1800

Thomas Jefferson and his Democratic Republicans approached the election of 1800 better organized and more determined than they had been four years earlier. Moreover, events in the months preceding the election worked in their favor. The Alien and Sedition Acts, the direct tax of 1798, and the Federalist military buildup were never popular. The army suppressed a minor tax rebellion led by Jacob Fries in Pennsylvania; prosecutions under the Sedition Act revealed its partisan origins; and the Federalists showed no sign of repealing the tax or abandoning the Alien and Sedition Acts and the new military even when peace seemed certain. Taken together, these events gave credence to the Republicans' allegation that the Federalists were using the crisis with France to increase their power, destroy their opposition, and overthrow the American republic. The Federalists' actions, charged the Republicans, were expensive, repressive, unwise, and unconstitutional; they also constituted the classic means by which despots destroyed liberty. The Federalists countered by warning that the election of Jefferson and his radical allies would release the worst horrors of the French Revolution onto the streets of American towns. Each side believed that its defeat in the election would mean the end of the republic.

The Democratic Republicans were strong in the South and weak in the Northeast; North Carolina was the one southern state in which Adams had significant support. Jefferson knew that in order to achieve a majority in the electoral college, he had to win New York, the state that had cost him the 1796 election. Jefferson's running mate, Aaron Burr, arranged a truce in New York between Republican factions led by the Clinton and Livingston families and chose candidates for the state legislature who were likely to win. In New York City, Burr played skillfully

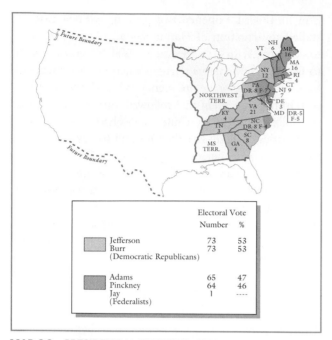

MAP 8.2   PRESIDENTIAL ELECTION, 1800

The electoral votes in 1800 split along starkly sectional lines. The South voted for Jefferson, New England voted for Adams, and the election was decided by close contests in Pennsylvania and New York.

on the interests and resentments of craftsmen and granted favors to merchants who worked outside the British trade, which was dominated by Federalist insiders. The strategy succeeded. The Republicans carried New York City and won a slight majority in the legislature; New York's electoral votes belonged to Jefferson. The election was decided in South Carolina, which, after a brisk campaign, cast its votes for Jefferson. (When it became clear that Jefferson had won, Hamilton suggested changing the law so that New York's electors would be chosen by popular vote; John Jay, the Federalist governor of New York, rejected the suggestion.)

When the electoral votes were counted, Jefferson and Burr had won with 73 votes each. Adams had 65 votes, and his running mate Charles Cotesworth Pinckney had 64. (In order to distinguish between their presidential and vice presidential candidates—and thus thwart yet another of Hamilton's attempts to rig the election—the Federalists of Rhode Island had withheld one vote from Pinckney.) Congress, which was still controlled by Federalists, would have to decide whether Jefferson or Burr was to be president of the United States. After 35 ballots, with most of the Federalists supporting Burr, a compromise was reached whereby some Federalists turned in blank ballots and thus avoided voting for the hated Jefferson. (In 1804, the 12th

Amendment, which requires electors to vote separately for president and vice president, was ratified to prevent a repetition of this situation.)

The Jeffersonians in Power

On the first Tuesday of March 1801, Thomas Jefferson left his rooms at Conrad and McMunn's boarding house in the half-built capital city of Washington and walked up Pennsylvania Avenue. He received military salutes along the way, but Jefferson forbade the pomp and ceremony that had ushered Washington into office. Accompanied by a few friends and a company of artillery from the Maryland militia (and not by the professional military of which Hamilton had dreamed), Jefferson walked up the street and into the unfinished capitol building. The central tower and the wing that would house Congress were only half completed. Jefferson joined Vice President Burr, other members of the government, and a few foreign diplomats in the newly finished Senate chamber.

The Republican Program

Jefferson took the oath of office from Chief Justice John Marshall, a distant relative and political opponent from Virginia. Then, in a small voice that was almost inaudible to those at a distance, he delivered his inaugural address. Referring to the political discord that had brought him into office, he began with a plea for unity, insisting that "every difference of opinion is not a difference of principle. We have called by different names brethren of the same principle. We are all Republicans, we are all Federalists."

Jefferson did not mean that he and his opponents should forget their ideological differences. He meant only to invite moderate Federalists into a broad Republican coalition in which there was no room for the statist designs of Alexander Hamilton and his High Federalist friends.

Jefferson went on to outline the kind of government a republic should have. Grateful that the Atlantic Ocean separated the United States from "the exterminating havoc" of Europe and that his countrymen were the possessors of "a chosen country, with room for our descendants to the thousandth and thousandth generation," he declared that Americans were a free people with no need for a national state built on European models. A people blessed with isolation, bountiful resources, and liberty needed only "a wise and frugal Government, which shall restrain men from injuring one another, shall leave them otherwise free to regulate their own pursuits of industry and improvement, and shall not take from the mouth of labor the bread it has earned. This is the sum of good government, and thus is necessary to close the circle of our felicities."

In particular, Jefferson's "wise and frugal" government would respect the powers of the individual states. It would also defend the liberties ensured by the Bill of Rights. It would be made smaller, and it would pay its debts without incurring new ones, thus ending the need for taxation and cutting the ground from beneath the burgeoning Federalist state. It would rely for defense on "a disciplined militia" that would fight invaders while regulars were being trained, thus getting rid of Hamilton's standing army. It would protect republican liberties from enemies at home and from the nations of Europe. And, Jefferson promised, it would ensure "the encouragement of agriculture, and of commerce as its handmaiden." Beyond the fostering of an agrarian republic and the maintenance of limited, frugal government, Jefferson promised little. Blessed with peace abroad and the defeat of the High Federalists at home, he believed that the United States could at last enter into its experiment with truly republican government.

The simplicity of Jefferson's inauguration set the social tone of his administration. The new president reduced the number and grandeur of formal balls, levees, and dinners. He sent his annual messages to Congress to be read by a clerk, rather than delivering them in person in the manner of English kings and Federalist presidents. He refused to ride about Washington in a carriage, preferring to carry out his errands on horseback. Abandoning the grand banquets favored by his predecessors, Jefferson entertained senators and congressmen at small dinners, which were served at a round table without formal seating, thus abandoning the fine-tuned hierarchy of the Federalists' old arrangements. Jefferson presided over the meals without wearing a wig and dressed in old homespun and a pair of worn bedroom slippers. The casualness (slovenliness, said some of his critics) did not extend to what was served at dinner, however. The food was prepared by expert chefs and accompanied by fine wines, and it was followed by brilliant conversation perfected by Jefferson while he was a diplomat and a visitor to the salons of Paris. The president's dinners set examples of the unpretentious excellence through which this cultivated country squire hoped to govern the republic that he claimed to have saved from monarchists.

Cleansing the Government

Jefferson's first order of business was to reduce the size and expense of government. The Federalists, despite their elitism and their statist dispositions, had left a surprisingly

---

LINK TO THE PAST

A Monarchist Looks at President Jefferson

In 1804, Sir John Augustus Foster took over his duties as Secretary of the British Legation in Washington. He kept diaries of his dealings with President Jefferson and with the new capital city of the United States, neither of which impressed him. Here is his description of Jefferson at a formal government function:

Having mentioned Mr. Jefferson, it may be interesting to the reader to have the following description of his person as he appeared to me on my arrival in the United States in the year 1804. He was a tall man with a very red freckled face and grey neglected hair, his manners goodnatured, frank and rather friendly though he had somewhat of a cynical expression of countenance. He wore a blue coat, a thick grey-coloured hairy waistcoat with a red under-waistcoat lapped over it, green velveteen breeches with pearl buttons, yarn stockings and slippers down at the heel, his appearance being very much like that of a tall large-boned farmer. He said he washed his feet as often as he did his hands in order to keep off cold, and appeared to think himself unique in so doing.

1. Compare President Jefferson's presidential persona with that of President Washington (in the other Link to the Past feature in this chapter). Why do you think they dressed, talked, and behaved so differently?
2. Were they simply different kinds of men, or did they wish to project different images of the president and the government that they headed?

For more of Foster's aristocratic reactions to the American capital, see Richard Beale Davis, ed., *Jeffersonian America: Notes on the United States of America Collected in the Years 1805–6–7 and 11–12 by Sir Augustus John Foster, Bart.* Westport, Conn.: Greenwood Press, 1954, Chapter II.

PORTRAIT OF JEFFERSON BY REMBRANDT PEALE, 1805

A self-consciously plain President Jefferson posed for this portrait in January 1805, near the end of his first term. He wears an unadorned fur-collared coat, is surrounded by no emblems of office, and gazes calmly and directly at the viewer.

explained, was to rely mainly on the militia for national defense but to maintain a small, well-trained professional army as well. (The same legislation that reduced the army created the military academy at West Point.) At Jefferson's urging, Congress also abolished the direct tax of 1798 and repealed the parts of the Alien and Sedition Acts that had not already expired. Jefferson personally pardoned the 10 victims of those acts who were still in jail and repaid with interest the fines that had been levied under them.

Thus with a few deft strokes, Jefferson dismantled the repressive apparatus of the Federalist state. By reducing government expenditures, he reduced the government's debt and the army of civil servants and "paper men" gathered around it. During Jefferson's administration, the national debt fell from $80 million to $57 million, and the government built up a treasury surplus, even after paying $15 million in cash for the Louisiana Purchase (discussed later in this chapter). Although some doubted

small federal establishment. Jefferson found only 316 employees who were subject to presidential appointment and removal. Those employees, together with 700 clerks and assistants and 3,000 post office workers, made up the entire federal civil service. Jefferson reduced the diplomatic corps and replaced officeholders who were incompetent, corrupt, or avowedly antirepublican. Even so, the rate of turnover was only about 50 percent during his first term. The replacements were not the violent revolutionaries that Federalists had warned against but Republican gentlemen who matched or exceeded the social status of the departed Federalists. Jefferson altered the politics of the civil service, but he left its size and shape intact.

Jefferson made more substantial cuts in the military. The Federalists had built a sizable army and navy to prepare for war and, if necessary, to put down opposition at home. Legislation passed in March 1802 reduced the army to two regiments of infantry and one of artillery—a total of 3,350 officers and men, most of whom were assigned to western posts far from the centers of white population. Similar cutbacks reduced the navy. The goal, Jefferson

"MAD TOM IN A RAGE"

This Federalist cartoon of 1801 portrays Jefferson, with the help of the devil and a bottle of brandy, pulling down the government that Washington and Adams had built.

the wisdom of such stringent economy, no one doubted Jefferson's frugality.

The Jeffersonians and the Courts

Jefferson's demands for a "wise and frugal" government applied to the federal judiciary as well as to other branches. The Constitution had created the Supreme Court but had left the creation of lesser federal courts to Congress. The First Congress had created a system of circuit courts presided over by the justices of the Supreme Court. Only Federalists had served on the Supreme Court under Washington and Adams, and Federalists on the circuit courts had extended federal authority into the hinterland—a fact that their prosecution of Jeffersonians under the Alien and Sedition Acts had made abundantly clear. Thus Jeffersonian Republicans had ample reason to distrust the federal courts. Their distrust was intensified by the Judiciary Act of 1801, which was passed just before Jefferson's inauguration by the lame-duck Federalist Congress. Coupled with President Adams's appointment of Federalist John Marshall as chief justice in January, the Judiciary Act ensured long-term Federalist domination of the federal courts. First, it reduced the number of associate justices of the Supreme Court from six to five when the next vacancy occurred, thus reducing Jefferson's chances of appointing a new member to the Court. The Judiciary Act also took Supreme Court justices off circuit and created a new system of circuit courts. This allowed Adams to appoint 16 new judges, along with a full array of marshals, federal attorneys, clerks, and justices of the peace. He worked until nine o'clock on his last night in office signing commissions for these new officers. All of them were staunch Federalists.

Republicans disagreed on what to do about the Federalists' packing of the courts. A minority distrusted the whole idea of an independent judiciary and wanted judges elected by popular vote. Jefferson and most in his party wanted the courts shielded from democratic control; at the same time, they deeply resented the uniformly Federalist "midnight judges" created by the Judiciary Act of 1801. Jefferson did replace the new federal marshals and attorneys with Republicans and dismissed some of the federal justices of the peace, but judges were appointed for life and could be removed only through impeachment. The Jeffersonians hit on a simple solution: They would get rid of the new judges by abolishing their jobs. Early in 1802, with some of Jefferson's supporters questioning the constitutionality of what they were doing, Congress repealed the Judiciary Act of 1801 and thus did away with the midnight appointees.

The Impeachments of Pickering and Chase

With the federal courts scaled back to their original size, Republicans in Congress, led by the Virginia agrarian John Randolph, went after High Federalists who were still acting as judges. As a first test of removal by impeachment, they chose John Pickering, a federal attorney with the circuit court of New Hampshire. Pickering was a highly partisan Federalist. He was also a notorious alcoholic and clearly insane. The Federalists who had appointed him had long considered him an embarrassment. The House drew up articles of impeachment, and Pickering was tried by the Senate, which, by a strict party vote, removed him from office.

On the same day, Congress went after bigger game: They voted to impeach Supreme Court Justice Samuel Chase. Chase was a much more prominent public figure than Pickering, and his "crimes" were not alcoholism or insanity but mere partisanship. He hated the Jeffersonians, and he had prosecuted sedition cases with real enthusiasm. He had also delivered anti-Jeffersonian diatribes from the bench, and he had used his position and his formidable legal skills to bully young lawyers with whom he disagreed. In short, Chase was an unpleasant, overbearing, and unashamedly partisan member of the Supreme Court. Even so, his faults did not add up to the "high crimes and misdemeanors" that are the constitutional grounds for impeachment.

Moderate Republicans in the government doubted the wisdom of the Chase impeachment, and their uneasiness grew when Congressman John Randolph took over the prosecution. Randolph led a radical states'-rights faction that violently disapproved of, among other things, the way Jefferson had settled a southern land controversy. A corrupt Georgia legislature had sold huge parcels in Mississippi and Alabama to the Yazoo Land Company, which in turn had sold them to private investors, many of them New England speculators. When a new Georgia legislature rescinded the sale and turned the land over to the federal government in 1802, Jefferson agreed to pay off the investors' claims with federal money.

As Randolph led the prosecution of Samuel Chase, he lectured in his annoying, high-pitched voice that Jefferson was double-crossing southern Republicans in an effort to win support in the Northeast. Most of the Republican senators disagreed, and some of them withdrew their support from the impeachment proceedings in order to isolate and humiliate Randolph and his friends. With Jefferson's approval, many Republicans in the Senate joined the Federalists in voting to acquit Samuel Chase.

Justice Marshall's Court

Chief Justice John Marshall probably cheered the acquittal of Justice Chase because it was clear that Marshall was next on the list. Secretary of state under John Adams, Marshall was committed to Federalist ideas of national power, as he demonstrated with his decision in the case of *Marbury* v. *Madison*. William Marbury was one of the justices of the peace whom Jefferson had eliminated in his first few days in office. He sued Jefferson's secretary of state, James Madison, for the nondelivery of his commission. Although Marbury never got his job, Marshall used the case to hand down several important rulings. The first ruling, which questioned the constitutionality of Jefferson's refusal to deliver Marbury's commission, helped convince Republican moderates to repeal the Judiciary Act of 1801. The last ruling, delivered in February 1803, laid the basis for the practice of judicial review—that is, the Supreme Court's power to rule on the constitutionality of acts of Congress. In arguing that Congress could not alter the jurisdiction of the Supreme Court, Marshall stated that the Constitution is "fundamental and paramount law" and that it is "emphatically the province and duty of the judicial department to say what law is."

Some Republicans saw Marshall's ruling as an attempt to arrogate power to the Court, but John Marshall was not a sinister man. As secretary of state under John Adams, he had helped end the undeclared war with France, and he had expressed doubts about the wisdom and necessity if not the constitutionality of the Alien and Sedition Acts. Of more immediate concern, although he disliked Congress's repeal of the 1801 legislation, he believed in Congress's right to make and unmake laws, and he was determined to accept the situation. The decision in *Marbury* v. *Madison* angered many Republicans, but Jefferson and the moderate Republicans noted that Marshall was less interested in the power of the judiciary than in its independence. Ultimately, they decided they trusted Marshall more than they trusted the radicals in their own party. With the acquittal of Justice Chase, Jeffersonian attacks on the federal courts ceased.

Justice Marshall demonstrated his strict constructionism (as well as his partisanship) in the treason trial of former Vice President Aaron Burr in 1807. Following his failed attempt at the presidency in 1801, Burr's further intrigues with northern Federalists broke down—a breakdown that helped lead to a duel in which Burr killed Alexander Hamilton. The disgraced Aaron Burr headed west and organized a cloudy conspiracy that may have involved (according to varying testimonies) an invasion of Mexico or Florida or the secession of Louisiana. President Jefferson heard that Burr had raised an army and ordered his arrest. He was tried for treason at Richmond, with the Chief Justice, who was riding circuit, on the bench. Kings had frequently used the charge of treason to silence dissent. Marshall stopped what he and other Federalists considered Jefferson's attempt to do the same thing by limiting the definition of treason to overt acts of war against the United States or to adhering to the republic's foreign enemies—and by requiring two witnesses to an overt act of treason. Under these guidelines, Burr went free. At the same time, the United States had formally separated internal dissent from treason.

Louisiana

It was Jefferson's good fortune that Europe remained at peace during his first term and stayed out of American affairs. The one development that posed an international threat to the United States turned into a grand triumph: the purchase of the Louisiana Territory from France in 1803.

By 1801, a half-million Americans lived west of the Appalachians. Although Federalists feared the barbaric

Architect of the Capitol.

JOHN MARSHALL

A Virginian and distant relative of Thomas Jefferson, John Marshall became chief justice of the Supreme Court in the last months of John Adams's administration. He used the Court as a conservative, centralizing force until his death in 1835.

westerners, Republicans saw westward expansion as the best hope for the survival of the republic. Social inequality and the erosion of yeoman independence would almost inevitably take root in the East, but in the vast lands west of the mountains, the republic could renew itself for many generations to come. To serve that purpose, however, the West needed ready access to markets through the river system that emptied into the Gulf of Mexico at New Orleans. "There is on the globe," wrote President Jefferson, "one single spot, the possessor of which is our natural and habitual enemy. It is New Orleans."

In 1801, Spain owned New Orleans and under Pinckney's Treaty allowed Americans to trans-ship produce from the interior. The year before, however, Spain had secretly ceded the Louisiana Territory (roughly, all the land west of the Mississippi drained by the Missouri and Arkansas rivers) to France. Napoleon Bonaparte had plans for a new French empire in America with the sugar island of Hispaniola (present-day Haiti and Dominican Republic) at its center, and with mainland colonies feeding the islands and thus making the empire self-sufficient. Late in 1802, the Spanish, who had retained control of New Orleans, closed the port to American commerce, creating rumors that they would soon transfer the city to France. To forestall such a move, which would threaten the existence of American settlements west of the Appalachians, President Jefferson sent a delegation to Paris early in 1803 with authorization to buy New Orleans for the United States.

By the time the delegates reached Paris, events had dissolved French plans for a new American empire. The slaves of Saint-Domingue (the French colony on Hispaniola) had revolted against the French and had defeated their attempts to regain control of the island (see chapter 7). At the same time, another war between Britain and France seemed imminent. Napoleon—reputedly chanting "Damn sugar, damn coffee, damn colonies"—decided to bail out of America and concentrate his resources in Europe. He astonished Jefferson's delegation by announcing that France would sell not only New Orleans but the whole Louisiana Territory—which would roughly double the size of the United States—for the bargain price of $15 million.

Jefferson, who had criticized Federalists whenever they violated the letter of the Constitution, faced a dilemma:

A View of New Orleans Taken from the Plantation of Marigny, November 1803 by Boqueto de Woiserie, Chicago Historical Society.

THE LOUISIANA PURCHASE

This panorama of New Orleans celebrates the Louisiana Purchase in 1803. The patriotic caption promises prosperity for the city and (by inference) for the American settlements upriver.

The president lacked the constitutional power to buy territory, but the chance to buy Louisiana was too good to refuse. It would ensure Americans access to the rivers of the interior; it would eliminate a serious foreign threat on America's western border; and it would give American farmers enough land to sustain the agrarian republic for a long time to come. Swallowing his constitutional scruples (and at the same time half-heartedly asking for a constitutional amendment to legalize the purchase), Jefferson told the American delegates to buy Louisiana. Republican senators, who shared few of Jefferson's doubts, quickly ratified the Louisiana treaty over Federalist objections that the purchase would encourage rapid settlement and add to backcountry barbarism and Republican strength. Most Americans agreed that the accidents of French and Haitian history had given the United States a grand opportunity, and Congress's ratification of the Louisiana Purchase met with overwhelming public approval. For his part, Jefferson was certain that the republic had gained the means of renewing itself through time. As he claimed in his second inaugural address, he had bought a great "empire of liberty."

As Jefferson stood for reelection in 1804, he could look back on an astonishingly successful first term. He had dismantled the government's power to coerce its citizens, and he had begun to wipe out the national debt. The Louisiana Purchase had doubled the size of the republic at remarkably little cost. Moreover, by eliminating France from North America, it had strengthened the argument for reducing the military and the debts and taxes that went

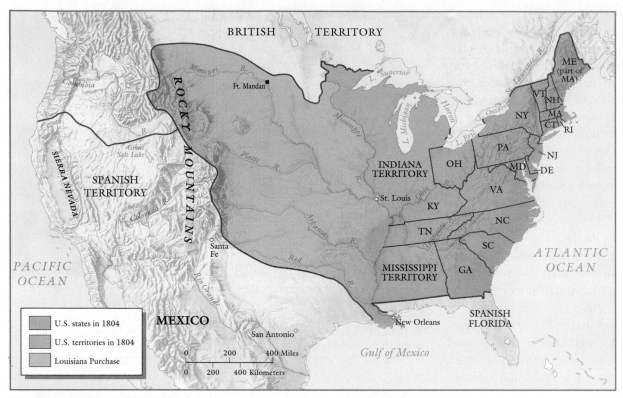

MAP 8.3 LOUISIANA PURCHASE

Jefferson's Louisiana Purchase nearly doubled the geographic size of the United States. It ended European competition for control of the North American interior and granted the United States the mouth of the Mississippi River, thus strengthening white settlements between the Appalachians and the Mississippi and increasing American control over those settlements.

with it. Jefferson was more certain than ever that the republic could preserve itself through peaceful expansion. The "wise and frugal" government he had promised in 1801 was becoming a reality.

The combination of international peace, territorial expansion, and inexpensive, unobtrusive government left the Federalists without an issue in the 1804 election. They went through the motions of nominating Charles Pinckney of South Carolina as their presidential candidate and then watched Jefferson capture the electoral votes of every state but Delaware and Connecticut. As he began his second term in 1805, Jefferson could assume that he had ended the Federalist threat to the republic.

🌐 The Republic and the Napoleonic Wars, 1804–1815

In spring 1803, a few weeks after closing the deal for Louisiana, Napoleon Bonaparte declared war on Great Britain. This 11-year war, like the wars of the 1790s, dominated the national politics of the United States. Most Americans wanted to remain neutral. Few Republicans supported Bonaparte as they had supported the French revolutionaries of 1789, and none but the most rabid Federalists wanted to intervene on the side of Great Britain, but neither France nor Britain would permit American neutrality.

The Dilemmas of Neutrality

At the beginning, both Britain and France, whose rural economies were disrupted by war, encouraged the Americans to resume their role as neutral carriers and suppliers of food. For a time, Americans made huge profits. Between 1803 and 1807, U.S. exports—mostly foodstuffs and plantation staples—rose from $66.5 million to $102.2 million. Reexports—goods produced in the British, Spanish, and French islands of the Caribbean, picked up by American vessels, and then reloaded in American ports onto American ships bound for Europe—rose even faster, from $13.5 million to $58.4 million.

In 1805, France and Great Britain began systematically to interfere with that trade. Also in 1805, the Royal Navy under Lord Nelson destroyed the French and Spanish fleets at the Battle of Trafalgar. Later that year, Napoleon's armies won a decisive victory over Austria and Russia at the Battle of Austerlitz and won effective control of Europe. The war reached a stalemate: Napoleon's army occupied Europe, and the British navy controlled the seas.

Britain decided to use its naval supremacy to blockade Europe and starve the French into submission. In the Essex Decision of 1805, the British ministry dusted off what was known as the Rule of 1756, which stated that a European country could not use a neutral merchant marine to conduct wartime trade with its colonies if its mercantile laws forbade such use during peacetime. Translated into the realities of 1805, the Essex Decision meant that the Royal Navy could seize American ships engaged in the reexport trade with France. In spring 1806, Congress, angered by British seizures of American ships, passed the Non-Importation Act forbidding the importation of British goods that could be bought elsewhere or that could be manufactured in the United States. A month after that, Britain blockaded long stretches of the European coast. Napoleon responded with the Berlin Decree, which outlawed all trade with the British Isles. The British answered with an Order in Council that demanded that neutral ships trading with Europe stop first for inspection and licensing in a British port. Napoleon responded with the Milan Decree, which stated that any vessel that obeyed the British decrees or allowed itself to be searched by the Royal Navy was subject to seizure by France. Beginning in 1805 and ending with the Milan Decree in December 1807, the barrage of European decrees and counterdecrees meant that virtually all American commerce with Europe had been outlawed by one or the other of the warring powers.

Trouble on the High Seas

Given British naval supremacy, French decrees were effective only against American ships that entered ports controlled by France. The Royal Navy, on the other hand, maintained a loose blockade of the North American coast and stopped and searched American ships as they left the major seaports. Hundreds of ships were seized, along with their cargoes and crews. Under British law, the Royal Navy could impress any British subject into service during wartime. The British were certain that many British subjects, including legions of deserters from the Royal Navy, were hiding in the American merchant marine, and they were right. The danger, low pay, bad food, and draconian discipline on British warships encouraged many British sailors to jump ship and take jobs as American merchantmen.

Many of the British warships that stopped American merchant ships on the high seas were undermanned; the sailors their officers commandeered often included Englishmen who had taken out U.S. citizenship (an act the British did not recognize) and, inevitably, native-born Americans. An estimated 6,000 American citizens were impressed into the Royal Navy between 1803 and 1812.

The kidnapping of American sailors, even more than maritime seizures of American property and other violations of American neutral rights, enraged the citizens of the United States and brought the country close to war in summer 1807. In June, the American naval frigate *Chesapeake*, which was outfitting in Norfolk, Virginia, signed on four English deserters from the British navy, along with some Americans who had joined the British navy and then deserted. The British warship H.M.S. *Leopard* was also docked at Norfolk, and some of the deserters spotted their old officers and taunted them on the streets. The *Leopard* left port and resumed its patrol of the American coast. Then, on June 21, its officers caught the *Chesapeake* off Hampton Roads and demanded the return of the British deserters. When the captain refused, the British fired on the *Chesapeake*, killing 3 Americans and wounding 18. The British then boarded the *Chesapeake*, seized the four deserters, and later hanged one of them. The *Chesapeake* limped back into port.

The *Chesapeake* affair set off huge anti-British demonstrations in the seaport towns and angry cries for war throughout the country. President Jefferson responded by barring British ships from American ports and American territorial waters and by ordering state governors to prepare to call up as many as 100,000 militiamen. The United States in 1807 stood at the brink of full-scale war with the most powerful nation in the world.

Embargo

Jefferson wanted to avoid war, which would inevitably bring high taxes, government debt, a bloated military and civil service, and the repression of dissent—precisely the evils that Jefferson had vowed to eliminate. Worse, war carried the danger of defeat and thus the possible failure of America's republican experiment.

Jefferson had one more card to play: He could suspend trade with Europe altogether and thus keep American ships out of harm's way. For many years, Jefferson had assumed that U.S. farm products and the U.S. market for imported goods had become crucial to the European economies. He could use trade as a means of "peaceable coercion" that would both ensure respect for American neutral rights and keep the country out of war. "Our commerce," he wrote just before taking office, "is so valuable to them, that they will be glad to purchase it, when the only price we ask is to do us justice." Convinced that America's yeoman republic could survive without European luxuries more easily than Europe could survive without American food, Jefferson decided to give "peaceable coercion" a serious test. Late in 1807, he asked Congress to suspend all U.S. trade with foreign countries.

Congress passed the Embargo Act on December 22. By the following spring, however, it was clear that peaceable coercion would not work. The British found other markets and other sources of food. They encouraged the smuggling of American goods into Canada. And American merchantmen who had been at sea when the embargo went into effect stayed away from their home ports and functioned as part of the British merchant marine. A loophole in the Embargo Act allowed U.S. ships to leave port in order to pick up American property stranded in other countries, and an estimated 6,000 ships set sail under that excuse. Hundreds of others, plying the coastal trade, were "blown off course" and found themselves thrust into international commerce. For his part, Napoleon seized American ships in European ports, explaining that, because the embargo kept all American ships in port, those trading under American flags must be British ships in disguise.

The embargo hurt American commerce badly. Its 1807 exports of $108 million dropped to $22 million in 1808. The economy slowed in every section of the country, but it ground to a halt in the cities of the Northeast. While the oceangoing merchant fleet rotted at anchor, unemployed sailors, dockworkers, and other maritime workers and their families sank to levels of economic

despair seldom seen in British North America. Northeastern Federalists branded Jefferson's embargo a "Chinese" (i.e., isolationist) solution to the problems of commerce and diplomacy. Commerce, they argued, was the great civilizer: "Her victories are over ferocious passions, savage manners, deep rooted prejudices, blind superstition and delusive theory." Federalists accused Jefferson of plotting an end to commerce and a reversion to rural barbarism, and they often took the lead in trying to subvert the embargo through smuggling and other means. In Connecticut, the Federalist governor flatly refused Jefferson's request to mobilize the militia to enforce the embargo.

The Federalists gained ground in the elections of 1808. James Madison, Jefferson's old ally and chosen successor, was elected president with 122 electoral votes to 47 for his Federalist opponent, C. C. Pinckney. Although Republicans retained control of both houses of Congress, Federalists made significant gains in Congress and won control of several state legislatures. Federalist opposition to the embargo, and to the supposed southern, agrarian stranglehold on national power that stood behind it, was clearly gaining ground.

The Road to War

When President Madison took office in spring 1809, it was clear that the embargo had failed to coerce the British. On the contrary, the embargo had created misery in the seaport cities, choked off the imports that provided 90 percent of federal revenue, and revived Federalist opposition to Republican dominance. Early in 1809, Congress passed the Non-Intercourse Act, which retained the ban on trade with Britain and France but reopened trade with other nations. It also gave President Madison the power to reopen trade with either Britain or France once they had agreed to respect American rights. Neither complied, and the Non-Intercourse Act proved nearly as ineffective as the embargo.

In 1810, Congress passed Macon's Bill No. 2, a strange piece of legislation that rescinded the ban on trade with France and Britain but also authorized the president to reimpose the Non-Intercourse Act on either belligerent if the other agreed to end its restrictions on U.S. trade. Napoleon decided to test the Americans. In September 1810, the French foreign minister, the Duc de Cadore, promised, with vague conditions, that France would repeal the Berlin and Milan Decrees. Although the proposal was a clear attempt to lead the United States into conflict with Great Britain, Madison saw no choice but to go along with it. He accepted the French promise and proclaimed in November 1810 that the British had three months to follow suit.

North Wind Picture Archives.

ANTIEMBARGO PROPAGANDA

A Federalist cartoonist heard the Embargo Act denounced as a "terrapin policy" and drew a snapping turtle seizing a tobacco smuggler by the seat of the pants. The man cries out "Oh! this cursed Ograbme"—*embargo* spelled backward.

"It promises us," he said of his proclamation, "at least an extrication from the dilemma, of a mortifying peace, or a war with both the great belligerents."

In the end, Madison's proclamation led to war. The French repealed only those sections of the Berlin and Milan Decrees that applied to the neutral rights of the United States. The British refused to revoke their Orders in Council and told the Americans to withdraw their restrictions on British trade until the French had repealed theirs. The United States would either have to obey British orders (thus making American exports and the American merchant marine a part of the British war effort—a neo-colonial situation that was utterly repugnant to most Americans) or go to war. When Congress reconvened in November 1811, it voted military measures in preparation for war with Great Britain.

The War Hawk Congress, 1811–1812

The Republicans controlled both houses of Congress in the 1811–12 session; however, although 75 percent of the House and 82 percent of the Senate identified themselves as members of President Madison's party, they were a divided majority. The Federalist minority, united against Madison, was joined on many issues by northeastern Republicans who followed the pro-British, Federalist line on international trade and by Republicans who wanted a more powerful military than other Republicans would allow. Also opposed to Madison were the self-styled Old Republicans of the South, led by John Randolph. Thus it was a deeply divided Congress that met the war crisis.

In this confused situation, a group of talented young congressmen took control. Nearly all of them were Republicans from the South or the West: Richard M. Johnson and Henry Clay of Kentucky, John C. Calhoun and William Lowndes of South Carolina, George M. Troup of Georgia, Peter B. Porter from the Niagara district of New York, and others. Called the War Hawks, these ardent nationalists were more than willing to declare war on England to protect U.S. rights. Through their organizational, oratorical, and intellectual power, they won control of Congress. Henry Clay, only 34 years old and serving his first term in Congress, was elected Speaker of the House. More vigorous than his predecessors, Clay controlled debate, packed key committees, worked tirelessly behind the scenes, and imposed order on his fellow congressmen. When John Randolph, one of the most feared members of the House, brought his dog into the House chamber, Speaker Clay pointedly ordered the dog removed. Earlier speakers had not dared give such an order.

North Wind Picture Archives.

HENRY CLAY

This portrait of Henry Clay was engraved at about the time the brilliant first-term congressman from Kentucky, as Speaker of the House, helped his fellow War Hawks steer the United States into the War of 1812.

In the winter and spring of 1811–12, the War Hawks led Congress into a declaration of war. In November they voted military preparations, and in April they enacted a 90-day embargo—not to coerce the British but to return American ships safely to port before war began. (As in 1807, the embargo prompted seaport merchants to rush their ships to sea.) On June 1, Madison sent a war message to Congress. This was to be the first war declared under the Constitution, and the president stayed out of congressional territory by not asking explicitly for a declaration of war. He did, however, present a list of British crimes that could be interpreted in no other way: the enforcement of the Orders in Council, even within the territorial waters of the United States; the impressment of American seamen; the use of spies and provocateurs within the United States; and the wielding of "a malicious influence over the Indians of the Northwest Territory." Madison concluded that war had in fact begun: "We behold . . . on the side of Great Britain a state of war against the United States; and on the side of the United States, a state of peace toward Great Britain."

Congress declared war on June 18. The vote was far from unanimous: 79 to 49 in the House of Representatives,

19 to 13 in the Senate. All 30 Federalists voted against the declaration, as did one in five Republicans, nearly all of them from the Northeast. Thus the war was declared by the Democratic Republican Party, more particularly by the Republicans of the South and the West. The Northeast, whose commercial rights were supposedly the issue at stake, opposed the declaration.

War Hawks and the War of 1812

The War Hawks declared a war to defend the sovereignty, the western territory, and the maritime rights of the United States. The war they planned and fought, however, bore the stamp of southern and western Republicanism. Federalists and many northeastern Republicans expected a naval war. After all, the British had committed their atrocities on the ocean, and some, remembering U.S. naval successes against France in the quasi-war of 1798–1800 (discussed earlier in this chapter), predicted similar successes against Great Britain. Yet when Madison asked Congress to prepare for war, the War Hawks led a majority that strengthened the U.S. Army and left the navy weak. Reasoning that no U.S. naval force could challenge British control of the seas, they prepared instead for a land invasion of British Canada.

The decision to invade Canada led the Federalists, along with many of Randolph's Old Republicans, to accuse Madison and the congressional majority of planning a war of territorial aggression. Some members of Congress did want to annex Canada to the United States, but most saw the decision to invade Canada as a matter of strategy. Lightly garrisoned and with a population of only one-half million (many of them French, and most of the others American émigrés of doubtful loyalties), Canada seemed the easiest and most logical place in which to damage the British. It was also from bases in Canada that the British armed Tecumseh's formidable Indian confederacy (see chapter 7). The western Republicans were determined to end that threat once and for all. Finally, Canada was a valuable colony of Great Britain. The American embargoes, coupled with Napoleon's control of Europe, had impaired Britain's ability to supply her plantation colonies in the West Indies, and Canadian farmers had begun to fill the gap. Thus Canada was both valuable and vulnerable, and American policy makers reasoned that they could take it and hold it hostage while demanding that the British back down on other issues. Although U.S. military strategy focused on Canada, maritime rights and national honor, along with the British-fed Indian threat west of the Appalachians, were the central issues in 1812. As John C. Calhoun, who was instrumental in taking the nation to war, concluded: "The mad ambition, the lust of power, and commercial avarice of Great Britain have left to neutral nations an alternative only between the base surrender of their rights, and a manly vindication of them."

The War with Canada, 1812–1813

The United States opened its offensive against Canada in 1812, with disastrous results. The plan was to invade Upper Canada (Ontario) from the Northwest, thus cutting off the Shawnee, Potawatomi, and other pro-British Indian tribes from their British support. When General William Hull, governor of Michigan Territory, took a poorly supplied, badly led army of militiamen and volunteers into Canada from a base in Detroit, he found that the British

AMERICAN TROOPS INVADE CANADA

In this painting, a Canadian artist depicts the failed American invasion at Queenston Heights in October 1812. British troops on the right are rushing to repel the Americans, who have occupied the cliffs at center.

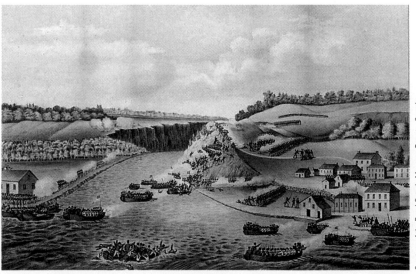

Courtesy of the Royal Ontario Museum, Toronto, Canada.

had outguessed him. The area was crawling with British troops and their Indian allies. With detachments of his army overrun and his supply lines cut, he retreated to the garrison at Detroit. Under siege, he heard that an Indian force had captured the garrison at Fort Dearborn. British General Isaac Brock, who knew that Hull was afraid of

Indians, sent a note into the fort telling him that "the numerous body of Indians who have attached themselves to my troops, will be beyond my controul the moment the contest commences." Without consulting his officers, Hull surrendered his army of 2,000 to the smaller British force. Although Hull was later court-martialed for cowardice,

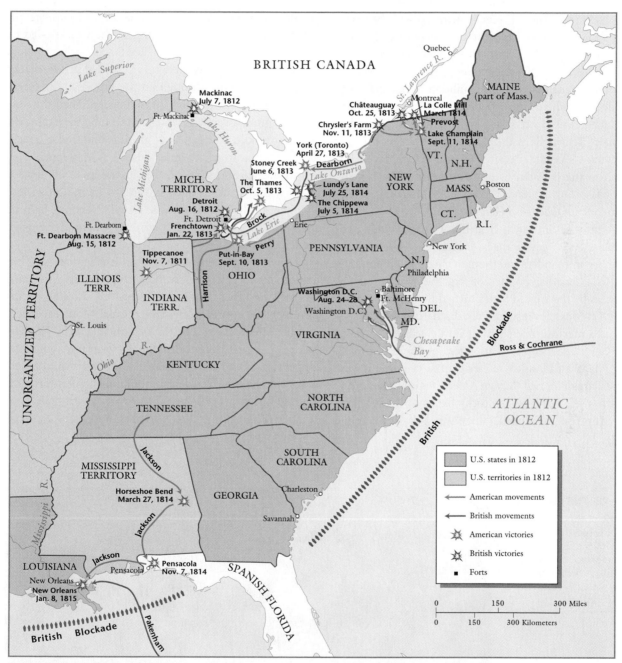

MAP 8.4 WAR OF 1812

Early in the war, Americans chose to fight the British in Canada, with costly and inconclusive results. Later, the British determined to blockade the whole coast of the United States and, late in the war, to raid important coastal towns. The results were equally inconclusive: Both sides could inflict serious damage, but neither could conquer the other. The one clear military outcome—one that the Americans were determined to accomplish—was the destruction of Indian resistance east of the Mississippi.

View an animated version of this map or related maps at http://history.wadsworth.com/murrin_LEP4e.

the damage had been done: The British and their Indian allies occupied many of the remaining American garrisons in the Northwest and transformed the U.S. invasion of Upper Canada into a British occupation of much of the Northwest.

The invasion of Canada from the east went no better. In October a U.S. force of 6,000 faced 2,000 British and Indians across the Niagara River separating Ontario from western New York. The U.S. regular army crossed the river, surprised the British, and established a toehold at Queenston Heights. While the British were preparing a counterattack, New York militiamen refused to cross the river to reinforce the regular troops. Ohio militiamen had behaved the same way when Hull invaded Canada, and similar problems had arisen with the New York militia near Lake Champlain. Throughout the war, citizen-soldiers proved that Jefferson's confidence in the militia could not be extended to the invasion of other countries. The British regrouped and slaughtered the outnumbered, exhausted U.S. regulars at Queenston Heights.

As winter set in, it was clear that Canada would not fall as easily as the Americans had assumed. The invasion, which U.S. commanders had thought would knife through an apathetic Canadian population, had the opposite effect: The attacks by the United States turned the ragtag assortment of American loyalist émigrés, discharged British soldiers, and American-born settlers into a self-consciously British Canadian people. Years later, an Englishwoman touring Niagara Falls asked a Canadian ferryman if it was true that Canadians had thrown Americans off Queenston Heights to their death on the rocky banks of the Niagara River. "Why yes," he replied, "there was a good many of

them; but it was right to show them that there was water between us, and you know it might help to keep the rest of them from coming to trouble us on our own ground."

Tecumseh's Last Stand

Tecumseh's Indian confederacy, bruised but not broken in the Battle of Tippecanoe (see chapter 7), allied itself with the British in 1812. On a trip to the southern tribes, Tecumseh found the traditionalist wing of the Creeks—led by prophets who called themselves Red Sticks—willing to join him. The augmented confederacy provided stiff resistance to the United States throughout the war. The Red Sticks chased settlers from much of Tennessee. They then attacked a group of settlers who had taken refuge in a stockade surrounding the house of an Alabama trader named George Mims. In what whites called the Massacre at Fort Mims, the Red Sticks (reputedly with the collusion of black slaves within the fort) killed at least 247 men, women, and children. In the Northwest, Tecumseh's warriors, fighting alongside the British, spread terror throughout the white settlements.

A wiser U.S. army returned to Canada in 1813. They raided and burned the Canadian capital at York (Toronto) in April, and then fought inconclusively throughout the summer. An autumn offensive toward Montreal failed, but the Americans had better luck on Lake Erie. The barrier of Niagara Falls kept Britain's saltwater navy out of the upper Great Lakes, and on Lake Erie the British and Americans engaged in a frenzied shipbuilding contest throughout the first year of the war. The Americans won. In September 1813, Commodore Oliver Hazard Perry cornered

BATTLE OF THE THAMES

The Battle of the Thames relieved the Northwest of the British and Indian threat. It became most memorable to Americans, however, as the battle in which Tecumseh was finally killed.

From the Collections of the Library of Congress.

and destroyed the British fleet at Put-in-Bay. Control of Lake Erie enabled the United States to cut off supplies to the British in the Northwest, and a U.S. army under William Henry Harrison retook the area and continued on into Canada. On October 5, Harrison caught up with a force of British and Indians at the Thames River and beat them badly. In the course of that battle, Richard M. Johnson, a War Hawk congressman acting as commander of the Kentucky militia, killed Tecumseh. Proud militiamen returned to Kentucky with pieces of hair and clothing and even swatches of skin torn from Tecumseh's corpse. Their officers reaped huge political rewards: The Battle of the Thames would eventually produce a president of the United States (Harrison), a vice president (Johnson), 3 governors of Kentucky, 3 lieutenant governors, 4 U.S. senators, and about 20 congressmen—telling evidence of how seriously the settlers of the interior had taken Tecumseh.

The following spring, General Andrew Jackson's Tennessee militia, aided by Choctaw, Creek, and Cherokee allies, attacked and slaughtered the Red Sticks, who had fortified themselves at Horseshoe Bend in Alabama. With the Battle of the Thames and the Battle of Horse Shoe Bend, the military power of the Indian peoples east of the Mississippi River was broken.

a doggerel poem that was later set to music and chosen as the national anthem in the 1930s. When a British offensive on Lake Champlain stalled during the autumn, the war reached a stalemate: Britain had prevented the invasion of Canada and had blockaded the American coast, but neither side could take and hold the other's territory.

The British now shifted their attention to the Gulf Coast, particularly to New Orleans, a city of vital importance to U.S. trans-Appalachian trade and communications. Peace negotiations had begun in August, and the British wanted to capture and hold New Orleans as a bargaining chip. A large British amphibious force landed and camped eight miles south of New Orleans. There they met an American army made up of U.S. regulars, Kentucky and Tennessee militiamen, clerks, workingmen, free blacks from the city, and about a thousand French pirates—all under the command of Andrew Jackson of Tennessee. Throughout late December and early January, unaware that a peace treaty had been signed on December 24, the armies exchanged artillery barrages and the British probed and attacked American lines. On January 8, the British launched a frontal assault. A formation of 6,000 British soldiers marched across open ground toward 4,000 Americans concealed behind breastworks. With the first American volley, it was clear that the British had made a

The British Offensive, 1814

The British defeated Napoleon in April 1814, thus ending the larger war from which the War of 1812 erupted. With both sides thinking about peace, the British decided to concentrate their resources on the American war and in 1814 went on the offensive. The British had already blockaded much of the American coast and had shut down ports from Georgia to Maine. During summer 1814, they began to raid the shores of Chesapeake Bay and marched on Washington, D.C. As retribution for the torching of the Canadian capital at York, they chased the army and politicians out of town and burned down the capitol building and the president's mansion. In September the British attacked the much larger city of Baltimore, but they could not blast their way past the determined garrison that commanded the harbor from Fort McHenry. This was the battle that inspired Francis Scott Key to write "The Star-Spangled Banner,"

Allyn Cox, 19741 Architect of the Capitol.

THE BURNING OF THE CAPITOL

The United States suffered one of its greatest military embarrassments ever when British troops burned the Capitol in 1814. This 1974 painting is on an archway in the present-day Capitol building.

mistake. Veterans of the bloodiest battles of the Napoleonic wars swore that they had never seen such withering fire; soldiers in the front ranks who were not cut down threw themselves to the ground and surrendered when the shooting stopped. The charge lasted half an hour. At the end, 2,000 British soldiers lay dead or wounded. American casualties numbered only 70. Fought nearly two weeks after the peace treaty, the Battle of New Orleans had no effect on the outcome of the war or on the peace terms, but it salved the injured pride of Americans and made a national hero and a political power of Andrew Jackson.

The Hartford Convention

While most of the nation celebrated Jackson's victory, events in Federalist New England went otherwise during the closing months of the war. New Englanders had considered themselves the victims of Republican trade policies, and their congressmen had voted overwhelmingly against going to war. The New England states seldom met their quotas of militiamen for the war effort, and some Federalist leaders had openly urged resistance to the war. The British had encouraged that resistance by not extending their naval blockade to the New England coast, and throughout the first two years of the war, New England merchants and farmers had traded freely with the enemy. In 1814, after the Royal Navy had extended its blockade northward and had begun to raid the towns of coastal Maine, some Federalists talked openly about seceding and making a separate peace with Britain.

In an attempt to undercut the secessionists, moderate Federalists called a convention at Hartford to air the region's grievances. The Hartford Convention, which met in late December 1814, proposed amendments to the Constitution that indicated New England's position as a self-conscious minority within the Union. First, the convention delegates wanted the "three-fifths" clause, which

---

HISTORY THROUGH FILM

The Buccaneer (1958)

Directed by Anthony Quinn. Starring Yul Brynner (Jean Lafitte), Charlton Heston (Andrew Jackson), Claire Bloom (Bonnie Brown), Inger Stevens (Annette Claiborne).

Here is one of the enduring legends of American history. Late in 1814, the British had attacked and burned Washington, D.C., and were moving a huge assault force toward the vital gulf port of New Orleans. Perhaps they wished to hold New Orleans as a bargaining chip in the peace negotiations already under way. Or perhaps they wished to conquer the whole Mississippi Valley. With the city in panic, Major General Andrew Jackson, at the head of a band of Tennessee squirrel shooters (the U.S. regulars and the local militia—including two battalions of free blacks—with him are seldom mentioned) rides in to save the day. The privateer Jean Lafitte controls the swamps and river channels that lead from the gulf to New Orleans, and the British try to win his allegiance. He turns them down and—despite an American naval assault on his stronghold and the imprisonment of many of his men—throws his men and munitions into the battle on the side of the victorious Americans. New Orleans is saved, Jackson becomes a national hero, and a pardoned Lafitte sails off into the sunset.

Hollywood took a good legend, added sentimental patriotism and a preposterous love story, and made The Buccaneer—with Yul Brynner as Jean Lafitte and Charlton Heston as Andrew Jackson. Brynner's Lafitte is a perfect swashbuckler: a fiery and fair-minded pirate who kills only when he has to, who has agreed not to attack American ships, and who is in love with the governor's daughter (Claire Bloom). Early on, he listens to the Declaration of Independence and wonders aloud if he would not prefer believing in a country to believing in the pirate brotherhood's code. (Another incentive: The governor's daughter refuses to marry him until he becomes respectable.) The dreams of citizenship and domesticity become doubtful, however, when one of Lafitte's (fictional) renegade captains loots and sinks the (fictional) American ship Corinthian, killing, along with 79 others, the governor's younger daughter. This remains secret while Lafitte joins Jackson to win the battle—with British automatons in kilts marching to their deaths, bagpipe players falling one by one until their terrifying wail is reduced to one dying note.

led to overrepresentation of the South in Congress and the electoral college (see chapter 6), stricken from the Constitution; they also wanted to deny naturalized citizens—who were strongly Republican—the right to hold office; they wanted to make it more difficult for new states—all of which sided with the Republicans and their southern leadership—to enter the Union; and finally, they wanted to require a two-thirds majority of both houses for a declaration of war—a requirement that would have prevented the War of 1812.

The Federalist leaders of the Hartford Convention, satisfied that they had headed off the secessionists, took their proposals to Washington in mid-January. They arrived to find the capital celebrating the news of the peace treaty and Jackson's stunning victory at New Orleans. When they aired their sectional complaints and their constitutional proposals, they were branded as negative, selfish, and unpatriotic. Although Federalists continued for a few years to wield power in southern New England, the

Hartford debacle ruined any chance of a nationwide Federalist resurgence after the war. Andrew Jackson had stolen control of American history from New England. He would do so again in the years ahead.

The Treaty of Ghent

Britain's defeat of Napoleon had spurred British and American efforts to end a war that neither wanted. In August 1814, they opened peace talks in the Belgian city of Ghent. Perhaps waiting for the results of their 1814 offensive, the British opened with proposals that the Americans were certain to reject. They demanded the right to navigate the Mississippi. Moreover, they wanted territorial concessions and the creation of the permanent, independent Indian buffer state in the Northwest that they had promised their Indian allies. The Americans ignored these proposals and talked instead about impressment and maritime rights. As the autumn wore on and the war reached

The Buccaneer **depicts the 1814 British attack on Washington, D.C., with plenty of sentimental patriotism and a love story thrown in for good measure.**

At the victory ball, Lafitte and his lady love announce their engagement; word of the *Corinthian* spreads through the room. Heston's Jackson (who looks exactly like the older Jackson on the $20 bill) stops a lynching and allows Lafitte and his men one hour to leave town. The marriage between the French rogue and the blonde American lady—

improbable in 1814 and impossible in the movies of the 1950s—is averted. Lafitte sails off to no particular destination (he died in Yucatán a few years later) with a pirate moll (Inger Stevens) at his side, and America has been saved in more ways than one.

stalemate, both sides began to compromise. The British knew that the Americans would grant concessions in the interior only if they were thoroughly defeated, an outcome that most British commanders thought impossible. For their part, the Americans realized that the British maritime depredations were by-products of the struggle with Napoleonic France. Faced with peace in Europe and a senseless military stalemate in North America, negotiators on both sides began to withdraw their demands. The Treaty of Ghent, signed on Christmas Eve 1814, simply put an end to the war. The border between Canada and the United States remained where it had been in 1812; Indians south of that border—defeated and without allies— were left to the mercy of the United States; and British maritime violations were not mentioned. The makers of the treaty stopped a war that neither side could win, trusting that a period of peace would resolve the problems created by two decades of world war.

Conclusion

In 1816, Thomas Jefferson was in retirement at Monticello, satisfied that he had defended liberty against the Federalists' love of power. The High Federalist attempt to consolidate power, militarize government, and jail their enemies had failed. Their direct taxes were repealed. Their debt and their national bank remained in place, but only under the watchful eyes of true republicans. And their attempt to ally the United States with the antirepublican designs of Great Britain had ended in what many called the Second War of American Independence. American independence was truly won, and Jefferson's vision of a union of independent republican states seemed to have been realized.

Yet for all his successes, Jefferson saw that he must sacrifice some of his longest-held dreams. Jefferson's republican vision was grounded in farmer-citizens whose vision was local and who wanted nothing more from government than protection of their property and rights. Jefferson's imagined yeomen traded farm surpluses for European manufactured goods—a system that encouraged rural prosperity, prevented the growth of cities and factories (the much-feared nurseries of corruption and dependence), and thus sustained the landed independence on which republican citizenship rested. Westward expansion, Jefferson had believed, would ensure the yeoman republic for generations to come. By 1816, that dream was ended. The British and French had "cover[ed] the earth and sea with robberies and piracies," disrupting America's vital export economy whenever it suited their whims. Arguing as Hamilton had argued in 1790, Jefferson insisted that "we must now place the manufacturer by the side of the agriculturalist." As he wrote, a Republican congress was taking steps that would help transform Jefferson's republic into a market society and a boisterous capitalist democracy.

SUGGESTED READINGS

Stanley Elkins and Eric McKitrick, *The Age of Federalism: The Early American Republic, 1788–1800* (1993) is definitive. **Henry Adams,** *History of the United States of America during the Administrations of Thomas Jefferson and James Madison,* 9 vols. (1889–1891; reprint, 2 vols., 1986) remains the fullest introduction to the Republican presidencies. **Thomas G. Slaughter,** *The Whiskey Rebellion: Frontier Epilogue to the American Revolution* (1986) is good on its subject. **Lance Banning,** *The Jeffersonian Persuasion: Evolution of a Party Ideology* (1980); **Drew R. McCoy,** *The Elusive Republic: Political Economy in*

Jeffersonian America (1980); and **Peter Onuf,** *Jefferson's Empire: The Language of American Nationhood* (2001) are insightful studies of Jeffersonianism. On relations with other countries, see **Lawrence Kaplan,** *"Entangling Alliances with None": American Foreign Policy in the Age of Jefferson* (1987); and **Donald R. Hickey,** *The War of 1812: A Forgotten Conflict* (1989). **Joseph J. Ellis,** *Founding Brothers: The Revolutionary Generation* (2000); and **Joanne B. Freeman,** *Affairs of Honor: National Politics in the New Republic* (2001) discuss the political culture of the founding generation.

AMERICAN JOURNEY ONLINE
AND
INFOTRAC COLLEGE EDITION

Visit the source collections at www.ajaccess.wadsworth.com and
infotrac.thomsonlearning.com and use the Search function with
the following key terms to explore documents, images, audio
and video clips, articles, and commentary related to the material
in this chapter.

George Washington   Thomas Jefferson
Alexander Hamilton   Louisiana Purchase
John Adams   *Marbury* v. *Madison*
Whiskey Rebellion   Aaron Burr
XYZ affair   Tecumseh

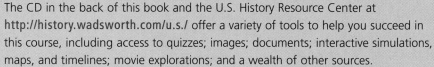

GRADE AIDS

**Visit the Liberty Equality Power Companion Web Site for resources specific to
this textbook:** http://history.wadsworth.com/murrin_LEP4e

The CD in the back of this book and the U.S. History Resource Center at
http://history.wadsworth.com/u.s./ offer a variety of tools to help you succeed in
this course, including access to quizzes; images; documents; interactive simulations,
maps, and timelines; movie explorations; and a wealth of other sources.

Chapter 9

The Market Revolution, 1815–1860

LOCKPORT
The Erie Canal was the first of the great public works projects that helped transform a wilderness continent into a 19th-century commercial society, and early travelers and publicists admired it not only as a feat of engineering but also as a work of art. The complex of locks at Lockport in particular became a symbol of the American triumph of civilization over nature. The town itself, filled with boatmen and construction workers, had a reputation for violence.

Jeffersonian Democrats had tied their hopes to the yeoman-artisan republic: Americans, they argued, could trade farm and plantation products for European manufactured goods, thus enjoying material comforts without sacrificing the landed independence on which Jefferson's republic rested. But two decades of world war demonstrated the vulnerability of American dependence on the export economy, and by 1816, Jefferson advised his countrymen to build enough factories to serve domestic needs.

The Americans went further than that, and after 1815, a Market Revolution transformed Jefferson's republic into the market-oriented, capitalist society it has been ever since. Improvements in transportation made that transformation possible, but thousands of farmers, planters, craftsmen, and merchants made the decisions that pulled farms and workshops out of old household and neighborhood arrangements and into production for distant markets.

By the 1830s and 1840s, the northern United States was experiencing a full-blown Market Revolution: New cities and towns provided financing, retailing, manufacturing, and markets for food; commercial farms traded food for what the cities made and sold. The South experienced a Market Revolution as well, but the region remained in its old colonial relationship to the centers of economic power. Away from the plantation belt, most southern farms remained marginal to the national and world economies. The wealthiest southerners, on the other hand, sent mountains of cotton, rice, and other plantation staples on to world markets. They remained provincial grandees who produced for distant markets and purchased shipping, financial services, and manufactured goods from outside the region, increasingly from the Northeast. They increased their wealth and local power and spread their plantation regime into vast new lands, and they maintained their old slaveholder's republic in the southern states. Now, however, they faced an aggressive and expanding capitalist democracy in the North.

Government and Markets

The 14th Congress met in the last days of 1815. Made up overwhelmingly of Jeffersonian Republicans, this Congress nevertheless would reverse many of the positions taken by Jefferson's old party. It would charter a national bank, enact a protective tariff, and debate whether to build a national system of roads and canals at federal expense. As late as 1811, the Republicans viewed such programs as heresy, but by 1815, the Republican majority in Congress had come to accept it as orthodox. The War of 1812 had demonstrated that the United States was unable to coordinate a fiscal and military effort. It had also convinced many Republicans that reliance on foreign trade rendered the United States dependent on Europe. The nation, they said, must abandon Jefferson's export-oriented agrarianism and encourage national independence through subsidies to commerce and manufactures.

The American System: The Bank of the United States

Nationalist Henry Clay retained his power in the postwar Congress and headed the drive for a neo-Federalist program of protective tariffs, internal improvements, and a national bank. He called his program the American System, arguing that it would foster national economic growth and a salutary interdependence between geographical sections, thus a happy and healthy republic.

In 1816, Congress chartered a Second Bank of the United States, headquartered in Philadelphia and empowered to establish branches wherever it saw fit. The government agreed to deposit its funds in the Bank, to accept the Bank's notes as payment for government land, taxes, and other transactions, and to buy one-fifth of the Bank's stock. The Bank of the United States was more powerful

than the one a Republican Congress had rejected as unconstitutional in 1811. The fiscal horrors of the War of 1812, however, had left most representatives in favor of moving toward a national currency and centralized control of money and credit. The alternative was to allow state banks—which had increased in number from 88 to 208 between 1813 and 1815—to issue unregulated and grossly inflated notes that might throw the anticipated postwar boom into chaos.

With no discussion of the constitutionality of what it was doing, Congress chartered the Bank of the United States as the sole banking institution empowered to do business throughout the country. Notes issued by the Bank would be the first semblance of a national currency (they would soon constitute from one-tenth to one-third of the value of notes in circulation). Moreover, the Bank could regulate the currency by demanding that state banknotes used in transactions with the federal government be redeemable in gold. In 1816, the Bank set up shop in Philadelphia's Carpenter's Hall, and, in 1824, moved around the corner to a Greek Revival edifice modeled after the Parthenon—a marble embodiment of the conservatism

The Library Company of Philadelphia.

THE BANK OF THE UNITED STATES

The classical Greek façade of the Bank of the United States reinforced its image as a conservative, centralizing—but still republican—financial force.

that directors of the Bank of the United States adopted as their fiscal stance. From that vantage point they would fight a running battle with state banks and local interests in an effort to impose direction on the transition to a market society.

The American System: Tariffs and Internal Improvements

In 1816, Congress drew up the first overtly protective tariff in U.S. history. Shepherded through the House by Clay and his fellow nationalist Calhoun, the Tariff of 1816 raised tariffs an average of 25 percent, extending protection to the nation's infant industries at the expense of foreign trade and American consumers. Again, wartime difficulties had paved the way: Because Americans could not depend on imported manufactures, Congress considered the encouragement of domestic manufactures a patriotic necessity. The tariff had strong support in the Northeast and the West and enough southern support to ensure its passage by Congress. Tariffs would rise and fall between 1816 and the Civil War, but the principle of protectionism would persist.

Bills to provide federal money for roads, canals, and other "internal improvements" had a harder time winning approval. The British wartime blockade had hampered coastal shipping and had made Americans dependent on the wretched roads of the interior. Many members of the 14th Congress, after spending days of bruising travel on their way to Washington, were determined to give the United States an efficient transportation network. Consensus was hard to reach. Some urged completion of the National Road linking the Chesapeake with the trans-Appalachian West. Some talked of an inland canal system to link the northern and southern coastal states. Others wanted a federally subsidized turnpike from Maine to Georgia.

Internal improvements, however, were subject to local ambitions and were of doubtful constitutionality as well. Congress agreed to complete the National Road, but President Madison and his Republican successor James Monroe both refused to support further internal improvements without a constitutional amendment. In 1822, Monroe even vetoed a bill authorizing repairs on the National Road, stating once again that the Constitution did not empower the federal government to build roads within the sovereign states.

With a national government squeamish about internal improvements, state governments took up the cause. The resulting transportation network after 1815 reflected the designs of the most ambitious states rather than the nationalizing dreams of men such as Henry Clay. New York's Erie Canal was the most spectacular accomplishment, but the canal systems of Pennsylvania and Ohio were almost as impressive. Before 1830, most toll roads were built and owned by corporations chartered by state governments, with the governments providing $5 million of the $30 million that it cost to build the roads. State expenditures on canals and railroads were even greater. Fully $41.2 million of the $58.6 million spent on the canals before 1834 came from state governments, as did more than one-third of the $137 million spend on railroads before 1843. Much of the rest came from foreign investors. Private entrepreneurs could not have built the transportation network that produced the market economy without the active support of state governments. States provided direct funding, bond issues, and corporate charters that gave the turnpike, canal, and railroad companies the privileges and immunities that made them attractive to private investors.

Markets and the Law

The Revolution replaced British courts with national and state legal systems based in English common law—systems that made legal action accessible to most white males. Thus many of the disputes generated in the transition to a market society ended up in court. The courts removed social conflicts from the public arena and brought them into a peaceful courtroom. There they dealt with the conflicts in language that only lawyers understood and resolved them in ways that tended to promote the entrepreneurial use of private property, the sanctity of contracts, and the right to do business shielded from neighborhood restraints and the tumult of democratic politics.

John Marshall, who presided over the Supreme Court from 1801 to 1835, took the lead. From the beginning, he saw the Court as a conservative hedge against the excesses of democratically elected legislatures. His early decisions protected the independence of the courts and their right to review legislation (see chapter 8). From 1816 onward, his decisions encouraged business and strengthened the national government at the expense of the states. Marshall's most important decisions protected the sanctity of contracts and corporate charters against state legislatures. For example, in *Dartmouth College* v. *Woodward* (1816), Dartmouth was defending a royal charter granted in the 1760s against changes introduced by a Republican legislature determined to transform Dartmouth from a privileged bastion of Federalism into a state college. Daniel Webster, who was both a Dartmouth alumnus and the school's highly paid lawyer, finished his argument before the Supreme Court on an emotional note: "It is, sir, as I have said, a small college. And yet there are those who

love it—." Reputedly moved to tears, Marshall ruled that a state legislature could not alter Dartmouth's corporate charter. Although in this case the Supreme Court was protecting Dartmouth's independence and its chartered privileges, Marshall and Webster knew that the decision also protected the hundreds of turnpike and canal companies, manufacturing corporations, and other ventures that held privileges under corporate charters granted by state governments. Once the charters had been granted, the states could neither regulate the corporations nor cancel their privileges. Thus corporate charters acquired the legal status of contracts, beyond the reach of democratic politics.

Two weeks after the *Dartmouth* decision, Marshall handed down the majority opinion in *McCulloch* v. *Maryland*. The Maryland legislature, nurturing old Jeffersonian doubts about the constitutionality of the Bank of the United States, had attempted to tax the Bank's Baltimore branch, and the Bank had challenged the legislature's right to do so. Marshall decided in favor of the Bank. He stated, first, that the Constitution granted the federal government "implied powers" that included chartering the Bank, and he denied Maryland's right to tax the Bank or any other federal agency: "The power to tax," he said, "involves the power to destroy." It was Marshall's most explicit blow

---

L I N K T O T H E P A S T

Charles Brockden Brown's American System

In 1809, Charles Brockden Brown, America's first professional literary man and a dedicated Jeffersonian, urged Congress to help create a national market society. The old Jeffersonian combination of agriculture and foreign trade, he said, kept Americans dependent on Europe and drew them into wars. As an alternative, he proposed a vision of national wealth and self-sufficiency:

W*hen we think on our helpless dependence, for the comforts and decencies of life, upon nations three thousand miles off, we may, without a crime, be disposed to wish that all intercourse of this kind, were at an end; that we should sit, quiet spectators of the storms that shake the rest of the world—employing all our vigor in building up an empire here in the West; and in cementing the members of our vast and growing nation, into one body.*

There is something charming too in the picture of a world within ourselves. . . . We should go on multiplying

persons and towns and cottages faster; and thus become much greater and more wealthy, if all our surplus products were consumed by mouths at home, and not abroad. If the millions who now weave and sow and hammer and file for us, were members of our own body, swelling by their gains and their experiences, the tide of circulation in our own community.

1. Here, in the words of a northern Jeffersonian, were the seeds of the American System. As of 1809, what were the motives for proposing that system?
2. How did arguments for that system grow and change over succeeding years? For clues, link to the works of Henry Clay (1810), Henry Niles (1823), Edward Everett (1830), and Daniel Webster (1836).

For additional sources related to this feature, visit the *Liberty, Equality, Power* Web site at:

http://history.wadsworth.com/murrin_LEP4e

against Jeffersonian strict constructionism. Americans, he said, "did not design to make their government dependent on the states." And yet many, particularly in Marshall's native South, remained certain that that was precisely what the founders had intended.

In *Gibbons* v. *Ogden* (1824) the Marshall Court broke a state-granted steamship monopoly in New York. The monopoly, Marshall argued, interfered with federal jurisdiction over interstate commerce. Like *Dartmouth College* v. *Woodward* and *McCulloch* v. *Maryland,* this decision empowered the national government in relation to the states. And like them, it encouraged private entrepreneurialism. Agreeing with congressmen who supported the American System, John Marshall's Supreme Court assumed that a natural and beneficial link existed between federal power and market society.

Meanwhile, the state courts were working quieter but equally profound transformations of American law. In the early republic, state courts had often viewed property not only as a private possession but as part of a neighborhood. Thus when a miller built a dam that flooded upriver farms or impaired the fishery, the courts might make him take those interests into account, often in ways that reduced the business uses of his property. By the 1830s, New England courts were routinely granting the owners of industrial mill sites unrestricted water rights, even when the exercise of those rights inflicted damage on their neighbors. As early as 1805, the New York Supreme Court in *Palmer* v. *Mulligan* had asserted that the right to develop property for business purposes was inherent in the ownership of property. A Kentucky court, asked to decide whether a railroad could come into downtown Louisville despite the protests of residents over the noise and the showers of sparks, decided that the public need for transportation outweighed the danger and annoyance to nearby residents. Railroads were necessary, and "private injury and personal damage . . . must be expected." "The onward spirit of the age," concluded the Kentucky court, "must, to a reasonable extent, have its way." In the courts of northern and western states, that "onward spirit" demanded legal protection for the business uses of private property, even when such uses conflicted with old common law restraints.

☛ The Transportation Revolution

After 1815, dramatic improvements in transportation—more and better roads, steamboats, canals, and finally railroads—tied old communities together and penetrated previously isolated neighborhoods. These improvements made the transition to a market society physically possible.

Transportation in 1815

In 1815, the United States was a rural nation stretching from the old settlements on the Atlantic coast to the trans-Appalachian frontier, with transportation facilities that ranged from primitive to nonexistent. Americans despaired of communicating, to say nothing of doing business on a national scale. In 1816, a Senate committee reported that $9 would move a ton of goods across the 3,000-mile expanse of the North Atlantic from Britain to the United States; the same $9 would move the same ton of goods only 30 miles inland. A year later, the cost of transporting wheat from the new settlement of Buffalo to New York City was three times greater than the selling price of wheat in New York. Farming for profit made sense only for farmers near urban markets or with easy river access to the coast.

West of the Appalachians, transportation was almost entirely undeveloped. Until about 1830, most westerners were southern yeomen who settled near tributaries of the Ohio-Mississippi River system—a network of navigable streams that reached the sea at New Orleans. Frontier farmers floated their produce downriver on jerry-built flatboats; at New Orleans it was trans-shipped to New York and other eastern ports. Most boatmen knocked down their flatboats, sold the lumber, and walked home to Kentucky or Ohio over the dangerous path known as the Natchez Trace.

Transporting goods to the western settlements was even more difficult. Keelboatmen such as the legendary Mike Fink could navigate upstream, using eddies and back currents, sailing when the wind was right, but usually poling their boat against the current. Skilled crews averaged only 15 miles per day, and the trip from New Orleans to Louisville took three to four months. (The downstream trip took a month.) Looking for better routes, some merchants dragged finished goods across Pennsylvania and into the West at Pittsburgh, but transport costs made these goods prohibitively expensive. Consequently, the trans-Appalachian settlements—home to one in five Americans by 1820—remained marginal to the market economy. By 1815, New Orleans was shipping about $5 million of western produce annually—an average of only $15 per farm family in the interior.

Improvements: Roads and Rivers

In 1816, Congress resumed construction of the National Road (first authorized in 1802) that linked the Potomac River with the Ohio River at Wheeling, Virginia. The smooth, crushed-rock thoroughfare reached Wheeling in 1818. At about the same time, Pennsylvania extended the

A RIVER STEAMBOAT IN 1826

By the mid-1820s, steamboats regularly plied the river systems of the United States. Businessmen and elite travelers rented nicely appointed cabins on the steamer and viewed the scenery as they strolled the comfortable (and usually uncrowded) passenger deck. Poorer passengers bought passage on the "Safety Barge" that was dragged behind the steamer.

Thomas L. McKenney, Sketches of a Tour to the Lakes (1827).

Lancaster Turnpike to make it run from Philadelphia to the Ohio River at Pittsburgh. These ambitious roads into the West, however, had few effects. The National Road made it easier for settlers and a few merchants' wagons to reach the West, but the cost of moving bulky farm produce over the road remained high. Eastbound traffic on the National Road consisted largely of cattle and pigs, which carried themselves to market. Farmers continued to float their corn, cotton, wheat, salt pork, and whiskey south by riverboat and thence to eastern markets.

The steamboat opened the West to commercial agriculture. Tinkerers and mechanics had been experimenting with steam-powered boats for a generation or more when an entrepreneur named Robert Fulton launched the *Clermont* on an upriver trip from New York City to Albany in 1807. Over the next few years, Americans developed flat-bottomed steamboats that could navigate rivers even at low water. The first steamboat reached Louisville from New Orleans in 1815. Two years later, with 17 steamboats already working western rivers, the *Washington* made the New Orleans–Louisville run in 25 days, a feat that convinced westerners that two-way river trade was possible. By 1820, 69 steamboats were operating on western rivers. The 60,000 tons of produce that farmers and planters had shipped out of the interior in 1810 grew to 500,000 tons in 1840. By the eve of the Civil War, two million tons of western produce—most of it southwestern cotton—reached the docks at New Orleans. The steamboat had transformed the interior from an isolated frontier into a busy commercial region that traded farm and plantation products for manufactured goods.

Improvements: Canals and Railroads

In the East, state governments created rivers where nature had made none. In 1817, Governor DeWitt Clinton talked the New York legislature into building a canal linking the Hudson River with Lake Erie, thus opening a continuous water route between the Northwest and New York City. The Erie Canal was a near-visionary feat of engineering: Designed by self-taught engineers and built by gangs of Irish immigrants, local farm boys, and convict laborers, it stretched 364 miles from Albany to Buffalo. Although "Clinton's Ditch" passed through carefully chosen level ground, it required a complex system of 83 locks, and it passed over 18 rivers on stone aqueducts. Construction began in 1819, and the canal reached Buffalo in 1825. It was clear even before then that the canal would repay New York state's investment of $7.5 million many times over, and that it would transform the territory it served.

The Erie Canal had its first and most powerful effects on western New York, which had been a raw frontier accessible to the East only over a notoriously bad state road. By 1830, the New York corridor of the Erie Canal, settled largely from hill-country New England, was one of the world's great grain-growing regions, dotted with market towns and new cities such as Syracuse, Rochester, and Buffalo.

The Erie Canal was an immense success, and legislators and entrepreneurs in other states joined a canal boom that lasted for 20 years. When construction began on the Erie Canal, there were fewer than 100 miles of canal in the

NEAR LOCKPORT ON THE ERIE CANAL

This engraving of the Deep Cut through hills near Lockport, New York, was commissioned for the official volume celebrating completion of the Erie Canal in 1825. It gives the canal a scale and an awesome beauty meant to rival and perhaps surpass the works of nature.

United States. By 1840, there were 3,300 miles, nearly all of them in the Northeast and Northwest. Northwestern states, Ohio in particular, built ambitious canal systems that linked isolated areas to the Great Lakes and thus to the Erie Canal. Northeastern states followed suit: A canal between Worcester and Providence linked the farms of central Massachusetts with Narragansett Bay. Another canal linked the coal mines of northeastern Pennsylvania with the Hudson River at Kingston, New York. In 1835, Pennsylvania completed a canal from Philadelphia to Pittsburgh, although at one point goods were shifted onto an unwieldy railroad that crossed a mountain.

The first American railroads connected burgeoning cities to rivers and canals. The Baltimore and Ohio Railroad, for example, linked Baltimore to the rivers of the West. Although the approximately 3,000 miles of railroads built between the late 1820s and 1840 helped the market positions of some cities, they did not constitute a national or even a regional rail network. A national system developed with the 5,000 miles of track laid in the 1840s and with the flurry of railroad building that gave the United States a rail network of 30,000 miles by 1860—a continuous, integrated system that created massive links between the East and the Northwest and that threatened to put canals out of business. In fact, the New York Central, which paralleled the Erie Canal, rendered that canal obsolete. Other railroads, particularly in the northwestern states, replaced canal and river transport almost completely, even though water transport remained cheaper. By 1860, few farmers in the North and West lived more than 20 road miles from railroads, canals, or rivers that could deliver their produce to regional, national, and international markets.

Time and Money

The transportation revolution brought a dramatic reduction in the time and money it took to move heavy goods. Turnpikes cut the cost of wagon transport in half between 1816 and 1860—from 30 cents per ton-mile to 15 cents. In 1816, freight rates on the Ohio-Mississippi system had been 1.3 cents per ton-mile for downriver travel and 5.8 cents for upriver travel; steamboats cut both costs to a bit more than a third of a cent. The Erie Canal and the Ohio canals reduced the distance between East and West and carried goods at about a cent per ton-mile; the railroads of the 1850s carried freight much faster, although at two to three times the cost. And the longer the haul, the greater the per-mile savings: Overall, the cost of moving goods across long distances dropped 95 percent between 1815 and 1860.

Improvements in speed were nearly as dramatic. The overland route from Cincinnati to New York in 1815 (by keelboat upriver to Pittsburgh, then by wagon the rest of the way) had taken a minimum of 52 days. Steamboats traveled from Cincinnati to New Orleans, then passed goods on to coasting ships that finished the trip to New York City in a total of 28 days. By the 1840s, upriver steamboats carried goods to the terminus of the Main Line Canal at Pittsburgh, which delivered them to Philadelphia, which sent them by train to New York City for a total transit time of 18 to 20 days. At about the same time, the Ohio

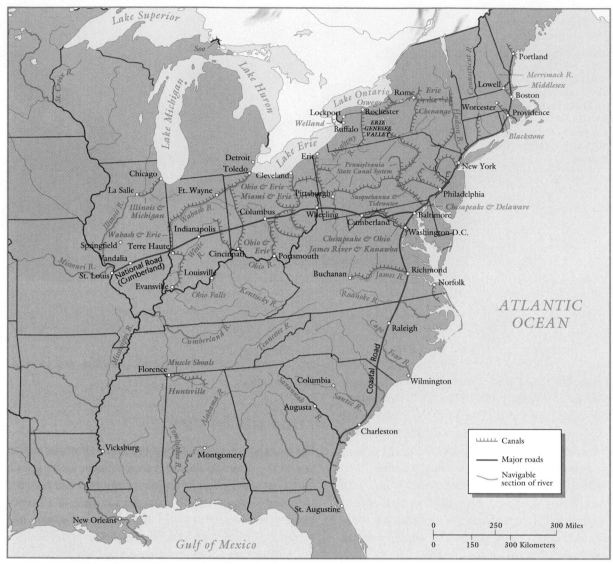

MAP 9.1   RIVERS, ROADS, AND CANALS, 1825–1860

In the second quarter of the 19th century, transportation projects linked the North and Northwest into an integrated economic and social system. There were fewer improvements in the South: farm produce traveled down navigable rivers from bottomland plantations to river and seaport towns, thence to New York for shipment overseas; southern legislatures and entrepreneurs saw little use for further improvements.

canal system enabled Cincinnati to send goods north through Ohio, across Lake Erie, over the Erie Canal, and down the Hudson to New York City—an all-water route that reduced costs and made the trip in 18 days. By 1852, the Erie Railroad and its connectors could make the Cincinnati–New York City run—although at a higher cost than water routes—in six to eight days. Similar improvements occurred in the densely settled and increasingly urbanized Northeast. By 1840, travel time between the big northeastern cities had been reduced to from one-fourth to one-eleventh of what it had been in 1790, with people, goods, and information traveling at an average of 15 miles

per hour. Such improvements in speed and economy made a national market economy possible.

By 1840, improved transportation had made a Market Revolution. Foreign trade, which had driven American economic growth up to 1815, continued to expand. In 1815, American exports totaled $52.6 million; imports totaled $113 million. Both rose dramatically in the years of the Market Revolution: Exports (now consisting more of southern cotton than of northern food crops) increased sixfold to $333.6 million by 1860; imports (mostly European manufactured goods) tripled to $353.6 million. Yet the increases in foreign trade represented vast reductions

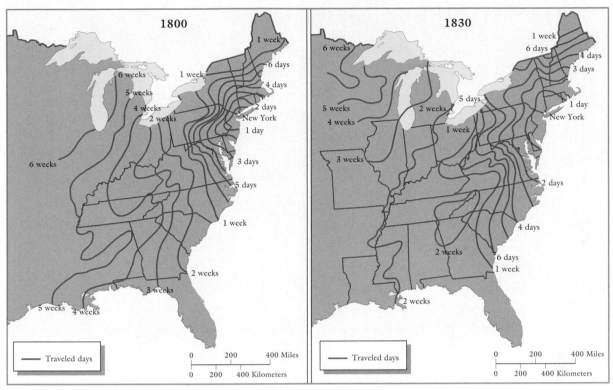

MAP 9.2 TIME REQUIRED TO TRAVEL FROM NEW YORK CITY, 1800 AND 1830
These maps illustrate the increasing ease of travel in the first third of the 19th century. In general, travelers could cover nearly twice as much territory in a day in 1830 than in 1800, although in both cases travel became more difficult as one left the densely settled east.

in the proportion of American market activity that involved other countries. Before 1815, Americans had exported about 15 percent of their total national product; by 1830, exports accounted for only 6 percent of total production. The reason for this shift was that after 1815, the United States developed self-sustaining domestic markets for farm produce and manufactured goods. The great engine of economic growth—particularly in the North and West—was not the old colonial relationship with Europe but a burgeoning internal market.

Markets and Regions

Henry Clay and other proponents of the American System dreamed of a market-driven economy that would transcend sectionalism and create a unified United States. Instead, until at least 1840, the Market Revolution produced greater results within regions than between them. The farmers of New England traded food for finished goods from Boston, Lynn, Lowell, and other towns in what was becoming an urban, industrial region. Philadelphia sold its manufactures to and bought its food from the farmers of the Delaware valley. Although the Erie Canal created a

huge potential for interregional trade, until 1839, most of its eastbound tonnage originated in western New York. In the West, market-oriented farmers fed such rapidly growing cities as Rochester, Cleveland, Chicago, and Cincinnati, which in turn supplied the farmers with locally manufactured farm tools, furniture, shoes, and other goods. Farther south, the few plantations that did not produce their own food bought surpluses from farmers in their own region. Thus until about 1840, the Market Revolution was more a regional than an interregional phenomenon.

In the 1840s and 1850s, however, the new transport networks turned the increasingly industrial Northeast and mid-Atlantic and the commercial farms of the Old Northwest into a unified market society. The earliest settlers in the Northwest were southerners who had carried on a limited trade through the river system that led to New Orleans. From the 1840s onward, produce left the Northwest less often by the old Ohio River route than by canal and railroad directly to the Northeast. Of the total produce exported from the Old Northwest in 1853, only 29 percent went by way of the river system, whereas 60 percent went by way of the Erie Canal alone. At the same time, canals and roads from New York, Philadelphia, and Baltimore

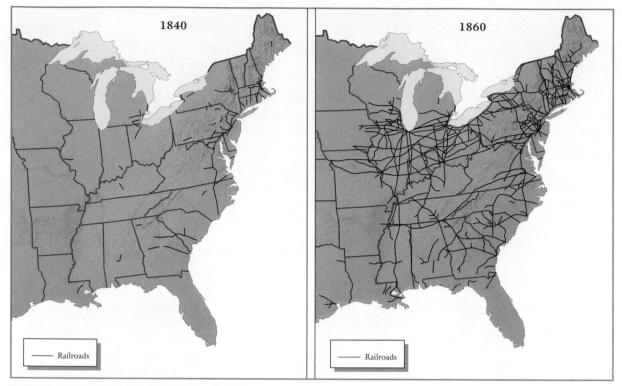

MAP 9.3 RAILROADS IN THE UNITED STATES, 1840 AND 1860

In these 20 years, both the North and South built railway systems. Northerners built rail lines that integrated the market economies of the Midwest and the East—both within sections and between them. For the most part, Southern railroads linked the plantation belt with the ocean. Revealingly, only a few lines connected the North and South.

became the favored passageways for commodities entering the West. As early as 1835, some 55 percent of the West's imported sugar, salt, iron, and coffee entered the region by the Great Lakes, Pennsylvania, or Wheeling routes. By 1853, that figure stood at 71 percent. In those years, the Ohio-Mississippi River system carried vastly increased amounts of goods, but that increase, particularly after 1840, added up to a shrinking share of the expanded total. In short, western farmers and northeastern businessmen and manufacturers were building a national market from which the South was largely excluded.

From Yeoman to Businessman: The Rural North and West

In the old communities of the Northeast, the Market Revolution sent some of the young people off to cities and factory towns and others to the West. Those who remained at home engaged in new forms of agriculture on a transformed rural landscape, while their cousins in the Northwest transformed a wilderness into cash-producing farms.

Shaping the Northern Landscape

An early 19th-century New England farm geared toward family subsistence required only 3 acres of cultivated land, 12 acres of pasture and meadow, another acre for the house, outbuildings, and vegetable garden, and a 30-acre woodlot to stoke the hearth that cooked the food and heated the house. Visitors to even the oldest towns found farmsteads, tilled fields, and pastures scattered across a heavily wooded landscape. In the 18th century, overcrowding had encouraged some farmers to turn woodlots into poor farmland. In the 19th century, however, millions of trees were stripped from the New England countryside and livestock raising replaced mixed farming. New Englanders who tried to grow grain on their rocky, worn-out soil could not compete with the farmers of western New York and the Old Northwest, who possessed fertile lands and ready access to markets. At the same time, however, the factories and cities of the Northeast provided Yankee farmers with a market for meat and other perishables. Beef became the great New England cash crop. Dairy products were not far behind, and the proximity to city markets encouraged the spread of poultry and egg farms, fruit orchards, and truck gardens. The burgeoning shoe industry bought leather from the farmers, and woolen mills created a demand for wool. In 1840, Vermont held 5.75 times more sheep than people.

The rise of livestock specialization reduced the amount of land under cultivation. Early in the century, New Englanders still tilled their few acres in the old three-year rotation: corn the first year, rye the second, fallow the third. By the 1820s and 1830s, as farmers raised more livestock and less grain, the land that remained in cultivation was farmed more intensively. Farmers saved manure and ashes for fertilizer, plowed more deeply and systematically, and tended their crops more carefully. These improved techniques, along with cash from the sale of their livestock and the availability of food at stores, encouraged Yankee farmers to allocate less land to growing food crops. In Concord, Massachusetts—the hometown of the agrarian republic—the portion of town land in tillage dropped from 20 percent to 7 percent between 1771 and 1850.

The transition to livestock raising transformed woodlands into open pastures. As farmers leveled the forests, they sold the wood to fuel-hungry cities. In 1829, a cord of wood sold for $1.50 in Maine and for $7 in Boston. Over the next decade, manufacturers began marketing cast-iron stoves that heated houses less expensively and more efficiently than open hearths, and canals brought cheap Pennsylvania anthracite to the Northeast. Farmers who needed pastureland could gain substantial one-time profits from the sale of cut wood. The result was massive deforestation. In 1790, in the central Massachusetts town of Petersham, forest covered 85 percent of the town lands. By 1830, the creation of pastureland through commercial woodcutting had reduced the forested area to 30 percent. By 1850, woods covered only 10 percent of the town, the pasturelands were overgrazed and ruined, and the landscape was dotted with abandoned farms. The pattern was the same throughout New England. At the beginning of European settlement, 95 percent of the region had been covered by forest. By 1850, forest covered only 30 percent of Connecticut, 32 percent of Rhode Island, 40 percent of Massachusetts, 45 percent of Vermont, and 50 percent of New Hampshire.

The Transformation of Rural Outwork

On that denuded landscape, poor families with many children continued to supplement their income with industrial outwork (see chapter 7). But the quickening of market activity brought new kinds of dependence. Before the 1820s, outworkers had used local raw materials such as wool, leather, and flax and had spent only their spare time on such work. Merchants who bought their finished products often complained that outworkers kept their best work for themselves and for exchange with their neighbors. In the 1820s, the manufacture of shoes and textiles began to be concentrated in factories, and outworkers who remained were reduced to dependence. Merchants now provided them with raw materials with which to make such items as cloth-covered buttons and palm-leaf hats (imported materials that only merchants could supply), and set the pace of labor and the quality of the finished goods. In the 1830s, fully 33,000 New England women were fashioning palm-leaf hats in their homes, far more than the 20,000 who worked in New England's much-publicized cotton mills. Although outwork still helped poor families to maintain their independence, control of their labor had passed to merchants and other agents of the regional economy.

Farmers as Consumers

With the shift to specialized market agriculture, New England farmers became customers for necessities that their forebears had produced themselves or had acquired through barter. They heated their houses with coal dug by Pennsylvania miners. They wore cotton cloth made by the factory women at Lowell. New Hampshire farm girls made straw hats for them, and the craftsmen of Lynn made their shoes. By 1830 or so, many farmers were even buying food. The Erie Canal and the western grain belt sent flour from Rochester into eastern neighborhoods where grain no longer grew. Many farmers found it easier to produce specialized crops for market, and to buy flour, butter, cheese, eggs, and vegetables at country stores—some of it from distant places, some of it produced by farm women in their own neighborhoods.

The turning point came in the 1820s. The storekeepers of Northampton, Massachusetts, for instance, had been increasing their stock in trade by about 7 percent per decade since the late 18th century. In the 1820s, they increased it 45 percent and now carried not only local farm products and sugar, salt, and coffee, but also bolts of New England cloth, sacks of western flour, a variety of necessities and little luxuries from the wholesale houses of New York City and Boston, and pattern samples from which to order silverware, dishes, wallpaper, and other household goods. Those goods were better than what could be made at home and were for the most part cheaper. The price of finished cloth, for instance, declined sixfold between 1815 and 1830; as a result, spinning wheels and hand-looms disappeared from the farmhouses of New England. Farm families preferred pies and bread made from western white flour to the old "Rye and Injun" (see chapter 7), and gladly turned their woodlands and unproductive grain

A NEW ENGLAND COUNTRY STORE

An 1830s Massachusetts country store was a community gathering place, a market for farm produce, and the source of a growing variety of commodities from the outside world.

fields into cash-producing pastures. Coal and cast-iron stoves replaced the family hearth. These consumer goods passed increased authority over the interior of rural households to women.

Material standards of living rose, but more families felt poor, and many more were incapable of feeding, clothing, and warming themselves in years when the market failed. By the 1820s and 1830s, northeastern farmers depended on markets in ways that their fathers and grandfathers would have considered dangerous not only to family welfare but also to the welfare of the republic.

The Northwest: Southern Migrants

One reason the Market Revolution in the Northeast went as smoothly as it did was that young people with little hope of inheriting land in the old settlements moved away to towns and cities or to the new farmlands of the Northwest. Between 1815 and 1840—precisely the years in which northeastern agriculture became a cash-crop business—migrants from the older areas transformed the Northwest Territory into a working agricultural landscape. In 1789, no Americans lived there. When the Treaty of Greenville made southern and eastern Ohio safe, settlers poured into the area. By 1800, the white population of Ohio numbered 45,365. In 1810, the population of Ohio, Indiana, and Illinois numbered 267,562, and settlement skyrocketed after the peace of 1815. By 1830, 1,438,379 whites lived in Ohio, Indiana, and Illinois. By 1860, the population of those three states, along with that of the new states of Wisconsin and

Michigan, numbered 6,926,884—22 percent of the nation's total population. (With the inclusion of the Old Southwest, nearly half of the population was west of the Appalachians; the geographic center of population was near Chillicothe, Ohio.)

In the Northwest until about 1830, most settlers were yeomen from Kentucky and Tennessee, usually a generation removed from Virginia, the Carolinas, and western Maryland. They moved along the Ohio and up the Muskingum, Miami, Scioto, Wabash, and Illinois rivers to set up farms in the southern and central counties of Ohio, Indiana, and Illinois. When southerners moved north of the Ohio River into territory that banned slavery, they often did so saying that slavery blocked opportunities for poor whites. The Methodist preacher Peter Cartwright left Kentucky with this thought: "I would get entirely clear of the evil of slavery," and "could raise my children to work where work was not thought a degradation." Similar hopes drew thousands of other southern yeomen north of the Ohio.

But even those who rejected slavery seldom rejected southern folkways. Like their kinfolk in Kentucky and Tennessee, the farmers of southern and central Ohio, Indiana, and Illinois remained tied to the river trade and to a mode of agriculture that favored free-ranging livestock over cultivated fields. The typical farmer fenced in a few acres of corn and left the rest of his land in woods to be roamed by southern hogs known as "razorbacks" and "land sharks." As late as 1860, southern-born farmers in the Northwest averaged 20 hogs apiece. These animals were thin and tough (they seldom grew to more than 200 pounds), and they could run long distances, leap fences, fend for themselves in the woods, and walk to distant markets. They were notoriously fierce; many more settlers were injured by their own hogs than by wild animals. When it was time to gather the hogs for slaughter, settlers often played it safe and hunted them with guns.

The southern-born pioneers of the Northwest, like their cousins across the Ohio River, depended more on their families and neighbors than on distant markets. Newcomers found that they could neither rent tools from their southern neighbors nor present them with "gifts" during hard times. Southerners insisted on repaying debts in kind and on lending tools rather than renting them, thus engaging outsiders in the elaborate network of "neighboring" through which transplanted southerners made their livings. As late as the 1840s, in the bustling town of Springfield, Illinois, barter was the preferred system of exchange. "In no part of the world," said a Scotsman in southern Illinois, "is good neighborship found in greater perfection than in the western territory."

The Northwest: Northern Migrants

Around 1830, a stream of northeasterners migrated to the Northwest via the Erie Canal and on Great Lakes steamboats. They filled the new lands of Wisconsin and Michigan and the northern counties of the older northwestern states. Most of them were New Englanders who had spent a generation in western New York (such settlers accounted for three-fourths of the early population of Michigan). The rest came directly from New England or—from the 1840s onward—from Germany and Scandinavia. Arriving in the Northwest along the market's busiest arteries, they duplicated the intensive, market-oriented farming they had known at home. They penned their cattle and hogs and fattened them up, making them bigger and worth more than those farther south. They planted their land in grain and transformed the region—beginning with western New York's Genesee Country in the 1820s and rolling through the Northwest—into one of the world's great wheat-producing regions. In 1820, the Northwest had exported only 12 percent of its agricultural produce. By 1840, that figure had risen to 27 percent, and it stood even higher among northern-born grain farmers. By 1860, the Northwest, intensively commercialized and tied by canals

and railways to eastern markets, was exporting 70 percent of its wheat. In that year it produced 46 percent of the nation's wheat crop, nearly all north of the line of southern settlement.

The new settlers were notably receptive to improvements in farming techniques. Even with plenty of southern proponents of "progress" and plenty of "backward" northerners, the line between new and old agricultural ways tended to separate northern grain farmers from corn, hogs, and southern settlers. In breaking new land, for instance, southerners still used the old shovel plow, which dug a shallow furrow and skipped over roots. Northerners preferred newer, more expensive cast-iron plows, which cut cleanly through oak roots 4 inches thick. By the 1830s, the efficient, expensive grain cradle had become the standard harvest tool in northwestern wheat fields. From the 1840s onward, even this advanced hand tool was replaced by mass-produced machinery such as the McCormick reaper. Instead of threshing their grain by driving cattle and horses over it, farmers bought new horse-powered and treadmill threshers and used hand-cranked fanning mills to speed the process of cleaning the grain.

Most agricultural improvements were tailored to grain and dairy farming and were taken up most avidly by the northern farmers. Others rejected them as expensive and "unnatural." They thought that cast-iron plows poisoned the soil and that fanning mills made a "wind contrary to nater," and thus offended God. John Chapman, an eccentric Yankee who earned the nickname "Johnny Appleseed" by planting apple tree cuttings in southern Ohio and Indiana before the settlers arrived, planted only

THE MCCORMICK REAPER

The boy Abraham Lincoln grew up on Indiana and Illinois farms on which cultivation was haphazard and tools were simple. Later, as a Whig and Republican politician, he rejected that world for the belief that intensive, mechanized farming improved not only crop yields but also intellectual, moral, and political standards, "whose course shall be onward and upward, and which, while the earth endures, shall not pass away." As he spoke, this factory in his hometown of Springfield, Illinois, churned out the implements that were bringing that new world into being.

low-yield, common trees; he regarded grafting, which farmers farther north and east were using to improve the quality of their apples, as "against nature." Southerners scoffed at the Yankee fondness for mechanical improvements, the systematic breeding of animals and plants, careful bookkeeping, and farm techniques learned from magazines and books. "I reckon," said one, "I know as much about farming as the printers do."

Conflict between intensive agriculture and older, less market-oriented ways reached comic proportions when the Illinois legislature imposed stiff penalties on farmers who allowed their small, poorly bred bulls to run loose and impregnate cows with questionable sperm, thereby depriving the owners of high-bred bulls of their breeding fees and rendering the systematic breeding of cattle impossible. When the poorer farmers refused to pen their bulls, the law was rescinded. A local historian explained that "there was a generous feeling in the hearts of the people in favor of an equality of privileges, even among bulls."

Households

The Market Revolution transformed 18th-century households into 19th-century homes. For one thing, Americans began to limit the size of their families. White women who married in 1800 gave birth to an average of 6.4 children. Those who married between 1800 and 1849 averaged 4.9 children. The decline was most pronounced in the North, particularly in commercialized areas. Rural birth rates remained at 18th-century levels in the southern uplands, in the poorest and most isolated communities of the North, and on the frontier. (As the New Yorker Washington Irving passed through the Northwest in the 1830s, he noted in his journal: "Illinois—famous for children and dogs— in house with nineteen children and thirty-seven dogs.") These communities practiced the old labor-intensive agriculture and relied on the labor of large families. For farmers who used newer techniques or switched to livestock, large families made less sense. Moreover, large broods hampered the ability of future-minded parents to provide for their children and conflicted with new notions of privacy and domesticity that were taking shape among an emerging rural middle class.

The commercialization of agriculture was closely associated with the emergence of the concept of housework. Before 1815, farm wives had labored in the house, the barnyard, and the garden while their husbands and sons worked in the fields. With the Market Revolution came a sharper distinction between "male work" that was part of the cash economy and "female work" that was not. Even such traditional women's tasks as dairying, vegetable gardening, and poultry raising became men's work once they became cash-producing specialties. (A Pennsylvanian who lived among market-oriented New Englanders in the Northwest was appalled at such tampering with hallowed gender roles and wrote the Yankees off as "a shrewd, selfish, enterprising, cow-milking set of men.")

At the same time, new kinds of women's work emerged within households. Although women had fewer children to care for, the culture began to demand forms of child-rearing that were more intensive, individualized, and mother-centered. Store-bought white flour, butter, and eggs and the new iron stoves eased the burdens of food preparation, but they also created demands for pies, cakes, and other fancy foods that earlier generations had only imagined. Although farm women no longer spun and wove their own cloth, the availability of manufactured cloth created the expectation that their families would dress more neatly and with greater variety than they had in the past—at the cost of far more time spent by women on sewing, washing, and ironing. Similar expectations demanded greater personal and domestic cleanliness,

A SOAP ADVERTISEMENT FROM THE 1850S
The rigors of "Old Washing Day" lead the mother in this advertisement to abuse the children and house pets, while her husband leaves the house. With American Cream Soap, domestic bliss returns: The children and cats are happy, the husband returns, and the wife has time to sew.

and farm women from the 1830s onward spent time planting flower beds, cleaning and maintaining prized furniture, mirrors, rugs, and ceramics, and scrubbing floors and children. The market and housework grew hand in hand: Among the first mass-produced commodities in the United States was the household broom.

Housework was tied to new notions of privacy, decency, and domestic comfort. Before 1820, farmers cared little about how their houses looked, often tossing trash and garbage out the door for the pigs and chickens that foraged near the house. In the 1820s and 1830s, as farmers began to grow cash crops and adopt middle-class ways, they began to plant shade trees and keep their yards free of trash. They painted their houses and sometimes their fences and outbuildings, arranged their woodpiles into neat stacks, surrounded their houses with flowers and ornamental shrubs, and tried to hide their privies from view. The new sense of refinement and decorum extended into other aspects of country life. The practice of chewing (and spitting) tobacco was gradually banned in churches and meeting halls, and in 1823, the minister in Shrewsbury, Massachusetts, ordered dogs out of the meetinghouse.

Inside, prosperous farmhouses took on an air of privacy and comfort. Separate kitchens and iron stoves replaced open hearths. Many families used a set of matched dishes for individual place settings, and the availability of finished cloth permitted the regular use of tablecloths, napkins, doilies, curtains, bedspreads, and quilts. Oil lamps replaced homemade candles, and the more comfortable families began to decorate their homes with wallpaper and upholstered furniture. Farm couples moved their beds away from the hearth and (along with the children's beds that had been scattered throughout the house) put them into spaces designated as bedrooms. They took the washstands and basins, which were coming into more common use, out of the kitchen and put them into the bedroom, thus making sleeping, bathing, and sex more private than they had been in the past. At the center of this new house stood the farm wife—apart from the bustling world of commerce, but decorating and caring for the amenities that commerce bought, and demanding that men respect the new domestic world that commerce had made possible.

Smithsonian Institution.

A WESTERN NEW YORK FARM

Here is a developer's rendition of a farm in western New York in the second quarter of the 19th century. The frame house (built onto the pioneer settler's log cabin) is fronted with a lawn, decorative shrubs, a shade tree, and dry walkways. Flanking the house are a vegetable garden and a well-tended orchard. Cash-crop fields stretch out behind the farmstead. A well-constructed fence marks off the home property and separates it from the road (another sign of progress) and the farm fields. The fence, the house, and a substantial barn are painted white. This was the rural comfort and respectability that northern farm families made for themselves from the 1820s onward.

Neighborhoods: The Landscape of Privacy

By the 1830s and 1840s, the Market Revolution had transformed the rural landscape of the Northeast. The forests had been reduced, the swamps had been drained, and most of the streams and rivers were interrupted by mill dams. Bears, panthers, and wolves had disappeared, along with the beaver and many of the fish. Now English cattle and sheep browsed on extensive pastures of English grasses dotted with English wildflowers such as buttercups, daisies, and dandelions. Next to the pastures lay neatly cultivated croplands that were regularly fertilized and seldom allowed to lie fallow. And at the center stood brightly painted houses and outbuildings surrounded by flowers and shrubs and vegetable gardens. Many towns, particularly in New England, had planted shade trees along the country roads, completing a rural landscape of straight lines and human cultivation—a landscape that made it easy to think of nature as a commodity to be altered and controlled.

Within that landscape, old practices and old forms of neighborliness fell into disuse. Neighbors continued to exchange goods and labor and to contract debts that might be left unpaid for years, but debts were more likely to be owed to profit-minded storekeepers and creditors, and even debts between neighbors often were paid in cash.

Traditionally, storekeepers had allowed farmers to bring in produce and have it credited to a neighbor/creditor's account—a practice that made the storekeeper an agent of neighborhood bartering. In 1830, half of the stores in rural Massachusetts carried accounts of this sort; by 1850, that figure had dropped to one in four. Storekeepers began to demand cash payment or to charge lower prices to those who paid cash.

The farm newspapers that appeared in these years urged farmers to keep careful records of the amount of fertilizer used, labor costs, and per-acre yields and discouraged them from relying on the old system of neighboring. Neighborly rituals such as parties, husking bees, barn-raisings—with their drinking and socializing—were scorned as an inefficient and morally suspect waste of time. The *Farmer's Almanac* of 1833 warned New England farmers: "If you love fun, frolic, and waste and slovenliness more than economy and profit, then make a husking."

Thus the efficient farmer after the 1820s concentrated on producing commodities that could be marketed outside the neighborhood and used his cash income to buy material comforts for his family and to pay debts and provide a cash inheritance for his children. Although much of the old world of household and neighborhood survived, farmers subsisted and maintained the independence of their households not through those spheres but through unprecedented levels of dependence on the outside world.

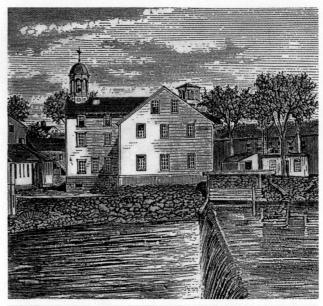

The Granger Collection, New York.

SAMUEL SLATER'S MILL AT PAWTUCKET, RHODE ISLAND

The first mill was small, painted white, and topped with a cupola. Set among craftsmen's workshops and houses, it looked more like a Baptist meetinghouse than a first step into industrialization.

The Industrial Revolution

In the 50 years following 1820, American cities grew faster than ever before or since. The old seaports—New York City in particular—grew rapidly in these years, but the fastest growth was in new cities that served commercial agriculture and in factory towns that produced for a largely rural domestic market. Even in the seaports, growth derived more from commerce with the hinterland than from international trade. Paradoxically, the Market Revolution and improved transportation in the countryside had produced the beginnings of industry and the greatest period of urban growth in U.S. history.

Factory Towns: The Rhode Island System

Jeffersonians held that the United States must always remain rural. Americans, they insisted, could expand into the rich new agricultural lands of the West, trade their farm surpluses for European finished goods, and thus avoid creating cities with their dependent social classes. Federalists argued that Americans, in order to retain their independence, must produce their own manufactured goods. Neo-Federalists combined those arguments after the War of 1812. Along with other advocates of industrial expansion, they argued that America's abundant water power—particularly the fast-running streams of the Northeast—would enable Americans to build their factories across the countryside instead of creating great industrial cities. Such a decentralized factory system would provide employment for country women and children and thus subsidize the independence of struggling farmers. The first American factories were built on those premises.

The American textile industry originated in industrial espionage. The key to mass-produced cotton and woolen textiles was a water-powered machine that spun yarn and thread. The machine had been invented and patented by the Englishman Richard Arkwright in 1769. The British government, to protect its lead in industrialization, forbade the machinery or the people who operated it to leave the country. Scores of textile workers, however, defied the law and made their way to North America. One of them was Samuel Slater, who had served an apprenticeship under Jedediah Strutt, a partner of Arkwright who had improved on the original machine. Working from memory while employed by Moses Brown, a Providence merchant, Slater built the first Arkwright spinning mill in America at Pawtucket, Rhode Island, in 1790.

Slater's first mill was a small frame building tucked among the town's houses and craftsmen's shops. It spun only cotton yarn, providing work for children in the mill and for women who wove yarn into cloth in their homes. Thus this first mill satisfied the neo-Federalists' requirements: It required no factory town, and it supplemented the household incomes of farmers and artisans. As his business grew and he advertised for widows with children, however, Slater encountered families headed by landless, impoverished men. Slater's use of children from these families prompted "respectable" farmers and craftsmen to pull their children out of Slater's growing complex of mills. More poor families arrived to take their places, and during the first years of the 19th century, Pawtucket grew rapidly into a disorderly mill town.

Soon Slater and other mill owners built factory villages in the countryside, where they could exert better control over their operations and their workers. The practice became known as the Rhode Island (or "family") system. At Slatersville, Rhode Island, at Oxford, Massachusetts, and at other locations in southern New England, mill owners built whole villages surrounded by company-owned farmland that they rented to the husbands and fathers of their mill workers. The workplace was closely supervised, and drinking and other troublesome prac-tices were forbidden in the villages. Fathers and older sons either worked on rented farms or as laborers at the mills.

By the late 1820s, Slater and most of the other owners were eliminating outworkers and were buying power looms, thus transforming the villages into disciplined, self-contained factory towns that turned raw cotton into finished cloth, but at great cost to old forms of household independence. When President Andrew Jackson visited Pawtucket in 1829, he remarked to Samuel Slater, "I understand you taught us how to spin, so as to rival Great Britain in her manufactures; you set all these thousands of spindles to work, which I have been delighted in viewing, and which have made so many happy, by a lucrative employment." "Yes sir," replied Slater, "I suppose that I gave out the psalm and they have been singing to the tune ever since."

Factory Towns: The Waltham System

A second act of industrial espionage was committed by a wealthy, cultivated Bostonian named Francis Cabot Lowell. Touring English factory districts in 1811, Lowell asked the plant managers questions and made secret drawings of the machines he saw. He also experienced a genteel distaste for the squalor of the English textile towns. Returning home, Lowell joined with wealthy friends to form the

Boston Manufacturing Company—soon known as the Boston Associates. In 1813, they built their first mill at Waltham, Massachusetts, and then expanded into Lowell, Lawrence, and other new towns near Boston during the 1820s. The company, operating under what became known as the Waltham system, built mills that differed from the early Rhode Island mills in two ways: First, they were heavily capitalized and as fully mechanized as possible; they turned raw cotton into finished cloth with little need for skilled workers. Second, the operatives who tended their machines were young, single women recruited from the farms of northern New England, which were switching to livestock raising, and thus had little need for the labor of daughters. The company housed the young women in carefully supervised boardinghouses and enforced rules of conduct both on and off the job. The young women worked steadily, never drank, seldom stayed out late, and attended church faithfully. They dressed neatly—often stylishly—and read newspapers and

American Textile History Museum. Lowell, Mass.

WOMEN IN THE MILLS

Two female weavers from a Massachusetts textile mill proudly display the tools of their trade. This tintype was made in about 1860, when New England farm women such as these were being replaced by Irish immigrant labor.

Francis Cabot Lowell in Manchester

In 1810, the Boston merchant Francis Cabot Lowell took his family on an extended trip to Great Britain. He enjoyed the glamour and cultural opportunities of London, but he also took an interest in British textile manufacturing technology. The ups and downs of commerce during the Napoleonic Wars, along with the likelihood that the United States would go to war, convinced important Americans—Lowell among them—that manufacturing within the United States would make a good investment. Lowell told his fellow Boston merchant Nathan Appleton that he had decided, "before his return to America, to visit Manchester, for the purpose of obtaining all possible information on the subject [of textile manufacturing], with a view to the introduction of the improved manufacture in the United States." Americans already possessed spinning mills that produced cotton yarn (thread) and farmed it out to handloom weavers. The British had developed a power loom that speeded production and allowed them to turn raw cotton into finished cloth under one roof. The British guarded their manufacturing secrets carefully, but Lowell, a rich American importer of British goods, gained access to factory floors, where he studied Manchester's power looms and tried to memorize what he saw. He also looked at the industrial city of Manchester and pronounced it full of "distress and poverty," reinforcing the Boston elite's notion that "operatives in the manufacturing cities of Europe, were notoriously of the lowest character, for intelligence and morals." Francis C. Lowell determined to build textile mills that would provide the benefits (and profits) of industrial production without creating the social, moral, and political dangers of industrial cities.

Back in Boston, Lowell hired the gifted mechanic Paul Moody, moved into a rented workshop in Boston, and tried—with Moody's mechanical acumen and his own memories of Manchester—to build a power loom. After several months, they succeeded, and the Boston Manufacturing Company (Lowell and his relatives and associates among the Boston mercantile elite) built integrated factories at Waltham and Lowell in 1813. With Manchester's exploited and angry workers (as well as, perhaps, his memories of the British model factory town of New Lanark) in mind, they built small cities with churches and well-regulated boardinghouses, set within pastoral landscapes, and invited young women from the farms of northern New England to come into the factories. The result, at least in the minds of Lowell and his friends, was a cadre of disciplined, respectable women workers whose moral character was preserved and even improved by factory labor. This Waltham System persisted into the 1840s, when the immigration of cheap Irish labor and the economics of factory production transformed the model towns near Boston into little Manchesters.

MANCHESTER

© Hulton-Deutsch Collection/Corbis.

attended lectures. They impressed visitors, particularly those who had seen factory workers in other places, as a dignified and self-respecting workforce.

The brick mills and prim boardinghouses set within landscaped towns and occupied by sober, well-behaved farm girls signified the Boston Associates' desire to build a profitable textile industry without creating a permanent working class. The women would work for a few years in a carefully controlled environment, send their wages back to their family, and return home to live as country housewives. These young farm women did in fact form an efficient, decorous workforce, but the decorum was imposed less by the owners than by the women themselves. In order to protect their own reputations, they punished misbehavior and shunned fellow workers whose behavior was questionable. Nor did they send their wages home or, as was popularly believed, use them to pay for their brothers' college education. Some saved their money to use as dowries that their fathers could not afford. More, however, spent their wages on themselves, particularly on clothes and books.

The owners of the factories expected that the young women's sojourn would reinforce their own paternalistic position and that of the girls' fathers. Instead, it produced a self-respecting sisterhood of independent, wage-earning women. Twice in the 1830s, the women of Lowell went out on strike, proclaiming that they were not wage slaves but "the daughters of freemen;" in the 1840s, they were among the leaders of a labor movement in the region. After finishing their stint in the mills, a good many Lowell women entered public life as reformers. Most of them married and became housewives, but not on the same terms their mothers had known. One in three of them married Lowell men and became city dwellers. Those who returned home to rural neighborhoods remained unmarried longer than their sisters who had stayed at home, and then married men about their own age who worked at something other than farming. Thus through the 1840s, the Boston Associates kept their promise to produce cotton cloth profitably without creating a permanent working class, but they failed to shuttle young women from rural to urban paternalism and back again. Wage labor, the ultimate degradation for agrarian-republican men, opened a road out of rural patriarchy for thousands of young women.

Urban Businessmen

The Market Revolution hit American cities—the old seaports as well as the new marketing and manufacturing towns—with particular force. Here was little concern for creating a classless industrial society. Vastly wealthy men of finance, a new middle class that bought and sold an ever-growing range of consumer goods, and the impoverished women and men who produced those goods lived together in communities that unabashedly recognized the reality of social class.

The richest men were seaport merchants who had survived and prospered during the world wars that ended in 1815. They carried on as importers and exporters, took control of banks and insurance companies, and made great fortunes in urban real estate. Those in Boston constituted an elite, urbane, and responsible cluster of families known as the Boston Brahmins. The elite of Philadelphia was somewhat less unified and perhaps less responsible; that of New York even less. These families continued in international commerce, profiting mainly from cotton exports and from a vastly expanded range of imports.

Below the old mercantile elite (or, in the case of the new cities of the interior, at the top of society) stood a growing middle class of wholesale and retail merchants, master craftsmen who had transformed themselves into manufacturers, and an army of lawyers, salesmen, auctioneers, clerks, bookkeepers, and accountants, who took care of the paperwork for the new market society. At the head of this new middle class were the wholesale merchants of the seaports who bought hardware, crockery, and other commodities from importers and then sold them in smaller lots to storekeepers from the interior. The greatest concentration of wholesale firms was on Pearl Street in New York City. Slightly below them were the large processors of farm products, including the meatpackers of Cincinnati and the flour millers of Rochester, and large merchants and real estate dealers in the new cities of the interior. Another step down were specialized retail merchants who dealt in books, furniture, crockery, or some other consumer goods. In Hartford, Connecticut, for instance, the proportion of retailers who specialized in certain commodities rose from 24 percent to 60 percent between 1792 and 1845.

Alongside the merchants stood master craftsmen who had become manufacturers. With their workers busy in backrooms or in household workshops, they now called themselves shoe dealers and merchant tailors. At the bottom of this new commercial world were hordes of clerks, most of them young men who hoped to rise in the world. Many of them—one study puts the figure at between 25 and 38 percent—did move up in society. Both in numbers and in the nature of the work, this white-collar army formed a new class created by the Market Revolution, particularly by the emergence of a huge consumer market in the countryside.

In the 1820s and 1830s, the commercial classes transformed the look and feel of American cities. As retailing and manufacturing became separate activities (even in firms that did both), the merchants, salesmen, and clerks now worked in quiet offices on downtown business streets. The seaport merchants built counting rooms and decorated their warehouses in the "new countinghouse style." Both in the seaports and the new towns of the interior, impressive brick and glass storefronts appeared on the main streets. Perhaps the most striking monuments of the self-conscious new business society were the handsome retail arcades that began going up in the 1820s. Boston's Quincy Market (1825), a two-story arcade on Philadelphia's Chestnut Street (1827), and Rochester's four-story Reynolds Arcade (1828) provided consumers with comfortable, gracious space in which to shop.

Metropolitan Industrialization

While businessmen were developing a new middle-class ethos, and while their families were flocking to the new retail stores to buy emblems of their status, the people who made the consumer goods were growing more numerous and at the same time disappearing from view. With the exception of textiles and a few other commodities, few goods were made in mechanized factories before the 1850s. Most of the clothes and shoes, brooms, hats, books, furniture, candy, and other goods available in country stores and city shops were made by hand. City merchants and master craftsmen met the growing demand by hiring more workers. The largest handicrafts—shoemaking, tailoring, and the building trades—were divided into skilled and semiskilled segments and farmed out to subcontractors, who could turn a profit only by cutting labor costs. The result was the creation of an urban working class, not only in the big seaports and factory towns but also in scores of milling and manufacturing towns throughout the North and the West.

The rise of New York City's ready-made clothing trade provides an example. In 1815, wealthy Americans wore tailor-made clothing; everyone else wore clothes sewn by women at home. In the 1820s, the availability of cheap manufactured cloth and an expanding pool of cheap—largely female—labor, along with the creation of the southern and western markets, transformed New York City into the center of a national market in ready-made clothes. The first big market was in "Negro cottons"—graceless, hastily assembled shirts, pants, and sack dresses with which southern planters clothed their slaves. Within a few years, New York manufacturers were sending dungarees and hickory shirts to western farmers and supplying shoddy, inexpensive clothing to the growing ranks of urban workers. By the 1830s, many New York tailoring houses, including the storied Brooks Brothers, were offer-

---

H I S T O R Y   T H R O U G H   F I L M

Gangs of New York (2002)

Directed by Martin Scorsese. Starring Leonardo DiCaprio (Amsterdam Vallon), Daniel Day-Lewis (Bill "The Butcher" Cutting), and Cameron Diaz (Jenny Everdeane).

This is Martin Scorsese's movie about the Five Points of New York—the most dangerous neighborhood in mid-19th-century North America. It is an operatic tragedy: An Irish boy (Leonardo DiCaprio) whose father, the leader of a gang called the Dead Rabbits, is killed by a nativist chieftain (Daniel Day-Lewis) in a gang fight spends his childhood in an orphanage, and then returns to the neighborhood to take revenge. He becomes part of the criminal entourage of his father's killer, falls in love with a beautiful and talented female thief (Cameron Diaz) who had been raised (and used) by the same gang boss, and bides his time—tortured all the while by the prospect of killing a second father figure. In the end, the Irish boy resurrects his father's gang and challenges the nativists to a battle for control of the Five Points. The battle coincides with the Draft Riots of 1863, and the film ends (as it had begun) in a horrendous bloodbath. The Irish thug kills the nativist thug, and the film ends with U2 singing about "We Who Built America."

For those who can stomach close-up fights with clubs and hatchets, it is a good enough melodrama. Unhappily, Scorsese casts his story against real history and gets most of it wrong. The film takes pains to "reconstruct" Manhat-

tan's Five Points, but our first view of the neighborhood is taken from a painting of a Brooklyn street. The oppressive noise and overcrowding that contemporary visitors describe are obliterated by a large public space at the center of the Points—historically nonexistent, but a fine field for the gang fights that begin and end the movie. Historically, the gangs were headquartered at saloons and firehouses, but Scorsese's operatic sensibilities move the Dead Rabbits into catacombs beneath the Old Brewery—complete with torchlight, a crude armory, and an untidy pyramid of skulls. The nativists, on the other hand, prefer an Asian motif, holding their get-togethers in an ornate Chinese theater and social house that lends an air of orientalist extravaganza to a neighborhood that knew nothing of such things. The catalogue of crimes against history could go on and on: The Dead Rabbits did not follow the cross into battle (Irish street gangs were not particularly religious), Irish priests did not look like Peter the Hermit, and Leonardo DiCaprio does not have a convincing Irish accent.

The "reformers" who minister to the Five Points receive equally silly treatment. The chief of the reformers are the aristocratic Schermerhorns. In fact, most Five Points

ing fancier ready-made clothes to members of the new middle class.

High rents and costly real estate, together with the absence of water power, made it impossible to set up large factories in cities. The nature of the clothing trade and the availability of cheap labor created a system of subcontracting that transformed needlework into the first "sweated" trade in America. Merchants kept a few skilled male tailors to take care of the custom trade and to cut cloth into patterned pieces for ready-made clothing. The pieces were sent out, often by way of subcontractors, to needleworkers, who sewed them together in their homes. Male tailors continued to do the finishing work on men's suits, but most of the work—on cheap goods destined for the South and West—fell to women, who worked long hours for piece rates that ranged from 75 cents to $1.50 per week. In 1860,

Brooks Brothers, which concentrated on the high end of the trade, kept 70 workers in its shops and used 2,000 to 3,000 outworkers, most of them women. Along with clothing, women in garrets and tenements manufactured the items with which the middle class decorated itself and its homes: embroidery, doilies, artificial flowers, fringe, tassels, fancy-bound books, and parasols. All provided work for ill-paid legions of female workers. In 1860, 25,000 women (about one-fourth of the total workforce) worked in manufacturing jobs in New York City; fully two-thirds of them were in the clothing trades.

Other trades followed similar patterns. For example, northeastern shoes were made in uniform sizes and sent in barrels all over the country. Like tailoring, shoemaking was divided into skilled operations and time-consuming unskilled tasks. The relatively skilled and highly paid work

Daniel Day-Lewis and his Five Points gang.

missionaries were middle-class evangelicals who had little to do with the Schermerhorns or the other old families of New York. The movie reformers hold a dance for the neighborhood; in fact, the evangelicals hated dancing and parties. The reformers also attend a public hanging, cheering as four innocent men are put to death. But New York had outlawed public executions a generation earlier; felons were now hanged within prison walls before small invited audiences. Even if public hangings had persisted, reformers would not have attended them (they had stopped going to such spectacles soon after 1815), and had they been dragged out of their parlors to witness an execution, they would not

have cheered. There is also an appearance by P. T. Barnum. Barnum had made his museum the premier middle-class entertainment spot in New York by eschewing low theater, cockfights, and other raucous and violent shows. Yet the movie has Barnum sponsoring a bare-knuckle prizefight— an act that would have cost him his reputation and his livelihood. The climactic riot includes another Barnum fabrication: Barnum's museum is set on fire; his menagerie escapes, and a terrified elephant romps through the burning streets. It almost certainly did not happen, but even the most fact-bound historian must bow to Scorsese's artistic license on that one.

The Library Company of Philadelphia.

CHARLES OAKFORD'S HAT STORE IN PHILADELPHIA, CIRCA 1855

Such specialized retail establishments (unlike the craftsmen's shops that preceded them) hid the process of manufacturing from customers' view.

of cutting and shaping the uppers was performed by men; the drudgery of sewing the pieces together went to low-paid women. In the shops of Lynn, Massachusetts, in the shoemakers' boardinghouses in Rochester and other new manufacturing cities of the interior, and in the cellars and garrets of New York City, skilled shoemakers performed the most difficult work for taskmasters, who passed the work along to subcontractors who controlled poorly paid, unskilled workers. Skilled craftsmen could earn as much as $2 per day making custom boots and shoes. Men shaping uppers in boardinghouses earned a little more than half of that; women binders could work a full week and earn as little as 50 cents. In this, as in other trades, wage rates and gendered tasks reflected the old family division of labor, which was based on the assumption that female workers lived with an income-earning husband or father. In fact, increasing numbers of them were young women living alone or older women who had been widowed, divorced, or abandoned—often with small children.

In their offices, counting rooms, and shops, members of the new middle class entertained notions of gentility based on the distinction between manual and nonmanual work. Lowly clerks and wealthy merchants prided themselves on the fact that they worked with their heads and not their hands. They fancied that their entrepreneurial and managerial skills were making the Market Revolution happen, while manual workers simply performed tasks thought up by the middle class. The old distinction between proprietorship and dependence—a distinction that had placed master craftsmen and independent tradesmen, along with farm-owning yeomen, among the respectable "middling sort"—disappeared. The men and women of

an emerging working class struggled to create dignity and a sense of public worth in a society that hid them from view and defined them as "hands."

The Market Revolution in the South

With the end of war in 1815, the cotton belt of the South expanded dramatically. The resumption of international trade, the revival of textile production in Britain and on the continent, and the emergence of factory production in the northeastern United States encouraged southern planters to extend the short-staple cotton lands of South Carolina and Georgia into a belt that would stretch—on Indian land from which the defeated natives were evicted—across the Old Southwest and beyond the Mississippi into Texas and Arkansas. The speed with which that happened startled contemporaries: By 1834, the new southwestern states of Alabama, Mississippi, and Louisiana grew more than half the U.S. cotton crop. By 1859, these states, along with Georgia, produced fully 79 percent of American cotton.

The southwestern plantation belt produced stupendous amounts of cotton. In 1810, the South produced 178,000 bales of ginned cotton—more than 59 times the 3,000 bales it had produced in 1790. By 1820, production stood at 334,000 bales. As southwestern cotton lands opened, production jumped to 1.35 million bales in 1840 and to 4.8 million on the eve of the Civil War. Over these years, cotton accounted for one-half to two-thirds of the value of all U.S. exports. The South produced three-fourths of the world supply of cotton—a commodity that, more than any other, was the raw material of industrialization in Britain and Europe and, increasingly, in the northeastern United States.

The Organization of Slave Labor

The plantations of the cotton belt were among the most intensely commercialized farms in the world. Although some plantations grew supplementary cash crops and produced their own food, many grew nothing but cotton—a practice that produced huge profits in good years but sent planters into debt and forced them to sell slaves and land in bad years. Nearly all of the plantation owners, from the proudest grandee to the ambitious farmer with a few slaves, organized their labor in ways that maximized production and reinforced the dominance of the white men who owned the farms.

Cotton, which requires a long growing season and a lot of attention, was well suited to slave labor and to the climate of the Deep South. After the land was cleared and plowed, it was set out in individual plants. Laborers weeded the fields with hoes throughout the hot, humid growing season. In the fall, the cotton ripened unevenly. In a harvest season that lasted up to two months, pickers swept through the fields repeatedly, selecting only the ripe bolls. Plantations that grew their own food cultivated large cornfields and vegetable gardens and kept large numbers of hogs. To cope with diverse growing seasons and killing times that overlapped with the cotton cycle, planters created complex labor systems.

On a large plantation in Louisiana in the 1850s, Frederick Law Olmstead, a New York landscape architect, watched a parade of slaves going into the fields. First came the hoe gang: "forty of the largest and strongest women I ever saw together: they were all in a single uniform dress of bluish check stuff, and skirts reaching little below the knee; their legs and feet were bare; they carried themselves loftily, each with a hoe sloping over the shoulder and walking with a free powerful swing, like Zouaves on the march." Following the hoe gang came the "cavalry, thirty strong, mostly men, but some women, two of whom rode astride, on the plow mules."

Although this slave force was larger than most, its organization was familiar to every southerner: Gangs of women wielded the hoes, and men did the plowing, accompanied, especially during the busiest times, by strong women who rode "astride" (and not, like white ladies, sidesaddle). The division of labor by sex was standard: Even at harvest festivals, teams of men shucked the corn while women prepared the meal and the after-supper dance. During the harvest, when every slave was in the fields, men tended to work beside men, women beside women. Most of the house slaves were women, and female slaves often worked under the direction of the plantation mistress—planters' wives, who were assuming greater control over their own domestic settings. Under the supervision of the mistress, female house slaves cared not only for the house, but for dairy cattle, chickens and geese, and vegetable gardens and orchards as well.

Although black women routinely worked in southern fields, white women did so only on the poorest farms and only at the busiest times of the year. Like their northern cousins, they took care of the poultry and cattle and the vegetable gardens—and not the profit-oriented fields. As the larger farms grew into plantations, white women took on the task of supervising the household slaves instead of doing the work. According to northern visitors, this association of labor with slavery encouraged laziness among southern whites and robbed work of the dignity it enjoyed in other parts of the country.

Paternalism

On the whole, the exploitation of slave labor after 1820 became both more systematic and more humane. An estimated 55 percent of southern slaves spent all of their time cultivating cotton, and it was brutal work by any standard. The arduous chore of transforming wilderness into cotton land demanded steady work in gangs, as did the yearly cotton cycle. Planters paid close attention to labor discipline: They supervised the work more closely than in the past, tried (often unsuccessfully) to substitute gang labor for the task system, and forcibly "corrected" slaves whose work

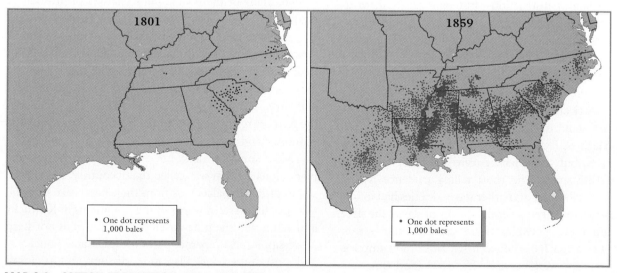

MAP 9.4   COTTON PRODUCTION, 1801 AND 1859
Short-staple cotton thrived wherever there was fertile soil, heat and humidity, low altitude, and a long growing season. As a result, a great belt of cotton and slavery took shape in the Lower South, from the midlands of South Carolina through East Texas.

HAULING THE WHOLE WEEK'S PICKING

William Henry Brown made this collage of a slave harvest crew near Vicksburg, Mississippi, in 1842. The rigors of the harvest put everyone, including small children, into the fields.

HAULING THE WHOLE WEEK'S PICKING

was slow or sloppy. At the same time, planters clothed the new discipline within a larger attempt to make North American slavery into a system that was both paternalistic and humane. Food and clothing seem to have improved, and individual cabins for slave families became standard. State laws often forbade the more brutal forms of discipline, and they uniformly demanded that slaves have Sundays off. More and more, the slaves spent that day listening to Christian missionaries provided by the planters.

The systematic paternalism on 19th-century farms and plantations sprang from both planter self-interest and a genuine attempt to exert a kindly, paternal control over slaves that planters uniformly called "our people" or "our family, black and white." The Louisiana planter Bennet H. Barrow insisted that the master must make the slave "as comfortable at home as possible, affording him what is essentially necessary for his happiness—you must provide for him your self and by that means creat[e] in him a habit of perfect dependence on you." On the whole, slaves endured the discipline and accepted the food, clothing, time off, and religious instruction—but used all of them to serve themselves and not the masters (see chapter 10).

Slaves' material standards rose. One rough indicator is physical height. On the eve of the Civil War, southern slaves averaged about an inch shorter than northern whites, but they were fully three inches taller than newly imported Africans, two inches taller than slaves on the Caribbean island of Trinidad, and one inch taller than British Marines. Slaves suffered greater infant mortality than whites, but those who survived infancy lived out "normal" life spans. The most telling evidence is that although Brazil, Cuba, and other slave societies had to import Africans to make up for the deaths of slaves, the slave population of the United States increased threefold—from 1,191,354 to 3,953,760—between 1810 and 1860. Imports of new Africans were banned after 1808 (and runaways outnumbered new Africans who were smuggled into the country); the increase reflected that—alone among slave populations of the Western Hemisphere—births outnumbered deaths among North American slaves.

Yeomen and Planters

Cotton brought economies of scale: Planters with big farms and many slaves operated more efficiently and more profitably than farmers with fewer resources. As the price of slaves and good land rose, fewer and fewer owners shared in the profits of the cotton economy, and wealth became more concentrated. Good farmland with ready access to markets was dominated by large plantations. By 1861, only one in four southern white households owned slaves. The Market Revolution had commercialized southern agriculture, but a shrinking proportion of the region's white population shared in the benefits. The result was not simply an unequal distribution of wealth, but the creation of a dual economy: plantations at the commercial center and a white yeomanry on the fringes.

Some small farmers remained in the plantation counties—most of them on poor, hilly land far from navigable rivers. They tended to be commercial farmers, growing a few bales of cotton with family labor and perhaps a slave or two. Many of them were poor relatives of prosperous plantation owners. They voted the great planters into office, and used their cotton gins and tapped into their marketing networks. Some of them worked as overseers for their wealthy neighbors, sold them food, and served on local slave patrols. Economic disparities between planters and farmers in the plantation belt continued to widen, but the farmers remained tied to the cotton economy and its economic and social imperatives.

Most small farmers, however, lived away from the plantations in what was called the upcountry: the eastern slopes of the Appalachians from the Chesapeake through Georgia, the western slopes of the mountains in Kentucky and Tennessee, the pine-covered hill country of northern Mississippi and Alabama, parts of Texas and Louisiana, and most of the Ozark Plateau in Missouri and Arkansas. All of these lands were too high, cold, isolated, and heavily wooded to support plantation crops. Here the farmers built a yeoman society that shared many of the characteristics of the 18th-century countryside, North and South (see chapter 7). While northern farmers commercialized, their southern cousins continued in a household- and neighborhood-centered agriculture until the Civil War and beyond.

Many southern farmers stayed outside the market almost entirely. The mountaineers of the southern Appalachians sent a trickle of livestock and timber out of their neighborhoods, but the mountains remained largely outside the market until the coming of big-business coal mines in the late 19th century. Moreover, farmers in large parts of the upcountry South preferred to raise livestock instead of growing cotton or tobacco. They planted cornfields and let their pigs run loose in the woods and on unfenced private land. In late summer and fall, they rounded up the animals and sold them to drovers, who conducted cross-country drives and sold the animals to flatland merchants and planters. These hill-country yeomen lived off a market with which they had little firsthand experience. It was a way of life that sustained some of the most fiercely independent neighborhoods in the country.

Yeomen and the Market

A larger group of southern yeomen practiced mixed farming for household subsistence and neighborhood exchange, with the surplus sent to market. Most of these farmers owned their own land. The settlement of new lands in the old backcountry and the southwestern states reversed the 18th-century growth of white tenancy (see chapter 7). Few of these farmers kept slaves. In the counties of upland Georgia, for instance, only 10 to 30 percent of households had slaves.

These farmers practiced a complicated system of "subsistence plus" agriculture. Northern yeomen before 1815 had grown grain and livestock with which they fed their families and traded with neighbors. Whatever was left over they sent to market, but cotton, like tobacco and other southern cash crops, was not a food; it contributed nothing to family subsistence. Most middling and poor farmers played it safe: They put most of their land into subsistence crops and livestock, cultivating only a few acres of cotton. They devoted more acreage to cotton as transportation made markets more accessible—particularly when railroads penetrated upland neighborhoods in the 1850s—but few southern yeomen allowed themselves to become wholly dependent on the market. The income from a few bales of cotton paid their debts and taxes and bought coffee, tea, sugar, tobacco, cloth, and shoes, but they continued to enter and leave the market at will, for their own purposes. The market served their interests; it seldom dominated them.

This way of life discouraged acquisitiveness and ambition. Because few farms were self-sufficient, the yeomen

farmers routinely traded labor and goods with each other. In the plantation counties, such cooperation tended to reinforce the power of planters who put some of their resources at the disposal of their poorer neighbors. In the upcountry, cooperation reinforced neighborliness. As one upland Georgian remarked, "Borrowing . . . was neighboring." Debts contracted within the network of kin and neighbors were generally paid in kind or in labor, and creditors often allowed their neighbors' debts to go unpaid for years.

Among southern neighborly restraints on entrepreneurialism, none was more distinctive than the region's attitude toward fences. Northerners never tired of comparing their neatly fenced farms with the dilapidated or absent fences of the South. In the bourgeois North, well-maintained fences were considered a sign of ambitious, hardworking farmers and the poor fences of the South were considered a sign of laziness. Actually, the scarcity of fences in most southern neighborhoods reflected local custom and state law. Georgia, for instance, required farmers to fence their planted fields but not the rest of their land. In country neighborhoods, where families fished and hunted for food, and where livestock roamed freely, fences conflicted with a local economy that required neighborhood use of privately owned land. In this sense, the northerners were right: The lack of fences in the South reflected neighborhood constraints on the private use of private property, and thus on individual acquisitiveness and ambition. Such constraints, however, were necessary to the subsistence of families and neighborhoods as they were organized in the upland South.

A Balance Sheet: The Plantation and Southern Development

The owners of the South's large farms were among the richest men in the Western Hemisphere. In 1860, the 12 wealthiest counties in the United States were in the South; the wealthiest of all was Adams County, Mississippi, on the Mississippi River. Southern wealth, however, was concentrating in fewer hands. The slaves whose labor created the wealth owned nothing. As much as one-third of southern white families lived in poverty, and a declining proportion of the others owned slaves. In 1830, some 36 percent of southern white households had owned at least one slave. By 1850, the percentage had dropped to 31 percent; by 1860, to 26 percent. And huge disparities existed even among the slaveholding minority; in 1860, only one-fifth of the slaveholders (1 in 20 white families) owned 20 or more slaves, thus crossing the generally acknowledged line that separated farmers from planters. At the apex of southern society were a few great planters: Between 2 and 3 percent of southern white men owned half of all the southern slaves.

The widening gap between planters and yeomen created a dangerous fault line in southern politics (see chapter 11). In economic terms, the concentration of wealth in the hands of a few planters had profound effects on how the Market Revolution affected the region. Much of the white population remained marginal to the market economy. A South Carolina yeoman who raised cattle claimed, "I never spent more than ten dollars a year, which was for salt, nails, and the like. Nothing to wear, eat or drink was purchased, as my farm provided all." Whereas in the North, the rural demand for credit, banking facilities, farm tools, clothing, and other consumer goods fueled a revolution in commerce, finance, and industry, the South remained a poor market for manufactured goods. The slaves wore cheap cloth made in the Northeast, and the planters furnished themselves and their homes with finery from Europe. In the North, the exchange of farm produce for finished goods was creating self-sustaining economic growth by the 1840s, but the South continued to export its plantation staples and to build only those factories, commercial institutions, and cities that served the plantation. In the North, the Market Revolution produced commercial agriculture, a specialized labor force, and technological innovation. In the South, it simply produced more slavery.

Not that the South neglected technological innovation and agricultural improvement. Southerners developed Eli Whitney's hand-operated cotton gin into equipment capable of performing complex milling operations; they made many significant improvements in steamboat design as well. They also developed—among other things—the cotton press, a machine with a huge wooden screw powered by horses or mules, used to compress ginned cotton into tight bales for shipping. Jordan Goree, a slave craftsman in Huntsville, Texas, won a reputation for being able to carve whole trees into perfect screws for these machines. Yet the few such innovations had to do with the processing and shipping of cotton rather than with its production. The truth is that cotton was a labor-intensive crop that discouraged innovation. Moreover, plantation slaves often resisted their enslavement by sabotaging expensive tools and draft animals, scattering manure in haphazard ways, and passively resisting innovations that would have added to their drudgery. Cotton fields continued to be cultivated by clumsy, mule-drawn plows that barely scratched the soil, by women wielding hoes, and by gangs who harvested the crop by hand.

Southern state governments spent little on internal improvements. A Virginia canal linked the flour mills at Richmond with inland grain fields, and another connected the Chesapeake Bay with the National Road, but planters in the cotton belt had ready access to the South's magnificent system of navigable rivers, while upland whites saw little need for expensive, state-supported internal improvements. Nor did the South build cities. In 1800, about 82 percent of the southern workforce and about 70 percent of the northern workforce were employed in agriculture. By 1860, only 40 percent of the northern workforce was so employed, but in the South the proportion had risen to 84 percent. The South used its canals and railroads mainly to move plantation staples to towns that trans-shipped them out of the region. Southern cities were located on the periphery of the region and served as transportation depots for plantation crops. River cities such as Louisville, Memphis, and St. Louis were little more than stopping places for steamboats. The great seaports of New Orleans, Charleston, and Baltimore sometimes shipped cotton directly to British and European markets. More often, however, they sent it by coasting vessel to New York City, where it was trans-shipped to foreign ports.

Thus while the North and the Northwest developed towns and cities throughout their regions, southern cities continued to be few and to perform the colonial functions of 18th-century seaport towns. Southern businessmen turned to New York City for credit, insurance, and coastal and export shipping. From New York they ordered finished goods for the southern market. *DeBow's Review,* the principal business journal of the South, reported that South Carolina storekeepers who bought goods from Charleston wholesalers concealed that fact and claimed they had bought them directly from New York City. For it was well known that New York provided better goods at lower prices than any supplier in the South. DeBow testified to the superior skill and diversification of the North when, after trying several New Orleans sources, he awarded the contract for his *Review* to a northern printer.

The Historic New Orleans Collection, Accension #1977.13734311.

A COTTON PRESS

Mule-driven presses such as the one shown here packed southern cotton into bales for easier transport to market. The cotton was pressed into a frame by a wooden screw carved from a whole tree.

That was not surprising in any case, because DeBow received three-fourths of his income from northern advertisers. In all, southerners estimated that 40 cents of every dollar produced by cotton remained in the Northeast.

Conclusion

In 1858, James H. Hammond, a slaveholding senator from South Carolina, asked:

> What would happen if no cotton was furnished for three years? . . . England would topple headlong and carry the whole civilized world with her save the South. No, you dare not make war on cotton. No power on earth dares to make war on cotton. Cotton is king.

Along with other planter-politicians, Hammond argued, as Jefferson had argued in 1807, that farmers at the fringes of the world market economy could coerce the commercial-industrial core. He was wrong. The commitment to cotton and slavery had not only isolated the South politically, but it had also deepened the South's dependence on the world's financial and industrial centers.

The North and West underwent a qualitative Market Revolution after 1815—a revolution that enriched both and that moved the Northeast from the old colonial periphery (the suppliers of food and raw materials) into the core (the suppliers of manufactured goods and financing) of the world market economy. In contrast, the South, by exporting plantation staples in exchange for imported goods, worked itself deeper and deeper into dependence—now as much on the American Northeast as on the old colonial rulers in London.

SUGGESTED READINGS

Works on the earlier phases of questions covered in this chapter are listed in the Suggested Readings for chapter 7. For a broad economic, cultural, and political synthesis, see **Charles G. Sellers, *The Market Revolution: Jacksonian America, 1815–1848*** (1991). **George Rogers Taylor, *The Transportation Revolution, 1815–1860*** (1951) remains the best single book on its subject. On legal and constitutional issues, see **R. Kent Newmeyer, *The Supreme Court under Marshall and Taney*** (1968); and **Morton J. Horwitz, *The Transformation of American Law, 1780–1860*** (1977). Changes in northern rural society are treated in **Christopher Clark, *The Roots of Rural Capitalism: Western Massachusetts, 1780–1860*** (1990); **Carolyn Merchant, *Ecological Revolutions: Nature, Gender, and Science in New England*** (1989); **Martin Bruegel, *Farm, Shop, Landing: The Rise of a Market Society in the Hudson Valley, 1780–1860*** (2002); and **John Mack Faragher, *Sugar Creek: Life on the Illinois Prairie*** (1986). Solid studies of industrial communities include **Thomas Dublin, *Women at Work: The Transformation of Work and Community in Lowell, Massachusetts, 1810–1860*** (1979); and **Anthony F. C. Wallace, *Rockdale: The Growth of an American Village in the Early Industrial Revolution*** (1978). On the plantation, see *Southern Honor: Ethics & Behavior in the Old South* (1982); and **Christine Leigh Heyerman, *Southern Cross: The Beginnings of the Bible Belt*** (1997). On the economics of slavery, see **Eugene D. Genovese, *The Political Economy of Slavery: Studies in the Economy and Society of the Slave South*,** 2d ed. (1989) and **R. W. Fogel, *Without Consent or Contract: The Rise and Fall of American Slavery*** (1989). On the southern yeomanry, see **Stephanie McCurry, *Masters of Small Worlds: Yeoman Households, Gender Relations, & the Political Culture of the South Carolina Lowcountry*** (1995); and **Steven Hahn, *The Roots of Southern Populism: Yeoman Farmers and the Transformation of the Georgia Upcountry, 1850–1890*** (1983).

AMERICAN JOURNEY ONLINE AND INFOTRAC COLLEGE EDITION

Visit the source collections at www.ajaccess.wadsworth.com and infotrac.thomsonlearning.com and use the Search function with the following key terms to explore documents, images, audio and video clips, articles, and commentary related to the material in this chapter.

Erie Canal   Robert Fulton
Francis Cabot Lowell   Cyrus McCormick
Henry Clay   John Marshall

Toward an American Culture

P. T. BARNUM AND TOM THUMB
Here is Phineas Taylor Barnum, America's greatest showman, together with the sprightly midget Tom Thumb, his first hugely successful attraction. The photograph conveys the combination of chicanery, farce, strangeness, and straight-faced respectability that made Barnum (but not Tom Thumb) a rich man.

CHAPTER OUTLINE

mericans after 1815 experienced wave after wave of social and cultural change. Territorial expansion, the Market Revolution, and the spread of plantation slavery uprooted Americans and broke old social patterns. Americans in these years reinvented family life. They created distinctively American forms of popular literature and art, and they found new ways of having fun. They flocked to evangelical revivals— meetings designed to produce religious conversions and led by preachers who were trained to that task—in which they revived and remade American religious life.

The emerging American culture was more or less uniformly republican, capitalist, and Protestant. Still, different kinds of Americans made different cultures out of the revolutionary inheritance, the Market Revolution, and revival religion. Southern farmers and their northern cousins thought differently about fatherhood, motherhood, and the proper way to make a family. Northeastern businessmen and southern planters agreed that economic progress was indeed progress, but they differed radically on its moral implications. Slaveholders, slaves, factory hands, rich and poor farmers, and middle-class women all heard the same Bible stories and learned different lessons. The result, visible from the 1830s onward, was an American national culture composed largely of subcultures based on region, class, and race.

CHAPTER FOCUS

♦ What were the central cultural maxims of the emerging middle class of the North?

♦ Within the North, what were the alternatives to middle-class culture?

♦ What was the nature of honor among southern whites, and how did it relate to southern families and southern religion?

♦ Describe the nature and limits of the cultural life that slaves made for themselves within the confines of slavery.

◗ The Northern Middle Class

"The most valuable class in any community," declared the poet-journalist Walt Whitman in 1858, "is the middle class." At that time, the term *middle class* (and the social group that it described) was no more than 30 or 40 years old. The Market Revolution since 1815 had created new towns and cities and transformed the old ones, and it had turned the rural North into a landscape of family-owned commercial farms. Those who claimed the title "middle class" were largely the new kinds of proprietors made by the market revolution—city and country merchants, master craftsmen who had turned themselves into manufacturers, and the mass of market-oriented farmers.

A disproportionate number of them were New Englanders. New England was the first center of factory production, and southern New England farms were thoroughly commercialized by the 1830s. Yankee migrants dominated the commercial heartland of western New York and the northern regions of the Northwest. Even in the seaport cities (New York's Pearl Street wholesale houses are a prime example), businessmen from New England were often at the center of economic innovation. This Yankee middle class invented cultural forms that became the core of an emerging business civilization. They upheld the autonomous and morally accountable individual against the claims of traditional neighborhoods and traditional families. They devised an intensely private, mother-centered domestic life. Most of all, they adhered to a reformed Yankee Protestantism whose moral imperatives became the foundation of American middle-class culture.

The Evangelical Base

In November 1830, the evangelist Charles Grandison Finney preached in Rochester, New York, to a church full of middle-class men and women. Most of them were transplanted New Englanders, the heirs of what was left of Yankee Calvinism. In their ministers' weekly sermons, in the formal articles of faith drawn up by their churches, and in the set prayers their children memorized, they reaffirmed the old Puritan beliefs in providence and original sin. The earthly social order (the fixed relations of power and submission between men and women, rich and poor, children and parents, and so on) was necessary because humankind was innately sinful and prone to selfishness and disorder. Christians must obey the rules governing their station in life; attempts to rearrange the social order were both sinful and doomed to failure.

Yet while they reaffirmed those conservative Puritan beliefs in church, the men and women in Finney's audience routinely ignored them in their daily lives. The benefits accruing from the Market Revolution were clearly the result of human effort. Just as clearly, they added up to "improvement" and "progress." And as middle-class Christians increasingly envisioned an improved material and social world, the doctrines of human inability and natural depravity, along with faith in divine providence, made increasingly less sense.

To such an audience, Charles Finney preached the organizing principle of northern middle-class evangelicalism: "God," he insisted, "has made man a moral free agent." Neither the social order, the troubles of this world, nor the spiritual state of individuals were divinely ordained. People would make themselves and the world better by choosing right over wrong, although they would choose right only after an evangelical conversion experience in which they submitted their rebellious wills to the will of God. It was a religion that valued individual holiness over a permanent and sacred social order. It made the spiritual nature of individuals a matter of prayer, submission, and choice. Thus it gave Christians the means—through the spread of revivals—to bring on the thousand-year reign of Christianity that they believed would precede the Second Coming of Christ. As Charles Finney told his Rochester audience, "If [Christians] were united all over the world the Millennium might be brought about in three months."

Charles Finney's Rochester revival—a six-month marathon of preaching and praying—was no isolated

CHARLES FINNEY

The evangelist, pictured here at the height of his preaching power in the 1830s, was remarkably successful at organizing the new middle-class culture into a millennial crusade.

© Bettmann/Corbis.

event. Yankee evangelists had been moving toward Finney's formulation since the turn of the 19th century. Like Finney, they borrowed revival techniques from the Methodists (weeklong meetings, meetings in which women prayed in public, an "anxious bench" for the most likely converts), but toned them down for their own more "respectable" and affluent audience. They used democratic methods and preached a message of individualism and free agency, but middle-class evangelicals retained the Puritans' Old Testament sense of cosmic history: They enlisted personal holiness and spiritual democracy in a fight to the finish between the forces of good and evil in this world. Building on the imperatives of the new evangelicalism, the entrepreneurial families of the East and Northwest constructed an American middle-class culture after 1825 based, paradoxically, on an intensely private and emotionally loaded family life and an aggressively reformist stance toward the world at large.

Domesticity

The Yankee middle class made crucial distinctions between the home and the world—distinctions that grew from the disintegration of the old patriarchal household economy. Men in cities and towns now went off to work, leaving wives and children to spend the day at home. Even commercializing farmers made a clear distinction between (male) work that was oriented toward markets and (female) work that was tied to household maintenance (see chapter 9). The new middle-class evangelicalism encouraged this division of domestic labor. The public world of politics and economic exchange, said the preachers, was the proper sphere of men; women, on the other hand, were to exercise new kinds of moral influence within households. As one evangelical put it:

> Each has a distinct sphere of duty—the husband to go out into the world—the wife to superintend the household. . . . Man profits from connection with the world, but women never; their constituents [sic] of mind are different. The one is raised and exalted by mingled association. The purity of the other is maintained in silence and seclusion.

The result was a feminization of domestic life. In the old yeoman-artisan republic, the fathers who owned property, headed households, and governed family labor were lawgivers and disciplinarians. They were God's delegated authorities on earth, assigned the task of governing women, children, and other underlings who were mired in original sin. Middle-class evangelicals raised new spiritual possibilities for women and children. Mothers replaced fathers as the principal child-rearers, and they enlisted the doctrines of free agency and individual moral responsibility in that task. Middle-class mothers raised their children with love and reason, not fear. They sought to develop the children's conscience and their capacity to love, to teach them to make good moral choices, and to prepare themselves for conversion and a lifetime of Christian service.

Middle-class mothers could take up these tasks because they could concentrate their efforts on household duties and because they had fewer children than their mothers or grandmothers had had. In Utica, New York, for example, women who entered their childbearing years in the 1830s averaged only 3.6 births apiece; those who had started families only 10 years earlier averaged 5.1 births. Housewives also spaced their pregnancies differently. Unlike their forebears, who gave birth to a child about once every two years throughout their childbearing years, Utica's middle-class housewives had their children at five-year intervals, which meant that they could give each child close attention. As a result, households were quieter and less crowded; children learned from their mothers how to govern themselves and seldom experienced the rigors of patriarchal family government. Thus mothers assumed responsibility for nurturing the children who would be carriers of the new middle-class culture—and fathers, ministers, and other authorities recognized the importance of that job. Edward Kirk, a minister in Albany, insisted that "the hopes of human society are to be found in the character, in the views, and in the conduct of mothers."

The new ethos of moral free agency was mirrored in the Sunday schools. When Sunday schools first appeared in the 1790s, their purpose was to teach working-class children to read and write by having them copy long passages from the Bible. Their most heavily publicized accomplishments were feats of memory: In 1823, Jane Wilson, a 13-year-old in Rochester, memorized 1,650 verses of scripture; Pawtucket, Rhode Island, claimed a mill girl who could recite the entire New Testament.

After the revivals of the 1820s and 1830s, the emphasis shifted from promoting feats of memory to preparing children's souls for conversion. Middle-class children were now included in the schools, corporal punishment was forbidden, and Sunday school teachers now tried to develop the moral sensibilities of their charges. They had the children read a few Bible verses each week and led them in a discussion of the moral lessons conveyed by the text. The proudest achievements of the new schools were children who made good moral choices. Thus Sunday schools became training grounds in free agency and moral accountability—a transformation that made sense only in a sentimental world where children could be trusted to make moral choices.

Sentimentality

Improvements in the printing, distribution, and marketing of books led to an outpouring of popular literature, much of it directed at the middle class. There were cookbooks, etiquette books, manuals on housekeeping, sermons, and sentimental novels—many of them written, and most of them read, by women. The works of popular religious writers such as Lydia Sigourney, Lydia Maria Child, and Timothy Shay Arthur found their way into thousands of middle-class homes. Sarah Josepha Hale, whose *Godey's Lady's Book* was the first mass-circulation

A MIDDLE-CLASS NEW ENGLAND FAMILY AT HOME, 1837

The room is carpeted and comfortably furnished. Father reads his newspaper; books rest on the table. Mother entertains their only child, and a kitten joins the family circle. This is the domestic foundation of sentimental culture on display.

magazine for women, acted as an arbiter of taste not only in furniture, clothing, and food but also in sentiments and ideas. Upon reviewing the cloying, sentimental literature read in middle-class homes, Nathaniel Hawthorne was not the only "serious" writer to deplore a literary marketplace dominated by "a damned mob of scribbling women."

Hawthorne certainly had economic reason for complaint. Sentimental novels written by women outsold by wide margins his *Scarlet Letter* and *House of Seven Gables*, Ralph Waldo Emerson's essays, Henry David Thoreau's *Walden*, Herman Melville's *Moby Dick*, Walt Whitman's *Leaves of Grass*, and other works of the American Renaissance of the 1850s. Susan Warner's *The Wide, Wide World* broke all sales records when it appeared in 1850. Harriet Beecher Stowe's *Uncle Tom's Cabin* (1852) broke the records set by Warner. In 1854, Maria Cummin's *The Lamplighter* (the direct target of Hawthorne's lament about scribbling women) took its place as the third of the monster best sellers of the early 1850s.

These sentimental novels upheld the new middle-class domesticity. They sacralized the middle-class home and the trials and triumphs of Christian women. The action in each takes place indoors, usually in the kitchen or parlor, and the heroines are women (in Stowe's book, docile slave Christians are included) who live under worldly patriarchy but who triumph through submission to God. The stories embody spiritual struggle, the renunciation of greed and desire, and mother love. The home is a shrine (and keeping it clean is a sacrament) that is juxtaposed to the marketplace and the world of competition, brutality, and power. Unlike the female characters in British and European novels of the time, the women in these American novels are intelligent, generous persons who grow in strength and independence. (The French visitor Alexis de Tocqueville commented that European women "almost think it a privilege to appear futile, weak, and timid. The women of America never lay claim to rights of that sort.")

In sentimental domestic fiction, women assume the role of evangelical ministers, demonstrating Christian living by precept, example, and moral persuasion. Female moral influence, wielded by women who had given themselves to God, is at war with the male world of politics and the marketplace—areas of power, greed, and moral compromise. Although few sentimental writers shared the views of the feminist Margaret Fuller, they would have agreed with her on the place of religion in women's lives. "I wish women to live first for God's sake," she wrote. "Then she will not make an imperfect man her God, and thus sink to idolatry."

The most successful sentimental novel of the 1850s was Harriet Beecher Stowe's *Uncle Tom's Cabin.* Stowe's book was also the most powerful antislavery tract of these years—in part because it successfully dramatized the moral and political imperatives of the northern middle class. At its core, *Uncle Tom's Cabin* indicts slavery as a system of absolute power at odds with domesticity and Christian love. The novel reverses the power relations of this world: In it, the home, and particularly the kitchen, is the ultimate locus of good, whereas law, politics, and the marketplace—the whole realm of men—are moved to the periphery and defined as unfeeling destroyers. Based solidly in revival Christianity, the novel lambastes the rational calculation, greed, and power hunger of the "real world" that was made and governed by white men and upholds domestic space filled with women, slaves, and children who gain spiritual power through submission to Christ. The two most telling scenes—the deaths of the Christian slave Uncle Tom and the perfect child Eva St. Claire—reenact the crucifixion of Jesus. Uncle Tom prays for his tormentors as he is beaten to death, and little Eva extracts promises of Christian behavior from her deathbed. Both are powerless, submissive characters who die in order to redeem a fallen humankind. Their deaths are thus Christian triumphs that convert the powerful and hasten the millennial day when the world will be governed by a feminized Christian love and not by male power.

Thus *Uncle Tom's Cabin* and other popular sentimental novels were not, as Hawthorne and his friends believed, frivolous fairytales into which housewives retreated from the real world. They were subversive depictions of a higher spiritual reality that would move the feminine ethos of the Christian home to the center of civilization. That vision drove an organized public assault on irreligion, drunkenness, prostitution, slavery, and other practices and institutions that substituted passion and force for Christian love (see chapter 11), an assault that tried to "domesticate" the world and shape it in the image of the middle-class evangelical home.

Fine Arts

Educated Americans of the postrevolutionary generation associated the fine arts with the sensuality, extravagance, and artificiality of European courts and European Catholicism. To them, the fine arts were the products of despotism and had nothing to offer the republicans of America. In making government buildings and monuments, building expensive homes, and painting portraits of wealthy and powerful men, American artists copied the classic simplicity of ancient Greece and Rome—republican styles tested by time and free of any hint of sensuality or luxury.

In the 1820s and 1830s, however, educated Americans began to view literature and the arts more favorably. American nationalists began to demand an American art that could compete with the arts of the despotic Old World. At the same time, evangelical Christianity and sentimental culture glorified a romantic cult of feeling that was, within its limits, far more receptive to aesthetic experience than Calvinism and the more spartan forms of republicanism had been. Finally, the more comfortable and educated Americans fell into a relationship with nature that called out for aesthetic expression. From the beginnings of English settlement, Americans had known that their civilization would be made in a contest with wilderness—wilderness they saw as dark, filled with demons, and implacably hostile to civilization. After 1815, with the Indians finally broken and scattered, with the agricultural frontier penetrating deep into the interior, and with improvements in transportation and communications annihilating distance, educated northeasterners became certain that Americans would win their age-old contest with nature—that civilization would supplant wilderness on the North American continent. The result was a multivoiced conversation about the relations between nature and civilization—a conversation that occupied a large portion of the new American art and literature that rose between 1830 and the Civil War.

Nature and Art

Much of the new American art was practical, to be lived in and used. Andrew Jackson Downing and other landscape designers and architects created beautiful country cottages surrounded by gardens—domestic environments that used art as an avenue to the grand lessons of nature. At the same time, cities began to build cemeteries in the surrounding countryside, replacing the old ill-tended graveyards at the center of town. In 1831, several wealthy Boston families put up the money to build Mount Auburn Cemetery, the first graveyard designed to serve as a cultural institution. Mount Auburn was situated on rolling ground, with footpaths following the contours of the land. Much of the natural vegetation was left untouched, and wildflowers were planted to supplement it. The headstones, which had to be approved by a board of directors, were small and dignified. Mount Auburn became a kind of public park in which nature's annual cycle of death and renewal taught chastening and reassuring lessons to the living. Copied in Brooklyn, Rochester, and other northern cities, the rural cemeteries embodied the faith that nature could teach moral lessons, particularly if nature was shaped and made available to humankind through art.

Not surprisingly, the leading artists of this generation were landscape painters. Thomas Cole, in his "Essay on American Scenery" (1835), reminded readers that the most distinctive feature of America was its wilderness:

> In civilized Europe the primitive features of scenery have long since been destroyed or modified. . . . And to this cultivated state our western world is fast approaching; but nature is still predominant, and there are those who regret that with the improvements of cultivation the sublimity of the wilderness should pass away; for those scenes of solitude from which the hand of nature has never been lifted, affect the mind with a more deep toned emotion than aught which the hand of man has touched. Amid them the consequent associations are of God the creator—they are his undefiled works, and the mind is cast into contemplation of eternal things.

In what became a manifesto of American intellectual and aesthetic life, Cole had found God in nature (previous generations had been taught to see wilderness as the devil's domain), and thus endowed art that depicted nature with religious purpose. Among educated persons, art was no longer subversive of the Protestant republic; done right, it was a bulwark of good citizenship and true religion. American housewives who planted and tended flower gardens were acting on that premise. So were the landscape architects who designed rural cemeteries and public and private gardens; the philosopher Ralph Waldo Emerson, who told Americans that "every natural process is a version of a moral sentence"; and Emerson's friend Henry David Thoreau, who lived in the woods and loved not only nature's beauties but also bad weather, wars between insects, and the corpses of horses in an attempt, as he put it, to live "deliberately" in a simple relationship with nature. These and thousands of educated middle- and upper-class northerners after 1830 built a cultural conversation in which Americans defined themselves by talking about American nature—a nature that had become Christianized and benign.

That conversation was strongest among urban northeasterners who benefited from the Market Revolution and who believed that theirs was an age of progress. Some would argue that the feminization of family life, the rise of sentimentality, and the romantic cult of nature could have appeared only when American civilization had turned the tide in its age-old battle with wilderness. The most sensitive and articulate northeasterners—Emerson, Thoreau, and Thomas Cole among them—warned that the victory might be too complete, and that the United States could become as "unnatural" and "artificial" as an overcultivated Europe. Similarly, ministers and mothers worried that the marketplace could corrupt the "natural" relations of family life, and middle-class women and men cultivated personal "sincerity" as a badge of moral status and as a hedge against the artificiality and dishonesty that thrived in an anonymous market society. At every level, middle-class culture was balanced, sometimes uncomfortably, between pride in economic and technological progress and veneration of what was natural.

Scenic Tourism: Niagara Falls

In the 1820s, rich Americans began to travel for the sole purpose of looking at scenery. Improved transportation and disposable time and money made such journeys possible, but just as important was the determination of the more affluent Americans to re-create themselves not only as a monied class but also as a community of sentiment and taste. They stood beside each other on steamboats and admired the picturesque farms and mountains of the Hudson Valley; they traveled to the Catskills and the White Mountains; but most of all, they descended on what became the most venerated spot in all of North America: Niagara Falls.

Niagara was a new attraction in the 1820s. The falls had become part of the border between the United States and British Canada in 1783, but few Americans visited the place, and even fewer settled there. The falls could be reached only by a difficult and expensive voyage up the St. Lawrence River and across Lake Ontario or, after 1804, over New York's notoriously bad state road. The Niagara frontier remained an unfriendly border, one of the principal battlegrounds of the War of 1812. The few Americans who wrote about Niagara Falls before the 1820s had stressed the power, wildness, and danger of the place along with its stunning beauty. These reactions aped literary convention that demanded terror as part of the apprehension of the sublime in nature; they also repeated old American fears of wilderness. In 1815, Niagara remained part of an unconquered American wilderness.

Completion of the Erie Canal in 1825 brought civilization to Niagara Falls. Every summer, crowds of genteel tourists traveled the easy water route to Buffalo, then took carriages to the falls, where entrepreneurs had built hotels, paths, and stairways and offered boat rides and guided tours. The falls quickly became surrounded by commerce and were viewed comfortably from various sites by well-dressed tourists. In early paintings of the falls, the foreground figure had usually been an Indian hunter or fisherman; now Indians were replaced by tourist couples, the women carrying parasols. The sublime experience of terror and wonder disappeared. Tourists read travel accounts before their trip and, once they arrived, bought guidebooks and took guided tours, aware that they were sharing their experience with thousands of others. Many of the tourists were women, and many men conceded that women possessed the "genuine emotion" that enabled them to experience Niagara Falls correctly. Niagara had become controlled, orderly, and beautiful, a grand sermon in which God revealed his benign plan to humankind. Young Harriet Beecher Stowe visited Niagara in the early 1830s and gushed, "Oh, it is lovelier than it is great; it is like the Mind that made it: great, but so veiled in beauty that we gaze without terror. I felt as if I could have gone over with the waters; it would be so beautiful a death." Niagara had become, for Stowe and thousands of others, a part of sentimental culture.

The Plain People of the North

From the 1830s onward, northern middle-class evangelicals proposed their religious and domestic values as a national culture for the United States, but even in their own region they were surrounded and outnumbered by Americans who rejected their cultural leadership. The plain people of the North were a varied lot: settlers in the lower Northwest who remained culturally southern; hill-country New Englanders, New Yorkers, and Pennsylvanians who had experienced little of what their middle-class cousins called "progress"; refugees from the countryside who had taken up urban wage labor; and increasing thousands of Irish and German immigrants. They did share a cultural conservatism—often grounded in the traditional, father-centered family—that rejected sentimentalism and reformist religion out of hand.

Religion and the Common Folk

Northern plain folk favored churches as doctrinally varied as the people themselves. These ranged from the voluntaristic "free grace" doctrines of the Methodists to the iron-bound Calvinism of most Baptists, from the fine-tuned hierarchy of the Mormons to the near-anarchy of the Disciples of Christ. They included the most popular faiths (Baptists and Methodists came to contain two-thirds of America's professing Protestants in both the North and the South) as well as such smaller sects as Hicksite Quakers,

Frederic Edwin Church NIAGARA, 1857. Oil on canvas, 42 1/2 x 90 1/2 in. (107.95 x 229.87 cm). In the Collection of the Corcoran Gallery of Art, Museum Purchase, Gallery Fund. 76.15.

NIAGARA FALLS
Frederic Edwin Church, one of the most renowned of American landscape artists, painted Niagara Falls in 1857. Church's Niagara is immense and powerful, yet somehow ordered, benign, and calming.

Universalists, Adventists, Moravians, and Freewill Baptists. Yet for all their diversity, these churches had important points in common. Most shared an evangelical emphasis on individual experience over churchly authority. Most favored democratic, local control of religious life and distrusted outside organization and religious professionalism, not only the declining colonial establishments but also the emerging missionary network created by middle-class evangelicals. They also rejected middle-class optimism and reformism, reaffirming God's providence and humankind's duty to accept an imperfect world even while waging war against it.

The most pervasive strain was a belief in providence—the conviction that human history was part of God's vast and unknowable plan, and that all events were willed or allowed by God. Middle-class evangelicals spoke of providence, too, but they seemed to assume that God's plan was manifest in the progress of market society and middle-class religion. Humbler evangelicals held to the older notion that providence was immediate, mysterious, and unknowable. They believed that the events of everyday life were parts of a vast blueprint that existed only in the mind of God—and not in the vain aspirations of women and men. When making plans, they added the caveat "the Lord willing," and they learned to accept misfortune with fortitude. They responded to epidemics, bad crop years, aches and pains, illness, and early death by praying for the strength to endure, asking God to "sanctify" their suffering by making it an opportunity for them to grow in faith. As a minister told the Scots Covenanters of Cambridge, New York, "It is through tribulation that all the saints enter into the kingdom of God. . . . The tempest sometimes ceases, the sky is clear, and the prospect is desirable, but by the by the gathering clouds threaten a new storm; here we must watch, and labor, and fight, expecting rest with Christ in glory, not on the way to it."

The providential worldview, the rejection of this world, and the notion that God granted spiritual progress only through affliction came directly into play when a member of a poor Protestant family died. Country Baptists and working-class Methodists mourned their dead but took care not to "murmur" against God. In a world governed by providence, the death of a loved one was a test of faith. Plain folk considered it a privilege to witness a death in the family, for it released the sufferer from the tribulations of this world and sent him or her to a better place. The death of children in particular called for heroic acts of submission to God's will; parents mourned the loss but stopped short of displaying grief that would suggest selfishness and lack of faith. Poor families washed and dressed the dead body themselves and buried it in a churchyard or on a hilltop plot on the family farm.

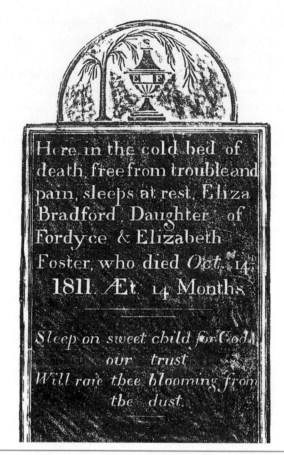

CHILD'S GRAVESTONE

Below the weeping willow on this baby girl's gravestone is an inscription affirming that death has set the child "free from trouble and pain" and has ushered her into a better life.

Whereas the urban middle class preferred formal funerals and carefully tended cemeteries, humbler people regarded death as a lesson in the futility of pursuing worldly goals and in the need to submit to God's will.

Popular Millennialism

The plain Protestants of the North seldom talked about the millennium. Middle-class evangelicals were *postmillennialists:* They believed that Christ's Second Coming would occur at the end of 1,000 years of social perfection that would be brought about by the missionary conversion of the world. Ordinary Baptists, Methodists, and Disciples of Christ, however, assumed that the millennium would arrive with world-destroying violence, followed by 1,000 years of Christ's rule on earth. Few, however, dwelled on this terrifying premillennialism, assuming that God would end the world in his own time. Now and then, however, the ordinary evangelicals of the North predicted the fiery end of the world. Prophets rose and fell, and thousands of people looked for signs of the approaching millennium in thunderstorms, shooting stars, eclipses, economic panics and depressions, and—especially—in hints that God had placed in the Bible.

An avid student of those hints was William Miller, a rural New York Baptist who, after years of systematic study, concluded that God would destroy the world during the year following March 1843. Miller publicized his predictions throughout the 1830s, and near the end of the decade, the Millerites (as his followers were called) accumulated thousands of believers—most of them conservative Baptists, Methodists, and Disciples in hill-country New England and in poor neighborhoods in New York, Ohio, and Michigan. As the end approached, the believers read the Bible, prayed, and attended meeting after meeting. A publicist named Henry Jones reported that a shower of meat and blood had fallen on Jersey City, and newspapers published stories alleging that the Millerites were insane and guilty of sexual license. Some of them, the press reported, were busy sewing "ascension robes" in which they would rise straight to heaven without passing through death.

When the end of the year—March 23, 1844—came and went, most of the believers quietly returned to their churches. A committed remnant, however, kept the faith, and by the 1860s founded the Seventh-Day Adventist Church. The Millerite movement was a reminder that hundreds of thousands of northern Protestants continued to believe that the God of the Old Testament governed everything from bee stings to the course of human history, and that one day he would destroy the world in fire and blood.

Family and Society

Baptists, Methodists, Disciples of Christ, and the smaller popular sects evangelized primarily among persons who had been bypassed or hurt by the Market Revolution. Many had been reduced to dependent, wage-earning status. Others had become market farmers or urban storekeepers or master workmen; few had become rich. Their churches taught them that the attractions and temptations of market society were at the center of the world they must reject.

Often their rhetoric turned to criticism of market society, its institutions, and its centers of power. The Quaker schismatic Elias Hicks, a Long Island farmer who fought the worldliness and pride of wealthy urban Quakers, listed the following among the mistakes of the early 19th century: railroads, the Erie Canal, fancy food and other luxuries, banks and the credit system, the city of Philadelphia, and the study of chemistry. The Baptist millenarian William Miller expressed his hatred of banks, insurance companies, stock-jobbing, chartered monopolies, personal greed, and the city of New York. In short, what the evangelical middle class identified as the march of progress, poorer and more conservative evangelicals often condemned as a descent into worldliness that would almost certainly provoke God's wrath.

Along with doubts about economic change and the middle-class churches that embraced it, members of the popular sects often held to the patriarchal family form in which they had been raised, and with which both the Market Revolution and middle-class domesticity seemed at war. Hundreds of thousands of northern Protestants considered the erosion of domestic patriarchy a profound cultural loss and not, as it seemed to the middle class, an avenue to personal liberation. Their cultural conservatism was apparent in their efforts to sustain the father-centered family of the old rural North or to revive it in new forms.

For some, religious conversion came at a point of crisis in the traditional family. William Miller, for example,

Courtesy American Antiquarian Society.

PROPHETIC CHART

A fixture at Millerite Adventist meetings, prophetic charts such as the one shown here displayed the succession of Biblical kingdoms and the prophecies of Daniel and John. Millerites revised their charts when the world failed to end in 1843.

had a strict Calvinist upbringing in a family in which his father, an uncle, and his grandfather were all Baptist ministers. As a young man he rejected his family, set about making money, and became a deist—actions that deeply wounded his parents. When his father died, Miller was stricken with guilt. He moved back to his hometown, took up his family duties, became a leader of the Baptist church, and (after reading a sermon entitled "Parental Duties") began the years of Bible study that resulted in his world-ending prophecies. Alexander Campbell, one of the founders of the Disciples of Christ, dramatized his filial piety when he debated the free-thinking socialist Robert Owen before a large audience in the Methodist meetinghouse in Cincinnati in 1828. He insisted that his white-haired father (himself a Scots Presbyterian minister) stand in the pulpit above the debaters.

The Prophet Joseph Smith

The weakening patriarchal family and attempts to shore it up were central to the life and work of one of the most unique and successful religious leaders of the period: the Mormon prophet Joseph Smith (see also chapter 13). Smith's father was a landless Vermont Baptist who moved his wife and nine children to seven rented farms within 20 years. Around 1820, when young Joseph was approaching manhood, the family was struggling to make mortgage payments on a small farm outside Palmyra, New York. That farm—Joseph referred to it as "my father's house"—was a desperate token of the Smith family's commitment to yeoman independence and an endangered rural patriarchy. Despite the efforts of Joseph and his brothers, a merchant cheated the Smith family out of the farm. With that, both generations of the Smiths faced lifetimes as propertyless workers. To make matters worse, Joseph's mother and some of his siblings began to attend an evangelical Presbyterian church in Palmyra, apparently against the father's wishes.

Before the loss of the farm, Joseph had received two visions warning him away from existing churches and telling him to wait for further instructions. In 1827, the Angel Moroni appeared to him and led him to golden plates that translated into *The Book of Mormon*. It told of a light-skinned people, descendants of the Hebrews, who had sailed to North America long before Columbus. They had had an epic, violent history, a covenanted relationship with God, and had been visited and evangelized by Jesus following his crucifixion and resurrection.

Joseph Smith later declared that his discovery of *The Book of Mormon* had "brought salvation to my father's house" by unifying the family. It eventually unified thousands of others under a patriarchal faith based on restored theocratic government, male dominance, and a democracy among fathers. The good priests and secular leaders of *The Book of Mormon* are farmers who labor alongside their neighbors; the villains are self-seeking merchants, lawyers, and bad priests. The account alternates between periods when the people obey God's laws and periods when they do not, each period accompanied by the blessings or punishments of a wrathful God. Smith carried that model of brotherly cooperation and patriarchal authority into the Church of Jesus Christ of Latter-Day Saints, which he founded in 1830.

The new church was ruled, not by professional clergy, but by an elaborate lay hierarchy of adult males. On top sat the father of Joseph Smith, rescued from destitution and shame, who was appointed Patriarch of the Church. Below him were Joseph Smith and his brother Hyrum, who were called First and Second Elders. The hierarchy descended through a succession of male authorities that finally reached the fathers of households. Smith claimed that this hierarchy restored the ancient priesthood that had disappeared over the 18 centuries of greed and error that he labeled the Great Apostasy of the Christian churches. Americans who knew the history of the Market Revolution and the Smith family's travails within it, however, might have noted similarities between the restored ancient order and a poor man's visionary retrieval of the social order of the 18th-century North.

◆ The Rise of Popular Culture

Of course, not all of the northern plain folk spent their time in church. Particularly in cities and towns, they became both producers and consumers of a nonreligious (sometimes irreligious) commercial popular culture. The sports and shows attended by northern plain folk, like the churches that they attended, were often grounded in an antisentimental view of the world and in traditional forms of patriarchy and masculinity.

Blood Sports

Urban working-class neighborhoods were particularly fertile ground for popular amusements. Young working men formed a bachelor subculture that contrasted with the piety and self-restraint of the middle class. They organized volunteer fire companies and militia units that spent more time drinking and fighting rival groups than drilling or putting out fires. Gathering at firehouses, saloons, and street corners, they drank, joked, and boasted, and nurtured notions of manliness based on physical prowess and coolness under pressure.

They also engaged in such "blood sports" as cock fighting, ratting, and dog fighting, even though many states had laws forbidding such activities. In 1823, an English tourist in New York City noted that "it is perfectly common for two or three cockfights to regularly take place every week." Such contests grew increasingly popular during the 1850s and often were staged by saloonkeepers doubling as sports impresarios. One of the best known was Kit Burns of New York City, who ran Sportsman Hall, a saloon frequented by prizefighters, criminals, and their hangers-on. Behind the saloon, however, was a space—reached through a narrow doorway that could be defended against the police—with animal pits and a small amphitheater that seated 250 but that regularly held 400 yelling spectators.

Although most of the spectators were working men, a few members of the old aristocracy who rejected middle-class ways also attended these events. In 1861, for instance, 250 spectators paid as much as $3 each to witness a fight between roosters belonging to the prizefighter John Morrissey and Mr. Genet, president of the New York City board of aldermen. A newspaper estimated bets on the event at $50,000. Frederick Van Wyck, scion of a wealthy old New York family, remembered an evening he had spent at Tommy Norris's livery stable, where he witnessed a fight between billy goats, a rat baiting, a cockfight, and a boxing match between bare-breasted women. "Certainly for a lad of 17, such as I," he recalled, "a night with Tommy Norris and his attraction was quite a night."

Boxing

Prizefighting emerged from the same subterranean culture that sustained cockfights and other blood sports. This sport, imported from Britain, called for an enclosed ring, clear rules, cornermen, a referee, and a paying audience. The early fighters were Irish or English immigrants, as were many of the promoters and spectators. Boxing's popularity rose during the 1840s and 1850s, a time of increasing immigration and violence in poor city neighborhoods. Many of the fighters had close ties with ethnic-based saloons, militia units, fire companies, and street gangs such as New York's (Irish) Dead Rabbits and (native) Bowery B'hoys, and many labored at occupations with a peculiarly ethnic base. Some of the best American-born fighters were New York City butchers—a licensed, privileged trade from which cheap immigrant labor was systematically excluded. Butchers usually finished work by 10 A.M. They could then spend the rest of the day idling at a firehouse or a bar and often were prominent figures in neighborhood gangs.

PRIZEFIGHTERS
The Irishman James "Yankee" Sullivan and the native-born Tom Hyer were immensely popular heroes of native and Irish workingmen, as well as of the street gangs and political factions of their respective ethnic groups.

A prizefight between an American-born butcher and an Irish day laborer would attract a spirited audience that understood its class and ethnic meaning.

Prizefighting was a way of rewarding courage and skill and, sometimes, of settling scores through fair contests limited to two combatants. Nonetheless, the fights were brutal. Boxers fought with bare knuckles, and a bout ended only when one of the fighters was unable to continue. In an infamous match in 1842, for instance, the Englishman Christopher Lilly knocked down his Irish opponent Thomas McCoy 80 times; the fight ended with round 119, when McCoy died in his corner.

Although boxing had close ties to ethnic rivalries, the contestants often exhibited a respect for one another that crossed ethnic lines. For example, native-born Tom Hyer, who had defeated Irishman James "Yankee" Sullivan in one of the great early fights, later bailed Sullivan out of jail. In 1859, when Bill Harrington, a retired native-born boxer, disappeared and left a wife and children, his former Irish-born opponent, John Morrisey, arranged a sparring match and sent the proceeds to Mrs. Harrington.

An American Theater

In the 18th and early 19th centuries, the only theaters were in the large seaport cities. Those who attended were members of the urban elite, and nearly all of the plays, managers, and actors were English. After 1815, however, improvements in transportation and communication, along with the rapid growth of cities, created a much broader audience. Theaters and theater companies sprang up not only in New York and Philadelphia but also in Cincinnati, St. Louis, San Francisco, Rochester, and dozens of other new towns west of the Appalachians, and traveling troupes carried theatrical performances to the smallest hamlets. Most of them catered to male, largely plebeian audiences. Before 1830, the poorer theatergoers—nearly all of them men—occupied the cheap balcony seats (with the exception of the second balcony, which was reserved for prostitutes); artisans and other workingmen filled benches in the ground-floor area known as "the pit"; wealthier and more genteel patrons sat in the boxes. Those sitting in the pit and balcony joined in the performance: They ate and drank, talked, and shouted encouragement and threats to the actors. The genteel New Yorker Washington Irving lamented the "discharge of apples, nuts, and gingerbread" flying out of the balconies "on the heads of honest folks" in the pit.

As time passed, however, rowdyism turned into violence. The less genteel members of theater audiences protested the elegant speech, gentlemanly bearing, and understated performances of the English actors, which happened to match the speech, manners, and bearing of the American urban elite. Thus the protests were directed not only at the English actors but also at the ladies and gentlemen in the orchestra who were seen as symbols of English culture unsuitable in a democratic republic.

The first theater riot occurred in 1817, when the English actor Charles Incledon refused a New York audience's demand that he stop what he was doing and sing "Black-Eyed Susan." Such assaults grew more common during the 1820s. By the 1830s, separate theaters offered separate kinds of performances for rich and poor, but violence continued. It culminated in the rivalry between the American actor Edwin Forrest and the English actor William Charles Macready. Macready was a trained Shakespearean actor, and his restrained style and attention to the subtleties of the text had won him acclaim both in Britain and in the United States. Forrest, on the other hand, played to the cheap seats. With his bombast and histrionics, he transformed Shakespeare's tragedies into melodramas. Forrest and Macready carried out a well-publicized feud that led to a mob attack on Macready in 1849. Led by E. Z. C. Judson (who, under the pen name Ned Buntline, wrote scores of dime novels), the mob descended on Macready's performance at the exclusive Astor Place Opera House. The militia was waiting for them, and 20 people died in the ensuing riot and gunfight.

Playhouses that catered to working-class audiences continued to feature Shakespearean tragedies (*Richard III*, played broadly and with a lot of swordplay, was the favorite), but they now shared the stage with works written in the American vernacular. The stage "Yankee," rustic but shrewd, appeared at this time, and so did Mose the Bowery B'hoy, a New York volunteer fireman who performed feats of derring-do. Both frequently appeared in the company of well-dressed characters with English accents—the Yankee outsmarted them; Mose beat them up.

Minstrelsy

The most popular form of theater was the blackface minstrel show. Although these shows conveyed blatant racism, they were the preferred entertainment of working men (again, the audience was overwhelmingly working class and male) in northern cities from 1840 to 1880. The first minstrel show was presented in 1831 when a white showman named Thomas Rice blacked his face and "jumped Jim Crow," imitating a shuffle-dance he had seen on the Cincinnati docks. Within a few years, a formula for these shows had emerged that every theatergoer knew by heart.

The minstrel shows lasted an hour and a half and were presented in three sections. The first consisted of songs and dances performed in a walkaround, in which

Edwin Forrest in Edinburgh:
The Hiss Heard Round The World

The American actor Edwin Forrest toured Great Britain in the mid-1840s. He was America's great native tragedian and a hero of American democratic nationalism—an imposing figure with a voice (according to the democratic press) like "the falls of Niagara," and powerful thighs "carved out of the American forest," with "nature" rather than culture as his teacher, and with a fine-tuned sense of what American democratic audiences wanted. In London he met with his great rival, the English tragedian William Charles Macready. Macready was engaged, both as an actor and a theater manager, in a campaign to rescue the theater from democracy. He argued that acting was a matter not only of native ability but also of study and formal training, and that plays be performed with fidelity to the text (Shakespeare the way Shakespeare wrote it) and before well-behaved, "tasteful" audiences that rewarded the best actors and the best plays. Macready saw Forrest, with his extravagant acting style, his noisy audiences, and his praise-heavy penny press reviews, as the opposite of high culture and good taste. Many years earlier, Macready had acknowledged Forrest's talent, but insisted that "if he would cultivate those powers and really study, where, as in England, his taste could be formed, he would make one of the very first actors of this or any other day. But I thought he would not do so, as his countrymen were, by their extravagant applause, possessing him with the idea . . . that it was unnecessary." Macready, in short, was a high-toned enemy of Edwin Forrest and democratic theater.

In early March 1846, Edwin Forrest and William Macready were both on tour in Scotland. Forrest decided to attend Macready's performance in Edinburgh. Macready acted Hamlet that night, and on one of his exits he performed "a most astounding pirouette, flicking his handkerchief in coquettish flourishes." From an upper box came a loud hiss—common fare in working-class theaters in both Britain and the United States, but shocking stuff for Macready's well-behaved audience. A week later, Edwin Forrest revealed himself as the man who had hissed Macready's cultured, effeminate flourish. Newspapers on both sides of the Atlantic played up the story, and the two actors stood at the center of a cultural cold war—one freighted with nationalism and social class.

When he came to America in 1849, William Macready was hissed in Boston and showered with rotten potatoes in New York, and he had to dodge half a sheep carcass that someone threw out of the audience in Cincinnati. The attacks on Macready came to a bad end when he played the elite Astor Place Opera House in New York in May. Handbills went up asking "WORKINGMEN: SHALL AMERICANS OR ENGLISH RULE," and telling true Americans to go to the "English Aristocratic Opera House." The militia was called to protect the theater, Macready, and his genteel audience, and the result was the worst theater riot in American history.

EDWIN FORREST

From the Collections of the Library of Congress.

the audience was encouraged to clap and sing along. This was followed by a longer middle section in which the company sat in a row with a character named Tambo at one end and a character named Bones at the other (named for the tambourine and bones, the instruments they played), with an interlocutor in the middle. The Tambo character, often called Uncle Ned, was a simple-minded plantation slave dressed in plain clothing; the Bones character, usually called Zip Coon, was a dandified, oversexed free black dressed in top hat and tails. The interlocutor was the straight man—fashionably dressed, slightly pretentious, with an English accent. This middle portion of the show consisted of a conversation among the three, which included pointed political satire, skits ridiculing the wealthy

AN EARLY PRINT OF "JIM CROW" RICE AT NEW YORK'S BOWERY THEATER

The caption reads "American Theatre, Bowery, New York, Nov. 25ᵗʰ 1833. The 57ᵗʰ Night of Mr. T. D. Jim Crow Rice."

and the educated, and sexual jokes that bordered on obscenity. The third section featured songs, dances, and jokes, most of them familiar enough so that the audience could sing along and laugh at the right places.

The minstrel shows introduced African American song and dance—in toned-down, Europeanized form—to audiences who would not have permitted black performers on the stage. They also reinforced racial stereotypes that were near the center of American popular culture. Finally, they dealt broadly with aspects of social and political life that other performers avoided.

Minstrel shows and other theatrical entertainments began to travel the new transportation network to rural America. The Grecian Dog Apollo, for example, arrived in New York from London in 1827; he played cards, solved problems in arithmetic "with the celerity of an experienced clerk," and answered questions on astronomy and geography. Apollo traveled the Erie Canal circuit, playing at Albany, Saratoga Springs, Utica, Rochester, Buffalo, and Niagara Falls before returning to Peale's Museum in New York for the 1828 season. Many actors traveled well-established circuits, calling on local amateurs for their supporting casts. Minstrel companies traveled the river system of the interior and played to enthusiastic audiences wherever the riverboats docked. Mark Twain recalled them fondly: "I remember the first Negro musical show I ever saw. It must have been in the early forties. It was a new institution. In our village of Hannibal [Missouri] . . . it burst upon us as a glad and stunning surprise." Among Americans who had been taught to distrust cities by cultural leaders ranging from Thomas Jefferson to Emerson and Thoreau to the evangelical preachers in their own neighborhoods, minstrel shows and other urban entertainments gave rural folk a sense of the variety and excitement of city life.

Novels and the Penny Press

Few of the commodities made widely available by the Market Revolution were more ubiquitous than newspapers and inexpensive books. Improvements in printing and paper making enabled entrepreneurs to sell daily newspapers for a penny. Cheap "story papers" became available in the 1830s, "yellow-back" fiction in the 1840s, and dime novels from the 1850s onward. Although these offerings were distributed throughout the North and the West, they found their first and largest audience among city workers.

Mass-audience newspapers carried political news and local advertisements, but they were heavily spiced with sensationalism. The *Philadelphia Gazette* in late summer 1829, for instance, treated its eager readers to the following: "Female Child with Two Heads," "Bats," "Another Shark," "Horrid Murder," "More Stabbing," "Steam Boat Robbery," "Fishes Travelling on Land," "Poisoning by Milk," "Dreadful Steam Boat Disaster," "Picking Pockets," "Raffling for Babies," "Combat with a Bear," "Lake Serpent," "Atrocious Murder," "Frauds on the Revenue," and much, much more. Henry David Thoreau commented on the "startling and monstrous events as fill the family papers," while his friend Ralph Waldo Emerson reported that Americans were "reading all day murders & railroad accidents." Even though such sensational stories are most remarkable for their variety, they all portrayed a haunted, often demonic nature that regularly produced monstrosities and ruined the works of humankind, as well as a human nature that, despite appearances, was often deceptive and depraved.

Working-class readers discovered a similarly untrustworthy world in cheap fiction. George Lippard's *Quaker City* (1845) sold 60,000 copies in its first year and 30,000 in each of the next five years, making it the best-selling American book before the sentimental blockbusters of the 1850s. Lippard's book was a fictional "exposé" of the hypocrisy, lust, and cruelty of Philadelphia's outwardly genteel and Christian elite. Lippard and other adventure writers (whose works accounted for 60 percent of all American fiction titles published between 1831 and 1860) indulged in a pornography of violence that included cannibalism, blood drinking, and murder by every imaginable means. They also dealt with sex in unprecedentedly explicit ways. The yellow-back novels of the 1840s introduced readers not only to seduction and rape but also to transvestitism, child pornography, necrophilia, miscegenation, group sex, homosexuality, and—perhaps most shocking of all— women with criminal minds and insatiable sexual appetites. The scenes of gore and sexual depravity were presented voyeuristically—as self-righteous exposés of the perversions of the rich and powerful and stories of the Founders' Republic trampled upon by a vicious elite that pretended virtue but lived only for its appetites.

Popular fictions—like most popular plays, Edwin Forrest's Shakespeare, and much of what went on in blood sports, the prize ring, and the penny press—were melodramatic contests between good and evil. Evil was described in terms reminiscent of original sin: It provided the background of all human action, and heroes met a demonic and chaotic world with courage and guile without hoping to change it. Melodramatic heroes frequently

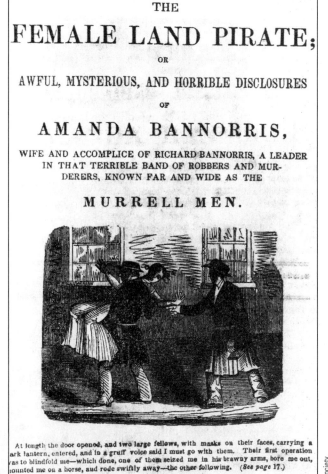

Courtesy American Antiquarian Society.

YELLOW-BACK NOVELS

Here are two pulp fiction hits of the 1840s: an erotic novel about the "amorous and lively" Mary Ann Temple and a crime story about robberies and murders committed by the "Female Land Pirate"—not the kinds of women encountered in middle-class sentimental fiction.

acknowledged evil in themselves while claiming moral superiority over the hypocrites and frauds who governed the world. A murderer in Ned Buntline's *G'hals of New York* (1850) remarks, "There isn't no *real* witue [virtue] and honesty nowhere, 'cept among the perfessional *dis-honest*." By contrast, in middle-class sentimental novels, the universe was benign; good could be nurtured, and evil could be defeated and transformed. Harriet Beecher Stowe's slave driver Simon Legree—the best-known villain in American literature—is evil not because of a natural disposition toward evil, but because he had been deprived of a mother's love during childhood.

🌀 Family, Church, and Neighborhood: The White South

Antebellum white southerners remained localistic and culturally conservative. Farm and plantation labor and the routines of family life still centered in the household, and prospects for most whites remained rooted in inherited land and family help. While the new northern middle class nourished a cosmopolitan culture and a domestic senti-mentalism that subverted traditional authority, southern-ers—planters and yeomen alike—distrusted outsiders and defended rural neighborhoods grounded in the authority of fathers and the integrity of families.

Southern Families

Most southern whites regarded them-selves less as individuals than as rep-resentatives of families that extended through time from the distant past to unborn generations. Southern boys often received the family names of heroes as their first names: Jefferson Davis, for example, or Thomas Jeffer-son (later, "Stonewall") Jackson. More often, however, they took the name of a related family—Peyton Randolph, Preston Brooks, Langdon Cheves— and carried them as proud and often burdensome badges of who they were. Children learned early on that their first duty was to their family's reputa-tion. When young Benjamin Tillman of South Carolina was away at school, his sister wrote, "Don't relax in your efforts to gain a good education. . . .

I want you to be an ornament to your family." Two years later, another sister wrote, "Do, Bud, study hard and make good use of your time. . . . I want you to do something for the Tillman name."

In the white South, reputation and the defense of family honor were everything. Boys and girls were taught to act as though everyone were watching them, ready to note any hint of inadequacy. A boy with a reputation for cowardice, for ineptness at riding or fighting, or for failure to control his emotions or hold his liquor was an embar-rassment to his family. Membership in the South's democ-racy of white men depended less on wealth than on the maintenance of personal and family integrity.

An "unsullied reputation," insisted Albert Gallatin Brown of Mississippi, placed a man "on a social level with all his fellows." As John Horry Dent, an Alabama slave-holder and bad amateur poet, put it:

> Honor and shame from all conditions rise;
> Act well your part and there the honor lies.

Among southern white men, wealth generally counted for less than did maintaining one's personal and family honor and thus winning membership in the democracy of hon-orable males.

The code of honor, although it forged ties of equality and respect among white men, made rigid distinctions be-tween men and women and whites and blacks. Women and girls who misbehaved—with transgressions ranging

COLONEL AND MRS. WHITESIDE

Colonel and Mrs. James Whiteside are pictured at home in their mansion on the heights above Chattanooga, Tennessee. The Colonel, Bible in hand, looks directly at his wife, while she looks shyly and indirectly back at him. Their infant son wears the traditional small child's dress, and the slaves are pictured as both subservient and comfortable. Here is southern patriarchy at its most genteel.

from simple gossip to poor housekeeping to adultery—damaged not only their own reputation but also the honor of the fathers, brothers, or husbands who could not control them. Such a charge could mean social death in a rural community made up of patriarchal households and watchful neighbors. In 1813, Bolling Hall of Alabama advised his daughter, "If you learn to restrain every thought, action, and word by virtue and religion, you will become an ornament." A "good man" or a "good woman" was someone who upheld the family by acting within a prescribed social role ("Act well your part. . . ."), and not, as the children of the northern middle class were being taught, by acting as an autonomous, self-governing individual.

The southern code of honor blunted attacks on social hierarchy and inherited status. When sentimental northerners attacked slavery because it denied the freedom of the individual, one southerner responded in a way that was meant to end the argument: "Do you say that the slave is held to involuntary service? So is the wife, [whose] relation to her husband, in the great majority of cases, is made for her and not by her." Few white southerners would have questioned the good sense of that response. Southern life was not about freedom, individual fulfillment, or social progress; it was about honoring the obligations to which one was born.

Southern Entertainments

Southerners of all classes and races were leisure-loving people, but the rural character of the South threw them upon their own resources rather than on commercial entertainments. They drank, told stories, engaged in wrestling and boxing matches, and danced. For evangelicals who withdrew from such entertainments, church socials and camp meetings filled the gap. Rural southerners both in and out of the churches engaged in corn-huskings, birthday celebrations, berry-picking expeditions, and so forth. Books were not as readily available as they were in the North. Whereas the big publishing houses produced many titles aimed at northern and western readers and at such specialized constituencies as commercial farmers or middle-class housewives, the southern literary market was too small to justify such special attention. Most southern families owned a Bible, and wealthier families often read histories, religious and political tracts, and English (seldom American) literature, with Shakespeare leading the way and Sir Walter Scott's tales of medieval chivalry not far behind. (Such stories exercised a strong fascination on some southerners; in the last years before the Civil War, jousting tournaments were held in which southern gentlemen clad in armor fought from horseback with lances and broadswords.) Hunting and fishing were passionate pursuits among southern men. Fox and deer hunts provided the gentry with an opportunity to display their skill with horses and guns, while the hunts of poorer whites and slaves both provided sport and enhanced their threatened roles as providers. Although state laws forbade slaves to own guns or dogs, thousands of slave owners found it wise to overlook the laws and to allow slaves to hunt as a favorite recreation.

The commercial entertainments in the South were concentrated in the larger towns and along the major rivers. Showboats brought theatrical troupes, minstrel shows, animal acts, and other entertainment to the river towns. The gentry's love of horses and competition made New Orleans the horse racing capital of the country; New Orleans also was the only southern city where one could watch a professional prizefight. Various violent contests appealed to New Orleans audiences. In 1819, a New Orleans impresario advertised a program that offered a bull versus six "of the strongest dogs in the country"; six bulldogs versus a Canadian bear; a "beautiful Tiger" versus a black bear; and 12 dogs versus a "strong and furious Opeloussas Bull." The advertisement further promised: "If the tiger is not vanquished in his fight with the Bear, he will be sent alone against the last Bull; and if the latter conquers all his enemies, several pieces of fireworks will be placed on his back, which will produce a very entertaining amusement." The impresario also stated that the premises had been inspected by the mayor of New Orleans, and that children would be admitted at half price. Although such events were outlawed in later years, they continued to be held on the sly. In 1852, a crowd of 5,000 gathered outside New Orleans to watch a bull and a grizzly bear fight to the death.

The Camp Meeting Becomes Respectable

The camp-meeting revivals of the early 19th century had transformed the South into an evangelical Bible belt (see chapter 7), although that label wouldn't be applied for another century. By 1860, 88 percent of southern church members were Methodist, Baptist, Presbyterian, or Disciples of Christ. Revival religion had spread from the frontier and upcountry yeomanry into both slave cabins and plantation mansions. Some evangelicals had risen into the slaveholding class, and many of the old families had been converted. As a result, the deist or indifferently Anglican gentry of the 18th century became outnumbered by earnest Baptist and Methodist planters who considered themselves the fathers of an inclusive southern Christian community.

Southern camp meetings continued throughout the antebellum years, but they were no longer the inclusive, ecstatic camp meetings of the past. They were often limited to a single denomination—usually Methodist—and were held on permanent campgrounds maintained by the churches. Conducted with more decorum than in the past, they were routine community events: Women began baking a week ahead of time and looked forward to visiting with neighbors and relatives as much as they did to getting right with God.

The goal of camp meetings was still to induce spiritual crisis and conversion, and sinners still wept and fell on their way to being saved, but such manifestations as the barking exercise and the jerks (see chapter 7) disappeared. Unfriendly observers after the 1820s could find nothing more offensive than simple breaches of decorum among the women. For instance, in 1828 an Englishwoman attended a meeting near Cincinnati at which nearly 100 women came forward to fall at the feet of Christ until "they were soon all lying on the ground in an indescribable confusion of heads and legs." The southern humorist George W. Harris described a fictional camp meeting at which his comic character Sut Lovingood put lizards up the preacher's pant leg. A fat woman fainted in the confusion, rolled down a hill, "tangled her laig an' garters in the top of a huckilberry bush, wif her head in the branch and jis' lay still."

The churches that grew out of southern revivals reinforced localistic neighborhoods and the patriarchal family. Some southern communities began when a whole congregation moved onto new land; others were settled by the chain migration of brothers and cousins, and subsequent revivals spread through family networks. Rural isolation limited most households to their own company during the week, but on Sundays, church meetings united the neighborhood's cluster of extended families into a community of believers. In most neighborhoods, social connections seldom extended beyond that. The word *church* referred ultimately to the worldwide community of Christians, and the war between the "church" and the "world" referred to a cosmic history that would end in millennial fire. In the day-to-day understandings of southern evangelicals, however, the church was the local congregation and the world was local sins and local sinners, many of whom were related to members of the church. Churches disciplined members for such worldly practices as drinking, gambling, dancing, swearing, fornication, and adultery, and even for giving the *impression* of sinful behavior. Mount Olive Baptist Church in North Carolina, for example, expelled Mary Bivens because she was "too thick with young men."

Religious Conservatism

Southern evangelicalism based itself, like religious conservatism in the North, on the sovereignty of God, a conviction of human sinfulness, and an acceptance of disappointment and pain as part of God's grand and unknowable design. "Oh man," lamented one slaveholder, "when will thou meekly submit to God without a murmur.... His will be done should be your constant prayer." Southern church people continued to interpret misfortune as divine punishment. When yellow fever was killing 1,000 people every week in New Orleans in 1853, the Episcopal bishop (and soon to be Confederate general) Leonidas Polk asked God to "turn us from the ravages of the pestilence, wherewith for our iniquities, thou are visiting us."

The same view held at home. When the young son of a planter family died, the mother was certain that God had killed the child because the parents had loved him more than God: "But God took him for he saw he was our idol." A grieving South Carolinian received this consolation from a relative: "Hope you are quite reconciled to the loss of your darling babe. As it was the will of God to take him, we must obey, and He will be angry at us if we go past moderate grief." Francis Pickens, another South Carolinian, wrote after losing his wife and child, "I had almost forgot there was a God, and now I stand the scattered . . . and blasted monument of his just wrath." It was a far cry from the middle-class North's garden cemeteries and the romantic, redemptive deaths of children in sentimental fiction.

Southern cultural conservatism was rooted in religion, in the family, and in a system of fixed social roles. Southern preachers assumed that patriarchal social relations were crucial to Christian living within an irredeemably imperfect and often brutal world. Southerners revered the patriarch and slaveholder Abraham more than any other figure in the Bible, and John C. Calhoun proclaimed "Hebrew Theocracy" the best government ever experienced by humankind. The father must—like Abraham—govern and protect his household; the mother must assist the father; and the women, children, and slaves must faithfully act out the duties of their stations. That meant a Christian must strive to be a good mother, a good father, a good slave; by the same token, a Christian never questioned his or her God-given social role.

Pro-slavery Christianity

In revolutionary and early national America, white southerners had been the most radical of republicans. Jeffersonian planter-politicians led the fights for equal rights and the absolute separation of church and state, and southern evangelicals were the early republic's staunchest opponents of slavery. By 1830, however, the South was an increasingly conscious minority within a democratic and capitalist nation. The northern middle classes proclaimed a link between material and moral progress, identifying both with individual autonomy and universal rights. A radical northern minority was agitating for the immediate abolition of slavery.

Southerners met this challenge with an "intellectual blockade" against outside publications and ideas and with a moral and religious defense of slavery. The Bible provided plenty of ammunition. Pro-slavery clergymen constantly stated that the Chosen People of the Old Testament had been patriarchs and slaveholders, and that Jesus had lived in a society that sanctioned slavery and never criticized the institution. Some ministers claimed that blacks were the descendants of Ham and thus deserved enslavement. The most common religious argument, however, was that slavery had given millions of heathen Africans the priceless opportunity to become Christians and to live in a Christian society. Thornton Stringfellow, a Virginia Baptist minister, insisted that "their condition . . . is now better than that of any equal number of laborers on earth, and is daily improving."

Like their northern counterparts, southern clergymen applauded the material improvements of the age, but they insisted that moral improvement occurred only when people embraced the timeless truths of the Bible. The South Carolinian William F. Hutson put it simply: "In religion and morals, we doubt all improvements, not known to certain fishermen who lived eighteen hundred years ago." Northern notions of progress through individual liberation, equal rights, and universal Christian love were wrong-headed and dangerous. The Presbyterian John Adger asserted that relations of dominance and submission (and not "barbarism and personal savage independence") were utterly necessary to both social and individual fulfillment, and that the distribution of rights and responsibilities was unequal and God-given. "The rights of the father are natural, but they belong only to the fathers. Rights of property are natural, but they belong only to those who have property," and such natural rights were coupled with the awesome duties of fatherhood and proprietorship. In the end, southern pro-slavery intellectuals rejected Jefferson's "self-evident" equality of man; Edmund Ruffin, for instance, branded that passage of the Declaration of Independence as "indefensible" as well as "false and foolish."

The Private Lives of Slaves

Some southern blacks, particularly in cities and town, were free. But the overwhelming majority were slaves. In law, in the census, and in the minds of planters, slaves were members of a plantation household over which the owner exercised absolute authority, not only as owner but also as paternal protector and lawgiver. Yet both slaveholders and slaves knew that slaves could not be treated like farm animals or little children. Wise slaveholders learned that the success of a plantation depended less on terror and draconian discipline (although whippings—and worse—were common) than on the accommodations by which slaves traded labor and obedience for some measure of privilege and autonomy within the bounds of slavery. After achieving privileges, the slaves called them their own: holidays, garden plots, friendships, and social gatherings both on and off the plantation; hunting and fishing rights; and so on. Together, these privileges provided some of the ground on which they made their own lives within slavery.

The Slave Family

The most precious privilege was the right to make and maintain families. As early as the Revolutionary War era, most Chesapeake slaves lived in units consisting of mother, father, and small children. On Charles Carroll's Maryland

From the Collections of the Library of Congress.

SLAVE CABINS ON A PLANTATION IN NORTHERN FLORIDA
Consisting of one room and set exactly 12 feet apart, this was minimal housing indeed. Yet it provided slaves with a place to live in families and the rudimentary sense of proprietorship exercised by these black workers sitting in front of their "own" houses.

farms in 1773, for example, 325 of the 400 slaves lived in such families. At Thomas Jefferson's Monticello, most slave marriages were for life, and small children almost always lived with both parents. The most common exceptions to this practice were fathers who had married away from their own plantations and who visited "broad wives" and children during their off hours. In Louisiana between 1810 and 1864, half the slaves lived in families headed by both parents; another one-fourth lived in single-parent families. Owners encouraged stable marriages because they made farms more peaceful and productive and because they flattered the owners' religious and paternalistic sensibilities. For their part, slaves demanded families as part of the price of their labor.

Yet slave families were highly vulnerable. Many slaveholders assumed that they had the right to coerce sex from female slaves; some kept slaves as concubines, and a few even moved them into the main house. They tended, however, to stay away from married women. While the slave community—in contrast to the whites—seldom punished sex before marriage, it took adultery seriously. Slaveholders knew that violations of married slave women could be enormously disruptive and strongly discouraged them. A far more serious threat to slave marriages was the death, bankruptcy, or departure of the slaveholders. Between one-fifth and one-third of slave marriages were broken by such events.

Slaveholders who encouraged slave marriages—even perhaps solemnizing them with a religious ceremony—

knew that marriage implied a form of self-ownership that conflicted with the slaves' status as property. Some conducted ceremonies in which couples "married" by jumping over a broomstick; others had the preacher omit the phrases "let no man put asunder" and "till death do you part" from the ceremony. Slaves knew that such ceremonies had no legal force. A Virginia slave remarked, "We slaves knowed that them words wasn't bindin'. Don't mean nothin' lessen you say, 'What God has jined, caint no man pull asunder.' But dey never would say dat. Jus' say 'Now you married.'" A black South Carolina preacher routinely ended the ceremony with "Till death or buckra [whites] part you."

Slaves modified their sense of family and kinship to accommodate such uncertainties. Because separation from father or mother was common, children spread their affection among their adult relatives, treating grandparents, aunts, and uncles almost as though they were parents. In fact, slaves often referred to all their adult relatives as parents. They also called nonrelatives "brother," "sister," "aunt," and "uncle," thus extending a sense of kinship to the slave community at large. Slaves chose as surnames for themselves the names of former owners, Anglicized versions of African names, or names that simply sounded good. They rarely chose the name of their current owner, however. Families tended to use the same given names from one generation to the next, naming boys after their father or grandfather, perhaps to preserve the memory of fathers who might be taken away. They seldom named

---

L I N K   T O   T H E   P A S T

A Slave Mother and the Slave Trade

In 1852, a slave mother from Virginia was caught up in the domestic slave trade. She wrote this to her husband:

D*ear Husband I write you a letter to let you know of my distress my master has sold Albert to a trader on Monday court day and myself and other child is for sale also and I want you to let [me] hear from you very soon before next cort if you can I don't know when I don't want you to wait till Christmas I want you to tell Dr. Hamilton your master if either will buy me then can attend to it know and then I can go afterwards*

I don't want a trader to get me they asked me if I had got any person to buy me and I told them no they told me to the court house too they never put me up A man buy the name of brady bought albert and is gone I don't know

whare they say he lives in scottsville my things is in several places some is in stanton and if I would be sold I don't know what will become of them I don't expect to meet with the luck to get that way till I am quite heart sick nothing more I am and ever will be your kind wife Marie Perkins.

---

1. Slaves uniformly feared the unpredictability and destructiveness of the domestic slave trade. Within this simple letter, how many social and personal injuries can you count?

For additional sources related to this feature, visit the *Liberty, Equality, Power* Web site at:

http://history.wadsworth.com/murrin_LEP4e

FIVE GENERATIONS OF A SLAVE FAMILY ON A SOUTH CAROLINA SEA ISLAND PLANTATION, 1862

Complex family ties such as those of the family shown here were among the most hard-won and vulnerable cultural accomplishments of enslaved blacks.

girls after their mother, however. Unlike Southern whites, slaves never married a first cousin, even though many members of their community were close relatives. The origins and functions of some of these customs are unknown. We know only that slaves practiced them consistently, usually without the knowledge of the slaveholders.

White Missions

A powerful aspect of planter paternalism was a widespread Christian mission to the slaves. By the 1820s, southern evangelicalism had long since abandoned its hostility toward slavery, and slaveholders commonly attended camp meetings and revivals. These prosperous converts faced conflicting duties. Their churches taught them that slaves had immortal souls and that planters were as responsible for the spiritual welfare of their slaves as they were for the spiritual welfare of their own children. One preacher remarked that it was difficult "to treat them as property, and at the same time render to them that which is just and equal as immortal and accountable beings, and as heirs of the grace of life, equally with ourselves." A planter on his deathbed told his children that humane treatment and religious instruction for slaves was the duty of slave owners; if these were neglected, "we will have to answer for the loss of their souls." After Nat Turner's bloody slave revolt in 1831 (to be discussed later in this chapter), missions to the slaves took on new urgency: If the churches were to help create a family-centered, Christian society in the South, that society would have to include the slaves. The

result after 1830 was a concerted attempt to Christianize the slaves.

To this end, Charles Colcock Jones, a Presbyterian minister from Georgia, spent much of his career writing manuals on how to preach to slaves. He taught that no necessary connection linked social position and spiritual worth—that there were good and bad slaveholders and good and bad slaves. He also taught, preaching from the Epistles of Paul ("Servants, obey your masters"), that slaves must accept the master's authority as God's, and that obedience was their prime religious virtue. Jones warned white preachers never to become personally involved with their slave listeners—to pay no attention to their quarrels, their complaints about their master or about their fellow slaves, or about working conditions on the plantation. "We separate entirely their religious from their civil condition," he said, "and contend that one may be attended to without interfering with the other." The catechism Jones prepared for slaves included the question, "What did God make you for?" The answer was, "To make a crop."

The evangelical mission to the slaves was not as completely self-serving as it may seem. For to accept one's worldly station, to be obedient and dutiful within that station, and to seek salvation outside of this world were precisely what the planters demanded of themselves and their own families. An important goal of plantation missions was, of course, to create safe and profitable plantations. Yet that goal was to be achieved by Christianizing both slaveholders and slaves—a lesson that some slaveholders learned when they were expelled from their churches for mistreating their slaves.

Slave Christians

The white attempt to Christianize slavery, however, depended on the acceptance of slavery by the slaves. But the biblical notion that slavery might be a punishment for sin and the doctrine of divinely ordained social orders never took root among the slaves. Hannah Scott, a slave in Arkansas, remarked on what she heard a white preacher say: "But all he say is 'bedience to de white folks, and we hears 'nough of dat without him telling us." One slave asked a white preacher, "Is us slaves gonna be free in heaven?" The preacher quickly changed the subject. As

one maid boldly told her mistress, "God never made us to be slaves for white people."

Although the slaves ignored much of what the missionaries taught, they embraced evangelical Christianity and transformed it into an independent African American faith. Some slave owners encouraged them by building "praise houses" on their plantations and by permitting religious meetings. Others tried to resist the trend, but with little success. After 1830, most of the southern states outlawed black preachers, but the laws could not be enforced. James Henry Hammond, a rich South Carolina planter, tried for 20 years to stop his slaves from holding religious meetings, but at night they would slip off to secret gatherings in the woods. Sometimes slaves met in a cabin—preaching, praying, and singing in a whisper. At their

HISTORY THROUGH FILM

Beloved (1998)

Directed by Jonathan Demme. Starring Danny Glover (Paul D), Oprah Winfrey (Sethe), Beah Richards (Baby Suggs).

Oprah Winfrey produced and starred in this adaptation of Toni Morrison's Pulitzer Prize–winning novel. It is a story of persisting personal and communal wounds inflicted by slavery, told from within a damaged black household near Cincinnati in 1873.

The action begins when Paul D (Danny Glover) walks up to the house of Sethe (Oprah Winfrey) and her daughter, Denver. As he enters, the house fills with a red glow and shakes itself into a storm of furniture and kitchen implements. The house is haunted by the ghost of Sethe's baby girl. Paul D is a former slave from Sweet Home, the horrific Kentucky plantation from which Sethe escaped. He moves in, the ghost moves out, and the film follows this household through the next year.

Peace lasts only a short time. A strange young woman named Beloved moves in and becomes Denver's sister, Sethe's daughter, and Paul D's mystical seducer. (The camera pans back from the seduction scene in the red glow that we remember from the initial haunting.) Paul D discovers that Sethe had killed her own baby in 1856 and he leaves. Beloved, now pregnant, demands (and gets) Sethe's time, money, and affection. Sethe loses her job and runs out of food and money, serving Beloved all the while. Denver begs work from an old teacher, and the community of black women, who have shunned Sethe and her family throughout the movie, begin leaving food.

In the climactic scene, Denver waits on the porch for her new white employer (a former abolitionist), when the black women arrive to sing and chant in an effort to exorcise ghosts from the house. Sethe, crazed, followed by naked and pregnant Beloved, comes onto the porch and attacks the employer with an ice pick. The women subdue her, Denver rides off (like her brothers before her) to another life, and Beloved disappears. The film ends with the return of Paul D, and we are left with the hope that Sethe may outlive her ghosts.

Although the action occurs in 1873, the explanation lies in slavery and in the 1856 escape attempt told—in conversation, dreams, and flashbacks—as memory. Love scenes between Sethe and Paul D display the scars of whippings, particularly on Sethe. She saw her mother hanged, she was whipped and beaten while pregnant, and her

meetings they rehearsed a faith that was at variance with the faith of the slaveholders. Reverend Anderson Edwards, a slave preacher from Texas, recalled that he "had to preach what Massa told me. And he say tell them niggers iffen they obeys the Massa they goes to heaven, but I knowed there's something better for them, but daren't tell them 'cept on the sly. That I done lots. I tells 'em iffen they keeps prayin' the Lord will set 'em free."

One way in which slave religion differed from what was preached to them by whites was in the practice of conjuring, folk magic, root medicine, and other occult knowledge, most of it passed down from West Africa. Such practices addressed areas in which Christianity was useless: curing illnesses, making people fall in love, ensuring a good day's fishing, or bringing harm to one's enemies.

Sometimes African magic competed with plantation Christianity. Just as often, slaves combined the two. For instance, slaves sometimes determined the guilt or innocence of a person accused of stealing by hanging a Bible by a thread, then watching the way it turned. The form was West African; the Bible was not. The slave root doctor George White boasted that he could "cure most anything," but added that "you got to talk wid God an' ask him to help out." Maum Addie, a slave in coastal South Carolina, dealt with the malevolent African spirits called plat-eyes with a combination of African potions, the Christian God, and a stout stick: "So I totes mah powder en sulphur en I carries mah stick in mah han en puts mah truss in Gawd."

Christianity could not cure sick babies or identify thieves, but it gave slaves something more important: a

owner's sons held her down and sucked the milk from her. (Sethe learns later that her husband, whom she thought had abandoned her, witnessed this scene from a hayloft and went hopelessly insane.) Her escape is botched and violent. Sethe secretly sends her two sons ahead to Baby Suggs (Beah Richards), her mother-in-law in Ohio. Sethe sets off alone, gives birth to Denver on the banks of the Ohio River, crosses the river, and spends one perfect month tending her children and going to Baby Suggs's church meetings in the woods—meetings at which Suggs demands that her people love themselves. Then the old master arrives to take them back to Kentucky, and Sethe grabs the children, takes them into an outbuilding, and tries to kill them, succeeding only with Denver's infant older sister.

It all works better in Morrison's novel than in Oprah Winfrey's movie, but both are terrible and disturbing dramatizations of the injury slavery inflicted and of African American attempts to both absorb and transcend the crimes committed against them.

Beloved (1998) stars Danny Glover and Oprah Winfrey and is based on Toni Morrison's Pulitzer Prize–winning novel.

Kobal Collection/Regan, Ken/Touchstone.

sense of themselves as a historical people with a role to play in God's cosmic drama. In slave Christianity, Moses the liberator (and not the slaveholders' Abraham) stood beside Jesus. The slaves' appropriation of the book of Exodus denied the smug assumption of the whites that they were God's chosen people who had escaped the bondage of despotic Europe to enter the promised land of America. To the slaves, America was Egypt, they were the chosen people, and the slaveholders were Pharaoh. Thomas Wentworth Higginson, a Boston abolitionist who went south during the Civil War to lead a Union regiment of freed South Carolina slaves, wrote that his men knew the Old Testament books of Moses and the New Testament book of Revelation. "All that lies between," he said, "even the life of Jesus, they hardly cared to read or to hear." He found their minds "a vast bewildered chaos of Jewish history and biography; and most of the events of the past, down to the period of the American Revolution, they instinctively attribute to Moses."

The slaves' religious songs, which became known as "spirituals," told of God's people, their travails, and their ultimate deliverance. In songs and sermons, the figures of Jesus and Moses were often blurred, and it was not always clear whether deliverance—accompanied by divine retribution—would take place in this world or the next. In any case, deliverance always meant an end to slavery, with the possibility that it might bring a reversal of relations between slaves and masters. "The idea of a revolution in the conditions of the whites and blacks," said the escaped slave Charles Ball, "is the corner-stone of the religion of the latter."

Religion and Revolt

Unlike slaves in Cuba, Jamaica, Brazil, and other New World plantation societies, North American slaves seldom went into organized, armed revolt. The environment of the United States was unfriendly to such events. American plantations were relatively small and dispersed, and the southern white population was large, vigilant, and well armed. Whites also enjoyed—until the cataclysm of the Civil War—internal political stability. The slaves encountered few promising opportunities to win their freedom by violent means. Thousands of slaves demonstrated their hatred of the system by running away. Others fought slave owners or overseers, sabotaged equipment and animals, stole from planters, and found other ways to oppose slavery, but most knew that open revolt was suicide.

Christianity convinced slaves that history was headed toward an apocalypse that would result in divine justice and their own deliverance, and thus held out the possibil-

ity of revolt. Slave preachers seldom indulged in prophecy and almost never told their congregations to become actively engaged in God's divine plan because they knew that open resistance was hopeless. Slave Christians believed that God hated slavery and would end it, but that their role was to have faith in God, take care of one another, preserve their identity as a people, and await deliverance. Only occasionally did slaves take retribution and deliverance into their own hands.

The most ambitious conspiracy was hatched by Denmark Vesey, a free black of Charleston, South Carolina. Vesey was a leading member of an African Methodist congregation that had seceded from the white Methodists and had been independent from 1817 to 1821. At its height, the church had 6,000 members, most of them slaves. Vesey and some of the other members read widely in political tracts, including the antislavery arguments in the Missouri debates (see chapter 12) and in the Bible. They talked about their delivery out of Egypt, with all white men, women, and children being cut off. They identified Charleston as Jericho and planned its destruction in 1822: A few dozen Charleston blacks would take the state armory, then arm rural slaves who would rise up to help them. They would kill the whites, take control of the city, commandeer ships in the harbor, and make their getaway, presumably to black-controlled Haiti. Word of the conspiracy spread secretly into the countryside, largely through the efforts of Gullah Jack, who was both a Methodist and an African conjurer. Jack recruited African-born slaves as soldiers, provided them with charms as protection against whites, and used his spiritual powers to terrify others into keeping silent.

In the end, the Vesey plot was betrayed by slaves. As one coerced confession followed another, white authorities hanged Vesey, Gullah Jack, and 34 other accused conspirators, 22 of them in one day. Even so, frightened whites knew that most of the conspirators (estimates ranged from 600 to 9,000) remained at large and unidentified.

Nat Turner

In August 1831, in a revolt in Southampton County, Virginia, some 60 slaves shot and hacked to death 55 white men, women, and children. Their leader was Nat Turner, a Baptist lay preacher. Turner was neither a conjurer like Gullah Jack (he violently opposed plantation conjurers) nor a republican revolutionary like Denmark Vesey or the Richmond slave Gabriel (see chapter 7). He was, he told his captors, an Old Testament prophet and an instrument of God's wrath. As a child, he had prayed and fasted often, and the spirit—the same spirit who had spoken to the

NAT TURNER

This contemporary woodcut depicts scenes from Nat Turner's rebellion. In this bloodiest of all North American slave revolts, 55 whites, most of them women and children, were shot and hacked to death.

prophets of the Bible—had spoken directly to him. When he was a young man, he had run away to escape a cruel overseer, but when God told him that he had not chosen Nat merely to have him run away, Nat returned. He justified his return by quoting one of the slave owners' favorite verses of scripture: "He who knoweth his master's will and doeth it not, shall be beaten with many stripes." But Turner made it clear that his Master was God, not a slave owner.

Around 1830, Turner received visions of the final battle in Revelation, recast as a fight between white and black spirits. He saw Christ crucified against the night sky, and the next morning he saw Christ's blood in a cornfield. Convinced by a solar eclipse in February 1831 that the time had come, Turner began telling other slaves about his visions, recruited his force, and launched a bloody and hopeless revolt that ended in mass murder, failure, and the execution of Turner and his followers.

The Vesey and Turner revolts, along with scores of more limited conspiracies, deeply troubled southern whites. Paternalistic slaveholders were increasingly committed to making slavery both domestic and Christian. For their part, slaves recognized that they could receive decent treatment and pockets of autonomy in return for outward docility. Vesey and Turner opened wide cracks

in that mutual charade. During the Turner revolt, slaves whose masters had been murdered joined the rebels without a second thought. A plantation mistress who survived by hiding in a closet listened to the murders of her husband and children and heard her house servants arguing over possession of her clothes. A Charleston grandee named Elias Horry, upon finding that his coachman was among the Vesey conspirators, asked him, "What were your intentions?" The formerly submissive slave replied that he had intended "to kill you, rip open your belly, and throw your guts in your face."

Such stories sent a chill through the white South—a suspicion that despite the appearance of peace, they were surrounded by people who would kill them in an instant. While northerners patronized plays and cheap fiction that dramatized the trickery and horror beneath placid appearances, the nightmares of slaveholding paternalists were both more savage and closer to home.

Conclusion

By the second quarter of the 19th century, Americans had made a patchwork of regional, class, and ethnic cultures. The new middle classes of the North and West compounded their Protestant and republican inheritance with a new entrepreneurial faith in progress. The result was a way of life grounded in the self-made and morally accountable individual and the sentimentalized (often feminized) domestic unit.

Their means of proposing that way of life as a national culture for the United States often offended others. The middle class met resistance, first of all, from poorer urban dwellers and the less prosperous farmers in their own sections—a northern and western majority that remained grimly loyal to the unsentimental, male-dominated families of their fathers and grandfathers, to new and old religious sects that continued to believe in human depravity and the mysterious workings of providence, and to the suspicion that perfidy and disorder lurked behind the smiling moral order of market economics and sentimental culture. They were also people who enjoyed dark and playful popular entertainments that often mocked middle-class sentimentalism. In the South, most white farmers persisted in a neighborhood-based, intensely evangelical, and socially conservative way of life; when asked their opinions, they often talked like classic Jeffersonian yeomen. Southern planters, although they shared in the northern elite's belief in material progress and the magic of the market, were bound by family values, a system of slave labor, and a code of honor that was strikingly at variance with middle-class faith in an orderly universe and perfectible individuals. Slaves in these years continued to make cultural forms of their own; and despite their exclusion from the white world of liberty and equality, they tied their aspirations to the family (although in broader and more flexible ways than most whites), to an evangelical Protestant God, and to the individual and collective dignity that republics promise to their citizens.

SUGGESTED READINGS

Stuart M. Blumin, *The Emergence of the Middle Class: Social Experience in the American City, 1760–1900* (1989) is a thorough study of work and material life among the urban middle class. Studies that treat religion, family, and sentimental culture include **Paul E. Johnson**, *A Shopkeeper's Millennium: Society and Revivals in Rochester New York, 1815–1837* (1978); **Mary P. Ryan**, *Cradle of the Middle Class: The Family in Oneida County, New York, 1790–1865* (1981); and **Jane Tompkins**, *Sensational Designs: The Cultural Work of American Fiction, 1790–1860* (1985). The works of **Jon Butler** and **Nathan Hatch** listed in the Suggested Readings for chapter 7 are the best overviews of religion in these years. Studies of popular literature and entertainments include **Elliott J. Gorn**, *The Manly Art: Bare-Knuckle Prize Fighting in America* (1986); **Eric Lott**, *Love & Theft: Blackface Minstrelsy and the American Working Class* (1993); **David S. Reynolds**, *Beneath the American Renaissance: The Subversive Imagination in the Age of Emerson and Melville* (1988); and **Paul E. Johnson**, *Sam Patch, the Famous Jumper* (2003). **Peter Kolchin**, *American Slavery, 1619–1877* (1993) is a good synthesis of the literature. Now-classic treatments of slave culture are **Eugene D. Genovese**, *Roll, Jordan, Roll: The World the Slaves Made* (1974); and **Lawrence W. Levine**, *Black Culture and Black Consciousness: Afro-American Folk Thought from Slavery to Freedom* (1977). Two essential books on the culture of southern whites are **Bertram Wyatt-Brown**, *Southern Honor: Ethics & Behavior in the Old South* (1982); and **Christine Leigh Heyerman**, *Southern Cross: The Beginnings of the Bible Belt* (1997). An enlightening counterpoint between black and white understandings of the slave trade (and, by extension, of the slave South generally) is presented in **Walter Johnson**, *Soul by Soul: Life Inside the Antebellum Slave Market* (1999).

AMERICAN JOURNEY ONLINE
A N D
 INFOTRAC COLLEGE EDITION

Visit the source collections at www.ajaccess.wadsworth.com and
infotrac.thomsonlearning.com and use the Search function with
the following key terms to explore documents, images, audio
and video clips, articles, and commentary related to the material
in this chapter.

Uncle Tom's Cabin	Nat Turner
Harriet Beecher Stowe	*The Book of Mormon*
Denmark Vesey	Joseph Smith
Sarah Josepha Hale	

GRADE AIDS

**Visit the Liberty Equality Power Companion Web Site for resources specific to
this textbook:** http://history.wadsworth.com/murrin_LEP4e

The CD in the back of this book and the U.S. History Resource Center at
http://history.wadsworth.com/u.s./ offer a variety of tools to help you succeed in
this course, including access to quizzes; images; documents; interactive simulations,
maps, and timelines; movie explorations; and a wealth of other sources.

Society, Culture, and Politics, 1820s–1840s

CANVASSING FOR A VOTE
Electioneering in Jacksonian America was continuous with everyday social and cultural life. Here, the Whig artist and politician George Caleb Bingham depicts four men talking outside a Missouri tavern. Although they could be talking about anything, Bingham tells us the man in the top hat at right is a politician, busily canvassing for a vote.

CHAPTER OUTLINE

Between 1820 and 1845, Thomas Jefferson's agrarian republic became Andrew Jackson's noisy and deeply divided mass democracy. Politicians who built the Whig and Democratic Parties, which helped bring about that change, participated in the economic and social transformations of those years as both consumers and producers of new forms of popular culture. In making their political appeals, they tapped skillfully into the national patchwork of aspiration, fear, and resentment. John Quincy Adams, Henry Clay, and their National Republican and Whig allies in the states concocted visions of smooth-running, government-sponsored transportation and monetary systems. Such visions echoed the faith in cosmic order, material progress, and moral improvement that had become cultural axioms for the more prosperous and cosmopolitan Americans. Democrats, on the other hand, defended Jefferson's republic of limited government and widespread equality and liberty. They portrayed a haunted political universe in which trickery, deceit, and special privilege lurked behind the promises and power-hunger of the Whigs.

Politicians constructed the Whig and Democratic coalitions largely at the neighborhood and state levels. Their arguments for and against state-supported internal improvements and state-chartered banks and corporations mirrored the ideological wars fought out nationally between Whigs and Jacksonian Democrats (see chapter 12). At the same time, national debates incorporated Democratic and Whig attitudes on family, religion, race, gender, ethnicity, class, and the proper functions of government that had been shaped by state-level debates. Those local and state issues and the social and cultural constituencies that argued them out are the subjects of this chapter.

CHAPTER FOCUS

♦ Which Americans were likely to support the Democratic Party in the 1830s and 1840s? Which Americans were likely to support the Whigs?

♦ What were Whig and Democratic conceptions of the duties and limits of government?

♦ What were the principal social reform movements of these years, and how did the political parties react to them?

♦ How did Whigs and Democrats differ on questions of gender and race?

CHRONOLOGY

1816	African Methodist Episcopal denomination founded in Philadelphia • American Colonization Society promises to repatriate blacks to Africa
1819	New York state builds the first prison under the Auburn system
1826	Reformers found the American Society for the Promotion of Temperance
1831	William Lloyd Garrison begins publication of the antislavery *Liberator* • New York Magdalen Society publishes its first annual report
1833	Abolitionists found the American Anti-Slavery Society
1834	Antiabolition mob riots in New York City • First major race riot breaks out in Philadelphia
1840	Working-class drinkers found the Washington Temperance Society
1848	First Women's Rights Convention held in Seneca Falls, New York
1851	Maine becomes the first of 17 states to enact statewide prohibition
1860	New York enacts the Married Women's Property Act

Constituencies

By the 1830s, support for the Democratic or Whig Party was a matter of personal identity as much as of political preference: A man's vote demonstrated his personal history, his cultural values, and his vision of the good society as clearly as it demonstrated his opinion on any particular political issue. Voters remained loyal to their parties in selecting officeholders ranging from local coroners and school board members to state legislators and presidents of the United States. Thus political parties reduced the stupendous diversity of American society to two political choices. Of course, limiting citizenship to white men narrowed diversity in the electorate, as did the fact that the youngest and poorest white men often failed to vote. But even with the deck stacked in favor of a homogeneous electorate, the Whig and Democratic Parties were national coalitions of ill-matched regional, economic, ethnic, and religious groups. They were united by Whig and Democratic political cultures—consistent attitudes toward government and politics embedded in religion, family, and economic life. For all their patchwork diversity, the Democratic and Whig Parties appealed to coherent constituencies and proposed coherent programs in every corner of the republic.

The North and West

In the North and West, the makers of what would become the Whig Party found their most loyal support at the centers of the Market Revolution and the Finneyite revival. The broad band of Yankee commercial farms stretching across southern New England, western New York, and the Old Northwest was the northern Whig heartland. Whigs also enjoyed support in northern cities and towns. The wealthiest men in cities were Whigs; more than 8 in 10 among the merchant elite of Boston and New York supported them. The new urban commercial classes created in the Market Revolution also supported the Whigs. Factory owners were solidly Whig, and native-born factory workers often joined them—partly because Whigs promised opportunities to rise in the world, partly because Whigs protected their jobs by encouraging domestic markets for what they made, and, increasingly, because Whigs pandered to their fears of immigrant labor. For similar reasons, many skilled urban artisans supported the Whigs, as did smaller numbers of dockworkers, day laborers, and others among the unskilled.

Northern Whiggery was grounded in the Market Revolution, but the Whig political agenda ranged far beyond economic life. The strongholds of Whiggery and the market were also the strongholds of the Finneyite revival. Among the urban middle class and in the more market-oriented rural neighborhoods, the inheritors of Puritan theocracy translated the spirit of the late 1820s and early 1830s revivals into an avowedly Christian Whig politics. Northern and western Whigs demanded that government actively encourage the transition to market society. At the same time, they called for moral legislation on such issues as Sabbath observance, temperance, and Bible-based public schools. Marching under the banner of activist government, economic development, and moral progress, Whigs set the political agenda in most northern states.

They met a determined Democratic opposition. Campaigning as defenders of the Jeffersonian republic, autonomous neighborhoods, and private conscience, Democrats found supporters among cultural traditionalists who had gained little from the expansion of national markets and who had no use for the moral agenda of the Whigs. The Butternuts (so named for the yellow vegetable dye with which they colored their homespun clothing) of the southern, river-oriented counties of the Northwest joined the Democratic Party. Farmers in the Allegheny Mountains of southern New York and northern Pennsylvania, in the declining (and non-Yankee) countryside of the Hudson River valley, and in the poor and isolated hill towns of northern and western New England also supported the Democrats.

In cities and towns, Democrats made up substantial minorities among businessmen, master craftsmen, and professionals, but most urban Democrats were wage earners. Perhaps the most overwhelmingly Democratic group in the country was immigrant Irish Catholics, who were filling the lower ranks of the urban workforce. Their presence in the Democratic Party pushed increasing numbers of native Protestant workers into the Whig ranks—a division that appeared in New York City in the early 1830s, in most cities and towns by the 1840s, and that pervaded the North and West in the 1850s.

When confronted with opposition to evangelical legislation, Whigs labeled the Democratic Party the party of atheism and immorality. Democrats responded that they opposed theocracy, not religion. True, most free-thinkers, atheists, and persons who simply did not care about religion supported the Democratic Party. So did immigrant Catholics, who rightfully feared the militant Protestantism of the Whigs. Democrats, however, won the support of hundreds of thousands of evangelical Protestants as well. At least half of Methodists, Baptists, Disciples of Christ, Old School Presbyterians, and members of Reformed churches put their faith in providence and individual piety, and deeply distrusted what they called "church and state" Whiggery and the mixing of politics and religion. "I am myself a candidate," said a Methodist Democrat in 1840, "but it is for eternal life. I aspire to a throne, but I must have one which will not perish." Evangelical Democrats were joined by sectarian Christians who looked to the Democrats for protection: Freewill Baptists, Universalists, Lutherans, Scots Covenanters, many Quakers, Mor-

The Saint Louis Art Museum, Purchase.

THE COUNTY ELECTION

The Whig artist-politician George Caleb Bingham said this election day scene was "illustrative of the manners of a free people and free institutions." It was a wry comment: Many of the figures are Missouri Democratic politicians who had, Bingham thought, cheated him in a contested election to the state legislature.

mons, and others. These Democratic churchgoers rejected Whig moral legislation as antirepublican and as Yankee cultural imperialism. George Washington Bethune, a Dutch Reformed minister and a New York Democrat, put the Democratic creed succinctly: "Religion is not to be advanced by civil power."

The South

Throughout the 1830s and 1840s, the southern states divided their votes equally between Whigs and Democrats, with most individual southern localities either solidly Democratic or solidly Whig. In the 1844 elections, for instance, the counties of Virginia and Alabama supported their favored candidates by margins of 23 and 27 percent, respectively—landslide margins by the standards of two-party politics. (The comparable figure for New York counties was 9 percent.) Much more than in the North, southern party preferences were tied to differences in economic life.

Isolationist southern neighborhoods tended to support the Democrats. Thus Democrats ran strongest in yeoman neighborhoods with few slaves and relatively little market activity—upcountry communities that valued household independence and the society of neighbors and that deeply distrusted intrusions from the outside. The more cosmopolitan southern communities tended to support the Whigs. In general, this meant that Whigs were strongest in plantation counties, where they commanded the votes not only of wealthy planters but also of smaller farmers, and of lawyers, storekeepers, and craftsmen in county-seat towns. Upland, nonplantation neighborhoods in which Whigs ran well (eastern Tennessee, western North Carolina, and parts of Virginia are examples) were places where Whigs promised state-sponsored internal improvements that would link ambitious but isolated farmers to outside markets. On the other hand, some plantation districts with easy access to markets, such as the South Carolina low-country, opposed expensive Whig projects that would benefit other areas.

Many other southern exceptions to the link between commerce and the Whig Party were grounded in the prestige and power of local leaders. Southern statesmen who broke with the Jacksonians in the 1830s—John C. Calhoun in South Carolina, Hugh Lawson White in Tennessee, and others—took personal and regional followings with them (see chapter 12). Political campaigners also had to contend with southerners such as George Reynolds of Pickens County, Alabama. Reynolds was a half-literate yeoman who fathered 17 children and had 234 direct descendants living in his neighborhood, which he delivered as a bloc to politicians who pleased him. Despite the vagaries of southern kinship and community, Whigs knew that their core constituency in the South was in communities that were or wanted to be linked to commercial society.

In sharp contrast with the North and West, southern political divisions had little to do with religion. The South was thoroughly evangelized by 1830, but southern Baptists, Methodists, and Presbyterians seldom combined religion and politics. The southern evangelical churches had begun as marginal movements that opposed the Anglican establishment; they continued to distrust ties between church and state. Although they enforced morality within their own households and congregations, southern evangelicals seldom asked state legislatures to pass moral legislation. In extreme cases, southern premillennialists rejected politics altogether, insisting that Jesus would soon return to take the reins of government. (One political canvasser faced with that argument responded, "I will bet one hundred dollars he can't carry Kentucky.") Southern evangelicals who embraced the world of the market assumed, along with their northern Whig counterparts, that the new economy encouraged a Christian, civilized life. Other southern churchgoers responded to the Jacksonians' denunciations of greed and the spirit of speculation. Thus, even though many southern communities were bitterly divided over religion, the divisions seldom shaped party politics.

The social, religious, cultural, and economic bases of party divisions formed coherent Whig and Democratic political cultures. Whig voters in the North and South either were or hoped to become beneficiaries of the Market Revolution and wanted government to subsidize economic development. In the North, they also demanded that government help shape market society into a prosperous, orderly, and homogeneous Christian republic. Democrats, North and South, demanded a minimal government that kept taxes low and that left citizens, their families, and their neighborhoods alone.

The Politics of Economic Development

Both Whigs and Democrats accepted the transition to market society, but they wanted to direct it into different channels. Whigs wanted to use government and the market to make an economically and morally progressive—albeit hierarchical—republic. Democrats viewed both government and the new institutions of market society with suspicion and vowed to allow neither to subvert the equal rights and rough equality of condition that were, in their view, the preconditions of republican citizenship. In language that echoed their Jeffersonian forebears, Jacksonian Democrats demanded that the market remain subservient to the republic.

Government and Its Limits

"The government," remarked a New York City Whig in 1848, "is not merely a machine for making wars and punishing felons, but is bound to do all that is within its power to promote the welfare of the People—its legitimate scope is not merely negative, representative, defensive, but also affirmative, creative, constructive, beneficent." *The American Review,* a Whig periodical, agreed: "Forms of government are instituted for the protection and fostering of virtue, and are valuable only as they accomplish this."

The Whigs insisted that economic development, moral progress, and social harmony were linked and that government should foster them. Market society, they argued, opened up opportunities for individual Americans. As long as people developed the work habits and moral discipline required for success, they would be rewarded. To poor farmers and city workers who believed that the Market Revolution undermined their independence, Whigs promised social mobility within a new system of interdependence—but only to deserving individuals. According to the New York *Herald* in 1836, "The mechanic who attends quietly to his business—is industrious and attentive—belongs to no club—never visits the porter-house—is always at work or with his family—such a man gradually rises in society and becomes an honor to himself, his friends, and to human nature." The *Herald* editor continued, "On the contrary, look at the Trade Unionist—the pot-house agitator—the stirrer-up of sedition—the clamorer for higher wages—After a short time, he ends his career in the Pen or State Prison." Whigs believed that the United States exhibited a harmony of class interests and an equality of opportunity that every virtuous person would recognize and that only resentful, mean-spirited, unworthy people would doubt. Pointing to self-made Whigs such as Daniel Webster and Abraham Lincoln, they demanded activist government that nurtured the economic, cultural, and moral opportunities provided by market society.

Democrats seldom praised or condemned market society per se. Instead, they argued for the primacy of citizenship: Neither government nor the market, they said, should be allowed to subvert the civil and legal equality among independent men on which the republic rested. Often sharing a view of human nature that was (in contrast to the Whigs' more optimistic views) a grim combination of classical republicanism and gothic romance, Democrats saw government not as a tool of progress but as a dangerous—although regrettably necessary—concentration of power in the hands of imperfect, self-interested men. The only safe course was to limit its power. In 1837, the *United States Magazine and Democratic Review* declared: "The best government is that which governs least," and went on to denounce the "natural imperfection, both in wisdom and judgment and purity of purpose, of all human legislation, exposed constantly to the pressure of partial interest; interests which, at the same time that they are essentially selfish and tyrannical, are ever vigilant, persevering, and subtle in all the arts of deception and corruption."

Democrats argued that the Whig belief in benign government and social harmony was absurd. Corporate charters, privileged banks, and subsidies to turnpike, canal, and railroad companies, they said, benefited privileged insiders and transformed republican government into an engine of inequality. Granting such privileges, warned one Democrat, was sure "to break up that social equality which is the legitimate foundation of our institutions, and the destruction of which would render our boasted freedom a mere phantom." George Bancroft, a radical Democrat from Massachusetts, concurred: "A republican people," he said, "should be in an equality in their social and political condition; . . . pure democracy inculcates equal rights—equal laws—equal means of education—and *equal means* of wealth also." By contrast, the government favored by the Whigs would enrich a favored few. Bancroft and other Democrats demanded limited government that was deaf to the demands of special interests.

Banks

Andrew Jackson's national administration destroyed the Bank of the United States (see chapter 12). As a result, regulation of banking, credit, and currency fell to the state governments. The proper role of banks emerged as a central political issue in nearly every state, particularly after the widespread bank failures following the crash of 1837. Whigs defended banks as agents of economic progress, arguing that they provided credit for roads and canals, loans to businessmen and commercial farmers, and the banknotes that served as the chief medium of exchange. Democrats, on the other hand, branded banks as agents of inequality dominated by insiders who controlled artificial concentrations of money, who enjoyed chartered privileges, and who issued banknotes and expanded or contracted credit to their own advantage. In short, they regarded banks as government-protected institutions that enabled a privileged few to make themselves rich at the public's expense.

The economic boom of the 1830s and the destruction of the national bank created a dramatic expansion in the number of state-chartered banks—from 329 in 1830 to 788 in 1837. Systems varied from state to state. South Carolina, Georgia, Tennessee, Kentucky, and Arkansas had state-owned banks. Many new banks in the Old Northwest were also partially state-owned. Such banks often operated as public-service institutions. Georgia's Central Bank, for example, served farmers who could not qualify for private loans, as did other state-owned banks in the South. The charter of the Agricultural Bank of Mississippi (1833) stipulated that at least half of the bank's capital be in long-term loans (farm mortgages) rather than in short-term loans to merchants.

Beginning in the 1820s, many states had introduced uniform banking laws to replace the unique charters previously granted to individual banks. The new laws tried to stabilize currency and credit. In New York, the Safety-Fund Law of 1829 required banks to pool a fraction of their resources to protect both bankers and small noteholders in the case of bank failures. The result was a self-regulating and conservative community of state banks. Laws in other states required that banks maintain a high ratio of specie (precious metals) to notes in circulation. Such laws, however, were often evaded. Michigan's bank inspectors, for instance, complained that the same cache of silver and gold was taken from bank to bank one step ahead of them. At one bank, an inspector encountered a bank teller who had 10 metal boxes behind his counter. The teller opened one of the boxes and showed that it was full of federal silver dollars. The wary inspector picked up another one and found that it was full of nails covered with a thin layer of silver dollars. All of the other boxes were the same, except for one that was filled with broken glass. Many Americans greeted such stories with a knowing wink until the Panic of 1837, when they presented state banknotes for redemption in specie and were turned down.

"Hard Money" Democrats (those who wanted to get rid of paper money altogether) regarded banks as centers of trickery and privilege and proposed that they be abolished. Banks, they claimed, with their manipulation of credit and currency, encouraged speculation, luxury, inequality, and the separation of wealth from real work. Jackson branded banks "a perfect humbug." An Alabama Democrat declared that banking was "in conflict with justice, equity, morality and religion" and that there was "nothing evil that it does not aid—nothing good that it is not averse to." Senator Bedford Brown of North Carolina doubted "whether banking institutions were at all compatible with the existence of a truly republican government," and Richard Swinton of Iowa dismissed banks as "a set of swindling machines." Samuel Medary of Ohio cast banks as the villains of Democratic melodrama. Banks possess, Medary wrote, "every inducement to attract the confidence of the unwary and seduce into their grasp the most watchful and shrewd, by the convenience and safety they hold out to the public through a thousand pretenses of being the exclusive friends and engines of trade and commerce."

In state legislatures, Whigs defended what had become a roughly standard system of private banks chartered by state governments. They had the right to circulate banknotes and had limited liability to protect directors and stockholders from debts incurred by their bank. Many Democrats proposed abolishing all banks. Others proposed reforms. They demanded a high ratio of specie reserves to banknotes as a guard against inflationary paper money. They proposed eliminating the issuance of banknotes in small denominations, thus ensuring that day-to-day business would be conducted in hard coin and protecting wage earners and small farmers from speculative ups and downs. Democrats also wanted to hold bank directors and stockholders responsible for corporate debts and bankruptcies; some proposed banning corporate charters altogether.

By these and other means, Democrats in the states protected currency and credit from the government favoritism, dishonesty, and elitism that, they argued, enriched Whig insiders and impoverished honest Democrats. Whigs responded that corporate privileges and immunities and an abundant, elastic currency were keys to economic development, and they fought Democrats every step of the way.

Internal Improvements

Democrats in Congress and the White House blocked federally funded roads and canals (see chapter 12). In response, the states launched the transportation revolution themselves, either by taking direct action or by chartering private corporations to do the work (see chapter 9). State legislatures everywhere debated the wisdom of direct state action, of corporate privileges, of subsidies to canals and

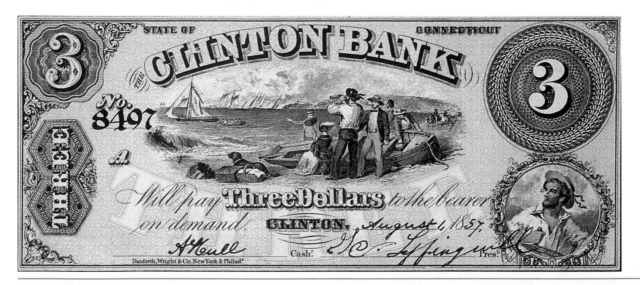

A THREE-DOLLAR BILL
This three-dollar bill was no joke. It was one of the small private banknotes that Democrats wanted to take out of circulation.

railroads, and of the accumulation of government debt. Whigs, predictably, favored direct action by state governments. Democrats were lukewarm toward the whole idea of internal improvements, convinced that debt, favoritism, and corruption would inevitably result from government involvement in the economy.

Whigs assumed a connection between market society and moral progress—and used that relationship as a basis of their argument for internal improvements. William H. Seward, the Whig governor of New York, supported transportation projects because they broke down neighborhood isolation and hastened the emergence of a market society with "all the consequent advantages of morality, piety, and knowledge." The historian Henry Adams, who grew up in a wealthy Whig household in Boston, later recalled that his father had taught him about a strong connection between good roads and good morals. In the minds of Whig legislators, a vote for internal improvements was a vote for moral progress and for individual opportunity within a prosperous and happily interdependent market society.

Democratic state legislators, although with less enthusiasm, supported at least some internal improvements, but they opposed "partial" legislation that would benefit part of their state at the expense of the rest. They also opposed projects that would lead to higher taxes and put state governments into debt—arguments that gathered force after the crash of 1837 bankrupted states that had overextended themselves in the canal boom of the 1830s. The Democrats made the same argument in every state: Beneath Whig plans for extensive improvements lay schemes to create special privilege, inequality, debt, and corruption—all at the expense of a hoodwinked people.

The Politics of Social Reform

In the North, the churchgoing middle class provided the Whig Party with a political culture, a reform-oriented social agenda, and most of its electoral support. Whig evangelicals believed that with God's help they could improve the world by improving the individuals within it, and they enlisted the Whig Party in that campaign. On a variety of issues, including prostitution, temperance, public education, and state-supported insane asylums and penitentiaries, Whigs used government to improve individual morality and discipline. Democrats, on the other hand, argued that attempts to dictate morality through legislation were both antirepublican and wrong. Questions of social reform provoked the most angry differences between Democrats and Whigs, particularly in the North.

Public Schools

During the second quarter of the 19th century, local and state governments built systems of tax-supported public schools, known as "common" schools. Before that time, most children learned reading, writing, and arithmetic at home, in poorly staffed town schools, in private schools, or in charity schools run by churches or other benevolent organizations. Despite the lack of any system of education, most children learned to read and write. That was, however, more likely among boys than among girls, among whites than among blacks, and among northeasterners than among westerners or southerners.

By the 1830s, Whigs and Democrats agreed that providing common schools was a proper function of government. And Democrats often agreed with Whigs that schools could equalize opportunity. Massachusetts Democrat Robert Rantoul, for example, believed that rich and poor children should "be brought equally and together up to the starting point at the public expense; after that we must shift for ourselves." More radical Democrats, however, wanted public schooling that would erase snobbery. A newspaper declared in 1828 that "the children of the rich and the poor shall receive a national education, calculated to make republicans and banish aristocrats." Marcus Morton, Democratic governor of Massachusetts, agreed that it was the job of the common schools to democratize children "before the pride of family or wealth, or other adventitious distinction has taken a deep root in the young heart."

The reformers who created the most advanced, expensive, and centralized state school systems were Whigs: Horace Mann of Massachusetts, Henry Barnard of Connecticut, Calvin Stowe (husband of Harriet Beecher) of Ohio, and others. These reformers talked more about character building and Whig Protestant culture than about the three R's, convinced that it was the schools' first duty to train youngsters to respect authority, property, hard work, and social order. They wanted schools that would downplay class divisions, but they were interested less in democratizing wealthy children than in civilizing the poor. Calvin H. Wiley, the Whig superintendent of schools in North Carolina, promised that proper schools would make Americans "homogeneous . . . intelligent, eminently republican, sober, calculating, moral and conservative." A Whig newspaper in Ohio declared in 1836 that character-building schools were essential in a democracy: "Other nations have hereditary sovereigns, and one of the most important duties of their governments is to take care of the education of the heir to their throne; these children all about your streets . . . are your future sovereigns." William Seward, the Whig governor of New York, insisted that "education

THE EUREKA SCHOOLHOUSE IN SPRINGFIELD, VERMONT
Mandated by state law and supported by local taxes, such one-room schools taught generations of American children the three R's.

North Wind Picture Archives.

tends to produce equality, not by leveling all to the condition of the base, but by elevating all to the association of the wise and good."

The schools taught a basic Whig axiom: that social questions could be reduced to questions of individual character. A textbook entitled *The Thinker, A Moral Reader* (1855) told children to "remember that all the ignorance, degradation, and misery in the world, is the result of indolence and vice." To teach that lesson, the schools had children read from the King James Bible and recite prayers acceptable to all of the Protestant sects. Such texts reaffirmed a common Protestant morality while avoiding divisive doctrinal matters. Until the arrival of significant numbers of Catholic immigrants in the 1840s and 1850s, few parents complained about Protestant religious instruction in the public schools.

Political differences centered less on curriculum than on organization. Whigs wanted state-level centralization and proposed state superintendents and state boards of education, normal schools (state teachers' colleges), texts chosen at the state level and used throughout the state, and uniform school terms. They also (often with the help of economy-minded Democrats) recruited young women as teachers. In addition to fostering Protestant morality in the schools, these women were a source of cheap labor: Salaries for female teachers in the northern states ranged from 40 to 60 percent lower than the salaries of their male coworkers. Largely as a result, the proportion of women among Massachusetts teachers rose from 56 percent in 1834 to 78 percent in 1860.

Democrats objected to the Whigs' insistence on centralization as elitist, intrusive, and expensive. They preferred to give power to individual school districts, thus enabling local school committees to tailor the curriculum, the length of the school year, and the choice of teachers and texts to local needs. Centralization, they argued, would create a metropolitan educational culture that served the purposes of the rich but ignored the preferences of farmers and working people. It was standard Democratic social policy: inexpensive government and local control. Henry Barnard, Connecticut's superintendent of schools, called his Democratic opponents "ignorant demagogues" and "a set of blockheads." Horace Mann denounced them as "political madmen." As early as 1826, Thaddeus Stevens, who would become a prominent Pennsylvania Whig, argued that voters must "learn to dread ignorance more than taxation."

Ethnicity, Religion, and the Schools

The argument between Whig centralism and Democratic parsimony dominated the debate over public education until the children of Irish and German immigrants began to enter schools by the thousands in the mid-1840s. Most immigrant families were poor and relied on their children to work and supplement the family income. Consequently, the children's attendance at school was irregular at best. Moreover, most immigrants were Catholics. The Irish regarded Protestant prayers and the King James Bible as heresies and as hated tools of British oppression. Some of the textbooks were worse. Olney's *Practical System of Modern Geography*, a standard textbook, declared that "the Irish in general are quick of apprehension, active, brave and hospitable; but passionate, ignorant, vain, and superstitious." A nun in Connecticut complained that Irish children in the public schools "see their parents looked upon as an inferior race."

Many Catholic parents simply refused to send their children to school. Others demanded changes in textbooks, the elimination of the King James Bible (perhaps to be replaced by the Douay Bible), tax-supported Catholic schools, or at least tax relief for parents who sent their children to parish schools. Whigs, joined by many native-born Democrats, saw Catholic complaints as popish assaults on the Protestantism that they insisted was at the heart of American republicanism.

Many school districts, particularly in the rural areas to which many Scandinavian and German immigrants found their way, created foreign-language schools and provided bilingual instruction. In other places, state support for church-run charity schools persisted. For example, both Catholic and Protestant schools received such assistance in New York City until 1825, and in Lowell, Massachusetts; Hartford and Middletown, Connecticut; and Milwaukee, Wisconsin, at various times from the 1830s through the 1860s. New Jersey extended state support to Catholic as well as other church schools until 1866. In northeastern cities, however, where immigrant Catholics often formed militant local majorities, such demands led to violence and to organized nativist (anti-immigrant) politics. In 1844, the Native American Party, with the endorsement of the Whigs, won the New York City elections. That same year in Philadelphia, riots that pitted avowedly Whig Protestants against Catholic immigrants, ostensibly over the issue of Bible reading in schools, killed 13 people. Such conflicts would severely damage the northern Democratic coalition in the 1850s (see chapter 13).

Prisons

From the 1820s onward, state governments built institutions to house orphans, the dependent poor, the insane, and criminals. The Market Revolution increased the numbers of such persons and made them more visible, more anonymous, and more separated from family and community resources. Americans in the 18th century (and many in the 19th century as well) had assumed that poverty, crime, insanity, and other social ills were among God's ways of punishing sin and testing the human capacity for both suffering and charity. By the 1820s,

however, reformers were arguing that deviance was the result of childhood deprivation. "Normal" people, they suggested, learned discipline and respect for work, property, laws, and other people from their parents. Deviants were the products of brutal, often drunken households devoid of parental love and discipline. The cure was to place them in a controlled setting, teach them work and discipline, and turn them into useful citizens.

In state legislatures, Whigs favored putting deviants in institutions for rehabilitation. Democrats, although they agreed that the states should care for criminals and dependents, regarded attempts at rehabilitation as wrongheaded and expensive; they favored institutions that isolated the insane, warehoused the dependent poor, and punished criminals. Most state systems were a compromise between the two positions.

Pennsylvania built prisons at Pittsburgh (1826) and Philadelphia (1829) that put solitary prisoners into cells to contemplate their misdeeds and to plot a new life. The results of such solitary confinement included few reformations and numerous attempts at suicide. Only New Jersey imitated the Pennsylvania system. Far more common were institutions based on the model developed in New York at Auburn (1819) and Sing Sing (1825). In the Auburn system, prisoners slept in solitary cells and marched in military formation to meals and workshops; they were forbidden to speak to one another at any time. The rule of silence, it was believed, encouraged both discipline and contemplation. The French writer Alexis de Tocqueville, visiting a New York prison in 1830, remarked that "the silence within these vast walls . . . is that of death. . . . There

Prisoners at the State Prison at Auburn.

The Granger Collection, New York.

AUBURN PRISON
Inmates at New York's Auburn Prison were forbidden to speak and were marched in lockstep between workshops, dining halls, and their cells.

were a thousand living beings, and yet it was a vast desert solitude."

The Auburn system was designed both to reform criminals and to reduce expenses, for the prisons sold workshop products to the outside. Between these two goals, Whigs favored rehabilitation. Democrats favored profit-making workshops, and thus lower operating costs and lower taxes. Robert Wiltse, named by the Democrats to run Sing Sing prison in the 1830s, used harsh punishments (including flogging and starving), sparse meals, and forced labor to punish criminals and make the prison pay for itself. In 1839, William Seward, as the newly elected Whig governor of New York, fired Wiltse and appointed administrators who substituted privileges and rewards for punishment and emphasized rehabilitation over profit making. They provided religious instruction; they improved food and working conditions; and they cut back on the use of flogging. When Democrats took back the statehouse in the 1842 elections, they discovered that the Whigs' brief experiment in kindness had produced a $50,000 deficit, so they swiftly reinstated the old regime.

Asylums

The leading advocate of humane treatment for people deemed to be insane was Dorothea Dix, a Boston humanitarian who was shocked by the incarceration and abuse of the insane in common jails. She traveled throughout the country urging citizens to pressure their state legislatures into building asylums committed to what reformers called "moral treatment." The asylums were to be clean and pleasant places, preferably outside the cities, and the inmates were to be treated humanely. Attendants were not to beat inmates or tie them up, although they could use cold showers as a form of discipline. Dix and other reformers wanted the asylums to be safe, nurturing environments in which people with mental illness could be made well.

By 1860, the legislatures of 28 of the 33 states had established state-run insane asylums. Whig legislators, with minimal support from Democrats, approved appropriations for the more expensive and humane moral treatment facilities. Occasionally, however, Dorothea Dix won Democratic support as well. In North Carolina, she befriended the wife of a powerful Democratic legislator as the woman lay on her deathbed; the dying woman convinced her husband to support building an asylum. His impassioned speech won the approval of the lower house for a state asylum to be named Dix Hill. In the North Carolina senate, however, the proposal was supported by 91 percent of the Whigs and only 14 percent of the Democrats—a partisan division that was repeated in state after state.

THE WHIPPING POST AND PILLORY AT NEW CASTLE, DELAWARE

Delaware was a slave state that continued to inflict public, corporal punishment on lawbreakers. Many of the witnesses to the whipping depicted here are small children, who are supposedly learning a lesson.

The South and Social Reform

On most economic issues, southern state legislatures divided along the same lines as northern legislatures: Whigs wanted government participation in the economy, Democrats did not. On social questions, however, southern Whigs and Democrats responded in distinctly southern ways. The South was a rural, culturally conservative region of patriarchal households that viewed every attempt at government intervention as a threat to independence. Most southern voters, Whigs as well as Democrats, perceived attempts at "social improvement" as expensive and wrong-headed.

The southern states enacted school laws and drew up blueprints for state school systems, but the culturally homogeneous white South had little need for schools to enforce a common culture. Moreover, the South had less money and less faith in government. Consequently, southern schools tended to be locally controlled, to be infused with southern evangelical culture, and to have a limited curriculum and a short school year. In 1860, northern children attended school for an average of more than 50 days a year; white children in the South attended school for an average of 10 days annually.

By 1860, every slave state except Florida (which had a tiny population) and the Carolinas operated prisons modeled on the Auburn system. Here, however, prisons stressed punishment and profits over rehabilitation. Although some southerners favored northern-style reforms, they knew that southern voters would reject them. Popular votes in Alabama in 1834 and in North Carolina in 1846 brought in resounding defeats for proposals to build or reform penitentiaries in those states. While northern evangelicals were preaching that criminals could be rescued, southern preachers demanded Old Testament vengeance, arguing that hanging, whipping, and branding were sanctioned by the Bible, inexpensive, and more effective than mere incarceration. Other southerners, defending the code of honor, charged that victims and their relatives would be denied vengeance if criminals were tucked away in prisons. Some southern prisons leased prison labor (and sometimes whole prisons) to private entrepreneurs, and dreams of reforming southern criminals were forgotten.

The South did participate in temperance—the all-consuming reform that is discussed in the next section. By the 1820s, Baptists and Methodists had made deep inroads into southern society. Southern ministers preached against dueling, fighting, dancing, gambling, and drinking, while churchgoing women discouraged their husbands, sons, and suitors from drinking. Many southern men either stopped drinking altogether or sharply reduced their consumption. Accordingly, the South contributed its share to the national drop in alcohol consumption. During the 1840s, the Washington Temperance Society and other voluntary temperance groups won a solid footing in southern towns, but southern religious and temperance organizations were based on individual decisions to abstain. Legal prohibition, which became dominant in the North, got nowhere in the South. In the 1850s, when one northern legislature after another passed statewide prohibition, the only slave state to follow was tiny, northern-oriented Delaware.

At bottom, southern resistance to social reform stemmed from a conservative, Bible-based acceptance of suffering and human imperfection and a commitment to the power and independence of white men who headed families. Any proposal that sounded like social tinkering or the invasion of paternal rights was doomed to failure. To make matters worse, many reforms—public schools, Sunday schools, prohibitionism, humane asylums—were seen as the work of well-funded and well-organized missionaries from the Northeast who wanted to fashion society in their own self-righteous image. The southern distrust of reform was powerfully reinforced after 1830, when northern reformers began to call for abolition of slavery and equality of the sexes—reforms most white southerners found unthinkable.

● Excursus: The Politics of Alcohol

Central to party formation in the North was the fight between evangelical Whigs who demanded that government regulate public (and often private) morality and Democrats who feared both big government and the Whig cultural agenda. The most persistent issue in the argument was the question of alcohol—so much so that in many places the temperance question defined the differences between Democrats and Whigs.

Ardent Spirits

Drinking had been a part of social life since the beginning of English settlement, but the withering of authority and the disruptions of the Market Revolution led to increased consumption, increased public drunkenness, and a perceived increase in alcohol-led violence and social problems (see chapter 7). Beginning in the 1790s, physicians and a few clergymen attacked not only habitual drunkenness but also alcohol itself. And for a short time after 1812, Federalist politicians and Congregational clergymen formed "moral societies" in New England that discouraged strong drink. Their imperious tone and their association with the old seats of authority, however, doomed them to failure.

The temperance crusade began in earnest in 1826, when northeastern evangelicals founded the American Society for the Promotion of Temperance (soon renamed the American Temperance Society). The movement's manifesto was Lyman Beecher's *Six Sermons on the Nature, Occasions, Signs, Evils, and Remedy of Intemperance* (1826). Addressing the churchgoing middle class, Beecher declared alcohol an addictive drug and warned that even moderate drinkers risked becoming hopeless drunkards. Thus temperance, like other evangelical reforms, was presented as a contest between self-control and slavery to one's appetites. By encouraging total abstinence, reformers hoped to halt the creation of new drunkards while the old ones died out. Even though Beecher pinned his hopes on self-discipline, he wanted middle-class abstainers to spread reform through both example and coercion. As middle-class evangelicals eliminated alcohol from their own lives, they would cease to offer it to their guests, buy or sell it, or provide it to their employees, and they would encourage their friends to do the same.

THE DRUNKARD'S PROGRESS

This popular print describes the drunkard's progression from social drinking to alcoholism, isolation, crime, and death by suicide. His desolate wife and daughter and his burning house are at bottom.

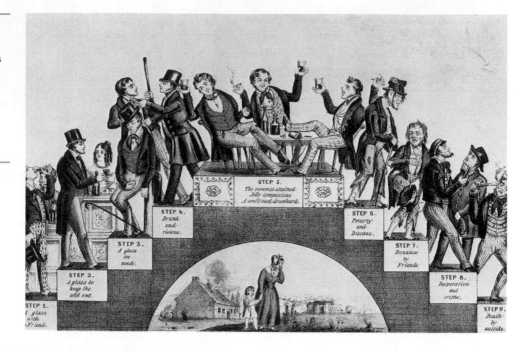

In the atmosphere surrounding the middle-class revivals of the 1820s and 1830s, Beecher's crusade gathered strength. Charles Grandison Finney (see chapter 10), in his revival at Rochester, made total abstinence a condition of conversion. Many other ministers and churches followed suit, and by the mid-1830s, members of the middle class had largely disengaged themselves from alcohol and from the people who drank it. Following a temperance lecture by Finney's coworker Theodore Dwight Weld, for instance, Rochester grocers Elijah and Albert Smith rolled their stock of whiskey out on the sidewalk, smashed the barrels, and let the liquor spill into the street. Other merchants threw their liquor into the Erie Canal or sold it off at cost. Hundreds of evangelical businessmen pledged that they would refuse to rent to merchants who sold liquor, sell grain to distillers, or enter a store that sold alcohol. Many of them made abstinence a condition of employment, placing ads that carried the line "None But Temperate Men Need Apply." Abstinence and opposition to the use of distilled spirits (people continued to argue about wine and beer) had become a badge of middle-class respectability.

Among themselves, the reformers achieved considerable success. By 1835, the American Temperance Society claimed 1.5 million members and estimated that 2 million Americans had renounced ardent spirits (whiskey, rum, and other distilled liquors); 250,000 had formally pledged to completely abstain from alcohol. The society further estimated that 4,000 distilleries had gone out of business, and that many of the survivors had cut back their production. Many politicians no longer bought drinks to win vot-

ers to their cause. The Kentucky Whig Henry Clay, once known for keeping late hours, began to serve only cold water when he entertained at dinner. And in 1833, members of Congress formed the American Congressional Temperance Society. The U.S. Army put an end to the age-old liquor ration in 1832, and increasing numbers of militia officers stopped supplying their men with whiskey. The annual consumption of alcohol, which had reached an all-time high in the 1820s, dropped by more than half in the 1830s (from 3.9 gallons of pure alcohol per adult in 1830 to 1.8 gallons in 1840).

The Origins of Prohibition

In the middle 1830s, Whigs made temperance a political issue. Realizing that voluntary abstinence would not put an end to drunkenness, Whig evangelicals drafted coercive, prohibitionist legislation. First, they attacked the licenses granting grocery stores and taverns the right to sell liquor by the drink and to permit it to be consumed on the premises. The licenses were important sources of revenue for local governments. They also gave local authorities the power to cancel the licenses of troublesome establishments. Militant temperance advocates, usually in association with local Whigs, demanded that the authorities use that power to outlaw all public drinking places. In communities throughout the North, the licensing issue, always freighted with angry divisions over religion and social class, became the issue around which local parties organized. The question first reached the state level in Massachusetts, when in 1838 a Whig legislature passed the

Fifteen-Gallon Law, which decreed that merchants could sell ardent spirits only in quantities of 15 gallons or more, thus outlawing every public drinking place in the state. In 1839, Massachusetts voters sent enough Democrats to the legislature to rescind the law.

The Whig attempt to cancel tavern licenses proved unenforceable because proprietors simply operated without licenses or found ways to get around the laws. While the Massachusetts Fifteen-Gallon Law was in effect, one Boston tavern keeper painted stripes on a pig and charged patrons an admission fee of six cents (the old price of a drink) to view the "exhibition." He then provided customers—who paid over and over to see the pig—with a "complimentary" glass of whiskey.

Leading Democrats agreed with Whigs that Americans drank too much, but whereas Whigs insisted that regulating morality was a proper function of government, Democrats warned that government intrusion into areas of private choice would violate republican liberties. The Democrats of Rochester, New York, responding to the license issue, made the following declaration:

> Anything which savours of restraint in what men deem their natural rights is sure to meet with opposition, and men convinced of error by force will most likely continue all their lives unconvinced in their reason. Whatever shall be done to stay the tide of intemperance, and roll back its destroying wave, must be done by suasive appeals to the reason, the interest, or the pride of men; but not by force.

In many communities, alcohol became the defining difference between Democrats and Whigs. In 1834, for instance, a Whig campaign worker ventured into a poor neighborhood in Rochester and asked a woman how her husband planned to vote. "Why, he has always been Jackson," she said, "and I don't think he's joined the Cold Water."

The Democratization of Temperance

Democratic voters held ambiguous attitudes toward temperance. Many of them continued to drink, while many others voluntarily abstained or cut down. Yet almost without exception they resented the coercive tactics of the Whigs and supported their party's pledge to protect them from evangelical meddling in their private lives. In 1830, when Lyman Beecher's Hanover Street Church in Boston caught fire, the volunteer fire companies (which doubled as working-class drinking clubs) arrived, noted that it was the hated Beecher's church, and made no effort to put out the fire. Unbeknownst to the Reverend Beecher, the church had rented basement space to a merchant who used it to store barrels of rum. According to a contemporary report,

the crowd that gathered to watch the church burn to the ground cheered as the barrels exploded one by one.

Democrats, despite their opposition to prohibition, often spoke out against drunkenness. Many craft unions denied membership to heavy drinkers, and hundreds of thousands of rural and urban Democrats quietly stopped drinking. (The sharp drop in alcohol consumption in the 1830s can be explained in no other way.) In the late 1830s, former antiprohibitionists launched a temperance movement of their own.

One evening in 1840—in the depths of a devastating economic depression—six craftsmen were drinking at Chase's Tavern in Baltimore. More or less as a joke, they sent one of their number to a nearby temperance lecture; he came back a teetotaler and converted the others. They then drew up a total abstinence pledge and promised to devote themselves to the reform of other drinkers. Within months, from this beginning a national movement had emerged, called the Washington Temperance Society. With a core membership of men who had opposed temperance in the 1830s, the Washingtonians differed from older temperance societies in several ways. First, they identified themselves as members of the laboring classes. Second, they were avowedly nonreligious: Although many of them were churchgoers (usually Methodist or Baptist), many were not, and the Washingtonians avoided religious controversy by avoiding religion. Third, the Washingtonians—at least those who called themselves True Washingtonians—rejected recourse to politics and legislation and concentrated instead on the conversion of drinkers through compassion and persuasion. Finally, they welcomed "hopeless" drunkards—who accounted for about 10 percent of the membership—and hailed them as heroes when they sobered up.

Temperance Schisms

Even though Whig reformers welcomed the Washingtonians at first, they soon had second thoughts. The nonreligious character of the movement disturbed those who saw temperance as an arm of evangelical reform. Previous advocates of temperance had assumed that sobriety would be accompanied by evangelical decorum. Instead, the meetings, picnics, and parades held by the Washingtonians were continuous with a popular culture that Whig evangelicals opposed. While the temperance regulars read pamphlets and listened to lectures by clergymen, lawyers, and doctors, the Washingtonians enjoyed raucous sing-alongs, comedy routines, barnyard imitations, dramatic skits, and even full-dress minstrel shows geared to temperance themes. Meetings featured experience speeches by reformed drunkards. Speaking extemporaneously, they omitted none of the horrors of an alcoholic life—attempts at suicide, friendships betrayed, fathers and mothers desolated, wives beaten and abandoned, children dead of starvation. Although Washingtonians had given up alcohol, their melodramatic tales, street parades, song books, and minstrel shows—even when presented with a Methodist or Baptist accent—were temperance, but not the temperance Lyman Beecher and the Whigs had had in mind.

Nowhere did the Washingtonians differ more sharply from the temperance regulars than in their visions of the reformed life. The Whig reformers tied abstinence to individual ambition and middle-class domesticity. They expected men who quit drinking to withdraw from the male world in which drinking was common and retreat into the comfort of the newly feminized middle-class family. Washingtonians, on the other hand, translated traditional male sociability into sober forms. Moreover, they called former drinkers back to the responsibilities of traditional fatherhood. Their experience stories began with the hurt drunkards had caused their wives and children and ended with their transformation into dependable providers and authoritative fathers. While the Whig temperance regulars tried to extend the ethos of individual ambition and the new middle-class domesticity into society at large, Washingtonians sought to rescue the self-respect and moral authority of working-class fathers.

The Washington Temperance Society collapsed toward the end of the 1840s, but its legacy survived. Among former drinkers in the North, it had introduced a new sense of domestic responsibility and a healthy fear of drunkenness. Consumption of pure alcohol dropped from 1.8 to 1.0 gallons annually in the 1840s. Along the way, the Washingtonians and related groups created a self-consciously respectable native Protestant working class in American cities.

Ethnicity and Alcohol

In the 1840s and 1850s, millions of Irish and German immigrants came pouring into neighborhoods stirred by working-class revivals and temperance agitation. The newcomers had their own time-honored relations to alcohol. The Germans introduced lager beer to the United States, thus providing a wholesome alternative for Americans who wished to give up spirits without joining the teetotalers. The Germans also built old-country beer halls

GERMAN BEER GARDEN

A German brewery and beer garden in antebellum Fort Wayne, Indiana. These were pleasant, landscaped establishments where patrons (most of them German immigrants) could bring their families to stroll the grounds, eat, socialize, listen to music—and drink.

From the Collections of the Library of Congress.

in American cities, complete with sausage counters, oompah bands, group singing, and other family attractions. For their part, the Irish reaffirmed their love of whiskey—a love forged in colonial oppression and in a culture that accepted trouble with resignation—a love that legitimized levels of male drunkenness and violence that Americans, particularly the temperance forces, found appalling. (Differences in immigrant drinking were given architectural expression. German beer halls provided seating arrangements for whole families. Irish bars, on the other hand, provided a bar but no tables or chairs. If a drinker had to sit down, they reasoned, it was time for him to go home.)

In the 1850s, native resentment of Catholic immigrants drove thousands of Baptist and Methodist "respectables" out of the Democratic coalition and into nativist Whig majorities that—beginning with Maine in 1851—established legal prohibition throughout New England, in the middle states, and in the Old Northwest. These often were the Democrats who became part of the North's Republican majority on the eve of the Civil War (see chapter 14).

⊛ The Politics of Race

Most whites in antebellum America believed in "natural" differences based on sex and race. God, they said, had given women and men and whites and blacks different mental, emotional, and physical capacities. And, as human-kind (female and nonwhite more than others) was innately sinful and prone to disorder, God ordained a fixed social hierarchy in which white men exercised power over others. Slaves and free blacks accepted their subordinate status only as a fact of life, not as something that was natural and just. Some women also questioned patriarchy. But before 1830, hierarchy based on sex and race was seldom questioned in public, particularly by persons who were in a position to change it.

In the antebellum years, as southerners and most northerners stiffened their defense of white paternalism, northern Whig evangelicals began to envision a world based on Christian love and individual worth, not inherited status. They transformed marriage from rank domination into a sentimental partnership—unequal, but a partnership nonetheless. They also questioned the more virulent forms of racism. From among the Whig evangelicals emerged a radical minority that envisioned a world without power. While conservative Christians insisted that relations based on dominance and submission were the lot of a sinful humankind, reformers argued that such relations interposed human power, too often in the form of brute force, between God and the individual spirit. They called for a world that substituted spiritual freedom and Christian love for every form of worldly domination. The result was a community of uncompromising radical reformers who attacked slavery and patriarchy as national sins.

Free Blacks

Before the American Revolution, sizable pockets of slavery existed in the northern states, but revolutionary idealism, and the growing belief that slavery was inefficient and unnecessary, led one northern state after another to abolish it. Vermont, with almost no slaves, outlawed slavery in its revolutionary constitution. By 1804, every northern state had taken some action, usually by passing laws that called for gradual emancipation. The first of such laws, and the model for others, was passed in Pennsylvania in 1780. This law freed slaves born after 1780 when they reached their 28th birthday. Slaves born before 1780 would remain slaves, and slave children would remain slaves through their prime working years. Some northern slave owners, in violation of the laws, sold young slaves into the South as their freedom dates approached. Still, the emancipation laws worked: By 1830, only a handful of aging blacks remained slaves in the North.

The rising population of northern free blacks gravitated to the cities. Most of those who had been slaves in cities stayed there. They were joined by thousands of free blacks who decided to abandon the declining northeastern countryside and move to the city. In many cities—Philadelphia and New York City in particular—they met a stream of free blacks and fugitive slaves from the Upper South, where the bonds of slavery were growing tighter, and where free blacks feared reenslavement. Thus, despite the flood of white immigrants from Europe and the American countryside, African Americans constituted a sizable minority in the rapidly expanding cities. New York City's black population, 10.5 percent in 1800, was still 8.8 percent in 1820; Philadelphia, the haven of thousands of southern refugees, was 10.3 percent African American in 1800 and 11.9 percent in 1820.

Blacks in the seaport cities tended to take stable, low-paying jobs. A few became successful (occasionally wealthy) entrepreneurs, and others practiced skilled trades. Many took jobs as waiters or porters in hotels, as barbers, and as butlers, maids, cooks, washerwomen, and coachmen for wealthy families. Others worked as dockworkers, laborers, and sailors. Still others became dealers in used clothing, or draymen with their own carts and horses, or food vendors in the streets and in basement shops (oysters in particular were a black monopoly).

A Black Oyster Seller in Philadelphia, 1814, Watercolor by John Lewis Krimmel. The Metropolitan Museum of Art, Rogers Fund, 1942. (42.95.18).

A BLACK STREET VENDOR, SELLING OYSTERS IN PHILADELPHIA, CIRCA 1814

In early 19th-century New York and Philadelphia, African Americans monopolized the public sale of oysters and clams.

Discrimination

From the 1820s onward, however, the growing numbers of white wage-workers began to edge blacks out of their jobs by underselling them, by pressuring employers to discriminate, and by outright violence. As a result, African Americans were almost completely eliminated from the skilled trades, and many unskilled and semiskilled blacks lost their jobs on the docks, in warehouses, and in the merchant marine. In 1834, a Philadelphian reported that "colored persons, when engaged in their usual occupations, were repeatedly assailed and maltreated, usually on the [waterfront]. Parties of white men have insisted that no blacks shall be employed in certain departments of labor." And as their old jobs disappeared, blacks were systematically excluded from the new jobs opening up in factories. By the 1830s, black workers in Philadelphia were noting "the difficulty of getting places for our sons as apprentices . . . owing to the prejudices with which we have to contend." In 1838 (during a depression that hit blacks first and hardest), an African American newspaper complained that blacks "have ceased to be hackney coachmen and draymen, and they are now almost displaced as stevedores. They are rapidly losing their places as barbers and servants. Ten families employ white servants now, where one did 20 years ago."

The depression was followed by waves of desperately poor Irish immigrants. By accepting low wages, and by rioting, intimidation, gunplay, and even murder, the Irish displaced most of the remaining blacks from their toehold in the economic life of the northeastern cities. An observer of the Philadelphia docks remarked in 1849 that "when a few years ago we saw none but Blacks, we now see none but Irish."

Meanwhile, official discrimination against blacks was on the rise. Political democratization for white men was accompanied by the disenfranchisement of blacks (see chapter 7). Cities either excluded black children from public schools or set up segregated schools. In 1845, when Massachusetts passed a law declaring that all children had the right to attend neighborhood schools, the Boston School Committee blithely ruled that the law did not apply to blacks. Blacks were also excluded from white churches or sat in segregated pews; even the Quakers seated blacks and whites separately.

African Americans responded by building institutions of their own. At one end were black-owned gambling houses, saloons, brothels, and dance halls—the only racially integrated institutions to be found in most cities. At the other end were black churches, schools, social clubs, and lodges. The first independent black church was the African Church of Philadelphia, founded in 1790; the African Methodist Episcopal Church, a national denomination still in existence, was founded in Philadelphia in 1816. Schools and relief societies, usually associated with churches, grew quickly. Black Masonic lodges attracted hundreds of members. Many of the churches and social organizations were given names that proudly called up the blacks' African origins. In Philadelphia, for instance, there were African Methodists, Abyssinian Baptists, and the African Dorcas Society, to name only a few.

Northern blacks also organized to fight slavery and discrimination. Perhaps the most radical of them was David Walker, a Boston used-clothing dealer whose *Appeal to the Colored Citizens of the World* (1829) urged blacks to revolt against slavery. (Soon thereafter, Walker was murdered under mysterious circumstances.) Others, including the escaped slave Harriet Tubman, operated the Underground Railroad, a system of antislavery activists and safe hiding places that smuggled runaway slaves out of the South, through the North, and into Canada. Some worked, like the former New York slave and religious mystic Sojourner Truth, to direct the attention of both black and white religious reformers to the problem of slavery. In Rochester, escaped Maryland slave Frederick Douglass published an antislavery newspaper and forayed throughout the North to lecture black and white audiences on the evils of slavery and discrimination. Thus from within the limited freedom provided by northern society, free blacks—sometimes alone, sometimes in combination with white abolitionists—combated southern slavery and northern discrimination.

Democratic Racism

Neither the Whigs nor the Democrats encouraged the aspirations of slaves or free blacks. But it was the Democrats, from their beginnings in the 1820s, who incorporated racism into their political agenda. Minstrel shows, for example, often reflected the Democratic line on current events, and Democratic cartoonists often featured minstrelsy's bug-eyed, woolly-haired caricatures of blacks. By the time of the Civil War, Democrats mobilized voters almost solely with threats of "amalgamation" and "Negro rule."

Democrats also contributed to the rising tide of antiblack violence. The Whigs had plenty of racists, but Democrats appear to have predominated when mobs moved into black neighborhoods, sometimes burning out whole areas. Many Democrats lumped together evangelical reformers, genteel Whigs, and blacks as a unified threat to the white republic. In July 1834, a New York City mob sacked the house of abolitionist Lewis Tappan, moved on to Charles Finney's Chatham Street Chapel, where aboli-

AMERICANS ABROAD

Frederick Douglass in Great Britain

The escaped slave and antislavery lecturer Frederick Douglass made a potentially dangerous move in 1845: To refute rumors that no one with his education and self-possession could ever have been a slave, he published a book detailing his experiences in bondage on Maryland's Eastern Shore. He and his abolitionist friends worried that he would be targeted by slave-catchers and returned to slavery under the laws of the United States. Early in 1845, he determined "to seek a refuge from republican slavery in monarchical England." He stayed in Britain, lecturing on slavery and meeting with writers and reformers, for 21 months.

On the ship going over (it was one of the early Cunard steamers), Douglass was excluded from the cabins and forced to travel in steerage. He was, however, invited to deliver an abolitionist lecture to the passengers. A few southerners ("under the inspiration of *slavery* and *brandy*," Douglass tells us) threatened to throw him overboard. The Captain prevented that, but the incident was publicized when the ship reached Britain, providing Douglass with large, curious, and sympathetic audiences that he might not otherwise have had. Douglass enjoyed Great Britain: well-heeled abolitionists escorted him to concerts, restaurants, and hotels. Gentlemen invited him into their great houses, and wealthy friends raised money to fund Douglass as an antislavery journalist and publisher upon his return to the United States. As a final gesture, they bought Douglass from his old master and gave him to himself. "Whatever may be said of the aristocracies here," said Douglass, "there is none based on the color of a man's skin. This species of belongs pre-eminently to 'the land of the free, and the home of the brave.'"

Proslavery Americans heard that Frederick Douglass was preaching against the republic to crowds of British monarchists. True, Douglass had written his abolitionist friend William Lloyd Garrison that "Instead of a democratic government, I am under a monarchical government. . . . I breathe, and lo! The chattel becomes a man." But he insisted that his British listeners were "about as good republicans as the mass of Americans, and with this decided advantage over the latter—they are lovers of republicanism for all men, for black men as well as for white men. They are the people who sympathize with . . . the oppressed and enslaved, of every color and nation, the world over." Douglass was an escaped slave and an internationalist democrat. He could not be an American patriot. "If I ever had any patriotism . . . it was whipped out of me long since, by the lash of the American soul-drivers." He knew that America was home, but "America will not allow her children to love her."

Douglass returned to America in spring 1847 on the same ship that had brought him to Britain. Again, he was barred from occupying a cabin.

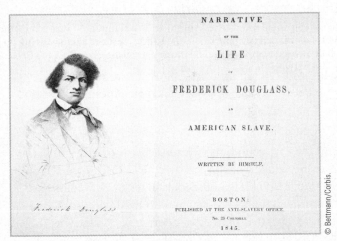

Frederick Douglass's 1845 autobiography.

---

tionists were said to be meeting, and finished the evening by attacking a British actor at the Bowery Theater. The manager saved his theater by waving two American flags and ordering an American actor to perform popular minstrel routines for the mob. In Jackson, Michigan, in 1839, after the local Sunday schools announced an outdoor meeting featuring temperance and antislavery speakers, antievangelical rowdies removed the benches from the meeting ground the night before and burned them in the town square. They then dug up the corpse of a black man who had been buried a few days earlier and propped him up in the pulpit of the Presbyterian church, where he greeted the Sunday school the next morning.

The first major American race riot broke out in Philadelphia in 1834 between working-class whites and blacks at a street carnival. Although blacks seemed to have

The Library Company of Philadelphia.

THE ATTACK ON THE CALIFORNIA HOUSE

In the big antebellum cities, volunteer fire companies were often ethnic clubs, and many were tied to street gangs. In 1849, a Philadelphia Irish gang called the Killers, some of them wearing their fire hats and carrying their fire horns, attacked a black-owned gambling and drinking establishment called the California House. The blacks (and apparently some of their white patrons) fought back with guns.

won the first round, the whites refused to accept defeat. Over the next few nights, they wrecked a black-owned tavern; broke into black households to terrorize families and steal property; attacked whites who lived with, socialized with, or operated businesses catering to blacks; wrecked the African Presbyterian Church; and destroyed a black church on Wharton Street by sawing through its timbers and pulling it down. Sporadic racial violence wracked the city throughout the 1830s and 1840s, reaching its height in 1849. That summer a firehouse gang of Irish immigrants calling themselves "the Killers" attacked the California House, a black-owned tavern and gambling hall. The black patrons had anticipated the attack and had armed themselves, and in the melee five Killers were shot. For two months, tempers simmered. Finally, the Killers set a fire at the California House that spread to nearby houses. They fought off neighborhood blacks, rival firemen, and the police. The riot ended only when the city sent in four companies of militia.

Conceptions of Racial Difference

Meanwhile, educated whites were being taught to think in racist terms. Among most scientists, biological determinism replaced historical and environmental explanations of racial differences; many argued that whites and blacks were separate species. Democrats welcomed that "discovery." John Van Evrie, a New York doctor and Democratic pamphleteer, declared that "it is a palpable and unavoidable fact that Negroes are a different species," and that the story of Adam and Eve referred only to the origin of white people. In 1850, the *Democratic Review* confided, "Few or none now seriously adhere to the theory of the unity of the races. The whole state of the science at this moment seems to indicate that there are several distinct races of men on the earth, with entirely different capacities, physical and mental."

As whites came to perceive racial differences as God-given and immutable, they changed the nature of those differences as well. In the 18th and early 19th centuries, whites had stereotyped blacks as ignorant and prone to drunkenness and thievery, but they had also maintained a parallel stereotype of blacks as loyal and self-sacrificing servants. From the 1820s onward, racists continued to regard blacks as incompetent, but they found it harder to distinguish mere carelessness from dishonesty. Now they saw all blacks as treacherous, shrewd, and secretive—individuals who only *pretended* to feel loyalty to white families and affection for the white children they took care of, while awaiting the chance to steal from them or poison them. The writer Herman Melville, a lifelong Democrat who shared little of his compatriots' racism but who helped codify their fascination with duplicity and deceit, dramatized these fears in *Benito Cereno,* a novel about slaves who commandeered a sailing ship and its captain and crew, then (with knives secretly at the throats of their captives) acted out a servile charade for unsuspecting visitors who came aboard.

Above all, Democratic ideologues pronounced blacks unfit to be citizens of the white man's republic. Whigs often supported various forms of black suffrage; Democrats uniformly opposed it. Their insistence that blacks were incapable of citizenship reinforced their concept of an equally natural white male political capacity. This exclusion of blacks (by Democrats whose own political competence was often doubted by wealthier and better-educated Whigs) was designed to protect the republic while extending citizenship to all white men. The most vicious racist assaults were often carried out beneath symbols of the revolutionary republic. Antiblack mobs in Baltimore, Cincinnati, and Toledo called themselves Minute Men and Sons of Liberty. Philadelphia blacks who gathered to hear the Declaration of Independence read on the Fourth of July were attacked for "defiling the government." The antiabolitionist mob that sacked Lewis Tappan's house rescued a portrait of George Washington and carried it as a banner during their later attacks on Finneyite evangelicals and English actors.

The Beginnings of Antislavery

Before 1830, only a few whites considered slavery a moral issue. Quakers, at their annual meeting in 1758, had condemned both the slave trade and slavery, and Methodists and some Baptists had done the same late in the century. Washington, Jefferson, and other Chesapeake gentlemen doubted the wisdom if not the morality of holding slaves; New England Federalists had condemned slavery in the course of condemning Jeffersonian masters. But there were too few Quakers to make a difference, and the movement to free slaves in the Upper South and the antislavery

sentiments of southern evangelicals both died out early in the 19th century. Southerners and most northerners—when they bothered to think about it at all—tended to accept slavery as the result of human (read "black") depravity and God's unknowable plan.

Organized opposition to slavery before 1831 was pretty much limited to the American Colonization Society, founded in 1816. Led by wealthy, generally conservative northern churchmen and a contingent of Chesapeake gentlemen, the society proposed the voluntary, gradual, and compensated emancipation of slaves and the "repatriation" of free blacks to West Africa. Although the society transported a few thousand blacks to Liberia, it never posed a serious threat to slavery. Southerners, who owned 2 million slaves by 1830, opposed emancipation whether compensated or not, and few free blacks were interested in moving to Africa. The society's campaign to deport them so disturbed many free blacks that they substituted "Colored" for "African" in naming their institutions. One black churchman explained that references to Africa provided "an available excuse for a powerful enemy, the American Colonization Society, to use . . . as a weapon of our own make, to expel ourselves from our beloved country."

Although few white Americans actively opposed slavery before 1830, the writing was on the wall. Emancipation in the North, although it came about quietly, constituted an implicit condemnation of slavery in the South. So did events outside the United States. Toussaint L'Ouverture's successful slave revolution in Haiti in 1804 threatened slavery everywhere (see chapter 7). The British, whose navy could enforce their dictates on the seas, outlawed the Atlantic slave trade in 1808. Mexico, Peru, Chile, Gran Colombia (present-day Colombia, Venezuela, Ecuador, and Panama), and other new republics carved out of the Spanish empire emancipated their slaves. The most powerful blow came in 1830 when the British Parliament emancipated the slaves of Jamaica, Bermuda, and other Caribbean islands ruled by Britain.

Abolitionists

Religious revivals during the late 1820s and early 1830s created a reform-minded evangelical culture in the northern United States. Radical abolitionism dates from 1831, when William Lloyd Garrison published the first issue of the *Liberator.* Already a veteran reformer, Garrison condemned slavery as a national sin and demanded immediate emancipation—or at least an immediate start toward emancipation. "I am in earnest," he declared in his first editorial; "I will not equivocate—I will not excuse—I will not retreat a single inch—and I will be heard!"

In 1833, Garrison and like-minded abolitionists formed the American Anti-Slavery Society. Some of them—Wendell Phillips, Thomas Wentworth Higginson, Theodore Parker—were Unitarians who opposed slavery as an affront to both humanity and rationality; others—most notably the poet John Greenleaf Whittier—were Quakers who were happy to join the movement. Abolitionists found their greatest support in southern New England, western New York, northern Ohio, and among the new middle classes of the northeastern cities—ground that Yankee settlement, the Market Revolution, and Finneyite revivals had turned into the heartland of the northern Whig Party.

Opposition to slavery was a logical extension of middle-class evangelicalism. Charles Finney, Lyman Beecher, and other Whig evangelicals retained a Puritan inheritance that demanded that God's people legislate the behavior of others. The new evangelicalism, however, was grounded in the morally accountable individual, and not in coercive institutions. Whig evangelicals posed a contest between Christian love and moral free agency on the one hand and every kind of passion, brutality, and force on the other. They often promised that their reforms would liberate the individual spirit from "slavery" to alcohol, lust, or ignorance—thus phrasing moral legislation as liberation, not coercion. Before long, some discovered that slavery itself, an institution that obliterated moral choice and encouraged the worst human passions, was America's great national sin.

The American Anti-Slavery Society demanded immediate emancipation of slaves and full civil and legal rights for blacks. Assuming that God had created blacks and

---

M U S I C A L   L I N K   T O   T H E   P A S T

The Grave of the Slave

**Composers: Francis Johnson (music),
Sarah Forten (lyrics)**
Title: "The Grave of the Slave" (1831)

"The Grave of the Slave," one of the rare abolitionist songs penned by African Americans, demonstrates the more active role blacks were beginning to take in the struggle against slavery. The lyrics of Sarah Forten, founder of the Philadelphia Anti-Slavery Society, were consistent with abolitionist arguments that, contrary to pro-slavery Southern propaganda, charged that slaves lived a miserable and unchristian existence that represented a worse fate than death: "Poor slave, shall we sorrow that Death was thy friend? / The last and the kindest that heaven could send? / The grave to the weary is welcome and blest / And death to the captive is freedom and rest."

In the early 1830s, the abolition movement reached a new political and emotional height, led by the uncompromising vision of William Lloyd Garrison (see pages 369–370). For many blacks, this represented a large improvement over the previous efforts of the white-led and largely unsuccessful American Colonization Society of the 1810s and 20s, which advocated shipping blacks to Africa. For the first time, significant numbers of black Americans in the north joined the abolitionist movement because of Garrison's tactics.

The composer, Francis Johnson, was one of the most famous and accomplished African Americans of the antebellum period. A prolific composer and world-famous orchestra leader, Johnson and his orchestra toured across North America (avoiding the Deep South), and were probably the first American band to give concerts abroad, including a command performance before Queen Victoria, at which she presented Johnson with a silver bugle. His orchestra performed both European classical music and American popular songs (Johnson published more than 200 pieces). Although most of his music served entertainment and dancing purposes, he also composed music with political and African American themes, including "Recognition March on the Independence of Hayti [sic]" (1825) and "The Grave of the Slave." Because recording technology did not yet exist, we will never know precisely how his music sounded, but his orchestra could very well have served as a major precedent for the jazz and blues that surfaced decades later.

1. Why do you think so many of the most famous and historically significant African American figures of the 19th and 20th centuries came from the worlds of religion and entertainment?

Listen to an audio recording of this music on the Musical Links to the Past CD.

Anti-Slavery Almanac.

[1840.]

"OUR *PECULIAR* DOMESTIC INSTITUTIONS."

Old Sturbridge Village, photo by Henry E. Peach.

AN ABOLITIONIST VIEW OF SLAVE SOCIETY

This provocative woodcut appeared in the *Anti-Slavery Almanac for 1840* (Boston, 1839). It pictures the lynching of slaves and their abolitionist allies by a southern mob. Surrounding the hanging tree are men (no women appear in the picture) engaged in other activities that northern reformers insisted grew from the brutal patriarchy of slave society. Men duel with pistols and knives, others engage in an eye-gouging wrestling match, others gamble and drink, and still others cheer for cock fights and horse races. The enemy here is not simply slavery but the debauchery and unbridled passions that abolitionists associated with it.

whites as members of one human family, abolitionists opposed the "scientific" racism spouted by Democrats and many Whigs. Moderates and latecomers to abolitionism spoke of inherent racial characteristics but still tended to view blacks in benign (if condescending) ways. Harriet Beecher Stowe, for instance, portrayed blacks as simple, innocent, loving people who possessed a capacity for sentiment and emotionalism that most whites had lost. In 1852, Horace Mann told an audience of blacks in Ohio that "in intellect, the blacks are inferior to the whites, while in sentiment and affections, the whites are inferior to the blacks." Radical abolitionists, however, remained committed environmentalists. Lydia Maria Child of New York City declared, "In the United States, colored persons have scarcely any chance to rise. But if colored persons are well treated, and have the same inducements to industry as others, they [will] work as well and behave as well."

Agitation

Antislavery, unlike other reforms, was a radical attack on one of the nation's central institutions, and the movement attracted a minority even among middle-class evangeli-

cals. Both Lyman Beecher and Charles Finney opposed the abolitionists in the 1830s, arguing that emancipation would come about sooner or later as a result of the religious conversion of slave owners; antislavery agitation and the denunciation of slaveholders, they argued, would divide Christians, slow the revival movement, and thus actually delay emancipation. Finney warned his abolitionist friend Theodore Dwight Weld that the logical end of antislavery was civil war.

Savoring its role as a beleaguered minority, the American Anti-Slavery Society staged a series of campaigns to force government and the public at large to confront the question of slavery. In 1835, the society launched its Postal Campaign, flooding the nation's postal system with abolitionist tracts that southerners and most northerners regarded as "incendiary." From 1836 onward, they petitioned Congress to abolish slavery and the slave trade in the District of Columbia and to deny the slaveholding Republic of Texas admission to the Union. These tactics forced President Andrew Jackson to permit southern postal workers to censor the mails; they also forced Democrats and southern Whigs to abridge the right of petition to avoid discussion of slavery in Congress (see chapter 12).

In these ways, a radical minority forced politicians to demonstrate the complicity of the party system (and the Democrats in particular) in the institution of slavery, brought the slavery question to public attention, and tied it to questions of civil liberties in the North and political power in the South. They were a dangerous minority indeed.

☙ The Politics of Gender and Sex

Whigs valued a reformed masculinity that was lived out in the sentimentalized homes of the northern business classes or in the Christian gentility of the Whig plantation and farm. Jacksonian voters, on the other hand, often defended domestic patriarchy. Whereas most were unimaginative paternalists, Democrats often made heroes of men whose flamboyant, rakish lives directly challenged Whig domesticity. Whigs denounced Andrew Jackson for allegedly stealing his wife from her lawful husband; Democrats often admired him for the same reason. Richard M. Johnson of Kentucky, who was vice president under Martin Van Buren, openly kept a mulatto mistress and had two daughters by her; with his pistols always at hand, he accompanied her openly around Washington, D.C. "Prince" John Van Buren, the president's son and himself a prominent New York Democrat, met a "dark-eyed, well-formed Italian lady" who called herself Amerigo Vespucci and claimed to be a direct descendant of the man for whom America was named. She became young Van Buren's "fancy lady," remaining with him until he lost her in a high-stakes card game.

Whigs made Democratic contempt for sentimental domesticity a political issue. William Crane, a Michigan Whig, claimed that Democrats "despised no man for his sins," and went on to say that "brothel-haunters flocked to this party, because here in all political circles, and political movements, they were treated as nobility." Much of the Whig cultural agenda (and much of Democratic hatred of that agenda) was rooted in contests between Whig and Democratic masculine styles.

Appetites

Many of the reforms urged by Whig evangelicals had to do with domestic and personal life rather than with politics. Their hopes for the perfection of the world hinged more on the character of individuals than on the role of institutions. Calvinism had taught that because human beings were innately selfish and subject to animal appetites, they must submit to godly authority. Evangelicals, on the other

hand, defined original sin as a *tendency* toward selfishness and sin that could be fought off—with God's help—through prayer and personal discipline. They hoped to perfect the world by filling it with godly, self-governing individuals.

It was not an easy task, for opportunities to indulge in vanity, luxury, and sensuality were on the rise. Charles Finney, for instance, preached long and hard against vanity. "A self-indulgent Christian," he said, "is a contradiction. You might as well write on your clothes 'NO TRUTH IN RELIGION,'" he told fashionably dressed women, for their dress proclaimed "GIVE ME DRESS, GIVE ME FASHION, GIVE ME FLATTERY, AND I AM HAPPY." Finney also worried about the effect of money, leisure time, and cheap novels on middle-class homes. He could not, he said, "believe that a person who has ever known the love of God can relish a secular novel" or open his or her home to "Byron, Scott, Shakespeare, and a host of triflers and blasphemers of God." Evangelicals also disdained luxury in home furnishings; they discouraged the use of silks and velvets and questioned the propriety of decorating the home with mahogany, mirrors, brass furnishings, and upholstered chairs and sofas.

Members of the evangelical middle class tried to define levels of material comfort that would separate them from the indulgences of those above and below them. They made similar attempts in the areas of food and sex. Sylvester Graham (now remembered for the wheat cracker that bears his name) gave up the ministry in 1830 to become a full-time temperance lecturer. Before long, he was lecturing on the dangers of excess in diet and sex. He claimed that the consumption of red meat, spiced foods, and alcohol produced bodily excitement that resulted in weakness and disease. Sex—including fornication, fantasizing, masturbation, and bestiality—affected the body in even more destructive ways, and the two appetites reinforced each other. (Graham admitted that marital sex, although it was physiologically no different from other forms of sex, was preferable, for it was the least exciting.)

Acting on Graham's concerns, reformers established a system of Grahamite boardinghouses in which young men who were living away from home were provided with diets that helped them control their other appetites. Oberlin College, when it was founded by evangelicals in 1832, banned "tea and coffee, highly seasoned meats, rich pastries, and all unholsome [sic] and expensive foods." Among others who heeded Graham's advice were such future feminists as Lucy Stone, Susan B. Anthony, and Amelia Bloomer. Reformers who did not actually adopt Graham's system shared his concern over the twin evils of rich food and sexual excess. John R. McDowall, a divinity student who headed a mission to New York City prostitutes, admitted, "Having eaten until I am full, lust gets the control of me." John Humphrey Noyes (another divinity student who turned to reform) set up a community in Oneida, New York, that indulged in plural marriage but at the same time urged sexual self-control; he also believed that a perfect Christian world would not allow meat-eating.

Moral Reform

Although most middle-class households failed to embrace Grahamism, simple food and sexual control became badges of class status. Men supposedly had the greatest difficulty taming their appetites. The old image—beginning with Eve and including Delilah and Jezebel and other dangerous women of the Old Testament—of woman as seductress persisted in the more traditionalist churches and in the pulp fiction from which middle-class mothers tried to protect their sons (see chapter 10). Whig evangelicals, on the other hand, had made the discovery that women were naturally free of desire and that only men were subject to the animal passions. "What terrible temptations lie in the way of your sex," wrote Harriet Beecher Stowe to her husband. "Tho I did love you with an almost insane love before I married you, I never knew yet or felt the pulsation which showed me that I could be tempted in that way. I loved you as I now love God." The middle-class ideal combined female purity and male self-control. For the most part it was a private reform, contained within the home. Sometimes, however, evangelical domesticity produced moral crusades to impose that ethos on the world at large. Many of these crusades were led by women.

In 1828, a band of Sunday school teachers—most of them women—initiated an informal mission to prostitutes that grew into the New York Magdalen Society. Taking a novel approach to an age-old question, the society argued that prostitution was created by brutal fathers and husbands who abandoned their young daughters or wives, by dandies who seduced them and turned them into prostitutes, and by lustful men who bought their services. Prostitution, in other words, was not the result of the innate sinfulness of prostitutes; it was the result of the brutality and lust of men. The solution was to remove young prostitutes from their environment, pray with them, and convert them to middle-class morality.

The Magdalen Society's *First Annual Report* (1831) inveighed against male lust and printed shocking life histories of prostitutes. Some men, however, read it as pornography; others used it as a guidebook to the seamier side of New York City. The wealthy male evangelicals who had bankrolled the Magdalen Society withdrew their support, and the organization fell apart. Thereupon many of the women reformers set up the Female Moral Reform Society, with a House of Industry in which prostitutes were taught morality and household skills to prepare them for new lives as domestic servants in pious middle-class homes. This effort also failed, largely because few prostitutes were interested in domestic service or evangelical religion. That fact became distressingly clear when in 1836 the society was obliged to close its House of Industry after the residents had taken it over during the caretaker's absence.

The Female Moral Reform Society was more successful with members of its own class. Its newspaper, the *Advocate of Moral Reform,* circulated throughout the evangelical North, eventually reaching 555 auxiliary societies with 20,000 readers. Now evangelical women fought prostitution by publishing the names of customers. They campaigned against pornography, obscenity, lewdness, and seduction and accepted the responsibility of rearing their sons to be pure, even when it meant dragging them out of brothels. Occasionally, they prosecuted men who took advantage of servant girls. They also publicized the names of adulterers, and they had seducers brought into court. In the process, women reformers fought the sexual double standard and assumed the power to define what was respectable and what was not.

Women's Rights

From the late 1820s onward, middle-class women in the North assumed roles that would have been unthinkable to their mothers and grandmothers. Evangelical domesticity made loving mothers (and not stern fathers) the principal rearers of children. Housewives saw themselves as missionaries to their families, responsible for the choices their children and husbands made between salvation or sin. In that role, women became arbiters of fashion, diet, and sexual behavior. Many joined the temperance movement and moral reform societies, where they became public reformers while posing as mothers protecting their sons from rum sellers and seducers. Such experiences gave them a sense of spiritual empowerment that led some to question their own subordinate status within a system of gendered social roles. Lydia Maria Child, a writer of sentimental fiction and manuals on household economy as well as a leading abolitionist and moral reformer, proclaimed, "Those who urged women to become missionaries and form tract societies . . . have changed the household utensil to a living, energetic being, and they have no spell to turn it into a broom again."

The antislavery movement turned many women into advocates of women's rights. Abolitionists, following the perfectionist implications of Whig evangelicalism to their

H I S T O R Y   T H R O U G H   F I L M

Not for Ourselves Alone (PBS, 1999)

Directed by Ken Burns.

In 1999, Ken Burns made a documentary film on the women's rights movement. Part One tells the story from about 1840 through the Civil War. It is vintage Ken Burns: old photographs scanned to give them the appearance of movies, period documents read over the pictures by actors (in this case, Sally Kellerman), modern-day experts speaking with authority, the same period music that Burns used in *The Civil War* and his other forays into the 19th century, and the same undercurrent of sentimentality. The film focuses on the collaboration and friendship between Susan B. Anthony and Elizabeth Cady Stanton, and through that medium and within its limits, it tells its story well.

Elizabeth Cady Stanton was descended, on her mother's side, from one of the great landholding families of colonial New York. Her father was a prosperous lawyer and judge. Young Elizabeth hungered for education, but no American college admitted women. She enrolled at Emma Willard's Female Seminary at Troy, New York, and shared her family's interest in the temperance and antislavery movements. She met lawyer and well-known antislavery speaker Henry B. Stanton through her cousin, wealthy abolitionist Gerrit Smith, and married Stanton in 1840. (Elizabeth excised the word "obey" from the ceremony.) The Stantons honeymooned at an antislavery convention in London that year. Organizers of the convention segregated women and men and forbade the women to speak. Stanton realized—as legions of women would realize—that the logic of antislavery applied to women as well as slaves, and that rights reform that was less than universal was badly flawed. The Stantons took up housekeeping in Boston, then moved to Seneca Falls in western New York. Henry Stanton was frequently away on lecture tours, and Elizabeth stayed at home, had babies, and grew weary of housework.

In 1848, after a visit with her friend and fellow activist Lucretia Mott, she helped organize the first Woman's Rights Convention in Seneca Falls. She authored the declaration demanding civil and legal equality for women, including the demand (truly shocking to contemporaries) that women be allowed to vote. Shortly after the Seneca Falls Convention, Stanton met Susan B. Anthony, another veteran reformer. Anthony, a Quaker, had been born into much humbler circumstances than Stanton, remained unmarried, and often upbraided other women reformers for marrying and having children. The differences between Stanton and Anthony added up to a lifelong collaboration: the educated and housebound Stanton wrote the manifestos, and the brave and unencumbered Anthony took them into lecture halls and the state legislature. They and their coworkers won some battles (in the area of women's property rights in particular), but could do little more than publicize their radical demands for the legal reform of marriage and for civil and political equality. This became painfully clear during the Civil War, when their fellow reformers told Stanton and Anthony to delay women's rights while slaves were freed and given the same rights for which the women's movement had fought. At the close of Part One, women's civil and legal equality remain far from realization.

Not for Ourselves Alone tells a familiar story clearly and entertainingly. Along the way, it portrays a friendship between women within the antebellum reform community and (intermittently) throws light on the workings of a reform culture that enlisted much of the zeal and intellect of the antebellum North.

Not for Ourselves Alone is a documentary by Ken Burns about the American women's suffrage movement.

logical ends, called for absolute human equality and a near-anarchist rejection of impersonal institutions and prescribed social roles. It became clear to some female abolitionists that the critique of slavery (a root-and-branch denunciation of patriarchy and prescribed hierarchy) applied as well to inequality based on sex.

Radical female abolitionists reached the conclusion that they were human beings first and women second. In 1837, Sarah Grimke announced, "The Lord Jesus defines the duties of his followers in his Sermon on the Mount . . . without any reference to sex or condition . . . never even referring to the distinction now so strenuously insisted upon between masculine and feminine virtues. . . . Men and women are CREATED EQUAL! They are both moral and accountable beings, and whatever is right for a man to do is right for woman." A women's rights convention put it just as bluntly in 1851: "We deny the right of any portion of the species to decide for another portion . . . what is and what is not their 'proper sphere'; that the proper sphere for all human beings is the largest and highest to which they are able to attain."

Beginning about 1840, women lobbied state legislatures and won significant changes in the laws governing women's rights to property, to the wages of their own labor, and to custody of children in cases of divorce. Fourteen states passed such legislation, culminating in New York's Married Women's Property Act in 1860.

The first Woman's Rights Convention met in Seneca Falls, New York, in 1848, and its ties to antislavery were clear. An argument over the right of women to deliver speeches and engage in other forms of public agitation had already split the American Anti-Slavery Society in 1840. Feminist abolitionists organized the Seneca Falls Convention. The only male delegate was the black abolitionist Frederick Douglass. Sojourner Truth, another prominent black opponent of slavery, also attended. Nearly all of the other delegates were white women who had worked within the abolition movement. Both as abolitionists and as feminists, they based their demands for equality not only on legal and moral arguments but also on the spirit of republican institutions. The principal formal document issued by the convention, a Declaration of Sentiments and Resolutions based on the Declaration of Independence, denounced "the repeated injuries and usurpations on the part of man toward woman."

Most of those "injuries and usurpations" were political. The central issue was the right to vote, for citizenship was central to the "democratic" pattern that granted liberty and equality to white men regardless of class and excluded Americans who were not white and male. Thus female participation in politics was a direct challenge to a male-ordained women's place. A distraught New York leg-

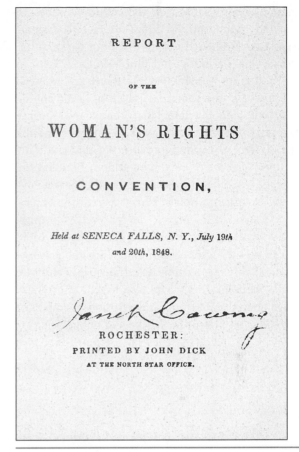

THE DECLARATION OF SENTIMENTS PUBLISHED BY THE FIRST WOMAN'S RIGHTS CONVENTION IN 1848

This account of the proceedings and list of resolutions announced that there was an organized women's rights movement in the United States. It also announced that women's rights activists knew how to organize a convention and how to publicize their activities in print. (Ties between the women's and antislavery movements led the women to have their report printed at the offices of the *North Star,* an abolitionist paper published by Frederick Douglass—the only male member of the convention—in Rochester.)

islator agreed: "It is well known that the object of these unsexed women is to overthrow the most sacred of our institutions. . . . Are we to put the stamp of truth upon the libel here set forth, that men and women, in the matrimonial relation, are to be equal?" Later, feminist Elizabeth Cady Stanton recalled such reactions: "Political rights," she said, "involving in their last results equality everywhere, roused all the antagonism of a dominant power, against the self-assertion of a class hitherto subservient."

Conclusion

By the 1830s, most citizens in every corner of the republic firmly identified with either the Whig or Democratic Party—so much so that party affiliation was recognized as an indicator of personal history and cultural loyalties. In the states and neighborhoods, Whigs embraced commerce and activist government, arguing that both would foster prosperity, social harmony, and moral progress. Faith in progress and improvement led Northern and western Whigs—primarily the more radical evangelicals among them—to entertain the hope that liberty and equality might apply to women and blacks. Democrats, on the other hand, were generally more localistic and culturally conservative. Like the Whigs, they seldom doubted the value of commerce, but they worried that the Market Revolution and its organization of banking, credit, and monetary supply was creating unprecedented levels of inequality and personal dependence among the republic's white male citizenry; they were certain that Whig public works projects and Whig taxation increased inequality and corrupted the republic. Democrats also looked with angry disbelief at attempts of Whigs (and rebellious members of Whig families) to govern the private and public behavior of their neighbors, and sometimes even to tinker with ancient distinctions of gender and race.

In sum, Whigs reformulated the revolutionary legacy of liberty and equality, moving away from classical notions of citizenship and toward liberty of conscience and equality of opportunity within a market-driven democracy. They often attempted to civilize that new world by using government power to encourage commerce, social interdependence, and cultural homogeneity. When Democrats argued that Whig "interdependence" in fact meant dependence and inequality, Whigs countered with promises of individual success for those who were morally worthy of it. Democrats trusted none of that. Theirs was a Jeffersonian formulation grounded in a fierce defense of the liberty and equality of white men, and in a minimal, inexpensive, decentralized government that protected the liberties of those men without threatening their independence or their power over their households and within their neighborhoods.

SUGGESTED READINGS

On party ideologies, see **John Ashworth, *'Agrarians & Aristocrats': Party Political Ideology in the United States, 1837–1846*** (1983), and **Daniel Walker Howe, *The Political Culture of the American Whigs*** (1979). Constituencies and state-level issues are addressed in **Lee Benson, *The Concept of Jacksonian Democracy: New York as a Test Case*** (1961); **Ronald P. Formisano, *The Transformation of Political Culture: Massachusetts Parties, 1790s–1840s*** (1983); and **Lacy K. Ford, Jr., *Origins of Southern Radicalism: The South Carolina Upcountry, 1800–1860*** (1988). **Richard J. Carwardine, *Evangelicals and Politics in Antebellum America*** (1993) is an insightful study of religion and politics in these years. On the politics of schools, see **Carl F. Kaestle, *Pillars of the Republic: Common Schools and American Society, 1780–1860*** (1983). Influential studies of prisons and asylums include **David J. Rothman, *The Discovery of the Asylum: Social Order and Disorder in the New Republic*** (1971) and **Michael Meranze, *Laboratories of Virtue: Punishment, Revolution, and Authority in Philadelphia, 1760–1835*** (1996).

Drinking and temperance are the subjects of **W. J. Rorabaugh, *The Alcoholic Republic: An American Tradition*** (1979). The standard study of free blacks is **Leon F. Litwack, *North of Slavery: The Negro in the Free States, 1790–1860*** (1960), which can be supplemented with **Gary B. Nash, *Forging Freedom: The Formation of Philadelphia's Black Community, 1720–1840*** (1988) and **Shane White, *Stories of Freedom in Black New York*** (2002). The literature on reform movements is synthesized in **Steven Mintz, *Moralists & Modernizers: America's Pre–Civil War Reformers*** (1995). Students might also consult **Robert H. Abzug, *Cosmos Crumbling: American Reform and the Religious Imagination*** (1994); **Jean Fagan Yellin, *Women & Sisters: The Antislavery Feminists in American Culture*** (1989); and **Lori D. Ginzberg, *Women and the Work of Benevolence: Morality, Politics, and Class in the 19th-Century United States*** (1990). The cultural and moral underpinnings of reform are a subtext of **Karen Halttunen's** subtle and important ***Murder Most Foul: The Killer and the American Gothic Imagination*** (1998).

AMERICAN JOURNEY ONLINE
 A N D
INFOTRAC COLLEGE EDITION

Visit the source collections at www.ajaccess.wadsworth.com and
infotrac.thomsonlearning.com and use the Search function with
the following key terms to explore documents, images, audio
and video clips, articles, and commentary related to the material
in this chapter.

Dorothea Dix	American Colonization Society
Free Blacks	American Anti-Slavery Society
Abolitionism	Seneca Falls
Herman Melville	Women's Rights
William H. Seward	Sarah Grimke

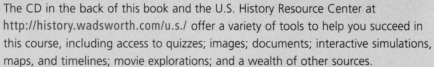

GRADE AIDS

**Visit the Liberty Equality Power Companion Web Site for resources specific to
this textbook:** http://history.wadsworth.com/murrin_LEP4e

The CD in the back of this book and the U.S. History Resource Center at
http://history.wadsworth.com/u.s./ offer a variety of tools to help you succeed in
this course, including access to quizzes; images; documents; interactive simulations,
maps, and timelines; movie explorations; and a wealth of other sources.

Jacksonian Democracy

JACKSON AS DEMOCRACY INCARNATE
Andrew Jackson struck a romantic military pose for this portrait painted in 1820.
Posing as the embodiment of democracy and as an extravagantly melodramatic hero,
Jackson imposed himself on his times as few Americans have done.

CHAPTER OUTLINE

N ational political leaders from the 1820s until the outbreak of the Civil War faced two persistent questions. First, a deepening rift between slave and free states threatened the very existence of the nation. Second, explosive economic development and territorial expansion made new demands on the political system—demands that raised the question of government participation in economic life.

The Whig Party proposed the American System as the answer to both questions. The national government, said the Whigs, should subsidize roads and canals, foster industry with protective tariffs, and maintain a national bank capable of exercising centralized control over credit and currency. The result would be a peaceful, prosperous, and truly national market society. If the South, the West, and the Northeast were profiting by doing business with each other, the argument went, sectional fears and jealousies would quiet down. Jacksonian Democrats, on the other hand, argued that the American System was unconstitutional, that it violated the rights of states and localities, and that it would tax honest citizens in order to benefit corrupt and wealthy insiders. Most dangerous of all, argued the Democrats, Whig economic nationalism would create an activist, interventionist national government that would anger and frighten the slaveholding South. To counter both threats, the Jacksonians resurrected Jefferson's agrarian republic of states' rights and inactive, inexpensive government—all of it deeply inflected in the code of white male equality, domestic patriarchy, and racial slavery that was being acted out in families, neighborhoods, and state legislatures.

CHAPTER FOCUS

♦ In terms of party development, what were the long-term results of the Missouri controversy and the Panic of 1819? Why?

♦ At the national level, how did Jacksonian Democrats and their opponents deal with widening differences between the northern and southern states during these years?

♦ How did they address issues raised by economic development?

♦ What was peculiarly "national" about the Second Party System?

🌐 Prologue: 1819

Jacksonian Democracy was rooted in two events that occurred in 1819. First, the angry debate that surrounded Missouri's admission as a slave state revealed the centrality and vulnerability of slavery within the Union. Second, a severe financial collapse led many Americans to doubt the Market Revolution's compatibility with the Jeffersonian republic. By 1820, politicians were determined to reconstruct the limited-government, states'-rights coalition that had elected Thomas Jefferson. By 1828, they had formed the Democratic Party, with Andrew Jackson at its head.

The West, 1803–1840s

When Jefferson bought the Louisiana Territory in 1803, he knew that he was giving future generations of Americans a huge "Empire for Liberty." He knew almost nothing, however, about the new land itself. Only a few French trappers and traders had traveled the plains between the Mississippi and the Rocky Mountains, and no white person had seen the territory drained by the Columbia River. In 1804, Jefferson sent an expedition under Meriwether Lewis, his private secretary, and William Clark, brother of the Indian fighter George Rogers Clark, to explore the land he had bought. To prepare for the expedition, Lewis studied astronomy, zoology, and botany; Clark was already an accomplished mapmaker. The two kept meticulous journals of one of the epic adventures in American history.

In May 1804, Lewis and Clark and 41 companions boarded a keelboat and two large canoes at the village of St. Louis. That spring and summer they poled and paddled 1,600 miles up the Missouri River, passing through rolling plains dotted by the farm villages of the Pawnee, Oto, Missouri, Crow, Omaha, Hidatsa, and Mandan peoples. The villages of the lower Missouri had been cut off from the western buffalo herds and reduced to dependence by mounted Sioux warriors, who had begun to establish their hegemony over the northern plains.

Lewis and Clark traveled through Sioux territory and stopped for the winter at the prosperous, heavily fortified Mandan villages at the big bend of the Missouri River in Dakota country. In the spring they hired Toussaint Charbonneau, a French fur trader, to guide them to the Pacific. Although Charbonneau turned out to be useless, his wife,

---

C H R O N O L O G Y

1804–06 Lewis and Clark explore the northern regions of the Louisiana Purchase

1819 Controversy arises over Missouri's admission to the Union as a slave state • Panic of 1819 marks the first failure of the national market economy

1820 Missouri Compromise adopted

1823 Monroe Doctrine written by Secretary of State John Quincy Adams

1824–25 Adams wins the presidency over Andrew Jackson • Adams appoints Henry Clay as secretary of state • Jacksonians charge a "Corrupt Bargain" between Adams and Clay

1827 Cherokees in Georgia declare themselves a republic

1828 Jackson defeats Adams for the presidency • "Tariff of Abominations" passed by Congress • John C. Calhoun's *Exposition and Protest* presents doctrine of nullification

1830 Congress passes the Indian Removal Act

1832 Jackson reelected over Henry Clay • *Worcester* v. *Georgia* exempts the Cherokee from Georgia law • Jackson vetoes recharter of the Bank of the United States

1833 Force Bill and Tariff of 1833 end the nullification crisis

1834 Whig Party formed in opposition to Jacksonians

1836 Congress adopts "gag rule" to table antislavery petitions • Van Buren elected president

1837 Financial panic ushers in a severe economic depression

1838 U.S. Army marches the remaining Cherokee to Indian Territory

1840 Whig William Henry Harrison defeats Van Buren for presidency

---

a teenaged Shoshone girl named Sacajawea, was an indispensable guide, interpreter, and diplomat. With her help, Lewis and Clark navigated the upper Missouri, crossed the Rockies to the Snake River, and followed that stream to the Columbia River. They reached the Pacific in November 1805 and spent the winter at what is now Astoria, Oregon. Retracing their steps the following spring and summer, they returned to St. Louis in September 1806. They brought with them many volumes of drawings and notes, along with assurances that the Louisiana Purchase had been worth many, many times its price.

As time passed, Americans began to settle the southern portions of the Louisiana Purchase. Louisiana itself, strategically crucial and already the site of sugar plantations and the town of New Orleans, entered the Union in 1812. Settlers were also filtering into northern Louisiana and the Arkansas and Missouri territories. Farther north and west, the Sioux extended their control over the northern reaches of the land that Jefferson had bought.

The Sioux were aided in their conquest by the spread of smallpox. The disease moved up the Missouri River periodically from the 1790s onward; by the 1830s, epidemics were ravaging the sedentary peoples of the Missouri. The Mandans, who had been so hospitable to Lewis and Clark, got the worst of it: They were almost completely wiped out. The Sioux and their Cheyenne allies, who lived in small bands and were constantly on the move, fared better. Their horse-raiding parties now grew into armies of mounted invaders numbering as many as 2,000, and they extended their hunting lands south into what is now southern Nebraska and as far west as the Yellowstone River. In the 1840s, white settlers began crossing the southern plains, while white politicians entered into a fateful debate on whether these lands would become the site of northern farms or southern plantations. At the same time, the newly victorious Sioux never doubted that the northern plains would be theirs forever.

The Argument over Missouri

Early in 1819, slaveholding Missouri applied for admission to the Union as the first new state to be carved out of the Louisiana Purchase. New York Congressman James Tallmadge, Jr., quickly proposed two amendments to the Missouri statehood bill. The first would bar additional slaves from being brought into Missouri (16 percent of Missouri's people were already slaves). The second would emancipate Missouri slaves born after admission when they reached their 25th birthday. Put simply, the Tallmadge amendments would admit Missouri only if Missouri agreed to become a free state.

The congressional debates on the Missouri question had nothing to do with humanitarian objections to slavery and everything to do with political power. Rufus King of New York, an old Federalist who led the northerners in the Senate, insisted that he opposed the admission of a new slave state "solely in its bearing and effects upon great political interests, and upon the just and equal rights of the freemen of the nation." Northerners had long chafed at the added representation in Congress and in the electoral college that the "three-fifths" rule granted to the slave states (see chapter 6). The rule had, in fact, added significantly to southern power: In 1790, the South, with 40 percent of the white population, controlled 47 percent of the votes in Congress—enough to decide close votes both in Congress and in presidential elections. Federalists pointed out that of the 12 additional electoral votes the three-fifths rule gave to the South, 10 had gone to Thomas Jefferson in 1800 and had given him the election. Without the bogus votes provided by slavery, they argued, Virginia's stranglehold on the presidency would have been broken with Washington's departure in 1796.

In 1819, the North held a majority in the House of Representatives. The South, thanks to the recent admissions of Alabama and southern-oriented Illinois, controlled a bare majority in the Senate. Voting on the Tallmadge amendments was starkly sectional: Northern congressmen voted 86 to 10 for the first amendment, 80 to 14 for the second; southerners rejected both, 66 to 1 and 64 to 2. In the Senate, a unanimous South defeated the Tallmadge amendments with the help of the two Illinois senators and three northerners. Deadlocked between a Senate in favor of admitting Missouri as a slave state and a House dead set against it, Congress broke off one of the angriest sessions in its history and went home.

The Missouri Compromise

The new Congress that convened in the winter of 1819–20 passed the legislative package that became known as the Missouri Compromise. Massachusetts offered its northern counties as the new free state of Maine, thus neutralizing fears that the South would gain votes in the Senate with the admission of Missouri. Senator Jesse Thomas of Illinois proposed the so-called Thomas Proviso: If the North would admit Missouri as a slave state, the South would agree to outlaw slavery in territories above 36°30′ N latitude—a line extending from the southern border of Missouri to Spanish (within a year, Mexican) territory. That line would open Arkansas Territory (present-day Arkansas and Oklahoma) to slavery and would close to slavery the remainder of the Louisiana Territory—land that would subsequently become all or part of nine states.

Congress admitted Maine with little debate, but the terms of the Thomas Proviso met northern opposition. A joint Senate-House committee finally decided to separate the two bills. With half of the southern representatives and nearly all of the northerners supporting it, the Thomas Proviso passed. Congress next took up the admission of Missouri. With the votes of a solid South and 14 compromise-minded northerners, Missouri entered the Union as a slave state. President James Monroe applauded the "patriotic devotion" of the northern representatives "who preferr'd the sacrifice of themselves at home" to endangering the Union. His words were prophetic: Nearly all of the 14 were voted out of office when they faced angry northern voters in the next election.

The Missouri crisis brought the South's commitment to slavery and the North's resentment of southern political power into collision, revealing an uncompromisable gulf between slave and free states. While northerners vowed to relinquish no more territory to slavery, southerners talked openly of disunion and civil war. A Georgia politician announced that the Missouri debates had lit a fire that "seas of blood can only extinguish." President Monroe's secretary of state, John Quincy Adams, saw the debates as an omen: Northerners would unanimously oppose the extension of slavery whenever the question came to a vote. Adams confided in his diary:

> Here was a new party ready formed, . . . terrible to the whole Union, but portentiously terrible to the South—threatening in its progress the emancipation of all their slaves, threatening in its immediate effect that Southern domination which has swayed the Union for the last twenty years.

Viewing the crisis from Monticello, the aging Thomas Jefferson was distraught:

> A geographical line, coinciding with a marked principle, moral and political, once conceived and held up to the angry passions of men, will never be obliterated; every new irritation will mark it deeper and deeper. . . . This momentous question, like a fire-bell in the night, awakened and filled me with terror. I considered it at once the knell of the Union.

The Panic of 1819

Politicians debated the Missouri question against a darkening backdrop of economic depression—a downturn that would shape political alignments as much as the slavery question. The origins of the Panic of 1819 were international and numerous: European agriculture was recovering from the Napoleonic wars, thereby reducing the demand for American foodstuffs; war and revolution in the New World had cut off the supply of precious metals (the base of the international money supply) from the mines of Mexico and Peru; debt-ridden European governments hoarded the available specie; and American bankers and businessmen met the situation by expanding credit and issuing banknotes that were mere dreams of real money. Coming in the first years of the Market Revolution, this speculative boom was encouraged by American bankers who had little experience with corporate charters, promissory notes, bills of exchange, or stocks and bonds.

Congress had in part chartered the Second Bank of the United States in 1816 (see chapter 9) to impose order on this situation, but the Bank itself under the presidency of the genial Republican politician William Jones became part of the problem. The western branch offices in Cincinnati and Lexington became embroiled in the speculative boom, and insiders at the Baltimore branch hatched criminal schemes to enrich themselves. With matters spinning out of control, Jones resigned early in 1819. The new president, Langdon Cheves of South Carolina, curtailed credit and demanded that state banknotes received by the Bank of the United States be redeemed in specie (precious metals). By doing so, Cheves rescued the Bank from the paper economy created by state-chartered banks, but at huge expense: When the state banks were forced to redeem their notes in specie, they demanded payment from their own borrowers, and the national money and credit system collapsed.

The depression that followed the Panic of 1819 was the first failure of the market economy. Local ups and downs had occurred since the 1790s, but this collapse was nationwide. Employers who could not meet their debts went out of business, and hundreds of thousands of wage workers lost their jobs. In Philadelphia, unemployment reached 75 percent; 1,800 workers in that city were imprisoned for debt. A tent city of the unemployed sprang up on the outskirts of Baltimore. Other cities and towns were hit as hard, and the situation was no better in the countryside. Thomas Jefferson reported that farms in his neighborhood were selling for what had earlier been a year's rent, and a single session of the county court at Nashville handled more than 500 lawsuits for debt.

Faced with a disastrous downturn that none could control and that few understood, many Americans directed their resentment onto the banks, particularly on the Bank of the United States. John Jacob Astor, a New York merchant and possibly the richest man in America at that time, admitted that "there has been too much Speculation and too much assumption of Power on the Part of the Bank Directors which has caused [sic] the institution to become unpopular." William Gouge, who would become the Jacksonian Democrats' favorite economist, put it more bluntly: When the Bank demanded that state banknotes be redeemed in specie, he said, "the Bank was saved and the people were ruined." By the end of 1819, the Bank of the United States had won the name that it would carry to its death in the 1830s: the Monster.

Republican Revival

The crises during 1819 and 1820 prompted demands for a return to Jeffersonian principles. President Monroe's happily proclaimed Era of Good Feelings—a new era of party-less politics created by the collapse of Federalism—was, according to worried Republicans, a disaster. Without opposition, Jefferson's dominant Republican Party had lost its way. The nationalist Congress of 1816 had enacted much of the Federalist program under the name of Republicanism;

the result, said the old Republicans, was an aggressive government that helped bring on the Panic of 1819. At the same time, the collapse of Republican Party discipline in Congress had allowed the Missouri question to degenerate into a sectional free-for-all. By 1820, many Republicans were calling for a Jeffersonian revival that would limit government power and guarantee southern rights within the Union.

Martin Van Buren Leads the Way

The busiest and the most astute of those Republicans was Martin Van Buren, leader of New York's Bucktail Republican faction, who took his seat in the Senate in 1821. An immensely talented man with no influential family connections (his father was a Hudson valley tavern keeper) and little formal education, Van Buren had built his political career out of a commitment to Jeffersonian principles, personal charm, and party discipline. He and his colleagues in New York, deploying group discipline oiled by the partisan use of government patronage, had begun to invent the modern political party—arguing that it was a necessary weapon in democracy's contests with the well-placed, well-educated gentlemen who had monopolized public office. Arriving in Washington in the aftermath of the Missouri debates and the Panic of 1819, he hoped to apply his new politics to what he perceived as a dangerous turning point in national public life.

Van Buren's New York experience, along with his reading of national politics, told him that disciplined political parties were necessary democratic tools. The Founding Fathers—including Jefferson—had denounced parties, claiming that republics rested on civic virtue, not competition. Van Buren, on the other hand, claimed that the Era of Good Feelings had turned public attention away from politics, allowing privileged insiders—many of them unreconstructed Federalists—to create a big national state and to reorganize politics along sectional lines. Van Buren insisted that competition and party divisions were inevitable and good, but that they must be made to serve the republic. He wrote:

> We must always have party distinctions, and the old ones are the best. . . . If the old ones are suppressed, geographical differences founded on local instincts or what is worse, prejudices between free & slave holding states will inevitably take their place.

Working with like-minded politicians, Van Buren reconstructed the coalition of northern and southern agrarians that had elected Thomas Jefferson. The result was the Democratic Party and, ultimately, a national two-party system that persisted until the eve of the Civil War.

The Election of 1824

With the approach of the 1824 presidential election, Van Buren and his friends supported William H. Crawford, Monroe's secretary of war and a staunch Georgia Republican. The Van Burenites controlled the Republican congressional caucus, the body that traditionally chose the party's presidential candidates. The public distrusted the caucus as undemocratic because it represented the only party in government and thus could dictate the choice of a president. Van Buren, however, continued to regard it as a necessary tool of party discipline. With most congressmen fearing their constituents, only a minority showed up for the caucus vote. They dutifully nominated Crawford.

With Republican Party unity broken, the list of sectional candidates grew. John Quincy Adams was the son of a Federalist president, successful secretary of state under Monroe, and one of the northeastern Federalist converts to Republicanism who, according to people like Van Buren and Crawford, had blunted the republican thrust of Jefferson's old party. He entered the contest as New England's favorite son. Henry Clay of Kentucky, a nationalist who claimed as his own the American System of protective tariffs, centralized banking, and government-sponsored internal improvements, expected to carry the West. John C. Calhoun of South Carolina announced his candidacy, but when he saw the swarm of candidates, he dropped out and put himself forth as the sole candidate for vice president.

The wild card was Andrew Jackson of Tennessee, who in 1824 was known only as a military hero—scourge of the southern Indians and victor over the British at New Orleans (see chapter 8). He was also a frontier nabob with a reputation for violence: He had killed a rival in a duel, had engaged in a shoot-out in a Nashville tavern, and had reputedly stolen his wife from her estranged husband. According to Jackson's detractors, such impetuosity marked his public life as well. As commander of U.S. military forces in the South in 1818, Jackson had led an unauthorized invasion of Spanish Florida, claiming that it was a hideout for Seminole warriors who raided into the United States and a sanctuary for runaway Georgia slaves. During the action, he had occupied Spanish forts, summarily executed Seminoles, and hanged two British subjects. Secretary of State John Quincy Adams had belatedly approved the raid, knowing that the show of American force would encourage the Spanish to sell Florida to the United States. Secretary of War Crawford, on the other hand, as an "economy" measure, had reduced the number of major generals in the U.S. Army from two to one, thus eliminating Jackson's job. After being appointed governor of newly acquired Florida in 1821, Jackson retired from public life

The Granger Collection.

JOHN QUINCY ADAMS

The politician enjoyed a remarkably productive career as Monroe's Secretary of State, then rode into the presidency in the conflicted and controversial election of 1824. The intelligence and erudition that the picture projects had served him well as a diplomat. As president, it marked him as aloof, aristocratic, and incapable of governing a democratic nation.

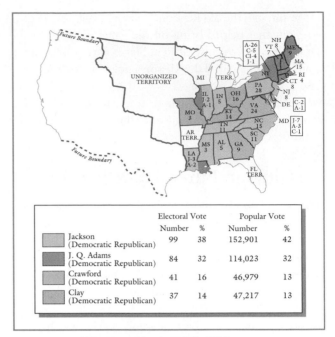

		Electoral Vote		Popular Vote	
		Number	%	Number	%
	Jackson (Democratic Republican)	99	38	152,901	42
	J. Q. Adams (Democratic Republican)	84	32	114,023	32
	Crawford (Democratic Republican)	41	16	46,979	13
	Clay (Democratic Republican)	37	14	47,217	13

MAP 12.1 PRESIDENTIAL ELECTION, 1824

Voting in the four-cornered contest of 1824 was starkly sectional. John Quincy Adams carried his native New England, while Crawford and Clay carried only a few states in their own sections. Only Andrew Jackson enjoyed national support: He carried states in every section but New England, and he ran a strong second in many of the states that were awarded to other candidates.

later that year. In 1824, eastern politicians knew Jackson only as a "military chieftain," "the Napoleon of the woods," a frontier hothead, and, possibly, a robber-bridegroom.

Jackson may have been all of those things, but the easterners failed to recognize his immense popularity, particularly in the new states of the South and the West. Thus, in the election of 1824, in the 16 states that chose presidential electors by popular vote (six states still left the choice to their legislatures), Jackson polled 152,901 votes to Adams's 114,023 and Clay's 47,217. Crawford, who suffered a crippling stroke during the campaign, won 46,979 votes. Jackson's support was not only larger but also more nearly national than that of his opponents. Adams carried only his native New England and a portion of New York. Clay's meager support was limited to the Northwest, and Crawford's to the Southeast and to the portions of New York that Van Buren was able to deliver. Jackson carried 84 percent of the votes of his own Southwest, and won victories in Pennsylvania, New Jersey, North Carolina, Indiana, and Illinois, and ran a close second in several other states.

"A Corrupt Bargain"

Jackson assumed that he had won the election: He had received 42 percent of the popular vote to his nearest rival's 33 percent, and he was clearly the nation's choice, but his 99 electoral votes were 32 shy of the plurality demanded by the Constitution. And so, acting under the 12th Amendment, the House of Representatives would select a president from among the top three candidates. As the candidate with the fewest electoral votes, Henry Clay was eliminated, but he remained Speaker of the House and had enough support to throw the election to either Jackson or Adams. Years later, Jackson told a dinner guest that Clay had offered to support him in exchange for Clay's appointment as secretary of state—an office that traditionally led to the presidency. When Jackson turned him down, according to Jacksonian legend, Clay went to Adams and made the same offer. Adams accepted what became known as the "Corrupt Bargain" in January 1825. A month later, the House of Representatives voted: Clay's supporters, joined by several old Federalists, switched to Adams, giving him a one-vote victory. Soon after becoming president, Adams appointed Henry Clay as his secretary of state.

From the Collections of the Library of Congress.

"THE SYMPTOMS OF A LOCKED JAW"

In 1827, Henry Clay published a rebuttal of Jacksonian charges that he had participated in a Corrupt Bargain to deliver the presidency to John Quincy Adams. Here, a pro-Clay cartoonist displays Clay as a tailor in the act of sewing Andrew Jackson's mouth shut. Neither the rebuttal nor the cartoon worked: the long-term suspicions of the bargain with Adams ruined Clay's chances to become president.

Jacksonian Melodrama

Andrew Jackson regarded the intrigues that robbed him of the presidency in 1825 as the culmination of a long train of corruption that the nation had suffered over the previous 10 years. Although in the campaign he had made only vague policy statements, he had firm ideas of what had gone wrong with the republic. In 1821, after having been "betrayed" by members of Monroe's cabinet over his raid into Florida, Jackson had retired to his plantation near Nashville to ponder the state of the nation and fill page after page with what he called "memorandums." (This was the kind of gaffe that appalled his educated eastern opponents and pleased nearly everyone else.)

A frontier planter with a deep distrust of banks, Jackson claimed that the Panic of 1819 had been brought on by self-serving miscreants in the Bank of the United States. He insisted that the national debt was another source of corruption; it must be paid off and never allowed to recur. The federal government under James Monroe was filled with swindlers, and in the name of a vague nationalism they were taking power for themselves and scheming against the liberties of the people. The politicians had been bought off, said Jackson, and had attempted—through "King Caucus"—to select a president by backstairs deals rather than by popular election. Finally, in 1825, they had stolen the presidency outright.

Like hundreds of thousands of other Americans, Jackson sensed that something had gone wrong with the republic—that selfishness and intrigue had corrupted the government. In the language of revolutionary republicanism, which Jackson had learned as a boy in the Carolina backwoods and would speak throughout his life, a corrupt power once again threatened to snuff out liberty.

In his "memorandums," Jackson set against the designs of that power the classic republican safeguard: a virtuous citizenry. Unlike most of his revolutionary forebears, however, he believed that government should follow the will of popular majorities. An aroused public, he said, was the republic's best hope: "My fervent prayers are that our republican government may be perpetual, and the people alone by their virtue, and independent exercise of their free suffrage can make it perpetual."

More completely than any of his rivals, Jackson had captured the rhetoric of the revolutionary republic. And, with his fixation on secrecy, corruption, and intrigues, he transformed both that rhetoric and his own biography into popular melodrama. Finally, with a political alchemy that his rivals never understood, Jackson submerged old notions of republican citizenship into a firm faith in majoritarian democracy: Individuals might become selfish and corrupt, he believed, but a democratic majority

Reaction to the alleged Corrupt Bargain between John Quincy Adams and Henry Clay dominated the Adams administration and gave rise to a rhetoric of intrigue and betrayal that nourished a rising democratic movement. Before the vote took place in the House of Representatives, Andrew Jackson remarked, "Rumors say that deep intrigue is on foot," and predicted a "bargain & sale" of the presidency. After the election, Jackson declared that the "gamester" Henry Clay has subverted the democratic will to his own purposes and that "the rights of the people have been bartered for promises of office." "So you see," Jackson said, "The *Judas* of the West has closed the contract and will receive the thirty pieces of silver. His end will be the same." Others in Washington were equally appalled. Robert Y. Hayne of South Carolina denounced the "monstrous union between Clay & Adams," and Louis McLane of Delaware declared the coalition of Clay and Adams utterly "unnatural & preposterous." (Eventually, Clay challenged Virginia Senator John Randolph, one of his nastiest critics, to a duel. Clay's shot passed harmlessly through Randolph's flowing coat, and Randolph fired a gentlemanly shot into the air, but the charge of corruption would follow Clay for the rest of his political life.)

was, by its very nature, opposed to corruption and governmental excess. Thus the republic was safe only when governed by the will of the majority. The Corrupt Bargain of 1825 had made that clear: Either the people or political schemers would rule.

Adams versus Jackson

While Jackson plotted revenge, John Quincy Adams assumed the duties of the presidency. He was well prepared. The son of a Federalist president, he had been an extraordinarily successful secretary of state under Monroe, guiding American diplomacy in the postwar world.

Nationalism in an International Arena

In the Rush-Bagot Treaty of 1817 and the British-American Convention of 1818, Secretary of State John Quincy Adams helped pacify the Great Lakes, restore American fishing rights off the coast of Canada, and draw the U.S.– Canadian boundary west to the Rocky Mountains—actions that transformed the Canadian–American frontier from a battleground into the peaceful border that it has been ever since. He pacified the southern border as well. In 1819, following Jackson's raid into Florida, the Adams-Onis Treaty procured Florida for the United States and defined the U.S.–Spanish border west of the Mississippi in ways that gave the Americans claims to the Pacific Coast in the Northwest.

Trickier problems had arisen when Spanish colonies in the Americas declared their independence. Spain could not prevent this, and the powers of Europe, victorious over Napoleon and determined to roll back the republican revolution, talked openly of helping Spain or of annexing South American territory for themselves. Both the Americans and the British opposed such a move, and the British proposed a joint statement outlawing the interference of any outside power (including themselves) in Latin America. Adams had thought it better for the United States to make its own policy than to "come in as cock-boat in the wake of the British man-of-war." In 1823, he wrote what became known as the Monroe Doctrine. Propounded at the same time that the United States recognized the new Latin American republics, it declared American opposition to any European attempt at colonization in the New World without (as the British had wanted) denying the right of the United States to annex new territory. Although the international community knew that the British navy, and not the Monroe Doctrine, kept the European powers out of the Americas, Adams had announced that the

United States was determined to become the preeminent power in the Western Hemisphere.

Nationalism at Home

As president, Adams tried to translate his fervent nationalism into domestic policy. Although the brilliant, genteel Adams had dealt smoothly with European diplomats, as president of a democratic republic he went out of his way to isolate himself and to offend popular democracy. In his first annual message to Congress, Adams outlined an ambitious program for national development under the auspices of the federal government: roads, canals, a national university, a national astronomical observatory ("lighthouses of the skies"), and other costly initiatives:

> The spirit of improvement is abroad upon the earth.... While foreign nations less blessed with ... freedom ... than ourselves are advancing with gigantic strides in the career of public improvement, were we to slumber in indolence or fold up our arms and proclaim to the world that we are palsied by the will of our constituents, would it not ... doom ourselves to perpetual inferiority?

Congressmen could not believe their ears as they listened to Adams's extravagant proposals. Here was a president who had received only one in three votes and who had entered office accused of intrigues against the democratic will. And yet at the first opportunity he was telling Congress to pass an ambitious program and not to be "palsied" by the will of the electorate. Even the many members of Congress who favored Adams's program were afraid to vote for it.

Adding to his reputation as an enemy of democracy whenever opportunity presented itself, Adams heaped popular suspicions not only on himself but also on his program. Hostile politicians and journalists never tired of joking about Adams's "lighthouses to the skies." More lasting, however, was the connection they drew between federal public works projects and high taxes, intrusive government, the denial of democratic majorities, and expanded opportunities for corruption, secret deals, and special favors. Congress never acted on the president's proposals, and the Adams administration emerged as little more than a long prelude to the election of 1828.

The Birth of the Democratic Party

As early as 1825, it was clear that the election of 1828 would pit Adams against Andrew Jackson. To the consternation of his chief supporters, Adams did nothing to prepare for the contest. He refused to remove even his noisiest enemies from appointive office, and he built no political organization for what promised to be a stiff contest for reelection.

Commodore David Porter, Commander of the Mexican Navy

Imperial wars and republican revolutions transformed the politics of the world in the late 18th and early 19th centuries. They also provided opportunities for international adventurers. Experienced naval officers were in particular demand, and some of them ended up in odd places: The Irishman William ("Admiral Guillermo") Brown sailed for revolutionary Buenos Aires; Thomas Cochrane, dismissed from the Royal Navy, became an admiral in the navies of Chile and Brazil; Admiral Murad Reis (a Scotsman named Lysle) sailed for the Tripoli pirates; and the American Commodore David Porter, for two tumultuous years beginning in 1826, commanded the naval forces of the Republic of Mexico.

David Porter was a brave and headstrong officer. He had spent two years in a Tripolitan prison; had pestered British commerce, the British whaling fleet, and the Royal Navy itself in the War of 1812; and was chasing pirates in the Caribbean when he launched an unauthorized raid into Puerto Rico (a Spanish possession) in 1824. (Porter did such things repeatedly: 10 years earlier, he had claimed the Marquesas Islands for an American government that had not authorized his action and did not want the islands.) John Quincy Adams, as secretary of state and then as president, was managing delicate relations with Spain, Spain's former mainland colonies, and the Spanish Caribbean. He encouraged the Navy as it court-martialed and suspended Porter for his Puerto Rican foray. Feeling betrayed, Porter offered his services to Mexico.

Mexico, along with Colombia and the Confederation of Central America, envisioned a grand republican fleet that would keep Spain off the mainland, destroy the Spanish fleet, and liberate Cuba. David Porter liked the idea. He went to Mexico City, agreed on a salary and a grant of land, set up headquarters in Veracruz, and began building the Mexican navy.

Nothing went right. The alliance of Latin American republics collapsed, and the Mexican government, embroiled in bankruptcy and intrigue, lost interest in its navy. Porter's officers were freebooters from England and Spain, and his sailors—many of whom were convicted felons—did not know how to sail. Still, he procured ships and trained crews, and in 1826 he sailed to the northern coast of Cuba to harass Spanish shipping. After a short, successful cruise, he took refuge in Key West (yet another flaunting of international boundaries) for much of 1827 and left only when the Mexican government, under subtle threats from Secretary of State Henry Clay, ordered him back to Veracruz.

Throughout 1828, he lobbied Mexico City (unsuccessfully) for his back pay and his land grant, and watched his ships rot and his sailors turn into vagrants on the streets of Veracruz. Worse, he ran afoul of General Antonio López de Santa Anna, who was emerging as the postrevolutionary strongman of Mexico. On one of Porter's trips to Mexico City, four assassins attacked him. He killed two and chased off the others, and was always certain that Santa Anna had sent them. Later, two more killers entered his bedroom in Veracruz, and Porter ran one of them through with his sword. It was time to leave Mexico.

President Andrew Jackson rescued him. Jackson did not value the niceties of diplomacy as did Adams and Clay; indeed, his own experience with military freelancing was similar to David Porter's. Porter sneaked out of Mexico and accepted appointment as Consul-General at Algiers, then as head of the American diplomatic mission to the Ottoman Empire. He built a grand orientalist mansion outside of Constantinople and died there in 1843.

U.S. Naval Historical Center Photograph.

COMMODORE DAVID PORTER

The opposition was much more active. Van Buren and like-minded Republicans (with their candidate Crawford hopelessly incapacitated) switched their allegiance to Jackson. They wanted Jackson elected, however, not only as a popular hero but as head of a disciplined and committed Democratic Party that would continue the states'-rights, limited-government positions of the old Jeffersonian Republicans.

The new Democratic Party Richmond *Enquirer* linked popular democracy with the defense of southern slavery. Van Buren began preparations for 1828 with a visit to John C. Calhoun of South Carolina. Calhoun was moving along the road from postwar nationalism to states'-rights conservatism; he also wanted to stay on as vice president and thus keep his presidential hopes alive. After convincing Calhoun to support Jackson and to endorse limited government, Van Buren wrote to Thomas Ritchie, editor of the *Enquirer* and leader of Virginia's Republicans, who could deliver Crawford's southern supporters to Jackson. In his letter, Van Buren proposed to revive the alliance of "the planters of the South and the plain Republicans of the North" that had won Jefferson the presidency. Reminding Ritchie of how one-party government had allowed the Missouri question to get out of hand, Van Buren insisted that "if the old [party loyalties] are suppressed, prejudices between free and slave holding states will inevitably take their place."

Thus a new Democratic Party, committed to an agrarian program of states' rights and minimal government and dependent on the votes of both slaveholding and non-slaveholding states (beginning, much like Jefferson's old party, with Van Buren's New York and Ritchie's Virginia), would ensure democracy, the continuation of slavery, and the preservation of the Union. The alternative, Van Buren firmly believed, was an expensive and invasive national state (Adams's "lighthouses to the skies"), the isolation of the slaveholding South, and thus mortal danger to the republic.

The Election of 1828

The presidential campaign of 1828 was an exercise in slander rather than a debate on public issues. Adhering to custom, neither Adams nor Jackson campaigned directly, but their henchmen viciously personalized the campaign. Jacksonians hammered away at the Corrupt Bargain of 1825 and at the dishonesty and weakness that Adams had supposedly displayed in that affair. The Adams forces attacked Jackson's character. They reminded voters of his duels and tavern brawls and circulated a "coffin handbill" describing Jackson's execution of militiamen during the Creek War. One of Henry Clay's newspaper friends circu-

lated the rumor that Jackson was a bastard and that his mother was a prostitute, but the most egregious slander of the campaign centered on Andrew Jackson's marriage. In 1790, Jackson had married Rachel Donelson, probably aware that she was estranged but not formally divorced from a man named Robards. Branding the marriage an "abduction," the Adams team screamed that Jackson had "torn from a husband the wife of his bosom," and had lived with her in a state of "open and notorious lewdness." They branded Rachel Jackson (now a deeply pious plantation housewife) an "American Jezebel," a "profligate woman," and a "convicted adulteress" whose ungoverned passions made her unfit to be First Lady of a "Christian nation."

The Adams strategy ultimately backfired. Many voters did agree that only a man who strictly obeyed the law was fit to be president and that Jackson's "passionate" and "lawless" nature disqualified him, but many others criticized Adams for making Jackson's private life a public issue. Some claimed that Adams's rigid legalism left no room for privacy or for local notions of justice. Whatever the legality of their marriage, Andrew and Rachel Jackson had lived as models of marital fidelity and romantic love for nearly 40 years; their neighbors had long ago forgiven whatever transgressions they may have committed. Thus,

The Hermitage: Home of President Andrew Jackson, Nashville, TN.

RACHEL DONELSON JACKSON AS A MATURE PLANTATION MISTRESS
Andrew Jackson supposedly wore this miniature portrait of his beloved Rachel over his heart after her death in 1828.

on the one hand, Jackson's supporters accused the Adams campaign of a gross violation of privacy and honor. On the other, they defended Jackson's marriage—and his duels, brawls, executions, and unauthorized military ventures—as a triumph of what was right and just over what was narrowly legal. The attempt to brand Jackson as a lawless man, in fact, enhanced his image as a melodramatic hero who battled shrewd, unscrupulous, legalistic enemies by drawing on his natural nobility and force of will.

The campaign caught the public imagination. Voter turnout was double what it had been in 1824, totaling 56.3 percent. Jackson won the election with 56 percent of the popular vote (a landslide unmatched until the 20th century) and with a margin of 178 to 83 in electoral votes. Adams carried New England, Delaware, and most of Maryland and took 16 of New York's 36 electoral votes. Jackson carried every other state. It was a clear triumph of democracy over genteel statesmanship, of limited government over expansive nationalism, and of the South and the West over New England. Just as clearly, it was a victory of popular melodrama over old forms of cultural gentility.

A People's Inauguration

Newspapers estimated that from 15,000 to 20,000 citizens (Duff Green's *United States Telegraph,* a Jackson paper, claimed 30,000) came to Washington to witness Jackson's

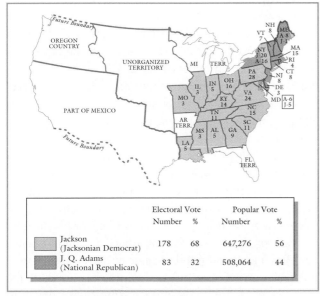

		Electoral Vote		Popular Vote	
		Number	%	Number	%
	Jackson (Jacksonian Democrat)	178	68	647,276	56
	J. Q. Adams (National Republican)	83	32	508,064	44

MAP 12.2 PRESIDENTIAL ELECTION, 1828

The 1828 presidential contest was a clear result of the organizing efforts that were building a national Democratic party under the name of Andrew Jackson. Jackson picked up all of the states that had gone for Crawford or Clay in 1824, leaving only New England and small portions of the mid-Atlantic for John Quincy Adams.

inauguration on March 4, 1829. They were "like the inundation of the northern barbarians into Rome," remarked Senator Daniel Webster. Many had traveled as much as 500 miles, and "they really seem to think that the country is rescued from some dreadful danger." As members of the Washington establishment watched uneasily, the crowd filled the open spaces and the streets near the east portico of the Capitol Building, where Jackson was to deliver his inaugural address.

Jackson arrived at the Capitol in deep mourning. In December, his wife Rachel had gone to Nashville to shop and had stopped to rest in a newspaper office. There, for the first time, she read the accusations that had been made against her. She fainted on the spot. Although she had been in poor health, no one would ever convince Jackson that her death in January had not been caused by his political enemies. As he arrived to assume the presidency, he wore a black suit and black tie, a black armband, and a black hatband that trailed down his neck in what was called a weeper.

Jackson's inaugural address was vague. He promised "proper respect" for states' rights and a "spirit of equity, caution, and compromise" on the question of the tariff, which was beginning to cause sectional controversy. He promised to reform the civil service by replacing "unfaithful or incompetent" officers, and he vowed to retire the national debt through "a strict and faithful economy." Beyond that, he said little, although he took every opportunity to flatter the popular majority. He had been elected "by the choice of a free people" (and not by King Caucus or Corrupt Bargains), and he pledged "the zealous dedication of my humble abilities to their service and their good." He finished—as he often finished an important statement—by reminding Americans that a benign providence looked over them. He then looked up to a roar of applause.

The new president traveled slowly from the Capitol to the White House, with the throng following and growing noisier along the way. The crowd followed him into the White House, where refreshments had been provided. Soon Jackson's well-wishers were ranging through the mansion, muddying the carpets, tipping things over, breaking dishes, and standing in dirty boots on upholstered chairs. Jackson had to retreat to avoid being crushed. The White House staff lured much of the crowd outside by moving the punch bowls and liquor to the lawn. A wealthy Washington matron who had admired the well-behaved crowd at the inaugural address exclaimed, "What a scene did we witness! *The Majesty of the People* had disappeared, and a rabble, a mob, of boys, negros, women, children, scrambling, fighting, romping. What a pity, what a pity." Another guest pronounced the occasion a "Saturnalia . . . of mud

THE PRESIDENT'S LEVEE
Robert Cruikshank drew Jackson's inaugural reception with men and women of all classes, children, dogs, and bucking horses celebrating the Old General's victory. Cruikshank subtitled his lithograph *All Creation Going to the White House.*

White House Collection.

and filth." A Democratic newspaper reported more favorably: "General Jackson is *their own* President. . . . He was greeted by them with an enthusiasm which bespoke him the Hero of a popular triumph."

The Spoils System

Jackson had begun to assemble his administration months before he took office. Martin Van Buren, who had mobilized much of the support Jackson gained between 1824 and 1828, was the new secretary of state—positioned to succeed Jackson as president. Van Buren quit his newly won post as governor of New York and came to Washington, where he became Jackson's most valued adviser. Other appointments were less promising, for Jackson filled the remaining cabinet posts with old friends and political supporters who in many cases proved unfit for their jobs. A critic looked at Jackson's cabinet and pronounced it—with the exception of Van Buren—"the Millennium of the Minnows."

Others were more concerned about what Jackson would do to the civil service than about whom he named to his cabinet. During the campaign, Jackson had vowed to fire corrupt officeholders—a term he applied to grafters, incompetents, long-term officeholders who considered their jobs personal property, and those who supported John Quincy Adams. Early in the administration, opponents complained that Jackson was replacing able, educated, patriotic public servants with some dubious appointments. They soon had convincing evidence: Samuel Swarthout, whom Jackson had appointed collector of the Port of New York (an office that handled $15 million dollars in tariff revenue annually), stole $1.2 million and took off for Europe.

Actually, much of the furor over Jackson's "spoils system" was overwrought and misdirected. He aimed, Jackson claimed, only to institute "rotation in office" and to eject officeholders who expected to hold lifetime appointments. Arguing that most government jobs could be performed by any honest, reasonably intelligent citizen, Jackson proposed ending the long tenures that, he said, turned the civil service into "support of the few at the expense of the many." Jackson removed about 1 in 10 executive appointees during his eight years in office, and his replacements (at least at the level of ambassadors, federal judges and attorneys, and cabinet members) were as wealthy and well-educated as their predecessors. They were, however, most decidedly *political* appointees. Acting out of his own need for personal loyalty and on the advice of Van Buren and other architects of the Democratic Party, Jackson filled vacancies—down to postmasters in the smallest towns—with Democrats who had worked for his election.

Jackson sought Van Buren's advice on appointments. Van Buren knew the political value of dispensing government jobs; one of his henchmen coined the phrase "To the victor belongs the spoils." In resorting to patronage to build the party, however, Jackson gave his opponents an important issue. Revolutionary republicans feared a government of lackeys dependent on a powerful executive, and congressional opponents argued that Jackson was using appointments to "convert the entire body of those in office into corrupt and supple instruments of power."

"A standing army," railed Henry Clay in the Senate, "has been, in all free countries, a just object of jealousy and suspicion. But is not a corps of one hundred thousand dependents upon government, actuated by one spirit, obeying one will, and aiming at one end, more dangerous than a standing army?" It became an anti-Jacksonian axiom that Jackson had made the federal civil service an arm of the Democratic Party and of despotic executive power.

Jacksonian Democracy and the South

In the 1828 election, even though Jackson ran strongly in every region but New England, the base of his support was in the South, where he won 8 of every 10 votes. Southerners had grown wary of an activist government in which they were in the minority. They looked to Jackson not only as a military hero but also as a Tennessee planter who talked about returning to republican fundamentals. Although southerners expected Jackson to look after southern interests, disagreement arose within the administration about how those interests should be protected. Some sided with Vice President Calhoun, who believed that any state had the right to veto federal legislation and even in extreme cases to secede from the Union. Others agreed with Secretary of State Van Buren that the Union was inviolable and that the South's best safeguard was in a political party committed to states' rights within the Union. The differences were fought out in the contest between Calhoun and Van Buren for the right to succeed Jackson as president, a contest that shaped every major issue of Jackson's first term.

Southerners and Indians

When Jackson entered office, a final crisis between frontier whites and the native peoples of the eastern woodlands was under way. By the 1820s, few Native Americans were left east of the Appalachians. The Iroquois of New York were penned into tiny reservations, and the tribes of the Old Northwest were broken and scattered. But in the Old Southwest, 60,000 Cherokees, Creeks, Choctaws, Chickasaws, and Seminoles were still living on their ancestral lands, with tenure guaranteed by federal treaties that (at least implicitly) recognized them as sovereign peoples. Congress had appropriated funds for schools, tools, seeds, and training to help these Civilized Tribes make the transition to farming. Most government officials assumed that the tribes would eventually trade their old lands and use their farming skills on new land west of the Mississippi.

Southwestern whites resented federal Indian policy as an affront to both white democracy and states' rights. The poorer farmers coveted the Indians' land, and states'-rights southerners denied that the federal government had the authority to make treaties or to recognize sovereign peoples within their states. Resistance centered in Georgia, where Governor George Troup brought native lands under the state's jurisdiction and then turned them over to poor whites by way of lotteries—thus tying states' rights to white hunger for Indian land. At one point, Troup sent state surveyors onto Creek territory before federal purchase from the Indians was complete, telling President Adams that if he resisted state authority he would be considered a "public enemy." The Cherokees in Georgia pressed the issue in 1827 by declaring themselves a republic with its own constitution, government, courts, and police, but at almost the same time, a gold discovery on their land made it even more attractive to whites. The Georgia legislature promptly declared Cherokee law null and void, extended Georgia's authority into Cherokee country, and began surveying the lands for sale. Hinting at the old connection between state sovereignty and the protection of slavery, Governor Troup warned that the federal "jurisdiction claimed over one portion of our population may very soon be asserted over *another*." Alabama and Mississippi quickly followed Georgia's lead by extending state authority over Indian lands and denying federal jurisdiction.

Indian Removal

President Jackson agreed that the federal government lacked the authority to recognize native sovereignty within a state and declared that he could not protect the Cherokees and the other Civilized Tribes from state governments. Instead, he offered to remove them to federal land west of the Mississippi, where they would be under the authority of the benevolent federal government. Congress made that offer official in the Indian Removal Act of 1830.

The Cherokees, with the help of New England missionaries, had taken their claims of sovereignty to court in the late 1820s. In 1830, John Marshall's Supreme Court ruled in *Cherokee Nation* v. *Georgia* that the Cherokees could not sue Georgia because they were not a sovereign people but "domestic dependent nations," thus dependents of the federal government, and not of the state of Georgia, although somehow "nations" as well. The Court's decision in *Worcester* v. *Georgia* (1832) declared that Georgia's extension of state law over Cherokee land was unconstitutional. President Jackson ignored the decision, however, reportedly telling a congressman, "John Marshall has made his decision: *now let him enforce it!*" In the end, Jackson sat back as the southwestern states encroached on

HISTORY THROUGH FILM

Amistad (1997)

Directed by Steven Spielberg. Starring Matthew McConaughey (Roger Baldwin), Morgan Freeman (Theodore Joadson), Anthony Hopkins (John Quincy Adams), Djimon Hounsou (Cinque).

In 1839, an American cruiser seized the Cuban slave ship *Amistad* off the shore of Long Island. The ship carried 41 Africans who had revolted, killed the captain and crew, and commandeered the ship—along with two Spanish slave dealers who bargained for their lives by promising to sail the ship east to Africa, then steered for North America. The Africans were imprisoned at New Haven and tried for piracy and murder in federal court. The government of Spain demanded their return, and southern leaders pressured President Van Buren for a "friendly" decision. The legal case centered on whether the Africans were Cuban slaves or kidnapped Africans. (The international slave trade was by then illegal.) The New Haven court acquitted them, the federal government appealed the case, and the Supreme Court freed them again. The Africans were returned to Sierra Leone.

The Africans spend most of the movie in a dark jail or in court, and the film centers on them and their experiences with two groups of Americans: the abolitionists who are trying to free them, and the political and legal officials who want to hang them—largely to keep their own political system intact. Spielberg's abolitionists are Lewis Tappan, a black activist (Morgan Freeman), an obscure young white lawyer (Matthew McConaughey), and, in the grand finale, Congressman and former President John Quincy Adams (played wonderfully by Anthony Hopkins). In the historical case, the defense was handled by veteran abolitionists or by persons who had been working with abolitionists for a long time. Spielberg shaped this group to tell his own story, beginning with reluctant and confused reformers and politicians who, along with the audience, gradually realize the moral imperatives of the case.

In one of the film's more powerful sequences, the Africans' leader, Cinque (Djimon Hounsou), through a translator, tells his story to the lawyer: his village life in Sierra Leone (the one scene filmed in bright sunlight), his capture by Africans, his transportation to the slave fort of Lomboko, the horrors of the passage on the Portuguese slaver *Tecora,* the slave market in Havana, and the bloody revolt on the *Amistad*—all of it portrayed wrenchingly on the screen. The Africans' story continues in jail, as they study pictures in a Bible and try to figure out the American legal, political, and moral system. In court, they finally cut through the mumbo-jumbo by standing and chanting "Give Us Free!"

In a fictive interview on the eve of the Supreme Court case, Cinque tells Adams that he is optimistic because he has called on the spirits of his ancestors to join him in court. This moment, he says, is the whole reason for their having existed at all. Adams, whose own father had helped lead the Revolution, speaks for his and Cinque's ancestors before the Supreme Court: to the prosecution's argument that the Africans are pirates and murderers and to southern arguments that slavery is a natural state, he answers that America is founded on the "self-evident truth" that the one natural state is freedom. It is a fine Hollywood courtroom speech: Adams has honored his ancestors, the justices and the audience see the moral rightness of his case, and the Africans are returned to Sierra Leone. (In a subscript, Spielberg tells us that Cinque returns to a village that had been destroyed in civil war, but the final ironic note is overwhelmed by the moral triumphalism of the rest of the movie.)

Amistad (1997) tells the story of 41 Africans who stage a revolt on the slave ship carrying them to Cuba and the trial that follows.

Kobal Collection/Cooper, Andrew/Dreamworks LLC.

the Civilized Tribes. In 1838, his successor, Martin Van Buren, sent the army to march the 18,000 remaining Cherokee to Oklahoma. Four thousand of them died along this Trail of Tears of exposure, disease, starvation, and white depredation.

Indian removal had profound political consequences. It violated Supreme Court decisions and thus strengthened Jackson's reputation as an enemy of the rule of law and a friend of local, "democratic" solutions; at the same time, it reaffirmed the link between racism and white democracy in the South and announced Jackson's commitment to state sovereignty and limited federal authority.

Southerners and the Tariff

In 1828, the Democratic Congress, acting under the direction of Van Buren and his congressional sidekick Silas Wright, set about writing a tariff that would win votes for Jackson in the upcoming presidential election. Assured of support in the South, the creators of the tariff bill fished for votes in the Middle Atlantic states and in the Old Northwest by including protective levies on raw wool, flax, molasses, hemp, and distilled spirits. The result was a patchwork tariff that pleased northern and western farmers but that worried the South and violated Jackson's own ideas of what a "judicious" tariff should be. Protective tariffs hurt the South by diminishing exports of cotton and other staples and by raising the price of manufactured goods. More ominous, they demonstrated the power of other sections to write laws that helped them and hurt the outnumbered South—a power, as southerners constantly reminded themselves, that might someday be used to attack slavery. Calling the new bill a Tariff of Abominations, the legislature of one southern state after another denounced it as (this was Virginia's formulation) "unconstitutional, unwise, unjust, unequal, and oppressive."

South Carolina, guided by Vice President Calhoun, took the lead in opposing the Tariff of 1828. During the War of 1812 and the ensuing Era of Good Feelings, Calhoun's South Carolina—confident of its future and deeply engaged in international markets for its rice and cotton—had favored the economic nationalism of the American

LINK TO THE PAST

Jackson and Indian Removal

In his second annual message to Congress in December 1830, President Jackson defended his policy of removing the remaining native peoples of the eastern woodlands to federal land west of the Mississippi:

Humanity has often wept over the fate of the aborigines of this country, and Philanthropy has been long busily employed in devising means to avert it, but its progress has never for a moment been arrested, and one by one have many powerful tribes disappeared from the earth. . . . Nor is there anything in this which, upon a comprehensive view of the general interests of the human race, is to be regretted.

Philanthropy could not wish to see this continent restored to the condition in which it was found by our forefathers. What good man would prefer a country covered with forests and ranged by a few thousand savages to our extensive Republic, studded with cities, towns and prosperous farms, embellished with all the improvements which art can devise or industry execute, occupied by

more than 12,000,000 happy people, and filled with all the blessings of liberty, civilization, and religion?

Jackson assumed that it was inevitable and good that white civilization would occupy North America, and that the history and lifeways of the Indians would end. These assumptions are offensive to modern sensibilities, and they were offensive to many Americans at the time. Yet Jackson and most of his contemporaries considered removal the best and most humane solution to the Native American "problem."

1. Can you think of other solutions to this problem?
2. What might the historical outcomes have been had your solutions been followed?

For additional sources related to this feature, visit the *Liberty, Equality, Power* Web site at:

http://history.wadsworth.com/murrin_LEP4e

Woolaroc Museum.

TRAIL OF TEARS

In 1838, the U.S. Army marched 18,000 Cherokee men, women, and children, along with their animals and whatever they could carry, out of their home territory and into Oklahoma. At least 4,000—most of them old or very young—died on the march.

System, but the Missouri debates had sent Carolinians looking for ways to safeguard slavery. The Denmark Vesey slave conspiracy of 1822 (see chapter 10) had stirred fears among the outnumbered whites of coastal South Carolina. Their fears grew more intense when federal courts shot down a state law forbidding black merchant seamen from moving about freely while their ships were docked at Charleston. Carolinians were disturbed too by persistent talk of gradual emancipation—at a time when their own commitment to slavery was growing stronger. Finally, southerners noted that in the congressional logrolling that made the Tariff of 1828, many western representatives had abandoned their old Jeffersonian alliance with the South to trade favors with the Northeast.

With the growth in the Northeast of urban markets for western produce, the American System's promise of interdependence among regions was beginning to work— but in ways that united the Northwest and Northeast against the export-oriented South. The Tariff of 1828 was the last straw: It benefited the city and commercial food producers at the expense of the plantation, and it demon-

strated that the South could do nothing to block the passage of such laws.

Nullification

As early as 1827, Calhoun concluded that southern states could protect themselves from national majorities only if they possessed the power to veto federal legislation within their boundaries. In 1828, in his anonymously published essay *Exposition and Protest,* he argued that the Constitution was a compact between sovereign states and that the states (not the federal courts) could decide the constitutionality of federal laws. A state convention (like the conventions that had ratified the Constitution) could nullify any federal law within state borders. "Constitutional government and the government of a majority," Calhoun argued, "are utterly incompatible." *Exposition and Protest* echoed the Virginia and Kentucky Resolves of 1798 and 1799 and anticipated the secessionist arguments of 1861: The Union was a voluntary compact between sovereign states, states were the ultimate judges of the validity of federal law, and states could break the compact if they wished.

Nullification was a dangerous measure, and Calhoun and his friends tried to avoid it. They knew that President Jackson was a states'-rights slaveholder who disliked the Tariff of 1828, and they assumed that Vice President Calhoun would succeed to the presidency in time and would protect southern interests. They were wrong on both counts. Jackson favored states' rights, but only within a perpetual and inviolable Union. His Indian policy, which had emboldened some southerners, was simply an acknowledgment of state jurisdiction over institutions within state boundaries. A tariff, on the other hand, was ultimately a matter of foreign policy, clearly within the jurisdiction of the federal government. To allow a state to veto a tariff would be to deny the legal existence of the United States.

Jackson revealed his views at a program celebrating Jefferson's birthday on April 13, 1830. Calhoun's southern friends dominated the speechmaking, and Jackson listened quietly as speaker after speaker defended the extreme states'-rights position. After the formal speeches were over, the president rose to propose an after-dinner toast. It was a powerful denunciation of what he had just heard: "Our Federal Union," he said in measured tones, *"It must be preserved."* Isaac Hill, a New Hampshire Democrat and a supporter of Van Buren, reported that "an order to arrest Calhoun where he sat would not have come with more blinding, staggering force." Dumb-struck, the southerners looked to Calhoun, who as vice president was to propose the second toast. Obviously shaken by Jackson's unqualified defense of the Union, Calhoun offered this toast: "The Union. Next to our liberties the most dear." They were strong words, but they had little meaning after Jackson's affirmation of the Union. A few days later, a South Carolina congressman on his way home asked the president if he had any message for him to take back. "Yes, I have," replied Jackson. "Please give my compliments to my friends in your state, and say to them, that if a single drop of blood shall be shed there in opposition to the laws of the United States, I will hang the first man I can lay my hand on engaged in such treasonable conduct, upon the first tree I can reach."

Having reaffirmed the Union and rejected nullification, Jackson asked Congress to reduce the tariff rates in the hope that he could isolate the nullifiers from southerners who simply hated the tariff. The resulting Tariff of 1832 lowered the rates on many items but still affirmed the principle of protectionism. That, along with the Boston abolitionist William Lloyd Garrison's declaration of war on slavery in 1831, followed by Nat Turner's bloody slave uprising in Virginia that same year (see chapter 10), led the whites of South Carolina and Georgia to intensify their distrust of outside authority and their insistence on the right to govern their own neighborhoods. South Carolina, now with Calhoun's open leadership and support, called a state convention that nullified the Tariffs of 1828 and 1832.

In Washington, President Jackson raged that nullification (not to mention the right of secession that followed logically from it) was illegal. Insisting that "Disunion . . . is *treason,*" he asked Congress for a Force Bill empowering him to personally lead a federal army into South Carolina. At the same time, however, he supported the rapid reduction of tariffs. When Democratic attempts at reduction bogged down, Henry Clay, who was now back in the Senate, took on the tricky legislative task of rescuing his beloved protective tariff while quieting southern fears. The result was the Compromise Tariff of 1833, which by lowering tariffs over the course of several years, gave southern planters the relief they demanded while maintaining moderate protectionism and allowing northern manufacturers time to adjust to the lower rates. Congress also passed the Force Bill. Jackson signed both into law on March 2, 1833.

With that, the nullification crisis came to a quiet end. No other southern state had joined South Carolina in nullifying the tariff, although some states had made vague pledges of support in the event that Jackson led his army to Charleston. The Compromise Tariff of 1833 isolated the South Carolina nullifiers. Deprived of their issue and most of their support, they declared victory and disbanded their convention—but not before nullifying the Force Bill. Jackson chose to overlook that last defiant gesture because he had accomplished what he wanted: He had asserted a perpetual Union, and he had protected southern interests within it.

The "Petticoat Wars"

The spoils system, Indian removal, nullification, and other heated questions of Jackson's first term were fought out against a backdrop of gossip, intrigue, and angry division within the inner circles of Jackson's government. The talk centered on Peggy O'Neal Timberlake, a Washington tavern keeper's daughter who, in January 1829, had married John Henry Eaton, Jackson's old friend and soon to be his secretary of war. Timberlake's former husband, a navy purser, had recently committed suicide; it was rumored that her affair with Eaton was the cause. Eaton was middle-aged; his bride was 29, pretty, flirtatious, and, according to Washington gossip, "frivolous, wayward, [and] passionate." Knowing that his marriage might cause trouble for the new administration, Eaton had asked for and received Jackson's blessings—and, by strong implication, his protection.

The marriage of John and Peggy Eaton came at a turning point in the history of both Washington society and elite sexual mores. Until the 1820s, most officeholders had left their families at home. They took lodgings at taverns and boardinghouses and lived in a bachelor world of shirtsleeves, tobacco, card-playing, and occasional liaisons with local women, but in the 1820s, the boardinghouse world was giving way to high society. Cabinet members, senators, congressmen, and other officials moved into Washington houses, and their wives presided over the round of dinner parties through which much of the government's business was done. As in other wealthy families, political wives imposed new forms of gentility and politeness on these affairs, and they assumed the responsibility of drawing up the guest lists. Many of them determined to exclude Peggy Eaton from polite society.

The exclusion of Peggy Eaton split the Jackson administration in half. Jackson was committed to protect her. He had met his own beloved Rachel while boarding at her father's Nashville tavern, and their grand romance (as well as the gossip that surrounded it) was a striking parallel to the affair of John and Peggy Eaton. That, coupled with Jackson's honor-bound agreement to the Eaton marriage, ensured that he would protect the Eatons to the bitter end. Always suspicious of intrigues, Jackson labeled the "dark and sly insinuations" about Peggy Eaton part of a "conspiracy" against his presidency. Motivated by chivalry, personal loyalty, grief and rage over Rachel's death, and angry disbelief that political intrigue could sully the private life of a valued friend, Jackson insisted to his cabinet that Peggy Eaton was "as chaste as a virgin!" Jackson noted that the rumor spreaders were not only politicians' wives but also prominent clergymen. Most prominent among the latter was Ezra Styles Ely of Philadelphia, who had recently called for an evangelical "Christian Party in politics." Jackson blamed the conspiracy on "females with clergymen at their head."

In fact, Mrs. Eaton's tormentors included most of the cabinet members as well as Jackson's own White House "family." Widowed and without children, Jackson had invited his nephew and private secretary, Andrew Jackson Donelson, along with his wife and her sister, to live in the White House. Donelson's wife, serving as official hostess, resolutely shunned Peggy Eaton. Jackson, who valued domestic harmony and personal loyalty, assumed that schemers had invaded and subverted his own household. Before long, his suspicions centered on Vice President Calhoun, whose wife, Floride Bonneau Calhoun, a haughty and powerful Washington matron, was a leader of the assault on Peggy Eaton. Only Secretary of State Van Buren,

a widower and an eminently decent man, included the Eatons in official functions. Sensing that Jackson was losing his patience with Calhoun, Van Buren's friends, soon after the Jefferson birthday banquet in spring 1830, showed Jackson a letter from William H. Crawford revealing that while serving in Monroe's cabinet Calhoun, contrary to his protestations, had favored censuring Jackson for his unauthorized invasion of Florida in 1818. An open break with Calhoun became inevitable.

The Fall of Calhoun

Jackson resolved the Peggy Eaton controversy, as he would resolve nullification, in ways that favored Van Buren in his contest with Calhoun. He sent Donelson, his wife, and his sister-in-law back to Tennessee and invited his friend W. B. Lewis and his daughter to take their place, but he pointedly made Peggy Eaton the official hostess at the

The Historical Society of Pennsylvania.

AN OPPOSITION CARTOON ON THE CABINET SHUFFLE OF 1831

The cabinet rats run from the falling house of government, while a bewildered Jackson retains Van Buren by standing on his tail.

White House. In spring 1831, Van Buren gave Jackson a free hand to reconstruct his tangled administration. He offered to resign his cabinet post and engineered the resignations of nearly all other members of the cabinet, thus allowing Jackson to remake his administration without firing anyone. Many of those who left were southern supporters of Calhoun. Jackson replaced them with a mixed cabinet that included political allies of Van Buren. Also at this time, President Jackson began to consult with an informal Kitchen Cabinet that included journalists Amos Kendall and Francis Preston Blair, along with Van Buren and a few others. The Peggy Eaton controversy and the resulting shakeup in the administration were contributing mightily to the success of Van Buren's southern strategy.

Van Buren's victory over Calhoun came to a quick conclusion. As part of his cabinet reorganization, Jackson appointed Van Buren minister to Great Britain—an important post that would remove him from the heat of Washington politics. Vice President Calhoun, sitting as president of the Senate, rigged the confirmation so that he cast the deciding vote against Van Buren's appointment—a petty act that turned out to be his last exercise of national power. Jackson replaced Calhoun with Van Buren as the vice presidential candidate in 1832 and let it be known that he wanted Van Buren to succeed him as president.

Petitions, the Gag Rule, and the Southern Mails

Van Buren and other architects of the Democratic Party promised to protect slavery with a disciplined national coalition committed to states' rights within an inviolable Union. The rise of a northern antislavery movement (see chapter 11) posed a direct challenge to that formulation. Middle-class evangelicals, who were emerging as the reformist core of the northern Whig Party, had learned early on that Jacksonian Democrats wanted to keep moral issues out of politics. In 1828 and 1829, when they petitioned the government to stop movement of the mail on Sundays, Jackson had turned them down. They next petitioned the government for humane treatment of the Civilized Tribes, whose conversion to Christianity had been accomplished largely by New England missionaries; again, the Jackson administration had refused. The evangelicals suspected Jackson of immorality, and they were appalled by his defense of Peggy Eaton and his attack on gentlewomen and preachers. Most of all, reformist evangelicals disliked the Democrats' rigid party discipline, which in each case had kept questions of morality from shaping politics.

In the early 1830s, a radical minority of evangelicals formed societies that were committed to the immediate abolition of slavery, and they devised ways of making the national government confront the slavery question. In 1835, abolitionists launched a "postal campaign," flooding the mail—both North and South—with antislavery tracts that southerners and most northerners considered incendiary. From 1836 onward, they bombarded Congress with petitions, most of them for the abolition of slavery and the slave trade in the District of Columbia (where Congress had undisputed jurisdiction), others against the interstate slave trade, slavery in the federal territories, and the admission of new slave states.

Some Jacksonians, including Jackson himself, wanted to stop the postal campaign with a federal censorship law. Calhoun and other southerners, however, argued that the states had the right to censor mail crossing their borders. Knowing that state censorship of the mail was unconstitutional and that federal censorship of the mail would be a political disaster, Amos Kendall, a Van Burenite who had become postmaster general in the cabinet shuffle, proposed an informal solution. Without changing the law, he would simply look the other way as local postmasters violated postal regulations and removed abolitionist materials from the mail. Almost all such materials were published in New York City and mailed from there. The New York postmaster, a loyal appointee, proceeded to sift them out of the mail and thus cut off the postal campaign at its source. The few tracts that made it to the South were destroyed by local postmasters. Calhoun and his supporters continued to demand that the states be given the power to deal with the mailings, but the Democrats had no intention of relinquishing federal control over the federal mail. They made it clear, however, that no abolitionist literature would reach the South as long as Democrats controlled the U.S. Post Office.

The Democrats dealt in a similar manner with antislavery petitions to Congress. Southern extremists demanded that Congress disavow its power to legislate on slavery in the District of Columbia, but Van Buren, who was preparing to run for president, declared that Congress did have that power but should never use it. In dealing with the petitions, Congress simply voted at each session from 1836 to 1844 to table them without reading them, thus acknowledging that they had been received but sidestepping any debate on them. This procedure, which became known as the "gag rule," was passed by southern Whigs and southern Democrats with the help of most (usually 80 percent or more) of the northern Democrats. Increasingly, abolitionists sent their petitions to ex-President John Quincy Adams, who had returned to Washington as a Whig congressman from Massachusetts. Like other northern Whigs, Adams openly opposed both slavery and the gag rule in Congress. Northern Whigs began calling him

Old Man Eloquent, while Calhoun dubbed him "a mischievous, bad old man." But most southerners saw what the Democrats wanted them to see: that their surest guarantee of safety within the Union was a disciplined Democratic Party determined to avoid sectional arguments.

Thus the Jacksonians answered the question that had arisen with the Missouri debates: how to protect the slave-holding South within the federal Union. Whereas Calhoun and other southern radicals found the answer in nullification and other forms of state sovereignty, Jackson and the Democratic coalition insisted that the Union was inviolable and that any attempt to dissolve it would be met with force. At the same time, a Democratic Party uniting northern and southern agrarians into a states'-rights, limited-government majority could guarantee southern rights within the Union. This answer to the southern question stayed in place until the breakup of the Democratic Party on the eve of the Civil War.

Jacksonian Democracy and the Market Revolution

Jacksonian Democrats cherished a nostalgic loyalty to the simplicity and naturalness of Jefferson's agrarian republic. They assumed power at the height of the Market Revolution, and they spent much of the 1830s and 1840s trying to reconcile the market and the republic. Like the Jeffersonians before them, Jacksonian Democrats welcomed commerce as long as it served the independence and rough equality of white men on which republican citizenship rested, but paper currency and the dependence on credit that came with the Market Revolution posed problems. The so-called paper economy separated wealth from "real work" and encouraged an unrepublican spirit of luxury and greed. Worst of all, the new paper economy required government-granted privileges that the Jacksonians, still speaking the language of revolutionary republicanism, branded "corruption." For the same reasons, the protective tariffs and government-sponsored roads and canals of the American System were antirepublican and unacceptable. The Jackson presidency aimed to curtail government involvement in the economy, to end special privilege, and thus to rescue the republic from the Money Power.

Jacksonians were opposed by those who favored an activist central government (by the mid-1830s they called themselves Whigs) that would encourage orderly economic development through the American System of protective tariffs, a federally subsidized transportation network, and a national bank. This system, they argued, would encourage national prosperity. At the same time, it would create a truly national market economy that would soften sectional divisions. Jacksonian rhetoric about the Money Power and the Old Republic, they argued, was little more than the demagoguery of unqualified, self-seeking politicians.

The Second Bank of the United States

The argument between Jacksonians and their detractors came to focus on the Second Bank of the United States, a mixed public-private corporation chartered by Congress in 1816 (see chapter 9). The national government deposited its revenue in the bank, thus giving it an enormous capital base. The government deposits also included state banknotes that had been used to pay customs duties or to buy public land; the Bank of the United States had the power to demand redemption of these notes in specie (gold and silver), thus discouraging state banks from issuing inflationary notes that they could not back up. The bank also issued notes of its own, and these served as the beginnings of a national paper currency. Thus with powers granted under its federal charter, the Bank of the United States exercised central control over the nation's monetary and credit systems.

Most members of the business community valued the Bank of the United States because it promised a stable, uniform paper currency and competent, centralized control over the banking system. But millions of Americans resented and distrusted the national bank, citing its role in the Panic of 1819 as evidence of the dangers posed by privileged, powerful institutions. President Jackson agreed with the latter. A southwestern agrarian who had lost money in an early speculation, he was leery of paper money, banks, and the credit system. He insisted that both the bank and paper money were unconstitutional and that the only safe, natural, republican currencies were gold and silver. Above all, Jackson saw the Bank of the United States as a government-sponsored concentration of power that threatened the republic.

The Bank War

The charter of the Bank of the United States ran through 1836, but Senators Henry Clay and Daniel Webster encouraged Nicholas Biddle, the Bank's brilliant, aristocratic president, to apply for recharter in 1832. Clay planned to oppose Jackson in the presidential election later that year, and he knew that Jackson hated the bank. He and his friends hoped to provoke the hot-tempered and supposedly erratic Jackson into a response they could use against him in the election.

Biddle applied to Congress for a recharter of the Bank of the United States in January 1832. Congress passed the recharter bill in early July and sent it on to the president. Jackson understood the early request for recharter as a political ploy. On July 4, Van Buren visited the White House and found Jackson sick in bed; Jackson took Van Buren's hand and said, "The bank, Mr. Van Buren, is trying to kill me, *but I will kill it!*" Jackson vetoed the bill.

Jackson's Bank Veto Message, sent to Congress on July 10, was a manifesto of Jacksonian Democracy. Written by Amos Kendall, Francis Preston Blair, and Roger B. Taney—republican fundamentalists who both hated the bank and understood the popular culture that shared their hatred—the message combined Jeffersonian verities with appeals to the public's prejudice. Jackson declared that the bank was "unauthorized by the Constitution, subversive of the rights of the states, and dangerous to the liberties of the people." Its charter, Jackson complained, bestowed special privilege on the bank and its stockholders, almost all of whom were northeastern businessmen or, worse, British investors. Having made most of its loans to southerners and westerners, the bank was a huge monster that sucked resources out of the agrarian South and West and poured them into the pockets of wealthy, well-connected northeastern gentlemen and their English friends. The granting of special privilege to such people (or to any others) threatened the system of equal rights that was essential in a republic. Jackson granted that differences in talents and resources inevitably created social distinctions, but he stood firm against "any prostitution of our Government to the advancement of the few at the expense of the many." He concluded with a call to the civic virtue and the conservative, God-centered Protestantism in which he and most of his agrarian constituency had been raised: "Let us firmly rely on that kind Providence which I am sure watches with peculiar care over the destinies of our Republic, and on the intelligence and wisdom of our countrymen. Through *His* abundant goodness and *their* patriotic devotion our liberty and Union will be preserved."

Henry Clay, Nicholas Biddle, and other anti-Jacksonians had expected the veto. And the Bank Veto Message was a long, rambling attack that, in their opinion, demonstrated Jackson's unfitness for office. "It has all the fury of a chained panther biting the bars of its cage," said Biddle, concluding that "it really is a manifesto of anarchy." So certain were they that the public shared their views that Clay's supporters distributed Jackson's Bank Veto Message as *anti*-Jackson propaganda during the 1832 campaign. They were wrong: A majority of the voters shared Jackson's attachment to a society of virtuous, independent producers and to republican government in its pristine form; they also agreed that the republic was in danger of subversion

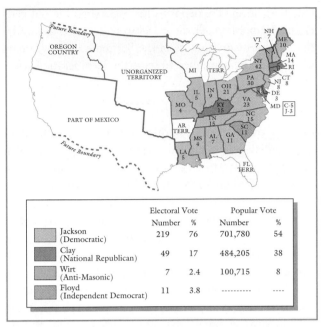

MAP 12.3 PRESIDENTIAL ELECTION, 1832

The election of 1832 was a landslide victory for Andrew Jackson. The National Republican Henry Clay carried only his native Kentucky, along with Delaware and southern New England. A defeated and resentful South Carolina ran its own candidate. Jackson, on the other hand, won in the regions in which he had been strong in 1828 and added support in New York and northern New England.

by parasites who grew rich by manipulating credit, prices, paper money, and government-bestowed privileges. Jackson portrayed himself as both the protector of the Old Republic and a melodramatic hero contending with illegitimate, aristocratic, privileged, secretive powers. With the bank and Jackson's veto as the principal issues, Jackson won reelection by a landslide in 1832.

Jackson began his second term determined to kill the Bank of the United States before Congress could reverse his veto. The bank would be able to operate under its old charter until 1836, but Jackson was determined to speed its death by withdrawing government deposits as they were needed and by depositing new government revenues in carefully selected state banks—soon to be called Pet Banks by the opposition. By law, the decision to remove the deposits had to be made by the secretary of the treasury, and Treasury Secretary Louis McLane, along with most of the cabinet, doubted the wisdom if not the legality of withdrawing these funds. Jackson in response transferred McLane to the vacant post of secretary of state and named William J. Duane as treasury secretary. Duane, too, refused to withdraw the deposits. Jackson fired him and appointed Roger B. Taney, the attorney general and a close adviser who had helped write the Bank Veto Message. A loyal Democrat who hated banks as much as Jackson did,

Taney withdrew the deposits. In 1835, when the old Federalist John Marshall died, Jackson rewarded Taney by making him Chief Justice of the Supreme Court—a post from which he continued to serve the Democratic Party.

The Beginnings of the Whig Party

Conflict over deposit removal and related questions of presidential power united opposers to the Jacksonian Democrats—most of them committed advocates of the American System—into the Whig Party in 1834. The name of the party, as everyone who knew the language of the republic immediately recognized, stood for legislative opposition to a power-mad executive. Jackson, argued the Whigs, had transformed himself from the limited executive described in the Constitution into King Andrew I. This had begun with Jackson's arbitrary uses of the executive patronage. It had become worse when Jackson began to veto congressional legislation. Earlier presidents had exercised the veto only nine times, usually on unimportant bills and always on the grounds that the proposed legislation was unconstitutional. Jackson used the veto often—too often, said the Whigs, when a key component of the American System was at stake. In May 1830, for instance, Jackson vetoed an attempt by Congress to buy stock in a turnpike to run from the terminus of the National Road at Louisville to Maysville, Kentucky. Jackson argued that because the road would be entirely in Kentucky, it was "partial" legislation that would take money from the whole people to benefit just one locality. He also questioned whether such federal subsidies were constitutional. Most important, however, Jackson announced that he was determined to reduce federal expenditures in order to retire the national debt—hinting strongly that he would oppose all federal public works.

The bank veto conveyed the same message even more strongly, and the withdrawal of the government deposits brought the question of "executive usurpation" to a head in 1834. Withdrawal of the deposits, together with Jackson's high-handed treatment of his treasury secretaries, caused uneasiness even among the president's supporters, and his enemies took extreme measures. Nicholas Biddle, announcing that he must clean up the affairs of the Bank of the United States before closing its doors, demanded that all its loans be repaid—a demand that undermined the credit system and produced a sharp financial panic. No doubt one reason for Biddle's action was to punish Andrew Jackson. While Congress received a well-orchestrated petition campaign to restore the deposits, Henry Clay led an effort in the Senate to censure the president, which it did in March 1834. Daniel Webster, the Bank's best friend

BORN TO COMMAND.

OF VETO MEMORY.

HAD I BEEN CONSULTED.

KING ANDREW THE FIRST.

KING ANDREW

THE FIRST,

" *Born to Command.*"

A **KING** who, possessing as much power as his Gracious Brother *William IV.*, makes a worse use of it.

A **KING** who has placed himself above the laws, as he has shown by his contempt of our judges.

A **KING** who would destroy our currency, and substitute *Old Rags.* payable by no one knows who, and no one knows where, instead of *good Silver Dollars.*

A **KING** born to command, as he has shown himself by appointing men to office contrary to the will of the People.

A **KING** who, while he was feeding his favourites out of the public money, denied a pittance to the *Old Soldiers* who fought and **bled** for our independence.

A **KING** whose *Prime Minister* and *Heir Apparent.* was thought unfit for the office of ambassador by the people:

Shall he reign over us,

Or shall the PEOPLE RULE?

KING ANDREW

In this widely distributed opposition cartoon, King Andrew, with a scepter in one hand and a vetoed bill in the other, tramples on internal improvements, the Bank of the United States, and the Constitution.

in government, and Clay, who had watched as Jackson denied one component after another of his American System, led the old National Republican coalition (the name that anti-Jacksonians had assumed since 1824) into the new Whig Party. They were joined by southerners (including Calhoun) who resented Jackson's treatment of the South Carolina nullifiers and Biddle's bank, and who distrusted his assurances on slavery. In any case, Jackson's war on the Bank of the United States did the most to separate parties. His withdrawal of the deposits chased lukewarm supporters into the opposition, while Democrats who closed ranks behind him could point to an increasingly sharp division between the Money Power and the Old Republic. Referring to Biddle's panic of 1834, James K. Polk of Tennessee, who led the Democrats in the House of Representatives, declared that "the question is in fact whether we shall have the Republic without the Bank or the Bank without the Republic."

A Balanced Budget

In part, Jackson removed the deposits because he anticipated a federal surplus revenue that, if handed over to Biddle's Bank of the United States, would have made it stronger than ever. The Tariffs of 1828 and 1832 produced substantial government revenue, and Jackson's frugal administration spent little of it. Even the Compromise Tariff of 1833 left rates temporarily high, and the brisk sale of

public lands was adding to the surplus. In 1833, for the only time in history, the United States paid off its national debt. Without Jackson's removal of the deposits, a growing federal treasury would have gone into the bank and would have found its way into the hated paper economy.

Early in his administration, Jackson had favored distributing surplus revenue to the states to be used for internal improvements, but he came to distrust even that minimal federal intervention in the economy, fearing that redistribution would encourage Congress to keep land prices and tariff rates high. Whigs, who by now despaired of ever creating a federally subsidized, coordinated transportation system, picked up the idea of redistribution. With some help from the Democrats, they passed the Deposit Act of 1836, which increased the number of banks receiving federal deposits (thus removing power from Jackson's Pet Banks) and distributed any federal surplus to the states to be spent on roads, canals, and schools. Jackson, who distrusted state-chartered banks as much as he distrusted the Bank of the United States, feared that the new deposit banks would use their power to issue mountains of new banknotes. He demanded a provision limiting their right to print banknotes. With that provision, he reluctantly signed the Deposit Act.

Jackson and many members of his administration had deep fiscal and moral concerns about the inflationary boom that accompanied the rapid growth of commerce, credit, roads, canals, new farms, and the other manifestations of

A MOCK BANKNOTE DECRYING THE DEMOCRATS' DESTRUCTION OF THE BANK OF THE UNITED STATES
A gang of officeholders pull Van Buren into perdition over the prostrate bodies of honest citizens. At right, Jackson, dressed as an old woman, watches.

the Market Revolution in the 1830s. After insisting that his hard-money, anti-inflationary provision be added to the Deposit Act, Jackson issued a Specie Circular in 1836, which provided that speculators could buy large parcels of public land only with silver and gold coins, and settlers could continue to buy farm-sized plots with banknotes. Henceforth, speculators would have to bring wagonloads of coins from eastern banks to frontier land offices. With this provision, Jackson hoped to curtail speculation and to reverse the flow of specie out of the South and West and into the Northeast. The Specie Circular was Jackson's final assault on the paper economy. It repeated familiar themes: It favored hard currency over paper, settlers over speculators, and the South and West over the Northeast.

The Second American Party System

In his farewell address in 1837, Jackson spoke once again of the incompatibility between the republic and the Money Power. He warned against a revival of the Bank of the United States and against all banks, paper money, the spirit of speculation, and every aspect of the "paper system." That system encouraged greed and luxury, which were at odds with republican virtue, he said. Worse, it thrived on special privilege, creating a world in which insiders meeting in "secret conclaves" could buy and sell elections. The solution, as always, was an arcadian society of small producers, a vigilant democratic electorate, and a chaste republican government that granted no special privileges.

"Martin Van Ruin"

Sitting beside Jackson as he delivered his farewell address was his chosen successor, Martin Van Buren. In the election of 1836, the Whigs had acknowledged that Henry Clay, the leader of their party, could not win a national election. Instead, they ran three sectional candidates—Daniel Webster in the Northeast, the old Indian fighter William Henry Harrison in the West, and Hugh Lawson White of Tennessee, a turncoat Jacksonian, in the South. With this ploy, the Whigs hoped to deprive Van Buren of a majority and throw the election into the Whig-controlled House of Representatives.

The strategy failed. Van Buren had engineered a national Democratic Party that could avert the dangers of sectionalism, and he questioned the patriotism of the Whigs and their sectional candidates, asserting that "true republicans can never lend their aid and influence in creating geographical parties." That, along with his associa-

tion with Jackson's popular presidency, won him the election. Van Buren carried 15 of the 26 states and received 170 electoral votes against 124 for his combined opposition. His popular plurality, however, was less than 51 percent.

Van Buren had barely taken office when the inflationary boom of the mid-1830s collapsed. Economic historians ascribe the Panic of 1837 and the ensuing depression largely to events outside the country. The Bank of England, concerned over the flow of British gold to American speculators, cut off credit to firms that did business in the United States. As a result, British demand for American cotton fell sharply, and the price of cotton dropped by half. With much of the speculative boom tied to cotton grown in the Southwest, the collapse of the economy was inevitable. The first business failures came in March 1837, just as Van Buren took office. By May, New York banks, unable to accommodate people who were demanding hard coin for their notes, suspended specie payments. Other banks followed suit, and soon banks all over the country—including Nicholas Biddle's newly renamed Bank of the United States of Pennsylvania—went out of business. Although few American communities escaped the economic downturn, the commercial and export sectors of

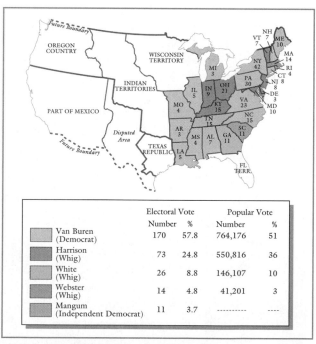

		Electoral Vote		Popular Vote	
		Number	%	Number	%
	Van Buren (Democrat)	170	57.8	764,176	51
	Harrison (Whig)	73	24.8	550,816	36
	White (Whig)	26	8.8	146,107	10
	Webster (Whig)	14	4.8	41,201	3
	Mangum (Independent Democrat)	11	3.7	----------	----

MAP 12.4 PRESIDENTIAL ELECTION, 1836

In 1836, the Whigs tried to beat the Democrats' national organization with an array of sectional candidates, hoping to throw the election into the House of Representatives. The strategy failed. Martin Van Buren, with significant support in every section of the country, defeated the three Whig candidates combined.

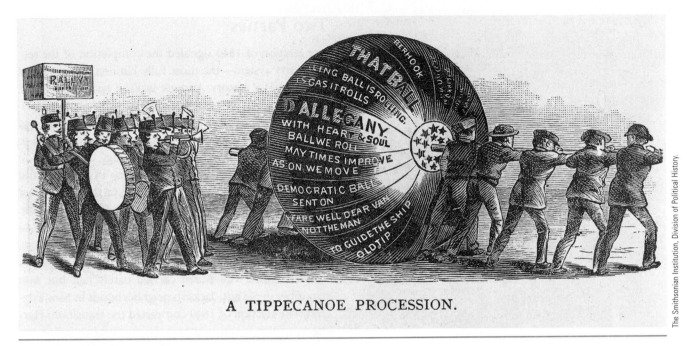

A TIPPECANOE PROCESSION.

The Smithsonian Institution, Division of Political History.

"A TIPPECANOE PROCESSION"

In 1840, the Whigs, who had earlier been repelled by the boisterous electioneering techniques of the Democrats, filled the campaign with humor and noise, beating the Democrats at their own game. Among many other things, the Whigs covered a great paper ball with slogans (none of which had anything to do with national issues) and rolled it across the midwestern and northeastern states—accompanied by brass bands and shouts of "Keep the ball rolling!"

the economy suffered most. In the seaport cities, one firm after another closed its doors, and about one-third of the workforce was unemployed. Wages for those who kept their jobs declined by some 30 to 50 percent. It was the deepest, most widespread, and longest economic depression Americans had ever faced.

Whigs blamed the depression on Jackson's hard-money policies, particularly his destruction of the Bank of the United States and his Specie Circular. With economic distress the main issue, Whigs scored huge gains in the midterm elections of 1838, even winning control of Van Buren's New York with a campaign that castigated the president as "Martin Van Ruin." Democrats blamed the crash on speculation, luxury, and Whig paper money. Whigs demanded a new national bank, but Van Buren proposed the complete divorce of government from the banking system through what was known as the Sub-Treasury, or Independent Treasury. Under this plan, the federal government would simply hold and dispense its money without depositing it in banks; it would also require that tariffs and land purchases be paid in gold and silver coins or in notes from specie-paying banks, a provision that allowed government to regulate state banknotes without resorting to a central bank. Van Buren asked Congress to set up the Independent Treasury in 1837, and Congress spent the rest of Van Buren's time in office arguing about it. The Independent Treasury Bill finally passed in 1840, completing the Jacksonian separation of bank and state.

The Election of 1840

Whigs were confident that they could blame Van Buren for the country's economic troubles and take the presidency away from him in the election of 1840. Trying to offend as few voters as possible, they passed over their best-known leaders, Senators Henry Clay and Daniel Webster, and nominated William Henry Harrison of Ohio as their presidential candidate. Harrison was the hero of the Battle of Tippecanoe (see chapter 7) and a westerner whose Virginia origins made him palatable in the South. He was also a proven vote-getter: As the Whigs' "western" candidate in 1836, he had carried seven states scattered across the Northwest, the Middle Atlantic, New England, and the Upper South. Best of all, he was a military hero who had expressed few opinions on national issues and who had no political record to defend. As his running mate, the Whigs chose John Tyler, a states'-rights Virginian who had joined the Whigs out of hatred for Jackson. To promote this baldly pragmatic ticket, the Whigs came up with a catchy slogan: "Tippecanoe and Tyler Too." Philip Hone, a wealthy New York City Whig, admitted that the slogan (and the ticket) had "rhyme, but no reason in it."

Early in the campaign, a Democratic journalist, commenting on Harrison's political inexperience and alleged unfitness for the presidency, wrote, "Give [Harrison] a barrel of hard cider, and settle a pension of two thousand a year on him, and my word for it, he will sit out the remainder of his days in his log cabin." Whigs who had been trying to shake their elitist image seized on the statement and launched what was known as the Log Cabin Campaign. The log cabin, the cider barrel, and Harrison's folksiness and heroism constituted the entire Whig campaign, while Van Buren was pictured as living in luxury at the public's expense. The Whigs conjured up an image of a nattily dressed President "Van Ruin" sitting on silk chairs and dining on gold and silver dishes while farmers and workingmen struggled to make ends meet. Whig doggerel contrasted Harrison the hero with Van Buren the professional politician:

> The knapsack pillow'd Harry's head
> The hard ground eas'd his toils;
> While Martin on his downy bed
> Could dream of naught but spoils.

Democrats howled that Whigs were peddling lies and refusing to discuss issues, but they knew they had been beaten at their own game. Harrison won only a narrow majority of the popular vote, but a landslide of 234 to 60 votes in the electoral college.

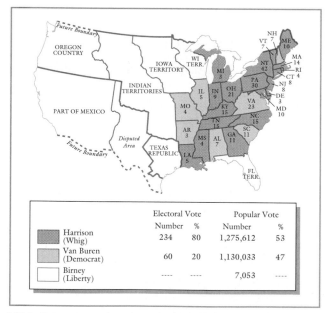

MAP 12.5 PRESIDENTIAL ELECTION, 1840

In 1840, the Whigs united under William Henry Harrison, the one Whig candidate who had won national support four years earlier. Borrowing campaign tactics from the Democrats and inventing many of their own, Whigs campaigned hard in every state. The result was a Whig victory and a truly national two-party system.

Two Parties

The election of 1840 signaled the completion of the second party system—the most fully national alignment of parties in U.S. history. Andrew Jackson had won in 1828 with Jefferson's old southern and western agrarian constituency; in 1832, he had carried his old voters and had won added support in the Middle Atlantic states and in northern New England. In 1836, Whigs capitalized on southern resentment of Jackson's defeat of Calhoun and nullification and on southern mistrust of the New Yorker Van Buren to break the Democratic hold on the South. Whigs came out of their old northeastern strongholds to carry Ohio, Illinois, Kentucky, Georgia, South Carolina, and even Jackson's Tennessee. Jackson had won 8 in 10 southern votes; Van Buren carried barely half but won majorities in old anti-Jackson neighborhoods in New England. The election of 1840 completed the transition: Harrison and Van Buren contested the election in nearly every state; perhaps most significantly, they received nearly equal levels of support in the slave and free states. Van Buren's dream of a national party system was realized. Ironically, the final pieces fell into place in an election that cost him the presidency.

The election of 1840 also witnessed the high-water mark of voter turnout. Whig and Democratic organizations focused on presidential elections, and prospective voters met a quadrennial avalanche of oratory, door-to-door canvassing, torchlight parades, and party propaganda. As the contests became national, Democrats or Whigs could take no state in the Union for granted. (In 1828, winning candidates carried individual states by an average of 36 percent; by 1840, that figure had dropped to 11 percent.) Both Whigs and Democrats maintained organizations and contested elections in nearly every neighborhood in the country, and the result was increased popular interest in politics. In 1824, about one in four adult white men had voted in the presidential election. Jackson's vengeful campaign of 1828 lifted the turnout to 56.3 percent, and it stayed at about that level in 1832 and 1836. The campaign of 1840 brought out 78 percent of the eligible voters, and the turnout remained at that high level throughout the 1840s and 1850s.

Conclusion

By 1840, American politics operated within a stable, national system of two parties, both of which depended on support in every section of the country. Whigs argued for the economic nationalism of the American System. Democrats argued for the limited, inexpensive government that since Jefferson's day had been a bulwark of both republicanism and slavery. The party system provided answers to the questions of sectionalism and economic development that had helped bring it into being. Democrats successfully fought off the American System: They dismantled the Bank of the United States, refused federal support for roads and canals, and revised the tariff in ways that mollified the export-oriented South. The result, however, was not the return to Jeffersonian agrarianism that many Democrats had wanted but an inadvertent experiment in laissez-faire capitalism. The stupendous growth of

the American economy between 1830 and 1860 became a question of state and local—not national—government action. On the growing political problems surrounding slavery, the two-party system did what Van Buren had hoped it would do: Because the Whig and (especially) Democratic Parties needed both northern and southern support, they were careful to focus national political debates on economic development, avoiding any discussion of sectional questions. It worked that way until the party system disintegrated on the eve of the Civil War.

SUGGESTED READINGS

Arthur M. Schlesinger, Jr., *The Age of Jackson* (1945) is a classic treatment of politics from the 1820s through the 1840s, whereas **Harry L. Watson,** *Liberty and Power: The Politics of Jacksonian America* (1990) is an excellent modern synthesis. On presidential elections, the best place to start is the essays in **Arthur M. Schlesinger, Jr., and Fred J. Israels, eds.,** *History of American Presidential Elections, 1789–1968,* 3 vols. (1971). **George Dangerfield,** *The Era of Good Feelings* (1953) and **Glover Moore,** *The Missouri Controversy, 1819–1821* (1953) are standard treatments of their subjects. On nullification, see **William W. Freehling,** *Prelude to Civil War: The Nullification Controversy in South Carolina, 1816–1836* (1965) and **Richard E. Ellis,** *The Union at Risk: Jacksonian Democracy, States' Rights and the Nullification Crisis* (1987). Two important accounts of slavery in national politics are **William Lee Miller,** *Arguing About Slavery: The Great Battle in the United States Congress* (1996) and **Don E. Fehrenbacher,** *The Slaveholding Republic: An Account of the United States Government's Relations to Slavery* (2001). On Jackson and Indian Removal, a good introduction is **Robert V. Remini,** *Andrew Jackson and His Indian Wars* (2001). On the Bank War, see **Bray Hammond,** *Banks*

and Politics in America from the Revolution to the Civil War (1957) and **Peter Temin,** *The Jacksonian Economy* (1967). The making of the party system is the subject of **Richard Hofstadter,** *The Idea of a Party System: The Rise of Legitimate Opposition in the United States, 1780–1840* (1969) and **Richard P. McCormick,** *The Second American Party System: Party Formation in the Jacksonian Era* (1966).

AMERICAN JOURNEY ONLINE AND INFOTRAC COLLEGE EDITION

Visit the source collections at www.ajaccess.wadsworth.com and infotrac.thomsonlearning.com and use the Search function with the following key terms to explore documents, images, audio and video clips, articles, and commentary related to the material in this chapter.

Lewis and Clark
Monroe Doctrine
Henry Clay

Missouri Compromise
Andrew Jackson
Indian Removal Act

GRADE AIDS

Visit the Liberty Equality Power Companion Web Site for resources specific to this textbook: http://history.wadsworth.com/murrin_LEP4e

The CD in the back of this book and the U.S. History Resource Center at http://history.wadsworth.com/u.s./ offer a variety of tools to help you succeed in this course, including access to quizzes; images; documents; interactive simulations, maps, and timelines; movie explorations; and a wealth of other sources.

Chapter 13

Manifest Destiny: An Empire for Liberty—or Slavery?

MANIFEST DESTINY
This painting portrays the self-serving symbolism of America's westward expansion in the mid-19th century. White pioneers on foot, on horseback, and in oxen-drawn wagons cross the plains, driving the Indians and buffalo before them while a farmer breaks the sod on the farming frontier. A stagecoach and puffing locomotives follow an ethereal Columbia in flowing raiment bearing a schoolbook and stringing telegraph wire across the continent.

When William Henry Harrison took the oath as the first Whig president on March 4, 1841, the stage seemed set for the enactment of Henry Clay's American System. Instead, Harrison contracted pneumonia after he delivered an interminable inaugural address outdoors in a sleet and snow storm. He died a month later, and John Tyler, a states-rights Virginian, became president. Tyler had become a nominal Whig only because of his hatred of Andrew Jackson. He proceeded to read himself out of the Whig Party by vetoing two bills to create a new national bank. Their domestic program a shambles, the Whigs lost control of the House in the 1842 midterm elections. Thereafter, the political agenda shifted to the Democratic program of territorial expansion. Through annexation, negotiation, and war, the United States increased its size by 50 percent in the years between 1845 and 1848, but this achievement reopened the issue of slavery's expansion and planted the bitter seeds of civil war.

CHAPTER FOCUS

♦ What impulses lay behind the Manifest Destiny of America's westward expansion?

♦ How did westward expansion relate to the issue of slavery?

♦ What were the causes and consequences of the Mexican-American War?

♦ What issues were at stake in the congressional debates that led to the Compromise of 1850?

♦ How successfully did the compromise resolve these issues?

🐢 Growth as the American Way

By 1850, older Americans had seen the area of the United States quadruple in their lifetime. During the 47 years since the Louisiana Purchase of 1803, the American population had also quadrupled. If those rates of growth had continued after 1850, the United States would have contained 1.8 *billion* people at the end of the 20th century and would have occupied every square foot of land on the globe. If the sevenfold increase in the gross national product that Americans enjoyed from 1800 to 1850 had persisted, today's U.S. economy would be larger than that of today's entire world economy.

Many Americans in 1850 took this prodigious growth for granted. They considered it evidence of God's beneficence to this virtuous republic. During the 1840s, a group of expansionists affiliated with the Democratic Party began to call themselves the Young America movement. They proclaimed that it was the Manifest Destiny of the United States "to overspread and to possess the whole of the continent which Providence has given us for the development of the great experiment of liberty," wrote John L. O'Sullivan, editor of the *Democratic Review*, in 1845.

Not all Americans considered this unbridled expansion good. For the earliest Americans, whose ancestors had arrived on the continent thousands of years before the Europeans, it was a story of defeat and contraction rather than of conquest and growth. By 1850, the white man's diseases and guns had reduced the Indian population north of the Rio Grande to fewer than half a million, a fraction of the population of two or three centuries earlier. The relentless westward march of white settlements had pushed all but a few thousand Indians beyond the Mississippi. In the 1840s, the U.S. government decided to create a "permanent Indian frontier" at about the 95th meridian (roughly the western borders of Iowa, Missouri, and Arkansas). But white emigrants were already violating that frontier on the overland trails to the Pacific, and settlers were pressing against the borders of Indian territory. In little more than a decade, the idea of "one big reservation" in the West would give way to the policy of forcing Indians onto small reservations. The government "negotiated" with Indian chiefs for vast cessions of land in return for annuity payments that were soon spent on the white man's firewater and other purchases from shrewd or corrupt traders. Required to learn the white man's ways or perish, many Indians perished—of disease, malnutrition, and alcohol, and in futile efforts to break out of the reservations and regain their land.

CHRONOLOGY

1844	Senate rejects Texas annexation • James K. Polk elected president
1845	Congress annexes Texas • Mexico spurns U.S. bid to buy California and New Mexico
1846	U.S. declares war on Mexico • U.S. forces under Zachary Taylor win battles of Palo Alto and Resaca de la Palma • U.S. and Britain settle Oregon boundary dispute • U.S. occupies California and New Mexico • House passes Wilmot Proviso • U.S. forces capture Monterrey, Mexico
1847	Americans win battle of Buena Vista • U.S. Army under Winfield Scott lands at Veracruz • Americans win battles of Contreras, Churubusco, Molino del Rey, and Chapultepec • Mexico City falls
1848	Treaty of Guadalupe Hidalgo ends Mexican War, fixes Rio Grande as border, cedes New Mexico and California to U.S. • Gold discovered in California • Spain spurns Polk's offer of $100 million for Cuba • Zachary Taylor elected president
1849	John C. Calhoun pens "Address of the Southern Delegates" • California seeks admission as a free state
1850	Taylor dies, Millard Fillmore becomes president • Bitter sectional debate culminates in Compromise of 1850 • Fugitive Slave Law empowers federal commissioners to recover escaped slaves
1851	Fugitive Slave Law provokes rescues and violent conflict in North • American filibusters executed in Cuba
1852	Uncle Tom's Cabin becomes best seller • Franklin Pierce elected president
1854	Anthony Burns returned from Boston to slavery • William Walker's filibusters invade Nicaragua • Pierce tries to buy Cuba • Ostend Manifesto issued
1856	William Walker legalizes slavery in Nicaragua
1860	William Walker executed in Honduras

Manifest Destiny and Slavery

If the Manifest Destiny of white Americans spelled doom for red Americans, it also presaged a crisis in the history of black Americans. By 1846, the Empire for Liberty that Thomas Jefferson had envisioned for the Louisiana Purchase seemed more an empire for slavery: Territorial acquisitions since 1803 had brought into the republic the slave states of Louisiana, Missouri, Arkansas, Florida, Texas, and parts of Alabama and Mississippi. Only Iowa, admitted in 1846, joined the ranks of the free states.

The division between slavery and freedom in the rest of the Louisiana Purchase had supposedly been settled by the Compromise of 1820. Although the issue frequently disturbed public tranquility for a quarter-century there-

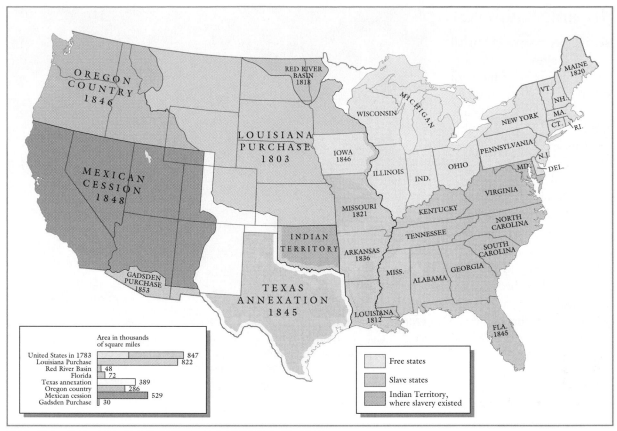

MAP 13.1 FREE AND SLAVE STATES AND TERRITORIES, 1848

Two developments of critical importance to the controversy over the expansion of slavery in the 1840s and 1850s are illustrated by this map: the larger number of slave than free states entering the Union from the territories acquired from France (Louisiana Purchase) and Spain (Florida) and the huge amount of new territory added by the acquisition of Texas and the Southwest from Mexico and the settlement of the Oregon boundary in the 1840s.

 View an animated version of this map or related maps at http://history.wadsworth.com/murrin_LEP4e.

after, as long as the controversy focused on the morality of slavery where it already existed, the two-party system—in which both major parties did their best to evade the issue—managed to contain its explosive potential. When the issue became the expansion of slavery into new territories, however, evasion and containment no longer sufficed. The issue first arose with the annexation of Texas, which helped provoke war with Mexico in 1846—a war that many antislavery northerners considered an ugly effort to expand slavery.

The Westering Impulse

Many Americans of European descent saw their future in the West. In the 1840s, Horace Greeley urged, "Go west, young man." And to the West they went in unprecedented numbers, driven in part by the depression of 1837–43 that prompted thousands to search for cheap land and better opportunity. "The West is our object, there is no other

hope left for us," declared one farmer as he and his family set out on the Oregon Trail. "There is nothing like a new country for poor folks."

An earlier wave of migration had populated the region between the Appalachians and the Missouri River, bringing a new state into the Union on an average of every three years. During those years, reports from explorers, fur traders, missionaries, and sailors filtered back from California and the Pacific Northwest, describing the bounteous resources and benign climates of those wondrous regions. Richard Henry Dana's *Two Years before the Mast* (1840), the story of his experience in the cowhide and tallow trade between California and Boston, alerted thousands of Americans to this new Eden on the Pacific. Guidebooks rolled off the presses describing the boundless prospects that awaited settlers who would turn "those wild forests, trackless plains, untrodden valleys" into "one grand scene of continuous improvements, universal enterprise, and unparalleled commerce."

The Hispanic Southwest

Of course, another people of partial European descent already lived in portions of the region west of the 98th meridian. The frontier of New Spain had pushed north of the Rio Grande early in the 17th century. By the time Mexico won its independence from Spain in 1821, some 80,000 Mexicans lived in this region. Three-fourths of them had settled in the Rio Grande Valley of New Mexico, and most of the rest in California. Centuries earlier, the Spaniards had introduced horses, cattle, and sheep to the New World. These animals became the economic mainstay of Hispanic society along New Spain's northern frontier. Later, Anglo-Americans would adopt Hispanic ranching methods to invade and subdue the lands of the arid western plains. Spanish words still describe the tools of the trade and the very land itself: *bronco, mustang, lasso, rodeo, stampede, canyon, arroyo, mesa.*

Colonial society on New Spain's northern frontier had centered on the missions and the presidios. Intended to Christianize Indians, the missions also became an instrument to exploit their labor, while the presidios (military posts) protected the settlers from hostile Indians. By the late 18th century, the mission system had fallen into decline, and a decade and a half after Mexican independence in 1821, it collapsed entirely. The presidios, underfunded and understaffed, also declined after Mexican independence, so that the defense of Mexico's far northern provinces increasingly fell to the residents. But by the 1830s, many residents of New Mexico and California were more interested in bringing American traders in than in keeping American settlers out. A flourishing trade over the Santa Fe Trail from Independence, Missouri, brought American manufactured goods to Santa Fe, New Mexico (and points south), in exchange for Mexican horses, mules, beaver pelts, and silver. New England ships carried American goods all the way around the horn of South America to San Francisco and other California ports in exchange for tallow and hides produced by *californio* ranchers. This trade linked the economies of New Mexico and California more closely to the United States than to the Mexican heartland. The trickle of Americans into California and New Mexico in the 1820s foreshadowed the flood that would engulf these regions two decades later.

North Wind Picture Archives.

EMIGRANTS MAKING CAMP IN THE SNOW

This drawing portrays the harsh conditions and dangers faced by many pioneers who crossed plains and mountains. Women often had to do a man's work as well as to cook and take care of children. One can only hope that this family did not suffer the fate of the Donner party, trapped by an early snowfall in the Sierra Nevada Mountains in October 1846. Nearly half of the 87 people in the Donner party died during the subsequent winter.

The Oregon and California Trails

In 1842 and 1843, Oregon fever swept the Mississippi Valley. Thousands of farm families sold their land, packed their worldly goods in covered wagons along with supplies for five or six months on the trail, hitched up their oxen, and headed out from Independence or St. Joseph, Missouri, for the trek of almost 2,000 miles to the river valleys of Oregon or California. On the way, they passed through regions claimed by three nations—the United States, Mexico, and Britain—and they settled on land owned by Mexico (California) or claimed jointly by the United States and Britain (Oregon, which then stretched north to the border of Russian Alaska). But no matter who claimed it, the land was occupied mostly by Indians, who viewed this latest intrusion with wary eyes. Few of the emigrants thought about settling down along the way, for this vast reach of arid plains, forbidding mountains, and burning wastelands was then known as the Great American Desert. White men considered it suitable only for Indians and the disappearing breed of mountain men who had roamed the region trapping beaver.

During the next quarter-century, half a million men, women, and children crossed a half continent in one of the great sagas of American history. After the migration of farm families to Oregon and California came the 1847 exodus of the Mormons to a new Zion in the basin of the Great Salt Lake and the 1849 gold rush to California. The stories of these migrants were of triumph and tragedy, survival and death, courage and despair, success and failure. Most of them reached their destinations; some died on the way—victims of disease, exposure, starvation, suicide, or homicide by Indians or by fellow emigrants. Of those who arrived safely, a few struck it rich, most carved out a modest although hard living, and some drifted on, still looking for the pot of gold that had thus far eluded them. Together, they generated pressures that helped bring a vast new empire—more than a million square miles— into the United States by 1848.

Migration was mostly a male enterprise. Adult men outnumbered women on the Oregon Trail and on the California Trail before the gold rush by more than 2 to 1, and in the gold rush by more than 10 to 1. The quest for new land, a new start, and a chance to make a big strike repre-

sented primarily masculine ideals. Women felt more rooted in family, home, and community, and less willing to pull up stakes to march into the wilderness. Yet even on the rough mining frontier of the West, men sought to replicate as soon as possible the homes and communities they had left behind. "We want families," wrote a Californian in 1858, "because their homes and hearth stones everywhere, are the only true and reliable basis of any nation." Except during the gold rush, and the figures for the absolute numbers of men and women notwithstanding, family groups predominated on the overland trails. Half of the emigrants were mothers and children, and some of the single men had relatives among the travelers.

Many of the women were reluctant migrants. Although middle-class urban families had made some small beginnings toward equal partnership in marriage, men still ruled the family on the midwestern farms from which most of the migrants came. Men made the decision to go;

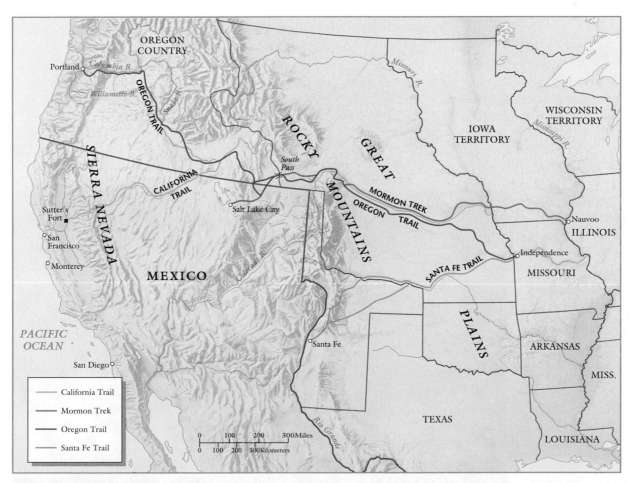

MAP 13.2 OVERLAND TRAILS, 1846
The Santa Fe Trail was mainly a route for trade between the United States and the Mexican province (before 1848) of New Mexico. The other three trails carried hundreds of thousands of Americans to new homes in the West.

women obeyed. Diaries kept by women on the trail testify to their unhappiness:

> What had possessed my husband, anyway, that he should have thought of bringing us away out through this God-forsaken country? . . . Oh, how I wish we never had started for the Golden Land. . . . I would make a brave effort to be cheerful and patient until the camp work was done. Then . . . I would throw myself down on the ground and shed tears, wishing myself back home with my friends and chiding myself for consenting to take this wild goose chase.

For some families it did turn out to be a wild goose chase, but for many of those who stayed the course and settled in the far West, it was a success story, made so in great measure by the women. They turned houses into homes, settlements into communities. The frontier did not break down the separate spheres of men and women. Woman's sphere in the West was still the home and the family, the bearing and nurturing of children, the management of the household economy. Man's sphere remained the world of public events and economic production.

The Mormon Migration

Patriarchal rule was strongest among those migrants with the most nearly equal sex ratio—the Mormons. Subjected to persecution that drove them from their original home in western New York to Ohio, Missouri, and eventually to Illinois, the Mormons established Nauvoo, Illinois, a thriving community of 15,000 souls, based on collective economic effort and theocratic discipline imposed by their founder and prophet, Joseph Smith. But the people of Illinois proved no more hospitable to the Mormons than the sect's previous neighbors had been. Smith did not make matters any easier. His insistence that God spoke through him, his autocratic suppression of dissent, and his assertion that the Mormons were the only true Christians and would inherit the earth provoked hostility. When a dissident faction of Mormons published Smith's latest revelation, which sanctioned polygamy, he ordered their printing press destroyed. The county sheriff arrested him, and in June 1844, a mob broke into the jail and killed him.

Smith's martyrdom prompted yet another exodus. Under the leadership of Smith's successor, Brigham Young, the Mormons began the long trek westward that would eventually lead them to the Great Salt Lake basin in a part of Mexican territory that soon was ceded to the United States in the wake of the Mexican War. A man of iron will and administrative genius, Young organized the migration down to the last detail. Arriving with the advance guard of Mormon pioneers at a pass overlooking the Great Basin on July 24, 1847, Young, who was ill with tick fever, struggled from his wagon and stared at the barren desert and mountains surrounding the lake. "This is the right place," he declared. Here the Mormons could build their Zion undisturbed.

JOSEPH MUSTERING THE NAUVOO LEGION

This painting depicts a self-defense force organized by Mormons in Nauvoo, Illinois, in the early 1840s. Beleaguered by neighbors, the Mormons decided to emigrate to Mexican territory in the West after Joseph Smith was murdered in 1844.

Joseph Mustering the Nauvoo Legion, C.C.A. Christensen.

They built a flourishing community, making the desert bloom with grain and vegetables irrigated by water they ingeniously diverted from mountain streams. Organizing the economy and the civil society as he had organized the exodus, Young reigned as leader of the church, and from 1850 to 1857 as governor of the newly created Utah Territory.

Zion, however, did not remain undisturbed. Relations with the government in Washington, D.C., and with those sent out as territorial officials were never smooth, especially after Young's proclamation in 1852 that authorized polygamy. (Although Young married a total of 55 women, most Mormon men could afford to support no more than one wife and her children; only about one-sixth of Mormon marriages were polygamous.) When conflict between the Mormons and the U.S. Army broke out in 1857, Young surrendered his civil authority and made an uneasy peace with the government.

The Republic of Texas

As the Mormons were starting west, a crisis between Mexico and the United States was coming to a boil. Although the United States had renounced any claim to Texas in a treaty with Spain negotiated in 1819, many Americans believed that Texas had been part of the Louisiana Purchase. By the time the treaty was ratified in 1821, Mexico had won its independence from Spain. The new Republic of Mexico wanted to develop its northern borderlands in Texas by encouraging immigration and settlement there. Thus, Stephen F. Austin, a Missouri businessman, secured a large land grant from Mexico to settle 300 families from the United States. Despite their pledge to become Roman Catholics and Mexican citizens, these immigrants and many who followed remained Protestants and Americans at heart. They also brought in slaves, in defiance of a recent Mexican law abolishing slavery. Despite Mexican efforts to ban any further immigration, 30,000 Americans lived in Texas by 1835, outnumbering Mexicans 6 to 1.

American settlers, concentrated in east Texas, initially had little contact with Mexican *tejanos* (Texans), whose settlements were farther south and west, but political events in Mexico City in 1835 had repercussions on the northern frontier. A new conservative national government seemed intent on consolidating its authority over the northern territories, including Coahuila-Texas. In response, the Anglo-American settlers and the *tejanos* forged a political alliance to protest any further loss of autonomy in their province. When the Mexican government responded militarily, many Texans—both Anglo and Mexican—fought back. Then, in March 1836, delegates from across Texas met at a village appropriately called Washington. They declared Texas an independent republic and adopted a constitution based on the U.S. model.

The American Revolution had lasted seven years; it took the Texans less than seven months to win and consolidate their independence. Mexican General Antonio López de Santa Anna led the Mexican army that captured the Alamo (a former mission converted to a fort) in San Antonio on March 6, 1836, killing all 187 of its defenders, including the legendary Americans Davy Crockett and Jim Bowie. Rallying to the cry "Remember the Alamo!" Texans swarmed to the revolutionary army commanded by Sam Houston. When the Mexican army slaughtered another force of more than 300 men after they had surrendered at Goliad on March 19, the Texans were further inflamed. A month later, Houston's army, aided by volunteers from southern U.S. states, routed a larger Mexican force on the San Jacinto River (near present-day Houston) and captured Santa Anna himself. Under duress, he signed a treaty granting Texas its independence. The Mexican congress later repudiated the treaty but could not muster enough strength to reestablish its authority north of the Nueces River. The victorious Texans elected Sam Houston president of their new republic and petitioned for annexation to the United States.

The Annexation Controversy

President Andrew Jackson, wary of provoking war with Mexico or quarrels with antislavery northerners who charged that the annexation of Texas was a plot to expand slavery, rebuffed the annexationists. So did his successor, Martin Van Buren. Although disappointed, the Texans turned their energies to building their republic. The British government encouraged the Texans, in the hope that they would stand as a buffer against further U.S. expansion. Abolitionists in England even cherished the notion that Britain might persuade the Texans to abolish slavery. Texas leaders made friendly responses to some of the British overtures, probably in the hope of provoking American annexationists to take action. They did.

Soon after Vice President John Tyler became president on the death of William Henry Harrison in 1841, he broke with the Whig Party that had elected him. Seeking to create a new coalition to reelect him in 1844, Tyler seized on the annexation of Texas as "the only matter that will take sufficient hold of the feelings of the South to rally it on a southern candidate."

Tyler named John C. Calhoun of South Carolina as secretary of state to negotiate a treaty of annexation. The southern press ran scare stories about a British plot to use Texas as a beachhead for an assault on slavery, and annexation became a popular issue in the South. Calhoun concluded a treaty with the eager Texans, but then he made a mistake: He released to the press a letter he had written to the British minister to the United States, informing him that, together with other reasons, Americans wanted to annex Texas in order to protect slavery, an institution "essential to the peace, safety, and prosperity" of the United States. This seemed to confirm abolitionist charges that annexation was a pro-slavery plot. Northern senators of both parties provided more than enough votes to defeat the treaty in June 1844.

By then, Texas had become the main issue in the forthcoming presidential election. Whig candidate Henry Clay had come out against annexation, as had the leading contender for the Democratic nomination, former president Martin Van Buren. Van Buren's stand ran counter to the rising tide of Manifest Destiny sentiment within the Democratic Party. It also angered southern Democrats, who were determined to have Texas. Through eight ballots at the Democratic national convention, they blocked Van Buren's nomination; on the ninth, the southerners broke the stalemate by nominating one of their own, James K. Polk of Tennessee. Polk, a staunch Jacksonian who had served as Speaker of the House of Representatives during Jackson's presidency, was the first "dark horse" candidate (not having been a contender before the convention).

HISTORY THROUGH FILM

The Alamo (1960)

The legendary actor John Wayne worked a decade to obtain backing for an epic film about the heroic but doomed defense of the Alamo. When the movie was finally released in 1960, Wayne not only played the lead role as Davy Crockett, but he was also the producer and director. Out of his depth in this last role, he received advice from the director of Wayne's best movies, John Ford, which helped overcome some but not all of the awkward, sentimental scenes in the film.

Three hours long, *The Alamo* begins with General Sam Houston, commander of the Texas revolutionary army, ordering Colonel William Travis to delay the Mexican regulars commanded by Santa Anna at the Alamo long enough for Houston to organize his ragtag volunteers in east Texas into an effective fighting force. Colonel Jim Bowie, a rival of Travis for command of the garrison, considers the Alamo (a mission converted into a fort) a trap and wants to pull out, because the Mexican army outnumbers the Texans 20 to 1.

Right away, Hollywood departs from historical reality. Houston had actually ordered Bowie to blow up the Alamo and retreat to join him. But Bowie and Travis agreed to stay and fight, supported by Davy Crockett and his fellow Tennessee volunteers who had come to Texas looking

Directed by John Wayne. Starring John Wayne (Davy Crockett), Richard Widmark (Jim Bowie), Laurence Harvey (William Travis).

for excitement. The tension between Travis and Bowie (with Crockett as a mediator) was real and is vividly portrayed if sometimes overdramatized in the film, but the tension concerned their relative authority, not strategy.

In wide-screen splendor, the film depicts the approach of the Mexican army, the artillery duels between the garrison and the Mexicans, and the infantry assaults that finally overpower the garrison after 13 days of resistance, killing them to the last man, sparing only the wife and child of a Texas lieutenant. The combat footage in the final attack is spectacular. Mexican artillery bombard the Alamo, infantry move forward taking heavy casualties, swarm over the wall, and overwhelm the doomed defenders. Bowie is wounded early in the fight and sent to an improvised hospital in the chapel, where he dies fighting from his bed. Travis is killed at the gate after dispatching several Mexicans with his sword. Crockett fights with fury until he is impaled by a Mexican lancer, but lives long enough to throw a torch into the powder magazine, blowing up the fort and hundreds of Mexicans.

In reality, none of it happened this way. Bowie had gone to bed with typhoid fever early in the siege; Travis was killed early in the final assault with a bullet through his

Southerners exulted in their victory. "We have triumphed," wrote one of Calhoun's lieutenants. "Polk is nearer to *us* than any public man who was named. He is a large Slave holder and [is for] Texas—States rights *out & out*." Polk's nomination undercut President Tyler's forlorn hope of being reelected on the Texas issue, so he bowed out of the race.

Polk ran on a platform that called not only for the annexation of Texas but also the acquisition of all of Oregon up to 54°40′ (the Alaskan border). That demand was aimed at voters in the western free states, who believed that bringing Oregon into the Union would balance the expansion of slavery into Texas with the expansion of free territory in the Northwest. Polk was more than comfortable with this platform. In fact, he wanted not only Texas and Oregon, but California and New Mexico as well.

Texas fever swept the South during the campaign. So powerful was the issue that Clay began to waver, stating that he would support annexation if it could be done without starting a war with Mexico. This concession won him a few southern votes but angered northern antislavery Whigs. Many of them voted for James G. Birney, candidate of the Liberty Party, which opposed any more slave territory. Birney probably took enough Whig votes from Clay in New York to give Polk victory there and in the electoral college.

John Wayne and Linda Cristal in an advertising poster for *The Alamo*.

head; and Crockett along with a few others surrendered but were executed on Santa Anna's orders. For Hollywood, and perhaps for most Americans, however, history is less important than legend. The Alamo became a heroic legend, a rallying cry for Texans in 1836, and a powerful symbol ever since. The film version dramatizes the legend better than an accurate version could have done.

The movie also reflects the cold-war mentality of the 1950s and Wayne's own full-blooded anti-Communism stance. Crockett's windy speeches about freedom and individual rights evoke the 1950s rhetoric of "better dead than red." Ironically, the Texans were fighting for an independent republic with slavery, in defiance of Mexico's recent abolition of the institution—an issue that the film virtually ignores.

Although The Alamo might have carried more punch if edited down to two hours, it nevertheless is visually powerful. It received seven Academy Award nominations, including one for Best Picture, but received only one Oscar—for sound.

Acquisition of Texas and Oregon

Although the election was extremely close (Polk won only a plurality of 49.5 percent of the popular vote), Democrats regarded it as a mandate for annexation. Eager to leave office in triumph, lame-duck President Tyler submitted to Congress a joint resolution of annexation, which required only a simple majority in both houses instead of the two-thirds majority in the Senate that a treaty would have required. Congress passed the resolution in March 1845. Texas thus bypassed the territorial stage and came in as the 15th slave state in December 1845. Backed now by the United States, Texans claimed a southern and western border beyond the Nueces River all the way to the Rio Grande, which nearly tripled the area that Mexico had formerly defined as Texas. Mexico responded by breaking off diplomatic relations with the United States. The stage was set for five years of bitter controversy that included a shooting war with Mexico and political warfare in the United States over the issue of slavery expansion.

Meanwhile, Polk lost no time in addressing his promise to annex Oregon. "Our title to the country of the Oregon is 'clear and unquestionable,'" he said in his inaugural address. "Already our people are preparing to perfect that title by occupying it with their wives and children." The

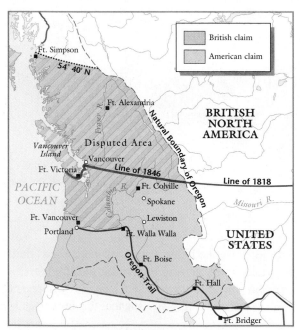

MAP 13.3 SETTLEMENT OF THE OREGON BOUNDARY DISPUTE, 1846

Before the 1840s, the only white residents of the Oregon country were fur traders and missionaries. Migration of Americans over the Oregon Trail created pressures to make all of Oregon part of the United States, but President Polk was not willing to go to war for the boundary of 54°40′.

problem was to persuade Britain to recognize the title. Both countries had jointly "occupied" Oregon since 1818, overseeing the fur trade carried on by British and American companies. Chanting the slogan "Fifty-four forty or fight!" many Americans in 1845 demanded all of Oregon, as pledged in the Democratic platform. But Polk proved unwilling to fight for 54°40′. So far, Americans had settled only in the region south of the Columbia River, at roughly the 46th parallel. In June 1846, Polk accepted a compromise treaty that split the Oregon country between the United States and Britain at the 49th parallel. Several Democratic senators from the Old Northwest (states north of the Ohio River and west of Pennsylvania) accused Polk of betrayal and voted against the treaty. They had supported Texas to the Rio Grande, and they had expected Polk to support Oregon to 54°40′. A sectional breach had opened in the Democratic Party that would soon grow wider.

The Mexican War

Having finessed a war with Britain, Polk provoked one with Mexico in order to gain California and New Mexico. In 1845, he sent a special envoy to Mexico City with an offer to buy California and New Mexico for $30 million. To help Mexico make the right response, he ordered federal troops to the disputed border area between Mexico and Texas, dispatched a naval squadron to patrol the Gulf Coast of Mexico, and instructed the American consul at Monterrey (the Mexican capital of California) to stir up annexation sentiment among settlers there. These strong-arm tactics provoked a political revolt in Mexico City that brought a militant anti-American regime to power.

Polk responded in January 1846 by ordering 4,000 soldiers under General Zachary Taylor to advance all the way to the Rio Grande. Recognizing that he could achieve his goals only through armed conflict, Polk waited for news from Texas that would justify a declaration of war, but none came. His patience having run out, on May 9, 1846, he began to draft a message to Congress asking for a declaration of war on general grounds of Mexican defiance. That evening, word finally arrived that two weeks earlier Mexican troops had crossed the Rio Grande and attacked an American patrol, killing 11 soldiers. Polk had what he wanted. He quickly revised his message and sent it to Congress on May 11.

Most Whigs opposed war with Mexico. But in the end, not wanting to be branded unpatriotic, all but a handful of them voted for the final declaration of war, which passed the House by 174 to 14 and the Senate by 40 to 2. Despite their continuing opposition to what they called "Mr. Polk's War," most Whigs voted supplies for the army. Having witnessed the demise of the Federalist Party after it had opposed the war in 1812, one Whig congressman said sarcastically that from then on he had decided to vote for "war, pestilence, and famine."

The United States went to war with a tiny regular army of fewer than 8,000 men, supplemented by 60,000 volunteers in state regiments, and an efficient navy that quickly established domination of the sea lanes. Mexican soldiers outnumbered American in most of the battles, but the Americans had higher morale, better leadership, and better weapons (especially artillery). They also enjoyed the backing of a more determined, stable government and a far richer, stronger economy. The U.S. forces won every battle—and the war—in a fashion that humiliated the proud Mexicans and left a legacy of national hostility and border violence. Especially remarkable was the prominent role played by junior American officers trained at West Point, for whom the Mexican War was a rehearsal for a larger conflict that would take place 15 years later: Robert E. Lee, Ulysses S. Grant, Pierre G. T. Beauregard, George B. McClellan, Braxton Bragg, George H. Thomas, Thomas J. Jackson, George G. Meade, Jefferson Davis, and others, whose names would become household words during the Civil War.

Yale Collection of Western Americana, Beinecke Rare Book and Manuscript Library.

AMERICAN FORCES IN SALTILLO, MEXICO

This posed photograph of General John E. Wool and his staff of Zachary Taylor's army on its march southward from Monterrey through Saltillo in November 1846 is the earliest known photograph of an American military force. Photography had recently been invented, and pictures such as this one were extremely rare before the 1850s.

Military Campaigns of 1846

The Mexican War proceeded through three phases. The first phase was carried out by Zachary Taylor's 4,000 regulars on the Rio Grande. In two small battles on May 8 and 9, at Palo Alto and Resaca de la Palma, they routed numerically superior Mexican forces even before Congress had declared war. Those victories made "Old Rough and Ready" Taylor a hero, a reputation he rode to the presidency two years later. Reinforced by several thousand volunteers, Taylor pursued the retreating Mexicans 100 miles south of the Rio Grande to the heavily fortified Mexican city of Monterrey, and took the city after four days of fighting in September 1846. Mexican resistance in the area crumbled, and Taylor's force settled down as an army of occupation.

Meanwhile, the second phase of American strategy had gone forward in New Mexico and California. In June 1846, General Stephen Watts Kearny led an army of 1,500 tough frontiersmen and regulars west from Fort Leavenworth toward Santa Fe. Kearny bluffed and intimidated the New Mexico governor, who fled southward without ever ordering the local 3,000-man militia into action. Kearny's army occupied Santa Fe on August 18 without firing a shot. With closer economic ties to the United States than to their own country, which taxed them well but governed them poorly, many New Mexicans seemed willing to accept American rule.

After receiving reinforcements, Kearny left a small occupation force and divided his remaining troops into two contingents, one of which he sent under Colonel Alexander Doniphan into the Mexican province of Chihuahua. In the most extraordinary campaign of the war, these 800 Missourians marched 1,500 miles, foraging supplies along the way; fought and beat two much larger enemy forces; and finally linked up with Zachary Taylor's army near Monterrey in spring 1847.

Kearny led the other contingent across deserts and mountains to California. Events there had anticipated his arrival. In June 1846, a group of American settlers backed by Captain John C. Frémont, a renowned western explorer with the army topographical corps, captured Sonoma and raised the flag of an independent California, displaying the silhouette of a grizzly bear. Marked by exploits both courageous and comic, this "bear-flag revolt" paved the way for the conquest of California by the *americanos*. The U.S. Pacific Fleet seized California's ports and the capital at Monterrey; sailors from the fleet and volunteer soldiers under Frémont subdued Mexican resistance. Kearny's weary and battered force arrived in December 1846, barely in time to help with the mopping up.

Military Campaigns of 1847

New Mexico and California had fallen into American hands, and Mexican armies had experienced nothing but defeat, but the Mexican government refused to admit that the war was over. A political maneuver by President Polk to secure a more tractable government in Mexico had backfired. In one of Mexico's many palace revolts, Santa Anna had been overthrown and forced into exile in Cuba in 1844. A shadowy intermediary convinced Polk in July 1846 that if Santa Anna returned to power, he would make peace on American terms in return for $30 million. Polk instructed the navy to pass Santa Anna through its blockade of Mexican ports. The wily Mexican general then rode in triumph to Mexico City, where yet another new government named him supreme commander of the army and president of the republic. Breathing fire, Santa Anna spoke no more of peace. Instead, he raised new levies and marched north early in 1847 to attack Taylor's army near Monterrey.

Taylor, 62 years old, was still rough but not as ready to withstand a counteroffensive as he had been a few weeks earlier. After capturing Monterrey in September 1846, he had let the defeated Mexican army go and had granted an eight-week armistice in the hope that it would allow time for peace negotiations. Angry at Taylor's presumption in making such a decision and suspicious of the general's political ambitions, Polk canceled the armistice and named General-in-Chief Winfield Scott to command the third phase of the war, a campaign against Mexico City. A large, punctilious man, Scott acquired the nickname "Old Fuss and Feathers" for a military professionalism that contrasted with the homespun manner of "Rough and Ready" Zach Taylor. Scott decided to lead an invasion of Mexico's heartland from a beachhead at Veracruz, and in January 1847 ordered the transfer of more than half of Taylor's troops to his own expeditionary force.

Left with fewer than 5,000 men, most of them untried volunteers, Taylor complained bitterly of political intrigue and military favoritism. Nevertheless, he marched out to meet Santa Anna's army of 18,000. In a two-day battle on February 22 and 23 at Buena Vista, Taylor's little force bent but never broke. They inflicted twice as many casualties as they suffered in a fierce struggle highlighted by the brilliant counterattack of a Mississippi regiment commanded by Jefferson Davis. The bloodied Mexican army retreated toward the capital. When news of the victory reached the East, Taylor's popularity soared to new heights. If Polk had wanted to quash a political rival by taking away most of his troops—as Taylor believed—he had achieved just the opposite.

But it was General Scott who actually won the war. With a combined army-navy force, he took the coastal fortress at Veracruz in March 1847. Over the next five months, his army, which never totaled more than 14,000 men (with considerable turnover because of expiring one-year enlistments), marched and fought its way over more than 200 miles of mountains and plains to Mexico City. It was a bold, high-risk action. When Scott's forces reached the fortifications of Mexico City, held by three times their numbers, the Duke of Wellington, who was following the campaign closely, predicted, "Scott is lost—he cannot capture the city, and he cannot fall back upon his base." But capture it he did, on September 14, after fierce hand-to-hand combat in the battles of Contreras, Churubusco, Molino del Rey, and Chapultepec. It was a brilliant success, even though it owed much to wrangling among Mexican leaders that forced Santa Anna to spend almost as much time facing down his internal enemies as fighting the Americans.

Antiwar Sentiment

The string of military victories prevented the significant U.S. antiwar sentiment from winning even wider support. The war had enthusiastic support in the South and West and among Democrats, but the Whigs and many people in the Northeast, especially in New England, considered it "a wicked and disgraceful war." Democrats and Whigs had different notions of progress. Democrats believed in expanding American institutions over *space*—in particular, the space occupied by Mexicans and Indians. Whigs, on the other hand, believed in improving American institutions over *time*. "Opposed to the instinct of boundless acquisition stands that of Internal Improvement," said Horace Greeley. "A nation cannot simultaneously devote its energies to the absorption of others' territories and the improvement of its own."

Antislavery people raised their eyebrows when they heard Manifest Destiny rhetoric about "extending the blessings of American liberty" to benighted regions. They suspected that the real reason was the desire to extend slavery. Hosea Biglow, the rustic Yankee philosopher created by the abolitionist poet James Russell Lowell, observed:

> They jest want this Californy
> So's to lug new slave-states in
> To abuse ye an' to scorn ye,
> And to plunder ye like sin.

The Wilmot Proviso

The slavery issue overshadowed all others in the debate over the Mexican War. President Polk could not understand the reason for the fuss. "There is no probability,"

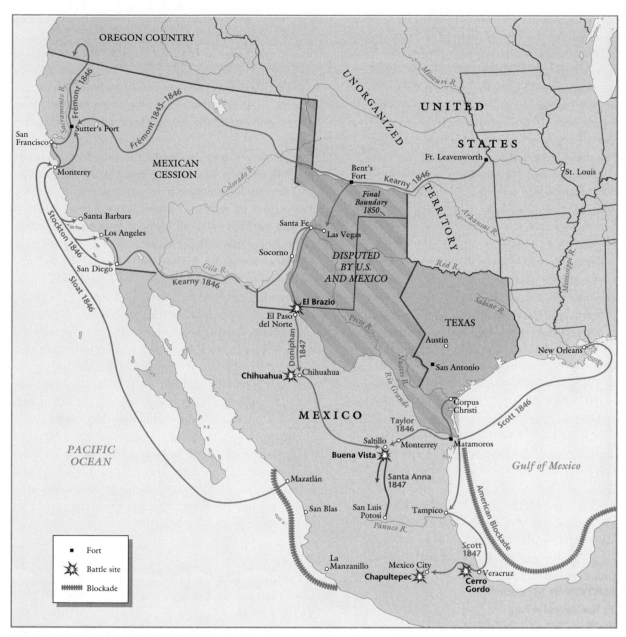

MAP 13.4 PRINCIPAL CAMPAIGNS OF THE MEXICAN WAR, 1846–1847

This map provides a graphic illustration of the vast territory over which the Mexican War was fought; the distance from Veracruz to San Francisco is 2,500 miles.

 View an animated version of this map or related maps at http://history.wadsworth.com/murrin_LEP4e.

he wrote in his diary, "that any territory will ever be acquired from Mexico in which slavery would ever exist." But other Americans were less sure. Many southerners hoped that slavery would spread into the fertile lowlands of Mexican territory. Many northerners feared that it might. Their fear was strengthened by an editorial in a Charleston newspaper: "California is peculiarly adapted for slave labor. The right to have [slave] property protected

there is not a mere abstraction." The issue came to a head early in the war. On August 8, 1846, Pennsylvania Democratic Congressman David Wilmot offered an amendment to an army appropriations bill: ". . . that, as an express and fundamental condition of the acquisition of any territory from the Republic of Mexico . . . neither slavery nor involuntary servitude shall ever exist in any part of said territory."

This famous Wilmot Proviso framed the national debate over slavery for the next 15 years. The House passed the amendment. Nearly all northern Democrats joined all northern Whigs in the majority, while southern Democrats and southern Whigs voted almost unanimously against it. (In the Senate, greater southern strength defeated the proviso.) This outcome marked an ominous wrenching of the party division between Whigs and Democrats into a *sectional* division between free and slave states. It was a sign that the two-party system might not successfully contain the convulsive question of slavery expansion.

Several factors underlay the split of northern Democrats from their own president on this issue. Ever since southern Democrats had blocked Van Buren's nomination in 1844, resentment had been growing in the party's northern wing. Polk's acceptance of 49° latitude for Oregon's northern boundary exacerbated this feeling. "Our rights to Oregon have been shamefully compromised," fumed an Ohio Democrat. "The administration is Southern, Southern, Southern! . . . Since the South have fixed boundaries for free territory, let the North fix boundaries for slave territories." The reduced rates of the Walker tariff in 1846 (sponsored by Robert J. Walker of Mississippi, Polk's secretary of the treasury) annoyed Democrats from Pennsylvania's industrial districts. Polk further angered Democrats from the Old Northwest by vetoing a rivers and harbors bill that would have provided federal aid for transportation improvements in their districts. The Wilmot Proviso was in part the product of these pent-up

frustrations over what northerners were increasingly calling "the slave power." "The time has come," said a Democratic congressman in 1846, "when the Northern Democracy should make a stand. Every thing has taken a Southern shape and been controlled by Southern caprice for years. . . . We must satisfy the Northern people . . . that we are not to extend the institution of slavery as a result of this war."

The slavery issue hung like the sword of Damocles over Polk's efforts to negotiate peace with Mexico. Polk also came under pressure from expansionist Democrats who, excited by military victory, wanted more Mexican territory, perhaps even "all Mexico." Polk had sent diplomat Nicholas Trist with Scott's army to negotiate the terms of Mexican surrender. Authorized to pay Mexico $15 million for California, New Mexico, and a Texas border on the Rio Grande, Trist worked out such a treaty. In the meantime, though, Polk had succumbed to the "all Mexico" clamor. He ordered Trist back to Washington, intending to replace him with someone who would exact greater concessions from Mexico. Trist ignored the recall, signed the treaty of Guadalupe Hidalgo on February 2, 1848, and sent it to Washington. Although angered by Trist's defiance, Polk nonetheless decided to end the controversy by submitting the treaty to the Senate, which approved it on March 10 by a vote of 38 to 14. Half the opposition came from Democrats who wanted more Mexican territory and half from Whigs who wanted none. As it was, the treaty sheared off half of Mexico and increased the size of the United States by one-fourth.

SLAVE AUCTION IN ST. LOUIS

The public buying and selling of human beings in cities such as St. Louis made a mockery of American boasts of liberty and gave a powerful impetus to the drive to prohibit the expansion of slavery into the territories acquired from Mexico. This painting hints at the ugliest dimension of the slave trade, the sale of mothers and children apart from fathers and sometimes apart from each other.

Margaret Fuller Fights for a Roman Republic

Margaret Fuller's father, a Massachusetts lawyer and congressman, taught her to read English at age three and Latin at age six. By the time she reached her twenties she was mixing with the New England Unitarian elite and Transcendentalist philosophers such as Ralph Waldo Emerson, to whom she taught German pronunciation. As a prolific essayist and editor of the Transcendentalist magazine *The Dial*, Fuller (1810–1850) urged the opening of wider intellectual and professional opportunities for women. In 1844, she became literary editor of Horace Greeley's *New York Tribune*, the first woman to hold such a position. In 1846, she went to Europe as foreign correspondent for the *Tribune*—also a first for a woman. She traveled from England through the continent to Italy, where she fell in love with Giovanni Angelo, the Marchese d'Ossoli, with whom she had a son in 1848. Whether they ever married officially is unclear; as a Catholic (albeit a liberal one), Ossoli technically could not marry a Protestant, but Margaret began calling herself Marchioness Ossoli.

She and the Marchese threw themselves into the fight for a Roman republic that was part of the revolutionary fervor sweeping across Europe in 1848–49. Fuller worked with Giuseppe Mazzini, Giuseppe Garibaldi, and other Italian liberals seeking to over-throw the old order. Her reports to the *Tribune* were infused with the ideals of liberty and equality she had carried from the New World to the Old. When the Roman republic was overthrown in July 1849, she fled with Ossoli and their son to Florence, where she began writing a history of the republic. A year later they were on a ship to the United States, which struck a sandbar in a storm off Fire Island, New York, and sank with the loss of all on board.

Fuller's formidable body of writings inspired women and men in both America and Europe with a vision of emancipation from repressive conventions of religion, thought, and gender.

James Smith Noel Collection, Noel Memorial Library.
Louisiana State University in Shreveport.

MARGARET FULLER

The Election of 1848

The treaty did nothing to settle the question of slavery in the new territory, however. Mexico had abolished the institution two decades earlier; would the United States reintroduce it? Many Americans looked to the election of 1848 to decide the matter. Four positions on the issue emerged, each identified with a candidate for the presidential nomination.

The Wilmot Proviso represented the position of those determined to bar slavery from all territories. The Liberty Party endorsed the proviso and nominated Senator John P. Hale of New Hampshire for president.

Southern Democrat John C. Calhoun formulated the "southern-rights" position. Directly challenging the Wilmot Proviso, Calhoun introduced resolutions in the Senate in February 1847 affirming the right of slave owners to take their human property into any territory. The Constitution protected the right of property, Calhoun pointed out; Congress could no more prevent a settler from taking his slaves to California than it could prevent him from taking his horses there.

Although most southerners agreed with Calhoun, the Democratic Party sought a middle ground. The Polk administration endorsed the idea of extending the old Missouri Compromise line of 36°30′ to the Pacific. This would have excluded slavery from present-day Washington, Oregon, Idaho, Utah, Nevada, and the northern half of California, but would have allowed it in present-day New Mexico, Arizona, and southern California. Secretary of State James Buchanan, also a candidate for the Democratic presidential nomination (Polk did not seek renomination), embraced this position.

Another compromise position became known as "popular sovereignty." Identified with Senator Lewis Cass of Michigan, yet another contender for the Democratic nomination, this concept proposed to let the settlers of each territory decide for themselves whether to permit slavery. This solution contained a crucial ambiguity: It did not specify *at what stage* the settlers of a territory could decide on slavery. Most northern Democrats assumed that a territorial legislature would make that decision as soon as it was organized. Most southerners assumed that it would not be made until the settlers had drawn up a state constitution. That would normally happen only after several years as a territory, during which time slavery might well have taken deep enough root to be implanted in the state constitution. So long as neither assumption was tested, each faction could support popular sovereignty.

The Democratic convention nominated Cass for president, thereby seeming to endorse popular sovereignty. In an attempt to maintain party unity, however, the platform made no mention of the matter. The attempt was not entirely successful: Two Alabama delegates walked out when the convention refused to endorse Calhoun's southern-rights position, and an antislavery faction from New York walked out when it failed to win a credentials fight.

The Whig convention tried to avoid a similar schism by adopting no platform at all, but the slavery issue would not die. In the eyes of many antislavery delegates who styled themselves Conscience Whigs, the party made itself ridiculous by nominating Zachary Taylor for president. Desperate for victory, the Whigs chose a hero from a war that most of them had opposed. But the fact that Taylor was also a large slaveholder who owned several plantations in Louisiana and Mississippi was too much for the Conscience Whigs. They bolted from the party and formed a coalition with the Liberty Party and antislavery Democrats.

The Free Soil Party

The Free-Soilers met in convention in August 1848. The meeting resembled a religious camp meeting more than a political gathering. Speakers proclaimed slavery "a great moral, social, and political evil—a relic of barbarism which must necessarily be swept away in the progress of Christian civilization." The convention did not say how

that would be done, but it did adopt a platform calling for "no more Slave States and no more Slave Territories." The Free Soil Party nominated former president Martin Van Buren, with Charles Francis Adams, the son and grandson of presidents, as his running mate.

The campaign was marked by the futile efforts of both major parties to bury the slavery issue. Free Soil pressure compelled both northern Democrats and Whigs to take a stand against slavery in the territories. Whigs pointed to their earlier support of the Wilmot Proviso, while Democrats said popular sovereignty would keep the territories free. In the South, though, the two parties presented other faces. There, the Democrats pointed with pride to their expansionist record that had brought to the nation hundreds of thousands of square miles of territory—territory into which slavery might expand. But Taylor proved the strongest candidate in the South because he was a southerner and a slaveholder. "Will the people of [the South] vote for a Southern President or a Northern one?" asked southern newspapers. "We prefer Old Zack with his sugar and cotton plantations and four hundred negroes to all their compromises."

Taylor carried 8 of the 15 slave states and increased the Whig vote in the South by 10 percent over 1844, while the Democratic vote declined by 4 percent. Although he did less well in the north, he carried New York and enough other states to win the election. The Free-Soilers won no electoral votes but polled 14 percent of the popular vote in the north. They also elected nine congressmen along with two senators who would be heard from in the future: Salmon P. Chase of Ohio, architect of the Free Soil coalition in 1848, and Charles Sumner of Massachusetts, leader of the Conscience Whigs.

The Gold Rush and California Statehood

About the time Nicholas Trist was putting the finishing touches on the treaty to make California part of the United States, workers building a sawmill on the American River near Sacramento discovered flecks of gold in the riverbed. The word gradually leaked out, reaching the East in August 1848, where a public surfeited with tall tales out of the West greeted this news with skepticism. But in December, Polk's final message to Congress confirmed the "extraordinary" discoveries of gold. Two days later, a tea caddy containing 320 ounces of pure gold from California arrived in Washington. Now all doubts disappeared. By spring 1849, 100,000 gold-seekers were poised to take off by foot on the overland trail or by ship—either around Cape Horn or to the isthmus of Central America, where

THE CALIFORNIA GOLD RUSH

Prospectors for gold in the foothills of California's Sierra Nevada came from all over the world, including China. This photograph shows American-born and Chinese miners near Auburn, California, a year or two after the initial gold rush of 1849. It illustrates the original technology of separating gravel from gold by panning or by washing the gravel away in a sluice box, leaving the heavier gold flakes behind.

ting forth its position. He eagerly complied, producing in January 1849 a document that breathed fire against "unconstitutional" northern efforts to keep slavery out of the territories. Calhoun reminded southerners that their "property, prosperity, equality, liberty, and safety" were at stake and prophesied secession if the South did not prevail.

But Calhoun's firebomb fizzled. Only two-fifths of the southern congressmen and senators signed it. The Whigs wanted nothing to do with it. They looked forward to good times in the Taylor administration and opposed rocking the boat. "We do not expect an administration which we have brought into power [to] do any act or permit any act to be done [against] our safety," said Robert Toombs of Georgia, a leading Whig congressman. "We feel *secure* under General Taylor," added his fellow Georgian Alexander H. Stephens.

after a land crossing, they could board another ship to take them up the Pacific Coast to the new boomtown of San Francisco. Eighty thousand actually made it that first year (5,000 succumbed to a cholera epidemic). Some of them struck it rich, most kept hoping to, and more came by the scores of thousands every year from all over the world, including China.

Political organization of California could not be postponed. The mining camps needed law and order; the settlers needed courts, land and water laws, mail service, and other amenities of established government. In New Mexico, the 60,000 former Mexican citizens, now Americans, also needed a governmental structure for their new allegiance. Nor could the growing Mormon community at Salt Lake be ignored.

Still, the slavery question paralyzed Congress. In December 1848, lame-duck president Polk recommended extension of the Missouri Compromise 36°30′ line to the Pacific. The Whig-controlled House defied him, reaffirmed the Wilmot Proviso, drafted a bill to organize California as a free territory, and debated abolishing the slave trade and even slavery itself in the District of Columbia. Fistfights flared in Congress; southerners declared that they would secede if any of those measures became law; the Democratic Senate quashed all the bills. A southern caucus asked Calhoun to draft an address set-

They were in for a rude shock. Taylor viewed matters as a nationalist, not as a southerner. New York's antislavery Senator William H. Seward became one of his principal advisers. A novice in politics, Taylor was willing to be guided by Seward. As a military man, he was attracted to the idea of vanquishing the territorial problem by outflanking it. He proposed to admit California and New Mexico (the latter comprising present-day New Mexico, Arizona, Nevada, Utah, and part of Colorado) immediately as *states*, skipping the territorial stage.

From the South came cries of outrage. Immediate admission would bring in two more free states because slavery had not existed under Mexican law, and most of the 49ers were Free Soil in sentiment. With the administration's support, Californians held a convention in October 1849, drew up a constitution excluding slavery, and applied to Congress for admission as a state. Taylor's end run would tip the existing balance of 15 slave and 15 free states in favor of the North, probably forever. The South would lose its de facto veto in the Senate. "For the first time," said freshman Senator Jefferson Davis of Mississippi, "we are about permanently to destroy the balance of power between the sections." Davis insisted that slave labor was suitable to mining and that slavery should be permitted in California. Southerners vowed never to "consent to be thus degraded and enslaved" by such a "monstrous trick and injustice" as admission of California as a free state.

The Compromise of 1850

California and New Mexico became the focal points of a cluster of slavery issues that faced the Congress of 1849–50. An earlier Supreme Court decision (*Prigg* v. *Pennsylvania,* 1842) had relieved state officials of any obligation to enforce the return of fugitive slaves who had escaped into free states, declaring that this was a federal responsibility. Southerners therefore demanded a strong national fugitive slave law (in utter disregard of their oft-stated commitment to states' rights). Antislavery northerners, on the other hand, were calling for an end to the disgraceful buying and selling of slaves in the national capital. And in the Southwest, a shooting war threatened to break out between Texas and New Mexico. Having won the Rio Grande as their southern border with Mexico, Texans insisted that the river must also mark their western border with New Mexico. (That would have given Texas more than half of the present state of New Mexico.) This dispute also involved slavery because the terms of Texas's annexation authorized the state to split into as many as five states, and the territory it carved out of New Mexico would create the potential for still another slave state.

These problems produced both a crisis and an opportunity. The crisis lay in the threat to break up the Union. From Mississippi had gone forth a call for a convention of southern states at Nashville in June 1850 "to devise and adopt some mode of resistance to northern aggression." Few doubted that the mode would be secession unless Congress met southern demands at least halfway. But Congress got off to an unpromising start. Sectional disputes prevented either major party from commanding a majority in electing a Speaker of the House. Through three weeks and 62 ballots, the contest went on while tempers shortened. Northerners and southerners shouted insults at each other, fistfights broke out, and a Mississippian drew a revolver during one heated debate. Southern warnings of secession became a litany: "If, by your legislation, you seek to drive us from the territories of California and New Mexico," thundered Toombs of Georgia, *"I am for disunion."* On the 63rd ballot, the exhausted legislators finally elected Howell Cobb of Georgia as Speaker by a plurality rather than a majority.

The Senate Debates

As he had in 1820 and 1833, Henry Clay hoped to turn the crisis into an opportunity. Seventy-two years old, a veteran of 30 years in Congress, three times an unsuccessful candidate for president, Clay was the most respected and still the most magnetic figure in the Senate. A nationalist from the border state of Kentucky, he hoped to unite North and South in a compromise. On January 29, 1850, he presented eight proposals to the Senate and supported them with an eloquent speech, the first of many to be heard in that body during what turned out to be the most famous congressional debate in U.S. history. Clay grouped the first six of his proposals into three pairs, each pair offering one concession to the North and one to the South. The first pair would admit California as a free state but would organize the rest of the Mexican cession without restrictions against slavery. The second would settle the Texas boundary dispute in favor of New Mexico but would compensate Texas to enable the state to pay off bonds it had sold when it was an independent republic. (Many holders of the Texas bonds were southerners.) The third pair of proposals would abolish the slave trade in the District of Columbia but would guarantee the continued existence of slavery there unless both Maryland and Virginia consented to abolition. Of Clay's final two proposals, one affirmed that Congress had no jurisdiction over the interstate slave trade; the other called for a strong national fugitive slave law.

At the end of a long, grueling bargaining process, the final shape of the Compromise of 1850 closely resembled Clay's package. The public face of this process featured set speeches in the Senate, the most notable of which were those of John C. Calhoun, Daniel Webster, and William H. Seward. Calhoun and Webster (along with Clay) represented the grand Senate triumvirate of the previous generation; Seward was the rising star of a new generation, whose speech catapulted him into renown. Each senator spoke for one of the three principal viewpoints on the issues.

Calhoun went first, on March 4. Suffering from consumption (he would die within a month), Calhoun sat shrouded in flannel as a colleague read his speech to a rapt audience. Unless northerners returned fugitive slaves in good faith, Calhoun warned, unless they consented to the expansion of slavery into the territories and accepted a constitutional amendment "which will restore to the South, in substance, the power she possessed of protecting herself before the equilibrium between the two sections was destroyed," southern states could not "remain in the Union consistently with their honor and safety."

Webster's famous "seventh of March" speech three days later was both a reply to Calhoun and an appeal to the North for compromise. In words that would be memorized by generations of schoolchildren, Webster announced his theme: "I wish to speak to-day, not as a Massachusetts man, nor as a Northern man, but as an American. I speak to-day for the preservation of the Union. Hear me for my cause." Although Webster had voted for the Wilmot Proviso, he now urged Yankees to forgo "taunt or reproach" of the South by insisting on the proviso. Nature would exclude slavery from New Mexico. "I would not take pains uselessly to reaffirm an ordinance of nature, nor to reenact the will of God." Believing that God helped those who helped themselves, many of Webster's former antislavery admirers repudiated his leadership—especially because he also endorsed a fugitive slave law.

On March 11, Seward expressed the antislavery position in what came to be known as his "higher law" speech. Both slavery and compromise were "radically wrong and essentially vicious," he said. In reply to Calhoun's arguments for the constitutional protection of slavery in the territories, Seward invoked "a higher law than the Constitution," the law of God in whose sight all persons were equal. Instead of legislating the expansion of slavery or the return of fugitive slaves, the country should be considering how to bring slavery peacefully to an end, for "you cannot roll back the tide of social progress."

Passage of the Compromise

While these speeches were being delivered, committee members worked ceaselessly behind the scenes to fashion compromise legislation. They were aided by lobbyists for Texas bondholders and for business interests that wanted an end to this distracting crisis. But, in reaching for a compromise, Clay chose what turned out to be the wrong tactic. He lumped most of his proposals together in a single bill, hoping that supporters of any given part of the compromise would vote for the whole in order to win the part they liked. Instead, most senators and representatives voted against the package in order to defeat the parts they disliked. President Taylor continued to insist on the immediate admission of California (and New Mexico, when it was ready) with no quid pro quo for the South. Exhausted and discouraged, Clay fled Washington's summer heat, leaving a young senator from Illinois, Stephen A. Douglas, to lead the forces of compromise.

Another rising star of the new generation, Douglas reversed Clay's tactics. Starting with a core of supporters made up of Democrats from the Old Northwest and Whigs from the upper South, he built a majority for each part of the compromise by submitting it separately and adding its supporters to his core: northerners for a free California, southerners for a fugitive slave law, and so on. This effort benefited from Taylor's sudden death on July 9 (of gastroenteritis, after consuming large quantities of iced milk and cherries on a hot Fourth of July). The new president, Millard Fillmore, was a conservative Whig from New York who gave his support to the compromise. One after another, in August and September, the separate measures became law: the admission of California as a free state; the organization of the rest of the Mexican cession

into the two territories of New Mexico and Utah without restrictions against slavery; the settlement of the Texas–New Mexico border dispute in favor of New Mexico and the compensation of Texas with $10 million; the abolition of the slave trade in the District of Columbia and the guarantee of slavery there; and the passage of a new fugitive slave law. When it was over, most Americans breathed a sigh of relief, the Nashville convention adjourned tamely, and President Fillmore christened the Compromise of 1850 "a final settlement" of all sectional problems. Calhounites in the South and antislavery activists in the North branded the compromise a betrayal of principle. But, for the time being, they seemed to be in a minority.

The compromise produced consequences different from what many anticipated. California came in as the 16th free state, but its senators during the 1850s were in fact conservative Democrats who voted with the South on most issues. California law even allowed slave owners to keep their slaves while sojourning in the state. The territorial legislatures of Utah and New Mexico legalized slavery, but few slaves were brought there. And the fugitive slave law generated more trouble and controversy than all the other parts of this final settlement combined.

The Fugitive Slave Law

The Constitution required that a slave who escaped into a free state must be returned to his or her owner, but failed to specify how that should be done. Under a 1793 law, slave owners could take their recaptured property before any state or federal court to prove ownership. This procedure worked well enough so long as officials in free states were willing to cooperate. As the antislavery movement gained momentum in the 1830s, however, some officials proved uncooperative. And professional slave-catchers sometimes went too far—kidnapping free blacks, forging false affidavits to "prove" they were slaves, and selling them south into bondage. Several northern states responded by passing antikidnapping laws that gave alleged fugitives the right of trial by jury. The laws also prescribed criminal penalties for kidnapping. In *Prigg* v. *Pennsylvania* (1842), the U.S. Supreme Court declared Pennsylvania's antikidnapping law unconstitutional.

But the Court also ruled that enforcing the Constitution's fugitive slave clause was entirely a federal responsibility, thereby absolving the states of any need to cooperate in enforcing it. Nine northern states thereupon passed personal liberty laws prohibiting the use of state facilities (courts, jails, police or sheriffs, and so on) in the recapture of fugitives.

Fugitive slaves dramatized the poignancy and cruelties of bondage more vividly than anything else. A man or woman risking all for freedom was not an abstract issue

KIDNAPPING AGAIN!

This is a typical poster printed by abolitionist opponents of the Fugitive Slave Law. It was intended to rally the citizens of Boston against the recapture and reenslavement of Anthony Burns, a fugitive slave from Virginia seized in Boston in May 1854.

but a real human being whose plight invited sympathy and help. Consequently, many northerners who were not necessarily opposed to slavery in the South nonetheless felt outrage at the idea of fugitives being seized in a land of freedom and returned to slavery. The "underground railroad" that helped spirit slaves out of bondage took on legendary status. Stories of secret chambers where fugitives were hidden, dramatic trips in the dark of the moon between stations on the underground, and clever or heroic measures to foil pursuing bloodhounds exaggerated the legend.

Probably fewer than 1,000 of a total 3 million slaves actually escaped to freedom each year. But to southerners the return of those fugitives, like the question of the legality of slavery in California or New Mexico, was a matter of *honor* and *rights*. "Although the loss of property is felt," said Senator James Mason of Virginia, sponsor of the Fugitive Slave Act, "the loss of honor is felt still more." The fugitive slave law, said another southern politician, was "the only measure of the Compromise [of 1850] calculated to secure the rights of the South." Southerners therefore regarded obedience to the law as a test of the North's good faith in carrying out the compromise.

The law's provisions were extraordinary. It created federal commissioners who could issue warrants for arrests of fugitives and before whom a slaveholder would bring a captured fugitive to prove ownership. All the slaveholder needed for proof was an affidavit from a slave-state court or the testimony of white witnesses. The fugitive had no right to testify on his or her own behalf. The commis-

sioner received a fee of $10 if he found the owner's claim valid, but only $5 if he let the fugitive go. (The difference was supposedly justified by the larger amount of paperwork required to return the fugitive to slavery.) The federal treasury would pay all costs of enforcement. The commissioner could call on federal marshals to apprehend fugitives, and the marshals in turn could deputize any citizen to help. A citizen who refused could be fined up to $1,000, and anyone who harbored a fugitive or obstructed his or her capture would be subject to imprisonment. Northern senators had tried in vain to weaken some of these provisions and to amend the law to give alleged fugitives the rights to testify, to habeas corpus, and to a jury trial.

Abolitionists denounced the law as draconian, immoral, and unconstitutional. They vowed to resist it. Opportunities soon came, as slave owners sent agents north to recapture fugitives, some of whom had escaped years earlier (the act set no statute of limitations). In February 1851, slave-catchers arrested a black man living with his family in Indiana and returned him to an owner who said he had run away 19 years before. A Maryland man tried to claim ownership of a Philadelphia woman who he said had escaped 22 years earlier; he also wanted her six children, all of whom were born in Philadelphia. In this case, the commissioner disallowed his claim to both mother and children. But statistics show that the law was rigged in favor of the claimants. In the first 15 months of its operation, 84 fugitives were returned to slavery and only 5 were released. (For the entire decade of the 1850s, the ratio was 332 to 11.)

The Slave-Catchers

Unable to protect their freedom through legal means, many blacks, with the support of white allies, resorted to flight and resistance. Thousands of northern blacks fled to Canada—3,000 in the last three months of 1850 alone. In February 1851, slave-catchers arrested a fugitive who had taken the name Shadrach when he escaped from Virginia a year earlier. They rushed him to the federal courthouse, where a few deputy marshals held him, pending a hearing. But a group of black men broke into the courtroom, overpowered the deputies, and spirited Shadrach out of the country to Canada. This was too much for the Fillmore administration. In April 1851, another fugitive, Thomas Sims, was arrested in Boston, and the president sent 250 soldiers to help 300 armed deputies enforce the law and return Sims to slavery.

Continued rescues and escapes kept matters at fever pitch for the rest of the decade. In the fall of 1851, a Maryland slave owner and his son accompanied federal mar-

THE UNDERGROUND RAILROAD

The Quaker merchant Levi Coffin was one of the principal "conductors" on the underground railroad. He is shown in this painting standing on the wagon wearing a broad-brimmed hat. His home in central Indiana (depicted here) and, after 1847, his home in Cincinnati were stations on the road for fugitive slaves escaping north to freedom.

"The Underground Railroad" painting by Charles T. Webber (1893) from the Cincinnati Art Museum (#1927.26).

shals to Christiana, Pennsylvania, a Quaker village, where two of the man's slaves had taken refuge. The hunters ran into a fusillade of gunfire from a house where a dozen black men were protecting the fugitives. When the shooting stopped, the slave owner was dead and his son was seriously wounded. Three of the blacks fled to Canada. This time Fillmore sent in the marines. They helped marshals arrest 30 black men and a half-dozen whites, who were indicted for treason. But the government's case fell apart, and the U.S. attorney dropped charges after a jury acquitted the first defendant, a Quaker.

Another white man who aided slaves was not so lucky. Sherman Booth was an abolitionist editor in Wisconsin who led a raid in 1854 to free a fugitive from custody. Convicted in a federal court, Booth appealed for a writ of habeas corpus from the Wisconsin Supreme Court. The court freed him and declared the Fugitive Slave Law unconstitutional. That assertion of states' rights prompted the southern majority on the U.S. Supreme Court to overrule the Wisconsin court, assert the supremacy of federal law, and order Booth back to prison.

Two of the most famous fugitive slave cases of the 1850s ended in deeper tragedy. In spring 1854, federal marshals in Boston arrested a Virginia fugitive, Anthony Burns. Angry abolitionists poured into Boston to save him. Some of them tried to attack the federal courthouse, where a deputy was killed in an exchange of gunfire. But the new president, Franklin Pierce, was determined not to back down. "Incur any expense," he wired the district attorney in Boston, "to enforce the law." After every legal move to free Burns had failed, Pierce sent a U.S. revenue cutter to carry Burns back to Virginia. While thousands of angry Yankees lined the streets under American flags hanging upside down to signify the loss of liberty in the cradle of the Revolution, 200 marines and soldiers marched this lone black man back into bondage.

Two years later Margaret Garner escaped from Kentucky to Ohio with her husband and four children. When a posse of marshals and deputies caught up with them, Margaret seized a kitchen knife and tried to kill her children and herself rather than return to slavery. She managed to cut her three-year-old daughter's throat before she was overpowered. After complicated legal maneuvers, the federal commissioner remanded the fugitives to their Kentucky owner. He promptly sold them down the river to Arkansas, and, in a steamboat accident along the way, one of Margaret Garner's sons drowned in the Mississippi.

Such events had a profound impact on public emotions. Most northerners were not abolitionists, and few of them regarded black people as equals. But millions of them moved closer to an antislavery—or perhaps it would be more accurate to say anti-Southern—position in response to the shock of seeing armed slave-catchers on their streets. "When it was all over," agreed two theretofore conservative Whigs in Boston after the Anthony Burns affair, "I put my face in my hands and wept. I could do nothing less. . . . We went to bed one night old-fashioned, conservative, compromise Union Whigs and waked up stark mad Abolitionists."

Several northern states passed new personal liberty laws in defiance of the South. Although those laws did not make it impossible to recover fugitives, they made it so difficult, expensive, and time consuming that many slave owners gave up trying. The failure of the North to honor the Fugitive Slave Law, part of the Compromise of 1850, was one of the South's bitter grievances in the 1850s. Several southern states cited it as one of their reasons for seceding in 1861.

Uncle Tom's Cabin

A novel inspired by the plight of fugitive slaves further intensified public sentiment. Harriet Beecher Stowe, author of *Uncle Tom's Cabin,* was the daughter of Lyman Beecher, the most famous clergyman-theologian of his generation, and the sister of Henry Ward Beecher, the foremost preacher of the next generation. Writing this book made her more famous than either of them. Having grown up in the doctrinal air of New England Calvinist notions of sin, guilt, and atonement, Harriet lived for 18 years in Cincinnati, where she became acquainted with fugitive slaves who had escaped across the Ohio River. During the 1840s, in spare moments that she carved out from the duties of bearing and nurturing seven children, Stowe wrote numerous short stories. Outraged by the Fugitive Slave Law in 1850, she responded to her sister-in-law's suggestion: "Hattie, if I could use a pen as you can, I would write something that will make this nation feel what an accursed thing slavery is."

In 1851, writing by candlelight after putting the children to bed, Stowe turned out a chapter a week for serial publication in an antislavery newspaper. When the installments were published as a book in spring 1852, *Uncle Tom's Cabin* became a runaway best seller and was eventually translated into 20 languages. Contrived in plot, didactic in style, steeped in sentiment, *Uncle Tom's Cabin* is nevertheless a powerful novel with unforgettable characters. Uncle Tom is not the fawning, servile Sambo of later caricature, but a Christlike figure who bears the sins of white people and carries the salvation of black people on his shoulders. The novel's central theme is the tragedy of the breakup of families by slavery—the theme most likely to pluck at the heartstrings of middle-class Americans of that generation. Few eyes remained dry as they read about Eliza fleeing across the ice-choked Ohio River to save her son from the slave trader, or about Tom grieving for the wife and children he had left behind in Kentucky when he was sold.

Although banned in some parts of the South, *Uncle Tom's Cabin* found a wide but hostile readership there. A measure of the defensiveness of southerners toward the book is the tone of the reviews that appeared in southern journals. The editor of the South's leading literary periodical instructed the reviewer: "I would have the review as hot as hellfire, blasting and searing the reputation of [this] vile wretch in petticoats." Pro-slavery authors rushed into print with more than a dozen novels challenging Stowe's themes, but all of them together made nothing like the impact of *Uncle Tom's Cabin.* The book helped shape a whole generation's view of slavery.

The Granger Collection, New York.

HARRIET BEECHER STOWE

A portrait of Harriet Beecher Stowe painted shortly after the publication of *Uncle Tom's Cabin* made her world famous.

Filibustering

If the prospects for slavery in New Mexico appeared unpromising, southerners could contemplate a closer region where slavery already existed—Cuba. Enjoying an economic boom based on slave-grown sugar, this Spanish colony only 90 miles from American shores had nearly 400,000 slaves in 1850—more than any American state except Virginia. President Polk, his appetite for territory not yet sated by the acquisition of Texas, Oregon, and half of Mexico, offered Spain $100 million for Cuba in 1848. The Spanish foreign minister spurned the offer, stating that he would rather see the island sunk in the sea than sold.

If money did not work, revolution might. Cuban planters, restive under Spanish rule, intrigued with American expansionists in the hope of fomenting an uprising on the island. Their leader was Narciso López, a Venezuelan-born Cuban soldier of fortune. In 1849, López recruited several hundred American adventurers for the first "filibustering" expedition against Cuba (from the Spanish *filibustero,* a freebooter or pirate). When President Taylor ordered the navy to prevent López's ships from leaving New York, López shifted his operations to the friendlier environs of New Orleans, where he raised a new force of filibusters, many of them Mexican War veterans. Port officials in New Orleans looked the other way when the expedition sailed in May 1850, but Spanish troops drove the filibusters into the sea after they had established a beachhead in Cuba.

Undaunted, López escaped and returned to a hero's welcome in the South, where he raised men and money for a third try in 1851. This time, William Crittenden of Kentucky, nephew of the U.S. attorney general, commanded the 420 Americans in the expedition. But the invasion ended in fiasco and tragedy. Spanish soldiers suppressed a local uprising timed to coincide with the invasion and then defeated the filibusters, killing 200 and capturing the rest. López was garroted in the public square of Havana, after which 50 American prisoners, including Crittenden, were lined up and executed by firing squad.

These events dampened southerners' enthusiasm for Cuba, but only for a time. "Cuba must be ours," declared Jefferson Davis, in order to "increase the number of slaveholding constituencies." In 1852, the Democrats nominated Franklin Pierce of New Hampshire for president. Although a Yankee, Pierce had a reputation as a "doughface"—a northern man with southern principles. Southern Democrats were delighted with his nomination. Pierce was "as reliable as Calhoun himself," wrote one, while another said that "a nomination so favorable to the South had not been anticipated." Especially gratifying was Pierce's support for annexing Cuba, which he made one of the top priorities of his new administration after winning a landslide victory over a demoralized Whig Party weakened by schism between its northern and southern wings.

Pierce covertly encouraged a new filibustering expedition to Cuba. This one was to be led by former Governor John Quitman of Mississippi. While Quitman was recruiting hundreds of volunteers, southerners in Congress introduced a resolution to suspend the neutrality law that prohibited American interference in the internal affairs of other countries. But, at the last moment, Pierce backed off, fearful of political damage in the North if his administration became openly identified with filibustering. The Quitman expedition never sailed.

Pierce again tried to buy Cuba, instructing the American minister in Madrid to offer Spain $130 million. The minister was Pierre Soulé, a flamboyant Louisianian who managed to alienate most Spaniards by his clumsy intriguing. Soulé's crowning act came in October 1854 at a meeting with the American ministers to Britain and France in Ostend, Belgium. He persuaded them to sign what came to be known as the Ostend Manifesto. "Cuba is as necessary to the North American republic as any of its present . . . family of states," declared this document. If Spain persisted in refusing to sell, then "by every law, human and divine, we shall be justified in wresting it from Spain."

LINK TO THE PAST

Demands for the Expansion of Slavery

Albert Gallatin Brown was a true fire-eater—a Southern-rights radical whose fiery secessionist rhetoric resonated through the 1850s. He had resisted the Compromise of 1850 because it admitted California as a free state: "We ask you to give us our rights" in California, he thundered in the House of Representatives; "if you refuse, I am for taking them by armed occupation." In 1851, he urged Mississippi's secession; when that did not happen, he threw his energy into the efforts to acquire Cuba and other tropical regions suitable for slavery. In 1858, as a United States senator, he spelled out his demands for Cuba and several additional Central American provinces in a speech to his Mississippi constituents.

I want Cuba, and I know that sooner or later we must have it. . . . I want Tamaulipas, Potosi, and one or two other Mexican States; and I want them all for the same reason—for the planting or spreading of slavery. And a foothold in Central America will powerfully aid us in acquiring those other States. . . . Yes, I want these Countries for the spread of slavery.

1. Do you think the South would have been well served if Brown's demands had been met?
2. Would the Civil War have been avoided?

For additional sources related to this feature, visit the CD accompanying this text or the *Liberty, Equality, Power* Web site at:

http://history.wadsworth.com/murrin_LEP4e

This "manifesto of the brigands," as antislavery Americans called it, caused an international uproar. The administration repudiated the Ostend Manifesto and recalled Soulé. Nevertheless, acquisition of Cuba remained an objective of the Democratic Party. The issue played a role in both the 1860 presidential election and the secession controversy during 1860 and 1861. Meanwhile, American filibustering shifted its focus 750 miles south of Havana to Nicaragua. There, the most remarkable of the *filibusteros*, William Walker, had proclaimed himself president and restored the institution of slavery.

The Gray-Eyed Man of Destiny

A native of Tennessee and a brilliant, restless man, Walker had earned a medical degree from the University of Pennsylvania and studied and practiced law in New Orleans before joining the 1849 rush to California. Weighing less than 120 pounds, Walker seemed an unlikely fighter or leader of men. But he fought three duels, and his luminous eyes, which seemed to transfix his fellows, won him the sobriquet "gray-eyed man of destiny."

Walker found his true calling in filibustering. At the time, numerous raids were taking place back and forth across the border with Mexico, some of them staged to seize more of that country for the United States. In 1853, Walker led a ragged "army" of footloose 49ers into Baja California and Sonora and declared the region an independent republic. Exhaustion and desertion depleted his troops, however, and the Mexicans drove the survivors back to California.

Walker decided to try again, with another goal. Many southerners eyed Nicaragua's potential for growing cotton, sugar, coffee, and other crops. The unstable Nicaraguan government offered a tempting target. In 1854, Walker signed a contract with rebel leaders in the civil war of the moment. The following spring, he led an advance guard of filibusters to Nicaragua and proclaimed himself commander-in-chief of the rebel forces. At the head of 2,000 American soldiers, he gained control of the country and named himself president in 1856. The Pierce administration extended diplomatic recognition to Walker's regime.

But things soon turned sour. The other Central American republics formed an alliance to invade Nicaragua and overthrow Walker. To win greater support from the southern states, Walker issued a decree in September 1856 reinstituting slavery in Nicaragua. A convention of southern economic promoters meeting in Savannah praised Walker's efforts "to introduce civilization in the States of Central America, and to develop these rich and productive regions by slave labor." Boatloads of new recruits arrived in Nicaragua from New Orleans. But in spring 1857, they succumbed to disease and to the Central American armies.

Walker escaped to New Orleans, where he was welcomed as a hero. He had no trouble recruiting men for another attempt, but the navy stopped him in November 1857. Southern congressmen condemned the naval commander and encouraged Walker to try again. He did, in December 1858, after a New Orleans jury refused to convict him of violating the neutrality law. On this third expedition, Walker's ship struck a reef and sank. Undaunted, he tried yet again. He wrote a book to raise funds for another invasion of Nicaragua, urging "the hearts of Southern youth to answer the call of honor. . . . The true field for the expansion of slavery is in tropical America." A few more southern youths answered the call, but they were stopped in Honduras. There, on September 12, 1860, the gray-eyed man met his destiny before a firing squad.

Conclusion

Within the three-year period from 1845 to 1848, the annexation of Texas, the settlement of the Oregon boundary dispute with Britain, and the acquisition by force of New Mexico and California from Mexico added 1,150,000 square miles to the United States. This expansion was America's "manifest destiny," according to Senator Stephen A. Douglas of Illinois. He further proclaimed:

> Increase, and multiply, and expand, is the law of this nation's existence. You cannot limit this great republic by mere boundary lines. Any one of you gentlemen might as well say to a son twelve years old that he is big enough, and must not grow any larger, and in order to prevent his growth put a hoop around him and keep him to his present size. Either the hoop must burst and be rent asunder, or the child must die. So it would be with this great nation.

But other Americans feared that the country could not absorb such rapid growth without strains that might break it apart. At the outbreak of the war with Mexico, Ralph Waldo Emerson predicted that "the United States will conquer Mexico, but it will be as the man swallows the arsenic, which brings him down in turn. Mexico will poison us." Emerson proved correct. The poison was the reopening of the question of slavery's expansion, which had supposedly been settled by the Missouri Compromise in 1820. The admission of Texas as a huge new slave state and the possibility that more slave states might be carved out of the territory acquired from Mexico provoked northern congressmen to pass the Wilmot Proviso. Southerners bristled at this attempt to prevent the further expansion of slavery. Threats of secession and civil war poisoned the atmosphere in 1849 and 1850.

The Compromise of 1850 defused the crisis and appeared to settle the issue once again, but events would soon prove that this compromise had merely postponed the crisis. The fugitive slave issue and filibustering expeditions to acquire more slave territory kept sectional controversies smoldering. In 1854, the Kansas-Nebraska Act would cause them to burst into a hotter flame than ever.

SUGGESTED READINGS

For the theme of Manifest Destiny, the best introduction is **Frederick Merk, *Manifest Destiny and Mission in American History*** (1963). See also the essays in **Samuel W. Haynes and Christopher Morris, eds., *Manifest Destiny and Empire*** (1997). Two good studies of the overland trails to California and Oregon and other points West are **John D. Unruh, Jr., *The Plains Across: The Overland Emigrants and the Trans-Mississippi West, 1840–1860*** (1979), and **John Mack Faragher, *Women and Men on the Overland Trail*** (1978). A fine introduction to the impact of American expansion on the Indians of the West is **Philip Weeks, *Farewell, My Nation: The American Indian and the United States 1820–1890*** (rev. ed., 2000). A good study of the relationship between American expansion and the coming of war with Mexico is **David Pletcher, *The Diplomacy of Annexation: Texas, Oregon, and the Mexican War*** (1973). For the Mexican War, a good narrative is **John S. D. Eisenhower, *So Far from God: The U.S. War with Mexico 1846–1848*** (1989). Opposition to and support for the war by different elements of the public are chronicled in **John H. Schroeder, *Mr. Polk's War: American Opposition and Dissent, 1846–1848*** (1973), and **Robert W. Johannsen, *To the Halls of the Montezumas: The Mexican War in the American Imagination*** (1985). For the conflict provoked by the issue of slavery's expansion into territory acquired from Mexico, see **David M. Potter, *The Impending Crisis 1848–1861*** (1976); **Richard H. Sewell, *Ballots for Freedom: Antislavery Politics in the United States 1837–1860*** (1976); **Michael A. Morrison, *Slavery and the American West: The Eclipse of Manifest Destiny and the Coming of the Civil War*** (1997); and **Leonard D. Richards, *The Slave Power: The Free North and Southern Domination, 1780–1860*** (2000). The best study of the Compromise of 1850 is **Holman Hamilton, *Prologue to Conflict: The Crisis and Compromise of 1850*** (1964). The passage and enforcement of the Fugitive Slave Act is the subject of **Stanley W. Campbell, *The Slave Catchers*** (1970). Still the best book on filibustering is **Robert E. May, *The Southern Dream of a Caribbean Empire 1854–1861*** (1971).

  ## AMERICAN JOURNEY ONLINE AND INFOTRAC COLLEGE EDITION

Visit the source collections at www.ajaccess.wadsworth.com and infotrac.thomsonlearning.com and use the Search function with the following key terms to explore documents, images, audio and video clips, articles, and commentary related to the material in this chapter.

Uncle Tom's Cabin	Mormons
Harriet Beecher Stowe	Manifest Destiny
Henry Clay	Texas Republic
Martin Van Buren	Battle of the Alamo
fugitive slave	Compromise of 1850
The Book of Mormon	Stephen Douglas

GRADE AIDS

Visit the Liberty Equality Power Companion Web Site for resources specific to this textbook: http://history.wadsworth.com/murrin_LEP4e

  The CD in the back of this book and the U.S. History Resource Center at http://history.wadsworth.com/u.s./ offer a variety of tools to help you succeed in this course, including access to quizzes; images; documents; interactive simulations, maps, and timelines; movie explorations; and a wealth of other sources.

Chapter 14

The Gathering Tempest, 1853–1860

The Granger Collection, New York.

THE 9:45 ACCOMMODATION
The railroad shrank distances and transformed the landscape in antebellum America.
The arrival of a train brought much of a town's population to the station to gape at the
iron horse belching smoke and sparks like a legendary dragon of old. By 1860, 31,000 miles
of railroad track crisscrossed the United States, more than in all of Europe combined.

The wounds caused by the 1850 battle over slavery in the territories had barely healed when they were reopened. This time the strife concerned the question of slavery in the Louisiana Purchase territory, an issue presumably settled 34 years earlier by the Missouri Compromise of 1820.

The Compromise of 1820 had admitted Missouri as a slave state but had banned slavery from the rest of the Purchase north of 36°30'. Senator Stephen Douglas, in search of southern support for organizing Kansas and Nebraska as territories, consented to the repeal of this provision of the Missouri Compromise. Northern outrage at this repudiation of a "sacred contract" killed the Whig Party and gave birth to the antislavery Republican Party. In 1857, the Supreme Court added insult to injury with the Dred Scott decision, which denied Congress the power to restrict slavery from the territories. The ominous reorientation of national politics along sectional lines was accompanied by a bloody civil war in Kansas and a raid on the federal arsenal at Harpers Ferry, Virginia, by John Brown and his followers.

CHAPTER FOCUS

♦ Why did the Whig party die, and why did the Republican rather than the American party emerge as the new majority party in the North?

♦ What were the origins of Nativism and how did this movement relate to the slavery issue?

♦ How did economic developments in the 1840s and 1850s widen the breach between North and South?

♦ What were the "free-labor ideology" and "herrenvolk democracy"? How did these concepts relate to the politics of the 1850s?

🌐 Kansas and the Rise of the Republican Party

By 1853, land-hungry settlers had pushed up the Missouri River to its confluence with the Kansas and Platte rivers, and entrepreneurs were talking about a railroad across the continent to San Francisco. But settlement of the country west of Missouri and land surveys for a railroad through it would require its organization as a territory. Accordingly, in 1853, the House passed a bill creating the Nebraska Territory, embracing the area north of Indian Territory (present-day Oklahoma) up to the Canadian border. But the House bill ran into trouble in the Senate. Under the Missouri Compromise, slavery would be excluded from the new territory. Having lost California, the pro-slavery forces were determined to salvage something from Nebraska. Missourians were particularly adamant, because a free Nebraska would leave them surrounded on three sides by free soil. Senator David R. Atchison of Missouri vowed to see Nebraska "sink in hell" before having it become free soil.

As president pro tem of the Senate, Atchison wielded great influence. A profane, gregarious man, he had inherited Calhoun's mantle as leader of the southern-rights faction. In the 1853–54 session of Congress, he kept raising the asking price for southern support of a bill to organize the Nebraska Territory.

The sponsor of the Senate bill was Stephen A. Douglas, chairman of the Senate Committee on Territories. Only 5 feet 4 inches tall, Douglas had earned the nickname Little Giant for his parliamentary skill, which he had demonstrated most dramatically in helping pass the Compromise of 1850 through Congress. In Douglas's opinion, the application of popular sovereignty to the slavery question in New Mexico and Utah had been the centerpiece of the compromise. The initial draft of his Nebraska bill merely repeated the language used for those territories, specifying that when any portion of the Nebraska Territory came in as a state, it could do so "with or without slavery, as its constitution may provide."

This was not good enough for Atchison and his southern colleagues. After talking with them, Douglas announced that because of a "clerical error," a provision calling for the territorial legislature to decide on slavery had been omitted from the draft. But Atchison raised the price once again, insisting on an explicit repeal of the Missouri Compromise. Sighing in response, Douglas stated that this action "will raise a hell of a storm," but he nevertheless agreed. He further agreed to divide the area in question into two territories: Kansas west of Missouri and Nebraska west of Iowa and Minnesota. To many northerners this looked suspi-

CHRONOLOGY

1852	Plenary Council of Catholic Church seeks tax support for parochial schools
1853	American Party emerges
1854	Crimean War begins • Congress passes Kansas-Nebraska Act • Republican Party organized • Antebellum immigration reaches peak
1855	Ethnic riots in several cities • "Border Ruffian" legislature in Kansas legalizes slavery
1856	Civil war in Kansas • Preston Brooks canes Charles Sumner on Senate floor • Crimean War ends • Buchanan wins three-way presidential election
1857	Supreme Court issues Dred Scott decision • Lecompton constitution written in Kansas • Congress enacts lower tariff • Panic of 1857 • Helper's *Impending Crisis* published
1858	Kansas voters reject Lecompton constitution • Lincoln-Douglas debates
1859	Congress defeats federal slave code for territories • John Brown's raid at Harpers Ferry
1860	Shoemakers' strike in New England • Buchanan vetoes Homestead Act

ciously like a scheme to mark Kansas out for slavery and Nebraska for freedom. Douglas then joined Jefferson Davis, Atchison, and other southern senators on a visit to the White House, where they twisted President Pierce's arm to give the revised Kansas-Nebraska bill the administration's support and to make its approval "a test of [Democratic] party orthodoxy."

The Kansas-Nebraska Act

The bill did "raise a hell of a storm." Contemporaries and historians have speculated endlessly on Douglas's motives. Some thought he wanted to win southern support for the presidential nomination in 1856. Perhaps, but he risked losing northern support. Others point out that Douglas's real estate holdings in Illinois would have risen in value if a transcontinental railroad were to traverse the Nebraska Territory and that southern opposition could block this route. The most likely reason, however, was Douglas's passionate belief in Manifest Destiny, in filling up the continent with American settlers and institutions. "The tide of immigration and civilization must be permitted to roll onward," he proclaimed. For this, he was willing to pay the South's price for support of his Kansas-Nebraska bill. He failed to recognize the depth of northern opposition to the "slave power" and to the expansion of slavery. Douglas had no firm moral convictions about slavery. He said that he

STEPHEN A. DOUGLAS

The Little Giant began his meteoric rise to leadership of the Democratic Party with his successful effort to have the Compromise of 1850 enacted by Congress. Having forestalled sectional schism in 1850, he drove a wedge more deeply than ever between North and South with the Kansas-Nebraska bill of 1854. Six years later, Douglas became a victim of sectional schism himself when the Democratic Party split into northern and southern factions and thereby ruined his chance of winning the presidency.

cared not whether the settlers voted slavery up or down; the important thing was to give them a chance to vote.

But many Americans did care. They regarded the expansion of slavery as a national question, and one that was too important to be left to territorial voters. One of them was an old acquaintance of Douglas, Abraham Lincoln. An antislavery Whig who had served four terms in the Illinois legislature and one term in Congress, Lincoln was propelled back into politics by the shock of the Kansas-Nebraska bill. He acknowledged the constitutional right to hold slave property in the states where it already existed, but he believed slavery was "an unqualified evil to

the negro, the white man, and to the state. . . . There can be no moral right in connection with one man's making a slave of another." Lincoln admitted he did not know how to bring this deeply entrenched institution to an end. He understood that race prejudice was a powerful obstacle to emancipation. Still, he believed that the country must face up to the problem. It must stop any further expansion of slavery as the first step on the long road to its "ultimate extinction."

Lincoln excoriated Douglas's "care not" attitude toward whether slavery was voted up or down: "I can not but hate [this] *declared* indifference, but as I must think, covert *real* zeal for the spread of [slavery]." The assertion that slavery would never be imported into Kansas anyway, because of the region's unsuitable climate, Lincoln branded as a "LULLABY argument." The climate of eastern Kansas was similar to that of the Missouri River Valley

RALLY

SPIRITS OF '76!

ALL CITIZENS OF

LEOMINSTER,

without distinction of party, who disapprove of the

"Nebraska Iniquity,"

are requested to meet at the

TOWN HALL,

Monday Evening, July 10th,

AT 7 O'CLOCK,

to choose delegates to meet in a

Mass Convention,

at Worcester, the 20th inst., to teach the "South" we have a "North," and will maintain our CONSTITUTIONAL RIGHTS.

CALEB C. FIELD, LEONARD BURRAGE, MERRITT WOOD.

Leominster, July 8, 1854.

BIRTH OF THE REPUBLICAN PARTY

The Kansas-Nebraska Act galvanized antislavery northerners of all parties into new anti-Nebraska organizations opposed to the repeal of the Missouri Compromise's ban on slavery in Louisiana Purchase territories north of 36°30′. Appealing to the "spirit of '76," these organizations coalesced into the Republican Party, which held its first convention at Pittsburgh on Washington's birthday in 1856 to organize a national party in preparation for the presidential nominating convention later that year.

in Missouri, where slaves were busily raising hemp and tobacco. Missouri slaveholders were already poised to take their slaves into the Kansas River valley. "Climate will not . . . keep slavery out of these territories," said Lincoln. "Nothing in *nature* will." Many of the founding fathers had looked forward to the day when slavery would no longer exist in republican America. Instead, the United States had become the world's largest slaveholding society, and Douglas's bill would permit slavery to expand even further. In a political speech at Peoria, Illinois, in October 1854, Lincoln insisted that "climate will not . . . keep slavery out of these territories. Nothing in *nature* will."

> The monstrous injustice of slavery [said Lincoln] deprives our republican example of its just influence in the world— enables the enemies of free institutions, with plausibility, to taunt us as hypocrites. . . . Let us re-adopt the Declaration of Independence, and with it, the practices, and policy, which harmonize with it. . . . If we do this, we shall not only have saved the Union; but we shall have so saved it, as to make, and to keep it, forever worthy of the saving.

With these eloquent words, Lincoln voiced the feelings that fostered an uprising against the Kansas-Nebraska bill. Abolitionists, Free-Soilers, northern Whigs, and even many northern Democrats held impassioned meetings to form anti-Nebraska coalitions, but they could not stop passage of the bill. It cleared the Senate easily, supported by a solid South and 15 of the 20 northern Democrats. In the House, where all of the northern Democrats would have to face the voters in the fall elections, the Pierce administration and the Democratic leadership still managed to wield the whip of patronage and party pressure and force half of them to vote for the bill, which passed by a vote of 113 to 100.

Death of the Whig Party

These proceedings completed the destruction of the Whigs as a national party. Southern Whigs had been disappearing ever since Zachary Taylor had "betrayed" them on the issue of a free California. After the presidential election of 1852, few Whigs remained in the cotton South. In that year, the Whig Party nominated General Winfield Scott for president. Although he was a Virginian, Scott, like Taylor, took a national rather than a southern view. He was the candidate of the northern Whigs in the national convention, which nominated him on the 53rd ballot after a bitter contest between the northern and southern wings of the party. A mass exodus of southern Whigs into the Democratic Party enabled Franklin Pierce to carry all but two slave states in the election. The unanimous vote of northern Whigs in Congress against the Kansas-Nebraska bill was the final straw. The Whig Party never recovered its influence in the South.

Whig strength seemed to be on its last legs in the North as well. Antislavery Whig leaders such as Seward and Lincoln hoped to channel the flood of anti-Nebraska sentiment through the Whig Party, an effort akin to containing Niagara Falls. Free-Soilers and antislavery Democrats spurned the Whig label. Political coalitions arose spontaneously in the North under various names: anti-Nebraska, Fusion, People's, Independent. The name that caught on evoked memories of America's first fight for freedom in 1776: Republican. The first use of this name seems to have occurred at an anti-Nebraska rally in a Congregational church at Ripon, Wisconsin, in May 1854. Soon, most of the congressional candidates fielded by anti-Nebraska coalitions ran their campaigns under the Republican banner.

The 1854 elections were disastrous for northern Democrats. One-fourth of Democratic voters deserted the party. The Democrats lost control of the House of Representatives when 66 of 91 incumbent free-state Democratic congressmen (including 37 of the 44 who had voted for the Kansas-Nebraska bill) went down to defeat. Combined with the increase in the number of Democratic congressmen from the South, where the party had picked up the pieces of the shattered Whig organization, this rout brought the party under southern domination more than ever.

But who would pick up the pieces of old parties in the North? The new Republican Party hoped to do so, but it suffered a shock in urban areas of the Northeast. Hostility toward immigrants created a tidal wave of nativism that threatened to swamp the anti-Nebraska movement. "Nearly everybody appears to have gone deranged on Nativism," reported a Pennsylvania Democrat, while a Whig in upstate New York warned that his district was "very badly infected with Knownothingism." Described as a "tornado," a "hurricane," a "freak of political insanity," the Know-Nothings won landslide victories in Massachusetts and Delaware, polled an estimated 40 percent of the vote in Pennsylvania, and did well elsewhere in the Northeast and border states. Who were these mysterious Know-Nothings? What did they stand for? What part did they play in the political upheaval of 1854?

Immigration and Nativism

During the early 19th century, immigration was less pronounced than in most other periods of U.S. history. The volume of immigration (expressed as the number of immigrants during a decade in proportion to the whole population at its beginning) was little more than 1 percent in the 1820s, increasing to 4 percent in the 1830s. Three-quarters of the newcomers were Protestants, mainly from Britain. Most of them were skilled workers, farmers, or members of white-collar occupations.

In the 1840s, a combination of factors abruptly quadrupled the volume of immigration and changed its ethnic and occupational makeup. The pressure of expanding population on limited land in Germany and successive failures of the potato crop in Ireland impelled millions of German and Irish peasants to emigrate. A majority came to the United States, where recovery from the depression of the early 1840s brought an economic boom with its insatiable demand for labor. During the decade after 1845, three million immigrants entered the United States— 15 percent of the total American population in 1845, the highest proportional volume of immigration in American history. Many of them, especially the Irish, joined the

unskilled and semiskilled labor force in the rapidly growing eastern cities and in the construction of railroads that proliferated to all points of the compass.

Most of them were also Roman Catholics. Anti-Catholicism had centuries-deep roots in Anglo-American Protestantism. Fear of the pope and of the Roman Church as autocratic and antirepublican was never far from the surface of American political culture, and scurrilous anti-Catholic literature circulated during the 1830s. Several ethnic riots between Protestant and Catholic workers over the years culminated in pitched battles and numerous deaths in Philadelphia in 1844. Short-lived nativist political parties that sprang up in several eastern cities in the early 1840s called for curbing the political rights of immigrants. Some of the nativists were actually immigrants from Britain and Northern Ireland who brought their anti-Catholicism with them.

Nativism appeared to subside with the revival of prosperity after 1844, but the decline was temporary because the vast increase of immigration proved too much for the country to absorb. Not only were most of the new immigrants Catholics, but many of them also spoke a foreign language and had alien cultural values. The temperance crusade had sharply curtailed drinking among native-born Protestants but had made little impact on the Irish and Germans, much of whose social and political life revolved around taverns and beer parlors (see chapter 11). Established Americans perceived more recent arrivals as responsible for an increase of crime and poverty in the cities. Cincinnati's overall crime rate tripled between 1846 and 1853; its murder rate increased sevenfold. Boston's expenditures for poor relief tripled during the same period.

Immigrants in Politics

The political power of immigrants also grew. In Boston, for example, the number of foreign-born voters (mostly Irish) increased by 200 percent from 1850 to 1855, whereas the number of native-born voters grew by only 14 percent. Most of the immigrants became Democrats, because that party welcomed or at least tolerated them and many Whigs did not. Foreign-born voters leaned toward the pro-slavery wing of the Democratic Party, even though seven-eighths of them settled in free states. Mostly working-class and poor, they rubbed shoulders against the small northern black population; Irish American mobs sometimes attacked black neighborhoods and rioted against black workers. They supported the Democratic Party as the best means of keeping blacks in slavery and out of the North. These attitudes sparked hostility toward immigrants among many antislavery people, some of whom equated slavery with Catholicism as a backward, despotic, repressive institution.

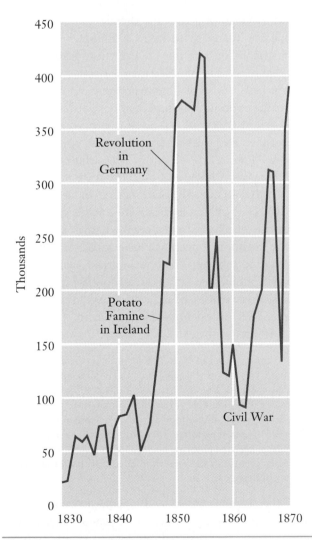

IMMIGRATION TO THE UNITED STATES

Source: From *Division and the Stresses of Reunion 1845–1876,* by David M. Potter. Copyright © 1973 Scott, Foresman and Company. Reprinted by permission.

The Roman Catholic hierarchy did little to allay that hostility. Pope Pius IX (1846–78) led the Church into a period of reaction against secular liberalism. The Church sided with the counterrevolutionary forces that crushed the European uprisings of 1848, which sought greater political and social democracy. In the United States, the leading Catholic prelate, Archbishop John Hughes of New York, taking his cue from the pope, attacked abolitionists, Free-Soilers, and various Protestant reform movements as akin to the Red Republicanism of Europe. In 1850, in a widely publicized address titled "The Decline of Protestantism and Its Causes," Hughes noted proudly that Catholic Church membership in the United States had grown three times faster than Protestant membership over the previous decade, and he predicted an eventual Catholic majority. "Protestantism is effete, powerless, dying out . . . and conscious that its last moment is come when it is fairly set, face to face, with Catholic truth."

Attitudes toward immigrants had political repercussions. Two of the hottest issues in state and local politics during the early 1850s were temperance and schools. The temperance crusaders had grown confident and aggressive enough to go into politics. The drunkenness and rowdiness they associated with Irish immigrants became one of their particular targets. Beginning with Maine in 1851, 12 states had enacted prohibition laws by 1855. Although several of the laws were soon weakened by the courts or repealed by legislatures, they exacerbated ethnic tensions.

So did battles over public schools versus parochial schools. Catholics resented the Protestant domination of public education and the reading of the King James Bible in schools. Archbishop Hughes flayed the public schools as purveyors of "Socialism, Red Republicanism, Universalism, Infidelity, Deism, Atheism, and Pantheism." The Church began to build parochial schools for the faithful, and in 1852, the first Plenary Council of American bishops decided to seek tax support for these schools or tax relief for Catholic parents who sent their children to them. This effort set off heated election contests in numerous northern cities and states. "Free school" tickets generally won by promising to defend public schools against the "bold effort" of this "despotic faith" to "uproot the tree of Liberty."

The Rise of the Know-Nothings

It was in this context that the Know-Nothings (their formal name was the American Party) burst onto the political scene. This party was the result of the merger in 1852 of two secret fraternal societies that limited their membership to native-born Protestants: the Order of the Star-Spangled Banner and the Order of United Americans.

Recruiting mainly young men in skilled blue-collar and lower white-collar occupations, the merged Order had a membership of 1 million or more by 1854. The Order supported temperance and opposed tax support for parochial schools. They wanted public office restricted to native-born men and sought to lengthen the naturalization period before immigrants could become citizens and voters from 5 to 21 years. Members were pledged to secrecy about the Order; if asked, they were to reply "I know nothing."

This movement swept through the Northeast in the 1854 elections, doing to the Whig Party in the Northeast what the slavery issue had done to it in the South. Although the American Party drew voters from both major parties, it cut more heavily into the Whig constituency. As a cultural force, nativism had found a more congenial home in the Whig Party than in the Democratic Party. When the American Party raised its banner in 1854, many northern Whigs who had not already gone over to the Republicans flocked to the Know-Nothings.

When the dust of the 1854 elections settled, it was clear that those who opposed the Democrats would control the next House of Representatives. But who would control the opposition—antislavery Republicans or nativist Americans? In truth, some northern voters and the congressmen they elected adhered to both political faiths. A Know-Nothing convention in Massachusetts resolved that "there can exist no real hostility to Roman Catholicism which does not also abhor slavery." In New England, several Know-Nothing leaders were actually Republicans in disguise who had jumped on the nativist bandwagon with the intention of steering it in an antislavery direction.

Many Republicans, however, warned against flirting with religious bigotry. "How can any one who abhors the oppression of negroes, be in favor of degrading classes of white people?" asked Abraham Lincoln in a letter to a friend. He further stated:

> As a nation, we began by declaring that "all men are created equal." We now practically read it "all men are created equal, except negroes." When the Know Nothings get control, it will read "all men are created equal, except negroes, and foreigners, and catholics." When it comes to this I should prefer emigrating to some country where they make no pretense of loving liberty—to Russia, for instance, where despotism can be taken pure, and without the base alloy of hypocrisy.

Other Republicans echoed Lincoln. Because "we are against Black Slavery, because the slaves are deprived of human rights," they declared, "we are also against . . . [this] system of Northern Slavery to be created by disfranchising the Irish and Germans." Many Republicans also considered nativism a red herring that diverted attention from

KNOW-NOTHINGS ON ELECTION DAY

In Baltimore, nativist political clubs called "Blood Tubs" and "Plug-Uglies" patrolled the streets at election time to intimidate foreign-born voters. An election riot in 1854 left 17 people dead in Baltimore; similar riots in St. Louis and Louisville also resulted in many deaths. This cartoon satirizes Baltimore's Know-Nothing street gangs.

the true danger confronting the country. "Neither the Pope nor the foreigners ever can govern the country or endanger its liberties," wrote the managing editor of the *New York Tribune,* "but the slavebreeders and slavetraders do govern it."

The Decline of Nativism

In 1855, Republican leaders maneuvered skillfully to divert the energies of northern Know-Nothings from their crusade against the pope to a crusade against the slave power. Two developments helped them. The first was turmoil in Kansas, which convinced many northerners that the slave power was a greater threat than the pope. The second was a significant shift southward in the center of nativist gravity. The American Party continued to do well in off-year elections in New England during 1855, but it also won elections in Maryland, Kentucky, and Tennessee and polled

at least 45 percent of the votes in five other southern states. Violence in several southern cities with large immigrant populations preceded or accompanied these elections. Riots left 10 dead in St. Louis, 17 in Baltimore, and 22 in Louisville, showing a significant streak of nativism in the South. But the American Party's success there probably owed a great deal to the search by former Whigs for a new political home outside the Democratic Party. Areas of American Party strength in seven or eight southern states more or less coincided with areas of former Whig strength.

These developments had important implications at the national level. Southern Know-Nothings were proslavery, whereas many of their Yankee counterparts were antislavery. Similar to the national Whig Party, so did the American Party founder on the slavery issue during 1855 and 1856. At the party's first national council in June 1855, most of the northern delegates walked out when southerners and northern conservatives joined forces to pass a resolution endorsing the Kansas-Nebraska Act. A similar scene occurred at an American Party convention in 1856. By that time, most northern members of the party had, in effect, become Republicans. When the House of Representatives elected in 1854 convened in December 1855, a protracted fight for the speakership again took place. The Republican candidate was Nathaniel P. Banks of Massachusetts, a former Know-Nothing who now considered himself a Republican. Banks finally won on the 133rd ballot with the support of about 30 Know-Nothings who thereby declared themselves Republicans. This marriage was consummated in summer 1856, when the "North Americans" endorsed the Republican candidate for president.

By that time, nativism had faded. The volume of immigration suddenly dropped by more than half in 1855 and stayed low for the next several years. Ethnic tensions eased, and cultural issues such as temperance and schools receded. Although the Republican Party took on some of the cultural baggage of nativism when it absorbed many northern Know-Nothings, party leaders shoved the baggage into dark corners. The real conflict was not the struggle between native and immigrant, or between Protestant and Catholic, but between North and South over the extension of slavery. That conflict led to civil war—and the war seemed already to have begun in the territory of Kansas.

Bleeding Kansas

When it became clear that southerners had the votes to pass the Kansas-Nebraska Act, William H. Seward stood up in the Senate and told his southern colleagues: "Since there is no escaping your challenge, I accept it in behalf of the cause of freedom. We will engage in competition for the virgin soil of Kansas, and God give victory to the side which is stronger in numbers as it is in right." Senator David Atchison of Missouri was ready for the expected influx of Free Soil settlers to the new Kansas Territory. "We are playing for a mighty stake," he wrote. "If we win we carry slavery to the Pacific Ocean; if we fail we lose Missouri, Arkansas, Texas and all the territories; the game must be played boldly."

Kansas State Historical Society, Topeka.

FREE-STATE MEN READY TO DEFEND LAWRENCE, KANSAS, IN 1856
After pro-slavery forces sacked the free-state capital of Lawrence in 1856, Northern settlers decided they needed more firepower to defend themselves. Somehow they got hold of a six-pound howitzer. This cannon did not fire a shot in anger during the Kansas troubles, but its existence may have deterred the "border ruffians."

Atchison did play boldly. At first, Missouri settlers in Kansas posted the stronger numbers. As the year 1854 progressed, however, settlers from the North came pouring in. Alarmed by this influx, bands of Missourians, labeled "border ruffians" by the Republican press, rode into Kansas prepared to vote as many times as necessary to install a pro-slavery government. In fall 1854, they cast at least 1,700 illegal ballots and sent a pro-slavery territorial delegate to Congress.

The following spring, when the time came to elect a territorial legislature, even greater efforts were needed because numerous Free Soil settlers had taken up claims during the winter. Atchison was equal to the task. He led a contingent of border ruffians to Kansas for the election. "There are eleven hundred coming over from Platte County to vote," he told his followers, "and if that ain't enough, we can send five thousand—enough to kill every God-damned abolitionist in the Territory."

His count was accurate. Nearly five thousand came—4,968 as determined by a congressional investigation—and voted illegally to elect a pro-slavery territorial legislature. The territorial governor pleaded with President Pierce to nullify the election. Pierce instead listened to Atchison and removed the governor. Meanwhile, the new territorial legislature legalized slavery and adopted a slave code that even authorized the death penalty for helping a slave to escape.

The so-called Free State party, outraged by these proceedings, had no intention of obeying laws enacted by this "bogus legislature." By fall 1855, they constituted a majority of bona fide settlers in Kansas. They called a convention, adopted a free-state constitution, and elected their own legislature and governor. By January 1856, two territorial governments in Kansas stood with their hands at each other's throats.

Kansas now became the leading issue in national politics. The Democratic Senate and President Pierce recognized the pro-slavery legislature meeting in the town of Lecompton, while the Republican House of Representatives recognized the antislavery legislature in the town of Lawrence. Southerners saw the struggle as crucial to their

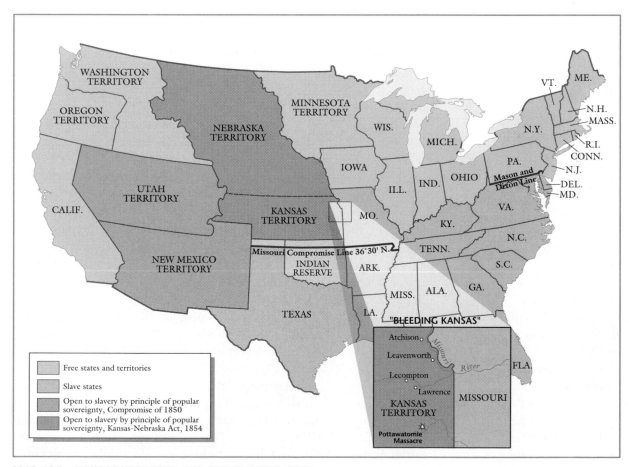

MAP 14.1 KANSAS-NEBRASKA AND THE SLAVERY ISSUE

On the main map, note how much territory was opened to slavery on the principle of popular sovereignty by the Compromise of 1850 and the Kansas-Nebraska Act. The enlarged inset map shows how close together were the centers of Free Soil and pro-slavery forces in Lawrence and Lecompton, respectively.

future. "The admission of Kansas into the Union as a slave state is now a point of honor," wrote Congressman Preston Brooks of South Carolina. "The fate of the South is to be decided with the Kansas issue." On the other side, Charles Sumner of Massachusetts gave a well-publicized speech in the Senate on May 19 and 20 entitled "The Crime against Kansas." "Murderous robbers from Missouri," charged Sumner, "from the drunken spew and vomit of an uneasy civilization" had committed the "rape of a virgin territory, compelling it to the hateful embrace of slavery." Among the southern senators whom Sumner singled out for special condemnation and ridicule was Andrew Butler of South Carolina, a cousin of Congressman Brooks. Butler was a "Don Quixote," said Sumner, "who had chosen a mistress to whom he has made his vows . . . the harlot, Slavery."

The Caning of Sumner

Sumner's speech incensed southerners, none more than Preston Brooks, who decided to avenge his cousin. He knew that Sumner would never accept a challenge to a duel. Anyway, dueling was for gentlemen, and even horse-whipping was too good for this Yankee blackguard. Two days after the speech, Brooks walked into the Senate chamber and began beating Sumner with a heavy cane. His legs trapped beneath the desk bolted to the floor, Sumner wrenched it loose as he stood up to try to defend himself, whereupon Brooks clubbed him so ferociously that Sumner slumped forward, bloody and unconscious.

News of the incident sent a thrill of pride through the South and a rush of rage through the North. Charleston newspapers praised Brooks for "standing forth so nobly in defense of . . . the honor of South Carolinians." Brooks resigned from Congress after censure by the House and was unanimously reelected. From all over the South came gifts of new canes, some inscribed with such mottoes as "Hit Him Again" and "Use Knock-Down Arguments." But, in the North, the Republicans gained thousands of voters as a result of the affair. It seemed to prove their contentions about "the barbarism of slavery." "Has it come to this," asked the poet William Cullen Bryant, editor of the *New York Evening Post,* "that we must speak with bated breath in the presence of our Southern masters? . . . Are we to be chastised as they chastise their slaves?" A veteran New York politician reported that he had "never before seen anything at all like the present state of deep, determined, & desperate feelings of hatred, & hostility to the further extension of slavery, & its political power."

Republicans were soon able to add "Bleeding Kansas" to "Bleeding Sumner" in their repertoire of winning issues. Even as Sumner was delivering his speech in Washington,

SOUTHERN CHIVALRY — ARGUMENT versus CLUB'S.

THE CANING OF SUMNER

This drawing by an antislavery Northerner shows pro-slavery Congressman Preston Brooks of South Carolina beating Senator Charles Sumner of Massachusetts with a heavy cane on the floor of the Senate on May 22, 1856. It portrays the inability of the South to respond to the power of Northern arguments, symbolized by the pen in Sumner's right hand and a speech in his left hand, except with the unthinking power of the club. Note other Southern senators in the background smiling on the scene or preventing Northern senators from coming to Sumner's aid. The caning of Sumner was the worst of several instances of North-South violence or threatened violence on the floor of Congress in the 1850s, presaging the violence on the battlefields of the 1860s.

an "army" of pro-slavery Missourians, complete with artillery, marched on the free-state capital of Lawrence, Kansas. On May 21, they shelled and sacked the town, burning several buildings. A rival force of free-state men arrived too late to intercept them. One of the free-state "captains" was John Brown, an abolitionist zealot who considered himself anointed by the Lord to avenge the sins of slaveholders. When he learned of the murder of several free-state settlers and the sack of Lawrence, he "went crazy—crazy," according to one of his followers. We must "fight fire with fire," Brown declared. "Something must be done to show these barbarians that we, too, have rights." Leading four of his sons and three other men to a pro-slavery settlement at Pottawatomie Creek on the night of May 24–25, 1856, Brown dragged five men from their cabins and split open their heads with broadswords.

Here was the Old Testament retribution of an eye for an eye. Brown's murderous act set off a veritable civil war in Kansas. One of Brown's sons was among the estimated 200 men killed in the bushwhackings and raids. Not until President Pierce sent a tough new territorial governor and 1,300 federal troops to Kansas in September 1856 did the violence subside—just in time to save the Democrats from possible defeat in the presidential election.

The Election of 1856

By 1856, the Republicans had become the largest party in the North. With the old Free-Soilers as their radical core, they had recruited about three-fourths of the former Whigs and one-fifth of the Democrats. They were also the first truly sectional party in American history because they had little prospect of carrying a single county in the slave states. At their first national convention, the Republicans wrote a platform that focused mainly on that "relic of barbarism," slavery. The platform also incorporated the old Whig program of federal aid to internal improvements, including a railroad to California. For its presidential nominee, the party steered away from its most prominent leaders, who were identified with the old parties, and turned instead to John C. Frémont. This "Pathfinder of the West" had a dashing image as an explorer and for his role in the acquisition of California. With little political experience, he had few political enemies and his antislavery credentials were satisfactory.

The Democrats chose as their candidate James Buchanan, a veteran of 30 years in various public offices. He had been minister to Britain during the Kansas-Nebraska controversy and so was not tainted with its unpopularity in the North, as were Pierce and Douglas, the other aspirants for nomination. The Democratic platform endorsed popular sovereignty and condemned the Republicans as a "sectional party" that incited "treason and armed resistance in the Territories."

This would be a three-party election because the American Party was still in the field. Having become mainly a waystation for former southern Whigs, the party nominated ex-Whig Millard Fillmore. The three-party campaign sifted out into a pair of two-party contests: Democrats versus Americans in the South; Democrats versus Republicans in the North. Fillmore, despite a good showing of 44 percent of the popular vote in the South, carried only Maryland. Considering Buchanan colorless but safe, the rest of the South gave him three-fourths of the electoral votes he needed for victory.

The real excitement in this election showed itself in the North. For many Republicans, the campaign was a moral cause, an evangelical crusade against the sin of slavery. Republican "Wide Awake" clubs marched in torchlight parades chanting "Free Soil, Free Speech, Free Men, Frémont!" A veteran politician in Indiana marveled: "Men, Women & Children all seemed to be out, with a kind of fervor I have never witnessed before in six Pres. Elections in which I have taken an active part." The turnout of eligible voters in the North was a remarkable 83 percent. One awestruck journalist, anticipating a Republican victory, wrote that "the process now going on in the United States is a *Revolution*."

Not quite. Although the Republicans swept New England and the upper parts of New York state and the Old Northwest—both settled by New Englanders, where evangelical and antislavery reform movements had taken hold—the contest in the lower North was close. Buchanan needed only to carry Pennsylvania and either Indiana or Illinois to win the presidency, and the campaign focused on those states. The immigrant and working-class voters of the eastern cities and the rural voters of the lower Midwest, descendants of upland southerners who had settled there, were antiblack and antiabolitionist in sentiment. They were ripe for Democratic propaganda that accused Republicans of favoring racial equality. "Black Republicans," declared an Ohio Democratic newspaper, intended to "turn loose . . . millions of negroes, to elbow you in the workshops, and compete with you in fields of honest labor." A Democrat in Pennsylvania told voters that "the one aim" of the Republicans was "to elevate the African race in this country to complete equality of political and economic condition with the white man." Indiana Democrats organized parades, with young girls in white dresses carrying banners inscribed "Fathers, save us from nigger husbands."

The Republicans in these areas denied that they favored racial equality. They insisted that the main reason for keeping slavery out of the territories was to enable white farmers and workers to make a living there without competition from black labor. But their denials were in vain. Support for the Republican Party by prominent black leaders, including Frederick Douglass, convinced hundreds of thousands of voters that the Black Republicans were racial egalitarians. For the next two decades, that sentiment

POPULAR AND ELECTORAL VOTES IN THE 1856 PRESIDENTIAL ELECTION

Candidate	Free States		Slave States		Total	
	Popular	Electoral	Popular	Electoral	Popular	Electoral
Buchanan (Democrat)	1,227,000	62	607,000	112	1,833,000	174
Frémont (Republican)	1,338,000	114	0	0	1,338,000	114
Fillmore (American)	396,000	0	476,000	8	872,000	8

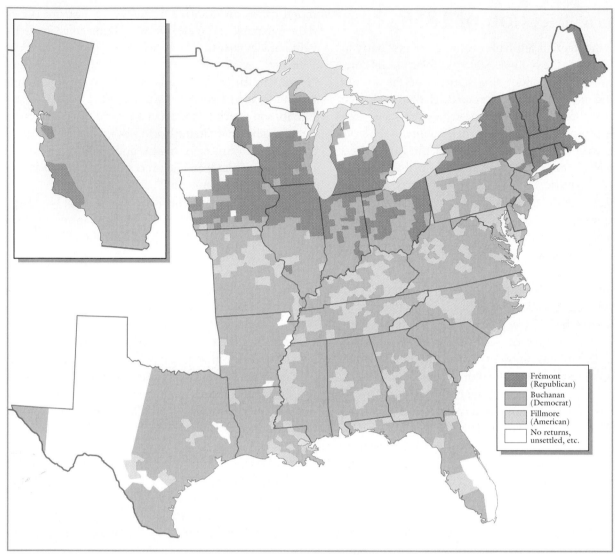

MAP 14.2   COUNTIES CARRIED BY CANDIDATES IN THE 1856 PRESIDENTIAL ELECTION

This map illustrates the sharp geographical division of the vote in 1856. The pattern of Republican counties coincided almost exactly with New England and the portions of other states settled by New England migrants during the two preceding generations.

 View an animated version of this map or related maps at http://history.wadsworth.com/murrin_LEP4e.

would be one of the most potent weapons in the Democratic arsenal.

In 1856, though, the charge that a Republican victory would destroy the Union was even more effective. Buchanan set the tone in his instructions to Democratic Party leaders: "The Black Republicans must be . . . boldly assailed as disunionists, and the charge must be re-iterated again and again." It was. And southerners helped the cause by threatening to secede if Frémont won. We "should not pause," said Senator James Mason of Virginia, "but proceed at once to 'immediate, absolute, and eternal separation.'" Fears of disruption caused many conservative ex-Whigs in the North to support Buchanan, who carried

Pennsylvania, New Jersey, Indiana, Illinois, and California and won the presidency.

But southerners did not intend to let Buchanan forget that he owed his election mainly to the South. "Mr. Buchanan and the Northern Democracy are dependent on the South," wrote a Virginian after the election. "If we can succeed in Kansas . . . and add a little more slave territory, we may yet live free men under the Stars and Stripes."

The Dred Scott Case

The South took the offensive at the outset of the Buchanan administration. Its instrument was the Supreme Court,

William and Ellen Craft Aid the Causes of Freedom and Union in England

William Craft (1824–1900) was born a slave in Georgia and learned the trade of cabinetmaker, which enabled him to save a little money when his master hired him out. Ellen (1826?–1897) was also born in slavery, the daughter of her master and his light-skinned concubine. At the age of 11, Ellen was separated from her mother and given by her master/father as a slave to her own white half-sister for a wedding present. William and Ellen met in Macon and were married in 1846. Unwilling to give birth to children who might be sold away from her, Ellen plotted with her husband to escape to the North. Light enough to pass for white, she sewed herself a pair of trousers and posed as a deaf-mute invalid young man traveling to Philadelphia for medical treatment attended by "his" slave William. After some close calls, they made it to Philadelphia at the end of 1848 and moved on to Boston in 1849, where William found work in his trade and Ellen as a seamstress.

After passage of the Fugitive Slave Law in 1850, however, two agents from Georgia appeared in Boston to recapture them. Local abolitionists spirited them away to Canada and then to England, where the Crafts lived for the next 19 years and had five children. Struggling at first in Surrey to make ends meet, Ellen nevertheless declared in 1852: "I had much rather starve in England, a free woman, than be a slave for the best man that ever breathed upon the American continent." Things soon improved for the Crafts, who became active in British antislavery circles and worked to counter pro-Confederate sentiment in England during the Civil War. William visited Dahomey, Africa, twice and founded a school there for native boys. In 1869, the Crafts returned to the United States and bought a farm in Georgia in 1871, where they established the Woodville Co-operative farm school for local freedpeople, which they conducted for several years until white hostility and financial problems forced them to close it. The Crafts were America's most famous fugitive slaves. Their story inspired other slaves and abolitionists on both sides of the Atlantic in their successful struggle for liberty.

WILLIAM AND ELLEN CRAFT

© The Granger Collection.

which had a majority of five justices from slave states led by Chief Justice Roger B. Taney of Maryland. Those justices saw the Dred Scott case as an opportunity to settle once and for all the question of slavery in the territories.

Dred Scott was a slave whose owner, an army surgeon, had kept him at military posts in Illinois and in the Wisconsin Territory for several years before taking him back to Missouri. After the owner's death, Scott sued for his freedom on the grounds of his prolonged stay in the Wisconsin Territory, where slavery had been outlawed by the Missouri Compromise. The case worked its way up from Missouri courts through a federal circuit court to the U.S. Supreme Court. There it began to attract attention as a test case of Congress's power to prohibit slavery in the territories.

The southern Supreme Court justices decided to declare that the Missouri Compromise ban on slavery in the territories was unconstitutional. To avoid the appearance of a purely sectional decision, they sought the concurrence of a northern Democratic justice, Robert Grier of Pennsylvania. President-elect Buchanan played an improper role by pressing his fellow Pennsylvanian to go along with the southern majority. Having obtained Justice Grier's concurrence, Chief Justice Taney issued the Court's ruling stating that Congress lacked the power to keep slavery out of a territory, because slaves were property and the Constitution protects the right of property. For good measure, Taney also wrote that the circuit court should not have accepted the Scott case in the first place because black men were not citizens of the United States and therefore had no standing in its courts. Five other justices wrote concurring opinions. The two non-Democratic northern justices (both former Whigs, one of them now a Republican) dissented vigorously. They stated that blacks were legal citizens in several northern states and were therefore citizens of the United States. To buttress their opinion that Congress could prohibit slavery in the territories, they cited Congress's Constitutional power to make "all needful rules and regulations" for the territories.

Modern scholars agree with the dissenters. In 1857, however, Taney had a majority, and his ruling became law. Modern scholars have also demonstrated that Taney was motivated by his passionate commitment "to southern life and values" and by his determination to stop "northern aggression" by cutting the ground out from under the hated Republicans. His ruling that their program to exclude slavery from the territories was unconstitutional was designed to do just that.

Republicans denounced Taney's "jesuitical decision" as based on "gross perversion" of the Constitution. The *New York Tribune* sneered that the Dred Scott decision was "entitled to just as much moral weight as would be the judgment of a majority of those congregated in any Washington bar-room." Several Republican state legislatures resolved that the ruling was "not binding in law and conscience." They looked forward to the election of a Republican president who could "reconstitute" the Court and secure a reversal of the decision. "The remedy," said the *Chicago Tribune*, "is the ballot box. . . . Let the next President be Republican, and 1860 will mark an era kindred with that of 1776."

The Lecompton Constitution

Instead of settling the slavery controversy, the Dred Scott decision intensified it. Meanwhile, pro-slavery advocates, having won legalization of slavery in the territories, moved to ensure that it would remain legal when Kansas became a state. That required deft maneuvering, because legitimate antislavery settlers outnumbered pro-slavery settlers by more than two to one. In 1857, the pro-slavery legislature (elected by the fraudulent votes of border ruffians two years earlier) called for a constitutional convention at Lecompton to prepare Kansas for statehood. Because the election for delegates was rigged, Free Soil voters refused to participate. One-fifth of the registered voters thereupon elected convention delegates, who met at Lecompton and wrote a state constitution that made slavery legal.

Then a nagging problem arose. Buchanan had promised that the Lecompton constitution would be presented to voters in a fair referendum. The problem was how to pass the pro-slavery constitution given the antislavery majority of voters. The convention came up with an ingenious solution. Instead of a referendum on the whole constitution, it would allow the voters to choose between a constitution "with slavery" and one "with no slavery." The catch was that the constitution "with no slavery" guaranteed slave owners' "inviolable" right of property in the 200 slaves already in Kansas and their progeny. It also did nothing to prevent future smuggling of slaves across the 200-mile border with Missouri. Once in Kansas, they, too, would become "inviolable" property.

Free-state voters branded the referendum a farce and boycotted it. One-quarter of the eligible voters went to the polls in December 1857 and approved the constitution "with slavery." Meanwhile, in a fair election policed by federal troops, the antislavery party won control of the new territorial legislature and promptly submitted both constitutions to a referendum that was boycotted by pro-slavery voters. This time, 70 percent of the eligible voters went to the polls and overwhelmingly rejected both constitutions.

Which referendum would the federal government recognize? That question proved even more divisive than the Kansas-Nebraska debate four years earlier. President Buchanan faced a dilemma. He had promised a fair referendum. But southerners, who dominated both the Democratic Party and the administration (the vice president and four of the seven cabinet members were from slave states), threatened secession if Kansas was not admitted to statehood under the Lecompton constitution "with slavery." "If Kansas is *driven out of the Union for being a Slave State*," thundered Senator James Hammond of South Carolina, "can any Slave State remain in it with honor?" Buchanan caved in. He explained to a shocked northern Democrat that if he did not accept the Lecompton constitution, southern states would "secede from the Union or take up arms against us." Buchanan sent the Lecompton constitution to Congress with a message recommending statehood. Kansas, said the president, "is at this moment as much a slave state as Georgia or South Carolina."

What would Stephen Douglas do? If he endorsed the Lecompton constitution, he would undoubtedly be defeated in his bid for reelection to the Senate in 1858. And he regarded the Lecompton constitution as a travesty of popular sovereignty. He broke with the administration on the issue. He could not vote to "force this constitution down the throats of the people of Kansas," he told the

Senate, "in opposition to their wishes and in violation of our pledges."

The fight in Congress was long and bitter. The South and the administration had the votes they needed in the Senate and won handily there, but the Democratic majority in the House was so small that the defection of even a few northern Democrats would defeat the Lecompton constitution. The House debate at one point got out of hand and a wild fistfight erupted between Republicans and southern Democrats. "There were some fifty middle-aged and elderly gentlemen pitching into each other like so many Tipperary savages," wrote a bemused reporter, "most of them incapable, from want of wind and muscle, from doing each other any serious harm."

When the vote was finally taken, two dozen northern Democrats defected, providing enough votes to defeat Lecompton. Both sides then accepted a compromise proposal to resubmit the constitution to Kansas voters, who decisively rejected it. This meant that while Kansas would not come in as a slave state, neither would it come in as a free state for some time yet. Nevertheless, the Lecompton debate had split the Democratic Party, leaving a legacy of undying enmity between southerners and Douglas. The election of a Republican president in 1860 was now all but assured.

The Economy in the 1850s

Beginning in the mid-1840s, the American economy enjoyed a dozen years of unprecedented growth and prosperity, particularly for the railroads. The number of miles in operation quintupled during those years. Railroad construction provided employment for many immigrants and spurred growth in industries that produced rails, rolling stock, and other railroad equipment. Most railroad construction took place in the Old Northwest, linking the region more closely to the Northeast and continuing the reorientation of transportation networks from a north-south river pattern to an east-west canal and rail pattern. By the mid-1850s, the east-west rail and water routes carried more than twice as much freight tonnage as the north-south river routes. This closer binding of the western and eastern states reinforced the effect of slavery in creating a self-conscious "North" and "South."

Although the Old Northwest remained predominantly agricultural, rapid expansion of railroads there laid the basis for its industrialization. During the 1850s, industrial output in the free states west of Pennsylvania grew at twice the rate of Northeast industrial output and three times as great as the rate in the South. The Northwest urban growth rate tripled that of the Northeast and quadrupled that of the South. Chicago became the terminus for 15 rail lines in the 1850s, during which its population grew by 375 percent. In 1847, two companies that contributed to the rapid growth of agriculture during this era built their plants in Illinois: the McCormick reaper works at Chicago and the John Deere steel-plow works at Moline.

According to almost every statistical index available from that period, economic expansion considerably outstripped even the prodigious pace of population increase. While the number of Americans grew by 44 percent during these 12 years (1844–56), the value of both exports and imports increased by 200 percent; mined coal tonnage by 270 percent; banking capital, industrial capital, and

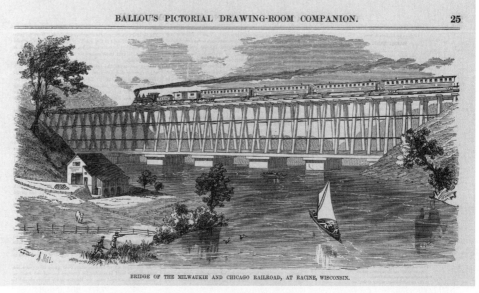

BRIDGE OF THE MILWAUKIE AND CHICAGO RAILROAD AT RACINE, WISCONSIN

By the 1850s, Chicago had become the hub for a dozen or more railroads that tied the fast-growing Midwest to the older South and East. This illustration shows the railroad bridge over the Root River between Chicago and Milwaukee.

BALLOU'S PICTORIAL DRAWING-ROOM COMPANION. 25

BRIDGE OF THE MILWAUKIE AND CHICAGO RAILROAD, AT RACINE, WISCONSIN.

© Corbis.

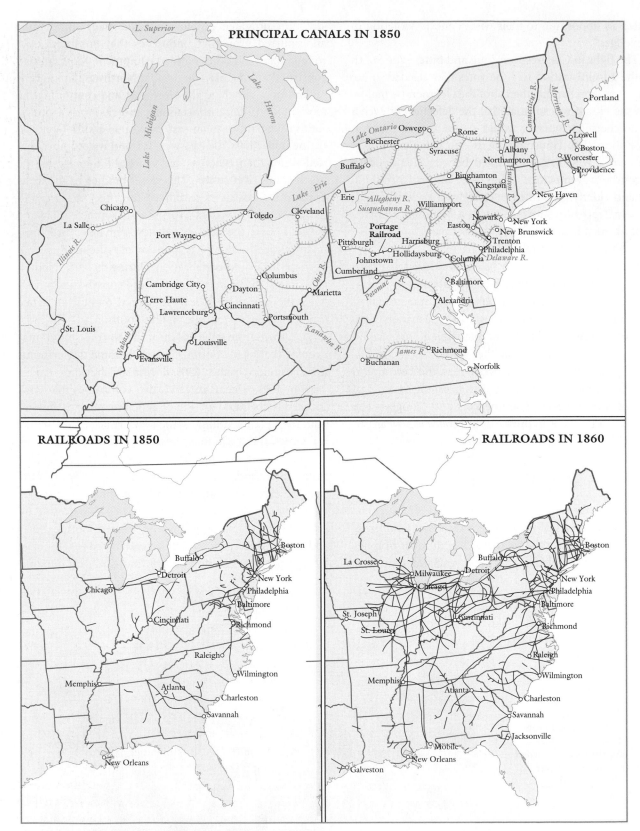

MAP 14.3 MAIN TRANSPORTATION ROUTES IN THE 1850S

These maps illustrate how the transportation networks by natural waterways (rivers and the Atlantic coastal waters) oriented commerce north and south while the canals and railroads linked east and west. By 1860, railroads tied the Midwestern states economically to the Northeast.

industrial output by approximately 100 percent; farmland value by 100 percent; and cotton, wheat, and corn harvests by about 70 percent. These advances meant a significant increase of per capita production and income, although the distance between rich and poor was widening—a phenomenon that has characterized all capitalist economies during stages of rapid industrial growth.

By the later 1850s, the United States had forged ahead of most other countries to become the second-leading industrial producer in the world, behind only Britain. But the country was still in the early stages of industrial development. Agricultural product processing and raw materials still played the dominant role. By 1860, the four leading industries, measured by value added in manufacturing, were cotton textiles, lumber products, boots and shoes, and flour milling. Iron and machinery, industries typical of a more mature manufacturing economy, ranked sixth and seventh.

"The American System of Manufactures"

The United States had pioneered in one crucial feature of modern industry: the mass production of interchangeable parts. This revolutionary concept had begun with the manufacture of firearms earlier in the 19th century and had spread to many products by the 1850s. High wages and a shortage of the skilled craftsmen who had traditionally fashioned guns, furniture, locks, watches, and other products had compelled American entrepreneurs to seek alternative methods. "Yankee ingenuity," already world-famous, came up with an answer: special-purpose machine tools that would cut and shape an endless number of parts that could be fitted together with other similarly produced parts to make whole guns, locks, clocks, and sewing machines in mass quantities.

These products were less elegant and less durable than products made by skilled craftsmen, but they were also less expensive and thus more widely available to the "middling classes" of a society that pro-

fessed to be more democratic than Europe in its consumer economy as well as in its politics.

Such American-made products were the hit of the first World's Fair, the Crystal Palace Exhibition at London in 1851. British manufacturers were so impressed by Yankee techniques, which they dubbed "the American system of manufactures," that they sent two commissions to the United States to study them. "The labouring classes are comparatively few," reported one commission in 1854, "and to this very want . . . may be attributed the extraordinary ingenuity displayed in many of these labour-saving machines." The British firearms industry imported American experts to help set up the Enfield Armoury in London to manufacture the new British army rifle.

The British also invited Samuel Colt of Connecticut, inventor of the famous six-shooting revolver, to set up a factory in England stocked with machinery from Connecticut. In testimony before a parliamentary committee in 1854, Colt summed up the American system of manufactures in a single sentence: "There is nothing that cannot be produced by machinery." Although the British had a half-century head start over Americans in the Industrial Revolution, Colt's testimony expressed a philosophy that would enable the United States to surpass Britain as the leading industrial nation by 1880.

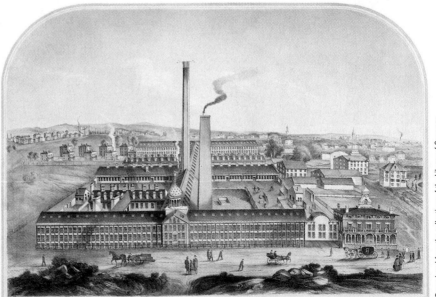

COLT ARMS PLANT IN HARTFORD, CONNECTICUT
Samuel Colt's factory for manufacturing firearms was a showpiece for the American system of manufactures in the 1850s. All of the processes for production of the famous Colt revolver were housed under one roof, with power-driven machinery cutting the metal and shaping the interchangeable parts. Hand filing was necessary, however, for a perfect fit of the parts because the tolerances of machine tools were not yet as finely calibrated as they later became.

The British industrial commissions also cited the American educational system as an important reason for the country's technological proficiency. "Educated up to a far higher standard than those of a much superior grade in the Old World," reported the 1854 commission, "every [American] workman seems to be continually devising some new thing to assist him in his work, and there is a strong desire . . . to be 'posted up' in every new improvement." By contrast, the British workman, trained by long apprenticeship "in the trade," rather than in school, lacked "the ductility of mind and the readiness of apprehension for a new thing" and was therefore "unwilling to change the methods he has been used to."

Whether this British commission was right in its belief that American schooling encouraged the "adaptative versatility" of Yankee workers, it was certainly true that public education and literacy were more widespread in the United States than in Europe. Almost 95 percent of adults in the free states were literate in 1860, compared with 65 percent in England and 55 percent in France. The standardization and expansion of public school systems that had begun earlier in New England had spread to the mid-Atlantic states and into the Old Northwest by the 1850s. Nearly all children received a few years of schooling, and most completed at least six or seven years.

This improvement in education coincided with the feminization of the teaching profession, which opened up new career opportunities for young women. The notion that the "woman's sphere" was in the home, rearing and nurturing children, ironically projected that sphere outside the home into the schoolroom when schools took over part of the responsibility of socializing and educating children. By the 1850s, nearly three-quarters of the public school teachers in New England were women (who worked for lower salaries than male teachers), a trend that was spreading to the mid-Atlantic states and the Old Northwest as well.

The Southern Economy

The feminization of teaching had not yet reached the South. Nor had the idea of universal public education taken deep root in the slave states. In contrast to the North, where 94 percent of the entire population could read and write, 80 percent of the free population and only 10 percent of the slaves in the South were literate. This was one of several differences between North and South that antislavery people pointed to as evidence of the backward, repressive, and pernicious nature of a slave society.

© Bettmann/Corbis.

THE COUNTRY SCHOOL

This famous painting by Winslow Homer portrays the typical one-room rural schoolhouse in which millions of American children learned the "three R's" (reading, writing, and arithmetic) in the 19th century. By the 1850s, teaching elementary school was a profession increasingly dominated by women, an important change from earlier generations.

Still, the South shared in the economy's rapid growth following recovery from the depression of 1837–43. Cotton prices and production both doubled between 1845 and 1855. Similar increases in price and output emerged in tobacco and sugar. The price of slaves, a significant index of prosperity in the southern economy, also doubled during this decade. Southern crops provided three-fifths of all U.S. exports, with cotton alone supplying more than half.

But a growing number of southerners deplored the fact that the "colonial" economy of the South was so dependent on the export of agricultural products and the import of manufactured goods. The ships that carried southern cotton were owned by northern or British firms; financial and commercial services were provided mostly by Yankees or Englishmen. In the years of rising sectional tensions around 1850, many southerners began calling for economic independence from the North. How could they obtain their rights, they asked, if they were "financially more enslaved than our negroes?" Yankees "abuse and denounce slavery and slaveholders," declared a southern newspaper in 1851, yet "we purchase all our luxuries and necessaries from the North. . . . Our slaves are clothed with Northern manufactured goods and work with Northern hoes, ploughs, and other implements. . . . The slaveholder dresses in Northern goods . . . and on Northern-made paper, with a Northern pen, with Northern ink, he resolves and re-resolves in regard to his rights."

Southerners must "throw off this humiliating dependence," declared James D. B. De Bow, the young champion of economic diversification in the South. In 1846, De Bow had founded in New Orleans a periodical eventually known as *De Bow's Review*. Proclaiming on its cover that "Commerce is King," the *Review* set out to make this slogan a southern reality. De Bow took the lead in organizing annual commercial conventions that met in various southern cities during the 1850s. In its early years, this movement encouraged southerners to invest in shipping lines, railroads, textile mills ("bring the spindles to the cotton"), and other enterprises. "Give us factories, machine shops, work shops," declared southern proponents of King Commerce, "and we shall be able ere long to assert our rights."

Economic diversification in the South did make headway during the 1850s. The slave states quadrupled their railroad mileage, increased the amount of capital invested in manufacturing by 77 percent, and boosted their output of cotton textiles by 44 percent. But like Alice in Wonderland, the faster the South ran, the farther behind it seemed to fall—for northern industry was growing even faster. The slave states' share of the nation's manufacturing capacity actually dropped from 18 to 16 percent during the decade. In 1860, the North had five times more industrial

output per capita than the South, and it had three times the railroad capital and mileage per capita and per thousand square miles. Southerners had a larger percentage of their capital invested in land and slaves in 1860 than they had had 10 years earlier. Some 80 percent of the South's labor force worked in agriculture—the same as 60 years earlier. By contrast, while farming remained, at 40 percent, the largest single occupation in the North, the northern economy developed a strong manufacturing and commercial sector whose combined labor force almost equaled that of agriculture by 1860.

The Sovereignty of King Cotton

A good many southerners preferred to keep it that way. "That the North does our trading and manufacturing mostly is true," wrote an Alabama planter in 1858. "We are willing that they should. Ours is an agricultural people, and God grant that we may continue so. It is the freest, happiest, most independent, and with us, the most powerful condition on earth." In the later 1850s, the drive for economic diversification in the South lost steam. King Cotton reasserted its primacy over King Commerce as cotton output *and* prices continued to rise, suffusing the South in a glow of prosperity. "Our Cotton is the most wonderful talisman on earth," declared a planter. "By its power we are transmuting whatever we choose into whatever we want." In a speech that became famous, James Hammond of South Carolina told his fellow senators in 1858 that "the slaveholding South is now the controlling power of the world. . . . No power on earth dares to make war on cotton. Cotton *is* king."

Even the commercial conventions in the South seemed to have embraced this gospel. In 1854, they merged with a parallel series of planters' conventions, and thereafter the delegates heard as much about cotton as they did about commerce. By the later 1850s, one of the main goals of these conventions was to reopen the African slave trade, prohibited by law since 1808. Many southerners rejected that goal, however, partly on moral grounds and partly on economic grounds. Older slave states such as Virginia, which profited from the sale of slaves to the booming cotton frontier of the Deep South, objected to any goal that would lower the price of their largest export. The conventions also lobbied for the annexation of Cuba, which would bring a productive agricultural economy and 400,000 more slaves into the United States.

Nowhere in the South, said defenders of slavery, did one see such "scenes of beggary, squalid poverty, and wretchedness" as one could find in any northern city. Black slaves, they insisted, enjoyed a higher standard of living than white "wage slaves" in northern factories.

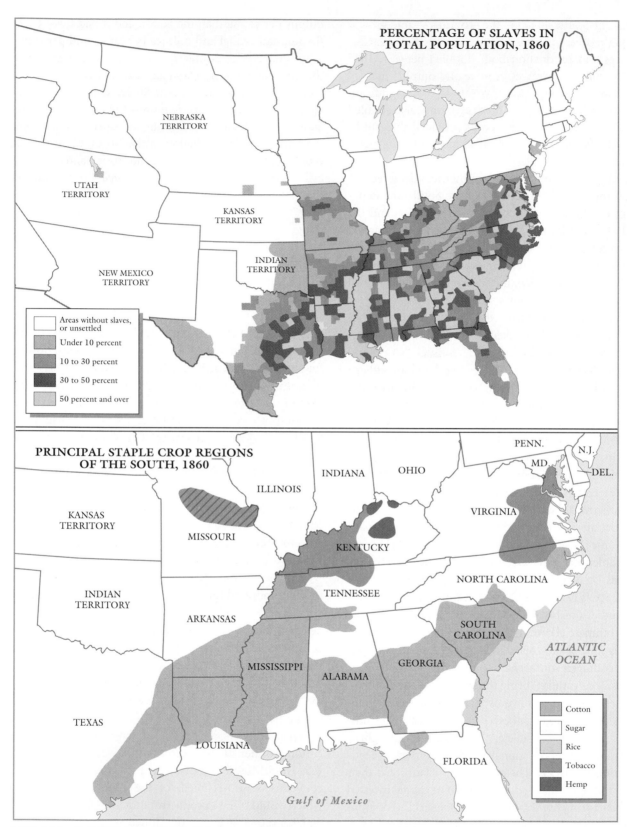

PERCENTAGE OF SLAVES IN TOTAL POPULATION, 1860

NEBRASKA TERRITORY

UTAH TERRITORY

KANSAS TERRITORY

NEW MEXICO TERRITORY

INDIAN TERRITORY

Areas without slaves, or unsettled

Under 10 percent

10 to 30 percent

30 to 50 percent

50 percent and over

PRINCIPAL STAPLE CROP REGIONS OF THE SOUTH, 1860

PENN.

N.J.

MD.

DEL.

INDIANA

OHIO

ILLINOIS

VIRGINIA

KANSAS TERRITORY

MISSOURI

KENTUCKY

NORTH CAROLINA

INDIAN TERRITORY

TENNESSEE

ARKANSAS

SOUTH CAROLINA

ATLANTIC OCEAN

MISSISSIPPI

ALABAMA

GEORGIA

TEXAS

LOUISIANA

FLORIDA

Gulf of Mexico

Cotton

Sugar

Rice

Tobacco

Hemp

MAP 14.4 SLAVERY AND STAPLE CROPS IN THE SOUTH, 1860

Note the close correlation between the concentration of the slave population and the leading cash crops of the South. Nothing better illustrates the economic importance of slavery.

 View an animated version of this map or related maps at http://history.wadsworth.com/murrin_LEP4e.

Black slaves never suffered from unemployment or wage cuts, they received free medical care, and they were taken care of in old age.

This argument reached its fullest development in the writings of George Fitzhugh, a Virginia farmer-lawyer whose newspaper articles were gathered into two books published in 1854 and 1857, *Sociology for the South* and *Cannibals All*. Free-labor capitalism, said Fitzhugh, was a competition in which the strong exploited and starved the weak. Slavery, by contrast, was a paternal institution that guaranteed protection of the workers. "Capital exercises a more perfect compulsion over free laborers than human masters over slaves," wrote Fitzhugh, "for free laborers must at all times work or starve, and slaves are supported

From the Collections of the Library of Congress.

The Granger Collection.

SOUTHERN PORTRAITS OF SLAVERY AND FREE LABOR

Romanticized images of happy, well-fed slaves enjoying their work picking cotton were common in pro-slavery literature. Such images were often contrasted with the supposed harshness of life in Northern tenement districts, as in this illustration of a communal pump that has run dry on a hot summer day in an immigrant neighborhood on New York's lower east side.

whether they work or not.... What a glorious thing is slavery, when want, misfortune, old age, debility, and sickness overtake [the slave]."

Labor Conditions in the North

How true was this portrait of poverty and starvation among northern workers? Some northern labor leaders did complain that the "slavery" of the wage system gave "bosses" control over the hours, conditions, and compensation of labor. Use of this wage-slavery theme in labor rhetoric declined during the prosperous years of the 1850s, and no evidence indicates that a northern working man ever offered to change places with a southern slave. Average per capita income was about 40 percent higher in the North than in the South. Although that average masked large disparities between rich and poor—even between the middle class and the poor—those disparities were no greater, and probably less, in the North than in the South.

To be sure, substantial numbers of recent immigrants, day laborers, and young single women in large northern cities lived on the edge of poverty—or slipped over the edge. Many women seamstresses, shoe binders, milliners, and the like, who worked 60 or 70 hours per week in the outwork system earned less than a living wage. Some of them resorted to prostitution in order to survive. The widespread adoption of the newly invented sewing machine in the 1850s did nothing to make life easier for seamstresses; it only lowered their per-unit piecework wages and forced them to turn out more shirts and trousers than before. Many urban working-class families could not survive on the wages of an unskilled or semiskilled father. The mother had to take in laundry, boarders, or outwork, and one or more children had to work. Much employment was seasonal or intermittent, leaving

---

M U S I C A L   L I N K   T O   T H E   P A S T

The Waltz—An Immoral Dance?

Composer: G. Jullien

Title: "Prima Donna Waltz" (c. late 1850s)

As tame and old-fashioned as the waltz may sound to modern ears, for many 19th-century observers, its arrival represented an alarming and morally dangerous development in American life. It did away with the niceties and social introductions of country dances, minuets, gavottes, and other dances championed previously in the American past. Those dances kept young people at a socially acceptable distance, constantly switching partners, never allowing a couple to concentrate on each other for an extended time. But couples who engaged in waltzing gripped each other in close embrace, intently gazed in each other's eyes at shockingly close range, and refused to share their partners or acknowledge other dancers on the floor. Worse yet, as reported by music historian Thornton Hagert, "The hypnotic effect of the unrelenting and mechanical turning, turning of the early waltz was thought to summon up uncontrollable passions that would surely lead to ridicule or even dishonor, disease and pregnancy." Despite numerous warnings of pernicious influence, waltz tempos steadily increased as the 19th century ambled forward, which presumably made dancers even dizzier and further clouded their personal judgment and morality. In addition, waltz steps were simplified as time went on, allowing more young people to participate in the waltz fad with little training.

The torrent of controversy surrounding the waltz presaged similar outcries against future American dance crazes such as the ragtime-influenced turkey trot of the 1910s, the jazz-inflected Charleston of the 1920s, the acrobatic lindy hop of the big band era, and the anarchic mosh pit chaos of the 1970s punk rock scene. American youth have often seized music as an outlet and excuse to exhibit and play out emotions and feelings normally excluded from public view, to the chagrin of some of their elders. Musical expression by the American youth of the mid-20th century often featured distorted and screeching electric guitars, but such contraptions and the music they accompanied were probably no more threatening to American parents of the 1950s than the graceful bugle-led strains of the "Prima Donna Waltz" were for American parents of the 1850s.

---

1. Why do you think popular dances became simpler and less formal as the 19th century unfolded?
2. What do you think such cultural changes said about the character of the maturing United States?

Listen to an audio recording of this music on the Musical Links to the Past CD.

workers without wages for long periods, especially during winter. The poverty, overcrowding, and disease in the tenement districts of a few large cities—especially New York City—seemed to lend substance to pro-slavery claims that slaves were better off.

But they were not—even apart from the psychological contrast between being free and being a slave. New York City's poverty, although highly concentrated and visible, was exceptional. In the North, only one-fourth of the people lived in cities or towns of more than 2,500 people. Wages and opportunities for workers were greater in the North than anywhere else in the world, including the South. That was why 4 million immigrants came to the United States from 1845 to 1860 and why seven-eighths of them settled in free states. It was also why twice as many white residents of slave states migrated to free states than vice versa. And it was one reason why northern farmers and workers wanted to keep slaves *and* free blacks out of the territories, where their cheaper labor would lower wages.

THE PANIC ON WALL STREET

This cartoon satirizes the consternation among New York investors and financiers when banks and businesses crashed in autumn 1857. Notice the smirk on the faces of two men in the foreground, who undoubtedly stood to benefit from foreclosures on defaulted property. The panic was no laughing matter, though, because it led to a short but sharp recession in 1857 and 1858.

The Panic of 1857

In fall 1857, the relative prosperity of the North was interrupted by a financial panic that caused a short-lived but intense depression. When the Crimean War in Europe (1854–56) cut off Russian grain from the European market, U.S. exports had mushroomed to meet the deficiency.

After the Crimean War ended, U.S. grain exports slumped. The sharp rise in interest rates in Britain and France, caused by the war, spread to U.S. financial markets in 1857 and dried up sources of credit. Meanwhile, the economic boom of the preceding years had caused the American economy to overheat: Land prices had soared, railroads had built beyond the capacity of earnings to service their debts, and banks had made too many risky loans.

This speculative house of cards came crashing down in September 1857. The failure of one banking house sent a wave of panic through the financial community. Banks suspended specie payments, businesses failed, railroads went bankrupt, construction halted, and factories shut down. Hundreds of thousands of workers were laid off, and others went on part-time schedules or took wage cuts, just as the cold winter months were arriving. The specter of class conflict such as had occurred during the European revolutions of 1848 haunted the public. Unemployed workers in several northern cities marched in parades carrying banners demanding work or bread. A mob broke into the shops of flour merchants in New York City. On November 10, a crowd gathered on Wall Street and threatened to break into the U.S. customs house and subtreasury vaults, where $20 million was stored. Soldiers and marines had to be called out to disperse the mob.

But the country got through the winter with little violence. No one was killed in the demonstrations—in contrast to the dozens who had been killed in ethnic riots a few years earlier and the hundreds killed in the guerrilla war in Kansas. Class conflict turned out to be the least threatening of the various discords that endangered society in the 1850s. Charity and public works helped tide the poor over the winter, and the panic inspired a vigorous religious revival. Spontaneous prayer meetings arose in many northern cities, bringing together bankers and seamstresses, brokers and streetsweepers. They asked God's forgiveness for the greed and materialism that, in a self-flagellating mood, they believed had caused the panic.

Perhaps God heeded their prayers. In any event, the depression was short-lived. By early 1858, banks had resumed specie payments; the stock market rebounded in the spring; factories reopened; railroad construction resumed; and by spring 1859, recovery was complete. The modest labor union activities of the 1850s revived after the depression, as workers in some industries went on strike to bring wages back to prepanic levels. In February 1860, the shoemakers of Lynn, Massachusetts, began the largest strike in U.S. history up to that time, eventually involving 20,000 workers in the New England shoe industry. Despite the organization of several national unions of skilled workers during the 1850s, less than 1 percent of the labor force was unionized in 1860.

Sectionalism and the Panic

The Panic of 1857 probably intensified sectional hostility more than it did class conflict. The South largely escaped the depression. Its export-driven economy seemed insulated from domestic downturns. After a brief dip, cotton and tobacco prices returned to high levels and production continued to increase: The cotton crop set new records in 1858 and 1859. Southern boasts about the superiority of the region's economic and labor systems took on added bravado. "Who can doubt, that has looked at recent events, that cotton is supreme?" asked Senator James Hammond in March 1858. "When thousands of the strongest commercial houses in the world were coming down," he told Yankees, "what brought you up? . . . We have poured in upon you one million six hundred thousand bales of cotton. . . . We have sold it for $65,000,000, and saved you."

Northerners were not grateful for their rescue. In fact, many of them actually blamed the South for causing the depression or for blocking measures to ease its effects in the North. Southern congressmen had provided most of the votes for a new tariff in 1857 that brought duties to their lowest levels in 40 years. Some northern Republicans blamed the tariff for causing the panic and wanted to revise certain duties upward to help hard-hit industries, especially Pennsylvania iron, which were being undercut by cheaper imports. They directed their arguments to workers as much as to manufacturers. "We demand that American laborers shall be protected against the pauper labor of Europe," they declared. Tariff revision would "give employment to thousands of mechanics, artisans, laborers, who have languished for months in unwilling idleness." In each session of Congress from 1858 through 1860, however, a combination of southerners and about half of the northern Democrats blocked Republican

efforts to raise tariffs. In the words of one bitter Pennsylvania Republican, this was proof that Congress remained "shamelessly prostituted, in a base subserviency to the Slave Power." Republicans made important gains in the Pennsylvania congressional elections of 1858, setting the stage for a strong bid in a state that they had to carry if they were to win the presidency in 1860.

Three other measures acquired additional significance after the Panic of 1857. Republicans supported each of them as a means to promote economic health and to aid farmers and workers. But southerners perceived all of them as aimed at helping *northern* farmers and workers and used their power to defeat them. One was a homestead act to grant 160 acres of public land to each farmer who settled and worked the land. Believing that this bill "would prove a most efficient ally for Abolition by encouraging and stimulating the settlement of free farms with Yankees," southern senators defeated it after the House had passed it in 1859. The following year both houses passed the homestead act, but Buchanan vetoed it and southern senators blocked an effort to pass it over his veto. A similar fate befell bills for land grants to a transcontinental railroad and for building agricultural and mechanical colleges to educate farmers and workers. In the Old Northwest, where these measures were popular, Republican prospects for 1860 were enhanced by southern and Democratic opposition to them.

The Free-Labor Ideology

By the later 1850s, the Republican antislavery argument had become a finely honed philosophy that historians have labeled a "free-labor ideology." It held that all work in a free society was honorable, but that slavery degraded the calling of manual labor by equating it with bondage. Slaves worked inefficiently, by compulsion; free men were stimulated to work hard and efficiently by the desire to get ahead. Social mobility was central to the free-labor ideology. Free workers who practiced the virtues of industry, thrift, self-discipline, and sobriety could move up the ladder of success. "I am not ashamed to confess," Abraham Lincoln told a working-class audience in 1860, "that twenty-five years ago I was a hired laborer, mauling rails, at work on a flat-boat—just what might happen to any poor man's son!" But in the free states, said Lincoln, a man knows that

> he can better his condition. . . . There is no such thing as a freeman being fatally fixed for life, in the condition of a hired laborer. . . . The man who labored for another last year, this year labors for himself, and next year will hire others to labor for him. . . . The free labor system opens the way for all—gives hope to all, and energy, and progress, and improvement of condition to all.

Lincoln drew too rosy a picture of northern reality, for large numbers of wage laborers in the North had little hope of advancing beyond that status. Still, he expressed a belief that was widely shared in the antebellum North. "There is not a working boy of average ability in the New England states, at least," observed a visiting British industrialist in 1854, "who has not an idea of some mechanical invention or improvement in manufactures, by which, in good time, he hopes to better his condition, or rise to fortune and social distinction." Americans could point to numerous examples of men who had achieved dramatic upward mobility. Belief in this "American dream" was most strongly held by Protestant farmers, skilled workers, and white-collar workers who had some real hope of getting ahead. These men tended to support the Republican Party and its goal of excluding slavery from the territories.

Slavery was the antithesis of upward mobility. Bondsmen were "fatally fixed in that condition for life," as Lincoln noted. Slaves could not hope to move up the ladder of success, nor could free men who lived in a society where they had to compete with slave labor. "Slavery withers and blights all it touches," declared an Iowa Republican. "It is a curse upon the poor, free, laboring white men." In the United States, social mobility often depended on geographic mobility. The main reason so many families moved into new territories was to make a new start, move ahead. But, declared a Republican editor, if slavery goes into the territories, "the free labor of all the states will not. If the free labor of the states goes there, the slave labor of the southern states will not, and in a few years the country will teem with an active and energetic population."

Southerners contended that free labor was prone to unrest and strikes. Of course it was, said Lincoln in a speech to a New England audience during the shoemakers' strike of 1860. "I am glad to see that a system prevails in New England under which laborers *can* strike when they want to (Cheers). . . . I like the system which lets a man quit when he wants to, and wish it might prevail everywhere (Tremendous applause)." Strikes were one of the ways in which free workers could try to improve their prospects. "I want every man," said Lincoln, "to have the chance—and I believe a black man is entitled to it—in which he can better his condition." That was why Republicans were determined to contain the expansion of slavery because if the South got its way in the territories, "free labor that can strike will give way to slave labor that cannot!"

The Impending Crisis

From the South came a maverick voice that echoed the Republicans. Hinton Rowan Helper considered himself a spokesman for the nonslaveholding whites of the South.

Living in upcountry North Carolina, a region of small farms and few slaves, he had brooded for years over slavery's retarding influence on southern development. In 1857, he poured out his bitterness in a book entitled *The Impending Crisis of the South.* Using selective statistics from the 1850 census, he pictured a South mired in economic backwardness, widespread illiteracy, poverty for the masses, and great wealth for the elite. He contrasted this dismal situation with the bustling, prosperous northern economy and its near-universal literacy, neat farms, and progressive institutions. What was the cause of this startling contrast? "Slavery lies at the root of all the shame, poverty, ignorance, tyranny, and imbecility of the South," he wrote. Slavery monopolized the best land, degraded all labor to the level of bond labor, denied schools to the poor, and impoverished all but "the lords of the lash [who] are not only absolute masters of the blacks [but] of all nonslaveholding whites, whose freedom is merely nominal, and whose unparalleled illiteracy and degradation is purposely and fiendishly perpetrated." The remedy? Nonslaveholding whites must organize and use their votes to overthrow "this entire system of oligarchical despotism."

No southern publisher dared touch this book. Helper lugged his bulky manuscript to New York City, where a printer brought it out in summer 1857. *The Impending Crisis* was virtually banned in the South, and few southern whites read it, but it made a huge impact in the North. Republicans welcomed it as confirmation of all they had been saying about the evils of slavery and the virtues of free labor. The Republican Party subsidized an abridged edition and distributed thousands of copies as campaign documents. During the late 1850s, a war of books (Helper's *Impending Crisis* versus Fitzhugh's *Cannibals All*) exacerbated sectional tensions. Fitzhugh's book circulated freely in the North, whereas the sale or possession of Helper's book was a criminal offense in many parts of the South. The New England Antislavery Society even invited Fitzhugh to New Haven to debate the abolitionist Wendell Phillips. Fitzhugh expressed surprise at his courteous reception in the North, aware that Phillips and other abolitionists could not set foot in the South without peril to their life. Northern spokesmen did not hesitate to point out the moral: A free society could tolerate free speech and a free press, but a slave society could not.

Southern Nonslaveholders

How accurate was Helper's portrayal of southern poor whites degraded by slavery and ready to revolt against it? The touchy response of many southern leaders suggested that the planters felt uneasy about that question. After all, slaveholding families constituted less than one-third of the

North Wind Picture Archives.

A SOUTHERN YEOMAN FARMER'S HOME
This modest log cabin on the edge of a small clearing, with the farmer's wife drawing water from a well in the foreground, was typical of nonslaveholders' farms in the backcountry of the South. Often stigmatized as poor whites, many of these families were in fact comfortable by the standards of the day. They did not feel the sense of oppression by the planter class that Hinton Rowan Helper believed they should feel.

white population in slave states, and the proportion was declining as the price of slaves continued to rise. Open hostility to the planters' domination of society and politics was evident in the mountainous and upcountry regions of the South. These would become areas of Unionist sentiment during the Civil War and of Republican strength after it.

But Helper surely exaggerated the disaffection of most nonslaveholders in the South. Three bonds held them to the system: kinship, economic interest, and race. In the Piedmont and the low-country regions of the South, nearly half of the whites were in slaveholding families. Many of the rest were cousins or nephews or in-laws of slaveholders in the South's extensive and tightly knit kinship network. Moreover, many young, ambitious nonslaveholders hoped to buy slaves eventually. Some of them *rented* slaves. And because slaves could be made to do the menial, unskilled labor in the South—the "mudsill" tasks, in Senator Hammond's language—white workers monopolized the more skilled, higher-paying jobs.

Most important, even if they did not own slaves, white people owned the most important asset of all—white skin. White supremacy was an article of faith in the South (and in most of the North, for that matter). Race

was a more important social distinction than class. The southern legal system, politics, and social ideology were based on the concept of "*herrenvolk* democracy" (the equality of all who belonged to the "master race"). Subordination was the Negro's fate, and slavery was the best means of subordination. Emancipation would loose a flood of free blacks on society and would undermine the foundations of white supremacy. Thus many of the poor whites in the South and immigrant workers or poorer farmers in the North supported slavery.

The *herrenvolk* theme permeated pro-slavery rhetoric. "With us," said John C. Calhoun in 1848, "the two great divisions of society are not the rich and the poor, but white and black; and all the former, the poor as well as the rich, belong to the upper class, and are respected and treated as equals." True freedom as Americans understood it required equality of rights and status (although not of wealth or income). Slavery ensured such freedom for all whites by putting a floor under them, a mudsill of black slaves that kept whites from falling into the mud of inequality. "Break down slavery," said a Virginia congressman, "and you would with the same blow destroy the great Democratic principle of equality among men."

◉ The Lincoln-Douglas Debates

Abraham Lincoln believed the opposite. For him, slavery and freedom were incompatible; the one must die that the other might live. This became the central theme of a memorable series of debates between Lincoln and Douglas in 1858, which turned out to be a dress rehearsal for the presidential election of 1860.

The debates were arranged after Lincoln was nominated to oppose Douglas's reelection to the Senate. State legislatures elected U.S. senators at that time, so the campaign was technically for the election of the Illinois legislature. The real issue, however, was the senatorship, and Douglas's prominence gave the contest national significance. Lincoln launched his bid with one of his most notable speeches. "'A house divided against itself cannot stand,'" he said, quoting the words of Jesus recorded in the Gospel of Mark (3:25). "I believe this government cannot endure, permanently half slave and half free. . . . It will become all one thing, or all the other." Under the Dred Scott decision, which Douglas had endorsed, slavery was legal in all of the territories. And what, asked Lincoln, would prevent the Supreme Court, using the same reasoning that had led it to interpret the Constitution as protecting property in slaves, from legalizing slavery in free states? (A case based on this question was then before the New York

HISTORY THROUGH FILM

Abe Lincoln in Illinois (1940)

Directed by John Cromwell. Starring Raymond Massey (Abraham Lincoln), Gene Lockhard (Stephen Douglas), Ruth Gordon (Mary Todd Lincoln).

Raymond Massey's portrayal of Abraham Lincoln in Robert Sherwood's Broadway play, which opened in 1938 and was made into a movie in 1940, launched this Canadian-born actor as the image and voice of Lincoln on stage, screen, and radio for a generation. More people saw or heard Massey as Lincoln than ever saw or heard the real Lincoln. Perhaps that was appropriate because Sherwood's Lincoln spoke more to the generation of the Second World War than to the generation of the Civil War.

In one of the film's most dramatic scenes of the Lincoln-Douglas debates, Massey/Lincoln delivers a speech against slavery that applied equally to Fascist totalitarianism and defended democracy in language resonant with the four freedoms that the Allies fought for in the Second World War. In an interview, Massey said that "If you substitute the word *dictatorship* for the word *slavery* throughout Sherwood's script, it becomes electric for our time." In the final scene, as Lincoln departs from Springfield to take up the burdens of the presidency, Massey's Lincoln sees beyond the challenge of disunion to the challenge to democracy in a world at war.

Sherwood skillfully wove together Lincoln's words with his own script to portray Lincoln's growth from the gawky youth of 1831 to the champion of freedom and democracy in 1861. Sherwood took many liberties, but what scriptwriter does not? He combined bits and pieces of several Lincoln speeches into one; he invented incidents and wrenched chronology in some of the 12 scenes from these 30 years of Lincoln's life.

Perhaps the film's sharpest departure from reality is the tension it depicts between "politics," which is bad, and "democracy," which is good. Sherwood's Lincoln doesn't want to play the dirty game of politics; early in the film, the homespun youth declares: "I don't want to be no politi-cian." It is Mary Todd Lincoln who is ambitious for her husband and pushes a reluctant Abraham toward his destiny. The real Lincoln, of course, loved the game of politics and played it masterfully. He was also as ambitious in his own right as Mary was for him; Lincoln's law partner William Herndon said that Abraham's ambition was "a little engine that knew no rest." Sherwood's Lincoln who transcends politics to become a great statesman could not have existed without the real Lincoln, the ambitious politician.

© Bettmann/Corbis.

Raymond Massey as the 23-year-old Abraham Lincoln just elected captain of a New Salem militia company in the Black Hawk War of 1832.

Courtesy of the Illinois State Historical Library.

THE LINCOLN-DOUGLAS DEBATES

The Lincoln-Douglas contest for the Senate in 1858 produced the most famous—and fateful—political debates in American history. At stake was nothing less than the future of the nation. Thousands of people crowded into seven towns to listen to these three-hour debates that took place outdoors from August to October in weather ranging from stifling heat to cold rain. Audiences were most friendly to Lincoln in antislavery northern Illinois, as portrayed in this illustration of the debate in Galesburg, home of Knox College and a hotbed of abolitionism.

courts.) The advocates of slavery, charged Lincoln, were trying to "push it forward, till it shall become lawful in all the States." But Republicans intended to keep slavery out of the territories, thus stopping its growth and placing it "where the public mind shall rest in the belief that it is in the course of ultimate extinction."

The seven open-air debates between Douglas and Lincoln focused almost entirely on the issue of slavery. Douglas asked: Why could the country not continue to exist half slave and half free as it had for 70 years? Lincoln's talk about the "ultimate extinction" of slavery would provoke the South to secession. Douglas professed himself no friend of slavery, but if people in the southern states or in the territories wanted it, they had the right to have it. Douglas did not want black people—either slave or free—in

Illinois. Lincoln's policy would not only free the slaves but would also grant them equality. "Are you in favor of conferring upon the negro the rights and privileges of citizenship?" Douglas called out to supporters in the crowd. "No, no!" they shouted back. He continued:

> Do you desire to strike out of our State Constitution that clause which keeps slaves and free negroes out of the State . . . in order that when Missouri abolishes slavery she can send one hundred thousand emancipated slaves into Illinois, to become citizens and voters on an equality with yourselves? ("Never," "no.") . . . If you desire to allow them to come into the State and settle with the white man, if you desire them to vote . . . then support Mr. Lincoln and the Black Republican party, who are in favor of the citizenship of the negro. ("Never, never.")

Douglas's demagoguery put Lincoln on the defensive. He responded with cautious denials that he favored "social and political equality" of the races. The "ultimate extinction" of slavery might take a century. It would require the voluntary cooperation of the South and would perhaps be contingent on the emigration of some freed slaves from the country. But come what may, freedom must prevail. Americans must reaffirm the principles of the founding fathers. In Lincoln's words, a black person was

> entitled to all the natural rights enumerated in the Declaration of Independence, the right to life, liberty and the pursuit of happiness. (Loud cheers.) I hold that he is as much entitled to these as the white man. I agree with Judge Douglas he is not my equal in many respects. . . . But in the right to eat the bread, without leave of anybody else, which his own hand earns, *he is my equal and the equal of Judge Douglas, and the equal of every living man.*
>
> (Great applause.)

Lincoln deplored Douglas's "care not" attitude whether slavery was voted up or down. He "looks to no end of the institution of slavery," said Lincoln. By endorsing the Dred Scott decision, Lincoln claimed, Douglas looks to its "perpetuity and nationalization." Douglas was thus "eradicating the light of reason and liberty in this American people." That was the real issue in the election, insisted Lincoln.

> That is the issue that will continue in this country when these poor tongues of Judge Douglas and myself shall be silent. It is the eternal struggle between these two principles—right and wrong—throughout the world. . . . The one is the common right of humanity and the other the divine right of kings. . . . No matter in what shape it comes, whether from a king who seeks to bestride the people of his own nation and live by the fruit of their labor, or from one race of men as an apology for enslaving another race, it is the same tyrannical principle.

The Freeport Doctrine

The popular vote for Republican and Democratic state legislators in Illinois was virtually even in 1858, but because apportionment favored the Democrats, they won a majority of seats and reelected Douglas. Lincoln, however, was the ultimate victor; his performance in the debates lifted him from political obscurity, while Douglas further alienated southern Democrats. In the Freeport debate, Lincoln had asked Douglas how he reconciled his support for the Dred Scott decision with his policy of popular sovereignty, which supposedly gave residents of a territory the power to vote slavery down. Douglas replied that even though the Court had legalized slavery in the territories, the enforcement of that right would depend on the people who lived there. This was a popular answer in the North, but it gave added impetus to southern demands for congressional passage of a federal slave code in territories such as Kansas, where the Free Soil majority had by 1859 made slavery virtually null. In the next two sessions of Congress after the 1858 elections, southern Democrats, led by Jefferson Davis, tried to pass a federal slave code for all territories. Douglas and northern Democrats joined with Republicans to defeat it. Consequently, southern hostility toward Douglas mounted as the presidential election of 1860 approached.

The 1859–60 session of Congress was particularly contentious. Once again a fight over the speakership of the House set the tone. Republicans had won a plurality of House seats, but lacking a majority could not elect a Speaker without the support of a few border-state representatives from the American (Know-Nothing) Party. The problem was that the Republican candidate for Speaker was John Sherman, who, along with 67 other congressmen, had signed an endorsement of Hinton Rowan Helper's *The Impending Crisis of the South* (without, Sherman later admitted, having read it). This was a red flag to southerners, even to ex-Whigs from the border states, who refused to vote for Sherman. Through 43 ballots and two months, the House remained deadlocked. Tensions escalated, and members came armed to the floor. One observer commented that "the only persons who do not have a revolver and knife are those who have two revolvers."

As usual, southerners threatened to secede if a Black Republican became Speaker. Several of them wanted a shootout on the floor of Congress. We "are willing to fight the question out," wrote one, "and to settle it right there." The governor of South Carolina told one of his state's congressmen: "If . . . you upon consultation decide to make the issue of force in Washington, write or telegraph me, and I will have a regiment in or near Washington in the shortest possible time." To avert a crisis, Sherman withdrew his candidacy and the House finally elected a conservative ex-Whig as Speaker on the 44th ballot.

John Brown at Harpers Ferry

Southern tempers were frayed even at the start of this session of Congress because of what had happened at Harpers Ferry, Virginia, the previous October. After his exploits in Kansas, John Brown had disappeared from public view but had not been idle. Like the Old Testament warriors he admired and resembled, Brown intended to carry his war against slavery into Babylon—the South. His favorite New Testament passage was Hebrews 9:22: "Without shedding of blood there is no remission of sin." Brown worked up a plan to capture the federal arsenal at Harpers Ferry, arm slaves with the muskets he seized there, and move southward along the Appalachian Mountains attracting more slaves to his army along the way until the "whole accursed system of bondage" collapsed.

Brown recruited five black men and seventeen whites, including three of his sons, for this reckless scheme. He also had the secret support of a half-dozen Massachusetts and New York abolitionists, who had helped him raise funds. On the night of October 16, 1859, Brown led his men across the Potomac River and occupied the sleeping town of Harpers Ferry without resistance. Few slaves flocked to his banner, but the next day state militia units poured into town and drove Brown's band into the fire-engine house. At dawn on October 18, a company of U.S. marines commanded by Colonel Robert E. Lee and Lieutenant J. E. B. Stuart stormed the engine house and captured the surviving members of Brown's party. Four townsmen, one marine, and 10 of Brown's men (including two of his sons) were killed; not a single slave was liberated.

John Brown's raid lasted 36 hours, but its repercussions resounded for years. Brown and six of his followers were promptly tried by the state of Virginia, convicted, and hanged. This scarcely ended matters. The raid sent a wave of revulsion and alarm through the South. Although no slaves had risen in revolt, it revived fears of slave insurrection that were never far beneath the surface of southern consciousness. Exaggerated reports of Brown's network of abolitionist supporters confirmed southern suspicions that a widespread northern conspiracy was afoot, determined to destroy their society. Although Republican leaders denied any connection with Brown and disavowed his actions, few southerners believed them. Had not Lincoln talked of the extinction of slavery? And had not William H. Seward, who was expected to be the next Republican presidential nominee, given a campaign speech in 1858 in

JOHN BROWN

This modern mural of John Brown is full of symbolism. Holding an open Bible, Brown bestrides the earth like an Old Testament prophet while dead Union and Confederate soldiers lie at his feet. Other soldiers clash behind him, slaves struggle to break free, and God's wrath at a sinful nation sends a destructive tornado to earth in the background.

which he predicted an irrepressible conflict between the free and slave societies?

Many northerners, impressed by Brown's dignified bearing and eloquence during his trial, considered him a martyr to freedom. In his final statement to the court, Brown said:

> I see a book kissed, which I suppose to be the Bible, which teaches me that all things whatsoever I would that men should do to me, I should do even so to them. It teaches me, further, to remember them that are in bonds as bound with them. I endeavored to act up to that instruction. . . . Now, if it is deemed necessary that I should forfeit my life for the furtherance of the ends of justice, and mingle my blood further with the blood of my children and with the blood of millions in this slave country whose rights are disregarded by wicked, cruel, and unjust enactments, I say, let it be done.

On the day of Brown's execution, bells tolled in hundreds of northern towns, guns fired salutes, and ministers preached sermons of commemoration. "The death of no man in America has ever produced so profound a sensation," commented one northerner. Ralph Waldo Emerson declared that Brown had made "the gallows as glorious as the cross."

This outpouring of northern sympathy for Brown shocked and enraged southerners and weakened the already frayed threads of the Union. "The Harper's Ferry invasion has advanced the cause of disunion more than any event that has happened since the formation of the

government," observed a Richmond, Virginia, newspaper. "I have always been a fervid Union man," wrote a North Carolinian, but "the endorsement of the Harper's Ferry outrage . . . has shaken my fidelity. . . . I am willing to take the chances of every possible evil that may arise from disunion, sooner than submit any longer to Northern insolence."

Something approaching a reign of terror now descended on the South. Every Yankee seemed to be another John Brown; every slave who acted suspiciously seemed to be an insurrectionist. Hundreds of northerners were run out of the South in 1860, some wearing a coat of tar and feathers. Several "incendiaries," both white and black, were lynched. "Defend yourselves!" Senator Robert Toombs cried out to the southern people. "The enemy is at your door . . . meet him at the doorsill, and drive him from the temple of liberty, or pull down its pillars and involve him in a common ruin."

Conclusion

Few decades in American history witnessed a greater disjunction between economic well-being and political upheaval than the 1850s. Despite the recession following the Panic of 1857, the total output of the American economy grew by 62 percent during the decade. Railroad mileage more than tripled, value added by manufacturing nearly doubled, and gross farm product grew by 40 percent. Americans were more prosperous than ever before.

Yet a profound malaise gripped the country. Riots between immigrants and nativists in the mid-1850s left more than 50 people dead. Fighting in Kansas between pro-slavery and antislavery forces killed at least 200. Fistfights broke out on the floor of Congress. A South Carolina congressman bludgeoned a Massachusetts senator to unconsciousness with a heavy cane. Representatives and senators came to congressional sessions armed with weapons as well as with violent words.

The nation proved capable of absorbing the large influx of immigrants despite the tensions and turmoil of the mid-1850s. It might also have been able to absorb the huge territorial expansion of the late 1840s had not the slavery issue been reopened in an earlier territorial acquisition, the Louisiana Purchase, by the Kansas-Nebraska Act of 1854. This legislation, followed by the Dred Scott decision in 1857, seemed to authorize the unlimited expansion of slavery. Within two years of its founding in 1854, however, the Republican Party emerged as the largest party in the North on a platform of preventing all future expansion of slavery. By 1860, the United States had reached a fateful crossroads. As Lincoln had said, it could not endure permanently half slave and half free. The presidential election of 1860 would decide which road America would take into the future.

SUGGESTED READINGS

For a detailed and readable treatment of the mounting sectional conflict in the 1850s, see **Allan Nevins, *Ordeal of the Union,*** 2 vols. (1947), and ***The Emergence of Lincoln,*** 2 vols. (1950). The Kansas-Nebraska Act and its political consequences are treated in **Gerald W. Wolff, *The Kansas-Nebraska Bill: Party, Section, and the Coming of the Civil War*** (1977). The conflict in Kansas itself is treated in **Nicole Etcheson, *Bleeding Kansas: Contested Liberty in the Civil War Era*** (2004). For the cross-cutting issue of nativism and the Know-Nothings, see **William E. Gienapp, *The Origins of the Republican Party, 1852–1856*** (1987), and **Tyler Anbinder, *Nativism and Politics: The Know Nothing Party in the Northern United States*** (1992). Two excellent studies of the role of Abraham Lincoln in the rise of the Republican Party are **Don E. Fehrenbacher, *Prelude to Greatness: Lincoln in the 1850s*** (1962), and **Kenneth Winkle, *The Young Eagle: The Rise of Abraham Lincoln*** (2003). The southern response to the growth of antislavery political sentiment in the North is the theme of **William J. Cooper, Jr., *The South and the Politics of Slavery 1828–1856*** (1978).

The year 1857 witnessed a convergence of many crucial events; for a stimulating book that pulls together the threads of that year of crisis, see **Kenneth M. Stampp, *America in 1857: A Nation on the Brink*** (1990). For economic developments during the era, an older classic is still the best introduction: **George Rogers Taylor, *The Transportation Revolution, 1815–1860*** (1951). An important dimension of the southern economy is elucidated in **Fred Bateman and Thomas Weiss, *A Deplorable Scarcity: The Failure of Industrialization in the Slave Economy*** (1981). Still the best study of the Republican free-labor ideology is **Eric Foner, *Free Soil, Free Labor, Free Men: The Ideology of the Republican Party before the Civil War*** (2nd ed., 1995). For southern yeoman farmers, a good study is **Stephanie McCurry, *Masters of Small Worlds: Yeoman Households, Gender Relations, and the Political Culture of the Antebellum South Carolina Low Country*** (1995). The best single study of the Dred Scott case is **Don E. Fehrenbacher, *The Dred Scott Case: Its Significance in American Law and Politics*** (1978), which was published in an abridged version with the title *Slavery, Law, and Politics: The Dred Scott Case in Historical Perspective* (1981).

AMERICAN JOURNEY ONLINE AND INFOTRAC COLLEGE EDITION

Visit the source collections at www.ajaccess.wadsworth.com and infotrac.thomsonlearning.com and use the Search function with the following key terms to explore documents, images, audio and video clips, articles, and commentary related to the material in this chapter.

Dred Scott

Lincoln-Douglas debates

Abraham Lincoln

Jefferson Davis

Harpers Ferry

John Brown

Kansas-Nebraska Act

Know-Nothings

GRADE AIDS

Visit the Liberty Equality Power Companion Web Site for resources specific to this textbook: http://history.wadsworth.com/murrin_LEP4e

The CD in the back of this book and the U.S. History Resource Center at http://history.wadsworth.com/u.s./ offer a variety of tools to help you succeed in this course, including access to quizzes; images; documents; interactive simulations, maps, and timelines; movie explorations; and a wealth of other sources.

Chapter 15

Secession and Civil War, 1860–1862

Thomas C. Linday, Hornet's Nest, Cincinnati Historical Society.

THE HORNET'S NEST AT SHILOH
In the bloody fighting on April 6 at the Battle of Shiloh, portions of three Union divisions held out along a sunken farm road for several hours. Virtually surrounded by Confederate attackers, the 2,200 Union survivors surrendered in midafternoon. This was a costly Confederate success because General Albert Sidney Johnston was mortally wounded while directing the attack. The volume of fire from Union defenders was so great that the Confederates called the enemy position the "hornet's nest" because of the whizzing bullets coming from it. The stubborn Union fighting at the hornet's nest bought Grant time to establish a defensive line, from which he launched a successful counterattack the next day.

CHAPTER OUTLINE

As the year 1860 began, the Democratic Party was one of the few national institutions left in the country. The Methodists and Baptists had split into Northern and Southern churches in the 1840s over the issue of slavery; several voluntary associations had done the same; the Whig Party and the nativist American Party had been shattered by sectional antagonism in the mid-1850s. Finally, in April 1860, even the Democratic Party, at its national convention in Charleston, South Carolina, split into Northern and Southern camps. This virtually ensured the election of a Republican president. Such a prospect aroused deep fears among Southern whites that a Republican administration might use its power to bring liberty and perhaps even equality to the slaves.

When Abraham Lincoln was elected president exclusively by Northern votes, the lower-South states seceded from the Union. When Lincoln refused to remove U.S. troops from Fort Sumter, South Carolina, the new Confederate States army opened fire on the fort. Lincoln called out the militia to suppress the insurrection. Four more slave states seceded. In 1861, the country drifted into a civil war whose immense consequences no one could foresee.

CHAPTER FOCUS

- ♦ Why did political leaders in the lower South think that Lincoln's election made secession imperative?
- ♦ Why did compromise efforts to forestall secession fail, and why did war break out at Fort Sumter?
- ♦ What were Northern advantages in the Civil War? What were Southern advantages?
- ♦ How did these advantages manifest themselves in the military campaigns and battles in 1861–62?

The Election of 1860

A hotbed of Southern-rights radicalism, Charleston, South Carolina, turned out to be the worst possible place for the Democrats to hold their national convention. Sectional confrontations took place inside the convention hall and on the streets. Since 1836, the Democratic Party had required a two-thirds majority of delegates for a presidential nomination, a rule that in effect gave Southerners veto power if they voted together. Although Stephen A. Douglas had the backing of a simple majority of the delegates, southern Democrats were determined to deny him the nomination. His opposition to the Lecompton constitution in Kansas and to a federal slave code for the territories had convinced pro-slavery Southerners that they would be unable to control a Douglas administration.

The first test came in the debate on the platform. Southern delegates insisted on a plank favoring a federal slave code for the territories. Douglas could not run on a platform that contained such a plank, and if the party adopted it, Democrats were sure to lose every state in the North. By a slim majority, the convention rejected the plank and reaffirmed the 1856 platform endorsing popular sovereignty. Fifty Southern delegates thereupon walked out of the convention. Even after they left, Douglas could not muster a two-thirds majority, nor could any other candidate. After 57 futile ballots, the convention adjourned to meet in Baltimore six weeks later to try again.

CHRONOLOGY

1860   Lincoln elected president (November 6) • South Carolina secedes (December 20) • Federal troops transfer from Fort Moultrie to Fort Sumter (December 26)

1861   Rest of lower South secedes (January–February) • Crittenden Compromise rejected (February) • Jefferson Davis inaugurated as provisional president of new Confederate States of America (February 18) • Abraham Lincoln inaugurated as president of the United States (March 4) • Fort Sumter falls; Lincoln calls out troops, proclaims blockade (April) • Four more states secede to join Confederacy (April–May) • Battle of Bull Run (Manassas) (July 21) • Battle of Wilson's Creek (August 10) • The *Trent* affair (November–December)

1862   Union captures Forts Henry and Donelson (February 6 and 16) • Congress passes Legal Tender Act (February 25) • Battle of Pea Ridge (March 7–8) • Battle of the *Monitor* and *Merrimac* (*Virginia*) (March 9) • Battle of Glorieta Pass (March 26–28) • Battle of Shiloh (April 6–7) • Union Navy captures New Orleans (April 25) • Stonewall Jackson's Shenandoah Valley campaign (May–June) • Seven Days' battles (June 25–July 1) • Second Battle of Manassas (Bull Run) (August 29–30) • Lee invades Maryland (September) • Battle of Corinth (October 3–4) • Battle of Perryville (October 8)

1863   Congress passes National Banking Act (February 25)

THE POLITICAL QUADRILLE

This cartoon depicts the four presidential candidates in 1860. Clockwise from the upper left are John C. Breckinridge, Southern Rights Democrat; Abraham Lincoln, Republican; John Bell, Constitutional Union; and Stephen A. Douglas, Democrat. All are dancing to the tune played by Dred Scott, symbolizing the importance of the slavery issue in this campaign. Each candidate's partner represents a political liability: for example, Breckinridge's partner is the disunionist William L. Yancey wearing a devil's horns, while Lincoln's partner is a black woman who supposedly gives color to Democratic accusations that Republicans believed in miscegenation.

By then the party was too badly shattered to be put back together. That pleased some pro-slavery radicals, who were convinced that the South would never be secure in a nation dominated by a Northern majority. The election of a Black Republican president, they believed, would provide the shock necessary to mobilize a Southern majority for secession. Two of the most prominent secessionists were William L. Yancey and Edmund Ruffin. In 1858, they founded the League of United Southerners to "fire the Southern heart . . . and at the proper moment, by one organized, concerted action, we can precipitate the Cotton States into a revolution." After walking out of the Democratic convention, the eloquent Yancey inspired a huge crowd in Charleston's moonlit courthouse square to give three cheers "for an Independent Southern Republic" with his concluding words: "Perhaps even now, the pen of the historian is nibbed to write the story of a new revolution."

The second convention in Baltimore reprised the first at Charleston. This time, an even larger number of delegates from Southern states walked out. They formed their own Southern Rights Democratic Party and nominated John C. Breckinridge of Kentucky (the incumbent vice president) for president on a slave-code platform. When regular Democrats nominated Douglas, the stage was set for what would become a four-party election. A coalition of former southern Whigs, who could not bring themselves to vote Democratic, and northern Whigs, who considered the Republican Party too radical, formed the Constitutional Union Party, which nominated John Bell of Tennessee for president. Bell had no chance of winning; the party's purpose was to exercise a conservative influence on a campaign that threatened to polarize the country.

The Republicans Nominate Lincoln

From the moment the Democratic Party broke apart, it became clear that 1860 could be the year when the dynamic young Republican Party elected its first president. The Republicans could expect no electoral votes from the 15 slave states. In 1856, however, they had won all but five northern states, and with only two or three of those five they could win the presidency. The crucial states were Pennsylvania, Illinois, and Indiana. Douglas might still carry them and throw the presidential election into the House, where anything could happen. Thus the Republicans had to carry at least two of the swing states to win.

As the Republican delegates poured into Chicago for their convention—held in a huge building nicknamed the Wigwam because of its shape—their leading presidential prospect was William H. Seward of New York. An experienced politician who had served as governor and senator, Seward was by all odds the most prominent Republican, but in his long career he had made many enemies. His antinativist policies had alienated some former members of the American Party, whose support he would need to carry Pennsylvania. His "Higher Law" speech against the Compromise of 1850 and his "Irrepressible Conflict" speech in 1858, predicting the ultimate overthrow of slavery, had given him a reputation for radicalism that might drive away voters in the vital swing states of the lower North.

Several of the delegates, uneasy about that reputation, staged a stop-Seward movement. The next candidate to the fore was Abraham Lincoln. Although he too had opposed nativism, he had done so less noisily than Seward. His "House Divided" speech had made essentially the same point as Seward's "Irrepressible Conflict" speech, but his reputation was still that of a more moderate man. He was from one of the lower-North states where the election would be close, and his rise from a poor farm boy and railsplitter to successful lawyer and political leader perfectly reflected the free-labor theme of social mobility extolled by the Republican Party. By picking up second-choice votes from states that switched from their favorite sons, Lincoln overtook Seward and won the nomination on the third ballot. Seward accepted the outcome gracefully, and the Republicans headed into the campaign as a united, confident party.

Their confidence stemmed in part from their platform, which appealed to many groups in the North. Its main plank pledged exclusion of slavery from the territories. Other planks called for a higher tariff (especially popular in Pennsylvania), a homestead act (popular in the Northwest), and federal aid for construction of a transcontinental railroad and for improvement of river navigation. This program was designed for a future in which the "house divided" would become a free-labor society modeled on Northern capitalism. Its blend of idealism and materialism proved especially attractive to young people; a large majority of first-time voters in the North voted Republican in 1860. Thousands of them joined Wide-Awake clubs and marched in huge torchlight parades through the cities of the North.

Southern Fears

Militant enthusiasm in the North was matched by fear and rage in the South. Few people there could see any difference between Lincoln and Seward—or for that matter

WIDE-AWAKE PARADE IN NEW YORK, OCTOBER 5, 1860

The Wide-Awakes were an organization of young Republicans who roused political enthusiasm by marching in huge torchlight parades during the political campaign of 1860. A year later, many of these same men would march down the same streets in army uniforms carrying rifles instead of torches on their way to the front.

From the Ralph E. Becker Collection of Political Americana, The Smithsonian Institution.

between Lincoln and William Lloyd Garrison. They were all Black Republicans and abolitionists. Had not Lincoln branded slavery a moral, social, and political evil? Had he not said that the Declaration of Independence applied to blacks as well as whites? Had he not expressed a hope that excluding slavery from the territories would put it on the road to ultimate extinction? To Southerners, the Republican pledge not to interfere with slavery in the states was meaningless.

A Republican victory in the presidential election would put an end to the South's political control of its destiny. Two-thirds of the time from 1789 to 1860, Southerners (all slaveholders) had been president of the United States. No northern president had ever won reelection. Two-thirds of the Speakers of the House and presidents

pro tem of the Senate had been Southerners. Southern justices had been a majority on the Supreme Court since 1791. Lincoln's election would mark an irreversible turning away from this Southern ascendancy. Even Southern moderates warned that the South could not remain in the Union if Lincoln won. "This Government and Black Republicanism cannot live together," said one of them. "At no period of the world's history have four thousand millions of property [that is, the slave owners] debated whether it ought to submit to the rule of an enemy." And what about the three-quarters of Southern whites who did not belong to slaveholding families? Lincoln's election, warned an Alabama secessionist, would show that "the North [means] to free the negroes and force amalgamation between them and the children of the poor men of

VOTING IN THE 1860 ELECTION

Candidate	All States		Free States (18)		Slave States (15)	
	Popular	Electoral	Popular	Electoral	Popular	Electoral
Lincoln	1,864,735	180	1,838,347	180	26,388	0
Opposition to Lincoln	2,821,157	123	1,572,637	3	1,248,520	120
"Fusion" Tickets*	595,846	—	580,426	—	15,420	—
Douglas	979,425	12	815,857	3	163,568	9
Breckinridge	669,472	72	99,381	0	570,091	72
Bell	576,414	39	76,973	0	499,441	39

* In several states, the two Democratic parties and the Constitutional Union Party arranged a single anti-Lincoln ballot. These "fusion" tickets carried several counties but failed to win any state.

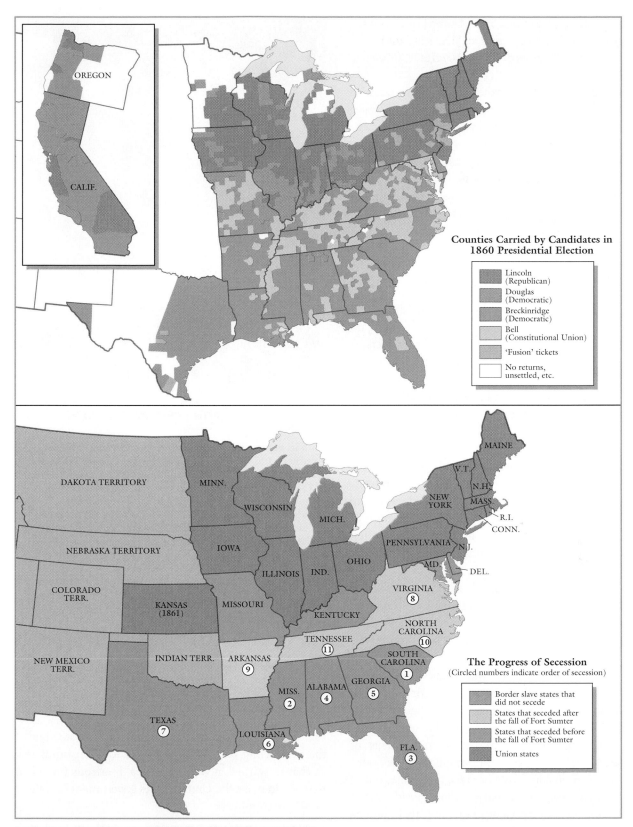

Counties Carried by Candidates in
1860 Presidential Election

Lincoln
(Republican)

Douglas
(Democratic)

Breckinridge
(Democratic)

Bell
(Constitutional Union)

'Fusion' tickets

No returns,
unsettled, etc.

OREGON

CALIF.

DAKOTA TERRITORY

MINN.

WISCONSIN

MICH.

MAINE

V.T.

N.H.

NEW
YORK

MASS.

R.I.

CONN.

NEBRASKA TERRITORY

IOWA

PENNSYLVANIA

N.J.

ILLINOIS

IND.

OHIO

MD.

DEL.

COLORADO
TERR.

KANSAS
(1861)

MISSOURI

KENTUCKY

VIRGINIA
⑧

NEW MEXICO
TERR.

INDIAN TERR.

ARKANSAS
⑨

TENNESSEE
⑪

NORTH
CAROLINA
⑩

SOUTH
CAROLINA
①

MISS.
②

ALABAMA
④

GEORGIA
⑤

TEXAS
⑦

LOUISIANA
⑥

FLA.
③

The Progress of Secession
(Circled numbers indicate order of secession)

Border slave states that
did not secede

States that seceded after
the fall of Fort Sumter

States that seceded before
the fall of Fort Sumter

Union states

MAP 15.1 ELECTION OF 1860 AND SOUTHERN SECESSION

Note the similarity of the geographical voting patterns in the upper map to the map on p. 444. Another striking pattern
shows the correlation between the vote for Breckinridge (upper map) and the first seven states to secede (lower map).

 View an animated version of this map or related maps at **http://history.wadsworth.com/murrin_LEP4e**.

the South." If Georgia remained in a Union "ruled by Lincoln and his crew," a secessionist in that state told non-slaveholders, "in TEN years or less our CHILDREN will be the *slaves* of negroes."

Most whites in the South voted for Breckinridge, who carried 11 slave states. Bell won the upper-South states of Virginia, Kentucky, and Tennessee. Missouri went to Douglas—the only state he carried, although he came in second in the popular vote. Although Lincoln received less than 40 percent of the popular vote, he won every free state and swept the presidency by a substantial margin in the electoral college (three of New Jersey's seven electoral votes went to Douglas).

The Lower South Secedes

Lincoln's victory provided the shock that Southern fire-eaters had craved. The tension that had been building up for years suddenly exploded like a string of firecrackers, as seven states seceded one after another. According to the theory of secession, when each state ratified the Constitution and joined the Union, it authorized the national government to act as its agent in the exercise of certain functions of sovereignty—but the states had never given away their fundamental underlying sovereignty. Any state, then, by the act of its own convention, could withdraw from its "compact" with the other states and reassert its individual sovereignty. Therefore, the South Carolina legislature called for such a convention and ordered an election of delegates to consider withdrawing from the United States. On December 20, 1860, the South Carolina convention did withdraw, by a vote of 169 to 0.

The outcome was closer in other lower-South states. Unconditional unionism was rare, but many conservatives and former Whigs, including Alexander H. Stephens of Georgia, shrank from the drastic step of secession. At the conventions in each of the next six states to secede, some delegates tried to delay matters with vague proposals for "cooperation" among all Southern states, or even with proposals to wait until after Lincoln's inauguration on March 4, 1861, to see what course he would pursue. Those minority factions were overridden by proponents of immediate secession. The conventions followed the example of South Carolina and voted to take their states out of the Union: Mississippi on January 9, 1861, Florida on the 10th, Alabama on the 11th, Georgia on the 19th, Louisiana on the 26th, and Texas on February 1. In those six states as a whole, 20 percent of the delegates voted against secession, but most of these, including Stephens, "went with their states" after the final votes had been tallied. Delegates from the seven seceding states met in Montgomery,

Courtesy of The South Carolina Historical Society.

BANNER OF THE SOUTH CAROLINA SECESSION CONVENTION

With its banner featuring a palmetto tree and a snake reminiscent of the American Revolution's "Don't Tread on Me" slogan, the South Carolina secession convention in 1860 looked forward to a grand new Southern republic composed of all 15 slave states and built on the ruins of the old Union. Note the large South Carolina keystone of the arch and the stones of free states lying cracked and broken on the ground.

Alabama, in February to create a new nation to be called the Confederate States of America.

Northerners Affirm the Union

Most people in the North considered secession unconstitutional and treasonable. In his final annual message to Congress, on December 3, 1860, President Buchanan insisted that the Union was not "a mere voluntary association of States, to be dissolved at pleasure by any one of the contracting parties." If secession was consummated, Buchanan warned, it would create a disastrous precedent that would make the United States government "a rope of sand." He continued:

> Our thirty-three States may resolve themselves into as many petty, jarring, and hostile republics. . . . By such a dread catastrophe the hopes of the friends of freedom throughout the world would be destroyed. . . . Our example for more than eighty years would not only be lost, but it would be quoted as proof that man is unfit for self-government.

European monarchists and conservatives were already expressing smug satisfaction at "the great smashup" of the republic in North America. They predicted that other disaffected minorities would also secede and that the United States would ultimately collapse into anarchy and revolution. That was precisely what Northerners and even some upper-South Unionists feared. "The doctrine of secession is anarchy," declared a Cincinnati newspaper. "If any minority have the right to break up the Government at pleasure, because they have not had their way, there is an end of all government." Lincoln denied that the states had ever possessed independent sovereignty before becoming part of the United States. Rather, they had been colonies or territories that never would have become part of the United States had they not accepted unconditional sovereignty of the national government. No government, said Lincoln, "ever had provision in its organic law for its own termination.... No State, upon its own mere motion, can lawfully get out of the Union.... They can only do so against law, and by revolution."

In that case, answered many Southerners, we invoke the right of revolution to justify secession. After all, the United States was born of revolution. The secessionists maintained that they were merely following the example of their forefathers in declaring independence from a government that threatened their rights and liberties. An Alabaman asked rhetorically: "[Were not] the men of 1776, who withdrew their allegiance from George III and set up for themselves . . . Secessionists?"

Northerners could scarcely deny the right of revolution: They too were heirs of 1776. But "the right of revolution, is never a legal right," said Lincoln. "At most, it is but a moral right, when exercised for a morally justifiable cause. When exercised without such a cause revolution is no right, but simply a wicked exercise of physical power." The South, in Lincoln's view, had no morally justifiable cause. In fact, the event that had precipitated secession was his own election by a constitutional majority. For Southerners to cast themselves in the mold of 1776 was "a libel upon the whole character and conduct" of the Founding Fathers, said the antislavery poet and journalist William Cullen Bryant. They rebelled "to establish the rights of man . . . and principles of universal liberty," whereas Southerners in 1861 were rebelling to protect "a domestic despotism. . . . Their motto is not liberty, but slavery."

Compromise Proposals

Bryant conveniently overlooked the fact that slavery had existed in most parts of the republic founded by the revolutionaries of 1776. In any event, most people in the North agreed with Lincoln that secession was a "wicked exercise

of physical power." The question was what to do about it. All kinds of compromise proposals came before Congress when it met in December 1860. To sort them out, the Senate and the House each set up a special committee. The Senate committee came up with a package of compromises sponsored by Senator John J. Crittenden of Kentucky. The Crittenden Compromise consisted of a series of proposed constitutional amendments: to guarantee slavery in the states perpetually against federal interference; to prohibit Congress from abolishing slavery in the District of Columbia or on any federal property (forts, arsenals, naval bases, and so on); to deny Congress the power to interfere with the interstate slave trade; to compensate slaveholders who were prevented from recovering fugitive slaves who had escaped to the North; and, most important, to protect slavery south of latitude 36°30′ in all territories "now held *or hereafter acquired.*"

Given the appetite of the South for more slave territory in the Caribbean and Central America, that italicized phrase, in the view of most Republicans, might turn the United States into "a great slavebreeding and slavetrading empire." But even though endorsement of the territorial clause in the Crittenden Compromise would require Republicans to repudiate the platform on which they had just won the election, some conservatives in the party were willing to accept it in the interest of peace and conciliation. Their votes, together with those of Democrats and upper-South Unionists whose states had not seceded, might have gotten the compromise through Congress. It is doubtful, however, that the approval of three-quarters of the states required for ratification would have been forthcoming. In any case, word came from Springfield, Illinois, where President-elect Lincoln was preparing for his inaugural trip to Washington, telling key Republican senators and congressmen to stand firm against compromise on the territorial issue. "Entertain no proposition for a compromise in regard to the *extension* of slavery," wrote Lincoln.

> Filibustering for all South of us, and making slave states would follow . . . to put us again on the high-road to a slave empire. . . . We have just carried an election on principles fairly stated to the people. Now we are told in advance, the government shall be broken up, unless we surrender to those we have beaten. . . . If we surrender, it is the end of us. They will repeat the experiment upon us *ad libitum.* A year will not pass, till we shall have to take Cuba as a condition upon which they will stay in the Union.

Lincoln's advice was decisive. The Republicans voted against the Crittenden Compromise, which therefore failed in Congress. Most Republicans, though, went along with a proposal by Virginia for a "peace convention" of all the states to be held in Washington in February 1861. Although the seven seceded states sent no delegates, hopes that the convention might accomplish something encouraged Unionists in the eight other slave states either to reject secession or to adopt a wait-and-see attitude. In the end, the peace convention produced nothing better than a modified version of the Crittenden Compromise, which suffered the same fate as the original.

Nothing that happened in Washington would have made any difference to the seven states that had seceded. No compromise could bring them back. "We spit upon every plan to compromise," said one secessionist. No power could "stem the wild torrent of passion that is carrying everything before it," wrote former U.S. Senator Judah P. Benjamin of Louisiana. Secession "is a revolution [that] can no more be checked by human effort . . . than a prairie fire by a gardener's watering pot."

Establishment of the Confederacy

While the peace convention deliberated in Washington, the seceded states focused on a convention in Montgomery, Alabama, that drew up a constitution and established a government for the new Confederate States of America. The Confederate constitution contained clauses that guaranteed slavery in both the states and the territories, strengthened the principle of state sovereignty, and prohibited its Congress from enacting a protective (as distinguished from a revenue) tariff and from granting government aid to internal improvements. It limited the president to a single six-year term. The convention delegates constituted themselves a provisional Congress for the new

LINK TO THE PAST

Cornerstone of the Confederacy

Alexander H. Stephens of Georgia had opposed the secession of his state in January 1861. But when Georgia seceded anyway, he "went with his state" as did so many other southerners who had initially counseled against secession. Stephens was subsequently elected vice president of the Confederate States of America. On March 21, 1861, he gave an address in Savannah, Georgia, which became known as the Cornerstone Speech, in which he proclaimed slavery to be the cornerstone of the new Confederacy.

The new Constitution [of the Confederate States] has put at rest forever all the agitating questions relating to our peculiar institution—African slavery as it exists among us—the proper status of the negro in our form of civilization. This was the immediate cause of the late rupture and present revolution.

[Thomas] Jefferson, in his forecast, had anticipated this, as the "rock upon which the old Union would split." He was right. . . . But whether he fully comprehended the great truth upon which that rock stood and stands, may be doubted. The prevailing ideas entertained by him and most of the leading statesmen at the time of the formation of the old Constitution were, that the enslavement of the African was in violation of the laws of nature; that it was wrong in principle, socially, morally,

and politically. It was an evil they knew not well how to deal with; but the general opinion of the men of that day was, that, somehow or other, in the order of Providence, the institution would be evanescent and pass away. . . . Those ideas, however, were fundamentally wrong. . . .

Our new Government is founded upon exactly the opposite ideas; its foundations are laid, its cornerstone rests, upon the great truth that the negro is not equal to the white man; that slavery, subordination to the superior race, is his natural and moral condition. This, our new Government, is the first, in the history of the world, based upon this great physical, philosophical, and moral truth.

1. After the Civil War, Stephens wrote a two-volume history titled *The War Between the States* in which he maintained that slavery was *not* the cornerstone of the Confederacy or the reason for secession. How might one explain the inconsistency between the Stephens of 1861 and the Stephens of 1868?

For additional sources related to this feature, visit the *Liberty, Equality, Power* Web site at:

http://history.wadsworth.com/murrin_LEP4e

nation until regular elections could be held in November 1861. For provisional president and vice president, the convention turned away from radical secessionists, such as Yancey, and elected Jefferson Davis, a moderate secessionist, and Alexander Stephens, who had originally opposed Georgia's secession but ultimately had supported it.

Davis and Stephens were two of the most able men in the South, with 25 years of service in the U.S. Congress between them. A West Point graduate, Davis had commanded a regiment in the Mexican War and had been secretary of war in the Pierce administration—a useful fund of experience if civil war became a reality. But perhaps the main reason they were elected was to present an image of moderation and respectability to the eight upper-South states that remained in the Union. The Confederacy needed those states—at least some of them—if it was to be a viable nation, especially if war came. Without the upper South, the Confederate states would have less than one-fifth of the population (and barely one-tenth of the free population) and only one-twentieth of the industrial capacity of the Union states.

Confederate leaders appealed to the upper South to join them because of the "common origin, pursuits, tastes, manners and customs [that] bind together in one brotherhood the ... slaveholding states." Residents of the upper South were indeed concerned about preserving slavery, but the issue was less salient there. A strong heritage of Unionism competed with the commitment to slavery. Virginia had contributed more men to the pantheon of Founding Fathers than any other state. Tennessee took pride in being the state of Andrew Jackson, who was famous for his stern warning to John C. Calhoun: "Our Federal Union—It must be preserved." Kentucky was the home of Henry Clay, the Great Pacificator, who had put together compromises to save the Union on three occasions. These states would not leave the Union without greater cause.

The Fort Sumter Issue

As each state seceded, it seized the forts, arsenals, customs houses, and other federal property within its borders. Still in federal hands, however, were two remote forts in the Florida keys, another on an island off Pensacola, and Fort Moultrie in the Charleston harbor. Moultrie quickly became a bone of contention. In December 1860, the self-proclaimed republic of South Carolina demanded its evacuation by the 84-man garrison of the U.S. Army. An obsolete fortification, Moultrie was vulnerable to attack by the South Carolina militia that swarmed into the area. On the day after Christmas 1860, Major Robert Anderson, commander at Moultrie, moved his men to Fort Sumter,

an uncompleted but immensely strong bastion on an artificial island in the channel leading into Charleston Bay. A Kentuckian married to a Georgian, Anderson sympathized with the South but remained loyal to the United States. He deplored the possibility of war and hoped that moving the garrison to Sumter would ease tensions by reducing the possibility of an attack. Instead, it lit a fuse that eventually set off the war.

South Carolina sent a delegation to President Buchanan to negotiate the withdrawal of the federal troops. Buchanan, previously pliable, surprised them by saying no. He even tried to reinforce the garrison. On January 9, the unarmed merchant ship *Star of the West*, carrying 200 soldiers for Sumter, tried to enter the bay but was driven away by South Carolina artillery. Loath to start a war, Major Anderson refused to return fire with Sumter's guns. Matters then settled into an uneasy truce. The Confederate government sent General Pierre G. T. Beauregard to take command of the troops ringing Charleston Bay with their cannons pointed at Fort Sumter, and waited to see what the incoming Lincoln administration would do.

When Abraham Lincoln took the oath of office as the 16th—and, some speculated, the last—president of the *United* States, he knew that his inaugural address would be the most important in American history. On his words would hang the issues of union or disunion, peace or war. His goal was to keep the upper South in the Union while cooling passions in the lower South, hoping that, in time, Southern loyalty to the Union would reassert itself. In his address, he demonstrated both firmness and forbearance: firmness in purpose to preserve the Union, forbearance in the means of doing so. He repeated his pledge not "to interfere with the institution of slavery where it exists." He assured the Confederate states that "the government will not assail *you*." His first draft had also included the phrase "unless you *first* assail it," but William H. Seward, whom Lincoln had appointed secretary of state, persuaded him to drop those words as too provocative. Lincoln's first draft had also stated his intention to use "all the powers at my disposal [to] reclaim the public property and places which have fallen." He deleted that statement as too warlike and said only that he would "hold, occupy, and possess the property, and places belonging to the government," without defining exactly what he meant or how he would do it. In his eloquent peroration, Lincoln appealed to Southerners as Americans who shared with other Americans four score and five years of national history. "We are not enemies, but friends," he said.

> Though passion may have strained, it must not break, our bonds of affection. The mystic chords of memory, stretching from every battlefield and patriot grave to every living

From the collections of the Library of Congress.

THE BOMBARDMENT OF FORT SUMTER, APRIL 12, 1861
This drawing shows the incoming shells from Confederate batteries at Fort Moultrie and Cummings Point, and Fort Sumter's return fire. Note that Confederate shells have set the fort's interior on fire, but the American flag is still flying. It would soon be lowered in surrender as the fire crept toward the powder magazine.

heart and hearthstone all over this broad land, will yet swell the chorus of the Union when again touched, as surely they will be, by the better angels of our nature.

Lincoln hoped to buy time with his inaugural address—time to demonstrate his peaceful intentions and to enable southern Unionists (whose numbers Republicans overestimated) to regain the upper hand. But the day after his inauguration, Lincoln learned that time was running out. A dispatch from Major Anderson informed him that provisions for the soldiers at Fort Sumter would soon be exhausted. The garrison must either be resupplied or evacuated. Any attempt to send in supplies by force would undoubtedly provoke a response from Confederate guns at Charleston. And by putting the onus of starting a war on Lincoln's shoulders, such an action would undoubtedly divide the North and unite the South, driving at least four more states into the Confederacy. Thus, most members of Lincoln's cabinet, along with the army's General-in-Chief Winfield Scott, advised Lincoln to withdraw the troops from Sumter. That, however, would bestow a great moral victory on the Confederacy. It would confer legitimacy on the Confederate government and would probably lead to

diplomatic recognition by foreign powers. Having pledged to "hold, occupy, and possess" national property, could Lincoln afford to abandon that policy during his first month in office? If he did, he would go down in history as the president who consented to the dissolution of the United States.

The pressures from all sides caused Lincoln many sleepless nights; one morning he rose from bed and keeled over in a dead faint. Finally he hit upon a solution that evidenced the mastery that would mark his presidency. He decided to send in unarmed ships with supplies but to hold troops and warships outside the harbor with authorization to go into action only if the Confederates used force to stop the supply ships. And he would give South Carolina officials advance notice of his intention. This stroke of genius shifted the decision for war or peace to Jefferson Davis. In effect, Lincoln flipped a coin and said to Davis, "Heads I win; tails you lose." If Confederate troops fired on the supply ships, the South would stand convicted of starting a war by attacking "a mission of humanity" bringing "food for hungry men." If Davis allowed the supplies to go in peacefully, the U.S. flag would continue to fly over Fort Sumter. The Confederacy would lose face at home and abroad, and southern Unionists would take courage.

Davis did not hesitate. He ordered General Beauregard to compel Sumter's surrender before the supply ships got there. At 4:30 A.M. on April 12, 1861, Confederate guns set off the Civil War by firing on Fort Sumter. After a 33-hour bombardment in which the rebels fired 4,000 rounds and the skeleton gun crews in the garrison replied with 1,000—with no one killed on either side—the burning fort lowered the U.S. flag in surrender.

Choosing Sides

News of the attack triggered an outburst of anger and war fever in the North. "The town is in a wild state of excitement," wrote a Philadelphia diarist. "The American flag is to be seen everywhere. . . . Men are enlisting as fast as possible." A Harvard professor born during George Washington's presidency was astounded by the public response. "The heather is on fire," he wrote. "I never knew what a popular excitement can be." A New York woman wrote that the "time before Sumter" seemed like another century. "It seems as if we were never alive till now; never had a country till now."

Because the tiny U.S. Army—most of whose 16,000 soldiers were stationed at remote frontier posts—was inadequate to quell the "insurrection," Lincoln called on the states for 75,000 militia. The free states filled their quotas immediately. More than twice as many men volunteered as Lincoln had requested. Recognizing that the 90 days' service to which the militia were limited by law would be too short a time, on May 3, Lincoln issued a call for three-year volunteers. Before the war was over, more than 2 million men would serve in the Union army and navy.

The eight slave states still in the Union rejected Lincoln's call for troops. Four of them—Virginia, Arkansas, Tennessee, and North Carolina—soon seceded and joined the Confederacy. Forced by the outbreak of actual war to choose between the Union and the Confederacy, most residents of those four states chose the Confederacy. As a former Unionist in North Carolina remarked, "The division must be made on the line of slavery. The South must go with the South. . . . Blood is thicker than Water."

Few found the choice harder to make than Robert E. Lee of Virginia. One of the most promising officers in the U.S. Army, Lee believed that Southern states had no legal right to secede. General-in-Chief Winfield Scott wanted Lee to become field commander of the Union army. Instead, Lee sadly resigned from the army after the Virginia convention passed an ordinance of secession on April 17. "I must side either with or against my section," Lee told a Northern friend. "I cannot raise my hand against my birthplace, my home, my children." Along with three sons and a nephew, Lee joined the Confederate army. "I foresee that the country will have to pass through a terrible ordeal," he wrote, "a necessary expiation perhaps for our national sins."

Most Southern whites embraced war against the Yankees with less foreboding and more enthusiasm. When news of Sumter's surrender reached Richmond, a huge crowd poured into the state capitol square and ran up the Confederate flag. "Everyone is in favor of secession [and] perfectly frantic with delight," wrote a participant. "I never in all my life witnessed such excitement." The London *Times* correspondent described crowds in North Carolina with "flushed faces, wild eyes, screaming mouths, hurrahing for 'Jeff Davis' and 'the Southern Confederacy.'" No one in those cheering crowds could know that before the war ended, at least 260,000 Confederate soldiers would lose their lives (along with 365,000 Union soldiers) and that the slave South they fought to defend would be utterly destroyed.

The Border States

Except for Delaware, which remained firmly in the Union, the slave states that bordered free states were sharply divided by the outbreak of war. Leaders in these states talked vaguely of neutrality, but they were to be denied that luxury—Maryland and Missouri immediately, and Kentucky in September 1861 when first Confederate and then Union troops crossed their borders.

SLAVERY AND SECESSION

The higher the proportion of slaves and slaveholders in the population of a southern state, the greater the intensity of secessionist sentiment.

	Percentage of Population Who Were Slaves	Percentage of White Population in Slaveholding Families
Seven states that seceded December 1860–February 1861 (South Carolina, Mississippi, Florida, Alabama, Georgia, Louisiana, Texas)	47%	38%
Four states that seceded after the firing on Fort Sumter (Virginia, Arkansas, Tennessee, North Carolina)	32	24
Four border slave states remaining in Union (Maryland, Delaware, Kentucky, Missouri)	14	15

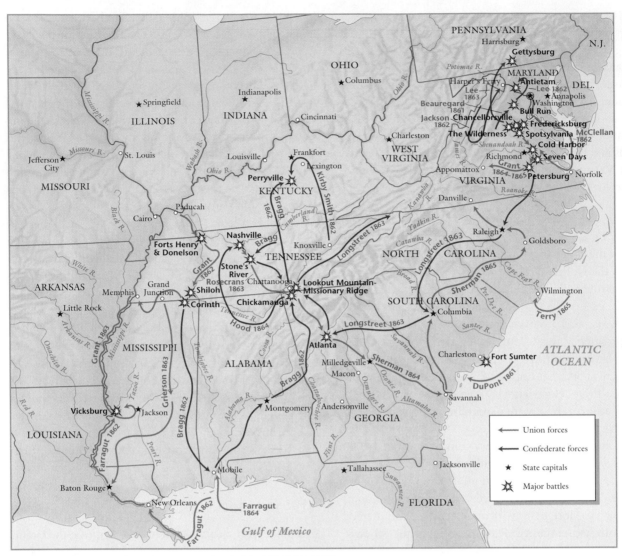

MAP 15.2 PRINCIPAL MILITARY CAMPAIGNS OF THE CIVIL WAR

This map vividly illustrates the contrast between the vast distances over which the armies fought in the western theater of the war and the concentrated campaigns of the Army of the Potomac and the Army of Northern Virginia in the East.

 View an animated version of this map or related maps at http://history.wadsworth.com/murrin_LEP4e.

The first blood was shed in Maryland on April 19, 1861, when a mob attacked Massachusetts troops traveling through Baltimore to Washington. The soldiers fired back, and, in the end, 12 Baltimoreans and 4 soldiers were dead. Confederate partisans burned bridges and tore down telegraph wires, cutting Washington off from the North for nearly a week until additional troops from Massachusetts and New York reopened communications and seized key points in Maryland. The troops also arrested many Confederate sympathizers, including the mayor and police chief of Baltimore, a judge, and two dozen state legislators. To prevent Washington from becoming surrounded by enemy territory, federal forces turned Maryland into an occupied state. Although thousands of Marylanders slipped into Virginia to join the Confederate army, a sub-

stantial majority of Maryland residents remained loyal to the Union.

The same was true of Missouri. Aggressive action by Union commander Nathaniel Lyon provoked a showdown between Unionist and pro-Confederate militia that turned into a riot in St. Louis on May 10 and 11, 1861, in which 36 people died. Lyon then led his troops in a summer campaign that drove the Confederate militia, along with the governor and pro-Southern legislators, into Arkansas, where they formed a Missouri Confederate government in exile. Reinforced by Arkansas regiments, these rebel Missourians invaded their home state, and on August 10 defeated Lyon (who was killed) in the bloody battle of Wilson's Creek in the southwest corner of Missouri. The victorious Confederates marched northward all the way to the Missouri River, capturing a Union garrison at Lexington 40 miles east of Kansas City on September 20. By then, Union forces made up of regiments from Iowa, Illinois, and Kansas as well as Missouri had regrouped and drove the ragged Missouri Confederates back into Arkansas.

From then until the war's end, Unionists maintained political control of Missouri through military power. Even so, continued guerrilla attacks by Confederate "bushwhackers" and counterinsurgency tactics by Unionist "jayhawkers" turned large areas of the state into a no-man's-land of hit-and-run raids, arson, ambush, and murder. During these years, the famous postwar outlaws Jesse and Frank James and Cole and Jim Younger rode with the notorious rebel guerrilla chieftains William Quantrill and "Bloody Bill" Anderson. More than any other state, Missouri suffered from a civil war within the Civil War, and its bitter legacy persisted for generations.

In elections held during summer and fall 1861, Unionists gained firm control of the Kentucky and Maryland legislatures. Kentucky Confederates, like those of Missouri, formed a state government in exile. When the Confederate Congress admitted both Kentucky and Missouri to full representation, the Confederate flag acquired its 13 stars. Nevertheless, two-thirds of the white population in the four border slave states favored the Union, although some of that support was undoubtedly induced by the presence of Union troops.

The Creation of West Virginia

The war produced a fifth Union border state: West Virginia. Most of the delegates from the portion of Virginia west of the Shenandoah Valley had voted against secession. A region of mountains, small farms, and few slaves, western Virginia's economy was linked more closely to nearby Ohio and Pennsylvania than to the South. Its largest city, Wheeling, was 330 miles from Richmond but only 60 miles from Pittsburgh. Delegates who had opposed Virginia's secession from the Union returned home determined to secede from Virginia. With the help of Union troops, who crossed the Ohio River and won a few small battles against Confederate forces in the area during summer 1861, they accomplished their goal. Through a complicated process of conventions and referendums—carried out in the midst of raids and skirmishes—they created the new state of West Virginia, which entered the Union in 1863.

Indian Territory and the Southwest

To the south and west of Missouri, civil war raged along a different border—between Southern states and territories—for control of the resources of that vast region. In the Indian Territory (present-day Oklahoma), the Native Americans, who had been resettled there from Eastern states in the generation before the war, chose sides and carried on bloody guerrilla warfare against each other as ferocious as the bushwhacking in Missouri. The more prosperous Indians of the five "civilized tribes" (Cherokees, Creeks, Seminoles, Chickasaws, and Choctaws), many of them of mixed blood and some of them slaveholders, tended to side with the Confederacy. Some tribes signed treaties of alliance with the Confederate government. Aided by white and black Union regiments operating out of Kansas and Missouri, the pro-Union Indians gradually gained control of most of the Indian Territory.

In the meantime, Confederates had made their boldest bid to fulfill antebellum Southern ambitions to win the Southwest. A small army composed mostly of Texans pushed up the Rio Grande valley into New Mexico in 1861. The following February, they launched a deeper strike to capture Santa Fe. With luck, they hoped to push even farther westward and northward to gain the mineral wealth of California and Colorado gold mines, whose millions were already helping to finance the Union war effort and could do wonders for Confederate finances. A good many Southerners lived in these Western territories and in California.

At first, the Confederate drive up the Rio Grande went well. The Texans won a victory over the Unionist New Mexico militia and a handful of regulars at the battle of Valverde, 100 miles south of Albuquerque, on February 21, 1862. They continued up the valley, occupied Albuquerque and Santa Fe, and pushed on toward Fort Union near Santa Fe. But Colorado miners who had organized themselves into Union regiments and had carried out the greatest march of the war, over the rugged Rockies in winter, met the Texans in the battle of Glorieta Pass on March 26–28. The battle was a tactical draw, but a unit of Coloradans destroyed the Confederate wagon train, forcing the Southerners into a disastrous retreat back to Texas. Of the 3,700 who had started out to win the West for the Confederacy, only 2,000 made it back. The Confederates had shot their bolt in this region; the West and Southwest remained safe for the Union.

The Balance Sheet of War

If one counts three-quarters of the border state population (including free blacks) as pro-Union, the total number of people in Union states in 1861 was 22.5 million, compared with 9 million in the Confederate states. The North's military manpower advantage was even greater because the Confederate population total included 3.7 million slaves compared with 300,000 slaves in Union areas. At first, neither side expected to recruit blacks as soldiers. Eventually, the Union did enlist 180,000 black soldiers and at least 10,000 black sailors; the Confederacy held out against that drastic step until the war was virtually over. Altogether, about 2.1 million men fought for the Union and 850,000 for the Confederacy. That was close to half of the North's male population of military age (18 to 40) and three-quarters of the comparable Confederate white population. Because the labor force of the South consisted mainly of slaves, the Confederacy was able to enlist a larger proportion of its white population.

The North's economic superiority was even greater. The Union states possessed nine-tenths of the country's industrial capacity and registered shipping, four-fifths of its bank capital, three-fourths of its railroad mileage and rolling stock, and three-fourths of its taxable wealth.

These statistics gave pause to some Southerners. In a long war that mobilized the total resources of both sides,

the North's advantages might prove decisive. But in 1861, few anticipated how long and intense the war would be. Both sides expected a short and victorious conflict. Confederates seemed especially confident, partly because of their vaunted sense of martial superiority over the "blue-bellied" Yankee nation of shopkeepers. Many Southerners really did believe that one of their own could lick three Yankees. "Let brave men advance with flintlocks and old-fashioned bayonets, on the popinjays of Northern cities," said ex-Governor Henry Wise of Virginia, now a Confederate general, and "the Yankees would break and run."

Although this turned out to be a grievous miscalculation, the South did have some reason to believe that its martial qualities were superior. A higher proportion of Southerners than Northerners had attended West Point and other military schools, had fought in the Mexican War, or had served as officers in the regular army. Volunteer military companies were more prevalent in the ante-

HISTORY THROUGH FILM

The Red Badge of Courage (1951)

Directed by John Huston. Starring Audie Murphy (The Youth) and Bill Mauldin (The Loud Soldier).

Stephen Crane's short novel *The Red Badge of Courage* became an instant classic when it was published in 1895. Civil War veterans praised its realistic descriptions of the confusion, terror, chaos, courage, despair, and adrenaline-driven rage of men in battle. A story of young Henry Fleming (The Youth) and his buddy Wilson (The Loud Soldier) in their first battle (Chancellorsville), the novel traces Henry's transition from boyhood to manhood, from raw recruit to veteran, over two days of violent combat. Intended by Crane as a portrait of soldiers facing the ultimate moment of truth in combat, the novel strives for universality rather than specificity as a Civil War story. Thus the battle is not actually named (although circumstances make clear that it is Chancellorsville, despite the film misleadingly dating it in 1862). The 304th New York regiment is fictional, and even the fact that it is a Civil War battle is scarcely mentioned. Crane did achieve a sort of universality; the novel is a story of men at war—not simply a story of the Civil War.

The film remains more faithful to the book than most movies based on novels. Most of the dialogue is taken directly from Crane. Henry Fleming's self-doubts, fears, and eventual heroism after he first runs away are brilliantly portrayed on the screen by action and dialogue against a background of a narrator's words. Fleming is played by Audie Murphy, America's most decorated soldier in the Second World War, and Wilson by Bill Mauldin, whose Willie and Joe cartoons provided the most enduring images of the American infantryman in that war. Virtually unknown as actors before this film, they make the characters come alive with moving performances.

Much of the credit for this success belongs to director John Huston, who brought out the best in his inexperienced actors. One of Hollywood's most prominent directors, Huston had lobbied Louis Mayer of MGM to produce the film. Believing that "Nobody wants to see a Civil War movie," Mayer finally gave in but provided Huston with a skimpy budget. When Huston flew to Africa immediately

THE BALANCE SHEET OF WAR ■ 479

bellum South than in the North. As a rural people, Southerners were proficient in hunting, riding, and other outdoor skills useful in military operations. Moreover, the South had begun to prepare for war earlier than the North. As each state seceded, it mobilized militia and volunteer military companies. On March 6, 1861, the Confederate Congress had authorized an army of 100,000 men. By the time Lincoln called for 75,000 militia after the fall of Fort Sumter, the Confederacy already had 60,000 men under arms. Not until summer 1861 would the North's greater manpower begin to make itself felt in the form of a larger army.

Strategy and Morale

Even when fully mobilized, the North's superior resources did not guarantee success. Its military task was much more difficult than that of the South. The Confederacy had come into being in firm control of 750,000 square miles—a vast territory larger than all of Western Europe and twice as large as the 13 colonies in 1776. To win the war, Union forces would have to invade, conquer, and occupy much of that territory, cripple its people's ability to sustain a war of independence, and destroy its armies. Britain had been unable to accomplish a similar task in the war for independence, even though it enjoyed a far greater superiority of resources over the United States in 1776 than the Union enjoyed over the Confederacy in 1861. Victory does not always ride with the heaviest battalions.

To "win" the war, the Confederacy did not need to invade or conquer the Union or even to destroy its armies; it needed only to stand on the defensive and prevent the North from destroying Southern armies—to hold out long enough to convince Northerners that the cost of victory was too high. Most Confederates were confident in 1861 that they were more than equal to the task. Most

Audie Murphy (Henry Fleming), Bill Mauldin (The Loud Soldier), and their comrades in *The Red Badge of Courage.*

© Springer/Corbis.

after the filming was completed to begin directing *The African Queen,* studio executives cut several of Huston's scenes and reduced the movie's length to 69 minutes. The studio also did little to promote the film, and because audiences failed to identify with its grim realism and mostly unknown cast, *The Red Badge of Courage* was a box-office failure. Like the novel, however, it has become a classic that is still, a half-century after it was filmed, one of the best cinematic portrayals of the psychology of men in combat.

European military experts agreed. The military analyst of the London *Times* wrote:

> It is one thing to drive the rebels from the south bank of the Potomac, or even to occupy Richmond, but another to reduce and hold in permanent subjection a tract of country nearly as large as Russia in Europe. . . . No war of independence ever terminated unsuccessfully except where the disparity of force was far greater than it is in this case. . . . Just as England during the revolution had to give up conquering the colonies so the North will have to give up conquering the South.

The important factor of morale also seemed to favor the Confederacy. To be sure, Union soldiers fought for powerful symbols: nation, flag, constitution. "We are fighting to maintain the best government on earth" was a common phrase in their letters and diaries. It is a "grate [sic] struggle for Union, Constitution, and law," wrote a New Jersey soldier. A Chicago newspaper declared that the South had "outraged the Constitution, set at defiance all law, and trampled under foot that flag which has been the glorious and consecrated symbol of American Liberty."

But Confederates, too, fought for nation, flag, constitution, and liberty—of whites. In addition, they fought to defend their land, homes, and families against invading "Yankee vandals" who many Southern whites quite literally believed were coming to "free the negroes and force amalgamation between them and the children of the poor men of the South." An army fighting in defense of its homeland generally has the edge in morale. "We shall have the enormous advantage of fighting on our own territory and for our very existence," wrote a Confederate leader. "All the world over, are not one million of men defending themselves at home against invasion stronger in a mere military point of view, than five millions [invading] a foreign country?"

Mobilizing for War

More than four-fifths of the soldiers on both sides were volunteers; in the first two years of the war, nearly all of them were. The Confederacy passed a conscription law in April 1862, and the Union followed suit in March 1863, but even afterward, most recruits were volunteers. In both North and South, patriotic rallies with martial music and speeches motivated local men to enlist in a company (100 men) organized by the area's leading citizens. The recruits elected their own company officers (a captain and two lieutenants), who received their commissions from the state governor. A regiment consisted of 10 infantry companies, and each regiment was commanded by a colonel, with a lieutenant colonel and a major as second and third in command—all of them appointed by the governor.

THE RICHMOND GRAYS

This photograph depicts a typical volunteer military unit that joined the Confederate army in 1861. Note the determined and confident appearance of these young men. By 1865, one-third of them would be dead and several others maimed for life.

Cook Collection, Valentine Museum, Richmond, Virginia.

Cavalry regiments were organized in a similar manner. Field artillery units were known as batteries, a grouping of four or six cannon with their caissons and limber chests (two-wheeled, horse-drawn vehicles) to carry ammunition; the full complement of a six-gun battery was 155 men and 72 horses.

Volunteer units received a state designation and number in the order of their completion—the 2nd Massachusetts Volunteer Infantry, the 5th Virginia Cavalry, and so on. In most regiments, the men in each company generally came from the same town or locality. Some Union regiments were composed of men of a particular ethnic group. By the end of the war, the Union army had raised about 2,000 infantry and cavalry regiments and 700 batteries; the Confederates had organized just under half as many. As the war went on, the original thousand-man complement of a regiment was usually whittled down to half or less by disease, casualties, desertions, and detachments. The states generally preferred to organize new regiments rather than keep the old ones up to full strength.

These were citizen soldiers, not professionals. They carried their peacetime notions of democracy and discipline into the army. That is why, in the tradition of the citizen militia, the men elected their company officers and sometimes their field officers (colonel, lieutenant colonel, and major) as well. Professional military men deplored the egalitarianism and slack discipline that resulted. Political influence often counted for more than military training in the election and appointment of officers. These civilians in uniform were extremely awkward and unmilitary at first, and some regiments suffered battlefield disasters because of inadequate training, discipline, and leadership. Yet this was the price that a democratic society with a tiny professional army had to pay to mobilize large armies almost overnight to meet a crisis. In time, these raw recruits became battle-hardened veterans commanded by experienced officers who had survived the weeding-out process of combat or of examination boards or who had been promoted from the ranks.

As the two sides organized their field armies, both grouped four or more regiments into brigades and three or more brigades into divisions. By 1862, they began grouping two or more divisions into corps and two or more corps into armies. Each of these larger units was commanded by a general appointed by the president. Most of the higher-ranking generals on both sides were West Point graduates, but others were appointed because they represented an important political, regional, or (in the North) ethnic constituency whose support Lincoln or Davis wished to solidify. Some of these "political" generals, like elected regimental officers, were incompetent, but as the war went on, they too either learned their trade or were weeded out. Some outstanding generals emerged from civilian life and were promoted up the ranks during the war. In both the Union and the Confederate armies, the best officers (including generals) *led* their men by example as much as by precept; they commanded from the front, not the rear. Combat casualties were higher among officers than among privates, and highest of all among generals, who died in action at a rate 50 percent higher than enlisted men.

Weapons and Tactics

In Civil War battles, the infantry rifle was the most lethal weapon. Muskets and rifles caused 80 to 90 percent of the combat casualties. From 1862 on, most of these weapons were "rifled"—that is, they had spiral grooves cut in the barrel to impart a spin to the bullet. This innovation was only a decade old, dating to the perfection in the 1850s of the "minié ball" (named after French army Captain Claude Minié, its principal inventor), a cone-shaped lead bullet with a base that expanded on firing to "take" the rifling of the barrel. This made it possible to load and fire a muzzle-loading rifle as rapidly (two or three times per minute) as the old smoothbore musket. Moreover, the rifle had greater accuracy and at least four times the effective range (400 yards or more) of the smoothbore.

Civil War infantry tactics adjusted only gradually to the greater lethal range and accuracy of the new rifle, however, for the prescribed massed formations had emerged from experience with the smoothbore musket. Close-order assaults against defenders equipped with rifles resulted in enormous casualties. The defensive power of the rifle became even greater when troops began digging into trenches. Massed frontal assaults became almost suicidal. Soldiers and their officers learned the hard way to adopt skirmishing tactics, taking advantage of cover and working around the enemy flank.

Logistics

Wars are fought not only by men and weapons but also by the logistical apparatus that supports and supplies them. The Civil War is often called the world's first modern war because of the role played by railroads, steam-powered ships, and the telegraph, which did not exist in earlier wars fought on a similar scale (those of the French Revolution and Napoleon). Railroads and steamboats transported supplies and soldiers with unprecedented speed and efficiency; the telegraph provided instantaneous communication between army headquarters and field commanders.

Yet these modern forms of transport and communications were extremely vulnerable. Cavalry raiders and guerrillas could cut telegraph wires, burn railroad bridges, and tear up the tracks. Confederate cavalry became particularly skillful at sundering the supply lines of invading Union armies and thereby neutralizing forces several times larger than their own. The more deeply the Union armies penetrated into the South, the more men they had to detach to guard bridges, depots, and supply dumps.

Once the campaigning armies had moved away from their railhead or wharfside supply base, they returned to dependence on animal-powered transport. Depending on terrain, road conditions, length of supply line, and proportion of artillery and cavalry, Union armies required one horse or mule for every two or three men. Thus a large invading Union army of 100,000 men (the approximate number in Virginia from 1862 to 1865 and in Georgia in 1864) would need about 40,000 draft animals. Confederate armies, operating mostly in friendly territory closer to

Photo by Timothy O'Sullivan, Chicago Historical Society, ICHi-08091.

UNION ARMY WAGON TRAIN IN VIRGINIA, 1863

By 1863, the productive power of farms and factories in the North had made the Union Army the best-fed and best-equipped army in history to that time. This supply wagon train testifies to the logistical efficiency of Union forces.

their bases, needed fewer. The poorly drained dirt roads typical of much of the South turned into a morass of mud in the frequently wet weather.

These logistical problems did much to offset the industrial supremacy of the North, particularly during the first year of the war when bottlenecks, shortages, and inefficiency marked the logistical effort on both sides. By 1862, though, the North's economy had fully geared up for war, making the Union army the best-supplied army in history up to that time.

Confederate officials accomplished impressive feats of improvisation in creating war industries, especially munitions and gunpowder, but the Southern industrial base was too slender to sustain adequate production. Particularly troublesome for the Confederacy was its inability to replace rails and rolling stock for its railroads. Although the South produced plenty of food, the railroads deteriorated to the point that food could not reach soldiers or civilians. As the war went into its third and fourth years, the Northern economy grew stronger and the Southern economy grew weaker.

Financing the War

One of the greatest defects of the Confederate economy was finance. Of the three methods of paying for a war—taxation, loans, and treasury notes (paper money)—treasury notes are the most inflationary because they pump new money into the economy. By contrast, taxation and loans (war bonds) soak up money and thus counteract inflation. Although Confederate treasury officials were quite aware of this difference, the Confederate Congress, wary of dampening patriotic ardor, was slow to raise taxes. And because most capital in the South was tied up in land and slaves, little was available for buying war bonds.

So, expecting a short war, the Confederate Congress authorized a limited issue of treasury notes in 1861, to be redeemable in specie (gold or silver) within two years after the end of the war. The first modest issue was followed by many more because the notes declined in value from the outset. The rate of decline increased during periods of Confederate military reverses, when people wondered whether the government would survive. At the end of

1861, the Confederate inflation rate was 12 percent every *month;* by early 1863, it took eight dollars to buy what one dollar had bought two years earlier; just before the war's end, the Confederate dollar was worth one U.S. cent.

In 1863, the Confederate Congress tried to stem runaway inflation by passing a comprehensive law that taxed income, consumer purchases, and business transactions and included a "tax in kind" on agricultural products, allowing tax officials to seize 10 percent of a farmer's crops. This tax was extremely unpopular among farmers, many of whom hid their crops and livestock or refused to plant, thereby worsening the Confederacy's food shortages. The tax legislation was too little and too late to remedy the South's fiscal chaos. The Confederate government raised less than 5 percent of its revenue by taxes and less than 40 percent by loans, leaving 60 percent to be created by the printing press. That turned out to be a recipe for disaster.

In contrast, the Union government raised 66 percent of its revenue by selling war bonds, 21 percent by taxes, and only 13 percent by printing treasury notes. The Legal Tender Act authorizing these notes—the famous "greenbacks," the origin of modern paper money in the United States—passed in February 1862. Congress had enacted new taxes in 1861—including the first income tax in American history—and had authorized the sale of war bonds. By early 1862, however, these measures had not yet raised enough revenue to pay for the rapid military buildup. To avert a crisis, Congress created the greenbacks. Instead of promising to redeem them in specie at some future date, as the South had done, Congress made them "legal tender"—that is, it required everyone to accept them as real money at face value. The North's economy suffered inflation during the war—about 80 percent over four years—but that was mild compared with the 9,000 percent inflation in the Confederacy. The greater strength and diversity of the North's economy, together with wiser fiscal legislation, accounted for the contrast.

The Union Congress also passed the National Banking Act of 1863. Before the war, the principal form of money had been notes issued by state-chartered banks. After Andrew Jackson's destruction of the Second Bank of the United States (chapter 12), the number and variety of bank notes had skyrocketed until 7,000 different kinds of state bank notes were circulating in 1860. Some were virtually worthless; others circulated at a discount from face value. The National Banking Act of 1863 resulted from the desire of Whiggish Republicans to resurrect the centralized banking system and create a more stable banknote currency, as well as to finance the war. Under the act, chartered national banks could issue bank notes up to 90 percent of the value of the U.S. bonds they held. This provision created a market for the bonds and, in combination with the greenbacks, replaced the glut of state bank notes with a more uniform national currency. To further the cause, in 1865, Congress imposed a tax of 10 percent on state bank notes, thereby taxing them out of existence.

National bank notes would be an important form of money for the next half-century. They had two defects, however: First, because the number of notes that could be issued was tied to each bank's holdings of U.S. bonds, the volume of currency available depended on the amount of federal debt rather than on the economic needs of the country. Second, the bank notes tended to concentrate in the Northeast, where most of the large national banks were located, leaving the South and West short. The creation of the Federal Reserve System in 1913 (chapter 21) largely remedied these defects, but Civil War legislation established the principle of a uniform national currency issued and regulated by the federal government.

🫖 Navies, the Blockade, and Foreign Relations

To sustain its war effort, the Confederacy needed to import large quantities of material from abroad. To shut off these imports and the exports of cotton that paid for them, on April 19, 1861, Lincoln proclaimed a blockade of Confederate ports. At first, the blockade was more a policy than a reality because the navy had only a few ships on hand to enforce it. The task was formidable; the Confederate coastline stretched for 3,500 miles, with two dozen major ports and another 150 bays and coves where cargo could be landed. The U.S. Navy, which since the 1840s had been converting from sail to steam, recalled its ships from distant seas, took old sailing vessels out of mothballs, and bought or chartered merchant ships and armed them. Eventually, the navy placed several hundred warships on blockade duty. But in 1861, the blockade was so thin that 9 of every 10 vessels slipped through it on their way to or from Confederate ports.

King Cotton Diplomacy

The Confederacy, however, inadvertently contributed to the blockade's success when it adopted King Cotton diplomacy. Cotton was vital to the British economy because textiles were at the heart of British industry—and three-fourths of Britain's supply of raw cotton came from the South. If that supply was cut off, Southerners reasoned, British factories would shut down, unemployed workers would starve, and Britain would face the prospect of revolution. Rather than risk such a consequence, people in the South believed that Britain (and other powers) would recognize the Confederacy's independence and then use the powerful British navy to break the blockade.

Southerners were so firmly convinced of cotton's importance to the British economy that they kept the 1861 cotton crop at home rather than try to export it through the blockade, hoping thereby to compel the British to intervene. But the strategy backfired. Bumper crops in 1859 and 1860 had piled up a surplus of cotton in British warehouses and delayed the anticipated "cotton famine" until 1862. In the end, the South's voluntary embargo of cotton cost them dearly. The Confederacy missed its chance to ship out its cotton and store it abroad, where it could be used as collateral for loans to purchase war matériel.

Moreover, the Confederacy's King Cotton diplomacy contradicted its own foreign policy objective: to persuade the British and French governments to refuse to recognize the legality of the blockade. Under international law, a blockade must be "physically effective" to be respected by neutral nations. Confederate diplomats claimed that the Union effort was a mere "paper blockade," yet the dearth of cotton reaching European ports as a result of the South's embargo suggested to British and French diplomats that the blockade was at least partly effective, and by 1862 it was. Slow-sailing ships with large cargo capacity rarely tried to run the blockade, and the sleek, fast, steam-powered "blockade runners" that became increasingly prominent had a smaller cargo capacity and charged high rates because of the growing risk of capture or sinking by the Union navy. Although most blockade runners got through, by 1862 the blockade had reduced the Confederacy's seaborne commerce enough to convince the British government to recognize it as legitimate. The blockade was also squeezing the South's economy. After lifting its cotton embargo in 1862, the Confederacy had increasing difficulty exporting enough cotton through the blockade to pay for needed imports.

Confederate foreign policy also failed to win diplomatic recognition by other nations. That recognition would have conferred international legitimacy on the Confederacy and might even have led to treaties of alliance or of foreign aid. The French Emperor Napoleon III expressed sympathy for the Confederacy, as did influential groups in the British Parliament, but Prime Minister Lord Palmerston and Foreign Minister John Russell refused to recognize the Confederacy while it was engaged in a war it might lose, especially if recognition might jeopardize relations with the United States. The Union foreign policy team of Secretary of State Seward and Minister to England Charles Francis Adams did a superb job. Seward issued blunt warnings against recognizing the Confederacy; Adams softened them with the velvet glove of diplomacy. Other nations followed Britain's lead; by 1862, it had become clear that Britain would withhold recognition until the Confederacy had virtually won its independence—but, of course, such recognition would have come too late to help the Confederacy win.

The *Trent* Affair

If anything illustrated the frustrations of Confederate diplomacy, it was the *Trent* Affair, which came tantalizingly close to rupturing British–American relations to Confederate advantage, but did not. In October 1861, Southern envoys James Mason and John Slidell slipped through the blockade. Mason hoped to represent the Confederacy in London and Slidell in Paris. On November 8, Captain Charles Wilkes of the U.S.S. *San Jacinto* stopped the British mail steamer *Trent*, with Mason and Slidell on board, near Cuba.

THE CONFEDERATE BLOCKADE RUNNER *ROBERT E. LEE*
Confederate armies depended heavily on supplies brought in from abroad on blockade runners, paid for by cotton smuggled out through the Union naval cordon by these same blockade runners. The sleek, narrow-beamed ships with raked masts and smokestacks (which could be telescoped to deck level) were designed for speed and deception to elude the blockade—a feat successfully accomplished on four-fifths of their voyages during the war. One of the most successful runners was the *Robert E. Lee,* photographed here after it had run the blockade 14 times before being captured on the 15th attempt.

Benjamin Moran Helps Prevent British Intervention in the Civil War

Learning the trade of printer as a young man in Philadelphia, Benjamin Moran (1820–1886) aspired to be a writer and in 1851 sailed for England, where two years later he published a book describing his walking tours of the island. He also met and married a British woman. In 1854, he began his career as a diplomat, serving as private secretary to James Buchanan, then the U.S. minister to Britain. For the next 20 years, Moran provided essential continuity for the American legation in London through five presidential administrations and six ministers. Moran was promoted to assistant secretary of legation in 1857 and secretary of legation in 1864. During the frequent absences of ministers, he served as charge d'affaires. In 1874, he was appointed minister to Portugal, where he remained until his retirement in 1882. In effect, he was the first professional foreign service officer of the United States before such a category officially existed.

Moran made his most important contribution during the Civil War, when his knowledge of British culture and politics plus his wide acquaintance with men of influence in England were of crucial assistance to Minister Charles Francis Adams in his efforts to prevent British intervention in the American war. During a House of Commons debate in July 1862 that seemed certain to result in a resolution calling for recognition of the Confederacy, Moran headed off the motion by producing a dispatch denying rumors of a Confederate capture of the Union Army of the Potomac.

During his years of service, Moran kept a detailed diary, which is an essential source for understanding Anglo-American relations. His acidulous comments on the anti-Union sympathies of large elements of the British press, Parliament, and the upper classes may overstate the case but are nevertheless enlightening. Professing to dislike slavery, many Britons initially sneered at Lincoln's Emancipation Proclamation, wrote Moran in October 1862, "thus showing the hollowness of the anti-slavery professions of this people." By January 1863, however, Moran could write: "The President's Proclamation continues to be productive of much good here. People now see that slavery is at the bottom of this war, and that the Government is fighting for freedom."

Historical Society of Pennsylvania.

BENJAMIN MORAN

Wilkes arrested the two Southerners, took them to Boston, and became an instant hero in the North. When the news reached England, the British government and public were outraged by Wilkes's "high-handed" action. Although the Royal Navy had acted in similar fashion during the centuries when Britannia ruled the waves, John Bull (England) would not take this behavior from his brash American cousin Jonathan (the United States). Britain demanded an apology and the release of Mason and Slidell. The popular press on both sides of the Atlantic stirred up war fever. Soon, however, good sense prevailed and Britain softened its demands. With a philosophy of "one war at a time," the Lincoln administration released Mason and Slidell the day after Christmas 1861, declaring that Captain Wilkes had acted "without instructions." The British accepted this statement in lieu of an apology, and the crisis ended.

The Confederate Navy

Lacking the capacity to build a naval force at home, the Confederacy hoped to use British shipyards for the purpose. Through a loophole in the British neutrality law, two fast commerce raiders built in Liverpool made their way into Confederate hands in 1862. Named the *Florida* and the *Alabama,* they roamed the seas for the next two years, capturing or sinking Union merchant ships and whalers. The *Alabama* was the most feared raider. Commanded by the leading Confederate sea dog, Raphael Semmes, she sank 62 merchant vessels plus a Union warship before another warship, the U.S.S. *Kearsarge* (whose captain, John A. Winslow, had once been Semmes's messmate in the old navy), sank the *Alabama* off Cherbourg, France, on June 19, 1864. Altogether, Confederate privateers and commerce raiders destroyed or captured 257 Union merchant vessels and drove at least 700 others to foreign registry. This Confederate achievement, although spectacular,

made only a tiny dent in the Union war effort, especially when compared with the 1,500 blockade runners captured or destroyed by the Union navy, not to mention the thousands of others that decided not to even try to beat the blockade.

The *Monitor* and the *Virginia*

Its inadequate shipbuilding facilities prevented the Confederate navy from challenging Union seapower where it counted most—along the coasts and rivers of the South. Still, though plagued by shortages on every hand, the Confederate navy department demonstrated great skill at innovation. Southern engineers developed "torpedoes"

THE MONITOR AND MERRIMAC

This black-and-white photograph shows the crew of the Union ironclad *Monitor* standing in front of its revolving two-gun turret. In action, the sun canopy above the turret would be taken down, and all sailors would be at their stations inside the turret or the hull, as shown in the color painting of the famed battle, on March 9, 1862, between the *Monitor* and the Confederate *Virginia* (informally called the *Merrimac* because it had been converted from the captured U.S. frigate *Merrimack*). There is no photograph of the *Virginia*, which was blown up by its crew two months later when the Confederates retreated toward Richmond because its draft was too deep to go up the James River.

From the Collections of the Library of Congress.

© Bettmann/Corbis.

(mines) that sank or damaged 43 Union warships in southern bays and rivers. The South also constructed the world's first combat submarine, the *H. L. Hunley,* which sank a blockade ship off Charleston in 1864 but then went down herself before she could return to shore. Another important innovation was the building of ironclad "rams" to sink the blockade ships. The idea of iron armor for warships was not new—the British and French navies had prototype ironclads in 1861—but the Confederacy built the first one to see action. It was the C.S.S. *Virginia,* commonly called (even in the South) the *Merrimac* because it was rebuilt from the steam frigate U.S.S. *Merrimack,* which had been burned to the waterline by the Union navy at Norfolk when the Confederates seized the naval base there in April 1861. Ready for its trial-by-combat on March 8, 1862, the *Virginia* steamed out to attack the blockade squadron at Hampton Roads. She sank one warship with her iron ram and another with her 10 guns. Other Union ships ran aground trying to escape, to be finished off (Confederates expected) the next day. Union shot and shells bounced off the *Virginia's* armor plate. It was the worst day the U.S. Navy would have until December 7, 1941.

Panic seized Washington and the whole northeastern seaboard. In almost Hollywood fashion, however, the Union's own ironclad sailed into Hampton Roads in the nick of time and saved the rest of the fleet. This was the U.S.S. *Monitor,* completed just days earlier at the Brooklyn navy yard. Much smaller than the *Virginia,* with two 11-inch guns in a revolving turret (an innovation) set on a deck almost flush with the water, the *Monitor* looked like a "tin can on a shingle." It presented a small target and was capable of concentrating considerable firepower in a given direction with its revolving turret. The next day, the *Monitor* fought the *Virginia* in history's first battle between ironclads. It was a draw, but the *Virginia* limped home to Norfolk never again to menace the Union fleet. Although the Confederacy built other ironclad rams, some never saw action and none achieved the initial success of the *Virginia.* By the war's end, the Union navy had built or started 58 ships of the *Monitor* class (some of them double-turreted), launching a new age in naval history that ended the classic "heart of oak" era of warships.

☙ Campaigns and Battles, 1861–1862

Wars can be won only by hard fighting. This was a truth that some leaders on both sides overlooked. One of them was Winfield Scott, General-in-Chief of the U.S. Army. Scott, a Virginian who had remained loyal to the Union,

evolved a military strategy based on his conviction that a great many Southerners were eager to be won back to the Union. The main elements of his strategy were a naval blockade and a combined army-navy expedition to take control of the Mississippi, thus sealing off the Confederacy on all sides and enabling the Union to "bring them to terms with less bloodshed than by any other plan." The Northern press ridiculed Scott's strategy as the Anaconda Plan, after the South American snake that squeezes its prey to death.

The Battle of Bull Run

Most Northerners believed that the South could be overcome only by victory in battle. Virginia emerged as the most likely battleground, especially after the Confederate government moved its capital to Richmond in May 1861. "Forward to Richmond," clamored Northern newspapers, and forward toward Richmond moved a Union army of 35,000 men in July, despite Scott's misgivings and those of the army's field commander, Irvin McDowell. McDowell believed his raw, 90-day Union militia were not ready to fight a real battle. They got no farther than Bull Run, a sluggish stream 25 miles southwest of Washington, where a Confederate army commanded by Beauregard had been deployed to defend a key rail junction at Manassas.

Another small Confederate army in the Shenandoah Valley under General Joseph E. Johnston had given a Union force the slip and had traveled to Manassas by rail to reinforce Beauregard. On July 21, the attacking Federals forded Bull Run and hit the rebels on the left flank, driving them back. By early afternoon, the Federals seemed to be on the verge of victory, but a Virginia brigade commanded by Thomas J. Jackson stood "like a stone wall," earning Jackson the nickname he carried ever after. By midafternoon, Confederate reinforcements—including one brigade just off the train from the Shenandoah Valley—had grouped for a screaming counterattack (the famed "rebel yell" was first heard here). They drove the exhausted and disorganized Yankees back across Bull Run in a retreat that turned into a rout.

Although the Battle of Manassas (or Bull Run, as Northerners called it) was small by later Civil War standards, it made a profound impression on both sides. Of the 18,000 soldiers actually engaged on each side, Union casualties (killed, wounded, and captured) were about 2,800 and Confederate casualties 2,000. The victory exhilarated Confederates and confirmed their belief in their martial superiority. It also gave them a morale advantage in the Virginia theater that persisted for two years. And yet, Manassas also bred overconfidence. Some in the South thought the war was won. Northerners, by contrast, were

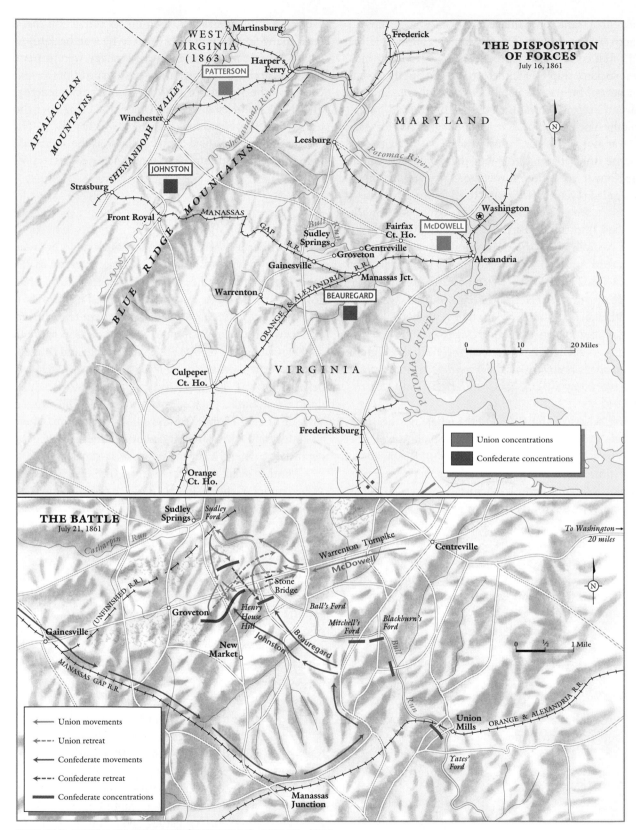

MAP 15.3 BATTLE OF BULL RUN (MANASSAS), JULY 21, 1861

The key to Confederate victory in the war's first major battle was the failure of Union General Robert Patterson to prevent the Confederate troops under General Joseph Johnston (upper map) from joining those under General Pierre G. T. Beauregard via the Manassas Gap Railroad (lower map) for a counterattack that won the battle.

jolted out of their expectations of a short war. A new mood of reality and grim determination gripped the North. Congress authorized the enlistment of up to 1 million three-year volunteers. Hundreds of thousands flocked to recruiting offices in the next few months. Lincoln called General George B. McClellan to Washington to organize the new troops into the Army of the Potomac.

An energetic, talented officer who was only 34 years old and small of stature but great with an aura of destiny, McClellan soon won the nickname "The Young Napoleon." He had commanded the Union forces that gained control of West Virginia, and he took firm control in Washington during summer and fall 1861. He organized and trained the Army of the Potomac into a large, well-disciplined, and well-equipped fighting force. He was just what the North needed after its dispiriting defeat at Bull Run. When Scott stepped down as General-in-Chief on November 1, McClellan took his place.

As winter approached, however, and McClellan did nothing to advance against the smaller Confederate army whose outposts stood only a few miles from Washington, his failings as a commander began to show. He was a perfectionist in a profession where nothing could ever be perfect. His army was perpetually *almost* ready to move. McClellan was afraid to take risks; he never learned the military lesson that no victory can be won without risking defeat. He consistently overestimated the strength of enemy forces facing him and used these faulty estimates as a reason for inaction until he could increase his own force. When newspapers began to publish criticism of McClellan from within the administration and among Republicans in Congress (he was a Democrat), he accused his critics of political motives. Having built a fine fighting machine, he was afraid to start it up for fear it might break. The caution that McClellan instilled in the Army of the Potomac's officer corps persisted for more than a year after Lincoln removed him from command in November 1862.

Naval Operations

Because of McClellan, no significant action occurred in the Virginia theater after the Battle of Bull Run until spring 1862. Meanwhile, the Union navy won a series of victories over Confederate coastal forts at Hatteras Inlet on the North Carolina coast, Port Royal Sound in South Carolina, and other points along the Atlantic and Gulf coasts. These successes provided new bases from which to expand and tighten the blockade. They also provided small Union armies with takeoff points for operations along the southern coast. In February and March 1862, an expeditionary force under General Ambrose Burnside won a string of victories and occupied several crucial ports on the North Carolina sounds. Another Union force captured Fort Pulaski at the mouth of the Savannah River, cutting off that important Confederate port from the sea.

One of the Union navy's most impressive achievements was the capture in April 1862 of New Orleans, the Confederacy's largest city and principal port. Most Confederate troops in the area had been called up the Mississippi to confront a Union invasion of Tennessee, leaving only some militia, an assortment of steamboats converted into gunboats, and two strong forts flanking the river 70 miles below New Orleans. That was not enough to stop Union naval commander David G. Farragut, a native of Tennessee who was still loyal to the U.S. Navy in which he had served for a half century. In a daring action on April 24, 1862, Farragut led his fleet upriver past the forts, scattering the Confederate fleet and fending off fire rafts. He lost four ships, but the rest won through and compelled the surrender of New Orleans with nine-inch naval guns trained on its streets. Fifteen thousand Union soldiers marched in and occupied the city and its hinterland.

Fort Henry and Fort Donelson

These victories demonstrated the importance of seapower even in a civil war. Even more important were Union victories won by the combined efforts of the army and fleets of river gunboats on the Tennessee and Cumberland rivers, which flow through Tennessee and Kentucky and empty into the Ohio River just before it joins the Mississippi. The unlikely hero of these victories was Ulysses S. Grant, who had failed in several civilian occupations after resigning from the peacetime military in 1854. Grant rejoined when war broke out. His quiet efficiency and determined will won him promotion from Illinois colonel to brigadier general and the command of a small but growing force based at Cairo, Illinois, in fall 1861. When Confederate units entered Kentucky in September, Grant moved quickly to occupy the mouths of the Cumberland and Tennessee rivers. Unlike McClellan, who had known nothing but success in his career and was afraid to jeopardize that record, Grant's experience of failure made him willing to take risks. Having little to lose, he demonstrated that willingness dramatically in the early months of 1862.

Military strategists on both sides understood the importance of these navigable rivers as highways of invasion into the South's heartland. The Confederacy had built forts at strategic points along the rivers and had begun to convert a few steamboats into gunboats and rams to back up the forts. The Union also converted steamboats into "timberclad" gunboats—so called because they were

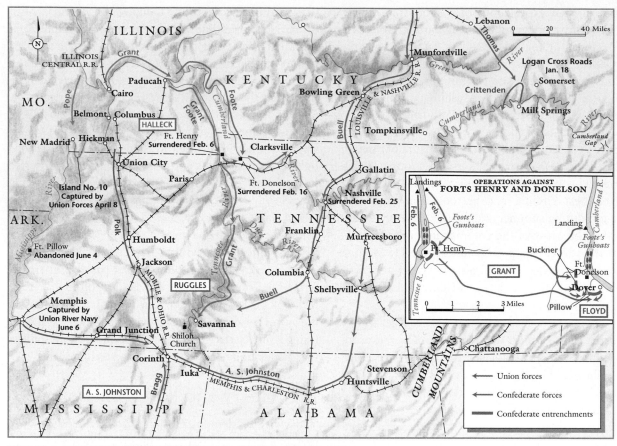

MAP 15.4 KENTUCKY–TENNESSEE THEATER, WINTER–SPRING 1862

This map illustrates the importance of rivers and railroads as lines of military operations and supply. Grant and Foote advanced up (southward) the Tennessee and Cumberland rivers while Buell moved along the Louisville and Nashville Railroad. Confederate divisions under the overall command of General Albert Sidney Johnston used railroads to concentrate at the key junction of Corinth.

armored just enough to protect the engine and the paddle wheels but not enough to impair speed and shallow draft for river operations. The Union also built a new class of ironclad gunboats designed for river warfare. Carrying 13 guns, these flat-bottomed, wide-beamed vessels drew only six feet of water. Their hulls and paddle wheels were protected by a sloping casemate sheathed in iron armor up to 2½ inches thick.

When the first of these strange-looking but formidable craft were ready in February 1862, Grant struck. His objectives were Forts Henry and Donelson on the Tennessee and Cumberland rivers just south of the Kentucky–Tennessee border. The gunboats knocked out Fort Henry on February 6. Fort Donelson proved a tougher nut to crack. Its guns repulsed a gunboat attack on February 14. The next day, the 17,000-man Confederate army attacked Grant's besieging army, which had been reinforced to 27,000 men. With the calm decisiveness that became his trademark, Grant directed a counterattack that penned the defenders back up in their fort. Cut off from support

by either land or river, the Confederate commander asked for surrender terms on February 16. Grant's reply made him instantly famous when it was published in the North: "No terms except an immediate and unconditional surrender can be accepted. I propose to move immediately upon your works." With no choice, the 13,000 surviving Confederates surrendered (some had escaped), giving Grant the most striking victory in the war thus far.

These victories had far-reaching strategic consequences. Union gunboats now ranged all the way up the Tennessee River to northern Alabama, enabling a Union division to occupy the region, and up the Cumberland to Nashville, which became the first Confederate state capital to surrender to Union forces on February 25. Confederate military units pulled out of Kentucky and most of Tennessee and reassembled at Corinth in northern Mississippi. Jubilation spread through the North and despair through the South. By the end of March 1862, however, the Confederate commander in the western theater, Albert Sidney Johnston (not to be confused with Joseph E. Johnston in Virginia), had built up an army of 40,000 men at Corinth. His plan was to attack Grant's force of 35,000, which had established a base 20 miles away at Pittsburg Landing on the Tennessee River just north of the Mississippi–Tennessee border.

The Battle of Shiloh

On April 6, the Confederates attacked at dawn near a church called Shiloh, which gave its name to the battle. They caught Grant by surprise and drove his army toward the river. After a day's fighting of unprecedented intensity, with total casualties of 15,000, Grant's men brought the Confederate onslaught to a halt at dusk. One of the Confederate casualties was Johnston, who bled to death when a bullet severed an artery in his leg—the highest-ranking

general on either side to be killed in the war. Beauregard, who had been transferred from Virginia to the West, took command after Johnston's death.

Some of Grant's subordinates advised retreat during the dismal night of April 6–7, but Grant would have none of it. Reinforced by fresh troops from a Union army commanded by General Don Carlos Buell, the Union counterattacked the next morning (April 7) and, after 9,000 more casualties to the two sides, drove the Confederates back to Corinth. Although Grant had snatched victory from the jaws of defeat, his reputation suffered a decline for a time because of the heavy Union casualties (13,000) and the suspicion that he had been caught napping the first day.

Union triumphs in the western theater continued. The combined armies of Grant and Buell, under the overall command of the top-ranking Union general in the

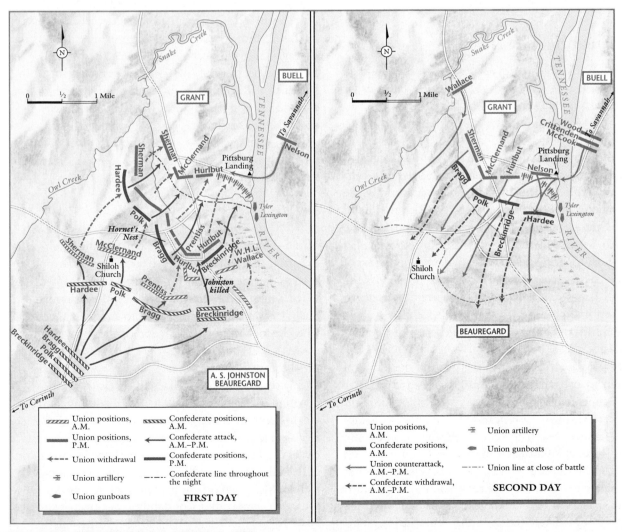

MAP 15.5 BATTLE OF SHILOH, APRIL 6–7, 1862

These two maps starkly illustrate the change of fortune from the first to the second day of the battle, with Confederates driving northward the first day and then being driven back over the same ground the second day.

West, Henry W. Halleck, drove the Confederates out of Corinth at the end of May. Meanwhile, the Union gunboat fleet fought its way down the Mississippi to Vicksburg, virtually wiping out the Confederate fleet in a spectacular battle at Memphis on June 6. At Vicksburg, the Union gunboats from the north connected with part of Farragut's fleet that had come up from New Orleans, taking Baton Rouge and Natchez along the way. The heavily fortified Confederate bastion at Vicksburg, however, proved too strong for Union naval firepower to subdue. Nevertheless, the dramatic succession of Union triumphs in the West from February to June—including a decisive victory at the battle of Pea Ridge in northwest Arkansas on March 7 and 8—convinced the North that the war was nearly won. "Every blow tells fearfully against the rebellion," boasted the leading Northern newspaper, the New York *Tribune.* "The rebels themselves are panic-stricken, or despondent. It now requires no very far reaching prophet to predict the end of this struggle."

The Virginia Theater

Even as the editorial writer wrote these words, affairs in Virginia were about to take a sharp turn in favor of the Confederacy. Within three months the Union, which had been so near a knockout victory that spring, was back on the defensive.

In the western theater, the broad rivers had facilitated the Union's invasion of the South, but in Virginia a half-dozen small rivers flowing west to east lay athwart the line of operations between Washington and Richmond and provided the Confederates with natural lines of defense. McClellan persuaded a reluctant Lincoln to approve a plan to transport his army down Chesapeake Bay to the tip of the Virginia peninsula, formed by the tidal portions of the York and James rivers. That would shorten the route to Richmond and give the Union army a seaborne supply line secure from harassment by Confederate cavalry and guerrillas.

This was a good plan—in theory. And the logistical achievement of transporting 110,000 men and all their equipment, animals, and supplies by sea to the jump-off point near Yorktown was impressive. But once again, McClellan's failings began to surface. A small Confederate blocking force at Yorktown held him for the entire month of April, as he cautiously dragged up siege guns to blast through defenses that his large army could have punched through in days on foot. McClellan slowly followed the retreating Confederate force up the peninsula to a new defensive line only a few miles east of Richmond, all the while bickering with Lincoln and Secretary of War

Edwin M. Stanton over the reinforcements they were withholding to protect Washington against a possible strike by Stonewall Jackson's small Confederate army in the Shenandoah Valley.

Jackson's month-long campaign in the Shenandoah (May 8–June 9), one of the most brilliant of the war, demonstrated what could be accomplished through deception, daring, and mobility. With only 17,000 men, Jackson moved by forced marches so swift that his infantry earned the nickname "Jackson's foot cavalry." Darting here and there through the valley, they marched 350 miles in the course of one month; won four battles against three separate Union armies, whose combined numbers surpassed Jackson's by more than 2 to 1 (but which Jackson's force always outnumbered at the point of contact); and compelled Lincoln to divert to the valley some of the reinforcements McClellan demanded.

Even without those reinforcements, McClellan's army substantially outnumbered the Confederate force defending Richmond, commanded by Joseph E. Johnston. As usual, though, McClellan overestimated Johnston's strength at double what it was and acted accordingly. Even so, by the last week of May, McClellan's army was within six miles of Richmond. A botched Confederate counterattack on May 31 and June 1 (the Battle of Seven Pines) produced no result except 6,000 Confederate and 5,000 Union casualties. One of those casualties was Johnston, who was wounded in the shoulder. Jefferson Davis named Robert E. Lee to replace him.

The Seven Days' Battles

That appointment marked a major turning point in the campaign. Lee had done little so far to earn a wartime reputation, having failed in his only field command to dislodge Union forces from control of West Virginia. His qualities as a commander began to manifest themselves when he took over what he renamed the Army of Northern Virginia. Those qualities were boldness, a willingness to take great risks, an almost uncanny ability to read the enemy commander's mind, and a charisma that won the devotion of his men. While McClellan continued to dawdle, Lee sent his dashing cavalry commander, J. E. B. "Jeb" Stuart, to lead a reconnaissance around the Union army to discover its weak points. Lee also brought Jackson's army in from the Shenandoah Valley and launched a June 26 attack on McClellan's right flank in what became known as the Seven Days' battles. Constantly attacking, Lee's army of 88,000 drove McClellan's 100,000 away from Richmond to a new fortified base on the James River. The offensive cost the Confederates 20,000 casualties (compared with 16,000

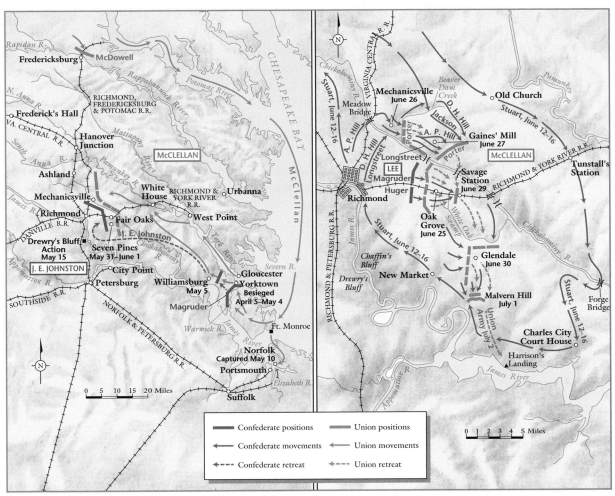

MAP 15.6 PENINSULA CAMPAIGN, APRIL–MAY 1862 [AND] SEVEN DAYS' BATTLES, JUNE 25–JULY 1, 1862
General McClellan used Union naval control of the York and James rivers to protect his flanks in his advance up the peninsula formed by these rivers (left map). When Robert E. Lee's Army of Northern Virginia counterattacked in the Seven Days' Battles (right map), McClellan was forced back to the James River at Harrison's Landing.

for the Union) and turned Richmond into one vast hospital. But it reversed the momentum of the war.

❧ Confederate Counteroffensives

Northern sentiments plunged from the height of euphoria in May to the depths of despair in July. "The feeling of despondency here is very great," wrote a New Yorker, while a Southerner exulted that "Lee has turned the tide, and I shall not be surprised if we have a long career of successes." The tide turned in the western theater as well, where Union conquests in the spring had brought 50,000 square miles of Confederate territory under Union control. To occupy and administer this vast area, however, drew many thousands of soldiers from combat forces,

which were left depleted and deep in enemy territory and vulnerable to cavalry raids. During summer and fall 1862, the cavalry commands of Tennesseean Nathan Bedford Forrest and Kentuckian John Hunt Morgan staged repeated raids in which they burned bridges, blew up tunnels, tore up tracks, and captured supply depots and the Union garrisons trying to defend them. By August the once-formidable Union war machine in the West seemed to have broken down.

These raids paved the way for infantry counteroffensives. After recapturing some territory, Earl Van Dorn's Army of West Tennessee got a bloody nose when it failed to retake Corinth on October 3 and 4. At the end of August, Braxton Bragg's Army of Tennessee launched a drive northward from Chattanooga through east Tennessee and Kentucky. It had almost reached the Ohio River in September but was turned back at the Battle of Perryville on October 8. Even after these defeats, the Confederate forces in the western theater were in better shape than they had been four months earlier.

The Second Battle of Bull Run

Most attention, though, focused on Virginia. Lincoln reorganized the Union corps near Washington into the Army of Virginia under General John Pope, who had won minor successes as commander of a small army in Missouri and Tennessee. In August, Lincoln ordered the withdrawal of the Army of the Potomac from the peninsula to reinforce Pope for a drive southward from Washington. Lee quickly seized the opportunity provided by the separation of the two Union armies confronting him, by the ill will between McClellan and Pope and their subordinates, and by the bickering among various factions in Washington. To attack Pope before McClellan could reinforce him, Lee shifted most of his army to northern Virginia, sent Jackson's foot cavalry on a deep raid to destroy its supply base at Manassas Junction, and then brought his army back together to defeat Pope's army near Bull Run on August 29 and 30. The demoralized Union forces retreated into the Washington defenses, where Lincoln reluctantly gave McClellan command of the two armies and told him to reorganize them into one.

MUSICAL LINK TO THE PAST

Wartime Music as Inspiration and Catharsis

Composers: Stephen C. Foster (music), James Sloan Gibbons (lyrics)

Title: "We Are Coming, Father Abraham, 300,000 More" (1862)

Composers: Stephen C. Foster (music), Cooper (lyrics)

Title: "Willie Has Gone to War" (1863)

"We Are Coming, Father Abraham, 300,000 More," with its marchlike beat and patriotic lift, captures the optimism some in the North felt at the start of the war, when many estimated that the confrontation would be finished within half a year. The song probably was also used to shore up sagging spirits in some northern areas. Although the song, and others with similar sentiments, sold well with its message of eager voluntarism on the part of soldiers united for the Union, it did not produce a corresponding effect on sluggish troop recruitment efforts in the North.

"Willie Has Gone To War," released a year later and popular in the South as well as the North, presents the more gloomy and death-obsessed nature of Civil War music that surfaced in the second half of the conflict. For months, press dispatches reported the crushing defeats and mortal losses on both sides with violent and gory detail. The occasion of a soldier going to the front was no longer viewed as a celebratory occasion. In "Willie," the notion of oncoming tragedy and death is never stated, but it unmistakably lingers over the song, both in its bittersweet melody and in the Victorian images of nature that are cast as a poetic counterpoint to the fact of Willie going to war: "The bluebird is singing his lay, to all the sweet flowers in the dale / The wild bee is roaming at play, and soft is the sigh of the gale / I stray by the brookside alone, where oft we have wandered before / And weep for my lov'd one, my own, My Willie has gone to the war / . . . Willie has gone to the war, Willie, my loved one is gone!" The last line quoted, part of the chorus of the song, is especially haunting, as the song drops into a minor chord and features a melody that combines mournful and patriotic elements simultaneously.

Although some at the time argued that such sad music eroded morale, perhaps it would have been even more damaging to ignore the kinds of welling emotions that "Willie" and songs like it documented. The catharsis these songs provided helped Americans face the loss and sacrifice of the war, which saw over 1 million people killed and wounded. Confederate General Robert E. Lee maintained that he could not imagine fighting a war without music. George F. Root, one of the most successful songwriters and publishers of the Civil War period, insisted that, as a songwriter, he was patriotically serving his country through the medium of song and that such contributions were as important as the contributions of a general.

---

1. Why do you think Lee and Root attached such importance to the role of music in fighting a war?

Listen to an audio recording of this music on the Musical Links to the Past CD.

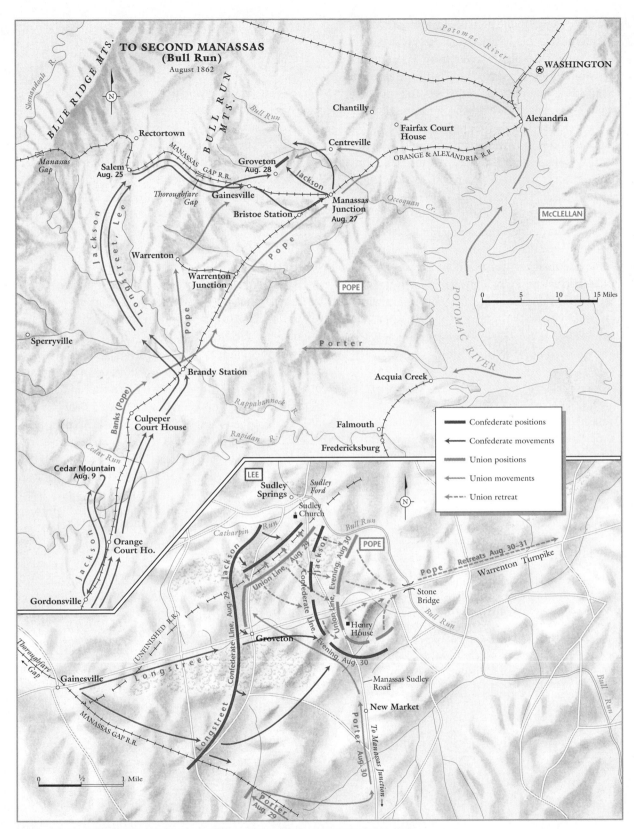

MAP 15.7 SECOND BATTLE OF MANASSAS (BULL RUN), AUGUST 29–30, 1862

Compare this map with the lower map on p. 488. Note that some of the heaviest fighting in both battles took place around the house owned by Judith Henry, which was destroyed and the elderly widow killed in her house in the first battle.

Lee decided to keep up the pressure by invading Maryland. On September 4, his weary troops began splashing across the Potomac 40 miles upriver from Washington. This move, which took place at the same time Braxton Bragg was invading Kentucky, presented several momentous possibilities: Maryland might be won for the Confederacy. Another victory by Lee might influence the U.S. congressional elections in November and help Democrats gain control of Congress, and might even force the Lincoln administration to negotiate peace with the Confederacy. Successful invasion of Maryland, coming on top of other Confederate successes, might even persuade Britain and France to recognize the Confederacy and offer mediation to end the war, especially since the long-expected cotton famine had finally materialized. In fact, in September 1862, the British and French governments were considering recognition and awaiting the outcome of Lee's invasion to decide whether to proceed. Great issues rode with the armies as Lee crossed the Potomac and McClellan cautiously moved north to meet him.

Conclusion

The election of 1860 had accomplished a national power shift of historic proportions. Through their domination of the Jeffersonian Republican coalition during the first quarter of the 19th century and of the Jacksonian Democrats thereafter, Southern political leaders had maintained effective control of the national government for most of the time before 1860. South Carolina's secession governor, Francis Pickens, described this leverage of power in a private letter to a fellow South Carolinian in 1857:

> We have the Executive [Buchanan] with us, and the Senate & in all probability the H[ouse of] R[epresentatives] too. Besides we have repealed the Missouri line & the Supreme Court in a decision of great power, has declared it . . . unconstitutional null and void. So, that before our enemies can reach us, they must first break down the Supreme Court—change the Senate & seize the Executive & . . . restore the Missouri line, repeal the Fugitive slave law &

change the whole govern[men]t. As long as the Govt. is on our side I am for sustaining it, & using its power for our benefit, & placing the screws upon the throats of our opponents.

In 1860, Pickens's worst-case scenario started to come true. With Lincoln's election as the first president of an antislavery party, the South lost control of the executive branch—and perhaps also of the House. They feared that the Senate and Supreme Court would soon follow. The Republicans, Southerners feared, would launch a "revolution" to cripple slavery and, as Lincoln had said in his "House Divided" speech two years earlier, place it "in course of ultimate extinction." The "revolutionary dogmas" of the Republicans, declared a South Carolina newspaper in 1860, were "active and bristling with terrible designs." Worst of all, the Northern Black Republicans would force racial equality on the South: "Abolition preachers will be on hand to consummate the marriage of your daughters to black husbands."

Thus the South launched a preemptive counterrevolution of secession to forestall a revolution of liberty and equality they feared would be their fate if they remained in the Union. As the Confederate secretary of state put it in 1861, the Southern states had formed a new nation "to preserve their old institutions [from] a revolution [that] threatened to destroy their social system."

Seldom has a preemptive counterrevolution so quickly brought on the very revolution it tried to prevent. If the Confederacy had lost the war in spring 1862, as appeared likely after Union victories from February to May of that year, the South might have returned to the Union with slavery intact. Instead, successful Confederate counteroffensives in summer 1862 convinced Lincoln that the North could not win the war without striking against slavery. Another issue that rode with Lee's troops as they crossed the Potomac into Maryland in September 1862 was the fate of an emancipation proclamation Lincoln had drafted two months earlier and then put aside to await a Union victory.

SUGGESTED READINGS

The most comprehensive one-volume study of the Civil War years is **James M. McPherson,** *Battle Cry of Freedom: The Civil War Era* (1988). The fullest and most readable narrative of the military campaigns and battles is **Shelby Foote,** *The Civil War: A Narrative,* 3 vols. (1958–1974). For the naval war, see **Ivan Musicant,** *Divided Waters: The Naval History of the Civil War* (1995). For the perspective of the soldiers and sailors who fought the battles, see **Bell I. Wiley's** two books: *The Life of Johnny Reb* (1943) and *The Life of Billy Yank* (1952). The motives of soldiers for enlisting and fighting are treated in **James M. McPherson,** *For Cause and Comrades: Why Men Fought in the Civil War* (1997).

For the home front in North and South, see **Phillip Shaw Paludan,** *"A People's Contest": The Union and Civil War, 1861–1865* (1988), and **Emory Thomas,** *The Confederate Nation, 1861–1865* (1979). For women and children, see **Elizabeth D. Leonard,** *Yankee Women: Gender Battles in the Civil War;* **George C. Rable,** *Civil Wards: Women and the Crisis of Southern Nationalism* (1989); and **James Marten,** *The Children's Civil War* (1998).

For biographical studies of leaders on both sides, consult the following: **Phillip S. Paludan,** *The Presidency of Abraham Lincoln* (1994); **William C. Cooper,** *Jefferson Davis, American* (2000); **Brooks D. Simpson,** *Ulysses S. Grant* (2000); and **Emory M. Thomas,** *Robert E. Lee* (1995). For a study of the Fort Sumter

crisis and the outbreak of the war that sets these events in their long-term context, see **Maury Klein,** *Days of Defiance: Sumter, Secession, and The Coming of the Civil War* (1997). For the guerrilla war in Missouri, the most useful of several books is *Michael Fellman, Inside War: The Guerrilla Conflict in Missouri during the Civil War* (1989). Of the many studies of diplomacy during the war, the most useful is **David P. Crook,** *The North, The South, and the Powers 1861–1865* (1974), an abridged version of which was published with the title *Diplomacy during the Civil War* (1975).

 AMERICAN JOURNEY ONLINE
A N D
INFOTRAC COLLEGE EDITION

Visit the source collections at www.ajaccess.wadsworth.com and infotrac.thomsonlearning.com and use the Search function with the following key terms to explore documents, images, audio and video clips, articles, and commentary related to the material in this chapter.

Fort Sumter	Stonewall Jackson
Abraham Lincoln	Battle of Bull Run (Manassas)
George B. McClellan	Battle of Shiloh
Robert E. Lee	

Chapter 16

A New Birth of Freedom, 1862–1865

Eastman Johnson 1824–1906 A RIDE FOR LIBERTY—THE FUGITIVE SLAVES, circa 1862. Oil on board.
The Brooklyn Museum 40.59. A Gift of Miss Gwendolyn O. L. Conkling.

A RIDE FOR LIBERTY
This splendid painting of a slave family escaping to Union lines during the Civil War dramatizes the experiences of thousands of slaves who thereby became "contrabands" and gained their freedom. Most of them came on foot, but this enterprising family stole a horse as well as themselves from their master.

CHAPTER OUTLINE

One of the great issues awaiting resolution as the armies moved into Maryland in September 1862 was emancipation of the slaves. The war had become a "total war," requiring the mobilization of every resource that might bring victory or the destruction of any resource that might inflict defeat. To abolish slavery would strike at a vital Confederate resource (slave labor) and mobilize that resource for the Union along with the moral power of fighting for freedom. Slaves had already made clear their choice by escaping to Union lines by the tens of thousands. Lincoln had made up his mind to issue an emancipation proclamation and was waiting for a Union victory to give it credibility and potency.

This momentous decision would radically enlarge the scope and purpose of the Union war effort. It would also polarize Northern public opinion and political parties. So long as the North fought simply for restoration of the Union, Northern unity was impressive, but the events of 1862 and 1863 raised the divisive question of what kind of Union was to be restored. Would it be a Union without slavery, as abolitionists and radical Republicans hoped? Or "the Union as it was, the Constitution as it is," as Democrats desired? The answer to this question would determine not only the course of the war but also the future of the United States.

CHAPTER FOCUS

♦ What factors led Lincoln to his decision to issue the Emancipation Proclamation?
♦ What were the sources of internal dissent and dissension in the Confederacy? In the Union?

◆ What contribution did women and African Americans make to the war efforts in both the North and South?

◆ Why did Lincoln expect to be defeated for reelection in August 1864? What changed to enable him to win reelection by a substantial margin?

Slavery and the War

At first, the leaders of both the Union and the Confederacy tried to keep the issue of slavery out of the war. For Southern leaders to proclaim that the defense of slavery was the aim of the war might prompt nonslaveholders to ask why they were risking their lives to protect their rich neighbors' property. Even more important, it might jeopardize Confederate efforts to win recognition and support from Britain. So the Confederates proclaimed liberty rather than slavery as their war aim—the same liberty their ancestors had fought for in 1776. The unspoken corollary of that aim was the liberty of whites to own blacks.

In the North, the issue of slavery was deeply divisive. Lincoln had been elected on a platform pledged to contain the expansion of slavery, but that pledge had provoked most of the Southern states to quit the Union. For the administration to take action against slavery in 1861 would be to risk the breakup of the fragile coalition Lincoln had stitched together to fight the war: Republicans, Democrats, and border-state Unionists. Spokesmen for the latter two groups served notice that, although they supported a war for the Union, they would not support a war against slavery. In July 1861, with Lincoln's endorsement, Congress passed a resolution affirming that Northern war aims included no intention "of overthrowing or interfering with the rights or established institutions of the States"— in plain words, slavery—but intended only "to defend and maintain the supremacy of the Constitution and to preserve the Union."

Many Northerners saw matters differently. They insisted that a rebellion sustained *by* slavery in defense *of* slavery could be suppressed only by striking *against* slavery. As the black leader Frederick Douglass stated, "To fight against slaveholders, without fighting against slavery, is but a halfhearted business, and paralyzes the hands engaged in it. . . . War for the destruction of liberty must be met with war for the destruction of slavery." A good many Union soldiers began to grumble about protecting the property of traitors in arms against the United States.

Wars tend to develop a logic and momentum that go beyond their original purposes. When Northerners discovered at Bull Run in July 1861 that they were not going to win an easy victory, many of them began to take a

CHRONOLOGY

1862	Confederacy enacts conscription (April 16) • Lincoln informs two cabinet members of intention to issue Emancipation Proclamation (July 13) • Battle of Antietam (September 17) • Lincoln issues preliminary Emancipation Proclamation (September 22) • Battle of Fredericksburg (December 13) • Battle of Stones River (December 31–January 2)
1863	Lincoln issues final Emancipation Proclamation (January 1) • Union enacts conscription (March 3) • Richmond bread riot (April 2) • Battle of Chancellorsville (May 1–5) • Battle of Gettysburg (July 1–3) • Vicksburg surrenders (July 4) • Port Hudson surrenders (July 9) • New York draft riot (July 13–16) • Assault on Fort Wagner (July 18) • Battle of Chickamauga (September 19–20) • Battles of Chattanooga (November 24–25)
1864	Battle of the Wilderness (May 5–6) • Battle of Spotsylvania (May 8–19) • Fighting at Petersburg leads to nine-month siege (June 15–18) • Fall of Atlanta (September 1) • Reelection of Lincoln (November 8) • Battle of Nashville (December 15–16)
1865	Capture of Fort Fisher (January 15) • Confederates evacuate Richmond (April 2) • Lee surrenders at Appomattox (April 9) • Booth assassinates Lincoln (April 14) • Last Confederate army surrenders (June 23) • 13th Amendment abolishing slavery ratified (December 6)

harder look at slavery. Slaves constituted the principal labor force in the South. They raised most of the food and fiber, built most of the military fortifications, worked on the railroads and in mines and munitions factories. Southern newspapers boasted that slavery was "a tower of strength to the Confederacy" because it enabled the South "to place in the field a force so much larger in proportion to her white population than the North." Precisely, responded abolitionists. So why not convert this Confederate asset to a Union advantage by confiscating slaves as enemy property and using them to help the Northern war effort? As the war ground on into 1862 and casualties mounted, this argument began to make sense to many Yankees.

The "Contrabands"

The slaves entered this debate in a dramatic fashion. As Union armies penetrated the South, a growing number of slaves voted for freedom with their feet. By twos and threes, by families, and eventually by scores, they escaped from their masters and came over to the Union lines. By obliging Union officers either to return them to slavery or accept them, these escaped slaves began to make the conflict a war for freedom.

Although some commanders returned escaped slaves to their masters or prevented them from entering Union camps, most increasingly did not. Their rationale was first expressed by General Benjamin Butler. In May 1861, three slaves who had been working for the Confederate army escaped to Butler's lines near Fortress Monroe at the mouth of the James River in Virginia. Butler refused to return them, on the grounds that they were "contraband of war." The phrase caught on. For the rest of the war, slaves who came within Union lines were known as contrabands. On August 6, 1861, Congress passed a confiscation act that authorized the seizure of all property, including slaves, that was being used for Confederate military purposes. The following March, Congress forbade the return of slaves who entered Union lines—even those belonging to owners loyal to the Union.

From the collections of the National Archives.

CONTRABANDS COMING INTO UNION LINES, VIRGINIA

This photograph portrays the arrival of several "contraband" families at Union lines in Virginia in 1862. Not yet legally freed, these people would never again be slaves.

The Border States

This problem of slavery in the loyal border states preoccupied Lincoln. On August 30, 1861, John C. Frémont, whose political influence had won him a commission as major general and command of Union forces in Missouri, issued an order freeing the slaves of all Confederate sympathizers in Missouri. This caused such a backlash among border-state Unionists, who feared it was a prelude to a general abolition edict, that Lincoln revoked the order, lest it "alarm our Southern Union friends, and turn them against us."

In spring 1862, Lincoln tried persuasion instead of force in the border states. At his urging, Congress passed a resolution offering federal compensation to states that voluntarily abolished slavery. Three times, from March to July 1862, Lincoln urged border-state congressmen to accept the offer. He told them that the Confederate hope that their states might join the rebellion was helping to keep the war alive. Adopt the proposal for compensated emancipation, he pleaded, and that hope would die. The pressure for a bold antislavery policy was growing stronger, he warned them in May. Another Union general had issued an emancipation order; Lincoln had suspended it, but "you cannot," Lincoln told the border-state congressmen, "be blind to the signs of the times."

They did seem to be blind. They complained that they were being coerced, bickered about the amount of com-

pensation, and wrung their hands over the prospects of economic ruin and race war, even if emancipation were to take place gradually over a 30-year period, as Lincoln had suggested. At a final meeting, on July 12, Lincoln, in effect, gave them an ultimatum: Accept compensated emancipation or face the consequences. In fact, thousands of slaves had already run away to Union camps in the border states. "The incidents of the war cannot be avoided," he said. "If the war continue long . . . the institution in your states will be extinguished by mere friction and abrasion . . . and you will have nothing valuable in lieu of it." Again they failed to see the light, and by a vote of 20 to 9, they rejected the proposal for compensated emancipation.

The Decision for Emancipation

That very evening, Lincoln decided to issue an emancipation proclamation in his capacity as commander-in-chief with power to order the seizure of enemy property. Several factors, in addition to the recalcitrance of the border states, impelled Lincoln to this fateful decision. One was a growing demand from his own party for bolder action: Congress had just passed a second confiscation act calling for seizure of the property of active Confederates. Another was rising sentiment in the Army to "take off the kid gloves" when dealing with "traitors." From General Henry

W. Halleck, who had been summoned to Washington as general-in-chief, went orders to General Grant in northern Mississippi instructing him on the treatment of rebel sympathizers inside Union lines: "Handle that class without gloves, and take their property for public use." Grant himself had written several months earlier that if the Confederacy "cannot be whipped in any other way than through a war against slavery, let it come to that." Finally, Lincoln's decision reflected his sentiments about the "unqualified evil" and "monstrous injustice" of slavery.

The military situation, however, rather than his moral convictions, determined the timing and scope of Lincoln's emancipation policy. Northern hopes that the war would soon end had risen after the victories of early 1862 but had then plummeted amid the reverses of that summer.

Three courses of action seemed possible. One, favored by the so-called Peace Democrats, urged an armistice and peace negotiations to patch together some kind of Union, but that would have been tantamount to conceding Confederate victory. Republicans therefore reviled the Peace Democrats as traitorous Copperheads, after the poisonous snake. A second alternative was to keep on fighting—in the hope that with a few more Union victories, the rebels would lay down their arms and the Union could be restored. Such a policy would leave slavery intact, a course of action that General McClellan strongly advocated. He wrote Lincoln an unsolicited letter of advice on July 7, 1862, warning him that "neither confiscation of property . . . [n]or forcible abolition of slavery should be contemplated for a moment." Yet that was precisely what Lincoln was contemplating. This was the third alternative: total war to mobilize all the resources of the North and to destroy all the resources of the South, including slavery—a war not to restore the old Union but to build a new one.

After his meeting with the border-state representatives convinced him that attempts at compromise were futile, Lincoln made his decision. On July 22, he formally notified the cabinet of his intention to issue an emancipation proclamation. It was "a military necessity, absolutely essential to the preservation of the Union," said Lincoln. "We must free the slaves or be ourselves subdued. The slaves [are] undeniably an element of strength to those who [have] their service, and we must decide whether that element should be with us or against us. . . . The Administration must set an example, and strike at the heart of the rebellion."

The cabinet agreed, except for Postmaster General Montgomery Blair, a resident of Maryland and a former Democrat, who warned that the border states and the Democrats would rebel against the proclamation and perhaps cost the administration the fall congressional elec-

tions as well as vital support for the war. Lincoln might have agreed—two months earlier. Now he believed that the strength gained from an emancipation policy—from the slaves themselves, from the dynamic Republican segment of Northern opinion, and in the eyes of foreign nations—would more than compensate for the hostility of Democrats and border-state Unionists. Lincoln did, however, accept the advice of Secretary of State Seward to delay the proclamation "until you can give it to the country supported by military success." Otherwise, Seward argued, it might be viewed "as the last measure of an exhausted government, a cry for help . . . our last shriek, on the retreat." Lincoln slipped his proclamation into a desk drawer and waited for a military victory.

New Calls for Troops

Meanwhile, Lincoln issued a call for 300,000 new three-year volunteers for the army. In July, Congress passed a militia act giving the president greater powers to mobilize the state militias into federal service and to draft men into the militia if the states failed to do so. Although not a national draft law, this was a step in that direction. In August, Lincoln called up 300,000 militia for nine months of service, in addition to the 300,000 three-year volunteers. (These calls eventually yielded 421,000 three-year volunteers and 88,000 nine-month militia.) The Peace Democrats railed against these measures and provoked antidraft riots in some localities. The government responded by arresting rioters and antiwar activists under the president's suspension of the writ of habeas corpus.[1]

Democrats denounced these "arbitrary arrests" as unconstitutional violations of civil liberties—and added this issue to others on which they hoped to gain control of the next House of Representatives in the fall elections. With the decline in Northern morale following the defeat at Second Bull Run and the early success of the Confederate invasion of Kentucky, prospects for a Democratic triumph seemed bright. One more military victory by Lee's Army of Northern Virginia might crack the North's will to

---

[1] A writ of habeas corpus is an order issued by a judge to law enforcement officers requiring them to bring an arrested person before the court to be charged with a crime so that the accused can have a fair trial. The U.S. Constitution, however, permits the suspension of this writ "in cases of rebellion or invasion," so that the government can arrest enemy agents, saboteurs, or any individual who might hinder the defense of the country, and hold such individuals without trial. Lincoln had suspended the writ, but political opponents charged him with usurping a power possessed only by Congress in order to curb freedom of speech of antiwar opponents and political critics guilty of nothing more than speaking out against the war. This issue of "arbitrary arrests" became a controversial matter in both the Union and Confederacy (where the writ was similarly suspended during part of the war).

continue the fight. It would certainly bring diplomatic recognition of the Confederacy by Britain and France. Lee's legions began crossing the Potomac into Maryland on September 4, 1862.

The Battle of Antietam

The Confederate invasion ran into difficulties from the start. Western Marylanders responded impassively to Lee's proclamation that he had come "to aid you in throwing off this foreign yoke" of Yankee rule. Lee split his army into five parts. Three of them, under the overall command of Stonewall Jackson, occupied the heights surrounding the Union garrison at Harpers Ferry, which lay athwart the Confederate supply route from the Shenandoah Valley. The other two remained on watch in the South Mountain passes west of Frederick. Then, on September 13, Union

commander George B. McClellan had an extraordinary stroke of luck. In a field near Frederick, two of his soldiers found a copy of Lee's orders for these deployments. Wrapped around three cigars, they had apparently been dropped by a careless Southern officer when the Confederate army passed through Frederick four days earlier. With this new information, McClellan planned to pounce on the separated segments of Lee's army before they could reunite. "Here is a paper," he exulted, "with which if I cannot whip 'Bobbie Lee,' I will be willing to go home."

But McClellan moved so cautiously that he lost much of his advantage. Although Union troops overwhelmed the Confederate defenders of the South Mountain passes on September 14, they advanced too slowly to save the garrison at Harpers Ferry, which surrendered 12,000 men to Jackson on September 15. Lee then managed to reunite most of his army near the village of Sharpsburg by

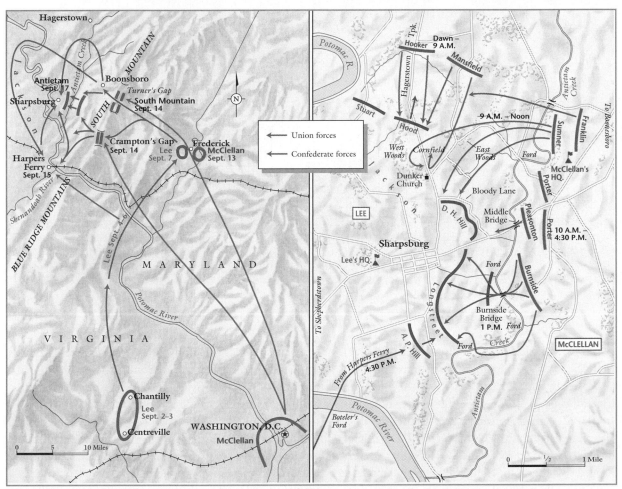

MAP 16.1 LEE'S INVASION OF MARYLAND, 1862 [AND] BATTLE OF ANTIETAM, SEPTEMBER 17, 1862
Both the advantages and disadvantages of Lee's defensive position in this battle are illustrated by the right-hand map. The Confederate flanks were protected by water barriers (the Potomac River on the left and Antietam Creek on the right), but the Confederates fought with their back to the Potomac and only Boteler's Ford as the single line of retreat across the river. If Burnside's attack on the Confederate right had succeeded before A. P. Hill's division arrived, Lee's forces could have been trapped north of the river.

CONFEDERATE DEAD ON THE BATTLEFIELD

The new technology of photography came into its own during the Civil War, providing us with the first realistic portrayal of the human cost of war. These photographs of Confederate dead at Antietam, taken two days after the battle, conveyed "the terrible reality and suffering of war," in the words of a *New York Times* reporter who saw the pictures at an exhibit in the city. But, he added, "one phase . . . escaped photographic skill . . . the background of widows and orphans. . . . Broken hearts cannot be photographed."

September 17, when McClellan finally crossed Antietam Creek to attack. Even so, the Union forces outnumbered the Confederates by almost 2 to 1 (75,000 to 40,000 men), but McClellan, as usual, believed that the enemy outnumbered *him*. Thus he missed several opportunities to inflict a truly crippling defeat on the Confederacy. The battle of Antietam (called Sharpsburg by the Confederates) nevertheless proved to be the single bloodiest day in American history, with more than 23,000 casualties (killed, wounded, and captured) in the two armies.

Attacking from right to left on a four-mile front, McClellan's Army of the Potomac achieved potential breakthroughs at a sunken road northeast of Sharpsburg

(known ever after as Bloody Lane) and in the rolling fields southeast of town. But fearing counterattacks from phantom reserves that he was sure Lee possessed, McClellan held back 20,000 of his troops and failed to follow through. Thus the battle ended in a draw. The battered Confederates still clung to their precarious line, with the Potomac at their back, at the end of a day in which more than 6,000 men on both sides were killed or mortally wounded—almost as many Americans as were killed or mortally wounded in combat during the entire seven years of the Revolutionary War.

Even though he received reinforcements the next day and Lee received none, McClellan did not renew the attack. Nor did he follow up vigorously when the Confederates finally retreated across the Potomac on the night of September 18.

The Emancipation Proclamation

Lincoln was not happy with this equivocal Union victory, despite its important consequences. Britain and France decided to withhold diplomatic recognition of the Confederacy. Northern Democrats failed to gain control of the House in the fall elections. And most significant of all, on September 22, Lincoln seized the occasion to issue his preliminary emancipation proclamation. This was less than a total surprise to the public because the president had already hinted that something of the sort might be in the offing. A month earlier, after Horace Greeley had written a strong editorial in the New York *Tribune* calling for action against slavery, Lincoln had responded with a public letter to Greeley (much as a president today might use a televised news conference). "My paramount object in this struggle," wrote Lincoln, "is to save the Union. . . . If I could

save the Union without freeing *any* slave I would do it, and if I could save it by freeing *all* the slaves I would do it; and if I could save it by freeing some and leaving others alone I would also do that." Knowing that the issue of Union united Northerners, while the prospect of emancipation still divided them, Lincoln had crafted these phrases carefully to maximize public support for his anticipated proclamation. He portrayed emancipation not as an end in itself—despite his personal convictions to that effect—but only as an instrument, a *means* toward saving the Union.

Lincoln's proclamation of September 22 did not go into effect immediately. Rather, it stipulated that if any state, or part of a state, was still in rebellion on January 1, 1863, the president would proclaim the slaves therein "forever free." Confederate leaders scorned this warning, and by January 1 no Southern state had returned to the Union. After hosting a New Year's Day reception at the White House, Lincoln signed the final proclamation as an "act of justice" as well as "a fit and necessary war measure for suppressing said rebellion."

Architect of the Capital.

THE EMANCIPATION PROCLAMATION

This famous contemporary painting by Francis Carpenter portrays Lincoln and his cabinet discussing the Emancipation Proclamation, which lies on the desk before Lincoln. The other members of the cabinet, from left to right, are Secretary of War Edwin M. Stanton, Secretary of the Treasury Salmon P. Chase, Secretary of the Navy Gideon Welles, Secretary of the Interior Caleb B. Smith, Secretary of State William H. Seward (seated facing Lincoln), Postmaster General Montgomery Blair, and Attorney General Edward Bates.

The Emancipation Proclamation exempted the border states, plus Tennessee and those portions of Louisiana and Virginia already under Union occupation because these areas were deemed not to be in rebellion, and Lincoln's constitutional authority for the proclamation derived from his power as commander-in-chief to confiscate enemy property. Although the proclamation could do nothing to liberate slaves in areas under Confederate control, it essentially made the Northern soldiers an army of liberation—however reluctant many of them were to risk their lives for that purpose. The North was now fighting for freedom as well as for Union. If the North won the war, slavery would die. But in the winter and spring of 1862–63, victory was far from assured.

A Winter of Discontent

Although Lee's retreat from Maryland and Braxton Bragg's retreat from Kentucky suggested that the Confederate tide might be ebbing, the tide soon turned. The Union could never win the war simply by turning back Confederate invasions. Northern armies would have to invade the South, defeat its armies, and destroy its ability to fight.

Displeased by McClellan's "slows" after Antietam, Lincoln replaced him on November 7 with General Ambrose E. Burnside. An imposing man whose muttonchop whiskers gave the anagram "sideburns" to the language, Burnside proposed to cross the Rappahannock River at Fredericksburg for a move on Richmond before bad weather forced both sides into winter quarters. Although Lee put his men into a strong defensive position on the heights behind Fredericksburg, Burnside nevertheless attacked on December 13. He was repulsed with heavy casualties that shook the morale of both the army and the public. When Lincoln heard the news, he said: "If there is a worse place than hell, I am in it."

News from the western theater did little to dispel the gloom in Washington. The Confederates had fortified Vicksburg on bluffs commanding the Mississippi River. This precaution gave them control of an important stretch of the river and preserved transportation links between the states to the east and west. Grant proposed to sever those links, and in November 1862, he launched a two-pronged drive against Vicksburg. With 40,000 men, he marched 50 miles southward from Memphis by land, while his principal subordinate William T. Sherman came down the river with 32,000 men accompanied by a gunboat fleet. Confederate cavalry raids destroyed the

LINK TO THE PAST

"We Cannot Escape History": Abraham Lincoln

In the closing passage of his annual message to Congress in December 1862, Lincoln soared to an eloquence that matched the later Gettysburg Address and Second Inaugural Address. In this passage, Lincoln was supporting a plan for gradual and compensated abolition of slavery everywhere by constitutional amendment. He did not expect Congress to pass such an amendment or the Confederate states to accept it even if Congress did pass it. The real reference point for this passage was the forthcoming Emancipation Proclamation, which Lincoln issued a month later.

The dogmas of the quiet past, are inadequate to the stormy present. The occasion is piled high with difficulty, and we must rise with the occasion. As our case is new, so we must think anew, and act anew. We must disenthrall our selves, and then, we shall save our country. Fellow-citizens, we cannot escape history. We of this Congress and this administration, will be remembered in spite of ourselves. No personal significance, or insignificance, can spare one or another of us. The fiery trial through which we pass, will light us down, in honor or dishonor, to the latest generation. . . . We—even we here— hold the power, and bear the responsibility. In giving freedom to the slave, we assure freedom to the free— honorable alike in what we give, and what we preserve. We shall nobly save, or meanly lose, the last best, hope of earth.

1. Why did Lincoln say that in giving freedom to the slave we assure freedom to the free?
2. What did he mean by "the last best, hope of earth"?

For additional sources related to this feature, visit the *Liberty, Equality, Power* Web site at:

http://history.wadsworth.com/murrin_LEP4e

railroads and supply depots in Grant's rear, however, forcing him to retreat to Memphis. Meanwhile, Sherman attacked the Confederates at Chickasaw Bluffs on December 29 with no more success than Burnside had enjoyed at Fredericksburg.

The only bit of cheer for the North came in central Tennessee at the turn of the year. There, Lincoln had removed General Don Carlos Buell from command of the Army of the Cumberland for the same reason he had removed McClellan—lack of vigor and aggressiveness. Buell's successor, William S. Rosecrans, had proved a fighter in subordinate commands. On the Confederate side, Davis stuck with Braxton Bragg as commander of the Army of Tennessee, despite dissension from some subordinate officers within his ranks.

On the day after Christmas 1862, Rosecrans moved from his base at Nashville to attack Bragg's force 30 miles to the south at Murfreesboro. The ensuing three-day battle (called Stones River by the Union and Murfreesboro by the Confederacy) resulted in Confederate success on the first day (December 31) but defeat on the last. Both armies suffered devastating casualties. The Confederate retreat to a new base 40 miles farther south enabled the North to call Stones River a victory. Lincoln expressed his gratitude to Rosecrans: "I can never forget . . . that you gave us a hard-earned victory which, had there been a defeat instead, the nation could scarcely have lived over."

As it was, the nation scarcely lived over the winter of 1862–63. Morale declined, and desertions rose so sharply in the Army of the Potomac that Lincoln replaced Burnside with Joseph Hooker, a controversial general whose nickname "Fighting Joe" seemed to promise a vigorous offensive. Hooker did lift morale in the Army of the Potomac, but elsewhere matters went from bad to worse.

Renewing the campaign against Vicksburg, Grant bogged down in the swamps and rivers that protected that Confederate bastion on three sides. Only on the east, away from the river, did he find high ground suitable for an assault on Vicksburg's defenses. Grant's problem was to get his army across the Mississippi to that high ground, along with supplies and transportation to support an assault. For three months, he floundered in the Mississippi-Yazoo bottomlands, while disease and exposure depleted his troops. False rumors of excessive drinking that had dogged Grant for years broke out anew, but Lincoln resisted pressures to remove him from command. "What I want," Lincoln said, "is generals who will fight battles and win victories. Grant has done this, and I propose to stand by him." Lincoln reportedly added that he would like to know Grant's brand of whiskey so that he could send some to his other generals.

The Rise of the Copperheads

Lincoln's reputation reached a low point during this Northern winter of discontent. A visitor to Washington in February 1863 found that "the lack of respect for the President in all parties is unconcealed. . . . If a Republican convention were to be held tomorrow, he would not get the vote of a State." In this climate, the Copperhead faction of the Democratic Party found a ready audience for its message that the war was a failure and should be abandoned. Having won control of the Illinois and Indiana legislatures the preceding fall, Democrats there called for an armistice and a peace conference. They also demanded retraction of the "wicked, inhuman, and unholy" Emancipation Proclamation.

In Ohio, the foremost Peace Democrat, Congressman Clement L. Vallandigham, was planning to run for governor. What had this wicked war accomplished, Vallandigham asked Northern audiences: "Let the dead at Fredericksburg and Vicksburg answer." The Confederacy could never be conquered; the only trophies of the war were "debt, defeat, sepulchres." The solution was to "stop the fighting. Make an armistice. Withdraw your army from the seceded states." Above all, give up the unconstitutional effort to abolish slavery.

Vallandigham and other Copperhead spokesmen had a powerful effect on Northern morale. Alarmed by a wave of desertions, the army commander in Ohio had Vallandigham arrested in May 1863. A military court convicted him of treason for aiding and abetting the enemy. The court's action raised serious questions of civil liberties. Was the conviction a violation of Vallandigham's First Amendment right of free speech? Could a military court try a civilian under martial law in a state such as Ohio where civil courts were functioning?

Lincoln was embarrassed by the swift arrest and trial of Vallandigham, which he learned about from the newspapers. To keep Vallandigham from becoming a martyr, Lincoln commuted his sentence from imprisonment to banishment—to the Confederacy! On May 15, Union cavalry escorted Vallandigham under a flag of truce to Confederate lines in Tennessee, where the Southerners reluctantly accepted their uninvited guest. He soon escaped to Canada on a blockade runner. There, from exile, Vallandigham conducted his campaign for governor of Ohio—an election he lost in October 1863, after the military fortunes of the Union had improved.

Economic Problems in the South

Low morale in the North followed military defeat. By contrast, Southerners were buoyed by their military success but were suffering from food shortages and hyperinflation. The tightening Union blockade, the weaknesses and imbalances of the Confederate economy, the escape of slaves to Union lines, and enemy occupation of some of the South's prime agricultural areas made it increasingly difficult to produce both guns and butter. Despite the conversion of hundreds of thousands of acres from cotton to food production, the deterioration of Southern railroads and the priority given to army shipments made food scarce in some areas. A drought in summer 1862 made matters worse. Prices rose much faster than wages. The price of salt, which was necessary to preserve meat in those days before refrigeration, shot out of sight. Even the middle class suffered, especially in Richmond, whose population had more than doubled since 1861. "The shadow of the gaunt form of famine is upon us," wrote a war department clerk in March 1863. "I have lost twenty pounds, and my wife and children are emaciated." The rats in his kitchen were so hungry that they nibbled bread crumbs from his daughter's hand "as tame as kittens. Perhaps we shall have to eat them!"

Poor people were worse off—especially the wives and children of nonslaveholders away in the army. By spring 1863, food supplies were virtually gone. Wrote a North Carolina farm woman to the governor in April 1863:

> A crowd of we Poor women went to Greenesborogh yesterday for something to eat as we had not a mouthful of meet nor bread in my house. What did they do but put us in gail in plase of giveing us aney thing to eat. . . . I have 6 little children and my husband in the armey and what am I to do?

Some women took matters into their own hands. Denouncing "speculators" who allegedly hoarded goods to drive up prices, they marched to stores, asked the price of bacon or cornmeal or salt, denounced such "extortion," and took what they wanted without paying. On April 2, 1863, a mob of more than 1,000 women and boys looted several shops in Richmond before the militia, under the personal command of Davis, forced them to disperse. The Confederate government subsequently released some emergency food stocks to civilians, and state and county governments aided the families of soldiers. Better crops in 1863 helped alleviate the worst shortages, but serious problems persisted.

The Wartime Draft and Class Tensions

In both South and North, the draft intensified social unrest and turned it in the direction of class conflict. The burst of patriotic enthusiasm that had prompted a million

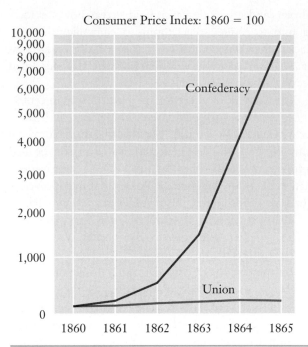

Consumer Price Index: 1860 = 100

WARTIME INFLATION IN THE CONFEDERACY AND THE UNION

men to join the colors in North and South during 1861 had waned by spring 1862. That April, the Confederacy enacted a draft that made all white men (with certain occupational exemptions) ages 18 to 35 liable to conscription. A drafted man could hire a substitute, but the price of substitutes soon rose beyond the means of the average Southern farmer or worker, giving rise to the bitter cry that it was "a rich man's war and a poor man's fight."

The cry grew louder in October 1862 when the Confederate Congress raised the draft age to 45 and added a clause exempting one white man from the draft on every plantation with 20 or more slaves. The purpose of this "overseer exemption" was to keep up production and prevent slave uprisings. It had been prompted by the complaints of planters' wives, who had been left alone to manage the slaves after the departure of husbands, sons, and overseers for the army. The so-called Twenty Negro Law was regarded as blatant discrimination by nonslaveholding farm families whose men were also at the front. In addition, raising the age limit to 45 took away many fathers of children too young to work the farm. The law provoked widespread draft-dodging and desertions.

Similar discontent greeted the enactment of a conscription law in the North. In summer 1863, some 30,000 Union soldiers—who had enlisted in 1861 for two years rather than the normal three—would be leaving military service, along with 80,000 of the nine-month militia called into service the preceding autumn. To meet the looming

The Library of Virginia.

THE RICHMOND BREAD RIOT

Illustrating the economic problems of the Confederacy and the suffering of poor civilians in overcrowded cities, the bread riot in Richmond involved 1,000 women and boys who broke into shops to take food and other goods on April 2, 1863. The rioters were white, although a few black children may have gotten into the act, as portrayed by the artist of this woodcut.

shortfall of men, Congress decreed in March that all male citizens ages 20 to 45 must enroll for the draft. Not all of them would necessarily be called (administrative policy exempted married men over 35), but all would be liable.

The law was intended more to encourage volunteers to come forward than to draft men directly into the army. In the president's four calls for troops under this law, the War Department set a quota for every congressional district and allowed 50 days for the quota to be met with volunteers before resorting to a draft lottery. Some districts avoided drafting anyone by offering large bounties to volunteers. The bounty system produced glaring abuses, including "bounty jumpers" who enlisted and then deserted as soon as they got their money—often to enlist again under another name somewhere else.

The drafting process was also open to abuse. Like the Confederate law, the Union law permitted hiring substitutes. To keep the price from skyrocketing as it had in the Confederacy, the law allowed a drafted man the alternative

of paying a "commutation fee" of $300 that exempted him from the current draft call (but not necessarily from the next one). That provision raised the cry of "rich man's war, poor man's fight" in the North as well. The Democratic Party nurtured this sense of class resentment and racism intensified it. Democrats in Congress opposed conscription, just as they opposed emancipation. Democratic newspapers told white workers, especially the large Irish American population, that the draft would force them to fight a war to free the slaves, who would then come north to take their jobs. This volatile issue sparked widespread violence when the Northern draft got under way in summer 1863. The worst riot occurred in New York City July 13–16, where huge mobs consisting mostly of Irish Americans demolished draft offices, lynched several blacks, and destroyed huge areas of the city in four days of looting and burning.

New York Historical Society.

THE NEW YORK CITY DRAFT RIOT

The worst urban violence in all of American history occurred in New York City July 13–16, 1863, when thousands of men and women, mostly poor Irish Americans, attacked draft offices, homes, businesses, and individuals. Black residents of the city were among the mob's victims because they symbolized labor competition to Irish Americans, who did not want to be drafted to fight a war to free the slaves. This illustration shows the burning of the Colored Orphan Asylum, a home for black orphans. More than 100 people were killed in the disturbance, most of them rioters shot down by police and soldiers.

Draft riots in the North and bread riots in the South exposed alarming class fissures that deepened with the strains of full-scale war. Although inflation was much less serious in the North than in the South, Northern wages lagged behind price increases. Labor unions sprang up in several industries and struck for higher wages. In some areas, such as the anthracite coal fields of eastern Pennsylvania, labor organizations dominated by Irish Americans combined resistance to the draft and opposition to emancipation with violent strikes against industries owned by Protestant Republicans. Troops sent in to enforce the draft sometimes suppressed the strikes as well. These class, ethnic, and racial hostilities provided a volatile mixture in several Northern communities.

A Poor Man's Fight?

The grievance that it was a rich man's war and a poor man's fight was more apparent than real. Property, excise, and income taxes to sustain the war bore proportionately more heavily on the wealthy than on the poor. In the South, wealthy property owners suffered greater damage and confiscation losses than did nonslaveholders. The war liberated 4 million slaves, the poorest class in America. Both the Union and Confederate armies fielded men from all strata of society in proportion to their percentage of the population. If anything, among those who volunteered in 1861 and 1862, the planter class was overrepresented in the Confederate army and the middle class in the Union forces because those privileged groups believed they had more at stake in the war and joined up in larger numbers during the early months of enthusiasm. Those volunteers—especially the officers—suffered the highest percentage of combat casualties.

Nor did conscription fall much more heavily on the poor than on the rich. Those who escaped the draft by decamping to the woods, the territories, or Canada were mostly poor. The Confederacy abolished substitution in December 1863 and made men who had previously sent substitutes liable to the draft. In the North, several city councils, political machines, and businesses contributed funds to pay the commutation fees of drafted men who were too poor to pay out of their own pockets. In the end, it was neither a rich man's war nor a poor man's fight. It was an American war.

🌐 Blueprint for Modern America

The 37th Congress (1861–63)—the Congress that enacted conscription, passed measures for confiscation and emancipation, and created the greenbacks and the national banking system (see chapter 15)—also enacted three laws that, together with the war legislation, provided what one historian has called "a blueprint for modern America": the Homestead Act, the Morrill Land-Grant College Act, and the Pacific Railroad Act. For several years before the war, Republicans and some northern Democrats had tried to pass these laws to provide social benefits and to promote economic growth, only to see them defeated by Southern opposition or by President Buchanan's veto. The secession of Southern states, ironically, enabled Congress to pass all three in 1862.

The Homestead Act granted a farmer 160 acres of land virtually free after he had lived on the land for five years and had made improvements on it. The Morrill Land-Grant College Act gave each state thousands of acres to fund the establishment of colleges to teach "agricultural and mechanical arts." The Pacific Railroad Act granted land and loans to railroad companies to spur building a transcontinental railroad from Omaha to Sacramento. Under these laws, the U.S. government ultimately granted 80 million acres to homesteaders, 25 million acres to states for land-grant colleges, and 120 million acres to several transcontinental railroads. Despite waste, corruption, and exploitation of the original Indian owners of this land, these laws helped farmers settle some of the most fertile land in the world, studded the land with state colleges, and spanned it with steel rails in a manner that altered the landscape of the western half of the country.

Women and the War

The war advanced many other social changes, particularly with respect to women. In factories and on farms, women replaced men who had gone off to war. Explosions in Confederate ordnance plants and arsenals killed at least 100 women, who were as surely war casualties as men killed in battle. The war accelerated the entry of women into the teaching profession, a trend that had already begun in the Northeast and now spread to other parts of the country. It also brought significant numbers of women into the civil service. During the 1850s, a few women had worked briefly in the U.S. Patent Office (including Clara Barton, who became a famous wartime nurse and founded the American Red Cross). The huge expansion of government bureaucracies after 1861 and the departure of male clerks to the army provided openings that were filled partly by women. After the war, the private sector began hiring women as clerks, bookkeepers, "typewriters" (the machine itself was invented in the 1870s), and telephone operators (the telephone was another postwar invention).

Women's most visible impact was in the field of medicine. The outbreak of war prompted the organization of soldiers' aid societies, hospital societies, and other volun-

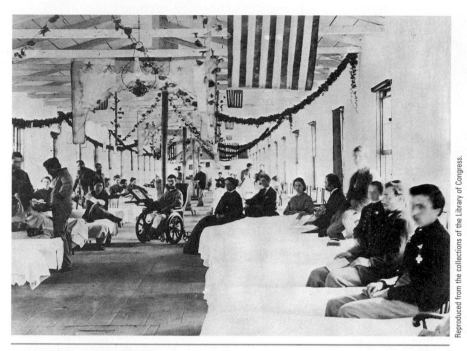

UNION ARMY HOSPITAL
The Armory Square military hospital in Washington, with its clean, cheerful wards apparently decorated for the Christmas holidays, showed Union medical care at its best.

thousands of women went to work, winning grudging and then enthusiastic admiration. One Confederate surgeon praised women nurses as far superior to the convalescent soldiers who had formerly done that job, "rough country crackers" who did not "know castor oil from a gun rod nor laudanum from a hole in the ground." In the North, the treasurer of the Sanitary Commission, who at first had disliked the idea of his wife working as a nurse, was converted by her performance as a volunteer for the Sanitary Commission during summer 1862. "The little woman has come out amazingly strong during these past two months," he wrote. "Have never given her credit for a tithe of the enterprise, pluck, discretion, and force of character that she has shown."

tary associations to provide home front support for the soldiers, and women played a leading role. Their most important function was to help—and sometimes to prod—the medical branches of the Union and Confederate armies to provide more efficient, humane care for sick and wounded soldiers. Dr. Elizabeth Blackwell, the first American woman to earn an M.D. (1849), organized a meeting of 3,000 women in New York City on April 29, 1861. They put together the Women's Central Association for Relief, which became the nucleus for the most powerful voluntary association of the war, the U.S. Sanitary Commission.

Eventually embracing 7,000 local auxiliaries, the Sanitary Commission was an essential adjunct of the Union army's medical bureau. Most of its local volunteers were women, as were most of the nurses it provided to army hospitals. Nursing was not a new profession for women, but it lacked respect as a wartime profession, being classed only slightly above prostitution. The fame won by Florence Nightingale of Britain during the Crimean War a half-dozen years earlier had begun to change that perception. As thousands of middle- and even upper-class women volunteers flocked to army hospitals, nursing began its transformation from a menial occupation to a respected profession.

The nurses had to overcome the deep-grained suspicions of army surgeons and the opposition of husbands and fathers who shared the cultural sentiment that the shocking, embarrassingly physical atmosphere of an army hospital was no place for a respectable woman. Many

The war also bolstered the fledgling women's rights movement. It was no coincidence that Elizabeth Cady Stanton and Susan B. Anthony founded the National Woman Suffrage Association in 1869, only four years after the war. Although a half century passed before women won the vote, this movement could not have achieved the momentum that made it a force in American life without the work of women in the Civil War.

The Confederate Tide Crests and Recedes

The Army of Northern Virginia and the Army of the Potomac spent the winter of 1862–63 on opposite banks of the Rappahannock River. With the coming of spring, Union commander Joe Hooker resumed the offensive with hopes of redeeming the December disaster at Fredericksburg. On April 30, instead of charging straight across the river, Hooker crossed his men several miles upriver and came in on Lee's rear. Lee quickly faced most of his troops about and confronted the enemy in dense woods, known locally as the Wilderness, near the crossroads hostelry of Chancellorsville. Nonplussed, Hooker lost the initiative.

The Battle of Chancellorsville

Even though the Union forces outnumbered the Confederates by almost two to one, Lee boldly went over to the

FEMALE SPIES AND SOLDIERS

In addition to working in war industries and serving as army nurses, some women pursued traditionally male wartime careers as spies and soldiers. One of the most famous Confederate spies was Rose O'Neal Greenhow, a Washington widow and socialite who fed information to officials in Richmond. Federal officers arrested her in August 1861 and deported her to Richmond in spring 1862. She was photographed with her daughter in the Old Capitol prison in Washington, D.C., while awaiting trial. In October 1864, she drowned in a lifeboat off Wilmington, North Carolina, after a blockade runner carrying her back from a European mission was run aground by a Union warship. The second photograph shows a Union soldier who enlisted in the 95th Illinois Infantry under the name of Albert Cashier and fought through the war. Not until a farm accident in 1911 revealed Albert Cashier to be a woman, whose real name was Jennie Hodgers, was her secret disclosed. Most of the other estimated 400 women who evaded the superficial physical exams and passed as men to enlist in the Union and Confederate armies were more quickly discovered and discharged—six of them after they had babies while in the army. A few, however, served long enough to be killed in action.

offensive. On May 2, Stonewall Jackson led 28,000 men on a stealthy march through the woods to attack the Union right flank late in the afternoon. As a result of the negligence of the Union commanders, the surprise was complete. Jackson's assault crumpled the Union flank as the sun dipped below the horizon. Jackson then rode out to scout the terrain for a moonlight attack but was wounded on his return by jittery Confederates who mistook him and his staff for Union cavalry. Nevertheless, Lee resumed the attack the next day. In three more days of fighting that caused 12,800 Confederate and 16,800 Union casualties (the largest number for a single battle in the war so far), Lee drove the Union troops back across the Rappahannock. It was a brilliant victory.

In the North, the gloom grew deeper. "My God!" exclaimed Lincoln when he heard the news of Chancellorsville. "What will the country say?" Copperhead opposition intensified. Southern sympathizers in Britain renewed efforts for diplomatic recognition of the Confederacy. Southern elation, however, was tempered by grief at the death on May 10 of Jackson, who had contracted pneumonia after amputation of his arm. Nevertheless, Lee decided to parlay his tactical victory at Chancellorsville into a strategic offensive by again invading the North. A victory on Union soil would convince Northerners and foreigners alike that the Confederacy was invincible. As his army moved north in June 1863, Lee was confident of success. "There never were such men in an army before," he

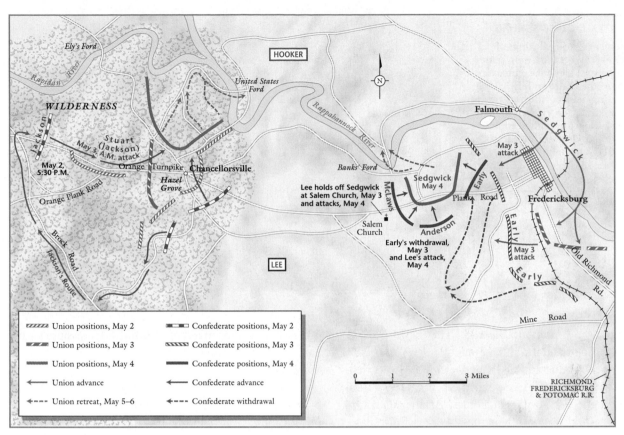

MAP 16.2   BATTLE OF CHANCELLORSVILLE, MAY 2–6, 1863
This map demonstrates the advantage of holding "interior lines," which enabled General Lee to shift troops back and forth to and from the Chancellorsville and Fredericksburg fronts over the course of three days while the two parts of the Union army remained separated.

wrote of his troops. "They will go anywhere and do anything if properly led."

The Gettysburg Campaign

At first, all went well. The Confederates brushed aside or captured Union forces in the northern Shenandoah Valley and in Pennsylvania. Stuart's cavalry threw a scare into Washington by raiding behind Union lines into Maryland and Pennsylvania. That very success led to trouble. With Stuart's cavalry separated from the rest of the army, Lee lost the vital intelligence that the cavalry garnered as the army's eyes. By June 28, several detachments of Lee's forces were scattered about Pennsylvania, far from their base and vulnerable.

At this point, Lee learned that the Army of the Potomac was moving toward him, now under the command of George Gordon Meade. Lee immediately ordered his own army to reassemble in the vicinity of Gettysburg, an agricultural and college town at the hub of a dozen roads leading in from all directions. There, on the morning of July 1,

the vanguard of the two armies met in a clash that grew into the greatest battle in American history.

As the fighting spread west and north of town, couriers pounded up the roads on lathered horses to summon reinforcements to both sides. The Confederates fielded more men and broke the Union lines late that afternoon, driving the survivors to a defensive position on Cemetery Hill south of town. General Richard Ewell, Jackson's successor as commander of the Confederate Second Corps, judging this position too strong to take with his own troops, chose not to press the attack as the sun went down on what he presumed would be another Confederate victory.

When the sun rose the next morning, however, the reinforced Union army was holding a superb defensive position from Culp's Hill and Cemetery Hill south to Little Round Top. Lee's principal subordinate, First Corps commander James Longstreet, advised against attack, urging instead a maneuver to the south, toward Washington, to force the Federals to attack Lee in a strong defensive position. But Lee believed his army invincible. After its victory on July 1, a move to the south might look like a retreat.

THE BATTLE OF GETTYSBURG
This is one of many paintings of Pickett's assault on the Union center on Cemetery Ridge at the climactic moment of the battle on July 3, 1863. The painting depicts "the high tide of the Confederacy" as Virginia and North Carolina troops pierce the Union line only to be shot down or captured— a fate suffered by half of the 13,000 Confederate soldiers who participated in Pickett's Charge.

National Park Service, Harpers Ferry Center.

Pointing to the Union lines, he said: "The enemy is there, and I am going to attack him there."

Longstreet reluctantly led the attack on the Union left. Once committed, his men fought with fury. The Union troops fought back with equal fury. As the afternoon passed, peaceful areas with names like Peach Orchard, Wheat Field, Devil's Den, and Little Round Top were turned into killing fields. By the end of the day, Confederate forces had made small gains at great cost, but the main Union line had held firm.

Lee was not yet ready to yield the offensive. Having attacked both Union flanks, he thought the center might be weak. On July 3, he ordered a frontal attack on Cemetery Ridge, led by a fresh division under George Pickett. After a two-hour artillery barrage, Pickett's 5,000 men and 8,000 additional troops moved forward on that sultry afternoon in a picture-book assault that forms our most enduring image of the Civil War. "Pickett's Charge" was shot to pieces; scarcely half of the men returned unwounded to their own lines. It was the final act in an awesome three-day drama that left some 50,000 men killed, wounded, or captured: 23,000 Federals and 25,000 to 28,000 Confederates.

Lee limped back to Virginia pursued by the Union troops. Lincoln was unhappy with Meade for not cutting off the Confederate retreat. Nevertheless, Gettysburg was a great Northern victory, and it came at the same time as other important Union successes in Mississippi, Louisiana, and Tennessee.

The Vicksburg Campaign

In mid-April, Grant had begun a move that would put Vicksburg in a vise. The Union ironclad fleet ran downriver past the big guns at Vicksburg with little dam-

age. Grant's troops marched down the Mississippi's west bank and were ferried across the river 40 miles south of Vicksburg.

There they kept the Confederate defenders off balance by striking east toward Jackson instead of marching north to Vicksburg. Grant's purpose was to scatter the Confederate forces in central Mississippi and to destroy the rail network so that his rear would be secure when he turned toward Vicksburg. It was a brilliant strategy, flawlessly executed. During the first three weeks of May, Grant's troops marched 180 miles, won five battles, and trapped 32,000 Confederate troops and 3,000 civilians in Vicksburg between the Union army on land and the Union gunboats on the river.

But the Confederate army was still full of fight. Confederate soldiers threw back Union assaults against the Vicksburg trenches on May 19 and 22. Grant then settled down for a siege. By late June, he had built up his army to 70,000 men to ward off a Confederate army of 30,000 scraped together by Joseph Johnston to try to rescue Vicksburg. Running out of supplies, the Vicksburg garrison surrendered on July 4. Grant then turned east and drove off Johnston's force. On July 9, the Confederate garrison at Port Hudson, 200 river miles south of Vicksburg, surrendered to a besieging Union army. Northern forces now controlled the entire length of the Mississippi River. "The Father of Waters again goes unvexed to the sea," said Lincoln. The Confederacy had been torn in two, and Lincoln knew who deserved the credit. "Grant is my man," he said, "and I am his the rest of the war."

Chickamauga and Chattanooga

Northerners had scarcely finished celebrating the twin victories of Gettysburg and Vicksburg when they learned of

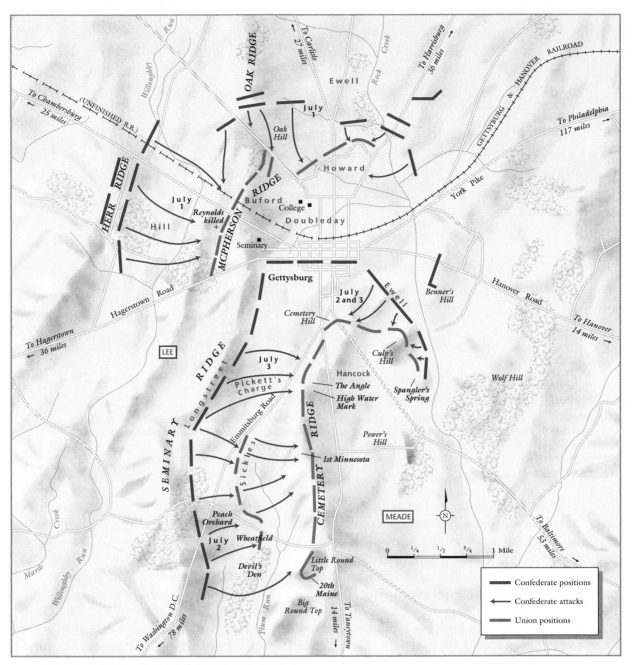

MAP 16.3 BATTLE OF GETTYSBURG, JULY 1–3, 1863
On July 2 and 3, the Union army had the advantage of interior lines at Gettysburg, which enabled General Meade to shift reinforcements from his right on Culp's Hill to his left near Little Round Top over a much shorter distance than Confederate reinforcements from one flank to the other would have to travel.

an important—and almost bloodless—triumph in Tennessee. After the traumatic Battle of Stones River at the end of 1862, the Union Army of the Cumberland and the Confederate Army of Tennessee had shadowboxed for nearly six months. On June 24, Union commander Rosecrans finally assaulted the Confederate defenses in the Cumberland foothills of east-central Tennessee. He used his cavalry and a mounted infantry brigade armed with new repeating rifles to get around the Confederate flanks while his infantry threatened the Confederate front. In the first week of July, the Confederates retreated all the way to Chattanooga.

After a pause for resupply, Rosecrans's army advanced again in August, this time in tandem with a smaller Union army in eastern Tennessee commanded by Burnside, who had come to this theater after being removed from command in Virginia. Again the outnumbered Confederates fell back, evacuating Knoxville on September 2 and Chattanooga on September 9. This action severed the South's only direct east-west rail link. Having sliced the

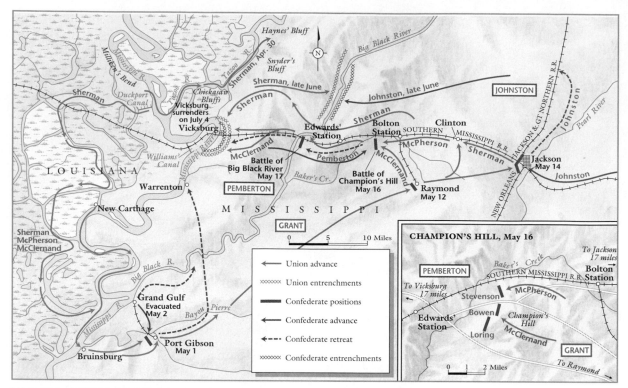

MAP 16.4 VICKSBURG CAMPAIGN, APRIL–JULY 1863

This map illustrates Grant's brilliant orchestration of the campaign that involved Sherman's feint at Haynes' Bluff (top of map) on April 30 while the rest of the Union forces crossed at Bruinsburg (bottom of map) and then cleared Confederate resistance out of the way eastward to Jackson before turning west to invest Vicksburg.

Confederacy in half with the capture of Vicksburg and Port Hudson, Union forces now stood poised for a campaign into Georgia that threatened to slice it into three parts. For the Confederacy, it was a stunning reversal of the situation only four months earlier, after Chancellorsville, when the Union cause had appeared hopeless.

Confederate General Braxton Bragg reached into his bag of tricks and sent fake deserters into Union lines with tales of a Confederate retreat toward Atlanta. He then laid a trap for Rosecrans's troops as they advanced through the mountain passes south of Chattanooga. To help him spring it, Davis approved the detachment of Longstreet with two divisions from Lee's army to reinforce Bragg. On September 19, the Confederates turned and counterattacked Rosecrans's now outnumbered army in the valley of Chickamauga Creek.

On that day and the next, in ferocious fighting that produced more casualties (35,000) than any other single battle save Gettysburg, the Confederates finally scored a victory. On September 20, after a confusion of orders left a division-size gap in the Union line, Longstreet's men broke through, sending part of the Union army reeling back to Chattanooga. Only a firm stand by corps commander George H. Thomas—a Virginian who had re-

mained loyal to the Union—prevented a Union rout. For this feat, Thomas earned the nickname "Rock of Chickamauga." Lincoln subsequently appointed Thomas commander of the Army of the Cumberland to replace Rosecrans, who was, in Lincoln's words, "confused and stunned like a duck hit on the head" after Chickamauga.

Lincoln also sent two army corps from Virginia under Hooker and two from Vicksburg under Sherman to reinforce Thomas, whose troops in Chattanooga were under virtual siege by Bragg's forces, which held most of the surrounding heights. More important, Lincoln put Grant in overall command of the beefed-up Union forces there. When Grant arrived in late October, he welded the various Northern units into a new army and opened a new supply line into Chattanooga. On November 24, Hooker's troops drove Confederate besiegers off massive Lookout Mountain.

The next day, an assault on Bragg's main line at Missionary Ridge east of Chattanooga won a smashing success against seemingly greater odds than Pickett had faced at Gettysburg. The Union troops that had been routed at Chickamauga two months earlier redeemed themselves by driving the Confederates off Missionary Ridge and 20 miles south into Georgia.

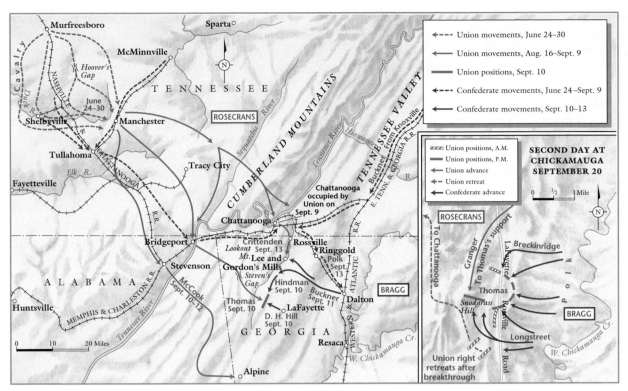

MAP 16.5 ROAD TO CHICKAMAUGA, JUNE–SEPTEMBER 1863
From Murfreesboro to Chattanooga, Rosecrans' campaign of maneuver on multiple fronts, as shown on this map, forced Bragg's Army of Tennessee all the way south into Georgia in a campaign with minimal casualties before Bragg counterattacked at Chickamauga.

These battles climaxed a string of Union victories in the second half of 1863, which made that year one of "calamity . . . defeat . . . utter ruin," in the words of a Confederate official. The Southern diarist Mary Boykin Chesnut found "gloom and unspoken despondency hang[ing] like a pall everywhere." Jefferson Davis removed the discredited Bragg from command of the Army of Tennessee and reluctantly replaced him with Joseph E. Johnston, in whom Davis had little confidence. Lincoln summoned Grant to Washington and appointed him general-in-chief of all Union armies in March 1864, signifying a relentless fight to the finish.

Black Men in Blue

The events of the second half of 1863 also confirmed emancipation as a Union war aim. Northerners had not greeted the Emancipation Proclamation with great enthusiasm. Democrats and border-state Unionists continued to denounce it, and many Union soldiers resented the idea that they would now be risking their lives for black freedom. The Democratic Party had hoped to capitalize on this opposition, and on Union military failures, to win

important off-year elections. Northern military victories knocked one prop out from under the Democratic platform, and the performance of black soldiers fighting for the Union knocked out another.

The enlistment of black soldiers was a logical corollary of emancipation. Free Negroes in the North had tried to enlist in 1861, but they were rejected. Proposals to recruit black soldiers, Democrats said, were part of a Republican plot to establish "the equality of the black and white races." In a way, that charge was correct. One consequence of black men fighting for the Union would be to advance the black race a long way toward equal rights. "Once let the black man get upon his person the brass letters, U.S.," said Frederick Douglass, "and a musket on his shoulder and bullets in his pocket, and there is no power on earth which can deny that he has earned the right to citizenship."

But it was pragmatism more than principle that pushed the North toward black recruitment. One purpose of emancipation was to deprive the Confederacy of black laborers and to use them for the Union. Putting some of those former laborers in uniform was a compelling idea, especially as white enlistments lagged and the North had to enact conscription in 1863. Some Union commanders in occupied portions of Louisiana, South Carolina, and Missouri began to organize black regiments in 1862. The Emancipation Proclamation legitimized this policy with its proposal to enroll able-bodied male contrabands in new black regiments—although these units would serve as labor battalions, supply troops, and garrison forces rather than as combat troops. They would be paid less than white soldiers, and their officers would be white. In other words, black men in blue would be second-class soldiers, just as free blacks in the North were second-class citizens.

Black Soldiers in Combat

Continuing pressure from abolitionists, as well as military necessity, partly eroded discrimination. Congress enacted equal pay in 1864. Officers worked for better treatment of their men. Above all, the regiments lobbied for the right to fight as combat soldiers. Even some previously hostile white soldiers came around to the notion that black men might just as well stop enemy bullets as white men. In May and June 1863, black regiments in Louisiana fought well in an assault on Port Hudson and in defense of a Union outpost at Milliken's Bend, near Vicksburg. "The bravery of the blacks in the battle of Milliken's Bend completely revolutionized the sentiment of the army with regard to the employment of negro troops," wrote the assistant secretary of war, who had been on the spot with Grant's army. "I heard prominent officers who formerly in private had sneered at the idea of the negroes fighting express themselves after that as heartily in favor of it."

Even more significant was the action of the 54th Massachusetts Infantry, the first black regiment raised in the North. Its officers, headed by Colonel Robert Gould Shaw, came from prominent New England antislavery families. Two sons of Frederick Douglass were in the regiment—one of them as sergeant major. Shaw worked hard to win the right for the regiment to fight. On July 18, 1863, he succeeded: The 54th was assigned to lead an assault on Fort Wagner, part of the network of Confederate defenses protecting Charleston. Although the attack failed, the 54th fought courageously, suffering 50 percent casualties, including Colo-nel Shaw, who was killed. This battle "made Fort Wagner such a name to the colored race as Bunker Hill had been for ninety years to the white Yankees," declared the New York *Tribune*.

The battle took place just after white mobs of draft rioters in New York had lynched blacks. Abolitionist and Republican commentators drew the moral: Black men who fought for the Union deserved more respect than white men who rioted against it. Lincoln made this point eloquently in a widely published letter to a political meeting in August 1863. When final victory was achieved, he wrote, "there will be some black men who can remember that, with silent tongue, and clenched teeth, and steady eye, and well-poised bayonet, they have helped mankind on to this great consummation; while, I fear, there will be some white ones, unable to forget that, with malignant heart, and deceitful speech, they have strove to hinder it."

Emancipation Confirmed

Lincoln's letter set the tone for Republican campaigns in state elections that fall. The party swept them all, including Ohio, where they buried Vallandigham under a 100,000-vote margin swelled by the soldier vote, which went 94 percent for his opponent. In effect, the elections were a powerful endorsement of the administration's

PART OF COMPANY E, 4TH U.S. COLORED INFANTRY
Organized in July 1863, most of the men were former slaves from North Carolina. The 4th fought in several actions on the Petersburg and Richmond fronts in 1864, helping to capture part of the Petersburg defenses on June 15. Of the 166 black regiments in the Union Army, the 4th suffered the fourth-largest number of combat deaths.

HISTORY THROUGH FILM

Glory (1989)

Directed by Edward Zwick. Starring Matthew Broderick (Robert Gould Shaw), Denzel Washington (Trip), Morgan Freeman (Rawlins).

Glory was the first feature film to treat the role of black soldiers in the Civil War. It tells the story of the 54th Massachusetts Volunteer Infantry from its organization in early 1863 through its climactic assault on Fort Wagner six months later. When the 54th moved out at dusk on July 18 to lead the attack, the idea of black combat troops still seemed a risky experiment. The New York *Tribune,* a strong supporter of black enlistment, had nevertheless observed in May 1863 that many Northern whites "have no faith" that black soldiers would stand and fight Southern whites who considered themselves a master race. The unflinching behavior of the regiment in the face of an overwhelming hail of lead and iron and its casualties of some 50 percent settled the matter. "Who now asks in doubt and derision 'Will the Negro fight?'" commented one abolitionist. "The answer comes to us from those graves beneath Fort Wagner's walls, which the American people will surely never forget."

Many did forget, but *Glory* revived their collective memory. Its combat scenes, climaxed by the assault on Fort Wagner, are among the most realistic and effective in any war movie. Morgan Freeman and Denzel Washington give memorable performances as a fatherly sergeant and a rebellious private who nevertheless picks up the flag when the color-bearer falls and carries it to the ramparts of Fort Wagner, where he too is killed. Matthew Broderick's portrayal of Colonel Robert Gould Shaw is less memorable because the real Shaw was more assertive and mature than Broderick's Shaw.

Except for Shaw, the principal characters in the film are fictional. There were no real Major Cabot Forbes; no tough Irish Sergeant Mulcahy; no black Sergeant John Rawlins; no brash, hardened Private Trip. A larger fiction is involved here. The movie gives the impression that most of the 54th's soldiers were former slaves. In fact, this atypical black regiment was recruited mainly in the North, so most of the men had always been free. The story that screenwriter Kevin Jarre and director Edward Zwick chose to tell is not simply about the 54th Massachusetts but about black soldiers in the Civil War. Most of the 179,000 African Americans in the Union army (and at least 10,000 in the navy) were slaves until a few months, even days, before they joined up. Fighting for the Union bestowed upon former slaves a new dignity, self-respect, and militancy, which helped them achieve equal citizenship and political rights—for a time—after the war.

Many of the events dramatized in *Glory* are also fictional: the incident of the racist quartermaster who initially refuses to distribute shoes to Shaw's men; the whipping Trip receives as punishment for going AWOL; Shaw's threat to expose his superior officer's corruption as a way of securing a combat assignment for the 54th; and the religious meeting the night before the assault on Fort Wagner. All of these scenes point toward a larger truth, however, most vividly portrayed symbolically in a surreal, and at first glance, irrelevant scene. During a training exercise, Shaw gallops his horse along a path flanked by stakes, each holding aloft a watermelon. Shaw slashes right and left with his sword, slicing and smashing every melon. The point becomes clear when we recall the identification of watermelons with the "darky" stereotype. The image of smashed melons drives home the essential message of *Glory*.

Kobal Collection/Tri Star.

A scene from *Glory* showing black soldiers of the 54th Massachusetts ready to fire at the enemy.

emancipation policy. If the Emancipation Proclamation had been submitted to a referendum a year earlier, observed a newspaper editor in November 1863, "the voice of a majority would have been against it. And yet not a year has passed before it is approved by an overwhelming majority."

Emancipation would not be assured of survival until it had been christened by the Constitution. On April 8, 1864, the Senate passed the 13th Amendment to abolish slavery, but Democrats in the House blocked the required two-thirds majority there. Not until after Lincoln's reelection in 1864 would the House pass the amendment, which became part of the Constitution on December 6, 1865. In the end, though, the fate of slavery depended on the outcome of the war. And despite Confederate defeats in 1863, that outcome was by no means certain. Some of the heaviest fighting lay ahead.

☙ The Year of Decision

Many Southerners succumbed to defeatism in the winter of 1863–64. "I have never actually despaired of the cause," wrote a Confederate War Department official in November, but "steadfastness is yielding to a sense of hopelessness." Desertions from Confederate armies increased. Inflation galloped out of control. According to a Richmond diarist, a merchant told a poor woman in October 1863 that the price of a barrel of flour was $70: "'My God!' exclaimed she, 'how can I pay such prices? I have seven children; what shall I do?' 'I don't know, madam,' said he, coolly, 'unless you eat your children.'"

The Davis administration, like the Lincoln administration a year earlier, had to face congressional elections during a time of public discontent, for the Confederate constitution mandated such elections in odd-numbered years. Political parties had ceased to exist in the Confederacy after Democrats and former Whigs had tacitly declared a truce in 1861 to form a united front for the war effort. Many congressmen had been elected without opposition in 1861. By 1863, however, significant hostility to Davis had emerged. Although it was not channeled through any organized party, it took on partisan trappings, as an inchoate anti-Davis faction surfaced in the Confederate Congress and in the election campaign of 1863.

Some antiadministration candidates ran on a quasi-peace platform (analogous to that of the Copperheads in the North) that called for an armistice and peace negotiations. The movement left unresolved the terms of such negotiations—reunion or independence—but any peace overture from a position of weakness was tantamount to

conceding defeat. The peace movement was especially strong in North Carolina, where for a time it appeared that the next governor would be elected on a peace platform (in the end, the "peace candidate" was defeated). Still, antiadministration candidates made significant gains in the 1863 Confederate elections, although they fell about 15 seats short of a majority in the House and two seats short in the Senate.

Out of the Wilderness

Shortages, inflation, political discontent, military defeat, high casualties, and the loss of thousands of slaves bent but did not break the Southern spirit. As spring 1864 came on, a renewed determination infused both home front and battle front. The Confederate armies no longer had the strength to invade the North or to win the war with a knockout blow, but they could still fight a war of attrition, as the patriots had done in the War of 1775–83 against Britain (chapter 6). If they could hold out long enough and inflict enough casualties on the Union armies, they might weaken the Northern will to continue fighting. And if they could just hold out until the Union presidential election in November, Northern voters might reject Lincoln and elect a Peace Democrat.

Northerners were vulnerable to this strategy of psychological attrition. Military success in 1863 had created a mood of confidence, and people expected a quick, decisive victory in 1864. The mood grew with Grant's appointment as general-in-chief. When Grant decided to remain in Virginia with the Army of the Potomac and to leave Sherman in command of the Union forces in northern Georgia, Northerners expected these two heavyweights to floor the Confederacy with a one-two punch. Lincoln was alarmed by this euphoria. "The people are too sanguine," he told a reporter. "They expect too much at once." Disappointment might trigger despair.

Lincoln was nearly proved right. Grant's strategic plan was elegant in its simplicity. While smaller Union armies in peripheral theaters carried out auxiliary campaigns, the two principal armies in Virginia and Georgia would attack the main Confederate forces under Lee and Johnston. Convinced that in years past Union armies in various theaters had "acted independently and without concert, like a balky team, no two ever pulling together," Grant ordered simultaneous offensives on all fronts, to prevent the Confederates from shifting reinforcements from one theater to another.

Grant's offensives began the first week of May. The heaviest fighting occurred in Virginia. When the Army of the Potomac crossed the Rapidan River, Lee attacked its flank in the thick scrub forest of the Wilderness, where

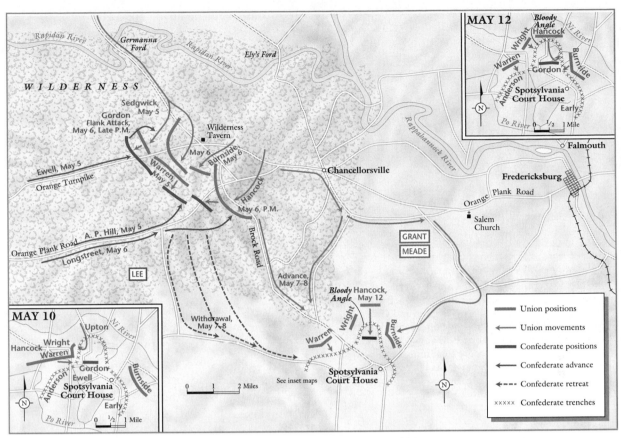

MAP 16.6   BATTLE OF THE WILDERNESS AND SPOTSYLVANIA, MAY 5–12, 1864

Four major battles with a total of more than 100,000 casualties to both sides were fought within a few miles of Fredericksburg between December 1862 and May 1864. Compare this map with the Chancellorsville map on p. 513. The first battle of Fredericksburg on December 13, 1862 (described p. 506) was fought in the same vicinity as the Fredericksburg fighting on May 3, 1863, shown on the Chancellorsville map.

Union superiority in numbers and artillery would count for little (and where Lee had defeated Hooker a year earlier at Chancellorsville). Lee's action brought on two days (May 5–6) of the most confused, frenzied fighting the war had yet seen. Hundreds of wounded men burned to death in brush fires set off by exploding shells or muzzle flashes. The battle surged back and forth, with the Confederates inflicting 18,000 casualties and suffering 12,000 themselves. Having apparently halted Grant's offensive, they claimed a victory.

Spotsylvania and Cold Harbor

Grant did not admit defeat, nor did he retreat, as other Union commanders in Virginia had done. Instead, he moved toward Spotsylvania Courthouse, a key crossroads 10 miles closer to Richmond. Skillfully, Lee pulled back to cover the road junction. Repeated Union assaults during the next 12 days (May 8–19) left another 18,000 Northerners and 12,000 Southerners killed, wounded, or cap-

tured. The Confederates fought from an elaborate network of trenches and log breastworks they had constructed virtually overnight. Civil War soldiers had learned the advantages of trenches, which gave the defense an enormous advantage and made frontal assaults almost suicidal.

Having achieved no better than stalemate around Spotsylvania, Grant again moved south around Lee's right flank in an effort to force the outnumbered Confederates into an open fight. Lee, however, anticipated Grant's moves and confronted him from behind formidable defenses at the North Anna River, Totopotomoy Creek, and near the crossroads inn of Cold Harbor, only 10 miles northeast of Richmond. Believing the Confederates must be exhausted and demoralized by their repeated retreats, Grant decided to attack at Cold Harbor on June 3—a costly mistake. Lee's troops were ragged and hungry but far from demoralized. Their withering fire inflicted 7,000 casualties in less than an hour. (By coincidence, this was the same number of casualties suffered during the same

Brown Brothers.

TRENCH WARFARE, 1864–1865

During the grueling campaigns of 1864 and 1865, the opposing armies entrenched wherever they paused. By the end of the war, hundreds of square miles in Virginia and Georgia looked like this, especially along a 35-mile line from a point east of Richmond to just southwest of Petersburg, where the armies confronted each other for more than nine months. Note not only the elaborate trench networks but also the absence of trees, cut down to provide firewood and to create open fields of fire for rifles and cannons.

length of time by the men in Pickett's Charge at Gettysburg exactly 11 months before.) "I regret this assault more than any other one I have ordered," said Grant.

Stalemate in Virginia

Now Grant moved all the way across the James River to strike at Petersburg, an industrial city and rail center 20 miles south of Richmond. If Petersburg fell, the Confederates could not hold Richmond. Once more Lee's troops raced southward on the inside track and blocked Grant's troops. Four days of Union assaults (June 15–18) produced another 11,000 Northern casualties but no breakthrough.

Such high Union losses in just six weeks—some 65,000 killed, wounded, and captured, compared with 37,000 Confederate casualties—cost the Army of the Potomac its offensive power. Grant reluctantly settled down for a siege along the Petersburg–Richmond front that would last more than nine grueling months.

Meanwhile, other Union operations in Virginia had achieved little success. Benjamin Butler bungled an attack up the James River against Richmond and was stopped by a scraped-together army under Beauregard. A Union thrust up the Shenandoah Valley was blocked at Lynchburg in June by Jubal Early, commanding Stonewall Jackson's old corps. Early then led a raid all the way to the outskirts of Washington on July 11 and 12 before being driven back to Virginia. Union cavalry under Philip Sheridan inflicted considerable damage on Confederate resources in Virginia—including the mortal wounding of Jeb Stuart in the battle of Yellow Tavern on May 11—but again failed to strike a crippling blow. In the North, frustration set in over failure to win the quick, decisive victory the public had expected in April.

The Atlanta Campaign

In Georgia, Sherman's army seemed to have accomplished more at less cost than Grant had in Virginia, but there too Union efforts had bogged down in apparent stalemate by August. The strategy and tactics of both Sherman and Johnston in Georgia contrasted with those of Grant and Lee in Virginia. Sherman forced Johnston south toward Atlanta by constantly flanking him to the Union right, generally without bloody battles. Grant constantly forced Lee back by flanking moves to the Union left, but only after bloody battles. By the end of June, Sherman had advanced 80 miles at the cost of 17,000 casualties to Johnston's 14,000—only one-third of the combined losses of Grant and Lee.

Davis grew alarmed by Johnston's apparent willingness to yield territory without a fight. Sherman again flanked the Confederate defenses (after a failed attack) at Kennesaw Mountain in early July. He crossed the Chattahoochee River and drove Johnston back to Peachtree Creek less than five miles from Atlanta. Fearing that Johnston would abandon the city, on July 17, Davis replaced him with John Bell Hood.

A fighting general from Lee's army who had lost a leg at Chickamauga, Hood immediately prepared to counterattack against the Yankees. He did so three times, in late July. Each time, the Confederates reeled back in defeat, suffering a total of 15,000 casualties to Sherman's 6,000. At last, Hood retreated into the formidable earthworks ringing Atlanta and launched no more attacks, although his army did manage to keep Sherman's cavalry and infantry from taking the two railroads leading into Atlanta from the south. Like Grant at Petersburg, Sherman seemed to settle down for a siege.

Peace Overtures

By August, the Confederate strategy of attrition seemed to be working. Union casualties on all fronts during the preceding three months totaled a staggering 110,000—double the number for any comparable period of the war. "Who shall revive the withered hopes that bloomed at the opening of Grant's campaign?" asked the leading Demo-

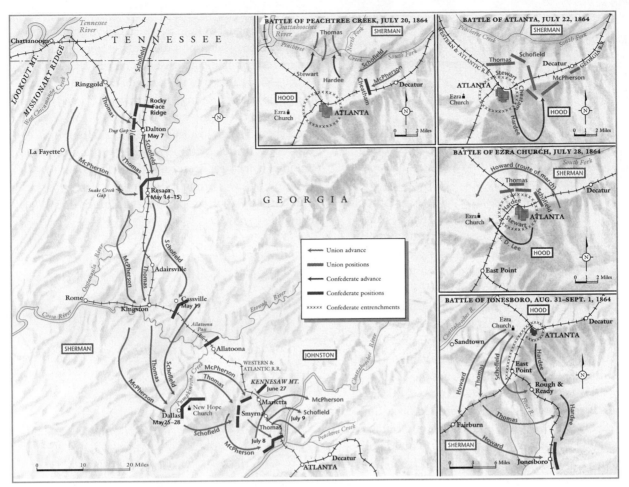

MAP 16.7   CAMPAIGN FOR ATLANTA, MAY–SEPTEMBER 1864
The main map illustrates Sherman's campaign of maneuver that forced Johnston back to Atlanta with relatively few battles.
The first three inset maps show the Confederate counterattacks launched by Hood and the fourth shows how the Union
army got astride the last two railroads entering Atlanta from the south and forced Hood to evacuate the city.

cratic newspaper, the *New York World.* "STOP THE WAR!" shouted Democratic headlines. "All are tired of this damnable tragedy."

Even Republicans joined the chorus of despair. "Our bleeding, bankrupt, almost dying country longs for peace," wrote Horace Greeley of the New York *Tribune.* Greeley became involved in abortive "peace negotiations" spawned by Confederate agents in Canada. Those agents convinced Greeley that they carried peace overtures from Davis, but Lincoln, aware that Davis's condition for peace was Confederate independence, was skeptical. Still, given the mood of the North in midsummer 1864, Lincoln could not reject any opportunity to stop the bloodshed. He deputized Greeley to meet with the Confederate agents in Niagara Falls on the Canadian side of the border. At almost the same time (mid-July), two other Northerners met under a flag of truce with Davis in Richmond. Lincoln had carefully instructed them—and Greeley—that his conditions

for peace were "restoration of the Union and abandonment of slavery."

Of course, Davis would no more accept those terms than Lincoln would accept his. Although neither of the peace contacts came to anything, the Confederates gained a propaganda victory by claiming that Lincoln's terms had been the only obstacle to peace. Northern Democrats ignored the Southern refusal to accept reunion as a condition of peace and focused on the slavery issue as the sole stumbling block. "Tens of thousands of white men must yet bite the dust to allay the negro mania of the President," ran a typical Democratic editorial. By August, even staunch Republicans such as national party chairman Henry Raymond and his associate Thurlow Weed were convinced that "the desire for peace" and the impression that Lincoln "is fighting not for the Union but for the abolition of slavery" made his reelection "an impossibility." Lincoln thought so, too. "I am going to be beaten," he told

John Bigelow Promotes
the Union Cause in France

A founder of the Free Soil and Republican parties, a skillful writer and journalist, and a friend of Secretary of State William H. Seward, John Bigelow (1817–1911) went to Paris in 1861 as consul general of the American legation. His actual role in American foreign policy during the Civil War far exceeded the vague authority suggested by his official title. The American minister, William L. Dayton, was a political appointee who did not speak French and had no diplomatic experience. Fluent in French, Bigelow became an essential partner with Dayton. Bigelow's journalistic experience also enabled him to establish important contacts with Parisian reporters and editors. With Seward's encouragement and secret service funds from the U.S. government, Bigelow bribed members of the notoriously corrupt French press and planted pro-Union or anti-Confederate articles in key journals. He also purchased information about Confederate efforts to build iron-clad ships and commerce raiders in French shipyards. His exposure of these efforts caused the French government to clamp down on them as a violation of French neutrality.

When Dayton died suddenly in late 1864, Bigelow became minister in name as well as in fact. He devoted his efforts after Appomattox to pressing Emperor Napoleon to remove from Mexico the 35,000 French troops who were propping up Ferdi-nand Maximilian, whom Napoleon had established as Emperor of Mexico in 1864. The U.S. government sent 50,000 veteran troops to Texas as a signal to France, which did withdraw the troops in 1866, whereupon the Mexican republicans captured Maximilian and executed him in 1867.

Bigelow returned to the United States in 1866, but during the rest of his long life he traveled abroad extensively, lived in Germany for several years, wrote several books about French history and about a famous predecessor in Paris, Benjamin Franklin, whose success in winning French support for the United States during the Revolution was brought full circle by Bigelow's role in preventing French support for the Confederacy during the Civil War.

JOHN BIGELOW

From the Collections of the Library of Congress.

---

a friend in August, "and unless some great change takes place, *badly* beaten."

Lincoln faced enormous pressure to drop emancipation as a condition of peace so the onus could be shifted to Jefferson Davis's insistence on Confederate independence. Lincoln refused to yield. He would rather lose the election than go back on the promise he had made in the Emancipation Proclamation. "No human power can subdue this rebellion without using the Emancipation lever as I have done," he told weak-kneed Republicans. Some 130,000 black soldiers and sailors were fighting for the Union.

They would not do so if they thought the North intended to forsake them:

> If they stake their lives for us they must be prompted by the strongest motive . . . the promise of freedom. And the promise being made, must be kept. . . . There have been men who proposed to me to return to slavery the[se] black warriors. . . . I should be damned in time & eternity for so doing. The world shall know that I will keep my faith to friends and enemies, come what will.

At the end of August, the Democrats nominated Mc-Clellan for president. The platform on which he ran declared that "after four years of failure to restore the Union by the experiment of war . . . [we] demand that immediate efforts be made for a cessation of hostilities." Southerners were jubilant. Democratic victory on that platform, said the *Charleston Mercury*, "must lead to peace and our independence [if] for the next two months *we hold our own and prevent military success by our foes.*"

The Prisoner-Exchange Controversy

The Democratic platform also condemned the Lincoln administration's "shameful disregard" of prisoners of war in Confederate prison camps. This raised another contentious matter. By midsummer 1864, the plight of Union and Confederate captives had become one of the most bitter issues of the war. The upcoming presidential election and the generally worse conditions in Southern prisons made it mainly a Northern political issue.

In 1862, the Union and Confederate armed forces had signed a cartel for the exchange of prisoners captured in battle. The arrangement had worked reasonably well for a year, making large prison camps unnecessary. When the Union army began to organize regiments of former slaves, however, the Confederate government announced that if they were captured, they and their white officers would be put to death for the crime of fomenting slave insurrections. In practice, the Confederate government did not enforce this policy because Lincoln threatened retaliation on Confederate prisoners of war if it did so, but Confederate troops sometimes murdered black soldiers and their officers as they tried to surrender—most notably at Fort Pillow, a Union garrison on the Mississippi north of Memphis, where cavalry commanded by Nathan Bedford Forrest slaughtered scores of black (and some white) prisoners on April 12, 1864.

In most cases, Confederate officers returned captured black soldiers to slavery or put them to hard labor on Southern fortifications. Expressing outrage at this treatment of soldiers wearing the United States uniform, the Lincoln administration in 1863 suspended the exchange of prisoners until the Confederacy agreed to treat white and black prisoners alike. The Confederacy refused. The South would "die in the last ditch," said the Confederate exchange agent, before "giving up the right to send slaves back to slavery as property recaptured."

There matters stood as the heavy fighting of 1864 poured many thousands of captured soldiers into hastily contrived prison compounds that quickly became death camps. Prisoners were subjected to overcrowding, poor sanitation, contaminated water, scanty rations, inadequate medical facilities, and exposure to deep-South summer heat and northern winter cold. The suffering of Northern prisoners was especially acute, because the deterioration of the Southern economy made it hard to feed and clothe even Confederate soldiers and civilians, let alone Yankee prisoners. Nearly 16 percent of all Union soldiers held in Southern prison camps died, compared with 12 percent of Confederate soldiers in Northern camps. Andersonville was the most notorious hellhole. A stockade camp of 26 acres with neither huts nor tents, designed to accommodate 15,000 prisoners, it held 33,000 in August 1864. They died at the rate of more than 100 per day. Altogether, 13,000 Union soldiers died at Andersonville.

The suffering of Union prisoners brought heavy pressure on the Lincoln administration to renew exchanges, but the Confederates would not budge on the question of exchanging black soldiers. After a series of battles on the Richmond–Petersburg front in September 1864, Lee proposed an informal exchange of prisoners. Grant agreed, on condition that black soldiers captured in the fighting be included "the same as white soldiers." Lee replied that

BURIAL OF UNION POWS AT ANDERSONVILLE

On many days during summer 1864, at least 100 Union prisoners of war died of disease, malnutrition, or exposure at Andersonville Prison in Georgia. This scene of burial in long trenches became so commonplace as to dull the sense of horror.

"negroes belonging to our citizens are not considered subjects of exchange and were not included in my proposition." No exchange, then, responded Grant. The Union government was "bound to secure to all persons received into her armies the rights due to soldiers." Lincoln backed this policy. He would not sacrifice the principle of equal treatment of black prisoners, even though local Republican leaders warned that many in the North "will work and vote against the President, because they think sympathy with a few negroes, also captured, is the cause of a refusal" to exchange prisoners.

The Issue of Black Soldiers in the Confederate Army

During the winter of 1864–65, the Confederate government quietly abandoned its refusal to exchange black prisoners, and exchanges resumed. One reason for this reversal was a Confederate decision to recruit slaves to fight for the South. Two years earlier, Davis had denounced the North's arming of freed slaves as "the most execrable measure recorded in the history of guilty man." Ironically, a few black laborers and body servants with Southern armies had taken up arms in the heat of battle and had unofficially fought alongside their masters against the Yankees. By February 1865, Southern armies were desperate for manpower, and slaves constituted the only remaining reserve. Supported by Lee's powerful influence, Davis pressed the Confederate Congress to enact a bill for recruitment of black soldiers. The assumption that any slaves who fought for the South would have to be granted freedom generated bitter opposition to the measure. "What did we go to war for, if not to protect our property?" asked a Virginia senator. By three votes in the House and one in the Senate, the Confederate Congress finally passed the bill on March 13, 1865. Before any Southern black regiments could be organized, however, the war ended.

🫖 Lincoln's Reelection and the End of the Confederacy

Despite Republican fears, battlefield events, rather than political controversies, had the strongest impact on U.S. voters in 1864. In effect, the election became a referendum on whether to continue fighting for unconditional victory. Within days after the Democratic national convention had declared the war a failure, the military situation changed dramatically.

The Capture of Atlanta

After a month of apparent stalemate on the Atlanta front, Sherman's army again made a large movement by the right flank to attack the last rail link into Atlanta from the south. At the battle of Jonesboro on August 31 and September 1, Sherman's men captured the railroad. Hood abandoned Atlanta to save his army. On September 3, Sherman sent a jaunty telegram to Washington: "Atlanta is ours, and fairly won."

This news had an enormous impact on the election. "VICTORY!" blazoned Republican headlines. "IS THE WAR A FAILURE? OLD ABE'S REPLY TO THE DEMOCRATIC CONVENTION." A New York Republican wrote that the capture of Atlanta, "coming at this political crisis, is the greatest event of the war." The *Richmond Examiner* glumly concurred. The fall of Atlanta, it declared, "came in the very nick of time [to] save the party of Lincoln from irretrievable ruin."

The Shenandoah Valley

If Atlanta was not enough to brighten the prospects for Lincoln's reelection, events in Virginia's Shenandoah Valley were. After Early's raid through the valley all the way to Washington in July, Grant put Philip Sheridan in charge of a reinforced Army of the Shenandoah and told him to "go after Early and follow him to the death." Sheridan infused the same spirit into the three infantry corps of the Army of the Shenandoah that he had previously imbued in his cavalry. On September 19, they attacked Early's force near Winchester, and after a day-long battle sent the Confederates flying to the south. Sheridan pursued them, attacking again on September 22 at Fisher's Hill 20 miles south of Winchester. Early's line collapsed, and his routed army fled 60 more miles southward.

Early's retreat enabled Sheridan to carry out the second part of his assignment in the Shenandoah Valley, which had twice served as a Confederate route of invasion and whose farms helped feed Confederate armies. Sheridan now set about destroying the valley's crops and mills so thoroughly that "crows flying over it for the balance of the season will have to carry their provender with them." Sheridan boasted that by the time he was through, "the Valley, from Winchester up to Staunton, ninety-two miles, will have little in it for man or beast."

But Jubal Early was not yet willing to give up. Reinforced by a division from Lee, on October 19, he launched a dawn attack across Cedar Creek, 15 miles south of Winchester. He caught the Yankees by surprise and drove them back in disorder. At the time of the attack, Sheridan was at Winchester, returning to his army from Washington, where he had gone to confer on future strategy. He jumped onto his horse and sped to the battlefield in a ride that became celebrated in poetry and legend. By sundown, Sheridan's charisma and tactical leadership had turned the battle from a Union defeat into another Confederate rout. The battle of Cedar Creek ended Confederate power in the valley.

Sherman's and Sheridan's victories ensured Lincoln's reelection on November 8 by a majority of 212 to 21 in the electoral college. Soldiers played a notable role in the balloting. Every Northern state except three whose legislatures were controlled by Democrats had passed laws allowing absentee voting by soldiers. Seventy-eight percent of the military vote went to Lincoln—compared with 54 percent of the civilian vote. The men who were doing the fighting had sent a clear message that they meant to finish the job.

From Atlanta to the Sea

Many Southerners got the message, but not Davis. The Confederacy remained "as erect and defiant as ever," he told his Congress in November 1864. "Nothing has changed in the purpose of its Government, in the indomitable valor of its troops, or in the unquenchable spirit

Reproduced from the collections of the Library of Congress.

SHERMAN'S SOLDIERS TEARING UP THE RAILROAD IN ATLANTA

One of the objectives of Sherman's march from Atlanta to the sea was to demolish the railroads so they could not transport supplies to Confederate armies. The soldiers did a thorough job. They tore up the rails and ties, made a bonfire of the ties, heated the rails in the fire, and then wrapped them around trees, creating "Sherman neckties."

of its people." It was this last-ditch resistance that Sherman set out to break in his famous march from Atlanta to the sea.

Sherman had concluded that "We are not only fighting hostile armies, but a hostile people." Defeat of the Confederate armies was not enough to win the war; the railroads, factories, and farms that supported those armies must also be destroyed. The will of the civilians who sustained the war must be crushed. Sherman expressed more bluntly than anyone else the meaning of total war and was ahead of his time in his understanding of psychological warfare. "We cannot change the hearts of those people of the South," he said, "but we can make war so terrible and make them so sick of war that generations would pass away before they would again appeal to it."

In Tennessee and Mississippi, Sherman's troops had burned everything of military value within their reach. Now Sherman proposed to do the same in Georgia. He urged Grant to let him march through the heart of Georgia, living off the land and destroying all resources not needed by his army—the same policy Sheridan was carrying out in the Shenandoah Valley. Grant and Lincoln were reluctant to authorize such a risky move, especially with Hood's army of 40,000 men still intact in northern Alabama. Sherman assured them that he would send George Thomas to take command of a force of 60,000 men in Tennessee, who would be more than a match for Hood. With another 60,000, Sherman could "move through Georgia, smashing things to the sea. . . . I can make the march, and make Georgia howl!"

Lincoln and Grant finally consented. On November 16, Sherman's avengers marched out of Atlanta after burning a third of the city, including some nonmilitary property. Southward they marched 280 miles to Savannah, wrecking everything in their path that could by any stretch of the imagination be considered of military value.

The Battles of Franklin and Nashville

They encountered little resistance. Instead of chasing Sherman, Hood invaded Tennessee with the hope of recovering that state for the Confederacy, a disastrous campaign that virtually destroyed his army. On November 30, the Confederates attacked part of the Union force at Franklin, a town 20 miles south of Nashville. The slaughter claimed no fewer than 12 Confederate generals and 54 regimental commanders as casualties. Instead of retreating, Hood moved on to Nashville, where on December 15 and 16 Thomas launched an attack that almost wiped out the

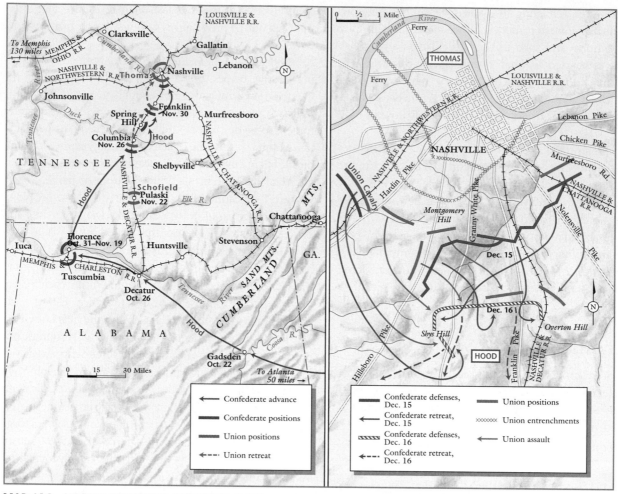

MAP 16.8   HOOD'S TENNESSEE CAMPAIGN, OCTOBER–NOVEMBER 1864 [AND] NASHVILLE, DECEMBER 15–16, 1864
The battle of Nashville on December 15–16, 1864, was the most carefully planned and decisive battle of the war. After Thomas's army drove the Confederates from their first line on December 15 (solid red line), they attacked again and overran the second position (striped red line) on the 16th. The Confederate army virtually disintegrated as it retreated.

Army of Tennessee. Its remnants retreated to Mississippi, where Hood resigned in January 1865.

Fort Fisher and Sherman's March through the Carolinas

News of Hood's defeat produced, in the words of a Southern diarist, "the darkest and most dismal day" of the Confederacy's short history, but worse was yet to come. Lee's army in Virginia drew its dwindling supplies overland from the Carolinas and through the port of Wilmington, North Carolina, the only city still accessible to blockade runners. Massive Fort Fisher guarded the mouth of the Cape Fear River below Wilmington, its big guns keeping blockade ships at bay and protecting the runners. The

Union navy had long wanted to attack Fort Fisher, but the diversion of ships and troops to the long, futile campaign against Charleston had delayed the effort. In January 1865, though, the largest armada of the war—58 ships with 627 guns—pounded Fort Fisher for two days, disabling most of its big guns. Army troops and marines landed and stormed the fort, capturing it on January 15. That ended the blockade running, and Sherman soon put an end to supplies from the Carolinas as well.

At the end of January, Sherman's soldiers headed north from Savannah, eager to take revenge on South Carolina, which to their mind had started the war. Here, they made even less distinction between civilian and military property than they had in Georgia and left even less of Columbia standing than they had of Atlanta. Seemingly invincible, Sherman's army pushed into North Carolina

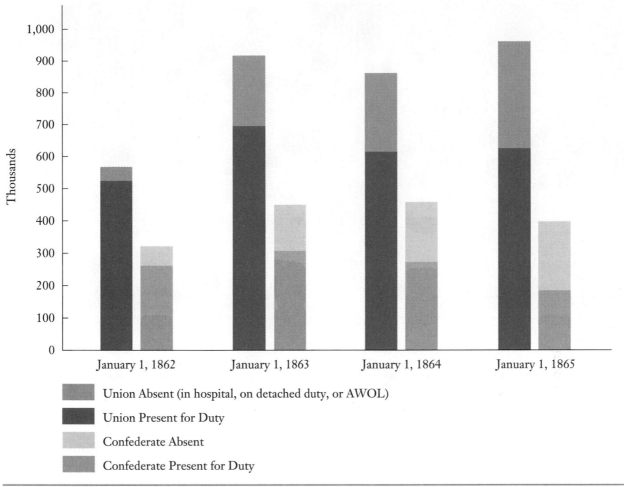

Union Absent (in hospital, on detached duty, or AWOL)

Union Present for Duty

Confederate Absent

Confederate Present for Duty

COMPARATIVE STRENGTH OF UNION AND CONFEDERATE ARMIES

and brushed aside the force that Joseph E. Johnston had assembled to stop them. The devastation left in their wake appalled Confederates. "All is gloom, despondency, and inactivity," wrote a South Carolinian. "Our army is demoralized and the people panic stricken. To fight longer seems to be madness."

But the war would not end until the Confederate armies surrendered, as Lincoln made clear in his second inaugural address on March 4, 1865. In the best-known words from that address, he urged a binding up of the nation's wounds "with malice toward none [and] charity for all." Even more significant, given that the conflict still raged, were these words:

> American Slavery is one of those offences which, in the providence of God . . . He now wills to remove [through] this terrible war, as the woe due to those by whom the offence came. . . . Fondly do we hope—fervently do we pray—that this mighty scourge of war may speedily pass away. Yet if God wills that it continue, until all the wealth piled by the bondman's two hundred and fifty years of

unrequited toil shall be sunk, and until every drop of blood drawn with the lash, shall be paid by another drawn with the sword, as was said three thousand years ago, so still it must be said "the judgments of the Lord, are true and righteous altogether."

The Road to Appomattox

The Army of Northern Virginia was now the only entity that kept the Confederacy alive, and it was on the verge of disintegration. Scores of its soldiers were deserting every day. On April 1, Sheridan's cavalry and an infantry corps smashed the right flank of Lee's line at Five Forks and cut off the last railroad into Petersburg. The next day, Grant attacked all along the line and forced Lee to abandon both Petersburg and Richmond. As the Confederate government fled its capital, its army set fire to all the military stores it could not carry. The fires spread and destroyed more of Richmond than the Northern troops had destroyed of Atlanta or Columbia.

THE FRUITS OF WAR

Several Southern cities suffered enormous damage in the Civil War from Union shelling and from the fires caused by Confederate soldiers when they destroyed everything of military value before evacuating the cities. Such was true of Charleston, where a Northern photographer who entered the city after it fell in February 1865 posed four black children amid the ruins to portray the symbolism of destruction and renewal.

Lee's starving men limped westward, hoping to turn south and join the remnants of Johnston's army in North Carolina. Sheridan's cavalry raced ahead and cut them off at Appomattox, 90 miles from Petersburg, on April 8. When the weary Confederates tried a breakout attack the next morning, their first probe revealed solid ranks of Union infantry arrayed behind the cavalry. It was the end. "There is nothing left for me to do," said Lee, "but to go and see General Grant, and I would rather die a thousand deaths." Lee met with Grant at the house of Wilmer McLean, who in 1861 had lived near Manassas, where a shell had crashed through his kitchen roof during the first battle of Bull Run. McLean had moved to the remote village of Appomattox to escape the war, only to have its final drama played out in his parlor. There, the son of an Ohio tanner dictated surrender terms to a scion of one of Virginia's First Families.

The terms were generous. Thirty thousand captured Confederates were allowed to go home on condition that they promise never again to take up arms against the

CASUALTIES IN CIVIL WAR ARMIES AND NAVIES

Confederate records are incomplete; the Confederate data listed here are therefore estimates. The actual Confederate totals were probably higher.

	Killed and Mortally Wounded in Combat	Died of Disease	Died in Prison	Miscellaneous Deaths*	Total Deaths	Wounded, Not Mortally	Total Casualties
Union	111,904	197,388	30,192	24,881	364,345	277,401	641,766
Confederate (estimated)	94,000	140,000	26,000	No Estimates	260,000	195,000	455,000
Both Armies (estimated)	205,904	337,388	56,192	24,881	624,365	472,401	1,096,766

*Accidents, drownings, causes not stated, etc.

ABRAHAM LINCOLN IN 1865

This is the last photograph of Lincoln, taken on April 10, 1865, four days before his assassination. Four years of war had left their mark on the 56-year-old president; note the lines of strain, fatigue, and sadness in his face.

Theatre. In the middle of the play, John Wilkes Booth broke into Lincoln's box and shot the president fatally in the head. A prominent actor, Booth was a native of Maryland and a frustrated, unstable egotist who hated Lincoln for what he had done to Booth's beloved South. As he jumped from Lincoln's box to the stage and escaped out a back door, he shouted Virginia's state motto at the stunned audience: "Sic semper tyrannis" ("Thus always to tyrants").

Lincoln's death in the early morning of April 15 produced an outpouring of grief throughout the North and among newly freed slaves in the South. The martyred president did not live to see the culmination of his great achievement in leading the nation to a victory that preserved its existence and abolished slavery. Within 11 days after Lincoln's death, his assassin was trapped and killed in a burning barn in Virginia (April 26). The remaining Confederate armies surrendered one after another (April 26, May 4, May 26, June 23), and Union cavalry captured the fleeing Jefferson Davis in Georgia (May 10). The trauma of civil war was over, but the problems of peace and reconstruction had just begun.

Conclusion

Northern victory in the Civil War resolved two fundamental questions of liberty and power left unresolved by the Revolution of 1776 and the Constitution of 1789: (1) whether this fragile republican experiment in federalism called the United States would survive as one nation; and (2) whether that nation, founded on a charter of liberty, would continue to exist as the largest slaveholding country in the world. Before 1861, the question of whether a state could secede from the Union had remained open. Eleven states did secede, but their defeat in a war that cost 625,000 lives resolved the issue: Since 1865, no state has seriously threatened secession. And in 1865, the adoption of the 13th Amendment to the Constitution confirmed the supreme power of the national government to abolish slavery and ensure the liberty of all Americans.

The Civil War also accomplished a regional transfer of power from South to North. From 1800 to 1860, the slave states had used their leverage in the Jeffersonian Republican and Jacksonian Democratic parties to control national politics most of the time. A Southern slaveholder was president of the United States during two-thirds of the years from 1789 to 1861. Most congressional leaders and Supreme Court justices during that period were Southerners.

United States. After completing the surrender formalities on April 9, Grant introduced Lee to his staff, which included Colonel Ely Parker, a Seneca Indian. As Lee shook hands with Parker, he stared for a moment at Parker's dark features and said: "I am glad to see one real American here." Parker replied solemnly: "We are all Americans." And indeed they now were.

The Assassination of Lincoln

Wild celebrations broke out in the North at news of the fall of Richmond, followed soon by news of Appomattox. Almost overnight, the celebrations turned to mourning. On the evening of April 14, the care-worn Abraham Lincoln sought to relax by attending a comedy at Ford's

In the 50 years after 1861, no native of a Southern state was elected president, only one served as Speaker of the House and none as president pro tem of the Senate, and only 5 of the 26 Supreme Court justices appointed during that half-century were from the South. In 1860, the South's share of the national wealth was 30 percent; in 1870, it was 12 percent.

The institutions and ideology of a plantation society and a caste system that had dominated half the country before 1861 went down with a great crash in 1865—to be replaced by the institutions and ideology of free-labor capitalism. Once feared as the gravest threat to liberty, the power of the national government sustained by a large army had achieved the greatest triumph of liberty in American history. With victory and peace in 1865, the reunited nation turned its attention to the issue of equality.

SUGGESTED READINGS

Several studies offer important information and insights about questions of strategy and command in military operations: **Joseph G. Glatthaar,** *Partners in Command: The Relationships between Leaders in the Civil War* (1993); **Richard M. McMurry,** *Two Great Rebel Armies* (1989); **Michael C. Adams,** *Our Masters the Rebels: A Speculation on Union Military Defeat in the East, 1861–1865* (1978), reissued under the title *Fighting for Defeat* (1992); **Mark Grimsley,** *The Hard Hand of War: Union Military Policy toward Southern Civilians, 1861–1865* (1995); and **Gary W. Gallagher,** *The Confederate War* (1997). Of the many books about black soldiers in the Union army, the most useful is **Joseph T. Glatthaar,** *Forged in Battle: The Civil War Alliance of Black Soldiers and White Officers* (1990). The Confederate debate about enlisting and freeing slave soldiers is chronicled in **Robert Durden,** *The Gray and the Black: The Confederate Debate on Emancipation* (1972). Conscription in the Confederacy and Union is treated in **Albert B. Moore,** *Conscription and Conflict in the Confederacy* (1924), and **James W. Geary,** *We Need Men: The Union Draft in the Civil War* (1991).

For the draft riots in New York, see **Adrian Cook,** *The Armies of the Streets: The New York Draft Riots of 1863* (1974). The best study of the civil liberties issue in the North is **Mark E. Neely, Jr.,** *The Fate of Liberty: Abraham Lincoln and Civil Liberties* (1990), and the same author has covered the same issue in the Confederacy in *Southern Rights: Political Prisoners and the Myth of Confederate Constitutionalism* (1999). For Civil War medicine, **Alfred Jay Bollet,** *Civil War Medicine: Challenges and Triumphs* (2002) is indispensable. A succinct account of the emancipation issue is **Ira Berlin, et al.,** *Slaves No More: Three Essays on Emancipation and the Civil War* (1992).

The activities of women in the U.S. Sanitary Commission, as spies, and even as soldiers, are covered in **Jeanie Attie,** *Patriotic Toil: Northern Women and the Civil War* (1998); **Elizabeth D. Leonard,** *All the Daring of a Soldier: Women of the Civil War Armies* (1999); and **Deanne Blanton and Lauren M. Cook,** *They Fought Like Demons: Women Soldiers in the American Civil War* (2002).

AMERICAN JOURNEY ONLINE
AND
INFOTRAC COLLEGE EDITION

Visit the source collections at www.ajaccess.wadsworth.com and
infotrac.thomsonlearning.com and use the Search function with
the following key terms to explore documents, images, audio
and video clips, articles, and commentary related to the material
in this chapter.

African American soldiers
Civil War women
Abraham Lincoln
George B. McClellan
Horace Greeley

Battle of Antietam
Battle of Chancellorsville
Battle of Gettysburg
Battle of Vicksburg

GRADE AIDS

Visit the Liberty Equality Power Companion Web Site for resources specific to this textbook: http://history.wadsworth.com/murrin_LEP4e

 The CD in the back of this book and the U.S. History Resource Center at http://history.wadsworth.com/u.s./ offer a variety of tools to help you succeed in this course, including access to quizzes; images; documents; interactive simulations, maps, and timelines; movie explorations; and a wealth of other sources.

Reconstruction, 1863–1877

SUNDAY MORNING IN VIRGINIA
This painting by Winslow Homer (1877) of four young black people and the grandmother of two of them is full of symbolism that illustrates important themes in both slavery and Reconstruction. The two lighter-skinned children, probably siblings, are reading the Bible while the dark-skinned children on either side—also probably brother and sister—follow along as they too learn to read. The grandmother listens with a wistful look into the distance, perhaps wishing that she was young enough to acquire the powerful tool of literacy denied to slaves. The religiosity of freedpeople, their humble homes, the partly white ancestry of some, and their thirst for education all are portrayed in this splendid painting.

CHAPTER OUTLINE

From the beginning of the Civil War, the North fought to "reconstruct" the Union. Lincoln first attempted to restore the Union as it had existed before 1861, but once the abolition of slavery became a Northern war aim, the Union could never be reconstructed on its old foundations. Instead, it must experience a "new birth of freedom," as Lincoln had said at the dedication of the military cemetery at Gettysburg.

But precisely what did "a new birth of freedom" mean? At the very least, it meant the end of slavery. The slave states would be reconstructed on a free-labor basis. But what would liberty look like for the 4 million freed slaves? Would they become citizens equal to their former masters in the eyes of the law? Would they have the right to vote? Should Confederate leaders and soldiers be punished for treason? On what terms should the Confederate states return to the Union? What would be the powers of the states and of the national government in a reconstructed Union?

CHAPTER FOCUS

♦ What were the positions of Presidents Abraham Lincoln and Andrew Johnson and of moderate and radical Republicans in Congress on the issues of restoring the South to the Union and protecting the rights of freed slaves?

♦ Why was Andrew Johnson impeached? Why was he acquitted?

♦ What were the achievements of Reconstruction? What were its failures?

♦ Why did a majority of the Northern people and their political leaders turn against continued federal involvement in Southern Reconstruction in the 1870s?

Wartime Reconstruction

Lincoln pondered the problems of Reconstruction long and hard. At first he feared that whites in the South would never extend equal rights to the freed slaves. After all, even most Northern states denied full civil equality to the few black people within their borders. In 1862 and 1863, Lincoln encouraged freedpeople to emigrate to all-black countries such as Haiti, where they would have a chance to get ahead without having to face the racism of whites. Black leaders, abolitionists, and many Republicans objected to that policy. Black people were Americans, they asserted. Why should they not have the rights of American citizens instead of being urged to leave the country?

Lincoln eventually acknowledged the logic and justice of that view, but in beginning the process of reconstruction, he first reached out to Southern *whites* whose allegiance to the Confederacy was lukewarm. On December 8, 1863, Lincoln issued his Proclamation of Amnesty and Reconstruction, which offered presidential pardon to Southern whites (with the exception of Confederate government officials and high-ranking military officers) who took an oath of allegiance to the United States and accepted the abolition of slavery. In any state where the number of white males aged 21 or older who took this oath equaled 10 percent of the number of voters in 1860, that nucleus could reestablish a state government to which Lincoln promised presidential recognition.

Because the war was still raging, this policy could be carried out only where Union troops controlled substantial portions of a Confederate state: Louisiana, Arkansas, and Tennessee in early 1864. Nevertheless, Lincoln hoped that once the process had begun in those areas, it might snowball as Union military victories convinced more and more Confederates that their cause was hopeless. In the end, those military victories were long delayed, and in most parts of the South, reconstruction did not begin until 1865.

Another problem that slowed the process was growing opposition within Lincoln's own party. Many Republicans believed that white men who had fought *against* the Union should not be rewarded with restoration of their political rights while black men who had fought *for* the Union were denied those rights. The Proclamation of Reconstruction had stated that

> any provision which may be adopted by [a reconstructed] State government in relation to the freed people of such State, which shall recognize and declare their permanent freedom, provide for their education, and which may yet be consistent, as a temporary arrangement, with their present condition as a laboring, landless, and homeless class, will not be objected to by the national Executive.

C H R O N O L O G Y

1863	Lincoln issues Proclamation of Amnesty and Reconstruction
1864	Congress passes Wade-Davis bill; Lincoln kills it by pocket veto
1865	Congress establishes Freedmen's Bureau • Andrew Johnson becomes president, announces his reconstruction plan • Southern states enact Black Codes • Congress refuses to seat Southern congressmen elected under Johnson's plan
1866	Congress passes civil rights bill and expands Freedmen's Bureau over Johnson's vetoes • Race riots in Memphis and New Orleans • Congress approves 14th Amendment • Republicans increase congressional majority in fall elections
1867	Congress passes Reconstruction acts over Johnson's vetoes • Congress passes Tenure of Office Act over Johnson's veto
1868	Most Southern senators and representatives readmitted to Congress under congressional plan of Reconstruction • Andrew Johnson impeached but not convicted • Ulysses S. Grant elected president • 14th Amendment is ratified
1870	15th Amendment is ratified
1871	Congress passes Ku Klux Klan Act
1872	Liberal Republicans defect from party • Grant wins reelection
1873	Economic depression begins with the Panic
1874	Democrats win control of House of Representatives
1875	Democrats implement Mississippi Plan • Congress passes civil rights act
1876	Centennial celebration in Philadelphia • Disputed presidential election causes constitutional crisis
1877	Compromise of 1877 installs Rutherford B. Hayes as president • Hayes withdraws troops from South
1883	Supreme Court declares civil rights act of 1875 unconstitutional

This seemed to mean that white landowners and former slaveholders could adopt labor regulations and other measures to control former slaves, so long as they recognized their freedom and made minimal provision for their education.

Radical Republicans and Reconstruction

These changes were radical advances over slavery, but for many Republicans they were not radical enough. Led by Thaddeus Stevens in the House and Charles Sumner in the Senate, the radical Republicans wanted to go much

LINCOLN'S FUNERAL PROCESSION IN CHICAGO, MAY 1, 1865

After a public funeral in Washington, D.C., on April 19, Lincoln's remains were transported by special train to New York City and then west to their final resting place in Springfield, Illinois, where Lincoln was buried on May 4, 1865. The funeral train stopped in major cities, where grieving citizens paid their last respects. An estimated 7 million people lined the tracks along the train's 1,000-mile journey, which reversed the route Lincoln had taken from Springfield to Washington, D.C., in February 1861.

further. If the freedpeople were landless, they said, provide them with land by confiscating the plantations of leading Confederates as punishment for treason. Radical Republicans also distrusted oaths of allegiance sworn by ex-Confederates. Rather than simply restoring the old ruling class to power, asked Charles Sumner, why not give freed slaves the vote, to provide a genuinely loyal nucleus of supporters in the South?

These radical positions did not command a majority of Congress in 1864. Yet the experience of Louisiana, the first state to reorganize under Lincoln's more moderate policy, convinced even nonradical Republicans to block Lincoln's program. With the protection of Union soldiers in the occupied portion of Louisiana (New Orleans and several parishes in the southern half of the state), enough white men took the oath of allegiance to satisfy Lincoln's

conditions. They adopted a new state constitution and formed a government that abolished slavery and provided a school system for blacks. But despite Lincoln's private appeal to the new government to grant literate blacks and black Union soldiers the right to vote, the reconstructed Louisiana legislature chose not to do so. It also authorized planters to enforce restrictive labor policies on black plantation workers. Louisiana's actions alienated a majority of congressional Republicans, who refused to admit representatives and senators from the "reconstructed" state.

At the same time, though, Congress failed to enact a reconstruction policy of its own. This was not for lack of trying. In fact, both houses passed the Wade-Davis reconstruction bill (named for Senator Benjamin Wade of Ohio and Representative Henry Winter Davis of Maryland) in July 1864. That bill did not enfranchise blacks, but it did impose such stringent loyalty requirements on Southern whites that few of them could take the required oath. Lincoln therefore vetoed it.

Lincoln's action infuriated many Republicans. Wade and Davis published a blistering "manifesto" denouncing the president. This bitter squabble threatened for a time to destroy Lincoln's chances of being reelected. Union military success in fall 1864, however, combined with sober second thoughts about the consequences of a Democratic electoral victory, reunited the Republicans behind Lincoln. The collapse of Confederate military resistance the following spring set the stage for compromise between the president and Congress on a policy for the postwar South. Two days after Appomattox, Lincoln promised that he would soon announce such a policy, which probably would have included voting rights for some blacks and stronger measures to protect their civil rights. But three days later, Lincoln was assassinated.

☙ Andrew Johnson and Reconstruction

In 1864, Republicans had adopted the name Union Party to attract the votes of War Democrats and border-state Unionists who could not bring themselves to vote Republican. For the same reason, they also nominated Andrew Johnson of Tennessee as Lincoln's running mate.

Of "poor white" heritage, Johnson had clawed his way up in the rough-and-tumble politics of east Tennessee. This region of small farms and few slaves held little love for the planters who controlled the state. Andrew Johnson denounced the planters as "stuck-up aristocrats" who had no empathy with the Southern yeomen for whom Johnson became a self-appointed spokesman. Johnson, although a Democrat, was the only senator from a seceding state who refused to support the Confederacy. For this stance, the Republicans rewarded him with the vice presidential nomination, hoping to attract the votes of pro-war Democrats and upper-South Unionists.

Booth's bullet therefore elevated to the presidency a man who still thought of himself as primarily a Democrat and a Southerner. The trouble this might cause in a party that was mostly Republican and Northern was not immediately apparent, however. In fact, Johnson's enmity toward the "stuck-up aristocrats" whom he blamed for leading the South into secession prompted him to utter dire threats against "traitors." "Treason is a crime and must be made odious," he said soon after becoming president. "Traitors must be impoverished. . . . They must not only be punished, but their social power must be destroyed."

Radical Republicans liked the sound of this pronouncement. It seemed to promise the type of reconstruction they favored—one that would deny political power to ex-Confederates and would enfranchise blacks. They envisioned a coalition between these new black voters and the small minority of Southern whites who had never supported the Confederacy. These men could be expected to vote Republican. Republican governments in Southern states would guarantee freedom and would pass laws to provide civil rights and economic opportunity for freed slaves. Not incidentally, they would also strengthen the Republican Party nationally.

Johnson's Policy

Radical Republicans, with a combination of pragmatic, partisan, and idealistic motives, prepared to implement a progressive reconstruction policy, but Johnson unexpectedly refused to cooperate. Instead of calling Congress into special session, he moved ahead on his own. On May 29, 1865, Johnson issued two proclamations. The first provided a blanket amnesty for all but the highest-ranking Confederate officials and military officers, and those ex-Confederates with taxable property worth $20,000 or more—the "stuck-up aristocrats." The second named a provisional governor for North Carolina and directed him to call an election of delegates to frame a new state constitution. Only white men who had received amnesty and taken an oath of allegiance could vote. Similar proclamations soon followed for other former Confederate states. Johnson's policy was clear: He would exclude both blacks and upper-class whites from the reconstruction process. The backbone of the new South would be yeomen whites who, like himself, had remained steadfastly loyal to the Union, along with those who now proclaimed themselves loyal.

Although at first many Republicans supported Johnson's policy, the radicals were dismayed. They feared that restricting the vote to whites would lead to oppression of the newly freed slaves and restoration of the old power structure in the South. They began to sense that Johnson (who had owned slaves) was as dedicated to white supremacy as any Confederate. "White men alone must govern the South," he told a Democratic senator. After a tense confrontation with a group of black men led by Frederick Douglass, who had visited the White House to urge black suffrage, Johnson told his private secretary: "Those damned sons of bitches thought they had me in a trap! I know that damned Douglass; he's just like any nigger, and he would sooner cut a white man's throat than not."

Moderate Republicans believed that black men should participate to some degree in the reconstruction process,

From the Collections of the Library of Congress.

From the Collections of the Library of Congress.

ANDREW JOHNSON AND FREDERICK DOUGLASS

By 1866, the president and the leading black spokesman for equal rights represented opposite poles in the debate about Reconstruction. Johnson wanted to bring the South back into the Union on the basis of white suffrage; Douglass wanted black men to be granted the right to vote. Johnson's resistance to this policy as Republicans tried to enact it was a factor in his impeachment two years later.

but in 1865, they were not yet prepared to break with the president. They regarded his policy as an "experiment" that would be modified as time went on. "Loyal negroes must not be put down, while disloyal white men are put up," wrote a moderate Republican. "But I am quite willing to see what will come of Mr. Johnson's experiment." If the new Southern state constitutions failed to enfranchise at least literate blacks and those who had fought in the Union army, said another moderate, "the President then will be at liberty to pursue a sterner policy."

Southern Defiance

As it happened, none of the state conventions enfranchised a single black. Some of them even balked at ratifying the 13th Amendment (which abolished slavery). The rhetoric of some white Southerners began to take on a renewed anti-Yankee tone of defiance that sounded like 1861 all over again. Reports from Unionists and army officers in the South told of neo-Confederate violence against blacks and their white sympathizers. Johnson seemed to encourage such activities by his own rhetoric,

which sounded increasingly like that of a Southern Democrat, and by allowing the organization of white militia units in the South. "What can be hatched from such an egg," asked a Republican newspaper, "but another rebellion?"

Then there was the matter of presidential pardons. After talking fiercely about punishing traitors, and after excluding several classes of them from his amnesty proclamation, Johnson began to issue special pardons to many ex-Confederates, restoring to them all property and political rights. Moreover, under the new state constitutions, Southern voters were electing hundreds of ex-Confederates to state offices. Even more alarming to Northerners, who thought they had won the war, was the election to Congress of no fewer than nine ex-Confederate congressmen, seven ex-Confederate state officials, four generals, four colonels, and even the former Confederate vice president, Alexander H. Stephens. To apprehensive Republicans, it appeared that the rebels, unable to capture Washington in war, were about to do so in peace.

Somehow the aristocrats and traitors Johnson had denounced in April had taken over the reconstruction process.

Instead of weapons, they had resorted to flattering the presidential ego. Thousands of prominent ex-Confederates or their tearful female relatives applied for pardons confessing the error of their ways and appealing for presidential mercy. Reveling in his power over these once-haughty aristocrats who had disdained him as a humble tailor, Johnson waxed eloquent on his "love, respect, and confidence" toward Southern whites, for whom he now felt "forbearing and forgiving." More effective, perhaps, was the praise and support Johnson received from leading Northern Democrats. Although the Republicans had placed him on their presidential ticket in 1864, Johnson was after all a Democrat. That party's leaders enticed Johnson with visions of reelection as a Democrat in 1868 if he could manage to reconstruct the South in a manner that would preserve a Democratic majority there.

The Black Codes

That was just what the Republicans feared. Their concern that state governments devoted to white supremacy would reduce the freedpeople to a condition close to slavery was confirmed in fall 1865, when some of those governments enacted "Black Codes."

One of the first tasks of the legislatures of the reconstructed states was to define the rights of 4 million former slaves. The option of treating them exactly like white citizens was scarcely considered. Instead, the states excluded black people from juries and the ballot box, did not permit them to testify against whites in court, banned interracial marriage, and punished blacks more severely than whites for certain crimes. Some states defined any unemployed black person as a vagrant and hired him out to a planter, forbade blacks to lease land, and provided for the apprenticing to whites of black youths who did not have adequate parental support.

These Black Codes aroused anger among Northern Republicans, who saw them as a brazen attempt to reinstate a quasi-slavery. "We tell the white men of Mississippi," declared the *Chicago Tribune,* "that the men of the North will convert the State of Mississippi into a frog pond before they will allow such laws to disgrace one foot of the soil in which the bones of our soldiers sleep and over which the flag of freedom waves." And, in fact, the Union army's occupation forces did suspend the implementation of Black Codes that discriminated on racial grounds.

Land and Labor in the Postwar South

The Black Codes, although discriminatory, were designed to address a genuine problem. The end of the war had left black-white relations in the South in a state of limbo. The South's economy was in a shambles. Burned-out plantations, fields growing up in weeds, and railroads without tracks, bridges, or rolling stock marked the trail of war. Nearly half of the livestock in the former Confederacy and most other tangible assets except the land itself had been destroyed. Many people, white as well as black, lived from meal to meal. Law and order broke down in many areas. The war had ended early enough in the spring to allow the planting of at least some food crops, but who would plant and cultivate them? One-quarter of the South's white farmers had been killed in the war; the slaves were slaves no more. "We have nothing left to begin anew with," lamented a South Carolina planter. "I never did a day's work in my life, and I don't know how to begin."

Despite all of this trouble, life went on. Soldiers' widows and their children plowed and planted. Slaveless planters and their wives calloused their hands for the first time. Confederate veterans drifted home and went to work. Former slave owners asked their former slaves to work the land for wages or shares of the crop, and many did so. Others refused, because for them to leave the old place was an essential part of freedom. In slavery times, the only way to become free was to run away, and the impulse to leave the scene of bondage persisted. "You ain't, none o' you, gwinter feel rale free," said a black preacher to his congregation, "till you shakes de dus' ob de Ole Plantashun offen yore feet" (dialect in original source).

Thus the roads were alive with freedpeople who were on the move in summer 1865. Many of them signed on to work at farms just a few miles from their old homes. Others moved into town. Some looked for relatives who had been sold away during slavery or from whom they had been separated during the war. Some wandered aimlessly. Crime increased as people, both blacks and whites, stole food to survive—and as whites organized vigilante groups to discipline blacks and force them to work.

The Freedmen's Bureau

Into this vacuum stepped the U.S. Army and the Freedmen's Bureau. Tens of thousands of troops remained in the South as an occupation force until civil government could be restored. The Freedmen's Bureau (its official title was Bureau of Refugees, Freedmen, and Abandoned Lands), created by Congress in March 1865, became the principal agency for overseeing relations between former slaves and owners. Staffed by army officers, the bureau established posts throughout the South to supervise free-labor wage contracts between landowners and freedpeople. The Freedmen's Bureau also issued food rations to 150,000 people daily during 1865, one-third of them to whites.

Southern whites viewed the Freedmen's Bureau with hostility. Without it, however, the postwar chaos and devastation in the South would have been much greater—as some whites privately admitted. Bureau agents used their influence with black people to encourage them to sign free-labor contracts and return to work.

In negotiating labor contracts, the bureau tried to establish minimum wages. Lack of money in the South, however, caused many contracts to call for share wages—that is, paying workers with shares of the crop. At first, landowners worked their laborers in large groups (called gangs) under direct supervision, but many black workers resented this arrangement as reminiscent of slavery. Thus, a new system evolved, called sharecropping, whereby a black family worked a specific piece of land in return for a share of the crop produced on it.

THE FREEDMEN'S BUREAU

Created in 1865, the Freedmen's Bureau stood between freed slaves and their former masters in the postwar South, charged with the task of protecting freedpeople from injustice and repression. Staffed by officers of the Union army, the bureau symbolized the military power of the government in its efforts to keep peace in the South.

Land for the Landless

Freedpeople, of course, would have preferred to farm their own land. "What's de use of being free if you don't own land enough to be buried in?" asked one black sharecropper. "Might juss as well stay slave all yo' days" (dialect in original). Some black farmers did manage to save up enough money to buy small plots of land. Demobilized black soldiers purchased land with their bounty payments, sometimes pooling their money to buy an entire plantation on which several black families settled. Northern philanthropists helped some freedmen buy land. Most ex-slaves found the purchase of land impossible. Few of them had money, and even if they did, whites often refused to sell their land because it would mean losing a source of cheap labor and encouraging notions of black independence.

Several Northern radicals proposed legislation to confiscate ex-Confederate land and redistribute it to freedpeople, but those proposals went nowhere. The most promising effort to put thousands of slaves on land of their own also failed. In January 1865, after his march through Georgia, General William T. Sherman had issued a military order setting aside thousands of acres of abandoned plantation land in the Georgia and South Carolina low

SHARECROPPERS WORKING IN THE FIELDS

After the war, former planters tried to employ their former slaves in gang labor to grow cotton and tobacco, with the only difference from slavery being the grudging payment of wages. Freedpeople resisted this system as being too reminiscent of slavery. They compelled landowners to rent them plots of land on which these black families struggled to raise corn and cotton or tobacco, paying a share of the crop as rent—hence "sharecropping." This posed photograph was intended to depict the family labor of sharecroppers; in reality, most black farmers had a mule to pull their plow.

country for settlement by freed slaves. The army even turned over some of its surplus mules to black farmers. The expectation of "40 acres and a mule" excited freedpeople in 1865, but President Johnson's Amnesty Proclamation and his wholesale issuance of pardons restored most of this property to pardoned ex-Confederates. The same thing happened to white-owned land elsewhere in the South. Placed under the temporary care of the Freedmen's Bureau for subsequent possible distribution to freedpeople, by 1866 nearly all of this land had been restored to its former owners by order of President Johnson.

Education

Abolitionists were more successful in helping freedpeople obtain an education. During the war, freedmen's aid societies and missionary societies founded by abolitionists had sent teachers to Union-occupied areas of the South to set up schools for freed slaves. After the war, this effort was expanded with the aid of the Freedmen's Bureau. Two thousand Northern teachers, three-quarters of them women, fanned out into every part of the South. There they trained black teachers to staff first the mission schools and later the public schools established by Reconstruction state governments. After 1870, the missionary societies concentrated more heavily on making higher education available to African Americans. Many of the traditionally black colleges in the South today were founded and supported by their efforts. This education crusade, which the black leader W. E. B. Du Bois described as "the most wonderful peace-battle of the nineteenth century," reduced the Southern black illiteracy rate to 70 percent by 1880 and to 48 percent by 1900.

☙ The Advent of Congressional Reconstruction

Political reconstruction shaped the civil and political rights of freedpeople. By the time Congress met in December 1865, the Republican majority was determined to control the process by which former Confederate states would regain full representation. Congress refused to admit the representatives and senators elected by the former Confederate states under Johnson's reconstruction policy and set up a special committee to formulate new

A BLACK SCHOOL DURING RECONSTRUCTION

In the antebellum South, teaching slaves to read and write was forbidden. Thus about 90 percent of the freedpeople were illiterate in 1865. One of their top priorities was education. At first, most of the teachers in the freedmen's schools established by Northern missionary societies were Northern white women. But as black teachers were trained, they took over the elementary schools, such as this one photographed in the 1870s.

terms. The committee held hearings at which Southern Unionists, freedpeople, and U.S. Army officers testified to abuse and terrorism in the South. Their testimony convinced Republicans of the need for stronger federal intervention to define and protect the civil rights of freedpeople. Many radicals wanted to go further and grant the ballot to black men, who would join with white Unionists and Northern settlers in the South to form a Southern Republican Party.

Most Republicans realized that Northern voters would not support such a radical policy, however. Racism was still strong in the North, where most states denied the right to vote to the few blacks living within their borders. Moderate Republicans feared that Democrats would exploit Northern racism in the congressional elections of 1866 if Congress made black suffrage a cornerstone of Reconstruction. Instead, the special committee decided to draft a constitutional amendment that would encourage Southern states to enfranchise blacks but would not require them to do so.

Schism between President and Congress

Meanwhile, Congress passed two laws to protect the economic and civil rights of freedpeople. The first extended the life of the Freedmen's Bureau and expanded its powers. The second defined freedpeople as citizens with equal legal rights and gave federal courts appellate jurisdiction to enforce those rights. To the dismay of moderates who were trying to heal the widening breach between the president and Congress, Johnson vetoed both measures. He followed this action with an intemperate speech to Democratic supporters in which he denounced Republican leaders as traitors who did not want to restore the Union

"PARDON, Columbia—'Shall I Trust These Men'?"

"FRANCHISE—'And Not This Man'?"

CARTOONS FOR FREEDOM

One of the best political cartoonists in American history, Thomas Nast drew scores of cartoons for *Harper's Weekly* in the 1860s and 1870s advocating the use of federal power to guarantee the liberty and enforce the equal rights of freed slaves. This illustration (1865) is an eloquent graphic expression of a powerful argument for giving freedmen the right to vote: black men who fought *for* the Union were more deserving of this privilege than white men who fought *against* it. Several of the kneeling figures are recognizable Confederate leaders: Alexander Stephens and Robert E. Lee in the foreground, Jefferson Davis to Lee's left, and John C. Breckinridge, Joseph E. Johnston, and Robert Toombs behind and to Davis's left.

except on terms that would degrade white Southerners. Democratic newspapers applauded the president for vetoing bills that would "compound our race with niggers, gypsies, and baboons."

The 14th Amendment

Johnson had thrown down the gauntlet to congressional Republicans, and they did not hesitate to take it up. With better than a two-thirds majority in both houses, they passed the Freedmen's Bureau and Civil Rights bills over the president's vetoes. Then on April 30, 1866, the special committee submitted to Congress its proposed 14th Amendment to the Constitution. After lengthy debate, the amendment received the required two-thirds majority in Congress on June 13 and went to the states for ratification. Section 1 defined all native-born or naturalized persons, including blacks, as American citizens and prohibited the states from abridging the "privileges and immunities" of citizens, from depriving "any person of life, liberty, or property without due process of law," and from denying to any person "the equal protection of the laws." Section 2 gave states the option of either enfranchising black males or losing a proportionate number of congressional seats and electoral votes. Section 3 disqualified a significant number of ex-Confederates from holding federal or state office. Section 4 guaranteed the national debt and repudiated the Confederate debt. Section 5 empowered Congress to enforce the 14th Amendment by "appropriate legislation." The 14th Amendment had far-reaching consequences. Section 1 has become the most important provision in the Constitution for defining and enforcing civil rights.

The 1866 Elections

Republicans entered the 1866 congressional elections campaign with the 14th Amendment as their platform. They made clear that any ex-Confederate state that ratified the amendment would be declared "reconstructed" and that its representatives and senators would be seated in Congress. Tennessee ratified the amendment, but Johnson counseled other Southern legislatures to reject the amendment, which they did. Johnson then prepared for an all-out campaign to gain a friendly Northern majority in the congressional elections.

Johnson began his campaign by creating a National Union Party made up of a few conservative Republicans who disagreed with their party, some border-state Unionists who supported the president, and Democrats. The inclusion of Democrats doomed the effort from the start. Many Northern Democrats still carried the taint of having opposed the war effort, and many Northern voters did not trust them. The National Union Party was further damaged by race riots in Memphis and New Orleans, where white mobs including former Confederate soldiers killed 80 blacks, among them several former Union soldiers. The riots bolstered Republican arguments that national power was necessary to protect "the fruits of victory" in the South. Perhaps the biggest liability of the National Union Party was Johnson himself. In a whistle-stop tour through the North, he traded insults with hecklers and embarrassed his supporters by comparing himself to Christ and his Republican adversaries to Judas.

Republicans swept the election: They gained a three-to-one majority in the next Congress. Having rejected the Reconstruction terms embodied in the 14th Amendment, Southern Democrats now faced far more stringent terms. "They would not cooperate in rebuilding what they destroyed," wrote an exasperated moderate Republican, so "we must remove the rubbish and rebuild from the bottom. Whether they are willing or not, we must compel obedience to the Union and demand protection for its humblest citizen."

The Reconstruction Acts of 1867

In March 1867, the new Congress enacted over Johnson's vetoes two laws prescribing new procedures for the full restoration of the former Confederate states (except Tennessee, which had already been readmitted) to the Union. These laws represented a complex compromise between radicals and moderates that had been hammered out in a confusing sequence of committee drafts, caucus decisions, all-night debates on the floor, and frayed tempers. The Reconstruction acts of 1867 divided the 10 Southern states into five military districts, directed army officers to register voters for the election of delegates to new constitutional conventions, and enfranchised males aged 21 and older (including blacks) to vote in those elections. The acts also disenfranchised (for these elections only) those ex-Confederates who were disqualified from holding office under the not-yet-ratified 14th Amendment—fewer than 10 percent of all white voters. When a state had adopted a new constitution that granted equal civil and political rights regardless of race and had ratified the 14th Amendment, it would be declared reconstructed and its newly elected congressmen would be seated.

These measures embodied a true revolution. Just a few years earlier, Southern whites had been masters of 4 million slaves and part of an independent Confederate nation. Now they were shorn of political power, with their former slaves not only freed but also politically empowered. To be sure, radical Republicans who warned that the

THE BURNING OF A FREEDMEN'S SCHOOL

Because freedpeople's education symbolized black progress, whites who resented and resisted this progress sometimes attacked and burned freedmen's schools, as in this dramatic illustration of a white mob burning a school during antiblack riots in Memphis in May 1866.

NEW YORK, SATURDAY, MAY 26, 1866.

Frank Leslie's Illustrated Newspaper.

revolution was incomplete as long as the old master class retained economic and social power turned out to be right in the end. In 1867, however, the emancipation and enfranchisement of black Americans seemed, as a sympathetic French journalist described it, "one of the most radical revolutions known in history."

Like most revolutions, the reconstruction process did not go smoothly. Many Southern Democrats breathed defiance and refused to cooperate. The presence of the army minimized antiblack violence, but thousands of white Southerners who were eligible to vote refused to do so, hoping that their nonparticipation would delay the process long enough for Northern voters to come to their senses and elect Democrats to Congress.

Blacks and their white allies organized Union leagues to inform and mobilize the new black voters into the Republican Party. Democrats branded Southern white Republicans as "scalawags" and Northern settlers as "carpetbaggers." By September 1867, the 10 states had 735,000 black voters and only 635,000 white voters registered. At least one-third of the registered white voters were Republicans.

President Johnson did everything he could to block Reconstruction. He replaced several Republican generals in command of Southern military districts with Democrats. He had his attorney general issue a ruling that interpreted the Reconstruction acts narrowly, thereby forcing a special session of Congress to pass a supplementary act

in July 1867. He encouraged Southern whites to obstruct the registration of voters and the election of convention delegates.

Johnson's purpose was to slow the process until 1868 in the hope that Northern voters would repudiate Reconstruction in the presidential election of that year, when Johnson planned to run as the Democratic candidate. Off-year state elections in fall 1867 encouraged that hope. Republicans suffered setbacks in several Northern states, especially where they endorsed referendum measures to enfranchise black men. "I almost pity the radicals," chortled one of President Johnson's aides after the 1867 elections. "After giving ten states to the negroes, to keep the Democrats from getting them, they will have lost the rest."

The Impeachment of Andrew Johnson

Johnson struck even more boldly against Reconstruction after the 1867 elections, despite warnings that he was risking impeachment. "What does Johnson mean to do?" an exasperated Republican asked another. "I am afraid his doings will make us all favor impeachment." In February 1868, Johnson took a fateful step. He removed from office Secretary of War Edwin M. Stanton, who had administered the War Department in support of the congressional Reconstruction policy. This appeared to violate the Tenure of Office Act, passed the year before over Johnson's veto, which required Senate consent for such removals. By a vote of 126 to 47 along party lines, the House impeached Johnson on February 24. The official reason for impeachment was that he had violated the Tenure of Office Act (which Johnson considered unconstitutional). The real reason was Johnson's stubborn defiance of Congress on Reconstruction.

Under the U.S. Constitution, impeachment by the House does not remove an official from office. It is more like a grand jury indictment that must be tried by a petit jury—in this case, the Senate, which sat as a court to try Johnson on the impeachment charges brought by the House. If convicted by a two-thirds majority of the Senate, he would be removed from office.

The impeachment trial proved long and complicated, which worked in Johnson's favor by allowing passions to cool. The Constitution specifies the grounds on which a president can be impeached and removed: "Treason, Bribery, or other high Crimes and Misdemeanors." The issue was whether Johnson was guilty of any of these acts. His able defense counsel exposed technical ambiguities in the Tenure of Office Act that raised doubts about whether

Johnson had actually violated it. Several moderate Republicans feared that the precedent of impeachment might upset the delicate balance of powers between the executive branch, Congress, and the judiciary that was an essential element of the Constitution. Behind the scenes, Johnson strengthened his case by promising to appoint the respected General John M. Schofield as secretary of war and to stop obstructing the Reconstruction acts. In the end, seven Republican senators voted for acquittal on May 16, and the final tally fell one vote short of the necessary two-thirds majority.

The Completion of Formal Reconstruction

The impeachment trial's end cleared the poisonous air in Washington, and Johnson quietly served out his term. Constitutional conventions met in the South during winter and spring 1867–68. Hostile whites described them as "Bones and Banjoes Conventions" and the Republican delegates as "ragamuffins and jailbirds." In sober fact, however, the delegates were earnest advocates of a new order, and the constitutions they wrote were among the

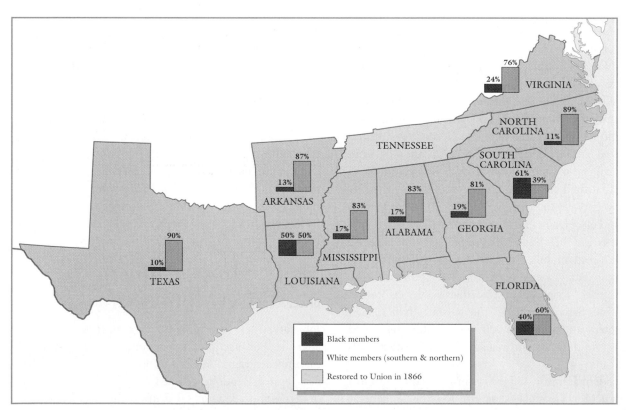

MAP 17.1 BLACK AND WHITE PARTICIPATION IN CONSTITUTIONAL CONVENTIONS, 1867–1868
Although black participation in these state constitutional conventions matched the African American percentage of the population only in South Carolina and Louisiana, the very presence of any black delegates in states where slavery had prevailed three years earlier was revolutionary.

most progressive in the nation. Three-quarters of the delegates to the 10 conventions were Republicans. About 25 percent of those Republicans were Northern whites who had relocated to the South after the war; 45 percent were native Southern whites who braved the social ostracism of the white majority to cast their lot with the despised Republicans; and 30 percent were blacks. Only in the South Carolina convention were blacks in the majority.

The new state constitutions enacted universal male suffrage, putting them ahead of most Northern states on that score. Some of the constitutions disenfranchised certain classes of ex-Confederates for several years, but by 1872, all such disqualifications had been removed. The constitutions mandated statewide public schools for both races for the first time in the South. Most states permitted segregated schools, but schools of any kind for blacks represented a great step forward. Most of the constitutions increased the state's responsibility for social welfare beyond anything previously known in the South.

Violence in some parts of the South marred the voting on ratification of these state constitutions. The Ku Klux Klan, a night-riding white terrorist organization, made its first appearance during the elections. Nevertheless, voters in seven states ratified their constitutions and elected new legislatures that ratified the 14th Amendment in spring 1868. That amendment became part of the U.S. Constitution the following summer, and the newly elected representatives and senators from those seven states, nearly all Republicans, took their seats in the House and Senate.

The 15th Amendment

The remaining three Southern states completed the reconstruction process in 1869 and 1870. Congress required them to ratify the 15th as well as the 14th Amendment. The 15th Amendment prohibited states from denying the right to vote on grounds of race, color, or previous condition of servitude. Its purpose was not only to prevent the reconstructed states from any future revocation of black suffrage, but also to extend equal suffrage to the border states and to the North. With final ratification of the 15th Amendment in 1870, the Constitution became truly color blind for the first time in U.S. history.

But the 15th Amendment still left half of the population disenfranchised. Many supporters of woman suffrage were embittered by its failure to ban discrimination on the grounds of gender as well as race. The radical wing of the suffragists, led by Elizabeth Cady Stanton and Susan B. Anthony, therefore opposed the 15th Amendment, causing a split in the woman suffrage movement.

This movement had shared the ideological egalitarianism of abolitionism since the Seneca Falls Convention of 1848. In 1866, male and female abolitionists formed the American Equal Rights Association (AERA) to work for both black and woman suffrage. Although some Republicans sympathized with the suffragists, they knew that no strong constituency among male voters favored granting the vote to women. A woman suffrage amendment to the state constitution of Kansas in 1867 suffered a lopsided defeat in a referendum. Most members of the AERA recognized that although Reconstruction politics made black enfranchisement possible, woman suffrage would have to wait until public opinion could be educated up to the standard of gender equality.

Stanton and Anthony refused to accept this reasoning. Why should illiterate Southern blacks have the right to vote, they asked, when educated Northern women remained shut out from the polls? It was "infinitely more important to secure the rights of 10 million women than to bring a million more men to the polls," declared Stanton. The 15th Amendment would establish "the most odious form of aristocracy the world has ever seen: an aristocracy of sex." When a majority of delegates at the 1869 convention of the AERA voted to endorse the 15th Amendment, several women led by Stanton and Anthony walked out and founded the National Woman Suffrage Association. The remainder reorganized themselves as the American Woman Suffrage Association. For the next two decades, these rival organizations, working for the same cause, remained at odds with each other.

The Election of 1868

Just as the presidential election of 1864 was a referendum on Lincoln's war policies, so the election of 1868 was a referendum on the Reconstruction policy of the Republicans. The Republican nominee was General Ulysses S. Grant. Although he had no political experience, Grant commanded greater authority and prestige than anyone else in the country. As general-in-chief of the army, he had opposed Johnson's Reconstruction policy in 1866 and had broken openly with the president in January 1868. That spring, Grant agreed to run for the presidency in order to preserve in peace the victory for Union and liberty he had won in war.

The Democrats turned away from Andrew Johnson, who carried too many political liabilities. They nominated Horatio Seymour, the wartime governor of New York, bestowing on him the dubious privilege of running against Grant. Hoping to put together a majority consisting of the South plus New York and two or three other Northern states, the Democrats adopted a militant platform denouncing the Reconstruction acts as "a flagrant usurpation of power ... unconstitutional, revolutionary, and void."

Dan Sickles Tries to Provoke War with Spain

A lawyer and Democratic politician associated with the Tammany Hall machine in New York City, Sickles (1819–1914) went to London in 1853 to become secretary of the legation, where he helped draft the notorious Ostend Manifesto, which called for American acquisition of Cuba from Spain (see p. 429). At a Fourth of July dinner in 1854, Sickles refused to stand when a toast was offered to Queen Victoria, an act that generated outrage in Britain.

Sickles returned to New York in 1854 and was elected to Congress in 1856. A conspicuous womanizer and philanderer, Sickles found the shoe on the other foot when he discovered that his beautiful young wife Teresa was having an affair in Washington with Philip Barton Key (son of the composer of "The Star-Spangled Banner"). In 1859, Sickles shot Key dead in Lafayette Square near the White House. After a celebrated murder trial, Sickles was acquitted, partly on grounds of temporary insanity—the first time that plea had been used in American jurisprudence.

Shunned by polite society, Sickles sought to retrieve his reputation by raising an entire infantry brigade (five regiments) in New York City when the Civil War broke out. Partly through political influence, he rose to the rank of major general in 1863. At Gettysburg, he moved his corps forward without orders from the main Union position on Cemetery Ridge on July 2, and lost his leg in the subsequent Confederate attack that wrecked his corps.

After the war, Sickles became a Republican, campaigned for Grant in 1868, and received appointment as minister to Spain as a reward. Teresa had died in 1867, and he married a Spanish woman in 1871, converted to Roman Catholicism, and had two children with her. During Sickles's tenure in Madrid, Spain experienced political upheaval. Queen Isabella had been deposed because of the scandals caused by her constant succession of lovers. Regents, military rulers, republican leaders, and dictators came and went from 1869 to 1874. Behind the scenes, Sickles was active in various intrigues associated with these changes of regime.

In 1873, the *Virginius,* a vessel flying the American flag and running guns to rebels in Cuba fighting against Spanish rule of that island, was seized by the Spanish navy, and 53 Americans and Cuban rebels were executed. Sickles used this incident to try to provoke a war between the United States and Spain to liberate Cuba, but Secretary of State Hamilton Fish bypassed his loose-cannon minister and negotiated a peaceful settlement with Spain, provoking Sickles to resign in 1874.

Sickles thereupon moved to Paris and renewed a torrid affair with deposed Queen Isabella, earning a satirical reputation as "the Yankee King of Spain." In 1879, he returned to the United States, where he lived out the rest of his long life—without his wife and children, who remained in Europe. In 1898, the United States went to war with Spain to liberate Cuba a quarter-century after Sickles had tried to provoke such a war.

© Corbis.

DANIEL SICKLES

The platform also demanded "the abolition of the Freedmen's Bureau, and all political instrumentalities designed to secure negro supremacy."

The vice presidential candidate, Frank Blair of Missouri, became the point man for the Democrats. In a public letter, he proclaimed, "There is but one way to restore the Government and the Constitution, and that is for the President-elect to declare these [Reconstruction] acts null and void, compel the army to undo its usurpations at the South, disperse the carpet-bag State Governments, [and] allow the white people to reorganize their own governments."

The only way to achieve this bold counterrevolutionary goal was to suppress Republican voters in the South. This the Ku Klux Klan tried its best to do. Federal troops failed to prevent much of the violence because martial law had been lifted in the states where civilian governments had been restored. In Louisiana, Georgia, Arkansas, and Tennessee, the Klan or Klan-like groups committed dozens of murders and intimidated thousands of black voters. The violence helped the Democratic cause in the South, but probably hurt it in the North where many voters perceived the Klan as an organization of neo-Confederate paramilitary guerrillas. In fact, many Klansmen were former soldiers, and such famous Confederate generals as Nathan Bedford Forrest and John B. Gordon held high positions in the Klan.

Seymour did well in the South, carrying five former slave states and coming close in others despite the solid Republican vote of the newly enfranchised blacks. Grant, however, swept the electoral vote 214 to 80. Seymour actually won a slight majority of the white voters nationally; without black enfranchisement, Grant would have had a minority of the popular vote.

🌑 The Grant Administration

A great military commander, Grant is usually branded a failure as president. That indictment is only partly correct. Grant's inexperience and poor judgment betrayed him into several unwise appointments of officials who were later convicted of corruption, and his back-to-back administrations (1869–77) were plagued by scandals. His secretary of war was impeached for selling appointments to army posts and Indian reservations, and his attorney general and secretary of the interior resigned under suspicion of malfeasance in 1875.

Although he was an honest man, Grant was too trusting of subordinates. He appointed many former members of his military family, as well as several of his wife's relatives, to offices for which they were scarcely qualified. In an

era notorious for corruption at all levels of government, many of the scandals were not Grant's fault. The Tammany Hall "Ring" of "Boss" William Marcy Tweed in New York City may have stolen more money from taxpayers than all of the federal agencies combined. It was said that the only thing the Standard Oil Company could not do with the Ohio legislature was refine it. In Washington, one of the most widely publicized scandals, the Credit Mobilier affair, concerned Congress rather than the Grant administration. Several congressmen had accepted stock in the Credit Mobilier, a construction company for the Union Pacific Railroad, which received loans and land grants from the government. In return, the company expected lax congressional supervision, thereby permitting financial manipulations by the company.

What accounted for this explosion of corruption in the postwar decade, which one historian has called "The Era of Good Stealings"? During the war, expansion of government contracts and the bureaucracy had created new opportunities for the unscrupulous. Following the intense sacrifices of the war years came a relaxation of tensions and standards. Rapid postwar economic growth, led by an extraordinary rush of railroad construction, further encouraged greed and get-rich-quick schemes of the kind satirized by Mark Twain and Charles Dudley Warner in their 1873 novel *The Gilded Age*, which gave its name to the era.

Civil Service Reform

Some of the apparent increase in corruption during the Gilded Age was more a matter of perception. During a civil service reform movement to purify the government bureaucracy and make it more efficient, reformers focused a harsh light into the dark corners of corruption that was hitherto unilluminated because of the nation's preoccupation with war and reconstruction. Thus reformers' publicity may have exaggerated the actual extent of corruption. In reality, during the Grant administration, several government agencies made real progress in eliminating abuses that had flourished in earlier administrations.

The chief target of civil service reform was the "spoils system." With the slogan "To the victor belongs the spoils," the victorious party in an election rewarded party workers with appointments as postmasters, customs collectors, and the like. The hope of getting appointed to a government post was the glue that kept the faithful together when a party was out of power. An assessment of 2 or 3 percent on the beneficiaries' government salaries kept party coffers filled when the party was in power. The spoils system politicized the bureaucracy and staffed it with unqualified personnel who spent more time working for their party than for the government. It also plagued every incoming president (and other elected officials) with the "swarm of office seekers" that loom so large in contemporary accounts (including those of the humorist Orpheus C. Kerr, whose nom de plume was pronounced "Office Seeker").

Civil service reformers wanted to separate the bureaucracy from politics by requiring competitive examinations for the appointment of civil servants. This movement gathered steam during the 1870s and finally achieved success in 1883 with the passage of the Pendleton Act, which established the modern structure of the civil service. When Grant took office, he seemed to share the sentiments of civil service reformers; several of his cabinet officers inaugurated examinations for certain appointments and promotions in their departments. Grant also named a civil service commission headed by George William Curtis, a leading reformer and editor of *Harper's Weekly*. But many congressmen, senators, and other politicians resisted civil service reform. Patronage greased the political machines that kept them in office and all too often enriched them and their political chums. They managed to subvert reform, sometimes using Grant as an unwitting ally and thus turning many reformers against the president.

Foreign Policy Issues

A foreign policy controversy added to Grant's woes. The irregular procedures by which his private secretary had negotiated a treaty to annex Santo Domingo (now the Dominican Republic) alienated leading Republican senators, who defeated ratification of the treaty. Politically inexperienced, Grant acted like a general who needed only to give orders rather than as a president who must cultivate supporters. The fallout from the Santo Domingo affair widened the fissure in the Republican Party between "spoilsmen" and "reformers."

The Grant administration had some solid foreign policy achievements to its credit, however. Hamilton Fish, the able secretary of state, negotiated the Treaty of Washington in 1871 to settle the vexing Alabama Claims. These were damage claims against Britain for the destruction of American shipping by the C.S.S. *Alabama* and other Confederate commerce raiders built in British shipyards. The treaty established an international tribunal to arbitrate the U.S. claims, thus creating a precedent for the peaceful settlement of disputes. It resulted in the award of $15.5 million in damages to U.S. shipowners and a British expression of regret.

The events leading to the Treaty of Washington also resolved another long-festering issue between Britain and the United States: the status of Canada. The seven separate British North American colonies were especially vulnerable to U.S. desires for annexation. In fact, many bitter Northerners demanded British cession of Canadian colonies to the United States as fair payment for the wartime depredations of the *Alabama* and other commerce raiders. Such demands tended to strengthen the loyalty of many Canadians to Britain as a counterweight to the aggressive Americans. In 1867, Parliament passed the British North America Act, which united most of the Canadian colonies into a new and largely self-governing Dominion of Canada.

Canadian nationalism was further strengthened by the actions of the Irish American Fenian Brotherhood. A secret society organized during the Civil War, the Fenians believed that an invasion of Canada would strike a blow for the independence of Ireland. Three times from 1866 to 1871, small "armies" of Fenians, composed mainly of Irish American veterans of the Union Army, crossed the border into Canada, only to be driven back after comic-opera skirmishes. The Fenian raids intensified Canadian anti-Americanism and complicated the negotiations leading to the Washington Treaty, but after its signing, Canadian-American tensions cooled. The treaty also helped resolve disputes over American commercial fishing in Canadian waters. U.S. troops prevented further Fenian raids, and American demands for annexation of Canada faded away. These events gave birth to the modern nation of Canada.

Reconstruction in the South

During Grant's two administrations, the Southern Question was the most intractable issue. A phrase in Grant's acceptance of the presidential nomination in 1868 had struck a responsive chord in the North: "Let us have peace." With the ratification of the 15th Amendment, many people breathed a sigh of relief at this apparent resolution of "the last great point that remained to be settled of the issues of the war." It was time to deal with other matters that had been long neglected. Ever since the annexation of Texas a quarter-century earlier, the nation had known scarcely a moment's respite from sectional strife. "Let us have done with Reconstruction," pleaded the New York *Tribune* in 1870. "LET US HAVE PEACE." But there was no peace. Reconstruction was not over; it had hardly begun. State governments elected by black and white voters were in place in the South, but Democratic violence against Reconstruction and the instability of the Republican coalition that sustained it portended trouble.

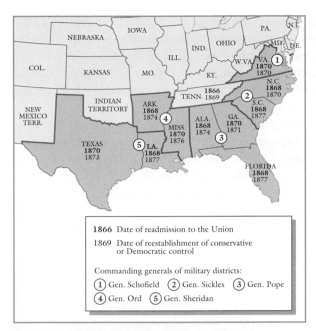

MAP 17.2   RECONSTRUCTION IN THE SOUTH

The dates for each state listed on this map show how short-lived "Radical Reconstruction" was in most Southern states.

Blacks in Office

Because the Republican Party had no antebellum roots in the South, most Southern whites perceived it as a symbol of conquest and humiliation. In the North, the Republican Party represented the most prosperous, educated, and influential elements of the population, but in the South, most of its adherents were poor, illiterate, and landless.

About 80 percent of Southern Republican voters were black. Although most black leaders were educated and many had been free before the war, most black voters were illiterate ex-slaves. Neither the leaders nor their constituents, however, were as ignorant or as venal as stereotypes have portrayed them. Of 14 black representatives and two black senators elected in the South between 1868 and 1876, all but three had attended secondary school and four had attended college. Several of the blacks elected to state offices were among the best-educated men of their day. Jonathan Gibbs, secretary of state in Florida from 1868 to 1872 and state superintendent of education from 1872 to 1874, was a graduate of Dartmouth College and Princeton Theological Seminary. Francis L. Cardozo, secretary of state in South Carolina for four years and treasurer for another four, was educated at the University of Glasgow and at theological schools in Edinburgh and London.

It is true that some lower-level black officeholders, as well as their constituents, could not read or write, but the fault for that situation lay not with them but with the slave regime that had denied them an education. Illiteracy did not preclude an understanding of political issues for them any more than it did for Irish American voters in the North, many of whom were also illiterate. Southern blacks thirsted for education. Participation in the Union League and the experience of voting were themselves forms of education. Black churches and fraternal organizations proliferated during Reconstruction and tutored African Americans in their rights and responsibilities.

Linked to the myth of black incompetence was the legend of the "Africanization" of Southern governments during Reconstruction. The theme of "Negro rule"—by which the "barbarous African" exercised "unbridled power" in the 10 Southern states—was a staple of Democratic propaganda. It was enshrined in folk memory and in generations of textbooks. In fact, blacks held only 15 to 20 percent of public offices, even at the height of Reconstruction in the early 1870s. No states had black governors (although the black lieutenant governor of Louisiana acted as governor for a month), and only one black man became a state supreme court justice. Nowhere except in South Carolina did blacks hold office in numbers anywhere near their proportion of the population; in that state, they constituted 52 percent of all state and federal elected officials from 1868 to 1876.

"Carpetbaggers"

Next to "Negro rule," carpetbagger corruption and scalawag rascality have been the prevailing myths of Reconstruction. Carpetbaggers did hold a disproportionate number of high political offices in Southern state governments during Reconstruction. More than half of the Republican governors and nearly half of the congressmen and senators were Northerners. A few did resemble the proverbial adventurer who came south with nothing but a carpetbag in which to stow the loot plundered from a helpless people. Most of the Northerners were Union army officers who stayed on after the war as Freedmen's Bureau agents, teachers in black schools, business investors, pioneers of a new political order—or simply because they liked the climate.

Like others who migrated to the West as a frontier of opportunity, those who settled in the postwar South hoped to rebuild its society in the image of the free-labor North. Many were college graduates at a time when fewer than 2 percent of Americans had attended college. Most brought not empty carpetbags but considerable capital, which they invested in what they hoped would become a new South. They also invested human capital—themselves—in a drive to modernize the region's social structure and democratize its politics. But they underestimated the hostility of Southern whites, most of whom regarded them as agents of an alien culture and leaders of an enemy army—as indeed they had been—in a war that for many Southerners was not yet over.

"Scalawags"

Most of the native-born whites who joined the Southern Republican Party came from the upcountry Unionist areas of western North Carolina and Virginia, eastern Tennessee, and elsewhere. Others were former Whigs who saw an opportunity to rebuild the South's economy in partnership with equally Whiggish Northern Republicans. Republicans, said a North Carolina scalawag, were the "party of progress, of education, of development. . . . Yankees and Yankee notions are just what we want in this country. We want their capital to build factories and work shops, and railroads."

But Yankees and Yankee notions were just what most Southern whites did not want. Democrats saw that the Southern Republican Party they abhorred was a fragile coalition of blacks and whites, Yankees and Southerners, hill-country yeomen and low-country entrepreneurs, illiterates and college graduates. The party was weakest along the seams where these disparate elements joined, especially the racial seam. Democrats attacked that weakness

HISTORY THROUGH FILM
The Birth of a Nation (1915)

Directed by D. W. Griffith. Starring Lillian Gish (Elsie Stoneman), Henry B. Walthall (Ben Cameron), Ralph Lewis (Austin Stoneman), George Siegmann (Silas Lynch).

Few, if any, films have had such a pernicious impact on historical understanding and race relations as *Birth of a Nation*. This movie popularized a version of Reconstruction that portrayed predatory carpetbaggers and stupid, brutish blacks plundering a prostrate South and lusting after white women. It perpetuated vicious stereotypes of rapacious black males. It glorified the Ku Klux Klan of the Reconstruction era, inspiring the founding of the "second Klan" in 1915, which became a powerful force in the 1920s (see chapter 24).

The first half of the film offers a conventional Victorian romance of the Civil War. The two sons and daughter of Austin Stoneman (a malevolent radical Republican who is a thinly disguised Thaddeus Stevens) become friends with the three sons and two daughters of the Cameron family of "Piedmont," South Carolina, through the friendship of Ben Cameron and Phil Stoneman at college. The Civil War tragically separates the families. The Stoneman and Cameron boys enlist in the Union and Confederate armies and—predictably—face each other on the battlefield. Two Camerons and one Stoneman are killed in the war, and Ben Cameron is badly wounded and captured, to be nursed back to health by—you guessed it—Elsie Stoneman.

After the war, the younger Camerons and Stonemans renew their friendship. During the Stonemans' visit to South Carolina, Ben Cameron and Elsie Stoneman, and Phil Stoneman and Flora Cameron, fall in love. If the story had stopped there, *Birth of a Nation* would have been just another Hollywood romance. But Austin Stoneman brings south with him Silas Lynch, an ambitious, leering mulatto demagogue who stirs up the animal passions of the ignorant black majority to demand "Equal Rights, Equal Politics, Equal Marriage." A "renegade Negro," Gus, stalks the youngest Cameron daughter, who saves herself from rape by jumping from a cliff to her death. Silas Lynch tries to force Elsie to marry him. "I will build a Black Empire," he tells the beautiful, virginal Elsie (Lillian Gish was the Hollywood beauty queen of silent films), "and you as my queen shall rule by my side."

Finally provoked beyond endurance, white South Carolinians led by Ben Cameron organize the Ku Klux Klan to save "the Aryan race." Riding to the rescue of embattled whites in stirring scenes that anticipated the heroic

with every weapon at their command, from social ostracism of white Republicans to economic intimidation of black employees and sharecroppers. The most potent Democratic weapon was violence.

The Ku Klux Klan

The generic name for the secret groups that terrorized the Southern countryside was the Ku Klux Klan, but some went by other names (the Knights of the White Camelia in Louisiana, for example). Part of the Klan's purpose was social control of the black population. Sharecroppers who tried to extract better terms from landowners, or black people who were considered too "uppity," were likely to receive a midnight whipping—or worse—from white-sheeted Klansmen. Scores of black schools, perceived as a particular threat to white supremacy, went up in flames.

The Klan's main purpose was political: to destroy the Republican Party by terrorizing its voters and, if necessary, by murdering its leaders. No one knows how many politically motivated killings took place—certainly hundreds, probably thousands. Nearly all of the victims were Republicans; most of them were black. In one notorious incident, the Colfax Massacre in Louisiana (April 18, 1873), a clash between black militia and armed whites left three whites and nearly 100 blacks dead. Half of the blacks were killed in cold blood after they had surrendered.

actions of the cavalry against Indians in later Hollywood Westerns, the Klan executes Gus, saves Elsie, disperses black soldiers and mobs, and carries the next election for white rule by intimidating black voters. The film ends with a double marriage that unites the Camerons and Stonemans in a symbolic rebirth of a nation that joins whites of the North and South in a new union rightfully based on the supremacy of "the Aryan race."

The son of a Confederate lieutenant colonel, David Wark (D. W.) Griffith was the foremost director of the silent movie era. He pioneered many precedent-setting cinematic techniques and profoundly influenced filmmaking throughout the world. *Birth of a Nation* was the first real full-length feature film, technically and artistically superior to anything before it. Apart from its place in the history of cinema, though, why should anyone today watch a movie that perpetuates such wrongheaded history and noxious racist stereotypes? Precisely *because* it reflects and amplifies an interpretation of Reconstruction that prevailed from the 1890s to the 1950s, and thereby shaped not only historical understanding but also contemporary behavior (as in its inspiration

Henry B. Walthall (Ben Cameron) kissing the hand of Elsie Stoneman (Lillian Gish) in *Birth of a Nation*.

© Bettmann/Corbis.

for the Klan of the 1920s). Although *Birth of a Nation* aroused controversy in parts of the North and was picketed by the NAACP, some 200 million people saw the film in the United States and abroad from 1915 to 1946. The story, and director Griffith, demonstrated in dramatic fashion how the South, having lost the Civil War, won the battle for how the war and especially Reconstruction would be remembered for more than half a century.

© Bettmann/Corbis.

TWO MEMBERS OF THE KU KLUX KLAN
Founded in Pulaski, Tennessee, in 1866 as a social
organization similar to a college fraternity, the Klan evolved
into a terrorist group whose purpose was intimidation of
Southern Republicans. The Klan, in which former Confederate
soldiers played a prominent part, was responsible for the
beating and murder of hundreds of blacks and whites alike
from 1868 to 1871.

In some places, notably Tennessee and Arkansas,
Republican militias formed to suppress and disarm the
Klan, but in most areas the militias were outgunned and
outmaneuvered by ex-Confederate veteran Klansmen.
Some Republican governors were reluctant to use black
militia against white guerrillas for fear of sparking a racial
bloodbath—as happened at Colfax.

The answer seemed to be federal troops. In 1870 and
1871, Congress enacted three laws intended to enforce
the 14th and 15th Amendments. Interference with voting rights became a federal offense, and any attempt to
deprive another person of civil or political rights became
a felony. The third law, passed on April 20, 1871, and popularly called the Ku Klux Klan Act, gave the president
power to suspend the writ of habeas corpus and send
in federal troops to suppress armed resistance to federal law.

Armed with these laws, the Grant administration
moved against the Klan. Because Grant was sensitive to
charges of "military despotism," he used his powers with
restraint. He suspended the writ of habeas corpus in only
nine South Carolina counties. Nevertheless, there and
elsewhere federal marshals backed by troops arrested
thousands of suspected Klansmen. Federal grand juries
indicted more than 3,000 members, and several hundred
defendants pleaded guilty in return for suspended sentences. To clear clogged court dockets so that the worst
offenders could be tried quickly, the Justice Department
dropped charges against nearly 2,000 others. About 600
Klansmen were convicted; most of them received fines or
light jail sentences, but 65 went to a federal penitentiary
for terms of up to five years.

The Election of 1872

These measures broke the back of the Klan in time for the
1872 presidential election. A group of dissident Republicans had emerged to challenge Grant's reelection. They
believed that conciliation of Southern whites rather than
continued military intervention was the only way to
achieve peace in the South. Calling themselves Liberal
Republicans, these dissidents nominated Horace Greeley,
the famous editor of the New York *Tribune*. Under the
slogan "Anything to beat Grant," the Democratic Party
also endorsed Greeley's nomination, although he had
long been their antagonist. On a platform denouncing
"bayonet rule" in the South, Greeley urged his fellow
Northerners to put the issues of the Civil War behind
them and to "clasp hands across the bloody chasm which
has too long divided" North and South.

This phrase would come back to haunt Greeley. Most
voters in the North were still not prepared to trust Democrats or Southern whites. Powerful anti-Greeley cartoons
by political cartoonist Thomas Nast showed Greeley shaking the hand of a Klansman dripping with the blood of a
murdered black Republican. Nast's most famous cartoon
portrayed Greeley as a pirate captain bringing his craft
alongside the ship of state, while Confederate leaders,
armed to the teeth, hid below waiting to board it.

Grant swamped Greeley on election day. Republicans
carried every Northern state and 10 of the 16 Southern
and border states. Blacks in the South enjoyed more freedom in voting than they would again for a century. This
apparent triumph of Republicanism and Reconstruction
would soon unravel.

The Panic of 1873

The U.S. economy had grown at an unprecedented pace since recovering from a mild postwar recession. In eight years, 35,000 miles of new railroad track were laid down, equal to all the track laid in the preceding 35 years. The first transcontinental railroad had been completed on May 10, 1869, when a golden spike was driven at Promontory Summit, Utah Territory, linking the Union Pacific and the Central Pacific. But the building of a second transcontinental line, the Northern Pacific, precipitated a Wall Street panic in 1873 and plunged the economy into a five-year depression.

Jay Cooke's banking firm, fresh from its triumphant marketing of Union war bonds, took over the Northern Pacific in 1869. Cooke pyramided every conceivable kind of equity and loan financing to raise the money to begin laying rails west from Duluth, Minnesota. Other investment firms did the same as a fever of speculative financing gripped the country. In September 1873, the pyramid of paper collapsed. Cooke's firm was the first to go bankrupt. Like dominoes, thousands of banks and businesses also collapsed. Unemployment rose to 14 percent, and hard times set in.

The Retreat from Reconstruction

It is an axiom of American politics that the voters will punish the party in power in times of economic depression. That axiom held true in the 1870s. Democrats made large gains in the congressional elections of 1874, winning a majority in the House for the first time in 18 years.

Public opinion also began to turn against Republican policies in the South. The campaign by Liberal Republicans and Democrats against "bayonet rule" and "carpetbag corruption" that left most Northern voters unmoved in 1872 found a growing audience in subsequent years. Intraparty battles among Republicans in Southern states enabled Democrats to regain control of several state governments. Well-publicized corruption scandals also discredited Republican leaders. Although corruption was probably no worse in Southern states than in many parts of the North, Southern postwar poverty made waste and extravagance seem worse. White Democrats scored propaganda points by claiming that corruption proved the incompetence of "Negro-carpetbag" regimes.

Northerners grew increasingly weary of what seemed to be the endless turmoil of Southern politics. Most of them had never had a strong commitment to racial equal-ity, and they were growing more and more willing to let white supremacy regain sway in the South. "The truth is," confessed a Northern Republican, "our people are tired out with this worn out cry of 'Southern outrages'!!! Hard times & heavy taxes make them wish the 'nigger,' 'everlasting nigger,' were in hell or Africa."

By 1875, only four Southern states remained under Republican control: South Carolina, Florida, Mississippi, and Louisiana. In those states, white Democrats had revived paramilitary organizations under various names: White Leagues (Louisiana), Rifle Clubs (Mississippi), and Red Shirts (South Carolina). Unlike the Klan, these groups operated openly. In Louisiana, they fought pitched battles with Republican militias in which scores were killed. When the Grant administration sent large numbers of federal troops to Louisiana, people in both North and South cried out against military rule. The protests grew even louder when soldiers marched onto the floor of the Louisiana legislature in January 1875 and expelled several Democratic legislators after a contested election. Was this America? asked Republican Senator Carl Schurz in a widely publicized speech: "If this can be done in Louisiana, how long will it be before it can be done in Massachusetts and Ohio? How long before a soldier may stalk into the national House of Representatives, and, pointing to the Speaker's mace, say 'Take away that bauble!'"

The Mississippi Election of 1875

The backlash against the Grant administration affected the Mississippi state election of 1875. Democrats there devised a strategy called the Mississippi Plan. The first step was to "persuade" the 10 to 15 percent of white voters still calling themselves Republicans to switch to the Democrats. Only a handful of carpetbaggers could resist the economic pressures, social ostracism, and threats that made it "too damned hot for [us] to stay out," wrote one white Republican who changed parties. "No white man can live in the South in the future and act with any other than the Democratic Party unless he is willing and prepared to live a life of social isolation and remain in political oblivion."

The second step in the Mississippi Plan was to intimidate black voters because even with all whites voting Democratic, the party could still be defeated by the 55 percent black majority. Economic coercion against black sharecroppers and workers kept some of them away from the polls, but violence was the most effective method. Democratic "rifle clubs" showed up at Republican rallies, provoked riots, and shot down dozens of blacks in the ensuing melees. Governor Adelbert Ames—a native of Maine, a Union general who had won a congressional

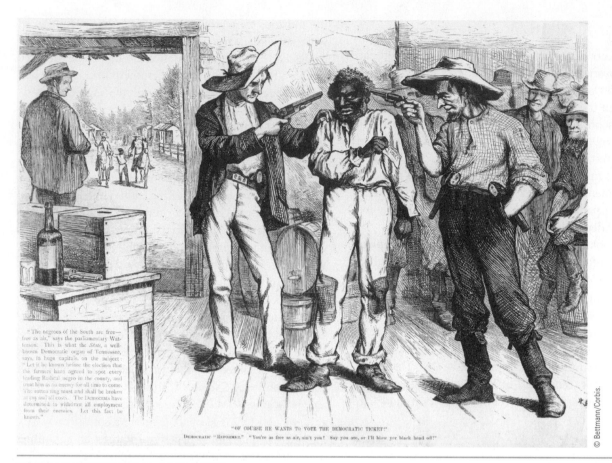

"The negroes of the South are free—free as air," says the parliamentary Watterson. This is what the *State*, a well-known Democratic organ of Tennessee, says, in huge capitals, on the subject: "Let it be known before the election that the farmers have agreed to spot every leading Radical negro in the county, and treat him as an enemy for all time to come. The rotten ring must and shall be broken at any and all costs. The Democrats have determined to withdraw all employment from their enemies. Let this fact be known."

"OF COURSE HE WANTS TO VOTE THE DEMOCRATIC TICKET!"
Democratic "Reformer." "You're as free as air, ain't you? Say you are, or I'll blow yer black head off!"

© Bettmann/Corbis.

HOW THE MISSISSIPPI PLAN WORKED

This cartoon shows how black counties could report large Democratic majorities in the Mississippi state election of 1875. The black voter holds a Democratic ticket while one of the men, described in the caption as a "Democratic reformer," holds a revolver to his head and says: "You're as free as air, ain't you? Say you are, or I'll blow your black head off!"

medal of honor in the war, and one of the ablest of Southern Republicans—called for federal troops to control the violence. Grant intended to comply, but Ohio Republicans warned him that if he sent troops to Mississippi, the Democrats would exploit the issue of "bayonet rule" to carry Ohio in that year's state elections. Grant yielded—in effect giving up Mississippi for Ohio. The U.S. attorney general replied to Ames's request for troops:

> The whole public are tired out with these annual autumnal outbreaks in the South, and the great majority are now ready to condemn any interference on the part of the government. . . . Preserve the peace by the forces in your own state, and let the country see that the citizens of Mississippi, who are . . . largely Republican, have the courage to fight for their rights.

Governor Ames did try to organize a loyal state militia, but that proved difficult—and in any case, he was reluctant to use a black militia for fear of provoking a race war. "No matter if they are going to carry the State," said

Ames with weary resignation, "let them carry it, and let us be at peace and have no more killing." The Mississippi Plan worked like a charm. In five of the state's counties with large black majorities, the Republicans polled 12, 7, 4, 2, and 0 votes, respectively. What had been a Republican majority of 30,000 in 1874 became a Democratic majority of 30,000 in 1875.

The Supreme Court and Reconstruction

Even if Grant had been willing to continue intervening in Southern state elections, Congress and the courts would have constricted such efforts. The new Democratic majority in the House threatened to cut any appropriations for the Justice Department and the army intended for use in the South. In 1876, the Supreme Court handed down two decisions that declared parts of the 1870 and 1871 laws for enforcement of the 14th and 15th Amendments unconstitutional. In *U.S.* v. *Cruikshank* and *U.S.* v. *Reese,* the Court ruled on cases from Louisiana and Kentucky. Both cases grew out of provisions in these laws authorizing federal officials to prosecute *individuals* (not states) for violations of the civil and voting rights of blacks. But, the Court pointed out, the 14th and 15th Amendments apply to actions by *states:* "No State shall . . . deprive any person of life, liberty, or property . . . nor deny to any person . . . equal protection of the laws": the right to vote "shall not be denied . . . by any State." Therefore, the portions of these laws that empowered the federal government to prosecute individuals were declared unconstitutional.

The Court did not say what could be done when states were controlled by white-supremacy Democrats who had no intention of enforcing equal rights. (In the mid-20th century, the Supreme Court would reverse itself and interpret the 14th and 15th Amendments much more broadly.)

Meanwhile, in another ruling, *Civil Rights Cases* (1883), the Court declared unconstitutional a civil rights law passed by Congress in 1875. That law, enacted on the eve of the Democratic takeover of the House elected in 1874, was a crowning achievement of Reconstruction. It banned racial discrimination in all forms of public transportation and public accommodations. If enforced, it would have effected a sweeping transformation of race relations—in the North as well as in the South. Even some of the congressmen who voted for the bill doubted its constitutionality, however, and the Justice Department had made little effort to enforce it. Several cases made their way to the Supreme Court, which in 1883 ruled the law unconstitutional—again on grounds that the 14th Amendment applied only to states, not to individuals. Several states—all in the North—passed their own civil rights laws in the 1870s and 1880s, but less than 10 percent of the black population resided in those states. The mass of African Americans lived a segregated existence.

The Election of 1876

In 1876, the remaining Southern Republican state governments fell victim to the passion for reform. The mounting revelations of corruption at all levels of government ensured that reform would be the leading issue in the presidential election. In this centennial year of the birth

LINK TO THE PAST

Frederick Douglass on the Supreme Court and Civil Rights

The Civil Rights Act of 1875 anticipated many of the provisions of the Civil Rights Act of 1964, which is the law of the land and has been upheld by the U.S. Supreme Court. But the law of 1875 was ahead of its time, or at least ahead of the Supreme Court of its time, which declared it unconstitutional on the grounds that the Fourteenth Amendment prohibited discrimination by states but not by individuals. The black civil rights leader Frederick Douglass denounced the Court's decision in language that anticipated the Supreme Court's reasoning in the last third of the 20th century.

This decision of the Supreme Court admits that the Fourteenth Amendment is a prohibition of the States. It admits that a State shall not abridge the privileges or immunities of citizens of the United States, but commits the seeming absurdity of allowing the people of a State to do what it prohibits the State itself from doing. . . . It is said that this decision will make no difference in the treatment of colored people; that the Civil Rights Bill was a dead letter, and could not be enforced. There is some truth in all this, but it is not the whole truth.

That bill, like all advance legislation, was a banner on the outer wall of American liberty, a noble moral standard, uplifted for the education of the American people. . . .

This law, though dead, did speak. It expressed the sentiment of justice and fair play. . . . If it is a bill for social equality, so is the Declaration of Independence, which declares that all men have equal rights; so is the Sermon on the Mount, so is the Golden Rule . . . so is the Constitution of the United States.

FREDERICK DOUGLASS
From a speech in Washington, D.C., October 22, 1883

1. What is Douglass's response to the argument that the Civil Rights Act was a dead letter even before the Supreme Court declared it so?

For additional sources related to this feature, visit the *Liberty, Equality, Power* Web site at:

http://history.wadsworth.com/murrin_LEP4e

of the United States, marked by a great exposition in Philadelphia, Americans wanted to put their best foot forward. Both major parties gave their presidential nominations to governors who had earned reform reputations in their states: Democrat Samuel J. Tilden of New York and Republican Rutherford B. Hayes of Ohio.

Democrats entered the campaign as favorites for the first time in two decades. It seemed likely that they would be able to put together an electoral majority from a "solid South" plus New York and two or three other Northern states. To ensure a solid South, they looked to the lessons of the Mississippi Plan. In 1876, a new word came into use to describe Democratic techniques of intimidation: *bulldozing*. To bulldoze black voters meant to trample them down or keep them away from the polls. In South Carolina and Louisiana, the Red Shirts and the White Leagues mobilized for an all-out bulldozing effort.

The most notorious incident, the Hamburg Massacre, occurred in the village of Hamburg, South Carolina, where a battle between a black militia unit and 200 Red Shirts resulted in the capture of several militiamen, five of

READING THE ELECTION BULLETIN BY GASLIGHT

In this drawing, eager voters scan the early returns, which seemed to give Samuel J. Tilden the presidency in 1876.

The Granger Collection, New York.

whom were shot "while attempting to escape." This time Grant did send in federal troops. He pronounced the Hamburg Massacre "cruel, blood-thirsty, wanton, unprovoked . . . a repetition of the course that has been pursued in other Southern States."

The federal government also put several thousand deputy marshals and election supervisors on duty in the South. Although they kept an uneasy peace at the polls, they could do little to prevent assaults, threats, and economic coercion in backcountry districts, which reduced the potential Republican tally in the former Confederate states by at least 250,000 votes.

Disputed Results

When the results were in, Tilden had carried four Northern states, including New York with its 35 electoral votes. Tilden also carried all of the former slave states except—apparently—Louisiana, South Carolina, and Florida, which produced disputed returns. Because Tilden needed only one of them to win the presidency, while Hayes needed all three, and because Tilden seemed to have carried Louisiana and Florida, it appeared initially that he had won the presidency. But frauds and irregularities reported from several bulldozed districts in the three states clouded the issue. For example, a Louisiana parish that had recorded 1,688 Republican votes in 1874 reported only 1 in 1876. Many other similar discrepancies appeared. The official returns ultimately sent to Washington gave all three states—and therefore the presidency—to Hayes, but the Democrats refused to recognize the results, and they controlled the House.

The country now faced a serious constitutional crisis. Armed Democrats threatened to march on Washington. Many people feared another civil war. The Constitution offered no clear guidance on how to deal with the matter. A count of the state electoral votes required the concurrence of both houses of Congress, but with a Democratic House and a Republican Senate, such concurrence was not forthcoming. To break the deadlock, Congress created a special electoral commission consisting of five representatives, five senators, and five Supreme Court justices split evenly between the two parties, with one member, a Supreme Court justice, supposedly an independent—but in fact a Republican.

Tilden had won a national majority of 252,000 popular votes, and the raw returns gave him a majority in the three disputed states. But an estimated 250,000 Southern Republicans had been bulldozed away from the polls. In a genuinely fair and free election, the Republicans might have carried Mississippi and North Carolina as well as

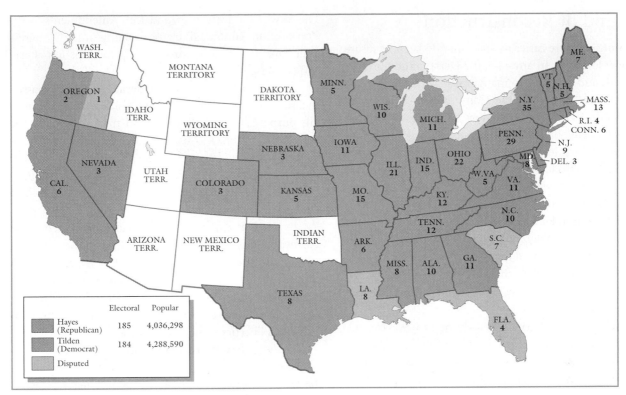

MAP 17.3 HAYES-TILDEN DISPUTED ELECTION OF 1876

A comparison of this map with those on pp. 546 and 551 shows the persistence of geographical voting patterns once Southern Democrats had overthrown most Republican state governments and effectively disenfranchised many black voters.

the three disputed states. While the commission agonized, Democrats and Republicans in Louisiana and South Carolina each inaugurated their own separate governors and legislatures (Republicans in Florida gave up the fight at the state level). Only federal troops in the capitals at New Orleans and Columbia protected the Republican governments in those states.

The Compromise of 1877

In February 1877, three months after voters had gone to the polls, the electoral commission issued its ruling. By a partisan vote of 8 to 7—with the "independent" justice voting with the Republicans—the commission awarded all of the disputed states to Hayes. The Democrats cried foul and began a filibuster in the House to delay the final electoral count beyond the inauguration date of March 4, so as to throw the election to the House of Representatives, an eventuality that threatened to bring total anarchy. But, behind the scenes, a compromise began to take shape. Both Northern Republicans and Southern Democrats of Whig heritage had similar interests in liquidating the sectional rancor and in getting on with the business of

economic recovery and development. Among these neo-Whigs were Hayes and his advisers. To wean Southern Whiggish Democrats away from a House filibuster, Hayes promised his support as president for federal appropriations to rebuild war-destroyed levees on the lower Mississippi and federal aid for a southern transcontinental railroad. Hayes's lieutenants also hinted at the appointment of a Southerner as postmaster general, who would have a considerable amount of patronage at his disposal—the appointment of thousands of local postmasters.

Most important, Southerners wanted to know what Hayes would do about Louisiana and South Carolina. Would he withdraw the troops and allow the Democrats who already governed those states in fact to do so in law as well? Hayes signaled his intention to end "bayonet rule," which he had for some time considered a bankrupt policy. He believed that the goodwill and influence of Southern moderates would offer better protection for black rights than federal troops could provide. In return for his commitment to withdraw the troops, Hayes asked for—and received—promises of fair treatment of freedpeople and respect for their constitutional rights.

The End of Reconstruction

Such promises were easier to make than to keep, as future years would reveal. In any case, the Democratic filibuster collapsed, and Hayes was inaugurated on March 4. He soon fulfilled his part of the Compromise of 1877: ex-Confederate Democrat David Key of Tennessee became postmaster general; in 1878, the South received more federal money for internal improvements than ever before; and federal troops left the capitals of Louisiana and South Carolina. The last two Republican state governments collapsed. The old abolitionist and radical Republican warhorses denounced Hayes's actions as a sellout of Southern blacks. His was a policy "of weakness, of subserviency, of surrender," in the words of the venerable crusader William Lloyd Garrison, a policy that sustained "might against right . . . the rich and powerful against the poor and unprotected."

Voices of protest could scarcely be heard above the sighs of relief that the crisis was over. Most Americans—including even most Republicans—wanted no more military intervention in state affairs. "I have no sort of faith in a local government which can only be propped up by foreign bayonets," wrote the editor of the New York *Tribune* in April 1877. "If negro suffrage means that as a permanency then negro suffrage is a failure."

Conclusion

Before the Civil War, most Americans had viewed a powerful government as a threat to individual liberties. That is why the first 10 amendments to the Constitution (the Bill of Rights) imposed strict limits on the powers of the federal government. During the Civil War and especially during Reconstruction, however, the national government had to exert an unprecedented amount of power to free the slaves and guarantee their equal rights as free citizens.

That is why the 13th, 14th, and 15th Amendments to the Constitution contained clauses stating that "Congress shall have power" to enforce these provisions for liberty and equal rights.

During the post–Civil War decade, Congress passed civil rights laws and enforcement legislation to accomplish this purpose. Federal marshals and troops patrolled the polls to protect black voters, arrested thousands of Klansmen and other violators of black civil rights, and even occupied state capitals to prevent Democratic paramilitary groups from overthrowing legitimately elected Republican state governments.

By 1875, many Northerners had grown tired of or alarmed by this continued use of military power to intervene in the internal affairs of states. The Supreme Court stripped the federal government of much of its authority to enforce certain provisions of the 14th and 15th Amendments. Traditional fears of military power as a threat to individual liberties came to the fore again.

The withdrawal of federal troops from the South in 1877 constituted both a symbolic and a substantive end of the 12-year postwar era known as Reconstruction. Reconstruction had achieved the two great objectives inherited from the Civil War: (1) to reincorporate the former Confederate states into the Union, and (2) to accomplish a transition from slavery to freedom in the South. That transition was marred by the economic inequity of sharecropping and the social injustice of white supremacy. A third goal of Reconstruction, enforcement of the equal civil and political rights promised in the 14th and 15th Amendments, was betrayed by the Compromise of 1877. In subsequent decades, the freed slaves and their descendants suffered repression into segregated, second-class citizenship. Not until another war hero-turned-president sent troops into Little Rock (chapter 28), 80 years after they had been withdrawn from New Orleans and Columbia, did the federal government launch a second Reconstruction to fulfill the promises of the first.

SUGGESTED READINGS

The most comprehensive and incisive history of Reconstruction is **Eric Foner, *Reconstruction: America's Unfinished Revolution 1863–1872*** (1988). For a skillful abridgement of this book, see Foner, *A Short History of Reconstruction* (1990). Also valuable is **Kenneth M. Stampp, *The Era of Reconstruction, 1865–1877*** (1965). Important for their insights on Lincoln and the reconstruction question are **Peyton McCrary, *Abraham Lincoln and Reconstruction: The Louisiana Experiment*** (1978) and **LaWanda Cox, *Lincoln and Black Freedom: A Study in Presidential Leadership*** (1981). A superb study of the South Carolina Sea Islands as a laboratory of Reconstruction is **Willie Lee Rose, *Rehearsal for Reconstruction: The Port Royal Experiment*** (1964).

Three important studies of Andrew Johnson and his conflict with Congress over Reconstruction are **Eric L. McKitrick, *Andrew Johnson and Reconstruction*** (1960); **Hans L. Trefousse, *The Radical Republicans: Lincoln's Vanguard for Racial Justice*** (1969); and **Michael Les Benedict, *The Impeachment and Trial of Andrew Johnson*** (1973). Two books by **Michael Perman** connect events in the South and in Washington during Reconstruction: ***Reunion without Compromise: The South and Reconstruction, 1865–1868*** (1973) and ***The Road to Redemption: Southern Politics 1868–1879*** (1984). For counter-Reconstruction violence in the South, see **George C. Rable, *But There Was No Peace: The Role of Violence in the Politics of Reconstruction*** (1984). The evolution of sharecropping and other aspects of the transition from slavery to freedom are treated in **Roger L. Ransom and Richard Sutch, *One Kind of Freedom: The Economic Consequences of Emancipation*** (1977).

Of the many books on African Americans in Reconstruction, the following are perhaps the most valuable: **Thomas Holt, *Black over White: Negro Political Leadership in South Carolina during Reconstruction*** (1977) and **Laura F. Edwards, *Gendered Strife and Confusion: The Political Culture of Reconstruction*** (1997). An excellent collection of essays on the Freedmen's Bureau is **Paul A. Cimbala and Randall Miller, eds., *The Freedmen's Bureau and Reconstruction*** (1999). Both black and white churches are the subject of **Daniel Stowell, *Rebuilding Zion: The Religious Reconstruction of the South, 1863–1877*** (1998).

AMERICAN JOURNEY ONLINE AND INFOTRAC COLLEGE EDITION

Visit the source collections at www.ajaccess.wadsworth.com and infotrac.thomsonlearning.com and use the Search function with the following key terms to explore documents, images, audio and video clips, articles, and commentary related to the material in this chapter.

Andrew Johnson	Transcontinental Railroad
Reconstruction	Ulysses S. Grant
Freedmen's Bureau	14th Amendment
Ku Klux Klan	15th Amendment

GRADE AIDS

Visit the Liberty Equality Power Companion Web site for resources specific to this textbook: http://history.wadsworth.com/murrin_LEP4e

The CD in the back of this book and the U.S. History Resource Center at http://history.wadsworth.com/u.s./ offer a variety of tools to help you succeed in this course, including access to quizzes; images; documents; interactive simulations, maps, and timelines; movie explorations; and a wealth of other sources.

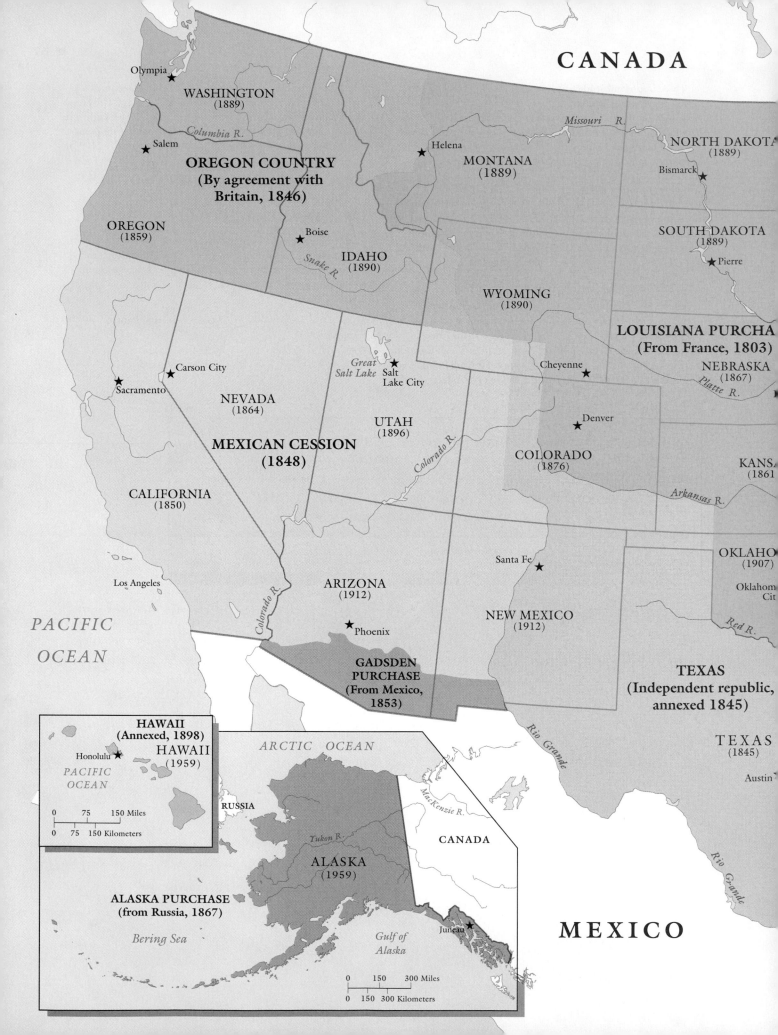

CANADA

Olympia ★
WASHINGTON
(1889)

Columbia R.

★ Salem

OREGON COUNTRY
(By agreement with
Britain, 1846)

OREGON
(1859)

Boise ★

IDAHO
(1890)

Snake R.

Helena ★
MONTANA
(1889)

Missouri R.

NORTH DAKOTA
(1889)

Bismarck ★

SOUTH DAKOTA
(1889)

★ Pierre

WYOMING
(1890)

LOUISIANA PURCHA
(From France, 1803)

NEBRASKA
(1867)

Platte R.

Great
Salt Lake

Salt ★
Lake City

Cheyenne ★

Carson City ★

Sacramento ★

NEVADA
(1864)

UTAH
(1896)

Colorado R.

Denver ★

COLORADO
(1876)

KANS
(1861)

Arkansas R.

MEXICAN CESSION
(1848)

CALIFORNIA
(1850)

Los Angeles

PACIFIC

OCEAN

Colorado R.

ARIZONA
(1912)

Phoenix ★

Santa Fe ★

NEW MEXICO
(1912)

OKLAHO
(1907)

Oklahom
Cit

Red R.

GADSDEN
PURCHASE
(From Mexico,
1853)

TEXAS
(Independent republic,
annexed 1845)

HAWAII
(Annexed, 1898)

Honolulu ★
PACIFIC
OCEAN

HAWAII
(1959)

0   75   150 Miles
0   75   150 Kilometers

ARCTIC OCEAN

RUSSIA

Yukon R.

MacKenzie R.

CANADA

ALASKA
(1959)

ALASKA PURCHASE
(from Russia, 1867)

Bering Sea

Gulf of
Alaska

Juneau ★

0   150   300 Miles
0   150   300 Kilometers

TEXAS
(1845)

Austin

Rio Grande

Rio Grande

MEXICO

UNITED STATES
Territorial Expansion

Lake of the Woods

Lake Superior

Lake Huron

Lake Michigan

Lake Ontario

Lake Erie

St. Lawrence R.

MAINE (1820)
★ Augusta

VT. (1791)
Montpelier ★

N.H. (1788)
★ Concord
Boston ★

NEW YORK (1788)
Albany ★

MASS. (1788)
★ Providence
R.I. (1790)

Hartford ★
CONN. (1788)

N.J. (1787)
★ Harrisburg
Trenton ★

PENN. (1787)

1800 ●
MD. (1788) ● 1790 ●
Annapolis ★ Dover
DEL. (1787)
Washington, D.C. ✪

MINNESOTA (1858)

St. Paul ★

WISCONSIN (1848)

Madison ★

MICHIGAN (1837)
★ Lansing

IOWA (1846)

★ Des Moines

ORIGINAL UNITED STATES
(By treaty with Britain, 1783)

OHIO (1803)

INDIANA (1816)

Indianapolis ★

ILLINOIS (1818)

Springfield ★
1900 ●

★ Columbus

1850 ●

VIRGINIA (1788)

Richmond ★

Chesapeake Bay

ATLANTIC OCEAN

ORIGINAL THIRTEEN COLONIES

Charleston ●
WEST VIRGINIA (1863)

MISSOURI (1821)
Missouri R.

Jefferson City ★
1950 ●

★ Frankfort

KENTUCKY (1792)

Ohio R.

2000 ●

Nashville ★

TENNESSEE (1796)

NORTH CAROLINA (1789)
★ Raleigh

ARKANSAS (1836)

Arkansas R.

Little Rock ★

Tennessee R.

SOUTH CAROLINA (1788)
Columbia ★

ALABAMA (1819)

Atlanta ★

GEORGIA (1788)

MISSISSIPPI (1817)

Montgomery ★

Jackson ★

Red R.

Baton Rouge ★

LOUISIANA (1812)

Mississippi R.

(Seized from Spain, 1810, 1813)

★ Tallahassee

FLORIDA
(By treaty with Spain, 1819)

FLORIDA (1845)

Lake Okeechobee

Gulf

of

Mexico

| ● | Geographical center of population per Census year |

PUERTO RICO
(From Spain, 1898)

ATLANTIC OCEAN

San Juan ★

★ Charlotte Amalie

VIRGIN ISLANDS
(From Denmark, 1917)

0   50   100 Miles
0   50   100 Kilometers

BAHAMAS

0   150   300 Miles
0   150   300 Kilometers

CUBA

Appendix

The Declaration of Independence

THE UNANIMOUS DECLARATION OF
THE THIRTEEN UNITED STATES OF AMERICA

When in the Course of human events it becomes necessary for one people to dissolve the political bands which have connected them with another, and to assume among the Powers of the earth, the separate and equal station to which the Laws of Nature and of Nature's God entitle them, a decent respect to the opinions of mankind requires that they should declare the causes which impel them to the separation.

We hold these truths to be self-evident, that all men are created equal, that they are endowed by their Creator with certain unalienable Rights, that among these are Life, Liberty and the pursuit of Happiness. That to secure these rights, Governments are instituted among Men, deriving their just Powers from the consent of the governed. That whenever any Form of Government becomes destructive of these ends, it is the Right of the People to alter or to abolish it, and to institute new Government, laying its foundation on such principles and organizing its Powers in such form, as to them shall seem most likely to effect their Safety and Happiness. Prudence, indeed, will dictate that Governments long established should not be changed for light and transient causes; and accordingly all experience hath shewn, that mankind are more disposed to suffer, while evils are sufferable, than to right themselves by abolishing the forms to which they are accustomed. But when a long train of abuses and usurpations, pursuing invariably the same Object evinces a design to reduce them under absolute Despotism, it is their right, it is their duty, to throw off such Government, and to provide new Guards for their future security. Such has been the patient sufferance of these Colonies; and such is now the necessity which constrains them to alter their former Systems of Government. The history of the present King of Great Britain is a history of repeated injuries and usurpations, all having in direct object the establishment of an absolute Tyranny over these States. To prove this, let Facts be submitted to a candid world.

He has refused his Assent to Laws, the most wholesome and necessary for the public good.

He has forbidden his Governors to pass Laws of immediate and pressing importance, unless suspended in their operation till his Assent should be obtained; and when so suspended, he has utterly neglected to attend to them.

He has refused to pass other Laws for the accommodation of large districts of people, unless those people would relinquish the right of Representation in the Legislature, a right inestimable to them and formidable to tyrants only.

He has called together legislative bodies at places unusual, uncomfortable, and distant from the depository of their Public Records, for the sole Purpose of fatiguing them into compliance with his measures.

He has dissolved Representative Houses repeatedly, for opposing with manly firmness his invasions on the rights of the People.

He has refused for a long time, after such dissolutions, to cause others to be elected; whereby the Legislative Powers, incapable of Annihilation, have returned to the People at large for their exercise; the State remaining in the mean time exposed to all the dangers of invasion from without, and convulsions within.

He has endeavoured to prevent the Population of these States; for that purpose obstructing the Laws for Naturalization of Foreigners; refusing to pass others to encourage their migrations hither, and raising the conditions of new Appropriations of Lands.

He has obstructed the Administration of Justice, by refusing his Assent to Laws for establishing Judiciary Powers.

He has made Judges dependent on his Will alone, for the tenure of their offices, and the amount and payment of their salaries.

He has erected a multitude of New Offices, and sent hither swarms of Officers to harass our People, and eat out their substance.

He has kept among us, in times of peace, Standing Armies without the Consent of our legislatures.

Text is reprinted from the facsimile of the engrossed copy in the National Archives. The original spelling, capitalization, and punctuation have been retained. Paragraphing has been added.

He has affected to render the Military independent of and superior to the Civil Power.

He has combined with others to subject us to a jurisdiction foreign to our constitution, and unacknowledged by our laws; giving his Assent to their Acts of pretended Legislation:

For Quartering large bodies of armed troops among us:

For protecting them, by a mock Trial, from Punishment for any Murders which they should commit on the Inhabitants of these States:

For cutting off our Trade with all parts of the world:

For imposing Taxes on us without our Consent:

For depriving us in many cases, of the benefits of Trial by Jury:

For transporting us beyond Seas to be tried for pretended offences:

For abolishing the free System of English Laws in a neighbouring Province, establishing therein an Arbitrary government, and enlarging its Boundaries so as to render it at once an example and fit instrument for introducing the same absolute rule into these Colonies:

For taking away our Charters, abolishing our most valuable Laws, and altering fundamentally the Forms of our Governments:

For suspending our own Legislatures, and declaring themselves invested with Power to legislate for us in all cases whatsoever.

He has abdicated Government here, by declaring us out of his Protection, and waging War against us.

He has plundered our seas, ravaged our Coasts, burnt our towns, and destroyed the lives of our people.

He is at this time transporting large Armies of foreign Mercenaries to compleat the works of death, desolation and tyranny, already begun with circumstances of Cruelty and perfidy scarcely paralleled in the most barbarous ages, and totally unworthy the Head of a civilized nation.

He has constrained our fellow Citizens taken Captive on the high Seas to bear Arms against their Country, to become the executioners of their friends and Brethren, or to fall themselves by their Hands.

He has excited domestic insurrections amongst us, and has endeavoured to bring on the inhabitants of our frontiers, the merciless Indian Savages, whose known rule of warfare, is an undistinguished destruction of all ages, sexes and conditions.

In every stage of these Oppressions We have Petitioned for Redress in the most humble terms: Our repeated Petitions have been answered only by repeated injury. A Prince, whose character is thus marked by every act which may define a Tyrant, is unfit to be the ruler of a free People.

Nor have We been wanting in attentions to our British brethren. We have warned them from time to time of attempts by their legislature to extend an unwarrantable jurisdiction over us. We have reminded them of the circumstances of our emigration and settlement here. We have appealed to their native justice and magnanimity, and we have conjured them by the ties of our common kindred to disavow these usurpations, which, would inevitably interrupt our connections and correspondence. They too have been deaf to the voice of justice and of consanguinity. We must, therefore, acquiesce in the necessity, which denounces our Separation, and hold them, as we hold the rest of mankind, Enemies in War, in Peace Friends.

WE, THEREFORE, the Representatives of the UNITED STATES OF AMERICA, in General Congress, Assembled, appealing to the Supreme Judge of the world for the rectitude of our intentions, do, in the Name, and by Authority of the good People of these Colonies, solemnly publish and declare, That these United Colonies are, and of Right ought to be FREE AND INDEPENDENT STATES; that they are Absolved from all Allegiance to the British Crown, and that all political connection between them and the State of Great Britain, is and ought to be totally dissolved; and that, as Free and Independent States, they have full Power to levy War, conclude Peace, contract Alliances, establish Commerce, and to do all other Acts and Things which Independent States may of right do. And for the support of this Declaration, with a firm reliance on the protection of divine Providence, we mutually pledge to each other our Lives, our Fortunes and our sacred Honor.

The Constitution of the United States of America

We the People of the United States, in Order to form a more perfect Union, establish Justice, insure domestic Tranquility, provide for the common defence, promote the general Welfare, and secure the Blessings of Liberty to ourselves and our Posterity, do ordain and establish this Constitution for the United States of America.

ARTICLE I.

SECTION 1. All legislative Powers herein granted shall be vested in a Congress of the United States, which shall consist of a Senate and House of Representatives.

SECTION 2. The House of Representatives shall be composed of Members chosen every second Year by the People of the several States, and the Electors in each State shall have the Qualifications requisite for Electors of the most numerous Branch of the State Legislature.

No Person shall be a Representative who shall not have attained to the Age of twenty five Years, and been seven Years a Citizen of the United States, and who shall not, when elected, be an Inhabitant of that State in which he shall be chosen.

Representatives and direct Taxes[1] shall be apportioned among the several States which may be included within this Union, according to their respective Numbers, which shall be determined by adding to the whole Number of free Persons, including those bound to Service for a Term of Years, and excluding Indians not taxed, three fifths of all other Persons.[2] The actual Enumeration shall be made within three Years after the first Meeting of the Congress of the United States, and within every subsequent Term of ten Years, in such Manner as they shall by Law direct. The Number of Representatives shall not exceed one for every thirty Thousand, but each State shall have at Least one Representative; and until such enumeration shall be made, the State of New Hampshire shall be entitled to chuse three; Massachusetts eight; Rhode Island and Providence Plantations one; Connecticut five; New York six; New Jersey four; Pennsylvania eight; Delaware one; Maryland six; Virginia ten; North Carolina five; South Carolina five; and Georgia three.

When vacancies happen in the Representation from any State, the Executive Authority thereof shall issue Writs of Election to fill such Vacancies.

The House of Representatives shall chuse their Speaker and other Officers; and shall have the sole Power of Impeachment.

SECTION 3. The Senate of the United States shall be composed of two Senators from each State, chosen by the Legislature thereof, for six Years; and each Senator shall have one Vote.[3]

Immediately after they shall be assembled in Consequence of the first Election, they shall be divided as equally as may be into three Classes. The Seats of the Senators of the first Class shall be vacated at the Expiration of the second Year, of the second Class at the Expiration of the fourth Year, and of the third Class at the Expiration of the sixth Year, so that one third may be chosen every second Year; and if Vacancies happen by Resignation, or otherwise, during the Recess of the Legislature of any State, the Executive thereof may make temporary Appointments until the next Meeting of the Legislature, which shall then fill such Vacancies.[4]

No Person shall be a Senator who shall not have attained to the Age of thirty Years, and been nine Years a Citizen of the United States, and who shall not, when elected, be an Inhabitant of that State for which he shall be chosen.

The Vice President of the United States shall be President of the Senate, but shall have no Vote, unless they be equally divided.

The Senate shall chuse their other Officers, and also a President pro tempore, in the Absence of the Vice President, or when he shall exercise the Office of President of the United States.

Text is from the engrossed copy in the National Archives. Original spelling, capitalization, and punctuation have been retained.

[1]Modified by the Sixteenth Amendment.
[2]Replaced by the Fourteenth Amendment.
[3]Superseded by the Seventeenth Amendment.
[4]Modified by the Seventeenth Amendment.

The Senate shall have the sole Power to try all Impeachments. When sitting for that Purpose, they shall be on Oath or Affirmation. When the President of the United States is tried, the Chief Justice shall preside: And no Person shall be convicted without the Concurrence of two thirds of the Members present.

Judgment in Cases of Impeachment shall not extend further than to removal from Office, and disqualification to hold and enjoy any Office of honor, Trust or Profit under the United States: but the Party convicted shall nevertheless be liable and subject to Indictment, Trial, Judgment and Punishment, according to Law.

SECTION 4. The Times, Places and Manner of holding Elections for Senators and Representatives, shall be prescribed in each State by the Legislature thereof, but the Congress may at any time by Law make or alter such Regulation, except as to the Places of chusing Senators.

The Congress shall assemble at least once in every Year, and such Meeting shall be on the first Monday in December, unless they shall by Law appoint a different Day.[5]

SECTION 5. Each House shall be the Judge of the Elections, Returns and Qualifications of its own Members, and a Majority of each shall constitute a Quorum to do Business; but a smaller Number may adjourn from day to day, and may be authorized to compel the Attendance of absent Members, in such Manner, and under such Penalties as each House may provide.

Each House may determine the Rules of its Proceedings, punish its Members for disorderly Behaviour, and, with the Concurrence of two thirds, expel a Member.

Each House shall keep a Journal of its Proceedings, and from time to time publish the same, excepting such Parts as may in their Judgment require Secrecy; and the Yeas and Nays of the Members of either House on any question shall, at the Desire of one fifth of those Present, be entered on the Journal.

Neither House, during the Session of Congress, shall, without the Consent of the other, adjourn for more than three days, nor to any other Place than that in which the two Houses shall be sitting.

SECTION 6. The Senators and Representatives shall receive a Compensation for their Services, to be ascertained by Law, and paid out of the Treasury of the United States. They shall in all Cases, except Treason, Felony and Breach of the Peace, be privileged from Arrest during their Attendance at the Session of their respective Houses, and in going to and returning from the same; and for any Speech or Debate in either House, they shall not be questioned in any other Place.

No Senator or Representative shall, during the Time for which he was elected, be appointed to any civil Office under the Authority of the United States, which shall have been created, or the Emoluments whereof shall have been encreased during such time; and no Person holding any Office under the United States, shall be a Member of either House during his Continuance in Office.

SECTION 7. All Bills for raising Revenue shall originate in the House of Representatives; but the Senate may propose or concur with Amendments as on other Bills.

Every Bill which shall have passed the House of Representatives and the Senate shall, before it become a Law, be presented to the President of the United States; If he approve he shall sign it, but if not he shall return it, with his Objections to that House in which it shall have originated, who shall enter the Objections at large on their Journal, and proceed to reconsider it. If after such Reconsideration two thirds of that House shall agree to pass the Bill, it shall be sent, together with the Objections, to the other House, by which it shall likewise be reconsidered, and if approved by two thirds of that House, it shall become a Law. But in all such Cases the Votes of both Houses shall be determined by yeas and Nays, and the Names of the Persons voting for and against the Bill shall be entered on the Journal of each House respectively. If any Bill shall not be returned by the President within ten Days (Sundays excepted) after it shall have been presented to him, the Same shall be a Law, in like Manner as if he had signed it, unless the Congress by their Adjournment prevent its Return, in which Case it shall not be a Law.

Every Order, Resolution, or Vote to which the Concurrence of the Senate and House of Representatives may be necessary (except on a question of Adjournment) shall be presented to the President of the United States; and before the Same shall take Effect, shall be approved by him, or being disapproved by him shall be repassed by two thirds of the Senate and House of Representatives, according to the Rules and Limitations prescribed in the Case of a Bill.

SECTION 8. The Congress shall have power To lay and collect Taxes, Duties, Imposts and Excises, to pay the Debts and provide for the common Defence and general Welfare of the United States; but all Duties, Imposts and Excises shall be uniform throughout the United States;

To borrow Money on the credit of the United States;

To regulate Commerce with foreign Nations, and among the several States, and with the Indian Tribes;

To establish an uniform Rule of Naturalization, and uniform Laws on the subject of Bankruptcies throughout the United States;

To coin Money, regulate the Value thereof, and of foreign Coin, and fix the Standard of Weights and Measures;

---

[5]Superseded by the Twentieth Amendment.

To provide for the Punishment of counterfeiting the Securities and current Coin of the United States;

To establish Post Offices and post Roads;

To promote the Progress of Science and useful Arts, by securing for limited Times to Authors and Inventors the exclusive Right to their respective Writings and Discoveries;

To constitute Tribunals inferior to the supreme Court;

To define and punish Piracies and Felonies committed on the high Seas, and Offences against the Law of Nations;

To declare War, grant Letters of Marque and Reprisal, and make Rules concerning Captures on Land and Water;

To raise and support Armies, but no Appropriation of Money to that Use shall be for a longer Term than two Years;

To provide and maintain a Navy;

To make Rules for the Government and Regulation of the land and naval Forces;

To provide for calling forth the Militia to execute the Laws of the Union, suppress Insurrections and repel Invasions;

To provide for organizing, arming, and disciplining, the Militia, and for governing such Part of them as may be employed in the Service of the United States, reserving to the States respectively, the Appointment of the Officers, and the Authority of training the Militia according to the discipline prescribed by Congress;

To exercise exclusive Legislation in all Cases whatsoever, over such District (not exceeding ten Miles square) as may, by Cession of particular States, and the Acceptance of Congress, become the Seat of the Government of the United States, and to exercise like Authority over all Places purchased by the Consent of the Legislature of the State in which the Same shall be, for the Erection of Forts, Magazines, Arsenals, dock-Yards, and other needful Buildings;—And

To make all Laws which shall be necessary and proper for carrying into Execution the foregoing Powers, and all other Powers vested by this Constitution in the Government of the United States, or in any Department or Officer thereof.

SECTION 9. The Migration or Importation of such Persons as any of the States now existing shall think proper to admit, shall not be prohibited by the Congress prior to the Year one thousand eight hundred and eight, but a Tax or duty may be imposed on such Importation, not exceeding ten dollars for each Person.

The Privilege of the Writ of Habeas Corpus shall not be suspended, unless when in Cases of Rebellion or Invasion the public Safety may require it.

No Bill of Attainder or ex post facto Law shall be passed.

No Capitation, or other direct, Tax shall be laid, unless in Proportion to the Census or Enumeration herein before directed to be taken.

No Tax or Duty shall be laid on Articles exported from any State.

No Preference shall be given by any Regulation of Commerce or Revenue to the Ports of one State over those of another: nor shall Vessels bound to, or from, one State, be obliged to enter, clear, or pay Duties in another.

No Money shall be drawn from the Treasury, but in Consequence of Appropriations made by Law, and a regular Statement and Account of the Receipts and Expenditures of all public Money shall be published from time to time.

No Title of Nobility shall be granted by the United States: And no Person holding any Office of Profit or Trust under them, shall, without the Consent of the Congress, accept of any present, Emolument, Office, or Title, of any kind whatever, from any King, Prince, or foreign State.

SECTION 10. No State shall enter into any Treaty, Alliance, or Confederation; grant Letters of Marque and Reprisal; coin Money; emit Bills of Credit; make any Thing but gold and silver Coin a Tender in Payment of Debts; pass any Bill of Attainder, ex post facto Law, or Law impairing the Obligation of Contracts, or grant any Title of Nobility.

No State shall, without the Consent of the Congress, lay any Imposts or Duties on Imports or Exports, except what may be absolutely necessary for executing its inspection Laws: and the net Produce of all Duties and Imposts, laid by any State on Imports or Exports, shall be for the Use of the Treasury of the United States; and all such Laws shall be subject to the Revision and Controul of the Congress.

No State shall, without the Consent of Congress, lay any Duty of Tonnage, keep Troops, or Ships of War in time of Peace, enter into any Agreement or Compact with another State, or with a foreign Power, or engage in War, unless actually invaded, or in such imminent Danger as will not admit of delay.

ARTICLE II.

SECTION 1. The executive Power shall be vested in a President of the United States of America. He shall hold his Office during the Term of four Years, and, together with the Vice President, chosen for the same Term, be elected, as follows:

Each State shall appoint, in such Manner as the Legislature thereof may direct, a Number of Electors, equal to the whole Number of Senators and Representatives to which the State may be entitled in the Congress: but no Senator or Representative, or Person holding an Office of Trust or Profit under the United States, shall be appointed an Elector.

The Electors shall meet in their respective States, and vote by Ballot for two Persons, of whom one at least shall not be an Inhabitant of the same State with themselves. And they shall make a List of all the Persons voted for, and of the Number of Votes for each; which List they shall sign and certify, and transmit sealed to the Seat of the Government of the United States, directed to the President of the Senate. The President of the Senate shall, in the Presence of the Senate and House of Representatives, open all the Certificates, and the Votes shall then be counted. The Person having the greatest Number of Votes shall be the President, if such Number be a Majority of the whole Number of Electors appointed; and if there be more than one who have such Majority, and have an equal Number of Votes, then the House of Representatives shall immediately chuse by Ballot one of them for President; and if no Person have a Majority, then from the five highest on the List the said House shall in like Manner chuse the President. But in chusing the President, the Votes shall be taken by States, the Representation from each State having one Vote; A quorum for this Purpose shall consist of a Member or Members from two thirds of the States, and a Majority of all the States shall be necessary to a Choice. In every Case, after the Choice of the President, the Person having the greatest Number of Votes of the Electors shall be the Vice President. But if there should remain two or more who have equal Votes, the Senate shall chuse from them by Ballot the Vice President.[6]

The Congress may determine the Time of chusing the Electors, and the Day on which they shall give their Votes; which Day shall be the same throughout the United States.

No Person except a natural born Citizen, or a Citizen of the United States, at the time of the Adoption of this Constitution, shall be eligible to the Office of President, neither shall any Person be eligible to that Office who shall not have attained to the Age of thirty five Years, and been fourteen Years a Resident within the United States.

In Case of the Removal of the President from Office, or of his Death, Resignation, or Inability to discharge the Powers and Duties of the said Office, the Same shall devolve on the Vice President, and the Congress may by Law provide for the Case of Removal, Death, Resignation or Inability, both of the President and Vice President, declaring what Officer shall then act as President, and such Officer shall act accordingly, until the Disability be removed, or a President shall be elected.[7]

The President shall, at stated Times, receive for his Services, a Compensation, which shall neither be encreased nor diminished during the Period for which he shall have been elected, and he shall not receive within that Period any other Emolument from the United States, or any of them.

Before he enter on the Execution of his Office, he shall take the following Oath or Affirmation:—"I do solemnly swear (or affirm) that I will faithfully execute the Office of President of the United States, and will to the best of my Ability, preserve, protect and defend the Constitution of the United States."

SECTION 2. The President shall be Commander in Chief of the Army and Navy of the United States, and of the Militia of the several States, when called into the actual Service of the United States; he may require the Opinion, in writing, of the principal Officer in each of the executive Departments, upon any Subject relating to the Duties of their respective Offices, and he shall have Power to grant Reprieves and Pardons for Offences against the United States, except in Cases of Impeachment.

He shall have Power, by and with the Advice and Consent of the Senate, to make Treaties, provided two thirds of the Senators present concur; and he shall nominate, and by and with the Advice and Consent of the Senate, shall appoint Ambassadors, other public Ministers and Consuls, Judges of the supreme Court, and all other Officers of the United States, whose Appointments are not herein otherwise provided for, and which shall be established by Law; but the Congress may by Law vest the Appointment of such inferior Officers, as they think proper, in the President alone, in the Courts of Law, or in the Heads of Departments.

The President shall have Power to fill up all Vacancies that may happen during the Recess of the Senate, by granting Commissions which shall expire at the End of their next Session.

SECTION 3. He shall from time to time give the Congress Information of the State of the Union, and recommend to their Consideration such Measures as he shall judge necessary and expedient; he may, on extraordinary Occasions, convene both Houses, or either of them, and in Case of Disagreement between them, with Respect to the Time of Adjournment, he may adjourn them to such Time as he shall think proper; he shall receive Ambassadors and other public Ministers; he shall take Care that the Laws be

---

[6]Superseded by the Twelfth Amendment.

[7]Modified by the Twenty-fifth Amendment.

faithfully executed, and shall Commission all the Officers of the United States.

SECTION 4. The President, Vice President and all civil Officers of the United States, shall be removed from Office on Impeachment for, and Conviction of, Treason, Bribery, or other high Crimes and Misdemeanors.

ARTICLE III.

SECTION 1. The judicial Power of the United States, shall be vested in one supreme Court, and in such inferior Courts as the Congress may from time to time ordain and establish. The Judges, both of the supreme and inferior Courts, shall hold their Offices during good Behaviour, and shall, at stated Times, receive for their Services, a Compensation, which shall not be diminished during their Continuance in Office.

SECTION 2. The judicial Power shall extend to all Cases, in Law and Equity, arising under this Constitution, the Laws of the United States, and Treaties made, or which shall be made, under their Authority;—to all Cases affecting Ambassadors, other public Ministers and Consuls;—to all Cases of admiralty and maritime Jurisdiction;—to Controversies to which the United States shall be a Party;—to Controversies between two or more States;—between a State and Citizens of another State;[8]—between Citizens of different States,—between Citizens of the same State claiming Lands under Grants of different States, and between a State, or the Citizens thereof, and foreign States, Citizens or Subjects.

In all Cases affecting Ambassadors, other public Ministers and Consuls, and those in which a State shall be Party, the supreme Court shall have original Jurisdiction. In all the other Cases before mentioned, the supreme Court shall have appellate Jurisdiction, both as to Law and Fact, with such Exceptions, and under such Regulations as the Congress shall make.

The Trial of all Crimes, except in Cases of Impeachment, shall be by Jury; and such Trial shall be held in the State where the said Crimes shall have been committed; but when not committed within any State, the Trial shall be at such Place or Places as the Congress may by Law have directed.

SECTION 3. Treason against the United States, shall consist only in levying War against them, or in adhering to their Enemies, giving them Aid and Comfort. No Person shall be convicted of Treason unless on the Testimony of two Witnesses to the same overt Act, or on Confession in open Court.

The Congress shall have Power to declare the Punishment of Treason, but no Attainder of Treason shall work Corruption of Blood, or Forfeiture except during the Life of the Person attainted.

ARTICLE IV.

SECTION 1. Full Faith and Credit shall be given in each State to the public Acts, Records, and judicial Proceedings of every other State. And the Congress may by general Laws prescribe the Manner in which such Acts, Records and Proceedings shall be proved, and the Effect thereof.

SECTION 2. The Citizens of each State shall be entitled to all Privileges and Immunities of Citizens in the several States.

A Person charged in any State with Treason, Felony, or other Crime, who shall flee from Justice, and be found in another State, shall on Demand of the executive Authority of the State from which he fled, be delivered up, to be removed to the State having Jurisdiction of the Crime.

No Person held to Service or Labour in one State, under the Laws thereof, escaping into another, shall, in Consequence of any Law or Regulation therein, be discharged from such Service or Labour, but shall be delivered up on Claim of the Party to whom such Service or Labour may be due.

SECTION 3. New States may be admitted by the Congress into this Union; but no new State shall be formed or erected within the Jurisdiction of any other State, nor any State be formed by the Junction of two or more States, or Parts of States, without the Consent of the Legislatures of the States concerned as well as of the Congress.

The Congress shall have Power to dispose of and make all needful Rules and Regulations respecting the Territory or other Property belonging to the United States; and nothing in this Constitution shall be so construed as to Prejudice any Claims of the United States, or of any particular State.

SECTION 4. The United States shall guarantee to every State in this Union a Republican Form of Government, and shall protect each of them against Invasion; and on Application of the Legislature, or of the Executive (when the Legislature cannot be convened) against domestic Violence.

ARTICLE V.

The Congress, whenever two thirds of both Houses shall deem it necessary, shall propose Amendments to this Constitution, or, on the Application of the Legislatures of

---

[8]Modified by the Eleventh Amendment.

two thirds of the several States, shall call a Convention for proposing Amendments, which, in either Case, shall be valid to all Intents and Purposes, as Part of this Constitution, when ratified by the Legislatures of three fourths of the several States, or by Conventions in three fourths thereof, as the one or the other Mode of Ratification may be proposed by the Congress; Provided that no Amendment which may be made prior to the Year One thousand eight hundred and eight shall in any Manner affect the first and fourth Clauses in the Ninth Section of the first Article; and that no State, without its Consent, shall be deprived of its equal Suffrage in the Senate.

ARTICLE VI.

All Debts contracted and Engagements entered into, before the Adoption of this Constitution, shall be as valid against the United States under this Constitution, as under the Confederation.

This Constitution, and the Laws of the United States which shall be made in Pursuance thereof; and all Treaties made, or which shall be made, under the Authority of the United States, shall be the supreme Law of the Land; and the Judges in every State shall be bound thereby, any Thing in the Constitution or Laws of any State to the Contrary notwithstanding.

The Senators and Representatives before mentioned, and the Members of the several State Legislatures, and all executive and judicial Officers, both of the United States and of the several States, shall be bound by Oath or Affirmation, to support this Constitution; but no religious Test shall ever be required as a Qualification to any Office or public Trust under the United States.

ARTICLE VII.

The Ratification of the Conventions of nine States, shall be sufficient for the Establishment of this Constitution between the States so ratifying the Same.

Done in Convention by the Unanimous Consent of the States present the Seventeenth Day of September in the Year of our Lord one thousand seven hundred and Eighty seven and of the Independence of the United States of America the Twelfth. In witness whereof We have hereunto subscribed our Names,

Articles in Addition to, and Amendment of, the Constitution of the United States of America, Proposed by Congress, and Ratified by the Legislatures of the Several States, Pursuant to the Fifth Article of the Original Constitution.

AMENDMENT I [9]

Congress shall make no law respecting an establishment of religion, or prohibiting the free exercise thereof; or abridging the freedom of speech, or of the press; or the right of the people peaceably to assemble, and to petition the Government for a redress of grievances.

AMENDMENT II

A well regulated Militia, being necessary to the security of a free State, the right of the people to keep and bear Arms shall not be infringed.

AMENDMENT III

No Soldier shall, in time of peace, be quartered in any house, without the consent of the Owner, nor in time of war, but in a manner to be prescribed by law.

AMENDMENT IV

The right of the people to be secure in their persons, houses, papers, and effects, against unreasonable searches and seizures, shall not be violated, and no Warrants shall issue, but upon probable cause, supported by Oath or affirmation, and particularly describing the place to be searched, and the persons or things to be seized.

AMENDMENT V

No person shall be held to answer for a capital or otherwise infamous crime, unless on a presentment or indictment of a Grand Jury, except in cases arising in the land or naval forces, or in the Militia, when in actual service in time of War or public danger; nor shall any person be subject for the same offence to be twice put in jeopardy of life or limb; nor shall be compelled in any criminal case to be a witness against himself, nor be deprived of life, liberty, or property, without due process of law; nor shall private property be taken for public use, without just compensation.

AMENDMENT VI

In all criminal prosecutions, the accused shall enjoy the right to a speedy and public trial, by an impartial jury of the State and district wherein the crime shall have been

---

[9]The first ten amendments were passed by Congress September 25, 1789. They were ratified by three-fourths of the states December 15, 1791.

committed, which district shall have been previously ascertained by law, and to be informed of the nature and cause of the accusation; to be confronted with the witnesses against him; to have compulsory process for obtaining witnesses in his favor, and to have the Assistance of Counsel for his defence.

AMENDMENT VII

In suits at common law, where the value in controversy shall exceed twenty dollars, the right of trial by jury shall be preserved, and no fact tried by a jury, shall be otherwise reexamined in any Court of the United States, than according to the rules of the common law.

AMENDMENT VIII

Excessive bail shall not be required, nor excessive fines imposed, nor cruel and unusual punishments inflicted.

AMENDMENT IX

The enumeration in the Constitution, of certain rights, shall not be construed to deny or disparage others retained by the people.

AMENDMENT X

The powers not delegated to the United States by the Constitution; nor prohibited by it to the States, are reserved to the States respectively, or to the people.

AMENDMENT XI[10]

The Judicial power of the United States shall not be construed to extend to any suit in law or equity, commenced or prosecuted against one of the United States by Citizens of another State, or by Citizens or Subjects of any Foreign State.

AMENDMENT XII[11]

The Electors shall meet in their respective States and vote by ballot for President and Vice-President, one of whom, at least, shall not be an inhabitant of the same State with themselves; they shall name in their ballots the person voted for as President, and in distinct ballots the person voted for as Vice-President, and they shall make distinct lists of all persons voted for as President, and of all persons voted for as Vice-President, and of the number of votes for each, which lists they shall sign and certify, and transmit sealed to the seat of the government of the United States, directed to the President of the Senate;—The President of the Senate shall, in the presence of the Senate and House of Representatives, open all the certificates and the votes shall then be counted;—The person having the greatest number of votes for President, shall be the President, if such number be a majority of the whole number of Electors appointed; and if no person have such majority, then from the persons having the highest numbers not exceeding three on the list of those voted for as President, the House of Representatives shall choose immediately, by ballot, the President. But in choosing the President, the votes shall be taken by states, the representation from each state having one vote; a quorum for this purpose shall consist of a member or members from two-thirds of the states, and a majority of all the states shall be necessary to a choice. And if the House of Representatives shall not choose a President whenever the right of choice shall devolve upon them, before the fourth day of March next following, then the Vice-President shall act as President, as in the case of the death or other constitutional disability of the President.—The person having the greatest number of votes as Vice-President, shall be the Vice-President, if such number be a majority of the whole number of Electors appointed, and if no person have a majority, then from the two highest numbers on the list, the Senate shall choose the Vice-President; a quorum for the purpose shall consist of two-thirds of the whole number of Senators, and a majority of the whole number shall be necessary to a choice. But no person constitutionally ineligible to the office of President shall be eligible to that of Vice-President of the United States.

AMENDMENT XIII[12]

SECTION 1. Neither slavery nor involuntary servitude, except as a punishment for crime whereof the party shall have been duly convicted, shall exist within the United States, or any place subject to their jurisdiction.

SECTION 2. Congress shall have power to enforce this article by appropriate legislation.

AMENDMENT XIV[13]

SECTION 1. All persons born or naturalized in the United States, and subject to the jurisdiction thereof, are citizens of the United States and of the State wherein they

---

[10]Passed March 4, 1794. Ratified January 23, 1795.
[11]Passed December 9, 1803. Ratified June 15, 1804.

[12]Passed January 31, 1865. Ratified December 6, 1865.
[13]Passed June 13, 1866. Ratified July 9, 1868.

reside. No State shall make or enforce any law which shall abridge the privileges or immunities of citizens of the United States; nor shall any State deprive any person of life, liberty, or property, without due process of law; nor deny to any person within its jurisdiction the equal protection of the laws.

SECTION 2. Representatives shall be apportioned among the several States according to their respective numbers, counting the whole number of persons in each State, excluding Indians not taxed. But when the right to vote at any election for the choice of electors for President and Vice-President of the United States, Representatives in Congress, the Executive and Judicial officers of a State, or the members of the Legislature thereof, is denied to any of the male inhabitants of such State, being twenty-one years of age, and citizens of the United States, or in any way abridged, except for participation in rebellion, or other crime, the basis of representation therein shall be reduced in the proportion which the number of such male citizens shall bear to the whole number of male citizens twenty-one years of age in such State.

SECTION 3. No person shall be a Senator or Representative in Congress, or elector of President and Vice-President, or hold any office, civil or military, under the United States, or under any State, who, having previously taken an oath, as a member of Congress, or as an officer of the United States, or as a member of any State legislature, or as an executive or judicial officer of any State, to support the Constitution of the United States, shall have engaged in insurrection or rebellion against the same, or given aid or comfort to the enemies thereof. But Congress may by a vote of two-thirds of each House, remove such disability.

SECTION 4. The validity of the public debt of the United States, authorized by law, including debts incurred for payment of pensions and bounties for services in suppressing insurrection or rebellion, shall not be questioned. But neither the United States nor any State shall assume or pay any debt or obligation incurred in aid of insurrection or rebellion against the United States, or any claim for the loss or emancipation of any slave; but all such debts, obligations, and claims shall be held illegal and void.

SECTION 5. The Congress shall have the power to enforce, by appropriate legislation, the provisions of this article.

AMENDMENT XV[14]

SECTION 1. The right of citizens of the United States to vote shall not be denied or abridged by the United States or by any State on account of race, color, or previous conditions of servitude—

SECTION 2. The Congress shall have power to enforce this article by appropriate legislation.

AMENDMENT XVI

The Congress shall have power to lay and collect taxes on incomes, from whatever source derived, without apportionment among the several States, and without regard to any census or enumeration.

AMENDMENT XVII[15]

The Senate of the United States shall be composed of two Senators from each State, elected by the people thereof, for six years; and each Senator shall have one vote. The electors in each State shall have the qualifications requisite for electors of the most numerous branch of the State legislatures.

When vacancies happen in the representation of any State in the Senate, the executive authority of such State shall issue writs of election to fill such vacancies: *Provided,* That the legislature of any State may empower the executive thereof to make temporary appointments until the people fill the vacancies by election as the legislature may direct.

This amendment shall not be so construed as to affect the election or term of any Senator chosen before it becomes valid as part of the Constitution.

AMENDMENT XVIII[16]

SECTION 1. After one year from the ratification of this article the manufacture, sale, or transportation of intoxicating liquors within, the importation thereof into, or the exportation thereof from the United States and all territory subject to the jurisdiction thereof for beverage purposes is hereby prohibited.

SECTION 2. The Congress and the several States shall have concurrent power to enforce this article by appropriate legislation.

SECTION 3. This article shall be inoperative unless it shall have been ratified as an amendment to the Constitution by the legislatures of the several States, as provided in the Constitution, within seven years from the date of the submission hereof to the States by the Congress.

---

[14]Passed February 26, 1869. Ratified February 2, 1870.

[15]Passed May 13, 1912. Ratified April 8, 1913.
[16]Passed December 18, 1917. Ratified January 16, 1919.

Amendment XIX[17]

The right of citizens of the United States to vote shall not be denied or abridged by the United States or by any State on account of sex.

Congress shall have power to enforce this article by appropriate legislation.

Amendment XX[18]

SECTION 1. The terms of the President and Vice-President shall end at noon on the 20th day of January, and the terms of Senators and Representatives at noon on the 3d day of January, of the years in which such terms would have ended if this article had not been ratified; and the terms of their successors shall then begin.

SECTION 2. The Congress shall assemble at least once in every year, and such meeting shall begin at noon on the 3d day of January, unless they shall by law appoint a different day.

SECTION 3. If, at the time fixed for the beginning of the term of the President, the President elect shall have died, the Vice-President elect shall become President. If a President shall not have been chosen before the time fixed for the beginning of his term, or if the President elect shall have failed to qualify, then the Vice-President elect shall act as President until a President shall have qualified; and the Congress may by law provide for the case wherein neither a President elect nor a Vice-President elect shall have qualified, declaring who shall then act as President, or the manner in which one who is to act shall be selected, and such person shall act accordingly until a President or Vice-President shall have qualified.

SECTION 4. The Congress may by law provide for the case of the death of any of the persons from whom the House of Representatives may choose a President whenever the right of choice shall have devolved upon them, and for the case of the death of any of the persons from whom the Senate may choose a Vice-President whenever the right of choice shall have devolved upon them.

SECTION 5. Sections 1 and 2 shall take effect on the 15th day of October following the ratification of this article.

SECTION 6. This article shall be inoperative unless it shall have been ratified as an amendment to the Constitution by the legislatures of three-fourths of the several States within seven years from the date of its submission.

Amendment XXI[19]

SECTION 1. The eighteenth article of amendment to the Constitution of the United States is hereby repealed.

SECTION 2. The transportation or importation into any State, Territory, or possession of the United States for delivery or use therein of intoxicating liquors, in violation of the laws thereof, is hereby prohibited.

SECTION 3. This article shall be inoperative unless it shall have been ratified as an amendment to the Constitution by conventions in the several States, as provided in the Constitution, within seven years from the date of the submission hereof to the States by the Congress.

Amendment XXII[20]

No person shall be elected to the office of the President more than twice, and no person who has held the office of President, or acted as President, for more than two years of a term to which some other person was elected President shall be elected to the office of the President more than once.

But this Article shall not apply to any person holding the office of President when this Article was proposed by the Congress, and shall not prevent any person who may be holding the office of President, or acting as President, during the term within which this Article becomes operative from holding the office of President or acting as President during the remainder of such term.

Amendment XXIII[21]

SECTION 1. The District constituting the seat of Government of the United States shall appoint in such manner as the Congress may direct:

A number of electors of President and Vice President equal to the whole number of Senators and Representatives in Congress to which the District would be entitled if it were a State, but in no event more than the least populous State; they shall be in addition to those appointed by the States, but they shall be considered, for the purposes of the election of President and Vice President, to be electors appointed by the State; and they shall meet in the District and perform such duties as provided by the twelfth article of amendment.

SECTION 2. The Congress shall have power to enforce this article by appropriate legislation.

---

[17]Passed June 4, 1919. Ratified August 18, 1920.
[18]Passed March 2, 1932. Ratified January 23, 1933.

[19]Passed February 20, 1933. Ratified December 5, 1933.
[20]Passed March 12, 1947. Ratified March 1, 1951.
[21]Passed June 16, 1960. Ratified April 3, 1961.

AMENDMENT XXIV[22]

SECTION 1. The right of citizens of the United States to vote in any primary or other election for President or Vice President, or for Senator or Representative in Congress, shall not be denied or abridged by the United States or any State by reason of failure to pay any poll tax or other tax.

SECTION 2. The Congress shall have power to enforce this article by appropriate legislation.

AMENDMENT XXV[23]

SECTION 1. In case of the removal of the President from office or of his death or resignation, the Vice President shall become President.

SECTION 2. Whenever there is a vacancy in the office of the Vice President, the President shall nominate a Vice President who shall take office upon confirmation by a majority vote of both Houses of Congress.

SECTION 3. Whenever the President transmits to the President pro tempore of the Senate and the Speaker of the House of Representatives his written declaration that he is unable to discharge the powers and duties of his office, and until he transmits them a written declaration to the contrary, such powers and duties shall be discharged by the Vice President as Acting President.

SECTION 4. Whenever the Vice President and a majority of either the principal officers of the executive department or of such other body as Congress may by law provide, transmit to the President pro tempore of the Senate and the Speaker of the House of Representatives their written declaration that the President is unable to discharge the powers and duties of his office, the Vice President shall immediately assume the powers and duties of the office of Acting President.

Thereafter, when the President transmits to the President pro tempore of the Senate and the Speaker of the House of Representatives his written declaration that no inability exists, he shall resume the powers and duties of his office unless the Vice President and a majority of either the principal officers of the executive department or of such other body as Congress may by law provide, transmit within four days to the President pro tempore of the Senate and the Speaker of the House of Representatives their written declaration that the President is unable to discharge the powers and duties of his office. Thereupon Congress shall decide the issue, assembling within forty-eight hours for that purpose if not in session. If the Congress, within twenty-one days after receipt of the latter written declaration, or, if Congress is not in session, within twenty-one days after Congress is required to assemble, determines by two-thirds vote of both Houses that the President is unable to discharge the powers and duties of his office, the Vice President shall continue to discharge the same as Acting President; otherwise, the President shall resume the powers and duties of his office.

AMENDMENT XXVI[24]

SECTION 1. The right of citizens of the United States, who are eighteen years of age or older, to vote shall not be denied or abridged by the United States or by any State on account of age.

SECTION 2. The Congress shall have power to enforce this article by appropriate legislation.

AMENDMENT XXVII[25]

No law, varying the compensation for the service of the Senators and Representatives, shall take effect, until an election of Representatives shall have intervened.

---

[22]Passed August 27, 1962. Ratified January 23, 1964.
[23]Passed July 6, 1965. Ratified February 11, 1967.

[24]Passed March 23, 1971. Ratified July 5, 1971.
[25]Passed September 25, 1789. Ratified May 7, 1992.

ADMISSION OF STATES

Order of admission	State	Date of admission	Order of admission	State	Date of admission
1	Delaware	December 7, 1787	26	Michigan	January 26, 1837
2	Pennsylvania	December 12, 1787	27	Florida	March 3, 1845
3	New Jersey	December 18, 1787	28	Texas	December 29, 1845
4	Georgia	January 2, 1788	29	Iowa	December 28, 1846
5	Connecticut	January 9, 1788	30	Wisconsin	May 29, 1848
6	Massachusetts	February 6, 1788	31	California	September 9, 1850
7	Maryland	April 28, 1788	32	Minnesota	May 11, 1858
8	South Carolina	May 23, 1788	33	Oregon	February 14, 1859
9	New Hampshire	June 21, 1788	34	Kansas	January 29, 1861
10	Virginia	June 25, 1788	35	West Virginia	June 20, 1863
11	New York	July 26, 1788	36	Nevada	October 31, 1864
12	North Carolina	November 21, 1789	37	Nebraska	March 1, 1867
13	Rhode Island	May 29, 1790	38	Colorado	August 1, 1876
14	Vermont	March 4, 1791	39	North Dakota	November 2, 1889
15	Kentucky	June 1, 1792	40	South Dakota	November 2, 1889
16	Tennessee	June 1, 1796	41	Montana	November 8, 1889
17	Ohio	March 1, 1803	42	Washington	November 11, 1889
18	Louisiana	April 30, 1812	43	Idaho	July 3, 1890
19	Indiana	December 11, 1816	44	Wyoming	July 10, 1890
20	Mississippi	December 10, 1817	45	Utah	January 4, 1896
21	Illinois	December 3, 1818	46	Oklahoma	November 16, 1907
22	Alabama	December 14, 1819	47	New Mexico	January 6, 1912
23	Maine	March 15, 1820	48	Arizona	February 14, 1912
24	Missouri	August 10, 1821	49	Alaska	January 3, 1959
25	Arkansas	June 15, 1836	50	Hawaii	August 21, 1959

POPULATION OF THE UNITED STATES

Year	Total population	Number per square mile	Year	Total population	Number per square mile	Year	Total population	Number per square mile
1790	3,929	4.5	1808	6,838		1826	11,580	
1791	4,056		1809	7,031		1827	11,909	
1792	4,194		1810	7,224	4.3	1828	12,237	
1793	4,332		1811	7,460		1829	12,565	
1794	4,469		1812	7,700		1830	12,901	7.4
1795	4,607		1813	7,939		1831	13,321	
1796	4,745		1814	8,179		1832	13,742	
1797	4,883		1815	8,419		1833	14,162	
1798	5,021		1816	8,659		1834	14,582	
1799	5,159		1817	8,899		1835	15,003	
1800	5,297	6.1	1818	9,139		1836	15,423	
1801	5,486		1819	9,379		1837	15,843	
1802	5,679		1820	9,618	5.6	1838	16,264	
1803	5,872		1821	9,939		1839	16,684	
1804	5,065		1822	10,268		1840	17,120	9.8
1805	6,258		1823	10,596		1841	17,733	
1806	6,451		1824	10,924		1842	18,345	
1807	6,644		1825	11,252		1843	18,957	

Figures are from *Historical Statistics of the United States, Colonial Times to 1957* (1961), pp. 7, 8; *Statistical Abstract of the United States: 1974*, p. 5, Census Bureau for 1974 and 1975; and *Statistical Abstract of the United States: 1988*, p. 7.

Note: Population figures are in thousands. Density figures are for land area of continental United States.

(continued)

Year	Total population	Number per square mile	Year	Total population[1]	Number per square mile	Year	Total population[1]	Number per square mile
1844	19,569		1897	72,189		1950	150,697	50.7
1845	20,182		1898	73,494		1951	154,878	
1846	20,794		1899	74,799		1952	157,553	
1847	21,406		1900	76,094	25.6	1953	160,184	
1848	22,018		1901	77,585		1954	163,026	
1849	22,631		1902	79,160		1955	165,931	
1850	23,261	7.9	1903	80,632		1956	168,903	
1851	24,086		1904	82,165		1957	171,984	
1852	24,911		1905	83,820		1958	174,882	
1853	25,736		1906	85,437		1959	177,830	
1854	26,561		1907	87,000		1960	178,464	60.1
1855	27,386		1908	88,709		1961	183,642	
1856	28,212		1909	90,492		1962	186,504	
1857	29,037		1910	92,407	31.0	1963	189,197	
1858	29,862		1911	93,868		1964	191,833	
1859	30,687		1912	95,331		1965	194,237	
1860	31,513	10.6	1913	97,227		1966	196,485	
1861	32,351		1914	99,118		1967	198,629	
1862	33,188		1915	100,549		1968	200,619	
1863	34,026		1916	101,966		1969	202,599	
1864	34,863		1917	103,414		1970	203,875	57.5[2]
1865	35,701		1918	104,550		1971	207,045	
1866	36,538		1919	105,063		1972	208,842	
1867	37,376		1920	106,466	35.6	1973	210,396	
1868	38,213		1921	108,541		1974	211,894	
1869	39,051		1922	110,055		1975	213,631	
1870	39,905	13.4	1923	111,950		1976	215,152	
1871	40,938		1924	114,113		1977	216,880	
1872	41,972		1925	115,832		1978	218,717	
1873	43,006		1926	117,399		1979	220,584	
1874	44,040		1927	119,038		1980	226,546	64.0
1875	45,073		1928	120,501		1981	230,138	
1876	46,107		1929	121,700		1982	232,520	
1877	47,141		1930	122,775	41.2	1983	234,799	
1878	48,174		1931	124,040		1984	237,001	
1879	49,208		1932	124,840		1985	239,283	
1880	50,262	16.9	1933	125,579		1986	241,596	
1881	51,542		1934	126,374		1987	234,773	
1882	52,821		1935	127,250		1988	245,051	
1883	54,100		1936	128,053		1989	247,350	
1884	55,379		1937	128,825		1990	250,122	70.3
1885	56,658		1938	129,825		1991	254,521	
1886	57,938		1939	130,880		1992	245,908	
1887	59,217		1940	131,669	44.2	1993	257,908	
1888	60,496		1941	133,894		1994	261,875	
1889	61,775		1942	135,361		1995	263,434	
1890	63,056	21.2	1943	137,250		1996	266,096	
1891	64,361		1944	138,916		1997	267,901	
1892	65,666		1945	140,468		1998	269,501	
1893	66,970		1946	141,936		1999	272,700	
1894	68,275		1947	144,698		2000	281,400	
1895	69,580		1948	147,208		2001	286,909	
1896	70,885		1949	149,767		2002	289,947	

[1]Figures after 1940 represent total population including armed forces abroad, except in official census years.

[2]Figure includes Alaska and Hawaii.

PRESIDENTIAL ELECTIONS

Year	Number of states	Candidates[1]	Parties	Popular vote	Electoral vote	Percentage of popular vote[2]
1789	11	**George Washington**	No party designations		69	
		John Adams			34	
		Minor Candidates			35	
1792	15	**George Washington**	No party designations		132	
		John Adams			77	
		George Clinton			50	
		Minor Candidates			5	
1796	16	**John Adams**	Federalist		71	
		Thomas Jefferson	Democratic-Republican		68	
		Thomas Pinckney	Federalist		59	
		Aaron Burr	Democratic-Republican		30	
		Minor Candidates			48	
1800	16	**Thomas Jefferson**	Democratic-Republican		73	
		Aaron Burr	Democratic-Republican		73	
		John Adams	Federalist		65	
		Charles C. Pinckney	Federalist		64	
		John Jay	Federalist		1	
1804	17	**Thomas Jefferson**	Democratic-Republican		162	
		Charles C. Pinckney	Federalist		14	
1808	17	**James Madison**	Democratic-Republican		122	
		Charles C. Pinckney	Federalist		47	
		George Clinton	Democratic-Republican		6	
1812	18	**James Madison**	Democratic-Republican		128	
		DeWitt Clinton	Federalist		89	
1816	19	**James Monroe**	Democratic-Republican		183	
		Rufus King	Federalist		34	
1820	24	**James Monroe**	Democratic-Republican		231	
		John Quincy Adams	Independent Republican		1	
1824	24	**John Quincy Adams**	Democratic-Republican	108,740	84	30.5
		Andrew Jackson	Democratic-Republican	153,544	99	43.1
		William H. Crawford	Democratic-Republican	46,618	41	13.1
		Henry Clay	Democratic-Republican	47,136	37	13.2
1828	24	**Andrew Jackson**	Democratic	647,286	178	56.0
		John Quincy Adams	National Republican	508,064	83	44.0
1832	24	**Andrew Jackson**	Democratic	687,502	219	55.0
		Henry Clay	National Republican	530,189	49	42.4
		William Wirt	Anti-Masonic ⎫	33,108	7	2.6
		John Floyd	National Republican ⎭		11	

[1]Before the passage of the Twelfth Amendment in 1804, the Electoral College voted for two presidential candidates; the runner-up became vice president. Figures are from *Historical Statistics of the United States, Colonial Times to 1957* (1961), pp. 682–83; and the U.S. Department of Justice.

[2]Candidates receiving less than 1 percent of the popular vote have been omitted. For that reason the percentage of popular vote given for any election year may not total 100 percent.

(continued)

PRESIDENTIAL ELECTIONS, CONTINUED

Year	Number of states	Candidates	Parties	Popular vote	Electoral vote	Percentage of popular vote[1]
1836	26	**Martin Van Buren**	Democratic	765,483	170	50.9
		William H. Harrison	Whig		73	
		Hugh L. White	Whig	739,795	26	
		Daniel Webster	Whig		14	
		W. P. Mangum	Whig		11	
1840	26	**William H. Harrison**	Whig	1,274,624	234	53.1
		Martin Van Buren	Democratic	1,127,781	60	46.9
1844	26	**James K. Polk**	Democratic	1,338,464	170	49.6
		Henry Clay	Whig	1,300,097	105	48.1
		James G. Birney	Liberty	62,300		2.3
1848	30	**Zachary Taylor**	Whig	1,360,967	163	47.4
		Lewis Cass	Democratic	1,222,342	127	42.5
		Martin Van Buren	Free Soil	291,263		10.1
1852	31	**Franklin Pierce**	Democratic	1,601,117	254	50.9
		Winfield Scott	Whig	1,385,453	42	44.1
		John P. Hale	Free Soil	155,825		5.0
1856	31	**James Buchanan**	Democratic	1,832,955	174	45.3
		John C. Frémont	Republican	1,339,932	114	33.1
		Millard Fillmore	American	871,731	8	21.6
1860	33	**Abraham Lincoln**	Republican	1,865,593	180	39.8
		Stephen A. Douglas	Democratic	1,382,713	12	29.5
		John C. Breckinridge	Democratic	848,356	72	18.1
		John Bell	Constitutional Union	592,906	39	12.6
1864	36	**Abraham Lincoln**	Republican	2,206,938	212	55.0
		George B. McClellan	Democratic	1,803,787	21	45.0
1868	37	**Ulysses S. Grant**	Republican	3,013,421	214	52.7
		Horatio Seymour	Democratic	2,706,829	80	47.3
1872	37	**Ulysses S. Grant**	Republican	3,596,745	286	55.6
		Horace Greeley	Democratic	2,843,446	[2]	43.9
1876	38	**Rutherford B. Hayes**	Republican	4,036,572	185	48.0
		Samuel J. Tilden	Democratic	4,284,020	184	51.0
1880	38	**James A. Garfield**	Republican	4,453,295	214	48.5
		Winfield S. Hancock	Democratic	4,414,082	155	48.1
		James B. Weaver	Greenback-Labor	308,578		3.4
1884	38	**Grover Cleveland**	Democratic	4,879,507	219	48.5
		James G. Blaine	Republican	4,850,293	182	48.2
		Benjamin F. Butler	Greenback-Labor	175,370		1.8
		John P. St. John	Prohibition	150,369		1.5
1888	38	**Benjamin Harrison**	Republican	5,477,129	233	47.9
		Grover Cleveland	Democratic	5,537,857	168	48.6
		Clinton B. Fisk	Prohibition	249,506		2.2
		Anson J. Streeter	Union Labor	146,935		1.3

[1]Candidates receiving less than 1 percent of the popular vote have been omitted. For that reason the percentage of popular vote given for any election year may not total 100 percent.

[2]Greeley died shortly after the election; the electors supporting him then divided their votes among minor candidates.

Year	Number of states	Candidates	Parties	Popular vote	Electoral vote	Percentage of popular vote[1]
1892	44	**Grover Cleveland**	Democratic	5,555,426	277	46.1
		Benjamin Harrison	Republican	5,182,690	145	43.0
		James B. Weaver	People's	1,029,846	22	8.5
		John Bidwell	Prohibition	264,133		2.2
1896	45	**William McKinley**	Republican	7,102,246	271	51.1
		William J. Bryan	Democratic	6,492,559	176	47.7
1900	45	**William McKinley**	Republican	7,218,491	292	51.7
		William J. Bryan	Democratic; Populist	6,356,734	155	45.5
		John C. Wooley	Prohibition	208,914		1.5
1904	45	**Theodore Roosevelt**	Republican	7,628,461	336	57.4
		Alton B. Parker	Democratic	5,084,223	140	37.6
		Eugene V. Debs	Socialist	402,283		3.0
		Silas C. Swallow	Prohibition	258,536		1.9
1908	46	**William H. Taft**	Republican	7,675,320	321	51.6
		William J. Bryan	Democratic	6,412,294	162	43.1
		Eugene V. Debs	Socialist	420,793		2.8
		Eugene W. Chafin	Prohibition	253,840		1.7
1912	48	**Woodrow Wilson**	Democratic	6,296,547	435	41.9
		Theodore Roosevelt	Progressive	4,118,571	88	27.4
		William H. Taft	Republican	3,486,720	8	23.2
		Eugene V. Debs	Socialist	900,672		6.0
		Eugene W. Chafin	Prohibition	206,275		1.4
1916	48	**Woodrow Wilson**	Democratic	9,127,695	277	49.4
		Charles E. Hughes	Republican	8,533,507	254	46.2
		A. L. Benson	Socialist	585,113		3.2
		J. Frank Hanly	Prohibition	220,506		1.2
1920	48	**Warren G. Harding**	Republican	16,143,407	404	60.4
		James N. Cox	Democratic	9,130,328	127	34.2
		Eugene V. Debs	Socialist	919,799		3.4
		P. P. Christensen	Farmer-Labor	265,411		1.0
1924	48	**Calvin Coolidge**	Republican	15,718,211	382	54.0
		John W. Davis	Democratic	8,385,283	136	28.8
		Robert M. La Follette	Progressive	4,831,289	13	16.6
1928	48	**Herbert C. Hoover**	Republican	21,391,993	444	58.2
		Alfred E. Smith	Democratic	15,016,169	87	40.9
1932	48	**Franklin D. Roosevelt**	Democratic	22,809,638	472	57.4
		Herbert C. Hoover	Republican	15,758,901	59	39.7
		Norman Thomas	Socialist	881,951		2.2

[1]Candidates receiving less than 1 percent of the popular vote have been omitted. For that reason the percentage of popular vote given for any election year may not total 100 percent.

(continued)

PRESIDENTIAL ELECTIONS, CONTINUED

Year	Number of states	Candidates	Parties	Popular vote	Electoral vote	Percentage of popular vote[1]
1936	48	**Franklin D. Roosevelt**	Democratic	27,752,869	523	60.8
		Alfred M. Landon	Republican	16,674,665	8	36.5
		William Lemke	Union	882,479		1.9
1940	48	**Franklin D. Roosevelt**	Democratic	27,307,819	449	54.8
		Wendell L. Willkie	Republican	22,321,018	82	44.8
1944	48	**Franklin D. Roosevelt**	Democratic	25,606,585	432	53.5
		Thomas E. Dewey	Republican	22,014,745	99	46.0
1948	48	**Harry S Truman**	Democratic	24,105,812	303	49.5
		Thomas E. Dewey	Republican	21,970,065	189	45.1
		J. Strom Thurmond	States' Rights	1,169,063	39	2.4
		Henry A. Wallace	Progressive	1,157,172		2.4
1952	48	**Dwight D. Eisenhower**	Republican	33,936,234	442	55.1
		Adlai E. Stevenson	Democratic	27,314,992	89	44.4
1956	48	**Dwight D. Eisenhower**	Republican	35,590,472	457	57.6
		Adlai E. Stevenson	Democratic	26,022,752	73	42.1
1960	50	**John F. Kennedy**	Democratic	34,227,096	303	49.9
		Richard M. Nixon	Republican	34,108,546	219	49.6
1964	50	**Lyndon B. Johnson**	Democratic	43,126,506	486	61.1
		Barry M. Goldwater	Republican	27,176,799	52	38.5
1968	50	**Richard M. Nixon**	Republican	31,785,480	301	43.4
		Hubert H. Humphrey	Democratic	31,275,165	191	42.7
		George C. Wallace	American Independent	9,906,473	46	13.5
1972	50	**Richard M. Nixon**	Republican	47,169,911	520	60.7
		George S. McGovern	Democratic	29,170,383	17	37.5
1976	50	**Jimmy Carter**	Democratic	40,827,394	297	50.0
		Gerald R. Ford	Republican	39,145,977	240	47.9
1980	50	**Ronald W. Reagan**	Republican	43,899,248	489	50.8
		Jimmy Carter	Democratic	35,481,435	49	41.0
		John B. Anderson	Independent	5,719,437		6.6
		Ed Clark	Libertarian	920,859		1.0
1984	50	**Ronald W. Reagan**	Republican	54,281,858	525	59.2
		Walter F. Mondale	Democratic	37,457,215	13	40.8
1988	50	**George H. Bush**	Republican	47,917,341	426	54
		Michael Dukakis	Democratic	41,013,030	112	46
1992	50	**William Clinton**	Democratic	44,908,254	370	43.0
		George H. Bush	Republican	39,102,343	168	37.4
		Ross Perot	Independent	19,741,065		18.9
1996	50	**William Clinton**	Democratic	45,628,667	379	49.2
		Robert Dole	Republican	37,869,435	159	40.8
		Ross Perot	Reform	7,874,283		8.5
2000	50	**George W. Bush**	Republican	50,456,062	271	47.9
		Albert Gore	Democratic	50,996,582	266	48.4
		Ralph Nader	Green	2,858,843		2.7

[1]Candidates receiving less than 1 percent of the popular vote have been omitted. For that reason the percentage of popular vote given for any election year may not total 100 percent.

PRESIDENTIAL ADMINISTRATIONS

President	Vice President	Secretary of State	Secretary of Treasury	Secretary of War	Secretary of Navy	Postmaster General	Attorney General
George Washington 1789–1797	John Adams 1789–1797	Thomas Jefferson 1789–1794 Edmund Randolph 1794–1795 Timothy Pickering 1795–1797	Alexander Hamilton 1789–1795 Oliver Wolcott 1795–1797	Henry Knox 1789–1795 Timothy Pickering 1795–1796 James McHenry 1796–1797		Samuel Osgood 1789–1791 Timothy Pickering 1791–1795 Joseph Habersham 1795–1797	Edmund Randolph 1789–1794 William Bradford 1794–1795 Charles Lee 1795–1797
John Adams 1797–1801	Thomas Jefferson 1797–1801	Timothy Pickering 1797–1800 John Marshall 1800–1801	Oliver Wolcott 1797–1801 Samuel Dexter 1801	James McHenry 1797–1800 Samuel Dexter 1800–1801	Benjamin Stoddert 1798–1801	Joseph Habersham 1797–1801	Charles Lee 1797–1801
Thomas Jefferson 1801–1809	Aaron Burr 1801–1805 George Clinton 1805–1809	James Madison 1801–1809	Samuel Dexter 1801 Albert Gallatin 1801–1809	Henry Dearborn 1801–1809	Benjamin Stoddert 1801 Robert Smith 1801–1809	Joseph Habersham 1801 Gideon Granger 1801–1809	Levi Lincoln 1801–1805 John Breckinridge 1805–1807 Caesar Rodney 1807–1809
James Madison 1809–1817	George Clinton 1809–1813 Elbridge Gerry 1813–1817	Robert Smith 1809–1811 James Monroe 1811–1817	Albert Gallatin 1809–1814 George Campbell 1814 Alexander Dallas 1814–1816 William Crawford 1816–1817	William Eustis 1809–1813 John Armstrong 1813–1814 James Monroe 1814–1815 William Crawford 1815–1817	Paul Hamilton 1809–1813 William Jones 1813–1814 Benjamin Crowninshield 1814–1817	Gideon Granger 1809–1814 Return Meigs 1814–1817	Caesar Rodney 1809–1811 William Pinkney 1811–1814 Richard Rush 1814–1817
James Monroe 1817–1825	Daniel D. Tompkins 1817–1825	John Quincy Adams 1817–1825	William Crawford 1817–1825	George Graham 1817 John C. Calhoun 1817–1825	Benjamin Crowninshield 1817–1818 Smith Thompson 1818–1823 Samuel Southard 1823–1825	Return Meigs 1817–1823 John McLean 1823–1825	Richard Rush 1817 William Wirt 1817–1825
John Quincy Adams 1825–1829	John C. Calhoun 1825–1829	Henry Clay 1825–1829	Richard Rush 1825–1829	James Barbour 1825–1828 Peter B. Porter 1828–1829	Samuel Southard 1825–1829	John McLean 1825–1829	William Wirt 1825–1829
Andrew Jackson 1829–1837	John C. Calhoun 1829–1833 Martin Van Buren 1833–1837	Martin Van Buren 1829–1831 Edward Livingston 1831–1833 Louis McLane 1833–1834 John Forsyth 1834–1837	Samuel Ingham 1829–1831 Louis McLane 1831–1833 William Duane 1833 Roger B. Taney 1833–1834 Levi Woodbury 1834–1837	John H. Eaton 1829–1831 Lewis Cass 1831–1837 Benjamin Butler 1837	John Branch 1829–1831 Levi Woodbury 1831–1834 Mahlon Dickerson 1834–1837	William Barry 1829–1835 Amos Kendall 1835–1837	John M. Berrien 1829–1831 Roger B. Taney 1831–1833 Benjamin Butler 1833–1837
Martin Van Buren 1837–1841	Richard M. Johnson 1837–1841	John Forsyth 1837–1841	Levi Woodbury 1837–1841	Joel R. Poinsett 1837–1841	Mahlon Dickerson 1837–1838 James K. Paulding 1838–1841	Amos Kendall 1837–1840 John M. Niles 1840–1841	Benjamin Butler 1837–1838 Felix Grundy 1838–1840 Henry D. Gilpin 1840–1841

(continued)

PRESIDENTIAL ADMINISTRATIONS, CONTINUED

President	Vice President	Secretary of State	Secretary of Treasury	Secretary of War
William H. Harrison 1841	John Tyler 1841	Daniel Webster 1841	Thomas Ewing 1841	John Bell 1841
John Tyler 1841–1845		Daniel Webster 1841–1843 Hugh S. Legaré 1843 Abel P. Upshur 1843–1844 John C. Calhoun 1844–1845	Thomas Ewing 1841 Walter Forward 1841–1843 John C. Spencer 1843–1844 George M. Bibb 1844–1845	John Bell 1841 John C. Spencer 1841–1843 James M. Porter 1843–1844 William Wilkins 1844–1845
James K. Polk 1845–1849	George M. Dallas 1845–1849	James Buchanan 1845–1849	Robert J. Walker 1845–1849	William L. Marcy 1845–1849
Zachary Taylor 1849–1850	Millard Fillmore 1849–1850	John M. Clayton 1849–1850	William M. Meredith 1849–1850	George W. Crawford 1849–1850
Millard Fillmore 1850–1853		Daniel Webster 1850–1852 Edward Everett 1852–1853	Thomas Corwin 1850–1853	Charles M. Conrad 1850–1853
Franklin Pierce 1853–1857	William R. King 1853–1857	William L. Marcy 1853–1857	James Guthrie 1853–1857	Jefferson Davis 1853–1857
James Buchanan 1857–1861	John C. Breckinridge 1857–1861	Lewis Cass 1857–1860 Jeremiah S. Black 1860–1861	Howell Cobb 1857–1860 Philip F. Thomas 1860–1861 John A. Dix 1861	John B. Floyd 1857–1861 Joseph Holt 1861
Abraham Lincoln 1861–1865	Hannibal Hamlin 1861–1865 Andrew Johnson 1865	William H. Seward 1861–1865	Salmon P. Chase 1861–1864 William P. Fessenden 1864–1865 Hugh McCulloch 1865	Simon Cameron 1861–1862 Edwin M. Stanton 1862–1865
Andrew Johnson 1865–1869		William H. Seward 1865–1869	Hugh McCulloch 1865–1869	Edwin M. Stanton 1865–1867 Ulysses S. Grant 1867–1868 John M. Schofield 1868–1869
Ulysses S. Grant 1869–1877	Schuyler Colfax 1869–1873 Henry Wilson 1873–1877	Elihu B. Washburne 1869 Hamilton Fish 1869–1877	George S. Boutwell 1869–1873 William A. Richardson 1873–1874 Benjamin H. Bristow 1874–1876 Lot M. Morrill 1876–1877	John A. Rawlins 1869 William T. Sherman 1869 William W. Belknap 1869–1876 Alphonso Taft 1876 James D. Cameron 1876–1877

Secretary of Navy	Postmaster General	Attorney General	Secretary of Interior
George E. Badger 1841	Francis Granger 1841	John J. Crittenden 1841	
George E. Badger 1841 Abel P. Upshur 1841–1843 David Henshaw 1843–1844 Thomas Gilmer 1844 John Y. Mason 1844–1845	Francis Granger 1841 Charles A. Wickliffe 1841–1845	John J. Crittenden 1841 Hugh S. Legaré 1841–1843 John Nelson 1843–1845	
George Bancroft 1845–1846 John Y. Mason 1846–1849	Cave Johnson 1845–1849	John Y. Mason 1845–1846 Nathan Clifford 1846–1848 Isaac Toucey 1848–1849	
William B. Preston 1849–1850	Jacob Collamer 1849–1850	Reverdy Johnson 1849–1850	Thomas Ewing 1849–1850
William A. Graham 1850–1852 John P. Kennedy 1852–1853	Nathan K. Hall 1850–1852 Sam D. Hubbard 1852–1853	John J. Crittenden 1850–1853	Thomas McKennan 1850 A. H. H. Stuart 1850–1853
James C. Dobbin 1853–1857	James Campbell 1853–1857	Caleb Cushing 1853–1857	Robert McClelland 1853–1857
Isaac Toucey 1857–1861	Aaron V. Brown 1857–1859 Joseph Holt 1859–1861 Horatio King 1861	Jeremiah S. Black 1857–1860 Edwin M. Stanton 1860–1861	Jacob Thompson 1857–1861
Gideon Welles 1861–1865	Horatio King 1861 Montgomery Blair 1861–1864 William Dennison 1864–1865	Edward Bates 1861–1864 James Speed 1864–1865	Caleb B. Smith 1861–1863 John P. Usher 1863–1865
Gideon Welles 1865–1869	William Dennison 1865–1866 Alexander Randall 1866–1869 William M. Evarts 1868–1869	James Speed 1865–1866 Henry Stanbery 1866–1868 O. H. Browning 1866–1869	John P. Usher 1865 James Harlan 1865–1866
Adolph E. Borie 1869 George M. Robeson 1869–1877	John A. J. Creswell 1869–1874 James W. Marshall 1874 Marshall Jewell 1874–1876 James N. Tyner 1876–1877	Ebenezer R. Hoar 1869–1870 Amos T. Akerman 1870–1871 G. H. Williams 1871–1875 Edwards Pierrepont 1875–1876 Alphonso Taft 1876–1877	Jacob D. Cox 1869–1870 Columbus Delano 1870–1875 Zachariah Chandler 1875–1877

(continued)

PRESIDENTIAL ADMINISTRATIONS, CONTINUED

President	Vice President	Secretary of State	Secretary of Treasury	Secretary of War	Secretary of Navy
Rutherford B. Hayes 1877–1881	William A. Wheeler 1877–1881	William M. Evarts 1877–1881	John Sherman 1877–1881	George W. McCrary 1877–1879 Alexander Ramsey 1879–1881	R. W. Thompson 1877–1881 Nathan Goff, Jr. 1881
James A. Garfield 1881	Chester A. Arthur 1881	James G. Blaine 1881	William Windom 1881	Robert T. Lincoln 1881	William H. Hunt 1881
Chester A. Arthur 1881–1885		F. T. Frelinghuysen 1881–1885	Charles J. Folger 1881–1884 Walter Q. Gresham 1884 Hugh McCulloch 1884–1885	Robert T. Lincoln 1881–1885	William E. Chandler 1881–1885
Grover Cleveland 1885–1889	T. A. Hendricks 1885	Thomas F. Bayard 1885–1889	Daniel Manning 1885–1887 Charles S. Fairchild 1887–1889	William C. Endicott 1885–1889	William C. Whitney 1885–1889
Benjamin Harrison 1889–1893	Levi P. Morton 1889–1893	James G. Blaine 1889–1892 John W. Foster 1892–1893	William Windom 1889–1891 Charles Foster 1892–1893	Redfield Procter 1889–1891 Stephen B. Elkins 1891–1893	Benjamin F. Tracy 1889–1893
Grover Cleveland 1893–1897	Adlai E. Stevenson 1893–1897	Walter Q. Gresham 1893–1895 Richard Olney 1895–1897	John G. Carlisle 1893–1897	Daniel S. Lamont 1893–1897	Hilary A. Herbert 1893–1897
William McKinley 1897–1901	Garret A. Hobart 1897–1899 Theodore Roosevelt 1901	John Sherman 1897–1898 William R. Day 1898 John Hay 1898–1901	Lyman J. Gage 1897–1901	Russell A. Alger 1897–1899 Elihu Root 1899–1901	John D. Long 1897–1901
Theodore Roosevelt 1901–1909	Charles Fairbanks 1905–1909	John Hay 1901–1905 Elihu Root 1905–1909 Robert Bacon 1909	Lyman J. Gage 1901–1902 Leslie M. Shaw 1902–1907 George B. Cortelyou 1907–1909	Elihu Root 1901–1904 William H. Taft 1904–1908 Luke E. Wright 1908–1909	John D. Long 1901–1902 William H. Moody 1902–1904 Paul Morton 1904–1905 Charles J. Bonaparte 1905–1906 Victor H. Metcalf 1906–1908 T. H. Newberry 1908–1909
William H. Taft 1909–1913	James S. Sherman 1909–1913	Philander C. Knox 1909–1913	Franklin MacVeagh 1909–1913	Jacob M. Dickinson 1909–1911 Henry L. Stimson 1911–1913	George von L. Meyer 1909–1913
Woodrow Wilson 1913–1921	Thomas R. Marshall 1913–1921	William J. Bryan 1913–1915 Robert Lansing 1915–1920 Bainbridge Colby 1920–1921	William G. McAdoo 1913–1918 Carter Glass 1918–1920 David F. Houston 1920–1921	Lindley M. Garrison 1913–1916 Newton D. Baker 1916–1921	Josephus Daniels 1913–1921

Postmaster General	Attorney General	Secretary of Interior	Secretary of Agriculture	Secretary of Commerce and Labor	
David M. Key 1877–1880 Horace Maynard 1880–1881	Charles Devens 1877–1881	Carl Schurz 1877–1881			
Thomas L. James 1881	Wayne MacVeagh 1881	S. J. Kirkwood 1881			
Thomas L. James 1881 Timothy O. Howe 1881–1883 Walter Q. Gresham 1883–1884 Frank Hatton 1884–1885	B. H. Brewster 1881–1885	Henry M. Teller 1881–1885			
William F. Vilas 1885–1888 Don M. Dickinson 1888–1889	A. H. Garland 1885–1889	L. Q. C. Lamar 1885–1888 William F. Vilas 1888–1889	Norman J. Colman 1889		
John Wanamaker 1889–1893	W. H. H. Miller 1889–1893	John W. Noble 1889–1893	Jeremiah M. Rusk 1889–1893		
Wilson S. Bissel 1893–1895 William L. Wilson 1895–1897	Richard Olney 1893–1895 Judson Harmon 1895–1897	Hoke Smith 1893–1896 David R. Francis 1896–1897	J. Sterling Morton 1893–1897		
James A. Gary 1897–1898 Charles E. Smith 1898–1901	Joseph McKenna 1897–1898 John W. Griggs 1898–1901 Philander C. Knox 1901	Cornelius N. Bliss 1897–1898 E. A. Hitchcock 1898–1901	James Wilson 1897–1901		
Charles E. Smith 1901–1902 Henry C. Payne 1902–1904 Robert J. Wynne 1904–1905 George B. Cortelyou 1905–1907 George von L. Meyer 1907–1909	Philander C. Knox 1901–1904 William H. Moody 1904–1906 Charles J. Bonaparte 1906–1909	E. A. Hitchcock 1901–1907 James R. Garfield 1907–1909	James Wilson 1901–1909	George B. Cortelyou 1903–1904 Victor H. Metcalf 1904–1906 Oscar S. Straus 1906–1909	

Postmaster General	Attorney General	Secretary of Interior	Secretary of Agriculture	Secretary of Commerce	Secretary of Labor
Frank H. Hitchcock 1909–1913	G. W. Wickersham 1909–1913	R. A. Ballinger 1909–1911 Walter L. Fisher 1911–1913	James Wilson 1909–1913	Charles Nagel 1909–1913	
Albert S. Burleson 1913–1921	J. C. McReynolds 1913–1914 T. W. Gregory 1914–1919 A. Mitchell Palmer 1919–1921	Franklin K. Lane 1913–1920 John B. Payne 1920–1921	David F. Houston 1913–1920 E. T. Meredith 1920–1921	W. C. Redfield 1913–1919 J. W. Alexander 1919–1921	William B. Wilson 1913–1921

(continued)

PRESIDENTIAL ADMINISTRATIONS, CONTINUED

President	Vice President	Secretary of State	Secretary of Treasury	Secretary of War	Secretary of Navy	Postmaster General	Attorney General
Warren G. Harding 1921–1923	Calvin Coolidge 1921–1923	Charles E. Hughes 1921–1923	Andrew W. Mellon 1921–1923	John W. Weeks 1921–1923	Edwin Denby 1921–1923	Will H. Hays 1921–1922 Hubert Work 1922–1923 Harry S. New 1923	H. M. Daugherty 1921–1923
Calvin Coolidge 1923–1929	Charles G. Dawes 1925–1929	Charles E. Hughes 1923–1925 Frank B. Kellogg 1925–1929	Andrew W. Mellon 1923–1929	John W. Weeks 1923–1925 Dwight F. Davis 1925–1929	Edwin Denby 1923–1924 Curtis D. Wilbur 1924–1929	Harry S. New 1923–1929	H. M. Daugherty 1923–1924 Harlan F. Stone 1924–1925 John G. Sargent 1925–1929
Herbert C. Hoover 1929–1933	Charles Curtis 1929–1933	Henry L. Stimson 1929–1933	Andrew W. Mellon 1929–1932 Ogden L. Mills 1932–1933	James W. Good 1929 Patrick J. Hurley 1929–1933	Charles F. Adams 1929–1933	Walter F. Brown 1929–1933	J. D. Mitchell 1929–1933
Franklin Delano Roosevelt 1933–1945	John Nance Garner 1933–1941 Henry A. Wallace 1941–1945 Harry S Truman 1945	Cordell Hull 1933–1944 E. R. Stettinius, Jr. 1944–1945	William H. Woodin 1933–1934 Henry Morgenthau, Jr. 1934–1945	George H. Dern 1933–1936 Harry H. Woodring 1936–1940 Henry L. Stimson 1940–1945	Claude A. Swanson 1933–1940 Charles Edison 1940 Frank Knox 1940–1944 James V. Forrestal 1944–1945	James A. Farley 1933–1940 Frank C. Walker 1940–1945	H. S. Cummings 1933–1939 Frank Murphy 1939–1940 Robert Jackson 1940–1941 Francis Biddel 1941–1945
Harry S Truman 1945–1953	Alben W. Barkley 1949–1953	James F. Byrnes 1945–1947 George C. Marshall 1947–1949 Dean G. Acheson 1949–1953	Fred M. Vinson 1945–1946 John W. Snyder 1946–1953	Robert P. Patterson 1945–1947 Kenneth C. Royall 1947	James V. Forrestal 1945–1947	R. E. Hannegan 1945–1947 Jesse M. Donaldson 1947–1953	Tom C. Clark 1945–1949 J. H. McGrath 1949–1952 James P. McGranery 1952–1953

Secretary of Defense

James V. Forrestal 1947–1949
Louis A. Johnson 1949–1950
George C. Marshall 1950–1951
Robert A. Lovett 1951–1953

President	Vice President	Secretary of State	Secretary of Treasury	Secretary of War	Secretary of Navy	Postmaster General	Attorney General
Dwight D. Eisenhower 1953–1961	Richard M. Nixon 1953–1961	John Foster Dulles 1953–1959 Christian A. Herter 1957–1961	George M. Humphrey 1953–1957 Robert B. Anderson 1957–1961	Charles E. Wilson 1953–1957 Neil H. McElroy 1957–1961 Thomas S. Gates 1959–1961		A. E. Summerfield 1953–1961	H. Brownell, Jr. 1953–1957 William P. Rogers 1957–1961
John F. Kennedy 1961–1963	Lyndon B. Johnson 1961–1963	Dean Rusk 1961–1963	C. Douglas Dillon 1961–1963	Robert S. McNamara 1961–1963		J. Edward Day 1961–1963 John A. Gronouski 1961–1963	Robert F. Kennedy 1961–1963
Lyndon B. Johnson 1963–1969	Hubert H. Humphrey 1965–1969	Dean Rusk 1963–1969	C. Douglas Dillon 1963–1965 Henry H. Fowler 1965–1968 Joseph W. Barr 1968–1969	Robert S. McNamara 1963–1968 Clark M. Clifford 1968–1969		John A. Gronouski 1963–1965 Lawrence F. O'Brien 1965–1968 W. Marvin Watson 1968–1969	Robert F. Kennedy 1963–1965 N. deB. Katzenbach 1965–1967 Ramsey Clark 1967–1969

Secretary of Interior	Secretary of Agriculture	Secretary of Commerce	Secretary of Labor	Secretary of Health, Education and Welfare	Secretary of Housing and Urban Development	Secretary of Transportation
Albert B. Fall 1921–1923 Hubert Work 1923	Henry C. Wallace 1921–1923	Herbert C. Hoover 1921–1923	James J. Davis 1921–1923			
Hubert Work 1923–1928 Roy O. West 1928–1929	Henry C. Wallace 1923–1924 Howard M. Gore 1924–1925 W. J. Jardine 1925–1929	Herbert C. Hoover 1923–1928 William F. Whiting 1928–1929	James J. Davis 1923–1929			
Ray L. Wilbur 1929–1933	Arthur M. Hyde 1929–1933 Roy D. Chapin 1932–1933	Robert P. Lamont 1929–1932 William N. Doak 1930–1933	James J. Davis 1929–1930			
Harold L. Ickes 1933–1945	Henry A. Wallace 1933–1940 Claude R. Wickard 1940–1945	Daniel C. Roper 1933–1939 Harry L. Hopkins 1939–1940 Jesse Jones 1940–1945 Henry A. Wallace 1945	Frances Perkins 1933–1945			
Harold L. Ickes 1945–1946 Julius A. Krug 1946–1949 Oscar L. Chapman 1949–1953	C. P. Anderson 1945–1948 C. F. Brannan 1948–1953	W. A. Harriman 1946–1948 Charles Sawyer 1948–1953	L. B. Schwellenbach 1945–1948 Maurice J. Tobin 1948–1953			
Douglas McKay 1953–1956 Fred Seaton 1956–1961	Ezra T. Benson 1953–1961	Sinclair Weeks 1953–1958 Lewis L. Strauss 1958–1961	Martin P. Durkin 1953 James P. Mitchell 1953–1961	Oveta Culp Hobby 1953–1955 Marion B. Folsom 1955–1958 Arthur S. Flemming 1958–1961		
Stewart L. Udall 1961–1963	Orville L. Freeman 1961–1963	Luther H. Hodges 1961–1963	Arthur J. Goldberg 1961–1963 W. Willard Wirtz 1962–1963	A. H. Ribicoff 1961–1963 Anthony J. Celebrezze 1962–1963		
Stewart L. Udall 1963–1969	Orville L. Freeman 1963–1969	Luther H. Hodges 1963–1965 John T. Connor 1965–1967 Alexander B. Trowbridge 1967–1968 C. R. Smith 1968–1969	W. Willard Wirtz 1963–1969	Anthony J. Celebrezze 1963–1965 John W. Gardner 1965–1968 Wilbur J. Cohen 1968–1969	Robert C. Weaver 1966–1968 Robert C. Wood 1968–1969	Alan S. Boyd 1966–1969

(continued)

PRESIDENTIAL ADMINISTRATIONS, CONTINUED

President	Vice President	Secretary of State	Secretary of Treasury	Secretary of Defense	Postmaster General[1]	Attorney General	Secretary of Interior	Secretary of Agriculture
Richard M. Nixon 1969–1974	Spiro T. Agnew 1969–1973 Gerald R. Ford 1973–1974	William P. Rogers 1969–1973 Henry A. Kissinger 1973–1974	David M. Kennedy 1969–1970 John B. Connally 1970–1972 George P. Schultz 1972–1974 William E. Simon 1974	Melvin R. Laird 1969–1973 Elliot L. Richardson 1973 James R. Schlesinger 1973–1974	Winton M. Blount 1969–1971	John M. Mitchell 1969–1972 Richard G. Kleindienst 1972–1973 Elliot L. Richardson 1973 William B. Saxbe 1974	Walter J. Hickel 1969–1971 Rogers C. B. Morton 1971–1974	Clifford M. Hardin 1969–1971 Earl L. Butz 1971–1974
Gerald R. Ford 1974–1977	Nelson A. Rockefeller 1974–1977	Henry A. Kissinger 1974–1977	William E. Simon 1974–1977	James R. Schlesinger 1974–1975 Donald H. Rumsfeld 1975–1977		William B. Saxbe 1974–1975 Edward H. Levi 1975–1977	Rogers C. B. Morton 1974–1975 Stanley K. Hathaway 1975 Thomas D. Kleppe 1975–1977	Earl L. Butz 1974–1976
Jimmy Carter 1977–1981	Walter F. Mondale 1977–1981	Cyrus R. Vance 1977–1980 Edmund S. Muskie 1980–1981	W. Michael Blumenthal 1977–1979 G. William Miller 1979–1981	Harold Brown 1977–1981		Griffin Bell 1977–1979 Benjamin R. Civiletti 1979–1981	Cecil D. Andrus 1977–1981	Robert Bergland 1977–1981
Ronald W. Reagan 1981–1989	George H. Bush 1981–1989	Alexander M. Haig, Jr. 1981–1982 George P. Shultz 1982–1989	Donald T. Regan 1981–1985 James A. Baker 1985–1988 Nicholas F. Brady 1988–1989	Caspar W. Weinberger 1981–1987 Frank C. Carlucci 1987–1989		William French Smith 1981–1985 Edwin Meese 1985–1988 Richard Thornburgh 1988–1989	James G. Watt 1981–1983 William P. Clark 1983–1985 Donald P. Hodel 1985–1989	John R. Block 1981–1986 Richard E. Lyng 1986–1989
George H. Bush 1989–1993	J. Danforth Quayle 1989–1993	James A. Baker 1989–1992 Lawrence S. Eagleburger 1992–1993	Nicholas F. Brady 1989–1993	Richard Cheney 1989–1993		Richard Thornburgh 1989–1990 William Barr 1990–1993	Manuel Lujan 1989–1993	Clayton Yeutter 1989–1990 Edward Madigan 1990–1993
William Clinton 1993–2001	Albert Gore 1993–2001	Warren M. Christopher 1993–1996 Madeleine K. Albright 1997–2001	Lloyd Bentsen 1993–1994 Robert E. Rubin 1994–1999 Lawrence H. Summers 1999–2001	Les Aspin 1993–1994 William J. Perry 1994–1996 William S. Cohen 1997–2001		Janet Reno 1993–2001	Bruce Babbitt 1993–2001	Mike Espy 1993–1994 Dan Glickman 1995–2001
George W. Bush 2001–	Richard B. Cheney 2001–	Gen. Colin L. Powell 2001–	Paul H. O'Neill 2001–2002 John W. Snow 2003–	Donald H. Rumsfeld 2001–		John Ashcroft 2001–	Gale A. Norton 2001–	Ann M. Veneman 2001–

[1]On July 1, 1971, the Post Office became an independent agency. After that date, the postmaster general was no longer a member of the Cabinet.

[2]Acting secretary.

Secretary of Commerce	Secretary of Labor	Secretary of Health, Education and Welfare	Secretary of Housing and Urban Development	Secretary of Transportation	Secretary of Energy	Secretary of Veterans Affairs	Secretary of Homeland Security
Maurice H. Stans 1969–1972 Peter G. Peterson 1972 Frederick B. Dent 1972–1974	George P. Shultz 1969–1970 James D. Hodgson 1970–1973 Peter J. Brennan 1973–1974	Robert H. Finch 1969–1970 Elliot L. Richardson 1970–1973 Caspar W. Weinberger 1973–1974	George W. Romney 1969–1973 James T. Lynn 1973–1974	John A. Volpe 1969–1973 Claude S. Brinegar 1973–1974			
Frederick B. Dent 1974–1975 Rogers C. B. Morton 1975 Elliot L. Richardson 1975–1977	Peter J. Brennan 1974–1975 John T. Dunlop 1975–1976 W. J. Usery 1976–1977	Caspar W. Weinberger 1974–1975 Forrest D. Matthews 1975–1977	James T. Lynn 1974–1975 Carla A. Hills 1975–1977	Claude S. Brinegar 1974–1975 William T. Coleman 1975–1977			
Juanita Kreps 1977–1981	F. Ray Marshall 1977–1981	Joseph Califano 1977–1979 Patricia Roberts Harris 1979–1980	Patricia Roberts Harris 1977–1979 Moon Landrieu 1979–1981	Brock Adams 1977–1979 Neil E. Goldschmidt 1979–1981	James R. Schlesinger 1977–1979 Charles W. Duncan, Jr. 1979–1981		

		Secretary of Health and Human Services	Secretary of Education				
		Patricia Roberts Harris 1980–1981	Shirley M. Hufstedler 1980–1981				

Secretary of Commerce	Secretary of Labor	Secretary of Health and Human Services	Secretary of Education	Secretary of Housing and Urban Development	Secretary of Transportation	Secretary of Energy	Secretary of Veterans Affairs	Secretary of Homeland Security
Malcolm Baldrige 1981–1987 C. William Verity, Jr. 1987–1989	Raymond J. Donovan 1981–1985 William E. Brock 1985–1987 Ann Dore McLaughlin 1987–1989	Richard S. Schweiker 1981–1983 Margaret M. Heckler 1983–1985 Otis R. Bowen 1985–1989	Terrell H. Bell 1981–1985 William J. Bennett 1985–1988 Lauro Fred Cavazos 1988–1989	Samuel R. Pierce, Jr. 1981–1989	Drew Lewis 1981–1983 Elizabeth H. Dole 1983–1987 James H. Burnley 1987–1989	James B. Edwards 1981–1982 Donald P. Hodel 1982–1985 John S. Harrington 1985–1989		
Robert Mosbacher 1989–1991 Barbara Franklin 1991–1993	Elizabeth Dole 1989–1990 Lynn Martin 1992–1993	Louis Sullivan 1989–1993	Lamar Alexander 1990–1993	Jack Kemp 1989–1993	Samuel Skinner 1989–1990 Andrew Card 1990–1993	James Watkins 1989–1993	Edward J. Derwinski 1989–1993	
Ronald H. Brown 1993–1996 William M. Daley 1997–2000 Norman Y. Mineta 2000–2001	Robert B. Reich 1993–1996 Alexis M. Herman 1997–2001	Donna E. Shalala 1993–2001	Richard W. Riley 1993–2001	Henry G. Cisneros 1993–1996 Andrew M. Cuomo 1997–2001	Federico F. Peña 1993–1996 Rodney E. Slater 1997–2001	Hazel O'Leary 1993–1996 Federico F. Peña 1997–1998 Bill Richardson 1998–2001	Jesse Brown 1993–1997 Togo D. West, Jr.[2] 1998–2001	
Donald L. Evans 2001–	Elaine L. Chao 2001–	Tommy G. Thompson 2001–	Roderick R. Paige 2001–	Melquiades R. Martinez 2001–	Norman Y. Mineta 2001–	Spencer Abraham 2001–	Anthony Principi 2001–	Tom Ridge 2001–

JUSTICES OF THE U.S. SUPREME COURT

Name	Term of Service	Years of Service	Appointed By	Name	Term of Service	Years of Service	Appointed By
John Jay	1789–1795	5	Washington	Rufus W. Peckham	1895–1909	14	Cleveland
John Rutledge	1789–1791	1	Washington	Joseph McKenna	1898–1925	26	McKinley
William Cushing	1789–1810	20	Washington	Oliver W. Holmes, Jr.	1902–1932	30	T. Roosevelt
James Wilson	1789–1798	8	Washington	William R. Day	1903–1922	19	T. Roosevelt
John Blair	1789–1796	6	Washington	William H. Moody	1906–1910	3	T. Roosevelt
Robert H. Harrison	1789–1790	—	Washington	Horace H. Lurton	1910–1914	4	Taft
James Iredell	1790–1799	9	Washington	Charles E. Hughes	1910–1916	5	Taft
Thomas Johnson	1791–1793	1	Washington	Willis Van Devanter	1911–1937	26	Taft
William Paterson	1793–1806	13	Washington	Joseph R. Lamar	1911–1916	5	Taft
John Rutledge[1]	1795	—	Washington	**Edward D. White**	1910–1921	11	Taft
Samuel Chase	1796–1811	15	Washington	Mahlon Pitney	1912–1922	10	Taft
Oliver Ellsworth	1796–1800	4	Washington	James C. McReynolds	1914–1941	26	Wilson
Bushrod Washington	1798–1829	31	J. Adams	Louis D. Brandeis	1916–1939	22	Wilson
Alfred Moore	1799–1804	4	J. Adams	John H. Clarke	1916–1922	6	Wilson
John Marshall	1801–1835	34	J. Adams	**William H. Taft**	1921–1930	8	Harding
William Johnson	1804–1834	30	Jefferson	George Sutherland	1922–1938	15	Harding
H. Brockholst Livingston	1806–1823	16	Jefferson	Pierce Butler	1922–1939	16	Harding
Thomas Todd	1807–1826	18	Jefferson	Edward T. Sanford	1923–1930	7	Harding
Joseph Story	1811–1845	33	Madison	Harlan F. Stone	1925–1941	16	Coolidge
Gabriel Duval	1811–1835	24	Madison	**Charles E. Hughes**	1930–1941	11	Hoover
Smith Thompson	1823–1843	20	Monroe	Owen J. Roberts	1930–1945	15	Hoover
Robert Trimble	1826–1828	2	J. Q. Adams	Benjamin N. Cardozo	1932–1938	6	Hoover
John McLean	1829–1861	32	Jackson	Hugo L. Black	1937–1971	34	F. Roosevelt
Henry Baldwin	1830–1844	14	Jackson	Stanley F. Reed	1938–1957	19	F. Roosevelt
James M. Wayne	1835–1867	32	Jackson	Felix Frankfurter	1939–1962	23	F. Roosevelt
Roger B. Taney	1836–1864	28	Jackson	William O. Douglas	1939–1975	36	F. Roosevelt
Philip P. Barbour	1836–1841	4	Jackson	Frank Murphy	1940–1949	9	F. Roosevelt
John Catron	1837–1865	28	Van Buren	**Harlan F. Stone**	1941–1946	5	F. Roosevelt
John McKinley	1837–1852	15	Van Buren	James F. Byrnes	1941–1942	1	F. Roosevelt
Peter V. Daniel	1841–1860	19	Van Buren	Robert H. Jackson	1941–1954	13	F. Roosevelt
Samuel Nelson	1845–1872	27	Tyler	Wiley B. Rutledge	1943–1949	6	F. Roosevelt
Levi Woodbury	1845–1851	5	Polk	Harold H. Burton	1945–1958	13	Truman
Robert C. Grier	1846–1870	23	Polk	**Fred M. Vinson**	1946–1953	7	Truman
Benjamin R. Curtis	1851–1857	6	Fillmore	Tom C. Clark	1949–1967	18	Truman
John A. Campbell	1853–1861	8	Pierce	Sherman Minton	1949–1956	7	Truman
Nathan Clifford	1858–1881	23	Buchanan	**Earl Warren**	1953–1969	16	Eisenhower
Noah H. Swayne	1862–1881	18	Lincoln	John Marshall Harlan	1955–1971	16	Eisenhower
Samuel F. Miller	1862–1890	28	Lincoln	William J. Brennan, Jr.	1956–1990	34	Eisenhower
David Davis	1862–1877	14	Lincoln	Charles E. Whittaker	1957–1962	5	Eisenhower
Stephen J. Field	1863–1897	34	Lincoln	Potter Stewart	1958–1981	23	Eisenhower
Salmon P. Chase	1864–1873	8	Lincoln	Byron R. White	1962–1993	31	Kennedy
William Strong	1870–1880	10	Grant	Arthur J. Goldberg	1962–1965	3	Kennedy
Joseph P. Bradley	1870–1892	22	Grant	Abe Fortas	1965–1969	4	Johnson
Ward Hunt	1873–1882	9	Grant	Thurgood Marshall	1967–1994	24	Johnson
Morrison R. Waite	1874–1888	14	Grant	**Warren E. Burger**	1969–1986	18	Nixon
John M. Harlan	1877–1911	34	Hayes	Harry A. Blackmun	1970–1994	24	Nixon
William B. Woods	1880–1887	7	Hayes	Lewis F. Powell, Jr.	1971–1987	15	Nixon
Stanley Matthews	1881–1889	7	Garfield	**William H. Rehnquist**[2]	1971–	—	Nixon
Horace Gray	1882–1902	20	Arthur	John P. Stevens III	1975–	—	Ford
Samuel Blatchford	1882–1893	11	Arthur	Sandra Day O'Connor	1981–	—	Reagan
Lucius Q. C. Lamar	1888–1893	5	Cleveland	Antonin Scalia	1986–	—	Reagan
Melville W. Fuller	1888–1910	21	Cleveland	Anthony M. Kennedy	1988–	—	Reagan
David J. Brewer	1890–1910	20	B. Harrison	David Souter	1990–	—	Bush
Henry B. Brown	1890–1906	16	B. Harrison	Clarence Thomas	1991–	—	Bush
George Shiras, Jr.	1892–1903	10	B. Harrison	Ruth Bader Ginsburg	1993–	—	Clinton
Howell E. Jackson	1893–1895	2	B. Harrison	Stephen G. Breyer	1994–	—	Clinton
Edward D. White	1894–1910	16	Cleveland				

Note: Chief justices appear in bold type.

[1]Acting chief justice; Senate refused to confirm appointment.

[2]Chief justice from 1986 on (Reagan administration).

Images not referenced below are in the public domain.

Chapter 1

p. 2 (left): © Bettmann/Corbis; **p. 2 (right):** Bibliotheque Nationale de France; **p. 10:** © Jon Adkins/National Geographic Society; **p. 11 (top):** © Genevieve Leaper; Ecoscene/Corbis; **p. 11 (bottom):** © Werner Forman/Art Resource, NY; **p. 13:** © Archivo Iconografico, S.A./Corbis; **p. 14:** Leonardo Torriani, Die Kanarischen Inseln und Ihre Urbewohner [1590], ed. Dominik Wolfel (Leipzig: K. F. Koehler, 1940), Plate X; **p. 18 (top left):** © North Wind Picture Archives; **p. 18 (top right):** © Stock Montage, Inc.; **p. 18 (bottom):** © Historical Picture Archive/Corbis; **p. 19 (top):** Courtesy of the John Carter Brown Library at Brown University; **p. 22 (bottom):** © Boltin Picture Library; **p. 22 (top):** © Werner Forman/Art Resource, NY; **p. 23 (top):** Reconstruction by Tatiana Proskouriakoff. From The Fall of the Ancient Maya by David Webster, published by Thames & Hudson, London and New York; **p. 23 (bottom):** © Boltin Picture Library; **p. 25 (left):** Image taken from exhibit produced by the Florida Museum of Natural History; **p. 25 (right):** © Boltin Picture Library; **p. 26 (bottom):** © Richard A. Cooke/Corbis; **p. 28:** Painting by Lloyd K. Townsend; **p. 29:** © David Muench; **p. 30:** North Wind Picture Archives; **p. 31:** Moctezuma's Mexico, by David Carrasco and Eduardo Mato Moctezuma, © 1992 University Press of Colorado. Photographs by Salvador Guil'liem Arroyo; **p. 32 (top):** Fray Bernardinode Sahagun, General History of the Things of New Spain; **p. 32 (bottom):** Folding Screen: The Encounter of Cortes and Moctezuma (obverse); The Four Continents (reverse) Collection Banco Nacional de Mexico, Mexico City; **p. 33:** York Public Library. Astor, Lenox and Tilden Foundations, Rare book Division; **p. 35:** © Picture Desk/Kobal Collection/Warner Bros; **p. 37:** © Hulton Archive/Getty Images

Chapter 2

p. 42: © SEF/Art Resource, NY; **p. 45:** Theodore DeBry; **p. 47:** © Picture Desk/Kobal Collection/Alliance/Goldwyn; **p. 48:** Theodore DeBry; **p. 56:** © Bettmann/Corbis; **p. 57:** William C. Clements Library, University of Michigan, Ann Arbor; **p. 59:** Courtesy of the John Carter Brown Library at Brown University; **p. 60:** Image courtesy of Historic St. Mary's City; **p. 62:** The Library Company of Philadelphia; **p. 64:** Museum of the American Indian/Heye Foundation, NY; **p. 68:** Photograph © 2003 Museum of Fine Arts, Boston; **p. 69:** From the Collection of the Library of Congress; **p. 70:** © Bettmann/Corbis; **p. 76:** North Wind Picture Archives; **p. 78:** © Bettmann/Corbis; **p. 79** (left): Hans Oswald Wild/TimePix; **p. 79** (right): From the Collections of the Library of Congress

Chapter 3

p. 82: © The Granger Collection, New York; **p. 90:** © The British Museum; **p. 92:** Houghton Library, Harvard University, Cambridge, Ma; **p. 94:** Courtesy, American Antiquarian Society; **p. 95:** Patrick M. Malone, The Skulking Way of War, Madison Books c 1991; **p. 97:** © Wendell Metzen/Bruce Coleman Inc.; **p. 98:** The Virginia Journals of Benjamin Henry Latrobe (2 vols., New Haven, 1977) I, 181-82, 247, plate 21; **p. 102 (left):** Thomas B. Macaulay, History of England from the Accession of James II, ed. by Charles H. Firth (London: Macmillan, 1914); **p. 10 (right):** Thomas B. Macaulay, History of England from the Accession of James II, ed. by Charles H. Firth (London: Macmillan, 1914); **p. 104:** PBS Home Video; **p. 105:** © Hulton Archive/Getty Images; **p. 108:** Yale University Art Gallery; **p. 109 (left):** Hampton Court Palace "A View of Hampton Court" by Leonard Knyff, c.1703 (detail). The Royal Collection © 1998 Her Majesty The Queen. The Royal Picture Library, Windsor Castle; **p. 109 (right):** Dixon Harvesters, c.1725. by English School, (18th century) Cheltenham Art Gallery & Museums, Gloucestershire, U.K./The Bridgeman Art Library; **p. 111:** Archives Nationales; **p. 115 (left):** Courtesy Massachusetts Historical Society; **p. 115 (right):** Illustrated London News

Chapter 4

p. 118: 1963.6.1 (1904)/PA: Copley, John Singelton, "Watson and the Shark", Ferdinand Lammot Belin Fund © 1998 Board of Trustees, National Gallery of Art, Washington, 1778, oil on canvas, 1.82 x 2.297 (71 3/4 x 90 1/2); framed: 2.413 x 2.642 x .101 (95 x 104 x 4); **p. 122:** Chicago Historical Society; **p. 123:** after John Barbot, from Churchill's Voyages; **p. 124:** © The Granger Collection; **p. 125:** North Wind Picture Archives; **p. 126:** © Corbis; **p. 128:** Copyright © 1965 by Edwin Tunis. Copyright renewed 1993 by David Hutton, Executor for the Estate of Edwin Tunis. Illustrations from Colonial Craftsmen and the beginnings of American Industry, now published by Johns Hopkins University Press. Reprinted by permission of Curtis Brown, Ltd.; **p. 130:** The Saint Louis Museum Purchase; **p. 131:** from the Collections of the Library of Congress; **p. 133:** Hargrett Rare Book and Manuscript Library/University of Georgia Libraries, Athens; **p. 138:** Colonial Williamsburg Foundation; **p. 142 (bottom):** Peabody Museum, Harvard University. Photograph by Hillel Burger; **p. 145:** Collection of the New-York Historical Society; **p. 147:** North Wind Picture Archives; **p. 149:** © Hulton Archive/Getty Images; **p. 151:** © Picture Desk/Kobal Collection/20th Century Fox/Morgan Creek; **p. 155:** Clements Library, University of Michigan, Ann Arbor

Chapter 5

p. 158: © The Granger Collection; **p. 163:** Colonial Williamsburg Foundation; **p. 165:** 05.003 New York Public Library; **p. 167:** © Philadelphia Museum of Art/Corbis; **p. 168:** Courtesy of the John Carter Brown Library at Brown University; **p. 171:** The Granger Collection, New York; **p. 173:** Colonial Williamsburg Foundation; **p. 179 (top):** From the Collections of the Library of Congress; **p. 179 (bottom):** American Antiquarian Society; **p. 180:** Courtesy of the John Carter Brown Library at Brown University; **p. 181:** Courtesy, American Antiquarian Society; **p. 182:** From the Collections of the Library of Congress; **p. 183 (left):** © North Wind Picture Archives; **p. 183 (right):** © The Granger Collection; **p. 185:** The Granger Collection, New York; **p. 189:** © Picture Desk/Kobal Collection/Columbia

Chapter 6

p. 192: Gift of the Owners of the Old Boston Museum Courtesy, Museum of Fine Arts, Boston © 2002/All Rights Reserved; **p. 197:** Lewis Walpole Library, Yale University; **p. 199:** Fairfield Historical Society; **p. 200:** © Alon Reininger/Woodfin Camp; **p. 205:** Courtesy, American Antiquarian Society; **p. 206:** National Archives of Canada/C-002001; **p. 207 (left):** Fenimore Art Museum, New York State Historical Association, Cooperstown, New York; **p. 207 (right):** Chicago Historical Society; **p. 209 (top):** Courtesy, American Antiquarian Society; **p. 209 (bottom):** Colonial Williamsburg; **p. 212:** Yale University Art Gallery, Gift of Ebenezer Baldwin, B.A. 1808; **p. 214:** From the Collections of the Library of Congress; **p. 217:** © J. Gilbert Harrington; **p. 219 (bottom):** Missouri Historical Society; **p. 224:**

© Bettmann/Corbis; **p. 225:** © North Wind Picture Archives

Chapter 7

p. 230: The Historical Society of Pennsylvania, Preparation for War to Defend Commerce, by William Russell Birch(BD61B531.2pl.29); **p. 235:** PBS Home Video; **p. 236:** Lewis Miller (1796-1882). The Historical Society of York County, The York County Heritage Trust, PA.; **p. 237:** New Bedford Whaling Museum; **p. 240:** The Granger Collection, New York; **p. 241:** "Old Homestead, Late Residence of R. H,. Constant." From Illustrated Atlas Map of Sangamon County, Ill. (Springfield, Ill.: Brink, McComrick & Co., 1874); **p. 243:** Abby Aldrich Rockefeller Folk Art Center, Williamsburg, VA; **p. 245:** Collection of the Maryland Historical Society, Baltimore; **p. 246:** The Granger Collection, New York; **p. 247:** Collection of the New-York Historical Society; **p. 248:** Courtesy, Gore Place; **p. 250:** The Historical Society of Pennsylvania, Procession of the Victuallers, by John Lewis Krimmel (Bc85 K89); **p. 251:** John Lewis Krimmel, American, 1786-1821 Village Tavern, 1813-14, oil on canvas, 16 7/8 x 22 1/2 in. (42.8 x 56.9 cm) The Toledo Museum of Art, Toledo, Ohio; Purchased with funds from the Florence Scott Libbey Bequest in Memory of her Father, Maurice A. Scott; **p. 257:** New Bedford Whaling Museum; **p. 258:** Historical Commission, Mother Bethel AME Church, Philadelphia, PA

Chapter 8

p. 262: collections of Davenport West, Jr.; **p. 265:** National Portrait Gallery/Smithsonian Institution/Art Resource, NY; **p. 269:** © Gianni Dagli/Corbis; **p. 273:** © North Wind Picture Archives; **p. 278 (top):** © Bettmann/Corbis; **p. 278 (bottom):** The Granger Collection, New York; **p. 280:** Architect of the Capitol; **p. 281:** A View of New Orleans Taken from the Plantation of Marigny, November, 1803 by Boqueto de Woiserie, Chicago Historical Society; **p. 284:** North Wind Picture Archives; **p. 285:** North Wind Picture Archives; **p. 286:** Courtesy of the Royal Ontario Museum, Toronto, Canada; **p. 288:** From the Collections of the Library of Congress; **p. 289:** Allyn Cox, 1974 Architect of the Capitol; **p. 291:** © Picture Desk/Kobal Collection/Paramount

Chapter 9

p. 294: from the Collections of the Library of Congress; **p. 297:** The Library Company of Philadelphia; **p. 300:** Thomas L. McKenney, Sketches of a Tour to the Lakes

(1827); **p. 301:** The Granger Collection; **p. 306:** Old Sturbridge Village, Photo by: Thomas Neill, #25.K74if.1994.2.1; **p. 307:** Chicago Historical Society; **p. 308:** © Bettmann/Corbis; **p. 309:** Smithsonian Institution; **p. 310:** The Granger Collection, New York; **p. 311:** American Textile History Museum. Lowell, Mass; **p. 312:** © Hulton-Deutsch Collection/Corbis; **p. 315:** © Kobal/Picture Desk; **p. 316:** The Library Company of Philadelphia; **p. 318:** The Historic New Orleans Collection, Accension #1975.931 & 2; **p. 320:** The Historic New Orleans Collection, Accension # 1977.13734311

Chapter 10

p. 322: National Portrait Gallery, Smithsonian Institution/Art Resource, NY; **p. 325:** © Bettmann/Corbis; **p. 326:** Abby Aldrich Rockefeller Folk Art Center, Williamsburg, VA; **p. 329:** Frederic Edwin Church NIAGARA, 1857. oil on canvas, 42 1/2 x 90 1/2 in. (107.95 x 229.87 cm) In the Collection of the Corcoran Gallery of Art, Museum Purchase, Gallery Fund. 76.15; **p. 331:** Courtesy American Antiquarian Society; **p. 335:** From the Collections of the Library of Congress; **p. 336:** © Museum of the City of New York/Corbis; **p. 337 (both):** Courtesy, American Antiquarian Society; **p. 338:** Hunter Museum of American Art, Chattanooga, Tennessee, Gift of Mr. and Mrs. Thomas B. Whiteside; **p. 341:** From the Collections of the Library of Congress; **p. 343:** Reproduced form the Collections of the Library of Congress; **p. 345:** © Picture Desk/Kobal Collection/Regan, Ken/Touchstone

Chapter 11

p. 350: The Nelson-Atkins Museum of Art, Kansas City, Missouri (Purchase: Nelson Trust) 54-9; **p. 353:** The Saint Louis Art Museum, Purchase; **p. 358:** North Wind Picture Archives; **p. 359:** The Granger Collection, New York; **p. 360:** North Wind Picture Archives; **p. 364:** From the Collections of the Library of Congress; **p. 365:** A Black Oyster Seller in Philadelphia, 1814, Watercolor by John Lewis Krimmel. The Metropolitan Museum of Art, Rogers Fund, 1942 (42.95.18) Photograph © 1989 The Metropolitan Museum of Art; **p. 367:** © Bettmann/Corbis; **p. 368:** The Library Company of Philadelphia; **p. 371:** Old Sturbridge Village, photo by Henry E. Peach; **p. 374:** PBS Home Video

Chapter 12

p. 378: National Portrait Gallery, Smithsonian Institution/Art Resource, NY; **p. 384:** The Granger Collection; **p. 385:** From the Collections of the Library of Congress; **p. 387:** U.S. Naval Historical Center Photograph; **p. 388:** The Hermitage: Home of President Andrew Jackson, Nashville, TN; **p. 390:** White House Collection; **p. 392:** © Picture Desk/Kobal Collection/Cooper, Andrew/Dreamworks LLC; **p. 394:** Woolaroc Museum; **p. 396:** From the Collection of the Library of Congress; **p. 400:** Collection of the New-York Historical Society; **p. 401:** North Wind Picture Archives; **p. 403:** Reproduced from the collections of the Library of Congress

Chapter 13

p. 406: From the collections of the Library of Congress; **p. 410:** North Wind Picture Archives; **p. 412:** Joseph Mustering the Nauvoo Legion, C.C.A. Christensen. © Courtesy Museum of Art, Brigham Young University. All Rights reserved. Photographer: David W. Hawkinson; **p. 415:** © John Springer Collection/Corbis; **p. 417:** Yale Collection of Western Americana, Beinecke Rare Book and Manuscript Library; **p. 420:** Missouri Historical Society. MHS art acc# 1939.3.1; **p. 421:** James Smith Noel Collection, Noel Memorial Library. Louisiana State University in Shreveport; **p. 423:** The Granger Collection, New York; **p. 426:** Courtesy of The Trustees of Boston Public Library; **p. 427:** "The Underground Railroad" painting by Charles T. Webber (1893) from the Cincinnati Art Museum (#1927.26); **p. 428:** The Granger Collection, New York

Chapter 14

p. 432: The Granger Collection, New York; **p. 435 (left):** Reproduced from the Collections of the Library of Congress; **p. 435 (right):** © Bettmann/Corbis; **p. 439:** Maryland Historical Society, Baltimore; **p. 440:** Kansas State Historical Society; **p. 442:** Prints Division, The New York Public Library. Astor, Lenox and Tilden Foundations; **p. 445:** © The Granger Collection; **p. 447:** © Corbis; **p. 449:** Reproduced from the Collections of the Library of Congress; **p. 450:** © Bettmann/Corbis; **p. 453 (top):** From the Collections of the Library of Congress; **p. 453 (bottom):** The Granger Collection; **p. 455:** © Bettmann/Corbis; **p. 458:** North Wind Picture Archives; **p. 459:** © Bettmann/Corbis; **p. 460:** Courtesy of the Illinois State Historical Library; **p. 462:** Kansas State Historical Society

Chapter 15

p. 464: Thomas C. Linday, Hornet's Nest, Cincinnati Historical Society; **p. 466:** Reproduced from the

Collections of the Library of Congress; **p. 468:** From the Ralph E. Becker Collection of Political Americana, The Smithsonian Institution; **p. 470:** Courtesy of The South Carolina Historical Society; **p. 474:** From the Collections of the Library of Congress; **p. 479:** © Springer/Corbis; **p. 480:** Cook Collection, Valentine Museum, Richmond, Virginia; **p. 482:** Photo by Timothy O'Sullivan, Chicago Historical Society, ICHi-08091; **p. 484:** From the Collections of the Library of Congress; **p. 485:** Historical Society of Pennsylvania; **p. 486 (top):** From the Collections of the Library of Congress; **p. 486 (bottom):** © Bettmann/Corbis

Chapter 16

p. 498: Eastman Johnson 1824-1906 A RIDE FOR LIBERTY-THE FUGITIVE SLAVES, circa 1862. Oil on board The Brooklyn Museum 40.59. A Gift of Miss Gwendolyn O.L. Conkling; **p. 501:** From the collections of the National Archives; **p. 504 (top):** Reproduced from the Collections of the Library of Congress; **p. 504 (bottom):** © Bettmann/Corbis; **p. 505:** Architect of the Capitol; **p. 509 (top):** The Library of Virginia; **p. 509 (bottom):** Collection of the New-York Historical Society; **p. 511:** Reproduced from the Collections of the Library of Congress; **p. 512 (left):** Reproduced from the Collections of the Library of Congress; **p. 512 (right):** Courtesy of the Illinois State Historical Library; **p. 514:** National Park Service, Harpers Ferry Center; **p. 518:** From the

Collections of the Library of Congress; **p. 519:** © Picture Desk/Kobal Collection/Tri Star; **p. 522:** Brown Brothers; **p. 524:** From the Collections of the Library of Congress; **p. 525:** Reproduced from the Collections of the Library of Congress; **p. 527:** Reproduced from the Collections of the Library of Congress; **p. 530:** Reproduced from the Collections of the Library of Congress; **p. 531:** Reproduced from the Collections of the Library of Congress

Chapter 17

p. 534: Winslow Homer, Sunday Morning in Virginia, 1877. Cincinnati Art Museum John J. Emery Fund. Acc.#1924.247; **p. 537:** Courtesy Chicago Historical Society; **p. 539 (left):** Reproduced from the Collections of the Library of Congress; **p. 539 (right):** Reproduced from the Collections of the Library of Congress; **p. 541 (top):** Reproduced from the Collections of the Library of Congress; **p. 541 (bottom):** © Bettmann/Corbis; **p. 542:** Reproduced from the Collections of the Library of Congress; **p. 543 (left):** © Stock Montage, Inc.; **p. 543 (right):** From the Collections of the Library of Congress; **p. 545:** From the Collections of the Library of Congress; **p. 548:** © Corbis; **p. 553:** © Bettmann/Corbis; **p. 554:** From the Collections of the Library of Congress; **p. 556:** © Bettmann/Corbis; **p. 558:** The Granger Collection, New York

Index